BOSTON MUSEUM

1841 · **1878**

Mr. R. M. Field, Manager.

THIRTY-SECOND WEEK OF THE 35th REGULAR DRAMATIC SEASON !

Mirth, Music and Magnificence

FOR A SHORT SEASON !

Commencing, Monday, April 8,

— WITH —

2 PERFORMANCES FAST DAY ! 2

Thursday, April 11,

A Grand, Glorious, Gorgeous, Glittering Spectacular Production of the old Fairy Tale, and Musical Extravaganza, of THE

ENCHANTED BEAUTY !

After months of very elaborate preparation,
Introducing

Entirely New and Appropriate Scenery

By Messrs. Thos. B. Glessing and E. Lamoss.

New Music, arranged by Mr. E. N. Catlin, new features, new artists, brilliant costumes, magnificent appointments, a very powerful chorus of male and female voices, and a world of fun.

THE CAST WILL BE AS FOLLOWS:

King of Noland	Mr. Alfred Hudson
	(Specially engaged for the part.)
Baron Factotum	Mr. E. A. McDowell
Prince Perfect	Miss Lizzie Harold
Larry O'Log	Mr. Geo. W. Wilson
Gentleman Usher	Mr. W. Morris
Colin Clump	Mr. W. Melbourne
Newspaper Imp	Little Gertrude
Prncess Is-a-Belle	Miss Venie Clancy
	(Specially engaged for the part.)
Lady Aurora Abigial	Miss Fannie Reeves
Fairy Baneful	Miss Laura Phillips
Queen Serina	Miss M. Parker
Fairy Antidote	Miss Jean Crozier
" Dewdrop	Miss Minnie Nolan
" Gossamer	Miss Jennie Calef
" Choreamusica	Mlle. M. Palardis
" Elegantia	Miss Willis
" Rosebud	Miss Carrie Perkins
" Philomel	Miss Bradford
Nurse	Mr. J. Nolan

Lords, Ladies, Pages, Servants, Huntsmen, Woodcutters, Guards, etc., by a double quartette of male and female voices, and ladies and gentlemen of the company.

Also in conjunction with above and for its *first representation*, a NEW COMEDIETTA, entitled

HEARTS ARE TRUMPS !

by Messrs. T. R. Sullivan (adaptor of PAPA PERRICHON, INDIAN SUMMER, etc.,) and W. W. Chamberlin.

Dudley Markham	Mr. F. G. Cotter
Wilder Harebrain	Mr. E. A. McDowell
Joseph	Mr. W. Morris
Mrs. Wetherington	Miss Annie Clarke
May Deering	Miss Fannie Reeves

LAST WEEK of Mr. LAWRENCE BARRETT

MONDAY and TUESDAY EVENINGS, at 7 3-4, and WEDNESDAY AFTERNOON, at 2, APRIL 1, 2 and 3, 1878.

FIRST PRODUCTION IN BOSTON

AND ONLY PERFORMANCES OF

Mr. W. D. HOWELL'S New Play, published by J. R. Osgood & Co., and entitled a

COUNTERFEIT PRESENTMENT

WILLIAM BARTLETT, a painter	MR. LAWRENCE BARRETT
ARTHUR CUMMINGS, a Minister	MR. F. G. COTTER
GENERAL WYATT	MR. F. McCLANNIN
CONSTANCE WYATT, his daughter	MISS ANNIE CLARKE
MRS. GENERAL WYATT	MRS. J. R. VINCENT
MRS. RANSOM, a landlady	MISS LAURA PHILLIPS
MARY, a maid	MISS J. CROZIER

ACT 1st.—UP AT THE HILLS.   ACT 2d.—LIKE AND UNLIKE.
ACT 3d.—A LESSON IN PAINTING.   ACT 4th.—NOT AT ALL LIKE.

THE ORCHESTRA, under the direction of MR. E. N. CATLIN, will perform Varied and Brilliant Selections.

Wednesday Eve., at 7 3-4, by request,	**MONEY !**
EVELYN	MR. LAWRENCE BARRETT
Graves	Mr. Wm. Warren | Clara	Miss Annie Clarke

Thursday Eve., at 7 3-4, by request,	**MARBLE HEART !**
RAPHAEL	MR. BARRETT | MARCO	MISS Annie Clarke

Friday Eve., at 7 3-4, BENEFIT OF MR. WM. WARREN,	**POOR GENTLEMAN !**

MR. BARRETT as FREDERICK BRAMBLE	Mr. Warren as Dr. Ollopod
Mr. King as Stephen Harrowby	Mrs. Vincent as Lucretia McTab

All of whom appeared in the same parts upon the occasion of Mr. Barrett's first appearance at the Boston Museum, Aug., 1858.

Also, the Shakespearean Comedy,

KATHARINE AND PETRUCHIO !

Grumio	Mr. Wm. Warren
Petruchio	Mr. Chas. Barron | Katharine	Miss Annie Clarke

Saturday Afternoon at 2, the great double bill,

MERCHANT OF VENICE ! and DAVID GARRICK !

SHYLOCK	MR. BARRETT | DAVID GARRICK	MR. BARRETT
PORTIA	MISS ANNIE CLARKE	

Saturday Eve., April 6th, BENEFIT AND FAREWELL APPEARANCE OF MR. LAWRENCE BARRETT.

The Performance for this occasion only, commencing at 7 1-2 o'clock, with W. G. Wills' Powerful Drama

Harebell, or The Man o' Airlie !

In consequence of its very great success, with

MR. LAWRENCE BARRETT as	HAREBELL
Mr. Warren as Saunders | Miss Annie Clarke as Kate Steelman

Also, first time in many years of the Glorious Comedy of

THE INCONSTANT; or, Wine Works Wonders !

MR. LAWRENCE BARRETT as YOUNG MIRABLE \| Miss Annie Clarke as Oriana

---

THE COMPLETE PLAYS OF W. D. HOWELLS

THE COMPLETE PLAYS

OF

W. D. Howells

WALTER J. MESERVE

Associate Professor of English, University of Kansas

Under the General Editorship of

WILLIAM M. GIBSON and GEORGE ARMS

NEW YORK UNIVERSITY PRESS   1960

The editor wishes to thank the following editors, publishers, and executors of literary estates for permission to publish copyrighted material in THE COMPLETE PLAYS OF W. D. HOWELLS:

The Literary Estate of W. D. Howells, William White Howells literary executor, for HER OPINION OF HIS STORY, copyright 1907 by Harper & Brothers; SAVED: AN EMOTIONAL DRAMA, copyright 1908 by Harper & Brothers; A TRUE HERO, copyright 1909 by Harper & Brothers; THE MOTHER AND THE FATHER, copyright 1909 by Harper & Brothers, copyright 1937 by John Mead Howells and Mildred Howells; THE IMPOSSIBLE, copyright 1910 by Harper & Brothers; PARTING FRIENDS, copyright 1911 by Harper & Brothers, copyright 1939 by John Mead Howells and Mildred Howells; THE DAUGHTER OF THE STORAGE AND OTHER THINGS IN PROSE AND VERSE, copyright 1916 by Harper & Brothers, copyright 1944 by John Mead Howells and Mildred Howells.

Mildred Howells for permission to quote from LIFE IN LETTERS OF WILLIAM DEAN HOWELLS, copyright 1928 by Mildred Howells.

Harper & Brothers, Publishers, for permission to quote from MARK TWAIN'S LETTERS by Albert Bigelow Paine, copyright 1917, by Mark Twain Company, copyright 1945, by Clara Clemens Samossoud; MARK TWAIN, A BIOGRAPHY, Vol. II, arranged with comment by Albert Bigelow Paine, copyright 1912, by Harper & Brothers, copyright 1940, by Dora L. Paine.

The Trustees of the Mark Twain Estate for permission to reprint the introductory material to COLONEL SELLERS AS A SCIENTIST, copyright 1958 by the Mark Twain Company, as published in MODERN DRAMA, December, 1958.

A. C. Edwards, editor of MODERN DRAMA, for permission to reproduce " 'Colonel Sellers As A Scientist,' a Play by S. L. Clemens and W. D. Howells," copyright 1958 by A. C. Edwards.

TYPOGRAPHIC DESIGN BY JOSEPH FRANCIS WEILER

For

VIRGINIA HAYNES MESERVE

Publication of this work was made possible by a partial subsidy from THE FORD FOUNDATION, *to whom the publishers make grateful acknowledgment.*

Acknowledgments

THE EDITING of any particular work is seldom a task that is accomplished alone. There are always those "without whose assistance" there might have been vastly different results. My debts are numerous, and to all of those who helped me I am deeply grateful.

Without the kindness and co-operation of Mr. William White Howells, executor of the Howells Literary Estate, this work could never have been completed. Not only did he give graciously of his time and his knowledge, but in a realistic yet romantic fashion that would have interested his grandfather he discovered in an old metal box the manuscript plays PRISCILLA: A COMEDY and A FOREGONE CONCLUSION. I am also indebted to John Mead Howells and to Mildred Howells.

To the University of Kansas, through the particular interest of Dr. John H. Nelson, Dean of the Graduate School, I owe a great debt for generous financial support for research and secretarial assistance during the years that I have been working on this project. I am also grateful to the University of Kansas for a Watkins Fellowship which allowed me to spend the summer of 1957 on research into Howells' plays. For innumerable kindnesses and for advice whenever I requested it I wish to thank Dr. George R. Waggoner, Dean of the College of Liberal Arts and Sciences, Dr. Robert Vosper, Director of Libraries, Dr. Clyde K. Hyder, Professor of English, and Dr. Edward F. Grier, Associate Professor of English—all of the University of Kansas.

For permission to include heretofore unpublished manuscripts and materials owned by particular individuals or libraries, I am grateful to the following people: William A. Jackson of the Houghton Library, Harvard University, for the vast resources of the Howells Collection; Henry Nash Smith (acting on behalf of the Mark Twain Estate) of the University Library, University of California, for manuscript versions of COLONEL SELLERS AS A SCIENTIST; Robert F. Metzdorf, Curator of Manuscripts, Yale University Library, for a version of COLONEL SELLERS AS A SCIENTIST; Clifton Waller Barrett, an extremely generous collector of Americana, for a version of COLONEL SELLERS AS A SCIENTIST; Mrs. Florence Wickham Lueder, literary executrix of the Paul Kester Estate, for THE RISE OF SILAS LAPHAM; Mrs. Emily H. Drake, widow of Francis C. Drake, for the Drake letters; Robert W. Hill, Keeper of Manuscripts, and Rutherford D. Rogers, Chief of the Reference Department, New York Public Library, also for the Drake letters; Lloyd A. Avidson, Curator of the American Literature Collection, University Library, University of Southern California, for the fragment, A HAZARD OF NEW FORTUNES; Miss Georgie Henschel, daughter of Sir George Henschel, for a page from the musical score of A SEA CHANGE; O. D. Savage, for William Poel's version of A FOREGONE CONCLUSION; The Lord Chamberlain's Office, London, for YORICK'S LOVE; Mary R. Keating of the Theatre Collection, Houghton Library, Harvard University, for the Boston Museum Program of A COUNTERFEIT PRESENTMENT (see Frontispiece).

Numerous librarians have helped me in numerous ways—by supplying information, by locating material, by providing microfilms of material, or by allowing me to publish extracts from letters owned by their libraries. To the following librarians and libraries I wish to express my thanks: Alice H. Bonnell, Butler Library, Columbia University; Frieda Thies, University Library, Johns Hopkins University; Watt P. Marchman, Director of the Rutherford B. Hayes

Library, Fremont, Ohio; Alice P. Hook, Historical and Philosophical Society of Ohio, Library of the University of Cincinnati; David C. Mearns, Chief of the Manuscript Division, Library of Congress; Carolyn E. Jakeman, Houghton Library, Harvard University; Ruth A. Kerr, Watkinson Library, Trinity College, Hartford, Connecticut; Clifford K. Shipton, American Antiquarian Society, Worcester, Massachusetts; Mrs. Graham D. Wilcox, Stockbridge Library Museum, Stockbridge, Massachusetts; Alexander Clark, Princeton University Library; Joyce McLeod, Watson Library, University of Kansas; Ethel J. McDowell, Ashtabula Public Library, Ohio; Zoltan Haraszti, Boston Public Library, Boston; Donald Gallup, Yale University Library; Herbert F. Smith, Library of Rutgers University; The Librarian, Huntington Library; Neda M. Westlake, Library of the University of Pennsylvania; Giles E. Dawson, Folger Shakespeare Library; H. G. Tupper, Brotherton Library, University of Leeds, England; M. St. Clare Byrne, Society for Theatre Research, London, England; G. W. Nash, Enthoven Theater Collection, Victoria & Albert Museum, London, England.

One's obligations to individuals can never really be tallied. I am indebted to Jerome W. Saphirstein, Manager of the Oceanside Hotel, Magnolia, Massachusetts, for a description of his hotel grounds as they compared with the scene in AN INDIAN GIVER; to James C. Davis of R. H. Stearns Company of Boston, for the location of that store at the time THE ALBANY DEPOT was written; to Henry F. Thoma of Houghton Mifflin Company, for the history of that publishing company. Napier Wilt of the University of Chicago gave me material from his files on American drama. John Reeves of Skidmore College constantly shared with me the pertinent results of his own research on Howells. As a group those scholars interested in W. D. Howells who feel a bond in THE HOWELLS SENTINEL have provided an invaluable sounding board for ideas concerning Howells. I should like to express my gratitude, in particular, to Clara M. and Rudolf Kirk, James Woodress, Edwin Cady, Louis Budd, and James Stronks.

To the general editors of this work, George Arms and William M. Gibson, I owe my greatest debt. Their innumerable helpful suggestions and criticisms of my work were, to me, a happy combination of their wisdom in scholarship and their patience with me.

In the years during which this book was being prepared I had the secretarial and research assistance of several students at the University of Kansas. To all of them I am grateful, and in particular I wish to thank Mary Emily Parsons Edwards, Karen Amell Linton and Joy Yeo Kitterman.

W.J.M.

Contents

ILLUSTRATIONS

Introduction

THE COMPLETE PLAYS OF W. D. HOWELLS

Introduction

As HE WROTE in his autobiography, W. D. Howells could scarcely remember when he was not interested in the theater. Plays had always fascinated him—reading them or seeing them performed—and during his youth he seldom missed the playgoing opportunities offered by the agents of the traveling theater companies who frequently paid his father for their newspaper advertisements and their handbills with free passes to their plays. According to his brother Joseph (Waldon Fawcett, "Mr. Howells and His Brother," *Critic* XXXV, November, 1899, [O.S.], 1027), Howells had written five plays by the time he was thirteen, one of which was a tragedy in rhyme, imitative of *The Lady of the Lake* (Howells, *A Boy's Town*, p. 63). At Dayton, Ohio, Howells got one of his early views of American drama, *A Glance at New York*, by B. A. Baker, a play which he disliked. While he was at Columbus as a correspondent for the Cincinnati *Gazette*, one of his few joys was the theater, an interest he shared with his fellow editor, Samuel R. Reed. This early attraction to the theater never left Howells; it grew slowly but steadily. Possibly some of the unsigned dialogues published in the Ashtabula *Sentinel*, such as "Busily Engaged. A Plot for a Farce" (October 3, 10, 1866) and "Why He Married" (October 31, 1866), were written by Howells. But it was not until 1874, when he was thirty-seven, that he made his first contribution to the theater.

Later to an old man writing of his youth, the years seemed to have gone remarkably fast. But he had accomplished a great deal: he had become one of the outstanding novelists of his century, and he had long been considered America's foremost critic. Advocating a truthful treatment of material, he championed and wrote works characterized by attention to everyday experiences seen in a perspective not easily mastered by a generation whose view of art was falsified by sentimentality. And partially satisfying the ambition of his youth, he had become a playwright of some reputation. It is true that his successes in the theater were few and that he had definite limitations as a dramatist; yet, as a part of his artistic contribution and in relation to the rest of American drama, his plays become significant in the rise of realism in the United States and in the development of American social comedy. However, this is a point of view of which Howells might not have been aware. Although during his lifetime his plays enjoyed a sympathetic audience, they were never justly appreciated by the critics. Friends such as Booth Tarkington told how Howells' plays "began to be acted everywhere within a week or two of their publication, and a college boy of the late eighties and 'golden nineties' came home at Christmas to be either in the audience at a Howells farce or in the cast that gave it" ("Mr. Howells," *Harper's Monthly*, CXLI [August, 1920], 348). Howells himself explained in *The House of Harper* (p. 320) that his dramas had made him "a very amiable public there with the youth who played in drawing-rooms and church parlors; they never got upon the stage though they were represented over the Union in private theatricals." In fact, the average person enjoyed these amusing little plays; but they held little attraction for theater managers, and since Howells' death they have slipped further and further away from critics and managers as well as audiences.

One could list many reasons why Howells' plays were not more widely accepted in the theater. But perhaps most important, he wrote mainly one-act plays, and as Augustin Daly told Howells in a letter (January 11, 1893, Harvard Library), ". . . one act pieces bring no profit & very little lasting reputation to authors, actors or managers." The theater managers wanted full-length plays and exciting, violent, passionate action. They wanted something compelling, something dramatic, or if not dramatic, at least theatrical. Joseph Jefferson made a significant observation when he criticized one of Howells' plays because it lacked the strong action the audience wanted (letter to Howells, January 22, 1880, Harvard Library).

One of the reasons why Howells was not more successful on the stage—his choice of scene, characters, and action—is the same reason why many of his plays are pleasant reading today. He wrote mainly of a Boston Back Bay aristocracy, a society which also formed a meaningful background for his ideas. There were the Robertses and the Campbells and Mr. and Mrs. Fountain (*The Night Before Christmas* and *The Impossible*), all members in good standing of this society. Other characters indicated their comparable social level by their manners and actions: they had summer residences (*A Previous Engagement, An Indian Giver*); they took trips abroad (*Parting Friends*); they gave afternoon receptions (*Bride Roses*); or they showed a particular sense of propriety (*Self-Sacrifice: A Farce Tragedy*). Against this social background Howells sometimes placed people from lower social levels, such as the Irishman McIlheny in *The Albany Depot*, the Maine girl in *The Smoking Car*, the tramps in *Out of the Question*, and the fellow passengers of *The Sleeping Car*. Another group of common but thoroughly respectable people hovered socially just below the Robertses and the Campbells. One sees them in *The Parlor Car* and *The Register* and perhaps at their worst in *Room Forty-Five*. Of all Howells' published plays there are only two—*A True Hero: Melodrama* and *Saved, An Emotional Drama*—that seem to utilize no particular social background, although even in these two satires on melodrama the general moral sense of Howells' society pervades.

Against this well-established social background Howells frequently gave his audience farce action with scarcely a serious thought in plays such as *The Sleeping Car, The Elevator,* and *The Smoking Car*. Because of this social atmosphere, however, more than a third of his published plays contain in both idea and execution some of the characteristics of social comedy. One often-repeated social-comedy theme is the ever-present struggle between man and woman. In these plays the initiating situations vary, but the result is always the same: The woman wins. With the exception of Willis Campbell and Dr. Lawton of the Roberts-Campbell plays, Howells' men generally lack those qualities which would make them even capable contenders in this universal struggle; and sometimes even Campbell and Lawton find themselves totally inadequate in coping with woman and her logic (*The Unexpected Guests*). *The Mouse Trap* and *A Likely Story* clearly show that there is no question concerning the superiority of women. In plays that do not feature the Robertses and the Campbells, Howells, in a kind of habitual behavior, treats this conflict between the sexes in a plot involving an engagement which is either being made for the first time or being remade after some confusion. No less than seven plays—*The Register, An Indian*

Giver, A Previous Engagement, Her Opinion of His Story, The Parlor Car, Parting Friends, Self-Sacrifice: A Farce Tragedy—have remarkably similar plots. In each instance the women are, in various degrees, charming and shrewd but always intelligent in knowing how to control men. These women may hate each other—and Howells seems to feel that women traditionally and instinctively dislike each other—but they understand men, at least Howells' men, and have few problems with them. The men, on the other hand, try to seem completely understanding when actually they understand nothing. Usually they are marked by a single-minded persistence which does not always do credit to their intelligence and by a blind devotion which romantic women admire.

In such plays Howells shows that the struggle of young love—much more complicated in women than in men—follows a definite pattern: The woman must know that the man loves her; then she must convince herself according to the rules of logic given only to women that she is in love with him. At least three plays evolve around the woman's ability to hold her young man secure while she persuades herself that he is the one. In *Self-Sacrifice: A Farce Tragedy* everyone knows that the heroine loves the man; nevertheless, she must go through a period of self-analysis and self-experimentation to prove this point to herself. Sometimes, as in *An Indian Giver*, she finds out very soon that she loves the man and has to use all her wiles to keep him from another woman. In *A Previous Engagement* the girl allows herself the pleasure of playing with her emotions for almost the entire drama. But the ending is always the same. It is perhaps romantic, but it is nonetheless truthful, and Howells' understanding of women is never so apparent as in these plays.

Through characters, social background, a concern for truth and realism, and some repeated themes, Howells' plays manifest a certain similarity, but it would be inaccurate to suggest anything like a unifying thematic structure running through his work. In most of his plays his major objective was obviously enjoyment—good fun; and while he attained this generally by poking fun at aspects of society, his method was chiefly farce. Techniques of humor in Howells' plays, therefore, assume some importance. Actually he shows no great originality, but his variety is interesting. The situation, of course, is an obvious technique: two doctors arrive simultaneously at a house and must be kept apart; a man knocks down a friend and takes his watch under the impression that he is recovering his own watch from a thief; a man cannot find his dress suit; a woman is afraid of a mouse. But without the farce intriguer the situation could not be effectively sustained; consequently Howells created Willis Campbell, an extremely clever character in that role. As one would expect in a farce, there is much physical humor, most noticeable in such plays as *Room Forty-Five* and *Evening Dress*. There is also a kind of vaudevillian humor of repetition in *The Elevator*, an obvious burlesque exaggeration of serious thought in *The Smoking Car*, an entertaining and humorous description in *Room Forty-Five*, and the humor of the ridiculous in most of the farce predicaments. Other techniques include understatement, overstatement, inconsistent behavior, minstrel-show humor, puns and other plays on words, gross exaggeration and even lies, gross stupidity, humor built around foreign character traits, and so on. Wit, too, has a prominent place in these plays. Howells wrote brilliant conversations, far more witty and clever than anything being written in American drama of his time. The dialogue of *Five O'clock Tea* is perhaps the most frequently quoted example, but the fast repartee in *A Letter of Introduction* is worthy of note, as well as the conversation in *The Garroters* and *The Unexpected Guests*. In such instances the dialogue raises the play above the limitations of farce and creates social comedy—a witty portrayal of a fashionable society.

Enhancing the wit of the plays and adding to the characteristics of social comedy is Howells' use of satire—essentially a means for producing enjoyment but frequently having serious implications. With a certain mischievousness, Howells satirized particularly the Boston woman of fashion. No doubt he admired the ladies and enjoyed their company, but one feels that he would not have appreciated them half so much if they had been as logical and consistent as men think they would like them to be. Plays such as *A Letter of Introduction*, probably his most successful satire, indicate the great pleasure he took in pointing out the ridiculous attitudes and foibles of society and the socially-acceptable person. In this play he manages to ridicule Englishmen, New Yorkers, American language and culture, critics, American artists, Boston snobbery, and the cultivated Bostonian family. Two of his plays are satiric in theme: *A True Hero: Melodrama* satirizes the traditional melodramatic hero, and *Saved, An Emotional Drama* satirizes the entire range of melodramatic techniques. More significant, however, are the two plays featuring Mr. and Mrs. Fountain, *The Night Before Christmas* and *The Impossible*. They not only contain bitter ironies concerning society and man—in contrast perhaps to the pathetic irony in *Bride Roses*—but also question meaning in society and ponder man's serious inadequacies.

Complementary to Howells' concern for social comedy is his interest in realism—his attention to details in dialogue and his numerous references to contemporary events and real persons; when new inventions appeared, such as the elevator, the phonograph, the telephone, the air brake, the Miller platform for railroad cars, and the motorcar, he frequently employed them in a farce. Often he mentioned contemporary artists and writers such as Bill Nye, Josh Billings, William Cullen Bryant, William Mallock, Sir Lawrence Alma-Tadema, Claude Monet, and Jean Baptiste Corot. If a popular topic of conversation or a particular current event took his fancy, the chances were it would appear in a play—for example, the fight between John L. Sullivan and Jake Kilrain, woman suffrage, the painting from the Casa d' Adonide Ferito in Pompeii, the District Messenger Service, the cholera epidemic in New York in 1893, Boston institutions such as the Provident Woodyard and the Boston Art Club, interest in Mars, and concern for psychical research. Language, too, was important in Howells' realism, and his actors' speeches are filled with commonplace phrases and the overused expressions of average conversation. The fact that several of the play situations come from his own or other people's experiences is further evidence of his concern for realism. In general, Howells' respect for minutiae of fact is considerable. For example, the Robertses and the Campbells had a train to catch in *The Albany Depot*, and the Boston-and-Albany train schedule of that time indicates that they took the right one. There was a difference in Howells' day between the operation of the steam elevator and the hydraulic elevator, and Howells makes central use of this difference in *The Elevator*. As in his fiction, then, Howells' use of realistic detail was a much-studied aspect of his art.

More important than these details in Howells' art, however, are the truthfulness and the moral value that accompanied his concern for reality. Observation is important, but art requires selection and imagination. In one Howells play a girl snaps her earring in place and then shakes her head slightly to assure herself that the jewelry is secure; in another, a woman will not allow the doctor to come to the sickbed until she makes her ailing child presentable and combs her own hair. The realistic details are surely effective, but to become art, to become nature with her capital N on, as Howells once described realism in *Criticism and Fiction,* the realism must be seen, as it is in these instances, through the creative imagination of the writer. There can be no question that a realistic but humorous view of life was Howells' main objective, although he was not consistently successful in achieving his goal. But his secondary purpose was to bring to his audience a greater understanding of life. Consequently, in a number of his plays, Howells directly posed a problem of real life in which truthfulness became either a central or an important contributory issue. *A True Hero: Melodrama,* for example, attempts to suggest a way in which man may equate truth and reality in life. Here truth is much more than a romantic, idealized concept; it is the function of Dr. Tolboy in this play to show the young hero that if twisted values and naïveté prompt one to lie in the name of truth, it will be morally impossible for him to be true to himself. The plot of another play, *The Unexpected Guests,* centers about the problem of the socially convenient lie, which in this instance is ineffective. Truth is all that remains at the climax of the play, and it is with truth that Mrs. Campbell has to deal, painful as this is to the people accustomed to the social code.

A large number of other plays make less extensive, but no less pointed, use of questions of truth and morality. In *The Albany Depot,* Willis Campbell tries to explain that one must sometimes give the truth a "slight twist in the right direction," resulting in the ideal truth rather than the real truth, but Howells is quick to show that the ideal truth is never adequate and that, as in this play, one is soon left with only the "bare truth." The confusion with which society sees truth is illustrated clearly in *Evening Dress.* One simply cannot tell the real truth in society and be acceptable; in fact, as the servant girl shows, a forthright lie is sometimes the most proper action. In this and other Howells plays—*A Likely Story, The Garroters, A Letter of Introduction, A Masterpiece of Diplomacy, Room Forty-Five,* and *An Indian Giver*—one is constantly impressed with the manner in which conventional society interprets truth. Yet Howells never lets the final curtain fall without assuring his audience that this society's concept of truth, though proper, is clearly false; it is a mark of their social maturity as well as an indication of their morality in the "larger sense" that certain of Howells' characters act to meet the real truth.

Perhaps more widely than in his other literary works, Howells' plays present a personal philosophy and an attitude toward social life. He was a man who liked to laugh, and he made fun an objective of his dramas. He was a man who held a thoughtful literary creed, and his best plays, sketches though they may be, suggest his basic critical theories. He was a man not always happy with the life that he saw around him, and in his plays, as well as in his fiction, he commented on human society as he saw it—superficial, proper, ridiculous, or truthful. Much of the time in his dramas he was playful, but he was also capable of great seriousness. There are, for example, few places in his writings where he talks about death and the mystery of what lies beyond with more beauty and feeling than in *The Mother and the Father. Bride Roses,* too, has a serious theme, as well as the two plays built around Mr. and Mrs. Fountain.

Although it is difficult to generalize about Howells' development as a dramatist, his humorous and serious plays divide quite clearly into two periods of his life. It is a fact, for example, that the twelve Roberts-Campbell comedies—all but two written in the 1880's—are his most humorous and stageworthy plays. After A *Masterpiece of Diplomacy* in 1893, Howells returned to his Robertses and Campbells only in *The Smoking Car*, a most inadequate play. His first original play with a serious theme, *Bride Roses*, was published (and probably written) in 1893. Thereafter he wrote thirteen short plays (counting the three parts of *The Mother and the Father*), of which seven have serious themes. Considering, then, some of the events of his own life during the half-dozen years surrounding 1890, one may draw certain conclusions about Howells' playwriting. The Robertses and the Campbells served him mainly as vehicles for fun and satire, and with them he reached his highest point as a dramatist in the theater. When life became more complicated, personally and philosophically, he abandoned these characters as such (although in essence the character types remained with him) and tried to express his ideas in another framework. The drama always remained a challenge to his creativity and an outlet for his realistic creed, but the late plays are much less consciously an attempt to appeal to the requirements of the stage and reflect more fully Howells' mature thought.

Perhaps the best way to understand Howells' entire dramatic production is first to set apart those dozen early one-act plays involving the same people. Certainly the best-known of Howells' dramas, these plays mainly explore some of the social emergencies suffered by Mr. and Mrs. Edward Roberts and Mr. and Mrs. Willis Campbell. But the plays do more than this: They form a rough chronological sketch covering a number of years in the lives of a group of socially conscious people. What may be called a twelve-act play, then, starts with Mrs. Roberts as she returns to her home in Boston on *The Sleeping Car* with her baby and her Aunt Mary, whom she has just visited in Albany. It is Christmas time, a time doubly meaningful that year because Mrs. Roberts' brother, Willis Campbell, is returning to Boston from California where he has lived for a number of years. Two Christmases later the Robertses entertain their friends at a dinner, and through an elevator mishap the reader is introduced to the people who belong to the Roberts-Campbell social group. By this time Willis is settled in Boston, and Aunt Mary has become a favorite of the Roberts children, the boy of *The Sleeping Car* and his baby sister. The following year Mrs. Roberts again invites her friends for Christmas dinner, and all are shocked and entertained by Roberts' garroting of old Mr. Bemis. Some of the group, the Millers and the Curwens, are unable to attend this dinner, but those present are more closely allied in their interests because Dr. Lawton's daughter Lou has recently married Mr. Bemis' son Alfred. (Although the publishing continuity of the plays was disturbed when *The Mouse Trap* appeared next before *Five O'clock Tea*, Howells explained his chronology in a footnote.) The next three plays follow the activities of Willis, first, as he becomes engaged to the young widow, Amy Somers, who has by *Five O'clock Tea* waited the proper period of time since the death of her husband; then, as he flirts with Amy's ire and adoration in *The Mouse Trap*; and finally, as he becomes involved in the problems of being a husband in A *Likely Story*. But Howells does not forget Mr. and Mrs. Roberts or the fact that their children are growing up as Roberts grows more absent-minded. He does, however, call the older Roberts child Jim in *The Unexpected Guests* and Bobby in A *Masterpiece of Diplomacy*. Although the same people appear throughout the plays at Howells' pleasure, different characters are emphasized with some effect on the value of the play. When the women are prominent, particularly Mrs. Campbell, the play, whether it is *Five O'clock Tea* or *The Unexpected Guests*, is much better as social comedy than those, such as *The Albany Depot, Evening Dress*, and *The Smoking Car*, in which the men assume primary roles.

As a group these plays are interesting because Howells obviously enjoyed these characters as he did the Marches in his novels and with them created his most effective satires and social comedies. It might be argued that the continuity of characterization carried through the several plays should provide some advantage in the portrayal of these people, but the advantage is slight because there is such disparity in the dramatic value of these sketches. Some are good comedies, and the characters are believable, interesting, and human, with likes and dislikes and various minor problems and quarrels. Dr. Lawton is a delightful talker, and Willis can be a charmer as well as a schemer. Other plays of the group are farces, and the characters are simple and one dimensional: Campbell, intriguer; Roberts, absent-minded foil to Campbell's wit; Mrs. Roberts, hysterical woman; Mrs. Campbell, semihysterical woman. Other characters in the plays vary from strong individuals to farce types. Although this group of people appears only in a dozen plays, Howells sometimes uses these character types in his other dramatic works. The personality of Dr. Lawton as wit and philosopher, for example, reappears as Grinnidge in *The Register*, as Mrs. Winton in *A Previous Engagement*, and as Dr. Tolboy in *A True Hero: Melo-drama*. Mr. and Mrs. Fountain are Mr. and Mrs. Campbell grown older. In contrast to the Roberts-Campbell entourage are those character types that do not appear in this series of plays. For example, with the exception of the minor plot in *A Likely Story*, there are no young lovers—Lou Lawton and Alfred Bemis are very inadequate and minor characters—yet of the remaining one-act plays, seven employ young love as a central theme. A major portion of Howells' dramatic output, the Roberts-Campbell plays show a mature, somewhat sophisticated, convention-bound society, where tradition has replaced thought, and action and words have become nearly equal in importance. In imagining such a group of people, Howells presents not only a truthful and charming scene but also a natural target for his satirical and humorous thrusts in the awkward situations which this society must produce.

In his "Letter to the Publisher" introducing *Minor Dramas*, Howells admitted that several of his plots and situations came from his own and his friends' experiences. It is not strange, then, that some of the people in his plays were also modeled from real life. Dr. Lawton, for example, might well have been created from certain traits of Dr. Oliver Wendell Holmes; they shared the same medical theories and enjoyed a similar capacity for wisdom and wit. Willis Campbell, as an adopted son of California, endowed with a lively sense of humor, a sharp wit, a taste for jokes, and a gift for dramatizing a situation, must certainly have been modeled on Mark Twain, with occasional touches from Bret Harte. The Robertses, particularly Mr. Roberts, seem a burlesque upon Howells himself and Elinor, his wife. Roberts is a writer, and there the comparison ends, but Howells exaggerates and Roberts becomes the conventional absent-minded intellectual with a quite unworldly view of life. Perhaps Howells, who was a short man, thought of himself when he made Walter Ashley of *Self-Sacrifice: A Farce Tragedy* a head shorter than the girl, and Camp in *A Previous Engagement* "not very tall." As a man who once studied law briefly because of the opportunities it offered, Howells chose law for a number of his young men:

Ashley and Camp, Grinnidge in *The Register*, and Holyford in *Her Opinion of His Story*. Even Campbell was a lawyer, although his profession has significance only in *The Mouse Trap*. All of this must remain only speculative, but one could probably draw more comparisons if one had more knowledge of Howells' immediate social group.

Along with his situations and characters Howells frequently took his scenes from his own surroundings. One interesting note on *An Indian Giver* concerns its setting. According to the records of the Oceanside Hotel, Magnolia, Massachusetts (courtesy of Jerome W. Saphirstein, present manager of the Oceanside Hotel), Howells was a guest there from August 24 through September 19, 1893, and from August 1 through September 5, 1894. Even today the landscape around the Oceanside Hotel is accurately described by Howells' introductory scene in *An Indian Giver*. For the Ponkwasset setting of *Out of the Question* and *A Counterfeit Presentment*, Howells probably chose either Mount Wachusett near Princeton, Massachusetts, or Mount Monadnock near Jaffrey, New Hampshire. Both areas are noted for their beautiful scenery and have lakes near the mountains. In the 1870's, when Howells perhaps visited these mountain scenes, there were summer hotels nearby that catered to writers and artists.

But the locale of Howells' plays is less significant than the social event or situation around which they are built. In the Roberts-Campbell plays, where the social background vitally affects both action and meaning, Howells chose social occasions which would give him the greatest opportunity to exploit through wit and satire the peculiarities of his society. One such occasion which he used several times in his novels as well as his plays was the formal dinner, which gathered people together and involved a maximum number of social conventions. At other times the event might be an afternoon tea, a garden party, a musicale, or a social visit. When such formality was not necessary to the temper of his play, Howells concerned himself with more modest situations. His people were real people who stayed in hotels, bought flowers, occasionally had to hire a cook, wrote letters of introduction, bemoaned the Christmas rush, perhaps took a train ride to a nearby city, and even had children whose unwise appetites warranted calling the doctor. This was all part of the everyday world of society, both at its back door and its front door, which Howells worked to make dramatic.

Whether the Roberts-Campbell plays and the other one-act dramas should be called farces or comedies is a difficult question. Howells subtitled most of them farces, but such able critics of the drama as G. B. Shaw, William Archer, Henry Arthur Jones, James A. Herne, and William Winter have found in some of his plays the essential characteristics of social comedy. On the other hand, Augustin Daly, Daniel Frohman, and Augustus Thomas spoke of Howells' plays mainly in terms of farce. Perhaps the wisest judgment, then, is that Howells wrote both types successfully: He could write effective farce, yet some of his plays also figure prominently in the rise of American social comedy.

Howells' longer published plays include two comedies, an operetta, a translation, and a series of dramatic dialogues. The translation, *Samson*, was a fortunate beginning for Howells because, although it was no more than a good translation, its success on the stage brought Howells to the attention of the theater people. Mark Twain immediately wrote to Augustin Daly of Howells' interest in the drama. James T. Fields introduced him to Lawrence Barrett, saying that he expected Howells to write a play (letter from Fields to Howells, June 8, 1875, Harvard Library). It was a good beginning, and it must have given

Howells confidence, for with only a pause to write *The Parlor Car*, he produced two long comedies, *Out of the Question* and *A Counterfeit Presentment*. The first is closet drama— a "middle form" between narrative and drama, Howells suggested—concerned with a problem of propriety: What constitutes a gentleman? This was a significant question for many Americans of that day, and Howells debated it effectively on different social levels. Many of his comments on Boston society and its mores clearly reveal his acute powers of observation, as well as the high degree of critical insight required of the social comedy dramatist, but he seemed unable to raise his material from simple argument to drama.

With *A Counterfeit Presentment* Howells began to write for Lawrence Barrett, an actor of the period, who during the next three or four years became a partial collaborator with Howells. It was an intense and sometimes grueling initiation into the theater for Howells, who learned a great deal from Barrett while earning more money as a result of Barrett's acting than he ever again received for his playwriting. Barrett's influence, however, marked by his acting in the theatrical traditions of his time, was not the kind to bring out the best in Howells, as *A Counterfeit Presentment* and *Yorick's Love* obviously show. Today *A Counterfeit Presentment* remains interesting primarily for Howells' social comments and for his scene introductions, a part of the literature of the play, in which Howells considered himself a pioneer and which foreshadowed the narrative comments of Shaw and Sir James M. Barrie. The remaining two full-length published plays represent, in one sense, extremes in Howells' writing. *A Sea Change*, Howells' comic operetta, features his enjoyment of low comedy and farce framed in an expansive plot sequence and embellished more by the ridiculous than the lyrical. In the manner of Gilbert and Sullivan, it is sufficiently imaginative and amusing in its scenes and ideas so that, properly adapted, the operetta might make a first-rate musical extravaganza even now. *The Mother and the Father*, on the other hand, is perhaps the most poignantly worded of Howells' expressed attitudes toward death and the power of love. It is dialogue rather than drama, but it contains more dramatic tension and force than many of his plays.

Howells' unpublished plays present a new view of him, as he tried seriously but with little success to reach the stage with a full-length play. *Samson* had been mildly successful. *A Counterfeit Presentment*, after being produced "some thirty times," had been dropped by Barrett; however, the actor still remained anxious for a Howells play, and in the fall of 1878 he was ready to tour with Howells' adaptation of Tamayo y Baus's *Un Drama Neuvo*. Within the next seven years Howells completed three more full-length plays: *Priscilla: A Comedy, Colonel Sellers as a Scientist* (in collaboration with Mark Twain), and *A Foregone Conclusion*, which he revised from William Poel's dramatization of his novel. There is strong evidence that he also worked on other plays during this time, if he did not actually complete them. On August 8, 1880 (Harvard Library), Howells wrote to his father that he was translating another play for Barrett, and later, in a note to C. E. Norton (August 29, 1880, Harvard Library), he wrote, "I've finished the Italian play I was translating." What became of this play, no one seems to know. Nor is there any trace of a Spanish play also adapted for Barrett, to whom Howells wrote (November 23, 1883, Princeton University Library): "I send you an outline of the new Spanish play, hastily and imperfectly done. The poetic beauty of the drama is very great, and Raimundo's is a noble part." This might have been another Tamayo y Baus play called *Juana de Arco*,

1847, but conclusive evidence is lacking. Barrett was not the only one interested in Howells' work. Augustin Daly made Howells an offer to which he responded (March 19, 1884, Harvard Library): "I will nationalize that German comedy for $2000 cash on delivery, if it is to appear without my name. If you want my name with yours you must pay me more." But here the matter was evidently left. The only thing certain is that Barrett's success with *Yorick's Love* spurred Howells on to make a decidedly more concentrated effort in the drama than previous historians of the drama or critics of Howells have known. Later, with the poor reception of *A Foregone Conclusion* and all the production problems of *Colonel Sellers as a Scientist*, Howells retired from the competition of the full-length drama and continued to write only one-act comedies and farces. He would probably have been content to do this for the rest of his life had he not become interested in the efforts of James A. Herne to do for the drama what he had been trying to do for fiction, and had he not been asked by Herne to dramatize *The Rise of Silas Lapham*. By this time, ten years had passed since his unpleasant experiences with the theater, and with Paul Kester he began the dramatization enthusiastically. Then he was confronted with an old problem: No producer would take his play and Herne lost interest. When a year later at the request of Francis Drake to dramatize *The Rise of Silas Lapham* he suggested they work on *A Hazard of New Fortunes*, one may surmise that he had no great illusions about the future of their adaptation.

For a well-known editor and novelist in the 1870's, 80's, and 90's to be a successful dramatist as well would have been a tremendous accomplishment. The list of those who tried and failed is long: Henry James, Mark Twain, Bret Harte, Hamlin Garland, Joseph Kirkland, Joaquin Miller, Thomas Bailey Aldrich, and others. But the attraction of the stage was almost irresistible, and the monetary rewards were high. Howells knew all this. Although he made only about $750 during the season that Barrett played *A Counterfeit Presentment*, *Yorick's Love* must have earned him several times that amount. But this was only a taste, a paltry amount compared to what could be made. Mark Twain averaged a thousand dollars a week with John T. Raymond's version of *The Gilded Age*, and Howells was anxious to make a lot of money. Perhaps if he had chosen his collaborators more wisely, he might have achieved his objective. If he had worked with Augustin Daly, for example, he might have written a successful play, but then again it might have been another of the dramatic caliber of *Yorick's Love*. At one time James A. Herne, who felt that Howells wrote the "most charming comedies" he had ever read (letter to Howells, June 1, 1890, Harvard Library), wanted to collaborate on a comedy. "A comedy in connection with a play like M[argaret] F[leming] will be a great power," he wrote to Howells (July 13 [?], Harvard Library); "it will add strength to both." Perhaps again Howells might have reached success, but the point is doubtful. In these longer, serious plays Howells refused to write what the theater demanded, and the drama he offered was neither copied after the best models nor made effective by the dramatic methods he chose. Hence the dramatization of *The Rise of Silas Lapham* failed; *A Foregone Conclusion* was generally inadequate, and reactions from the clergy might have added to its difficulties with playgoers; and *Priscilla: A Comedy* was never produced.

The Mark Twain-Howells collaboration, *Colonel Sellers as a Scientist*, however, was entirely different. It was an exciting adventure for the two friends, who thought of their labor of love and enjoyment primarily in terms of a theatrical and financial success. As a play it may lack dramatic and artistic effectiveness, but it boasts episodes of hilarious humor. Flinging all dramatic theory to the winds and indulging themselves extravagantly, the two writers produced a play which is quite impossible for the stage but very pleasant reading. The only other of his longer plays in which Howells put aside his creed was *Yorick's Love,* adapted with the help of Lawrence Barrett. The result is a play which is extremely difficult to read but which was highly regarded by literary men and theatergoers who retained a taste for high-flown rhetoric and sentiment in a rather unusual plot. Just as he dismissed the sentimental in fiction, Howells generally avoided the poor dramatic conventions of nineteenth-century American drama, but when he did submit to these conventions, as in *Yorick's Love,* he showed an inability to handle them effectively. It is a strange combination of the old and the new in the American theater that Howells' dramas, both one-act and full-length, provide. His best one-act plays show the new drama in the rise of realism and the development of social comedy; on the other hand, *Yorick's Love,* his greatest stage success, is a feeble and late remnant of the extravagant poetic drama that reached its height in mid-nineteenth-century America.

Among Howells' unpublished manuscripts there is further evidence of his interest in the drama—a sketch of a court-martial scene, an outline of a play, and the beginning of a masque. These are, of course, only fragments, perhaps deserving no more than passing comment. The masque exists (Harvard Library) only in a single sheet in Howells' handwriting, without title or comment. On the typed copy of this sheet is penciled, presumably by Mildred Howells, the remark: "Masque of Diseases by Edmund Gosse and W. D. Howells." It would seem to be the introduction for a traditional masque, and it is unfortunate that the two writers went no further with their project and that neither Philip Gosse, son of Edmund Gosse, nor the Howells family has any further information concerning the writers' intention regarding it.

Jocund Palsy led the train,
Pouring o'er the enameled plain,
Where beneath the purling brook,
The joyous nymphs of Ague shook,
Ague, ever fair and young,
Purple-lipt and wan of cheek,
High above the others sung,
And calm Delirium meek
Afar her sweetness flung,
Where dewy eyed Malaria came,
And Fever, winged with flame.

II

Tricksy, blithe Obesity,
Rheumatism, footing free
Through the dance where Bright's disease,
Formed to flatter and to please
Moves like some melodious star
That in creation's morning sang
Ere human stomachs felt a pang.

Another manuscript of four sheets in the Harvard Library indicating Howells' concern for dramatic possibilities in material is a brief outline of a scene labeled only "Court Martial at Fort P. Jan. 26." As an observer, Howells describes in fragmentary prose the courtroom, the officers and the judge advocate, the prisoners and the witnesses, and the atmosphere of the trial, as it is conducted. The trial concerns a soldier who, when ordered to shovel snow by an offensive sergeant, answered: "I want you to distinctly understand that you are speaking to a man and not to a damned dog." It is further brought out at the trial that the soldier had been up two nights in a row and had just returned at 5 A.M. from a dance at which he had drunk "several beers." The evidence presented and the witnesses examined, the court dismisses the prisoner and the witnesses, but Howells admits that "I could not tell which side Court leaned to." The final sentence of the court also disturbs him: "Take him out and reason with him, serg't. Give him a damned good thrashing." Consistent with his concern for truth, Howells stresses at two points in his précis that it was the business of the judge advocate not to convict but to find the truth. The last comment of this fragment, however, suggestive of a melodramatic stage direction, presents another aspect of Howells' playwriting. "Snowing without; drifting. Cruel sounding calls in hall across court." The whole episode is extremely fragmentary in both expression and continuity, but it is clear that Howells thought of it as action to be dramatized rather than narrated.

The third fragment (Harvard Library) is an unfinished outline of a three-act comedy called *Conley's Uncle*, which Howells once sent to Henry Alden of Harper's staff. It is a confused and sketchy outline indicating little originality in idea or plot, and Alden, who was frank in his criticism of Howells' contributions, probably rejected it immediately. Briefly, the play concerns a rich old man living in California, loved and respected for his public spirit and private generosity. The great cross that he has to bear is a nephew who wants to be a painter and whose studies in Paris the old man has been supporting. As the play opens, the nephew, Conley, returns to New York, where he becomes prosperous and enters society. Soon he becomes engaged to a "rich and lovely girl," after which he goes to California with the brother of his betrothed to visit his uncle, who has never been able to rid himself of the idea that Conley is a "poor devil of a painter, next to a beggar." As a joke, the two young friends arrange to deceive the uncle when he comes East to visit them. In New York (Act II), the uncle finds Conley and his friend in dire poverty and offers to save him and support him if he will give up his painting. But when Conley tells him that he makes enough through his pictures, the old man's sense of family pride becomes confused with suspicions regarding his nephew. Although Howells does not elaborate his few comments on this act, there is the implication that a kind old man in New York being deceived by his prosperous nephew would occasion many comic situations. In Act III Conley has become sorry for his deceptions and tries to raise himself in his uncle's esteem, but the old man is now extremely suspicious. When he catches Conley kissing the girl to whom he is engaged, he sees Conley as a "scoundrel who is guilty of the basest treachery" in betraying a heart of innocence. Presumably, before the final curtain and by some contrivance, the uncle would discover his error and forgive his nephew. A marriage would then take place and all would end happily. But this is mere supposition because Howells did not complete his plot idea. It all seems quite different from Howells' usual dramas; however, even from this meager outline there is the Howellsian concern for truthfulness inherent in the old man and developing in Conley, as well as an opportunity for a comedy portrayal of New York society.

In all these plays and attempts at drama, published or unpublished, completed or fragmentary, there is something of Howells as writer and man. An artist and literary rebel, though sometimes a reticent rebel, Howells was also a businessman who earned his living by writing, and as such he was one of the shrewdest literary men in American history. His contracts with publishers were his daily bread, and he acted accordingly—bargaining for his works, requesting higher salaries, fighting for better payments for his stories and plays. As an editor he sometimes made or suggested changes in manuscripts that angered his contributors. Also, as a writer he made requests that occasionally irritated his editors, but he seems to have had a real gift for smoothing over personal feelings, and usually he had his own way. A good critic of his own work and aware of his value as a writer, he continually capitalized on his reputation in making contracts with his publishers.

Late in his life he wrote to Bliss Perry (April 9, 1907, Harvard Library): "In the days before my inclusive salary I used to make the people pay shocking prices for my things." But although he was independent at times with his publishers, he was also anxious to further the sale of his books. To add to his independence and increase his bargaining power and therefore his royalties, he frequently contracted to pay for the printing plates of a play or story. By doing this he could switch publishers if it seemed advantageous. He also watched his contract rights carefully and consistently retained the dramatic rights to his plays and other works. To enhance the sales of his books he concerned himself with the format of the work, the illustrations, the advertising methods, and even the time of publication. On occasion he suggested that inexpensive editions of his plays be printed, that some of his plays be published together, or that the sales promotion program be changed. A pioneer in copyright reform, he was careful to arrange British publication of his works, supplying the printing plates for David Douglas, his publisher in Scotland.

Four of Howells' plays never appeared in book form, and toward the end of his life Howells started bargaining with Sergel of Chicago, a publisher of farces, for an American collection of his plays. Unfortunately, he was not able to complete the arrangements before his death, and although Mildred Howells continued for nearly five years to urge the publication of the plays, she was unsuccessful. Almost from the beginning, his plays became a part of his bargaining power, and as they grew in popularity among his readers, their value increased. Early in his career he received $400 for a play. When Alden offered him $600 (letter, December 29, 1884, Harvard Library), Howells requested $750. Finally Alden suggested two classes of farces (letter, April 25, 1885, Harvard Library): "First, the more complex sort like these you have hitherto contributed which involve treatment at considerable length, and second, a simpler work based on a simple idea and really having but one situation like the *Mouse Trap*. I would suggest that while the price of the former would be $750 as per agreement, the latter might be rated a third lower." The point is that Howells was both businessman and literary artist, and by handling his literary affairs with intelligence and shrewdness he was usually able to promote his own welfare with marked success.

With the exception of the unpublished plays, which are printed here in what seems the most readable form, the texts of the plays in this volume are taken from the last American versions which Howells had an opportunity to revise. Sometimes it is evident that he made revisions and sometimes it is not. The form in which the plays are printed, although designed more for reading than acting drama, is only slightly different from Howells' requirements. In an undated note to Ticknor (Harvard Library) Howells wrote: "I wish them [the compositors] to follow the magazine copy. I wrote the *Sleeping Car* in the same way, and the proofreaders changed this style in my absence without my consent." In *Harper's Christmas* (1882), *The Sleeping Car* had been published in the traditional fashion of the acting play.

There are no significant bibliographical problems for Howells' plays, although the fact that many had several different publishers may require some explanation. A number of times the plays came out under the imprints of James R. Osgood, Ticknor and Company, and Houghton Mifflin & Company with identical texts. The background of this seeming confusion can be found in Henry A. Laughlin's *An Informal Sketch of the History of Houghton Mifflin Company* (1957). It is necessary here only to point out the succession of Howells' publishers. When in 1878 Osgood, a man of real brilliance in the publishing world, although frequently lacking in judgment and stability, found himself in financial difficulties, he saved his company—then called James R. Osgood and Company —by joining with Henry O. Houghton. The new firm, known as Houghton, Osgood and Company, lasted only until 1880, when two new companies were formed: Houghton Mifflin Company, Houghton keeping young George Mifflin with him, and James R. Osgood and Company, Benjamin Ticknor and Thomas Ticknor staying with Osgood. This second partnership was dissolved in 1885 when Osgood failed and was immediately reestablished as Ticknor and Company, which lasted until 1889, when this firm sold its best books to Houghton Mifflin Company and ceased to publish. Howells followed these changes. Only one other problem concerning copyright dates should be noted. Early in 1885 Henry Alden provided Howells with a contract for three plays which were to be delivered during the next three years. But Howells' correspondence indicates that the plays—*The Mouse Trap, Five O'clock Tea*, and *A Likely Story*—were all written in 1885, hence the 1885 copyright date for each play and publication dates of 1886, 1887, and 1888 respectively.

One other aspect of Howells' work must be considered in any study of Howells and the drama: that is Howells' ability as a dramatic critic. In *Criticism and Fiction* Howells concerned himself mainly with his theory of realism as it applied to the novel; he had little to say about the drama. But over the many years that he wrote for periodicals— starting with an essay in the *North American Review*, October, 1864, on "Recent Italian Comedy"—Howells had a great deal to say about plays, dramatists, and the theater. From these many essays and reviews, one may easily piece together Howells' theory of the drama, which was simply a logical extension of his theory of fiction with those added qualifications made necessary by the limitations of the dramatic form. In "The Recent Dramatic Season" (*North American Review*, CLXXII [March, 1901], 478), Howells declared that "the drama is distinctly a literary form; in fact, it is the supreme form." "The primal purpose of the play," he wrote in an essay on Eugene Brieux (*North American Review*, CCI [March, 1915], 407), "is to illustrate life or to reproduce it. This done, the secondary or moral purposes fulfill themselves—that is, to teach. . . ." Here was truth, moral intention, and literary quality, to which Howells added objectivity.

His comments on truthfulness in the drama are particularly interesting because they show distinct development in his understanding of truth. First, there was Carlo Goldoni, "the diligent student of human nature," whose truthfulness with his Venetian characters influenced Howells' criticism of truth in the sketches of Harrigan and Hart and in *The Old Homestead* by Denman Thompson. Then came the late 1880's, a tremendously disturbing period for Howells. His letter addressed to the *Tribune*, November 12, 1887, but never sent (Harvard Library), concerning the Chicago anarchists was entitled "A Word for the Dead. 'They died in the prime of the freest Republic the world has ever known for their opinion's sake.' " Ill-health plagued Howells during these years, and he became tired of his public and tired of writing. "If I could live without writing, I don't believe I should write any more," he told his father (letter, December 1, 1889, Harvard Library). Nine months after the death of his daughter Winifred, he wrote to James Parton (January 3, 1890, Harvard Library): "And where is she, and shall I ever see her again? The world has largely resolved itself into this question for me." It was a "dark riddle" which compounded all other problems. "Someday," he confided to his father (letter, October 7, 1888, Harvard Library), "I should like to write the tragedy of a man trying to escape from his circumstances. It would be funny." That a man should work hard all his life and then be troubled about his livelihood was "blasphemous, insulting to God," Howells thought (letter to his father, June 9, 1891, Harvard Library). One consequence of this period was a deepening of Howells' entire critical outlook. Twice during the 1890's (1894 and 1899) Howells saw Ibsen's *Ghosts* on the stage. The second performance he called one of his life's greatest experiences; in contrast to other critics, Howells' comments on the play show a thoughtful and mature view which penetrated beyond the truthfulness of character and action that he had enjoyed in the sketches of Goldoni and Harrigan to the fundamental truthfulness of idea.

All dramatists, Howells once noted, are also moralists, and morality is "the soul of all things." The play could be concerned with simply propriety or it could penetrate to the universal problem of values—morality in "the larger and the lesser sense"—but it should not subjectively preach, nor could morality in the "larger" sense, as "an affair of being rather than doing," ever become the chief interest in a play. It was also important to Howells that the drama which proposed to be a faithful representation of the lives of men and women should not be written in verse form. "Prose is now undisputably the dialect of the stage," he stated from "The Easy Chair" in 1902. For similar reasons Howells was opposed to the soliloquy, "the most discouraging thing in the work of the playwright for it ought never to be, and the smallest art would eliminate it"; to the asides, "those poor crutches, those futile props of the drama"; and to the *deus ex machina*. People did not speak in soliloquies or asides, and certainly there was no *deus ex machina* to free them from the problems of the real world.

These were Howells' precepts for the drama, and he would have been more successful himself had he followed them more carefully and at the same time been gifted with a greater sense of the dramatic. The reason for his failure at times to live up to his own dramatic standards is not easy to formulate, although perhaps it may be phrased this way: He did not seriously consider himself a playwright, but he did take his writing of individual plays seriously. "One thing," A. H. Quinn once wrote (letter to the author, August 14, 1950), "you may be sure that Howells took his playwriting seriously. . . . He earnestly desired to write for the theatre." Yet Clara and Rudolf Kirk in the "American Writers

Series" volume on Howells conclude that Howells was "a novelist and not a dramatist, and he never seriously mistook his vocation." However these statements appear, they are not contradictory, and to understand Howells as a playwright one must sense the complementary features of these two views. Howells did not consider the drama his primary genre of expression because in most of his plays his foremost objective was to entertain; consequently, as he wrote in *Criticism and Fiction*, such literature which seeks only to entertain need not be held so strictly to the tenets of realistic fiction.

The greater portion of Howells' dramatic criticism was directed toward American plays; in particular he was concerned with the conflict between dramatic art and the commercial theater in America. There were, on the one hand, the few worthwhile American playwrights; on the other, the managers and playwrights who wanted only to make money; and between the two groups, always ready to discourage the first and taunt the second, a body of dramatic critics whose chief equipment was their "traditional ignorance of the essence and nature of drama." From this confusion Howells tried to select the best plays, but he sadly admitted that it was a difficult task. Excellent plays were few, particularly those with the typically American emphasis that he wanted.

The nearest thing to a distinctly American drama for Howells were the dramatic sketches of New York City life by Edward Harrigan—the American Goldoni, as Howells described him in the *Harper's* "Editor's Study" of July, 1886—who emphasized a certain homely realism. Howells became his lifelong admirer, sometimes losing himself in expansive and indiscriminate praise, and saw in his plays "the spring of a true American comedy, the beginning of things which may be great things." Two other playwrights whom he obviously enjoyed for similar reasons were Denman Thompson and Charles Hoyt. Howells referred to Thompson's *The Old Homestead* again and again as one of the "sweetest and simplest" of American dramas. "On a wider plane than anyone else has yet attempted, Mr. Thompson gives us in this piece a representation of American life" ("Editor's Study," *Harper's Monthly*, LXXIX [July, 1889], 317). All these dramatists he considered originators of a typically American drama; but, he noted, they were first of all sketch writers and were not expected to produce dramas in the traditional sense with well-formed plots and adequately developed characters.

Although Howells saw the beginning of an American comedy in Harrigan's work, there is no question but that he considered James A. Herne the foremost American dramatist of his time. Through the years he commented on several of Herne's dramas, but he had most to say about *Margaret Fleming*, which he perceptively catalogued as an "epoch-marking" rather than an "epoch-making" play. It was, he wrote, a piece of "great realism in its whole effect." The only other American dramatist whose plays he liked to read as well as to watch was Augustus Thomas, in whom he found a literary quality— and this before *The Witching Hour*, which is usually considered to mark the turning point in Thomas' change from melodrama to more serious comedy. Clyde Fitch he ranked with, or slightly higher than, Thomas because he felt that at least two of Fitch's plays, *The Girl with the Green Eyes* and *Her Own Way*, would compare well with the best of the contemporary English comedy. Fitch's gift for capturing the spirit of New York and the essential ingredients of its people impressed Howells, although he did not comment on *The Truth* or *The City*. For a number of other American dramatists Howells showed some interest. Bronson Howard's *One of Our Girls* he thought "a well-knit, thoroughly right-minded play with a literary quality," and he noted that *Shenandoah* was a very successful play, but beyond that he did not concern himself with the work of the man whom Montrose Moses called the Dean of American Drama. He did have a great deal of praise for William Gillette as both actor and dramatist. *Held by the Enemy* he thought the best of the war plays, and *Secret Service*, with its regard for a unity of time and its forcibly drawn characters, seemed to Howells a play that would be good literature as well as good drama. When the century changed and a new crop of younger dramatists started to write, Howells had little to say in spite of his reputation as one who favored younger writers. He seemed to lack his previous enthusiasm, although he still professed vital interest in American drama. He stopped writing plays, too, during the last ten years of his life. Perhaps it seemed to him that a part of his theater was dead, as were all his favorite dramatists— Harrigan, Herne, Hoyt, and Fitch.

As a critic of American drama, Howells was a very kind promoter of the features that interested him; fortunately, his standards were those which contributed to modern American drama. He wanted to like American plays, wanted to find them good; but since he realized that only a few could measure up to English and European plays, he diluted his critical standards and tried to find the great American dramatist among the sketch writers of the stage and the beginning realists in the drama. He was right in finding some contemporary and some permanent value in the works of Howard, Thomas, Gillette, Fitch, and Herne; in fact, every man whom Howells praised has some significance in American drama in the area in which Howells catalogued him. The relative grouping Howells gave to the American dramatists of that period still holds, although the entire drama of that period is considered generally lower and inferior when compared with its contemporary foreign drama and with the plays of previous centuries as well as our modern drama.

At his seventy-fifth birthday dinner in New York, Howells made a speech which is significant for this study in that a proportionately large part of it was concerned with the drama. It may perhaps be taken as his final comment on American drama:

> Not less wonderful to me than the growth of the American novel . . . is the growth of the American play. . . . Before the great Civil War . . . we had no drama which was essentially American except the wretched stage travesty of that most essentially American novel *Uncle Tom's Cabin*. But now already we have a drama which has touched our life at many characteristic points, which has dealt with our moral and material problems and penetrated the psychological regions which it seemed impossible an art so objective should reach. Mainly it has been gay as our prevalent mood is; mainly it has been honest as our habit is in cases where we believe we can afford it; and now that Ibsen no longer writes new plays, I would rather take my chance of pleasure and profit with a new American play than with any other sort of new play. (*North American Review*, CCXII [July, 1920], 12.)

"To go from American to English plays," Howells wrote, "is to pass from clever sketches, from graphic studies, brilliant suggestion, to finished pictures." ("The Recent Dramatic Season," *North American Review*, CLXXII [March, 1901], 477.) As the best of the English dramatists Howells chose Henry Arthur Jones, whose plays he commented on in several letters and four essays, finding the dramatist a master craftsman who searched for truth. Closely behind Jones he rated Sir Arthur Wing Pinero, a dramatist who took his art seriously, produced admirable pieces of literature, and worked in the interest of morality. Howells also admired Oscar Wilde for what he considered Wilde's moral truthfulness and "his wide prospect of human nature." But in spite of his praise of these dramatists, his comments on the works of Sir James M. Barrie are among his most enthusiastic criticisms of foreign playwrights. He felt a sort of poetic "sweetness" in Barrie's work, and yet he was shrewd enough to see beneath Barrie's saccharine-coated fantasies and discover an insight into human nature and a truthfulness of idea that more than compensated for the unrealistic whimsey. On the Continent the dramatists who interested him were Ibsen and Brieux; the others, such as Bjørnson, Sudermann, Hauptmann, Maeterlinck, and Rostand, he mentioned, but only in passing. Rostand he enjoyed, but questioned. His plays, he wrote, "leave one without doubt that he . . . is a deft and skillful playwright, but with question whether he is so much more as to be a dramatist of great promise." ("The New Poetic Drama," *North American Review*, CLXXII [May, 1901], 497.) But Brieux he did not question. ("The Plays of Eugene Brieux," *North American Review*, CCI [March, 1915], 402–11.) "He is a great dramatist," Howells concluded; "he has given faithful reports of life. . . ."

There is no doubt, however, that Howells' most penetrating and brilliant venture in dramatic criticism is his defense of Ibsen and his comparison of Ibsen and G. B. Shaw. During his career he had occasion to comment on Shaw's work several times, but one essay stands out above the rest ("Editor's Easy Chair," *Harper's Monthly*, CXXVI [May, 1913], 958–61). "Mr. Shaw," he wrote, "is the comic analogue of the tragic Ibsen and goes no further than to make the witness look where he stands, even while cutting the ground from under his feet." Long before this time, through the storm of protest from an enraged public and an unenlightened body of critics, Howells had stood forth to proclaim Ibsen as the "greatest of the moderns." In addition to numerous brief comments, Howells devoted three articles to Ibsen: the "Editor's Easy Chair," *Harper's Monthly*, CXII (May, 1906), 958–59, 961; "The Ibsen Influence," *Harper's Monthly*, XXXIX (April 27, 1895), 390; and "Henrik Ibsen," *North American Review*, CLXXXIII (July, 1906), 1–14. His summation was simply that "no greater mind, no perfecter art" had revealed itself in his time. He recognized Ibsen's thorough knowledge of stage techniques, his masterly dramatic form, his fidelity to natural conditions, his ability as a dramatist of ideas, his capacity to create characters and atmosphere, and his great moral force. But far more than the value of Ibsen's plays, he found Ibsenism the greatest influence on modern drama.

As critic of the drama and as playwright, Howells has substance that has never been adequately evaluated either in relation to his artistry or to the American drama. Howells' position as novelist and critic during the rise of realism in America is more or less fixed, although it is not yet fully understood. On the other hand, historians of nineteenth-century American drama have sometimes exaggerated his importance, while later critics have been too quick to disparage all Howells' dramatic efforts. In spite of the theatrical weaknesses brought to Howells' plays by his desire to dramatize the commonplace, and in addition to his interest in farce, Howells' contribution to the rise of realism in drama and to the development of a social comedy is of primary importance. His plays achieve their individual value largely in terms of these two strains of American drama. No passing fancy, his playwriting does not belong to a particular period of his career but becomes a significant aspect, in amount and value, of his literary output—thirty-six plays written during the most productive years of his life. For the student of Howells, for the investigator of the rise of realism, for the historian of American drama, these plays have importance. Perhaps the modern reader of plays may also find in the best of them the pleasure they brought to earlier generations of American and English readers.

WALTER J. MESERVE

THE COMPLETE PLAYS OF W. D. HOWELLS

Samson

[1874]

At the suggestion of the actor Charles Pope, Howells started his career as a dramatist with a translation from the Italian of D'Aste's *Sansone*. Unlike his later play *Yorick's Love*, *Samson* is a reasonably straightforward translation, scholarly and faithful. Interestingly enough, most of the newspaper critics who reviewed it seemed impressed with the translation and commented on the "literary finish" of the play (Boston *Herald*, August 13, 1895), the dignity of the English (Philadelphia *Telegraph*, December 3, 1889), and the superiority of the diction compared to most versions of foreign plays (Boston *Post*, November 7, 1889). Howells himself was enthusiastic about *Samson*. The more he worked on the play the more he enjoyed it, and on August 12, 1874 (Harvard Library), he wrote to Pope:

> I have this day finished the translation of the *Sansone*, and have now merely to copy it. . . . In making this version I have of course gone deeply into the spirit of this play, and I shall annotate some of the passages . . . giving my notion of the author's conception. . . . I must say that I am more and more impressed with the *acting* qualities of the play, and I have a higher opinion of it as literature than I had at first, though I always respected it.

One significant aspect of this letter is Howells' reference to the play as literature. Throughout the many years during which he criticized plays, he distinguished between the popular stage success and the drama that would last and achieve some stature in the world of the stage and of literature. One of his criteria for the best drama was that it must have a literary quality; the play must be good reading, good literature, as well as good theater.

The poetry in *Samson* varies markedly in value. Portions are weak and ineffective; some speeches rise to a certain dignity and grandeur. Although most of the play is in blank verse, Howells does employ other meters. Manoah's prayer, for example, early in Act I, is written in trochaic tetrameter, and the effect is not unsucccessful, for the shorter line and the periodic rhyming suggest a hymn. Howells used this form again, in Act III, for Delilah's chant but here the lyric mood becomes sophomoric and jinglelike, completely lacking the controlled rhythmic power necessary in a chant. With his blank verse Howells is sometimes irregular and uneven. In places he shows a habit of breaking almost every line with a strong caesura, thus producing choppy speech and a most unpleasing rhythm, ill-fitted to the mood of the scene. However, there is much passably good blank verse in *Samson*. Usually the speeches of Delilah, Lamech, and Samson are the best, but Howells also relates stories well in poetry—stories such as that of Samson and the lion, which is told in blank verse that flows smoothly and well, easily adapting to the pace and excitement of the situation.

When Howells was a young man, he was introduced both in the United States and abroad by Lowell and the rest of his Brahmin admirers as the coming young poet rather than as a novelist or a journalist. And this reputation had some basis in his writings of that period. Most certainly it must have influenced his choice of a poetic drama—at least his acceptance of Pope's commission to translate a poetic drama—for his first attempt in the dramatic field.

Samson was played on the stage with some success from time to time for twenty-five years. Three actors used it at various times as a vehicle

1

for their theatrical talents. For Pope, who had noted the success of Tommaso Salvini in D'Aste's original, the play became one of the greatest hits of his later years on the stage. During 1874 and 1875 he toured the country with *Samson*, playing, among other cities, New Orleans (John S. Kendall, *The Golden Age of The New Orleans Theater* [Baton Rouge: Louisiana State University Press, 1952], p. 460), St. Louis (October 5, 1874, Olympic Theatre—a performance that A. H. Quinn called successful [A *History of The American Drama* (2nd ed.; New York: Appleton–Century–Crofts, Inc., 1936), I, 68]), Chicago (May 17 and 22, 1875, McVicker's Theatre), and points west as far as California. Two years later Pope had an extremely successful week at the Varieties Theater in New Orleans starting February 5, 1877. The play was not again revived for an extensive run until the theater season of 1889–90, when Salvini made his farewell American tour. At that time A. M. Palmer initiated the production at his New York theater on October 11 and 13, 1889, and the play drew significant critical approval. Salvini then toured with the play, producing it, among other places, at the Tremont Theatre in Boston, November 7, 1889, and the Broad Street Theatre in Philadelphia, December 3, 1889, receiving good reviews throughout. For his Chicago production, January 8, 11, 14 (matinee), and 16, 1890, at the Columbia Theatre, Salvini spoke his lines in Italian while the rest of the cast used the Howells version. The third actor to use the play extensively was J. Walter Kennedy, who starred in it over a period of several years. During the 1894–95 season, Kennedy toured with *Samson*, playing at the Walnut Street Theatre, Philadelphia, December 18, 1894, and at the People's Theatre (on the Bowery, in New York), April 30, 1895; and giving a performance in Chicago that the Chicago *Post* reviewed favorably in its May 6, 1895 issue.

Samson [1]

1 A *Tragedy* in five acts, by Ippolito D'Aste. Translated by W. D. Howells. This play was published only by Charles D. Koppel, New York, 1889.

THE ARGUMENT

The Jews languish under one of their periodical subjections to foreign dominations, as a penalty for their sins. This time the Philistines are their oppressors and taskmasters.

The action opens with a sacrifice by Manoah and other pious Hebrews. Manoah chants a rhythmic prayer. The leading Jews bewail the distresses of the people and express their disappointment in Samson, who was to have been the regenerator and deliverer. Manoah justifies his son, and narrates the miraculous circumstances of his birth. Samson himself appears, rebukes his detractors and tells how he had been engaged to marry a Philistine woman; how, on his way, he had been assailed by a lion, which, unarmed, he had fought and killed; how he had, at his wedding festival, proposed a riddle with a heavy wager, and how his wife had wheedled him out of the answer and told it to his friends and companions, who had thus cheated him. He now declares his intention to go to Askelon and there take his wager by force from other Philistines. We learn, subsequently, that he has done this; and that, in so doing, he has killed several Philistines, and thus excited public indignation. Delilah is arrested, having been found in his company; but she is released by Lamech, a Philistine prince, who directs the crowd against Samson's house. Presently Samson reappears and reviles his enemies, announces that he has paid his wager, and, when the Philistines, not daring to attack him, seize his father, Samson rescues the old man, and retires with threats of revenge and retribution.

The next action takes place in Delilah's house. Here Lamech persuades her to make use of her influence with Samson, and to find out the secret of his great strength. She admits her duty to her country, but pleads her love for Samson and refuses. Meanwhile news is brought of his terrible slaughter of Philistines, with the jaw-bone of an ass. Lamech again urges her, she repeats her refusal; but on Lamech's solemnly assuring her that no harm is intended against Samson's life, she reluctantly consents to act with her countrymen, and to deliver Samson into captivity. Melcah, a slave woman, whose son had been one of the victims at Askelon, and who acts from motives of vengeance, is introduced into Delilah's house as a spy on both Delilah and Samson. Samson now appears; he drinks wine, and, in his drunkenness, tells Delilah that his strength lies in his hair. Delilah would withhold the secret, but Melcah betrays it to the exulting Philistines. When he awakes he finds that he has been shorn; he is set on by the Philistines and taken to prison. Delilah abandons herself to passionate grief, rejects the homage of her people, and reviles Lamech for his perfidy; and Manoah tells the narrative of his sufferings, and of his eyes being destroyed.

The last act takes place in front of the temple of Dagon, the fish-god and tutelar of the Philistines. Ordered to exhibit himself at the games, Samson submits. He prays for Divine help, and becomes conscious of the miraculous restoration of his strength. He is visited by his father and Delilah, who persuade him to escape. He refuses. Delilah retires. The father leads him to the outer pillars of the temple, the Philistines being inside. He bows himself, strains on the supports, and brings down the whole structure, burying himself in the ruins, while the cries and shrieks within show the havoc he has wrought.

ACT I

SCENE

A high table-land in Zorah, surrounded and shaded by trees, and accessible by a craggy path, R. Thebni, Neriah and many Israelites, of both sexes, discovered assembled around a blazing pyre, in the manner of the ancient sacrifices. Manoah, standing alone, intones the following prayer:

MANOAH

Rise, rise, sweet smell of sacrifice, ascend
To the Eternal!

THEBNI

To the throne of God,
Rise fragrant smoke of spices and of gums,
And humbly bear His people's prayer to Him!

MANOAH

Let us pray, and let us scatter
Ashes on our foreheads bent
In the dust; let crag and cavern
Echo with our sore lament,
Till from Engardi to the cedars
Of high Lebanon, far abroad
From the Red Sea unto Jordan

3

All bow down before our God!
We have sinned against the Almighty,
At whose frown the universe
Trembles, and who stays and launches
Every peril, every curse.
Thou, who mad'st the constellations,
Taught'st the Cherubin their flight,
Holdest in thy fist the thunders,
Givest life to Day and Night:
In the temples of their idol
With the Amorites knelt we;
Yea, but Ashtaroth henceforward
Unto us as dust shall be!
From the depth of our abasement
Hath our faith arisen free:
Lord, upon the wings of angels
Take our penitent prayers to Thee.
Pardon us, Oh, God, whose vengeance
So hath chastened us, and subdued;
Help thy children, succor, save us,
From our cruel servitude;
In the tents, among our women
Rise another Jael and dwell;
Be our enemies rent and scattered
By the Lion of Israel!

[All rise.]

THEBNI

Vain hope, vain hope! The Lion of Israel,
The bold and valorous youth, upon whose brow,
Jehovah's fire hath blazed from the first hour
Of childhood, now hath turned his face away
From his own people.

NERIAH
                Zorah's mighty cedar
Transplanted, strikes into Philistine soil
Its roots, and spreads them far abroad, perchance
Unto our hurt.

MANOAH
                Nay, such iniquity
Is not in my son's heart!

THEBNI
                Samson was chosen
To be our judge; in Samson's hand we placed
All rule and power, that he might crush our foes;
But Samson houses with our enemies;
He is their friend, he feasts and riots with them;
Yea, and as if our Israel were barren
Of fair and virtuous daughters, he has chosen
Among the wanton Amoritish girls,
A woman for his wife. Are these, Manoah,
Are these the promises, the prophecies,
Thine Elema dreamt?

MANOAH
                Mine Elema dreamed not,
Mine eyes betrayed me not; and the Almighty,

He hath not lied. Is it unknown to you,
Perchance, how face to face, my wife and I
Beheld the Eternal here? Ah, yes, Jehovah's voice
Is strange to you, I know, but not to us,
Who in this place, upon yon loftiest steep,
The sacred footprints of God's holy angel
Kissed with glad lips!·The will of the Most High
Fell deep into our hearts, and in my soul
It burneth yet, so that I can repeat
All, word for word, to you: "Wife of Manoah!"
Thundered the Angel, "Thou art barren now,
And bearest not, but thou shalt yet conceive
And bear a son. Therefore, beware, I pray thee,
And drink not wine, nor any potent drink,
And eat not anything that is unclean;
For lo, thou shalt conceive and bear a son,
Upon whose head never let nazor come;
For he, thy child shall be a Nazarite
To God, even from the womb, and shall begin
To succor Israel from the Philistine's hand."
So spake the angelic lips, and in this place,
Here, where before the King of Kings we offer
Sacred and solemn vows, I sacrificed
With grateful heart a poor ewe-lamb upon
This lowly stone. The humble sacrifice
Was, with as strange a miracle, accepted:
The spilt libations and the fragrant herbs,
The lustral waters, in the whirl of fire
Rose from the ashes, and before our eyes
Within that column of vapor and of flame
The Angel vanished, while through all the heaven
Rang loud hosannas to the promised child.

THEBNI

The fame of that portent has gone throughout
All Zorah; and thou knowest well, Manoah,
What honor and what reverence and what faith
Have ever followed thee, thy wife, thy child,
From Israel's fathers. But what recompense
Have we yet had from thee?

NERIAH
                Have we received
Our freedom from our promised liberator?

THEBNI

We are condemned to harder servitude,
And from the race of Dan hath risen, not a Lion
Fearless and free, but a poor crawling worm
That licks the right hand of our enemy.

NERIAH

He is a traitor, and I hold him such.

MANOAH

And by what right? My son. . . .

NERIAH
                Yea, I proclaim it:
The head of Judah, the elect of Zorah,
Must not and should not riot with the wicked

In their lewd orgies. Not a fault, I hold it,
But horrible sin and blackest crime in him
That he betrothed himself unto a vile
Idolatrous girl.

THEBNI
O, light of Zorah, how,
How art thou faded! How thy lovely dawns
Are turned to darkness! How the lilies lie
Broken among thy valleys. Naught remains
But idle tears!

NERIAH
Whom shall we trust?

THEBNI
O, what
Shall be our refuge now?

SAMSON
My breast!

THEBNI
'Tis Samson!

MANOAH
My son!

NERIAH
Thou!

SAMSON
Thou hast hurled at me
The name of traitor. But no renegade
Is Samson, for if he were false, I here,
Your judge would punish him for treason, yea,
Even I myself.

NERIAH
Haply thou comest not
From our foes' borders?

THEBNI
And art not betrothed
Unto a maiden of the Amorites?

SAMSON
[Appearing on rocks.]
Nay, it is true: I seek not to conceal it.
What matters it? Plucking a flower up
Out of an alien field, have I plucked forth
All fealty to you from my breast? Have I
Betrayed the faith of our forefathers? No!
My country went with me, the only God
That sits above the Heavens guided me;
The God that in my cradle woke in me
This wondrous sense of life. He led my steps
Unto Philistia.—He breathed into me
A spark divine, and straight I felt myself

Become all steel within, and my limbs throbbed,
And all my pulses, nerves, and sinews grew
In strength gigantic!

THEBNI
Well, and wherefore?

SAMSON
My nuptials were appointed that the pride
Of the Philistines might be broken.

MANOAH
How?

SAMSON
I am stronger than the fiercest beast. Behold
My savage mantle in witness.

MANOAH
What mean'st thou?

THEBNI
Speak clearly!

SAMSON
Hardly had I set foot among
Timnath's thick vineyard when I heard a stir
Upon a sudden in the vines, and then
A growl, and then a roar so terrible,
So loud and deep that all the vales and caverns
Of Timnath bellowed back, and as in fear
The echoes fled.—The spirit of the Lord
Came mightily upon me. Firm and bold
I searched the vines, when, swifter than my words,
Leaped forth a lion with distended jaws,
Wild tossing mane, and ranks of teeth agrin,
And mad with famine. Full in front of me
He crouched and bounded at my breast, but I
Slipped lightly backward, while he roared and raged,
Then lightning-like he sprang upon my side,
But I, more supple than a serpent, twisted
And turned myself, and seized him by the mane
And clutched his throat, and with a mighty shock
I hurled him down and held him with my foot,
Nailed to the earth. In vain his flaming eyes
Shot fire at me, in vain he writhed and showed
His ravening teeth, for I more fierce than he
Into the hollow of his reeking throat
Plunged deep my fist, and then with both hands tore
And rent him as I would a kid, and sat me down
Victor upon the dead king of the desert.

MANOAH
God shielded thee, my son!

THEBNI
What divine power
Compassed thee 'round?

SAMSON
                    The sacred star of Moses
Protected me. And, as of old, he turned
The rivers into blood, and bade the floods
Storm·back upon our pathway through the sea,
By the help of the Most High did I draw forth
Meat from the eater, sweetness from the strong one.

THEBNI
Thy words are like a riddle.

SAMSON
                        Thou sayest well;
For in these very words the riddle lies
With which I baffled all my wedding guests
The sennight that we feasted. Ye all know
It is an ancient usage, handed down
From our forefathers, for the bridegroom thus
To banquet with his comrades. The Philistines
Numbered not less than thirty, and I put
This riddle forth to them, and we agreed
That if they could not guess it they should give
Thirty rich change of garments. But if they
Could read my riddle within those same days,
Then I should give as many robes to them.
They knew not that the eater symbolized
The lion in his strength, and that the meat
Was but the honey that the wild-bees stored
Within his carcass, and that I drew forth
And ate, and made my father, and my mother
To eat thereof. And they never could have guessed
Save for their treachery. They beset my wife
With threats to burn her and her father's house
With fire. And so, for seven whole days, my wife
Came weeping unto me, and cried, and said
I hated her, and loved her not, for I
Had spoken her people a riddle and not told her
The secret. Therefore, on the seventh day,
Because her weeping wearied me, I told her,
And she betrayed me. And that treason of theirs
Rankles within my heart. I swear to you,
Who gnaw the chain of slavery with me,
I swear to fall upon the accursed race
Born of the Chaldees, as the fire from Heaven
Destroying fell on Sodom and Gomorrah!
I will lay waste their houses and their lands,
Their flocks and herds, and fields of standing corn,
And I will slay their wives and little ones,
And overthrow their idols till God's people
Rise from their suffering and their infamy.

NERIAH
Would it were as thou sayest.

THEBNI
                        Even now the fields
Of our fierce enemies whiten to the harvest,
While ours are laid in ashes and in smoke,
Or trampled by the Assyrian horse.

NERIAH
                                The curse
Of Cain has fallen upon us.

THEBNI
                        Like the serpent
We feed our famine in the dust and grass,
Under their feet.

SAMSON
                    But in the days to come
Their corn shall feast you, and ye shall not crawl
Like serpents then. But blessed among men
With the eagle's fire, your eyes upon the sun
Whose brightness is the radiance of the Lord
Shedding the light of faith into your souls—
The light of that faith which in other times,
Armed with a pebble a weak woman's hand
To beat the greatness of Abimelech down;
The immortal faith that in the wilderness
Sustained our fathers, and that now I feel
Fill all my soul, and give me strength beyond
The might of man to bring Philistia low.

THEBNI
We trust in thee!

                                [Enter Salem.]

SALEM
                    A band of lawless youths,
Out of the country of the Amorites,
Come with loud yells and cries, and call upon
The name of Samson.

SAMSON
                    They demand the prize
Of the solved riddle. I will pay it, friends.
These ruffians have won from me their thirty
Rich change of garments, and I go to slay
Yet other thirty of their kind to clothe them.

THEBNI
We go with thee.

SAMSON
                    Let no one follow,
I go down alone to Askelon.

MANOAH
                    Upon thy footsteps I—

SAMSON
Nay, father, I shall see thee soon again
In Timnath. Meanwhile mid our people bowed
Before the Lord, with prayers and vows entreat
That in my right hand I may grasp and wield
The omnipotent and unseen sword of God.

CURTAIN

ACT II

SCENE

The Valley of Timnath, at the foot of Mount Ephraim.
Enter Zambres and Lamech.

LAMECH
It matters little. Israel deserves
To be subjected unto us.

ZAMBRES
                    Nay, then,
Gaza shall scarce rejoice if Zorah's children
Rapine and murmur.

LAMECH
                    The great torch of Ammon
Keeps vigil over us. Ashtaroth is stronger
Than that archangel of the fiery sword,
Who as men dreamed or fabled in old time,
Thrust our first parents out of Paradise.
She hath made us lords over all Israel,
New glory springs from the Etean stock
In us.

ZAMBRES
            The people go no longer bent
Like beasts of burden; from the servile glebe
Starts the free growth, and from a wretched rabble
Of wandering shepherds, heralded by prophets,
A hero comes.

LAMECH
                    Thou mean'st that pitiful wretch,
The Judge of Zorah—him whose mighty limbs
Put his weak soul to shame—thou mean'st Samson,
From whom the soft note of a woman's pleading
Had power to lure the secret that his heart
Should have kept locked within it.

ZAMBRES
                                    Fatal riddle,
That cost us far more tears than it cost him!

LAMECH
Thou viewest the present with the eye o' the herd.
I pierce the future's darkness and discern,
Amidst the private sorrows of the few,
The overwhelming public good. And who
Are we to fly before the apparition
Of this phantasmal hero? We shall see,
Though he hath slain a young lion, as he boasts,
With naked hand, whether when fully armed,
He will know how to front the angry pride
Of the Philistine princes.

ZAMBRES
                    Thou knowest well
What he hath done in Askelon.

LAMECH
                    I know
That like a coward he laid violent hands
Upon the flower of the illustrious youth
Of Askelon, and would have robbed them; but,
That he hath vanquished thirty of their number,
I'll not believe.

ZAMBRES
                    A moment since there came
Bereav'd mothers and disconsolate widows
To witness it with tears.

LAMECH
                    Their blood shall be
Avenged; and to avenge it thou shalt see
Our people rise like the long waves that beat
The shores of Askelon. Ah, woe to Samson,
If he return! I swear to Ashtaroth,
His bridal bed shall be his tomb; his wife
And his wife's kindred all shall share the ruin
Of this vile Hebrew robber whom she wed.
            [*Enter Guards, Gomer, and Delilah.*]

GOMER
We found this woman not far off from here
With Samson.

DELILAH
                    I can hardly be a stranger
To the Philistine prince. Why hide myself?
If haply unknown to you, am I not known
Too well in my own Sorek?

LAMECH
                    O, Delilah,
What joy thy coming brings me! Hospitable
Be all our land unto the beautiful
And lovely lady that the vale of Sorek
Rejoices in. Let no one lift his voice
Against her here—it is the sovereign will
And mandate of your prince!

GOMER
                    And shall we, then,
Become her safeguard? Nay, let us revenge
Our wrongs upon his paramour!

LAMECH
                    I will,
And I command ye that ye pay her honor!
How hath 't offended you, this loveliness
That draws so many lovers after it?

DELILAH
                    In every woman born
Dwelleth a spirit that, openly or in secret,
Controls her impulses. Mine, boldly broke
The rein; and like some wilding, wayside flower

That any passer plucks, and having breathed
Its sweetness, casts aside forgotten, bloomed
My beauty in the world. Within the arms
Of many, in the heart of none; 'mid loves
Unbridled, loving overmuch, I never
Loved any truly; and in this I am guilty.

LAMECH

She hath told you all. And woe be unto him
That offers her offense! Are ye so blind
As not to see the true source of our sorrows?
Hath he no fields, hath he no kindred here,
That treacherous Judean? There let your revenge
Glut itself.

ZAMBRES

Haste! before the impious Samson
Come again, go ye to his house.

GOMER

Yea, there,
There fall our hate; and in the pitiless flames
Let his house crumble, and amidst the ashes
There let him find his wife.

LAMECH

I will not baulk
Your generous fury. Go!

[Exit Gomer with populace.]
[Aside.]
And I shall have

No longer a rival.

DELILAH

What say'st thou?

LAMECH

Delilah,
Remain here, if thou wilt in perfect safety,
Nor let the tumult of the mob affright thee.

DELILAH

My life hath schooled me against every chance:
Born by the waters of the Dead Sea, I,
From my first years, was blown about the world
Like a leaf played with by the restless winds!
Bereft of friends and home, in Palestine,
My beauty ripened, and the multitudes
That thronged about me, when with fire divine,
I sang, and struck the psalter in the dance,
Called me alluring, called me beautiful!—
Ah, fataller the sorcery of applause
Than the mob's fury that thou speakest of!
The heart grows hard amid delights like mine:
Their flatteries were as draughts of Sorek wines;
The pomps of Sidon dazzled me; and I,
Child of the desert, dreamt of palaces!—
Hither I came, and here will I remain,
As careless of the future as the present.

LAMECH

And so live, for so
The prince of the Philistines wills. Thou, Zambres,
Open thy house to her; and let her be used
With every honor.

ZAMBRES

Trust in me.

LAMECH

[Aside, to him.]
Perchance
We may avail ourselves of her.

ZAMBRES

[Aside to Lamech.]
I hope so.
[Exit.]

LAMECH

I have known thee long, Delilah, by the fame
Of thy fair face, and of thy life, and all
The charm that clothes thee; but the witchery,
The exquisite sweetness of thy voice, hath now
Won such a sweet dominion over me
That here I offer thee the full assurance
Of a true friendship.

DELILAH

Thou! my lord.

LAMECH

Ere long
I shall return to thee. Others have trampled
Upon thy name—I'll lift it to the throne!
[Exit.]

DELILAH

Dreams of an hour; alluring promises,
Desire created and the sated wish
Destroyeth! Ah, I drift upon the sea
Of life, and though the deep is smooth and fair,
I drive to shipwreck still, I fear. So be it!
I will still live my fill of pleasure.
[Enter Manoah.]

MANOAH

Woman,
Is this the vale of Timnath?

DELILAH

Thou hast but now
Her lofty height descended. From what land
Art thou, old man? Judea, perchance?

MANOAH

I am,
Thou hast guessed right. I left my native fields
Yesterday morn at dawn, and I have wandered
By day and night among the rocks and brambles,

Hither and thither, till my aching limbs
Do crave repose.

DELILAH
The aspect of age is ever
Sacred to me. Come, venerable man,
And sit thee here.

MANOAH
I thank thee. May the Lord
Make his face shine upon thee.

DELILAH
Wilt thou not
Refresh thee with a friendly cup?

MANOAH
'Twere idle.
I keep my life from all the vaunted juices
Of the glad vine, and in the limpid springs
Alone I slake my thirst.
Jehovah's messenger did so command my wife,
And I fulfill his sovereign will.

DELILAH
Our gods
Are less austere.

MANOAH
I venerate the law
Of the God of Abraham, and evermore
I bless the Lord whose grace hath made me father
Of my great son. Well were my toil repaid
If I could reach yon steep, and see myself
In my son's eyes and kiss him on the brow,
And smooth the long waves of his flowing hair.

DELILAH
Thy son? Thou—

MANOAH
I am Samson's father—

DELILAH
Hush!
Speak not his name! Woe to thee if they heard thee!
The wrath of the Philistines is poured out
Against thy house. Thy life—

VOICES
[From within.]
There, on the mountains!
[Enter Gomer, Zambres, Populace, and Soldiers.
Samson is seen upon the heights above, descend-
ing.]

GOMER
Up there, upon the cliff!

ZAMBRES
What? Who?

GOMER
There, yonder,
The impious Hebrew stood! Up, follow him!

SAMSON
Cease—cease these coward yells! Whom do you shout
for?
Am I unknown to you?

ZAMBRES
Too well we know thee!

MANOAH
My son—

DELILAH
Do not reveal thyself!

SAMSON
I come
To pay the debts I owed. Where is the throng
Of my bold comrades who were chosen to guess
My riddle out? Let them come forward, here,
That company of heroes! I promised them
Thirty rich change of raiment, and already
True to my word I've placed them in their houses.

ZAMBRES
Those mantles reek with the fraternal blood
That thou has shed.

SAMSON
One only have I kept,
And I would fain bestow it with mine own hand
Upon your most illustrious warrior. Tell me
Where is your prince? Is he in conclave yet
With Samson's bride? Is he perchance extorting
New secrets from her? Or is he desecrating
The absent husband's fireside?

ZAMBRES
The fireside
O' the alien robber is no longer his;
No longer is the ill-starred woman thine
That was thy wife.

SAMSON
Born of your own, she ever
Was loth and cold with me. I thank you more
For taking her away than giving her.

ZAMBRES
Yea, and she shall be taken from thee!

SAMSON
I will first see her.
[Enter Lamech.]

LAMECH
Nay, thou shalt embrace
Only her ashes!

SAMSON
What sayest thou?

LAMECH
Unlooked-for,
Illustrious guest, to pay thee honor
We had lighted certain bonfires. See, the sun
Hath scarcely light enough t' eclipse the flame,
Vivid and fierce, that yonder swells and rises
In smoky columns. O, but look—for thine,
Thine are those fields, thine are those blazing harvests,
Thine are those slaughtered flocks and herds, and thine
That desolate hearthstone!

SAMSON
And my wife?

LAMECH
Thy ruin
Is thy wife's sepulcher.

SAMSON
Oh, monstrous villain!
Was it not then enough that you had lured her
Into your dark designs? Was death the guerdon
Ye gave her faith? Filthy idolaters,
Now—now I know you! But she shall not rest
Long unavenged! As the Lord showed himself
In Horeb's lightning, so in yonder flames
He shows himself. I see him, feel him—filled
With wrath divine I proclaim war against you!

LAMECH
Thou darest so much? Ah, traitor!

SAMSON
Hearken, Philistine,
Unto my words. The measure of thy crimes
Is full to overflowing; thou hast heaped
Insult and outrage on us, and hast made
Power the heavy load of misery
That crushed my father's people. Thou hast profaned
The altars of our God—trampled the ark
O' the covenant under foot, and dragged the flower
Of our chaste virgins into thy lewd harem—
I know it well. And who and whence art thou
Who sit thee in dominion over us?
What heritage did thine ancestors bequeath thee
Among us? A heritage of hate, and hate
Shall be between us ever, for thou bearest
Upon thy forehead written, ALIEN, Oh,
We sprang not from the mire of Egypt, we!
The seed of Jacob beareth fruit in us;
He wrestled with the angel of the Lord
Upon Periel for us, and prophesying

He spoke of Dan that he should judge his people,
And be a basilisk in their foeman's path
To bite the horses. But that horse and rider
Should fall and perish in their agony
Together! Hearken to me! I am of Dan
And I will be the basilisk in thy path—

LAMECH
But thou shalt first in chains—

SAMSON
Let no man lay
His hand upon the Nazarite.

LAMECH
Fall upon him
With stones, and beat him down; let the wretch die
Beneath the scourge. On, on! what do ye, slaves?
Cowards!
[The Philistines draw back terrified.]

ZAMBRES
My lord—

SAMSON
Oh, they are worthy of thee,
Lamech. Here, take this mantle to adorn thy limbs.
[Tosses a tunic to Lamech.]

LAMECH
O, scorn.

MANOAH
My son!

LAMECH
Art thou his father?

MANOAH
It is my boast!

LAMECH
Ho, let this hoary wretch
Die in his stead!

GOMER
Kill him!

DELILAH
Ah no!—

GOMER
No man
Shall save him!
[Advancing upon Manoah.]

SAMSON
But the hand of God shall do it—
He wills that he be saved.—Under this burden

I swear to scatter ruin where I go
Throughout the land of the Philistine; I,
Terrible as the Lion of my tribe,
Swear to mark my way with blood and death.

CURTAIN

ACT III

SCENE

Interior of Delilah's house; a room furnished with luxurious divans; vases of perfume in various places; a harp on its pedestal, etc. Lamech discovered, with Melcah at his feet.

LAMECH

Slave, hast thou heard me?

MELCAH

Deep within my heart
Thy words are graven.

LAMECH

And thou swearest?

MELCAH

I swear,
Here in the dust, a blind obedience
To thee, my lord, as I do hope to have
Vengeance for my dead son—by Dagon; I swear!

LAMECH

Rise, then, and hearken unto me. Be thou
Delilah's shadow; be all humbleness
With her, but be thou prompt and fierce to act
When the hour comes! Thou knowest how Delilah
Plunges more deeply into her wild orgies;
And there is not one breath of true love in her:
She sells her favors and she changes lovers
As lightly as the fashion of her garment.
Look thou to take her, therefore, in some lapse
Of variable love fever, that her lover
May die through her.

MELCAH

Yea, he *shall* die through her!

LAMECH

Use Zambres for thy purpose.

MELCAH

I will be cautious.
[*Enter Delilah.*]

DELILAH

About my threshold thronged but now glad youth
And beauty, with the sounds of ministrelsy
And singing—but thou wast not there, my lord:
Why wert thou absent?

LAMECH

I awaited here
The splendor of the fairest star of all—
Thou bringest it!

DELILAH

Oh, very kind!

LAMECH

I've heard
Thy praises from the faithful Melcah, here;
I'm glad thou lik'st so well the slave I offered.

DELILAH

It was a gift indeed.

MELCAH

I hope to prove
Worthy, Delilah.
[*Aside.*]
And I will!
[*Exit.*]

LAMECH

I came
Hither for no light purpose. Thou dost know
How much thou hast promised me?

DELILAH

And have I not
Kept faith with thee?

LAMECH

Blinded by love, thou see'st
A friend in yonder Hebrew, and thou know'st not
The venom of the serpent in his kiss.
Ay, he spoke truly unto thee! Canst thou
Call thyself mistress of his heart?

DELILAH

Nay, then,
Have I not twice entreated him to tell me
Where lurked the might of his strong limbs?

LAMECH

And twice
Hath he not mocked at thee and told thee lies?
And when thou cried'st, "The Philistines be
Upon thee, Samson!" he did break the withes,
As flax is broken when it toucheth fire.
"Tie me," he said, "with seven new ropes that never
Were used before, and I shall be as weak
As other men," and when thou called'st them
That lay in ambush in thy chamber, straight
He burst the ropes from off his arms like thread.
An insolent jest this ruffian puts upon us
And thou must suffer it no longer.
One last attempt is to be made. Delilah,
Is thy soul equal to the work?

DELILAH
Why not?

LAMECH
Dost thou love Samson with thy wonted love,
Or hath he touched thy heart?

DELILAH
With manly love
Samson loves me; and I—

LAMECH
Thou lovest him
With love as great?

DELILAH
I cannot answer no.

LAMECH
Ah, idle hopes, ah, empty dreams! The gods
Did seem to shower from full hands upon thee
Their gifts of beauty and of genius, that
This curs'd serpent of the tribe of Zorah
Might die upon a bed of flowers through thee.
But thou dost pity him and hold him dear,
Thou lovest him! O blind! Thine own hand shuts
The gates of a bright future in thy face.
The nobles and the people vied together
To hail thee savior of our nation; sang
Thy praises with the harp, and would have strewn
Thy path with gems and gold; and thou, Delilah,
Thou scornest all their love.

DELILAH
The name of traitress
Fills me with loathing.

LAMECH
And was she not, then,
A traitress whom the tribe of Judah boasts
Bless'd above the women in the tent?
She did betray, not thou.—Our Sisera
Fled from the slaughter unto Heber's tent,
And Jael, Heber's wife, came forth to him;
"Turn in," she said, "my lord, turn in to me:
Fear nothing," and he turned into her tent.
"Give me, I pray, a little water to drink,
For I am very thirsty," so he prayed her.
He asked for water and she gave him milk,
She brought him butter in a lordly dish;
She put her right hand to the workman's hammer,
And softly went in unto him and smote
The tent-pin through his temples to the ground,
For he was fast asleep, and weary. So
He died. "He bowed before her feet, he fell,
There where he bowed him, there he fell down dead."
So sang their prophet-woman, Deborah,
Exulting in the treachery of Jael.
And dost thou hesitate to deliver up
Thy country's foe? He comes a conqueror,

And not a fugitive; he comes to thee
Followed by hate and tears; he only comes
To bring disgrace on thee, to make a jest
Of the Philistine blood that he hath shed.
And thou thyself must fly before his scorn,
Unless thou learnest soon to arm thy soul
With patriot hate. Arouse thyself, Delilah;
Wake, wake! And since thou needs must live by love,
Let love of country kindle in thy heart;
Burn in thy kiss and kill in thine embrace!

DELILAH
Thou dost ask too much!

LAMECH
I can ask no less.

DELILAH
My lord—O, no!

[Enter Zambres.]

ZAMBRES
He flouts at us beyond
All sufferance!

LAMECH
Samson?

ZAMBRES
Such might is in him
That he seems more than mortal.

LAMECH
What
Hath he done now?

ZAMBRES
He hath shown such valor,
So strange and marvellous are his deeds, that words
Of mine could never tell them. He hath blighted
The glory of our fertile fields, and burned
Our standing corn, our vineyards, and our olives;
His hand hath smitten us sorer than the whirlwind;
Our lands are turned to savage wastes; the rock
Of Etam is our sepulcher.

LAMECH
Accursed wretch! And did not hundreds rise
For every ten that fell? Had ye no swords
Within your scabbards?

ZAMBRES
Terror-struck, the most
Fled from his face, and whosoever drew
His weapon bit the dust.

DELILAH
Oh, from his eyes
There flashes such a supernatural fire,

Such force, that human eye cannot endure
To meet it. Yea, the grandeur of a god
Is his, a god's sublimity and splendor
Dwell in his love and hate! And he is surely
Sent of the gods: it is impossible
To fight against the gods! Let us appease
This mighty one with humble supplications,
Let us disarm his wrath with tenderness
And love.

LAMECH

   Not so! Let us oppose his craft
With craft as pitiless! Delilah, thou
Shalt overcome him, thou shalt break the spell
That guards him, thou shalt pierce the cunning mesh
That wraps him round. What gods, what powers have
  sent him?
Phantoms to awe the vulgar, empty masks
To frighten children! Samson is no god,
But common clay, the idol of an hour.
Deliver in my hands that wretch, and thou
Shalt have from every prince of the Philistines,
A thousand and a hundred silver pieces!
I promise it, I swear to pour out gold
From overflowing hands upon thee, cover thee
With gems, if thou canst, by thy subtle arts,
Steal me his fatal secret.

DELILAH

   Steal his secret?—
I!

LAMECH

What! Dost thou still hesitate?

DELILAH

    Our hearts
Are blent in one, and she who loveth Samson
Cannot betray him! Thou set'st terrible war
In me; for I can see the thing that I should do
As a Philistine woman, and I feel
The shame of my abject condition; yet,
Why wilt thou plunge me into this abyss?—
Doom me to sacrifice my lover? No!
I will not ope his tomb; he shall not taste
Death in my kiss!

LAMECH

   What death? Who talks of death?
Woe be to him who even thinks of death
To Samson! Do not fear. We only seek
To take his strength away. His life shall be
Sacred to us; we will preserve his life
And keep it for thy love.

DELILAH

   And dost thou promise
All this to me, O prince?

LAMECH

I swear 't!

DELILAH

     And I—

LAMECH

Speak!

DELILAH

I—I will content thee!

       [Enter Samson.]

ZAMBRES

    He!

DELILAH

Oh! Samson!

LAMECH

       [Aside.]
  Villain!

SAMSON

I scarcely recognize Delilah's house
Since it became the haunt of princes!

DELILAH

      Samson,
The prince—

SAMSON

I took away the gates of Gaza, prince,
That when thou dost return there thou mayest find
An easy entrance.

LAMECH

   And I trust to meet thee
In Gaza soon.

SAMSON

  I will not fail.

DELILAH

     How glad
I am to have thee here, my love, my hero!
How glorious is thy name! Oh, though I know
Thy laurels drip with my Philistine blood,
I cannot weep for it, for my pride in thee
O'ercomes my pity and my duty. Oh,
How I rejoice to see thee once again!
The sun that beat upon thee in the fields,
Hath only made the more beautiful
Thy tawny face! Who can compare with thee,
My lover? Who can stand so tall and strong
Beside thee? None! The man of my heart's love
Is first of men.

SAMSON

   As in the fight I share
My perils and my triumphs with no other,

So would I be; I only, I alone,
Lord of my love, for I would make my love
A temple where I could devote the honors
In sacred battles won, and hide the secrets
Of my inmost soul; and I would rest myself
From every trouble in my love's embrace,
As on a mother's breast, and yield my brow
That she might wipe the sweat of strife away.

DELILAH

Let me be all this to thee—

SAMSON

Thou? born Philistine!

DELILAH

What matters it?

SAMSON

But I could ne'er endure
The shadow of a rival, and *thy* lover
Must suffer many rivals. Ah, Delilah,
If—

DELILAH

I was that thing; An orphan flung
From Dead Sea shores, even as a stone is cast
Out of a sling. I fell into the mire
O' the wayside ditch. But I have washed me clean
At the pure fount! Love hath redeemed itself!
The roses bloomed beneath my feet; their sweet
Was as the breath of serpents to my soul—
I lived a poisoned life. Its joys have passed
Like the heat lightning; naught but shame remains
Of all my delights. Forget, forget my past!
Read not my infamy there!— Oh look—she's dead
The false Delilah of others! *Thy* Delilah
She alone lives!

SAMSON

And mine thou art forever!
I would drink deep the draft of love with thee.
Oh, rapture—oh, how the thick cloud of ills
That weighs on mortals vanishes before
The light of love!— Oh, warlike panoply,
Ye noble steeds, and ye victorious cars,
Ye trumpets, and ye trophies and laurels,
What are ye all, if ye be not endeared
And consecrated by love's smile? There is
No life where love is not. And I do love thee,
My own Delilah!

DELILAH

Where love is, is trust;
And hast thou faith in me? And wilt thou pour
The secrets of thy soul into my breast?

SAMSON

I will ope wide to thee its inmost chamber:
Thou shalt know all its mysteries.

DELILAH

Not all!

SAMSON

I will keep none from thee.

DELILAH

Thou wilt keep one!

SAMSON

Ask it!

DELILAH

What power, what fate, or magic science
Gave thee the strength that makes thee mightier
Than beast or man?

SAMSON

The Lord. He gave it me.

DELILAH

But where doth't lie in thee?

SAMSON

There where it pleased
The Eternal Maker to conceal it. I
Was born to do miraculous deeds. The Lord
Did smile upon my birth, and breathed in me
His strength divine. Woe to any babbling tongue
If it betray the mystery he bequeathed me,
Accursed among all the sons of men,
I were the most accursed.

DELILAH

Old wives' tales!
Nay, tell me not Jehovah is the cause.
Thou keep'st thy secret from me. I know well
Another reason!

SAMSON

What is that?

DELILAH

The doubt
Thou hast of me, that am Philistine born.

SAMSON

Hearts have no country, we are one in love.

DELILAH

Ah, thou canst not deceive me; for thy silence
Confirms my fear.

SAMSON

Delilah!

DELILAH

Keep thy secret,
Nay, keep it! Go, go, Israelite, and find
Some fairer, dearer, worthier one than I—
Get thee to her, and tell it—

SAMSON
None shall know,
If thou know not the secret of my soul.
For the Lord never made a woman yet,
So wonderfully beautiful as thou!
Eve, first of women, never had the charm
Of thy fair form, and never shone her eyes,
As bright as thine.—Oh, turn them not away!
Nay, do not go! Listen to me! Love burns
Like fever in my blood! Delilah, clasp thy hand
In mine—Oh, stay—what a sweet flood of life
Breaks over the fierce lion of Judah now!
One kiss—one kiss—Oh, rapture of the skies,
I am in paradise!

DELILAH
Ho!—wine of Sorek!

SAMSON
Thou wouldst—

DELILAH
Sing thee a glorious song of love!

SAMSON
Yea, sing.

[Enter Melcah with vase and cups.]

MELCAH
Here are the cups.

DELILAH
But ere I sing.
Taste thou this Sorek wine.

SAMSON
I must not drink it.

DELILAH
I offer thee the cup of Noah; and my hero
Refuses the gift of bliss! Wilt thou not drink
The nuptials of our souls?

SAMSON
I!—if—

DELILAH
This is
The dawn of love.—Come, let us pledge each other
Eternal truth and fealty. Swear!

SAMSON
I swear.

DELILAH
[Chants following verses.]
In the land of his foes, without arms, without steed,
    My love is the boldest to do and to dare;
Like the crest of high Carmel he lifteth his head,

Like the myrrh and the saffron he perfumes the air.
Sweet star of my soul! Like honey his words;
    His limbs are like columns of steel and of gold;
His looks pierce like lances, they fright the wild pards;
    In ruin before him his foemen are rolled.

SAMSON
Cry aloud to thy people, and repeat
That which thou singest. Israel has suffered
Sorely. But Gideon's unconquered seed
Survives in me.
[Shows signs of drunkenness.]

MELCAH
[Aside.]
Insolent!

DELILAH
Rest thou here.
[Leads him to ottoman.]

SAMSON
Ah, my love!

DELILAH
Wilt thou still conceal from me
Where thy strength lies?

SAMSON
Search thou the tangled mane
O' the lion for his might, O my heart's queen!

DELILAH
[Chants again.]
O'er the dead and the dying he sendeth his roar,
    The lion of Judah, my Samson, my own;
On my lap stream his locks that the steel never shore,
    And there hides the secret of none ever known!

SAMSON
Thou sayest well—The Lord did hide his might
Within my locks.

MELCAH
O, joy!

SAMSON
Delilah!
[Sleeps.]

DELILAH
Samson! Have I betrayed thee?
[Sees Melcah.]
O, alas!

MELCAH
[Coming forward.]
He lieth sunk in deepest slumber!

DELILAH
What!
Thou hast heard?

MELCAH

I have heard everything!

DELILAH

And thou would'st—

MELCAH

Wreak my vengeance on him!

DELILAH

No!

MELCAH

Ay, so! My murdered son's blood cries to me
From his new grave!

DELILAH
[*Flinging herself upon Samson.*]
Never!

MELCAH
[*Dragging her away.*]
Away with thee!
Mine is the man thou hast betrayed. The mother
Arises from the slave! Philistines—come!
[*Enter Zambres and other Philistines.*]
CURTAIN

ACT IV

SCENE

*Same as end of Act III. Samson asleep on ottoman.
Melcah standing beside him. Zambres and the other
Philistines form a circle around him. Delilah prostrate
in intense self-abasement at foot of ottoman.*

ZAMBRES

He slumbers long.

MELCAH
He fell asleep in joy,
Let him awake in shame!

ZAMBRES
Ay, now at last
This Israelitish terror of our race
Shall be our scoff and scorn.

MELCAH
Ay, now at last
Oh, pent up hate that so hath swelled my heart,
Thou may'st burst forth, and sweet shall be the vengeance
That I shall taste!

ZAMBRES

We shall all share thy vengeance.

DELILAH

It is a coward's trick!

MELCAH
The trick was thine!
Poor fool! Thou hast sown love and reaped contempt
Till now; but now thou shalt reap glory; thou,
Once idol of the populace, shall be
The pride of princes. Thou didst well fulfill
Thy task and thou shalt have a worthy guerdon.

DELILAH

Melcah—

MELCAH

Art thou not glad?

DELILAH
I am ashamed
Of my misdeed; would that this night could hide me
Deep in its blackness evermore!

MELCAH
The sun
Shall show thee as thou art!
[*Pause.*]

SAMSON

Delilah!

DELILAH

Oh! He speaks!

SAMSON

Oh, my Delilah, where, where art thou?
Dost thou not hear me? Let me look on thee.

ZAMBRES
[*Advancing.*]
Nay, look on the Philistines!

SAMSON
Ye, and so few
Of you? Have you forgotten Askelon?
The hundreds and the thousands that I slew there
With my own hand?

ZAMBRES
That which thou wast thou art
No longer.

SAMSON
Villain—dost thou dare so far?

ZAMBRES

Yea, the wings of Zorah's eagle are clipped,
And thou art but a croaking raven now.

SAMSON

I am a Lion.—But what unknown languor
Seizes on me?

ZAMBRES

What is it stays thee, Samson?

SAMSON

My feet, why do they stagger? Am not I
A Nazarite, perchance? I am—Great God!!
My hair—my hair!

MELCAH

We've shorn it from thy head!

ZAMBRES

This woman-warrior trusted in a woman;
Let's mock him to his face!

ALL

Accursed!

SAMSON

The air around me hisses in my ears,
"Thou art accursed!" From the frailest leaf
Unto the mighty cedar; from the pool,
Stagnant and foul, unto the shoreless sea,
From the sun fronting eagle to the signet,
From earth to heaven, all things, everywhere,
Heap curses on me!— Guiltier than Cain
Am I, for Cain shed but *one* brother's blood,
I could have rescued thousands upon thousands,
Redeemed a nation from its servitude,—
And I have infamously doomed my people
To pitiless slavery evermore.

MELCAH

Ah, how his pride is broken!

ZAMBRES

Felon, stretch
Thine arm out for the manacle. The dungeons
Of Gaza now shall be thy home.

SAMSON

I, captive?
I—no! Delilah! Oh, where is she? I'd see her
Yet once again! Where art thou? Dost not hear
My voice? Why dost thou hide thee in the night,
The fatal night? I'll find thee—oh, thanks—thanks!
Spirit of hell, why dost thou fly from me?
Come—come—thou perjurers! I'd have wreathed thy
  life
With flowers; and thou dost garland mine with thorns.
It well becomes me: on my naked skull
Here, lay thy chaplet of my infamy!
Huckster of filthy kisses, for what sum
Hast sold me?

DELILAH

O, in mercy!—Remorse
Tears at my heart!

SAMSON

At dawn and in thy dreams,
At table, in the dance, even in the hour
When thou invokest thy God, may my form flame
Before thy eyes.

DELILAH

No more!

SAMSON

Beneath thy feet
May the paths break in ruin, and may serpents
Gender along thy way, and with their hisses
Hush the lascivious music of thy harp!
Under a sky of brass live thou, and wander, like
The greedy worm, and on thy lips thy food
Be ashes; may the gold-wrought borders of thy robes
Distill salt tears, and every gem of thine
Dash thy false visage with my blood:
Go—Go!

DELILAH

Pardon!

SAMSON

Philistines—I am yours!

DELILAH

Bound up in thee I follow.

SAMSON

A horrible barrier divideth us
Forever and forever! Thou shalt see
The firmament crumble, and the most high god
In league with hell, or ever Samson stoop
To lift thee from the dust, accursed woman!
                              [*Rushes off.*]

DELILAH

Oh, was it me? So dost thou leave me? Ah,
Stay! Listen! O, heaven, his life—

MELCAH

And dost thou pray
For him?

DELILAH

What hath my heart in it, but him?
Do I not love him with a love that hath
No like nor bound?

MELCAH

And when hast thou before
Spoken of love? 'Tis woman's vanity
That thou call'st love.

DELILAH

It is a flame, a fire,
The whirlwind could not fan to greater fierceness,
The Red Sea could not quench! Oh, Melcah, Melcah,
Thou hast plunged a dagger in my breast, and broken
My roof above me, poured out on my head
The inexhaustible cup of human woes,
And so with sorrow choked my soul in me
That speech dies on my lips!

MELCAH

A keener anguish
Hath pierced my heart—a sacred grief that turned
To hate.

DELILAH

Hate! Thou—

MELCAH

Yea, I! A mother's fury
Rages in me! A poor despis'd slave,
I sheltered in my heart a tender germ,
And when it grew into the light of day,
I fed it with my tears more than my milk;
In fasting, and in vigilance and fear
I reared my boy. And he grew strong and bold.
And in his hand I placed the warrior's sword.
I saw the prosperous star of the Philistines
Burn on his brow, and proud of my brave boy,
I pitied in my slavery those free women
Who were not mothers. Ah, the day of sorrow
Dawned upon me! The mother's smile was banished
Forever from my lips, and he, thy Samson,
Thy treacherous Hebrew, there in Askelon
Bathed his right hand in my son's blood, and flung
His fatal garment reeking in my face,
And bade me keep it for his winding-sheet.

DELILAH

Alas, what memories!

[On ottoman L.]

MELCAH

In that baleful hour
Upon that sacred spot where my son fell
I did devote my life to vengeance; then,
To compass it, I came to thee, and feigned
To be the friend of thy lewd paramour,
And made the closest secrets of your hearts
My prey!—But now at last the hour of justice
Hath struck, and now the mother from the slave
Hath risen, and the man of death shall die!

DELILAH

[Rises.]

Oh, fell spirit!

[Enter Lamech with slaves, bearing gifts.]

LAMECH

To the beauteous lady, whom
The realm of the Philistines owes so much,
To fair Delilah, every prince of Gaza
Sends salutation—

DELILAH

Oh!—but Samson—

LAMECH

In
The hearts of all Delilah hath a place;
Thy name is praised of all, and all desire
To do thee honor. To the price we fixed,
Of many thousand shekels, here we add
Jewels and gold untold—

DELILAH

Gold!—gold!

LAMECH

Present
Our offerings humbly, slaves!

[Two slaves present the gifts, kneeling.]

DELILAH

To me?

MELCAH

[Ironically.]
Fling this necklace
Of lucent stones upon thy breast of snow;
Put on these purple robes; twine in thy hair
These India pearls and beauteous sapphires; ay,
Let thy proud beauty clothe itself in all
These lustrous gems and gold!—

DELILAH

Oh, your gifts reek
With tears! Oh, hide them!—I abhor myself.
Keep, keep your splendid offerings, my lord,
And give me back again my peace of soul!
Thy solemn oaths, thy promise,—hast kept them?

LAMECH

What did I promise thee?

DELILAH

Shall I behold
Samson alive?

LAMECH

I am the guaranty
Of Samson's life.

[Enter Manoah.]

MANOAH

Delilah, oh, Delilah,
What has thou done unto my son?

DELILAH
[*Aside.*]
Oh, what?

MANOAH

Dost thou stand here in idle talk? 'Twas true,
That horrible rumor, then? Within these walls
Was Israel's mighty champion bought and sold?
Thou art silent? Drop'st thine eye? Thou tremblest,
     weepest?
Weep, weep, thou cruel wretch! I have shed tears
Of blood.

DELILAH
Oh, speak! What meanest thou?

MANOAH
                              I saw
My son chained hand and foot, and dragged along
Like a wild beast, amid the yells and jeers
Of the Philistine mob. I followed fast
As age would suffer me, the drunken rabble,
That flung itself down like an avalanche
Into the valley where the satraps sat
In sinister conclave round, I came, I called,
I wept, I shrieked in vain! Horrible sight!
Helpless, there Samson stood, the prey and sport
Of the unpitying mulitude that swarmed
About him, stoning, scourging him with rods—
And not yet glutted with their cruelties
I saw them plunge sharp, red-hot points of steel
Into his eyes and quench their light forever!

DELILAH

Oh, agony, oh, death! Merciless fiends!
And I did trust thy word! Away! The furies
Of hell awake in me! Give me, thou, villain,
My Samson's life!

LAMECH
I've paid for it with gold.

DELILAH

I trample on thy gold. I crush, I scatter
The wages of my crime!

LAMECH
Woman!

DELILAH
                              Away
From me! Where's Samson? Oh, what darkness
Is this that wraps me round? What baleful star
Strikes its fierce flame into my face? What moan
Incessant as if mortal anguish fills
Mine ear? It is the roar of Zorah's lion!
They steep their fingers in his blood, and write
Upon my forehead, Bought! Ah, no, no, no!

I am not bought! The hate of the Philistines
Hath made me guilty; but henceforth I trample
Upon the tombs and altars of my sires.
For him who is my country and my God
I do here renounce them all!
                              [*Kneels.*]

LAMECH
Woman, thou'rt mad!

DELILAH
                              [*Rises.*]
Begone! I am not mad, but desperate!
Go, go!
                              [*To Manoah.*]
     Holy old man, let me lie at thy feet!
CURTAIN

ACT V

SCENE

*Vestibule under the temple of Dagon. The rising of the
curtain reveals many Israelites crouching together.
Among them are Thebni and Neriah and Samson, blind.
Gomer and other Philistines are keeping watch.*

GOMER

Make your choice quickly. The temple is adorned
For a high festival against your coming.
But no one of your captive crew may be
Admitted to its solemn rites, unless
He bow to Dagon. Children of Israel,
Choose ye between him and your dungeons!

NERIAH
                              Haste!
Drag me back to my cell!

THEBNI
                    Double my chains,
Increase my pains a hundredfold, for I
Kneel not to heathen idols!

GOMER
                    Oh, your hero
Is not so haughty!

THEBNI
Who?

GOMER
                    The judge of Zorah,
The invincible, the mighty Samson, he
Who hath been chosen to make the people sport
Before our Dagon.

THEBNI
He!

NERIAH
            Did I err, then,
When I denounced thee as a traitor, there
In Zorah?

GOMER
            Drive these to their cells again;
Let *him* remain and rave here in the dust!

NERIAH
He hath earned his reward.

THEBNI
                                    [*To Samson.*]
            Stay thou!
                                    [*Exit.*]

SAMSON
            I crawl and writhe here like a wounded worm
Under my foemen's feet, more vilely wretched
Than even the loathesome charnel worm, for he
Through some small crevice of the tomb enjoys
A glimmer of the day and lives secure
And unmolested! I, loaded down with chains,
Slave of mine enemies, under the vast cope
Of heaven and amidst the noonday stream
Of the all-bathing light imortal, lie
In darkness blacker than the sepulchers!
Miserable Samson! In the flower of life
How art thou broken! Ah, how hath thy greatness
Vanished, and left no memory behind,
Save such as tarnishes thy mighty deeds.
Wearisome, solitary, horrible
The future glooms before me! Oh, where are ye,
Ye beauteous dawn, and ye effulgent noons
Of my youth's strength, ye fair wide fields of Lebi,
Ye billow-beaten shores of Askelon,
Ye echoing caves of Etam, where are you?
Night, only night remains. Oh, vales of Timnath,
Keep, keep my name! Keep it, ye perishing years,
And say to aftertimes that I was born
To trample on the seed of Pharaoh,—
Say that the Lord endowed me with his might
That I should break the fetters of his people!
And wilt thou suffer that thy glory, Lord,
Be mocked in me? And wilt thou not destroy
Yon idol of theirs? Oh, give me back once more
My bounding pulses, and my growing locks
Strengthen anew! And give me sight again,
My sight, that I may fall a thunderbolt,
A meteor of death upon them.
                        [*Enter Delilah and Manoah.*]

MANOAH
                                    Oh,
How do I find him?

DELILAH
            It makes me afraid
To look on him!

SAMSON
                        Methinks, thou God of justice,
That in Thy silence I can read and feel,

By Thy miraculous grace, Thy spirit coming
Mightily upon me! I grow, and all my limbs
Throb with the strength of old. My broken spirit
Thrills with gigantic courage. I am—I am
That which I was.

MANOAH
                                    [*Comes down.*]
            The Everlasting God
Hath not forsaken thee.

SAMSON
            What voice!

MANOAH
                                    My son!

SAMSON
Oh, father! Thou—

MANOAH
Embrace me!

SAMSON
                        Oh, the bliss
To feel once more my father's arm around me,
To kiss his wrinkled brow.

MANOAH
                        Life's supreme hour
Is this for us!—and thou wilt not refuse
A father's counsel?

SAMSON
            I?

MANOAH
                        Here, in the temple
The lords of the Philistines and the people
Are met to offer sacrifice to Dagon—
A countless multitude,—and on the roof
Thousands of men and women sit to look.
Their hearts are merry with the fumes of wine;
They cry, "Our Dagon hath delivered Samson
Into our hands—our enemy, who destroyed
Our country and who slew our mighty men.
Bring us forth Samson to make sport for us."
And they would force thee to profane thy faith,
The holy faith of Israel, and thou—

SAMSON
I keep the faith of my forefathers pure.

MANOAH
But they will send their guards to drag thee thither.

SAMSON
No force can do it.

MANOAH
                        I have come with gold,
With gold abundant and with precious stones,
To pay thy ransom.

SAMSON

      And will Samson's father
Bow down to the Philistines?

MANOAH

      No!

SAMSON

          Who then
Will pay them for me?

DELILAH

         [*Coming down L.*]
      The unhappiest,
The guiltiest of women!

SAMSON

      Thou?

DELILAH

          My shame
Hath eaten deep into my soul, and men
Shall never see me lift my face again;
I hope for nothing now but that my torment
May bring me death!

SAMSON

      But thou should'st lift thy face
And triumph in thy victim. Look on me.

DELILAH

Have pity, have pity on me!

SAMSON

      The ghost of Samson
Standeth before thee! Look here, where the light
Of life once shone. See how the darkness thickens
In the empty sockets. They were quenched for thee,
For thee the Nazarite's sacred locks were shorn.
Art thou not satisfied? Feed full thy heart
Upon the sight! But what hast thou to do
Here with my misery? Who bade thee buy
My safety with the gold for which thou sold'st me?

DELILAH

Be not so wroth with me—

SAMSON

      My father's presence
Shall be thy shield, and I will speak no more
In anger with thee! Young in years, I stand
Upon the brink of death, and I would fain
Wash all the stains of dust away, that I
Guiltless may pass to the eternal truth
That veils itself beyond. Mine now, not thine
The unpardonable fault hath been, and I
Must bear the penalty in patience. Keep
The guerdon, thou! Mingle with the Philistines,

Seek Dagon's altar and perfume thyself
With the sweet incense burning at his shrine,
Yea, deck thy temples with his wreaths, for they
Should be thy badge, and he should share his altar
With great Delilah.

DELILAH

      Nay, my badge shall be
A crown of thorns. Oh, I was rather weak
Than guilty. But I will implore no longer
Thy pardon.—Thy just wrath should strike me dead
Before thy face.—The evil fate that choked
All virtue in me, from my mother's breast,
And gifted me with infamy and beauty,
That evil destiny bewildered me,
And I became the weapon of thy foes:
I am the fountain of thy woes; 'twas I
That lured thee on, and thou shalt punish me:
I do beseech thee, kill me with thy hand!

MANOAH

O let us fly, while yet 'tis time—

SAMSON

      My father,
Thy will is sacred unto me, but never
Shall I set foot beyond this threshold more.
The will of the Eternal stays me here,
And from yon vault methinks I hear the voice
Of God speak unto me.

DELILAH

      O, fly—

MANOAH

      My son!
        [*Enter Lamech.*]

LAMECH

The multitude call on Delilah's name!

SAMSON

Why runnest thou not to meet the well earned praise?

DELILAH

Samson—

SAMSON

      The harps of the Philistines praise thee,
And worthy of song is Sorek's beauteous lady!
Bow down before her feet, Princes of Gaza,
Upon your altars lift your heroine.

LAMECH

Woe unto thee, if thou dost not refrain
Thine insolent raillery. Thou hast suffered him
Too long, Delilah. Leave the impious Hebrew
Here to his shame.

DELILAH

      No, no; I cannot leave him!

LAMECH

Then I will tear thee from the coward's breast
With my own hands. Come!

DELILAH

No!

LAMECH

Prepare thyself,
Thou mountebank, to make us sport;
If thou shalt fall below our expectations,
Or thy strength fail thee!—

SAMSON

It shall rise gigantic.

LAMECH

Woe unto thee if thou—

DELILAH

For mercy's sake!

LAMECH

Go thou before me into the temple.

DELILAH

[*Moving toward temple door.*]
Alas!

[*Exit.*]

LAMECH

The multitude awaits thee; all are eager
To look upon thee; I grant thee but a moment.

[*Exit.*]

SAMSON

An instant were enough.

MANOAH

What sayest thou?

SAMSON

Dost thou not hear a heavenly harmony
That drowns the yells of yon idolaters?
Dost thou not see as on Sinai of old
The sword of God's eternal justice gleam?
It blazes on the sightless sockets, and I—
I seize it to avenge the everlasting.
Are we alone?

MANOAH

We are alone.

SAMSON

There, yonder—
Beside the stairway to the temple's door
Place me, my father. Let me feel the pillars
That the house stands on.

MANOAH

Here, this is the base
Of the two pillars.

SAMSON

Lo! I bow myself
Under the guilty roof, and I implore
Thy blessing.

MANOAH

Yea, I bless thee; but what thought
Is thine, my son? Tell me!—

SAMSON

My locks are grown
Again, and in my veins the hot blood boils
Like molten lava.

VOICES

[*Within the temple.*]
Bring us Samson, to make us sport!—

SAMSON

Take flight,
My father—save thee! [1]

MANOAH

What?

[*Enter Zambres.*]

ZAMBRES

Patience can endure
No more. Old man, leave the slave to his duty.

SAMSON

Leave me forever!

MANOAH

The Lord keep thee and help thee.
[*Exit Manoah.*]

VOICES

[*Within.*]
Samson, bring Samson!

SAMSON

God is all with me!
He fills me with the power of His Hosts.
Remember me, oh, Lord, remember, I pray Thee
Only this once! Oh, God, that I may be
Avenged on the Philistines for mine eyes!
Now fall, fall, thou temple of iniquity—
Oh, joy—I feel it shake on its foundations!
I hear the shriek of the idolaters
Already. Let them all die—
Crumble, walls—down—down,
And let me die with the Philistines,
I pray thee, Lord, and let my people live.
[*The temple falls, and Samson is buried in the ruins.*]
CURTAIN

[1] The translation of this speech is editorially supplied.
Howells' version was by some mischance omitted from
the one printed edition.

The Parlor Car

[1876]

With this first of his twenty-five one-act dramas, Howells was plainly hopeful of writing a play of literary quality that would also be acceptable for stage production. Realizing, however, that *The Parlor Car* differed from the plays then popular, he asked a number of persons to read it before it was published. Mark Twain, as might be expected, was most enthusiastic. A more important critical opinion is that of William Winter, who wrote to Howells (February 18, 1876, Hayes Memorial Library):

> I thank you much for your letter and the accompanying copy of your farce of the Parlor Car. The farce is delicate and will require cleverness of a peculiar kind in the acting: but, if rightly presented, it will surely please. The invention is happily whimsical: the language is piquant; the situations indicate much and good comic business; and the lovers are clearly and neatly sketched. I should judge it would be a point of policy for Mr. D[aly] to produce the farce, and, for that reason, I think he will keep the promise which you inform me he has made. I will, at all events, make such allusion to the subject as will neither hurt nor offend any interest. I am sure that you know you have, at all times, my best wishes.

Later, when Edmund Gosse, one of Howells' first English admirers, read the play, he wrote to Howells (October 12, 1882, Harvard Library): "We are all talking about you. I see ladies giggling over little books in the trains, and then I know they must be reading 'The Parlour Car.' "

Of course not all readers have agreed with Howells' friends that he displayed dramatic talent and discerning powers of observation. Oscar Firkins has little good to say about the play. "The

Parlor Car," Firkins writes (*William Dean Howells, A Study* [Cambridge: Harvard University Press, 1924], p. 245), "explains in needless detail how a girl whom we strongly dislike renews her broken engagement with a man whom we barely tolerate." A less witty but more substantial criticism is that of John M. Robertson (*Essays Toward a Critical Method* [London: T. F. Unwin, 1889], p. 189): "The farce consists in the conduct of the young lady, who is a charming goose, while the young man is drawn respectfully enough, and endowed with sense and delicacy. . . ."

From a professional standpoint *The Parlor Car* had drawbacks. Daly considered it too slight for his use. Mark Twain, an unsuccessful dramatist himself, thought the play should have more humor to lessen its argumentative quality. He suggested that Howells introduce one of those instinctively obnoxious train butchers into the play and have him intrude at inopportune moments. Undoubtedly this would have added a typical Mark Twain type of humor, but Howells did not take the suggestion. Possibly, however, he was impressed with it, since in later plays he used a somewhat intuitively mischievous character in the person of Willis Campbell, who, after *The Sleeping Car*, could be counted on to supply comic wit and farcical humor when the action dragged. But in spite of numerous inadequacies, *The Parlor Car* gave evidence of some facility in framing a one-act play, and for what Howells was trying to do, it was a good beginning. Many found it enjoyable reading.

Howells, of course, would have been more pleased if people had also found the play enjoyable as a stage production, but the stage history of this farce was not a happy one for Howells. Mark Twain first suggested that Augustin Daly ask

Howells to write a play, and in his answer to Daly (M. J. Moses, *The American Dramatist* [Boston: Little, Brown & Co., 1911], pp. 180–81; letter, November 14, 1874), Howells mentioned that he did have a "notion of a play" which had been approved by Mark Twain, but he was not sure that its "rather tragical" nature would make it a success. However, in the same letter he said, "I have also the idea of a farce or vaudeville of strictly American Circumstances." This was evidently to be *The Parlor Car*. On April 24, 1876, Howells again wrote to Daly (J. F. Daly, *The Life of Augustin Daly* [New York: The Macmillan Co., 1917], p. 232), reminding him of his invitation to send him any play he might write and enclosing *The Parlor Car*. Howells' final comment in his letter was: "If by any chance it should please you and you should feel like bringing it out on some off-night when nobody will be there, pray tell me whether it will hurt or help it, for your purpose, to be published in the *Atlantic*."

Daly did like the play, and on May 9, 1876

(*Daly*, p. 233), Howells wrote to say that it was at his disposal and he hoped that if this one failed, he might still write plays for Daly. Then nothing happened. Later, Mark Twain wrote to Howells suggesting that they go to New York together to see the production, for evidently the news of its acceptance was spreading. Howells' reply (June 8, 1876, Mildred Howells [ed.], *Life in Letters*, I [Garden City: Doubleday, Doran & Co., 1928], 221–22) is indicative of the gloom that was later to cloud his relations with theater managers. "It [*The Parlor Car*] has not yet been given and I have not heard from Daly anything about it. I have heard from others, however, that he promises rashly; and I dare say that it's quite likely that on second thought he doesn't find the play desirable. Small blame to him in any case. I shall quietly pass it down to posterity in the September *Atlantic*." Although Daly announced the play for the 1876–77 season, it was explained (*Daly*, p. 231) that other requirements prevented production; in point of fact, Daly never did produce it.

The Parlor-Car [1]

SCENE: *A Parlor-Car on the New York Central Railroad. It is late afternoon in the early autumn, with a cloudy sunset threatening rain. The car is unoccupied save by a gentleman, who sits fronting one of the windows, with his feet in another chair; a newspaper lies across his lap; his hat is drawn down over his eyes, and he is apparently asleep. The rear door of the car opens, and the conductor enters with a young lady, heavily veiled, the porter coming after with her wraps and travelling-bags. The lady's air is of mingled anxiety and desperation, with a certain fierceness of movement. She casts a careless glance over the empty chairs.*

CONDUCTOR: Here's your ticket, madam. You can have any of the places you like here, or *(glancing at the unconscious gentleman, and then at the young lady)* if you prefer, you can go and take that seat in the forward car.

MISS LUCY GALBRAITH: Oh, I can't ride backwards. I'll stay here, please. Thank you.

The porter places her things in a chair by a window, across the car from the sleeping gentleman, and she throws herself wearily into the next seat, wheels round in it, and lifting her veil gazes absently out at the landscape. Her face, which is very pretty, with a low forehead shadowed by thick blond hair, shows the traces of tears. She makes search in her pocket for her handkerchief, which she presses to her eyes. The conductor, lingering a moment, goes out.

PORTER: I'll be right here, at de end of de cah, if you should happen to want anything, miss *(making a feint of arranging the shawls and satchels)*. Should you like some dese things hung up? Well, dey'll be jus' as well in de chair. We's pretty late dis afternoon; more'n four hours behin' time. Ought to been into Albany 'fore dis. Freight train off de track jus' dis side o' Rochester, an' had

to wait. Was you going to stop at Schenectady, miss?

MISS GALBRAITH, *absently*: At Schenectady? *(After a pause)* Yes.

PORTER: Well, that's de next station, and den de cahs don't stop ag'in till dey git to Albany. Anything else I can do for you now, miss?

MISS GALBRAITH: No, no, thank you, nothing. *The Porter hesitates, takes off his cap, and scratches his head with a murmur of embarrassment. Miss Galbraith looks up at him inquiringly and then suddenly takes out her portemonnaie, and fees him.*

PORTER: Thank you, miss, thank you. If you want anything at all, miss, I'm right dere at de end of de cah.

He goes out by the narrow passage-way beside the smaller enclosed parlor. Miss Galbraith looks askance at the sleeping gentleman, and then, rising, goes to the large mirror, to pin her veil, which has become loosened from her hat. She gives a little start at sight of the gentleman in the mirror, but arranges her headgear, and returning to her place looks out of the window again. After a little while she moves about uneasily in her chair, then leans forward, and tries to raise her window; she lifts it partly up, when the catch slips from her fingers, and the window falls shut again with a crash.

MISS GALBRAITH: Oh, *dear*, how provoking! I suppose I must call the porter. *(She rises from her seat, but on attempting to move away she finds that the skirt of her polonaise has been caught in the falling window. She pulls at it, and then tries to lift the window again, but the cloth has wedged it in, and she cannot stir it.)* Well, I certainly think this is beyond endurance! Porter! Ah,— Porter! Oh, he'll never hear me in the racket that these wheels are making! I wish they'd stop—I

The gentleman stirs in his chair, lifts his head, listens, takes his feet down from the other seat, rises abruptly, and comes to Miss Galbraith's side.

[1] The text is from *The Sleeping-Car and Other Farces*.

MR. ALLEN RICHARDS: Will you allow me to open the window for you? (*Starting back*) Miss Galbraith!

MISS GALBRAITH: Al— Mr. Richards!

There is a silence for some moments, in which they remain looking at each other; then—

MR. RICHARDS: Lucy—

MISS GALBRAITH: I forbid you to address me in that way, Mr. Richards.

MR. RICHARDS: Why, you were just going to call me Allen!

MISS GALBRAITH: That was an accident, you know very well—an impulse—

MR. RICHARDS: Well, so is this.

MISS GALBRAITH: Of which you ought to be ashamed to take advantage. I wonder at your presumption in speaking to me at all. It's quite idle, I can assure you. Everything is at an end between us. It seems that I bore with you too long; but I'm thankful that I had the spirit to act at last, and to act in time. And now that chance has thrown us together, I trust that you will not force your conversation upon me. No gentleman would, and I have always given you credit for thinking yourself a gentleman. I request that you will not speak to me.

MR. RICHARDS: You've spoken ten words to me for every one of mine to you. But I won't annoy you. I can't believe it, Lucy; I can *not* believe it. It seems like some rascally dream, and if I had had any sleep since it happened, I should think I *had* dreamed it.

MISS GALBRAITH: Oh! You were sleeping soundly enough when I got into the car!

MR. RICHARDS: I own it; I was perfectly used up, and I *had* dropped off.

MISS GALBRAITH, *scornfully*: Then perhaps you *have* dreamed it.

MR. RICHARDS: I'll think so till you tell me again that our engagement is broken; that the faithful love of years is to go for nothing; that you dismiss me with cruel insult, without one word of explanation, without a word of intelligible accusation, even. It's too much! I've been thinking it all over and over, and I can't make head or tail of it. I meant to see you again as soon as we got to town, and implore you to hear me. Come, it's a mighty serious matter, Lucy. I'm not a man to put on heroics and that; but I believe it'll play the very deuce with me, Lucy—that is to say, Miss Galbraith—I do indeed. It'll give me a low opinion of woman.

MISS GALBRAITH, *averting her face*: Oh, a very high opinion of woman you have had!

MR. RICHARDS, *with sentiment*: Well, there was one woman whom I though a perfect angel.

MISS GALBRAITH: Indeed! May I ask her name?

MR. RICHARDS, *with a forlorn smile*: I shall be obliged to describe her somewhat formally as— Miss Galbraith.

MISS GALBRAITH: Mr. Richards!

MR. RICHARDS: Why, you've just forbidden me to say *Lucy*! You must tell me, dearest, what I have done to offend you. The worst criminals are not condemned unheard, and I've always thought you were merciful if not just. And now I only ask you to be just.

MISS GALBRAITH, *looking out of the window*: You know very well what you've done. You can't expect me to humiliate myself by putting your offence into words.

MR. RICHARDS: Upon my soul, I don't know what you mean! I *don't* know what I've done. When you came at me, last night, with my ring and presents and other little traps, you might have knocked me down with the lightest of the lot. I was perfectly dazed; I couldn't say anything before you were off, and all I could do was to hope that you'd be more like yourself in the morning. And in the morning, when I came round to Mrs. Philips's, I found you were gone, and I came after you by the next train.

MISS GALBRAITH: Mr. Richards, your personal history for the last twenty-four hours is a matter of perfect indifference to me, as it shall be for the next twenty-four hundred years. I see that you are resolved to annoy me, and since *you* will not leave the car, I must do so. (*She rises haughtily from her seat, but the imprisoned skirt of her polonaise twitches her abruptly back into her chair. She bursts into tears.*) Oh, what *shall* I do?

MR. RICHARDS, *dryly*: You shall do whatever you like, Miss Galbraith, when I've set you free; for I see your dress is caught in the window. When it's once out, I'll shut the window, and you can call the porter to raise it. (*He leans forward over her chair, and while she shrinks back the length of her tether, he tugs at the window-fastening.*) I can't get at it. Would you be so good as to stand up—all you can? (*Miss Galbraith stands up, droopingly, and Mr. Richards makes a movement towards her, and then falls back.*) No, that won't do. Please sit down again. (*He goes round her chair and tries to get at the window from that side.*) I can't get any purchase on it. Why don't you cut out that piece? (*Miss Galbraith stares at him in dumb amazement.*) Well, I don't see what we're to do. I'll go and get the porter. (*He goes to the end of the car, and returns.*) I can't find the porter—he must be in one of the other cars. But—(*brightening with the fortunate conception*) I've just thought of something. Will it unbutton?

MISS GALBRAITH: Unbutton?

MR. RICHARDS: Yes; this garment of yours.

MISS GALBRAITH: My polonaise? (*Inquiringly*) Yes.

MR. RICHARDS: Well, then, it's a very simple matter. If you will just take it off I can easily—

MISS GALBRAITH, *faintly*: I can't. A polonaise isn't like an overcoat—

MR. RICHARDS, *with dismay*: Oh! Well, then—
    He remains thinking a moment in hopeless perplexity.

MISS GALBRAITH, *with polite ceremony*: The porter will be back soon. Don't trouble yourself any further about it, please. I shall do very well.

MR. RICHARDS, *without heeding her*: If you could kneel on that foot-cushion, and face the window—.

MISS GALBRAITH, *kneeling promptly*: So?

MR. RICHARDS: Yes, and now—(*kneeling beside her*) if you'll allow me to—to get at the window-catch—(*he stretches both arms forward; she shrinks from his right into his left, and then back again*) and pull, while I raise the window—

MISS GALBRAITH: Yes, yes; but do hurry, please. If any one saw us, I don't know what they would think. It's perfectly ridiculous! (*Pulling*) It's caught in the corner of the window, between the frame and the sash, and it won't come! Is my hair troubling you? Is it in your eyes?

MR. RICHARDS: It's in my eyes, but it isn't troubling me. Am I inconveniencing you?

MISS GALBRAITH: Oh, not at all.

MR. RICHARDS: Well, now then, pull hard!
    He lifts the window with a great effort; the polonaise comes free with a start, and she strikes violently against him. In supporting the shock he cannot forbear catching her for an instant to his heart. She frees herself, and starts indignantly to her feet.

MISS GALBRAITH: Oh, what a cowardly—subterfuge!

MR. RICHARDS: Cowardly? You've no idea how much courage it took. (*Miss Galbraith puts her handkerchief to her face, and sobs.*) Oh, don't cry! Bless my heart—I'm sorry I did it! But you know how dearly I love you, Lucy, though I do think

you've been cruelly unjust. I told you I never should love any one else, and I never shall. I couldn't help it; upon my soul, I couldn't. Nobody could. Don't let it vex you, my—
    He approaches her.

MISS GALBRAITH: Please not touch me, sir! You have no longer any right whatever to do so.

MR. RICHARDS: You misinterpret a very inoffensive gesture. I have no idea of touching you, but I hope I may be allowed, as a special favor, to—pick up my hat, which you are in the act of stepping on. (*Miss Galbraith hastily turns, and strikes the hat with her whirling skirts; it rolls to the other side of the parlor, and Mr. Richards, who goes after it, utters an ironical*) Thanks! (*He brushes it, and puts it on, looking at her where she has again seated herself at the window with her back to him, and continues.*) As for any further molestation from me—

MISS GALBRAITH: If you *will* talk to me—

MR. RICHARDS: Excuse me, I am not talking to you.

MISS GALBRAITH: What were you doing?

MR. RICHARDS: I was beginning to think aloud. I—I was soliloquizing. I suppose I may be allowed to soliloquize?

MISS GALBRAITH, *very coldly*: You can do what you like.

MR. RICHARDS: Unfortunately that's just what I can't do. If I could do as I liked, I should ask you a single question.

MISS GALBRAITH, *after a moment*: Well, sir, you may ask your question.
    She remains as before, with her chin in her hand, looking tearfully out of the window; her face is turned from Mr. Richards, who hesitates a moment before he speaks.

MR. RICHARDS: I wish to ask you just this, Miss Galbraith: if you couldn't ride backwards in the other car, why do you ride backwards in this?

MISS GALBRAITH, *burying her face in her handkerchief, and sobbing*: Oh, oh, oh! This is too bad!

MR. RICHARDS: Oh, come now, Lucy. It breaks my heart to hear you going on so, and all for nothing. Be a little merciful to both of us, and listen to me. I've no doubt I can explain everything if I once understand it, but it's pretty hard explaining a thing if you don't understand it yourself. Do turn round. I know it makes you sick to ride in that way, and if you don't want to face me—there!—(*wheeling in his chair so as to turn his back upon her*) you needn't. Though it's rather trying to a fellow's politeness, not to mention his other feelings. Now, what in the name—

PORTER, *who at this moment enters with his step-ladder, and begins to light the lamps*: Going pretty slow ag'in, sah.

MR. RICHARDS: Yes; what's the trouble?

PORTER: Well, I don't know exactly, sah. Something de matter with de locomotive. We sha'n't be into Albany much 'fore eight o'clock.

MR. RICHARDS: What's the next station?

PORTER: Schenectady.

MR. RICHARDS: Is the whole train as empty as this car?

PORTER, *laughing*: Well, no, sah. Fact is, *dis* cah don't belong on dis train. It's a Pullman that we hitched on when you got in, and we's taking it along for one of de Eastern roads. We let you in 'cause de Drawing-rooms was all full. Same with de lady *(looking sympathetically at her, as he takes his steps to go out)*. Can I do anything for you now, miss?

MISS GALBRAITH, *plaintively*: No, thank you; nothing whatever.

She has turned while Mr. Richards and The Porter have been speaking, and now faces the back of the former, but her veil is drawn closely. The Porter goes out.

MR. RICHARDS, *wheeling round so as to confront her*: I wish you would speak to me half as kindly as you do to that darky, Lucy.

MISS GALBRAITH: He is a *gentleman!*

MR. RICHARDS: He is an urbane and well-informed nobleman. At any rate, he's a man and a brother. But so am I. *(Miss Galbraith does not reply, and after a pause Mr. Richards resumes.)* Talking of gentlemen, I recollect, once, coming up on the day-boat to Poughkeepsie, there was a poor devil of a tipsy man kept following a young fellow about, and annoying him to death—trying to fight him, as a tipsy man will, and insisting that the young fellow had insulted him. By and by he lost his balance and went overboard, and the other jumped after him and fished him out. *(Sensation on the part of Miss Galbraith, who stirs uneasily in her chair, looks out of the window, then looks at Mr. Richards, and drops her head.)* There was a young lady on board, who had seen the whole thing—a very charming young lady indeed, with pale blond hair growing very thick over her forehead, and dark eyelashes to the sweetest blue eyes in the world. Well, this young lady's papa was amongst those who came up to say civil things to the young fellow when he got aboard again, and to

ask the honor—he said the *honor*—of his acquaintance. And when he came out of his state-room in dry clothes, this infatuated old gentleman was waiting for him, and took him and introduced him to his wife and daughter; and the daughter said, with tears in her eyes, and a perfectly intoxicating impulsiveness, that it was the grandest and the most heroic and the noblest thing that she had even seen, and she should always be a better girl for having seen it. Excuse me, Miss Galbraith, for troubling you with these facts of a personal history, which, as you say, is a matter of perfect indifference to you. The young fellow didn't think at the time he had done anything extraordinary; but I don't suppose he *did* expect to live to have the same girl tell him he was no gentleman.

MISS GALBRAITH, *wildly*: O Allen, Allen! You *know* I think you are a gentleman, and I always did!

MR. RICHARDS, *languidly*: Oh, I merely had your word for it, just now, that you didn't. *(Tenderly)* Will you hear me, Lucy?

MISS GALBRAITH, *faintly*: Yes.

MR. RICHARDS: Well, what is it I've done? Will you tell me if I guess right?

MISS GALBRAITH, *with dignity*: I am in no humor for jesting, Allen. And I can assure you that though I consent to hear what you have to say, or ask, *nothing* will change my determination. All is over between us.

MR. RICHARDS: Yes, I understand that, perfectly. I am now asking merely for general information. I do not expect you to relent, and, in fact, I should consider it rather frivolous if you did. No. What I have always admired in your character, Lucy, is a firm, logical consistency; a clearness of mental vision that leaves no side of a subject unsearched; and an unwavering constancy of purpose. You may say that these traits are characteristic of *all* women; but they are pre-eminently characteristic of you, Lucy. *(Miss Galbraith looks askance at him, to make out whether he is in earnest or not; he continues, with a perfectly serious air.)* And I know now that if you're offended with me, it's for no trivial cause. *(She stirs uncomfortably in her chair.)* What I have done I can't imagine, but it must be something monstrous, since it has made life with me appear so impossible that you are ready to fling away your own happiness—for I know you *did* love me, Lucy—and destroy mine. I will begin with the worst thing I can think of. Was it because I danced so much with Fanny Watervliet?

MISS GALBRAITH, *indignantly*: How can you insult me by supposing that I could be jealous of such a *perfect* little goose as that? No, Allen! Whatever I think of you, I *still* respect you too much for *that*.

MR. RICHARDS: I'm glad to hear that there are yet depths to which you think me incapable of descending, and that Miss Watervliet is one of them. I will now take a little higher ground. Perhaps you think I flirted with Mrs. Dawes. I thought, myself, that the thing might begin to have that appearance, but I give you my word of honor that as soon as the idea occurred to me, I dropped her—rather rudely, too. The trouble was, don't you know, that I felt so perfectly safe with a *married* friend of yours. I couldn't be hanging about you all the time, and I was afraid I might vex you if I went with the other girls; and I didn't know what to do.

MISS GALBRAITH: I think you behaved rather silly, giggling so much with her. But—

MR. RICHARDS: I own it, I know it was silly. But—

MISS GALBRAITH: It wasn't that; it wasn't that!

MR. RICHARDS: Was it my forgetting to bring you those things from your mother?

MISS GALBRAITH: No!

MR. RICHARDS: Was it because I hadn't given up smoking yet?

MISS GALBRAITH: You *know* I never asked you to give up smoking. It was entirely your own proposition.

MR. RICHARDS: That's true. That's what made me so easy about it. I knew I could leave it off *any* time. Well, I will not disturb you any longer, Miss Galbraith. (*He throws his overcoat across his arm, and takes up his travelling-bag.*) I have failed to guess your fatal—conundrum; and I have no longer any excuse for remaining. I am going into the smoking-car. Shall I send the porter to you for anything?

MISS GALBRAITH: No, thanks.

She puts up her handkerchief to her face.

MR. RICHARDS: Lucy, do you send me away?

MISS GALBRAITH, *behind her handkerchief*: You were going, yourself.

MR. RICHARDS, *over his shoulder*: Shall I come back?

MISS GALBRAITH: I have no right to drive you from the car.

MR. RICHARDS, *coming back, and sitting down in the chair nearest her*: Lucy, dearest, tell me what's the matter.

MISS GALBRAITH: O Allen! your not *knowing* makes it all the more hopeless and killing. It shows me that we *must* part; that you would go on, breaking my heart, and grinding me into the dust as long as we lived. (*She sobs.*) It shows me that you never understood me, and you never will. I know you're good and kind and all that, but that only makes your not understanding me so much the worse. I do it quite as much for your sake as my own, Allen.

MR. RICHARDS: I'd much rather you wouldn't put yourself out on my account.

MISS GALBRAITH, *without regarding him*: If you could mortify me before a whole roomful of people, as you did last night, what could I expect after marriage but continual insult?

MR. RICHARDS, *in amazement*: How did I mortify you? I thought that I treated you with all the tenderness and affection that a decent regard for the feelings of others would allow. I was ashamed to find I couldn't keep away from you.

MISS GALBRAITH: Oh, you were *attentive* enough, Allen; nobody denies that. Attentive enough in non-essentials. Oh, yes!

MR. RICHARDS: Well, what vital matters did I fail in? I'm sure I can't remember.

MISS GALBRAITH: I dare say! I dare say they won't appear vital to you, Allen. Nothing does. And if I had told you, I should have been met with ridicule, I suppose. But I knew *better* than to tell; I respected myself too *much*.

MR. RICHARDS: But now you mustn't respect yourself *quite* so much, dearest. And I promise you I won't laugh at the most serious thing. I'm in no humor for it. If it were a matter of life and death, even, I can assure you that it wouldn't bring a smile to my countenance. No, indeed! If you expect me to laugh, *now*, you must say something particularly funny.

MISS GALBRAITH: I was not going to say anything *funny*, as you call it, and I will say nothing at all, if you talk in that way.

MR. RICHARDS: Well, I won't, then. But do you know what I suspect, Lucy? I wouldn't mention it to everybody, but I will to you—in strict confidence: I suspect that you're rather ashamed of your grievance, if you have any. I suspect it's nothing at all.

MISS GALBRAITH, *very sternly at first, with a rising hysterical inflection*: Nothing, Allen! Do you call it *nothing*, to have Mrs. Dawes come out with all that about your accident on your way up the river, and ask me if it didn't frighten me terribly to hear of it, even after it was all over; and I had to say you hadn't told me a word of it? "Why, Lucy!" (*angrily mimicking Mrs. Dawes*) "you must teach him better than that. I make Mr. Dawes tell *me* everything." Little simpleton! And then to have them all laugh—Oh, dear, it's too much!

MR. RICHARDS: Why, my dear Lucy—

MISS GALBRAITH, *interrupting him*: I saw just how it was going to be, and I'm thankful, *thankful* that it happened. I saw that you didn't care enough for me to take me into your whole life; that you despised and distrusted me, and that it would get worse and worse to the end of our days; that we should grow farther and farther apart, and I should be left moping at home, while you ran about making confidantes of other women whom you considered *worthy* of your confidence. It all *flashed* upon me in an *instant*; and I resolved to break with you, then and there; and I did, just as soon as ever I could go to my room for your things, and I'm glad—yes—Oh, hu, hu, hu, hu, hu!—*so* glad I did it!

MR. RICHARDS, *grimly*: Your joy is obvious. May I ask—

MISS GALBRAITH: Oh, it wasn't the *first* proof you had given me how little you really cared for me, but I was determined it should be the last. I dare say you've forgotten them! I dare say you don't remember telling Mamie Morris that you didn't like embroidered [1] cigar-cases, when you'd just *told* me that you did, and let me be such a fool as to commence one for you; but I'm thankful to say *that* went into the fire,—oh, yes, *instantly!* And I dare say you've forgotten that you didn't tell me your brother's engagement was to be kept, and let me come out with it that night at the Rudges', and then looked perfectly aghast, so that everybody thought I had been blabbing! Time and again, Allen, you have made me suffer agonies, yes, *agonies*; but your power to do so is at an end. I am free and happy at last.

She weeps bitterly.

MR. RICHARDS, *quietly*: Yes, I *had* forgotten those crimes, and I suppose many similar atrocities. I own it, I *am* forgetful and careless. I was wrong about those things. I ought to have told you why I said that to Miss Morris: I was afraid she was going to work me one. As to that accident I told Mrs. Dawes of, it wasn't worth mentioning.

[1] All texts except *Minor Dramas* and *The Parlor-Car and The Sleeping-Car* read "crocheted."

Our boat simply walked over a sloop in the night, and nobody was hurt. I shouldn't have thought twice about it, if she hadn't happened to brag of their passing close to an iceberg on their way home from Europe; then I trotted out *my* pretty-near disaster as a match for hers—confound her! I wish the iceberg had sunk them! Only it wouldn't have sunk her—she's so light; she'd have gone bobbing about all over the Atlantic Ocean, like a cork; she's got a perfect life-preserver in that mind of hers. (*Miss Galbraith gives a little laugh, and then a little moan.*) But since you are happy, I will not repine, Miss Galbraith. I don't pretend to be very happy myself, but then, I don't deserve it. Since you are ready to let an absolutely unconscious offence on my part cancel all the past; since you let my devoted love weigh as nothing against the momentary pique that a malicious little rattle-pate—she was vexed at my leaving her—could make you feel, and choose to gratify a wicked resentment at the cost of any suffering to me, why, *I* can be glad and happy too. (*With rising anger*) Yes, Miss Galbraith. All *is* over between us. You can go! I renounce you!

MISS GALBRAITH, *springing fiercely to her feet*: Go, indeed! Renounce me! Be so good as to remember that you haven't got me *to* renounce!

MR. RICHARDS: Well, it's all the same thing. I'd renounce you if I had. Good-evening, Miss Galbraith. I will send back your presents as soon as I get to town; it won't be necessary to acknowledge them. I hope we may never meet again. (*He goes out of the door towards the front of the car, but returns directly, and glances uneasily at Miss Galbraith, who remains with her handkerchief pressed to her eyes.*) Ah—a—that is—I shall be obliged to intrude upon you again. The fact is—

MISS GALBRAITH, *anxiously*: Why, the cars have stopped! Are we at Schenectady?

MR. RICHARDS: Well, no; not *exactly*; not exactly at *Schenectady*—.

MISS GALBRAITH: Then what station is this? Have they carried me by? (*Observing his embarrassment*) Allen, what is the matter? What has happened? Tell me instantly! Are we off the track? Have we run into another train? Have we broken through a bridge? Shall we be burnt alive? Tell me, Allen, tell me—I can bear it!—are we telescoped?

She wrings her hands in terror.

MR. RICHARDS, *unsympathetically*: Nothing of the kind has happened. This car has simply come uncoupled, and the rest of the train has gone on ahead, and left us standing on the track, nowhere in particular.

He leans back in his chair, and wheels it round from her.

MISS GALBRAITH, *mortified, yet anxious*: Well?

MR. RICHARDS: Well, until they miss us, and run back to pick us up, I shall be obliged to ask your indulgence. I will try not to disturb you; I would go out and stand on the platform, but it's raining.

MISS GALBRAITH, *listening to the rain-fall on the roof*: Why, so it is! *(Timidly)* Did you notice when the car stopped?

MR. RICHARDS: No.

He rises and goes out at the rear door, comes back, and sits down again.

Miss Galbraith rises, and goes to the large mirror to wipe away her tears. She glances at Mr. Richards, who does not move. She sits down in a seat nearer him than the chair she has left.

MISS GALBRAITH, *after some faint murmurs and hesitations*: Will you please tell me why you went out just now?

MR. RICHARDS, *with indifference*: Yes. I went to see if the rear signal was out.

MISS GALBRAITH, *after another hesitation*: Why?

MR. RICHARDS: Because, if it wasn't out, some train might run into us from that direction.

MISS GALBRAITH, *tremulously*: Oh! And was it?

MR. RICHARDS, *dryly*: Yes.

Miss Galbraith returns to her former place, with a wounded air, and for a moment neither speaks. Finally she asks very meekly,

MISS GALBRAITH: And there's no danger from the front?

MR. RICHARDS, *coldly*: No.

MISS GALBRAITH, *after some little noises and movements meant to catch Mr. Richards's attention*: Of course, I never meant to imply that you were *intentionally* careless or forgetful.

MR. RICHARDS, *still very coldly*: Thank you.

MISS GALBRAITH: I always did justice to your good-heartedness, Allen; you're perfectly lovely that way; and I know that you would be sorry if you *knew* you had wounded my feelings, however accidentally. *(She droops her head so as to catch a sidelong glimpse of his face, and sighs, while she nervously pinches the top of her parasol, resting the point on the floor. Mr. Richards makes no answer.)* That about the cigar-case might have been a mistake; I saw that myself, and, as you

explain it, why, it was certainly very kind and very creditable to—to your thoughtfulness. It *was* thoughtful!

MR. RICHARDS: I am grateful for your good opinion.

MISS GALBRAITH: But do you think it was exactly—it was quite—nice, not to tell me that your brother's engagement was to be kept, when you know, Allen, I can't bear to blunder in such things? *(Tenderly)* Do you? You *can't* say it was?

MR. RICHARDS: I never said it was.

MISS GALBRAITH, *plaintively*: No, Allen. That's what I always admired in your character. You always owned up. Don't you think it's easier for men to own up than it is for women?

MR. RICHARDS: I don't know. I never knew any woman to do it.

MISS GALBRAITH: Oh, yes, Allen! You know I *often* own up.

MR. RICHARDS: No, I don't.

MISS GALBRAITH: Oh, how can you bear to say so? When I'm rash, or anything of that kind, you know I acknowledge it.

MR. RICHARDS: Do you acknowledge it now?

MISS GALBRAITH: Why, how can I, when I haven't *been* rash? *What* have I been rash about?

MR. RICHARDS: About the cigar-case, for example.

MISS GALBRAITH: Oh! *that!* That was a great while ago! I thought you meant something quite recent. *(A sound as of the approaching train is heard in the distance. She gives a start, and then leaves her chair again for one a little nearer his.)* I thought perhaps you meant about—last night.

MR. RICHARDS: Well.

MISS GALBRAITH, *very judicially*: I don't think it was *rash*, exactly. No, not *rash*. It might not have been very *kind* not to—to—trust you more, when I knew that you didn't mean anything but— No, I took the only course I could. *Nobody* could have done differently under the circumstances. But if I caused you any pain, I'm very sorry; oh, yes, very sorry indeed. But I was not precipitate, and I know I did right. At least I *tried* to act for the best. Don't you believe I did?

MR. RICHARDS: Why, if you have no doubt upon the subject, my opinion is of no consequence.

MISS GALBRAITH: Yes. But what do you think? If you think differently, and can make me see it differently, oughtn't you to do so?

MR. RICHARDS: I don't see why. As you say, all is over between us.

MISS GALBRAITH: Yes. *(After a pause)* I should

suppose you would care enough for *yourself* to wish me to look at the matter from the right point of view.

MR. RICHARDS: I don't.

MISS GALBRAITH, *becoming more and more uneasy as the noise of the approaching train grows louder*: I think *you* have been very quick with *me* at times, quite as quick as I could have been with you last night. (*The noise is more distinctly heard.*) I'm sure that if I could once see it as you do, *no* one would be more willing to do anything in their power to atone for their rashness. Of course I know that everything is over.

MR. RICHARDS: As to that, I have your word; and, in view of the fact, perhaps this analysis of motive, of character, however interesting on general grounds, is a little—

MISS GALBRAITH, *with sudden violence*: Say it, and take your revenge! I have put myself at your feet, and you do right to trample on me! Oh, this is what women may expect when they trust to men's generosity! Well, it *is* over now, and I'm thankful, thankful! Cruel, suspicious, vindictive, you're all alike, and I'm glad that I'm no longer subject to your heartless caprices. And I don't care what happens after this, I shall always— Oh! You're sure it's from the front, Allen? Are you sure the rear signal is out?

MR. RICHARDS, *relenting*: Yes, but if it will ease your mind, I'll go and look again.

He rises, and starts towards the rear door.

MISS GALBRAITH, *quickly*: Oh, no! Don't go! I can't bear to be left alone! (*The sound of the approaching train continually increases in volume.*) Oh, isn't it coming very, very, *very* fast?

MR. RICHARDS: No, no! Don't be frightened.

MISS GALBRAITH, *running towards the rear door*: Oh, I *must* get out! It will kill me, I know it will. Come with me! Do, do! (*He runs after her, and her voice is heard at the rear of the car.*) Oh, the outside door is locked, and we are trapped, trapped, trapped! Oh, quick! Let's try the door at the other end. (*They re-enter the parlor, and the roar of the train announces that it is upon them.*) No, no! It's too late, it's too late! I'm a wicked, wicked girl, and this is all to punish me! Oh, it's coming, it's coming at full speed! (*He remains bewildered, confronting her. She utters a wild cry, and as the train strikes the car with a violent concussion, she flings herself into his arms.*) There, there! Forgive me, Allen! Let us die together, my own, own love!

She hangs fainting on his breast. Voices are heard without, and after a little delay The Porter comes in with a lantern.

PORTER: Rather more of a jah than we meant to give you, sah! We had to run down pretty quick after we missed you, and the rain made the track a little slippery. Lady much frightened?

MISS GALBRAITH, *disengaging herself*: Oh, not at all! Not in the least. We thought it was a train coming from behind, and going to run into us, and so—we—I—

PORTER: Not quite so bad as that. We'll be into Schenectady in a few minutes, miss. I'll come for your things.

He goes out at the other door.

MISS GALBRAITH, *in a fearful whisper*: Allen! What will he ever think of us? I'm sure he saw us!

MR. RICHARDS: I don't know what he'll think now. He *did* think you were frightened; but you told him you were not. However, it isn't important what he thinks. Probably he thinks I'm your long-lost brother. It had a kind of family [1] look.

MISS GALBRAITH: Ridiculous!

MR. RICHARDS: Why, he'd never suppose that I was a jilted lover of yours!

MISS GALBRAITH, *ruefully*: No.

MR. RICHARDS: Come, Lucy, (*taking her hand*) you wished to die with me a moment ago. Don't you think you can make one more effort to live with me? I won't take advantage of words spoken in mortal peril, but I suppose you were in earnest when you called me your own—own—

Her head droops; he folds her in his arms a moment, then she starts away from him, as if something had suddenly occurred to her.

MISS GALBRAITH: Allen, where are you going?

MR. RICHARDS: Going? Upon my soul, I haven't the least idea.

MISS GALBRAITH: Where *were* you going?

MR. RICHARDS: Oh, I *was* going to Albany.

MISS GALBRAITH: Well, don't! Aunt Mary is expecting me here at Schenectady—I telegraphed her—and I want you to stop here, too, and we'll refer the whole matter to her. She's such a wise old head. I'm not sure—

MR. RICHARDS: What?

MISS GALBRAITH, *demurely*: That I'm good enough for you.

MR. RICHARDS, *starting, in burlesque of her movement, as if a thought had struck him*: Lucy! how came you on this train when you left Syracuse on the morning *express*?

[1] All texts except *Minor Dramas* and *The Parlor-Car and The Sleeping-Car* read "familiar."

MISS GALBRAITH, *faintly*: I waited over a train at Utica.

She sinks into a chair, and averts her face.

MR. RICHARDS: May I ask why?

MISS GALBRAITH, *more faintly still*: I don't like to tell. I—

MR. RICHARDS, *coming and standing in front of her, with his hands in his pockets*: Look me in the eye, Lucy! (*She drops her veil over her face, and looks up at him.*) Did you—did you expect to find *me* on this train?

MISS GALBRAITH: I was afraid it never *would* get along—it was so late!

MR. RICHARDS: Don't—tergiversate.

MISS GALBRAITH: Don't *what*?

MR. RICHARDS: Fib.

MISS GALBRAITH: Not for worlds!

MR. RICHARDS: How did you know I was in this car?

MISS GALBRAITH: Must I? I thought I saw you through the window; and then I made sure it was you when I went to pin my veil on—I saw you in the mirror.

MR. RICHARDS, *after a little silence*: Miss Galbraith, do you want to know what *you* are?

MISS GALBRAITH, *softly*: Yes, Allen.

MR. RICHARDS: You're a humbug!

MISS GALBRAITH, *springing from her seat, and confronting him*: So are you! You pretended to be asleep!

MR. RICHARDS: I—I—I was taken by surprise. I had to take time to think.

MISS GALBRAITH: So did I.

MR. RICHARDS: And you thought it would be a good plan to get your polonaise caught in the window?

MISS GALBRAITH, *hiding her face on his shoulder*: No, no, Allen! That I never *will* admit. No woman would!

MR. RICHARDS: Oh, I dare say! (*After a pause*) Well, I am a poor, weak, helpless man, with no one to advise me or counsel me, and I have been cruelly deceived. How could you, Lucy, how could you? I can never get over this.

He drops his head upon her shoulder.

MISS GALBRAITH, *starting away again, and looking about the car*: Allen, I have an idea! Do you suppose Mr. Pullman could be induced to *sell* this car?

MR. RICHARDS: Why?

MISS GALBRAITH: Why, because I think it's perfectly lovely, and I should like to live in it always. It could be fitted up for a sort of summer-house, don't you know, and we could have it in the garden, and you could smoke in it.

MR. RICHARDS: Admirable! It would look just like a travelling photographic saloon. No, Lucy, we won't buy it; we will simply keep it as a precious souvenir, a sacred memory, a beautiful dream—and let it go on fulfilling its destiny all the same.

PORTER, *entering, and gathering up Miss Galbraith's things*: Be at Schenectady in half a minute, miss. Won't have much time.

MISS GALBRAITH, *rising, and adjusting her dress, and then looking about the car, while she passes her hand through her lover's arm*: Oh, I do *hate* to leave it. Farewell, you dear, kind, good, lovely car! May you never have another accident!

She kisses her hand to the car, upon which they both look back as they slowly leave it.

MR. RICHARDS, *kissing his hand in the like manner*: Good-by, sweet chariot! [1] May you never carry any but bridal couples!

MISS GALBRAITH: Or engaged ones!

MR. RICHARDS: Or husbands going home to their wives!

MISS GALBRAITH: Or wives hastening to their husbands.

MR. RICHARD: Or young ladies who have waited one train over, so as to be with the young men they hate.

MISS GALBRAITH: Or young men who are so indifferent that they pretend to be asleep when the young ladies come in! (*They pause at the door and look back again.*) And must I leave thee, Paradise? [2] (*They both kiss their hands to the car again, and, their faces being very close together, they impulsively kiss each other. Then Miss Galbraith throws back her head, and solemnly confronts him.*) Only think, Allen! If this car hadn't broken *its* engagement, we might never have mended ours.

1 "Swing Low, Sweet Chariot" was first made known by the Fisk University Jubilee Singers in 1871.
2 Milton, *Paradise Lost*, Bk. XI, l. 269. (Incorrectly quoted.)

Out of the Question

[1877]

Out of the Question is Howells' first original full-length drama, and with it he tried something new. Writing to John Hay on February 22, 1877 (*Life in Letters*, I, 230), he said: "The play is too short to have any strong effect, I suppose, but it seems to me to prove that there is a middle form between narrative and drama, which may be developed into something very pleasant to the reader, and convenient to the fictionist. At any rate my story wouldn't take any other shape." Although "middle form" is rather difficult to define, obviously *Out of the Question* is not material for a stage production. In fact, it is much more like a debate concerning the question of social equality. Resolved: A class-conscious gentleman's daughter should marry only a man who is a gentleman according to society. But after the last rebuttal, the negative wins. In the process, Howells manages to give several definitions of a gentleman and to satirize the pattern of Boston's snobbish society in much the same way that John P. Marquand was to do later in *The Late George Apley*. There are several striking parallels between the two works.

Indicative of the degree of Howells' sympathetic insight into society are his characters. He manages to show clearly three different strata of Boston society. There is Mrs. Murray as the opinionated, forthright old warrior of Louisburg Square society viewing life through an opaque lorgnette, who demands everything befitting her place in society and refuses to recognize anything of value below her own level. Mrs. Bellingham, although ostensibly a member of the same society as Mrs. Murray, has a wider outlook on life through her association with her daughter, yet has no appreciable feeling of life's difficulties. Because her vista of life is rendered quite useless by the proprieties of her age, she is scarcely better off than Mrs. Murray, but she is vastly more understanding. Leslie represents young society—not so set in her ways that she cannot learn, and not so blinded by the demands of her social level that she cannot see some good outside of it. She has the beauty, the background, the intelligence, and the love and tolerance that Howells liked to imagine were the basic qualities of the American girl. Into this social group he introduces Blake, the modern democratic gentleman, before whom the old, rigid social standards crumble.

There are, of course, many dramatic inadequacies in the play, although, since it is an attempt at "middle form," it should not be criticized too minutely from the perspective of traditional drama. In a way this "middle form" is a novelist's attempt to avoid some of the distinctive difficulties that the drama presents. One of the better features of the whole play is the literary quality of the stage directions. New characters arriving on the scene are described in great detail, and scenes are frequently introduced in a similarly pleasurable fashion—the beginning of the tramp scene, for example. Howells foreshadowed Shaw and Barrie with his literary stage directions and took considerable pride in this part of his playwriting. Perhaps it gives some evidence for his theory that there might be a "middle form" between narrative and drama.

Out of the Question[1]

I.

In the Parlor of the Ponkwasset Hotel

The Ponkwasset Hotel stands on the slope of a hill and fronts the irregular mass of Ponkwasset Mountain, on which the galleries and northern windows of the parlor look out. The parlor is furnished with two hair-cloth sofas, two hair-cloth easy-chairs, and cane-seated chairs of divers patterns; against one side of the room stands a piano, near either end of which a door opens into the corridor; in the center of the parlor a marble-topped table supports a state-lamp of kerosene,—a perfume by day, a flame by night,—and near this table sit two young ladies with what they call work in their hands and laps.

MISS MAGGIE WALLACE, *with her left wrist curved in the act of rolling up a part of her work, at which she looks down with a very thoughtful air and a careworn little sigh*: I don't think I shall cut it bias, after all, Lilly.

MISS LILLY ROBERTS, *letting her work fall into her lap, in amazement*: Why, Maggie!

MAGGIE: No. Or at least I shan't decide to do so till I've had Leslie's opinion on it. *She has perfect* taste, and she could tell at a glance whether it would do.

LILLY: I wonder she isn't here, now. The stage must be very late.

MAGGIE: I suppose the postmaster at South Herodias waited to finish his supper before he "changed the mail," as they call it. I *was* so in hopes she would come while they were at *tea!* It will *so* disgust her to see them all strung along the piazza and staring their eyes out at the arrivals, when the stage drives up,—

A horrible picture which Miss Wallace dreamily contemplates for a moment in mental vision.

LILLY: Why don't you go down, too, Maggie? Perhaps she'd find a familiar face a relief.

MAGGIE, *recalled to herself by the wild suggestion*: Thank you, Lilly. I'd rather not be thought so vulgar as *that*, by Leslie Bellingham, if it's quite the same to other friends. Imagine her catching sight of me in that crowd! I should simply wither away.

LILLY, *rebelliously*: Well, I don't see why she should feel authorized to overawe people in that manner. What does she do to show her immense superiority?

MAGGIE: Everything! In the first place she's so refined and cultivated, you can't live; and then she takes your breath away, she's so perfectly lovely; and then she kills you dead with her style, and all that. She isn't the least stiff. She's the kindest to other people you ever saw, and the carefullest of their feelings; and she has the grandest principles, and she's *divinely* impulsive! But somehow you feel that if you do anything that's a little vulgar in her presence, you'd better die at once. It was always so at school, and it always will be. Why, you would no more dare to do or say anything just a little common, don't you know, with Leslie Bellingham—(*A young lady, tall, slender, and with an air of delicate distinction, has appeared at the door of the parlor. She is of that type of beauty which approaches the English, without losing the American fineness and grace; she is fair, and her eyes are rather gray than blue; her nose is slightly aquiline; her expression is serious, but becomes amused as she listens to Miss Wallace. She wears one of those blonde traveling-costumes, whose general fashionableness she somehow subdues into character with herself; over her arm she carries a shawl. She drifts lightly into the room. At the rustling of her dress Miss Wallace looks up, and with a cry of surprise and ecstasy springs from her chair, scattering the contents of her work-box in every direction over the floor, and flings herself into Miss Leslie Bellingham's embrace. Then she starts away from her and gazes rapturously into her face, while they prettily clasp hands and hold each other at arm's length.*) Leslie! You heard every word!

[1] The text used is the Houghton, Mifflin and Company edition.

MISS LESLIE BELLINGHAM: Every syllable, my child. And when you came to my grand principles, I simply said to myself, "Then listening at key-holes is heroic," and kept on eavesdropping without a murmur. Had you quite finished?

MAGGIE: Oh Leslie! You know I *never* can finish when I get on that subject! It inspires me to greater and greater flights every minute. Where is your *mother?* Where *is* Mrs. Murray? Where is the *stage?* Why, excuse me! This is Miss Roberts. Lilly, it's Leslie Bellingham! *Oh,* how glad I am to see you together at last! Didn't the stage—

LESLIE, *having graciously bowed to Miss Roberts*: No, Maggie. The stage didn't bring me here. I walked.

MAGGIE: Why, Leslie! How perfectly ghastly!

LESLIE: The stage has done nothing but disgrace itself ever since we left the station. In the first place it pretended to carry ten or twelve people and their baggage, with two horses. Four horses oughtn't to drag such a load up these precipices; and wherever the driver would stop for me, I insisted upon getting out to walk.

MAGGIE: How like you, Leslie!

LESLIE: Yes; I wish the resemblance were not so striking. I'm here in character, Maggie, if you like, but almost nothing else. I've nothing but a hand-bag to bless me with for the next twenty-four hours. Shall you be very much ashamed of me?

MAGGIE: Why, you don't mean to say you've lost your trunks? Horrors!

LESLIE: No. I mean that I wasn't going to let the driver add them to the cruel load he had already, and I made him leave them at the station till to-morrow night.

MAGGIE, *embracing her*: Oh, you dear, good, grand, generous Leslie! How— Why, but Leslie! He'll have *just* as many people to-morrow night, and your trunks besides theirs!

LESLIE, *with decision*: Very well! Then I shall not be there to see the outrage. I will not have suffering or injustice of any kind inflicted in my presence, if I can help it. That is all.

Nevertheless, Miss Bellingham sinks into one of the armchairs with an air of some dismay, and vainly taps the toe of her boot with the point of her umbrella in a difficult interval of silence.

MAGGIE, *finally*: But where is your hand-bag?

LESLIE, *with mystery*: Oh, *he's* bringing it.

MAGGIE: He?

LESLIE, *with reviving spirits*: A young man, the good genius of the drive. He's bringing it from the foot of the hill; the stage had its final disaster there; and I left him in charge of mamma and Aunt Kate, and came on to explore and surprise, and he made me leave the bag with him, too. But that isn't the worst. I shall know what to do with the hand-bag when it gets here, but I shan't know what to do with the young man.

MAGGIE: With the young man? Why, Leslie, a young man is worth a *thousand* hand-bags in a place like this! You don't know what you're talking about, Leslie. A young man—

LESLIE, *rising and going toward the window*: My dear, he's out of the question. You may as well make up your mind to that, for you'll see at once that he'll never do. He's going to stop here, and as he's been very kind to us it makes his never doing all the harder to manage. He's a hero, if you like, but if you can imagine it he isn't quite —well, what you've been used to. Don't you see how a person could be everything that was unselfish and obliging, and yet not—not—

MAGGIE, *eagerly*: Oh yes!

LESLIE: Well, he's that. It seems to me that he's been doing something for mamma, or Aunt Kate, or me, ever since we left the station. To begin with, he gave up his place inside to one of us, and when he went to get on top, he found all the places taken there; and so he had to sit on the trunks behind—whenever he rode; for he walked most of the way, and helped me over the bad places in the road when I insisted on getting out. You know how Aunt Kate is, Maggie, and how many wants she has. Well, there wasn't one of them that this young man didn't gratify: he handed her bag up to the driver on top because it crowded her, and handed it down because she couldn't do without it; he got her out and put her back so that she could face the front, and then restored her to her place because an old gentleman who had been traveling a long way kept falling asleep on her shoulder; he buttoned her curtain down because she was sure it was going to rain, and rolled it up because it made the air too close; he fetched water for her; he looked every now and then to see if her trunks were all right, and made her more and more ungrateful every minute. Whenever the stage broke down—as it did twice before the present smash-up—he befriended everybody, encouraged old ladies, quieted children, and shamed the other men into trying to be of some use; and if it hadn't been for him, I don't see how the stage would ever have got out of its troubles; he always knew just what was the matter, and just how to mend it. Is that the window that commands a magnificent prospect of Ponkwasset Mountain—in the advertisement?

MAGGIE: The very window!

LESLIE: Does it condescend to overlook so common a thing as the road up to the house?

MAGGIE: Of course; but why?

LESLIE, *going to the open window, and stepping through it upon the gallery, whither the other young ladies follow her, and where her voice is heard:* Yes, there they come! But I can't see my young man. Is it possible that he's riding? No, there he is! He was on the other side of the stage. Don't you see him? Why, he needn't *carry* my hand-bag! He certainly might have let *that* ride. I do wonder what he means by it! Or is it only absent-mindedness? *Don't* let him see us looking! It would be altogether too silly. *Do* let's go in!

MAGGIE, *on their return to the parlor:* What a great pity it is that he won't do! Is he handsome, Leslie? Why won't he do?

LESLIE: You can tell in a moment, when you've seen him, Maggie. He's perfectly respectful and nice, of course, but he's no more social perspective than—the man in the moon. He's never obtrusive, but he's as free and equal as the Declaration of Independence; and when you did get up some little perspective with him, and tried to let him know, don't you know, that there was such a thing as a vanishing point somewhere, he was sure to do or say something so unconscious that away went your perspective—one simple crush.

MAGGIE: How ridiculous!

LESLIE: Yes. It was funny. But not just in that way. He isn't in the least common or uncouth. Nobody could say that. But he's going to be here two or three weeks, and it's impossible not to be civil; and it's very embarrassing, don't you see?

LILLY: Let me comfort you, Miss Bellingham. It will be the simplest thing in the world. We're all on the same level in the Ponkwasset Hotel. The landlord will bring him up during the evening and introduce him. Our table girls teach school in the winter and are as good as anybody. Mine calls me "Lilly," and I'm so small I can't help it. They dress up in the afternoon, and play the piano. The cook's as affable, when you meet her in society, as can be.

MAGGIE: Lilly!

LESLIE, *listening to Miss Roberts with whimsical trepidation:* Well, this certainly complicates matters. But I think we shall be able to manage. (*At a sound of voices in the hall without, Miss*

Bellingham starts from her chair and runs to the corridor, where she is heard.) Thanks ever so much. So very good of you to take all this trouble. Come into the parlor, mamma—there's nobody there but Maggie Wallace and Miss Roberts—and we'll leave our things there till after tea.

She reënters the parlor with her mother and her Aunt Kate, Mrs. Murray; after whom comes Stephen Blake with Leslie's bag in his hand, and the wraps of the other ladies over his arm. His dress, which is evidently a prosperous fortuity of the clothing-store, takes character from his tall, sinewy frame; a smile of somewhat humorous patience lights his black eyes and shapes his handsome moustache, as he awaits in quiet self-possession the pleasure of the ladies.

MRS. BELLINGHAM, *a matronly, middle-aged lady of comfortable, not cumbrous bulk, taking Miss Wallace by the hand and kissing her:* My dear child, how pleasant it is to see you so strong again! You're a living testimony to the excellence of the air! How well you look!

LESLIE: Mamma,—Miss Roberts.

Mrs. Bellingham murmurously shakes hands with Miss Roberts, and after some kindly nods and smiles, and other shows of friendliness, provisionally and expectantly quiesces into a corner of the sofa, while her sister-in-law comes aggressively forward to assume the burden of conversation.

MRS. MURRAY: Well, a more fatiguing drive I certainly never knew! How do you do, Maggie? (*She kisses Miss Wallace in a casual, uninterested way, and takes Lilly's hand.*) Isn't this Miss Roberts? I am Mrs. Murray. I used to know your family—your uncle George, before that dreadful business of his. I believe it all came out right; he wasn't to blame; but it was a shocking experience. (*Mrs. Murray turns from Lilly, and refers herself to the company in general.*) It seems as if I should expire on the spot. I feel as if I had been packed away in my own hat-box for a week, and here, just as we arrive, the landlord informs us that he didn't expect us till to-morrow night, and he hasn't an empty room in the house!

MAGGIE: No room! To-morrow night! What nonsense! Why, it's perfectly frantic! How could he have misunderstood? Why, it seems to me that I've done *nothing* for a week past but tell him you were coming to-night!

MRS. MURRAY, *sharply:* I have no doubt of it. But it doesn't alter the state of the case. You may tell us to leave our things till *after tea,* Leslie. If they can't make up beds on the sofas and the piano, I don't know where we're going to pass the night.

In the moment of distressful sensation which follows Miss Wallace whispers something eagerly to her friend, Miss Roberts.

MAGGIE, *with a laughing glance at Leslie and her mother, and then going on with her whispering*: Excuse the little confidence!

MRS. BELLINGHAM: Conspiracy, I'm afraid. What are you plotting, Maggie?

MAGGIE, *finishing her confidence*: Oh, we needn't make a mystery of such a little thing. We're going to offer you one of our rooms.

MRS. BELLINGHAM: My dear, you are going to do nothing of the kind. We will never allow it.

MAGGIE: Now, Mrs. Bellingham, you break my heart! It's nothing, it's less than nothing. *I* believe we can make room for all three of you.

MRS. MURRAY, *promptly*: Let me go with you, young ladies. I'm an old housekeeper, and I can help you plan.

MAGGIE: Oh do, Mrs. Murray. You can tell which room you'd better take, Lilly's or mine. Lilly's is—

MRS. MURRAY: Oh! I had forgotten that we were detaining you! (*Mrs. Murray is about to leave the room with the two young girls, when her eye falls upon Blake, who is still present, with his burden of hand-bags and shawls.*) Leave the things on the table, please. We are obliged to you.

Mrs. Murray speaks with a certain finality of manner and tone which there is no mistaking; Blake stares at her a moment, and then, without replying, lays down the things and turns to quit the room; at the same instant Leslie rises with a grand air from her mother's side, on the sofa, and sweeps towards him.

LESLIE, *very graciously*: Don't let our private afflictions drive you from a public room, Mr.—

BLAKE: Blake.

LESLIE: Mr. Blake. This is my mother, Mr. Blake, who wishes to thank you for all your kindness to us.

MRS. BELLINGHAM: Yes, indeed, Mr. Blake, we are truly grateful to you.

LESLIE, *with increasing significance*: And my aunt, Mrs. Murray; and my friend, Miss Wallace; and Miss Roberts. (*Blake bows to each of the ladies as they are named, but persists in his move-ment to quit the room; Leslie impressively offers him her hand.*) Must you go? Thank you, ever, ever so much!

She follows him to the door in his withdrawal, and then turns and confronts her aunt with an embattled front of defiance.

MAGGIE, *with an effort breaking the embarrassing silence*: Come, Lilly. Let us go and take a look at our resources. We'll be back in a moment, Mrs. Bellingham.

LESLIE, *coming abruptly forward as her aunt goes out with the two young girls, and drooping meekly in front of her mother, who remains seated on the sofa*: Well, mamma!

MRS. BELLINGHAM, *tranquilly contemplating her for a moment*: Well, Leslie! (*She pauses, and again silently regards her daughter.*) Perhaps you may be said to have overdone it.

LESLIE, *passionately*: I can't help it, mother! I couldn't see him sent away in that insolent manner, I don't care who or what he is. Aunt Kate's tone was outrageous, atrocious, hideous! And after accepting, yes, *demanding* every service he could possibly render, the whole afternoon! It made me blush for her, and I wasn't going to stand it.

MRS. BELLINGHAM: If you mean by all that that your poor aunt is a very ungracious and exacting woman, I shall not dispute you. But she's your father's sister; and she's very much older than you. You seem to have forgotten, too, that your mother was present to do any justice that was needed. It's very unfortunate that he should have been able to do us so many favors, but that can't be helped now. It's one of the risks of coming to these out-of-the-way places, that you're so apt to be thrown in with nondescript people that you don't know how to get rid of afterwards. And now that he's been so cordially introduced to us all! Well, I hope you won't have to be crueller in the end, my dear, than your aunt meant to be in the beginning. So far, of course, he has behaved with perfect delicacy; but you must see yourself, Leslie, that even as a mere acquaintance he's quite out of the question; that however kind and thoughtful he's been, and no one could have been more so, he isn't a gentleman.

LESLIE, *impatiently*: Well, then, mother, I am! And so are you. And I think we are bound to behave like gentlemen at any cost. I didn't mean to ignore you. I didn't consider. I acted as I thought Charley would have done.

MRS. BELLINGHAM: Oh, my dear, my dear!

Don't you see there's a very important difference? Your brother is a man, and he can act without reference to consequences. But you are a young lady, and you can't be as gentlemanly as you like without being liable to misinterpretation. I shall expect you to behave very discreetly indeed from this time forth. We must consider now how our new friend can be kindly, yet firmly and promptly, dropped.

LESLIE: Oh, it's another of those embarrassments that Aunt Kate's always getting me into! I *was* discreet about it till she acted so horridly. You can ask Maggie if I didn't talk in the wisest way about it; like a perfect—owl. I saw it just as you do, mamma, and I *was* going to drop him, and so I will, yet; but I couldn't see him so ungratefully trampled on. It's *all* her doing! Who wanted to come here to this out-of-the-way place? Why, Aunt Kate,—when I was eager to go to Conway! I declare it's too bad!

MRS. BELLINGHAM: That will do, Leslie.

LESLIE: And now she's gone off with those poor girls to crowd them out of house and home, I suppose. It's a shame! Why did you let her, mamma?

MRS. BELLINGHAM: For the same reason that I let you talk on, my dear, when I've bidden you stop.

LESLIE: Oh, you dear, kind old mamma, you! *You're* a gentleman, and you always were! I only wish I could be half like you! (*She throws her arms round her mother's neck and kisses her.*) I know you're right about this matter, but you mustn't expect me to acknowledge that Aunt Kate is. If you both said exactly the same thing, you would be right and she would be wrong, you'd say it so differently!

MRS. MURRAY, *who returns alone with signs of discontent and perplexity, and flings herself into a chair*: Their rooms are mere coops, and I don't see how even two of us are to squeeze into one of them. It's little better than impertinence to offer it to us. I've been down to see the landlord again, and you'll be pleased to know, Marion, that the only vacant room in the house had been engaged by the person to whom we've all just had the honor of an introduction. (*Leslie makes an impetuous movement, as if she were about to speak, but at a gesture from her mother she restrains herself, and Mrs. Murray continues.*) Of course, if he had been a gentleman, in the lowest sense of the word, he would have offered his room to ladies

who had none, at once. As long as he could make social capital out of his obtrusive services to us he was very profuse with them, but as soon as it came to a question of real self-sacrifice—to giving up his own ease and comfort for a single night—

A bell rings, and at the sound Mrs. Bellingham rises.

MRS. BELLINGHAM: I suppose that's for supper. I think a cup of tea will put a cheerfuller face on our affairs. I don't at all agree with you about Mr. Blake's obligation to give up his room, nor about his services to us this afternoon; I'm sure common justice requires us to acknowledge that he was everything that was kind and thoughtful. Oh, you good child! (*as Miss Wallace appears at the door*) have you come to show us the way to supper? Are you quite sure you've not gone without tea on our account as well as given up your room?

She puts her arm fondly round the young girl's waist, and presses her cheek against her own breast.

MAGGIE, *with enthusiasm*: Oh, Mrs. Bellingham, you know I wouldn't ask anything better than to starve on your account. I wish I *hadn't* been to tea! I'm afraid that you'll think the room is a very slight offering when you come to see it —it *is* such a little room; why, when I took Mrs. Murray into it, it seemed all at once as if I saw it through the wrong end of an opera-glass—it did dwindle so!

LESLIE: Never mind, Maggie; you're only too good, as it is. If your room was an inch bigger, we couldn't bear it. I hope you may be without a roof over your head yourself, some day! Can I say anything handsomer than that? Don't wait for me, mamma; I'll find the dining-room myself. I'm rather too crumpled even for a houseless wanderer. (*She opens her bag where it stands on the table.*) I am going to make a flying toilet at one of these glasses. Do you think any one will come in, Maggie?

MAGGIE: There isn't the least danger. This is the parlor of the "transients," as they call them, —the occasional guests,—and Lilly and I have it mostly to ourselves when there are no transients. The regular boarders stay in the lower parlor. Shan't I help you, Leslie?

LESLIE, *rummaging through her bag*: No, indeed! It's only a question of brush and hair-pins. Do go with mamma! (*As Maggie obeys, Leslie finds her brush, and going to one of the mirrors touches the blonde masses of her hair, and then remains a moment, lightly turning her head from side to side to get the effect. She suddenly claps her hand to one ear.)* Oh, horrors! That ear-drop's gone again! *(She runs to the table, reopens her bag, and searches it in every part, talking rapidly to herself.)* Well, really, it seems as if sorrows would never end! To think of that working out a third time! To think of my coming away without getting the clasp fixed! And to think of my not leaving them in my trunk at the station! Oh dear me, I shall certainly go wild! What *shall* I do? It isn't in the bag at all. It *must* be on the floor. *(Keeping her hand in helpless incredulity upon the ear from which the jewel is missing, she scrutinizes the matting far and near, with a countenance of acute anguish. Footsteps are heard approaching the door, where they hesitatingly arrest themselves.)* Have you come back for me? Oh, I've met with *such* a calamity! I've lost one of my ear-rings. I could cry. Do come and help me mouse for it. *(There is no response to this invitation, and Leslie, lifting her eyes, in a little dismay confronts the silent intruder.)* Mr. Blake!

BLAKE: Excuse me. I expected to find your mother here. I didn't mean to disturb—

LESLIE, *haughtily*: There's no disturbance. It's a public room: I had forgotten that. Mamma has gone to tea. I thought it was my friend Miss Wallace. I— *(With a flash of indignation)* When you knew it wasn't, why did you let me speak to you in that way?

BLAKE, *with a smile*: I couldn't know whom you took me for, and I hadn't time to prevent your speaking.

LESLIE: You remained.

BLAKE, *with a touch of resentment tempering his amusement*: I couldn't go away after I had come without speaking to you. It was Mrs. Bellingham I was looking for. I'm sorry not to find her, and I'll go, now.

LESLIE, *hastily*: Oh no! I beg your pardon. I didn't mean—

BLAKE, *advancing toward her, and stooping to pick up something from the floor, near the table*: Is this what you lost?—if I've a right to know that you lost anything.

LESLIE: Oh, my ear-ring! Oh, thanks! How did you see it? I thought I had looked and felt everywhere. *(A quick color flies over her face as she takes the jewel from the palm of his hand. She turns to the mirror, and, seizing the tip of her delicate ear between the thumb and forefinger of*

one hand, hooks the pendant into place with the other, and then gives her head a little shake; the young man lightly sighs. She turns toward him, with the warmth still lingering in her cheeks.)* I'm ever so much obliged to you, Mr. Blake. I wish I had your gift of doing all sorts of services —favors—to people. I wish I could find something for you.

BLAKE: I wish you could—if it were the key to my room, which I came back in hopes of finding. I've mislaid it somewhere, and I thought I might have put it down with your shawls here on the table. *(Leslie promptly lifts one of the shawls, and the key drops from it.)* That's it. Miss Bellingham, I have a favor to ask: will you give this key to your mother?

LESLIE: This key?

BLAKE: I have found a place to sleep at a farmhouse just down the road, and I want your mother to take my room; I haven't looked into it yet, and I don't know that it's worth taking. But I suppose it's better than no room at all; and I know you have none.

LESLIE, *with cold hauteur, after looking absently at him for a moment*: Thanks. It's quite impossible. My mother would never consent.

BLAKE: The room will stand empty, then. I meant to give it up from the first,—as soon as I found that you were not provided for,—but I hated to make a display of it before all the people down there in the office. I'll go now and leave the key with the landlord, as I ought to have done, without troubling you. But—I had hardly the chance of doing so after we came here.

LESLIE, *with enthusiasm*: Oh, Mr. Blake, do you really mean to give us your room after you've been so odiously— Oh, it's too bad; it's too bad! You mustn't; no, you shall not.

BLAKE: I will leave the key on the table here. Good night. Or—I shall not see you in the morning: perhaps I had better say good-by.

LESLIE: Good-by? In the morning?

BLAKE: I've changed my plans, and I'm going away to-morrow. Good-by.

LESLIE: Going— Mamma will be very sorry to— Oh, Mr. Blake, I hope you are not going because— But indeed— I want you to believe—

BLAKE, *devoutly*: I believe it. Good-by!

He turns away to go, and Leslie, standing bewildered and irresolute, lets him leave the room; then she hastens to the door after him, and encounters her mother.

MRS. BELLINGHAM: Well, Leslie. Are you quite

ready? We went to look at Maggie's room before going down to tea. It's small, but we shall manage somehow. Come, dear. She's waiting for us at the head of the stairs. Why, Leslie!

LESLIE, *touching her handkerchief to her eyes*: I was a little overwrought, mamma. I'm tired. *(After a moment)* Mamma, Mr. Blake—

MRS. BELLINGHAM, *with a look at her daughter*: I met him in the hall.

LESLIE: Yes, he has been here; and I thought I had lost one of my ear-rings; and of course he found it on the floor the instant he came in; and—

MRS. MURRAY, *surging into the room, and going up to the table*: Well, Marion, the tea— What key is this? What in the world is Leslie crying about?

LESLIE, *with supreme disregard of her aunt, and adamantine self-control*: Mr. Blake had come— *(She hands the key to Mrs. Bellingham.)*—to offer you the key of his room. He asked me to give it.

MRS. BELLINGHAM: The key of his room?

LESLIE: He offers you his room; he had always meant to offer it.

MRS. BELLINGHAM, *gravely*: Mr. Blake had no right to know that we had no room. It is too great a kindness. We can't accept it, Leslie. I hope you told him so, my dear.

LESLIE: Yes, mamma. But he said he was going to lodge at one of the farm-houses in the neighborhood, and the room would be vacant if you didn't take it. I couldn't prevent his leaving the key.

MRS. BELLINGHAM: That is all very well. But it doesn't alter the case, as far as we are concerned. It is very good of Mr. Blake, but after what has occurred, it's simply impossible. We can't take it.

MRS. MURRAY: Occurred? Not take it? Of *course* we will take it, Marion! I certainly am astonished. The man will get a much better bed at the farmer's than he's accustomed to. You talk as if it were some act of self-sacrifice. I've no doubt he's made the most of it. I've no doubt he's given it an effect of heroism—or tried to. But that you should fall in with his vulgar conception of the affair, Marion, and Leslie should be affected to tears by his magnanimity, is a little too comical. One would think, really, that he had imperiled life and limb on our account. All this sentiment about a room on the third floor! Give the key to me, Marion. *(She possesses herself of it from Mrs. Bellingham's passive hand.)* Leslie will wish to stay with you, so as to be near her young friends. *I* will occupy this vacant room.

II.

"IN FAYRE FOREST" [1]

Under the shelter of some pines near a lonely by-road, in the neighborhood of the Ponkwasset Hotel, lie two tramps asleep. One of them, having made his bed of the pine-boughs, has pillowed his head upon the bundle he carries by day; the other is stretched, face downward, on the thick brown carpet of pine-needles. The sun, which strikes through the thin screen of the trees upon the bodies of the two men, is high in the heavens. The rattle of wheels is heard from time to time on the remoter highway; the harsh clatter of a kingfisher, poising over the water, comes from the direction of the river near at hand. A squirrel descends the trunk of an oak near the pines under which the men lie, and at sight of them stops, barks harshly, and then, as one of them stirs in his sleep, whisks back into the top of the oak. It is the luxurious tramp on the pine-boughs who stirs, and who alertly opens his eyes and sits up in his bed, as if the noisy rush of the squirrel had startled him from his sleep.

FIRST TRAMP, *casting a malign glance at the top of the oak*: If I had a fair shot at you with this club, my fine fellow, I'd break you of that trick of waking people before the bell rings in the morning, and I'd give 'em broiled squirrel for breakfast when they did get up. *(He takes his bundle into his lap, and, tremulously untying it, reveals a motley heap of tatters; from these he searches out a flask, which he holds against the light, shakes at his ear, and inverts upon his lips.)* Not a drop; not a square smell, even! I dreamt it. *(He lies down with a groan, and remains with his head pillowed in his hands. Presently he reaches for his stick, and again rising to a sitting posture strikes his sleeping comrade across the shoulders.)* Get up!

SECOND TRAMP, *who speaks with a slight brogue, briskly springing to his feet, and rubbing his shoulders*: And what for, my strange bedfellow?

FIRST TRAMP: For breakfast. What do people generally get up for in the morning?

SECOND TRAMP: Upon my soul, I'd as soon have had mine in bed; I've a day of leisure before me. And let me say a word to you, my friend: the

1 Chaucer, *Canterbury Tales*, "Tale of Sir Thopas," l. 1944.

next time you see a gentleman dreaming of one of the most elegant repasts in the world, and just waiting for his stew to cool, don't you intrude upon him with that little stick of yours. I don't care for a stroke or two in sport, but when I think of the meal I've lost, I could find it in my heart to break your head for you, you ugly brute. Have you got anything to eat there in your wardrobe?

FIRST TRAMP: Not a crumb.

SECOND TRAMP: Or to drink?

FIRST TRAMP: Not a drop.

SECOND TRAMP: Or to smoke?

FIRST TRAMP: No.

SECOND TRAMP: Faith, you're nearer a broken head than ever, me friend. Wake a man out of a dream of that sort!

FIRST TRAMP: I've had enough of this. What do you intend to do?

SECOND TRAMP: I'm going to assume the character of an impostor, and pretend at the next farm-house that I haven't had any breakfast, and haven't any money to buy one. It's a bare-faced deceit, I know, but— (*looking down at his broken shoes and tattered clothes*) I flatter myself that I dress the part pretty well. To be sure, the women are not as ready to listen as they were once. The tramping-trade is overdone; there's too many in it; the ladies can't believe we're all destitute; it don't stand to reason.

FIRST TRAMP: I'm tired of the whole thing.

SECOND TRAMP: I don't like it myself. But there's worse things. There's work, for example. By my soul, there's nothing disgusts me like these places where they tell you to go out and hoe potatoes, and your breakfast will be ready in an hour. I never could work with any more pleasure on an empty stomach than a full one. And the poor devils always think they've done something so fine when they say that, and the joke's so stale! I can tell them I'm not to be got rid of so easy. I'm not the lazy, dirty vagabond I look, at all; I'm the inevitable result of the conflict between labor and capital; I'm the logical consequence of the prevailing corruption. I read it on the bit of newspaper they gave me round my dinner, yesterday; it was cold beef of a quality that you don't often find in the country.

FIRST TRAMP, *sullenly*: I'm sick of the whole thing. I'm going out of it.

SECOND TRAMP: And what'll you do? Are ye going to work?

FIRST TRAMP: To work? No! To steal.

SECOND TRAMP: Faith, I don't call that going out of it, then. It's quite in the line of business. You're no bad dab at a hen-roost, now, as I know very well; and for any little thing that a gentleman can shove under his coat, while the lady of the house has her back turned buttering his lunch for him, I don't know the man I'd call master.

FIRST TRAMP: If I could get a man to tell me the time of day by a watch I liked, I'd as lief knock him over as look at him.

SECOND TRAMP: Oh, if it's high-way robbery you mean, partner, I don't follow you.

FIRST TRAMP: What's the difference?

SECOND TRAMP: Not much, if you take it one way, but a good deal if you take it another. It's the difference between petty larceny and grand larceny; it's the difference between three months in the House of Correction and ten years in the State's Prison, if you're caught, not to mention the risks of the profession.

FIRST TRAMP: I'd take the risks if I saw my chance.

He lies down with his arms crossed under his head, and stares up into the pine. His comrade glances at him, and then moves stiffly out from the shelter of the trees, and, shading his eyes with one hand, peers down the road.

SECOND TRAMP: I didn't know but I might see your chance, partner. You wouldn't like an old gentleman with a load of potatoes to begin on, would ye? There's one just gone up the cross-road. And yonder goes an umbrella-mender. I'm afraid we shan't take any purses to speak of, in this neighborhood. Whoosh! Wait a bit—here's somebody coming this way. (*The first tramp is sufficiently interested to sit up.*) Faith, here's your chance at last, then, if you're in earnest, my friend; but it stands six feet in its stockings, and it carries a stick as well as a watch. I won't ask a share of the plunder, partner; I've rags enough of my own without wanting to divide your property with the gentleman coming.

He goes back and lies down at the foot of one of the trees, while the other, who has risen from his pine-boughs, comes cautiously forward; after a glance at the approaching wayfarer he flings away his cudgel, and, taking a pipe from his pocket drops into a cringing attitude. The Irishman grins. In another moment Blake appears from under the cover of the woods and advances with long strides, striking with his stick at the stones in the road as he comes on, in an absent-minded fashion.

FIRST TRAMP: I say, mister! (*Blake looks up, and his eye falls upon the squalid figure of the tramp; he stops.*) Couldn't you give a poor fellow a little tobacco for his pipe? A smoke comes good, if you don't happen to know where you're going to get your breakfast.

SECOND TRAMP, *coming forward, with his pipe in his hand*: True for you, partner. A little tobacco in the hand is worth a deal of breakfast in the bush.

Blake looks from one to the other, and then takes a paper of tobacco from his pocket and gives it to the first tramp, who helps himself and passes it to his comrade; the latter offers to return it after filling his pipe; Blake declines it with a wave of his hand, and walks on.

SECOND TRAMP, *calling after him*: God bless you! May you never want it!

FIRST TRAMP: Thank you, mister. *You're a* gentleman!

BLAKE: All right. (*He goes out of sight under the trees down the road, and then suddenly reappears and walks up to the two tramps, who remain where he left them and are feeling in their pockets for a match.*) Did one of you call me a gentleman?

FIRST TRAMP: Yes, I did, mister. No offense in that, I hope?

BLAKE: No, but why did you do it?

FIRST TRAMP: Well, you didn't ask us why we didn't go to work; and you didn't say that men who hadn't any money to buy breakfast had better not smoke; and you gave us this tobacco. I'll call any man a gentleman that'll do that.

BLAKE: Oh, that's a gentleman, is it? All right.

He turns to go away, when the second tramp detains him.

SECOND TRAMP: Does your honor happen to have ever a match about you? (*Blake takes out his match-case and strikes a light.*) God bless your honor. You're a *real* gentleman.

BLAKE: Then this makes me a gentleman past a doubt?

SECOND TRAMP: Sure, it does that.

BLAKE: I'm glad to have the matter settled.

He walks on absently as before, and the tramps stand staring a moment in the direction in which he has gone.

SECOND TRAMP, *who goes back to the tree where he has been sitting and stretches himself out with his head on one arm for a quiet smoke*: That's a queer genius. By my soul, I'd like to take the road in *his* company. Sure, I think there isn't the woman alive would be out of cold victuals and old clothes when he put that handsome face of his in at the kitchen window.

FIRST TRAMP, *looking down the road*: I wonder if that fellow could have a drop of spirits about him! I say, mister! (*Calling after Blake*) Hello, there, I say!

SECOND TRAMP: It's too late, my worthy friend. He'll never hear you; and it's not likely he'd come back to fill your flask for you, if he did. A gentleman of his character'd think twice before he gave a tramp whiskey. Tobacco's another thing. (*He takes out the half-paper of tobacco, and looks at the label on it.*) What an extravagant dog! It's the real cut-cavendish; and it smells as nice as it smokes. This luxury is what's destroying the country. "With the present reckless expenditure in all classes of the population, and the prodigious influx of ignorant and degraded foreigners, there must be a constant increase of tramps." True for you, Mr. Newspaper. 'Twould have been an act of benevolence to take his watch from him, partner, and he never could tell how fast he was going to ruin. But you can't always befriend a man six feet high and wiry as a cat.

He offers to put the tobacco into his pocket again, when his comrade slouches up, and makes a clutch at it.

FIRST TRAMP: I want that.

SECOND TRAMP: Why, so ye do!

FIRST TRAMP: It's mine.

SECOND TRAMP: I'm keeping it for ye.

FIRST TRAMP: I tell you the man gave it to me.

SECOND TRAMP: And he wouldn't take it back from me. Ah, will you, ye brute? (*The other seizes the wrist of the hand with which the Irishman holds the tobacco; they wrestle together, when women's voices are heard at some distance down the road.*) Whoosh! Ladies coming. (*The first tramp listens, kneeling. The Irishman springs to his feet and thrusts the paper of tobacco into his pocket, and, coming quickly forward, looks down the road.*) Fortune favors the brave, partner! Here comes another opportunity—three of them, faith, and pretty ones at that! Business before pleasure; I'll put off that beating again; it's all the better for keeping. Besides, it's not the thing, quarreling before ladies.

He is about to crouch down again at the foot of the tree as before, when his comrade hastily gathers up his bundle, and seizing him by the arm drags him back into the thicket behind the pine-trees. After a moment or two, three young ladies come sauntering slowly along the road.

LILLY, *delicately sniffing the air*: Fee, fi, fo, fum; I smell the pipe of an Irishman.

LESLIE: Never! I know the flavor of refined tobacco, thanks to a smoking brother. Oh, what a lonely road!

LILLY: This loneliness is one of the charms of the Ponkwasset neighborhood. When you're once out of sight of the hotel and the picnic-grounds you'd think you were a thousand miles away from civilization. Not an empty sardine-box or a torn paper collar anywhere! This scent of tobacco is an unheard-of intrusion.

MAGGIE, *archly*: Perhaps Mr. Blake went this way. Does he smoke, Leslie?

LESLIE, *coldly*: How should I know, Maggie? A gentleman would hardly smoke in ladies' company—strange ladies. (*She sinks down upon a log at the wayside, and gazes slowly about with an air of fastidious criticism that gradually changes to a rapture of admiration.*) Well, I certainly think that, take it all in all, I never saw anything more fascinating. It's wonderful! This little nook itself, with that brown carpet of needles under the pines, and that heavy fringe of ferns there, behind those trunks; and then those ghostly birches stretching up and away, yonder—thousands of them! How tall and slim and stylish they are. And how they do march into the distance! I never saw such multitudes; and their lovely paleness makes them look as if one saw them by moonlight. Oh, oh! How perfectly divine! If one could only have their phantom-like procession painted! But Corot himself couldn't paint them. Oh, I *must* make some sort of memorandum—I won't have the presumption to call it a sketch. (*She takes a sketch-book from under her arm, and lays it on her knees, and then with her pencil nervously traces on the air the lines of the distant birches.*) Yes; I *must*. I never shall see them so beautiful again! Just jot down a few lines, and wash in the background when I get to the hotel. But girls; you mustn't stay! Go on and get the flowers, and I'll be done by the time you're back. I couldn't bear to have you overlooking me; I've all the sensitiveness of a great artist. Do go! But don't be gone long.

She begins to work at her sketch, without looking at them.

MAGGIE: I'm *so* glad, Leslie. I knew you'd be perfectly fascinated with this spot, and so I didn't tell you about it. I wanted it to *burst* upon you.

LESLIE, *with a little impatient surprise, as if she had thought they were gone*: Yes, yes; never mind. You did quite right. Don't stay long.

She continues to sketch, looking up now and then at the scene before her; but not glancing at her companions, who walk away from her some paces, when Miss Wallace comes back.

MAGGIE: What time is it, Leslie? Leslie!

LESLIE, *nervously*: Oh! What a start you gave me. (*Glancing at her watch*) It's nine minutes past ten—I mean ten minutes past nine. (*Still without looking at her*) Be back soon.

MAGGIE: Oh, it isn't far.

Again she turns away with Miss Roberts, but before they are quite out of sight Leslie springs to her feet and runs after them.

LESLIE: Oh, girls—girls!

MAGGIE, *anxiously, starting back toward her*: What? What?

LESLIE, *dreamily, as she returns to her place and sits down*: Oh, nothing. I just happened to think. (*She closes her eyes to a narrow line, and looks up at the birches.*) There are so many horrid stories in the papers. But of course there can't be any in this out-of-the-way place, so far from the cities.

MAGGIE: Any *what*, Leslie?

LESLIE, *remotely*: Tramps.

MAGGIE, *scornfully*: There never was such a thing heard of in the whole region.

LESLIE: I thought not. (*She is again absorbed in study of the birches; and, after a moment of hesitation, the other two retreat down the road once more, lingering a little to look back in admiration of her picturesque devotion to art, and then vanishing under the flickering light and shadow. Leslie works diligently on, humming softly to herself, and pausing now and then to look at the birches, for which object she rises at times, and, gracefully bending from side to side, or stooping forward to make sure of some effect that she has too slightly glimpsed, resumes her seat and begins anew.*) No, that won't do! (*Vigorously plying her india-rubber on certain lines of the sketch*) How stupid! (*Then beginning to draw again, and throwing back her head for the desired distance on her sketch*) Ah, that's more like. Still, nobody could accuse it of slavish fidelity. Well! (*She sings.*)

"Through starry palm-roofs on Old Nile
The full-orbed moon looked clear;
The bulbul sang to the crocodile,
'Ah, why that bitter tear?'

'With thy tender breast against the thorn,
Why that society-smile?'
The bird was mute. In silent scorn
Slow winked the crocodile."

How perfectly ridiculous! *Slow winked—(Miss Bellingham alternately applies pencil and rubber) slow winked the croco*—I never shall get that right; it's too bad!—*dile.*

While she continues to sketch, and sing da capo, the tramps creep stealthily from their covert. Apparently in accordance with some preconcerted plan, the surlier and huger ruffian goes down the road in the direction taken by Leslie's friends, and the Irishman stations himself unobserved at her side and supports himself with both hands resting upon the top of his stick, in an attitude of deferential patience and insinuating gallantry. She ceases singing and looks up.

SECOND TRAMP: Not to be interrupting you, miss,—*(Leslie stares at his grinning face in dumb and motionless horror)* would ye tell a poor traveler the time of day, so that he needn't be eating his breakfast prematurely, if he happens to get any?

FIRST TRAMP, *from his station down the road, in a hoarse undertone*: Snatch it out of her belt, you fool! Snatch it! He's coming back. Quick!

Leslie starts to her feet.

SECOND TRAMP: Ye see, miss, my friend's impatient. *(Soothingly)* Just let me examine your watch. I give ye my honor I won't hurt you; don't lose your presence of mind, my dear; don't be frightened.

As she shrinks back, he clutches at her watch-chain.

LESLIE, *in terror-stricken simplicity*: Oh, oh, no! Don't! Don't take my watch. My father gave it to me—and he's dead.

SECOND TRAMP: Then he'll never miss it, my dear. Don't oblige me to be rude to a lady. Give it here, at once, that's a dear.

FIRST TRAMP: Hurry, hurry! He's coming!

As the Irishman seizes her by the wrist, Leslie utters one wild shriek after another, to which the other young girls respond, as they reappear under the trees down the road.

MAGGIE: Leslie, Leslie! What is it?

LILLY, *at sight of Leslie struggling with the tramp*: Oh, help, help, help, somebody—do!

MAGGIE: Murder!

FIRST TRAMP, *rushing past them to the aid of his fellow*: Clap your hand over her mouth! Stop her noise, somehow! Choke her!

He springs forward, and while the Irishman stifles her cries with his hands, the other tears the watch-chain loose from its fastening. They suddenly release her, and as she reels gasping and swooning away, some one has the larger villain by the throat, who struggles with his assailant backward into the undergrowth, whence the crash of broken branches, with cries and curses, makes itself heard. Following this tumult comes the noise of a rush through the ferns, and then rapid footfalls, as of flight and pursuit on the hard road, that die away in the distance, while Maggie and Lilly hang over Leslie, striving to make out from her incoherent moans and laments what has happened.

MAGGIE: Oh, Leslie, Leslie, Leslie, what was it? Do try to think! Do try to tell! Oh, I shall go wild if you don't tell what's the matter.

LESLIE: Oh, it was—Oh, oh, I feel as if I should never be clean again! How *can* I endure it? That filthy hand on my mouth! Their loathsome rags, their sickening faces! Ugh! Oh, I shall dream of it as long as I live! Why, why did I ever come to this horrid place?

MAGGIE: Leslie,—dear, good Leslie,—what *was* it all?

LESLIE, *panting and sobbing*: Oh, two horrid, disgusting men! Don't ask me! And they told me to give them my watch, and I begged them not to take it. And one was a hideous little Irish wretch, and he kept running all round me, and oh, dear! the other was worse than he was; yes, worse! And he told him—oh, girls!—to choke me! And he came running up, and then the other put one of his hands over my mouth, and I couldn't breathe; and I thought I should die; but I wasn't going to let the wretches have my watch, if I could help it; and I kept struggling; and all at once they ran away, and—*(Putting her hand to her belt)* Oh, it's gone, it's gone, it's gone! Oh, papa, papa! The watch you gave me is gone!

She crouches down upon the log, and leaning her head upon her hands against the trunk of a tree gives way to her tears and sobs, while the others kneel beside her in helpless distress. On this scene Blake emerges from the road down which the steps were heard. His face is pale, and he advances with his right arm held behind him, while the left clasps something which he extends as he speaks.

BLAKE, *after a pause in which he stands looking at Leslie unheeded by the others*: Here is your watch, Miss Bellingham.

LESLIE, *whirling swiftly round to her feet*: My watch? Oh, where did you find it? (*She springs towards him and joyfully seizing it from his hand scans it eagerly, and then kisses it in a rapture.*) Safe, safe, safe! Not hurt the least! My precious gift! Oh, how glad I am! It's even going yet! How did you get it? Where did you get it?

BLAKE, *who speaks with a certain painful effort while he moves slowly away backward from her*: I found it—I got it from the thief.

LESLIE, *looking confusedly at him*: How did you know they had it?

MAGGIE: Oh, it was you, Mr. Blake, who came flying past us, and drove them away! Did you have to fight them? Oh, did they hurt you?

LESLIE: It was you— Why, how pale you look! There's blood on your face! Why, where were you? How did it all happen? It was you that drove them away? You? And I never thought of you! And I only thought about myself—my watch! I never can forgive myself.

She lets fall the watch from her heedless grasp, and he mechanically puts out the hand which he has been keeping behind him; she impetuously seizes it in her own and, suddenly shrinking, he subdues the groan that breaks from him to a sort of grasp and totters to the log where Leslie has been sitting.

LILLY: Oh, see, Miss Bellingham; they've broken his wrist!

BLAKE, *panting*: It's nothing; don't—don't—

MAGGIE: Oh dear, he's going to faint! What *shall* we do if he does? I didn't know they *ever* fainted! (*She wrings her hands in despair, while Leslie flings herself upon her knees at Blake's side.*) Oughtn't we to support him, somehow? Oh yes do let's support him, all of us!

LESLIE, *imperiously*: Run down to the river as fast as ever you can, and wet your handkerchiefs to sprinkle his face with. (*She passes her arm round Blake's, and tenderly gathers his broken wrist into her right hand.*) One can support him.

III.

A SLIGHT MISUNDERSTANDING

Three weeks after the events last represented Mrs. Bellingham and her sister-in-law are once more seated in the hotel parlor, both with sewing, to which the latter abandons herself with an apparently exasperated energy, while the former lets her work lie in her lap, and listens with some lady-like trepidation to what Mrs. Murray is saying.

MRS. MURRAY: From beginning to end it has been quite like a sensation play. Leslie must feel herself a heroine of melodrama. She is sojourning at a country inn, and she goes sketching in the woods, when two ruffians set upon her and try to rob her. Her screams reach the ear of the young man of humble life but noble heart, who professed to have gone away but who was still opportunely hanging about; he rushes on the scene and disperses the brigands, from whom he rends their prey. She seizes his hand to thank him for his sublime behavior, and discovers that his wrist has been broken by a blow from the bludgeon of one of the wicked ruffians. Very pretty, very charming, indeed; and so appropriate for a girl of Leslie's training, family, and station in life. Upon my word I congratulate you, Marion. To think of being the mother of a heroine! It was fortunate that you let her snub Mr. Dudley. If she had married him probably nothing of this kind would have happened.

MRS. BELLINGHAM, *uneasily*: I ought to be glad the affair amuses you, but I don't see how even *you* can hold the child responsible for what has happened.

MRS. MURRAY: Responsible! I should be the last to do that, I hope. No, indeed. I consider her the victim of circumstances, and since the hero has been thrown back upon our hands, I'm sure every one must say that her devotion is most exemplary. I don't hold her responsible for that, even. (*As Mrs. Murray continues, Mrs. Bellingham's uneasiness increases, and she drops her hands with a baffled look upon the work in her lap.*) It's quite en règle that she should be anxious about him; it would be altogether out of character otherwise. It's a pity that he doesn't lend himself more gracefully to being petted. When I saw her bringing him a pillow, that first day, after the doctor set his wrist and she had got him to repose his exhausted frame on the sofa, I was almost melted to tears. Of course it can end only in one way.

MRS. BELLINGHAM: Kate, I will not have any more of this. It's intolerable, and you have no right to torment me so. You know that I'm as much vexed as you can be. It annoys me beyond endurance, but I don't see what, as a lady, I can do about it. Mr. Blake is here again by no fault of his own, certainly, and neither Leslie nor I can treat him with indifference.

MRS. MURRAY: I don't object to *your* treating him as kindly as you like, but you had better leave as little kindness as possible to Leslie. You must sooner or later recognize one thing, Marion, and take your measures accordingly. I advise you to do it sooner.

MRS. BELLINGHAM: What do you mean?

MRS. MURRAY: I mean what you know well enough: that Leslie is interested in this Mr. Blake. I saw that she was, from the very first moment. He's just the kind of man to fascinate a girl like Leslie; you know that. He's handsome, and he's shown himself brave; and all that unconventionality which marks him of a different class gives him a charm to a girl's fancy, even when she has recognized, herself, that he isn't a gentleman. She soon forgets that, and sees merely that he is clever and good. She would very promptly teach a girl of his traditions her place, but a young man is different.

MRS. BELLINGHAM: I hope Leslie would treat even a woman with consideration.

MRS. MURRAY: Oh, consideration, consideration! You may thank yourself, Marion, and your impossible ideas, if this comes to the worst. You belong to one order of things or you belong to another. If you believe that several generations of wealth, breeding, and station distinguish a girl so that a new man, however good or wise he is, can never be her equal, you must act on your belief, and in a case like this you can't act too promptly.

MRS. BELLINGHAM: What should you do?

MRS. MURRAY: Do? I should fling away all absurd ideas of consideration, to begin with. I should deal frankly with Leslie; I should appeal to her pride and her common sense; and I should speak so distinctly to this young man that he couldn't possibly mistake my meaning. I should tell him—I should advise him to try change of air for his wound; or whatever it is.

MRS. BELLINGHAM, *after a moment's dreary reflection*: That's quite impossible, Kate. I will speak to Leslie, but I can never offer offense to any one we owe so much.

MRS. MURRAY: Do you wish *me* to speak to him?

MRS. BELLINGHAM: No, I can't permit that, either.

MRS. MURRAY: Very well; then you must abide by the result.

Mrs. Murray clutches her work together, stooping to recover dropping spools and scissors with an activity surprising in a lady of her massive person, and is about to leave the room, when the sound of steps and voices arrests her; a moment after Miss Bellingham and Blake, with his right arm in a sling, enter the room, so intent upon each other as not to observe the ladies in the corner.

LESLIE: I'm afraid you've let me tire you. I'm such an insatiable walker, and I never thought of your not being perfectly strong, yet.

BLAKE, *laughing*: Why, Miss Bellingham, it isn't one of my ankles that's broken.

LESLIE, *concessively*: No; but if you'd only let me *do* something for you. I can both play and sing, and really not at all badly. Shall I play to you? (*She goes up and strikes some chords on the piano, and with her hand on the keys glances with mock gravity round at Blake, who remains undecided. She turns about.*) Perhaps you'd rather have me read to you?

BLAKE: Do you really wish me to choose?

LESLIE: I do. And ask something difficult and disagreeable.

BLAKE: I'd rather have you talk to me than either.

LESLIE: Is that your idea of something difficult and disagreeable?

BLAKE: I hope you won't find it so.

LESLIE: But I shan't feel that it's anything, then! Shall I begin to talk to you here? Or where?

BLAKE: This is a good place, but if I'm to choose again, I should say the gallery would be better.

LESLIE: Oh, you're choosing that because I said I wondered how people could come into the country and sit all their time in stuffy rooms!

BLAKE, *going to the window and looking out*: There are no seats.

He returns, and putting the backs of two chairs together, lifts them with his left hand to carry them to the gallery.

LESLIE, *advancing tragically upon him and re-*

proachfully possessing herself of the chairs: Never! Do you think I have *no* sense of shame? *(She lifts a chair in either hand and carries them out, while Blake in a charmed embarrassment follows her, and they are heard speaking without.)* There! Or no! That's in a draught. You mustn't sit in a draught.

BLAKE: It won't hurt me. I'm not a young lady.

LESLIE: That's the very reason it *will* hurt you. If you were a young lady you could stand anything. Anything you *liked*.

> There are indistinct murmurs of further feigned dispute, broken by more or less conscious laughter, to which Mrs. Bellingham listens with alarm and Mrs. Murray with the self-righteousness of those who have told you so, and who, having thus washed their hands of an affair, propose to give you a shower-bath of the water.

MRS. MURRAY: Well, Marion?

MRS. BELLINGHAM, *rising, with a heavy sigh*: Yes, it's quite as bad as you could wish.

MRS. MURRAY: As bad as *I* could wish? This is too much, Marion. What are you going to do?

> Mrs. Bellingham is gathering up her work as if to quit the room, and Mrs. Murray's demand is pitched in a tone of falling indignation and rising amazement.

MRS. BELLINGHAM: We can't remain to overhear their talk. I am going to my room.

MRS. MURRAY: Why, Marion, the child is your own daughter!

MRS. BELLINGHAM: That is the very reason why I don't wish to feel that she has cause to be ashamed of me; and I certainly should if I stayed to eavesdrop.

MRS. MURRAY: How in the world should she ever know it?

MRS. BELLINGHAM: I should tell her. But that isn't the point, quite.

MRS. MURRAY: This is fantastic! Well, let her marry her—Caliban! Why don't you go out and join them? *That* needn't give her cause to blush for you. Remember, Marion, that Leslie is an ignorant, inexperienced child, and that it's your duty to save her from her silliness.

MRS. BELLINGHAM: My daughter is a lady, and will remember herself.

MRS. MURRAY: But she's a woman, Marion, and will forget herself!

MRS. BELLINGHAM, *who hesitates in a brief perplexity, but abruptly finishes her preparations for going out*: At any rate, I can't dog her steps, nor play the spy upon her. I wish to know only what she will freely tell me.

MRS. MURRAY: And are you actually going? Well, Marion, I suppose I mustn't say what I think of you.

MRS. BELLINGHAM: It isn't necessary that you should.

MRS. MURRAY: If I *were* to speak, I should say that your logic was worthy of Bedlam, and your morality of—of—the millenium!

> She whirls furiously out of the parlor, and Mrs. Bellingham, with a lingering glance at the door opening upon the balcony, follows her amply eddying skirts. A moment after their disappearance, Leslie comes to the gallery door and looks exploringly into the parlor.

LESLIE, *speaking to Blake without*: I was sure I heard voices. But there's nobody. *(She turns, and glancing at the hills which show their irregular mass through the open window, sinks down into a chair beside the low gallery rail.)* Ah, this is a better point still. *(And as Blake appears with his chair and plants it vis-à-vis with her)* Why old Ponkwasset, I wonder? But people always say old of mountains:[1] old Wachusett, old Agamenticus, old Monadnock, old Ponkwasset. Perhaps the young mountains have gone West and settled down on the prairies, with all the other young people of the neighborhood. Wouldn't that explain it? *(She looks with openly-feigned seriousness at Blake, who supports in his left hand the elbow of his hurt arm.)* I'm sure it's paining you.

BLAKE: No, no; not the least. The fact is—*(he laughs lightly)* I'm afraid I wasn't thinking about the mountains just now, when you spoke.

LESLIE: Oh, well, neither was I—very much. *(They both laugh.)* But why do you put your hand under your arm, if it doesn't pain you?

BLAKE: Oh!—I happened to think of the scamp who broke it for me.

LESLIE, *shuddering*: Don't speak of it! Or yes, do! Tell me about it; I've *wanted* to ask you. I ought to know about it; I hoped you would tell without asking. I can never be thankful enough that your walk happened to bring you back the same way. Why must you leave me to imagine all the rest?

BLAKE: Oh, those things are better imagined than described, Miss Bellingham.

[1] These are New England mountains: Wachusett Mountain by Princeton, Massachusetts; Mt. Monadnock near Jaffrey, New Hampshire; Mt. Agamenticus, a short distance from York Beach, Maine.

LESLIE: But I want it described. I must hear it, no matter how terrible it is.

BLAKE: It wasn't terrible; there was very little of it, one way or the other. The big fellow wouldn't give up your watch; and I had to—urge him; and the little Irishman came dancing up, and made a pass at us with his stick, and my wrist caught it. That's all.

LESLIE, with effusion: All? You risked your life to get me back my watch, and I asked about that first, and never mentioned you.

BLAKE: I hadn't done anything worth mentioning.

LESLIE: Then getting my watch wasn't worth mentioning!

BLAKE: Where is it? I haven't seen you wear it.

LESLIE: I broke something in it when I threw it down. It doesn't go. Besides, I thought perhaps you wouldn't like to see it.

BLAKE: Oh, yes, I should.

LESLIE, starting up: I'll go get it.

BLAKE: Not now!

They are both silent. Leslie falters and then sits down again, and folds one hand over the other on the balcony rail, letting her fan dangle idly by its chain from her waist. He leans forward a little, and taking the fan, opens and shuts it, while she looks down upon him with a slight smile; he relinquishes it with a glance at her, and leans back again in his chair.

LESLIE: Well, what were you thinking about that hideous little wretch who hurt you?

BLAKE: Why, I was thinking, for one thing, that he didn't mean to do it.

LESLIE: Oh! Why did he do it, then?

BLAKE: I believe he meant to hit his partner, though I can't exactly say why. It went through my mind. And I was thinking that a good deal might be said for tramps.

LESLIE: For tramps that steal watches and break wrists? My philanthropy doesn't rise to those giddy heights, quite. No, decidedly, Mr. Blake, I draw the line at tramps. They never look clean, and why don't they go to work?

BLAKE: Well, they couldn't find work just now, if they wanted it, and generally I suppose they don't want it. A man who's been out of work three months is glad to get it, but if he's idle a year he doesn't want it. When I see one of your big cotton mills standing idle, I know that it means just so much tramping, so much starving and stealing, so much misery and murder. We're

all part of the tangle; we're all of us to blame, we're none of us to blame.[1]

LESLIE: Oh, that's very well. But if you pity such wretches, what becomes of the deserving poor?

BLAKE: I'm not sure there are any deserving poor, as you call them, any more than there are deserving rich. So I don't draw the line at tramps. The fact is, Miss Bellingham, I had just been doing those fellows a charity before they attacked you,—given them some tobacco. You don't approve of that?

LESLIE: Oh, I like smoking!

BLAKE, laughing: And I got their idea of a gentleman.

LESLIE, after a moment: Yes? What was that?

BLAKE: A man who gives you tobacco, and doesn't ask you why you don't go to work. A real gentleman has matches about him to light your pipe with afterwards. Is that your notion of a gentleman?

LESLIE, consciously: I don't know; not exactly.

BLAKE: It made me think of the notion of a gentleman I once heard from a very nice fellow years ago: he believed that you couldn't be a gentleman unless you began with your grandfather. I was younger then, and I remember shivering over it, for it left me quite out in the cold, though I couldn't help liking the man; he was a gentleman in spite of what he said,—a splendid fellow, if you made allowance for him. You have to make allowances for everybody, especially for men who have had all the advantages. It's apt to put them wrong for life; they get to thinking that the start is the race. I used to look down on that sort of men, once—in theory. But what I saw of them in the war taught me better; they only wanted an emergency, and they could show themselves as good as anybody. It isn't safe to judge people by their circumstances; besides, I've known too many men who had all the disadvantage and never came to anything. Still I prefer the tramp's idea—perhaps because it's more flattering—that you are a gentleman if you choose to be so. What do you think?

LESLIE: I don't know. (After an interval long enough to vanquish and banish a disagreeable consciousness) I think it's a very unpleasant subject. Why don't you talk of something else?

BLAKE: Oh, I wasn't to talk at all, as I understood. I was to be talked to.

[1] These suggested economic problems refer to the consequences in New England of the Panic of 1873.

LESLIE: Well, what shall I talk to you about? You must choose that, too.

BLAKE: Let us talk about yourself, then.

LESLIE: There *is* nothing about me. I'm just like every other girl. Get Miss Wallace to tell you about herself, some day, and then you'll know my whole history. I've done everything that she's done. We had the same dancing, singing, piano, French, German, and Italian lessons; we went to the same schools and the same lectures; we have both been abroad, and can sketch, and paint on tiles. We're as nearly alike as the same experiences and associations could make us, and we're just like all the other girls we know. Isn't it rather monotonous?

BLAKE: I don't know all the other girls that you know. If I can judge from Miss Wallace, I don't believe you're like them; but they may be like you.

LESLIE, *laughing*: That's too fine a distinction for me. And you haven't answered my question.

BLAKE, *gravely*: No, it isn't monotonous to me; it's all very good, I think. I'm rather old-fashioned about women; I like everything in their lives to be regular and ordered by old usage.

LESLIE: Then you don't approve of originality?

BLAKE: I don't like eccentricity.

LESLIE: Oh, I do. I should like to do all sorts of odd things, if I dared.

BLAKE: Well, your not daring is a great point. If I had a sister, I should want her to be like all the other girls that are like you.

LESLIE: You compliment! She couldn't be like me.

BLAKE: Why?

LESLIE: Why? Oh, I don't know. (*She hesitates, and then with a quick glance at him.*) She would have dark eyes and hair, for one thing.

They both laugh.

BLAKE: Was that what you meant to say?

LESLIE: Isn't it enough to say what you mean, without being obliged to say what you meant?

BLAKE: Half a loaf is better than no bread; beggars mustn't be choosers.

LESLIE: Oh, if you put it so meekly as that you humiliate me. I must tell you now: I meant a question.

BLAKE: What is it?

LESLIE: But I can't ask it, yet. Not till I've got rid of some part of my obligations.

BLAKE: I suppose you mean what I—what happened.

LESLIE: Yes.

BLAKE: I'm sorry that it happened, then; and

I had been feeling rather glad of it, on the whole. I shall hate it if it's an annoyance to you.

LESLIE: Oh,—not annoyance, exactly.

BLAKE: What then? Should you like a receipt in full for all gratitude due me?

LESLIE: I should like to feel that we had done something for you in return.

BLAKE: You can cancel it all by giving me leave to enjoy being just what and where I am.

LESLIE, *demurely*, *after a little pause*: Is a broken wrist such a pleasure, then?

BLAKE: I take the broken wrist for what it brings. If it were not for that I should be in New York breaking my heart over some people I'm connected with in business there, and wondering how to push a little invention of mine without their help. Instead of that—

LESLIE, *hastily*: Oh! Invention? Are you an inventor, too, Mr. Blake? Do tell me what it is.

BLAKE: It's an improved locomotive driving-wheel. But you'd better let me alone about that, Miss Bellingham; I never stop when I get on my driving-wheel. That's what makes my friends doubtful about it; they don't see how any brake can check it. They say the Westinghouse air-brake would exhaust the atmosphere of the planet on it without the slightest effect. You see I *am* rather sanguine about it.

He laughs nervously.

LESLIE: But what have those New York people to do with it?

BLAKE: Nothing, at present. That's the worst of it. They were partners of mine, and they got me to come on all the way from Omaha, and then I found out that they had no means to get the thing going.

LESLIE: Oh! How could they do it?

BLAKE: Well, I used language to that effect myself, but they didn't seem to know; and I ran up here to cool off and think the matter over for a fresh start. You see, if I succeed it will be an everlasting fortune to me; and if I fail,—well, it will be an everlasting *mis*fortune. But I'm not going to fail. There; I'm started! If I went on a moment longer, no power on earth could stop me. I suppose you're not much used to talking about driving-wheels, Miss Bellingham?

LESLIE: We don't *often* speak of them. But they must be very interesting to those that understand them.

BLAKE: I can't honestly say they are. They're like railroads; they're good to get you there.

LESLIE: Where?

BLAKE: Well, in my case, away from a good deal of drudgery I don't like, and a life I don't altogether fancy, and a kind of world I know too well. I should go to Europe, I suppose, if the wheel succeeded. I've a curiosity to see what the apple is like on the other side; whether it's riper or only rottener. And I always believed I should quiet down somewhere, and read all the books I wanted to, and make up for lost time in several ways. I don't think I should look at any sort of machine for a year.

LESLIE, *earnestly*: And would all that happen if you had the money to get the driving-wheel going?

BLAKE, *with a smile at her earnestness*: I'm not such a driving-wheel fanatic as that. The thing has to be fully tested, and even after it's tested, the roads may refuse to take hold of it.

LESLIE, *confidently*: They can't—when they see that it's better.

BLAKE: I wish I could think so. But roads are human, Miss Bellingham. They prefer a thing that's just as well to something that's much better —if it costs much to change.

LESLIE: Well, then, if you don't believe the roads will take hold of it, why do you want to test it? Why don't you give it up at once?

BLAKE: It won't give me up. I do believe in it, you know, and I can't stop where I am with it. I must go on.

LESLIE: Yes. I should do just the same. I should never, *never* give it up. I know you'll be helped. Mr. Blake, if this wheel—

BLAKE: Really, Miss Bellingham, I feel ashamed for letting you bother yourself so long with that ridiculous wheel. But you wouldn't stick to the subject: we were talking about you.

LESLIE, *dreamily*: About me? (*Then abruptly*) Mamma will wonder what in the world has become of me. (*She rises, and Blake, with an air of slight surprise, follows her example. She leads the way into the parlor, and lingeringly drawing near the piano, she strikes some chords, and as she stands over the instrument, she carelessly plays an air with one hand. Then, without looking up*) Was that the air you were trying to remember?

BLAKE, *joyfully*: Oh yes, that's it; that's it, at last!

LESLIE, *seating herself at the piano and running over the keys again*: I think I can play it for you; it's rather old-fashioned, now.

She plays and sings, and then rests with her hands on the keys, looking up at Blake where he stands leaning one elbow on the corner of the piano.

BLAKE: I'm very much obliged.

LESLIE, *laughing*: And I'm very much surprised.

BLAKE: Why?

LESLIE: I should think the inventor of a driving-wheel would want something a great deal more stirring than this German sentimentality and those languid, melancholy things from Tennyson that you liked.

BLAKE: Ah, that's just what I don't want. I've got stir enough of my own.

LESLIE: I wish I could understand you.

BLAKE: Am I such a puzzle? I always thought myself a very simple affair.

LESLIE: That's the difficulty. I wish—

BLAKE: What?

LESLIE: That I could say something wrong in just the right way!

BLAKE, *laughing*: How do you know it's wrong?

LESLIE: It isn't, if you don't think so.

BLAKE: I don't, so far.

LESLIE: Ah, don't joke. It's a very serious matter.

BLAKE: Why should I think it was wrong?

LESLIE: I don't know that you will. Mr. Blake—

BLAKE: Well?

LESLIE: Did you know— If I begin to say something, and feel like stopping before I've said it, you won't ask questions to make me go on?

Very seriously.

BLAKE, *with a smile of joyous amusement, looking down at her as he lounges at the corner of the piano*: I won't even ask you to begin.

Leslie passes her hand over the edges of the keys, without making them sound; then she drops it into her lap and there clasps it with the other hand, and looks up at Blake.

LESLIE: Did you know I was rich, Mr. Blake?

BLAKE: No, Miss Bellingham, I didn't.

His smile changes from amusement to surprise, and he colors faintly.

LESLIE, *blushing violently*: Well, I am,—if being rich is having a great deal more money to do what you please than you know what to do with. (*Blake listens with a look of deepening mystification; she hurries desperately on.*) I have this money in my own right; it's what my uncle left me, and I can give it all away if I choose. (*She pauses again, as if waiting for Blake to ask her to go on, but he remains loyally silent; his smile has died away, and an embarrassment increases upon both of them. She looks up at him again, and implores.*) What *will* you think of what I'm going to say?

BLAKE, *breaking into a troubled laugh*: I can't imagine what you're going to say.

LESLIE: Don't laugh! I know you won't—O Mr. Blake, you said you liked girls to be just like everybody else, and old-established, and that; and I know this is as eccentric as it can be. It isn't at all the thing, I know, for a young lady to say to a gentleman; but you're not like the others, and— Oh, it doesn't seem possible that I should have begun it! It seems perfectly monstrous! But I know you won't misinterpret; I must, I must go on, and the bluntest and straightforwardest way will be the best way. (*She keeps wistfully scanning Blake's face as she speaks, but apparently gathers no courage or comfort from it.*) Mr. Blake!

BLAKE, *passively*: Well?

LESLIE, *with desperate vehemence*: I want— Oh, what will you think of me! But no, you're too good yourself not to see it in just the right way. I'm sure that you won't think it—unlady-like— for me to propose such a thing, merely because— because most people wouldn't do it; but I shall respect your reasons—I shall know you're right— even if you refuse me; and— O Mr. Blake, I want to go into partnership with you!

BLAKE, *recoiling a pace or two from the corner of the piano, as Leslie rises from the stool and stands confronting him*: To—to—go into—

LESLIE: Yes, yes! But how dreadfully you take it; and you promised— Oh, I *knew* you wouldn't like it! I know it seems dreadfully queer, and not at all delicate. But I thought—I thought—from what you said— You said those people had no money to push your invention, and here I have all this money doing nobody any good—and you've done nothing but heap one kindness after another on us—and why *shouldn't* you take it, as much as you want, and use it to perfect your driving-wheel? I'm sure I believe in it; and— (*She has followed him the pace or two of his withdrawal; but now, at some changing expression of his face, she hesitates, falters, and remains silent and motionless, as if fixed and stricken mute by the sight of some hideous apparition. Then with a wild incredulity*) Oh! (*and indignation*) Oh! (*and passionate reproach and disappointment*) Oh! How cruel, how shameless, how horrid!

She drops her face into her hands, and sinks upon the piano-stool, throwing her burdened arms upon the keys with a melodious crash.

BLAKE: Don't, don't! For pity's sake, don't, my—Miss Bellingham! (*He stands over her in helpless misery and abject self-reproach.*) Good heavens, I didn't— It was all—

LESLIE, *springing erect*: Don't speak to me. Your presence, your being alive in the same world after that is an insufferable insult! For you to dare! Ah! No woman could say what you thought. No lady—

BLAKE: Wait! (*He turns pale, and speaks low and steadily.*) You must listen to me now; you must hear what I never dreamt I should dare to say. I loved you! If that had not bewildered me I could not have thought—what was impossible. It was a delusion dearer than life; but I was ashamed of the hope it gave me even while it lasted. Don't mistake *me*, Miss Bellingham; I could have died to win your love, but if your words had said what they seemed to say, I would not have taken what they seemed to offer. But that's past. And now that I have to answer your meaning, I must do it without thanks. You place me in the position of having told my story to hint for your help—

LESLIE, *in vehement protest*: Oh, no, no, no! I never dreamt of such a thing! I couldn't!

BLAKE: Thank you at least for that; and— Good-by!

He bows and moves away toward the door.

LESLIE, *wildly*: Oh, don't go, don't go! What have I done, what shall I do?

BLAKE, *pausing, and then going abruptly back to her*: You can forgive me, Miss Bellingham; and let everything be as it was.

LESLIE, *after a moment of silent anguish*: No, no. That's impossible. It can never be the same again. It must all end. I can forgive you easily enough; it was nothing; the wrong was all mine. I've been cruelly to blame, letting you—go on. Oh, yes, very, very much. But I didn't know it; and I didn't mean anything by anything. No, I couldn't. Good-by. You are right to go. You mustn't see me any more. I shall never forget your goodness and patience. (*Eagerly*) You wouldn't want me to forget it, would you?

BLAKE, *brokenly*: Whatever you do will be right. God bless you, and good-by.

He takes up her right hand in his left, and raises it to his lips, she trembling, and as he stands holding it Mrs. Bellingham enters with an open letter.

MRS. BELLINGHAM: Leslie—

LESLIE, *who withdraws her hand, and after a momentary suspense turns unashamed to her mother:* Mr. Blake is going away, mamma—

Mrs. Bellingham faintly acknowledges his parting bow. Leslie watches him go, and then turns away with a suppressed sob.

IV.
MRS. MURRAY'S TRIUMPH

LESLIE: Well, mamma, what will you say to me now?

Without the inspiration of Blake's presence, she stands drearily confronting her mother in Mrs. Bellingham's own room, where the latter, seated in her easy-chair, looks up into Leslie's face.

MRS. BELLINGHAM: Nothing, Leslie. I am waiting for you to speak.

LESLIE: Oh, I can't speak unless you ask me.

She drops into a chair, and hiding her face in her handkerchief weeps silently. Her mother waits till her passion is spent and she has wiped her tears, and sits mutely staring toward the window.

MRS. BELLINGHAM: Is he coming back again, Leslie?

LESLIE: No.

MRS. BELLINGHAM: Was it necessary that you should let him take leave of you in that way?

LESLIE, *sighing:* No, it wasn't necessary. But—it was inevitable.

MRS. BELLINGHAM: What had made it inevitable? Remember, Leslie, that you asked me to question you.

LESLIE: I know it, mamma.

MRS. BELLINGHAM: And you needn't answer if you don't like.

LESLIE: I don't like, but I will answer, all the same, for you have a right to know. I had been saying something silly to him.

MRS. BELLINGHAM, *with patient hopelessness:* Yes?

LESLIE: It seems so, now; but I know that I spoke from a right motive,—a motive that you wouldn't disapprove of yourself, mamma.

MRS. BELLINGHAM: I'm sure of that, my dear.

LESLIE: Well, you see— Couldn't you go on and ask me, mamma?

MRS. BELLINGHAM: I don't know what to ask, Leslie.

LESLIE: It's so hard to tell, without! *(Desperately)* Why, you see, mamma, Mr. Blake had told me about a thing he had been inventing, and how some people in New York had promised him money to get it along,—push it, he said,—and when he came on all the way from Omaha, he found that they had no money; and so—and so—I—I offered him some.

MRS. BELLINGHAM: Oh, Leslie!

LESLIE: Yes, yes, it seems horrid, now,—perfectly hideous. But I did so long to do something for him because he had done so much for us, and I think he is so modest and noble, and I felt so sorry that he should have been so cruelly deceived. Wasn't that a good motive, mamma?

MRS. BELLINGHAM: Oh, yes, my poor headlong child! But what a thing for a young lady to propose! I can't imagine how you could approach the matter.

LESLIE: That's the worst of it,—the very worst. Of course, I never *could* have approached such a thing with any other young man; but I thought there was such a difference between us, don't you know, in everything, that it would be safe; and I thought it would be better—he would like it better—if there was no beating about the bush; and so I said—I said—that I wanted to go into partnership with him.

MRS. BELLINGHAM, *with great trouble in her voice, but steadily:* What answer did he make you, Leslie?

LESLIE: Oh, I was justly punished for looking down upon him. At first he blushed in a strange sort of way, and then he turned pale and looked grieved and angry, and at last repeated my words in a kind of daze, and I blundered on, and all at once—I saw what he thought I had meant; he thought— Oh dear, dear,—he thought— *(she hides her face again, and sobs out the words behind her handkerchief)* that I w-w-anted to—to—to marry him! Oh, how shall I ever endure it? It was a thousand times worse than the tramps,—a thousand times. *(Mrs. Bellingham remains silently regarding her daughter, who continues to bemoan herself, and then lifts her tearstained face.)* Don't you think it was ungratefully, horridly, cruelly vulgar?

MRS. BELLINGHAM: Mr. Blake can't have the refinement of feeling that you've been used to in the gentlemen of your acquaintance; I'm glad that you've found that out for yourself, though you've had to reach it through such a bitter mortification. If such a man misunderstood you—

LESLIE, *indignantly*: Mr. Blake is quite as good as the gentlemen of my acquaintance, mamma; he couldn't help thinking what he did, I blundered so, and when I flew out at him, and upbraided him for his—ungenerosity, and hurt his feelings all I could, he excused himself in a perfectly satisfactory way. He said—

MRS. BELLINGHAM: What, Leslie?

LESLIE, *with a drooping head*: He said—he used words more refined and considerate than I ever dreamt of—he said he was always thinking of me in that way without knowing it, and hoping against hope, or he could never have misunderstood me in the world. And then he let me know that he wouldn't have taken me, no matter how much he liked me, if what he thought for only an instant had been true; and he could never have taken my money, for that would have made him seem like begging, by what he had told me. And he talked splendidly, mamma, and he put me down, as I deserved, and he was going away, and I called him back, and we agreed that we must never see each other again; and—and I couldn't help his kissing my hand.

She puts up her handkerchief and sobs, and there is an interval before her mother speaks in a tone of compassion, yet of relief.

MRS. BELLINGHAM: Well, Leslie, I'm glad that you could agree upon so wise a course. This has all been a terribly perplexing and painful affair; and I have had my fears, my dear, that perhaps it had gone so far with you that—

LESLIE, *vehemently*: Why, so it had! I didn't know I liked him so, but I do; and I give him up —I gave him up—because you all hate him, yes, *all*; and you shut your eyes, and *won't* see how kind and brave and good he is; and I can't hold out against you. Yes, he must go; but he takes my broken heart with him.

MRS. BELLINGHAM, *sternly*: Leslie, this is absurd. You know yourself that he's out of the question.

LESLIE, *flinging herself down and laying her head in her mother's lap with a desolate cry*: O mamma, mamma, don't speak so harshly to me, or I shall die. I *know* he's out of the question; yes, yes, I do. But how? How, mamma? How is he out of the question? That's what I can't understand!

MRS. BELLINGHAM: Why, to begin with, we know nothing about him, Leslie.

LESLIE, *eagerly*: Oh yes, I do. He's told me all about himself. He's an inventor. He's a genius. Yes, he knows everything, indeed he does; and in the war he was an engineer. If you could only hear him talk as I do—

MRS. BELLINGHAM: I dare say. But even a civil engineer—

LESLIE: A *civil* engineer! I should hope *not*. I should be ashamed of a man who had been a civilian during the war. He always had this great taste for mechanics, and he studied the business of a machinist—I don't know what it is, exactly; but he knows all about steam, and he can build a whole engine, himself; and he happened to be a private soldier going somewhere on a Mississippi gunboat when the engineer was killed, and he took charge of the engine at once, and was in the great battles with the boat afterwards. He's a military engineer.

MRS. BELLINGHAM: He's a *steamboat* engineer, Leslie.

LESLIE: He was an officer of the boat—an officer—

MRS. BELLINGHAM, *with a groan*: Oh, he wasn't an officer of the sort you think; he had no military rank; he had the place of a clever artisan.

LESLIE: I don't understand.

MRS. BELLINGHAM: He looked after the machinery, and saw that the boiler didn't burst,—I don't know what. But you might as well marry a locomotive-driver, as far as profession goes.

LESLIE, *aghast*: Do you mean that when Mr. Blake was an engineer, he didn't wear any coat, and had his sleeves rolled up, and went about with a stringy wad of oily cotton in his hand?

MRS. BELLINGHAM: Yes.

LESLIE: Oh!

She excludes the horrible vision by clasping both hands over her eyes.

MRS. BELLINGHAM, *very gravely*: Now listen to me, Leslie. You know that I am not like your Aunt Kate,—that I never talk in that vulgar way about classes and stations, don't you?

LESLIE, *still in a helpless daze*: Oh, yes, mamma. I've always been a great deal worse than you, myself.

MRS. BELLINGHAM: Well, my dear, then I hope that you will acquit me of anything low or snobbish in what I have to say. There is a fitness in all things, and I speak out of respect to that. It is simply impossible that a girl of your breeding and ideas and associations should marry a man of his. Recollect that no one belongs entirely to themselves. You are part of the circle in which you have always moved, and he is part of the circumstances of his life. Do you see?

LESLIE: Yes.

She lapses from a kneeling to a crouching posture, and resting one elbow on her mother's knee poises her chin on her hand, and listens drearily.

MRS. BELLINGHAM: We may say that it is no matter what a man has been; that we are only concerned with what Mr. Blake is now. But the trouble is that every one of us is what they have been. If Mr. Blake's early associations have been rude and his business coarse, you may be sure they have left their mark upon him, no matter how good he may be naturally. I think he is of a very high and sweet nature; he seems so—

LESLIE: Oh, he is, he is!

MRS. BELLINGHAM: But he can't outlive his own life. Isn't that reasonable?

LESLIE, *hopelessly*: Yes, it seems so.

MRS. BELLINGHAM: You can't safely marry any man whose history you despise. Marriage is a terrible thing, my dear; young girls can never understand how it searches out the heart and tries and tests in every way. You mustn't have a husband whom you can imagine with a wad of greasy cotton in his hand. There will be wicked moments in which you will taunt and torment each other.

LESLIE: O mamma, mamma!

MRS. BELLINGHAM: Yes, it is so! The truest love can come to that. And in those moments it is better that all your past and present should be of the same level as his; for you wouldn't hesitate to throw any scorn in his teeth; you would be mad, and you must not have deadly weapons within reach. I speak very plainly.

LESLIE: Terribly!

MRS. BELLINGHAM: But that is the worst. There are a thousand lighter trials, which you must meet. Where would you live, if you married him? You have a fortune, and you might go to Europe—

LESLIE: I *never* would sneak away to Europe with him!

MRS. BELLINGHAM: I should hope not. But if you remained at home, how would you introduce him to your friends? Invention isn't a profession; would you tell them that he was a machinist or a steamboat engineer by trade? And if they found it out without your telling?

LESLIE, *evasively*: There are plenty of girls who marry men of genius, and it doesn't matter what

the men have done,—how humble they have been. If they're geniuses—

MRS. BELLINGHAM: O Leslie, such men have won all the honors and distinctions before they marry. Girls like you, my dear, don't marry geniuses in their poverty and obscurity. Those men spend years and years of toil and study, and struggle through a thousand difficulties and privations, and set the world talking about them, before they can even be asked to meet the ordinary people of our set in society. Wait till Mr. Blake has shown—

LESLIE: But he'd be an old man by that time, and then I shouldn't want him. If I know *now* that he's going to be great—

MRS. BELLINGHAM: My dear, you know nothing whatever about him, except that his past life has been shabby and common.

LESLIE, *with sudden spirit*: Well, then, mamma, at least I don't know anything horrid of him, as some girls must know of the young men they marry,—and the old men, too. Just think of Violet Emmons's match with that count, there in Paris! And Aggy Lawson's, with that dreadful old Mr. Lancaster, that everybody says has been so wicked! I'd rather marry Mr. Blake, a thousand times, if he had been a—I don't know what!

MRS. BELLINGHAM: You have no right to take things at their worst, Leslie. Remember all the girls you know, and the accomplished men they have married in their own set; men who are quite their equals in goodness as well as station and wealth and breeding. That's what I want you to do.

LESLIE: Do you wish me to marry somebody I don't like?

MRS. BELLINGHAM: Be fair, Leslie. I merely wish you to like somebody you ought to marry,—when the proper time comes. How do you know that Mr. Blake isn't quite as bad as the count or Mr. Lancaster?

LESLIE, *with a burst of tears*: Oh, mamma, you just now said yourself that you believed he was good and sweet, and you have seen the beautiful delicacy he behaves towards women with. Well, well,— (*she rises, and catches in her hand a long coil of her hair which has come loose from the mass, and stands holding it while she turns tragically toward her mother*) let it all go. I will never marry at all, and then at least I can't displease you. I give him up, and I hope it will make you happy, mamma.

MRS. BELLINGHAM, *rising*: Leslie, is this the way you reward my anxiety and patience? I have reasoned with you as a woman of sense, and the return you make is to behave as a petulant child. I will never try to control you in such a matter as this, but you know now what I think, and you can have your own way if you like it better or believe it is wiser than mine. Oh, my poor child!— (*clasping Leslie's head between her hands and tenderly kissing the girl's hair*) don't you suppose your mother's heart aches for you? Marry him if you will, Leslie, and I shall always love you. I hope I may never have to pity you more than I do now. All that I ask of you, after all, is to make sure of yourself.

LESLIE: I will, mamma, I will. He must go; oh, yes, he must go! I see that it wouldn't do. It would be too unequal,—I'm so far beneath him in everything but the things I ought to despise. No, I'm not his equal, and I never can be, and so I must not think of him any more. If *he* were rich, and had been brought up like me, and I were some poor girl with nothing but her love for him, he would never let the world outweigh her love, as I do his. Don't praise me, mother; don't thank me. It isn't for you I do it; it isn't for anything worthy, or true, or good; it's because I'm a coward, and afraid of the opinions of people I despise. You've shown me what I am. I thought I was brave and strong; but I am weak and timid, and I shall never respect myself any more. Send him away; tell him what an abject creature I am! It will kill me to have him think meanly of me, but oh, it will be a thousand times better that he should have a right to scorn me now, than that I should ever come to despise myself for having been ashamed of him, when—when— That I *couldn't* bear!

She drops into a chair near the table and lets fall her face into her hands upon it, sobbing.

MRS. BELLINGHAM: Leslie, Leslie! Be yourself! How strangely you act!

LESLIE, *lifting her face, to let it gleam a moment upon her mother before she drops it*: Oh, yes, I *feel* very strangely. But now I won't distress you any more, mother. (*Lifting her face again and impetuously drying her eyes with her handkerchief*) I will be firm, now, and no one shall ever hear a murmur from me,—not a murmur. I think that's due to you, mamma; you have been so patient with me. I've no right to grieve you by going on in this silly way, and I won't. I will be firm, firm, firm!

She casts herself into her mother's arms, and as she hangs upon her neck in a passion of grief, Mrs. Murray appears in the door-way, and in spite of Mrs. Bellingham's gesticulated entreaties to retire, advances into the room.

MRS. MURRAY: Why, what in the world does all this mean?

LESLIE, *raising her head and turning fiercely upon her*: It means that I'm now all you wish me to be,—quite your own ideal of ingratitude and selfishness, and I wish you joy of your success!

She vanishes stormily from the room and leaves Mrs. Murray planted.

MRS. MURRAY: Has she dismissed him? Has she broken with him?

MRS. BELLINGHAM, *coldly*: I think she meant you to understand that.

MRS. MURRAY: Very well, then, Charles can't come a moment too soon. If things are at this pass, and Leslie's in this mood, it's the most dangerous moment of the whole affair. If she should meet him now, everything would be lost.

MRS. BELLINGHAM: Don't be troubled. She won't meet him; he's gone.

MRS. MURRAY: I shall believe that when I see him going. A man like that would never leave her, in the world, because she bade him,—and I should think him a great fool if he did.

V.
BLAKE'S SAVING DOUBT

LESLIE: But it's all over,—it's all over. I shall live it down; but it will make another girl of me, Maggie. (*Along the road that winds near the nook where the encounter with the tramps took place, Leslie comes languidly pacing with her friend Maggie Wallace, who listens, as they walk, with downcast eyes and an air of reverent devotion, to Leslie's talk. Her voice trembles a little, and as they pause a moment Maggie draws Leslie's head down upon her neck, from which the latter presently lifts it fiercely.*) I don't *wish* you to pity me, Maggie, for I don't deserve any pity. I'm not suffering an atom more than I ought. It's all my own fault. Mamma really left me quite free, and if I cared more for what people would say and think and *look* than I did for him, I'm rightfully punished, and I'm not going to whimper about it. I've thought it all out.

MAGGIE: O Leslie, you always *did* think things out so clearly!

LESLIE: And I hope that I shall get my reward, and be an example. I hope I shall never marry at all, or else some horrid old thing I detest; it would serve me right and I should be glad of it!

MAGGIE: Oh no, no! Don't talk in that way, Leslie. Do come back with me to the house and lie down, or I'm sure you'll be ill. You look perfectly worn out.

LESLIE, *drooping upon the fallen log where she had sat to sketch the birch forest*: Yes, I'm tired. I think I shall never be rested again. It's the same place,— *(looking wistfully round)* and yet how strange it seems. You know we used to come here, and sit on this log and talk. What long, long talks! Oh me, it will never be again! How weird those birches look! Like ghosts. I wish I was one of them. Well, well! It's all over. Don't wait here, Maggie, dear. Go back to the house; I will come soon; you mustn't let me keep you from Miss Roberts. Excuse me to her, and tell her I'll go some other time. I can't, now. Go, Maggie!

MAGGIE: O Leslie; I hate to leave you here! After what's happened, it seems such a dreadful place.

LESLIE: After what's happened, it's a sacred place,—the dearest place in the world to me. Come, Maggie, you mustn't break your appointment. It was very good of you to come with me at all, and now you must go. Say that you left me behind a little way; that I'll be there directly.

MAGGIE: Leslie!

LESLIE: Maggie!

They embrace tenderly, and Maggie, looking back more than once, goes on her way, while Leslie sits staring absently at the birches. She remains in this dreary reverie till she is startled by a footfall in the road, when she rises in a sudden panic. Blake listlessly advances toward her; at the sight of her he halts, and they both stand silently regarding each other.

LESLIE: Oh! You said you were going away.

BLAKE: Are you in such haste to have me gone? I had to wait for the afternoon stage; I couldn't walk. I thought I might keep faith with you by staying away from the house till it was time to start.

LESLIE, *precipitately*: Do you call that keeping faith with me? Is leaving me all alone keeping— Oh, yes, yes, it is! You have done right. It's I who can't keep faith with myself. Why did you come here? You knew I would be here! I didn't think you could be guilty of such duplicity.

BLAKE: I had no idea of finding you here, but if I had known you were here perhaps I couldn't have kept away. The future doesn't look very bright to me, Miss Bellingham. I had a crazy notion that perhaps I might somehow find something of the past here that I could make my own. I wanted to come and stand here, and think once more that it all really happened—that here I saw the pity in your face that made me so glad of my hurt.

LESLIE: No; stop! It wasn't pity! It was nothing good or generous. It was mean regret that I should be under such an obligation to you; it was a selfish and despicable fear that you would have a claim upon my acquaintance which I must recognize. *(Blake makes a gesture of protest and disbelief, and seems about to speak, but she hurries on.)* You mustn't go away with one good thought of me. Since we parted, three hours ago, I have learned to know myself as I never did before, and now I see what a contemptible thing I am. I flattered myself that I had begged you to go away because I didn't like to cross the wishes of my family, but it wasn't that. It was—oh, listen! and try if you can imagine such vileness: I'm so much afraid of the world I've always lived in, that no matter how good and brave and wise and noble you were, still if any one should laugh or sneer at you because you had been—what you have been —I should be ashamed of you. There! I'm so low and feeble a creature as that; and that's the real reason why you must go and forget me; and I must not think and you must not think it's from any good motive I send you away.

BLAKE: I don't believe it!

LESLIE: What!

BLAKE: I don't believe what you say. Nothing shall rob me of my faith in you. Do you think that I'm not man enough to give up what I've no right to because it's the treasure of the world? Do you think I can't go till you make me believe that what I'd have sold my life for isn't worth a straw? No! I'll give up my hope, I'll give up my love,—poor fool I was to let it live an instant!— but my faith in you is something dearer yet, and I'll keep that till I die. Say what you will, you are still first among women to me: the most beautiful, the noblest, the best!

LESLIE, *gasping, and arresting him in a movement to turn away*: Wait, wait; don't go! Speak; say it again! Say that you don't believe it; that it isn't true!

BLAKE: No, I don't believe it. No, it isn't true. It's abominably false!

LESLIE, *bursting into tears*: Oh yes, it is. It's abominable, and it's false. Yes, I *will* believe in myself again. I *know* that if I had cared for—any one, as—as you cared, as you said you cared for me, I could be as true to them as you would be through any fate. Oh, thank you, thank you! (*At the tearful joy of the look she turns on him he starts toward her.*) Oh! (*she shrinks away*) you mustn't think that I—

BLAKE: I don't think anything that doesn't worship you!

LESLIE: Yes, but what I said sounds just like the other, when you misunderstood me so heartlessly.

BLAKE: I don't misunderstand you now. You *do* tell me that you love me, don't you? How should I dare hope without your leave?

LESLIE: You said you wouldn't have taken me as a gift if I had. You said you'd have hated me. You said—

BLAKE: I was all wrong in what I thought. I'm ashamed to think of that; but I was right in what I said.

LESLIE: Oh, *were* you! If you could misunderstand me then, how do you know that you're not misunderstanding me now?

BLAKE: Perhaps I am. Perhaps I'm dreaming as wildly as I was then. But you shall say. Am I?

LESLIE, *demurely*: I don't know; I— (*Staying his instantaneous further approach with extended arm*) No, no! (*She glances fearfully round.*) Wait; come with me. Come back with me—that is, if you will.

BLAKE, *passionately*: If I will!

LESLIE, *with pensive archness*: I want you to help me clear up my character.

BLAKE, *gravely*: Leslie, may I—

LESLIE: I can't talk with you here.

BLAKE, *sadly*: I will not go back with you to make sorrow for you and trouble among your friends. It's enough to know that you don't forbid me to love you.

LESLIE: Oh no, it isn't enough—for everybody.

BLAKE: Leslie—

LESLIE: Miss Bellingham, please!

BLAKE: Miss Bellingham—

LESLIE: Well?

BLAKE, *after a stare of rapturous perplexity*: Nothing!

LESLIE, *laughing through her tears*: If you don't make haste you will be too late for the stage, and then you can't get away till to-morrow.

VI.
MR. CHARLES BELLINGHAM'S DIPLOMACY

In the parlor with Mrs. Bellingham and Mrs. Murray sits a gentleman no longer young, but in the bloom of a comfortable middle life, with blonde hair tending to baldness, accurately parted in the middle, and with a handsome face, lazily shrewd, supported by a comely substructure of double chin, and traversed by a full blonde mustache. He is simply, almost carelessly, yet elegantly dressed in a thin summer stuff, and he has an effect of recent arrival. His manner has distinction, enhanced and refined by the eye-glasses which his near-sightedness obliges him to wear. He sits somewhat ponderously in the chair in which he has planted a person just losing its earlier squareness in the lines of beauty; his feet are set rather wide apart in the fashion of gentlemen approaching a certain weight; and he has an air of amiable resolution as of a man who having dined well yesterday means to dine well to-day.

CHARLES BELLINGHAM, *smiling amusement and indolently getting the range of his aunt through his glasses*: So I have come a day after the fair.

MRS. MURRAY: That is your mother's opinion.

MRS. BELLINGHAM: Yes, Charles, Leslie had known what to do herself, and had done it, even before I spoke to her. I'm sorry we made you drag all the way up here, for nothing.

BELLINGHAM: Oh, I don't mind it, mother. Duty called, and I obeyed. My leisure can wait for my return. The only thing is that they've got a new fellow at the club now, who interprets one's ideas of planked Spanish mackerel with a sentiment that amounts to genius. I suppose you plank horn-pout, here. But as to coming for nothing, I'd much rather do that than come for something, in a case like this. You say Leslie saw herself that it wouldn't do?

MRS. BELLINGHAM: Yes, she had really behaved admirably, Charles; and when I set the whole matter before her, she fully agreed with me.

BELLINGHAM: But you think she rather liked him?

MRS. BELLINGHAM, *sighing a little*: Yes, there is no doubt of that.

BELLINGHAM, *musingly*: Well, it's a pity. Behaved rather well in that tramp business, you said?

MRS. BELLINGHAM: Nobly.

BELLINGHAM: And hasn't pushed himself, at all?

MRS. BELLINGHAM: Not an instant.

BELLINGHAM: Well, I'm sorry for him, poor fellow, but I'm glad the thing's over. It would have been an awkward affair, under all the circumstances, to take hold of. I say, mother,— (*with a significant glance at Mrs. Murray*) there hasn't been anything—ah—abrupt in the management of this matter? You ladies sometimes forget the limitations of action in your amiable eagerness to have things over, you know.

MRS. BELLINGHAM: I think your mother would not forget herself in such a case.

BELLINGHAM: Of course, of course; excuse my asking, mother. But you're about the only woman that wouldn't.

MRS. MURRAY, *bitterly*: Oh, your mother and Leslie have *both* used him with the greatest tenderness.

BELLINGHAM, *dryly*: I'm glad to hear it; I never doubted it. If the man had been treated by any of my family with the faintest slight after what had happened, I should have felt bound as a gentleman to offer him any reparation in my power,—to make him any apology. People of our sort can't do anything shabby. (*Mrs. Murray does not reply, but rises from her place on the sofa and goes to the window.*) Does Leslie know I'm here?

MRS. BELLINGHAM, *with a little start*: Really, I forgot to tell her you were coming to-day; we had been keeping it from her, and—

BELLINGHAM: I don't know that it matters. Where is she?

MRS. BELLINGHAM: I saw her going out with Maggie Wallace. I dare say she will be back soon.

BELLINGHAM: All right. Where is the young man? Has he gone yet?

MRS. BELLINGHAM: No, he couldn't go till the afternoon stage leaves. He's still here.

BELLINGHAM: I must look him up, and make my acknowledgments to him. (*He rises.*) By the way, what's his name?

MRS. MURRAY, *standing with her face toward the window, leans forward and inclines to this side and that, as if to make perfectly sure before speaking of some fact of vivid interest which seems to have caught her notice, and at the moment Bellingham puts his question summons her sister-in-law in a voice of terrible incrimination and triumph*: Marion, did you say Leslie had gone out with Maggie Wallace?

MRS. BELLINGHAM, *indifferently*: Yes.

MRS. MURRAY: Will you be kind enough to step here? (*Mrs. Bellingham, with a little lady-like surprise, approaches, and Mrs. Murray indicates with a stabbing thrust of her hand, the sight which has so much interested her.*) Does *that* look as if it were all over?

BELLINGHAM, *carelessly, as Mrs. Bellingham with great evident distress remains looking in the direction indicated*: What's the matter now?

MRS. MURRAY: Nothing. I merely wished your mother to enjoy a fresh proof of Leslie's discretion. She is returning to tell us that it's out of the question in company with the young man himself.

BELLINGHAM: Wha—ha, ha, ha!—W*hat*?

MRS. MURRAY: She is returning with the young man from whom she had just parted forever.

BELLINGHAM, *approaching*: Oh, come now, aunt.

MRS. MURRAY, *fiercely*: Will you look for yourself, if you don't believe me?

BELLINGHAM: Oh, I believe you, fast enough, but as for looking, you know I couldn't tell the man in the moon at this distance, if Leslie happened to be walking home with him. But is the —ah—fat necessarily in the fire, because— (*Mrs. Murray whirls away from Bellingham where he remains with his hands on his hips peering over his mother's shoulder, and pounces upon a large opera-glass which stands on the centre-table, and returning with it thrusts it at him.*) Eh? What?

MRS. MURRAY, *excitedly*: It's what we watch the loons on the lake with.

BELLINGHAM: Well, but I don't see the application. They're not loons on the lake.

MRS. MURRAY: No; but they're loons on the land, and it comes to the same thing.

She vehemently presses the glass upon him.

BELLINGHAM, *gravely*: Do you mean, aunt, that you actually want me to watch my sister through an opera-glass, like a shabby Frenchman at a watering-place? Thanks. I could never look Les in the face again. It's a little too much like eavesdropping.

He folds his arms, and regards his aunt with reproachful amazement, while she dashes back to set the glass on the table again.

MRS. BELLINGHAM, *in great trouble*: Wait, Kate. Charles, dear, I—I think you must.

BELLINGHAM: What?

MRS. BELLINGHAM: Yes, you had better look. You will have to proceed in this matter now, and you must form some conclusions beforehand.

BELLINGHAM: But mother—

MRS. BELLINGHAM, *anxiously*: Don't worry me, Charles. I think you must.

BELLINGHAM: All right, mother. (*He unfolds his arms and accepts the glass from her.*) I never knew you to take an unfair advantage, and I'll obey you on trust. But I tell you I don't like it. I don't like it at all— (*Getting the focus, with several trials*) I've never stolen sheep, but I think I can realize, now, something of the self-reproach which misappropriated mutton might bring. *Where* did you say they were? Oh, over there! I was looking off here, at that point. They're coming this way, aren't they? (*With a start*) Hollo! She's got his arm! Oh, *that* won't do. I'm surprised at Les doing that, unless— (*Continuing to look*) By Jove! He's not a bad-looking fellow, at all. He— Why, confound it! No, it can't be! Why, yes—no—yes, it is, it *is*—by Heaven, it is—by all that's strange it is—BLAKE!

He lets the glass fall; and stands glaring at his aunt and mother, who confront him in speechless mystification.

MRS. BELLINGHAM: Blake? Why, of course it's Blake. We *told* you it was Mr. Blake!

BELLINGHAM: No, I beg your pardon, mother, you didn't! You never told me it was anybody—by name.

MRS. BELLINGHAM: Well?

BELLINGHAM: Why, don't you understand, mother? It's *my* Blake!

MRS. BELLINGHAM: *Your* Blake? *Your*—Charles, what *do* you mean?

BELLINGHAM: Why, I mean that this is the man— (*giving his glasses a fresh pinch on his nose with his thumb and forefinger*) that fished me out of the Mississippi. I flatter myself he couldn't do it now. "The grossness of my nature would have weight to drag him down,"—*both* of us down. But he'd try it, and he'd have the pluck to go down with me if he failed. Come, mother, you see I can't do anything in this matter. It's simply impossible. It's out of the question.

MRS. MURRAY: *Why* is it out of the question?

BELLINGHAM: Well, I don't know that I *can* explain, Aunt Kate, if it isn't clear to you, already.

MRS. BELLINGHAM, *recovering from the dismay in which her son's words have plunged her*: Charles, Charles! Do you mean that this Mr. Blake is the person who saved you from—

BELLINGHAM: From a watery grave? I do, mother.

MRS. BELLINGHAM: There *must* be some mistake. You can't tell at this distance, Charles.

BELLINGHAM: There's no mistake, mother. I should know Blake on the top of Ponkwasset. He was rather more than a casual acquaintance, you see. By Jove, I can't think of the matter with any sort of repose. I can see it all now, just as if it were somebody else: I was weighted down with my accoutrements, and I went over the side of the boat like a flash, and under that yellow deluge like a bullet. I had just leisure to think what a shame it was my life should go for nothing at a time when we needed men so much, when I felt a grip on my hair. (*Rubbing his bald spot*) It couldn't be done now! Then I knew I was all right, and waited for developments. The only development was Blake. He fought shy of me, if you'll believe it, after that, till I closed with him one day and had it out with him, and convinced him that he had done rather a handsome thing by me. But that was the end of it. I couldn't get him to stand anything else in the way of gratitude. Blake had a vice: he was proud.

MRS. BELLINGHAM: And what became of him?

BELLINGHAM: Who? Blake? He was the engineer of the boat, I ought to explain. He was transferred to a gunboat after that, and I believe he stuck to it throughout the fighting on the Mississippi. It's—let me see—it's five years now since I saw him in Nebraska, when I went out there to grow up with the country, and found I couldn't wait for it. (*After a pause*) I don't know what it was about Blake; but he somehow made everybody feel that there was stuff in him. In the three weeks we were together we became great friends, and I must say I never liked a man better. Well, that's why, Aunt Kate.

MRS. MURRAY: I don't see that it has anything whatever to do with the matter. The question is whether you wish Leslie to marry a man of his station and breeding, or not. His goodness and greatness have nothing to do with it. The fact remains that he is not at all her equal—that he isn't a gentleman—

BELLINGHAM: Oh, come now, Aunt Kate. You're not going to tell me that a man who saved my life isn't a gentleman?

MRS. MURRAY: And you're not going to tell me that a steamboat engineer is a gentleman?

BELLINGHAM, *disconcerted*: Eh?

MRS. MURRAY: The question is, are you going

to abandon that unhappy girl to her fancy for a man totally unfit to be her husband simply because he happened to save your life?

BELLINGHAM: Why, you see, Aunt Kate—

MRS. MURRAY: Do you think it would be gentlemanly to do it?

BELLINGHAM: Well, if you put it that way, no, I don't. And if you want to know, I don't see my way to behaving like a gentleman in this connection, whatever I do. (*He scratches his head ruefully.*) The fact is that the advantages are all on Blake's side, and he'll have to manage very badly if he doesn't come out the only gentleman in the business. (*After a moment*) How was it you didn't put the name and the—a—profession together, mother, and reflect that this *was* my Blake?

MRS. BELLINGHAM, *with plaintive reproach*: Charles, you know how uncommunicative you were about all your life as a soldier. You never told me half so much about this affair before, and you never—it seems very heartless now that I didn't insist on knowing, but at the time it was only part of the nightmare in which we were living—you never told me his name before.

BELLINGHAM: Didn't I? Well! I supposed I had, of course. Um! That was too bad. I say, mother, Blake has never let anything drop that made you think he had ever known me, or done me any little favor, I suppose?

MRS. BELLINGHAM: No, not the slightest hint. If he had only—

BELLINGHAM: Ah, that was like him, confound him! (*Bellingham muses again with a hopeless air, and then starts suddenly from his reverie.*) Why, the fact is, you know, mother, Blake is really a magnificent fellow; and you know—well, I *like* him!

MRS. MURRAY: Oh! That's Leslie's excuse!

BELLINGHAM: Eh?

MRS. MURRAY: If you are going to take Leslie's part, it's fortunate you have common ground. *Like* him!

BELLINGHAM: Mother, what is the unhallowed hour for dinner in these wilds? One o'clock? I've a fancy for tackling this business after dinner.

MRS. BELLINGHAM: I'm afraid, my dear, that it can't be put off. They must be here, soon.

BELLINGHAM, *sighing*: Well! Though they didn't seem to be hurrying.

MRS. MURRAY, *bitterly*: If they could only know what a friendly disposition there was towards him here, I'm sure they'd make haste!

BELLINGHAM: Um!

MRS. BELLINGHAM, *after a pause*: You don't know anything about his—his—family, do you, Charles?

BELLINGHAM: No, mother, I don't. My impression is that he *has* no family, any more than —Adam; or—protoplasm. All I know about him is that he was from first to last one of those natural gentlemen that upset all your preconceived notions of those things. His associations must have been commoner than—well it's impossible to compare them to anything satisfactory; but I never saw a trait in him or heard a word from him that wasn't refined. He gave me the impression of a very able man, too, as I was just saying, but where his strength lay, I can't say.

MRS. BELLINGHAM: Leslie says he's an inventor.

BELLINGHAM: Well, very likely. I remember, now: he was a machinist by trade, I believe, and he was an enlisted man on the boat when the engineer was killed; and Blake was the man who could step right into his place. It was considered a good thing amongst those people. He was a reader in his way, and most of the time he had some particularly hard-headed book in his hand when he was off duty,—about physics or metaphysics; used to talk them up now and then, very well. I never had any doubt about his coming out all right. He's a baffler, Blake is,—at least he is, for me. Now I suppose Aunt Kate, here, doesn't find him baffling, at all. She takes our little standards, our little weights and measures, and tests him with them, and she's perfectly satisfied with the result. It's a clear case of won't do.

MRS. MURRAY: Do you say it isn't?

BELLINGHAM: No; I merely doubt if it is. You don't doubt, and there you have the advantage of me. You always were a selected oyster, Aunt Kate, and you always knew that you couldn't be improved upon. Now, I'm a selected oyster, too, apparently, but I'm not certain that I'm the best choice that could have been made. I'm a *huitre de mon siècle*; I am the ill-starred mollusk that doubts. Of course we can't go counter to the theory that God once created people and nopeople, and that they have nothing to do but to go on reproducing themselves and leave him at leisure for the rest of eternity. But really, Aunt Kate, I have seen some things in my time— and I don't mind saying Blake is one of them— that made me think the Creator was still—active. I admit that it sounds — (*fitting his glasses on*) rather absurd for an old diner-out like myself to say it.

MRS. MURRAY, *with energy*: All this is neither here nor there, Charles, and you know it. The simple question is whether you wish your sister to marry a man whose past you'll be ashamed to be frank about. I'll admit, if you like, that he's quite our equal,—our superior; but what are you going to do with your ex-steamboat engineer in society?

BELLINGHAM, *dubiously*: Well, it would be rather awkward.

MRS. MURRAY: How will you introduce him, and what will you say to people about his family and his station and business? Or do you mean to banish yourself and give up the world which you find so comfortable for the boon of a brother-in-law whom you don't really know from Adam?

BELLINGHAM: Well, I must allow the force of your argument. Yes,— (*after a gloomy little reverie*) you're right. It won't do. It *is* out of the question. I'll put an end to it,—if it doesn't put an end to me. That "weird seizure" as of misappropriated mutton oppresses me again. Mother, I think you'd better go away,—you and Aunt Kate,—and let me meet him and Leslie here alone, when they come in. Or, I say: if you could detach Les, and let him come in here by himself, somehow? I don't suppose it can be done. Nothing seems disposed to let itself be done.

MRS. BELLINGHAM: Charles, I'm sorry this disagreeable business should fall to you.

BELLINGHAM: Oh, don't mind it, mother. What's a brother for, if he can't be called upon to break off his sister's love affairs? But I don't deny it's a nasty business.

MRS. MURRAY, *in retiring*: I sincerely hope he'll make it so for you, and cure you of your absurdities.

BELLINGHAM: O Parthian shaft! Wish me well out of it, mother!

MRS. BELLINGHAM, *sighing*: I do, Charles; I do with all my heart. You have the most difficult duty that a gentleman ever had to perform. I don't see how you're to take hold of it; I don't, indeed.

BELLINGHAM: Well, it *is* embarrassing. But it's a noble cause, and I suppose Heaven will befriend me. The trouble is, don't you know, I haven't got any—any point of view, any tenable point of view. It won't do to act simply in our own interest; *we* can't do *that*, mother; we're not the sort. I must try to do it in Blake's behalf, and that's what I don't see my way to, exactly. What I wish to do is to make my interference a magnanimous benefaction to Blake,—something that he'll recognize

in after years with gratitude as a—a mysterious Providence. If I've got to be a snob, mother, I wish to be a snob on the highest possible grounds.

MRS. BELLINGHAM: Don't use that word, Charles. It's shocking.

BELLINGHAM: Well, I won't, mother. I say: can't you think of some disqualifications in Leslie, that I could make a *point d'appui* in a conscientious effort to serve Blake?

MRS. BELLINGHAM: Charles!

BELLINGHAM: I mean, isn't she rather a worldly, frivolous, fashionable spirit, devoted to pleasure, and incapable of sympathizing with—with his higher moods, don't you know? Something like that?

Bellingham puts his thumbs in his waistcoat pockets and inclines towards his mother with a hopeful smile.

MRS. BELLINGHAM: No, Charles; you know she is nothing of the kind. She's a girl and she likes amusement, but I should like to see the man whose moods were too lofty for Leslie. She is everything that's generous and true and high-minded.

BELLINGHAM, *scratching his head*: That's bad! Then she isn't—ah—she hasn't any habits of extravagance that would unfit her to be the wife of a poor man who—ah—had his way to make in the world?

MRS. BELLINGHAM: She never spends half her allowance on herself; and besides, Charles, (how ridiculously you talk!) she has all that money your uncle left her, and if she marries him, he won't be poor any longer.

BELLINGHAM, *eagerly*: And that would ruin his career! Still— (*after a moment's thought*) I don't see how I'm to use that idea, exactly. No, I shall have to fall back on the good old ground that it's simply—out of the question. I think that's good; it has a thorough, logical, and final sound. I shall stick to that. Well, leave me to my fate! —Hollo! That's Blake's voice, now. I don't wonder it takes Leslie. It's the most sympathetic voice in the world. They're coming up here, aren't they? You'd better go, mother. I wish you could have got Leslie away—

LESLIE, *without*: Wait for me, there. I must go to mamma's room at once, and tell her everything.

BLAKE, *without*: Of course. And say that I wish to see her.

LESLIE: Good-by.

BLAKE: Good-by.

LESLIE: We won't keep you long. *Good*-by.

BLAKE: *Good*-by.

As he enters one of the parlor doors, flushed and radiant, Mrs. Bellingham retreats through the other.

BELLINGHAM, *coming promptly forward to greet Blake, with both hands extended*: Blake!

BLAKE, *after a moment of stupefaction*: Bellingham!

BELLINGHAM: My dear old fellow! (*He wrings Blake fervently by the left hand.*) This is the most astonishing thing in the world! To find you here—in New England—with my people; it's the most wonderful thing that ever was! They've been—ah—been telling me all about you, my mother has; and I want to thank you—you look uncommonly well, Blake, and not a day older! Do you mean to go through life with that figure?—thank you for all you've done for them; and—I don't know: what does a man say to a fellow who has behaved as you did in that business with the tramps?— (*Wringing Blake's left hand again and gently touching his right arm in its sling*) By Jove, old fellow! I don't know what to say, to *you*; I— Do you think it was quite the thing, though, not to intimate that you'd known *me*? Come, now; that wasn't fair. It wasn't frank. It wasn't like *you*, Blake. Hey?

He affectionately presses Blake's hand at every emphatic word.

BLAKE, *releasing himself*: I didn't like it: but I couldn't help it. It would have seemed to claim something, and I should have had to allow—they would have found out—

BELLINGHAM: That you happened to save my life, once. Well, upon my word, I don't think it was a thing to be ashamed of; at least, at that time; I was in the army, then. At present—I don't know that I should blame you for hushing the matter up.

BLAKE, *who has turned uneasily away, and has apparently not been paying the closest attention to Bellingham's reproaches, but now confronts him*: I suppose you're a gentleman, Bellingham.

BELLINGHAM, *taking the abruptness of Blake's question with amiable irony*: There have been moments in which I have flattered myself to that degree; even existence itself is problematical, to my mind, at other times: but—well, yes, I suppose I am a gentleman. The term's conventional. And then?

BLAKE: I mean that you're a fair-minded, honest man, and that I can talk to you without the risk of being misunderstood or having any sort of meanness attributed to me?

BELLINGHAM: I should have to be a much shabbier fellow than I am, for anything of that sort, Blake.

BLAKE: I didn't expect to find you here; I was expecting to speak with your mother. But I don't see why I shouldn't say to you what I have to say. In fact, I think I can say it better to you.

BELLINGHAM: Thanks, Blake; you'll always find me your—That is—well, go ahead!

BLAKE: You don't think I'm a man to do anything sneaking, do you?

BELLINGHAM: Again? My dear fellow, that goes without saying. It's out of the question.

BLAKE, *walking up and down, and stopping from time to time while he speaks in a tone of passionate self-restraint*: Well, I'm glad to hear that, because I know that to some the thing might have a different look. (*After a pause, in which Blake takes another turn round the room and arrives in front of Bellingham again*) If your people have been telling you about me, I suppose they've hinted—but I don't care to know it—that they think I'm in love with Miss Bellingham, your sister. I am! (*He looks at Bellingham, who remains impassive behind the glitter of his eyeglasses.*) Do you see any reason why I shouldn't be?

BELLINGHAM, *reluctantly*: N-no.

BLAKE: I believe—no, I *can't* believe it!—but I *know* that Miss Bellingham permits it; that she— I can't say it! Is there any—any reason why I shouldn't ask her mother's leave to ask her to be my wife? Why, of course, there is!—a thousand, million reasons in my unworthiness; I know that. But is there—

BELLINGHAM, *abruptly*: Blake, my dear fellow—my dear, good old boy—it won't do; it's out of the question! It is, it is indeed! It won't do at all. Confound it, man! You know I like you, that I've always wanted to be a great deal more your friend than you would ever let me. Don't ask me why, but take my word for it when I tell you it's out of the question. There are a thousand reasons, as you say, though there isn't one of them in any fault of yours, old fellow. But I can't give them. It won't do!

Bellingham in his turn begins to walk up and down the room with a face of acute misery and hopelessness, and at the last word he stops and stares helplessly into Blake's eyes, who has remained in his place.

BLAKE, *with suppressed feeling*: Do you expect me to be satisfied with that answer?

BELLINGHAM, *at first confused and then with a burst of candor*: No; I wouldn't, myself. (*His head falls, and a groan breaks from his lips.*) This is the roughest thing I ever knew of. Hang it, Blake, don't you see what a—a—box I'm in? People pulling and hauling at me, and hammering away on all sides, till I don't know which end I'm standing on! You wouldn't like it yourself. Why do you ask? Why must you be—ah—satisfied? Come! Why don't you let it all—go?

BLAKE: Upon my word, Bellingham, you talk—

BELLINGHAM: Like a fool! I know it. And it's strictly in character. At the present moment I *feel* like a fool! I *am* a fool! By Jove, if I ever supposed I should get into such a tight place as this! Why, don't you see, Blake, what an extremely unfair advantage you have of me? Deuce take it, man, *I* have some rights in the matter, too, I fancy!

BLAKE, *bewildered*: Rights? Advantage? I don't understand all this.

BELLINGHAM: How not understand?

BLAKE, *gazing in mystified silence at Bellingham for a brief space, and then resuming more steadily*: There's some objection to me, that's clear enough. I don't make any claim, but you would think I ought to know what the matter is, wouldn't you?

BELLINGHAM: Y-yes, Blake.

BLAKE: I know that I'm ten years older than Miss Bellingham, and that it might look as if—

BELLINGHAM, *hastily*: Oh, not in the least—not in the least!

BLAKE: Our acquaintance wasn't regularly made, I believe. But you don't suppose that I urged it, or that it would have been kept up if it hadn't been for their kindness and for chances that nobody foresaw?

BELLINGHAM: There isn't a circumstance of the whole affair that isn't perfectly honorable to you, Blake; that isn't *like* you. Confound it—

BLAKE: I won't ask you whether you think I thought of her being rich?

BELLINGHAM: No, sir! That would be offensive.

BLAKE: Then what is it? Is there some personal objection to me with your family?

BELLINGHAM: There isn't at all, Blake, I assure you.

BLAKE: Then I don't understand, and— (*with rising spirit*) I want to say once for all that I think your leaving me to ask these things and put myself on the defensive in this way, begging you for this reason and for that, isn't what I'm used to. But I'm like a man on trial for his life, and I stand it. Now, go on and say what there is to say. Don't spare my feelings, man! I have no pride where *she* is concerned. What do you know against me that makes it impossible?

BELLINGHAM: O Lord! It isn't *against* you. It's nothing personal; personally we've all reason to respect and honor you; you've done us nothing but good in the handsomest way. But it won't do for all that. There's an incompatibility—a—a—I don't know what to call it! Confound it, Blake! You know very well that there's none of that cursed nonsense about me. *I* don't care what a man is in life; I only ask what he is in himself. I accept the American plan in good faith. I know all sorts of fellows; devilish good fellows some of them are, too! Why, I had that Mitchell, who behaved so well at the Squattick Mills disaster, to dine with me; went down and looked him up, and had him to dine with me. Some of the men didn't think it was the thing; but I can assure you that he talked magnificently about the affair. I drew him out, and before we were done we had the whole room about us. I wouldn't have missed it on any account. That's *my* way.

BLAKE, *dryly*: It's a very magnanimous way. The man must have felt honored.

BELLINGHAM: What?—Oh, deuce take it! I don't mean any of that patronizing rot, you know I don't. You know I think such a man as that ten times as good as myself. What I mean is that it's different with women. They haven't got the same—what shall I say?—horizons, social horizons, don't you know. *They* can't accept a man for what he is in himself. They have to take him for what he *isn't* in himself. They have to have their world carried on upon the European plan, in short. I don't know whether I make myself understood—

BLAKE, *with hardness*: Yes, you do. The objection is to my having been—

BELLINGHAM, *hastily interposing*: Well—ah—no! I can't admit that. It isn't the occupation. We've all been occupied more or less remotely in—in some sort of thing; a man's a fool who tries to blink that. But I don't know that I can make it clear how our belonging, now, to a different order of things makes our women distrustful—I won't say skeptical, but anxious—as to the influence of—ah—other social circumstances. They're mere creatures of tradition, women are, and where you or I, Blake,— (*with caressing good comradeship and the assumption of an impartial high-mindedness*) wouldn't care a straw for a man's trade or profession, *they* are more disposed to—ah—particularize, and—don't you know—distinguish!

BLAKE, *gravely*: I tried to make Miss Bellingham understand from the first just what I was and had been. I certainly never concealed anything. Do you think she would care for what disturbs the other ladies of your family?

BELLINGHAM: Leslie? Well, she's still a very young girl, and she has streaks of originality that rather disqualify her for appreciating—ah—She's romantic! I'm sure I'm greatly obliged to you, Blake, for taking the thing in this reasonable way. You know how to sympathize with one's extreme reluctance—and—ah—embarrassment in putting a case of the kind.

BLAKE, *with a sad, musing tone*: Yes, God knows I'm sorry for you. I don't suppose you like to do it.

BELLINGHAM: Thanks, thanks, Blake. It was quite as much on your own account that I spoke. They would make it deucedly uncomfortable for you in the family,—there's no end to the aunts and grandmothers, and things, and you'd make them uncomfortable too, with your—history. (*Mopping his forehead with his handkerchief*) You have it infernally hot, up here, don't you?

BLAKE, *still musingly*: Then you think that Miss Bellingham herself wouldn't be seriously distressed?

BELLINGHAM: Leslie's a girl that will go through anything she's made up her mind to. And if she likes you well enough to marry you—

BLAKE: She says so.

BELLINGHAM: Then burning plowshares wouldn't have the smallest effect upon her. But—

BLAKE, *quietly*: Then I won't give her up.

BELLINGHAM: Eh?

BLAKE: I won't give her up. It's bad enough as it is, but if I were such a sneak as to leave the woman who loved me because my marrying her would be awkward for her friends, I should be ten thousand times unworthier than I am. I am going to hold to my one chance of showing myself worthy to win her, and if she will have me I will have *her*, though it smashes the whole social structure. Bellingham, you're mistaken about this thing; her happiness won't depend upon the success of the aunts and cousins in accounting for me to the world; it'll depend upon whether I'm man enough to be all the world to her. If she thinks I am, I *will* be!

BELLINGHAM: Oh, don't talk in that illogical way, Blake. Confound it! I know; I can account for your state of feeling, and all that; but I do assure you it's mistaken. Let me put it to you. You don't see this matter as I do; you can't. The best part of a woman's life is social—

BLAKE: I don't believe that.

BELLINGHAM: Well, no matter: it's so; and whether you came into Leslie's world or took her out of it, you'd make no end of—of—row. She'd suffer in a thousand ways.

BLAKE: Not if she loved me, and was the kind of girl I take her to be.

BELLINGHAM: Oh, yes, she would, my dear fellow; Leslie's a devilish proud girl; she'd suffer in secret, but it would try her pride in ways you don't know of. Why, only consider: she's taken by surprise in this affair; she's had no time to think—

BLAKE: She shall have my whole lifetime to make up her mind in; she shall test me in every way she will, and she may fling me away at any moment she will, and I will be her slave forever. She may give me up, but I will not give her up.

BELLINGHAM: Well, well! We won't dispute about terms, but I'll put it to you, yourself, Blake, —yourself. I want you to see that I'm acting for your good; that I'm your friend.

BLAKE: You're her brother, and you're my friend, whatever you say. I've borne to have you insinuate that I'm your inferior. Go on!

Blake's voice trembles.

BELLINGHAM: Oh, now! Don't take that tone! It isn't fair. It makes me feel like—like the very devil. It does, indeed. I don't mean anything of the kind. I mean simply that—that—ah—remote circumstances over which you had—ah—no control have placed you at a disadvantage,—social disadvantage. That's all. It isn't a question of inferiority or superiority. And I merely put it to you—as a friend, mind—whether the happiness of—ah—all concerned couldn't be more promptly —ah—secured by your refusing to submit to tests that might—Come now my dear fellow! She's flattered—any woman might be—by your liking her; but when she went back to her own associations—

BLAKE: If she sees any man she likes better than me, I won't claim her. But I can't judge her by a loyalty less than my own. She will never change. (*Bellingham essays an answer, but after some preliminary ahs and ums, abruptly desists, and guards an evidently troubled silence, which*

Blake assails with jealous quickness.) What do you mean? Out with it, man!

BELLINGHAM: Don't take it in that way! My dear fellow—

BLAKE: If I'm her caprice and not her choice, I want to know it! I won't be killed by inches. Speak!

BELLINGHAM: Stop! I owe you my life, but you mustn't take that tone with me.

BLAKE: You owe me nothing,—nothing but an answer. If you mean there has been some one before me— *She* has told me that she never cared for any one but me; I believe her, but I want to know what you mean.

BELLINGHAM: She's my sister! What do *you* mean?

LESLIE: Oh, what *does* it mean? (*She enters the room, as if she had been suddenly summoned by the sound of their angry voices from a guiltless ambush in the hall. At the sight of their flushed faces and defiant attitudes she flutters, electrically attracted, first toward one and then toward the other, but at last she instinctively takes shelter at Blake's elbow.*) Charles, what are you saying? What are you both so angry for? Oh, I hoped to find you such good friends, and here you are quarreling! Charles, what have you been doing? O Charles, I always thought you were so generous and magnanimous, and have *you* been joining that odious conspiracy against *us*? For shame! And what have you found to say, I should like to know? I should *like* to know what you've found to say— what a *gentleman* COULD say, under the circumstances! (*She grows more vehement as their mutual embarrassment increases upon the men, and Bellingham fades into a blank dismay behind the glitter of his eye-glasses.*) Have you been saying something you're ashamed of, Charles? You *couldn't* say anything about *him*, and so you've been trying to set him against *me*. What have you said about your sister, Charles?—and always pretending to be so fond of *me*! Oh, oh, oh!

Miss Bellingham snatches her handkerchief from her pocket and hides her grief in it, while her brother remains in entire petrifaction at her prescience.

BELLINGHAM, *finally*: Why, Leslie— Deuce take it all, Blake, why don't *you* say something? I tell you, I haven't *said* anything against you, Les. Blake will tell you himself that I was merely endeavoring to set the thing before him from different points of view. I wanted him to consider the shortness of your acquaintance—

LESLIE, *in her handkerchief*: It's fully three weeks since we met,—you *know* it is.

BELLINGHAM: And I wanted him to reflect upon how very different all your associations and—traditions—were—

LESLIE, *still in her handkerchief*: Oh, *that* was delicate—very!

BELLINGHAM: And to—ah—take into consideration the fact that returning to another—atmosphere—surroundings, you might—ah—change.

LESLIE, *lifting her face*: You did! Charles, did I *ever* change?

BELLINGHAM: Well, I don't know. I don't know whether you'd call it *changing*, exactly; but I certainly got the impression from Aunt Kate that there was some hope on Dudley's part last summer—

LESLIE, *quitting her refuge and advancing fiercely upon the dismayed but immovable Bellingham with her right hand thrust rigidly down at her side, and her left held behind her clutching her hankerchief*: Charles, have you *dared* to intimate that I ever cared the least thing about that —that—horrid—little—reptile? When you *knew* that my life was made perfectly ghastly by the way Aunt Kate forced him on me, and it was as much as I could ever do to treat him decently! I never encouraged him for an *instant,* and you know it. Oh, Charley, Charley, how could you? It isn't for myself I care; it's for you, for you're a *gentleman,* and you let yourself do that! How painfully strange that low, mean, shabby feeling must have been to you! I don't wonder you couldn't face me or speak to me. I don't—

BELLINGHAM, *desperately*: Here; hold on! Good Lord! I can't stand this! Confound it, I'm not made of granite—or gutta-percha. I'll allow it was sneaking,—Blake will tell you I looked it,—but it was a desperate case. It was a family job, and I had to do my best—or my worst—as the head of the family; and Blake wouldn't hear reason, and—

LESLIE: And so you thought you'd try *fraud!*

BELLINGHAM: Well, I shouldn't use that word. But it's the privilege of your sex to call a spade a pitchfork, if you don't like the spade. I tell you I never professed to know anything personally about the Dudley business and I didn't *say* anything about it; when Blake caught me up so, I was embarrassed to think how I might have mentioned it in—in the heat of argument. Come, Blake—

LESLIE, *turning and going devoutly up to Blake*: Yes, *he* will defend you. *He* must save your honor since he saved your life.

BELLINGHAM, *with a start*: Eh?

LESLIE: Oh, I know about it! Mamma told me. She thinks just as I do, now, and she has been feeling dreadfully about this shabby work she'd set you at; but I comforted her. I told her you would never do it in the world; that you would just shuffle about in your way—

BELLINGHAM: Oh, thanks!

LESLIE: But that you had too good a heart, too high a spirit, to breathe a syllable that would wound the pride of a brave and generous man to whom you owed life itself: that you would rather *die* than do it! (*To Blake*) Oh, I've always been a romantic girl,—you won't mind it in me, will you?—and I've had my foolish dreams a thousand times about the man who risked his life to save my brother's; and I hoped and longed that some day we should meet. I promised myself that I should know him, and I always thought how sweet and dear a privilege it would be to thank him. I want to thank you for his life as I used to dream of doing, but I cannot yet. I cannot till you tell me that he has not said one word unworthy of you,—unworthy of a gentleman!

BLAKE, *smiling*: He's all right!

LESLIE, *impetuously clinging to him*: Oh, thanks, thanks, thanks!

BELLINGHAM, *accurately focusing the pair with freshly adjusted glasses*: If you'll both give me your blessing, now, I'll go away, feeling perfectly rehabilitated, in the afternoon stage.

MRS. BELLINGHAM, *entering the parlor door*: Stage? Why, Mr. Blake isn't going away!

BELLINGHAM: Oh, no, Mr. Blake has kindly consented to remain. It was I who thought of going. I can't bear to be idle!

MRS. BELLINGHAM, *apart from the others*: Charles, dear, I'm sorry I asked you to undertake that disagreeable business, and I'd have come back at once with Leslie to relieve you,—to tell you that you needn't speak after all,—but she felt sure that you wouldn't, and she insisted upon leaving you together and then stealing back upon you and enjoying—

BELLINGHAM, *solemnly*: You little knew me, mother. I have the making of an iron-hearted parent in me, and I was crushing all hope out of Blake when Leslie came in.

MRS. BELLINGHAM: Charles, you don't mean that you said anything to wound the feelings of a man to whom you owed your life,—to whom we *all* owe so much?

BELLINGHAM: I don't know about his *feelings*. But I represented pretty distinctly to him the social incompatibility.

MRS. BELLINGHAM: Charles, I wonder at you!

BELLINGHAM: Oh, yes! So do I. But if you'll take the pains to recall the facts, that's exactly what you left me to do. May I ask what has caused you to change your mind?

MRS. BELLINGHAM, *earnestly*: I found that Leslie's happiness really depended upon it; and in fact, Charles, when I came to reflect, I found that I myself liked him.

BELLINGHAM: The words have a familiar sound, —as if I had used them myself in a former existence. (*Turning from his mother and looking about*) I seem to miss a—a support—moral support—in those present. Where is Aunt Kate?

MRS. MURRAY, *appearing at the door*: Marion! Ma—

She hesitates at sight of the peaceful grouping.

BELLINGHAM: Ah, this is indeed opportune! Come in, Aunt Kate, come in! This is a free fight, as they say in Mr. Blake's section. Any one can join. (*Mrs. Murray advances wonderingly into the room, and Bellingham turns to his sister, where she stands at Blake's side.*) Leslie, you think I've behaved very unhandsomely in this matter, don't you?

LESLIE, *plaintively*: Charley, you know I hate to blame you. But I never could have believed it if any one else had told me.

BELLINGHAM: All right. Mother, I understand that you would have been similarly incredulous?

MRS. BELLINGHAM: I know that you acted from a good motive, Charles, but you certainly went to an extreme that I could never have expected.

BELLINGHAM: All right, again. Blake, if the persons and relations had all been changed, could you have said to me what I said to you?

BLAKE: That isn't a fair question, Bellingham.

BELLINGHAM: All right, as before. Now, Aunt Kate, I appeal to you. You know all the circumstances in which I was left here with this man who saved my life, who rescued Leslie from those tramps, who has done you all a thousand kindnesses of various sorts and sizes, who has behaved with the utmost delicacy and discretion throughout, and is in himself a thoroughly splendid fellow. Do you think I did right or wrong to set plainly before him the social disadvantages to which his marrying Leslie would put us?

MRS. MURRAY, *instantly and with great energy*: Charles, I say—and every person in society, *except* your mother and sister, would say—that you did exactly right!

BELLINGHAM: That settles it. Blake, my dear old fellow, I beg your pardon with all my heart; and I ask you to forget, if you can, every word I said. Confound society!

He offers his hand to Blake, who seizes it and wrings it in his own.

LESLIE, *as she flings her arms round his neck, with a fluttering cry of joy*: Oh, Charley, Charley, I've got my ideal back again!

BELLINGHAM, *disengaging her arms and putting her hand into Blake's*: Both of them. (*Turning to Mrs. Murray*) And now, aunt, I beg *your* pardon. What do you say?

MRS. MURRAY, *frozenly*: Charles, you know my principles.

BELLINGHAM: They're identical on all points with my own. Well?

MRS. MURRAY, *grimly*: Well, then, you know that I never would abandon my family, whatever happened!

BELLINGHAM: By Jove, that isn't so bad. We must be satisfied to take your forgiveness as we get it. Perhaps Leslie might object to the formulation of—

LESLIE, *super-joyously*: Oh, no! I object to nothing in the world, now, Charles. Aunt Kate is *too* good! I never should have thought of asking her to remain with us.

BELLINGHAM: *That* isn't so bad, either! You are your aunt's own niece. Come, Blake, we can't let this go on. Say something to allay the ill feeling you've created in this family.

BLAKE: I think I'd better not try. But if you'll give me time, I'll do my best to live down the objections to me.

BELLINGHAM: Oh, you've done that. What we want now—as I understand Aunt Kate—is that you should live down the objections to us. One thing that puzzles me— (*thoughtfully scratching the sparse parting of his hair*) is that our position is so very equivocal in regard to the real principle involved. It seems to me that we are begging the whole question, which is, if Blake—

LESLIE: There, there! I *knew* he would!

BELLINGHAM, *severely*: Mother, you will allow that I have been left to take the brunt of this little affair in a—well, somewhat circuitous manner?

MRS. BELLINGHAM: Charles, I am very, very sorry—

BELLINGHAM: And that I am entitled to some sort of reparation?

LESLIE: Don't allow that, mamma! I know he's going to say something disagreeable. He looks just as he always does when he has one of his ideas.

BELLINGHAM: Thanks, Miss Bellingham. I am going to have this particular satisfaction out of *you*. Then I will return to my habitual state of agreeable vacancy. Mother—

LESLIE: Mamma, don't answer him! It's the only way.

BELLINGHAM: It is not necessary that I should be answered. I only wish to have the floor. The question is, if Blake were merely a gentleman somewhat at odds with his history, associations, and occupation, and not also our benefactor and preserver in so many ways,—whether we should be so ready to—ah—

MRS. BELLINGHAM: Charles, dear, I think it is unnecessary to enter into these painful minutiæ.

MRS. MURRAY: I feel bound to say that I know we should not.

BELLINGHAM: This is the point which I wished to bring out. Blake, here is your opportunity: renounce us!

BLAKE: What do you say, Leslie?

LESLIE: I say that I don't believe it, and I know that I like you for yourself,—not for what you've done for us. I did from the first moment, before you spoke or saw me. But if you doubt me, or should ever doubt me—

BLAKE, *taking in his left both the little hands that she has appealingly laid upon his arms*: That's out of the question!

A Counterfeit Presentment

[1877]

As a play enjoying moderate success on the stage, *A Counterfeit Presentment* shares honors with the heretofore unpublished *Yorick's Love.* Evidently in the spring of 1877 Howells interested the well-known actor Lawrence Barrett in his play, for Mark Twain wrote to Howells (June 6, 1877, Harvard Library): "I am more delighted about Barrett & the play than I can express. I hope you get good terms out of him, & have drawn your contract from the standpoint that he is the blackest-livered scoundrel on earth." Answering, Howells wrote (June 9, 1877, *Life in Letters*, I, 237) that Barrett had offered $25 a night for the play anywhere outside New York and $50 a night in that city, adding that his surprise caused him to accept immediately. On August 13, 1877 (Harvard Library), Howells wrote to C. E. Norton: "You have seen perhaps that my new comedy is to be played. The actor professes great faith in its success; but I profess to wait and see. If some actress of intuition and sympathy could be found for Constance I should feel safer about it."

With the various successful performances of *A Counterfeit Presentment*, Howells held high hopes that his plays might be hailed as a contribution to American drama, but his hopes never materialized. *A Counterfeit Presentment* was eventually a disappointment to him, but no playwright could have asked for more support from his friends. Clemens, Aldrich, Lowell, Longfellow, Whittier—all were enthusiastic in their praise. Nor were the critics in the main unkind, although they were naturally more severe than his friends. The book reviewer for the New York *Daily Tribune* (October 19, 1877, p. 6, col. 1) suggests the response of the contemporary literary world:

[*A Counterfeit Presentment*] will be a great gain if our theatre-going public can be led to appreciate the superiority of light, graceful, refined humor, picturesque contrasts of character and the charm of probable incidents, over the extravagant and vulgar forms of farce which are threatening to usurp our stage. "A Counterfeit Presentment" has not the compactness and the brilliant succession of deceitful devices which we find in Mr. Howells' "Parlor Car"; both the incidents and the manifestations of character are more improbable—too much so, indeed, for a story meant only to be read, but not for the sharper perspective which the stage requires.

Later critics have pointed out the literary effectiveness and the dramatic deficiencies of this play when compared to contemporary dramas and have emphasized its significance in the development of American drama. John M. Robertson (*Essays Towards a Critical Method*, pp. 173, 197) called both *A Counterfeit Presentment* and *Out of the Question* semidramatic sketches, explaining that "though they have a species of delicacy that raises them above contemporary drama, [they] can only be classed as specimens of dainty confectionery." Nevertheless, ". . . despite this confectionery quality, it is impossible not to perceive the delicacy and ingenuity with which our palates are titillated." Even Oscar Firkins (*William Dean Howells, A Study*, p. 236), who successfully contained his enthusiasm for Howells' plays, praised *A Counterfeit Presentment*, calling it one of Howells' "most fortunate grades of seriousness: the coincidence is inherently light; the situation of Constance is essentially tragic; but the treatment occupies a middle zone, lightening and darkening as the occasion deserves." Both Montrose Moses and A. H. Quinn in their histories of American drama note the historical significance of the play in the rise of social comedy; and

Margaret Mayorga (*A Short History of the American Drama* [New York: Dodd Mead & Co., 1932], pp. 266–67), after describing the play as a piece of psychological comedy in tune with the modern spirit, states that Howells was "the precursor of the Anglo-American school, his *A Counterfeit Presentment* in the light comedy vein which the English so well enjoy, having had a very definite effect on a number of other American writers."

During the 1877–78 theatrical season, Lawrence Barrett toured the country with *A Counterfeit Presentment*. His letters to his wife (Theatre Collection, Harvard Library) have indicated in many instances the city where the play was produced, but the following itinerary must remain only suggestive of more numerous performances.

On October 11, 1877, Barrett opened the play at the Grand Opera House in Cincinnati, Ohio, and repeated it at a matinee two days later, both times to full houses. Immediately Barrett telegraphed to Howells that the play was a success, and the critics for the Cincinnati *Gazette* and the *Commercial* were enthusiastic in their praise. The *Commercial* critic gave a very lengthy review of the plot, with numerous quotations from the Osgood text and little censure of any part of the play. From this performance on through the production the following April in Boston, Barrett made suggestions for revisions, and Howells tried to satisfy him, as well as to exploit his own ideas toward revision. Frequently they differed, and James R. Osgood served as a sympathetic intermediary, although Howells always gave Barrett credit for the play's success and lavishly praised his acting and management (e.g., his letter to Barrett of October 19, 1877, now in the Harvard Library). From Cincinnati, Barrett went to Cleveland and then to Franklyn and Pittsburgh, Pennsylvania, where the critics were unanimous in their praise of *A Counterfeit Presentment*—one calling Howells "the long awaited messiah of American Comedy" (James A. Laurie, "A History of the Pittsburgh Stage [1861–1891]," [unpublished thesis] I, 133). But Barrett was not easily satisfied, and in a letter to Osgood, November 4, 1877, dated from Pittsburgh (Harvard Library), he frankly stated his opinion of the play: Its success "has been owing to friendly and cultured audiences, but it must now please the popular taste which will not accept fine writing and pretty dialogue in a thin plot. He [Howells] talks of adding a new act—that would be fatal. I want

him to add new characters and revamp his dramatic personae—and add new incidents—not more fine talk."

It would seem, however, that although things were not always smooth, Howells handled his temperamental actor very well. On November 14, 1877 (Princeton University Library), he wrote to Barrett:

> I mail you herewith the new act. I need not lecture upon it. You will see what it is. Understand that I don't hold you bound to like it, and above all that I don't expect or desire you to accept it if you don't like it. I have worked with the idea of telling the story more fully and of developing Bartlett's character by certain situations in which I have left almost everything to your acting. . . . Of course I want all the suggestions and criticism you can give.

As a realist Howells was interested in details, and in this and other letters, he wrote about such things as the canvas on which Constance was to paint, her technique in painting, and the General's snore—"Pray have it a snore of the utmost possible refinement."

Barrett's tour continued, and in Indianapolis *A Counterfeit Presentment* "made its usual hit" with a select audience (Barrett to Osgood, November 24, 1877, Harvard Library), but the actor had not inserted the new act because he thought it less attractive the more he read it. Later in Detroit he tried the new act and found it successful. From Chicago he wrote to Osgood (December 2, 1877, Harvard Library): "Sold again!—the new act made a good impression and by many who saw it I am told that it is now nearly complete as a play which fills me with joy." Although in his letter to Osgood from St. Louis (December 13, 1877, Harvard Library) he complained of "my sense of being Father, Son, and Holy Ghost" to the play, it continued successful in production. The year ended with performances at Providence, Rhode Island (December 28), and Springfield, Massachusetts (December 31). The reviewer for the Providence *Evening Bulletin*, December 29, 1877, recorded his impressions: "*A Counterfeit Presentment* is a genuine comedy in the pure sense. . . . It is a picture from the American society of to-day as perfect in tone and spirit as can be. Its humor is delightful, fresh and easy, and the happy surprises of the dialogue are as natural and unforced as they are unexpected." The performance, the reviewer mentioned, was very little changed from Osgood's edition of the play—except for the added act—which indicates that the various beginnings to the play and added characters had been disposed of by this time.

With the new year Lester Wallack, manager of Wallack's Theatre in New York, considered A Counterfeit Presentment and later rejected it (Howells to Sedgwick, January 1, 1878, C. W. Barrett Collection, New York). Barrett still toured New England but with poor houses, and Howells began to feel "awfully discouraged about the thing" (Howells to Osgood, January 5, 1878, Harvard Library). Then on April 1, 1878, Barrett presented A Counterfeit Presentment in the Boston Museum. Howells attended both rehearsals and the performance and wrote to his father on April 3 (Life in Letters, I, 250–51) that the play had been most successful. "The first night was a superb emotion: a gurgle of laughter from beginning to end, a constant clapping of hands. They called me up at the end of their third act, and roared at me. I never had my popularity at arm's length before, and it was very pleasant." The play did not go on to New York as Howells had hoped, but one consequence of the Boston performance was a request by Augustin Daly for Howells to adapt a German play for him; however, Howells did not think the suggested play worth his time, and after some counter-recommendations the matter was dropped (The Life of Augustin Daly, p. 367).

After the April performance in Boston Barrett continued on to the West Coast with the play in his repertoire, but he did not use it frequently. The following year Howells wrote to James R. Lowell (June 22, 1879, Harvard Library): "My comedy was played some thirty times but is now in abeyance—not to use a harsher expression. They played it charmingly at the Museum, to packed houses, and I in my simple soul thought it beautiful. There is no delight like seeing one's play acted." But because Barrett did not produce the play often, Howells started looking for other means of getting his drama upon the stage. Soon he asked William Winter's help with the actor Joseph Jefferson, and on January 11, 1880 (Harvard Library), Winter wrote to Howells: "I had a talk with Jefferson, last Sunday, about your comedy. He said he had read it carefully, . . . but that he did not think he could act Bartlett, and deemed the part unsuitable to him." Later (January 22, 1880, Harvard Library), Jefferson offered his opinion to Howells concerning the play. "I would say," he wrote, "that while it is charmingly written it seems to lack that thing action—which the audiences of the present day continually demand." After this failure to interest Jefferson, Howells tried William Gillette, actor and manager, who replied to Howells on February 26, 1881 (Harvard Library), after having read the play: "We do not think the comedy one we could use during what is known as the regular season but think well of it for a summer or preliminary season where light comedy is more suitable than pieces of considerable weight and dramatic intensity." But there is no record that the summer or preliminary production was ever given, and Howells, who soon had no illusions about his chances for success in the theater, became interested in other plays and other works. A Counterfeit Presentment disappeared from the stage.

A Counterfeit Presentment[1]

(The Scene is always in the Parlor of the Ponkwasset Hotel.)

I.
AN EXTRAORDINARY RESEMBLANCE [2]

*On a lovely day in September, at that season
when the most sentimental of the young
maples have begun to redden along the hidden
courses of the meadow streams, and the elms,
with a sudden impression of despair in their
languor, betray flecks of yellow on the green
of their pendulous boughs,—on such a day
at noon, two young men enter the parlor of
the Ponkwasset Hotel, and deposit about the
legs of the piano the burdens they have been
carrying: a camp-stool, namely, a field-easel,
a closed box of colors, and a canvas to which,
apparently, some portion of reluctant nature
has just been transferred. These properties
belong to one of the young men, whose general look and bearing readily identify him as
their owner: he has a quick, somewhat furtive
eye, a full brown beard, and hair that falls in
a careless mass down his forehead, which as
he dries it with his hankerchief, sweeping the
hair aside, shows broad and white; his figure
is firm and square, without heaviness, and in
his movement as well as in his face there is
something of stubbornness, with a suggestion
of arrogance. The other, who has evidently
borne his share of the common burdens from
a sense of good comradeship, has nothing of
the painter in him, nor anything of this painter's peculiar temperament: he has a very ab-
stracted look and a dark, dreaming eye; he is
pale, and does not look strong. The painter*

---

[1] The text used here is the Houghton, Mifflin and
Company edition. The act entitled "Dissolving Views,"
placed between the second and third acts of the original
play, was added after the play was published by James R.
Osgood & Company. Title: *Hamlet,* III, 4:54.

[2] Houghton Library at Harvard University holds a
prompt copy—three acts, two kinds of type and changes
in two hands—which has two beginnings distinct from
the one published. Both beginnings contrive to leave
Constance's hat and shawl on the scene.

*flings himself into a rocking-chair and draws
a long breath.*

CUMMINGS, *for that is the name of the slighter
man, who remains standing as he speaks:* It's
warm, isn't it?

*His gentle face evinces a curious and kindly
interest in his friend's sturdy demonstrations
of fatigue.*

BARTLETT: Yes, hot—confoundedly. (*He rubs
his handkerchief vigorously across his forehead,
and then looks down at his dusty shoes, with
apparently no mind to molest them in their dusti-
ness.*) The idea of people going back to town in
this weather! However, I'm glad they're such asses;
it gives me free scope here. Every time I don't
hear some young woman banging on that piano,
I fall into transports of joy.

CUMMINGS, *smiling:* And after to-day you won't
be bothered even with me.

BARTLETT: Oh, I shall rather miss you, you
know. I like somebody to contradict.

CUMMINGS: You can contradict the ostler.

BARTLETT: No, I can't. They've sent him away;
and I believe you're going to carry off the last
of the table-girls with you in the stage to-morrow.
The landlord and his wife are to run the concern
themselves the rest of the fall. Poor old fellow!
The hard times have made lean pickings for him
this year. His house wasn't full in the height of
the season, and it's been pretty empty since.

CUMMINGS: I wonder he doesn't shut up altogether.

BARTLETT: Well, there are a good many transients, as they call them, at this time of year,—
fellows who drive over from the little hill-towns
with their girls in buggies, and take dinner and
supper; then there are picnics from the larger
places, ten and twelve miles off, that come to the
grounds on the pond, and he always gets something out of them. And as long as he can hope
for anything else, my eight dollars a week are
worth hanging on to. Yes, I think I shall stay here
all through October. I've got no orders, and it's
cheap. Besides, I've managed to get on confidential terms with the local scenery; I thought we

should like each other last summer, and I feel now that we're ready to swear eternal friendship. I shall do some fairish work here, yet. Phew!

He mops his forehead again, and springing out of his chair he goes up to the canvas, which he has faced to the wall, and turning it about retires some paces, and with a swift, worried glance at the windows falls to considering it critically.

CUMMINGS: You've done some fairish work already, if I'm any judge. *(He comes to his friend's side, as if to get his effect of the picture.)* I don't believe the spirit of a graceful elm that just begins to feel the approach of autumn was ever better interpreted. There is something tremendously tragical to me in the thing. It makes me think of some lovely and charming girl, all grace and tenderness, who finds the first gray hair in her head. I should call that picture The First Gray Hair.

BARTLETT, *with unheeding petulance*: The whole thing's too infernally brown!—I beg your pardon, Cummings: what were you saying? Go on! I like your prattle about pictures; I do, indeed. I like to see how far you art-cultured fellows can miss all that was in a poor devil's mind when he was at work. But I'd rather you'd sentimentalize my pictures than moralize them. If there's anything that makes me quite limp, it's to have an allegory discovered in one of my poor stupid old landscapes. But The First Gray Hair isn't bad, really. And a good, senseless, sloppy name like that often sells a picture.

CUMMINGS: You're brutal, Bartlett. I don't believe your pictures would own you, if they had their way about it.

BARTLETT: And I wouldn't own *them* if I had *mine*. I've got about forty that I wish somebody else owned—and I had the money for them; but we seem inseparable. Glad you're going to-morrow? You *are* a good fellow, Cummings, and I *am* a brute. Come, I'll make a great concession to friendship: it struck me, too, while I was at work on that elm, that it was something like—an old girl! *(Bartlett laughs, and catching his friend by either shoulder twists him about in his strong clutch, while he looks him merrily in the face.)* I'm not a poet, old fellow; and sometimes I think I ought to have been a painter and glazier instead of a mere painter. I believe it would have paid better.

CUMMINGS: Bartlett, I hate to have you talk in that way.

BARTLETT: Oh, I know it's a stale kind.

CUMMINGS: It's worse than stale. It's destructive. A man can soon talk himself out of heart with his better self. You can end by really being as sordid-minded and hopeless and low-purposed as you pretend to be. It's insanity.

BARTLETT: Good! I've had my little knock on the head, you know. I don't deny being cracked. But I've a method in my madness.

CUMMINGS: They all have. But it's a very poor method; and I don't believe you could say just what yours is. You think because a girl on whom you set your fancy—it's nonsense to pretend it was your heart—found out she didn't like you as well as she thought, and honestly told you so in good time, that your wisest course is to take up that rôle of misanthrope which begins with yourself and leaves people to imagine how low an opinion you have of the rest of mankind.

BARTLETT: My dear fellow, you know I always speak well of that young lady. I've invariably told you that she behaved in the handsomest manner. She even expressed the wish—I distinctly remember being struck by the novelty of the wish at the time—that we should remain friends. You misconceive—

CUMMINGS: How many poor girls have been jilted who don't go about doing misanthropy, but mope at home and sorrow and sicken over their wrong in secret,—a wrong that attacks not merely their pride, but their life itself. Take the case I was telling you of: did you ever hear of anything more atrocious? And do you compare this little sting to your vanity with a death-blow like that?

BARTLETT: It's quite impossible to compute the number of jilted girls who take the line you describe. But if it were within the scope of arithmetic, I don't know that a billion of jilted girls would comfort me or reform me. I never could regard myself in that abstract way—a mere unit on one side or other of the balance. My little personal snub goes on rankling beyond the reach of statistical consolation. But even if there were any edification in the case of the young lady in Paris, she's too far off to be an example for me. Take some jilted girl nearer home, Cummings, if you want me to go round sickening and sorrowing in secret. I don't believe you can find any. Women are much tougher about the pericardium than we give them credit for, my dear fellow,—much. I don't see why it should hurt a woman more than a man to be jilted. We shall never truly philosophize this important matter till we regard women with something of the fine penetration and impartiality with which they regard each other. Look at the stabs they give and take—they would kill men! And the graceful ferocity with which they dispatch any of their number who happens to be down is quite unexampled in natural history. How much do you suppose her lady friends have left of that poor girl whose case wrings your foolish bosom all the way from Paris? I don't believe so much as a boot-button. Why, even your correspondent—a very lively woman, by the way—can't conceal under all her indignation her little satisfaction that so *proud* a girl as Miss What's-her-name should have been jilted. Of course, she doesn't say it.

CUMMINGS, *hotly*: No, she doesn't say it, and it's not to your credit to imagine it.

BARTLETT, *with a laugh*: Oh, I don't ask any praise for the discovery. You deserve praise for not making it. It does honor to your good heart. Well, don't be vexed, old fellow. And in trying to improve me on this little point—a weak point, I'll allow, with me—do me the justice to remember that I didn't flaunt my misanthropy, as you call it, in your face; I didn't force my confidence upon you.

CUMMINGS, *with compunction*: I didn't mean to hurt your feelings, Bartlett.

BARTLETT: Well, you haven't. It's all right.

CUMMINGS, *with anxious concern*: I wish I could think so.

BARTLETT, *dryly*: You have *my* leave—my request, in fact. (*He takes a turn about the room, thrusting his fingers through the hair on his forehead, and letting it fall in a heavy tangle, and then pulling at either side of his parted beard. In facing away from one of the sofas at the end of the room, he looks back over his shoulder at it, falters, wheels about, and picks up from it a lady's shawl and hat.*) Hallo! (*He lets the shawl fall again into picturesque folds on the sofa.*) This is the spoil of no local beauty, Cummings. Look here; I don't understand this. There has been an arrival.

CUMMINGS, *joining his friend in contemplation of the hat and shawl*: Yes; it's an arrival beyond all question. Those are a *lady's* things. I should think that was a Paris hat.

They remain looking at the things some moments in silence.

BARTLETT: How should a Paris hat get here? I know the landlord wasn't expecting it. But it can't be going to stay; it's here through some caprice. It may be a transient of quality, but it's a transient. I suppose we shall see the young woman belonging to it at dinner. (*He sets the hat on his fist, and holds it at arm's length from him.*) What a curious thing it is about clothes—

CUMMINGS: Don't, Bartlett, don't!

BARTLETT: Why?

CUMMINGS: I don't know. It makes me feel as if you were offering an indignity to the young lady herself.

BARTLETT: You express my idea exactly. This frippery has not only the girl's personality but her very spirit in it. This hat looks like her; you can infer the whole woman from it, body and soul. It has a conscious air, and so has the shawl, as if they had been eavesdropping and had understood everything we were saying. They know all about my heart-break, and so will she as soon as she puts them on; she will be interested in me. The hat's in good taste, isn't it?

CUMMINGS, *with sensitive reverence for the millinery which his friend handles so daringly*: Exquisite, it seems to me; but I don't know about such things.

BARTLETT: Neither do I; but I feel about them. Besides, a painter and glazier sees some things that are hidden from even a progressive minister. Let us interpret the lovely being from her hat. This knot of pale-blue flowers betrays her a blonde; this lace, this mass of silky, fluffy, cobwebby what-do-you-call-it, and this delicate straw fabric show that she is slight; a stout woman would kill it, or die in the attempt. And I fancy—here pure inspiration comes to my aid—that she is tallish. I'm afraid of her! No—wait! The shawl has something to say. (*He takes it up and catches it across his arm where he scans it critically.*) I don't know that I understand the shawl, exactly. It proves her of a good height,—a short woman wouldn't, or had better not, wear a shawl,—but this black color: should you think it was mourning? Have we a lovely young widow among us?

CUMMINGS: I don't see how it could go with the hat, if it were.

BARTLETT: True; the hat is very pensive in tone, but it isn't mourning. This shawl's very light, it's very warm; I construct from it a pretty invalid. (*He lets the shawl slip down his arm to his hand, and flings it back upon the sofa.*) We return from the young lady's heart to her brain—where she carries her sentiments. She has a nice taste in perfumes, Cummings: faintest violet; that goes with the blue. Of what religion is a young lady who uses violet, my reverend friend?

CUMMINGS: Bartlett, you're outrageous. Put down that hat!

BARTLETT: No, seriously. What is her little æsthetic specialty? Does she sketch? Does she scribble? Tell me, thou wicked hat, does she flirt? Come; out with the vows that you have heard poured into the shelly ear under this knot of pale-blue flowers! Where be her gibes now, her gambols, her flashes of merriment? Now get you to my lady's chamber, and tell her, let her paint an inch thick, to this favor she must come; make her laugh at that. Dost thou think, Horatio Cummings, Cleopatra looked o' this fashion? And smelt so?— (*He presses the knot of artificial flowers to his mustache.*) Pah!

He tosses the hat on the sofa and walks away.

CUMMINGS: Bartlett, this is atrocious. I protest—

BARTLETT: Well, give me up, I tell you. (*He returns, and takes his friend by the shoulders, as before, and laughs.*) I'm not worth your refined pains. I might be good, at a pinch, but I never could be truly lady-like.

CUMMINGS: You like to speak an infinite deal of nothing, don't you?

BARTLETT: It's the only thing that makes conversation.

As he releases Cummings, and turns away from him, in the doorway he confronts an elderly gentleman, whose white hair and white mustache give distinction to his handsome florid face. There is something military in his port, as he stands immovably erect upon the threshold, his left hand lodged in the breast of his frock-coat, and his head carried with an officer-like air of command. His visage grows momently redder and redder, and his blue eyes blaze upon Bartlett with a fascinated glare that briefly preludes the burst of fury with which he advances toward him.

GENERAL WYATT: You infernal scoundrel! What are you doing here? (*He raises his stick at Bartlett, who remains motionlessly frowning in wrathful bewilderment, his strong hand knotting itself into a fist where it hangs at his side, while Cummings starts toward them in dismay, with his hand raised to interpose.*) Didn't I tell you if I ever set eyes on you again, you villain—didn't I warn you that if you ever crossed my path, you— (*He stops with a violent self-arrest, and lets his stick drop as he throws up both his hands in amaze.*) Good Heavens! It's a mistake! I beg your pardon, sir;

I do, indeed. (*He lets fall his hands, and stands staring into Bartlett's face with his illusion apparently not fully dispelled.*) A mistake, sir, a mistake. I was misled, sir, by the most prodigious resemblance—

At the sound of voices in the corridor without, he turns from Bartlett, and starts back toward the door.

A VOICE, *very sweet and weak, without*: I left them in here, I think.

ANOTHER VOICE: You must sit down, Constance, and let me look.

THE FIRST VOICE: Oh, they'll be here.

GENERAL WYATT, *in a loud and anxious tone*: Margaret, Margaret! Don't bring Constance in here! Go away!

At the moment he reaches the door by which he came in, two ladies in black enter the parlor by the other door, the younger leaning weakly on the arm of the elder, and with a languidly drooping head letting her eyes rove listlessly about over the chairs and sofas. With an abrupt start at sight of Bartlett, who has mechanically turned toward them, the elder lady arrests their movement.

MRS. WYATT: Oh, in mercy's name!

The young lady wearily lifts her eyes; they fall upon Bartlett's face, and a low cry parts her lips as she approaches a pace or two nearer, releasing her arm from her mother's.

CONSTANCE: Ah!

She stops; her thin hands waver before her face, as if to clear or to obstruct her vision, and all at once she sinks forward into a little slender heap upon the floor, almost at Bartlett's feet. He instantly drops upon his knees beside her, and stoops over her to lift her up.

MRS. WYATT: Don't touch her, you cruel wretch! Your touch is poison; the sight of you is murder!

Kneeling on the other side of her daughter, she sets both her hands against his breast and pushes him back.

GENERAL WYATT: Margaret, stop! Look! Look at him again! It isn't *he*!

MRS. WYATT: Not he? Don't tell me! What? (*She clutches Bartlett's arm, and scans his face with dilating eyes.*) Oh! it isn't, it isn't! But go away,—go away, all the same! You may be an innocent man, but she would perish in your presence. Keep your hands from her, sir! If your wicked heart is not yet satisfied with your wicked work— Excuse me; I *don't* know what I'm saying! But if you have any pity in your faithless soul—

I—oh, *speak* for me, James, and send him—implore him to go away!

> *She bows her face over her daughter's pale visage, and sobs.*

GENERAL WYATT: Sir, you must pardon us, and have the great goodness to be patient. You have a right to feel yourself aggrieved by what has happened, but no wrong is meant,—no offense. You must be so kind as to go away. I will make you all the needed apologies and explanations. *(He stoops over his daughter, as Bartlett, in a sort of daze, rises from his knees and retires a few steps.)* I beg your pardon, sir,— *(addressing himself to Cummings)* will you help me a moment? *(Cummings, with delicate sympathy and tenderness, lifts the arms of the insensible girl to her father's neck, and assists the General to rise with his burden.)* Thanks! She's hardly heavier, poor child, than a ghost. *(The tears stand in his eyes, as he gathers her closer to him and kisses her wan cheek.)* Sir,— *(as he moves away he speaks to Bartlett)* do me the favor to remain here till I can return to offer you reparation.

> *He makes a stately effort to bow to Bartlett in leaving the room, while his wife, who follows with the young lady's hat and shawl, looks back at the painter with open abhorrence.*

BARTLETT, *turning to his friend from the retreating group on which he has kept his eyes steadfastly fixed*: Where are their keepers?

> *He is pale with suppressed rage.*

CUMMINGS: Their keepers?

BARTLETT, *savagely*: Yes! Have they escaped from them, or is it one of the new ideas to let lunatics go about the country alone? If that old fool hadn't dropped his stick, I'd have knocked him over that table in another instant. And that other old maniac,—what did she mean by pushing me back in that way? How do you account for this thing, Cummings? What do you make of it?

CUMMINGS: I don't know, upon my word. There seems to be some mystery,—some painful mystery. But the gentleman will be back directly, I suppose, and—

BARTLETT, *crushing his hat over his eyes*: I'll leave you to receive him and his mystery. I've had enough of both.

> *He moves toward the door.*

CUMMINGS, *detaining him*: Bartlett, you're surely not going away?

BARTLETT: Yes, I am!

CUMMINGS: But he'll be here in a moment. He said he would come back and satisfy the claim which you certainly have to an explanation.

BARTLETT, *furiously*: Claim? I've a perfect Alabama Claim to an explanation. He can't satisfy it; he shall not try. It's a little too much to expect me to be satisfied with anything he can say after what's passed. Get out of the way, Cummings, or I'll put you on top of the piano.

CUMMINGS: You may throw me out of the window, if you like, but not till I've done my best to keep you here. It's a shame, it's a crime to go away. You talk about lunatics: you're a raving madman, yourself. Have one glimmer of reason, do; and see what you're about. It's a mistake; it's a misunderstanding. It's his right, it's your duty, to have it cleared up. Come, you've a conscience, Bartlett, and a clean one. Don't give way to your abominable temper. What? You won't stay? Bartlett, I blush for you!

BARTLETT: Blush unseen, then!

> *He thrusts Cummings aside and pushes furiously from the room. Cummings looks into the corridor after him, and then returns, panting, to the piano, and mechanically rearranges the things at its feet; he walks nervously away, and takes some turns up and down the room, looking utterly bewildered, and apparently uncertain whether to go or stay. But he has decided upon the only course really open to him by sinking down into one of the arm-chairs, when General Wyatt appears at the threshold of the door on the right of the piano. Cummings rises and comes forward in great embarrassment to meet him.*

GENERAL WYATT, *with a look of surprise at not seeing Bartlett*: The other gentleman—

CUMMINGS: My friend has gone out. I hope he will return soon. He has—I hardly know what to say to you, sir. He has done himself great injustice; but it was natural that under the circumstances—

GENERAL WYATT, *with hurt pride*: Perfectly. I should have lost my temper, too; but I think I should have waited at the request—the prayer of an older man. I don't mind his temper; the other villain had *no* temper. Sir, am I right in addressing you as the Rev. Arthur Cummings?

CUMMINGS: My name is Arthur Cummings. I am a minister.

GENERAL WYATT: I thought I was not mistaken this time. I heard you preach last Sunday in Boston; and I know your cousin, Major Cummings of the 34th Artillery. I am General Wyatt.

CUMMINGS, *with a start of painful surprise and sympathy*: General Wyatt?

GENERAL WYATT, *keenly*: Your cousin has mentioned me to you?

CUMMINGS: Yes,—oh yes, certainly; certainly, very often, General Wyatt. But—(*endeavoring to recover himself*) your name is known to us all, and honored. I—I am glad to see you back; I—understood you were in Paris.

GENERAL WYATT, *with fierce defiance*: I was in Paris three weeks ago.

> *Some moments of awkward silence ensue, during which General Wyatt does not relax his angry attitude.*

CUMMINGS, *finally*: I am sorry my friend is not here to meet you. I ought to say, in justice to him, that his hasty temper does great wrong to his heart and judgment.

GENERAL WYATT: Why, yes, sir; so does mine, —so does mine.

CUMMINGS, *with a respectful smile lost upon the General*: And I know that he will certainly be grieved in this instance to have yielded to it.

GENERAL WYATT, *with sudden meekness*: I hope so, sir. But I am not altogether sorry that he has done it. I have not only an explanation but a request to make,—a very great and strange favor to ask,—and I am not sure that I should be able to treat him civilly enough throughout an entire interview to ask it properly. (*Cummings listens with an air of attentive respect, but makes, to this strange statement, no response other than a look of question, while the General pokes about on the carpet at his feet with the point of his stick for a moment before he brings it resolutely down upon the floor with a thump, and resumes, fiercely again.*) Sir, your friend is the victim of an extraordinary resemblance, which is so much more painful to us than we could have made it to him that I have to struggle with my reason to believe that the apology should not come from his side rather than mine. He may feel that we have outraged him, but every look of his, every movement, every tone of his voice, is a mortal wound, a deadly insult to us. He should not live, sir, in the same solar system! (*The General deals the floor another stab with his cane, while his eyes burn vindictively upon the mild brown orbs of Cummings, wide open with astonishment. He falters, with returning consciousness of his attitude.*) I— I beg your pardon, sir; I am ridiculous. (*He closes his lips pathetically, and lets fall his head. When he lifts it again, it is to address Cummings with a singular gentleness.*) I know that I speak to a gentleman.

CUMMINGS: I try to be a good man.

GENERAL WYATT: I had formed that idea of you, sir, in the pulpit. Will you do me the great kindness to answer a question, personal to myself, which I must ask?

CUMMINGS: By all means.

GENERAL WYATT: You spoke of supposing me still in Paris. Are you aware of any circumstances —painful circumstances—connected with my presence there? Pardon my asking; I wouldn't press you if I could help.

CUMMINGS, *with reluctance*: I had just heard something about—a letter from a friend—

GENERAL WYATT, *bitterly*: The news has traveled fast. Well, sir, a curious chance—a pitiless caprice of destiny—connects your friend with that miserable story. (*At Cummings's look of amaze*) Through no fault of his, sir; through no fault of his. Sir, I shall not seem to obtrude my trouble unjustifiably upon you when I tell you how; you will see that it was necessary for me to speak. I am glad you already know something of the affair, and I am sure that you will regard what I have to say with the right feeling of a gentleman,—of, as you say, a good man.

CUMMINGS: Whatever you think necessary to say to me shall be sacred. But I hope you won't feel that it is necessary to say anything more. I am confident that when my friend has your assurance from me that what has happened is the result of a distressing association—

GENERAL WYATT: I thank you, sir. But something more is due to him; how much more you shall judge. Something more is due to us: I wish to preserve the appearance of sanity, in his eyes and your own. Nevertheless— (*the General's tone and bearing perceptibly stiffen*) if you are reluctant—

CUMMINGS, *with reverent cordiality*: General Wyatt, I shall feel deeply honored by whatever confidence you repose in me. I need not say how dear your fame is to us all. (*General Wyatt, visibly moved, bows to the young minister.*) It was only on your account that I hesitated.

GENERAL WYATT: Thanks. I understand. I will be explicit, but I will try to be brief. Your friend bears this striking, this painful resemblance to the man who has brought this blight upon us all; yes, sir,— (*at Cummings's look of deprecation*) to a scoundrel whom I hardly know how to characterize aright—in the presence of a clergyman. Two years ago—doubtless your correspond-ent has written—my wife and daughter (they were then abroad without me) met him in Paris; and he won the poor child's affection. My wife's judgment was also swayed in his favor,—against her first impulse of distrust; but when I saw him, I could not endure him. Yet I was helpless: my girl's happiness was bound up in him; all that I could do was to insist upon delay. He was an American, well related, unobjectionable by all the tests which society can apply, and I might have had to wait long for the proofs that an accident gave me against him. The man's whole soul was rotten; at the time he had wound himself into my poor girl's innocent heart, a woman was living who had the just and perhaps the legal claim of a wife upon him; he was a felon besides,—a felon shielded through pity for his friends by the man whose name he had forged; he was of course a liar and a coward: I beat him with my stick, sir. Ah! I made him confess his infamy under his own hand, and then— (*the General advances defiantly upon Cummings, who unconsciously retires a pace*) and then I compelled him to break with my daughter. Do you think I did right?

CUMMINGS: I don't exactly understand.

GENERAL WYATT: Why, sir, it happens often enough in this shabby world that a man gains a poor girl's love, and then jilts her. I chose what I thought the less terrible sorrow for my child. I could not tell her how filthily unworthy he was, without bringing to her pure heart a sense of intolerable contamination; I could not endure to speak of it even to my wife. It seemed better that they should both suffer such wrong as a broken engagement might bring them, than that they should know what I knew. He was master of the part, and played it well; he showed himself to them simply a heartless scoundrel, and he remains in my power, an outcast now and a convict when-ever I will. My story, as it seems to be, is well known in Paris; but the worst is unknown. I choose still that it shall be thought my girl was the victim of a dastardly slight, and I bear with her and her mother the insolent pity with which the world visits such sorrow. (*He pauses, and then brokenly resumes.*) The affair has not turned out as I hoped, in the little I could hope from it. My trust that the blow, which must sink so deeply into her heart, would touch her pride, and that this would help her to react against it, was mis-taken. In such things it appears a woman has no pride; I did not know it; we men are different.

The blow crushed her; that was all. Sometimes I am afraid that I must yet try the effect of the whole truth upon her; that I must try if the knowledge of all his baseness cannot restore to her the self-respect which the wrong done herself seems to have robbed her of. And yet I tremble lest the sense of his fouler shame—I may be fatally temporizing; but in her present state, I dread any new shock for her; it may be death—I— (*He pauses again, and sets his lips firmly; all at once he breaks into a sob.*) I—I beg your pardon, sir.

CUMMINGS: Don't! You wrong yourself and me. I have seen Miss Wyatt; but I hope—

GENERAL WYATT: You have seen her ghost. You have not seen the radiant creature that was once alive. Well, sir; enough of this. There is little left to trouble you with. We landed eight days ago, and I have since been looking about for some place in which my daughter could hide herself; I can't otherwise suggest her morbid sen-sitiveness, her terror of people. This region was highly commended to me for its healthfulness; but I have come upon this house by chance. I under-stood that it was empty, and I thought it more than probable that we might pass the autumn months here unmolested by the presence of any one belonging to our world, if not in entire se-clusion. At the best, my daughter would hardly have been able to endure another change at once; so far as anything could give her pleasure, the beauty and the wild quiet of the region had pleased her, but she is now quite prostrated, sir,—

CUMMINGS, *definitively*: My friend will go away at once. There is nothing else for it.

GENERAL WYATT: That is too much to ask.

CUMMINGS: I won't conceal my belief that he will think so. But there can be no question with him when—

GENERAL WYATT: When you tell him our story? (*After a moment*) Yes, he has a right to know it— as the rest of the world knows it. You must tell him, sir.

CUMMINGS, *gently*: No, he need know nothing beyond the fact of this resemblance to some one painfully associated with your past lives. He is a man whose real tenderness of heart would revolt from knowledge that could inflict further sorrow upon you.

GENERAL WYATT: Sir, will you convey to this friend of yours an old man's very humble apology, and sincere prayer for his forgiveness?

CUMMINGS: He will not exact anything of that

sort. The evidence of misunderstanding will be clear to him at a word from me.

GENERAL WYATT: But he has a right to this explanation from my own lips, and— Sir, I am culpably weak. But now that I have missed seeing him here, I confess that I would willingly avoid meeting him. The mere sound of his voice, as I heard it before I saw him, in first coming upon you, was enough to madden me. Can you excuse my senseless dereliction to him?

CUMMINGS: I will answer for him.

GENERAL WYATT: Thanks. It seems monstrous that I should be asking and accepting these great favors. But you are doing a deed of charity to a helpless man utterly beggared in pride. (*He chokes with emotion, and does not speak for a moment.*) Your friend is also—he is not also—a clergyman?

CUMMINGS, *smiling*: No. He is a painter.

GENERAL WYATT: Is he a man of note? Successful in his profession?

CUMMINGS: Not yet. But that is certain to come.

GENERAL WYATT: He is poor?

CUMMINGS: He is a young painter.

GENERAL WYATT: Sir, excuse me. Had he planned to remain here some time, yet?

CUMMINGS, *reluctantly*: He has been sketching here. He had expected to stay through October.

GENERAL WYATT: You make the sacrifice hard to accept—I beg your pardon! But I must accept it. I am bound hand and foot.

CUMMINGS: I am sorry to have been obliged to tell you this.

GENERAL WYATT: I obliged you, sir; I obliged you. Give me your advice, sir; you know your friend. What shall I do? I am not rich. I don't belong to a branch of the government service in which people enrich themselves. But I have my pay; and if your friend could sell me the pictures he's been painting here—

CUMMINGS: That's quite impossible. There is no form in which I could propose such a thing to a man of his generous pride.

GENERAL WYATT: Well, then, sir, I must satisfy myself as I can to remain his debtor. Will you kindly undertake to tell him?

AN ELDERLY SERVING-WOMAN, *who appears timidly and anxiously at the right-hand door*: General Wyatt.

GENERAL WYATT, *with a start*: Yes, Mary! Well?

MARY, *in vanishing*: Mrs. Wyatt wishes to speak with you.

GENERAL WYATT, *going up to Cummings*: I must go, sir. I leave unsaid what I cannot even try to say.

He offers his hand.

CUMMINGS, *grasping the proffered hand*: Everything is understood. (*But as Mr. Cummings returns from following General Wyatt to the door, his face does not confirm the entire security of his words. He looks anxious and perturbed, and when he has taken up his hat and stick, he stands pondering absent-mindedly. At last he puts on his hat and starts briskly toward the door. Before he reaches it, he encounters Bartlett, who advances abruptly into the room.*) Oh! I was going to look for you.

BARTLETT, *sulkily*: Were you?

He walks, without looking at Cummings, to where his painter's paraphernalia are lying, and begins to pick them up.

CUMMINGS: Yes. (*In great embarrassment*) Bartlett, General Wyatt has been here.

BARTLETT, *without looking round*: Who is General Wyatt?

CUMMINGS: I mean the gentleman who—whom you wouldn't wait to see.

BARTLETT: Um!

He has gathered the things into his arms, and is about to leave the room.

CUMMINGS, *in great distress*: Bartlett, Bartlett! Don't go! I implore you, if you have any regard for me whatever, to hear what I have to say. It's boyish, it's cruel, it's cowardly to behave as you're doing!

BARTLETT: Anything more, Mr. Cummings? I give you benefit of clergy.

CUMMINGS: I take it—to denounce your proceeding as something that you'll always be sorry for and ashamed of.

BARTLETT: Oh! Then, if you have quite freed your mind, I think I may go.

CUMMINGS: No, no! You mustn't go. Don't go, my dear fellow. Forgive me! I know how insulted you feel, but upon my soul it's all a mistake,—it is, indeed. General Wyatt— (*Bartlett falters a moment and stands as if irresolute whether to stay and listen or push on out of the room*) the young lady—I don't know how to begin!

BARTLETT, *relenting a little*: Well? I'm sorry for *you*, Cummings. I left a very awkward business to you, and it wasn't yours, either. As for General Wyatt, as he chooses to call himself—

CUMMINGS, *in amaze*: *Call* himself? It's his name!

BARTLETT: Oh, very likely! So is King David

his name, when he happens to be in a Scriptural craze. What explanation have you been commissioned to make me? What apology?

CUMMINGS: The most definite, the most satisfactory. You resemble in a most extraordinary manner a man who has inflicted an abominable wrong upon these people, a treacherous and cowardly villain—

BARTLETT, *in a burst of fury*: Stop! Is that your idea of an apology, an explanation? Isn't it enough that I should be threatened, and vilified, and have people fainting at the sight of me, but I must be told by way of reparation that it all happens because I look like a rascal?

CUMMINGS: My dear friend! Do listen to me!

BARTLETT: No, sir, I won't listen to you! I've listened too much! What right, I should like to know, have they to find this resemblance in me? And do they suppose that I'm going to be placated by being told that they treat me like a rogue because I look like one? It's a little too much. A man calls "Stop Thief" after me and expects me to be delighted when he tells me I look like a thief! The reparation is an additional insult. I don't choose to know that they fancy this infamous resemblance in me. Their pretending it is an outrage; and your reporting it to me is an offense. Will you tell them what I say? Will you tell this General Wyatt and the rest of his Bedlam-broke-loose, that they may all got to the—

CUMMINGS: For shame, for shame! You outrage a terrible sorrow! You insult a trouble sore to death! You trample upon an anguish that should be sacred to your tears!

BARTLETT, *resting his elbow on the corner of the piano*: What—what do you mean, Cummings?

CUMMINGS: What do I mean? What you are not worthy to know! I mean that these people, against whom you vent your stupid rage, are worthy of angelic pity. I mean that by some disastrous mischance you resemble to the life, in tone, manner, and feature, the wretch who won that poor girl's heart, and then crushed it; who—Bartlett, look here! These are the people—this is the young lady—of whom my friend wrote me from Paris; do you understand?

BARTLETT, *in a dull bewilderment*: No, I don't understand.

CUMMINGS: Why, you know what we were talking of just before they came in; you know what I told you of that cruel business.

BARTLETT: Well?

CUMMINGS: Well, this is the young lady—

BARTLETT, *dauntedly*: Oh, come, now! You don't expect me to believe that! It isn't a stage-play.

CUMMINGS: Indeed, indeed, I tell you the miserable truth.

BARTLETT: Do you mean to say that *this* is the young girl who was jilted in that way? Who— Do you mean— Do you intend to tell me— Do you suppose—Cummings—

CUMMINGS: Yes, yes, yes!

BARTLETT: Why, man, she's in Paris, according to your own showing!

CUMMINGS: She was in Paris three weeks ago. They have just brought her home, to help her hide her suffering, as if it were her shame, from all who know it. They are in this house by chance, but they are here. I mean what I say. You *must* believe it, shocking and wild as it is.

BARTLETT, *after a prolonged silence in which he seems trying to realize the fact*: If you were a man capable of such a ghastly joke—but that's impossible. (*He is silent again, as before.*) And I— What did you say about me? That I look like the man who— (*He stops and stares into Cummings's face without speaking, as if he were trying to puzzle the mystery out; then, with fallen head, he muses in a voice of devout and reverent tenderness.*) That—that—broken—lily! Oh! (*With a sudden start he flings his burden upon the closed piano, whose hidden strings hum with the blow, and advances upon Cummings.*) And you can *tell* it? Shame on *you*! It ought to be known to no one upon earth! And you—you show that gentle creature's death-wound to teach something like human reason to a surly dog like me? Oh, it's monstrous! I *wasn't* worth it. Better have let me go, where I would, how I would. What did it matter what I thought or said? And I—I look like that devil, do I? I have his voice, his face, his movement? Cummings, you've over-avenged yourself.

CUMMINGS: Don't take it that way, Bartlett. It *is* hideous. But I didn't make it so, nor you. It's a fatality, it's a hateful chance. But you see now, don't you, Bartlett, how the sight of you must affect them, and how anxious her father must be to avoid you? He most humbly asked your forgiveness, and he hardly knew how to ask that you would not let her see you again. But I told him there could be no question with you; that of course you would prevent it, and at once. I know it's a great sacrifice to expect you to go—

BARTLETT: Go? What are you talking about? (*He breaks again from the daze into which he had relapsed.*) If there's a hole on the face of the earth where I can hide myself from them, I want to find it. What do you think I'm made of? Go? I ought to be shot away out of a mortar; I ought to be struck away by lightning! Oh, I can't excuse you, Cummings! The indelicacy, the brutality of telling me that! No, no,—I can't overlook it. (*He shakes his head and walks away from his friend; then he returns, and bends on him a look of curious inquiry.*) Am I really such a ruffian— (*he speaks very gently, almost meekly now*) that you didn't believe anything short of that would bring me to my senses? Who told you this of her?

CUMMINGS: Her father.

BARTLETT: Oh, that's too loathsome! Had the man no soul, no mercy? Did he think me such a consummate beast that nothing less would drive me away? Yes, he did! Yes, I made him think so! Oh!

He hangs his head and walks away with a shudder.

CUMMINGS: I don't know that he did you that injustice; but I'm afraid *I* did. I was at my wits' end.

BARTLETT, *very humbly*: Oh, I don't know that you were wrong.

CUMMINGS: I suppose that his anxiety for her life made it comparatively easy for him to speak of the hurt to her pride. She can't be long for this world.

BARTLETT: No, she had the dying look! (*After a long pause, in which he has continued to wander aimlessly about the room*) Cummings, is it necessary that you should tell him you told me?

CUMMINGS: You know I hate concealments of any kind, Bartlett.

BARTLETT: Oh, well; do it, then!

CUMMINGS: But I don't know that we shall see him again; and even if we do, I don't see how I can tell him unless he asks. It's rather painful.

BARTLETT: Well, take that little sin on your conscience, if you can. It seems to me too ghastly that I should know what you've told me; it's indecent. Cummings,— (*after another pause*) how does a man go about such a thing? How does he contrive to tell the woman whose heart he has won that he doesn't care for her, and break the faith that she would have staked her life on? Oh, I know,—women do such things, too; but it's different, by a whole world's difference. A man comes and a man goes, but a woman *stays*. The world is before him after that happens, and we don't think him much of a man if he can't get

over it. But she, she has been sought out; she has been made to believe that her smile and her looks are heaven, poor, foolish, helpless idol! her fears have been laid, all her pretty maidenly traditions, her proud reserves overcome; she takes him into her inmost soul,—to find that his love is a lie, a lie! Imagine it! She can't do anything. She can't speak. She can't move as long as she lives. She must stay where she has been left, and look and act as if nothing had happened. Oh, good Heaven! And I, *I* look like a man who could do that! (*After a silence*) I feel as if there were blood on me! (*He goes to the piano, and gathering up his things, turns about towards Cummings again.*) Come, man; I'm going. It's sacrilege to stay an instant,—to exist.

CUMMINGS: Don't take it in that way, Bartlett. I blame myself very much for not having spared you in what I said. I wouldn't have told you of it, if I could have supposed that an accidental resemblance of the sort would distress you so.

BARTLETT, *contritely*: You had to tell me. I forced you to extreme measures. I'm quite worthy to look like him. Good Lord! I suppose I should be capable of his work.

He moves towards the door with his burden, but before he reaches it General Wyatt, from the corridor, meets him with an air of confused agitation. Bartlett halts awkwardly, and some of the things slip from his hold to the floor.

GENERAL WYATT: Sir, I am glad to see you. (*He pronounces the civility with a manner evidently affected by the effort to reconcile Bartlett's offensive personal appearance with his own sense of duty.*) I—I was sorry to miss you before; and now I wish— Your friend— (*referring with an inquiring glance to Cummings*) has explained to you the cause of our very extraordinary behavior, and I hope you—

BARTLETT: Mr. Cummings has told me that I have the misfortune to resemble some one with whom you have painful associations. That is quite enough and entirely justifies you. I am going at once, and I trust you will forgive my rudeness in absenting myself a moment ago. I have a bad temper; but I never could forgive myself if I had forced my friend— (*he turns and glares warningly at Cummings, who makes a faint pantomime of conscientious protest as Bartlett proceeds*) to hear anything more than the mere fact from you. No, no,— (*as General Wyatt seems about to speak*) it would be atrocious in me to seek to go behind it. I wish to know nothing more. (*Cummings gives signs of extreme unrest at being made a party to this tacit deception, and General Wyatt, striking his palms hopelessly together, walks to the other end of the room. Bartlett touches the fallen camp-stool with his foot.*) Cummings, will you be kind enough to put that on top of this other rubbish? (*He indicates his armful, and as Cummings complies, he says in a swift, fierce whisper*) Her secret is mine. If you dare to hint that you've told it to me, I'll—I'll assault you in your own pulpit. (*Then to General Wyatt, who is returning toward him*) Good morning, sir.

GENERAL WYATT: Oh! Ah! Stop! That is, don't go! Really, sir, I don't know what to say. I must have seemed to you like a madman a moment ago, and now I've come to play the fool. (*Bartlett and Cummings look their surprise and General Wyatt hurries on.*) I asked your friend to beg you to go away, and now I am here to beg you to remain. It's perfectly ridiculous, sir, I know, and I can say nothing in defense of the monstrous liberties I have taken. Sir, the matter is simply this: my daughter's health is so frail that her life seems to hang by a thread, and I am powerless to do anything against her wish. It may be a culpable weakness, but I cannot help it. When I went back to her from seeing your friend, she immediately divined what my mission had been, and it had the contrary effect from what I had expected. Well, sir! Nothing would content her but that I should return and ask you to stay. She looks upon it as the sole reparation we can make you.

BARTLETT, *gently*: I understand that perfectly; and may I beg you to say that in going away I thanked her with all my heart, and ventured to leave her my best wishes?

He bows as if to go.

GENERAL WYATT, *detaining him*: Excuse me— thanks—but—but I am afraid she will not be satisfied with that. She will be satisfied with nothing less than your remaining. It is the whim of a sick child—which I must ask you to indulge. In a few days, sir, I hope we may be able to continue on our way. It would be simply unbearable pain to her to know that we had driven you away, and you must stay to show that you have forgiven the wrong we have done you.

BARTLETT: That's nothing, less than nothing. But I was thinking—I don't care for myself in the matter—that Miss Wyatt is proposing a very unnecessary annoyance for you all. My friend can remain and assure her that I have no feeling

whatever about the matter, and in the mean time I can remove—the embarrassment—of my presence.

GENERAL WYATT: Sir, you are very considerate, very kind. My own judgment is in favor of your course, and yet—

CUMMINGS: I think my friend is right, and that when he is gone—

GENERAL WYATT: Well, sir! well, sir! It may be the best way. I think it *is* the best. We will venture upon it. Sir,— (*to Bartlett*) may I have the honor of taking your hand? (*Bartlett lays down his burden on the piano, and gives his hand.*) Thank you, thank you! You will not regret this goodness. God bless you! May you always prosper.

BARTLETT: Good-by; and say to Miss Wyatt—

At these words he pauses, arrested by an incomprehensible dismay in General Wyatt's face, and turning about he sees Cummings transfixed at the apparition of Miss Wyatt advancing directly toward himself, while her mother coming behind her, exchanges signals of helplessness and despair with the General. The young girl's hair, thick and bronze, has been heaped in hasty but beautiful masses on her delicate head; as she stands with fallen eyes before Bartlett, the heavy lashes lie dark on her pale cheeks, and the blue of her eyes shows through their transparent lids. She has a fan with which she makes a weak pretense of playing, and which she puts to her lips as if to hide the low murmur that escapes from them as she raises her eyes to Bartlett's face.

CONSTANCE, *with a phantom-like effort at hauteur*: I hope you have been able to forgive the annoyance we caused you, and that you won't let it drive you away.

She lifts her eyes with a slow effort, and starts with a little gasp as they fall upon his face, and then remains trembling before him while he speaks.

BARTLETT, *reverently*: I am to do whatever you wish. I have no annoyance—but the fear that— that—

CONSTANCE, *in a husky whisper*: Thanks!

As she turns from him to go back to her mother, she moves so frailly that he involuntarily puts out his hand.

MRS. WYATT, *starting forward*: No!

But Constance clutches his extended arm with one of her pale hands, and staying herself for a moment lifts her eyes again to his, looks steadily at him with her face half turned upon him, and then, making a slight, sidelong inclination of the head, releases his arm and goes to her mother, who supports her to one of the easy-chairs and kneels beside her when she sinks into it. Bartlett, after an instant of hesitation, bows silently and withdraws, Cummings having already vanished. Constance watches him going, and then hides her face on her mother's neck.

II.
DISTINCTIONS AND DIFFERENCES

CONSTANCE: And he is still here? He is going to stay on, mother?

She reclines in a low folding chair, and languidly rests her head against one of the pillows with which her mother has propped her; on the bright-colored shawl which has been thrown over her lie her pale hands loosely holding her shut fan. Her mother stands half across the parlor from her, and wistfully surveys her work, to see if some touch may not yet be added for the girl's comfort.

MRS. WYATT: Yes, my child. He will stay. He told your father he would stay.

CONSTANCE: That's very kind of him. He's very good.

MRS. WYATT, *seating herself before her daughter*: Do you really wish him to stay? Remember how weak you are, Constance. If you are taking anything upon yourself out of a mistaken sense of duty, of compunction, you are not kind to your poor father or to me. Not that I mean to reproach you.

CONSTANCE: Oh, no. And I am not unkind to you in the way you think. I'm selfish enough in wishing him to stay. I can't help wanting to see him again and again,—it's so strange, so strange. All this past week, whenever I've caught a glimpse of him, it's been like an apparition; and whenever he has spoken, it has been like a ghost speaking. But I haven't been afraid since the first time. No, there's been a dreary comfort in it; you won't understand it; I can't understand it myself; but I know now why people are glad to see their dead in dreams. If the ghost went, there would be nothing.

MRS. WYATT: Constance, you break my heart!

CONSTANCE: Yes, I know it; it's because I've none. (*She remains a little space without speaking, while she softly fingers the edges of the fan lying in her lap.*) I suppose we shall become more acquainted, if he stays?

MRS. WYATT: Why, not necessarily, dear. You need know nothing more of him than you do now. He seems very busy, and not in the least inclined to intrude upon us. Your father thinks him a little odd, but very gentlemanly.

CONSTANCE, *dreamily*: I wonder what he would think if he knew that the man whom I would have given my life did not find my love worth having? I suppose it *was* worthless; but it seemed so much in the giving; it was that deceived me. He was wiser. Oh, me! (*After a silence*) Mother, why was I so different from other girls?

MRS. WYATT: So different, Constance? You were only different in being lovelier and better than others.

CONSTANCE: Ah, that's the mistake! If that were true, it could never have happened. Other girls, the poorest and plainest, are kept faith with, but I was left. There must have been something about me that made him despise me. Was I silly, mother? Was I too bold, too glad to have him care for me? I was so happy that I couldn't help showing it. May be that displeased him. I must have been dull and tiresome. And I suppose I was somehow repulsive, and at last he couldn't bear it any longer and had to break with me. Did I dress queerly? I know I looked ridiculous at times; and people laughed at me before him.

MRS. WYATT: Oh, Constance, Constance! Can't you understand that it was his unworthiness alone, his wicked heartlessness?

CONSTANCE, *with gentle slowness*: No, I can't understand that. It happened after we had learned to know each other so well. If he had been fickle, it would have happened long before that. It was something odious in me that he didn't see at first. I have thought it out. It seems strange now that people could ever have tolerated me. (*Desolately*) Well, they have their revenge.

MRS. WYATT: Their revenge on *you*, Constance? What harm did you ever do them, my poor child? Oh, you mustn't let these morbid fancies overcome you. Where is our Constance that used to be,—our brave, bright girl, that nothing could daunt, and nothing could sadden?

CONSTANCE, *sobbing*: Dead, dead!

MRS. WYATT: I can't understand! You are so young still, and with the world all before you. Why will you let one man's baseness blacken it all and blight your young life so? Where is your pride, Constance?

CONSTANCE: Pride? What have I to do with pride? A thing like me!

MRS. WYATT: Oh, child, you're pitiless! It seems as if you took a dreadful pleasure in torturing those who love you.

CONSTANCE: You've said it, mother. I do. I know now that I am a vampire, and that it's my hideous fate to prey upon those who are dearest to me. He must have known, he must have felt the vampire in me.

MRS. WYATT: Constance!

CONSTANCE: But at least I can be kind to those who care nothing for me. Who is this stranger? He must be an odd kind of man to forgive us. What is he, mother?—if he is anything in himself; he seems to me only a likeness, not a reality.

MRS. WYATT: He is a painter, your father says. (Mrs. Wyatt gives a quick sigh of relief, and makes haste to confirm the direction of the talk away from Constance.) He is painting some landscapes, here. That friend of his who went to-day is a cousin of your father's old friend, Major Cummings. He's a minister.

CONSTANCE: What is the painter's name? Not that it matters. But I must call him something if I meet him again.

MRS. WYATT: Mr. Bartlett.

CONSTANCE: Oh, yes, I forgot. (She falls into a brooding silence.) I wonder if he will despise me—if he will be like in that, too? (Mrs. Wyatt sighs patiently.) Why do you mind what I say, mother? I'm not worth it. I must talk on, or else go mad with the mystery of what has been. We were so happy; he was so good to me, so kind; there was nothing but papa's not seeming to like him; and then suddenly, in an instant, he turns and strikes me down! Yes, it was like a deadly blow. If you don't let me believe that it was because he saw all at once that I was utterly unworthy, I can't believe in anything.

MRS. WYATT: Hush, Constance; you don't know what you're saying.

CONSTANCE: Oh, I know too well! And now this stranger, who is so like him—who has all his looks, who has his walk, who has his voice,— won't he have his insight, too? I had better show myself for what I am, at once—weak, stupid, selfish, false; it'll save me the pain of being found out. Pain? Oh, I'm past hurting! Why do you cry, mother? I'm not worth your tears.

MRS. WYATT: You're all the world to us, Constance; you know it, child. Your poor father—

CONSTANCE: Does papa really like me?

MRS. WYATT: Constance!

CONSTANCE: No; but why should he? He never liked him; and sometimes I've wondered, if it wasn't papa's not liking him that first set him against me. Of course, it was best he should find me out, but still I can't keep from thinking that if he had never begun to dislike me! I noticed from the first that after papa had been with us he was cold and constrained. Mother, I had better say it: I don't believe I love papa as I ought. There's something in my heart—some hardness— against him when he's kindest to me. If he had only been kinder to him—

MRS. WYATT: Kinder to him? Constance, you drive me wild! Kind to a wolf, kind to a snake! Kind to the thief who has robbed us of all that made our lives dear; who stole your love, and then your hope, your health, your joy, your pride, your peace! And you think your father might have been kinder to him! Constance, you were our little girl when the war began,—the last of brothers and sisters that had died. You seemed given to our later years to console and comfort us for those that had been taken; and you were so bright and gay! All through those dreadful days and months and years you were our stay and hope, —mine at home, his in the field. Our letters were full of you,—like young people's with their first child; all that you did and said I had to tell him, and then he had to talk it over in his answers back. When he came home at last after the peace —can you remember it, Constance?

CONSTANCE: I can remember a little girl that ran down the street, and met an officer on horseback. He was all tanned and weather-beaten; he sat his horse at the head of his troop like a statue of bronze. When he saw her come running, dancing down the street, he leaped from his horse and caught her in his arms, and hugged her close and kissed her, and set her all crying and laughing in his saddle, and walked on beside her; and the men burst out with a wild yell, and the ragged flags flapped, over her, and the music flashed out— (She rises in her chair with the thrill of her recollection; her voice comes free and full, and her pale cheeks flush; suddenly she sinks back upon the pillows.) Was it really I, mother?

MRS. WYATT: Yes, it was you, Constance. And do you remember all through your school-days, how proud and fond he was of you? what presents and feasts and pleasures he was always making you? I thought he would spoil you; he took you everywhere with him, and wanted to give you everything. When I saw you growing up with his pride and quick temper, I trembled, but I felt safe when I saw that you had his true and tender heart, too. You can never know what a pang it cost him to part with you when we went abroad, but you can't forget how he met you in Paris?

CONSTANCE: Oh, no, no! Poor papa!

MRS. WYATT: Oh, child! And I could tell you something of his bitter despair when he saw the man—

CONSTANCE, *wearily*: You needn't tell me. I knew it as soon as they met, without looking at either of them.

MRS. WYATT: And when the worst that he feared came true, he was almost glad, I believe. He thought, and I thought, that your self-respect would come to your aid against such treachery.

CONSTANCE: My self-respect? Now I know you've not been talking of me.

MRS. WYATT, *desperately*: Oh, what shall I do?

MARY, *the serving-woman, at the door*: If you please, Mrs. Wyatt, I can't open Miss Constance's hat-box.

MRS. WYATT, *rising*: Oh, yes. There's something the matter with the lock. I'll come, Mary.

She looks at Constance.

CONSTANCE: Yes, go, mother. I'm perfectly well here. I like being alone well enough.

As Mrs. Wyatt, after a moment's reluctance, goes out, the girl's heavy eyelids fall, and she lies motionless against her pillows, while the fan, released from her careless hold, slides slowly over the shawl, and drops with a light clash upon the floor. She starts at the sound, and utters a little involuntary cry at sight of Bartlett, who stands irresolute in the doorway on her right. He makes as if to retreat, but at a glance from her he remains.

BARTLETT, *with a sort of subdued gruffness*: I'm afraid I disturbed you.

CONSTANCE, *passively*: No, I think it was my fan. It fell.

BARTLETT: I'm glad I can lay the blame on the fan.

He comes abruptly forward and picks it up for her. She makes no motion to receive it, and he lays it on her lap.

CONSTANCE, *starting from the abstraction in which she has been gazing at him*: Oh! Thanks.

BARTLETT, *with constraint*: I hope you're better this morning?

CONSTANCE: Yes.

She has again fallen into a dreamy study of him, as unconscious, apparently, as if he were a picture before her, the effect of which is to reduce him to a state of immovable awkwardness. At last he tears himself loose from the spot on which he has been petrifying, and takes refuge in the business which has brought him into the room.

BARTLETT: I came to look for one of my brushes. It must have dropped out of my traps here, the other day. (*He goes up to the piano and looks about the floor, while Constance's gaze follows him in every attitude and movement.*) Ah, here it is! I knew it would escape the broom under the landlady's relaxed régime. If you happen to drop anything in this room, Miss Wyatt, you needn't be troubled; you can always find it just where it fell. (*Miss Wyatt's fan again slips to the floor, and Bartlett again picks it up and restores it to her.*) A case in point.

CONSTANCE, *blushing faintly*: Don't do it for me. It isn't worth while.

BARTLETT, *gravely*: It doesn't take a great deal of time, and the exercise does me good. (*Constance faintly smiles, but does not relax her vigilance.*) Isn't that light rather strong for you?

He goes to the glass doors opening on the balcony and offers to draw down one of their shades.

CONSTANCE: It doesn't make any difference.

BARTLETT, *bluffly*: If it's disagreeable it makes some difference. Is it disagreeable?

CONSTANCE: The light's strong— (*Bartlett dashes the curtain down*) but I could see the mountain.

He pulls the curtain up.

BARTLETT: I beg your pardon.

He again falls into statue-like discomposure under Miss Wyatt's gaze, which does not seek the distant slopes of Ponkwasset, in spite of the lifted curtain.

CONSTANCE: What is the name? Do you know?

BARTLETT: Whose? Oh! Ponkwasset. It's not a pretty name, but it's aboriginal. And it doesn't hurt the mountain.

Recovering a partial volition, he shows signs of a purpose to escape, when Miss Wyatt's next question arrests him.

CONSTANCE: Are you painting it, Mr.—Bartlett?

BARTLETT, *with a laugh*: Oh, no, I don't soar so high as mountains; I only lift my eyes to a tree here and there, and a bit of pasture and a few of the lowlier and friendlier sort of rocks.

He now so far effects his purpose as to transfer his unwieldly presence to a lateral position as regards Miss Wyatt. The girl mechanically turns her head upon the pillow and again fixes her sad eyes upon him.

CONSTANCE: Have you ever been up it?

BARTLETT: Yes, half a dozen times.

CONSTANCE: Is it hard to climb—like the Swiss mountains?

BARTLETT: *You* must speak for the Swiss mountains after you've tried Ponkwasset, Miss Wyatt. I've never been abroad.

CONSTANCE, *her large eyes dilating with surprise*: Never been abroad?

BARTLETT: I enjoy that distinction.

CONSTANCE: Oh! I thought you had been abroad.

She speaks with a slow, absent, earnest, accent, regarding him, as always, with a look of wistful bewilderment.

BARTLETT, *struggling uneasily for his habitual lightness*: I'm sorry to disappoint you, Miss Wyatt. I will go abroad as soon as possible. I'm going out in a boat this morning to work at a bit on the point of the island yonder, and I'll take lessons in sea-faring.

Bartlett, managing at last to get fairly behind Miss Wyatt's chair, indulges himself in a long, low sigh of relief, and taking out his handkerchief rubs his face with it.

CONSTANCE, *with sudden, meek compunction*: I've been detaining you.

BARTLETT, *politely coming forward again*: Oh, no, not at all! I'm afraid I've tired *you.*

CONSTANCE: No, I'm glad to have you stay.

In the unconscious movement necessary to follow Bartlett in his changes of position, the young girl has loosened one of the pillows that prop her head. It slowly disengages itself and drops to the floor. Bartlett, who has been crushing his brush against the ball of his thumb, gives a start of terror, and looks from Constance to the pillow, and back again to Constance in despair.

CONSTANCE: Never mind.

She tries to adjust her head to the remaining pillows, and then desists in evident discomfort.

BARTLETT, *in great agony of spirit*: I—I'm afraid you miss it.

CONSTANCE: Oh, no.

BARTLETT: Shall I call your mother, Miss Wyatt?

CONSTANCE: No. Oh, no. She will be here presently. Thank you so much.

Bartlett eyes the pillow in renewed desperation.

BARTLETT: Do you think—do you suppose I could— (*Recklessly*) Miss Wyatt, let *me* put back that pillow for you!

CONSTANCE, *promptly, with a little flush*: Why, you're very good! I'm ashamed to trouble you.

As she speaks, she raises her head, and lifts herself forward slightly by help of the chair-arms; two more pillows topple out, one on either side, unknown to her.

BARTLETT, *maddened by the fresh disaster*: Good Lord! (*He flings himself wildly upon the first pillow, and crams it into the chair behind Miss Wyatt; then without giving his courage time to flag, he seizes the others, and packs them in on top of it.*) Will that do?

He stands hot and flushed, looking down upon her, as she makes a gentle attempt to adjust herself to the mass.

CONSTANCE: Oh, perfectly.

She puts her hand behind her and feebly endeavors to modify Bartlett's arrangement.

BARTLETT: What is it?

CONSTANCE: Oh—nothing. Ah—would—would you draw this one a little—toward you? So! Thanks. And that one—out a little on the—other side? You're very kind; that's right. And this one under my neck—lift it up a little? Ah, thank you ever so much. (*Bartlett, in a fine frenzy, obeying these instructions, Miss Wyatt at last reposes herself against the pillows, looks up into his embarrassed face, and deeply blushes; then she turns suddenly white, and weakly catching up her fan she passes it once or twice before her face, and lets it fall.*) I'm a little—faint.

Bartlett seizes the fan, and after a moment of silent self-dedication kneels down beside her chair, and fans her.

CONSTANCE, *after a moment*: Thanks, thanks. You are very good. I'm better now. I'm ashamed to have troubled you. But I seem to live only to give trouble.

BARTLETT, *with sudden deep tenderness*: Oh, Miss Wyatt, you mustn't say that. I'm sure I— we all—that is—shall I call your mother *now*, Miss Wyatt?

CONSTANCE, *after a deep breath, firmly*: No. I'm quite well, now. She is busy. But I know I'm keeping *you* from your work— (*With ever so slight a wan little smile*) I mustn't do that.

BARTLETT: Oh, you're not *keeping* me! There's no hurry. I can work later just as well.

CONSTANCE: Then,— (*with a glance at his devout posture, of which Bartlett has himself become quite unconscious*) won't you sit down, Mr. Bartlett?

BARTLETT, *restored to consciousness and confusion*: Thanks; I think it will be better. (*He rises, and in his embarrassment draws a chair to the spot on which he has been kneeling and sits down very close to her. He keeps the fan in his hand, as he talks.*) It's rather nice out there, Miss Wyatt, —there on the island. You must be rowed out as soon as you can stand it. The General would like it.

CONSTANCE: Is it a large place, the island?

BARTLETT: About two acres, devoted exclusively to golden-rod and granite. The fact is, I was going to make a little study of golden-rod and granite, there. You shall visit the Fortunate Isle in my sketch, this afternoon, and see whether you'd like to go, really. People camp out there in the summer. Who knows, but if you keep on—gaining—this way, you may yet feel like camping out there yourself before you go away? You do begin to feel better, don't you? Everybody cries up this air.

CONSTANCE: It's very pleasant; it seems fine and pure. Is the island a pretty place?

BARTLETT, *glancing out at it over his shoulder*: Well, you get the best of it from the parlor window, here. Not that it's so bad when you're on it; there's a surly, frugal, hard-headed kind of beauty about it,—like the local human nature,—and it has its advantages. If you were camping out there, you could almost provision yourself from the fish and wild fowl of the surrounding waters,—supposing any of your party liked to fish or shoot. Does your father like shooting?

CONSTANCE: No, I don't believe he cares for it.

BARTLETT: I'm glad of that. I shall be spared the painful hospitality of pointing out the best places for ducks. (*At an inquiring look from Constance*) I'm glad for their sakes, not mine; *I* don't want to kill them.

CONSTANCE, *with grave mistrust*: Not like shooting?

BARTLETT: No, I think it's the sneakingest sort of assassination; it's the pleasure of murder without the guilt. If you must kill, you ought to be man enough to kill something that you'll suffer remorse for. Do you consider those atrocious sentiments, Miss Wyatt? I assure you that they're entirely my own.

CONSTANCE, *blankly*: I wasn't thinking— I was thinking— I supposed you liked shooting.

BARTLETT, *laughing uneasily*: How did you get that impression?

CONSTANCE, *evasively*: I thought all gentlemen did.

BARTLETT: They do, in this region. It's the only thing that can comfort them in affliction. The other day our ostler's brother lost his sweetheart —she died, poor girl,—and the ostler and another friend had him over here to cheer him up. They took him to the stable, and whittled round among the stalls with him half the forenoon, and let him rub down some of the horses; they stood him out among the vegetables and let him gather some of the new kind of potato-bugs; they made him sit in the office with his feet on top of the stove; they played billiards with him; but he showed no signs of resignation till they borrowed three squirrel-guns and started with him to the oak woods yonder. That seemed to "fetch" him. You should have seen them trudging off together with their guns all aslant,—this way,—the stricken lover in the middle! (*Bartlett rises to illustrate, and then at the deepening solemnity of Constance's face he desists in sudden dismay.*) Miss Wyatt, I've shocked you!

CONSTANCE: Oh, no—no!

BARTLETT: It *was* shocking. I wonder how I could do it! I—I thought it would amuse you.

CONSTANCE, *mournfully*: It did, thank you, very much. (*After a pause*) I didn't know you liked— joking.

BARTLETT: Ah! I don't believe I do—all kinds. Good Lord—I beg your pardon. (*Bartlett turns away, with an air of guilty consciousness, and goes to the window and looks out, Constance's gaze following him.*) It's a wonderful day! (*He comes back toward her.*) What a pity you couldn't be carried there in your chair!

CONSTANCE: I'm not equal to that, yet. (*Presently*) Then you—like—nature?

BARTLETT: Why, that's mere shop in a landscape painter. I get my bread and butter by her. At least I ought to have some feeling of gratitude.

CONSTANCE, *hastily*: Of course, of course. It's very stupid of me, asking.

BARTLETT, *with the desperate intention of grappling with the situation*: I see you have a passion for formulating, classifying people, Miss Wyatt. That's all very well, if one's characteristics were not so very characteristic of everybody else. But I generally find in my moments of self-consciousness, when I've gone round priding myself that such and such traits are my peculiar property, that the first man I meet has them all and as many more, and isn't the least proud of them. I dare say you don't see anything very strange in them, so far.

CONSTANCE, *musingly*: Oh, yes; very strange indeed. They're all—wrong!

BARTLETT: Well! I don't know—I'm very sorry— Then you consider it wrong not to like shooting and to be fond of joking and nature, and—

CONSTANCE, *bewilderedly*: Wrong? Oh, no!

BARTLETT: Oh, I'm glad to hear it. But you just said it was.

CONSTANCE, *slowly recalling herself, with a painful blush, at last*: I meant—I meant I didn't expect any of those things of you.

BARTLETT, *with a smile*: Well, on reflection, I don't know that I did, either. I think they must have come without being expected. Upon my word, I'm tempted to propose something very ridiculous.

CONSTANCE, *uneasily*: Yes? What is that?

BARTLETT: That you'll let me try to guess *you* out. I've failed so miserably in my own case, that I feel quite encouraged.

CONSTANCE, *morbidly*: I'm not worth the trouble of guessing out.

BARTLETT: That means no. You always mean no by yes, because you can't bear to say no. That is the mark of a very deep and darkling nature. I feel that I *could* go on and read your mind perfectly, but I'm afraid to do it. Let's get back to myself. I can't allow that you've failed to read my mind aright; I think you were careless about it. Will you give your intuitions one more chance?

CONSTANCE, *with an anxious smile*: Oh, yes.

BARTLETT: All those traits and tastes which we both find so unexpected in me are minor matters at the most. The great test question remains. If you answer it rightly, you prove yourself a mind-reader of wonderful power; if you miss it— The question is simply this: Do I like smoking?

CONSTANCE, *instantly, with a quick, involuntary pressure of her hankerchief to her delicate nostrils*: Oh, yes, indeed.

BARTLETT, *daunted and reddening*: Miss Wyatt, you have been deluding me. You are really a mind-reader of great subtlety.

CONSTANCE: I don't know—I can't say that it was *mind*-reading exactly. (*She lifts her eyes to his, and in his embarrassment he passes his hand over his forehead and then feels first in one pocket and then in the other for his handkerchief; suddenly he twitches it forth, and with it a pipe, half a dozen cigars, and a pouch of smoking tobacco, which fly in different directions over the floor. As he stoops in dismay and sweeps together these treasures, she cries*) Oh, it didn't need all *that* to prove it! (*and breaks into a wild, helpless laugh, and striving to recover herself with many little moans and sighs behind her handkerchief, laughs on and on.*) Oh, don't! I oughtn't! Oh dear, oh dear!

> When at last she lies spent with her reluctant mirth, and uncovers her face, Bartlett is gone, and it is her mother who stands over her, looking down at her with affectionate misgiving.

MRS. WYATT: Laughing, Constance?

CONSTANCE, *with a burst of indignant tears*: Yes, yes! Isn't it shocking? It's horrible! He made me.

MRS. WYATT: He?

CONSTANCE, *beginning to laugh again*: Mr. Bartlett; he's been here. Oh, I *wish* I *wouldn't* be so silly!

MRS. WYATT: Made you? How could he make *you* laugh, poor child?

CONSTANCE: Oh, it's a long story. It was all through my bewilderment at his resemblance. It confused me. I kept thinking it was *he*,—as if it were some dream,—and whenever this one mentioned some trait of his that totally differed from *his*, don't you know, I got more and more confused, and—mamma!— (*With sudden desolation*) I know he knows all about it!

MRS. WYATT: I am sure he doesn't. Mr. Cummings only told him that his resemblance was a painful association. He assured your father of this, and wouldn't hear a word more. I'm certain you're wrong. But what made you think he knows?

CONSTANCE, *solemnly*: He behaved just as if he didn't.

MRS. WYATT: Ah, you can't judge from that, my dear. (*Impressively*) Men are very different.

CONSTANCE, *doubtfully*: Do you think so, mamma?

MRS. WYATT: I'm certain of it.

CONSTANCE, *after a pause*: Mamma, will you help take this shawl off my feet? I am so warm. I think I should like to walk about a little. Can you see the island from the gallery?

MRS. WYATT: Do you think you'd better try to leave your chair, Constance?

CONSTANCE: Yes, I'm stronger this morning. And I shall never gain, lounging about this way. *(She begins to loose the wraps from her feet, and Mrs. Wyatt coming doubtfully to her aid she is presently freed. She walks briskly toward the sofa, and sits down quite erectly in the corner of it.)* There! that's pleasanter. I get so tired of being a burden.

She is silent, and then she begins softly and wearily to laugh again.

MRS. WYATT, *smiling curiously*: What is it, Constance? I don't at all understand what made you laugh.

CONSTANCE: Why, don't you know? Several times after I had been surprised that he didn't like this thing, and hadn't that habit and the other, he noticed it, and pretended that it was an attempt at mind-reading, and then all at once he turned and said I must try once more, and he asked, "Do I like smoking?" and I said instantly, "Oh, yes!" Why, it was like having a whole tobacconist's shop in the same room with you from the moment he came in; and of course he understood what I meant, and blushed, and then felt for his handkerchief, and pulled it out, and discharged a perfect volley of pipes and tobacco, that seemed to be tangled up in it, all over the floor, and then I began to laugh—so silly, so disgusting, so perfectly flat! and I thought I should *die*, it was so ridiculous! and— Oh, dear, I'm beginning again! *(She hides her face in her handkerchief and leans her head on the back of the sofa.)* Say something, *do* something to stop me, mother!

She stretches an imploring left hand toward the elder lady, who still remains apparently but half convinced of any reason for mirth, when General Wyatt, hastily entering, pauses in abrupt irresolution at the spectacle of Constance's passion.

CONSTANCE: *Oh*, ha, ha, ha! Oh, *ha*, ha, ha, ha!

GENERAL WYATT: Margaret! Constance!

At the sound of his voice, Constance starts up with a little cry, and stiffens into an attitude of ungracious silence, without looking at her father, who turns with an expression of pain toward her mother.

MRS. WYATT: Yes, James. We were laughing at something Constance had been telling me about Mr. Bartlett. Tell your father, Constance.

CONSTANCE, *coldly, while she draws through her hand the handkerchief which she has been press-ing to her eyes*: I don't think it would amuse papa.

She passes her hand across her lap, and does not lift her heavy eyelashes.

MRS. WYATT, *caressingly*: Oh, yes, it would; I'm sure it would.

CONSTANCE: You can tell it then, mamma.

MRS. WYATT: No; you, my dear. You tell it so funnily; and—*(In a lower tone)* it's so long since your father heard you laugh.

CONSTANCE: There was nothing funny in it. It was disgusting. I was laughing from nervousness.

MRS. WYATT: Why, Constance—

GENERAL WYATT: Never mind, Margaret. Another time will do. *(He chooses to ignore the coldness of his daughter's bearing toward himself.)* I came to see if Constance were not strong enough to go out on the lake this morning. The boats are very good, and the air is so fine that I think she'll be the better for it. Mr. Bartlett is going out to the island to sketch, and—

CONSTANCE: I don't care to go.

MRS. WYATT: Do go, my daughter! I know it will do you good.

CONSTANCE: I am not strong enough.

MRS. WYATT: But you said you were better, just now; and you should yield to your father's judgment.

CONSTANCE: I will do whatever papa bids me.

GENERAL WYATT: I don't bid you. Margaret, I think I will go out with Mr. Bartlett. We will be back at dinner.

He turns and leaves the room without looking again at Constance.

MRS. WYATT: Oh, Constance! How can you treat your father so coldly? You will suffer some day for the pain you give him!

CONSTANCE: Suffer? No, I'm past that. I've exhausted my power of suffering.

MRS. WYATT: You haven't exhausted your power of making others suffer.

CONSTANCE, *crouching listlessly down upon the sofa*: I told you that I lived only to give pain. But it's my fate, not my will. Nothing but that can excuse me.

MRS. WYATT, *wringing her hands*: Oh, oh! Well, then, give *me* pain if you must torment somebody. But spare your father,—spare the heart that loves you so tenderly, you unhappy girl.

CONSTANCE, *with hardness*: Whenever I see papa, my first thought is, If he had not been so harsh and severe, it might never have happened! What can I care for his loving me when he hated *him*? Oh, *I* will do my duty, mother; I will obey;

I *have* obeyed, and I know how. Papa can't demand anything of me *now* that isn't easy. I have forgiven everything, and if you give me time I can forget. I *have* forgotten. I have been laughing at something so foolish, it ought to make me cry for shame.

MRS. WYATT: Constance, you try me beyond all endurance! You talk of forgiving, you talk of forgetting, you talk of that wretch! Forgive *him*, forget *him*, if you can. If he had been half a man, if he had ever cared a tithe as much for you as for himself, all the hate of all the fathers in the world could not have driven him from you. You talk of obeying—

MARY, *the serving woman, flying into the room*: Oh, please, Mrs. Wyatt! There are four men carrying somebody up the hill. And General Wyatt just went down, and I can't see him anywhere, and—

MRS. WYATT: You're crazy, Mary! He hasn't been gone a moment; there isn't time; it can't be he!

Mrs. Wyatt rushes to the gallery that overlooks the road to verify her hope or fear, and then out of one of the doors into the corridor, while Constance springs frantically to her feet and runs toward the other door.

CONSTANCE: Oh, yes, yes! It's papa! It's my dear, good, kind papa! He's dead; he's drowned; I drove him away; I murdered him! Ah-h-h-h! (*She shrinks back with a shriek at sight of Bartlett, whose excited face appears at the door.*) Go! It was you, *you* who made me hate my father! You made me kill him and now I abhor you! I—

BARTLETT: Wait! Hold on! What is it all?

CONSTANCE: Oh, forgive me! I didn't mean— I didn't know it was you, sir! But where *is* he? Oh, take me to him! Is he dead?

She seizes his arm, and clings to it trembling.

BARTLETT: Dead? No, he isn't dead. He was knocked over by a team coming behind him down the hill, and was slightly bruised. There's no cause for alarm. He sent me to tell you; they've carried him to your rooms.

CONSTANCE: Oh, thank Heaven! (*She bows her head with a sob, upon his shoulder, and then lifts her tearful eyes to his.*) Help me to get to him! I am weak. (*She totters and Bartlett mechanically passes a supporting arm about her.*) Help me, and don't—don't leave me!

She moves with him a few paces toward the door, her head drooping; but all at once she raises her face again, stares at him, stiffly re-

leases herself, and with a long look of reproach walks proudly away to the other door, by which she vanishes without a word.

BARTLETT, *remaining planted, with a bewildered glance at his empty arm*: Well, I wonder who and what and where I am!

III.
DISSOLVING VIEWS [1]

In the parlor stands an easel with a canvas of inordinate dimensions upon it, and near this a small table, with a fresh box of colors in tubes, and a holiday outfit of new brushes, pallet, and other artist's materials, evidently not the property of Bartlett. Across the room from this apparatus is stretched Constance's easy-chair, towards which General Wyatt, bearing some marks of his recent accident in a bandaged wrist and a stiff leg, stumps heavily, supported by Mrs. Wyatt. Beside this chair is the centre-table of the parlor, on which are an open box of cigars, and a pile of unopened newspapers.

GENERAL WYATT, *dropping into the chair with a groan*: Well, my dear! I feel uncommonly ashamed of myself, taking Constance's chair in this manner. Though there's a great consolation in thinking she doesn't need it any longer. (*Settling himself more comfortably in the chair, and laying his stick across his knees*) Margaret, I begin to be very happy about Constance. I haven't had so light a heart for many a long day. The last month has made a wonderful change in her. She is almost like her old self again.

MRS. WYATT, *sighing*: Yes, it seems almost too good to be true. I don't know quite what to make of it. Sometimes, I almost fear for her mind. I'm sure that half the time she forgets that Mr. Bartlett isn't that wretch, and I can see her awake with a start to the reality every little while, and then willfully lull her consciousness to sleep again. He's terribly like. I can hardly keep from crying out at times; and yesterday I did give way: I was *so* ashamed, and he looked so *hurt*. I see Constance restrain herself often, and I dare say there are times that we don't know of when she doesn't.

1 In the Houghton Library at Harvard there are five cue parts, indicating a play of four acts, for the following characters: Mrs. Wyatt, Mary, Landlady, and Mrs. Ransom. The parts of Mary and Mrs. Ransom show that this act once began with the traditional servant scene.

GENERAL WYATT: Well, all that may be. But it's a thing that will right itself in time. We must do our best not to worry him. This painter is a fine fellow, my dear. I took a great fancy to him at the beginning. I liked him from the moment I saw him.

MRS. WYATT: James! You were going to strike him with your cane.

GENERAL WYATT: That was before I saw *him*. I was going to strike the other one. But that's neither here nor there. We must be careful not to hurt his feelings; that's all. We've got our Constance back again, Margaret. Impossible as it seems, we have got her back by his help. Isn't it wonderful to see that killing weight lifted from her young life? It's like a miracle.

MRS. WYATT: It isn't lifted *all* the time, James.

GENERAL WYATT: No matter—no matter. It isn't crushing her all the time, either. I'm glad for what relief there is, and I feel that all is going well. Do you hear that step, Margaret? Listen! That's *like* the old bounding tread of our little girl. Where is the leaden-footed phantom that used to drag along that hall? Is she coming this way?

MRS. WYATT, *listening*: No, she is going to our rooms. Has Mr. Bartlett been here yet?

GENERAL WYATT: Not yet. He was to come when he got back from his sketching. What a good fellow, to take so much trouble for Constance's amusement! It was uncommonly kind of Mr. Bartlett, Margaret, offering to give her these lessons.

MRS. WYATT: Yes, it worries me.

GENERAL WYATT: Why in the world should it worry you, Margaret?

MRS. WYATT: You can't offer him any compensation for his instructions.

GENERAL WYATT: Of course not. That would be offensive. Well?

MRS. WYATT: Well, James, can't you see how it complicates everything? He is conferring another obligation. He might almost think we tried to throw them together.

GENERAL WYATT, *fiercely*: He had better not! Why, Margaret, he's a gentleman! He can't think that.

MRS. WYATT: No, I suppose not. I suppose it's our trouble that has made me suspicious of every one.

She goes sadly about the room, rearranging, with a housekeeper's instinct, everything in it.

GENERAL WYATT: You needn't trouble yourself with the room, Margaret; Mary told me that she and the landlady had put it in order.

MRS. WYATT: That's just why I need. (*After a moment*) Are you going to be here, James?

GENERAL WYATT: Yes, I thought I should stay. It's a cheerful place to read and smoke. It won't disturb them, will it?

MRS. WYATT: Oh, no! It's quite necessary some one should stay. I'm very glad you can, for I've got a few little things to do.

GENERAL WYATT: All right. I'll stay and do the dragon, or whatever it is. But I wish you hadn't put it in that light, Margaret. I was proposing to enjoy myself.

MRS. WYATT: Enjoy yourself, James? With such a terribly perplexing affair before you!

GENERAL WYATT: I don't see anything perplexing about it. It's perfectly simple, to my mind. Mr. Bartlett kindly proposes to give Constance a few lessons in drawing,—or painting; I don't know which it is. That's the beginning and the end of it.

MRS. WYATT, *with a heavy sigh*: Yes, that's the *beginning*.

GENERAL WYATT, *impatiently*: Well?

MRS. WYATT: Nothing. Are you quite comfortable, here? Have you got everything you wish?

GENERAL WYATT, *with a glance at the things on the table at his elbow*: Here are my cigars, and —yes, here are the papers. Yes, I'm all right. But what do you mean by "nothing"? What— Ah, here's Mr. Bartlett! (*As Bartlett comes into the room, the General, since he cannot conveniently rise, makes a demonstration of welcome with his hands. Bartlett has his color box under his arm, and a canvas in his hand.*) You've been improving the shining hour, I see. What have you there?

BARTLETT, *with a smile and nod inclusive of Mrs. Wyatt*: Nothing worth looking at. (*He goes and faces it against the wall.*) Have I kept Miss Wyatt waiting?

MRS. WYATT, *anxiously*: It's too bad you should waste your time upon her, Mr. Bartlett. I don't know why we let you.

BARTLETT: You can't help yourself, Mrs. Wyatt. The wrong is owing to circumstances beyond your control. If I have any virtue it is a particularly offensive form of stubbornness. Besides,—(*more seriously*) I feel myself honored to do it—to contribute anything to Miss Wyatt's—ah—ah— In short, if she can stand it I can.

GENERAL WYATT: It's immensely kind of you.

By the way, you won't mind my staying here, will you, to read my papers, while you're at work? Because if you do, I can clear out at once. (*Mrs. Wyatt, with mute but lively tokens of dismay, attends the General's further remarks.*) I don't want to stay here and be a bore and a nuisance, you know.

Mrs. Wyatt vanishes from the scene in final despair.

BARTLETT, *going up to the easel and dragging it into an entirely new position*: Not in the least. Some woman been putting this room in order, hasn't there?

GENERAL WYATT: Three.

BARTLETT: I thought so. (*He continues to disarrange all the preparations for his work. His operations bring him in the vicinity of General Wyatt, upon whose box of cigars his eye falls.*) Oh, I say, General! Smoking?

GENERAL WYATT: Certainly. Why not?

BARTLETT: Well, I don't know. I thought perhaps—I supposed—I imagined somehow from something she said, or that happened—it was offensive to Miss Wyatt.

GENERAL WYATT: Why, bless your heart, man, she minds it no more than I do!

BARTLETT: You don't say so! Why, I haven't smoked any for the last two weeks, because— because— And I'm almost dead for a pipe!

GENERAL WYATT: Why, poor fellow! Why, here! Take a cigar!

BARTLETT, *significantly shaking his head*: Oh, no, no! I said a *pipe*. (*He rushes to an old studio jacket which the landlady has hung for him on the back of a chair; he dives in one pocket and gets out a pipe, plunges into another and extracts a pouch of tobacco. He softly groans and murmurs with impatience while he makes these explorations. Upon their success*) So lucky Mrs. Ransom brought down that coat. I couldn't have lived to get up-stairs after it!

Stuffing his pipe in a frenzy, he runs to the General for a match; that veteran has already lighted it, and extends it toward him. Bartlett stoops over the flame, pipe in mouth. As the General drops the extinct match upon the floor, the painter puffs a great cloud, in which involved he is putting on his studio jacket when Constance appears at the door. He instinctively snatches his pipe from his lips and puts it in his pocket.

CONSTANCE, *fighting her way through the smoke to the General's chair*: Why, papa, how you *have* been smoking!

GENERAL WYATT, *with a queer look*: Yes; I find it rests me after a bad night. I didn't sleep well.

CONSTANCE: Oh, poor papa! How do *you* do, Mr. Bartlett?

She gives him her hand for good-morning.

BARTLETT: Oh, quite well, quite well *now* thank you. I—I—had been a little off my—diet.

CONSTANCE: Oh!

BARTLETT: Yes. But I've gone back now, and I'm all right again. (*He retires to the easel, and mechanically resumes his pipe, but takes it from his mouth again, and, after an impatient glance at it, throws it out of the window.*) When you're ready, Miss Wyatt, we can begin any time. There's no hurry, though.

CONSTANCE: I'm ready now. Is everything in reach, papa?

GENERAL WYATT: Yes, my dear. I'm so perfectly comfortable that one touch more would make me miserable.

CONSTANCE: Can't I do something for you?

GENERAL WYATT: Not a thing. I'm a prodigy of content.

CONSTANCE: Not lift up this last fold of the chair, so your foot won't rest so heavily on the floor?

GENERAL WYATT: Was it resting heavily? I hadn't noticed. Yes, it was; how you see everything, my dear! Yes—

Constance stoops to put up the chair to its last extension, and Bartlett runs forward to anticipate her.

BARTLETT: Miss Wyatt, let me do that!

CONSTANCE: No, no! No one must touch papa but me. There, is that right, papa?

GENERAL WYATT: Exactly. That makes me plu-perfectly comfortable. I haven't a wish in the world, and all I ask now is to—

CONSTANCE: Get at your newspapers? Let me take off the wrappers for you.

GENERAL WYATT: Not on any account. (*He gently withdraws from her the newspaper she has taken up.*) That is truly a kindness that kills. Open my papers for me? I'd as lief you'd put on my hat for me, my dear.

BARTLETT: That's the one thing that can't be done for any man!

CONSTANCE: Why not? A woman can put on another woman's bonnet for her.

GENERAL WYATT: Ah, that's a different thing. A man doesn't wear his hat for looks.

CONSTANCE: That's true, papa,—*some* of them. (*She turns gayly from her father, and looks up at Bartlett, who has smilingly listened. She gives a start, and suppresses a cry; she passes her hand quickly over her eyes, and then staying herself a moment with one hand on the back of a chair resumes with forced calm.*) Shall we begin, now— ah—Mr.—Bartlett?

An awkward silence ensues, in which Bartlett remains frowning and the General impatiently flings open a newspaper. Then Bartlett's frown relaxes into a compassionate response to her appealing look.

BARTLETT: Yes, I'm quite ready. But it's you who are to begin, Miss Wyatt. I am to assume the safe and eligible position of art critic. I wish I had some of those fellows who write about my pictures before an easel; I'd stand their unpleasant company a while for the sake of taking the conceit out of them. Not but what my pictures *are* bad enough,—as bad as any critic says, for that matter. Well, Miss Wyatt; here is the charcoal, and yonder out-doors is the mountain.

CONSTANCE: Excuse me a moment. Papa, will our talking disturb you? (*To Bartlett*) I suppose we will have to talk a little?

BARTLETT: A little.

GENERAL WYATT, *from behind his paper*: It won't disturb me if you don't talk to me.

CONSTANCE: We'll try not. (*To Bartlett*) Well?

BARTLETT, *as Constance places herself before the canvas, and receiving the charcoal from his fingers, glances out at Ponkwasset*: May I ask why you chose such a capacious canvas?

CONSTANCE, *in meek surprise*: Why, the mountain being a large object—

BARTLETT: A large canvas was necessary. I see. There's reason in that. But were you going to do it life size?

CONSTANCE, *as before*: Why, no!

BARTLETT: What was your idea?

CONSTANCE: I don't know. I thought—I thought I would have the mountain in the background, with some clouds over it, and a few figures in the foreground, to give it a human interest.

BARTLETT: Yes, that's a good notion. Well, now begin. First get your distance—No; better strike in a horizon line first. That will keep you right. Draw the line straight across the middle of the canvas. (*Constance retires a few steps from the canvas, measures its spaces with her eye, and then with a glance at the horizon outside draws. Bart-*

lett, looking over her shoulder) Straight, straight! The line should be straight. Don't you see?

CONSTANCE, *falteringly*: I meant that for a straight line.

BARTLETT: Oh! Well! Yes! I see. However, now you've got it in, hadn't you better use it for a *curved* line? Say for that wavering outline of the hills beyond Ponkwasset?

CONSTANCE: Why, if you think so, Mr. Bartlett.

BARTLETT: And I'll just strike in the horizon line here. (*He draws rapidly, steps back a pace, approaches, and touches Constance's line at different points. Then he gives her the chalk again.*) Now, scratch in the outline of Ponkwasset. (*Constance begins to draw.*) Ah! Wait a moment, please. You're not quite getting it. Will you let me? (*Constance offers him the charcoal, which he declines with a gesture.*) No, no! *You* must do it. I meant—

CONSTANCE: What?

BARTLETT: That if you would allow me to—to —guide your hand—

CONSTANCE, *frankly*: Why, of course. Do what you like with it—

BARTLETT: Oh!

CONSTANCE: So that you teach it a little of the skill of yours. (*He gently, and after some delicate hesitations, takes her hand, as it grasps the charcoal, and slowly guides it in forming the outline of the mountain. Constance, in admiration of his cleverness*) What a delicious touch you have!

BARTLETT, *confusedly*: Yes?

CONSTANCE, *regarding the outline after he has released her hand, while Bartlett, with a gesture of rapturous fondness, looks at the fingers that have guided hers, and tenderly kisses them*: Oh, yes; I'd give anything if I had your hand!

BARTLETT: It's at your service always, Miss Wyatt.

CONSTANCE, *still regarding the picture*: Ah, but I should need your mind, too!

BARTLETT: Well?

CONSTANCE: I couldn't rob you of everything. *She begins to draw again, and then, in pretty, unconscious imitation of Bartlett, throws back her head.*

BARTLETT, *breaking forth in rapture at her movement and attitude*: Oh, divine!

CONSTANCE, *innocently beaming upon him*: Do you think so? I didn't suppose I could get it so at once. Is it really good?

BARTLETT, *recalled to himself*: Who? What? Yes, yes; it isn't bad. Not at all bad. That is—

CONSTANCE, *disappointedly*: I thought you liked it. (*Gravely*) Why did you say it was divine?

BARTLETT: Because—I—I—thought so!

CONSTANCE, *with mystification*: I'm afraid I don't understand. Shall I let this outline remain for Ponkwasset, or shall I use it for something else?

BARTLETT: Yes, let it remain for Ponkwasset; if it needs changing that can easily be done afterwards. Now block out your middle distance. So! (*He takes the charcoal from her and draws.*) Now, then, sketch in your figures.

CONSTANCE, *timidly*: How large shall I make them?

BARTLETT: Oh, as large as you like. How large did you think?

CONSTANCE: I don't know. About a foot high.

BARTLETT: Well, try them.

Constance draws, and Bartlett regards the operation with gestures and contortions of countenance expressive of mingled tenderness for Constance and extreme suffering from her performance. She turns about, and surprises him with his hands clutched in his shaggy hair.

CONSTANCE, *with dignity*: What is the matter, Mr. Bartlett?

BARTLETT, *forcing an imbecile smile*: Nothing. I was just thinking—I should—like to venture to make a remark.

CONSTANCE: You *know* I wish you to speak to me about everything.

BARTLETT: Did you mean that lady to be in the middle distance?

CONSTANCE: Yes.

BARTLETT: Well, there is a slight, a very slight, error in the perspective. She is as tall as Ponkwasset, you see, and could touch the top of it with the point of her parasol.

CONSTANCE, *dejectedly*: I see. I can never do it.

BARTLETT: Oh, yes, you can, Miss Wyatt; you mustn't lose patience with me.

CONSTANCE: It's you who won't be able to keep your patience with my stupidity.

BARTLETT: That's not the name for it. I shall think more of your failures than of anybody's successes—that *is*—I mean—if you don't let this thing be a pain instead of a pleasure to you. Remember, I hoped it would amuse you.

CONSTANCE: Oh, yes. You have been only *too* kind, in that and everything.

BARTLETT: Well, now, let us begin again. This lady is very well as a lady; you understand the figure better than perspective; but she's out of place here, a little; and a flower out of place, you

know, is a weed. Suppose we— (*he takes up the charcoal, and makes a few dashes at the canvas*) treat her as a clump of tall birch-trees,—that clump over there in the edge of the meadow; that will bring her into the foreground, and entitle her to be three inches high; we can't really allow her more, even as a clump of birches. Eh?

CONSTANCE: Oh, yes; that's better, decidedly. (*Smiling*) Being under instruction, this way makes me think of my school-days.

BARTLETT, *impressively*: I hope they were happy days.

CONSTANCE: Oh, the happiest of my life.

BARTLETT: I am *so* glad. (*Constance stares at him in surprise, but finally says nothing.*) I mean since this is like them.

CONSTANCE, *pensively*: Yes, it's pleasant to go back to that time. (*With more animation*) Papa, I wonder if you remember Madame Le May, who used to teach me French when you came home after the war?

GENERAL WYATT, *behind his newspaper*: Eh? What? What's that? Some difficulty in the drawing? You must both have patience,—patience—

CONSTANCE: Why, papa! Oh, well, I won't worry him. I suppose he's found something about cutting down the army appropriations; that always absorbs him. What shall I try next, Mr. Bartlett?

BARTLETT: You can rub in your middle distance.

CONSTANCE, *laughing*: I'll try. But I think I should be at my best beyond the vanishing point.

BARTLETT: Oh, I don't believe *that*! Perhaps it annoys you to have me looking over your shoulder while you work?

CONSTANCE: No. Oh, no.

BARTLETT: I see that it does.

CONSTANCE: It makes me a little nervous. I'm afraid of you, you know.

BARTLETT: I didn't know I was so terrible. How far off shall I go, to be agreeable?

CONSTANCE, *laughing*: Across the room.

BARTLETT: Shall you like me better at that distance?

CONSTANCE: I can't let you make a joke of our liking for you.

BARTLETT: You defend me, even in my presence. What kindness I must miss when I'm absent! Well, I will go and see what interests General Wyatt.

GENERAL WYATT: Madame Le May? Yes, certainly. Remember her perfectly. False hair, false teeth, false—

CONSTANCE: Why, what *are* you talking of, papa?

GENERAL WYATT: Mayo. Capital cavalry officer —cutting down the pay of such a man—

CONSTANCE: What *are* you reading?

The General makes no answer.

BARTLETT: Don't disturb him. I'll walk off here at this end of the room. (*He paces softly up and down, while Constance returns to her drawing, to which she diligently applies herself. A thought seems to strike Bartlett as his wandering eye falls upon General Wyatt, who still sits with his head buried in his newspaper. He approaches, and remarks in a low tone*) I believe I *will* take a cigar now, Gen—

The newspaper falls slightly, and Bartlett makes a discovery. The General has dropped off into a doze. With a gesture of amusement, Bartlett restores the paper to its place, and resumes his walk in a quiet rapture, interrupting it now and then to dwell in silent adoration on the young lady's absorption in the fine arts.

CONSTANCE: Mr. Bartlett—

BARTLETT, *halting*: Recalled from exile already? Well?

CONSTANCE: I'm afraid I can't get by this point alone.

BARTLETT: Yes? Let's see it.

He eagerly crosses the room, takes his stand behind her, and throws up his hands in despair. Constance indicates her difficulties.

CONSTANCE: The question is how to get in some idea of those slopes of the mountain. These things seem to crowd everything out.

BARTLETT, *hopelessly regarding the work*: I see. You have been composing a little,—idealizing. Well, I don't object to that. Though perhaps it had better come later. This long stretch of rocky cliff—

CONSTANCE: Rocky cliff?

BARTLETT: Isn't in nature, but it might have a good effect if properly utilized—

CONSTANCE: But it isn't rocky cliff, Mr. Bartlett. It's—

BARTLETT, *looking a second time, and more closely*: Why, of course! It's that stretch of broken woodland at the foot of the mountain. Very good; very good indeed; very boldly treated. Still, I should say—

CONSTANCE, *in desperation*: Oh, Mr. Bartlett, it *isn't* rocks, and it isn't *woods*; it's—hay-stacks!

BARTLETT: Hay-stacks?

CONSTANCE, *desolately*: Yes, hay-stacks.

BARTLETT: But hay-stacks at the foot of the mountain, Miss Wyatt—

CONSTANCE, *inconsolably*: They're *not* at the foot of the mountain. They're those hay-stacks just out there in the meadow. I thought it would be nice to have them in near that clump of birches you drew.

BARTLETT: Oh-h-h-h! (*He scratches his head in visible stupefaction. Then with reanimation*) I see. It was my error. *I* was looking for middle distance, and *you* had been working on the foreground. Very good; very— Oh, gracious powers— No, no! Don't be discouraged, Miss Wyatt; remember it's the first time you've attempted anything of the sort, and you've really done very well. Here! (*He seizes the pencil and draws.*) We will just sink these hay-stacks,—which are very good in their way, but not perhaps sufficiently subordinated,—just sink them into the lake yonder. They will serve very well for the reflections of those hills beyond, and now you can work away at some of the details of the foreground; they will interest you more. (*He retires a pace.*) It's really not a bad start, as it is.

CONSTANCE, *ruefully*: But it's all yours, Mr. Bartlett.

BARTLETT: Eh?

CONSTANCE: You drew every line in it.

BARTLETT: No, you drew the line of the distant hills.

CONSTANCE: But I didn't mean it for that!

BARTLETT: Well, well; but the lady's figure, that was good—

CONSTANCE: You turned her into a clump of birches.

BARTLETT: True. A mere exigency of the perspective. The hay-stacks—

CONSTANCE: You've just sunk them into the lake!

BARTLETT: Well, well. Perhaps I may have helped in the execution of the picture, a little. But my dear Miss Wyatt, the *drawing* is nothing; it's the *design* is what makes the picture, and that's *entirely* yours; the ideas were all *yours*. Come! Try your hand now at the shore line of the lake, just here.

CONSTANCE: I'm afraid I'm a little tired. My hands are cold.

BARTLETT: Oh, I'm sorry! (*He takes one of them and places it between either of his.*) That shows you've been working too hard. I can't allow that. All the art in the world isn't worth—I mustn't forget that you have not been well; and I want these little lessons to be a pastime and not a burden to you. The picture's sufficiently advanced now— *(he mechanically puts her hand under his left arm, and keeps his own right hand upon it, while he takes his station with her in front of the easel)* to warrant us in trying a little color to-morrow. You'll be very much more interested in color. It *is* refreshing to get at the brushes after you've tired yourself out with the black and white. You've got a very pretty outfit, there, Miss Wyatt.

He indicates her colors on the little table.

CONSTANCE: I didn't mean to refuse the offer of your paints, but I thought it would be better to have the colors *perfectly fresh*, you know.

BARTLETT: Quite right. Quite right. Now you see— Rest on *me*, Miss Wyatt, or I shall be afraid of fatiguing you by standing; and I'd like to point out a few things for you to begin on here to-morrow.

CONSTANCE: Oh, I'm not *very* tired. But I *will* keep your arm, if you will let me.

BARTLETT, *making her sustain her weight more distinctly on his arm*: By all means. Now, here, at this point, I think I'd better sketch you in that old oak down there at the foot of our hill, with its grape-vine, and you can work away at these without reference to Ponkwasset. The line of that clinging vine is one of the most graceful things that Nature—and Nature *does* know a thing or two, Miss Wyatt; she's particularly good at clinging vines—ever drew. *(He looks at her over his shoulder with an involuntary sigh. Then)* Suppose— *(he takes up the charcoal)* I do it now. No, don't disturb yourself. *(They lean forward, and as he sketches, their faces, drawn together, almost touch. Bartlett drops the pencil, and starts away, releasing his arm.)* Oh, no, no!

CONSTANCE, *simply*: Can't you do it?

BARTLETT, *in deep emotion*: No, no; I can't do it—I mustn't—it would be outrageous—I—I— *(Regaining his self-possession at sight of Constance's astonished face)* You said yourself just now that I had drawn everything in the picture. I can't do any more. *You* must do the clinging vine!

CONSTANCE, *innocently*: Very well, I'll try. If you'll do the oak for me. I'll let you do *that* much more.

They regard each other, she with her innocent smile, he with a wild rapture of hope, doubt, and fear. Then Bartlett draws a long, despairing sigh, and turns away.

BARTLETT: To-morrow, to-morrow! *(He walks away, and returns to her.)* Have you read—have you ever read The Talking Oak, Miss Wyatt?

CONSTANCE: Tennyson's? A thousand times. Isn't it charming?

BARTLETT: It's absurd, I think. Do you remember where he makes the oak say of the young lady,—

> "And in a fit of frolic mirth,
>   She strove to span my waist, ...
> I wished myself the fair young beech
>   That here beside me stands,
> That round me, clasping each in each,
>   She might have locked her hands"? [1]

CONSTANCE: Why, that's lovely,—that attribution of human feeling to the tree. Don't you think so?

BARTLETT, *absently*: Yes, yes; beautiful. But it's terrible, too; terrible. Supposing the oak really had human feeling; or supposing that a man had been meant in the figure of an oak— *(He has drawn near Constance again; but now he retreats.)* Ah, I can't work out the idea.

CONSTANCE: What idea? I can't imagine what you mean.

BARTLETT: Ah! I can. My trouble is, I can't *say* what I mean! This was sometime a paradox.

CONSTANCE: Oh! I should think, a riddle.

BARTLETT: Some day I hope you'll let me read it to you.

CONSTANCE: Why not now?

BARTLETT, *impetuously*: If you only meant what you said, it would be—so much better than if I said what I meant!

CONSTANCE: You are dealing in mysteries to-day.

BARTLETT: Oh, the greatest of them! But don't mind. Wait! I'll try to tell you what I mean. I won't make you stand, while I talk. Here! *(He wheels up in front of the picture one of the hair-cloth sofas; Constance mechanically sinks down upon it, and he takes his place at her side; she bends upon him a look of smiling amusement.)* I can put my meaning best, I think, in the form of allegory. Do you like allegory, Miss Wyatt?

CONSTANCE: Yes. That is, not very much.

BARTLETT: Oh! You don't like allegory! Upon second thoughts, I don't myself. We will not try allegory. We will try a supposed case. I think that's always the best way, don't you?

---

[1] Tennyson, "The Talking Oak," lines 1 and 2 of stanza 35, complete stanza 36.

CONSTANCE: No, I don't like any sort of indirection. I believe the straightforward way is the best.

BARTLETT: Yes, so do I; but it's impossible. We *must* try a supposed case.

CONSTANCE, *laughing*: Well!

BARTLETT: Ah! I can't say anything if you laugh. It's a serious matter.

CONSTANCE, *with another burst of laughter*: I should never have thought so. (*With a sudden return of her old morbid mood*) I beg your pardon for laughing. What right have I to laugh? Go on, Mr. Bartlett, and I will listen as I should have done. I am ashamed.

BARTLETT: No, no! That won't do! You mustn't take me so seriously as that! Oh, Miss Wyatt, if I could only be so much your friend, your fool,— I don't care what,—as to banish that look, that tone from you forever!

CONSTANCE: Why do you care?

BARTLETT: Why do I care?

CONSTANCE: Yes. Why should you mind whether so weak and silly a thing as I is glad or sad? I can't understand. Why have you had so much patience with me? Why do you take all this trouble on my account, and waste your time on me? Why—

BARTLETT, *starting up*: *Why* do I do it? (*He walks away to the other side of the room with signs of great inward struggle; then he swiftly returns to her side where she has risen and stands near the sofa, and seizes her hand.*) Well, I will tell you why. No, no! I can't! It would be—

GENERAL WYATT, *behind his newspaper*: Outrageous! Gross violation of good faith! Infernal shame!

The General concludes these observations with a loud, prolonged, and very stertorous respiration.

CONSTANCE, *running to him*: Why papa, what *do* you mean? Oh poor papa! He's asleep, and in *such* a wretched position! (*From which she hastens to move him, while Bartlett, recovering from the amaze in which the appositeness of the General's remarks had plunged him, breaks into a harsh "Ha! ha!" Constance turns and advances upon him in threatening majesty.*) Did you *laugh*, Mr. Bartlett?

BARTLETT, *after a moment's dismay*: Well, I don't know whether you call it laughing. I smiled.

CONSTANCE, *with increasing awfulness*: *Why* did you laugh, Mr. Bartlett?

BARTLETT: I—I—I can't say.

CONSTANCE: You were laughing at General Wyatt!

BARTLETT: Was there nothing to laugh at?

CONSTANCE: For children! For vulgar, silly boys! For a gentleman, nothing!

BARTLETT, *with rising wrath*: Then I have no excuse, unless I say that I am no gentleman.

CONSTANCE: *I* shall not dispute you in anything; and I will leave you to the enjoyment of your mirth.

BARTLETT: Very well. As you like. I am sorry to have offended you. I shall take care never to offend you again.

Constance sweeps towards one door, at the threshold of which she pauses to look round and see Bartlett dashing her box of colors together as if it were his own, and thrusting it under his arm, seizing with a furious hand the canvas on the easel and his coat from the chairback, and then rushing from the room. She drops her face into her hands and vanishes, and the next moment Mrs. Wyatt enters.

MRS. WYATT: What is the matter with Constance, James? Have you been— (*She goes up to the General and discovers his vigilance.*) Asleep! (*Waking him*) James, James! Is *this* the way you do the dragon, as you call it?

GENERAL WYATT, *starting awake*: Dragon? Dragon? What dragon? I dreamt I was a perfect fiery dragon, and went about breathing flame and smoke. How long have I slept, Margaret? Where is Mr. Bartlett? Where is Constance?

MRS. WYATT: Oh, you may well ask that, James. I just met Constance at the door, in tears. Oh, I hope nothing dreadful has happened.

GENERAL WYATT: Nonsense, Margaret. Here, help me up, my dear. My nap hasn't done me any good. I'm stiff all over.

MRS. WYATT, *anxiously*: I'm afraid you have taken cold, James.

GENERAL WYATT, *with impatience*: Cold? No! Not in the least. I'm perfectly well. But that was a very unpleasant dream. Margaret, I'm afraid that I breathed rather—explosively, at one time.

MRS. WYATT: Oh, James, this is worse and worse. It must have mortified Constance, dreadfully.

GENERAL WYATT, *taking his wife's arm, and limping from the scene*: Well, well! Never mind! I'll make it right with Bartlett. He's a man of sense, and will help me laugh it off with her. It will be all right, Margaret; don't worry over a trifle like that.

MRS. WYATT, *as they disappear*: Trifle? Her whole happiness may depend upon it.

At the instant of their withdrawal, Constance and Bartlett, hastily entering by opposite doors, encounter each other in the middle of the room.

BOTH, *at once*: I came to—

BARTLETT: Restore you your box of colors and your canvas, which I carried off by mistake.

CONSTANCE: To say that I am very, very sorry for my rudeness to you, and to entreat you to forget my abominable words, if you can.

BARTLETT, *with a generous rush of emotion, dropping the canvas on the floor at one side and the box of colors on the other, and snatching her extended hand to his lips*: Don't say that. I deserved a thousand times more. You were right.

CONSTANCE: No, no! I can't let you blame yourself to save me from self-reproach. I know papa was ridiculous. But what made me angry was this thought that you were laughing at *him*. I couldn't bear that. I shouldn't have minded your laughing at me; but at papa!

BARTLETT, *sadly*: I happened to be laughing much more at myself than your father. Where is the General?

CONSTANCE: He has gone with mamma. They wondered where you were, and I said you were coming back again.

BARTLETT: How did you know?

CONSTANCE: I thought you would come,—that you would upbraid yourself for my bad behavior, and return to excuse it to me. You see what perfect faith I—we—have in you.

BARTLETT, *earnestly*: Have you indeed perfect faith in me?

CONSTANCE: Perfect!

BARTLETT, *vehemently*: But why, *why* do you trust me? You see that I am hasty and rude.

CONSTANCE: Oh, no, not rude.

BARTLETT: But I assure you that I am so; and you have seen that I laughed—that I am wanting in delicacy, and—

CONSTANCE, *devoutly*: How can you say that to *us*, when every day, every hour, every instant of the last month has given us proof of unimaginable kindness in you! (*He eagerly approaches and takes her hands, which she frankly yields him.*) Your patience, your noble forbearance, which we so sorely tried, has made us all forget that you are a stranger, and—and—to me it's as if we had always known you—(*her head droops*) as if you were a—an old friend, a—brother—

BARTLETT, *dropping her hands*: Oh!

He turns away, and pacing the length of the room reapproaches her hastily.

CONSTANCE, *with a little cry*: Mr. Bartlett! Do look! Did you intend to trample my canvas and colors under foot?

She makes as if to stoop for them.

BARTLETT, *his manner undergoing a total change as if he had been suddenly recalled to himself at a critical moment*: Don't! (*He hastily picks them up, and puts the canvas on the easel and the colors on the table. With a glance at the canvas*) Ponkwasset doesn't seem to have been seriously injured by his violent usage. Shall you like to try your hand at him again to-morrow?

CONSTANCE: Oh, yes. But on one condition.

BARTLETT: Yes.

CONSTANCE: That you have a little faith in *me*, too.

BARTLETT: Oh, Miss Wyatt—

CONSTANCE: I used to have a bad temper, and now that I'm getting better it seems to be getting worse. Try to believe in me enough to know that when I do or say some violent thing, I'm ashamed of it; and that when I wounded you, I really meant to hurt myself; that I— Oh, you know, Mr. Bartlett, how much you've borne from us, and how much we owe you; and if you did anything now to make us think less of your unselfish goodness, we never could forgive you! (*Bartlett remains with bowed head.*) I must go, now. (*Gayly*) Perhaps to-morrow, when we resume our lessons, you'll tell me what you meant to-day, when you couldn't explain yourself.

BARTLETT, *vehemently*: No, I can never tell you.

CONSTANCE: I can't believe that! At any rate, we shall talk the matter over, and I may say something to help you. You know how one thing leads to another.

BARTLETT: But nothing you can ever say now will lead to what I wanted to say.

CONSTANCE, *laughing*: Don't be sure. If you rouse my curiosity, I shall be a powerful aid to expression. With a woman's wit to help you out with your meaning, how can you help making it clear?

BARTLETT: Because—because it wants something more than wit in you to make it clear.

CONSTANCE: Well, you shall have sympathy, if sympathy is what you need. Is it something like sympathy?

BARTLETT: Something like sympathy; but—not—not exactly sympathy.

CONSTANCE, *with another laugh*: How difficult you make it! I see! You want compassion.

BARTLETT, *quickly*: Oh, no! I would sooner have contempt!

CONSTANCE: But that's the one thing you can't have. Try to think of something else you want, and let me know to-morrow.

She nods brightly to him, and he follows her going with a gaze of hopeless longing. As she vanishes through the door-way, he lifts his hand to his lips, and reverently kisses it to her.

BARTLETT, *alone*: Try to *think* what I want and let you know! Ah, my darling, my darling! Your faith in me kills my hope. If you only dared a little less with me how much more I might dare with you; and if you were not so sisterly sweet how much sweeter you might be! Brother? Forty thousand brothers could not with all their quantity of love make up my sum! You drive me farther than your worst enemy from you with that fatal word. Brother? I hate brother! If it had been cousin— And kind? Oh, I would we were "A little less than kin, and more than kind!" [1]

IV.
NOT AT ALL LIKE

BARTLETT: Six weeks since you were here? I shouldn't have thought that. (*Bartlett's easel stands before the window, in the hotel parlor; he has laid a tint upon the canvas, and has retired a few paces for the effect, his palette and mahl-stick in hand, and his head carried at a critical angle. Cummings, who has been doing the duty of art-culture by the picture, regards it with renewed interest. Bartlett resumes his work.*) Pretty good, Cummings?

CUMMINGS: Capital! The blue of that distance—

BARTLETT, *with a burlesque sigh*: Ah, I looked into my heart and painted for *that*! Well, you find me still here, Cummings, and apparently more at home than ever. The landlord has devoted this parlor to the cause of art,—makes the transients use the lower parlor, now,—and we have this all to ourselves: Miss Wyatt sketches, you know. Her mother brings her sewing, and the General his bruises; he hasn't quite scrambled up, yet, from that little knock-down of his; a man doesn't, at his time of life, I believe; and we make this our family-room; and a very queer family we

1 See *Hamlet*, I, 2:65.

are! Fine old fellow, the General; he's behaved himself since his accident like a disabled angel, and hasn't sworn,—well, anything worth speaking of. Yes, here I am. I suppose it's all right, but for all I know it may be all wrong. (*Bartlett sighs in unguarded sincerity.*) I don't know what I'm here for. Nature began shutting up shop a fortnight ago at a pretty lively rate, and edging loafers to the door, with every sign of impatience; and yet, here I am, hanging round still. I suppose this glimpse of Indian Summer is some excuse just now; it's a perfect blessing to the landlord, and he's making hay—rowen crop—while the sun shines; I've been with him so long now, I take quite an interest in his prosperity, if eight dollars a week of it *do* come out of me! What is talked of in "art-circles" down in Boston, brother Cummings?

CUMMINGS: Your picture.

BARTLETT, *inattentively, while he comes up to his canvas, and bestows an infinitesimal portion of paint upon a destitute spot in the canvas*: Don't be sarcastic, Cummings.

CUMMINGS: I'm not, I assure you.

BARTLETT, *turning toward him incredulously*: Do you mean to say that The First Gray Hair is liked?

CUMMINGS: I do. There hasn't been any picture so much talked of this season.

BARTLETT: Then it's the shameless slop of the name. I should think you'd blush for your part in that swindle. But clergymen have *no* conscience, where they've a chance to do a fellow a kindness, I've observed. (*He goes up to Cummings with his brush in his mouth, his palette on one hand, and his mahl-stick in the other, and contrives to lay hold of his shoulders with a few disengaged fingers. As Cummings shrinks a little from his embrace*) Oh, don't be afraid; I shan't get any paint on you. You need a whole coat of whitewash, though, you unscrupulous saint! (*He returns to his easel.*) So The Old Girl—that's what I shall call the picture—is a success, is she? The admiring public ought to see the original elm-tree now; she hasn't got a hair, gray or green, on her head; she's perfectly bald. I say, Cummings, how would it do for me to paint a pendant, *The Last Gray Hair*? I might look up a leaf or two on the elm, somewhere: stick it on to the point of twig; they wouldn't know any better.

CUMMINGS: The leafless elm would make a good picture, whatever you called it. (*Bartlett throws back his shaggy head and laughs up at the ceiling.*) The fact is, Bartlett, I've got a little surprise for you.

BARTLETT, *looking at him askance*: Somebody wanting to chromo The Old Girl? No, no; it isn't quite so bad as that!

CUMMINGS, *in a burst*: They *did* want to chromo it. But it's sold. They've got you two hundred dollars for it.

Bartlett lays down his brush, palette, and mahl-stick, dusts his fingers, puts them in his pockets, and comes and stands before Cummings, on whom, seated, he bends a curious look.

BARTLETT: And do you mean to tell me, you hardened atheist, that you don't believe in the doctrine of future punishments? What are they going to do with *you* in the next world? And that picture dealer? And *me*? Two hund— It's an outrage! It's— The picture wasn't worth fifty, by a stretch of the most charitable imagination! Two hundred d— Why, Cummings, I'll paint no end of Old Girls, First and Last Gray Hairs— I'll flood the market! Two— Good Lord! (*Bartlett goes back to his easel, and silently resumes his work. After a while*) Who's been offered up?

CUMMINGS: What?

BARTLETT: Who's the victim? My patron? The noble and discriminating and munificent purchaser of The Old Girl?

CUMMINGS: Oh! Mrs. Bellingham. She's going to send it out to her daughter in Omaha.[1]

BARTLETT: Ah! Mrs. Blake wishes to found an art-museum with that curiosity out there? Sorry for the Omaha-has. (*Cummings makes a gesture of impatience.*) Well, well; I won't then, old fellow! I'm truly obliged to you. I accept my good fortune with compunction, but with all the gratitude imaginable. I say, Cummings!

CUMMINGS: Well?

BARTLETT: What do you think of my taking to high art,—mountains twelve hundred feet above the sea, like this portrait of Ponkwasset?

CUMMINGS: I've always told you that you had only to give yourself scope,—attempt something worthy of your powers—

BARTLETT: Ah, I thought so. Then you believe that a good big canvas and a good big subject would be the making of me? Well, I've come round to that idea myself. I used to think that if there was any greatness in me, I could get it into a small picture, like Meissonier or Corot.

But I can't. I must have room, like the Yellowstone and Yo-Semite fellows. Don't you think Miss Wyatt is looking wonderfully improved?

CUMMINGS: Wonderfully! And how beautiful she is! She looked lovely that first day, in spite of her ghostliness; but now—

BARTLETT: Yes; a *phantom* of delight is good enough in its way, but a *well woman* is the prettiest, after all. Miss Wyatt sketches, I think I told you.

CUMMINGS: Yes, you mentioned it.

BARTLETT: Of course. Otherwise, I couldn't possibly have thought of her while I was at work on a great picture like this. She sketches — (*Bartlett puts his nose almost on the canvas in the process of bestowing a delicate touch*) she sketches about as badly as any woman I ever saw, and *that's* saying a good deal. But she looks uncommonly well while she's at it. The fact is, Cummings,— (*Bartlett retires some feet from the canvas and squints at it*) this very picture which you approve of so highly is—Miss Wyatt's. I couldn't attempt anything of the size of Ponkwasset! But she allows me to paint at it a little when she's away. (*Bartlett steals a look of joy at his friend's vexation, and then continues seriously.*) I've been having a curious time, Cummings. (*The other remains silent.*) Don't you want to ask me about it?

CUMMINGS: I don't know that I do.

BARTLETT: Why, my dear old fellow, you're hurt! It *was* a silly joke, and I honestly ask your pardon. (*He lays down his brush and palette, and leaves the easel.*) Cummings, I don't know what to do. I'm in a perfect deuce of a state. I'm hit —awfully hard; and I don't know what to do about it. I wish I had gone at once—the first day. But I had to stay,—I had to stay.

He turns and walks away from Cummings, whose eyes follow him in pardon and sympathy.

CUMMINGS: Do you really mean it, Bartlett? I didn't dream of such a thing. I thought you were still brooding over that affair with Miss Harlan.

BARTLETT: Oh, child's play! A prehistoric illusion! A solar myth! The thing never was. (*He rejects the obsolete superstition with a wave of his left hand.*) I'm in love with this girl, and I feel like a sneak and a brute about it. At the very best it would be preposterous. Who am I, a poor devil of a painter, the particular pet of Poverty, to think of a young lady whose family and position could command her the best? But putting that aside,— putting that insuperable obstacle lightly aside, as

---

[1] This is a reference to *Out of The Question.*

a mere trifle,—the thing remains an atrocity. It's enormously indelicate to think of loving a woman who would never have looked twice at me if I hadn't resembled an infernal scoundrel who tried to break her heart; and I've nothing else to commend me. I've the perfect certainty that she doesn't and can't care anything for me in myself; and it grinds me into the dust to realize on what terms she tolerates me. I could carry it off as a joke, at first; but when it became serious, I had to look it in the face; and that's what it amounts to, and if you know of any more hopeless and humiliating tangle, *I* don't.

Bartlett, who has approached his friend during this speech, walks away again; and there is an interval of silence.

CUMMINGS, *at last, musingly*: *You* in love with Miss Wyatt? I can't imagine it!

BARTLETT, *fiercely*: You can't imagine it? What's the reason you can't imagine it? Don't be offensive, Cummings! (*He stops in his walk and lowers upon his friend.*) Why shouldn't I be in love with Miss Wyatt?

CUMMINGS: Oh, nothing. Only you were saying—

BARTLETT: I was saying! Don't tell me what *I* was saying. Say something yourself.

CUMMINGS: Really, Bartlett, you can't expect me to stand this sort of thing. You're preposterous.

BARTLETT: I know it! But don't blame me. I beg your pardon. Is it because of the circumstances that you can't imagine my being in love with her?

CUMMINGS: Oh, no; I wasn't thinking of the circumstances; but it seemed so out of character for you—

BARTLETT, *impatiently*: Oh, love's always out of character, just as it's always out of reason. I admit freely that I'm an ass. And then?

CUMMINGS: Well, then, I don't believe you have any more reason to be in despair than you have to be in love. If she tolerates you, as you say, it *can't* be because you look like the man who jilted her.

BARTLETT: Ah! But if she still loves *him?*

CUMMINGS: You don't know that. That strikes me as a craze of jealousy. What makes you think she tolerates you for that reason or no-reason?

BARTLETT: What makes me think it? From the very first she interpreted *me* by what she knew of *him*. She expected me to be this and not to be that; to have one habit and not another; and I could see that every time the fact was different, it was a miserable disappointment to her, a sort of shock. Every little difference between me and that other rascal gave her a start; and whenever I looked up I found her wistful eyes on me as if they were trying to puzzle me out; they used to follow me round the room like the eyes of a family portrait. You wouldn't have liked it yourself, Cummings. For the first three weeks I simply existed on false pretenses,—involuntary false pretenses, at that. I wanted to explode; I wanted to roar out, "If you think I'm at all like that abandoned scoundrel of yours in anything but looks, I'm *not!*" But I was bound by everything that was decent, to hold my tongue, and let my soul be rasped out of me in silence and apparent unconsciousness. That was *your* fault. If you hadn't told me all about the thing I could have done something outrageous and stopped it. But I was tied hand and foot by what I knew. I had to let it go on.

CUMMINGS: I'm very sorry, Bartlett, but—

BARTLETT: Oh, I dare say you wouldn't have done it if you hadn't had a wild ass of the desert to deal with. Well, the old people got used to some little individuality in me, by and by, and beyond a suppressed whoop or two from the mother when I came suddenly into the room, they didn't do anything to annoy me directly. But they were anxious every minute for the effect on *her;* and it worried me as much to have *them* watching *her* as to have *her* watching *me*. Of course I knew that she talked this confounded resemblance over with her mother every time I left them, and avoided talking it over with the father.

CUMMINGS: But you say the trouble's over now.

BARTLETT: Oh—*over!* No, it isn't over. When she's with me a while she comes to see that I am not a mere *doppelgänger*. She respites me to that extent. But I have still some small rags of self-esteem dangling about me; and now suppose I should presume to set up for somebody on my own account; the first hint of my caring for her as I do, if she could conceive of anything so atrocious, would tear open all the old sorrows. Ah! I can't think of it. Besides, I tell you, it isn't all over. It's only not so bad as it was. She's subject to relapses, when it's much worse than ever. Why—

Bartlett stands facing his friend, with a half-whimsical, half-desperate smile, as if about to illustrate his point, when Constance and her mother enter the parlor.

CONSTANCE, *with a quick, violent arrest*: Ah! Oh!

MRS. WYATT: Constance, Constance, darling! What's the matter?

CONSTANCE: Oh, nothing—nothing. (*She laughs, nervously.*) I thought there was nobody —here; and it—startled me. How do you do, Mr. Cummings? She goes quickly up to that gentleman, and gives him her hand. Don't you think it wonderful to find such a day as this, up here, at this time of year?

She struggles to control the panting breath in which she speaks.

CUMMINGS: Yes, I supposed I had come quite too late for anything of the sort. You must make haste with your Ponkwasset, Miss Wyatt, or you'll have to paint him with his winter cap on.

CONSTANCE: Ah, yes! My picture. Mr. Bartlett has been telling you. (*Her eyes have already wandered away from Cummings, and they now dwell, with a furtive light of reparation and imploring upon Bartlett's disheartened patience.*) Good morning.

It is a delicately tentative salutation, in a low voice, still fluttered by her nervous agitation.

BARTLETT, *in dull despair*: Good morning.

CONSTANCE: How is the light on the mountain this morning?

She drifts deprecatingly up to the picture, near which Bartlett has stolidly kept his place.

BARTLETT, *in apathetic inattention*: Oh, very well, very well, indeed, thank you.

CONSTANCE, *after a hesitating glance at him*: Did you like what I had done on it yesterday?

BARTLETT, *very much as before*: Oh, yes; why not?

CONSTANCE, *with meek subtlety*: I was afraid I had vexed you—by it. (*She bends an appealing glance upon him, to which Bartlett remains impervious, and she drops her eyes with a faint sigh. Then she lifts them again.*) I was afraid I had— made the distance too blue.

BARTLETT: Oh, no; not at all.

CONSTANCE: Do you think I had better try to finish it?

BARTLETT: Oh, certainly. Why not? If it amuses you!

CONSTANCE, *perplexedly*: Of course. (*Then with a sad significance*) But I know I am trying your patience too far. You have been so kind, so good, I can't forgive myself for annoying you.

BARTLETT: It doesn't annoy me. I'm very glad to be useful to you.

CONSTANCE, *demurely*: I didn't mean painting;

I meant—screaming. (*She lifts her eyes to Bartlett's face, with a pathetic, inquiring attempt at lightness, the slightest imaginable experimental archness in her self-reproach, which dies out as Bartlett frowns and bites the corner of his mustache in unresponsive silence.*) I ought to be well enough now to stop it; I'm quite well enough to be ashamed of it.

She breaks off a miserable little laugh.

BARTLETT, *with cold indifference*: There's no reason why you should stop it—if it amuses you. (*She looks at him in surprise at this rudeness.*) Do you wish to try your hand at Ponkwasset this morning?

CONSTANCE, *with a flash of resentment*: No; thanks. (*Then with a lapse into her morbid self-abasement*) I shall not touch it again. Mamma!

MRS. WYATT: Yes, Constance.

Mrs. Wyatt and Cummings, both intent on Bartlett and Constance, have been heroically feigning a polite interest in each other, from which pretense they now eagerly release themselves.

CONSTANCE: Oh—nothing. I can get it of Mary. I won't trouble you.

She goes toward the door.

MRS. WYATT: Mary isn't up from her breakfast, yet. If you want anything, let me go with you, dear. (*She turns to follow Constance.*) Good morning, Mr. Cummings; we shall see you at dinner. Good morning—

With an inquiring glance at Bartlett. Constance slightly inclines towards the two gentlemen without looking at them, in going out with her mother; and Cummings moves away to the piano, and affects to examine the sheet-music scattered over it. Bartlett remains in his place near the easel.

BARTLETT, *harshly, after a certain silence which his friend is apparently resolved not to break*: Sail in, Cummings!

CUMMINGS: Oh, I've got nothing to say.

BARTLETT: Yes, you have. You think I'm a greater fool and a greater brute than you ever supposed in your most sanguine moments. Well, I am! What then?

CUMMINGS, *turning about from the music at which he has been pretending to look, and facing Bartlett, with a slight shrug*: If you choose to characterize your own behavior in that way, I shall not dispute you at any rate.

BARTLETT: Go on!

CUMMINGS: Go on? You saw yourself, I suppose,

how she hung upon every syllable you spoke, every look, every gesture?

BARTLETT: Yes, I saw it.

CUMMINGS: You saw how completely crushed she was by your tone and manner. You're not blind. Upon my word, Bartlett, if I didn't know what a good, kind-hearted fellow you are, I should say you were the greatest ruffian alive.

BARTLETT, *with a groan*: Go on! That's something like.

CUMMINGS: I couldn't hear what was going on—I'll own I tried—but I could see; and to see the delicate *amende* she was trying to offer you, in such a way that it should not seem an *amende*,—a perfect study of a woman's gracious, unconscious art,—and then to see your sour refusal of it all, it made me sick.

BARTLETT, *with a desperate clutch at his face, like a man oppressed with some stifling vapor*: Yes, yes! I saw it all, too! And if it had been for *me*, I would have given anything for such happiness. Oh, gracious powers! How dear she is! I would rather have suffered any anguish than give her pain, and yet I gave her pain! I knew how it entered her heart: I felt it in my own. But what could I do? If I am to be myself, if I am not to steal the tenderness meant for another man, the *love* she shows to me because I'm like somebody else, I *must* play the brute. But have a little mercy on me. At least, I'm a *baited* brute. I don't know which way to turn, I don't know what to do. She's so dear to me,—so dear in every tone of her voice, every look of her eyes, every aspiration or desire of her transparent soul, that it seems to me my whole being is nothing but a thought of her. I loved her helplessness, her pallor, her sorrow; judge how I adore her return to something like life! Oh, you blame me! You simplify this infernal perplexity of mine and label it brutality, and scold me for it. Great heaven! And yet you saw, you heard how she entered this room. In that instant the old illusion was back on her, and *I* was nothing. All that I had been striving and longing to be to her, and hoping and despairing to seem, was swept out of existence; I was reduced to a body without a soul, to a shadow, a counterfeit! You think I resented it? Poor girl, I *pitied* her so; and my own heart all the time like lead in my breast,—a dull lump of ache! I swear, I wonder I don't go mad. I suppose—why, I suppose I *am* insane. No man in his senses was ever bedeviled by such a maniacal hallucination. Look here, Cummings: tell me that this damnable

coil isn't simply a matter of my own fancy. It'll be some little relief to know that it's *real*.

CUMMINGS: It's real enough, my dear fellow. And it *is* a trial,—more than I could have believed such a fantastic thing could be.

BARTLETT: Trial? Ordeal by fire! Torment! I can't stand it any longer.

CUMMINGS, *musingly*: She *is* beautiful, isn't she, with that faint dawn of red in her cheeks,—not a color, but a colored light like the light that hangs round a rose-tree's boughs in the early spring! And what a magnificent movement, what a stately grace! The girl must have been a goddess!

BARTLETT: And now she's a saint—for sweetness and patience! You think she's had nothing to suffer before from me? You know me better. Well, I'm going away.

CUMMINGS: Perhaps it will be the best. You can go back with me to-morrow.

BARTLETT: To-morrow? Go back with you to-morrow? What are you talking about, man? (*Cummings smiles.*) I can't go to-morrow. I can't leave her hating me.

CUMMINGS: I knew you never meant to go. Well, what will you do?

BARTLETT: Don't be so cold-blooded! What would *you* do?

CUMMINGS: I would have it out, somehow.

BARTLETT: Oh, you talk! How?

CUMMINGS: I am not in love with Miss Wyatt.

BARTLETT: Oh, don't try to play the cynic with me! It doesn't become you. I know I've used you badly at times, Cummings. I behaved abominably in leaving you to take the brunt of meeting General Wyatt that first day; I said so then, and I shall always say it. But I thought you had forgiven that.

CUMMINGS, *with a laugh*: You make it hard to treat you seriously, Bartlett. What do you want me to do? Do you want me to go to Miss Wyatt and explain your case to her?

BARTLETT, *angrily*: No!

CUMMINGS: Perhaps to Mrs. Wyatt?

BARTLETT, *infuriate*: No!

CUMMINGS: To the General?

BARTLETT, *with sudden quiet*: You had better go away from here, Cummings—while you can.

CUMMINGS: I see you don't wish me to do anything, and you're quite right. Nobody *can* do anything but yourself.

BARTLETT: And what would you advise me to do?

CUMMINGS: I've told you that I would have it

out. You can't make matters worse. You can't go on in this way indefinitely. It's just possible that you might find yourself mistaken,—that Miss Wyatt cares for you in your own proper identity.

BARTLETT: For shame!

CUMMINGS: Oh, if you like!

BARTLETT, *after a pause*: Would you—would you see the General?

CUMMINGS: If I wanted to marry the General. Come, Bartlett; don't be ridiculous. You know you don't want my advice, and I haven't any to give. I must go to my room a moment.

BARTLETT: Well, go! You're of no advantage here. You'd have it out, would you? Well, then, I wouldn't. I'm a brute, I know, and a fool, but I'm not such a brute and fool as that!

Cummings listens with smiling patience, and then goes without reply, while Bartlett drops into the chair near the easel, and sulkily glares at the picture. Through the window at his back shows the mellow Indian summer landscape. The trees have all dropped their leaves, save the oaks which show their dark crimson banners among the deep green of the pines and hemlocks on the hills; the meadows, verdant as in June, slope away toward the fringe of birches and young maples along the borders of the pond; the low-blackberry trails like a running fire over the long grass limp from the first frosts, which have silenced all the insect voices. No sound of sylvan life is heard but the harsh challenge of a jay, answered from many trees of the nearest wood-lot. The far-off hill-tops are molten in the soft azure haze of the season; the near slopes and crests sleep under a grayer and thinner veil. It is to this scene that the painter turns from the easel, with the sullen unconsciousness in which he has dwelt upon the picture. Its beauty seems at last to penetrate his mood; he rises and looks upon it; then he goes out on the gallery, and, hidden by the fall of one of the curtains, stands leaning upon the rail and rapt in the common revery of the dreaming world. While he lingers there, Cummings appears at the door, and looks in; then with an air of some surprise, as if wondering not to see Bartlett, vanishes again, to give place to General Wyatt, who after a like research retires silently and apparently disconcerted. A few moments later Mrs. Wyatt comes to the threshold, and calling gently into the room, Constance! waits briefly and goes away. At last, the young girl herself appears, and falters in the doorway an instant, but finally comes forward and drifts softly and indirectly up to the picture, at which she glances with a little sigh. At the same moment Bartlett's voice, trolling a snatch of song, comes from the gallery without:—

ROMANCE

I

Here apart our paths, then, lie:
This way you wend, that way I;
Speak one word before you go:
Do not, do not leave me so!

II

What is it that I should say?
Tell me quick; I cannot stay;
Quick! I am not good at guessing:
Night is near, and time is pressing.

III

Nay, then, go! But were I you,
I will tell you what I'd do:
Rather than be baffled so,
I would never, never go!

As the song ends, Bartlett reappears at the gallery door giving into the parlor, and encounters Constance turning at his tread from the picture on which she has been pensively gazing while he sang. He puts up a hand on either side of the door.

BARTLETT: I didn't know you were here.

CONSTANCE: Neither did I—know you were, till I heard you singing.

BARTLETT, *smiling ironically*: Oh, you didn't suppose I sang!

CONSTANCE, *confusedly*: I—I don't know—

BARTLETT: Ah, you thought I did! I don't. I was indulging in a sort of modulated howling which I flatter myself is at least one peculiarity that's entirely my own. I was baying the landscape merely for my private amusement, and I'd not have done it, if I'd known you were in hearing. However, if it's helped to settle the fact one way or other, concerning any little idiosyncrasy of mine, I shan't regret it. I hope not to disappoint you in anything, by and by.

He drops his hands from the doorposts and steps into the room, while Constance, in shrinking abeyance, stands trembling at his harshness.

CONSTANCE, *in faltering reproach*: Mr. Bartlett!

BARTLETT: Constance!

CONSTANCE, *struggling to assert herself, but breaking feebly in her attempt at hauteur*: Constance? What does this mean, Mr. Bartlett?

BARTLETT, *with a sudden burst*: What does it mean? It means that I'm sick of this nightmare masquerade. It means that I want to be something to you—all the world to you—in and for myself. It means that I can't play another man's part any longer and live. It means that I love you, love you, love you, Constance!

He starts involuntarily toward her with outstretched arms, from which she recoils with a convulsive cry.

CONSTANCE: You love me? *Me?* Oh, no, no! How can you be so merciless as to talk to me of love?

She drops her glowing face into her hands.

BARTLETT: Because I'm a man. Because love is more than mercy—better, higher, wiser. Listen to me, Constance!—yes, I will call you so now if never again: you are so dear to me that I must say it at last if it killed you. If loving you is cruel, I'm pitiless! Give me some hope, tell me to breathe, my girl!

CONSTANCE: Oh go, while I can still forgive you.

BARTLETT: I won't go; I won't have your forgiveness; I will have all or nothing; I want your love!

CONSTANCE, *uncovering her face and turning its desolation upon him*: My love? I have no love to give. My heart is dead.

BARTLETT: No, no! That's part of the ugly trance that we've both been living in so long. Look! You're better now than when you came here; you're stronger, braver, more beautiful. My angel, you're turned a woman again! Oh you can love me if you will; and you will! Look at me, darling!

He takes her listless right hand in his left, and gently draws her toward him.

CONSTANCE, *starting away*: You're wrong; you're all wrong! You don't understand; you don't know— Oh, listen to me!

BARTLETT, *still holding her cold hand fast*: Yes, a thousand years. But you must tell me first that I may love you. That first!

CONSTANCE: No! That never! And since you speak to me of love, listen to what it's my right you should hear.

BARTLETT, *releasing her*: I don't care to hear. Nothing can ever change me. But if you bid me, I will go!

CONSTANCE: You shall not go now till you know what despised and hated and forsaken thing you've offered your love to.

BARTLETT, *beseechingly*: Constance, let me go while I can forgive myself. Nothing you can say will make me love you less; remember that; but I implore you to spare yourself. Don't speak, my love.

CONSTANCE: Spare myself? Not speak? Not speak what has been on my tongue and heart and brain, a burning fire, so long?— Oh, I was a happy girl once! The days were not long enough for my happiness; I woke at night to think of it. I was proud in my happiness and believed myself, poor fool, one to favor those I smiled on; and I had my vain and crazy dreams of being the happiness of some one who should come to ask for— what you ask now. Some one came. At first I didn't care for him, but he knew how to make me. He knew how to make my thoughts of him part of my happiness and pride and vanity till he was all in all, and I had no wish, no hope, no life but him; and then he—left me!

She buries her face in her hands again, and breaks into a low, piteous sobbing.

BARTLETT, *with a groan of helpless fury and compassion*: The fool, the sot, the slave! Constance, I knew all this,—I knew it from the first.

CONSTANCE, *recoiling in wild reproach*: You *knew* it?

BARTLETT, *desperately*: Yes, I knew it—in spite of myself, through my own stubborn fury I knew it, that first day, when I had obliged my friend to tell me what your father had told him, before I would hear reason. I would have given anything not to have known it then, when it was too late, for I had at least the grace to feel the wrong, the outrage of my knowing it. You can never pardon it, I see; but you must feel what a hateful burden I had to bear, when I found that I had somehow purloined the presence, the looks, the voice of another man—a man whom I would have joyfully changed myself to any monstrous shape *not* to resemble, though I knew that my likeness to him, bewildering you in a continual dream of him, was all that ever made you look at me or think of me. I lived in the hope—Heaven only knows why I should have had the hope!—that I might yet be myself to you; that you might wake from your dream of him and look on me in the daylight, and see that I was at least an honest man, and pity me and may be love me at last, as I loved you at first, from the moment I saw your dear, pale face, and heard your dear, sad voice. (*He follows up her slow retreat and again possesses himself of her hand.*) Don't cast me off! It was monstrous, out of all decency, to know your sorrow; but I never tried to know it; I tried *not* to know it. (*He keeps fast hold of her hand, while she remains with averted head.*) I love you, Constance; I loved you; and when once you had bidden me stay, I was helpless to go away, or I would never be here now to offend you with the confession of that shameful knowledge. Do you think it was no trial to me? It gave me the conscience of an eavesdropper and a spy; yet all I knew was sacred to me.

CONSTANCE, *turning and looking steadfastly into his face*: And you could care for so poor a creature as I—so abject, so obtuse as never to know what had made her intolerable to the man that cast her off?

BARTLETT: Man? He was *no* man! He—

CONSTANCE, *suddenly*: Oh, wait! I—I love him yet.

BARTLETT, *dropping her hand*: You—

CONSTANCE: Yes, yes! As much as I live, I love him! But when he left me, I seemed to die; and now it's as if I were some wretched ghost clinging for all existence to the thought of my lost happiness. If that slips from me, then I cease to be.

BARTLETT: Why, this is still your dream. But I won't despair. You'll wake yet, and care for me: I know you will.

CONSTANCE, *tenderly*: Oh, I'm not dreaming now. I know that you are not he. You are everything that is kind and good; and some day you will be very happy.

BARTLETT, *desolately*: I shall never be happy without your love. (*After a pause*) It will be a barren, bitter comfort, but let me have it if you can: if *I* had met you first, could you have loved *me*?

CONSTANCE: I might have loved you if—I had —lived.

She turns from him again, and moves softly toward the door; his hollow voice arrests her.

BARTLETT: If you are dead, then I have lived too long. Your loss takes the smile out of life for me. (*A moment later*) You are cruel, Constance.

CONSTANCE, *abruptly facing him*: I cruel? To *you*?

BARTLETT: Yes, you have put me to shame before myself. You might have spared me! A treacherous villain is false in time to save you from a life of betrayal, and you say your heart is dead. But that isn't enough. You tell me that you cannot care for me because you love that treacherous villain still. That's my disgrace, that's my humiliation, that's my killing shame. I could have borne all else. You might have cast me off however you would, driven me away with any scorn, whipped me from you with the sharpest rebuke that such presumption as mine could merit; but to drag a decent man's self-respect through such mire as that poor rascal's memory for six long weeks, and then tell him that you prefer the mire—

CONSTANCE: Oh, hush! I can't let you reproach him! He was pitilessly false to me, but I will be true to him forever. How do I know—I *must* find some reason for that, or there is no reason in anything!—how do I know that he did not break his word to me at my father's bidding? My father never liked him.

BARTLETT, *shaking his head with a melancholy smile*: Ah, Constance, do you think I would break my word to you at your father's bidding?

CONSTANCE, *in abject despair*: Well, then I go back to what I always knew; I was too slight, too foolish, too tiresome for his life-long love. He saw it in time, I don't blame him. You would see it, too.

BARTLETT: What devil's vantage enabled that infernal scoundrel to blight your spirit with his treason? Constance, is this my last answer?

CONSTANCE: Yes, go! I am so sorry for you,— sorrier than I ever thought I could be for anything again.

BARTLETT: Then if you pity me, give me a little hope that sometime, somehow—

CONSTANCE: Oh, I have no hope, for you, for me, for any one. Good-by, good, kind friend! Try, —you won't have to try hard—to forget me. Unless some miracle should happen to show me that it was all his fault and none of mine, we are parting now forever. It has been a strange dream, and nothing is so strange as that it should be ending so. Are you the ghost or I, I wonder! It confuses me as it did at first; but if you are he, or only you— Ah, don't look at me so, or I must believe he has never left me, and implore you to stay!

BARTLETT, *quietly*: Thanks. I would not stay a moment longer in his disguise, if you begged me on your knees. I shall always love you, Constance, but if the world is wide enough, please Heaven,

I will never see you again. There are some things dearer to me than your presence. No, I won't take your hand; it can't heal the hurt your words have made, and nothing can help me, now I know from your own lips that but for my likeness to *him* I should never have been anything to you. Good-by!

CONSTANCE: Oh!

She sinks with a long cry into the arm-chair beside the table, and drops her head into her arms upon it. At the door toward which he turns Bartlett meets General Wyatt, and a moment later Mrs. Wyatt enters by the other. Bartlett recoils under the concentrated reproach and inquiry of their gaze.

MRS. WYATT, *hastening to bow herself over Constance's fallen head*: Oh, what is it, Constance?

As Constance makes no reply, she lifts her eyes again to Bartlett's face.

GENERAL WYATT, *peremptorily*: Well, sir!

BARTLETT, *with bitter desperation*: Oh, you shall know!

CONSTANCE, *interposing*: I will tell! You shall be spared that, at least. (*She has risen, and with her face still hidden in her handkerchief, seeks her father with an outstretched hand. He tenderly gathers her to his arms, and she droops a moment upon his shoulder; then, with an electrical revolt against her own weakness, she lifts her head and dries her tears with a passionate energy.*) He—Oh, speak *for* me!

Her head falls again on her father's shoulder.

BARTLETT, *with grave irony and self-scorn*: It's a simple matter, sir; I have been telling Miss Wyatt that I love her, and offering to share with her my obscurity and poverty. I—

GENERAL WYATT, *impatiently*: Curse your poverty, sir! I'm poor myself. Well!

BARTLETT: Oh, that's merely the beginning; I have had the indecency to do this, knowing that what alone rendered me sufferable to her it was a cruel shame for me to know, and an atrocity for me to presume upon. I—

GENERAL WYATT: I authorized this knowledge on your part when I spoke to your friend, and before he went away he told me all he had said to you.

BARTLETT, *in the first stages of petrifaction*: Cummings?

GENERAL WYATT: Yes.

BARTLETT: Told you that I knew whom I was like?

GENERAL WYATT: Yes.

BARTLETT, *very gently*: Then I think that man will be lost for keeping his conscience *too* clean. Cummings has invented a new sin.

MRS. WYATT: James, James! You told me that Mr. Bartlett didn't know.

GENERAL WYATT, *contritely*: I let you think so, Margaret; I didn't know what else to do.

MRS. WYATT: Oh, James!

CONSTANCE: Oh, papa!

She turns with bowed head from her father's arms, and takes refuge in her mother's embrace. General Wyatt, released, fetches a compass round about the parlor, with a face of intense dismay. He pauses in front of his wife.

GENERAL WYATT: Margaret, you must know the worst, now.

MRS. WYATT, *in gentle reproach, while she softly caresses Constance's hair*: Oh, is there anything *worse*, James?

GENERAL WYATT, *hopelessly*: Yes: I'm afraid I have been to blame.

BARTLETT: General Wyatt, let me retire. I—

GENERAL WYATT: No, sir. This concerns you, too, now. Your destiny has entangled you with our sad fortunes, and now you must know them all.

CONSTANCE, *from her mother's shoulder*: Yes, stay,—whatever it is. If you care for me, nothing can hurt you any more, now.

GENERAL WYATT: Margaret,—Constance! If I have been mistaken in what I have done, you must try somehow to forgive me; it was my tenderness for you both misled me, if I erred. Sir, let me address my defense to you. You can see the whole matter with clearer eyes than we. (*At an imploring gesture from Bartlett, he turns again to Mrs. Wyatt.*) Perhaps you are right, sir. Margaret, when I had made up my mind that the wretch who had stolen our child's heart was utterly unfit and unworthy—

CONSTANCE, *starting away from her mother with a cry*: Ah, you *did* drive him from me, then! I knew, I knew it! And after all these days and weeks and months that seem years and centuries of agony, you tell me that it was *you* broke my heart! No, no, I never *will* forgive you, father! Where is he? Tell me that! Where is my husband —the husband you robbed me of? Did you kill him, when you chose to crush my life? Is he dead? If he's living I will find him wherever he is. No distance and no danger shall keep me from him.

I'll find him and fall down before him, and implore *him* to forgive you, for I never can! Was this your tenderness for me—to drive him away, and leave me to the pitiless humiliation of believing myself deserted? Oh, great tenderness!

GENERAL WYATT, *confronting her storm with perfect quiet*: No, I will give better proof of my tenderness than that. (*He takes from his pocket-book a folded paper which he hands to his wife.*) Margaret, do you know that writing?

MRS. WYATT, *glancing at the superscription*: Oh, too well! This is to you, James.

GENERAL WYATT: It's for you, now. Read it.

MRS. WYATT, *wonderingly unfolding the paper and then reading*: "I confess myself guilty of forging Major Cummings's signature, and in consideration of his and your own forbearance, I promise never to see Miss Wyatt again. I shall always be grateful for your mercy; and"—James, James! It isn't possible!

CONSTANCE, *who has crept nearer and nearer while her mother has been reading, as if drawn by a resistless fascination*: No, it isn't possible! It's false; it's a fraud! I *will* see it. (*She swiftly possesses herself of the paper and scans the handwriting for a moment with a fierce intentness. Then she flings it wildly away.*) Yes, yes, it's true! It's his hand. It's true, it's the only true thing in this world of lies!

> She totters away toward the sofa. Bartlett makes a movement to support her, but she repulses him, and throws herself upon the cushions.

GENERAL WYATT: Sir, I am sorry to make you the victim of a scene. It has been your fate, and no part of my intention. Will you look at this paper? You don't know all that is in it yet.

> He touches it with his foot.

BARTLETT, *in dull dejection*: No, I won't look at it. If it were a radiant message from heaven, I don't see how it could help me now.

MRS. WYATT: I'm afraid you've made a terrible mistake, James.

GENERAL WYATT: Margaret! Don't say that!

MRS. WYATT: Yes, it would have been better to show us this paper at once,—better than to keep us all these days in this terrible suffering.

GENERAL WYATT: I was afraid of greater suffering for you both. I chose sorrow for Constance rather than the ignominy of knowing that she had set her heart on so base a scoundrel. When he crawled in the dust there before me, and whined for pity, I revolted from telling you or her how vile he was; the thought of it seemed to dishonor you; and I had hoped something, everything, from my girl's self-respect, her obedience, her faith in me. I never dreamed that it must come to this.

MRS. WYATT, *sadly shaking her head*: I know how well you meant; but oh, it was a fatal mistake!

CONSTANCE, *abandoning her refuge among the cushions, and coming forward to her father*: No, mother, it was no mistake! I see now how wise and kind and merciful you have been, papa. You can never love me again, I've behaved so badly; but if you'll let me, I will try to live my gratitude for your mercy at a time when the whole truth would have killed me. Oh, papa! What shall I say, what shall I do to show how sorry and ashamed I am? Let me go down on my knees to thank you. (*Her father catches her to his heart, and fondly kisses her again and again.*) I don't deserve it, papa! You ought to hate me, and drive me from you, and never let me see you again. (*She starts away from him as if to execute upon herself this terrible doom, when her eye falls upon the letter where she had thrown it on the floor.*) To think how long I have been the fool, the slave of that—felon! (*She stoops upon the paper with a hawk-like fierceness; she tears it into shreds, and strews the fragments about the room.*) Oh, if I could only tear out of my heart all thoughts of him, all memory, all likeness!

> In her wild scorn she has whirled unheedingly away toward Bartlett, whom, suddenly confronting, she apparently addresses in this aspiration; he opens wide his folded arms.

BARTLETT: And what would you do, then, with this extraordinary resemblance?

> The closing circle of his arms involves her and clasps her to his heart, from which beneficent shelter she presently exiles herself a pace or two and stands with either hand pressed against his breast while her eyes dwell with rapture on his face.

CONSTANCE: Oh, *you're* not like him, and you *never* were!

BARTLETT, *with light irony*: Ah?

CONSTANCE: If I had not been blind, blind, blind, I never could have seen the slightest similarity. Like *him*? Never!

BARTLETT: Ah! Then perhaps the resemblance, which we have noticed from time to time, and which has been the cause of some annoyance and embarrassment all round, was simply a disguise which I had assumed for the time being to accomplish a purpose of my own?

CONSTANCE: Oh, don't jest it away! It's your soul that I see now, your true and brave and generous heart; and if you pardoned me for mistaking you a single moment for one who had neither soul nor heart, I could never look you in the face again!

BARTLETT: You seem to be taking a good provisional glare at me beforehand, then, Miss Wyatt. I've never been so nearly looked out of countenance in my life. But you needn't be afraid; I shall not pardon your crime.

Constance abruptly drops her head upon his breast, and again instantly repels herself.

CONSTANCE: No, you must not if you could. But you can't—you can't care for me after hearing what I could say to my father—

BARTLETT: That was in a moment of great excitement.

CONSTANCE: After hearing me rave about a man so unworthy of—any one—you cared for. No, your self-respect—everything—demands that you should cast me off.

BARTLETT: It does. But I am inexorable,—you must have observed the trait before. In this case I will not yield even to my own colossal self-respect. (*Earnestly*) Ah, Constance, do you think I could love you the less because your heart was too true to swerve even from a traitor till he was proved as false to honor as to you? (*Lightly again*) Come, I like your fidelity to worthless people; I'm rather a deep and darkling villain myself.

CONSTANCE, *devoutly*: You? Oh, you are as nobly frank and open as—as—as papa!

BARTLETT: No, Constance, you are wrong, for once. Hear my dreadful secret: I'm not what I seem,—the light and joyous creature I look,—I'm an emotional wreck. Three short years ago, I was frightfully jilted— (*they all turn upon him in surprise*) by a young person who, I'm sorry to say, hasn't yet consoled me by turning out a scamp.

CONSTANCE, *drifting to his side with a radiant smile*: Oh, I'm so glad.

BARTLETT, *with affected dryness*: Are you? I didn't know it was such a laughing matter. I was always disposed to take those things seriously.

CONSTANCE: Yes, yes! But don't you see? It places us on more of an equality.

She looks at him with a smile of rapture and logic exquisitely compact.

BARTLETT: Does it? But you're not half as happy as I am.

CONSTANCE: Oh, yes, I am! Twice.

BARTLETT: Then that makes us just even, for so am I.

They stand ridiculously blest, holding each other's hand a moment, and then Constance, still clinging to one of his hands, goes and rests her other arm upon her mother's shoulder.

CONSTANCE: Mamma, how wretched I have made you, all these months!

MRS. WYATT: If your trouble's over now, my child,— (*she tenderly kisses her cheek*) there's no trouble for your mother in the world.

CONSTANCE: But I'm not happy, mamma. I can't be happy, thinking how wickedly unhappy I've been. No, no! I had better go back to the old wretched state again; it's all I'm fit for. I'm so ashamed of myself. Send him away!

She renews her hold upon his hand.

BARTLETT: Nothing of the kind. I was requested to remain here six weeks ago, by a young lady. Besides, this is a public house. Come, I haven't finished the catalogue of my disagreeable qualities yet. I'm jealous. I want you to put that arm on my shoulder. (*He gently effects the desired transfer, and then, chancing to look up, he discovers the Rev. Arthur Cummings on the threshold in the act of modestly retreating. He detains him with a great melodramatic start.*) Hah! A clergyman! This is indeed ominous!

Yorick's Love

[1878]

During the fall theater season of 1877 when Lawrence Barrett was touring sections of the midwest with *A Counterfeit Presentment*, Howells was already beginning a translation and adaptation of *Un Drama Nuevo* (1867) by Manuel Tamayo y Baus (1829–98). Obviously Howells had Barrett in mind while he worked on the Spanish tragedy, and he occasionally mentioned his progress on the play when he wrote to the actor (November 14, 1877, Princeton University Library): "I have broken ground on the Spanish play." By the end of summer, 1878, Howells had finished his adaptation, and in September his letters to Barrett indicated that he was then beginning to make revisions according to the actor's suggestions. On September 9, 1878, for example, he wrote (Princeton University Library): "I send you by express Act II, which I have gone over very carefully. The longer speeches of Yorick I have let now into blank verse, which they did naturally; but I have kept the prose, so that you have two lists to choose from." And the revisions went on and on, sometimes to a point of confusion for Howells. In response to John Hay's letter concerning the play's première in Cleveland, he wrote (*Life in Letters*, I, 259): "Do tell me one thing: Is there a second part of the last act in which Yorick loses himself in the character of Count Octavio? And does the play close with a speech of Yorick's? I'm glad Shakespeare was kept out." Barrett himself sometimes made changes in the play. In this same letter to Hay, Howells complained: "I haven't the least idea how far Barrett has let my work alone. He wrote me in Chicago three weeks ago, in quite a panic, that it was all bad, and that he should have to 'take it into his workshop' and do it over."

Barrett *was* difficult to please; revision seemed always necessary, and Howells continued his work far into 1879, completing his last major revision of the play in April. With this, Barrett seemed delighted. He wrote to his wife from Cincinnati, April 12, 1879 (Harvard Library): "Howells sent me the new act today. It was wonderfully fine— the best thing he ever did and is just the thing." But he evidently had some suggestions which Howells complied with as rapidly and as well as he could. His letter to Barrett of April 22, 1879 (Princeton University Library), shows something of the detail and scope of his reworking:

> Here is the new act amended, as nearly as I could mend it after your wishes. I *could not* put that talk of Gregory's into dialogue for Yorick and Alice, and that is the only point on which I have wholly failed. I give you here seventeen pages of fresh matter, and I have got you several new turns that work out Yorick as a humorist. There is also *click* at the close of the act, which it wanted before. I now suggest that the second act (old first) begin with the enclosed lines spoken in soliloquy by Heywood while he briefly waits Yorick's entry.
>
> Of course, the diction of the act is not yet as I should *print* it; but its very roughness is a merit, in some respects. I want you in acting to make . . . turns that will improve it, and we will fight over them in the summer.

It is, of course, impossible to know the many ways in which Howells revised his work before it reached the stage in the form in which it is printed in this volume or whether he did all of the revision himself. In an article, "Tracking Down Two Lost Manuscripts," in the New York *Post, Literary Review* (October 10, 1925), A. H.

Quinn tells of three versions of *Yorick's Love* by Howells, Barrett, and William Seymour, Barrett's stage manager. Existing letters indicate, however, that Howells did much of the rewriting. Newspaper reviews that report the plot of the play also suggest the general evolution of *Yorick's Love*.

The original play by Tamayo y Baus takes its thesis from *Hamlet*, Act II, scene 2, line 574 ff., as Hamlet exclaims:

> What would he do,
> Had he the motive and the cue for passion
> That I have?

It was an ingenious and striking stage production, if not a particularly profound work. Sensing the passion of the play, Augustin Daly had it translated in 1874, but his work, produced December 5, 1874, at the New Fifth Avenue Theatre in New York, failed, whereas Howells' adaptation, perhaps more fortunate in having the suggestions of Lawrence Barrett, was successful. Obviously, there must have been reasons. Daly's version (typed script, Harvard Library) is simply a close translation of the Spanish play. At first Howells, too, stayed reasonably close to his Spanish model; then he began to elaborate. By the time of the Cleveland première he had added a servant to the cast of characters, substituted Heywood, manager of the Globe Theatre, for Shakespeare—undoubtedly at the suggestion of Barrett, who would want Yorick to be the principal part—embellished the climax of Act II by having Yorick hurl Walton to the floor for his stubborn villainy, and given the final speech in the play to Yorick rather than to Shakespeare-Heywood. But in spite of these changes, the production was seriously criticized for its unrelieved tragedy, and one of Howells' first problems of revision after this performance was to enliven the play.

He attempted to do this in three ways: by adding light characters, by making his climaxes more theatrical, and by writing more beauty and poetry into his lines. But he did not do these things all at once. In Cleveland he had used one servant, Adam. Soon Adam became two servants, Gregory and Dorothy, who introduced Acts I and II and whose gay banter added humor and lightness to the play. In the third act the added egotism of Woodford, the author, and his remonstrances with the actors in his play also provided some humor. Later, some time before 1882,

Howells added two more servants, Philip and Tobias, to enliven the beginning of the play. Except for these servants, Howells' first act is much like the action in the Spanish original, but he freely deletes or adds lines and extends speeches throughout the play. Particularly does he improve the effect of his adaptation by adding strengthening climaxes. In the Spanish play, Act II ends with emphasis on the love of Alice and Edmund and with some suspenseful indication of subsequent action; Howells, however, builds on the pathos and tragedy in Yorick's character and situation. (Quinn notes this ending in "Barrett's version of the Howells version," but evidence suggests that Howells revised *with* Barrett until the final acting draft was produced.) The final act of *Un Drama Nuevo* closes simply by having Shakespeare recite what has happened to Edmund and Walton and urge the audience: "Rogad por los muertos. Ay, rogad tambien por los matadores!" Howells adds the theatrical touch by extending Yorick's part and emphasizing his tragedy. In the Spanish drama, only Yorick's lines in the play within the play are in poetry—a rhymed iambic verse of sometimes three, sometimes five feet. Howells added dignity and beauty by turning many of Yorick's long speeches into blank verse. In consequence of these changes, then, in added characters, dramatic climaxes, poetry and humor—although they may have been suggested and perhaps partially written by Barrett—the success of this play must largely be attributed to Howells.

The text of *Yorick's Love* used in this volume is Lawrence Barrett's manuscript version from the Lord Chamberlain's Office in London, where Barrett sent it for licensing early in 1884. This seems to be the only complete extant version that, considering its date, constitutes a reliable text for publication. There are, however, existing fragments of other slightly variant texts. The Princeton University Library has three manuscript pages, and the Harvard Library has an incomplete manuscript version of Acts I and III (in two hands, neither of which is Howells' or Barrett's) which was written sometime after the Cleveland performance in 1878 but before the St. Louis performance of 1882. This text includes Act I, complete except for one page, and a version of Act III that omits the parts of Yorick and Heywood except for final cue phrases in their speeches. As the text in this volume stands, it is reasonable to suggest that Howells would have thought at least twice before printing it, but for the sake of completeness and the play's value as representative of a certain kind of drama prevalent in nineteenth-century America, *Yorick's Love* is included. Obviously, a version copied in Howells' hand would have been preferable to Barrett's copy, admittedly a slipshod job, but this could not be found. It has been necessary, therefore, to make certain changes in capitalization, spelling, and punctuation in order to produce a consistent and fairly readable text.

There is no evidence that Howells copyrighted this drama either as *A New Play* or as *Yorick's Love*, the title that Barrett finally gave to the play. In 1874 Daly had copyrighted his unsuccessful translation as *Yorick*, and there was some confusion when Barrett first advertised Howells' play as *Yorick*—in spite of a note from Howells (September 16, 1878, Princeton University Library) telling the actor that the play could not be produced with this title. Daly was somewhat upset by this event, but Howells immediately apologized to him (October 18, 1878, Harvard Library) and explained that it was his understanding from Barrett and his intention that the play should be advertised as *A New Play*—a simple translation of the Spanish title. There the matter ended.

At odd intervals Howells commented on his writing of *Yorick's Love*. Barrett, of course, had helped him considerably both with *A Counterfeit Presentment* and *Yorick's Love*, and Howells clearly recognized this aid as contributing to his success. But with regard to his own work he usually mentioned it obliquely as "conveying" the play from the Spanish—a play with "Spanish passion and Northern conscience in it"—with some effort to disguise his theft (letter to C. D. Warner, March 5, 1880, Watkinson Library, Hartford). In his letter to Hay, previously noted, he confessed that he had "blank-versified the more touching and noble speeches, and here and there . . . helped the Spaniard out a little." At other times his attitude toward his work seemed somewhat changed. On December 27, 1880, he wrote to A. C. Sedgwick about *Yorick's Love* (*Life in Letters*, I, 291–92):

I wish it to be authoritatively said that the play is *not* mine, as many suppose, but merely my translation and modification. Above all, it is the Spaniard's idea (which I heartily agree with) that it isn't necessary for the young

people to be 'criminal' in order to feel badly; though some of the newspapers think that without carnal sin they have no occasion to be troubled.

Un Drama Nuevo is considered by most critics to be Tamayo y Baus' best work; it was extremely successful when it was first produced on the stage and went through four published editions rapidly. Yet the modern reader of Howells' adaptation may find it difficult to view the play seriously— a comment on the condition of the American stage during the Gilded Age as well as on Howells' willingness to abort his talents to such ends.

From the point of view of stage history, however, *Yorick's Love* is Howells' most successful work. For its première it opened at the Euclid Avenue Opera House in Celeveland, Ohio, on the evening of October 25, 1878. According to the newspapers the play enjoyed a qualified success. The Cleveland *Herald* was most enthusiastic, seeing the play as "one of the greatest events in Cleveland's history of the drama" and Howells' work as a "wonderful contrast to the usual modern drama" with "elegant and refined" language "at times even rising to grandeur." The critic for the Cleveland *Leader* admired the play as a "passion poem" but found it incomplete as a drama and "open to the objection, from an artistic standpoint, of being a one-part play, the greater portion of the lines and action being assigned to Yorick." "Mr. Howells," this writer continued, "has translated it [the play] in beautiful blank verse, embodying exquisite language and diction; everything has been made of it which the theme and plot will warrant. The former is of the highest order. . . . The plot, it will be seen, is slight, with neither intrigue nor counterplot of sufficient prominence to be called such!" All accounts of the performance lauded the efforts of Barrett and had kind words for Howells' literary art.

Probably the most constructive critical comment on this first performance came from John Hay, who in a letter from Cleveland dated October 26, 1878 (*Life in Letters*, I, 258), gave Howells his opinion. He wrote, in part:

It was a great tragedy, nobly played, in short, and it had last night an honest and legitimate success. . . . It was the best written play I have heard for a long time. Now, shall I go on with the hateful candor of a friend, and tell you the farther impression it made on me? I do not believe that as the play stands it will ever have great runs, or make you much money. The plot is so simple, the story so somber and heart breaking, that after the play becomes known, few people will go to see it except those who enjoy the very best things in writing and in acting. It is too concentrated, too intense. The five people in it are in such a prolonged agony that an ordinary audience would grow nervous. They must laugh once in a while, and if you do not give them the chance to do it legitimately, they will do it in the wrong places. I do not know how the Greeks managed with their awful simplicity and terror, but Shakespeare had to throw in a good deal of what I dare not call padding. Perhaps I am croaking in vain, after all. The play is magnificent —I wonder how any contemporary Spaniard could have done it. Your part of the work is, it seems to me, faultless, and Barrett's is unquestionably the stoutest piece of work I ever saw him do.

During 1879, *A New Play* with Lawrence Barrett as Yorick enjoyed its most active and probably its most successful season on the stage. For three weeks, closing on February 8, 1879, audiences at the Boston Museum had an opportunity to see Howells' tragedy. The Boston *Advertiser*, February 8, 1879, lauded Howells' skill but criticized the lack of suspense, progress, and developed secondary characters in the play, finding some portions "monotonously grim and black." Yet E. P. Whipple could write to Howells (February 8, 1879, Harvard Library): "I congratulate you on your glory as a tragic dramatist. For effectiveness the play cannot be exceeded. The close of the second act, especially, is effective beyond anything I have witnessed for a long time on the stage."

At the time of these productions, early in 1879, Howells and Barrett were constantly trying to make the play better, and with some success; Barrett became more and more excited over the part of Yorick as time went on and produced the play more frequently. After playing Yorick throughout the Middle West, he performed before enthusiastic audiences in Sacramento, California (Sacramento *Daily-Record-Union*, May 17, 1879), San Francisco (San Francisco *Bulletin*, June 10, 1879), Salt Lake City,

and Denver. From Denver he wrote to his wife (July 17, 1879, Harvard Library) that he had "decided to pin my future to *A New Play* next year."

By 1880 the play was being billed under its present title, *Yorick's Love*. In the spring Barrett played New England; on October 12 *Yorick's Love* opened for two performances at the McVicker's Theatre in Chicago. Then on December 20 it started a four weeks' engagement, advertised as an "unabated success," at Abbey's (New) Park Theatre in New York. But the critic of the *Dramatic Mirror* (December 25, 1880), in contrast to the *New York Times*'s mildly favorable review, was bored; he saw the play as neither a success nor a failure. Barrett returned to the Park Theatre the next November for at least one performance of *Yorick's Love* before playing it again in Chicago at McVicker's.

On April 12, 14–19, and 21–26, 1884, Barrett presented *Yorick's Love* to the English at the Lyceum Theatre in London. As might be expected its reception was varied. One of Howells' friends in London, Edmund Gosse, wrote his impressions to the author on Easter Sunday, 1884 (Harvard Library): "Your beautiful poem was played last night to a crowded audience at the Lyceum. . . . It left upon my mind, then, the impression of a *great popular success*. The writing told well, the situations were sharply and brightly defined, and Barrett, though painfully nervous, was superb. . . . It was very exciting to us— my wife and me—to see your tragedy." On the other hand, Clement Scott could not respond kindly to the play in spite of Barrett's acting (*The Theatre*, III [May 1, 1884], 259–60). "We could not see its poetry," he wrote, "or detect its passion. . . . The antiphonal anguish, the strophe and antistrophe of sorrow, would in England have made a stage manager tear his hair and throw the text at the head of the author." Generally the English critics were unimpressed; nor was the play a financial success.

Until his death on March 20, 1891, Lawrence Barrett continued to perform in *Yorick's Love*. Much of the time Louis James, who had played in Daly's version, acted the part of Master Walton, the villain. The rest of the cast changed occasionally, although Marie Wainwright played the feminine lead for a number of years, and at least once, in the St. Louis Grand Opera House, April 19, 1882, Otis Skinner performed as Master Edmund. During the last years of his life, Barrett probably performed *Yorick's Love* a number of times. The following productions are representative: McVicker's Theatre in Chicago, November 17, 18, 22, and December 1, 1884; Star Theatre in New York, February 14, 1885, August 30, 31, and September 1, 4, 7, 1886; Chestnut Street Opera House in Philadelphia, October 13–20, 1886; Boston Theatre in Boston, March 20, 1885, and February 16, 1889; Broadway Theatre in New York, February 21, 1891.

For a few years after Barrett's death, *Yorick's Love* seems to have been neglected. Then for the 1895–96 theatrical season, Louis Morrison made the play a part of his repertoire. His performance at the Bowdoin Square Theatre on September 20,

1895, was received favorably by a half-dozen Boston newspapers. Commenting on a production of the play in the Alcazan Theatre, May 23, 1898, the San Francisco *Chronicle* praised Morrison and remembered the play as "one of Lawrence Barrett's favorite pieces and one of the most popular in his repertoire." There is no reason to believe that this engagement was the play's final performance, but it probably was not played much longer. Although it attracted a great actor who made it successful, it is hardly a great play; but a tragedy translated and reworked by Howells and which remained on the stage for twenty years has historical interest and a place in theater history.

Yorick's Love [1]

A Tragedy in three Acts. Adapted and translated from the Spanish of Estabenez by W. D. Howells.

ACT I

SCENE: *A room in Yorick's house. Enter Gregory. L. 2. E. preceding the two servants. One of them bears Alice's portrait heavily framed. The other, an easel.*

GREGORY: Hither, hither! This way, I say. Look that you mar it not, or woe upon your lives. 'Twere the same in my master's eyes as if you offered wrong to Mistress Alice herself.

PHILLIP, *with easel*: Nay, we know our part. Master Warrener hath given us our charges. (*Placing and arranging easel R. H. near window. R. 2. E.*) Here, brother, set it here.

GREGORY, *regarding easel*: And what manner of strange three-legged beast is that, pray thee?

TOBIAS, *setting picture upon the easel*: Ay! A beast, indeed! Well said, Goodman Gregory, for it's called by the Frenchman "a little horse"—and by your Italian—"a pony"—and by your high Dutchman—"an ass." "It will not kick, it will not shy," quoth our master. "Fear not, 'twill bear you safely." Said he not so, brother?

PHILLIP: Ay, that he did. And then we laughed, ha! ha! ha! We know how to laugh at his sayings. Then he gave us each a sixpence and bade us go drink a mug of ale to his good health.

TOBIAS, *significantly to Gregory*: Ah, he gave us sixpence each—

PHILLIP: And bade us go drink—

TOBIAS: Ay, to your fair mistress' health.

PHILLIP: He gave us—

TOBIAS: Truly, 'twas sixpence each. No less—

GREGORY: O, a plague o' ye. Think ye that ye should leave Yorick's roof without remembrance on Yorick's birthday? There! There! Ye varlets! (*Gives them money.*) Get ye gone.

TOBIAS, *crossing to R. L.*: Save you, Goodman Gregory.

PHILLIP, *crossing to L.*: My service to you, master.
Exeunt, L. 2. E.

GREGORY: Master! Master! Well! 'tis a good lad! He meant no harm, though I am but Yorick's poor old serving man: "Master!" Ay! He meant well. 'Twas a good face. I liked not the other, with his bold "goodman" and his "Gregory's."
Enter Dorothy. R. 2. E.

DOROTHY: What art thou moping and mowing at now, Gregory?

GREGORY: A saucy knave, I say, to call me goodman.

DOROTHY: A saucy knave, indeed! I would never call thee, "goodman." 'Twas the same as I should say "husband," and that were too bold.

GREGORY, *flattered*: Not in thee, sweet Dorothy. Not in *thy* mouth.

DOROTHY: Nay! Nay! I know the respect that should be paid to age and its infirmities. I would call thee "Gaffer." Ha! ha! ha! (*Gregory goes indignantly and places himself before the easel.*) What hast thou there, Gaffer Gregory, that I partly spy through the ribs of thy skeleton?

GREGORY: Never ask aught of me, thou jade! Look for thyself if thou mayst face the effigy of one that is a daily reproof to all lightness and folly.

DOROTHY, *going to picture*: O, Mistress Alice's picture sent home! I care not for Mistress Alice's picture.

GREGORY: And why, Mistress Malapert?

DOROTHY: Because I care not for the moonlight when the sun shines, or for a death's head when thou art by. (*Coaxingly.*) Wilt thou marry me, Gaffer Gregory? 'Tis the fashion of the house for old men to mate with young wives. And I would mourn for thee truly when thou madest me a widow. (*A knock.*) There! Thou art called! Stay not to woo. Fly! fly! thou spectre! Ha! ha! ha! Is the picture for Master Edmund?

GREGORY: No, chatterer! for Master Yorick.

DOROTHY: Oh! Methought Master Edmund might at least have the shadow. Poor Master Edmund! *He* should be an old man.

GREGORY: What dost thou mean? Thou—
Knocking heard again.

DOROTHY: Dost thou stay yet? Why, thou wilt linger when Death knocks for thee. Run—limp—crawl. (*Exit Gregory L. 2. E. She goes to portrait.*) Oh! Dost thou think I am blind, Mistress? *Thou*, a reproof to folly!
Re-enter Gregory, ushering in Heywood.

GREGORY: Good Master Heywood. You have come upon the instant.
Dorothy R. C. curtsies to Heywood.

HEYWOOD: For what, Gregory? For what?

GREGORY, *indicating portrait*: To welcome Mistress Alice home.

HEYWOOD, *crossing to picture*: So Master Warrener

[1] This play has not been published previously.

hath finished his work in time! (*To Dorothy.*) Let thy mistress know my coming, pretty Dorothy. (*She curtsies and exits R. 2 E. Heywood turns lightly away and laughs.*) Well! 'tis a quaint fancy, and like Yorick to make himself a gift of his wife's portrait on his birthday.

GREGORY: 'Tis all his love of her. 'Tis like father and daughter to see them together. His hair just touched with frost and hers all sunshine. 'Tis like April and October. I can think of nothing else.

HEYWOOD, *absently*: And Yorick is five and forty today!

GREGORY: Truly! Truly! You are right, Master Heywood! And Mistress Alice is a good child—a good child —and she hath never turned to look at any of the fine court gallants that go mad of her beauty and write themselves blind upon her eyebrows.

ALICE, *who has entered R. 3. E. unknown to Gregory*: Thanks, good Gregory! But defend me not to every one or thou wilt make the world suspect me.

GREGORY: Nay, never fear for me, Mistress Alice. I am no fool!

ALICE, *laughing*: Well! Well! Go now, and make ready against thy master's coming. He will be here anon. (*Exit Gregory. L. 2. E.*) I have made you wait, Master Heywood. Cry you mercy! (*Drops a curtsy in mock humility.*)

HEYWOOD, *indicating portrait with exaggerated compliment*: Nay! You have been here ever since I came; only I marvel you did not speak before.

ALICE, *archly*: Was it too long for a woman to keep silence? You think the picture is not like, then?

HEYWOOD: Like? Oh! a good map.

ALICE, *crossing to portrait*: "Map"—do you call it? That's a phrase for Master Warrener, the limner, when I shall tell him the terms of Master Heywood's praise. You shall see the painter's pencil to a rapier turn—his palette to a buckler—and woe to thee when you encounter. Come, now! Some kinder word. Is it not alive? Doth it not breathe? Doth it not follow you with its eyes about the room? Is there not somewhat of Apelles here? Oh! Apelles at the very least. You can not say less than Apelles.

HEYWOOD: Well! Well! Say Apelles. And all the other masters of antiquity to boot. Truly, if Warrener was not inspired, he should have been.

ALICE: What should have been our painter's inspiration?

HEYWOOD: Thy goodness, child, that shines through every word; all slaves of thine, transfiguring all thy life. There, I have made thee blush.

ALICE, *evasively*: I am sorry Yorick is not here.

HEYWOOD: Nay! My errand was half to you. I came to wish you joy—both you and Yorick—of this happy day.

ALICE, *trying to recover herself*: Only to wish us joy?

HEYWOOD: Oh! Ay! And to temper his raptures a little with some talk of affairs.

ALICE: I might have known it. Atlas is ever bearing up the globe. You have come to talk of the new play, I warrant me! Cannot you leave us poor fictions of your stage one little day of real life? I was trying to feign myself the happy wife of a happy husband—in and for myself—not in a play—but in very truth—and here you come—

HEYWOOD: Is it so difficult a fancy then, that you cannot resume it afterwards when we have spoken of the play?

ALICE: Difficult? What mean you, Master Heywood?

HEYWOOD: I? I? I meant nothing.

YORICK, *entering L. 2. E.*: Nothing whatever, I will dare be sworn. What was he saying?

ALICE, *embarrassed*: Oh! Nothing! Nothing!

YORICK: Why, so I said!

HEYWOOD: Yorick, I came to wish you many happy days like this, but happier and brighter each, till your round century makes you last of us.

YORICK

Oh! Do not wish me to outlive my friends!
But I'll live on another fifty years
In friendly memories, if thou wilt, as one
That made men laugh, till not one bitter drop
Lurked in his blood for any one on earth.

HEYWOOD

Not even Walton!

YORICK

Nay, not even Walton.

HEYWOOD

Well! I believe it. And die when thou wilt,
I will write down these words thy epitaph.
There's nothing that I should enjoy so much
As writing Yorick's epitaph.

YORICK

                              [*Laughing.*]
                    Why, that
Is like a friend, indeed.

ALICE

                         Oh! Do not talk
Of epitaphs on such a day as this.
     [*Places herself before the portrait as if to hide it.*]

YORICK

Nay, thou say'st well.
Our talk should be, methinks, of lofty themes,
Of beauty made immortal! Of sweet eyes
Bidden shine with fadeless luster when ours
Are dim with dust.
Our talk should be of fine arts— Of the art
The limner hath to mirror loveliness
And the art of loveliness to hide itself.

Ah! What art can equal thine?
Hast seen it, Heywood?

HEYWOOD
Ay, I have seen it, Yorick.

YORICK
Well! What dost thou think of it, then?

ALICE
Oh! You should have heard him only now
Lording it with fine phrases—bidding me
Tell Master Warrener 'twas a good *map.*

YORICK
Map? And why, sweetheart—so it is a map.
It is the world—the world in which I live—
The pleasant country where my soul abides.
Map is not so ill, and yet a better word
Methinks he might have chosen—say, a landscape.
There are your golden harvest fields of hair.
Here your white brow—a buckwheat field in bloom,
And here those lovely blue, twin lakes—your eyes—
From which like rounded shores do rise your cheeks,
A wilderness of roses and of lilies.
And here your lips—and here your lips—

ALICE
Oh! Come! Come! Get you to my lips.

YORICK
                                        [*Kissing her.*]
Why so I will.

ALICE
Nay—nay, I meant not that.
You shall not cheat me of the proper phrase—
Come, now, begin again. My hair is like
A wheatfield or a haystack—and my brow
As brown as buckwheat meal—ah! And my eyes—
Pale watery green like two dull pools— My cheeks
Purple as thistles—and my lips—my lips.

YORICK
                                        [*Rapturously.*]
The praise of them is inarticulate.
A bird might chirp out something like the sound.

ALICE
Or a door creak it.

YORICK
Heywood, you have not wished me half the joy
That is my due this day.

HEYWOOD
                    Then take the rest
With all my heart.

YORICK
                And didst thou not remember
My birthday also was our wedding day?

HEYWOOD
I do remember now, but on my word
I had forgotten. I wish you joy again.

YORICK
Two years ago a fair and trusting girl
Laid her dear hand in mine, who might have been
Her father—but that the youth within my love
Made me the youngest husband in the land.
If I should tell thee how she hath blessed my life,
'Twould seem such profanation as if I
Should boast of Heaven, and I will not speak.

ALICE
O Yorick.

YORICK
There is no speck. No fear in my content.
I am so wholly, absolutely happy,
Except—except— Why is not Edmund here?
Is it my fancy that I find him cold?
This is his home, and Edmund is my son.
And yet I rarely see him at my board
And never more a night beneath my roof.

HEYWOOD: The boy is steeped in study.
ALICE: Yes—Yorick—'tis his study—do not think of it. (*Knock is heard L. 2 E.*) Why, that's his knock!
YORICK: The time hath been he hath not stayed to knock.

Enter Gregory L. 2 E.
GREGORY: Master Yorick—
YORICK: Is Edmund there?
GREGORY: Master Yorick—
YORICK: Does he wait to be announced? Ha! Ha! Ha! Let me usher in this Sir Punctilio!
Runs into Woodford's arms who enters.
GREGORY: There! There! I told you 'twas not Master Edmund.
YORICK: You might have told me in the course of time, but never mind. (*Exit Gregory L. 2 E. To Woodford.*) You, sir! Whom I have taken so warmly to my heart. You shall not say I drove you from my door. Welcome!
HEYWOOD: This is the author of our new play. Brave Master Woodford, whom a fortnight hence, I shall not need to name to any one.
They salute and Yorick leads him up to portrait of Alice.

YORICK
And this is Mistress Alice, Yorick's wife.
                    [*Woodford stares confusedly.*]

HEYWOOD

[*Laughing.*]

Yorick! Yorick! What a mad wag thou art!

YORICK

And this is her picture painted in oils
After the new Venice fashion, and but now
Sent home by Master Warrener, the limner.
Is it not like, sir? How cunningly
The painter hath counterfeited nature
In those eyes that seem to move and
To have speculation in them. See this
Smiling mouth that might at any moment
Break in laughter.

ALICE

For shame! Yorick—for shame.

YORICK

Good sir! I do entreat your pardon
For my error for which the painter's skill
Is much to blame. I see more clearly now,
And I do assure you that yonder
Is the portrait, and this is the Lady.
Trust me, 'tis so—this—this is Mistress Alice.

WOODFORD

The heroine, I hope, in my new play.

ALICE

Why, that shall be as Master Heywood wills.
We are but puppets in his sovereign hands.
We rage, we languish, burn with hate or love,
Kiss—kill—weep—live—die—or walk as ghosts
Just as he chooses to appoint our parts.
He is a pitiless tyrant to us players.
I hope his poets find him merciful.

WOODFORD

Why, truly, Madame, I have nothing
To lament in Master Heywood's usage.
My play coming to him as it hath
With Master Shakespeare's praise, 'tis not as if
It were unfriended—and 'tis not as if
I approached him without authority.

YORICK

Hath Master Shakespeare praised it? Then I warrant me
He hath not indulged his envious wont
Of striking all the good things from your pages.

WOODFORD

Why, truly, as to that, good Master Yorick,
We have not agreed as I could wish
On certain passages. At his insistence,
I have greatly reduced the speeches.

YORICK

Oh! Shameful!

WOODFORD

And several scenes I have suppressed.

ALICE

Oh! Cruel!

WOODFORD

And some of the highest languaged encounters
Where I had spent my very best on verse,
I have, at his instance, resolved to native prose.

ALICE: Why, this is sacrilege!

HEYWOOD: Come, Mistress Alice, if you embroil me with this poet again, whom, after this endeavor, I have brought to know his place under the manager's feet, I swear you shall play his whole tragedy yourself.

WOODFORD: Ha! ha! ha! Very good, i' faith! Very good, good—m'lady! If Mistress Alice might but play it all.

HEYWOOD: See to what a pass you have flattered him already! Yorick, will you not use a husband's authority?

YORICK: Nay, she does my pleasure, whatever she may do. But let us hear Master Woodford expound the argument of his play— How runs it, sir?

WOODFORD: The manner of my tragedy is this— The Count Octavio hath a young wife, and his son loves her— This is known to all.

ALICE: What?

WOODFORD: That the young man loves his adoptive father's wife. This is known to all—to all—but the Count Octavio, of course. It ever befalls so— Ha! ha! ha!

YORICK: 'Tis true—'tis a good point—'tis nature.

WOODFORD: Then the Count hath a familiar, one Landolfo, who by means of a letter acquaints him with the guilt of his son and his wife.

ALICE: Horrible!

WOODFORD: Ay! 'tis strong! And so they fight. And the young man is slain.

ALICE: Slain?

WOODFORD: By his father's hand. I had a touch there that Shakespeare pronounced the best in the play.

YORICK: 'Tis a good argument. And these are the chief persons: the count and his son— What call you him?

WOODFORD: Manfredo. 'Tis in Spanish taste.

YORICK: Ay! And the wife—

WOODFORD: Beatrice.

YORICK: Very good! And then this villain, Landolfo. Master Heywood, of whom think you for the part of Beatrice?

HEYWOOD: Mistress Alice, with your leave.

YORICK: Excellent. And whom have you chosen for Manfredo? Edmund!

HEYWOOD: You have guessed.

YORICK: I could not have erred. There are no such lovers as they to be found in any theatre. Excellent well! And the villain goes to Walton.

HEYWOOD: Why, there I have been given pause. Walton is a good villain.

YORICK: Nature framed him so.

HEYWOOD: Nay, you said but now you had no unkindness even for Walton.

YORICK: Said I so? I lied. I did but wish I had none.

HEYWOOD: Well! Here comes the rub. Walton is our first player—and the Count Octavio is the principal part. If I give him the villain, who will play Octavio?

YORICK: Ah! (*Pause.*) Is there no part in the new play for me, Master Woodford?

WOODFORD: Sir, you honor me past all deserving. But my poor play is a tragedy.

YORICK: Ay, So!— And yet methinks—or am I wrong to think it?—Shakespeare writ tragedy?

WOODFORD: The highest.

YORICK: And still he put some light heart jester in.

WOODFORD: Oh, there by your leave—I have thought Master Shakespeare out of taste.

YORICK

I do remember me that once the Master
Would have me walk with him in London streets
Where oft he loved to note the passing crowd
And make his studies from the life. It chanced
That, as we went, we talked of tragedy.
And "Pray thee, what is tragedy?" I cried.
We had stopped to hear a strolling mountebank
Making the crowd roar with his cap and bells
When, on a sudden, there arose a shriek
And a wild mother caught her dead child up
From under flying wheels. The fool who noted not
Capered and babbled on. But the great Master
Seized on my arm and pointed "There! There!"
'Twas all he said.

WOODFORD: Grant you that! But we do not copy life. We but choose—banish—and reject.

YORICK: Ay! So! Well, I would fain see your play though I be elected—chosen—banished—and rejected out of it. By your favor, Master Woodford, you will stay dinner with us—will you not?

WOODFORD: Good Master Yorick, hold me excused for on a day of private merry making I must not stay. Pray, Madame, let me commend to your special kindness the part you are to bear in my tragedy. Without your interest in Beatrice the best Octavio and Landolfo in the world cannot save it—fail it must. And though it be so opposite, Madame, to your natural frame, to play the part of a lady who loves not her lord, let it not displease you, for at the worst she is innocent and doth take—

ALICE: Enough! Enough! I understand!

WOODFORD: You shall see the delicacy with which I have endeavored it. A lawless and unhappy love so treated—the son to love his benefactor's wife.

ALICE: It is too terrible.

WOODFORD: And yet loving her not willingly—

ALICE: No more—no more—

WOODFORD: Ay! It kindles your fancy. I'm glad of that. And for Master Edmund! He will not play his part—he will live it.

ALICE: Merciful Heaven!

WOODFORD: There is a scene where the lovers are together, and the husband comes suddenly upon them.

ALICE: Prithee, no more—

Yorick touches her arm.

WOODFORD: 'Tis the very action—'tis marvellous fine. If you can do it—so in my play they shall 'plaud you to the skies. 'Tis the very truth of nature!

YORICK: Truth! You do well to praise her in that word. The secret of her art—the secret of her life is truth.

ALICE: Good Master, you see how the mere argument of your tragedy plays upon a weak woman's nerves. Think what havoc it shall work upon the scenes—and write comedy hereafter.

DOROTHY, *entering* R. 2. E.: Mistress Alice! The cook hath sent me.

ALICE: Ay! Ay! Master Woodford, the Tenth Muse calls me. Fare you well. Write comedy hereafter.

She curtsies and goes out with Dorothy.

HEYWOOD: By my soul, she is herself all the muses in one—ten or ten thousand.

WOODFORD: How prettily she mocked away the effect of my tragedy!

YORICK: Yet not the less her soul abhorred the guilty cases and her loathing of the treachery will teach her how to paint it best.

WOODFORD: If she but paint it to the world, as now she colored it for us, she will make me immortal. But she shall not make you wish my death now in defect of my absence. Farewell, Master Yorick, Master Heywood. I will await you at the Mitre? Give you good day, gentlemen.

YORICK: Save you, Master Woodford, to write many tragedies.

Woodford goes off L. 2. E.

HEYWOOD: Now, Yorick! Is this some new jest?

YORICK: Not unless you make a jest of it, old friend.

HEYWOOD: What wilt thou with me?

YORICK: Honestly, what think you of this drama that you are going to play?

HEYWOOD: Honestly, then, I like it very much.

YORICK: And is it the youngster's first play?

HEYWOOD: His first. He showed it to Shakespeare, who commended it to me. And now, what thinkest thou the vain fool saith? That Shakespeare feared to dispraise it.

YORICK: I think very well of it, too. Though I note some blemishes in it.

HEYWOOD: Oh! Let the envious find the blemishes. We will look only at the beauties.

YORICK: Ay, thou who hast never felt the sting of envy—thou who hast not to envy others—

HEYWOOD: The envious never lack for something to envy.

YORICK: I should know something of envy in such a

hot bed of envy as the theatre. But thou hast done well, Master, to lay down the actor's part and keep only the poet.

HEYWOOD: Nay, there are noble exceptions to the rule.

YORICK: Surely! My wife and Edmund are living proof of that. Heaven has given me the great happiness of seeing in this life the reward of whatever good I have done. Because I have striven to be faithful and generous, He hath given me in Alice a wife of angelic truth and in Edmund a friend—a friend? A son—full of the noblest qualities. And what talent—what genius they have! How they play Romeo and Juliet together! The lovers whom Shakespeare gave being are marvellous creatures, but how much more wonderful they are when Alice and Edmund lend their human form and souls. What gestures! What glances! What passionate embodiment of love! 'Tis his very truth of nature!

HEYWOOD, *aside*: Alas! Poor Yorick! *(To Yorick.)* And now may I retire?

YORICK: Nay, Master, not yet. Not until I have said a word to the manager of our theatre—the laurelled poet—to—

HEYWOOD: By Heaven! These sugared endearments cloy me. I might have known thou hadst something to ask me—and wast striving to pay me for the favor in advance.

YORICK: Yes, truly, I have a favor to ask.

HEYWOOD: Ask it then.

YORICK: That is what I would like to do if only I knew how.

HEYWOOD: Why, man! Speak out.

YORICK: Have you decided finally—who is to play the part of Octavio?

HEYWOOD: I think it will go to Walton, who is incomparable in that way.

YORICK: I knew it. To whom should any great part go, except to Walton? What luck the bitter rascal has!

HEYWOOD: Walton was very unhappy in his youth; he should have your pity. For the last time, farewell.

YORICK: But I have not yet said—

HEYWOOD: Say on then.

YORICK: I would like—I would like— But you are not to mock at me.

HEYWOOD: By Heaven, if you do not speak—

YORICK: I would like—

HEYWOOD: What! Speak! Or I shall vanish through the trap.

YORICK: I should like to play that part.

HEYWOOD: What part?

YORICK: That in the new play.

HEYWOOD: But which?

YORICK: That of the Count Octavio.

HEYWOOD: That of the husband?

YORICK: That—

HEYWOOD: Thou?

YORICK: I.

HEYWOOD: Good heavens! Take physic, Yorick, for thou art perilously ill.

YORICK: Why, so the fools talk. And I talking like a fool that knew only thy tragedies would have said thou wert incapable of writing comedy. Because I have done nothing till now but interpret jest and merriment, must I be condemned never to leave the beaten path?

HEYWOOD: To leave it for the unknown mountain-top? Why, thou hast been so long the very type, and arch-conceit of mirth that when Shakespeare cast about him for some name by which the sweetest and dearest wit should be known—the jester who enthralled the memory of his melancholy Dane with tenderness and delight, he could not but make free with thine and call him Yorick. If Hamlet live to after-time—and sometimes I think the poor Prince will survive us both in spite of Laertes' venomed point—thou shalt go down with him, the bright foil of his dark sadness to remotest fame.

YORICK: I thank our Master for an immortality for which I shall be none the happier—but do thou grant me the favor of a present triumph.

HEYWOOD: Yorick, Yorick, till now thou hast tried to make people laugh and they have laughed. Woe to thee when thou seekest to make them weep, and they continue to laugh.

YORICK: Ungracious Master, deny so slight a boon to one who was ever thy loyal friend? Very well, give the Count's part then to another, but then we are no longer friends and next year I will quit your theatre, and with me goes Alice—and Edmund, too. We shall see then which of the two is the greater loser.

HEYWOOD: And there is really no one in the world contented with his lot.

YORICK: Must one forever be amused with the business of amusing others?

HEYWOOD: Didst thou speak seriously? Couldst thou in truth abandon me?

YORICK: Abandon thee! I said it, and thou didst not believe me. When thou didst doubt my talent, nothing more was wanting but that thou shouldst doubt my heart. No, I will not abandon thee! Yorick may not know how to feign what he feels, but he knows how to feel. Thou woundest him—thou puttest him to shame—and he—look, Master—he opens his arms to thee.

HEYWOOD: Good heavens! Tears?

YORICK: I weep because it is not Walton alone who holds me for a gross buffoon, fit only to make fools burst into stupid laughter. Because I see that thou, too— Heaven help me! What an unhappy wretch I am.

HEYWOOD: Oh, devil take thee. Dost thou wish the part of the husband? 'Tis thine, then, and much good may it do thee.

YORICK: Truly? Thou speakest truly?

HEYWOOD: Ay, glut this cursed fancy from which I have vainly endeavored to wean thee.

YORICK: But if I should succeed in the part—

HEYWOOD: And if they strike thee dead with hisses.

YORICK: Nothing ventured—nothing gained. I should like to do it well if only in thy despite, Master.

HEYWOOD: I hope thou wilt not do it ill in thine own.

YORICK: Go, friend, and take the air.

HEYWOOD: I desire nothing so much.

YORICK: In good sooth, Master, if they should applaud me in the part—

HEYWOOD: Well!

YORICK: My joy would be very great.

HEYWOOD: And mine, Yorick, no less.

Gives his hand and goes out L. 2. E.

YORICK: "Oh! It's easy to make people laugh," I heard Walton say to his friends the other night. But they shall see that with this part of the Count Octavio I know how to make them weep when there is need. They shall see—and they shall rage to see. And as I have hitherto poured mirth, I can pour pity and terror into every heart. But I must go carefully. This part of the Count Octavio hath its difficulties, and at the slightest misstep I should fall and break my neck. "Tremble, faithless woman! Tremble!" Ah! Here is the heart of it. "Tremble, unfaithful woman! Tremble, ingrate, Who robbest me of mine honor and my peace, Vain all thy subtleties. Here stands thy guilt revealed." To begin with, he opens the letter, "My blood is frozen in my veins." "Thou art the villain—thou!" Oh! If I could only do it as I feel it.

EDMUND, *outside*: Very well, Gregory.

Enters.

YORICK: Ah! Ingrate! Thou to be the last to wish me joy upon this happy day. But never mind, my boy! Dost thou not know I am to have a great part in the new play?

EDMUND: I rejoice to hear it, sir.

YORICK, *earnestly*: Edmund, for some time past, thou hast called me "Sir" instead of "Father" and I have reprehended thee in vain. "Tremble, unfaithful woman!" Is it for some fault of mine that thou deniest me the dearer name?

EDMUND: I am not worthy to pronounce that name.

YORICK: Since when? Ah! Edmund! Thou art losing the old tenderness that thou hadst for me.

EDMUND: Oh! No! What has made you fancy that?

YORICK: Thou wouldst be less reserved with me if thou didst love me still.

EDMUND: And how am I reserved with you?

YORICK: In not telling me the cause of thy sadness.

EDMUND: I, sad?

YORICK: Sad, and full of disquiet. Can it be thou art in love?

EDMUND: In love? I? Do you think—

YORICK: So I think? It would seem that I had accused thee of a crime. Ah! love may be a crime. Dost thou love another's wife?

EDMUND, *starts*: Oh!

YORICK: Thou art pale. Thy hand trembles.

EDMUND: Yes—surely—you look at me in such a way.

YORICK: Infirm must be thy conscience when a look can startle thee. Consider well. He who steals a man's money does him no such harm as the thief who steals his honor—nor he who wounds his body as the assassin who strikes at his soul. Edmund, do not do this! Ah! My son! for the love of Heaven! forbear!

EDMUND: You suspect me without cause. I do assure you.

YORICK: I believe thee— Thou wouldst not deceive me. And is it not droll that Alice should be going to play the guilty wife, and thou the gay seducer in this new drama?

EDMUND, *dissembling*: Yes—

YORICK: And I—I—I am to do the injured husband.

EDMUND: You?

YORICK: Yes, I! Does it surprise thee?

EDMUND: No!

YORICK: Oh! Art thou, too, one of those who think I cannot play a serious part?

EDMUND: No—sir—no—unless—that is—

YORICK: Faith! I have no slight task before me. In the first place, no part could suit me less than a jealous husband's, for I have not an idea what kind of animal a jealous man is. Alice—as thou knowest well—has never caused me a pang of jealousy, and never will as long as I live. It is not possible to doubt so high and pure a creature.

EDMUND: No, sir! It is not possible.

YORICK: Thou speakest coldly, Edmund. Thou dost ill to try to hide what I have now some time noted.

EDMUND: Have you noted anything? What? What have you noted?

YORICK: That while Alice is no less thy friend than ever, thou sometimes lookest on her with aversion.

EDMUND: You have noted that?

YORICK: And I understand the reason. Thou didst reign alone in my heart before Alice became my wife, and it vexes thee to share thy empire with her. Egotist! Promise me to make thy peace with her this very day, and hereafter thou must call her simply "Alice." It were even better thou shouldst call her "sister," for brother and sister you should be since you have both the same father.

EDMUND, *aside*: What misery!

YORICK: Dost thou know what I think? If thou art so jealous as a son, thou shouldst be something terrible as a jealous lover. They say that there is no passion so potent as this same jealousy—that it dominates the whole soul—and makes one forget everything else.

EDMUND: Everything, sir. Ay, everything.

YORICK: Of whom hast thou been jealous? And for what woman's sake? Why, thou shalt study the part of the jealous husband with me, and explain how this passion, unknown to me, unfolds itself—what kind of torments it occasions—and by what outward signs it may be recognized—all, in fine, that thou hast felt and known. Begin by reading me this scene here. From this point—go on.

EDMUND: "Wert thou the villain, thou?"

YORICK: That is what I am to say to thee.

EDMUND, *reading in dull dismay*: "Wert thou the cunning and perfidious knave?"

YORICK: My lad! Thou couldst not possibly have done that worse. More spirit! More vehemence!

EDMUND: "The infamous seducer thou—that durst—"

YORICK: More soul—more life—

EDMUND: "Pierce thus the bosom of thine ancient friend."

YORICK: Thou art not in the humor for it today. (*Taking manuscript.*) Listen! "Wert thou the cunning and perfidious knave?"

Walton enters L. 2. E.

WALTON: Who is raving here?

YORICK: Walton!

WALTON: Wert thou quarrelling with Edmund?

YORICK: I was quarrelling with no one.

WALTON: Methought as I came in—

YORICK, *aside*: He knows of it already, and is seeking some pretext for a quarrel.

WALTON: It seemed to me thou receivest me with little pleasure.

YORICK: I divine thy motives.

WALTON: Truly, 'tis divination.

YORICK: Let us have no idle words. What brings thee here?

WALTON: As thou hast already divined my motives, why should I tell thee? But what dost thou on foot, good Master Walton? Here is a chair. Thanks!

Sits.

YORICK: Dost thou gird at me with a mock of civilities that pertain to me? If thou seekest to annoy me?

WALTON: Ah! This is a pleasant greeting! Why, he has the spirits of the tiger. Eh, Edmund?

EDMUND: Eh? Dost thou make a jest of him?

WALTON: 'Tis well thou shouldst defend thy friend, Yorick—thy protector—thy second father. This boy's a jewel. How pleasant it is to meet agreeable people.

EDMUND: Walton!

WALTON: My compliments incommode you!

YORICK: What is thy intent?

WALTON: You are both out of temper today. Fare you well. But thou art the loser.

YORICK: I? Loser! I?

WALTON: I came here to seek a friend. I find a fool and I am going away.

YORICK: Dost thou call me fool?

WALTON: I would not if I could think of a better word.

YORICK: Hast thou seen our Master Heywood?

WALTON: No! Only the author of the new play.

YORICK: Well!

WALTON: The Master met him at the Mitre as he came away from you, and told him that you were to do the part of the husband.

YORICK: Ah! Now we understand each other.

WALTON: The author came to me in a frenzy, to beg that I should reclaim a part that fitted me—and—

YORICK: And thou— Well! and thou—

WALTON: I—I wish you to know the truth. At first I was furious—then I saw that I was wrong—and I said to the author— But why should I trouble myself to tell you?

YORICK: No! I listen— Come! What didst thou say to him?

WALTON: I told him that you were my friend—that an actor of your merit and experience could do well any part that he attempted if he would but throw himself into it—that I would play the part of the confidant—which is difficult, though detestable—that I would aid you with my advice, if you would accept it and—Farewell!

YORICK: Nay! Come hither, man! Come hither! Didst thou say that?

WALTON: And when I come here very well pleased with myself, I am received with looks of vinegar and words of gall. By my faith! I should pay you back in the same coin! I have mistaken.

Going again.

YORICK: No! Thou shalt not go. This is all very strange.

WALTON: And why is it so strange? Come! Let us hear.

YORICK: It would seem more natural thou shouldst be vexed to lose the occasion of a new triumph—to see me—

WALTON: Tut! Tut! The temple of fame is so vast that it never yet was filled and never will be.

YORICK: Ay, but that bitter humor of thine—

WALTON: You think me bitter because I know not how to feign or lie.

YORICK: And thou art not pained that I should have the part of Count Octavio?

WALTON: I have told you—no.

YORICK: And thou wilt play the part of the confidant?

WALTON: I have told you—yes.

YORICK: And thou wilt study this part for me?

WALTON: You insult one with your doubts.

YORICK, *to Edmund*: Edmund! Dost thou hear this? (*To Walton.*) To be frank with thee—I have always held thee till now a subtle rogue.

WALTON: So the world judges men.

YORICK: Confession is the beginning of repentance— If thou art in the humor now to give me half a dozen honest thumps about the head—

WALTON: Faith! I owe thee as many—

YORICK: Begin, then! And I pray thee in charity, let them be well laid on.

WALTON: Enough of this.

YORICK: Then give me thy hand.

WALTON: Ay, that I will.

YORICK: And—I—I could have sworn— Hast thou aught to do at present?

WALTON: Nothing.

YORICK: I would fain hear thee read the part before I begin to study it.

WALTON: Why, and if thou wilt—

YORICK: If I will? Have I not good reason to wish it? I wish nothing so much. Thou hast astonished me by thy unmeasured goodness and nobleness. Who would ever have imagined that thou—

WALTON: Wilt thou return to thy offense?

YORICK: No—no—on the contrary, I meant— But come with me to my study. We will lock ourselves in and— Frankly, the part of outraged husband seems to me rather difficult.

WALTON: Thou are deceived. The part of outraged husband is played without the slightest difficulty. What does Edmund think?

EDMUND: I? I? (Aside.) What does this man mean?

YORICK: It will be easy to me with thy instructions. And wilt thou teach me something of those inflections of the voice, with which thou makest such effect?

WALTON: Assuredly.

YORICK: And some of those sudden transitions that every one applauds?

WALTON: Without doubt.

YORICK: And that touch of feigning tears that makes the public weep?

WALTON: Yes—man—yes—everything that thou wilt.

YORICK: And thinkest thou that I shall succeed?

WALTON: Thou wilt triumph.

YORICK: Truly?

WALTON: Thou dost not know what thou canst do.

YORICK: But—but—

WALTON: Oh, I plume myself on knowing actors.

YORICK: I could fly for joy. Come in! Come in! But Edmund, is it possible that seeing me mad with joy, thou dost not rejoice? Rejoice with me, in Heaven's name. I would have the whole world glad. "Wert thou the villain, thou?"

WALTON: Come! Come! We are losing time.

YORICK: Yes, let us go and not lose time, since I have already lost my wits for joy. Dost thou hear, Edmund? Walton is going over the part with me. But I depend upon thee, too, boy. I must have thy help, thy counsel, thy criticism—ay! Even thy derision when I go wrong. With two such masters, and Heywood in addition—and I am no fool. "Tremble, unfaithful woman! Tremble, ingrate." Oh! Without question I shall do it divinely. I could dance like a child.

WALTON: But thou dost not come.

YORICK: Yes! Yes! I come.

Exeunt. R. C.

EDMUND: What to think? What to believe? Does Walton know my secret? Did he speak without malice —without insinuation? Oh! This perpetual concealment! This perpetual terror! What hideous unrest in guilt?

Alice enters L. 2 E. goes to Edmund.

ALICE: What is the matter, Edmund? What has happened to thee? What is it?

EDMUND: Thou, too! Poor child, dost thou tremble, too?

ALICE: And why should I not tremble? One does not defy one's conscience without terror.

EDMUND: And must we always live thus? Tell me, in pity, is this life?

ALICE: Dost thou ask me? It is possible to number the moments of a day, but not to count the pangs and agonies I suffer in a day. If any one looks at me, I say, "He knows it." If any one accosts my husband, I say, "He is going to tell it him." In every face I see a threat. The simplest word strikes like a menace on my heart. The light makes me afraid lest it reveal my evil conscience; the dark frightens me; in the night my guilt shows all the blacker. At times I seem to feel a brand of shame upon my face. It is as if I could touch it with my hand, and my mirror scarce can bid the stubborn illusion vanish. My strength forsakes me. My sore heart scarcely beats and the blessed hour of rest comes only with new terrors for me; I dread to sleep lest I should dream of thee—lest thy name should escape my lips—lest I should say, "I love thee!" And if— worn out with misery—I sleep at last, then am I more unhappy, for then the vague terror of the day takes on a hideous embodiment. And, again, the morning comes, and the bitterness of yesterday that seemed unsurpassable, and the bitterness of another morrow when it comes then surpasses that of today. Tears? Groans? There are no tears or groans of all I spend that bring relief to me. When thou comest to me, what anguish? What unrest till thou art gone? When thou goest, what agony? What longing till thou art returned? And when I speak to thee alone, as I speak now, my words seem to fill the world—world—the buzzing of a fly sends the blood to my heart. All ears seem to listen— all eyes to look— And I know not where to turn my own. And— Ah!

With a cry, falls.

EDMUND, *starting*: What? Speak!

ALICE: Nothing! My shadow! My shadow that seemed to me an accusing witness. And thou askest me if this is life? What is it to be alive, Edmund? No! This is not life—it is perpetual death.

EDMUND: Calm thyself, Alice. If thou wert guilty, thou wouldst think thyself less so. Sin never seems so foul as when virtue shines beside it.

ALICE: Do not talk to me of virtue. In loving thee I violate all duties. I offend heaven and earth. Save me! Save me! As a strong man may save a weak woman.

EDMUND: Oh! Yes! We must needs save each other. But how? See—and not speak to thee? Speak to thee, and not tell thee that I love thee? Cease to love thee— having loved thee once? What folly! What madness! I pass my days in forming good purposes with no intention to fulfil them—a thing to make the devil laugh. I do as everyone has done in such a case; I dream of turning love into friendship. And love—striving to diminish itself—only grows the more. Love cannot turn to friendship though it may turn to hate as fierce and deep. The thought of loving thee less than I love thee—affronts—infuriates me. Love thee to delirium, or abhor thee to frenzy. There is no middle course. Tell me—teach me—how shall I abhor thee?

ALICE: And I—I, too, pass whole days imagining means to overcome this passion that enslaves me. Sometimes I think if thou shouldst love some other woman all would be well, but when I think of thee beside some other woman, I tremble with hate. And there is no other pang that is not bliss to the agony I suffer. I kneel down to pray God that thou mayst forget me, and I find myself asking Him for thy love. It is vain to struggle longer. I know my ingratitude to the best of men—I love thee! I know my baseness—I love thee! I bade thee save me. My safety is not loving thee—thou canst not save me. I love thee!

EDMUND: Alice! My soul!

ALICE: Edmund.

HEYWOOD, *entering L. 2. E.*: Alice.

ALICE: Oh! Fly! Fly!

HEYWOOD: Thank Heaven! I find you alone. I came to look for you.

EDMUND, *suspiciously*: For whom? For me?

HEYWOOD: For thee and her.

ALICE: Both?

HEYWOOD: Both.

EDMUND, *aside*: Heavens!

ALICE, *aside*: My God!

HEYWOOD: Can I speak here without fear of being overheard?

EDMUND: Is what you have to say so secret?

HEYWOOD: So secret that I would that I myself might not hear it.

EDMUND: Speak, but look to what you say.

HEYWOOD: Look thou to what thou sayst.

EDMUND: I will not suffer you.

HEYWOOD: Cease and listen!

EDMUND: Oh! Master!

HEYWOOD: Time was when I should have taken voluntarily this step to which necessity now forces me. I was a coward, cursed by the pitying weakness that makes a coward of an honest man. I hesitate no longer. Edmund, thou lovest this woman.

EDMUND: I!

HEYWOOD: Alice! Thou lovest this man.

ALICE: Ah!

EDMUND: By what right do you accuse us?

HEYWOOD: By the right of a friend to the husband of Alice—the benefactor of Edmund.

EDMUND: But if this is not true—if you have been deceived.

ALICE: Oh! Do not doubt it. You have been deceived.

HEYWOOD: Hypocrisy and guilt are twin sisters. Come hither! *(To Alice.)* Come hither! *(To Edmund.)* Lift thy head, Edmund, and lift thou thine. Look each other in the face with the calm of innocence. Look! Oh! You were white a moment since. And now what makes you so red? You wore the color of remorse. You wear the hue of shame.

ALICE: Mercy, Master.

EDMUND: Enough!

ALICE: We have struggled hard.

EDMUND: I will tell you the truth.

ALICE: Oh! Yes! He loves me— I love him.

EDMUND: Be merciful—Master—be generous.

ALICE: Have pity on two hapless wretches.

EDMUND: Do not add to our misery.

ALICE: Save us—defend us from ourselves.

HEYWOOD: Courage—my children.

ALICE: His children! Didst thou hear him?

EDMUND: Oh! Let us fall at your feet, Master!

ALICE: Yes!

HEYWOOD: You were better in my arms.

EDMUND: Master!

ALICE: Can it be!

HEYWOOD: Come!

EDMUND: Save us.

Throws himself into his arms.

ALICE, *same action*: Save us for mercy's sake!

HEYWOOD: Yes, I will save you with the help of God.

ALICE: Edmund, Heaven hath sent us a protector, and we would have deceived him. How blind is misery! Oh, happiness! I breathe again. Ay, Edmund, this is life.

HEYWOOD: There is no time to lose. Speak. I must know all.

Music tremolo.

EDMUND: Alice came to our theatre two years ago. I saw her then for the first time. Oh! If I had never seen her!

ALICE: Oh! If we had never met.

EDMUND: I saw her. I trembled—I loved her.

ALICE: And I loved him.

EDMUND: The days passed. I did not tell my love—impossible.

ALICE: Yorick had already shown his regard for me.

EDMUND: My rival was the man to whom I owed everything.

ALICE: My mother fell sick; we had no one to help us. Yorick seemed a friend sent by Heaven. "Alice," my mother said to me one day, "wed Yorick; he loves thee so much and is so kind."

EDMUND: Yorick had taken me naked and starving from the street to give me love and shelter and fortune and a place in the world.

ALICE: Yorick crowned with peace my mother's last days on earth.

EDMUND: To have destroyed the happiness of such a man would have been villainy without parallel.

ALICE: My mother besought me on her deathbed.

EDMUND: I did what he who adds reverence to gratitude must do.

ALICE: I answered as one must answer a dying mother's prayers.

EDMUND: I strove in my heart to forget her.

ALICE: I strove to love him less and loved him more.

EDMUND: The struggle was vain.

ALICE: I said, "Edmund is Yorick's son."

EDMUND: "Yorick is my father," I said.

ALICE: And when I marry Yorick, my love for Edmund will cease.

EDMUND: And I believed that when she became Yorick's wife my love for her would end.

ALICE: At last the hour came.

EDMUND: They were married.

ALICE: And in the hour of its despair, love, instead of dying in our hearts—

EDMUND: Rose mightier than ever, inexorable—resistless.

ALICE: And yet, we did not speak.

EDMUND: In spite of Yorick's tears and prayers I refused to live under his roof.

ALICE: We saw each other daily, and yet we did not speak.

EDMUND: We passed whole hours together, yet we did not speak.

ALICE: At last, one night, as we were playing Romeo and Juliet—

EDMUND: Moved by the beautiful story—

ALICE: Blent in passionate fire—the fire of truth—

EDMUND: When all eyes were fixed upon us—

ALICE: When all ears waited upon our words—

EDMUND: Then, tongue—mind—heart—asked in the same low whisper, "Dost thou love me?"

ALICE: And tongue—mind—heart—responded faintly, "Yes."

EDMUND: That was our sin.

ALICE: Our punishment has been to fear everyone— to suspect everything.

EDMUND: Inappeasable remorse.

ALICE: Comfort—none!

EDMUND: Refuge! One—only—

ALICE: Death!

EDMUND: And our sole crime is to have spoken.

ALICE: We swear it.

EDMUND: By Yorick's life.

ALICE: By his life.

EDMUND: This is all.

ALICE: All.

EDMUND AND ALICE: All!

Stop music.

HEYWOOD: Poor humanity! Daunted by a molehill and ready to leap a mountain! You love! It is necessary that you should not love.

ALICE: But in pity, tell me, what shall one do who loves and would not love?

HEYWOOD: *Will* not to love.

EDMUND: To will is not enough.

HEYWOOD: Enough—unless the will be feigned.

ALICE: How can you be sure of that?

HEYWOOD: By an unimpeachable witness.

EDMUND: What witness?

HEYWOOD: Your own conscience. If you were not responsible for your wrong, why these terrors—these tears —this remorse? You must part with Alice forever.

EDMUND: I have thought of that a thousand times. But we cannot accomplish impossibilities.

HEYWOOD: In the process of every crime there is a moment to recede or advance.

ALICE: Edmund will obey you. With you for our protector, you will see how truth and strength will spring up in us again.

EDMUND: Oh! Yes! With your help, Master, nothing will be impossible.

HEYWOOD: I confide in the promise of a man and of a wife.

EDMUND AND ALICE: Yes.

HEYWOOD: Then, till the day comes that Edmund goes, never be alone together, never exchange a glance in the presence of others. Duty—necessity demands it. I had vainly fancied myself the sole possessor of your secret. I was a fool. Love can never be hidden.

ALICE: What say you?

EDMUND: Speak!

HEYWOOD: This horrible secret is known to a man from whom some villainy is deeply to be feared.

Music tremolo.

EDMUND: What man?

HEYWOOD: On account of the distribution of the parts in the new play, Walton is furious against Yorick.

EDMUND: Walton!

HEYWOOD: I know it from the author of the play, who came to me from Walton and repeated the talk they had had together.

EDMUND: Alice! We are lost—lost beyond all hopes.

HEYWOOD: Not yet. I am going to look for him. You will have nothing to fear.

EDMUND: Alice! Alice!

ALICE: What is the matter? Why are you so affected?

HEYWOOD: Courage, Edmund! I will come again presently to calm your fears.

EDMUND: For Heaven's sake, do not leave us—do not go.

HEYWOOD: Not go? Wherefore!

EDMUND: Walton is not at home.

HEYWOOD: How knowest thou this?

ALICE: Oh! Save us from this horrible suspense.

HEYWOOD: Where is the man?

EDMUND: Here.

HEYWOOD: Heavens!

ALICE: With him?

EDMUND: With him.

HEYWOOD: Thou hast seen him?

EDMUND: He began to disclose his purpose in my presence.

ALICE: Oh! What shall we do? What shall we do?

HEYWOOD: What a fatality!

ALICE: Do not abandon us—defend us. Save us, Master.

EDMUND: In pity, find some way—some hope—

HEYWOOD: Let us keep our wits about us—be calm— be quiet.

Yorick enters at back with Walton.

EDMUND: What have you decided?

ALICE: Tell us, Master.

YORICK: "Tremble, thou faithless woman, tremble."

ALICE: Oh! God! Mercy—

She faints.

YORICK: Mercy! She cried me mercy! Why should she cry me mercy?

HEYWOOD: Seest thou not how delicate and slight she is?

YORICK: Oh! Ay! But mercy! Why should she cry me mercy?

HEYWOOD: Startled by the sudden accusation.

YORICK: Ay—so—but—mercy—

WALTON: A singular accident!

YORICK: Mercy—mercy!

CURTAIN

ACT II

SCENE: *Garden of Yorick's house. Arbor in garden. Dorothy and Gregory discovered.*

DOROTHY: Hast thou Master Yorick's part there, Gregory?

GREGORY: Ay! Here 'tis! But wilt thou set thyself in authority here, too, Mistress—in the arbor that these hands have built for Master Yorick's more quiet study and better inspiration? Away with thee and thy brooms and brushes! Wilt thou put his table here, where the light strikes him full in the eyes? An thou knewest how to read, thou'dst know thou couldst never read so.

DOROTHY: And how should it be, good Gregory? Prythee, teach me, and reproach me not. I am no scholar, that I know.

GREGORY: Why, an thou wilt truly learn—look! Yorick should sit so—with the part before him, on the table, thus. Then will the light fall over his shoulder, and strike the pages and he shall read you sweetly and smoothly by the hour, like any clock ticking.

DOROTHY: Oh! if thou wouldst but read a little of the part to me, Gregory!

GREGORY: Nay! Nay! 'Tis not for young maids to hear.

DOROTHY: Oh! fie, Gregory! Shall they not hear it in the theatre! Sweet Gregory, read me a verse or two! Thou canst not think how I do long to know this new tragical part of Master Yorick's, and if 'tis not fit I hear it, all the more should I listen—and know how to shun such things hereafter.

GREGORY: Well! Well! An thou wilt. There is a trick of holding the book this way or that—that I have well nigh forgotten. If you hold it in one fashion— you can read it like a clock, but if you hold it otherwise, you were as well dumb and blind. Wait! There is another trick. If you hold it near, you cannot see, and if you hold it afar off the wording is not plain, and between the two tricks—faith! Stay, I will tell thee the story of the part, pretty Dorothy, an thou wilt not say it again to any living soul.

DOROTHY: Nay, trust me. I will not breathe it till thou rememberest those two tricks of reading.

GREGORY: Well! Well! say no more, then, and thou shall hear. Dost thou remember in that tragedy of Master Shakespeare's where that pretty white maid of Venice is married to that blackamoor— I cannot remember his name.

DOROTHY: No matter for his name. That he was a blackamoor were quite enough for me. Ha! I would rather wed an old man white, than the youngest black-amoor [there] ever was.

GREGORY: He was both black and old—and this one in the new play is old.

DOROTHY: Oh! Then, truly 'tis not fit.

GREGORY: Nay! I will guard thy sensibilities against the worst. And then, when they go to that island—that island— I can never remember the name of that island. Where is it that the wine of Venice comes from?

DOROTHY: From Cyprus.

GREGORY: Oh! Ay! Cyprus—Cyprus 'tis. He! he! he! Methought at first 'twas sack. But sack, quoth I, is a Spanish wine—and there is no island called sack, quoth I—and this wine of Venice is both wine and island, quoth I. So it ran in my mind and still I should not bethink me of—what saidst thou it was called?

DOROTHY: Cyprus!

GREGORY: Ay, Cyprus 'tis. Well! And then he grows jealous of his young wife—

DOROTHY: Prythee, good gaffer Gregory, is Master Yorick to have the part of Othello in the new play?

GREGORY: No!

DOROTHY: Then, thou silly dotard, why dost thou waste thy time and mine with talk of blackamoors and sack and islands? Get thee to the marrow of the subject and leave mumbling these dry bones of argument. What is Yorick's part in the new play?

GREGORY, *flinging down the part*: That, thou mayst learn for thyself when thou hast learned to read. To *me*—gaffer? To *me*, silly? To *me*—dotard?

Walton enters L. 2 E.

WALTON: Did she speak so of her master? A saucy minion! Where is he? He sent for me hither.

DOROTHY, *going R.*: I am sorry that Master Yorick should not know better how to choose his company.

WALTON: Wilt thou answer me, baggage?

DOROTHY: Thou *art* answered, brute!

Exit R.

WALTON: Cursed jade! *(Sees manuscript.)* What is this litter under foot? A sluttish careless wench!

GREGORY, *picking up manuscript*: 'Tis Master Yorick's part in the new play.

WALTON: Ay, truly! And what bower is this where I am sent to wait the new tragedian's pleasures?

GREGORY: 'Tis an arbor that my poor skill hath contrived for Master Yorick's quiet study of his part. Doth it please thee, Master Walton?

WALTON: Excellently. And when Yorick hath it not in use, Edmund and Alice might sweetly study here together. Would I might come upon them here!

GREGORY: Ay! 'Tis a pretty sight, Master Walton, and one that ever delights my master.

WALTON: He is lightly pleased. 'Tis something he can have his fill of. Well! Why dost thou stay?

GREGORY: I but stayed your bidding, Master Walton.

WALTON: Get thee gone, then, and tell thy master that he keeps me waiting. Here, take thy master's part.

GREGORY: Ay! I will take my master's part against all the knaves in Christendom.

Exit Gregory R. 2. E.

WALTON: He passes more than three hours with me at rehearsal, and then he comes to my house to look for me! What can he want with me? And I—what do I want with him? The thing we hate attracts us like the thing we love. Tonight they give the new play. Tonight Yorick plays the part he has vilely robbed me of. Will he do it well? To let him, ay, to encourage him in attempting impossible things—to play an inferior part beside him better than his own, this seemed the best means of assuring the keenest shame for him, the most satisfactory revenge for me. But now I fear I have erred. Everyone expects him to fail—except myself. Moreover, the vulgar applaud from habit. Yorick is their idol—even the fact of his exchanging the comic for the tragic mask will recommend him. And my enemies will not lose the occasion to injure me. Oh! Fame! My only hope and comfort, since my heart received the wound that will never be healed—thou comest with leaden feet! Thou hast eagle wings for flight! We suffer when we desire thee—more when we enjoy thee—more yet a thousand times when we lose thee! How often does thy worshipper stifle in his heart the voice of honor and of truth? When Yorick sought to wrong me, I resolved to strike him dead with the knowledge of his shame. The quickest and the surest revenge is best, and there is no doubt but Yorick is jealous. He strives to hide it in his heart—but jealousy always mounts to the eye. Accident has done for me in part what I would have done, and this barbed suspicion once fixed in his soul, he cannot rest till he puts his hand upon the truth. And who knows but the actor in his feigned jealousy may be inspired by the real jealousy of the man! It lacks but this—that the misery of my enemy should recoil on my head. *(Enter Yorick.)* Ah! Is it thou?

YORICK: Thou here!

WALTON: I knew thou wast at my house after rehearsal, and I came to see how I could serve thee.

YORICK: It is true. I was there. I thank thee for thy courtesy.

WALTON: Bah! Between friends and comrades—What wilt thou?

YORICK: I merely wished— I will tell thee—

WALTON, *aside*: What can it be?

YORICK: I have walked far and I am half dead with fatigue.

WALTON: Well, rest thee, then.

YORICK: I thought to find relief in the open air of the fields, but I found none.

WALTON: Thou art not well? Thou art—

YORICK: Restless— Ill—

WALTON: Thou art heated. Methinks thou art feverish.

YORICK: 'Tis possible.

WALTON: And why dost thou not send word to Heywood?

YORICK: Heywood! Wherefore?

WALTON: Perhaps thou wilt not be able to play tonight; perhaps the performance should be postponed.

YORICK: 'Tis not so bad as that.

WALTON: Come, come. I will go to the Master myself, and—

YORICK: I tell thee I will not see him. I tell thee I will play tonight.

WALTON: But how canst thou hope for a triumph tonight, if—

YORICK: A triumph? Yes—a triumph! Walton.

WALTON: Well!

YORICK: Walton!

WALTON: That is my name.

YORICK: Nay! Do not jest at me!

WALTON: By my faith! I think thou art mad!

YORICK: I have a failing that I must correct.

WALTON: Only one? Happy thou.

YORICK: I am a slave to curiosity.

WALTON: Adam and Eve were the parents of mankind.

YORICK: This morning thou wast speaking with Heywood in private at the theatre, and as I passed near by accident I heard thee say—

WALTON: What?

YORICK, *aside*: He changes countenance. *(To Walton.)* I heard thee say, "I have not broken my promise. Yorick knows nothing from me."

WALTON: And what else didst thou hear?

YORICK: Only what I have told thee.

WALTON: Well!

YORICK: And, as I am so curious, I long to know what thing it was Heywood made thee promise not to tell me.

WALTON: On my word, thou art curious, indeed.

YORICK: I began by confessing that.

WALTON: Thou hast another little foible also.

YORICK: What?

WALTON: That of dreaming in broad day.

YORICK: What dost thou mean?

WALTON: Thou thinkest thou hast heard me speak words that never passed my lips.

YORICK: No!

WALTON: No.

YORICK: This is sorcery.

WALTON: If thou hast no other commands—

YORICK, *aside*: I cannot believe him. *(To Walton.)* Walton!

WALTON: Thou callest me?

YORICK: To wish thee joy.

WALTON: Of what?

YORICK: Of lying very ill.

WALTON: Neither ill nor well. I do not lie.

YORICK: Thou liest.

WALTON: Yorick!

YORICK: Thou liest!

WALTON: Art thou beside thyself?

YORICK: It seems not, since I see that thou hast lied.

WALTON: I will give thee another proof of my regard by turning my back upon thee.

Going.

YORICK: Thou shalt not go till thou hast told me what thou didst promise to conceal.

WALTON: Why, fool! If I promised to conceal it, how should I tell it thee?

YORICK: Ah! Then I did not dream! Then I did hear the words thou hast just denied!

WALTON: Leave me in peace! Farewell!

YORICK: Walton, in pity—speak!

WALTON: Yorick, in pity, I will not speak.

YORICK: Is it some misfortune that thou hidest from me?

WALTON: If thou couldst but know how foolish is thy persistence, and how generous my silence.

YORICK: By my soul, thou shalt speak!

WALTON: By thy soul, I will not speak.

YORICK: Speak!

WALTON: Ah! No!

YORICK: No!

WALTON, *coldly*: No!

YORICK: I give thee an hour to think of it.

WALTON: Dost thou threaten me?

YORICK: Ay, methinks.

WALTON: Listen!

YORICK: Within an hour I will seek thee to know thy last decision.

WALTON: And if thou dost not find—

YORICK: I shall say thou art afraid.

WALTON: Of whom? Of thee?

YORICK: Of me.

WALTON: I will be here within an hour.

YORICK: Thou wilt come?

WALTON: Be sure of it.

YORICK: To tell me what thou dost now refuse?

WALTON: No. To see what thou wilt do when I refuse thee again.

YORICK: 'Tis ill playing with fire, Walton. Worse, a thousand times, to jest with the misery of a desperate man.

WALTON: Art thou a desperate man?

YORICK: I know not. Leave me.

WALTON: Farewell, then. Do we part friends?

YORICK: No— Yes.

WALTON: Yes or no?

YORICK: No!

WALTON: Then I will not offer thee my hand.

YORICK: We were friends for life. Didst thou change thy purpose?

WALTON: Within an hour, Yorick.

YORICK: Walton, within an hour. (*Going—meets Edmund who enters L. 2 E.*) Good morrow, Edmund.

EDMUND: Good morrow.

WALTON, *aside*: Since he is resolved to know it, 'twill be the easier for me to keep silence.

Exit Walton L. 2. E.

YORICK: Ah! Master Edmund! By what miracle do I see thee here at last?

EDMUND: This morning you reproached me for not coming.

YORICK: And thou art come because I reproached thee? For that alone?

EDMUND: No— I meant to say—

YORICK: Do not weary thyself in contriving an excuse.

EDMUND: You seem preoccupied—disturbed. Doubtless the rehearsal of the play—

YORICK: The rehearsal of the play—certainly—that is—

EDMUND: As regards you—there is nothing to be feared. The public loves you blindly. Tonight it will recognize your talent as it always does, and—

YORICK: What art thou saying? Speak! I hear thee.

EDMUND, *aside*: He must know everything at last; there is no help.

YORICK: Thou dost not speak.

EDMUND: Yes, sir, I was saying that the play tonight—

YORICK: Thou hast not asked for Alice! Why hast thou not asked for Alice?

EDMUND: Having seen her at rehearsal this morning—

YORICK: Yes, it is true—

EDMUND, *aside*: His doubts grow momently—they have reached their height?

YORICK: And the play tonight—

EDMUND: It will please, I think. It has interest and movement; the author is unknown, and therefore unenvied—

YORICK: It shall not be.

EDMUND: Oh!

YORICK: What? Did I say anything? Words escape me without my knowing. I am not well these days.

EDMUND: You are ill? What is the matter?

YORICK: A long and difficult part—the rehearsals—excessive study— But there is nothing serious. It will pass, it has passed. Let us talk here together awhile. (*Sits.*) We were talking of— What? Ah! Yes—of the new play. Thou wilt do thy part wonderfully well—and—Alice— How dost thou find her in the part of the disloyal wife?

EDMUND: Good, very good.

YORICK: Good!

EDMUND: Yes, sir, I think—

YORICK: And thou seest how happy I am that thou— Edmund, come hither!

There is a furious tempest of the heart
Whose lurid lightnings and whose thunder peals,
Whose wild tornado blasts, the heart in vain
Struggles to hide and hush. Yes, there is torment
That from the stoutest and the bravest breast
Can drag forth pitiful groans, and there is sorrow

Whose burden is so great that if it find not
Help in the heart of some compassionate friend,
It grows intolerable. Edmund, methinks
That thou shouldst be my friend. Even more than
My son.

EDMUND: Ah! Yes! I am thy son.

YORICK: Love me a little then, my son, for I—
I have dire need of some one's love, now. Thou must
know, Edmund, that Alice— Oh! How my tongue
shrinks from uttering the words that I abhor to hear
even more than speak. She loves me not.

EDMUND: Heavens!

YORICK: Thou seest the greatness of my misery. Could
there be greater? Ay. There can be greater, vaster than
mind can measure. She loves another.

EDMUND: But surely you deceive yourself. How do
you know that your wife— Who has persuaded you
to believe?

YORICK: Hearing one call her "faithless wife" in the
words of that accursed play that seemed my own, she
was so stricken that she swooned away.

EDMUND: Is it strange? She, being so delicate and
sensitive that the lightest sudden noise startles and
convulses her? Did not Heywood say—

YORICK: Ay! He said so! Alice, in her dismay, prayed
for mercy.

EDMUND: Startled by the sudden accusation her mind
followed the impulse received like a blind machine.
Did not Heywood tell you?

YORICK

He told me that, also, in effect,
It left a barb to rankle in my heart—
A little barb that has waxed greater since,
Till now, it is a red hot bolt! Oh! Edmund!
I had seen nothing—had suspected nothing—
The light of happiness dazzles like the sun,
But the sweet Heaven of my bliss o'ercast,
I saw, all things so vaguely fair before,
Distinct and terrible within the shadow.
Then I remembered tears untimely shed,
Then I remembered groundless fears and terrors.
I saw her younger, lovelier than ever,
Myself grown suddenly hideous and old,
And Alice seeks not to deceive or feign.
The burden of her guilt palsies her will. She shows
Such anguish when I chance to look upon her.
She is so moved and stricken that I marvel
If my regard have supernatural power
To pierce her inmost soul. Her trembling lips
Betray the tumult of her conscience. When
She speaks to me, sometimes, rebellious tears
Spring to her eyes and tremble 'neath the lids
That vainly struggle to imprison them.
It wrings my heart. And if she ever laugh,
Her laughter is sadder than her tears to me.
Yes, I would swear it before God in Heaven
Alice is hiding in her soul once pure
A secret foul as sin. Oh! I have learned

To know it with such terror as the wretch
Should feel who saw the blue Heaven rent asunder
And in the rift the lurid fires of Hell.
Who is the thief that robbed me of my peace?
Who is the thief that stole her innocence?
Speak! Do not tell me that thou dost not know.
'Twere idle! I would not believe thee! Speak!
Thou dost not speak! Thou wilt not speak! My God,
Is all the world in league with guilt against me?

EDMUND: To see you suffer such bitter anguish leaves
me almost powerless to open my lips. But I repeat that
your suspicions are unfounded, that I know nothing.

YORICK: Why hast thou ever been so disdainful of
Alice? Because thou knewest she had betrayed thy
more than friend, because thou wouldst not countenance
with thy presence thy benefactor's shame.

EDMUND: Oh! Do not believe it! It is a hideous illusion.

YORICK: I tell thee that my eyes are purged and my
brain is clear at last. Dost thou know my rival?

EDMUND: Your rival does not exist. Alice is guiltless.

YORICK: I will solve my doubts this instant. I am going to know whether she is guilty or no!

EDMUND: What do you mean?

YORICK: Nothing! The most natural thing in the
world—to ask her the question.

EDMUND: No! No! In mercy, no!

YORICK: And wherefore no? Can I do less than trust
her word?

EDMUND: But, if you accuse her without cause? If
she be innocent?

YORICK: If she be innocent! Why should she tremble? Why should I tremble? Why shouldst thou tremble?

EDMUND: Time will solve all your doubts.

YORICK: Ah! Time, that seems to fly so swiftly,
pauses at terrible moments, and appalls the soul with
the image of an eternity of pain. For some days past,
time has stood still with me. I would fain live again.

EDMUND: Wait for another day. Wait one day
more.

YORICK: Not a day more—not an hour more. Not
an instant more—off!

EDMUND: Oh! Consider what you are doing.

YORICK: The boy is stubborn.

EDMUND: Listen.

YORICK: And a fool to boot! Away!

EDMUND: Oh! Oh!

YORICK: There is no help! I must know all.

EDMUND: Mercy.

YORICK: As if I would not have mercy.

Exit into House R.

Enter Alice by window.

EDMUND, *seeing her*: Oh! Heavens! Didst thou hear?

ALICE: Yes.

EDMUND: Tomorrow a ship sails at daybreak. The
captain is our friend. Let us escape.

ALICE: No!

EDMUND: By night everything could be ready for our flight.

ALICE: No!

EDMUND: If there be no other means to reach thee, thou wilt receive a letter tonight at the theatre telling thee what I have done and what we have both to do.

ALICE: No!

EDMUND: Thy husband will soon know all.

ALICE: God's will be done!

EDMUND: And what will become of thee?

ALICE: Why should I care?

EDMUND: And what will become of us both?

ALICE: Fly thou.

EDMUND: Alone! Never!

ALICE: Fly!

EDMUND: With thee?

ALICE: No—no—a thousand times! No!

YORICK, *without*: Alice! Alice!

EDMUND: Dost thou hear? Already thou art faint and breathless.

ALICE: He is looking for me.

EDMUND: To ask thee if thou art guilty. What wilt thou say?

ALICE: What will I say? "Yes."

EDMUND: And then?

ALICE: And then? Oh! Dost thou think he will kill me?

EDMUND: His fury, or thine own anguish will be thy death.

ALICE: Oh! Rapture!

EDMUND: Thou seekest not thy death alone—but mine as well.

ALICE: Thine!

YORICK, *without*: Alice!

EDMUND: He comes.

ALICE: I will be silent. I will lie to him. I cannot be more unhappy but do not fear— I can be more despicable.

YORICK, *nearer*: Alice!

ALICE: Here! I am here!

Enter Yorick.

YORICK: Ah!

ALICE: You were looking for me, and I for you, and it seems we were running from each other.

YORICK, *aside to Edmund*: I wish to speak with Alice alone for a moment. Wait for me in my room.

EDMUND, *aside*: At least, I shall be at hand.

Exit R. 3. C.

YORICK: Come hither, Alice! Nearer, Alice! Sit here beside me. Art thou afraid of me?

ALICE, *sitting*: Afraid? Wherefore? What do you wish with me?

YORICK, *aside*: She tranquil! I perturbed! (*To Alice.*) Alice, there is a guilty conscience here. Is it thine or mine?

ALICE: A guilty conscience? Thine—or—

YORICK

Alice! Men commonly awake to love
In the fast dawn of youth, and recklessly,
Press in pursuit of the divine allure
Shining before them, and involve themselves
In passion after passion—foul or futile.
Leaving along life's thorny labyrinth
Bits of their hearts on every briar. My heart
Was whole and virgin when I saw and loved thee.
And, oh, how potent is the sore felt first,
In the autumnal years to which can come
No second love. Thus, Alice, I have loved thee!
Dost thou love me as thou shouldst love me? Speak!

ALICE: Oh! Surely, I owe you so much for the benefits—

YORICK: Benefits? Who spake of benefits? Dost thou love me?

ALICE: Love you? Am I not your wife?

YORICK: Dost thou love me?

ALICE: Yes, sir. Yes, I love you.

YORICK: In very truth? Yes? Shall I believe it? For God's sake, tell me the truth. Dost thou love none but me? None?

ALICE: What is it you ask me?

YORICK: Dost thou love another?

ALICE: No sir! No!

YORICK

I think, I fear, thou art deceiving me.
Perchance thou lov'st another—and hast not
Yet told thy love. Alice, if this be true,
Fear not to own thy secret before me.
Humbly will [I] accept the penalty
Of taking for my wife a child who might
Have been my daughter. Tenderly, like a father,
Not harshly like a husband will I listen
To thy confession. I will make thee see
The difference between the adulterous love
That makes Hell laugh—and that pure wedded love
For which Heaven keeps its crown and palms. For thee.
I will redouble all my arts and worship,
And I will never cease to supplicate
Thy guardian angel that he hold thee safe
Within his hand. And do not doubt, my love,
Alice, my soul, but I shall yet prevail
Against my rival, and shall win thy heart
And lead thee once again into the path
Of duty and happiness. For thou art good,
Thy heart is noble and generous. Thou couldst sin
Through error but not through willfulness and when
Thou hadst seen the ugliness of sin
Must fly it in horror, and when thou hadst known
All my tenderness— Oh! Believe me, child,
Some little love is surely due to him
Who loves thee so much.

ALICE, *aside*: The air chokes me. If I could die—

YORICK

Thou answerest nothing! Thou art silent still!

Thou lovest another, and thy love is known!
As little shouldst thou hide it from me, then,
For well thou knowest that so black a sin
Could not remain unpunished. Sully thy name!
And drag thy husband's honor through the mire!
And if that husband's only care had been
To save his wife from every slightest sorrow
His very happiness in adoring her,
And if he had no life but hers, no hope
Of Heaven but in her love and, losing that,
Only despair and death. And if she knew
All this, and doomed him to the pangs of Hell
In this world and the next, then were her guilt
Too great for thought to grasp, and though as proved
As Holy Writ, it needs must seem a lie
Incredible! I will not think that thou—
Such treachery with me—that thou has been—
No! No! I do not—cannot—will not think it.

Kneeling? Were she innocent she would not kneel! Infamous woman! Then I have not been deceived! What is it? What? What hast thou? Speak! Weep! Art thou dying? Oh! What's to me whether she die or live? Her suffering may be feigned. All is deceit, and vileness in her! Nay, the woman knows not even the name of truth.

ALICE: Oh!

Falls forward on floor.

YORICK, *raising her*: Alice, calm thyself! Tomorrow we shall see what's to be done! Today we must think of other things. The play tonight. Alice, for God's sake, rouse thyself. *(Heywood appears.)* Ha! Who is it? Who is there? Who dares to enter here?

HEYWOOD: So blind thou didst not know me?

YORICK: Thou?

HEYWOOD: Rise, Alice.

YORICK: Do not touch her.

HEYWOOD, *lifting Alice*: Twice thou hast taken this fancy for tragedy. Thou art grown insufferable.

YORICK: Did I not bid thee touch her not?

HEYWOOD: Stand aside.

YORICK: Am I dreaming?

HEYWOOD: I would swear thou wert, or else drunk or mad. Come to thy chamber, Alice.

YORICK: What! Thou!

HEYWOOD: Wait a moment! I would speak with thee.

YORICK: I tell thee, Alice must not leave me.

HEYWOOD: I tell thee to wait a little.

Exit with Alice.

YORICK: What is it? Has the reality of my life turned to some fantastic dream whose end cannot be foreseen? Am I the sport of some black sorcery? Heywood! Yes! There is no doubt! No! Impossible! What misery to live forever in this darkness! Light! Light! Eternal Heaven! He is with her! They are together! I will part them.

Going.

Enter Walton L.

WALTON: The hour is passed and here I am.

YORICK: Oh! Walton! Welcome Walton! Thrice welcome! This is surely keeping one's promise.

WALTON: I always keep my promises.

YORICK: And thou art come to tell me thou wilt not satisfy my curiosity!

WALTON: Precisely.

YORICK: Since I threatened thee, thou wilt show me that thou dost not fear me!

WALTON: Even so.

YORICK: Why, I like that. There shall be no quarrel between us. Away with these punctilios.

WALTON: As thou wilt. But, in good faith, I had not hoped to find thee so reasonable.

YORICK: Ay, there is no need that thou shouldst tell me anything. On the contrary, I have an amusing story for thee.

WALTON: For me?

YORICK: There was once a youngster—all vehemence —all fire. He fell furiously in love with a lady nearly twice his age, but of irrisistible beauty. *(Walton starts.)* His love was returned. What rapture! They were married, bliss beyond measure!

WALTON: Wilt thou cease?

YORICK: These loving turtles had passed the honeymoon in peace, when one night the youngster returning home unexpectedly found his wife—

WALTON: It is false, it is a lie.

YORICK: Found his wife in the arms of another.

WALTON: I swear to Heaven.

YORICK: Oh! He swore to Heaven, too, and fancy what he must have said when he found that this man, a gentleman of lofty lineage, was an old lover, with whom she had often sinned.

WALTON: It is a lie—peace!

YORICK: He resolved to take vengeance on his wife, and his wife disappeared as if by magic.

WALTON: Wilt thou be silent?

YORICK: He resolved to take vengeance on the lover, and the lover had him well cudgelled by his lackeys.

WALTON: Wilt thou cease!

YORICK: Wilt thou begin! Ha! ha! ha! The little story amuses thee! Ha! ha! ha! Well, thou must know that twenty years after, the cudgelled husband under another name and far from the scene of the event, which he believed buried in oblivion— But, look you, he deceived himself. He was known to bear a false name that he might hide the dishonor of his own.

WALTON: What art thou doing, Yorick?

YORICK: And there were not wanting those who pointed their fingers at him.

WALTON: Oh! Fury!

YORICK: And when they saw him pass, cried, "There goes a poltroon!" For the outraged husband who does not avenge himself is infamous.

WALTON: Then who more infamous than thou.

YORICK: Ah! Ha! At last, thou wilt speak!

WALTON: I, at least, discovered the intrigue!

YORICK: Speak.

WALTON: I, at least, tried to avenge myself.

YORICK: And I? Speak! And I?

WALTON: Thou art blind.

YORICK: Speak.

WALTON: Thou livest in peace with thy dishonor.

YORICK: Speak.

WALTON: Thy wife—

YORICK: My wife! Speak! Nay, cease! Why heaven! I'll tear thy tongue from thy throat!

WALTON: Ah! Thou seest now. Thou art more infamous than I.

YORICK: My wife?

WALTON: Has betrayed thee!

YORICK: Betrayed me! Prove it! Give me silent proof proof—clearer than the sun in heaven! Thou dost not launch this terrible accusal without the power to make it good by proofs; then give me them. Why dost thou delay? Thou shouldst have them. Thou hast them not. I knew it. This man tells me that an angel is a devil, and expects me to believe it on his word.

WALTON: I say that Alice is unfaithful to thee.

YORICK: And I say that thou must prove it. And, if thou dost not prove it now, upon this instant, confess that thou hast lied. Say that Alice is an honest wife. Say that she loves none but me. Say that the world reveres her and worships her. Say that the heavens rejoice to look down upon her. Say it! If thou wilt not—

WALTON: I say that Alice has a lover.

YORICK: Thou sayst it?

WALTON: Yes.

YORICK: And provest it not? Villain! Thou shalt never say it more.

Seizes him. Enter Heywood, Alice, and Edmund.

WALTON: Yorick!

HEYWOOD: My friend!

YORICK: I have no friend.

EDMUND: My father!

YORICK: I have no son.

ALICE: My husband!

YORICK: My God! I have no wife.

Rushes out.

TABLEAU

CURTAIN

ACT III

SCENE I

SCENE: *Green room of the theatre. Large table, with cover—two small mirrors. Two cornices from which hang ample curtains that touch the ground. Chair C. Door on R. Woodford and Thomas enter at rise.*

THOMAS: There ought to be some water here for Mistress Alice.

WOODFORD: Yes—in a bottle.

THOMAS: Take some.

Pours from bottle.

WOODFORD, *drinks*: Ah! I breathe again! I had my heart all doubled up in a knot. I thought they were going to— So many emotions—such joy— Oof—*(Takes a paper from table and fans himself.)* Well! Master Thomas! What think you of my play, now?

THOMAS: What do I think? Come. Mighty pretty! And this last act in my opinion is going to please as much as the others.

WOODFORD: Certainly. If one were at all vain, some men in my place would fancy that they rivalled Shakespeare. I do not. Out of sheer modesty, I go about doing him homage. But poor soul, I pity him tonight, for he must feel that the new author is bearding him. But how can it be helped! He cannot expect to be always the first.

Enter Edmund as Manfredo. R.

EDMUND: Tell me, Thomas! Does Mistress Alice come off before I go on?

THOMAS: No, sir!

EDMUND: And I am on the stage till the end?

THOMAS: Did you not know it?

EDMUND, *aside*: The play over, it will be impossible to reach her. What a fatality!

Going.

WOODFORD: Master Edmund, in that challenge scene —to tell the truth— I thought you—well! You were better at the rehearsal! Ah!

EDMUND: Yes, sir! Yes!

Exit absent-mindedly.

WOODFORD: He scarcely deigned to answer me. I rack my brains making plays like this in order that an impertinent little actor—

Enter Walton as Landolfo.

WALTON, *to Thomas*: Edmund has just gone?

THOMAS: Yes, sir!

WALTON: What did he want?

THOMAS: Nothing! To know when Mistress Alice came off.

WOODFORD: Master Walton, do you not think that Edmund is playing pretty badly tonight?

THOMAS: Something must have happened to him.

WOODFORD: Twice, when I went to his room I found him talking with Dervil in a low voice, and when they saw me they changed the subject of their conversation. Actors should not be allowed to receive visitors behind the scenes.

WALTON: And this Dervil—who is he?

WOODFORD: The captain of a ship that sails tomorrow.

THOMAS: As soon as the captain went away, Edmund asked me for ink and wrote a letter.

WOODFORD: Writing letters during the representation of a play!

WALTON, *aside*: A letter! A ship that sails tomorrow!

THOMAS: And talking of letters, here is this one you are to take with you on the stage and give to Count Octavio.

Gives letter.

WALTON: Well!

Puts letter in pocket of dress. Applause heard without.

WOODFORD: What's that? Whom is that for?

THOMAS: Whom? Whom else but Yorick!
Running out R.
WOODFORD: How that man is playing tonight! Why, when they told me he was to do the Count, I was ready to dash my head against the wall. But so it goes. Who would have imagined that an actor used only to the part of the buffoon— Why, he has left all the actors in the world behind him. Why, he does better than thou.
WALTON: Really!
WOODFORD: Much better!
WALTON: And if that is your opinion, does it seem civil or prudent to tell it me, face to face?
WOODFORD: Pardon, I thought—the glory of a fellow actor.
WALTON: You are a fool!
WOODFORD: How? What! A fool? I—
Enter Thomas.
THOMAS: It was just as I said—the applause was for Yorick.
WOODFORD, *aside*: Walton is consumed with envy. *(Aloud.)* Bravo! Yorick! Bravo! *(Aside.)* Digest that, you sour-stomached ruffian!
Exit R.
THOMAS: And what think you of Yorick?
WALTON: Thou art a good boy, Thomas. Look well to thy duty, and I will make Heywood increase thy wages.
THOMAS: Oh! If I do not! I will be greatly beholden to you.
WALTON: Thou askest me what I think of Yorick?
THOMAS: Yes, sir!
WALTON: Well, and what thinkest thou?
THOMAS: I?
WALTON: Yes, tell me! This morning thou saidst he would do very badly.
THOMAS: How often I said so!
WALTON: And now thou thinkest?
THOMAS: I do not think; I am sure.
WALTON: What?
THOMAS: That I talked nonsense.
WALTON: Ah!
THOMAS: He has played us all a fine trick. In the first act, you know—he was—well—somewhat embarrassed, but he soon—ay, faith—he came mighty well out of some scenes even then! I stood there gaping and staring at him till I forgot to call Mistress Alice, and if the author had not given me a good pinch to bring me to my senses, the play would have ended there. Look you, Master Walton! When I saw you play Macbeth, I thought that nothing could be better, but now—
WALTON: Come! Come! Don't fall into a new blunder—
THOMAS, *startled and looking at manuscript*: Eh! No! This scene is very long. We may be sure after this that as long as Yorick is in the company no one else will have the first parts. Who could rival him in them?
WALTON: Faith! Thou art a chatterer.
THOMAS: Enthusiasm was always a great talker, and

I am enthusiastic for Yorick. Everyone is! The principal actors grumble under their breath, but it is envy, pure envy.
WALTON: Wilt thou leave me in peace?
THOMAS, *aside*: What a gesture! What a look! Oh! What a fool I am! Hold thy tongue, my good friend Thomas.
WALTON: What art thou muttering?
THOMAS: Nay, I did not mutter—on the contrary.
WALTON: Away with thee, or I swear—
THOMAS: Going—going—*(Walton turns away.)* Rage—rage—and eat thy bitter heart!
Exit Thomas.
WALTON, *alone*: Yes! Yorick applauded with enthusiasm! What a triumph! What a glory! Greater than mine! A thousand times greater! If I could not pardon him the injury he did me before, how can I pardon him this? I will have revenge—equal to the offense—revenge! *(Shouts without.)* More applause! *(Goes to door.)* Ah! For Alice! She's coming off! Edmund is going on by the same side! They exchange glances! Yes! without question, the act was quick as thought, but I saw it. Edmund gave her something as he passed. What could it be? Perhaps that letter—the proof that Yorick demands. If it were only a letter. If fate should favor me! Hither she comes! Ah!
Hides behind the curtains.
Enter Alice. Looks around, closes door—then goes to dressing table and opens paper.
WALTON, *aside*: Yes, it is Edmund's letter.
ALICE, *reads letter*: " 'Till now I did not know with certainty that we could fly tomorrow, but all is ready. At five in the morning I will await thee in the street. We will never part—my love will last my life. Fly with me—there is no other hope— Fly, Alice! My soul —and—'" Fly? Abandon my unhappy husband? Make my wrong irremediable? An eternal shame? Never! Death were better. *(Puts letter to flame. Walton seizes her arm.)* Oh! *(She changes letter to other hand.)* Walton!
WALTON: Ay—Walton!
ALICE: Where were you?
WALTON: Behind the curtains.
ALICE: What is your purpose here?
WALTON: I want Edmund's letter which you hold in your hand there.
ALICE: Mercy!
WALTON: Give it me!
ALICE: Do not come near me!
WALTON: Why should I not?
ALICE: I will cry out.
WALTON: Oh! Very well! That will serve my purpose even better.
ALICE: Oh! What is your purpose?
WALTON: You shall see.
ALICE: Would you betray him to my husband?
WALTON: Perchance.
ALICE: Tonight? Here? During the play? But that were infamous—base beyond example. There is no

name for such a horrible deed. Oh, be mericiful—a little mercy—for him—for him alone—I implore you. Whom do you love? What words will soonest touch your heart? Tell me what I must do to move you?

WALTON: You can do nothing. I must be revenged.

ALICE: And why should you not be revenged? But must you be revenged tonight? Tomorrow I will give you the paper I crush in my hand—believe me—I swear it. Tomorrow my husband shall know the truth. You shall be present. You shall slake your thirst of vengeance with his agony and mine. It will not vex you then to have waited till tomorrow. Leave me. You will grant the favor that I ask! You will grant it, will you not? Why should it be so hard to say "yes"?

WALTON: No! And a thousand times No!

ALICE: Ah! I took him for a man and he is a demon.

WALTON: I am a man, a man with a wrong to be revenged.

ALICE: Oh!

Sees Yorick, who enters.

YORICK, *seeing Walton*: Thou here! 'Twere better we did not meet tonight except upon the stage.

WALTON: Truly, thou art right but when thou knowest what has happened—

YORICK: No matter. Tonight we belong to the public. Go!

WALTON: Is the greed of glory so great in thee that thou has forgotten all else?

YORICK: Greed for glory? Prythee! Go!

WALTON: As thou didst once ask me for a certain proof—

YORICK: Proof? What sayest thou?

ALICE, *aside*: Can this be reality?

YORICK: See! She is here! Beware thou dost not slander her. Where is it? In her presence. Proof!

WALTON: Bid thy wife show thee her hands.

ALICE: Do not heed him.

YORICK: Go! Leave us!

WALTON: In one of her hands she holds a paper.

ALICE: He is a villain.

YORICK: A paper? Go.

WALTON: That paper is a letter from her lover.

ALICE: Ah!

Crushing paper.

YORICK: Give me that letter, Alice.

ALICE: It is not a letter. Did he say it was a letter? He lied. Do not believe him.

YORICK: He accuses thee. Thou mayst refute the slanderer. Do so.

ALICE: It is—I will tell thee—this letter.

YORICK: I must see it.

ALICE: It is impossible.

YORICK: Impossible! Give it me.

ALICE: Ah!

Starts towards door.

YORICK: Wouldst thou make my dishonor public?

ALICE: Pity me, thou mother of the friendless!

WALTON: Resistance is useless. You had better yield at once.

Knocking at door.

THOMAS, *without*: Yorick!

YORICK: You hear them! They are calling me. I must go on the stage.

ALICE: Go—go—for Heaven's sake.

THOMAS, *without*: Yorick!

YORICK: Do not force me to use violence with a woman.

THOMAS, *without*: Yorick, you are keeping the scene waiting.

YORICK: Dost thou not hear them?

ALICE: I shall go mad.

YORICK: Dost thou despise my threats?

WOODFORD, *without*: Open— Open— The stage is all prepared.

YORICK: Oh! I must put an end to this.

ALICE: Mercy! Mercy!

YORICK: The letter! The letter!

ALICE: Have pity on me.

HEYWOOD, *without*: Will you open here, I say!

ALICE: Master, master!

YORICK: The letter!

ALICE: No! My life first. (*Walton seizes letter.*) Ah!

WALTON: Here it is!

YORICK: Give it me.

THOMAS, *without*: Yorick! Yorick!

YORICK: You will not?

ALICE: What does he say?

Doors burst open. Enter Heywood, Thomas, Woodford.

HEYWOOD: Walton!

WOODFORD: You have ruined me.

THOMAS: The stage has been waiting two minutes.

YORICK: Will you give me that letter?

WALTON: I have told you not now.

WOODFORD: What are you doing? (*Shouts outside.*) Don't you hear?

THOMAS, *prompting Yorick*: "Heaven help me at last. And now I burst the prism of my doubt."

YORICK: Oh! I am not an actor now. I am a man His name! At least his name.

WALTON: Presently.

HEYWOOD: The public is waiting, Yorick.

THOMAS: The public is furious.

WOODFORD: Oh, my poor play!

YORICK: That letter! Wilt thou give it me?

WALTON: It shall not leave my hands except for thine.

WOODFORD: Come!

THOMAS: "Heaven help me at last."

HEYWOOD: Duty before everything.

YORICK: A curse upon duty—a curse upon me!

Exit.

THOMAS, *to Alice*: You now!

ALICE, *whispers to Heywood*: A letter from Edmund.

WOODFORD: And she won't go either.

ALICE, *as before*: If my husband sees it—

HEYWOOD: He shall not see it.

WOODFORD: Madam!

ALICE, *to Woodford*: Support me! Lead me—

WOODFORD: Willingly, Madam. Lean on me. I shall go like Atlas bearing up the world, or the envy of the world. We are come now to the point that Shakespeare chiefly praised. If you could imagine that you were really betraying your husband—

WALTON: Do not fear, master poet! She will play your false wife to the life.

WOODFORD: Doubtless! Rest on me, Madam. Faith, 'tis a play that seems to prosper both before and behind the scenes. Players and spectators all are alike frenzied by it.

ALICE: Merciful Heaven! Can I endure?

WOODFORD: Madam, you must. Else my play is ruined.

Exeunt R.

THOMAS, *to Walton*: Did I hand you the letter you are to give the Count?

WALTON: Yes.

THOMAS: I don't know whether I am standing on my head or on my feet.

Exit.

HEYWOOD: Walton, that paper does not belong to thee.

WALTON: Nor to thee.

HEYWOOD: The owner has charged me to reclaim it from thee.

WALTON: Let me see, then, how thou wilt reclaim it.

HEYWOOD: How? *(Restrains himself.)* Walton! Brave and generous hearts feel only compassion for the misfortunes of others. Have pity on Yorick! Have pity on Alice! Save her, if it be possible. Her fault is not so grave as thou thinkest—and can be easily repaired. Let us destroy that paper.

WALTON: Yorick has wronged me.

HEYWOOD: Yorick has wronged thee? Then take thy revenge, but take it nobly. Thou canst not heal thy honor by committing a villainy. If Alice has offended thee in nothing, why shouldst thou make her the victim of thy resentment? To wound, at the same stroke, the innocent and the guilty is the act of a savage or a madman. And even if this unhappy woman had done thee wrong, thou couldst not avenge thyself on her without cowardice. Men avenge themselves on men—not on women.

WALTON: Ask me whatever you will, so you do not ask me for that letter.

HEYWOOD: Do not think me ignorant of the cause of thy hate for Yorick. Thou hatest him not because he has wronged thee, but because thou enviest him.

WALTON: What! Darest thou say?

HEYWOOD: I have called thee villain and coward—thou art worse yet—thou art envious.

WALTON: I! Envious? Nothing could pain me so much as that!

HEYWOOD: Because thou most deservest it. Yes! Envy holds thy soul within its clutch. Envy that laughs at others' evil and bewails their good! Envy is the most pitiable of afflictions—if it were not the most repulsive of vices. Envy! The shame and dishonor of the mind! the leprosy of the heart!

Applause heard.

WALTON: Duty calls me. As thou saidst to Yorick, "duty before everything."

HEYWOOD: They are applauding him. Hear them. Dost thou tremble to hear them? There is no sound in the world so deadly to the envious soul as the applause a rival wins.

Enter Woodford, jubilant.

WOODFORD: Hurrah! Hurrah! The public is ours again! The verses certainly are not bad, but then how Yorick spoke them! What gestures! What intonation! *(Shouts.)* More applause—more—admirable! divine!

Clapping his hands.

WALTON, *starting to go*: I shall be late if you keep me here.

HEYWOOD, *interposing*: Give me the letter.

WOODFORD: What is the matter with everyone tonight? Is Master Heywood gone mad, too? This is the error of writing too forcibly.

Enter Thomas.

THOMAS, *to Walton*: Come, you are to go on in a minute.

WOODFORD: Oh well, then, lose no time. Have you got the letter?

WALTON: I have the letter, and I will keep it.

WOODFORD: No—no—you must not keep it! You are mad. You must give the letter to Master Yorick.

WALTON: Never fear. Yorick shall duly have the letter. *(To Thomas.)* Go! I am coming.

HEYWOOD: Stop, I say! I will tear it from thee with thy life if needs must.

WOODFORD: Tear the letter from him? Oh, merciful heavens! Heywood is as mad as all his players, and he isn't in the piece either. But, here alone, I will appeal to Shakespeare himself.

WALTON, *with sudden resolution*: Ah!

HEYWOOD: Well!

WOODFORD: Only five verses more.

WALTON: Duty is stronger than will— Take it.

Gives wrong letter.

HEYWOOD, *taking letter*: At last!

Exit Walton.

WOODFORD, *urging him*: Run!

THOMAS, *prompting him*: "My Lord, behold me here."

Exeunt all but Heywood.

HEYWOOD, *opens letter*: A piece of blank paper. Ah! The one he was to give Yorick in the play! And the other! Great heavens! He is already on the stage.

Rushes off.

CURTAIN

SCENE LAST

SCENE: *Magnificent hall in the palace of Count Octavio. Yorick as Octavio, Edmund as Manfredo, Alice as Beatrice, Walton as Landolfo, discovered. The Prompter in his place. The Count and Landolfo speak together without being heard by Beatrice and*

Manfredo who are at the back of the stage, their attitudes and faces betraying dismay and sorrow.

YORICK
[*As Count.*]

"Landolfo, though a deep anxiety
Preyed on my mind when thou wert absent, yet,
Thy presence causes me still greater sorrow.
Prythee, if thou hast that letter still
Give it me now, and end at least my doubts."

LANDOLFO, *giving him Edmund's letter*: "Take it!"
COUNT: "Oh!"
LANDOLFO: "I am avenged."
COUNT: "Go, Landolfo!"
    Landolfo bows and retires, looking back at Yorick with malicious joy.
ALICE, *as Beatrice, in a low tone*: "Manfredo!"
EDMUND, *as Manfredo*: "Beatrice!"
BEATRICE: "The hour has come."

COUNT

"Now I shall know at least thy lover's name.
Tremble, faithless woman! Tremble, ingrate,
Who has robbed me of my honor and my peace.
Vain all thy cunning, for here stands revealed
Thy guilt."
[*Opens letter.*]
    "My blood is frozen in my veins.
Here let it burn like fire! Woe to the wretch
For whose vile sake thou bringest this shame upon me."
[*Fixes his eyes on paper—starts violently.*]

How! What!
    Overwhelmed with amazement, he speaks in his own voice, forgetting play. Edmund and Alice look in dismay.
PROMPTER: "Oh! What do I behold?"
YORICK: What is this?
PROMPTER: "What do I behold?"
YORICK: Ah! Merciful God! (*Falls into chair—after a pause, starts up.*) "Here there is no escape in doubt. The truth imprisons me. Come!" (*Alice and Edmund approach. Drops again into chair—and stares at table—and then.*) Look!
    Shows letter.
EDMUND AND ALICE: Oh!
    Shrinking back.
YORICK: "Oh, that the earth might swallow us up." (*Drops again into chair—and stares at table—and then, with desperate effort, flings himself threateningly towards Edmund—checks himself—looks at the audience, giving them to understand the tumult of emotion in his soul—turns his eyes away. They fall on Alice. He rushes towards her—again checks himself—goes up stage —pressing hands to forehead and heart alternately.*) "Oh, that the earth might swallow us up."
    Edmund and Alice in terror.

PROMPTER: "Wert thou the villain—thou?" (*Pauses, and repeats.*) "Wert thou the villain—thou?"

YORICK, *yielding to the circumstances and unable to master his fury, makes the situation of the play his own, and speaks to Edmund in the words of the person he represents. From this point the dramatic fiction merges into reality and Alice, Edmund and Yorick lose themselves in its character:*

Why, what accursed coil is this, thou knave?
Thou mock'st me with a mimic misery.
So apt with that which eats into my soul
That I could well believe your Poet made
My wretchedness the mirror of his art.
His words spring to my lips. They speak my hate,
My fury, my despair. Thou painted Count!
Thou poor, unreal thing! Thou effigy!
Yorick and thou art one in wretchedness!
Let us be one in language—and speak thou
For me, that else were speechless in amaze
Before this devil's miracle of falsehood.
I make thy griefs my own, and from this point
I'll be no longer Yorick but Octavio!
And, oh, let them beware whose guilt has turned
This shadow of sorrow into living shame,
When Yorick and Octavio unite to right this wrong.
Now, prompter, what was the word?

PROMPTER: "Wert thou the villain—thou?"
YORICK: Ay! well—

"Wert thou the villain—thou? The faithless wretch,
The infamous seducer, thou, whose hand
Could strike his benefactor to the heart?
And art thou then the thief
That robbed me of my wife? And wert thou he
That put this mark of shame upon my brow?
To make me, while I live, a mock of men,
A hissing and a by-word?
My God! Is this the recompense he earns
Who pities and who loves the friendless? No!
On the betrayer fall the dishonor and the disgrace.
To the betrayed be all respect."

EDMUND

Oh! Father!

YORICK

"Do I dream?
Thy father, I? Then, may a father's curse
Be the more on such a son as thou."

EDMUND

Oh! No! No! What hast thou said?

YORICK
[*To Alice.*]
    "And thou.
Unhappy woman! What shall I say to thee?

Thou standest there so breathless and so mute,
To all immovable with thy gaze so fixed
That I could swear thou wert carved out of marble,
But that I hear the violent palpitation
With which thy heart responds to mine.
Oh! Where is the light, that, in a fatal hour,
Shone on me from those beauteaus eyes of thine,
Whose timorous softness shamed the evening star?
Where is that face divine, wherein, together,
The red rose and the orange blossom glowed.
I saw thee—would I had never seen thee—
When sad and wayworn, I drew near the bounds
Of middle life and unto me thou wast
A ray of sunshine from a clouded heaven!
My sadness turned to rapture! I adored thee
With all my soul—as men look up to angels.
Now I can see that thou wert false as fair,
And I can hate thee! No! I do not know
Whether I hate or love thee—Woe to thee!
For love turned madness knows not how to pardon
And if thou wouldst I should not strike thee dead,
Look at me, face to face, and die of shame."

ALICE
"O! Mercy!"

YORICK
          "In vain thou criest me mercy—
Thou shalt have none."

EDMUND
          "And yet she merits it."

YORICK
"Not she nor thou."

ALICE
          "My life belongs to thee!
Oh! Have a little pity— Kill me quickly!"

EDMUND
"I alone wronged thee and on me alone
Let your wrath fall."

YORICK
          "The guilt belongs to both.
And both of you shall render me account!"

EDMUND
"She, too? And will you kill her with your hand?"

YORICK
"Fool! For such a guilt as hers, could I do less
Than kill her?"

ALICE
          "Ay, let him, and make an end.
My blood can give him back his name unstained.
My blood alone can wash away his shame."

YORICK
Oh! Thou wouldst die content if he were spared!
But his blood shall be shed as well as thine!
And his blood first.
          [*Gets sword from wall.*]

EDMUND
          O, fatal night!

ALICE
                    O, Heaven!

YORICK
Choose thy sword.

EDMUND
          Yes, to sheathe it in my breast.
          [*Chooses sword and turns point to his breast.*]

YORICK
          [*Turning his sword against Alice.*]
And I sheathe mine in thy paramour.

EDMUND
          [*Throws himself before Alice.*]
                    Hold!

YORICK
Then defend! And remember well
It is the hand of vengeance threatens her.

ALICE
No, in the name of pity let me die.

EDMUND
As long as I have life thou shalt not die.

YORICK
Then thou art ready to defend her and
Wilt fight with me?

EDMUND
I will.

YORICK
                    In very earnest!
Regardless who I am and who thou art?

EDMUND
Yes!

YORICK
And thou'lt do thy best to kill me?

EDMUND
Yes! By Heaven, I will.

ALICE
          O, stay!

EDMUND

No! Never!

ALICE

Listen!

EDMUND

This man is thy enemy.

ALICE

Eternal Heaven!

YORICK

Good! Then we fight this quarrel to the death?

EDMUND

Crime cries for crime, and Hell is all too good
For such as thou.

[*They fight.*]

ALICE

[*Clinging to Edmund.*]

Oh, hold!

EDMUND

Unhand me!

ALICE

Wait!

YORICK

Thou makest him lose heart.

ALICE

[*Clinging to Yorick.*]

Then do thou be merciful!

YORICK

Thou aidest him against me!

ALICE

O, cruel!

[*Fight resumed.*]

EDMUND

[*Wounded—drops sword.*]

Heavens!

YORICK

Look!

[*To Alice.*]

ALICE

Ah!

EDMUND

[*Dying.*]

God forgive me!

ALICE

Help! Mercy!

YORICK

Silence!

[*Enter Heywood.*]

HEYWOOD

Yorick! What hast thou done?

[*Enter Woodford, Thomas, and the actors and
the employees. They crowd around, hiding
bodies from audience. Alice is taken away.*]

HEYWOOD, *to Audience*: The play cannot go on!
Carried away by his part, the comedian, Yorick, has
seriously wounded the actor who was playing Manfredo.
(*To Prompter.*) Bring down the curtain!

*The small curtain descends, and what follows is
seen and heard through this transparent curtain.*

WOODFORD: But where is Walton?

HEYWOOD: He has been found in the street, dead!
(*Seeing Yorick.*) Stand aside.

YORICK

Oh! My boy, my boy! Why, look you, Master,
He was a little lad when first I saw him,
Tattered and wan with hunger—with such eyes
Full of such silent histories of want and sorrow,
Orphanage and all the world's unkindness
They went straight to my heart. I took him home.
And there I kept him ever since—and he
Lies dead within my heart. Oh, I could
Tell you such things of him. I used to
Watch him in the night and rise
And listen to his breathing—feel his pulse
To know if any sickness threatened him.
His childish joys made me a happy man.
You all can hear me witness how I loved him.
My love has made me many a time the laugh
Of all of you. Oh! now methinks I dream
And am not I, or was not what I am!
And now this hand, to which thy little hand
So oft hath clung for safety in the dark—
This hand hath murdered thee! No! No!
Master! Tell me how could I kill my boy?
It must have been an accident—
A slip of the foot—an error of the hand.
Lend me thy sword, good Master.
Since mine hath pierced his heart
I cannot touch it.

[*Snatches sword.*]

Why, be not afraid!
You are thinking of that blackamoor of Venice
And surely not of this poor merry Yorick
That never yet was apt for tragedy.
I shall not harm myself. I am past all harm.
It must have happened thus.

[*Turns point—to breast—all start.
He laughs and removes it.*]

Nay, do not fear.
If I should pass this rapier through my heart,
It would not harm me. I am dead within!

HEYWOOD

He is mad!

YORICK

No! Was mad!

[*Kneeling to Edmund.*]

Oh! My boy, my boy! Kiss me once more!
My boy! Thy lips as yet
Warm with the life, shall redden there no more!
Oh! Edmund! Edmund! Edmund!
Oh! My son! My hope! My pride!
My hero among men! My good
Sweet boy! My little loving lad!

[Kisses him.]

Dead! Dead! Dead!
Here, Master, take thy sword.
It tempts me!

[Stabs himself.]

Pray for us, Master—for him—for her!
But most of all for me.
"Vengeance is the Lord's. I will repay,"
He said. How dark it grows.
Ring down the curtain. So! So!
Master! Master—

[Dies.]

HEYWOOD

Alas! Poor Yorick!

CURTAIN FALLS

END

Priscilla: A Comedy

[1879–82]

Sometime between October of 1879 and the summer of 1882, Howells dramatized *The Courtship of Miles Standish.* On October 22, 1879 (*Life in Letters,* I, 277), he wrote to H. W. Longfellow that "Mr. Barrett continues urgent for the drama of *Miles Standish,* and with your kind leave I am coming soon to look over the poem with you." Five days later he sent a hurried note to Longfellow (*Life in Letters,* I, 278): "I am extremely vexed—for your sake—to find a newspaper paragraph stating that 'Mr. Longfellow and Mr. Howells are writing a play for Lawrence Barrett on the subject of Miles Standish.' I suppose I need not say that I have never given anyone the slightest ground for making this extraordinarily foolish statement and that I am quite mystified by it. It is too bad that your kind permission for the use of this poem should be tormented into this annoying shape." Presumably with little delay, Howells started dramatizing the Miles Standish poem, but his completion date can only be surmised. References to the play in his letters are very few.

On August 7, 1880, Howells mentioned his work on this play in a letter to Rutherford B. Hayes (Hayes Memorial Library). Within the next twelve months he finished his dramatization and turned the script over to Lawrence Barrett, but the actor did nothing with it immediately, although Howells must have prodded him as he did other actors who showed interest in his plays. "Has Barrett concluded to do anything with the Miles Standish this fall?" Howells asked Osgood in a letter dated October 1, 1882 (Harvard Library). Apparently Barrett had not, and the following year Howells tried to publish his play in the *Atlantic Monthly.* Thomas Bailey Aldrich had already read the manuscript of *Priscilla* when on September 30, 1883, Howells wrote to Ernest Longfellow requesting publication permission (Harvard Library). For some reason, however, the play was never published, and, as Mildred Howells (*Life in Letters,* I, 277) points out, there is no record of its ever being acted.

Probably this play was in typescript form at one time, for Howells would most likely have sent a typed copy to Aldrich. But the only existing copy (in the files of Mr. William White Howells) is a manuscript of 129 pages—all in Howells' handwriting with the exception of three typed pages containing corrections in Howells' hand and three manuscript pages in an unidentified hand of copied dialogue from the Longfellow poem. At least twice—once in pencil and once in ink—Howells revised this manuscript play by adding or crossing out lines and speeches. The text printed here attempts to present Howells' revised version. In one instance, four pages concerning Alden's endeavor to place Standish's proposal before Priscilla's father have been omitted because the material was not consistent with the rest of the play.

The plot of the play follows Longfellow's poem, although Howells adds both characters and action for his drama. The dialogue is occasionally taken directly from the poem, but most of it is Howells' work. Poetic dialogue in comedy, however, was not popular at this date, and the language of this drama generally detracts from its over-all effect. Particularly successful in the play are the creation of Billington as a garrulous and comic character, and Howells' effective bits of dramatic irony.

Priscilla: A Comedy[1]

ACT I

SCENE I

GOODWIFE MARTIN

Still at your writing, Master Alden? Methought you had finished
Long before this. Well! There is something worse than being a widow:
That is, being a clerk! I am glad that I never learned writing!

ALDEN

[Writing.]

I shall have finished anon. What is it you would with me, goodwife?

GOODWIFE MARTIN

Nay, my business can wait. Well-a-day, when I look at this cabin,
And remember then the goodly hall of Sir Thurston of Standish,
With our brave captain in it, and sweet Mistress Rose there beside him,
As I have often seen them sitting—her hand held in his hand—
By the great fire in the hearth, and all his ancestors round him,
Looking down from their frames, and painted so pretty and life-like,
Knights with their shields and blazons, and ladies smelling to lilies,
Truly, it makes my heart ache for him, though he never murmurs!
Here to be sure is part of the armor—and how he scours and rubs it,
Half the day, dear heart, to keep it bright and in order!
But, will you tell me where are Mistress Rose and the portraits?

ALDEN

[Writing.]

She is with God, and they are still in their frames in the mansion
Where the Standishes dwelt of old, and where Captain Miles Standish
Would be now, had he not been wrongfully meted.

[Starting up.]

Why look, now!
If you have not made me put all that in my letter!
Will you be done and begone? I do implore and beseech you,
Do not molest me now: the Mayflower sails in the morning,
And I am near the close of my fortieth letter, and last one.

[Sits down and writes.]

GOODWIFE MARTIN

Is it so many, in sooth? Well, I will not trouble you further;
I will come again presently.

[Exit.]

[1] This play has not been published previously.

141

ALDEN

[*Writing.*]

Presently, aye. There, 'tis ended!
Let me see what 'tis I have written.

[*He comes forward, letter in hand, and reads.*]

Honored and dear my cousin:
You will learn from others whom I have greeted by letter,
How it hath fared with us here: how half our number lies buried
On the bleak seaward cliff at whose foot we touched land last December,
And lest the heathen around us should know how heavy our loss is,
How their graves have been leveled and planted. Already the young corn
Springeth above the faces of friends and kindred. It needs not
I should tax your pity with tidings so often repeated
That both the hand and the heart of the writer are sore with the telling.
Only this you must know, that she whose eyes drew me hither,
More than the will of the Lord, as you profest in your mocking—
God send you soberer mind!—is now—

[*Ceases reading, and with the paper stretched between his fallen hands, lifts his eyes passionately.*]

Oh, Priscilla, Priscilla!

[*Enter Miles Standish suddenly. Alden starts and
crushes the paper between his hands.*]

STANDISH

Have I broken in upon thee untimely?

ALDEN

[*Stupidly.*]

Untimely?

STANDISH

Aye. I can come at another season.

ALDEN

Nay, I have finished.
I have only this last of my letters to seal.

[*He smooths out the sheet in confusion.*]

STANDISH

[*Ironically.*]

And the good folk,
There, beyond the sea, find thy writing so fair they can read it when folded
As it were meant to be fired upon them out of a musket?

[*Alden makes some unintelligible murmurs; Standish approaches, and putting one hand affectionately
on his shoulder, points to the paper with the
other.*]

Or is this letter intended for certain eyes that could read it,
Were it but writ in kisses and signed with the name of John Alden?
Hast thou a sweetheart in England? Poor boy! Keep thy secret!
It shall be safe and sacred e'en from the love that I bear thee.
Fold up thy letter and seal it.

[*Alden hastily obeys, Standish walking up and
down the room; when Alden has finished the two
come forward together.*]

Look at these weapons,
Hanging here burnisht and bright and clean as if for parade and inspection!
This is the sword of Damascus I fought with in Flanders. This breastplate—
Well I remember the day!—it once saved my life in a skirmish.
Here in front you can see the very dent of the bullet
Fired pointblank at my heart by a Spanish arcabucero.

ALDEN

It was the breath of the Lord that slackened the speed of the bullet.
He in his mercy preserved you to be our shield and our weapon.

STANDISH

That may very well be. I can see my face in this armor.
That is because I clean it myself and do not leave it to others.
Serve yourself, would you be well served, is an excellent adage.
Then, too, there are my soldiers, the mighty army of Plymouth.
Twelve men, all equipped, having each his rest and his matchlock;
Eighteen shillings a month, together with diet and pillage.
And, like Caesar, I know the name of each of my soldiers.

ALDEN

Hail, our Caesar! Hail, our Captain of Plymouth!

STANDISH

Nay, mock not.
[Takes a volume from the shelf.]
You are a writer, and I am a fighter; but here was this Caesar,
Who could both write and fight and in both was equally skilful.

ALDEN

Somewhere I have read—but where I forget—he could dictate
Seven letters at once, at the same time writing his memoirs.

STANDISH

Truly a wonderful man was this Caius Julius Caesar.
He was married twice before he was twenty, and many times after.

ALDEN

There I think he was wrong. One love for one life is sufficient.

STANDISH

Spoken like one who has known but a first love! A great life
May be ample for loves more than one, only so they be honest;
Or for more than one marriage. But what was I saying of Caesar?
He, too, fought in Flanders, as he himself has recorded.
Finally, he was stabbed by his friend, the orator Brutus.

ALDEN

He should rather have had for his friend the scrivener Alden:
Then he had not been stabbed.

STANDISH

Nay, it irketh me somehow to hear thee
Jesting in that sort. Have you never heard what this Caesar
Did on a certain occasion in Flanders? When the rear guard
Of his army retreated, the front giving way, too,
And the immortal Twelfth Legion was crowded so closely together
There was no room for their swords? He seized a shield from a soldier,
Put himself straight at the head of his troops and commanded the captains,
Calling each by his name, to order forward the ensigns;
Then to widen their ranks, and give more room for their weapons.
So he won the day—the battle of something or other.
That's what I always say: if you wish a thing to be well done,
You must do it yourself, you must not leave it to others.

[Goes to window.]

Look! You can see from this window how I've had my howitzer planted
High on the roof of the church—a preacher who speaks to the purpose—
Steady, straight forward, and strong, with irresistible logic
Orthodox, flashing conviction right into the heart of the heathen.
Now we are ready, I think, for any assault of the Indians!
Let them come if they will, and the sooner they try it the better.
Let them come, if they like; be it sagamore, sachem or pow-wow,
Aspinet, Samoset, Corbitant, Squanto, or Tokamarhamon!

ALDEN

[Joining him at window.]

All the sunshine is gone that brightened the morning. How dreary
All the landscape lies in the chill of the afternoon shadow—
Forest, and meadow, and hill, and yon steel blue rim of the ocean!

STANDISH

Aye, and there on the hill by the sea lies buried Rose Standish.
She was the first to die of all who came in the Mayflower!

[Sighs and walks away.]

'Tis not good for man to be alone, say the Scriptures.
Every hour in the day I think it, and feel it, and say it,
Since Rose Standish died!

ALDEN

Can I ever forget her?
She was so gracious and fair, the godly and beautiful lady,
When I beheld you together, she withering moment by moment
Unto all eyes but your own, "And how will it be with Miles Standish,
When she is gone?" I thought. "And where shall he find such another
Apt for the place in the generous heart that she shall leave empty?

STANDISH

[Coming to him, and placing a hand on either of his shoulders.]

Aye, didst thou now, John Alden? I thank thee.

[He makes a turn about the room.]

Thy letters—hadst truly
Made an end ere I came?

ALDEN

Aye, truly. But wherefore—

STANDISH

Tell me—and if I ask amiss, then mayst freely deny me—
Art thou in love?

[*He scans Alden keenly, taking him by both arms.*]

Nay, spare thyself! I am answered. That letter—
Was it for her, as I guessed?

ALDEN

Nay, nay! She dwells not in England—
She—

STANDISH

Is sweet, comely damsel, then, of Holland! The letter,
Of her, not *for* her goes to some friend who knoweth thy secret!
Guess I right?

ALDEN

Yes—no! (The Lord forgive me the half-lie!)

[*Hastily.*]

Aye, the letter is meant for my cousin at Bristol. *She* dwelleth,
As I have said, not in England. She dwelleth, that is, she abideth,
That is to say, she presently tarrieth—stayeth—remaineth—
That is to say, her home, if one may call it her home—

STANDISH

That sufficeth.
I will inquire no farther. Be she in Holland or elsewhere,
There thy heart is with her, and thou canst conceive as a lover
All that I speak as a friend and thou canst do me an office
That I would trust to no other man. For I know thee, John Alden,
Leal and good and true, and I do believe that thou lovst me.

ALDEN

Aye, as I would my own father!

STANDISH

Well, not as thy *father*, precisely.
Say, as thy elder brother, thy comrade?

ALDEN

In what-wise soever,
You would rather be loved, I love you, Miles Standish.

[*Offers his hand.*]

STANDISH

Then hearken!

[*He takes Alden's hand and draws him close to him.*]

Why dost thou think that Caesar did ill to take more than one wife?

ALDEN

Ha, ha, ha, ha! And is this the service you want thee rendered,
Answering you such a question?

STANDISH

[*Embarrassed.*]

Nay, it leadeth, it leadeth!

Prythee, answer me why; and no more laughing, I pray thee.
I am not in the vein.

ALDEN

[*Soberly.*]

Why, then, you are answered, already.

By your own words: I spoke as a youth in his first love.

STANDISH

Was that all?

ALDEN

Verily, that was all. For the rest, why Caesar, at twenty,
Certainly was not too old to marry again. His baldness
Which is now a part of his fame could scarce have begun, then.
When I spoke, I must have had a grizzled beard in my mind's eye—

STANDISH

[*Regarding him fixedly.*]

When thou spokest thou hadst a grizzled beard in thy mind's eye!

[*Then he adds after a moment.*]

Whose?

ALDEN

[*Startled.*]

Of a truth, I had no one in my thought.

STANDISH

[*Severely.*]

The Book saith

It is not good for man to be alone. Doth the Book, peradventure,
Make an exception of men with grizzled beards?

ALDEN

[*As before.*]

Nay, truly.

STANDISH

Haply it biddeth a man, if he be past his boyhood when smitten
With the despair and desolation befalling the widower, rest so.

Letting the void in his heart and life go unfilled, be an outcast
From the joys and comforts of other men, homeless and hopeless?

[He walks away and then rushes stormily back.]

Was it, perchance, *my* grizzled beard that thou hadst in thy mind's eye?

ALDEN

No, on my soul! And I say it no whit for the fury that shameth
All your nobler part, and well might embitter thy kindness
That hath past between us, did I not know you far better
Than you would let me believe.

STANDISH

Forgive me! I wronged thee.
Dreaming that thou canst wrong me.

[After a moment of misgiving.]

And if I had thoughts of a marriage,
What wouldst thou say?

ALDEN

If you had thoughts of a marriage?

STANDISH

Aye, marriage.
Marriage concrete, not abstract, my scholar. A man and a woman united
Presently, here, at once, in the bonds of wedlock.

ALDEN

[Confusedly.]

At once, sir?

STANDISH

[Hotly.]

Aye, wherefore not? Why delay? If a thing is to do, let us do it
Out of hand, I say.

ALDEN

I had not spoken—

STANDISH

Why speak, then;
That is the thing I would have thee do!

ALDEN

But I fear me—I know not
Even if she do love me—

STANDISH

Thou? *Who* love thee? What coil art thou weaving?
What hast thou conceived from my words?

ALDEN

That you intended my marriage

With—with—her I love; that you—

STANDISH

[*With a gesture of disgust and rejection.*]

Oh!

ALDEN

I see; I have blundered.

Frankly, then, I will own, that when you spoke of a marriage
I could think of but one, and that was mine. My tongue spoke
Out of the fullness of my heart. But you can forgive me
When you remember how it was with yourself, once—

STANDISH

Remember?

Once? What new offence is this?

ALDEN

[*Warmly.*]

Now, truly. But, since I am human,

And have mine own infirmities, being perplexed with a temper
Often pushing control, I do implore and beseech you.
Use what patience you can, and in what you would say be explicit.

STANDISH

Then, I will be explicit, so plain that none can mistake me.
Wayfaring man or fool, or lover, or all three together:
I, Miles Standish, gentleman, lately of Duxbury Park, and at present,
Captain of Plymouth Colony, wish to be married.

ALDEN

[*With a great start.*]

You! Married!

STANDISH

[*Advancing upon him.*]

Wilt thou wholly rend the work of God's grace in my spirit
With this unseemly behavior, this shameless surprise, this indecent—
Wherefore should I not wish to be married?

[*Alden is silent; after a moment Standish resumes
in a wholly different tone.*]

I know what thou meanest.

Scarce three months are past since my Rose was laid in the snow-drifts,
Whiter and purer than they, and colder! Think not that another
Ever may know such love as I bore her! This second affection,
Moving me to fulfill the duty I owe and to give an example
Unto all that have been bereaved in this terrible winter
Not to remain unwed in barren sorrow, but duly
Bow to the will of the Lord, and where all are alone and in exile,

Mend as they may the ravage of death in orderly marriage—
This affection I say is like the love of a parent
Or a compassionate friend, than the love that I bore Rose Standish.
Aye, for the damsel is young enough to be my daughter, and she, too,
Hath been stripped of all, of father and mother and brother—

ALDEN

[With a start.]

Oh!

STANDISH

Aye. None of her kith or kin is left.

ALDEN

[Wildly.]

And her name is—

STANDISH

All in good time thou shalt know. Dost thou think that she might esteem me,
Haply, too old?

ALDEN

No, truly—

STANDISH

Or in my visage ill-favored?

ALDEN

Yours is a soldier's visage, scarred in battle and sunburnt,
Such as men envy and women think beautiful—

STANDISH

I might seem little of stature?

ALDEN

Nay, then, if I know not the maiden
How can I know her likings? But some that were godliest in old times
Were but little of stature, and he that was hugest, Goliath,
Died by the sling of a stripling. But I say if I know not the maiden—

STANDISH

Nay, thou knowest her well; thou hast seen her going and coming
All through the days and nights of this winter, as I have,
Now to the grave of the dead, and now to the bed of the dying—
Patient, courageous and strong.

ALDEN

And beautiful—lovely—

Aye!

STANDISH

Passing all others,
And in thy heart then hast said, as I have said in my own heart,
If there be angels on earth, as there are angels in heaven—

ALDEN

Heaven—aye—

STANDISH

She is an angel surely.

ALDEN

Surely—

STANDISH

And worthy

ALDEN

Worthy—

STANDISH

Worthy even of Rose Standish's place is this maiden Priscilla.

[*Walks away.*]

ALDEN

[*Like one in a dream.*]

Oh, I knew it, I knew it, I knew it! I knew that it must be!

STANDISH

Then thou dost approve? And thou wilt grant what I ask thee?
Go to Priscilla, then, the loveliest maiden of Plymouth,
Say that a blunt old Captain, a man not of words but of actions,
Offers his hand and his heart, the hand and the heart of a soldier.
Not in these words, thou knowest, but this in short is my meaning;
I am a maker of war, and not a maker of phrases.
You, who are bred as a scholar, can say it in elegant language,
Such as you read in your books of the pleadings and wooings of lovers,
Such as you think best adapted to win the heart of a maiden—
Why, man, what is the matter? Why standst thou aghast and bewildered,
With that sickly smile on thy visage as senseless and soulless
As the face of a clock that stops in a house struck by lightning!
Speak! And say no, if thou wilt.

ALDEN

[*With a great effort.*]

I would not deny you—
But such a message as that, I am sure I should mangle and mar it;
If you would have it well done—I am only repeating your maxim—
You must do it yourself, you must not leave it to others!

STANDISH

Truly, the maxim is good, and I do not mean to gainsay it;
But we must use it discreetly, and not waste powder for nothing.
Now, as I said before, I was never a maker of phrases.
I can march up to a fortress, and summon the place to surrender,
But march up to a woman with such a proposal, I dare not.
I'm not afraid of bullets, nor shot from the mouth of a cannon,
But of a thundering *No!* point-blank from the mouth of a woman
That I confess I'm afraid of, nor am I ashamed to confess it!
So, you must grant my request for you are an elegant scholar,
Having the graces of speech, and skill in the turning of phrases.

ALDEN

Nay, not in such a case. I have no wisdom in wooing.
I should find it hard to woo for myself, I too am timid
When it concerneth women; but oh! to ask for another—
Bid a damsel lay bare the sacred secret she hideth
Even from her own heart, and give it into my keeping,
Like a parcel to carry to him that would not come for it
In his own person—think of the profanation!

STANDISH

                                    I know naught,
I, of these fine-spun reluctancies. I am a soldier;
I know what I would, and I leave the why and the wherefore
Unto her: she is free to take or reject me. I ask thee
What I have asked in the name of our friendship. Wilt do it?
Yea or nay, then; wilt thou?

ALDEN

                    The name of friendship is sacred;
What you demand in that name I had not power to deny you,
But for that which I may not utter—

STANDISH

                    Which thou mayst not utter

ALDEN

Never, since you have asked me this service. I cannot serve you.
But in the name of our friendship I can be silent forever!

STANDISH

Silent? Not utter? Never? What mystery are thou concealing?

ALDEN

                    I would not gainsay you.
But, but—I was thinking—

STANDISH

            What?

ALDEN
Methought—

STANDISH

Well, what, man?
What wast thou thinking?

[*After a pause, furiously.*]
Knowest thou aught against the fame of the maiden?
Out with it, then! Or nay, if thou darest to breathe it in secret
Unto thyself alone by night in the depths of the forest
That breath were thy last!

[*Seizes him.*]

ALDEN

[*Loosing himself.*]
What madness! *I* to defame her?
I to feel or think or dream or imagine aught of Priscilla
That might not worship a saint? You, *you* are guilty to doubt it!
You are unworthy of her, if you let the faintest conjecture
Cloud, not her purity, no, but the soul that reflects her perfection,
And I might well refuse to bear your message, for her sake!

STANDISH

Nay, forgive me! I do confess that I was wrong to have questioned—
Yet—yet—yet and yet, what was it thou mightest not have uttered?
Speak, for thou knowest that I am hot, and quick to be jealous,
Not enduring the sting of a doubt that festers and rankles,
Fain to pluck it forth, though I pluck forth my life with it. Is there,
Haply, aught— Dost thou know or fear or think that Priscilla
Loveth some other—

ALDEN

[*With a sigh.*]
I know not; nor can I say that I think it.

STANDISH

Then—such a thing may happen—perchance thou art privy
Unto the love of some other for her?

[*Alden starts.*]
I see. I have guessed it!
Let me embrace thee!

[*Alden awkwardly submits.*]
And know that Miles Standish can honor thy feeling,
Though it be fatal to him, that forbiddeth thee to betray him.
If thou art anywise bound, in terms explicit or tacit,
Unto him whose name I would scorn to ask of thee, say so,
And thou art straightway absolved from all that I hoped or dreamed.
Speak!

ALDEN

[*Faintly.*]
I am nowise bound to him. Rather—

STANDISH

                    Is he more worthy,
Trustier, abler than I to guard and cherish Priscilla
In these tremulous times?

ALDEN

                    He cannot be paralleled for a moment
With you in either of these regards!

STANDISH

                    He is younger?

ALDEN

Younger—aye!

STANDISH

          And comelier?

ALDEN

                    Nay, that I think not.
There is not a comelier man than Miles Standish,
Not in Plymouth alone, but—

STANDISH

          Mayhap this other is taller?

ALDEN

                              [Looking at him.]
Taller—aye.

STANDISH

                              [Thoughtfully.]
          Thou art nowise bound, and he is no better nor fitter.
                              [Gayly.]
Then, for the few years less and the few inches more, let us risk them!
All is not in complexion nor all in cubits of stature.
I can conceive why at first thou shouldst halt and consider it fairly,
Thou mightest plead my cause when thou knowest the love of another;
And I had been the last to ask aught that sullied thy honor,
Or that would tax thy tender conscience hereafter with treason.
Yet I am a foe to overfine spinning of scruples;
And I urge my request again withouten misgiving,
Either for my sake or thy sake. Wilt go for me to Priscilla?

ALDEN

                              [Sadly.]
Aye, I will go—I will go.

STANDISH

          Then say to her all that I bade thee.
                    [Alden starts precipitately and absent-mindedly
                    toward the door.]
Nay—stay!
                              [Very earnestly.]
          Canst thou not tell me the name of this other?

ALDEN

I cannot.

STANDISH

Neither give me any clue whereby I might guess it?

ALDEN

Trust me, I may not!

STANDISH

I will not press thee further. My meaning,
Thou wilt well believe, was not to seize an advantage.

ALDEN

Surely!

STANDISH

But I would not cross the path of a friend, if I knew it.
All is fair in love they say, but I never heard it of friendship.
Is this rival some friend of mine?

ALDEN

There is no one among us,
Who is not the friend of Miles Standish.

STANDISH

Thou lovst me,
That I know. But do not glaze the matter in kindness.
Answer me fairly.

ALDEN

[Desperately.]

Then, I say that the other is no one
Having a special claim on your mercy, but he rather remaineth
After the worst be done, your debtor. Let this suffice thee!
Also let me go in pity!

STANDISH

Go and God speed thy errand.
Wilt thou not wear thy hat?

ALDEN

[Coming back for it.]

Oh!

[Starts again.]

STANDISH

Best take thy doublet. 'Tis chilly!

[Alden comes back and gets it from him.]

How distraught are you scholars! And take this last charge from Miles Standish:

Look you well in all you say for me not to disadvantage yon other;
Be to my rival however he is, *more* than just, and defraud him
Not by a word or a look, or a thought, and if the claim of my friendship
Tempt thee to aught that is more or less than noble, remember,
He who would serve him ignobly is not the friend of Miles Standish.
Wilt thou promise?

ALDEN

O, aye, I promise, I promise, I promise.

[*They go out of separate side doors.*]

SCENE II

*Alden, seated alone, on a fallen tree in the forest. At the bottom of the scene is
Priscilla's house. The early twilight has begun, and a light appears at her casement.
While Alden soliloquizes, a spring snow begins but all in large clots.*

ALDEN

Oh, what a heavy burden is laid upon me! Surely,
Surely, methought he must have understood that *I* was the other!
Could it have been that he *did* understand, and would punish,
By a feint in turn my own hypocritical feigning?
Then were I justly punished! This conflict within me,
How can I bear it longer? And yet, in what sort shall I end it?
Shall I seek safety in flight? Conceal myself in the Mayflower,
And, from my hope and despair together sail in the morning?
I should leave only hope behind! Shall I rather go to Priscilla,
Speak my love and implore her to fly with me? Never!
Nothing but sorrow and shame could wait on such cowardly treason!
Then, shall I go to her and give her the message I promised,
And be the bearer from her again— O my soul! of what answer?

[*He hides his face in his hands. Priscilla is heard
within singing the Hundredth Psalm.*]

PRISCILLA

Be thou exalted, O my God!
Above the heavens where angels dwell;
Thy power on earth be known abroad,
And land to land thy wonders tell.
My heart is fixed; my song shall raise
Immortal honors to thy name.

Awake, my tongue, to sound his praise,
My tongue, the glory of my frame.
High o'er the earth his mercy reigns,
And reaches to the utmost sky;
His truth to endless years remains,
When lower worlds dissolve and die.[1]

ALDEN

It is her voice, and it bringeth me peace. It bids me,
Honor the truth at whatever cost; to seek and think of that only.

[*He goes to the cottage door and knocks. The
scene parts, and he is discovered within at the
threshold. Priscilla, singing at her wheel in the
chimney corner, sees him, and rising, comes forward to give him her hand.*]

1 See Psalm 108, verses 1–5.

PRISCILLA

[*Joyfully.*]

John! Is it you? How kind of you, when you were so weary
Writing all those letters that Goodwife Martin left you intent on!
Have you finished at last? Sit down by the fire and rest you,
Then. Here, take my father's chair—

[*Scanning him closely.*]
You are covered with snowflakes!

Is it snowing without?

ALDEN

[*Looking at his coat, absently.*]
It must be! Methought it was snowing

Only within!

PRISCILLA

Within? You are pleased to speak in a riddle.

ALDEN

Riddle?

PRISCILLA

I do profess, if you parrot me, after this fashion.
I shall be angry with you. Your hair and mustachio are grizzled
As your great Captain yonder—

ALDEN

[*Quickly.*]
You like not grizzled mustachios?

PRISCILLA

If they shall change to yellow again by the fire—

[*Demurely.*]
Why ask you?

Such a strange question to ask!

ALDEN

Aye, is it so? Something

Stranger still I was to ask—

PRISCILLA

[*Tenderly.*]
What was it?

ALDEN

I cannot!

It is too much. No, no! I never can ask it! I cannot!

PRISCILLA

[*Ironically.*]
Then will you be seated? Or, if it be not your pleasure,
Stand! Nay, John, you are ill! What is it hath crossed you?

ALDEN

[With an effort.]

Nothing has crossed me. I am quite well.

PRISCILLA

[Returning to her wheel.]

I must go to my spinning.
If it diverteth you less to talk than to stand and stare straight before you
Like a man who has looked on a ghost—

ALDEN

I have looked on the Mayflower.

PRISCILLA

[Coming quickly back to him.]

Ah, you are homesick, too! I might have remembered! Forgive me!

ALDEN

Ah, Priscilla!

PRISCILLA

You were thinking of England; I knew it:
That is what makes you so sad. Is this like April in England?
Do you believe that there the snow is falling this evening
Into the half-finished nests that the birds began in the morning?
No, the English April is no such deceiver and mocker.
She may be fickle enough with her freaks of sunshine and shower
But she has no delight to play at hide and seek with December
Like this squaw April here, this faithless, pitiless savage.

ALDEN

Are you loath to be here?

PRISCILLA

Are you?

ALDEN

I am weak and a sinner.
Aye, I will own that my heart, too, hath ached all day.

PRISCILLA

Nay, it cannot be sinful, John, to wish ourselves back in England.
Those that I live with here are kind, and I love my religion.
Here are the nameless graves of my father and brother and mother;
This should be my home; but I wish myself back in Old England.
You will say it is wrong; but I cannot help it: I almost
Wish myself back in Old England, I feel so lonely and wretched.

ALDEN

Lonely, Priscilla?

PRISCILLA

Nay, I am not so ungrateful. I meant not
Lonely, when friends like you are with me.

ALDEN

Priscilla! Oh—

PRISCILLA

[*Sympathetically.*]

What, John?

ALDEN

Can I believe—is it true—then you would forgive me— Oh heaven!
What was I going to say?

PRISCILLA

I profess, I cannot imagine.
But let me hear what it was.

ALDEN

[*Gravely controlling himself.*]
I do not condemn you, Priscilla—

PRISCILLA

I am so glad. I feared you would blame my womanly weakness—

ALDEN

Stouter hearts than a woman's have quailed in this terrible winter.
Yours is tender and trusting—

PRISCILLA

It trusts the friends it has proven.

ALDEN

Nay, do not break in upon me!

PRISCILLA

I will not speak.

ALDEN

'Tis not easy,
At the best. Where was I?

PRISCILLA

My heart was tender and trusting—

ALDEN

Aye, I remember now!
So I have come to you, with an offer and proffer of marriage—

PRISCILLA

[*Starting rapturously toward him.*]

John!

ALDEN

Hold, hold! Do not speak! With an offer and proffer of marriage
Made by a good man and true, Miles Standish, the Captain of Plymouth!

PRISCILLA

[*Retreating, with a look of reproach and amaze.*]

You come with this offer to me! Do not answer! You've said it!
It is enough. You cannot undo it!

ALDEN

Priscilla, hear me, in pity!

PRISCILLA

[*Proudly.*]

Hear you? Oh, certainly, Master Alden. Why should I not hear you?
Though methinks that having once delivered your message
You might rather hear me. But what have you now to rage further?

ALDEN

[*Stupidly.*]

Nothing.

PRISCILLA

Nothing in explanation from him, or excusal?
If the great Captain of Plymouth is so very eager to wed me,
Why does not he come himself and take the trouble to woo me?
If I am not worth the wooing I surely am not worth the winning.
Bear him this answer from me.

[*She goes to her wheel and sits down at it, while
Alden stands silent in the middle of the floor.*]

Why did he not come in person?

ALDEN

He—he—is busy with public affairs. I ought to have told you—
He has no time for such things—

PRISCILLA

For such things! Ha, ha, ha! He bade you,
Tell me he had no *time?*

ALDEN

No, no; but I knew it—

PRISCILLA

Indeed, sir!
Then this gracious excuse is your own skilful contrivance!
Go back again to your mighty Captain of Plymouth and tell him

That he has erred first of all in his ambassador. Tell him
That the dexterous writer he chose to deliver his message,
Did not embellish his theme or array it in beautiful phrases
But came straight to the point, and blurted it out like a school boy.
Even the Captain himself could scarcely have said it more bluntly.

[*Spins.*]

ALDEN

That was my fault, not his. I do beseech you, Priscilla—

PRISCILLA

Mistress Mullins, please you. If I must to be courted by proxy,
Like a princess, let me be used with state.

ALDEN
Mistress Mullins,

Will you let me speak?

PRISCILLA

[*Coming forward again.*]
Aye, more than you will, Master Alden.

What would you say?

ALDEN
Alas, I know not.

PRISCILLA
Mayhap you can tell me.

If he has no time for such things before he is married,
How he is likely to find it or make it after the wedding?

ALDEN

Truly, I cannot tell you that. But—

PRISCILLA
You are like all the others.

All you men are alike; you don't understand us, you cannot.
Doubtless you think it is quite enough for your Captain of Plymouth
When he has made up his mind after thinking of this one and that one,
Choosing, selecting, rejecting, comparing one with another,
Only to send to me word of his decision, and—

ALDEN
No! On my life, no!

PRISCILLA

Doubtless were you in his place, you would be amazed and indignant
That I did not respond with "Aye, and my duty and thanks, sir!"
Unto a love that I never suspected. You would not?

ALDEN

No!

PRISCILLA

Then, if you were in love with a woman—I merely suppose it,
For such a thing could not be!—you would not send to apprize her
By your friend, but would come yourself—

ALDEN

                                Through fire and water!
I would throw myself at her feet, and— Oh!
                                *[Launches himself towards her, and then recol-
                                lects himself.]*

PRISCILLA

                                Mighty pretty!
Then, sir, how durst you come to me on an errand you never
Would have presumed to send another upon? Tell your Captain,
One does not send to say one loves, but comes and declares it!
Had he but waited a while, had he only showed that he loved me,
Even this Captain of yours—who knows?—at last might have won me,
Old and rough as he is; but now it never can happen!
                                [Returns to her wheel.]

ALDEN

Do not say that, I implore you, or I must hold myself traitor—
False to his cause, or cold. Consider how I have suffered
In this service for him—

PRISCILLA

Why, then, did you do it?
He has not done it for you, and you, you say, would not ask it.

ALDEN

Ah, but there is no equal ground whereon to compare us—
Me a penniless scholar, with him who is famous and gentle.
Surely you must have heard of all his battles in Flanders—

PRISCILLA

Aye, we heard nothing else for weeks in our voyaging hither.

ALDEN

How with the people of God he chose to suffer affliction—

PRISCILLA

That I have heard of, too, from the Captain himself, on occasion.

ALDEN

How, in return for his zeal they made him Captain of Plymouth;

He is a gentleman born, can trace his pedigree plainly
Back to Hugh Standish of Duxbury Hall in Lancaster, England,
Who was the son of Ralph, and the grandson of Thurston de Standish;
Heir to vast estates of which he was basely defrauded,
Still bears the family arms, and hath for his crest a cock argent,
Combed and wattled gules, and all the rest of the blazon.

PRISCILLA

Ah, a wondrous bird, that family cock! Methinks I have heard it
Crowing night and morn, and early and late, for a year past—
Captain Standish never opens his mouth but I hear it.
Give me some other reasons.

ALDEN
                    Nay, there are plenty of others.
He is a man of honor, of noble and generous nature.
Though he is rough, he is kindly. You know how all through the winter
He has attended the sick, with a hand as kind as a woman's.

PRISCILLA

Aye, that is true. But so hath the meanest among us. Go on, sir.

ALDEN

He is hasty and hot, I cannot deny it, and headstrong;
Stern as a soldier may be, but hearty and placable always.
And he is not to be laughed at because he is little of stature,
For he is great of heart, magnanimous, courtly, courageous.
Any woman in Plymouth, nay, any woman in England
Might be happy and proud to be called the wife of Miles Standish.

PRISCILLA
        [While Alden speaks she has been gathering her
        wool into her apron; as he stops, she rises and
        goes towards the door in the back, and puts her
        hand on it.]

Why, and so well she might—if only she loved him! I quit you,
Now of all coldness in his behalf. You have argued it well, and persuaded
Till you are hot and red in the cause of this wonderful hero.
He should be pleased with you. You have done yourself and him honor,
And I am much to blame that I do not yield to such wooing.
But when you were talking, and celebrating his merits
With a zeal so single, I thought in my heart, what a pity
All this should be for another: Why don't you speak for yourself, John!
        [She slips through the door, and casts a laughing
        look at him over her shoulder. He stands trans-
        fixed, gazing after her, and crushing his hat be-
        tween his hands.]

CURTAIN

ACT II

SCENE

The house of Miles Standish as in the first act. Standish discovered reading a huge volume open on his knees. As Alden enters furtively, he looks up, noisily closes the book, and rising, comes briskly forward to meet him.

STANDISH

[*Speaking, cheerily.*]

Ah, thou hast come at last! Thou hast been a long time on thy errand.
Though the woods are between us, Priscilla's house is not far off;
But thou hast lingered so long, that while thou wert coming and going
I have had leisure to read half the Commentaries of Caesar;
I have fought ten battles and sacked and demolished a city
In the space thou hast taken to storm and carry one damsel.
Come, sit down, and tell me in order all that has happened.
Down, I say; sit down, man!

[*Pushes him into a chair.*]

And do not delay with the answer.
Out with it, straight! Say first what she answered and after
How she answered. Speak! God's mercy! Where is thy tongue, man?
Art thou dumb, or mad, with that hang-dog look of thine! I tell thee
Time was when if a man had so mocked my importance
I had unlocked his lips with my dagger. Dost hear me?
Hast thou seen the maiden, dead or alive, well or ailing?

ALDEN

I have seen her, live and well.

STANDISH

So far, so good. And her answer?

ALDEN

Presently. Let me take thought.

STANDISH

Let thee take thought, to deliver
Plain yes or no! Or stay! Thou art right. For when did a woman
Answer plain yes or no! But there is no need to support it
With her circumlocutions. Come straight to the pith of the matter
Like a man with a man.

ALDEN

I must be silent forever
If you will not let me tell it all as it happened.

STANDISH

God grant me patience, then. But beware and dispatch as thou mayst!
Well!

[*Sinking into a chair in front of Alden.*]

ALDEN

She was singing, as I drew near the cottage.

STANDISH

Was singing!
Mighty important! Perchance can tell me *what* she was singing?

ALDEN

It was the Hundredth Psalm.

STANDISH

[*Fuming with impatience.*]
The Lord have mercy upon me!
Well, thou didst knock at the door—

ALDEN

Nay, I lifted the latch without knocking.

STANDISH

[*Furiously.*]
'S blood!

ALDEN

And she came to meet me from where she sat at her spinning
In the chimney corner with both hands outstretched to receive me.

STANDISH

Fire and fury!

ALDEN

Saying she knew it was I—

STANDISH

God's compassion!
I shall burst!

ALDEN

And that all the afternoon she was thinking—
No, that came afterwards! But she had been thinking that moment
How in the first great snow I broke a path to her threshold,
And she let me in with the snow upon my mustachio
White as any old man's. And I asked if a gray bread displeased her,
And she said, nay, if it melted to gold in the chimney corner.
[*Standish rises and stamps about the room.*]
So we fell talking of this and that, and how she was homesick,
And how she had been thinking the whole afternoon of Old England.
And she told me that she feared it was wrong to be homesick;
And I told her, not so, for many stronger than women
Had been sorely discouraged by such a terrible winter.
And so I brought it about to say that she in her weakness

Needed a stay and protector, and then without further preamble
Told her that I had come from you with an offer of marriage—

STANDISH

[Rushing upon him.]

Now, by the beard of Mars! If thou do not report what she answered,
Straight as a bullet out a gun, I swear I will kill thee!
What did she answer?

ALDEN

She answered nothing. She asked me,
Why you had not come yourself with your offer of marriage.

STANDISH

[Thoughtfully.]

She had a right to ask that. And then, what didst thou make answer?

ALDEN

That you were busy with public affairs, and had no time for such matters.

STANDISH

Well!

ALDEN

Then she said if she was not worth wooing she was not worth winning.
Bade me go back and tell you that I had mismanaged my message
And that you could not have done it worse yourself.

STANDISH

She said that?

ALDEN

That and more of the same effect; so that being wounded and smitten
With her reproach and the fear that perchance I had bungled the business,
Out I launched in your praise. I will not repeat what I uttered
From a heart full of love for you. But she sat at her spinning
Listening to every word, and rose up when I had finished,
Gathered her work in her apron and slid to the door of her chamber
And with her hand upon it said I had quitted me well of my errand,
And that she took back all she had said of my being awkward and lukewarm
In your behalf; and pushed open her door, but or ever she vanished
Looked at me over her shoulder, and laughed—methinks I can see her
Now, how she laughed—and said—

STANDISH

And said— Speak now, or by Caesar

Never speak more!

ALDEN

And said, why don't you speak for yourself, John?

STANDISH

[Stamping on the floor, and wildly shouting.]

You have betrayed me, John Alden! Supplanted, defrauded, betrayed me!
One of my ancestors ran his sword through the heart of Wat Tyler;
Who shall prevent me from running mine through the heart of a traitor?
Viler traitor than he, for you art a traitor to friendship!

ALDEN

No, on my life, not so! You may drive your sword through my bosom,
But you shall draw it forth with no drop of treason upon it.
Listen to me! She scarcely spoke, I rushed from the cottage,
Rushed like a man insane, and wandered alone by the seaside.
Like an awakened conscience, the sea was moaning and tossing,
And in my soul was the struggle and tumult of passions contending;
Love triumphant and crowned, and friendship wounded and bleeding,
Passionate cries of desire, and importunate pleadings of duty.
"Is it my fault," I said, "that the maiden has chosen between us?
Is it my fault that he failed—my fault that I am the victor?"
Then within me there thundered a voice, like the voice of the Prophet,
It hath displeased the Lord! and I thought of David's transgression,
Bathsheba's beautiful face, and his friend in the front of the battle.[1]
Shame and guilt overwhelmed me, abasement and self condemnation
But I lifted my head and looked at the sea, and beheld there
Dim in the gathering night the Mayflower riding at anchor,
Rocked on the rising tide, and ready to sail in the morning.
Here was rescue, escape! And I said I will go to Miles Standish,
Tell him all and sail with the ship back to England tomorrow.
So shalt Priscilla be his. Farewell, Miles Standish; be happy;
And hereafter judge more leniently him who can never be happy.

STANDISH

I shall judge you then as now, for a hypocrite, knave, and a traitor.
Think you to seal my lips with this pretence of devotion?
Think you I'd want a maiden who had offered herself to another?
Shame upon you both!

ALDEN

No, not upon her!

STANDISH

Upon you, then,
Doubly and triply on you! I will not rail at a woman.
You were that other, then, to whose love you were privy,
When you first faltered at going to her and when I besought you
If there were aught in honor that hindered your doing my errand,
Not to do it, for my sake? Why could you have not spoken frankly,
Said that you loved her and spared me this disgrace and confusion?

1 See II Samuel, 11:1–12:25.

ALDEN

[Proudly.]

If it appear not why, I cannot make it apparent.

STANDISH

No, but you rather went with this secret sapping your fealty,
And having set my claim before her, with laughter and mocking,
Come back to me·with this tale of "Why don't you speak for yourself, John?"

ALDEN

Oh, you wrong me, Miles Standish!

STANDISH

And you have wronged me, traitor Alden,
You, who lived under my roof, whom I cherished and loved as a brother;
You, who have fed at my board, and drunk at my cup, to whose keeping
I have intrusted my honor, my thoughts the most sacred and secret,
You too, Brutus! Ah, woe to the name of friendship hereafter!
Brutus was Caesar's friend and you were mine, but hereafterward
Let there be nothing between us but war and implacable hatred.
Here!

[He runs to the wall and takes down two of the swords hanging there.]

You shall take my Damascus blade, and I will take this Toledo
Wrenched from an old Castilian who fell by my hand before Bruges.

[He thrusts it into Alden's hand.]

Come, you say I have wronged you, and though by birth you are simple,
You shall have a gentleman's satisfaction. Have at me!
I have given you lessons in fence, and if you be not a coward
You can stand to me fairly, and I will take no advantage.
On! Now!

ALDEN

[Flinging the sword from him.]

No!

STANDISH

You will not?

ALDEN

No, you may kill me.
But I will never lift hand upon you!

STANDISH

I will make you then, sirrah!
If not in your defence, then in hers—in that of the maiden
Whom you would kindly bestow upon me—of that hoyden,
Yonder bold-faced—

ALDEN

[With a cry of rage, running to pick up the sword.]

Oh!

STANDISH

[As they fly at each other.]

Methought I should make you!

*[They fight, and just as Standish disarms Alden,
the door opens and enter John Billington.]*

BILLINGTON

Gallantly done, I profess! Methought when I opened upon you,
Here was very war, instead of a lesson in fencing!
You did send Master Alden's weapon flying in such sort,
That I looked next to see you plunge your blade in his midriff.

STANDISH

[Lowering his point.]

Why, there was danger of it! You see, I give way to my fancy,
When I take the sword in hand, as in like manner Master Alden
Doth when he takes up his pen, and I fancied there stood there a traitor!
One that had surely wronged me where he should have been fastest and truest,
And on a sudden I felt in my blade such an itching and tingling
That I knew not what might have chanced if it had not been for your coming.

[To Alden.]

Hang the swords up, Master Alden. I will resume your instruction
Presently.

[To Billington.]

Well, Goodman Billington, what is your errand?

BILLINGTON

Under the Lord, it seems, to save Master Alden's life, sir.
But if you ask the purpose methought I had in my coming,
Worshipful Captain, 'tis this.

STANDISH

What is it?

BILLINGTON

It needs, sir,

That I go back a little.

STANDISH

Go back, then, in God's name. But haste you,
Or I may not have patience to wait your returning.

BILLINGTON

Sir, I know my duty and will dispatch. You remember
How one month ago, I lost myself in the forest?

STANDISH

Surely, Goodman Billington! None is allowed to forget it.

BILLINGTON

How, for five long days and nights, I wandered and wandered,

Up and down in the woods, and lived upon roots and wild berries,
Such as I could find?

STANDISH
I remember that equally, goodman.
Well.

BILLINGTON
And worshipful Captain, perchance you also remember,
How the Indians found me and fed me, but held me captive
Until his worship, Governor Carver, sent and paid them my ransom;
Forty pounds of codfish: salted and dried?

STANDISH
I remember!
Some thought you dear at half the cost. But I charge you,
Tell me now without further preamble your business! There lately
[*He glances at Alden.*]
Came to me one with a disagreeable message, who told it
Out to me word by word till methought I had stifled
In my impatience. 'Twas a story of infamous treason
Which he thought with time he could paint of another complexion,
But it grew only the blacker. Now, Goodman Billington, look you!
If you have aught to tell me, good or bad, why, out with it.
Straight! Else, yet you get gone. I have no leisure for gossip.

BILLINGTON
There you are right, Master Standish. And knowing how scant was your leisure,
All the way to your door I was studying how to discharge me
Quickest. You must know that while I abode with the heathen,
Being a man wont to note what passeth before him and ponder
Much upon this and that, I studied their customs and manners;
And one day there came from another tribe to the people
That I was captive with till they sent my ransom of codfish—
Do you follow me, worshipful Captain?

STANDISH
So sharply, goodman,
That I can scarce keep my dagger from pricking you onward.

BILLINGTON
Where was I? Oh! Aye! Codfish! There came as I told you,
From another tribe a messenger, feathered and painted;
And in his hand he bore a serpent-skin, filled like a quiver,
Full of arrows. There, methought, is something fit to be noted.
So I asked one of the heathen that knew a few words of our English,
What they meant, and he said it meant a challenge to battle:
'Twas a sign that the tribe who sent it had taken the warpath,
So he said, against the tribe that held me a captive

Until the codfish came. And I said to myself 'twas a matter
Worthy of note, and I set it down in my mind.

STANDISH

Is that all?

BILLINGTON

Aye.

STANDISH

Why, thou fool, overbought with a tithe of the codfish
That thy ramson cost, dost thou come to me then with this
Tedious story passing all suffrance? Hast thou a fondness for putting
That thick pate of thine in the jaws of the lion to prove them
If they have strength to crush it? Be off, sir, or ever—

BILLINGTON

Worshipful Captain! Stay! I have only told you my story.
Now for the application. What should I see in the forest,
Just before nightfall this e'en upon the skirts of the village
But a pair of the heathen and one of them bearing a snake-skin
Filled as full as 'twould hold with arrows, just like that other.
Captain, I do profess that from that day yonder to this day,
I had not thought of that snake-skin of arrows. It went like the lightning
Through my brain that war was somewhere intended. I hasted
After the twain, and followed them straight to the council,
Where with our godly Elder Brewster, the magistrates all are assembled
And where they stay your presence. Aye, they sent me to pray you
Make what haste you could, sir.

[Exit.]

STANDISH

Merciful Providence, keep me
From the offence of blasphemy! Alden, my breast-plate and buckler,
Here! And give me my blade of Damascus, and fasten my gorget.
Now, my morion! So! Let the savages see that a soldier,
Aye, and a gentleman leads the forces of Plymouth. I'm ready
If they have come for war to give them war on the instant.
Yet, do not think you have done services to me as your friend, sir.
When this public danger is over, we will return to our quarrel.

[He rushes toward the door, which opens and admits Brewster, Carver, and citizens.]

Welcome, gentlemen! But you put me to shame by your coming
Hither to me. 'Twas my duty to go to you, and my pleasure
To have been with you ere this, but that your envoy kept me
While he discoursed of his estrayal, his capture and ransom,
Ignorant quite till now that you have desired to see me.
Sirs, will you sit? I have a chair for his worship, Governor Carver,
And for his reverence, Elder Brewster. As for the others,

I am grieved that my house affords me no means of expressing
That high sense of their worth that my heart doth not lack in toward them.

[*He places chairs for Carver and Brewster at either end of the table, and bows low to the rest.*]

Gentlemen, what good chance am I to thank for this visit?

CARVER

Would that the chance were good, indeed! But we come, worthy Captain,
Rather than wait for you. It matters not, here in Plymouth,
Where all houses are humble alike, in which we assemble for council,
Nay, since it seems we are to receive a belligerent message,
No place can be more fit than the house of our Captain. Without, here,
Standeth an ambassador sent by the heathen, and with him,
Our good friend and interpreter, Hobomok.

STANDISH

Hath he
Yet delivered his message?

CARVER

We would not receive it,
Save in your presence, Captain.

STANDISH

So much the better. Admit him.
You that stand next to the door.

[*They open; enter with a musketeer on either side, Corbitant and Hobomok; the former naked to the waist. He advances haughtily to the table, and lays down upon it the snake-skin filled with arrows, retires a pace or two and with folded arms defiantly regards Standish.*]

Well, Hobomok, who is this warrior?

HOBOMOK

This is the great chief, Corbitant.

STANDISH

Who are his people?

HOBOMOK

To the westward,
Dwell the Pocanawkits, his people.

STANDISH

What is his errand?

HOBOMOK

War.

BILLINGTON

[*Coming eagerly forward.*]

War, quotha! Said I not right, Captain Standish? I knew it;
When I saw that serpent-skin filled with arrows, I knew it!

I was not lost in the forest, nor lived upon roots and wild berries
Till the heathen took me, and our good governor bought me
With forty weight of salt codfish—for nothing, eh, Captain.
Truly, I was a man to learn something even from the heathen.

STANDISH

You should have also learnt from the savages, how to be silent
When your betters would speak.

[*To Hobomok.*]

Why declare they war against us?

HOBOMOK

Two years ago an English shipman came to their borders for traffic.
But when he had got their people on board of his vessel,
He commanded his people to fire upon them, and slew them.
Some leaped into the sea and escaped. They that were murdered,
Ever since then have cried aloud in the dreams of their kindred
For revenge. The Pocanawkits can bear it no longer.
Therefore they send you this message of war. So Corbitant sayeth.
Hobomok only repeats the words of Corbitant.

STANDISH

[*Retiring.*]

Governor Carver,

'Tis for the civil offices to test herein the will of the people.

CARVER

[*Rising.*]

What do you say, my masters? Any person in here is permitted
Frankly to speak his mind.

[*Sits.*]

BILLINGTON

Most worship governor, I say

And I will utter my sense without either fear or affection,
That before you sent and paid my ransom with codfish,
Forty weight, salted and dried, I heard much talk from the heathen,
Touching these Pocanawkits, and that, from all I could gather,
They are a parlous crew! There you have my opinion upon it,
Neither minced nor mimicked.

CARVER

[*Without heeding him.*]

You, Master Winslow, what say you?

WINSLOW

[*Coming forward.*]

Only this, your worship: that we have done naught to these heathen
Worthy of war. And as to their tale they have told you,
Touching the slaughter of kindred of theirs on an Englishman's vessel,
I'll not believe it.

THE OTHERS
Never!

WINSLOW
Englishmen never were traitors.
Either the heathen were slain in seeking to capture his vessel,
Or 'twas some Spaniard murdered them so, and the Frenchmen among them—
Spies and foes to us—have abused their simpleness, feigning
It was an Englishman's work. Or, else, as seemeth more likely
'Tis, from beginning to end, a lie of the savages, knowing
How the fever hath wasted away our numbers and willing,
When occasion lacks, to invent occasion against us.
Therefore, I say, since they send to make war without reason,
Let them have war without mercy.

THE OTHERS
So do we all say!

WINSLOW
Enfeebled,
Few, and alone as we are on this rock on the edge of desert
Stretching in limitless solitude westward how far, none knoweth
Saving the Prince of the Powers of the Air, whose minions possess it,
Yet are we Englishmen still and undismayed by all forces
Darkness can league against us. Let them come in what guise so-ever,
We will meet them like Englishmen!
[Retires.]

THE OTHERS
We will so.

ELDER BREWSTER
[Rising.]
Aye, and like Christians.
Are we not Christians, first, and Englishmen after, my brethren?
Fled we as Englishmen out of England to Holland, and over
Yonder sea to this desert rock, or as Christians? Who drove us
Forth from our country? Englishmen! Who oppressed and pursued us
Even to foreign lands, and at last would have kept us,
When we would have escaped in peace, for further tormenting?
Englishmen, Englishmen always! Dear are kindred and country!
Dearer yet is God's law, and Christ hath ransomed and bought us,
With the price of his blood, and first of all, we are Christians.
Wherefore let us behave like Christians unto these heathen.
Render not evil for evil, for thence is continual evil.
Good for evil and peace for war is our duty. This savage,
Plumed and painted for fight, who comes with his people's defiance,
Let us entreat him kindly, and send not unto them soldiers,
Bidden to burn and kill, but send some Christian teacher
With the word of the Lord in his hand for a weapon. Better,

Better far that ten were converted than fifty were slaughtered.
Wiser, now and hereafter. For we are not here as sojourners,
But we are come to possess the land, and if we possess it
Bloodily and by violence, woe to us and our children!

[*Sits.*]

STANDISH

[*Coming forward.*]

All this is very well, and incontrovertible doctrine
But will you answer me, reverend sir, a question that pricks me?
Is it to shoot red squirrels you have your howitzer planted
There on the roof of the church or is it to shoot red devils?

THE OTHERS

Hear him!

STANDISH

The only tongue that is understood by a savage
Is the tongue of fire that speaks from the mouth of the cannon.

BREWSTER

As for your question, which some might well imagine to savor
Of an irreverence scarcely due from yours to mine office, I answer,
You, not I it was, who planted the gun on my church-roof.
As for the rest, not so thought Paul and the other Apostles.
Not from the cannon's mouth were the tongues of fire *they* spoke with.

STANDISH

What knew the Apostles of war, with such as these heathen?
Paul, to be sure, was a maker of tents, but I never
Heard that he pitched or struck a tent; much less that he ever
Stood in the front of the battle. Go back to those heroes,
Like the great Hebrew for whom the sun stood still while he slaughtered
Them that denied the Lord, and I am with you in Scripture.
Go back to Moses, who slew the Egyptian for smiting a Hebrew:
Back to Gideon, to Jephthah, to Samson, to David,
In their wars with Jonathan, the Philistines, and with the children of Ammon;
Joab, who drove his dart through the rebel's heart when he found him
Hung by his hair in the oak tree; to Samuel, also the prophet,
When he hewed Agag in pieces before the Lord; and I follow.
They were not men to fight with milk and water of roses.
Neither should you, pious sir, transcend your office to argue
Matters that in their very nature are alien to you and beyond you.

[*Advances to the table.*]

Leave this affair to me, for to me by right it pertaineth.
War is a terrible trade; but in the cause that is righteous,
Sweet is the smell of powder! And thus I answer this challenge.

[*He seizes the snake-skin and contemptuously flinging the arrows upon the floor, speaks to Corbitant.*]

Get you back to your people, your dread Pocanawkits, and tell them

How I emptied your bolts on the ground; and how I filled up your serpent
Unto the very jaws with the Englishman's thunder

[Pouring in powder.]

and then with his lightning.

[Putting in bullets, and handing it to Corbitant.]

This is your answer! Take it and get you into the forest,
With your serpent's skin: the one that you bear, and the one that you wear, and
warn them.
We shall not wait for your people to come and make vile war upon us!
You black and treacherous serpent!

[Exit Corbitant.]

THE PEOPLE

Well done! Rightly answered and like the Captain of Plymouth.

CURTAIN

ACT III

SCENE

*The seashore at sunrise; the Mayflower lying at anchor; Miles Standish marching
at the head of his men with Hobomok, beside whom marches Billington, as a
volunteer guide.*

STANDISH

Forward! Forward! Halt!

*[He stops, and leaning upon his sword, gazes at
the ship, and speaks sadly.]*

Look your last, my men, on the Mayflower!
There she lies, ready to sail, and before we have marched through the forest
Half a league hence we shall hear her signal gun of departure.
All our friends will be here to see her set sail for Old England.
Aye, and many a true heart will ache to sail in her for England—
England, however cruel, inalienably our mother.
How the people will come thronging hither with letters and packets
And with each one word of mouth to send home to their kindred.
Ah, how hard the parting will be! I am glad that I shall not behold it.

[The sun shows above the sea-view.]

Look, the sun is rising. The sea seems to laugh at his coming,
And in his heavenly light, the poor old Mayflower yonder,
Battered and blackened and worn by all the storms of the winter,
With her canvas rent by the gales and patched by the sailors,
Loosely flapping against her mast, is like a vessel transfigured
In a vision of sleep. Oh beautiful!

[Musingly.]

She was my home for a half-year,
Hallowed to me for age by Rose Standish's presence! Farewell,
Farewell, beautiful ship! I feel as if still I should find her
Waiting for me, on your deck. But if she were living and beckoned,
Waved me her hand to come with her and abandon this people,

I could not obey her! With them lies my fate and my duty.
Farewell, Rose, my love, if indeed you sail in the Mayflower!

> [*He walks down to the water's edge, and kisses his gauntlet to the ship.*]

BILLINGTON

What is this talk of a dead woman sailing away in the Mayflower?
Doth the Captain see her ghost on board? It maketh my flesh creep!

A SOLDIER

Peace, thou fool!

STANDISH

> [*Returning.*]

My men, if any among you be minded
Here to remain, and claim his right to return in the Mayflower,
Let him freely remain! He shall not have letting or hindrance,
Nay, not a word of reproach!

A SOLDIER

We be true men all, Captain Standish.
We would rather die than do it. Pray you, lead onward.

STANDISH

Be it so. Forward, then! Halt!

> [*The vessel fires a gun.*]

The first gun of parting, already!
Men, we have no powder to waste, and every bullet is precious,
As it were gold. Yet methinks it were churlish in us not to answer
Yonder farewell! Make ready! Aim! Fire!

> [*They fire, and when the smoke clears away Alden is discovered standing by the shore with a bundle in his hand.*]

John Alden,
What do you here? Oh, I see now! You have made up your fardel,
And you are ready to leave us. I hear that some of the women,
And of the sickly old men may bear you company homeward.

ALDEN

> [*Sadly.*]

You know why I go, Miles Standish.

STANDISH

Forward, men, forward!
I will o'ertake you, anon!

BILLINGTON

> [*Running to their head.*]

I know the way, worshipful Captain.
I will lead them. Forward!

> [*The foremost soldier jerks him away, and exeunt.*]

Go on and be lost in the woods, then;
Live as I did upon roots and wild berries; be ta'en by the heathen,

And be ransomed with codfish if there be codfish sufficient
At the rate of forty pound a man to ransom so many,
Left in the whole Plymouth Colony. I could have led ye
Straight as an arrow unto the land of the Pocanawkits.
Now go your ways and alone, and let us see if you find 'em!

[Lurks at the back of the scene.]

ALDEN

You know why I go and that I would rather be marching
Into the wilderness with you than sail in the Mayflower.

STANDISH

Why, are you not content with one treason? Or would you betray me,
Unto some ambush of savages e'en as you did with Priscilla?
No, we want no traitors with us!

ALDEN

I do implore and beseech you,
Let me go with you, and make the heart you wring so a target
For the first Indian arrow that else were aimed at Miles Standish.

STANDISH

You? Nay, I dare not adventure your softness among them.
We are presently going forth to make war, and not love, sir.
Wait till peace is restored, and then go unto their women.
And if you have not courage even then, the squaws shall bridle and ask you,
Why don't you speak for yourself, John? Out on you, traitor!
See that for once you are true, and keep me your promise!
Get back to England and leave her here as you promised,
Or let the curse of Miles Standish, dead or living, be on you!

[Exit.]

BILLINGTON

[Following.]

Well said, worshipful Captain! Very justly and well said.
I never liked that scrivener's face, with his inkhorn and goose-quills.

[Exit.]

ALDEN

Even yonder poor half-wit scouts me!

*[Sobs, his face in his hands; when he lifts it he
discovers Priscilla before him with one hand kept
behind her.]*

Priscilla!

PRISCILLA

John Alden!

[Then, after a pause.]

Are you so much offended, John, that you will not speak to me?
Am I so much to blame, that yesterday, when you were pleading
Warmly the cause of another, my heart, impulsive and wayward
Pleaded your own, and spake out, forgetful perhaps of decorum?

Certainly you can forgive me for speaking so frankly, for saying
What I ought not to have said, yet now I cannot gainsay it;
For there are moments in life, when the heart is so full of emotion,
That if by chance it be shaken, or into its depths like a pebble
Drops some careless word, it overflows, and its secret,
Spilt on the ground like water, can never be gathered together.
Yesterday I was shocked when I heard you speak of Miles Standish,
Praising his virtues, transforming his very defects into virtues,
Praising his courage and strength, and even his fighting in Flanders,
As if by fighting alone you could win the heart of a woman,
Quite overlooking yourself and the rest, in exalting your hero.
Therefore I spake as I did, by an irresistible impulse.
You will forgive me, I hope, for the sake of the friendship between us,
Which is too true and too sacred to be so easily broken.

ALDEN

I was not angry with you, with myself alone I was angry,
Seeing how badly I managed the matter I had in my keeping.

PRISCILLA

No; you were angry at me for speaking so frankly and freely.
It was wrong, I acknowledge; for it is the fate of a woman
Long to be patient and silent, to wait like a ghost that is speechless,
'Till some questioning voice dissolves the spell of its silence.
Hence is the inner life of so many suffering women
Loveless and silent and deep, like subterranean rivers
Running through caverns of darkness, unheard, unseen, and unfruitful,
Chafing their channels of stone, with endless and profitless murmurs.

ALDEN

Heaven forbid it, Priscilla; and truly they seem to me always
More like the beautiful rivers that watered the garden of Eden,
More like the river Euphrates, through deserts of Havilah flowing
Filling the land with delight, and memories sweet of the garden.

PRISCILLA

Ah, by these words I can see how very little you prize me,
When from the depths of my heart, with pain and with secret misgiving
Frankly I speak to you, asking for sympathy only and kindness,
Straightway you take up my words, that are plain and direct and in earnest,
Turn them away from their meaning, and answer with flattering phrases.
This is not right, is not just, is not true to the best that is in you;
For I know and esteem you, and feel that your nature is noble,
Lifting mine up to a higher, a more ethereal level.
Therefore I value your friendship, and feel it perhaps the more keenly
If you say aught that implies I am only as one among many,
If you make use of those common and complimentary phrases
Most men think so fine, in dealing and speaking with women,
But which women reject as insipid, if not as insulting.

Let us, then, be what we are, and speak what we think, and in all things
Keep ourselves loyal to truth, and the sacred professions of friendship.
It is no secret I tell you, nor am I ashamed to declare it:
I have liked to be with you, to see you, to speak to you always.
So I was hurt at your words, and a little affronted to hear you
Urge me to marry your friend, though he were the Captain Miles Standish.
For I must tell you the truth: much more to me is your friendship
Than all the love he can give, were he twice the hero you think him.

ALDEN

Yes, we must ever be friends; and of all who offer you friendship
Let me be ever the first, the truest, the nearest and dearest.
So, farewell, Priscilla!

PRISCILLA

Farewell?

ALDEN

[Bringing his hand from behind him with his bundle in it.]
I am going to sail in the Mayflower.

PRISCILLA

[Bringing her hand and bundle forward, with precisely the same action.]
I—and I—am going to sail in the Mayflower.

ALDEN

[Dropping his bundle.]
You!

PRISCILLA

[Dropping hers.]
I.

Never! It must not, it cannot be!

PRISCILLA
And why, Master Alden?

ALDEN

Why? Because last night when I told him all that had happened,
Stricken through with remorse and the fear that I had betrayed him,
I did promise him I would depart and leave him to wed you
When I was gone; and now, only now, he went from me,
Leaving me his curse if I kept not my promise. Priscilla,
Can you not see that if we sailed in the Mayflower together,
I were doubly false to him?

PRISCILLA
Nay, I cannot see it.
But, if it seems so to you, rest you here. *I* will sail in the Mayflower.

ALDEN

You? Alone!

PRISCILLA

Not more alone than if you left me unfriended
In the wilderness here, or left me worse than unfriended
To the pursuit of Miles Standish. It may have been all well for you, sir,
Thus to give what never was yours to another, and promise
That you would go away and leave Miles Standish to wed me,
But it was cruel to me. And know once for all, Master Alden,
Were he the last man alive I never would marry Miles Standish!
Oh, I fear and abhor him! A man of blood and of carnage!
Therefore, go or stay, as you will.

ALDEN

Sail you, then, Priscilla.
Others besides may go who will watch over you. Farewell!
Haply in England, you will find a worthier lover,
And when John Alden returns, years hence you will show him your husband.

PRISCILLA

[*With a reproachful cry.*]

Oh!

ALDEN

Priscilla!

[*They suddenly open their arms and fly together.*]

What are we doing?

PRISCILLA

The will of the Lord, John.

ALDEN

[*Pushing her from him, and keeping his hands on her shoulders.*]

I am no traitor, then, in your eyes? You do not think me a traitor?

PRISCILLA

You are the truest-hearted man in the world!

ALDEN

I believe you,
Rather than him! Farewell to England! Here then, together,
We will abide whatever betides.

[*They clasp each other again; but at the sound of a gun from the ship they start asunder.*]

The signal for parting.
Look! They are lowering a boat from the ship. 'Tis the captain,
Coming ashore the last time. And here come the people to meet him.
Ladies with missions and messages. Let them not see us, Priscilla,
With these fardels of ours, lest some of the weaklier-hearted

Lose all courage to stay, and return with him in the Mayflower.
Here let us hide them both in the rushes.

> [*He hides the bundles; then he and Priscilla go apart on each side of the scene, as in Boughton's[1] picture. As the boat arrives, the people flock to her, and hand the captain letters and packages. He stands with one foot on shore and one in the boat, and receives them.*]

CAPTAIN

                    Good folk, which among you,
Goes with me back to England? Where are my passengers? Gaffer,
Will you not bear me company?

AN OLD MAN

                    Give my love to my children.
Tell them I fain would see them before I die. But hither
They must come, for I shall never set foot again in Old England.
Where the Lord led me, I rest.

CAPTAIN

                    But you, my pretty young mistress,
With that letter you bring for me to give to your sweetheart,
It were better come tell him in person how much you have missed him.

A YOUNG GIRL

You are too bold, sir. But if this letter were meant for a sweetheart,
'Twere but to tell him he loves not me who loves not my people,
Or will not follow me hither.

CAPTAIN

You, poor Mistress Martin, will come, I know, and abandon this country,
Where the hand of death hath stripped you of husband and children.
Come back to good old England with me to your brothers and sisters.
It shall not cost you a stiver.

A WIDOW

                    I thank you with all my heart, sir.
Here are my dead and here is my God, and I rest here.

CAPTAIN

What, will none of you come? Not one?

THE PEOPLE

                    No! Fare you well, Captain!

CAPTAIN

Why, that little man you have presently sent to make war on the heathen
Hath a stout heart enow, but one of those big Pocanawkits

---

[1] George Henry Boughton, 1833–1905, English painter who depicted many scenes of American Colonial life.

Would not make a mouthful of him and his army together.
What will you do then?

THE PEOPLE

Whatever willeth the Lord. He giveth.
Yea, He taketh away.

CAPTAIN

The Lord keep you! You do not lack courage!
Good-bye, all ye doughty souls! For me, I'm glad to be going—
Glad to be gone from a land of sand, and sickness and sorrow,
Short allowance of victual, and plenty of nothing but Gospel!
But if you like it, stay!

THE PEOPLE

Farewell! Captain!

CAPTAIN

[To his oarsmen.]
Give way, men!
[A gun from the ship.]

THE SAILORS

[Hauling up the sails.]
Yo, heave, yo! Yo, heave, yo! Hurrah, my hearties, for England!

ELDER BREWSTER

O, strong hearts and true! Not one goes back in the Mayflower!
Brethren and sisters, Let us pray, and thank God for his mercies!
[They all kneel, and the ship sails away.]

CURTAIN

ACT IV

SCENE

A grassy space in front of Priscilla's cottage. She sits near the threshold, spinning. Alden leaning on the back of a chair, reaches a bunch of flowers towards her.

PRISCILLA

[Taking the flowers.]
Mayflowers! Mayflowers still! Can you never come here without them?
Might one be jealous of flowers, I well might begin to be jealous!
First you think of them, and you only think of me after!
Oh, what beautiful flowers! you say to yourself when you find them.
Um—um—! Let me see! They mind me of some one, or something
That I cannot rightly recall— Oh, I have it! Priscilla!
Yes, that is it! They make me think of my sweetheart Priscilla,
Whom I had quite forgotten, else!

ALDEN

[*Fondly.*]

Ah, sweetheart, your mocking
Doth divine the truth. They *do* make me think of Priscilla—

PRISCILLA

Whom you had else forgotten? Oh, well-a-day!

[*Sighs in burlesque.*]

ALDEN

Not so, sweet!
But because I am so full of you that I find you about me
Not in the Mayflowers but in all that is lovely.

PRISCILLA

Oh, but that is the thing which redoubles the wrong, to my thinking!
Last week, I was like the fawn that you saw, coming hither,
In your woodland path—

ALDEN

And art thou not tender and graceful—

PRISCILLA

Saturday, like a certain thrush that you heard a singing.

ALDEN

Only that you out-sing for sweetness, even the thrushes!

PRISCILLA

Monday, you thought you saw a likeness 'twixt me and the ocean!

ALDEN

Nay, that was like our love!—eternal, fathomless, boundless!

PRISCILLA

Well, then, say it was our love you said. Was that any reason.
Why, on Tuesday, a wild plum in blossom, a rabbit, a quail,
Not to mention a dove, a straight young pine, and a streamlet,
All made you think of me! Then, as if that could not suffice you,
You could not rest content till you saw a resemblance in my eyes
To the eyes of your white bull, Raghorn. Think you 'twas pretty,
Lik'ning the eyes of a bull to the eyes of a maid?

ALDEN

I confess it!
Nay, I defend it. Those things resemble you in my fancy.
Most of all do these Mayflowers favor you! Oh, my Priscilla,
Last of the letters I wrote to send by the Mayflower to England,
Was a letter for one that had suspected my secret,
Heaven grant not my unworthy hope! in following hither,

Her whom I durst not think I loved. 'Twas my cousin;
And in my letter I sent him one of these flowers to show him,
As I best knew how the thing that was likest Priscilla!

PRISCILLA

*[Tenderly, while she puts the flowers to her breast,
and drops her lips on them.]*

Did you, John? I forgive them, then!

ALDEN

And me, too!

PRISCILLA

And you, too?

How was there question of you?

[As he offers to come round the chair to her.]
Nay, nay! Keep your distance, I pray you!
I cannot have you spoiling my work with your silliness. Go to!
I must finish all the wool that you see here, this morning.

[Spins.]

ALDEN

Truly, Priscilla, when I see you always spinning and spinning,
Never idle a moment but thrifty and thoughtful of others,
Suddenly you are transformed, are visibly changed in a moment,
You are no longer Priscilla, but Bertha, the Beautiful Spinner.[1]
You are the beautiful Bertha, the spinner, the queen of Helvetia;
She whose story I read at a stall in the streets of Southampton
Who, as she rode on her palfrey o'er valley, meadow and mountain,
Ever was spinning her thread from a distaff fixed to her saddle.
She was so thrifty and good, that her name passed into a proverb.
So shall it be with your own, when the spinning wheel shall no longer
Hum in the house of the farmer, and fill its chambers with music.
Then, shall the mothers, reproving, relate how it was in their childhood,
Praising the good old times, and the days of Priscilla the spinner!

PRISCILLA

[Rising and taking a hank of yarn.]
Well, you must not be idle; if I am a pattern of housewives,
Show yourself equally worthy of being the model of husbands.
Hold this skein on your hands, while I wind it ready for knitting;
Then, who knows but hereafter, when fashions have changed, and the manners,
Fathers may talk to their sons of the good old times of John Alden.
Here, sit you down, and hold out your arms.

[He does it awkwardly.]
But do not do it so stiffly!
[She takes hold of them, and puts them right.]
So! But flexibly! lightly! 'Tis not such a task as you'd make it.
[She passes the yarn over his hands.]

---

[1] See *Proverbs Français*, II, 28, edited by Leroux De Lincy.

Oh! but stiffen your thumbs, or my yarn will slip over them! Mercy!
There!

[Seizes his thumbs and stiffens them.]

ALDEN

I profess I know not your pleasure, Priscilla! You tell me
First, not to hold my arms so stiffly, but flexibly, lightly!
Then you lay hold my thumbs, and set them up like two brazen
Statues erected in memory of us! The right thumb is Alden
And the left is—

PRISCILLA

[Touching the right one.]

Nay! I will not have it! *This* is Priscilla.

ALDEN

[Starting.]

Oh, but have a care! For when you touch me, Priscilla,
Something thrills through all my nerves as if it were lightning.

PRISCILLA

[Laughing.]

Why, so it doth through mine the same. But *I* never mind it!

ALDEN

Well, then, neither will I.

PRISCILLA

Now go on with what you were saying,
While I am winding my yarn.

[She winds.]

ALDEN

I? I was saying nothing.

PRISCILLA

[Busily winding.]

What were you doing, then?

ALDEN

I suppose I must have been thinking.

PRISCILLA

Thinking of what?

ALDEN

Of you! And how lovely you are and how graceful,
Standing so slim and straight and swaying before me so lightly,
With your head like a lily upon the stem of the lily!

PRISCILLA

Fie!

ALDEN

And I thought what a pity that arms so set for embracing
Should hold nothing but empty air!

PRISCILLA

Oh fie upon you, John Alden!
I do not like you when you are bold, but when you are timid
As when you came to see me a fortnight ago from the Captain.

ALDEN

Only a fortnight ago!

PRISCILLA

Has the time passed so heavy it seemeth
Longer than that?

ALDEN

Oh no! but I seem to have lived a whole lifetime
Since that night. When I came through the woods it was snowing. The winter,
Scarcely seemed broken and now! What a rapture of springtime is with us!
What do you say of the squaw April, now?

PRISCILLA

Nothing but praises,
Since she hath turned Christian from being a heathen.

ALDEN

Is it not almost as if we had died, my love, and awakened
In some other world, whither none of the earth's canker or sorrow
More than its weather had followed us?

[*After a moment he sighs and drops his head.*]
Ah!

PRISCILLA

[*Tenderly.*]
Would no trouble,
Truly had followed us! Thou at least, I see, art still mortal.
Tell me what ails thee, John?

ALDEN

Alas! Thou knowest, Priscilla.

PRISCILLA

Is it thy same foolish scruple?

ALDEN

Aye.

PRISCILLA

Then I have no patience with thee.

ALDEN

Nay, but thou must have patience with me—patience and pity.
When I am not thinking of thee in heavenly rapture,
I am thinking of him in the pangs of perdition. Priscilla,
All that night after I had seen you I lay without slumber,
Turning and tossing about in the heat and unrest of my fever.
He had returned to our cottage long after midnight. I heard him
Stalking into the room, and heard him mutter and murmur,
Sometimes it seemed a prayer, and sometimes it sounded like swearing—

PRISCILLA

I will be bound it was swearing! 'Twere a great deal more like a soldier!
Who, indeed, knows him save from himself, this Captain Miles Standish?
Some will have it that he is a papist, a Jesuit, haply!
With that leathern visage of his he *looks* like a Spaniard!
I never liked his looks.

ALDEN

Oh, do not mis-speak him, Priscilla,
Or, thou will break my heart!

PRISCILLA

[*Piqued.*]
One would almost believe that you loved him
More than you love me. Well, well! I am rightfully punished!
Maids must not be lightly won if they would be prized. But I trusted
When I spoke as I did, in a generous soul—

ALDEN

Oh, Priscilla!
Do not reproach me, dearest! Or truly methinks I must perish
Under the double weight of his displeasure and yours!

[*Clasps his hands.*]

PRISCILLA

[*Starting forward.*]
A mercy!
How you are tangling my yarn! Can you never rest quiet, John Alden?

ALDEN

Aye, if thou wilt quietly hear me!

PRISCILLA

[*Winding.*]
I will have patience.

ALDEN

[Sighing.]

Once he came to my bed, and stood there a moment in silence;
Then he turned away, and said: "I will not awake him:
Let him sleep on, it is best; for what is there use of more talking!"

PRISCILLA

That is the wisest thing that I ever heard of your Captain.
That is what I say too: for what is the use of more talking?

ALDEN

[Reproaching.]

Did you not promise not to interrupt me, Priscilla?

PRISCILLA

[Winding.]

No, I only said that I would have patience. I *never*
Promised that I would be silent.

ALDEN

Then let me beseech thee,
Try to be a *little* silent, now and then, love, for *my* sake!

PRISCILLA

Well, I will try.

Go on.

[Winds.]

ALDEN

He threw himself down on his pallet,
Dressed as he was, and ready to start at the break of the morning—
Covered himself with the cloak he had worn in his campaigns in Flanders,
Slept as a soldier sleeps in his bivouac, ready for action.
But with the dawn he rose, and in the twilight I saw him
Put on his corselet of steel, and all the rest of his armor,
Buckle about his waist his trusty blade of Damascus,
Take from the corner his musket, and so stride out of the chamber.
Often my heart had burned within me, and yearned to embrace him,
Often my lips had essayed to speak, imploring for pardon;
All the old friendship came back with its tender and grateful emotions;
But my pride overmastered the better nature within me,
Pride and the sense of my wrong, and the burning fire of the insult.
So I beheld my friend departing in anger and spoke not,
Saw him go forth to danger, perhaps to death, and I spoke not!

[Drops his head on his hands.]

PRISCILLA

Oh, my yarn, beware! This comes of my keeping silent!

[She adds earnestly.]

John, dost thou prize at aught the love that thou didst not ask for?

ALDEN

Nay, do not wrong thyself! I only lacked courage for asking.
I longed more for thy love than my salvation, Priscilla.
What dost thou intend?

PRISCILLA

Thou trustest the heart of a woman,
Where it loves and honors that it hath instinct and insight,
How to know the right and the truth?

ALDEN

Far more than man's wisdom!

PRISCILLA

Hearken to me then, John Alden! Thou has no reason for grieving
Over aught that hath passed 'twixt thee and thy friend. He only,
He alone hath been false to your friendship and cruel. He only,
He alone is to blame. Thou hast been as leal and honest,
Through it all, as a man can be, not answering insult with insult,
Taunt for taunt, or wrong for wrong; and if thou hast erred 'twas in being
Only too meek with that violent man, and so I would tell him
If I should meet him coming back in triumph tomorrow!
Oh, thou tender heart and true! Dost thou doubt that I know thee?
Dost thou not believe I know what thou hast suffered in conscience,
Blamelessly for his sake, as I should not falter to tell him,
Were his furious spirit discharged from his furious body
Like a bomb from a mortar to drop here this moment between us!
Yes, I would defy his very ghost to gainsay me!

ALDEN

Oh, Priscilla! Not his ghost! Speak not of his dying!
Were he to die without sending me his forgiveness, believe me,
I could never be happy again!

PRISCILLA

Nay, be not afflicted.
He will come back in the flesh and forgive you. Your Captain,
He is a little chimney, and heated through in a moment!
But when the fire is out, be sure he will hearken to reason.
I will reason with him.

[Gaily.]

See! I have almost finished!
Only a turn or two more! And then canst thou tell me what follows?

ALDEN

Nay, that I cannot.

PRISCILLA

[Swiftly finishing and dropping the ball.]
Why, then, I put up my palms against thy palms.

ALDEN

So! Aye.

PRISCILLA

Then I lean forward and thou leanest forward—

ALDEN

Aye.

PRISCILLA

And then—dost thou not know then what should follow?

ALDEN

No, truly!

PRISCILLA

[Suddenly kissing him.]

John, thou art *almost* a goose! But la! I forgive thee.

ALDEN

But sweetheart,

Only now thou saidst that thou likest me not to be bold.

PRISCILLA

[With her head on his shoulder.]

And was it,

Thou who wast bold, in this case?

BILLINGTON

[Who had come on them unperceived.]

Kissing a damsel in secret?

Is this lawful?

[They fly asunder.]

What! Under Providence, we shall have dicing,

Next, or carding, among us; or dancing, or stage-plays. I take it,

Kissing a damsel is not too removed from a stage-play!

PRISCILLA

[Coming forward.]

Wilt thou swear thou sawest him kiss me?

BILLINTON

Aye.

PRISCILLA

Thou art perjured!

It was I who kissed him!

BILLINGTON

[Scratching his head in bewilderment.]

'Tis different, truly.

PRISCILLA

And further,

We are betrothed.

BILLINGTON

You!

PRISCILLA

We! And almost the same as if married.

We have been cried, already, and are to be married tomorrow.

BILLINGTON

'Tis a main difference!

PRISCILLA

Aye! And 'twere best thou kept thyself quiet.

Touching that thou hast seen lest another and worse thing befall thee!

BILLINGTON

I will not speak.

PRISCILLA

But tell me now where hast thou ever been, goodman,

Not to have heard this news? Wert thou lost again in the forest?

BILLINGTON

Lost, quotha? Lost! Ha, ha! Know you, mistress, I have been leader,

Guide, and as it were, captain of Captain Standish's foray

Into the Pocanawkits' country.

ALDEN

[Coming forward.]

I remember now. I did see him,

Going forth with the rest—

BILLINGTON

Ah ha! You remember, my master!

Hearken you, mistress, he remembers. And I, too, remember

How Captain Standish rated him that morning! Ah! I remember!

Heaven is over all! Well!

[Shakes his head.]

'Tis full soon to fall kissing,

Aye, or to being kissed.

ALDEN

[Agitated.]

Why, how doth the Captain? What tidings

Bringest thou from him?

BILLINGTON

Great and wonderful tidings, my master!

ALDEN

Well!

BILLINGTON

Seven days and nights we marched through the forest, where no man,
Were he not lost therein and ransomed after with codfish,
Might find the way! But I led them straight to the Pocanawkit's encampment,
Into an ambush of heathen, under Providence. Truly,
That I did. And the first thing we knew came their arrows!
Pitter patter! Like raindrops through the leaves.

ALDEN

And the Captain,
Was he slain?

BILLINGTON

Nay, truly.

ALDEN

What happened?

BILLINGTON

A parley. The Captain
Fought them like any minister touching their souls and the devil.
But, they would none of it!
Where they would fain have bartered their peltries for powder and muskets,
Captain Standish bade Hobomok tell them they should have blankets,
And he would send teachers to teach them our English religion,
So that they should become as great and strong as the English;
If they would receive the Bible they would be prospered,
But if they did not receive the Bible, the devil would get them.
But they made answer they would not, and one of their sachems, Pecksuot
Flung himself on the captain, but ere I could say it the captain
Plucked the knife of the heathen out of his girdle and plunged it—
But have ye heard what Hobomok said?

ALDEN

No matter!

BILLINGTON

Nay, *tis* matter.
Pecksuot bragged very loud, of his courage, his strength, and his stature,—
Mocked the great Captain, and called him a little man; but he said now,
"Big enough have you been to lay him dead here before you!"
Was it not well said for Hobomok, who was so lately
Snatched, as it were, a brand from the burning?

ALDEN

But after,
What happened after?

BILLINGTON
More arrows; a volley of musketry.

ALDEN
                                                        Was he—
Was the Captain hurt!

BILLINGTON
                    Nay! Wattawamat, the sachem,
He was hurt, and you might say was killed. And the heathen
Fled before us!

ALDEN
            Was that all?

BILLINGTON
                        Aye. I hacked off the heads of the sachems,
Then, I hurried away. I have them here in the forest,
Ready to be set up, by the governor's grace on the church roof.
For a terror to traitors and evil-doers of all sorts.
I will fetch them and show you.

                                            [Offers to go.]

PRISCILLA
                                    [With a shriek.]
            Ah! Horrible! Bid him begone, John!
He is a bloodier wretch than ever your blood-bestained Captain!
Send him away!

                                            [Hides her face.]

BILLINGTON
            Why, mistress, but for me they had never
Known that the arrow was poisoned—

ALDEN
                        What arrow was poisoned?

BILLINGTON
What! Why, this is best of all! Know you then, that the Captain,
Being somehow smit at the sight of the squaw and papooses
Of the heathen he slew that he should chance to have slain him
In the face and eyes as 'twere of his wife and his children,
Stood lamenting his fortune when a bolt from the forest,
Found a hole in his corselet. He plucked it forth and had flung it
From him when I marked it and saw that 'twas poisoned,
After the Indian manner. Well! We all must die, sometime!

ALDEN
What! Is Miles Standish dead?

BILLINGTON

I make haste home with my burden—

ALDEN

Is Miles Standish dead?

BILLINGTON

Six days and nights ago, master,
At the very least. Fare you well, I must onward
Into the village.

[*As he goes out, Alden hides his face in Priscilla's shoulder.*]

ALDEN

Oh, Priscilla, banish me from thee!
I have slain my friend, after playing the robber and stealing
That which made life dear to him. I am a wretch past forgiving
Yet—yet tell me once more that thou didst love me, Priscilla,
And that I once seemed a just man and blameless!

PRISCILLA

[*Consolingly.*]

And wilt thou
Quite give way, then? Wilt thou not believe me, his dying
Nowise hath changed thy act? Thou art blameless or guilty,
Neither more nor less now, than ever! Nay, what shall *I* do,
If thou will forsake me? And wilt thou kill me, too?
Will thy killing me perchance bring him back to the living?
Nay, dear heart! Thou shalt not go! I banish thee from me?
Nothing shall part us but death, since death hath joined us together.
Come—come—come within, lest others should see thee unmanned, so.

[*They go out, she keeping his head pressed on her shoulder.*]

[*Enter Standish leaning upon Winslow, who supports him to Priscilla's door.*]

STANDISH

Do you conceive that a soldier, like any civilian Christian,
Lieth under the law to forgive his enemies?

WINSLOW

Truly
That is a nice inquiry. I never considered the matter.
Yet, methinks that 'twixt *kinds* of enemies we should distinguish.
There be enemies public and enemies private. For instance,
Saving due respect to Elder Brewster's opinion,
It were a kind of sin to pardon the Pocanawkits,
Till we had thoroughly beaten them, and it were folly,
Meeting them in battle to stop, and propose to forgive them.
After a round or two of musketry, *then* you might offer
Truly a pardon for all their offenses committed against us.

Certes, a soldier lieth under no law of forgiveness
With such foes as the Pocanawkits.

STANDISH

[*Musingly.*]

What saith the Scripture?

WINSLOW

Touching what matter, Captain?

STANDISH

The matter of injuries private.

WINSLOW

[*Thoughtfully.*]

There be divers texts. If thy brother trespass against thee,
Go and tell him his fault between thyself and him only.

STANDISH

That have I done, and roundly: he cannot lay *that* up against me!
Well!

WINSLOW

Forgive us our debts as we forgive also our debtors.

STANDISH

Aye, that is in the prayer. Well!

WINSLOW

Bless them that curse you,
Pray for them that despitefully use you and persecute you.

STANDISH

Doth it say so?

WINSLOW

Aye, and more. For when Peter asked of his Master,
How many times shall I forgive my brother's trespass against me?
Seven times? Aye, seven times seventy; so he was answered.

STANDISH

[*Rising quickly to his feet, and walking uneasily
up and down.*]

That could never have been intended to govern a soldier!

WINSLOW

Truly, there seemeth reason, Captain, in your supposition.
Were we for instance to act on the mandate, Resist not evil;
But whosoever shall smite thee on the right cheek, turn also
Unto him the other—where were wars? Where were soldiers?

These are texts, I opine, should be read in the light of some others—
In the light of the Chronicles, and of the Kings and the Hebrews.

STANDISH

Such was my mind when I answered Elder Brewster. But, Winslow,
Here comes another question. If these texts touch injuries private,
Only injuries private, can one whose life is devoted,
Like, for example, my own, to the state, receive any trespass
That is of private effect?

WINSLOW

Do you mean that a soldier
Ought to have no foes but those of the public?

STANDISH

Not quite that.
But can any one trespass against the commonwealth's servant,
And not become thereby the general foe of the public—
Not to be pardoned, but punished implacably, and without mercy?

WINSLOW

That is a *nicer* inquiry, captain, than even the first one.
There is no text of Scripture that I can remember, would solve it.

STANDISH

Aye, you are right. That must rest for every man's conscience to deal with.
[*He looks at the cottage and resumes after a
pause.*]
After all, I have scarce the heart to see her, good Winslow,
Now that I stand at her door. I never had courage with women,
And to confront a woman whom I had widowed more truly
Than if her husband had died by my sword—that I cannot and may not!
Winslow, let me put the question once more to thy judgment,
And, do thou answer me honestly, sparing me nothing,
Be the truth hard as it will. I have had evil visions,
In my sleep these three nights past, of the Mayflower: I saw her
Wallowing in the sea, a wreck, the sport of the tempest,
And on her wave-swept deck, a figure hopelessly clinging
Unto the stump of a mast, that turned his visage upon me—
Alden's visage!

WINSLOW

'Twas an effect of the poison.

STANDISH

Nay, Winslow,
Had it happened but once I might have thought so. But three times!
It was a warning! The vessel was old, and scarce sea-worthy. Battered,
As she was, by our voyage hither, she should not have ventured

On the homeward voyage. And he alone of our number,
He whom I loved like a son, the sacrifice of my fury,
He hath gone to his death in her! How he implored me, that morning,
When we parted to let him come with me! And how I denied him.
How did I mock and insult him! But if we grant 'twas the poison
Working still in my brain, and no real vision or warning,
Am I not guilty the same before the maiden I widowed
Ere she was wedded, by banishing from her the lover
Whom her heart had chosen? They were most fit to be mated,
Young and comely both, and good—who was I, to put them asunder?
Leave me, Winslow, to make my peace as I may with the damsel!
Naught can avail me here, but full and humble confession
And a complete surrender, if even *that* can avail me!
Go, and stay for me with my men hard by. In this peril,
All the legions of Caesar were useless!

[*Exit Winslow.*]

How shall I meet her?
What shall I say to Priscilla? How shall I frame my confession?
How best sue for pardon? And if she received me in anger,
What should I do? Or what, if she wept? Gracious Power!
Would that John Alden were here, to intercede for me! Alden!
I must be going mad! John Alden present to ask her
Pardon for me that he is absent! It is the fever
Working still in my brain from that poisonous arrow. O, Alden,
Couldst thou but come to my aid, here fondly I'd hail thee
Ev'n if thou camest in her arms!

[*Re-enter Alden and Priscilla, he with his head on her shoulder, as they went out.*]

PRISCILLA
Now, sweetheart, say thou art better!
Or I shall hold hereafter there is no virtue in kisses,
And I will not come to thee for comfort when I am in trouble.
Promise me thou wilt think no more of that violent soldier,
He who butchered fathers before the eyes of their children!
Is it not written that they who take the sword, they shall perish
By the sword? And if he is dead, then hath he not perished
As it was written he should? I pity the squaw and papooses
Whom he hath bereft of their husband and father. But, never,
Never will I shed a tear for him. I always abhorred him.
Nor shall you grieve either for such a pestilent tyrant!

[*They move towards a seat.*]

STANDISH
[*Who after the first shock of surprise, has heard Priscilla with mounting fury, bursts forth, drawing his sword.*]
Villain!

PRISCILLA
[*With a shriek, flinging herself on Alden's breast.*]
Save me, save me, John! 'Tis his spirit!

STANDISH

[*To Alden.*]

No spirit!

No, but flesh and blood and fire! Whereto thou shall answer the outrage
That this woman's tongue hath spoken! Draw, traitor and villain!
Oh, thou hast even abused my dreams! Thou art he, then,
Whom these three nights past I have dreamt of as shipwrecked
In the vessel that thou didst promise to sail in. I might have known thee,
O thou traitor, bitter! I might have known that or ever
I had marched a mile away thou hadst broken thy promise.
Coward! I mourned thee dead. Let me not have sorrowed for nothing!
Draw!

ALDEN

[*Putting Priscilla aside.*]

And *I* too have mourned you for dead. Were I weaponed,
Thou shouldst not challenge me twice! But weaponless, naked against you,
Here I stand, and I tell you that he is a villain and liar
Dares attaint my truth and honesty.

STANDISH

What! Wilt thou tell me,

Thou art no traitor?

ALDEN

Aye!

STANDISH

Then why art thou here? Didst thou not promise
That thou wouldst sail in the Mayflower and leave me this damsel?

ALDEN

I did so promise.

STANDISH

And hast thou kept thy promise?

ALDEN

Alas, no!

STANDISH

Why hast thou not kept thy promise?

ALDEN

[*Confusedly.*]

I—I may not tell you.

STANDISH

Then, mayst thou tell me why thou art not a traitor to friendship?

PRISCILLA

[Coming between them.]

I will answer for him. He is no traitor to friendship!
Friendship! I am sick of the word alike in your mouth and his mouth.
Friendship! Is there naught else hath a claim on his fealty?
Is there no other—feeling—no—no—something that rises
Far above friendship as heaven from earth?

STANDISH

No, there is nothing!

PRISCILLA

Aye, there is something higher! And he was most faithful to friendship,
When he was truest to that. For if when he came to demand me,
At your imperious suit, he had been in the least less than loyal
In his endeavor for you, I had counted him doubly a traitor
Unto the love that I knew he bore me in secret,
And I had been ashamed as now I am proud that he loved me.
Nay, if you would be answered, too, why he sailed not for England,
As he vainly promised, I will tell you.

STANDISH

Well, wherefore?

PRISCILLA

[Aghast at herself.]

I will not tell you!

STANDISH

Then he shall!

ALDEN

No, never. I will not.

STANDISH

What, you defy me?

PRISCILLA

[Twisting her fingers into Alden's.]
We never will tell you! We *never*,
Never will tell you! You, who are so outrageous and cruel,
You would condemn him for what I did—

ALDEN

I will answer
Unto all the world for what thou doest, dear Priscilla,
But Miles Standish never was cruel.

PRISCILLA

Not cruel, but—hasty—
Violent—so—in manner. I meant not in heart! If the Captain
Would but be patient—

STANDISH

Well, mistress, I will be patient. Say on, now.

PRISCILLA

'Tis not so easy, saying on!

[*To Alden.*]

Shall I tell him?

ALDEN

'Tis nothing,
Sweetheart, that I am ashamed to have known.

PRISCILLA

He sailed not,
As he promised and wished, because I met him and told him,
After he parted with you that I was not his to be given.

STANDISH

Well, how should that have kept him?

PRISCILLA

Or left to another.
That, too, I told him!

STANDISH

But that was no reason for staying. Why staid he?

PRISCILLA

[*Desperately.*]
If you will know then, I said that if he sailed in the Mayflower,
[*She suddenly hides her face in Alden's shoulder.*]
I would sail with him! And shame to you for making me tell you!

STANDISH

[*Furiously.*]
This is the way I was cozened—

PRISCILLA

[*Turning quickly about.*]
You said, if I told you,
You would be patient, and you are a gentleman, Captain—

STANDISH

[*After a pause.*]
And I must keep my word. You are right, fair Mistress Priscilla.
I will be patient from this time forth.

[*Calls.*]
Leftenant! Leftenant!
Winslow, I say!

WINSLOW

[*Coming.*]
Here, Captain.

STANDISH

March my musketeers hither!
Then go you with two of them straight to the village.
Wait on their worships, Elder Brewster and Governor Carver,
And with their good leave assemble all of the people.
Then return at their head to me.

WINSLOW

They have not stayed to be sent for,
Captain. The whole of Plymouth, even, women and children,
Here are met to welcome you home and back to the living.
Billington had preceded us with news of your death by the arrow,
And, but for one who chanced upon us here in the forest,
And whom I sent straightway to deny before Governor Carver
Billington's dismal tidings, all the colony now had been mourning
Where they are madly rejoicing. They press so hard to be with you
That we have scarcely withstood them.

STANDISH

Withstand them no longer.
Let them come hither.

[Exit Winslow.]

I fain would have as many for witness
As I may, to what I intend.

*[Re-enter Winslow with his men; then Governor
Carver, Elder Brewster, and the colonists. To
Carver and Brewster.]*

Good sirs, you have sought me,
As you did once before, when I should have come to you.

CARVER

[Shaking his hand.]
'Tis our pleasure,
Wheresoever we may, to welcome you, Captain! 'Tis but a moment
Since we all were plunged in grief at the terrible tidings
Goodman Billington brought us.

BREWSTER

Believe me, worshipful Captain,
When I heard the tale of that venomed and treacherous arrow,
I did greatly misdoubt but reason and Scripture were wasted
On such desperate heathen, and truly I grieved to remember
How I had answered you in argument touching their treatment.
Blest be the name of the Lord! that you are alive and are with us!

STANDISH

Reverend sir, your kindness moveth me. I have had my misgivings,
Likewise! Whereof, anon!

*[The colonists all crowd round him with cries of
welcome, shaking his hand and embracing him. He
breaks from them at last with a laugh.]*

I do profess, I would rather have fallen
Into another ambush of Pocanawkits! Will you unhand me?
Or must I order my musketeers to fire upon you?

CARVER

Will you not [go] back with us to the village, Captain, and tell us,
There in public meeting minutely all that hath happened,
Since you marched away?

BREWSTER

It shall pass for a sermon
If you will deliver your tale in the church.

STANDISH

I thank you.
Later, I will rehearse my story there before all the people.
But for the present I ask the church for another occasion,
Good your reverence.

*[He parts the crowd, and going back through it
leads forward by either hand Alden and Priscilla.]*

Here are a youth and maid who have wrought me
Grievous wrong, and I ask for justice upon them.

BREWSTER

Priscilla!

CARVER

Alden!

STANDISH

Aye, and I ask that first the ill-doers be punished.
Afterward, let them be tried. I say let them straightway be married!
On to the church with the culprits!

ALDEN

[Rapturously.]

Miles Standish!

PRISCILLA

[Demurely.]

Oh, Captain!

Not—not just at once!

STANDISH

Not a moment, mistress, of respite!
What! Do you think to escape me!

[He doffs his hat, bows low and kisses her hand.]

A moment ago when you thought me
Deaf enough to your words, you spoke certain things of Miles Standish,
Called him—

PRISCILLA

'Twas in the heat of argument, Captain! I ever
Held you in honor, until you sent John to tell me—

STANDISH

Content you!
I can well believe you. I should have remembered the adage,
If you would be well served, you must serve yourself; and moreover,
No man can gather cherries in Kent at the season of Christmas!
I was too old; and I knew it then as well as I know it
Now. You have chosen wisely and well. I wish you joy and long life!
There is no better nor truer man in the world than John Alden.

[Turning to Alden.]
What shall I say to you? Let all be forgotten between us!
All save the dear old friendship, and that shall grow older and dearer.

ALDEN

[Pressing his hand.]
Oh, there never was aught in my heart save kindness for you!

STANDISH

Aye,
Now I believe you. Your worships, masters and goodmen,
Let us on to the church—

BILLINGTON

[Bursting through the crowd.]
Aye, 'tis in perfect repentance.
While you all were away, I have prettily trimmed the two gables
With the heads of Pecksuot and Wattawamat—

BREWSTER

Good Captain!
You will not suffer them to remain?

STANDISH

'Tis a fortress,
Sir, as well as a church.

BREWSTER

I must submit!

PRISCILLA

But not I!
I will die a maid ere I consent to be wedded
Under that roof! 'Tis horrible! Ugh!

STANDISH

What! Fire and fury!
Must I still be denied then, whether I *would* have you married
Or I would *not?*

BREWSTER

The damsel hath reason, good Captain,
On her side, methinks; and in the generations to follow,
Many, I doubt not, will hold that even a church that's half fortress
Is not meetly adorned with the heads of heathen. I pray you,
Take them down!

STANDISH

Well, let her be contented.

[*To Winslow.*]
Send forward,

And let the heads be removed.

PRISCILLA

I cannot go! I shall see them,
Whether they be there or no, now!

STANDISH

This truly passeth endurance!
Shall I not see you married?

PRISCILLA

I know not!

BREWSTER

Governor Carver,
Let them join hands before you here and repeat their betrothal
Taking each other for husband and wife in the magistrate's presence
After the Puritan way, and the laudable custom of Holland;
Then I will ask the blessing of God on their marriage.

STANDISH

[*To Winslow, as he leads Priscilla forward and
places her hand in Alden's before the governor.*]
Leftenant,
Bid my men wish them joy from the iron throats of their matchlocks! [1]

1 This ending seems abrupt, and the final page of the play manuscript may be missing.

Colonel Sellers as a Scientist

[1883]

W. D. Howells and S. L. Clemens

As interesting and as revealing of personality and artistic characteristics as anything the two friends did together is the venture of Clemens and Howells into the world of the drama and the theater. Their interest in a combined dramatic work started during the summer of 1875 when Clemens proposed that Howells dramatize *Tom Sawyer*, but as Howells explained that he had no time and that Clemens should do it anyway, nothing came of the suggestion (July 19, 1875, *Life in Letters*, I, 208). Earlier that year Clemens had sent a Mr. Haskins, an actor with a plot, to Howells thinking that a play might result, but Howells was unimpressed. "I have seen Haskins," he wrote to Clemens (July 3, 1875, *Life in Letters*, I, 207). "His *plot* was a series of stage *situations*, which no mortal ingenuity could harness together."

Actually, a number of years passed before the two writers completed a play together, but in the meantime Clemens tried to interest Howells in writing a play about his brother Orion Clemens. "You *must* put him in a book or play right away," he wrote (February 9, 1879, *Mark Twain Letters*, arranged with comment by Albert Bigelow Paine, [New York: Harper & Brothers, copyright 1917, by Mark Twain Company; copyright 1945, by Clara Clemens Samossoud], I, 352). "You are the only man capable of doing it. You might die at any moment and your very greatest work would be lost to the world." As time passed, Clemens' imagination worked more graphically on the subject. "Orion is a field which grows richer and richer the more he mulches it with each new top dressing of religion or other guano. Drop me an immediate line about this, won't you? I imagine I see Orion on the stage, always gentle, always melancholy, always trying to reform the world, always inventing something and losing a limb by a new kind of explosion at the end of each of the four acts. Poor old chap, he is good material" (September 15, 1879, *Mark Twain Letters*, I, 361). Howells, however, protested that he had "a compunction or two about helping to put your brother into a drama" (September 17, 1879, *Life in Letters*, I, 276), but they must have put some work into this play idea before Howells' sense of propriety overcame his desire to write drama. On January 21, 1879 (*Mark Twain Letters*, I, 346), Clemens wrote to Howells: "I have always been sorry that we threw up that play embodying Orion which you began. It was a mistake to do that. Do keep that MS and tackle it again."

The play that Clemens and Howells finally wrote together concerned Colonel Sellers, the dreamer of *The Gilded Age*, and was referred to in their letters as *The Steam Generator* or *Orme's Motor*. It was a failure, but, as Howells said, they had a lot of fun writing it. The idea originated with Clemens, who wrote to Howells just before the latter left for Europe (September 5, 1881, Harvard Library):

Osgood says something about your projecting a play. Now I think that the play for you

This introduction was previously published in *Modern Drama*, I (December, 1958), 151–56.

to write would be one entitled "Col. Mulberry Sellers in Age" (75) with that fool of a Lafayette Hawkins (aged 50) still sticking to him & believing in him & calling him "My Lord" (S. being America's earl of Durham) & has cherished his delusion until he & his chuckleheaded household believe he *is* the rightful earl & that he is being shamefully treated by the House of Lords. He is a "specialist" & a "scientist" in various ways, makes collections of pebbles & brickbats & discourses garrulously & ignorantly over them & projects original geological "theories" etc. A selfish old hog & hypocrite, surrounded by sap-headed worshippers. Has a lot of impossible inventions, which cost somebody a good deal & then blow up & cripple disinterested parties or poison them. Let the patent for his earldom actually arrive from England just as he is dying.

Your refined people & purity of speech would make the best possible background for this coarse old ass. And when you were done, I could take your MS & re-write the Colonel's speeches & make him properly vulgar & extravagant. For this service I would require only ¾'s of the pecuniary result. (How liberal, how lavish, I seem to grow these days!) And I would let the play to Raymond, & bind him up with a contract that would give him the bellyache every time he read it. (I made $70,000 out of that devil with the other play.)

Shall we think this over?—or drop it, as being nonsense.

Howells did think this idea over, and several months later when the Mallory brothers of the Madison Square Theatre in New York asked him for a play, he told them of Clemens' plot (Howells to Clemens, July 14, 1882, *Life in Letters*, I, 313). Money was immediately mentioned and both writers became interested. From Switzerland (October 17, 1882, Harvard Library), Howells imparted his enthusiasm to Clemens, inviting him to Florence, where they could work on the "great American comedy of *Orme's Motor* which is to enrich us both beyond the dreams of avarice." (It should be noted that the steam generator, the motor, and the earldom are all used in *Colonel Sellers As A Scientist*.) But for some reason this did not work out, and Clemens suggested another time (May 18, 1883, Harvard Library): "Next

October you will come here and roost with me, and we will lock ourselves up from all the world and put the great American comedy through." When the time came, October was not long enough, and the two were still at work in November. "I'll send you the play today," Clemens wrote November 31, 1883 (Harvard Library), "& while you are working on it, introduce more people on the stage, or new incidents, where they seem necessary. And another turn or so of the phonograph. And maybe Sellers with his robe of the garter & his coronet." Howells, in *My Mark Twain* (New York: Harper & Bros., 1910), described their joy as they took the plot scene by scene and constructed the play, which he thought "extremely funny." Although each contributed some scenes, the characters were for the most part Clemens'. "No dramatists ever got greater joy out of their creations, and when I reflect that the public never had the chance of sharing our joy, I pity the public from a full heart."

Although they had been ostensibly writing their play with the blessings of the Madison Square people, when it was completed Clemens immediately set out to find an actor who could do the part of Colonel Sellers. But even before he started this search, so great was his pleasure in playwriting that he thought of doing more plays with Howells. On December 20, 1883 (Harvard Library), he wrote: "Now let's write a tragedy." And he included a draft of the closing scene of his "possible tragedy" based on an incident in Carlyle's life of Cromwell. Two months later he had another play on his mind (Clemens to Howells, February 26, 1884, Harvard Library): "Have you blocked out the Sandwich Island play yet? I'm mulling over that old sea-captain in my mind, but I don't exactly see how to get him in. In my mind, he is a bachelor (as the *real* man was—Capt. Smith of New Bedford and Honolulu) & the heroine is a half-white, & his adopted child." But neither play idea produced a finished manuscript.

The result of the Howells-Clemens collaboration was a dramatic revival of Colonel Sellers, the character that John T. Raymond had made popular on the stage in a dramatization of *The Gilded Age*. But in their play Howells and Clemens had allowed their imaginations to run so rampant that a stage production was almost unthinkable. The enthusiastic playwrights soon made this discovery when they began to approach prospective managers and actors. Clemens wanted a "specialist" to handle the Sellers part, and he first thought of Nat Goodwin. Probably the Mallorys would have produced the play with Goodwin, but they wanted thirds—managers, authors, actor—and Clemens thought he could deal directly with Goodwin (Clemens to Howells, February 13, 1884, Harvard Library). Howells, however, objected to something in Goodwin's character, and although Clemens argued that their reputations would not be harmed if the Mallorys produced the play (February 18, 1884, Harvard Library), Goodwin was dropped as a possibility. In the meantime the Mallorys took the play and resumed the search for an actor (Clemens to Howells, February 26, 1884, Harvard Library). The most logical choice, of course, was Raymond, who was at first favorably impressed with the play, but in September, 1884, rejected it because it presented a lunatic rather than the stageworthy Sellers and because the authors refused the extensive revision he requested. This was, indeed, a low point for the authors. For a while they seemed to accept their failure, and Clemens got the manuscript from Howells so that he could "get some truck out of it for the platform readings" (Clemens to Howells, October 18, 1884, Harvard Library).

During 1885, the playwrights seemed to continue losing interest in this play, although Goodwin remained anxious for the Sellers part (Clemens to Howells, February 27, 1885; July, 1885, Harvard Library). Then in the spring of 1886, A. P. Burbank, a popular lecture-platform ventriloquist and elocutionist, convinced Clemens that he could produce the play successfully by impersonating Raymond in the role of Sellers and thereby effecting a double burlesque. But Howells was not pleased; he agreed with Raymond that the play could not succeed, that there was nothing in it but "the idea of Sellers' character, and a lot of comic situations" (Howells to Clemens, May 5, 1886, Life in Letters, I, 381). Clemens, however, was reluctant to let it drop; he had faith in Burbank, whom he considered a "pretty live man." "He had made an incredible lot of arrangements with people," Clemens wrote to Howells (May 13, 1886, Harvard Library); "he had gone personally to Mr. Edison & got him so interested that he said, 'Leave that invention museum to me; give yourself no uneasiness; I will make it the completest thing of the kind you ever saw; you shall have a phonograph that will

need only that you turn the crank—it shall do its own talking & singing, & to the satisfaction of the audience, too; I'll invent some new curiosities; yes, I will furnish you a museum of inventions which shall be memorable in annals of the stage; & I'll do it all at my own expense.' " In fact, according to Clemens, who was angry with Howells for allowing them to become involved in production plans that Howells privately opposed, Burbank had his performance schedule all set up starting May 17, 1886. Although Howells admired Burbank and offered to do "literary tinkering" for him on any play (Howells to Clemens, May 18, 1886, Life in Letters, I, 383), he now declared his point of view firmly. After a sleepless night he wrote to Clemens: "Here's a play which every manager has put out-of-doors and which every actor known to us has refused, and now we go and give it to an elocutioner. We are fools." (Albert Bigelow Paine, Mark Twain: A Biography, II, [New York: Harper & Brothers, copyright 1912, by Harper & Brothers; copyright 1940, by Dora L. Paine], 762). With this kind of opposition, Clemens succumbed and with a $3,000 limit bought off their obligations to Burbank, Frohman, and the Lyceum Theatre, where the play was to have been produced. Eventually Howells shared the loss with Clemens equally.

But this was not the end for the play. Howells was not interested, but Clemens went ahead with Burbank and his company, rewrote portions of the play, and produced the play for one-night stands at his own expense. After performances at New Brunswick, New Jersey, and Syracuse and Rochester, New York, it finally played a trial matinee at the Lyceum Theatre, New York, September 23, 1887, as The American Claimant or Mulberry Sellers Ten Years Later (Odell, Annals of the New York Stage, XIII, 426). The play at this performance was probably similar to the Yale version—both of which omit Uncle Daniel from the cast of characters. But the play was not successful. The critic for the New York Tribune (September 24, 1887, p. 4, col. 5) saw little good in the performance, and the reviewer for The Theatre (III [October 11, 1887], 267) called it "a miserable lot of twaddle with neither dramatic construction nor reason. . . ." Howells recognized this, of course, as did a great many others, and Daniel Frohman's comment (Memories of a Manager [New York: Doubleday, Page & Co., 1911], p. 50) indicates from the producer's point of view the kind of overenthusiastic playwriting in which Howells and Clemens had indulged themselves: "The piece was full of humor. The hero was an inventor. One of the inventions was a fire-extinguisher. With this machine he makes his first entrance on the stage, and with it almost sets fire to the apartment. Rehearsals showed that the work was not likely to prove successful."

One might think that such overwhelming opposition to the play would completely discourage the authors, but it evidently did not. And the next time, Howells seems to have initiated the renewed interest. In a long and characteristic letter (February 9, 1889, Harvard Library), James A. Herne answered a Howells suggestion that he and Clemens write a play for Herne. The scene mentioned in the letter was Washington, and Sellers was the main character; hence, it would seem that the play for Herne was a suggested revision of *Colonel Sellers As A Scientist*. But nothing came of these negotiations, although the authors relieved Burbank of whatever control he still possessed over the play (Clemens to Howells, January 31, 1890, Harvard Library). Once again, many years later, Howells wrote to his daughter for the play manuscript (November 21, 1915, Harvard Library): "An actor man provoked to madness by Booth Tarkington thinks he wants to produce Mark Twain's and my Sellers play. . . . The actor man is capable of saying he thought the play was a tragedy, and he doesn't want it." But that seems to have been the end of it. Years after the collaboration, when he wrote *My Mark Twain*, Howells looked fondly back at their playwriting, still believing that it should have been successful—"So hard does the faith of the unsuccessful dramatist in his work die." Of course, the work was not all lost. Clemens used parts of it in his story of *The American Claimant*—begun in February, 1891—but, ironically enough, even he could not use the play as he had thought. It "couldn't be fitted to the new conditions," he wrote to Howells (May 20, 1891, Harvard Library), and it saved him only half a day's work. Certainly this was an unhappy conclusion for such illustrious collaborators.

The text of *Colonel Sellers As A Scientist* as published in this volume comes from three sources: (1) An incomplete manuscript from the Mark Twain Estate, with a synopsis of the play in Howells' hand; a working draft of the play in both Howells' and Clemens' hands, about two-thirds Howells'; and "Fragments of Sellers play" in Clemens' hand. The longest of these fragments is another Act I in Clemens' hand. The scene is a Washington hotel where first Mary and Aunt Sally discuss Mary's love problem, and later the De Bohun cousins talk about the girl one of them loves and the strange American Claimant the other has recently met. The hotel fire ends the act. In another fragment De Bohun, knowing that he is believed dead in the fire, decides to stay "dead," meets Sellers, "appears" at a Sellers seance as his real self, and listens to a most confusing and absurd history of the Earldom of Dover. (2) An incomplete typescript from the collection of C. Waller Barrett, New York City, with corrections in Howells' hand, lacking a conclusion to Act III. (3) A complete typescript with additional scenes, from the Yale University Library, listed as "Twain's own personal copy with pencilled notes in his hand."

A comparison of these three texts indicates that the Barrett copy was typed from the manuscript in the Mark Twain Estate and then worked over by Howells; the ending of the third act, however, which did not appear in the Barrett typescript, is in the manuscript. Because Howells lost interest in the play after the Burbank episode, the Yale version, which included some manuscript insertions and corrections from the Barrett version, may be considered less a product of the collaboration of the two writers than a revision by Clemens without Howells' countercomments. Therefore the text in this volume primarily follows the Barrett version, omitting minor changes inserted in the Yale copy, such as the Hawkins–Mary love theme, but adding, with notation, major scenes that appear only in the Yale version, and in two instances showing two endings to an act when one seems a product of the collaboration and the other a distinct change by Clemens.

Colonel Sellers as a Scientist[1]

A COMEDY

By S. L. Clemens and W. D. Howells

ACT I

SCENE 1: *A large room in Colonel Sellers' house in Washington; a large parlor, with folding doors, cheaply but very showily furnished, equipped with all manner of fantastic inventions, lying on chairs, scattered over the floor, hanging from the walls, and heaped in the corners, various cheap chromos on the walls. At the bottom of the scene is a grotesque arrangement of numerous batteries and other apparatus for generating electricity. Mary Sellers and the old nurse moving about and trying to evoke a little order from the chaos, with Mrs. Sellers looking on.*

AUNT SALLY: It don't seem just right, Miss Mary, to hear you talk about your Paw the way you do.

MRS. SELLERS: No indeed, that it don't! I wonder at you!

MARY: Oh no, you don't, mother! And nobody else would that knew how he had pulled us about from pillar to post, all our lives, and kept us getting poorer and poorer. I don't see how such a good, kind man as father can bear to do it.

MRS. SELLERS: You know, you ungrateful child, that he does it all for your sake. What else made him break up at Hannibal, where we had got so comfortably settled, and come on to Washington at his time of life?

MARY: Oh, I know he did it for me; and don't you suppose I love him the more, the more he makes us suffer? There isn't a dun comes into the house, and they're about the only visitors we have except the newspaper interviewers, that I don't fire up on father's account, and believe just as he does that we are coming into our everlasting fortune to-morrow morning. But we've lived on faith so long—and dressed in it! Look at yourself,

mother, in that ridiculous dressing-gown while I've got on the only decent dress we have left between us! I shall wear it till eleven o'clock, and you'll be "dressing" till that time; then you'll put it on, and I'll turn into the kitchen in my beautiful flour-sack peignoir, and be "Engaged" and let you have the dress. And here are all these blessed inventions and scientific discoveries, with millions in every one of them, littering up the whole house! Oh, if I didn't know father was the best man in the world, I should say he was the worst. (*Playfully.*) Well, go along, mother, you're as bad as Aunt Sally about him, every bit and grain. One would think he had kept you rolling in the lap of luxury all your days.

MRS. SELLERS: He's kept me happy, child, and that's a great deal better and the luxury is coming along too, in good time.

MARY: Oh, yes, to-morrow morning before breakfast, as usual. Just at present there's nothing to eat in the house but dried apples, and nothing to cook them with. Don't stand round in the way, mother; that doesn't help any.

She playfully takes her mother by the shoulders and pushes her out of the door.

MRS. SELLERS: Oh, you ridiculous girl. You're as full of spirits as your father.

MARY: Am I? Then I'll be just as rich as he is before I die.

Her mother goes out, and Mary turning from the door, suddenly bursts into tears.

AUNT SALLY: Oh don' you cry, honey; don' you take on so!

MARY: Oh, I can't help it! It's no use, Aunt Sally; I might as well give up at once. (*She drops into a chair and leaning forward seizes the back of another with her hand and rests her head wearily on her arm.*) You do what you can, Aunt Sally. The gentleman to see the motor won't be here till one o'clock. All that I wanted was to have the place looking a little less crazy! Oh, poor father! Poor mother! Oh dear me!

She drops a feather duster with which she has been operating to the floor.

AUNT SALLY, *sweeping vigorously between the*

[1] This play has not been published previously.

piles of inventions: Don' you min', honey; don' you min'. Aunt Sally gwine to put all dis to rights. You jes sit still dare and res' yourse'f. De Lord knows you need it in dis house. I don' know what Marse Sellers thinkin' about, de life he leads you and yo' mother, honey, wid dis thing and dat thing, change, change, change from morning till night, and no res'.

MARY, *lifting her head*: No, none for me! Oh, I wish it was all a dream, and then I could try to forget it.

AUNT SALLY: Yes, we'd all been better off dis minute if it hadn't happened—if we'd all stayed at home in old Missouri, 'stead o' comin' on here, and reskin' life and limb to get here, and scapin' by de skin o' your teeth from fire and flood on the way—smashed up on the railroad and drownded in de Mississippi. It's perplexing, honey, it's ridiculous, all dem accidents.

MARY, *springing to her feet*: Oh, no, no, Aunt Sally! Don't speak against the accidents. They're my only comfort now! They are all I have left of *him*—all that there is to prove that he ever lived, or spoke to me, or touched me. When shall I ever see him again. Oh, never, never!

AUNT SALLY: What you talkin' 'bout, Miss Mary? Is it dot young man wot—wot—wot—why Miss Mary, you ain't in love with him?

MARY: No, no, Aunt Sally! Not in love with him, not in love, but—interested. Yes, and very anxious to know what happened to him. Oh, I wish I had gone down in the water in his place— or with him! Oh, oh, if we could only have been drowned together!

AUNT SALLY: Drownded? You think he got drownded? Fine, strong, active, young man like dat?

MARY: Oh, he was strong, wasn't he, Aunt Sally? And beautiful wasn't he; and so noble, and brave, and unselfish. Don't you remember how he worked to get those poor creatures out of the wreck of the train—how quiet he was, how gentle, how thoughtful, and then when the boat went down—

AUNT SALLY: I lay ef I git my han's on him I take en tar de lights out'n him.

MARY, *horrified*: Aunt Sally!

AUNT SALLY: I bet I'll do it. I'll take en mop up de flo' wid him—I'll—

MARY, *indignantly*: Hush—I won't have it!

AUNT SALLY, *shaking her head threateningly and muttering broken sentences*: Nemmine—nemmine —any man dat go back on you—

MARY: Will you be still, you dreadful old thing? What—how did he go back on me, as you call it? He is dead, and I won't let any one speak a word against him! Was it his fault, I should like to know, if I was so silly as to take a fancy to a perfect stranger on the cars, before I had spoken a word to him?

AUNT SALLY: No, no, it won't do, honey.

MARY: And was it his fault, if he showed mother and me all those little attentions and took care of us while father was addressing a mass meeting of the gentlemen passengers in the smoking-car, and drawing up a constitutional amendment authorizing the President to declare war against any power excluding American pork? Was that his fault?

AUNT SALLY: No, it wasn't dat.

MARY: And was—was it my darling's fault— Oh, he is my darling, my dear, dead only love! Was it his fault that he seemed like a ministering angel to me when he was helping those bruised and mangled creatures out of the wreck?

AUNT SALLY: No, it wasn't dat.

MARY: And was it—you cruel old thing—was it his fault that the little hour after chance brought us together on the boat, the next day, and we stood there talking by the guard before the boat went down, and we didn't know each other's names, and we didn't care, because we knew each other's hearts—was it his fault that he made that hour a whole long eternity of bliss for me?

AUNT SALLY: No, honey, I ain't blamin' him for dat.

MARY: Very well, then, you wicked old creature, do you blame him when he found me at the last gasp in the river, and pulled me up on *that* piece of the wreck, and told me there in the horror and darkness that he would rather be there with me in the presence of death than in the midst of the brightest and gladdest scene on earth without me! Oh, that moment, Aunt Sally! That happy, happy time that out-heavened the wildest, fondest dream of bliss! Do you blame him for giving me that moment?

AUNT SALLY: De Lord knows I ain't blamin' him for dat.

MARY, *falling from her rapturous key, and speaking brokenly and doubtfully*: And then when that miserable thing came floating by—I know she floated as near as she could on purpose, because I saw her watching us before the boat struck— Do you blame him for leaving me to save her?

AUNT SALLY, *doggedly*: No.

MARY: For giving up his own place on the piece of wreck to her, and for pushing us to the shore, and then in the dark and confusion getting separated from me?

AUNT SALLY: No, I ain't blamin' him for dat.

MARY: Then what—what are you blaming him for?

AUNT SALLY, *very severely*: What am I blamin' him for? For goin' off with dat oder woman after you got separated. *What's* de reason when your paw come and fin' you he couldn't fin' *dem?* What's de reason, honey? What's de reason day never turn up again? You think he got drownded, hey? You think she got drownded? No, honey! No such thing! Dey lit out togeder, and de sooner you make up your mind to dat, de better, and de sooner you'll git cured of him. Oh, if I git my han's on him!

MARY: Oh, he never did it, he never did it! Oh yes, he did, he did, he did, he left me! Oh, he went away with her, and I shall never see him any more! Oh, my poor false, lost darling! Oh, my love, my cruel love! (*She drops her face in her hands and sinks sobbing to the floor. At the sound of steps outside, she springs to her feet again.*) What's that, who's there?

A VOICE WITHOUT: All right, Mrs. Sellers. Don't trouble yourself. I'll go right in. She won't mind me.

As Lafayette Hawkins enters one door, Mary with a cry escapes through the other.

SCENE II: *Hawkins and Aunt Sally*

HAWKINS: Is that you, Aunt Sally? Why, I wouldn't have known you, you have changed so.
He takes her hand.

AUNT SALLY: Yes, it's me, Marse Lafayette, it's me, I reckon, but sometimes I ain't shore. Oh, laws, de goin's on in dis house! You see de ole Missus?

HAWKINS: No, she couldn't see me. She sent me in here to see Mary— Where is Mary? Mrs. Sellers called down from up stairs that she couldn't see me because she was dressing. Fashionable hours—not dressed at eleven in the morning.

AUNT SALLY: No, nor at three in the afternoon. She ain't dressed, cause she ain't got nothin to dress in. I reckon the poor soul's pinnin' a few rags together, so's to look a little 'spectable before she comes down to see you. Poor Miss Mary run out soon's she heard your voice, po' thing, she's

been a crying here, Marse Lafayette, and I bin a tryin' to comfort her. But don' you min', Marse Lafayette. When she comes back, don' you seem to notice nothin'. I'm powerful glad to see you again, powerful glad. You're gittin' gray too, Marse Lafayette. You ain't so young as you was. Well, we've all got to die sometime. Don' you min' Miss Mary when you see her. She's ben cryin' a little—jis kin' o' mortified to think you ketch her in such ornery lookin' clo'es. Don' you 'pear to notice when she comes in. She's been kin' o' downhearted, but I done what I could to cheer her up, and I reckon she'll get along. I'll call her. Jis' set down— (*She looks around the bare room for a chair, but finds none.*) Jis' set down on—on—on some dese yer flyin' machines, or percussion bombshells, or 'lectric batories, and I'll go and send Miss Mary to you. (*Goes out calling.*) Miss Mary, oh Miss Mary, yer cousin, Marse Lafayette Hawkins, is in de parlor.

HAWKINS, *alone, going about, inspecting the inventions, and gingerly handling them*: This—this —seems to be some sort of dining-table. (*He places his hand on the top and the table suddenly opens and drops to the floor in the form of an oblong punt or boat. He reads a label pasted in the bottom.*) "The Sellers' convertible marine ship's table and life boat. Patent applied for." Well, I declare to goodness what a man the Colonel is! Just as full of ideas as he was when I first knew him thirty years ago. And all his thoughts run to benevolent enterprises; he still devotes himself to the amelioration and advancement of his species! What's this? (*He picks up a tin can like an oyster can and reads in the bottom.*) "Sellers' corn beef can for the supply of contraband provisions during time of the war. Dynamite charge inserted under the label 'Open here.'" My gracious, how can I get this out of my hands quick enough without dropping it? (*He changes it from one hand to the other with the greatest tenderness.*) Where is a soft place to put it? (*In stepping backward in this search, he trips on a string which pulls the trigger of a spring-gun, and sets off an alarm clock, which continues to ring after the discharging of the gun.*) Hello! Hello the house! Mary! Aunt Sally! Uncle Daniel! Mary, Cousin Mary! (*He stands upright in the center of the room, and repeats these cries, while the clock rattles on. Mary enters in the midst of the hubbub, and runs to stop the alarm.*) Cousin Mary, what does all this mean?
Quaking and afraid to move.

MARY, *approaching and throwing her arms around him*: It's nothing but father's burglar alarm—patent applied for. Oh, Cousin Lafayette, how glad I am to see you! When did you come? Have you seen mother yet?

HAWKINS: No, no. I haven't seen anybody yet, but Aunt Sally. Is it safe to—to—step about here, freely? Perhaps you'd like to take me to some other room. I'm afraid I might—disarrange some of your father's inventions.

MARY: Don't be troubled. You can't hurt them. We have them all right in the family and don't mind them any more. (*Desperately.*) You can sit down on them and kick them about the room if you choose.

HAWKINS, *eagerly*: Oh no, thank you, I can stand. I'm not tired—I've been sitting so long in the cars—all the way from Hannibal. It's a long way from Missouri. But Mary, my dear little cousin— You don't look very well or very happy. And Aunt Sally tells me—

MARY: Oh don't mind Aunt Sally; she's a silly cross old thing. I'm very well, and I'm perfectly happy.

HAWKINS, *looking doubtfully at her*: Well, I'm glad of that—very glad.

MARY, *incoherently*: Yes, I knew you would rejoice with us. I knew—ughhoo! Ughhoo!

> *Sobbing and then suddenly arresting herself, and looking defiantly at him.*

HAWKINS, *after a pause*: And is your mother well?

MARY: Oh perfectly well.

HAWKINS: And your father?

MARY: Ughhoo. He's always pro-pros-perous—ugh hoo, ugh hoo! And you know it Cousin Lafayette!

HAWKINS: Well, well, I thought he must be so, to be able to send me such a long message as he did when he telegraphed me to come here.

MARY, *astounded*: Father telegraphed you to come on here?

HAWKINS: Yes, here's the dispatch I got in Hannibal, Monday morning and here I am in Washington, at eleven A.M. Wednesday. Pretty quick work! But I never stopped a moment after I heard from your father. Here's his telegram. "Come on to Washington immediately. The heir of the Earl of Dover will be here Tuesday night as the guest of the British minister. Everything in train for a successful interview. Lose no time. If Jones still wants your house, sell out to him at any sacrifice. All my enterprises flourishing— The motor as

good as disposed of to parties in New York. Come at once, and charge all expenses to me. Bring all that documentary evidence that we drew up together in reference to my claim to the Earldom. Sellers. P. S. Turn all your property into cash. You mustn't return to Hannibal. Bring your family." The first time I ever had a telegram with a postscript.

MARY: He sent you all that by telegraph! Why it must have cost him ten or fifteen dollars!

HAWKINS: Well, I suppose he thought I could put that into the general account against him.

MARY, *aghast*: He didn't let you pay it?

HAWKINS: Oh never mind. I know your father's ways, but I've never lost confidence in him through thick and thin. I've always pinned my faith to the Colonel. So I just let Jones take the house at his own price—lost about fifteen hundred dollars on it; but I was glad to do it if I could be of any use to the Colonel. And he seems to feel that he's got a sure thing this time. (*Looking about the room.*) This is a pleasant house, Mary. You seem to be living in fine style here.

MARY, *giving over to prolonged fit of sobbing, and at last recovering her voice*: Didn't Aunt Sally tell you—tell—

HAWKINS: O, yes, she got off some nonsense, but I didn't pay any particular attention to it. I knew that if Colonel Sellers telegraphed on to me in that way, he knew what he was about. I didn't care what Aunt Sally said about your circumstances, I—

MARY: Well then, I tell you that we are as poor as poverty, and that we are head over ears in debt, and we haven't a decent thing to wear, nor hardly raw turnips any more to eat, and if father has got you to waste your money coming on here to share our wretchedness, it's a cruel, cruel shame and I don't care who knows it! If those New York people who are coming to see the electric motor to-day don't do something about it—and of course they won't—we are ruined—that's all.

HAWKINS, *incredulously*: Oh, you mustn't feel that way, Mary. Your father's got some plan you don't know about. Don't be troubled. He's going to come out all right, yet. I'm not afraid. I suppose he's got as many schemes on hand as ever?

MARY, *with bitter coldness*: Oh, quite!

HAWKINS: Then some of them *must* prosper. You must cheer up. Your mother isn't discouraged, is she?

MARY: She isn't when father's with her, but when he's away, she does nothing but cry over our troubles. Father could cheer up a lost soul, but that's neither here nor there. He even cheers me up.

HAWKINS: I wish he were here to cheer you up now. Where *is* your father?

MARY: Oh, I don't know, he's out somewhere trying his latest invention.

HAWKINS: *Latest?* Then the motor isn't his latest?

MARY: There have been a *dozen* since the motor. The very last latest is a fire extinguisher. He'll explain it to you. He goes about all day with it strapped on his back and he sleeps with it at his bedside, so as to be able to run at the first alarm of fire. It makes me frantic to see him. Of course, at his age, he can't get to the fires before they're all put out, and so he goes about indoors and out with that ridiculous thing on his back and every now and then at the table or when he's getting into bed, it shoots off—

HAWKINS: Shoots off, Mary?

MARY: Yes, fireballs, like a roman candle—it's a new principle of fire extinguishing—and scares us almost out of our wits—or would if we had any left, and—there! There he is now—out on the fire-escape!

Sound of shuffling and scraping outside, with incoherent exclamations growing gradually more distinct.

HAWKINS: On the fire-escape! Cousin Mary?

MARY: Yes, yes! Didn't you notice father's fire-escape on the outside of the house? He always comes and goes by it, so as to advertise it, and keep it before the people. There is always a crowd following him.

HAWKINS: Well, I never did hear of coming *up* a fire-escape before!

A voice outside and below.

VOICE: Three cheers for the Colonel.

The cheers are given.

SELLERS, *without*: I thank you gentlemen for this reception. At another time I will address you more fully. But now, I am exhausted from the efforts which have proved my fire extinguisher a complete success, and have scored another triumph in the cause of humanity! Gentlemen, for the present I bid you good day! (*He appears at the window which he throws up.*) Mary, is that you, and—what! Not Lafayette Hawkins! Lafayette, my dear boy, my faithful friend, my generous ally, my— (*He shows himself in profile at the window with the extinguisher strapped on his back and in the effort to spring into the room,*

catches his toe on the sill, and tumbles forward, but is saved from falling by Hawkins who runs forward and catches him in his arms.) All right! All right! In your arms, my friend, my more than son and brother! I accept the omen! (*Hot and swabbing his face.*) Why, this is delightful! (*Shakes both his hands.*) It's a breath of old Missouri to see you. Sit down—sit down. (*Sits.*) How'd you leave everything? And when did you come? (*Lafayette tries to get in answers, but doesn't succeed.*) Mary, my dear, where's your mother? Your mother ought to be here to welcome Lafayette! Go and call her, my family—her own child, as it were—tell her to throw on anything—any—little sort of negligee thing. Lafayette won't mind.

MARY, *in a responsive aside*: Any little negligee thing! My floursack peignoir, or the dressing gown I made her out of my old water-proof and faced with the silk of the worn out family umbrella!

Exit.

SELLERS: Well, well, well! Here we are in Washington again, after all these years! How it brings back the old times, the Goose Run appropriation that didn't get through; and the Tennessee land appropriation that broke down in the Senate; and the noble Senator Dilworthy—ah! There was a grand man, a *grand* man, Lafayette—there are all too few like him in these days—he's keeping a butcher shop, now, in Kansas. Ah, yes, you'll find things changed here, Lafayette, since you were a youth. Well, let bygones be bygones. By accident —purely by accident—I made some little failures in those days and your father's family suffered some of the consequences. But our sun is rising now, Lafayette—certain and prodigious prosperity right ahead, and imminent—and as soon as I was perfectly sure of that, I telegraphed for you—for I mean that you and yours shall share the coming good fortune as freely as you've shared in the former disasters. (*Laying his hand on his shoulder. Impressively.*) Lafayette, I've got the world in my grip—the world, understand—and I am going to divide it with you!

HAWKINS, *with sincerity*: Ah, that's like you, Colonel. You've not changed at any rate.

SELLERS: I'm glad you believe in me still, Lafayette.

HAWKINS: I always have believed in you; and I always shall, as long as I live.

SELLERS: Thank you, my boy. You shan't repent it. You *can't*. Why, cast your eyes around this room—what do you see? Apparently a junk-shop; apparently a hospital connected with a patent office—in reality, the mines of Golconda in disguise! [1] We live in the sum total of time, Lafayette. The elements are crowded full of beneficent forces—always have been—and ours is the first generation to turn them to account and make them work for us. Has Mary been telling you about some of my little contrivances?

HAWKINS: Yes, but I had no idea how fast you had been throwing them off lately. I supposed that you were still working at the electric motor.

SELLERS: Of course, of course. I didn't write you, I suppose, I got the motor off my hands two weeks ago, and parties from New York are coming to take it away to-day. I don't know what they're going to do with it, but I've an idea, Lafayette, that they're going to employ it in the application of stored electricity to the grip cars on the Brooklyn bridge.

HAWKINS: Why of course! The very thing! There's a mint in that thing—

SELLERS: A few millions. I shall take a royalty, probably, on the cars passed over the bridge. But look here! (*Turning himself around so as to show the extinguisher, which covers his whole back and is strapped round his shoulders and thighs.*) There! There is a trifle I threw off a few weeks ago between whiles. What do you think of that?

HAWKINS, *lost in admiration*: Well, of course, Colonel! Anything you've given your mind to—

SELLERS: A child could use this extinguisher. (*Seized with an idea and coming forward to the audience.*) I'll have children's sizes introduced at once with chambers to replace the old-fashioned school satchels and offer special terms to schools. I'll write a manual of my extinguisher drill for the use of—of—of—your ladies' seminaries, I will have a ladies' style out at once. Old ladies—I'll get out a pattern for elderly and timid people. I'll—

HAWKINS, *still looking at the machine*: But what's the principle, Colonel Sellers? Is it a chemical vapor, or—

SELLERS: Chemical vapor! No, sir! *Fire!* A principle as old as the Christian civilization! *Greek* fire! Why, Lafayette, I claim nothing in this case, as an inventor. I merely apply ideas that have always existed but haven't been developed because the world wasn't ripe for them. Fire and vaccina-

tion—that is the strange device of my banner, Lafayette. The principle of vaccination has always existed. They're applying it now to everything in France. They're inoculating for scarletina and consumption and erysipelas—they don't stop at smallpox. I apply the principle to fire. And when you inoculate for fire, what do you want? The strongest form of virus! You want *Greek* fire. That combustion, in-extinguishable by water, with which the Greeks of old Byzantium destroyed the galleys of their enemies—that devouring element which they employed against the Turks at the battle of Navarino—Greek fire! Wherever it strikes, it simply obliterates and annihilates every other form of combustion. No conflagration can stand before it a moment—not an instant. If they had twelve— or half a dozen of my instruments, even the old common unimproved kind, when Chicago burned down—wait, I'll just show you! (*Begins to fool about his machine.*) See that button? Well that's the key to a chamber where I have twenty-five charges of Greek fire stored. By simply touching that button—by pressing it thus—don't be alarmed! I fired off the entire series of charges into a vacant lot on my way home—thus— (*He touches the button, and the extinguisher fires off a ball, which whizzes past Hawkins' face, and Sellers rushes after it and dashes a bucket of sand on it.*) There! If I hadn't had that bucket of sand left over from my last experiment, nothing could have saved this house!

HAWKINS: My goodness!

SELLERS: No, sir! Water has no effect on it— makes it worse—makes it burn fiercer! This destroys the original fire, and concentrates the element wherever it strikes.

HAWKINS: Well, but how—if the engines can't put out the fire when you've concentrated it—

SELLERS: The *water*-engines can't put it out, but the *sand*-blast engines can! And here comes in a third great principle. What causes the greatest ravage by fire? The limited supply of water! The cisterns give out—you're always reading of it. But the supply of earth is simply inexhaustible! As long as there's a handful left of this distracted globe, you can put out a fire. No more Chicago fires—no more Boston fires [2]—they're obsolete. Lafayette, I threw off the idea of a little sand-blast engine the other day—or wait, I'll show you! (*He begins rumaging among the different piles of inventions.*) I declare, if those women don't

---

[1] In the C. W. Barrett version the material on the "adaptations of the phonograph to the Marine service" was inserted at this point. The later Yale version places it in Act III.

[2] Boston fire, November 9–10, 1872; Chicago fire, October 8, 1871.

stop putting those things in order—(Desists.) Well, never mind! Why do I waste your time with these trifles? This will do well enough to pass an idle hour—to kill time, but the extinction of fire after all is such a small matter—

HAWKINS: Small matter?

SELLERS: Compared with materialization—

HAWKINS: Materialization?

SELLERS: With the restoration of the dead to all the necessary functions of life—so small a matter that I feel like apologizing to you, Lafayette, for talking to you about it. I do, indeed. The *great* thing—the great *thing*—is materialization! Mark my words. Ma-te-ri-al-ization.

HAWKINS, *aghast*: Why Uncle Mulberry, I didn't know you were a spiritualist.

SELLERS, *with the greatest contempt*: Spiritualist! Who? *I*? I a spiritualist? Do *I* look like one of those crazy, rapping, table-tipping, planchette, music in the air, hand-tying, parafine candle-moulding frauds? Why should any relative of *mine*, any blood-relation, why should you who have known me from the cradle, and know what a plain, practical, straightforward common-sense man I have been all my days, imagine that in the very prime of life, the ripe wisdom of my years, I should sink so low as that.

Deeply affected.

HAWKINS: But Uncle Mulberry— Don't take on about it— I didn't mean anything— I only mean that I thought I had heard that this materialization was one of the latest discoveries of spiritualization—

SELLERS: No *spiritualization* about it. The principle is as old as the everlasting hills. (Softening into confidentiality.) Why, Lafayette, this thing has *always* existed. It's an old *thing*. Only the world wasn't prepared for it. It's just like steam and electricity—the principle *always* has been understood and practiced in a small way, off in holes and corners. But now it comes out in the full light of day because the world's ripe for it—wants it—needs it—must have it. It's a plain practical thing—and I wouldn't take hold of it as a man of science, if it wasn't. I can explain it to you in half a minute. The spiritualists materialize one little pitiful specter—or part of a specter—a leg, or an arm! Or a forefinger, or a big toe! They do it by taking substance from each person in the circle. Now I propose to do it on a large scale. I propose to reclothe the departed spirits and bring them back solid and substantial by simply using the enormous waste of human substance that's always going on; by employing the lost weight and vitality thrown off in breathing, by utilizing what we lose through hunger every day between breakfast and dinner, by applying the insensible perspiration of living men.

HAWKINS, *dazed*: It is immense, it is prodigious —but it sounds so impossible.

SELLERS: Nothing impossible about it!

HAWKINS: But—but—you only propose to do it; as I understand, you; you only hope—

SELLERS: No, I don't merely *propose* to do it, I can *do* it. The thing has finished and completed itself in my mind—the final and essential details flashed upon me this very day. Lafayette. (Impressively.) I can actually make a dead man rise up and live.

HAWKINS: Live? You don't mean actually?

SELLERS: Yes sir, live. This is the thing I was referring to a while ago—for this is the grandest invention of the age, of all the ages, as you said. There's no end of money in it.

HAWKINS: How? Why, where is there money in it? It's certainly a much bigger wonder than materializing a mere plaster of Paris leg in a dim light, but you know the public have grown so suspicious of all that sort of thing, that now even an entire dead man walking about in the impressive twilight of a seance would hardly draw, I'm afraid.

SELLERS, *compassionately*: Ah, dear me, you— why Lafayette, did you suppose I had anything so paltry as an *exhibition* in my mind? (Earnestly.) No, sir! I have a far nobler object in bringing these dead people back to life. I shall make them useful.

HAWKINS: Useful? How?

SELLERS, *pauses—reflecting gravely*: For one thing I shall put them on the police. (Hawkins breaks into a laugh. With rebuking seriousness.) It is not a laughing matter, Lafayette.

HAWKINS, *sincerely*: You must excuse me, Colonel—I meant no harm—I did not know you were in earnest.

SELLERS: I am in earnest. I shall rehabilitate these dead men and put them on the police. I have thought it all out, and it is perfectly rational, perfectly feasible. And mints of money in it. It's full of sense. You take the average policeman. Look at that animal yonder, (pointing out of the window) asleep—against a lamp-post—moss growing on his back and probably barnacles— is he better than a dead man? I mean a dead man that's been dead 500 *years* and *had a rest*. Of course he isn't; he's not half so good—not half as lively. You wait—you'll see how it'll freshen them up—

my process, I mean. I don't care how long a man's been dead; the longer he's been dead the better—he's more rested. I have been inquiring around privately, among officials and politicians; and I find that by a judicious distribution of money I can get a contract to supply Washington with a police force of this kind. Now look at the thing calmly. What does the present force cost this town, in the mere item of wages alone? Two hundred men at, say, an average of $100 a month apiece, $20,000 a month—$240,000 a year. Very good—now listen. A materialized policeman costs nothing for his keep—not a cent; because he doesn't eat anything, he doesn't drink anything. Very good; I can materialize a very good article of policeman at eight cents apiece—that will cover my expenses, wear and tear of machinery, etc.—and I can turn out the very best A.1. article that ever was seen at nine or ten cents—say $13 a gross. Suppose I let them to the city at $50 a month—200 of them— A hundred and twenty thousand dollars a year clear profit, ain't it? Now do you begin to see any money in it?

HAWKINS: Money? Why it takes a body's breath away!

SELLERS: Does *that* take your breath away? Why, Lafayette, that is nothing but the mere poverty-stricken preliminary.

HAWKINS: You don't mean to say—

SELLERS: I mean to say just what I—why look here! There's New York, Philadelphia, Boston, Baltimore, Chicago, St. Louis, Cincinnati, San Francisco, and a hundred and fifty other cities—I'll supply them all—they've got to come to it, they can't help themselves. Why? Because if they'll give me a monopoly, I'll let them have policemen at club terms. There are 30,000 policemen in the U.S. I'll furnish the entire lot at $5 a month apiece. Just figure on that; $150,000 a month, ain't it? Eighteen hundred thousand dollars a year, ain't it?

HAWKINS: It's too stupendous!

SELLERS, *indifferently*: Yes—yes—it's well enough for a beginning.

HAWKINS: For a beginning!

SELLERS: That's all—merely a beginning. The rest of the world—

HAWKINS: The rest of the world?

SELLERS, *calmly*: Certainly. I have thought it all out and I have made the necessary calculations. (*Taking a paper from his pocket.*) I find that in Europe and the rest of the world there are 500,000 policemen employed—at a perfectly ruinous ex-

pense. From my works, when I get them fully equipped, I shall supply all these men. I shall let them go at, say $2 a month apiece; a million dollars a month, you see—twelve millions a year. Lafayette, I will make policemen cheaper than any other kind of meat in the world. This thing is so sure; these grand results are so absolutely certain, that if a man was to come in here now, and say "Colonel Sellers, could you let me have five million dollars for a few—" (*Knocking at the door.*) Come in. (*Enter a man—he and Sellers step aside and talk together inaudibly, Sellers feeling in all his pockets in vain and saying.*) Two dollars—um—two dollars—I meant to pay it six weeks ago—but my capital is so engrossed by— look here I'll tell you what I'll do. (*Leading him to a picture.*) You shall take this work of art temporarily until I can—and please be very careful with it. (*Brushing it with handkerchief.*) It's a marvelous thing, marvelous—it's the best battle-field pastoral that ever—why just look at these drums— you can hear them—and observe the tone of the middle distance, and the extraordinary attitude of the high lights—and the feeling—ah, just observe the feeling that's in that picture. I regard it as altogether the finest work in my collection. One of the Vanderbilts said to me, said he, "Sellers, people may talk about a railroad being the one possession that can round and complete a human life, and satisfy the tender and nameless longings that breathe their plaintive sighings through the mysterious chambers of the soul, but I would rather own that Meissonnier of yours than—"

MAN: Meissonnier? Why, it's chromo!

SELLERS, *undisturbed*: Why of course it is. Do you suppose you'll ever see another original painting in the U.S. while the national idiot asylum yonder in the capital levies a 30 per cent duty on them?

MAN, *gratefully*: Let me shake you by the hand. Give me the chromo. I'm not going to draw business lines too rigidly with a man who is animated by such honorable sentiments as that. (*Shaking hands.*) Good day, sir, good day—take your own time.

SELLERS: Good day. (*Man leaves with picture. Calling after him.*) Keep it in a dry place—don't let the temperature get below seventy. (*Resuming with Lafayette.*) It's better he should have it, anyway, till I can build a gallery—bound to get injured here. (*Brushing another chromo with handkerchief and holding it at arm's length in different lights.*) He's got a fine feeling for art, that man.

(Brush.) The finest I ever saw, *(Brush.)* in a gas fitter. I'm glad he didn't get his eye on this old Rembrandt. *(Re-hanging picture and sitting down.)* Let me see—where was I? Oh, the policemen.

HAWKINS: Yes, that was it.

SELLERS: Now as to detectives. There's always been an ineradicable defect about detectives. I have recalled and set down, here, *(Referring to document)* upwards of a hundred cases where they would have ferreted out a crime if they had lived long enough. Now I can fix all that. I can get up an article of detective that'll last like the joke about the church sociable oyster. There's no reason in the world why if proper pains are taken in the materializing the materialized detective shouldn't remain perfectly sound and sweet a thousand years. Just the same with policemen. For a reasonable premium I'll make 'em immortal.

HAWKINS: It's a grand idea—grand!

SELLERS: The more this thing opens up to me, the more marvelously its possibilities expand. Think of it. Why, these now idle, useless myriads of dead men can be employed in a thousand ways. District telegraph messengers, consuls—Congressmen—why look here. Why shouldn't we have a permanent set of dead congressmen? Instead of always turning out one lot that were just beginning to learn something and electing a new lot that didn't know anything. Why, man, it would entirely stop this ignorant tampering with the tariff—because any dead man of ordinary intelligence knows that those mistakes were all committed ages ago. And moreover it—why, Lafayette, I could give this country its pick and choice out of its dead statesmen—think of that, now!

HAWKINS, *going to Sellers:* Your materialization plan beats immigration if it will work!

SELLERS: It will work and I will work sometime! And take the case of Europe. I can furnish Europe a set of kings that can *eat* dynamite if they want to—it won't hurt them. Lafayette, I can do a splendid trade in misfit kings—just as one does in carpets—for a reasonable brokerage, take an Alphonse[1] off their hands and furnish them the old original! Solomon in his place, Solomon ought to fetch a slashing figure. What should you think I ought to ask for Solomon, Lafayette?

HAWKINS: I believe you could get anything you chose to charge.

SELLERS, *meditatively, telling off his fingers:*

[1] The reference is probably to Alphonso XII, 1857–1885, king of Spain.

Say a million a year—dirt cheap—million for Charlemagne—million for—a million's too cheap, Lafayette—we can do better; we can do a great deal better. You write to some of those governments—let 'em bid; that's the best way. Or if you think it's better, you can try an auction. I really believe an auction's the correct thing. It excites competition, you know. And everybody likes auctions, anyway. It's human—it's a human failing. I believe there's thirty or forty millions a year just in kings alone. But you musn't be too hasty—you want to make sure of the best way before you break ground. Now if you could get some advice from the British minister—I'll leave the whole thing in your hands—get the best terms you can, and—

HAWKINS: But in such an important matter as this, I should think you yourself—

SELLERS, *impressively:* If it were an important thing, I should of course give it my personal attention—but in view of the greater matter at stake, it will be necessary for me to occupy myself exclusively with the wholesale end of the business, so to speak, and entrust the retail trade to you.

HAWKINS: Why, how can there be anything bigger than—

SELLERS: Peddling kings? Why, Lafayette, have you forgotten that the nations of the earth have got to be supplied with armies?

HAWKINS: Good land!

SELLERS: Can they afford to carry their custom anywhere else? I would like you to answer me that? What chance would an entire army of living soldiers stand against a single brigade of my dead ones— My immortal ones? None at all. Lafayette, the combined armies of the European and Asiatic world aggregate 16,000,000 men. To these we add our own army, which, including deserters, amounts to nearly 20,000. I will supply 16,020,000 men for $200,000,000 a year or I will sell the entire crop, and warrant them to outlast the solar system, for the bagatelle of sixty billion dollars cash on the nail.

HAWKINS: Good heavens!

SELLERS: But there's not got to be any higgling. They've got to take me up now—right on the spot —or I'll put up the rate to a hundred billions. *(Knock at the door.)* Come in! *(Enter another creditor and talks with Sellers aside who searches his pockets and says presently.)* One dollar and a half—um—I thought it was a dollar and forty cents—but you're right—I remember now. You lent me a couple of car tickets—yes, it was a dollar and a half. (*Reflects, then takes down picture and brushes it off, occasionally wiping away a tear.*) Take it along, there's no other way.

MAN, *ruefully*: If you've got anything else, I'd infinitely rather—

SELLERS, *interrupting and gently pushing him out with the chromo*: No, it will break my heart, but I've got to submit to the heavy blow—for the present—for a couple of days—but I know you'll take good care of it—do guard it as you would your own life—it's the only Rembrandt that's in this country.

MAN, *casting his eyes toward Heaven*: Rembrandt!

Exit.

HAWKINS, *hesitatingly*: I suppose, Colonel, that necessarily in view of these new and colossal interests, the business which you called me here about, is no longer of sufficient importance to—

SELLERS: What, the Earldom! The Earldom not important! Why, now it's a hundred times more important than it was before. Why, Lafayette, do you know what it is to be an English earl? Why it's a grander thing, it's a sublimer thing, it's a more enviable thing to be an English earl than to be a materialized Solomon, with all his unapproachable paraphernalia of wisdom including his eight hundred materialized wives; that's an ordinary earl. Think what an earl I shall be, with these billions at my back. No, indeed, the Earldom's a hundred times more important now, than it was before. You know all about our family claim and how the matter stands, don't you?

HAWKINS: In general terms, yes—but that is all.

SELLERS: Well, it's very simple. Our branch of the family came over to this country about a hundred years ago. Several times, since, the Earldom has come near falling to the American tribe but always missed fire at the last moment. By the extinction of my Uncle Abner's family ten years ago I became the head of the American House. Well, our chances have become good again. For instance—there's the present Earl, now in possession. He's old and feeble and likely to go any time. After him comes his young bachelor son, Reginald De Bohun, his heir. If Reginald should die unmarried, his cousin Rupert, also a bachelor, would inherit. If he should die unmarried, I walk into the Earldom with none to dispute. Very well; Rupert is here in Washington at this moment. I haven't seen him, but he's here—arrived lately. Now, my idea is to buy out his claim.

HAWKINS: But why don't you buy out the immediate heir?

SELLERS: Well, for the present I can't get at him. He's in England; so I will buy out Rupert, and as soon as that's all fixed, you will proceed to England and negotiate with Reginald. As soon as you've fixed Reginald, go ahead and buy out the old gentleman, telegraph me, and I'll come along with the family.

HAWKINS: O, Colonel, I shall never know how to be grateful enough to you for choosing me for this service; for all my life I have so longed to travel to foreign lands, but I never could afford it before.

SELLERS: Well, you can afford it, now, and you shall go in style, too—style that'll make your head swim. I don't want you to spare any expense —just make the money fly. I'll foot the bills.

HAWKINS: O, it'll be delightful. And what do you think I had better pay for Reginald and the old Earl?

SELLERS: O, pay what you like—it isn't any matter.

HAWKINS: But will they sell? Will an Englishman's pride allow him to sell such a thing?

SELLERS: Well, how you talk! An Englishman's pride allows him to sell the succession to a pulpit to the highest bidder, don't it? Do you reckon the pride that don't stick at peddling places in the immediate service of the Deity for cash, will stick at peddling little sham dignities pertaining to the fictitious service of an earthly king? Don't you see that would be idiotic?

HAWKINS: Certainly—I see it now—now that you've put it so that a body can't help seeing it —but I hadn't thought of it before.

SELLERS, *reflectively*: In a week—or at most, two weeks—the lightnings will be carrying my stupendous achievement all around the globe.

HAWKINS, *concerned*: Won't that make Reginald and the Earl put up their price?

SELLERS: Yes—that's true. By the time you get there, they'll have it up a billion.

HAWKINS, *despairing gasp*: Aw!

SELLERS: As far as I am personally concerned I don't mind it, for it is not a sum of consequence; but what I am troubled about is the effect upon my country. No, Lafayette, as a patriot I—to suddenly remove this money from the veins and arteries of commerce— (*Walking the floor in distress.*) Why—why—true, the sum is nothing to us, but the United States can't stand it. We've got to look out for our country first and ourselves afterward.

HAWKINS, *with enthusiasm*: That's just like you, Colonel Sellers—and I'm proud of you for it. Well, then—

SELLERS: Well, then—um, um. (*Walking and puzzling over it—then cheerfully.*) I've got it! You'll hold that auction there!

HAWKINS: Good! I see! Take money out of Europe!

SELLERS: That's the idea. Now as soon as your money begins to pile in, pay those people their billion and square the thing up, and make the proper preparations for my reception right away. Go down to the House of Lords and have my seat upholstered fresh. (*Knock at the door.*) Buy me a few country seats in good localities—Warwick and Hampton Court and one or two others —and buy Kenilworth and fix it up and put a mansard on it—white-wash it and put in a burglar alarm— (*Louder knock.*) And when you've got everything ready for me, send a ship.

HAWKINS: A ship? A whole one?

SELLERS: Yes— What could I do with a half a one?

HAWKINS: What kind of one shall—

SELLERS: Why, the best of course—what other kind would you have me use?

HAWKINS: Very well, then—I—

SELLERS: Get the great Eastern.

HAWKINS: What, charter the gr—

SELLERS: No. (*Loud knock.*) Buy her. Come in. (*Enter creditor.*) Blast these people, they annoy a body to death. (*Talking all the time, and removing watch guard from around his neck.*) Get her properly repaired. (*Handing large silver watch to creditor who starts away.*) There, I know what you want—hold that a couple of days—I'll redeem it— (*Exit creditor.*) Man her with a picked crew of five hundred men, get an admiral for captain, and send her along—and I'll go to England in a style befitting my rank. (*Pause.*) Well, I believe everything's settled and understood, now— (*Pause. Meditatively, slowly, absendmindedly.*) Windsor Castle—um— If Windsor Castle were just a shade nearer town—

Mrs. Sellers bursts in with the newspaper. She is shabbily dressed in the gown that Mary had on when she left the room.

MRS. SELLERS: Lafayette Hawkins, I'm glad to see you. You don't need to have me tell you *how* glad. How are all your family? And Sarah and the girls? And your mother? Is she well? I'm ashamed to keep you waiting so long—I was just trying on a dress, and I couldn't come any sooner, and I'm so flustered about this fire—

HAWKINS: Oh, that's all right, Mrs. Sellers. Don't mention it at all. How young you look! Why when you came in I thought it was Mary right over again. You don't look a bit older.

MRS. SELLERS, *looking fearfully down at her dress*: I reckon it's the dress partly. We always dress off the same piece—when we can. You come at a sad time, Lafayette, but you're welcome all the same! You're a Sellers by blood too, and you've a right to share our family affliction. I suppose the Colonel has told you of our bereavement. Oh, it don't seem as if I could bear it.

Pulls out her handkerchief.

SELLERS: What affliction? What bereavement? Are you crazy, Polly? What are you talking about?

MRS. SELLERS: Why, don't you know about it? Haven't you seen the paper? Haven't you been at the fire?

Hands paper.

SELLERS: Of course I've been at the fire! I got there as usual just as they had put it out but I illustrated the principle of the extinguisher to a magnificent audience in a vacant lot on the way home. (*Mrs. Sellers continues to weep.*) But what in the world has the conflagration of a woodshed in Georgetown got to do with our family troubles? I thought—

MRS. SELLERS: It wasn't a woodshed—it was the Tolliver House, last night—it's all in the paper! I just happened to see it as I came along through the hall—

SELLERS: Fire at the Tolliver House, and I not there with my extinguisher? Oh, this is a calamity! Where—where is the account? (*Looking over the paper.*) Oh, here it is! Here— (*Reads.*) "Destructive fire at the Tolliver House last night. Three lives lost." Oh dear, dear! This is terrible—um— um— (*Reading.*) "The three victims taken from the burnt wing of the hotel are charred and consumed beyond recognition but it is ascertained that one of them was undoubtedly the Hon. R. De Bohun, guest at the dinner of—the—British— minister—and—oom—oom—oom— (*Whimpering.*) Nephew of the—Earl of Dover!" My poor cousin! (*He drops the paper and lets his head fall on Lafayette's shoulder.*) Lafayette! Lafayette! This is a blow! A great blow! Only think how such a thing would be felt in Newport! Or in the clubs of New York, and the coaching circles! Or in the best society of Boston! Or Philadelphia! Or anywhere that the moral worth and amiable manners of the travelling English nobleman have endeared him to our wealthy countrymen! And they are merely strangers! And I am a c—c—c—cousin! The ties of blood are strangely powerful when they bind us to the British aristocracy. The voice of nature when it cries from the dust of an earl's nephew is singularly piercing. Forgive—forgive this weakness, my boy! I—I—trust that these are not unmanly tears!

He continues to sob on Lafayette's shoulder.

MRS. SELLERS: Oh, Berry dear, don't take on so! Indeed you must not! Remember that he was only your thirteenth or fourteenth cousin.

SELLERS, *brokenly*: I know. But he was an English nobleman.

MRS. SELLERS: You never saw him you know.

SELLERS: But his father and mine fought on opposite sides at Nasby!

MRS. SELLERS: And the poor young man's death does bring you one step nearer the Earldom.

SELLERS, *lifting his head*: No matter, Heaven knows, my dear, that I should be unworthy of you, unworthy of the name which my ancestors bore in common with this young man, and the brave knight Richard Lion Heart, who invented a horse-power auger for boring through the walls of Jerusalem, if I could allow a moment's selfish exultation to alloy my grief for my poor cousin. *(Folding up the paper with sorrowful dignity.)* But I can at least claim a kinsman's privilege with regard to the—the—mortal coil, so to speak, of this De Bohun. He shall not feel that he is a stranger among us. *(Breaking again.)* I—I—will have his ashes—properly—prepared—and sent home to his—heart-broken uncle—the lonely old man who sits nephewless in his halls of pride among the cinque ports of Dover! *(He gradually allows his feelings to overcome him, and hides his face, then he commands himself again.)* Come—come—Lafayette. You will go with me to the scene of this disaster and help me to identify the—

MRS. SELLERS: But Mulberry dear, the paper says the victims are indistinguishable!

SELLERS, *taken aback and then recovering himself*: Then we will send them all!

MRS. SELLERS: Oh, don't go, my dear. Remember how very, very poor we are! I know we are going to be rich, and very very soon, but now we are absolutely destitute, and how will you meet the expense? I know your good and noble heart, Mulberry, and how much you like to do

magnanimous things, and it's natural you should feel as you do about your cousin, but, indeed, indeed, you can't afford this.

SELLERS, *strongly moved*: You are right, my dear. I must, I *must* forego this luxury. Yes, I must. I must leave to the British minister, who has never admitted me to his house, and has contemptuously ignored me, both as a Southern gentleman and potential English nobleman— I must let him, a stranger, intervene, where a kinsman's pious hands— *(Suddenly brightening.)* Why Polly! What am I thinking of? I will send these—these—ashes to the Earl of Dover C.O.D. and let the expense follow the package! The Earl is rich, he is proud. I freely give my time, and if he knew it, he would demand to defray the mere pecuniary cost of the transaction.

He is rushing from the room when his wife gets between him and the door and stops him.

MRS. SELLERS: But wait—think—consider! You don't know anything about this young man; or what terms he was on with his uncle. He and the Earl may not have been friends—

SELLERS: That is true, Polly, very true. *(Returning and speaking with great enthusiasm.)* And the only way to find out is to ask the young man himself!

MRS. SELLERS: The young man himself! Why, how—

SELLERS: By simply materializing and interrogating his departed spirit, his ghost.

MRS. SELLERS: Ghost?

HAWKINS: Ghost!

SELLERS: His ghost, which I shall summon visibly and tangibly here before us by my new process. *(He attempts to take off his coat, but the extinguisher only allows him to get his arms out and the sleeves hang dangling and flapping.)* Let me get at these poles and batteries, my dear, and you fix your mind firmly on the thought of De Bohun.

MRS. SELLERS: Ow! Never!

She rushes from the room.

SELLERS: No matter! You will do quite as well, Lafayette! Fix your mind on him.

HAWKINS: But I never saw him!

SELLERS: Then think of nothing—the subway or the silver dollar—think of nothing and my mortality will act on yours— *(Continues to fuss about the machinery.)* Now, are you ready? Well then, one, two, three, think!

HAWKINS: Of nothing?

SELLERS: This current of electricity which I'm

now generating here will take the direction of your thoughts. Your thoughts in fixing themselves upon a given person, collect the idea of him from all space. Understand?

HAWKINS: Yes—yes—

SELLERS: And the electricity takes up unorganized matter wherever it finds it, and clothes the spirit of the departed in it. Understand? [1]

HAWKINS: Y—e—s—

SELLERS: Well, then, think! (*The door opens and Uncle Daniel puts his head in.*) Don't come in, Uncle Daniel! Don't you see I'm busy? Go away—go away, you old fool. I can't see anybody now!

UNCLE DANIEL: De gentleman give me his card and said he was shore you'd see him!

SELLERS: I can't, I can't indeed! I'm very sorry. Tell him to call again—well here, give me his card. (*Takes it and then falls back against the wall.*) Look—look here, Lafayette. Read—read—read—that!

HAWKINS, *reading*: Mr. R. De Bohun! Is it possible!

SELLERS: It must be—it must! But who could have dreamt that it would operate so soon? Why, I hadn't hardly commenced! And sending up his card! Well, he's gentleman to the last! Yes, this is the right way! The clothes materialized just as well as the flesh. Even the spiritualists have found that out—this is a materialized card. Of course—of course—I must see him, Lafayette. Yes, and don't go! Don't go! (*With ill-concealed alarm.*) I'd prefer to have you present—all in the family you know. And this is the first one I've ever materialized—you might be able to offer some suggestions if we didn't know how to get on, at first. You're a good man, Lafayette. You needn't be afraid. And I've always tried to do what was right, too. Not very regular at church, but sent the children and Mrs. Sellers as long as she had anything decent to wear and—I suppose I'm all right if I treat him just like any other gentleman, Lafayette? I won't need to—to—to—oh, Lord! Angels and ministers of gr—show this gentleman in—Daniel!

1 The Yale copy continues from this point to the end of Act I as follows:
  Hawkins retreats in alarm up L.C. to L.D., exit; R.D. opens and enter De Bohun.
SELLERS, *regarding him in surprise and alarm*: De Bohun! Sweet spirit! So soon!
CURTAIN
  Tableau. Enter R.D. Mrs. Sellers, L.D. Hawkins startled by apparition—tableaux.

Glimpse of the "Materializee" solemnly entering.

CURTAIN

ACT II

SCENE I: *Sellers and De Bohun discovered standing and talking.*

SELLERS, *aside*: He's superbly materialized; it's beautiful! (*Aloud.*) Ah, by the way—can you sit down? There—careful, careful—not too fast—because there's really nothing to you, you know, till your parts harden.

DE BOHUN, *dazed—aside*: What can the man mean?

SELLERS: There— How do you feel? Pretty solid?

DE BOHUN: O, quite, thank you.

SELLERS: Voice is very good—very good indeed. A little light, yet a while, maybe—but that's natural, perfectly natural. (*Getting heavy object.*) You want anything on you to hold you down?

DE BOHUN, *bewildered*: To hold me down? Bless my soul!

SELLERS: Now that is beautiful! (*Blowing on him—perhaps with bellows.*) Why, it don't stir you a bit! (*Blowing again.*) Joggle you!

DE BOHUN, *starts a little each time—says, aside*: Bless my soul, this person's a lunatic.

SELLERS: My friend, it's the grandest success in the world! And mind, you'll get solider and solider, right along—by my process. But these ordinary mediumistic arms and feet and things don't amount to anything—no substance in them—you strike a light or fetch in a skeptic, and pff! They disappear. Because the principle's wrong. You don't mind the light in the least, do you?

DE BOHUN: Not in the least.

SELLERS: It doesn't keep you from solidifying?

DE BOHUN: Solidifying?

SELLERS: Because you know, that mustn't proceed too fast. (*Making some passes.*) If it goes too fast you might petrify. You don't feel petrified, do you?

DE BOHUN: Bless my soul, no! How extraordinary! I'm perfectly comfortable, thank you.

SELLERS: Well, then, that's all right. But if you should begin to petrify, you speak because it isn't good to let it get a start. Now honestly—do you feel in all respects just as you did before you—you—as you did before?

DE BOHUN: Why—why—exactly the same.

SELLERS: No! How odd that is! Now ain't it?

DE BOHUN: Is it odd?

SELLERS: Well I should say so. And you don't regret being here—would just as soon be here as—as—where you were?

DE BOHUN, *aside*: The man's mad—I've got to humor him—till I can escape. (*Aloud.*) O, much rather.

SELLERS, *musing—aside*: Why how strange that is. He would rather be here than in Heaven. I certainly couldn't have understood right. (*To De Bohun.*) Reflect now—do you seriously mean to say you would rather be here than—than—that you'd rather?

DE BOHUN, *with effusion*: A hundred thousand times rather!

SELLERS, *staring at him a few moments in stupefied surprise—then aside*: Why, good land, he was in *he*— He wasn't *in* Heaven! (*Pause.*) Why, there's advantages about this thing I hadn't thought of. (*Hesitatingly to De Bohun.*) Pardon me—don't be offended—I wouldn't hurt you for—don't you feel any—er—any remains of discomfort? Don't feel any overheated?

DE BOHUN: Overheated? Why no—of—course I don't. (*Aside.*) Now what in the world does the man mean? What kind of a craze is he in?

SELLERS, *aside—with enthusiasm*: I'll empty perdition! I'll do it as sure as guns! It's the grandest invention of the age—of all the ages! If I can keep him cool—I wouldn't take billions for it. Yes, sir, I'll empty per—

DE BOHUN, *rising*: I beg your pardon, Colonel Sellers, for interrupting your—ah—meditations—and perhaps I've come inopportunely—

SELLERS: Oh, not at all, not at all—I had sent for you.

DE BOHUN, *mystified*: Sent for me?

SELLERS: Yes—to the hotel, you know.

DE BOHUN: Ah, I didn't know they got the names in the papers so soon.

SELLERS: Oh, they're all there! A full account of it.

DE BOHUN: I really don't understand you, my dear sir. But I don't know that it matters. If you sent for me, it was very kind and hospitable.

SELLERS: Oh, not at all!

DE BOHUN: And it relieves my mind, in regard to what I was afraid might seem an intrusion.

But the fact is, I've wished to make your acquaintance ever since I came into the country, and I first visited Missouri for that purpose.

SELLERS: Sir, I appreciate—

DE BOHUN: When I found that you had recently left Hannibal—Hamilcar, or Regulus Hannibal or some of those punic characters— It's very extraordinary calling a town after an elephant! I assure you that I didn't know where to turn. Besides my personal wish to meet the American claimant to the Earldom of Dover, and to make the acquaintance of a cousin, whose rights, such as they are, we all acknowledge—

SELLERS, *with spirit*: Oh, you do! Then, sir, may I ask, why my cousin, the Earl of Dover, has taken no notice whatever of the letters I have addressed to him? Three letters a week for the last two years at the lowest calculation—letters proffering him the hospitality of my Missouri home, if he should come out our way, and attempting to establish a—a—cousinly reciprocity with him on the—the questions of the day, and—

DE BOHUN: Well, the fact is, you know, the Earl is a very poor correspondent, and he's an irascible old man, gouty, and perhaps always a little hot tempered. And one thing I had in mind was to beg you not to expose yourself to the ignominy of having letters put into the fire by the footman as fast as they arrived—

SELLERS: The infernal, insolent old scoundrel!

DE BOHUN: Ah, I dare say you're quite right. The Earl *is* old, and he's insolent, so far as I've been able to observe, and he's the greatest scoundrel alive. (*Suggestively.*) But he's the head of the house, you know.

SELLERS: Well, sir, I'm a Southern gentleman, and I am the head of the house, in right.

DE BOHUN: I dare say—I've no doubt you're quite right; but the present Lord Dover is in possession. However, that's neither here nor there. Besides the wish to meet you as a kinsman, I have had another motive in coming here this morning. I have ventured to hope that you would be willing to assist me in a matter which concerns me very deeply.

SELLERS, *with bland dignity*: You may command me, sir. My house, my person, and my purse are at your disposal. You must allow me to introduce you to my wife and daughter. (*Aside.*) I don't know how they'll manage about that one good dress, between them. But I could have them appear on the installment plan.

DE BOHUN: You're very good, I'm sure. The matter is simply this! When I left Hamilcar, Missouri, after my disappointment in failing to find you there, three months ago, I met with what I suppose were some common incidents of travel in your country! I was in a railway smash-up —I think you call it—and I was carried down in a sinking steamboat in the Mississippi.

SELLERS: Oh, every day occurrences, sir, in our country. Something of the sort happened to *us* on our way east.

DE BOHUN: When I came up, I had the pleasure of saving the life of a young lady, to whom I had spoken on the train just before the smash-up, and whom I had met again on board. In the darkness we were separated, and I have never seen her again. My life since then has been merely a search for her. Can you aid me to find her?

SELLERS: I can and will, with great pleasure. What was her name?

DE BOHUN: I never knew.

SELLERS: Well, no matter. Not the least matter. I can arrange all that. I will simply materialize one of the people who were lost on that boat, and ascertain her whereabouts. You see this electric apparatus? With the aid of this simple affair, I can materialize any body who ever died, have done it— *(Aside.)* My goodness, I forgot that I had materialized *him.*

DE BOHUN: I can't refuse to try. It's a desperate extremity. But it's only fair to tell you I haven't the least faith in spiritualism.

SELLERS: Spiritualism? No spiritualism about it, sir. A purely scientific operation— *(Cautiously.)* But may I ask, sir, why you wish to meet this young lady again?

DE BOHUN: I may as well be frank with you; I love her.

SELLERS, *aghast:* You—love—her?

DE BOHUN: We pledged each other there on the bit of wreck to which we clung, and I hope to meet her as my betrothed, and—in short—to marry her.

SELLERS: Marry her! Oh, good Lord! You mustn't! You can't! It isn't permissible—it isn't possible! No, sir! You mustn't think of it.

UNCLE DANIEL, *at the door:* Yere's dat gentleman from New York wants to see you, Marse Sellers. He's waitin' down in de hall, an' he says he mus' see you right away.

SELLERS, *to De Bohun:* Ah, excuse me a moment! Just—just amuse yourself here till I come back—I won't detain you—unavoidable engagement.

Exit.

SCENE II: *De Bohun alone.*

DE BOHUN: Really, this is a most extraordinary old gentleman. He surpasses all that the American claimant should be in eccentricity and originality. I fancy he can't be in his right mind—if he has one, as his country-men would say. Most extraordinary! What does he mean by his jargon about my buoyancy? I never felt less buoyant in the whole course of my life! And why does he expect me to petrify? Bless my soul, it's very odd, very strange! I can't understand this! I've visited a good many parts of this remarkable country and I've met a great many remarkable men in it, but my American cousin is certainly the most remarkable. What a very curious old den it is! It looks like the collection of some cheap Jack who had gone into the business at second hand. *(He walks about the room, examining the various objects through his eye-glass till he comes to the ship's phonograph. He reads the label.)* "The Sellers Ship's Phonograph for the application of stored Profanity to the working of Vessels during storms. Adapted to the use of Foremen in Boiler Manufactories, and Large Press-Rooms. Patent applied for." My kinsman is certainly one of the most—

He turns the crank of the phonograph.

THE PHONOGRAPH: Drop that, drop that, you infernal lubber, or I'll knock you off that yard with a belaying pin!

DE BOHUN: Very extraordinary.

Turns.

THE PHONOGRAPH: Turn out o' there, you lousy hound. Going to be all night— If you don't jump I'll wow, wow, wow, you low lived wow, wow, wow, of a wow.

DE BOHUN: Really, this is a most amazing implement!

Turns.

THE PHONOGRAPH: Where's that Portagee Joe? Go aloft, go aloft, you wow, wow, or I'll heave your carcass overboard to the sharks.

DE BOHUN: Very truculent language, upon my word. I wonder if my ingenious cousin charged this instrument himself?

Turns.

THE PHONOGRAPH: I could whittle a better sailor than you out of a pine stick, you miserable Portagee, wow, wow, wow. I could go ashore at Cape Ann and dig up a man out of the grave-yard that could reef a sail better than that.

DE BOHUN: This is the true American touch, upon my word. I must get one of these for the old Earl, and have it charged with profanity here in America. The Earl runs to quantity rather than quality in his blasphemy. He'll be glad of a thing like this!

Turns the crank.

THE PHONOGRAPH: [1] O, I wish I had gone down in the water in his place—or with him!

DE BOHUN: Ha! High! What's this? This means another voice—non-professional.

Turns.

THE PHONOGRAPH: Oh, oh! If we could only have been drowned together!

DE BOHUN: Why—why—I know that voice—can it be? It can't be—

Turns wildly.

THE PHONOGRAPH, *confusedly*: You think he got drowned—poor creatures out of the train—git my hands on him—tar de lights out'n him—mop de floor wid him—fancy to a perfect stranger in the cars—American pork— Oh, he is my dear, dead only love—talking by the guard before the boat went down—pulled me up on that piece of wreck and told me there in the horror and darkness that he would rather be there with me in the presence of death—

DE BOHUN: Gracious powers! What is all this? I distinguish two voices! And one I know. It is her voice! Yes, it is! And these last words were the last I spoke to her— Oh, my lost love!

Turns.

THE PHONOGRAPH: Than in the midst of the brightest and gladdest scene on earth without me.

DE BOHUN: Yes, my words!

Turns.

THE PHONOGRAPH: Then in the darkness and confusion—

DE BOHUN: Oh, something lost here!

THE PHONOGRAPH: Dey lit out together and de sooner you make up your mind. Oh, yes he did, he left me and went away with her—poor lost false—my love, my cruel love!

DE BOHUN, *staggering back from the phonograph*: Merciful Heaven, what can it mean? Wait,

1 This section with De Bohun and the other voices on the phonograph appears only in the Yale version.

let me think? This is the story of my luckless love—it can't be any other! One of the voices is hers—no other! This machine, they say, gathers up and records every sound uttered in its presence— Then—yes, it must be so! She spoke those words here—in this room— She is in this house now, perhaps—oh!

MARY, *within*: Uncle Daniel, will you let that phonograph alone? (*Entering.*) Oh, I beg your pardon, sir. I thought it was our old servant. Whenever he gets provoked at anything, he comes in here and swears through the phonograph till we have no peace of our lives. (*Recognizing De Bohun.*) Oh!

DE BOHUN: You! (*She makes a step towards him; then arrests herself; he rushes upon her, and clasps her in his arms.*) Oh, my darling; is it you at last! Have I found you again? How did I lose you that night? Where have you been? What—but now I have you once more, and nothing but death shall part us! Oh, my dear, my love! Wake! Look at me! It's I— I, your—

MARY, *rousing herself from the faintness that has crept over her and feebly struggling to repel him*: Let me go! Leave—leave—let me— (*She lifts her face and looks into his and then before blissfully relapsing into his embrace.*) No, no! I can't! I do love you, whatever you have been or done! Stay with me now, and let the past go! I have you again, and I have been so true to you that it shall be enough for both!

DE BOHUN: But I have been true to you, dearest, in every word and thought since we parted—

MARY: And that—*that woman*—whom you gave your place upon the wreck? That—

DE BOHUN: Poor old lady! When I lost you, it was my sole drop of comfort that I could restore her to her grand-children.

MARY: Her grand-children! Oh, bless, bless you, my darling for that word! (*Wildly clasping and clinging to him.*) Oh, forgive me, love! Oh, hate me—hate me for my wicked doubt of you.

Kissing him.

DE BOHUN: Well, under the circumstances it's a little difficult. And I have been looking for you ever since that fatal night for a very different purpose! You must try to be coherent, my love—you must, indeed, for I've quite lost my senses, and there ought to be some slight method in the madness of such lovers as we. I don't know what to make of it all. How is it you happen to be in this house?

MARY: This house?

DE BOHUN: This private bedlam, if you like—

MARY: Oh, it is a bedlam indeed!

DE BOHUN: I found my way here in the hope that I might chance to learn something of you or get some hint or help in tracing you from my remarkable cousin, Colonel Sellers—

MARY, *starting from him*: Cousin? Who—who—

DE BOHUN: My co-heir to the dream of being Earl of Dover, the American claimant—

MARY: Then you are—

DE BOHUN: Rupert De Bohun.

MARY, *wildly*: But you are dead!

DE BOHUN, *astounded*: I beg your pardon. I think there must be some error.

MARY: No, no! There is none—none! You were burnt to death last night in the Tolliver House! It was all in the papers! Haven't you seen it?

DE BOHUN: No, I haven't seen any paper to-day. I arrived this morning at half-past eight—and—

His eye follows Mary as she bustles about the room, looking at the newspapers scattered over the floor.

MARY: Here it is! Fire at the Tolliver House. There! Can you deny it, now? What does it mean? (*She clasps her hands before him, while he quietly reads.*) Who—who are you?

DE BOHUN, *quietly folds the paper*: Rupert De Bohun, as I told you. It's my poor cousin, Reginald De Bohun who was burned last night. He was a cad, and we weren't on terms; but I'm sorry for him—I'm sorrier for my uncle—I had no idea Reginald was in America. Poor boy! I must go—

MARY, *throwing her arms around him*: And leave me! Oh, no! Not yet—not—

DE BOHUN: Not instantly, of course. I've no doubt that everything has been done that can be done. I'll leave you when you bid me. There's no haste.

MARY: Yes, you must go and go at once! It is your duty! Wait! My father will wish to go with you.

DE BOHUN: Your father? Is your father—

MARY: Colonel Sellers, the American claimant. I'm Mary.

DE BOHUN: You are my cousin then?

MARY: Yes, cousin.

DE BOHUN: How sweet the word is on your lips! And that remarkable old gentleman is your father?

MARY: He is.

DE BOHUN: I might as well take it all coolly. A miracle more or less don't greatly matter! And may I ask, my pretty cousin, what theory your father is treating me upon?

MARY: Why, how does he treat you?

DE BOHUN: He seems to have some doubt whether I can sit down, and when I've sat down, he seems to doubt whether I can get up. He begs me not to get into a current of air for fear I shall be carried out of the window, and he hopes next I'm not solidifying too rapidly. Sometimes he claps me on the knee with the greatest possible friendliness; then he treats me with the deepest awe, and then he suddenly seizes me by the coat lapel and pulls me about—I beg your pardon my love, but if I were you—I hope you'll excuse my saying it, but really I think some physician ought to see your father. He seems to be over-excited, and—

MARY: Does he know your name?

DE BOHUN: Certainly.

MARY: Then he thinks you're dead!

DE BOHUN: Bless my soul, how extremely unpleasant!

MARY: Yes. And he believes that he's materialized you. That's his latest invention.

DE BOHUN: Materialized, as the spiritualists do? Is your father—excuse me—a spiritualist?

MARY: No, indeed! He's a man of science! He has materialized you by stored electricity! He was talking of trying it yesterday.

DE BOHUN: Dear me! And at present I am—an—an—apparition?

MARY: Exactly. He thinks you were burnt last night, and when you called here to-day, I suppose he must have been trying to materialize you, and thought he had succeeded.

DE BOHUN: Ah, that accounts for it. It's very simple when you understand it. But still, my dear, I think you'd better have a physician see your father—*two* of them!

SELLERS, *without*: In a minute, in a minute, in just one minute. (*Entering.*) Ah, Mary, I'm glad to see you've found our—our honored guest here. Do you still find yourself pretty well, sir? No great change I suppose? Mary, my dear, I've got a little surprise for you. You must prepare yourself for a *great* surprise. This is our cousin, Mary, our cousin from England, Mr. De Bohun, one of my fellow heirs to the Earldom of Dover.

MARY: Father!

SELLERS: Yes, I knew I should astonish you. Mr. De Bohun, my daughter.

DE BOHUN, *with some embarrassment*: Why, the fact is, I had been making—Miss Sellers had allowed me to make—her acquaintance before you came in.

SELLERS: Is that so? Well, so much the better—so much the better. I want Mary to take you and introduce you to her mother. Better go right to the dining room with Cousin De Bohun, Mary. I've got to meet that New York gentleman here; he wants to examine the motor as I *used* to call it. But I'll join you directly at lunch. We make a light lunch, cousin, about this hour—a few dried apples desiccated by my own process—I'll explain it to you—dried apples and pure cold water—you can go with Cousin De Bohun, Mary. It's all right—no cause for anxiety—no trouble—he's just like one of ourselves—

DE BOHUN: I beg your pardon, but I ought to disabuse you—I'm really not at all what you take me for. I'm not the De Bohun who—

SELLERS: Oh, it's all right. I'll follow right along down. Just tell your mother, Mary, that he's our late cousin—our cousin lately from England—she'll understand—(*He gets them out of the room, familiarly caressing De Bohun and at times starting back. Then he opens the other door to admit the New Yorker.*) Walk right in—sorry to keep you waiting, sir. There, sir, there it is. (*He points to the motor, and stands with his arms akimbo admiring it while the New York gentleman picks his way about the room inspecting the mechanism from different points. He steps on a sugared almond which explodes with the report of an ironclad torpedo.*) Ah, a little idea of mine, that I threw off at an odd moment—little improvement on the Nihilist bomb— There's getting to be a grand demand for those things, in Europe, among people of advanced opinions. You see I put the dynamite up in the form of these little sugarplums, (*Picks one up from the floor.*) which may be introduced in the dessert at the Royal or Imperial table— I told my servant to sweep these things up, but you can't place any dependence upon the negro. He's left them scattered all over the floor, just where they fell. Well, sir, there's the motor.

NEW YORK MAN, *looking about his feet*: Yes, yes, it's very intricate—it's—

SELLERS: The mechanism is intricate, but the principle is one of the simplest known to science. In five minutes I can make the whole thing clear to you. You observe this battery—but I prefer to know first what your idea for the employment of the motor is?

NEW YORK MAN: Why, in the application of

stored electricity to the street cars on the Brooklyn bridge—

SELLERS: Yes, yes. All very well. No harm in that idea. That is the *old* idea!

NEW YORK MAN: Old idea! Isn't that what you telegraphed me to come on for, yesterday?

SELLERS: I may have put that idea forth yesterday—advanced it tentatively, experimentally, suggestively, so to speak; but this motor was *built* for an entirely different purpose. Be careful, there—that little cylinder contains a new explosive I've been amusing myself with—perfectly safe if you don't touch it. This machine was invented and designed exclusively for materialization!

NEW YORK MAN: Materialization?

SELLERS: Yes, sir, for absorbing and condensing the enormous waste of vital force with which our atmosphere is filled from the dissolution of the human race—computed at nine-thousand millions of square feet of gaseous matter. This has hitherto been entirely lost, except as it has been applied in a small one-horse way by the necromancers of former ages and the spiritualists of ours for the materialization of a few sporadic spectres here and there, to delude their ignorant votaries.

NEW YORK MAN: And are you—you are a spiritualist?

SELLERS: Not at all, sir! The question is perfectly natural. My nephew, Major Lafayette Hawkins, of Hannibal, Missouri, a shrewd and long-headed operator in real estate, out there, asked me the same question in this room not an hour ago; and I replied to General Hawkins, one of the greatest financiers of the west—as I now reply to you; not at all. I am a plain straightforward man of science, dealing with a well-ascertained scientific fact. I claim no merit in the matter, nor any supernatural power; I apply natural forces on a large scale, that have always existed. I have only to press this button here, and I fill this room with the disembodied—no sir—the *re*-embodied spirits of the dead of all ages!

NEW YORK MAN, *edging towards the door, backwards, and looking carefully to his feet*: Is it possible?

SELLERS: You may have your doubts, sir—it's natural you should. It would detain you too long, perhaps, if I were to attempt this experiment, now; but I can inform you in confidence that there is now a gentleman in the dining room with my wife and daughter, whom I materialized by my process not three quarters of an hour ago.

NEW YORK MAN, *still edging away*: Is it possible!

SELLERS: I prefer not to give names—these things get into the papers so soon—but this gentleman was one of the victims of the Tolliver House fire, last night—cousin of mine, distant cousin; so there's no deception—no possible deception. I materialized that man in five minutes—five seconds! I hadn't started a full current from those batteries before that man sent in his card! Yes, sir! And a minute afterwards he stood before me here, perfectly materialized down to the minutest detail of the clothes that were consumed last night on his person.

NEW YORK MAN: Great heavens!

SELLERS: A fact, sir, a simple fact! Why, pshaw! I'll call him up here. He can excuse himself to the ladies half a minute, and I can show you what a perfect article of materialization this machine can turn out. Just amuse yourself with the morning paper a moment, while I get the gentleman to step up. There—there's the account of the fire in this paper; you can see there's no deception about it! *Starting for the door.*

NEW YORK MAN, *excitedly*: No, no! Don't go! Not this morning, please. I'll look in again in the course of the day. I've got an appointment. *(Taking out his watch.)* I promised to see a man at half-past twelve, and I've only got five minutes. I'll stop in towards evening, if you'll allow me. I'll be back—

The door opens, and Uncle Daniel puts his head in. The New Yorker improves his opportunity to slip out.

SELLERS: Well, what is it, Daniel?

UNCLE DANIEL: De deputation of temperance ladies.

SELLERS: What deputation of what temperance ladies?

UNCLE DANIEL: I don't know. Dey said you'd know. Dey said you promised to 'dress 'em and dey's come for you to go at de head of de possession to de hall.

SELLERS: It's a mistake. I remember now, I made a partial promise to address a temperance meeting on Thursday. But this is Wednesday.

UNCLE DANIEL: No, it ain't, Marse Sellers; it's Thursday, shore enuff. Dey said dey'd wait outside till you was ready. De possession ain't all formed yet. But it's formin'—formin' in front o' de house. Dey ain't many ladies yit; but dey's lots o' boys and dogs. I guess dey's pretty near all de boys and dogs dere *is.*

SELLERS, *fuming about*: Well, well. I must go, I suppose. I must go. It's a matter of public duty.

Where is Lafayette? Send Lafayette to me. *(Uncle Daniel goes out.)* I'm not at all prepared. I've forgotten all about this address. What shall I do? I must say something—perhaps Lafayette can suggest something. Dear, oh dear! *(He hunts aimlessly about the room, and takes a bottle from the mantel-piece at random.)* Alcohol! The subtle spirit of alcohol! Yes, something like that! Oh, that a man should put—put—*(Uncorks the bottle and smells it.)* an enemy in his mouth to steal away his brains! [1] Good Iago—*(Smelling.)* Prythee tell me, *(Smelling.)* I am unused to the soothing mood,[1] *(Smelling.)* and the big wars that make ambition virtue.[1] *(Smelling.)* Be thou a spirit of health or goblin damned.[1] *(Smelling.)* Out damned spot! [1] *(Smelling.)* Not all the perfumes of Araby [1]—I've got it! I've got it! *But pure alcohol won't do! (Replacing the bottle, he turns about and confronts Hawkins.)* Lafayette, my son, how long is it since you were drunk?

HAWKINS: Why, Colonel Sellers, I don't know what you mean. You know I never was drunk in my life.

SELLERS: Ah, that's a great pity—a terrible pity!

HAWKINS: Pity? But say what about this English chap with Mary; they seem to be old acquaintances.

SELLERS: Don't mind him. He's only a materialization and if he doesn't mind will soon dematerialize. Ah—hum—yes—there's a procession of ladies forming in front of this house, to conduct me to the hall of the Sisters of Siloam, where I've promised to deliver a lecture on temperance. And I've just got a great idea for my address—something that will carry my name throughout the land, and make it a means of good in every household. But your inexperience spoils everything. How have you been brought up? Never been drunk!

HAWKINS: But I don't see what my never having been drunk has to do with it, Colonel.

SELLERS: That's because you don't take a practical view of things. What makes the average temperance lecturer an utter failure? What saps the cause at its fountainhead? Simply the fact that its advocates can speak so little from their own experience. This is what gives Goff [2] his im-

[1] *Othello,* II, 3:289–291; *Othello,* V, 2:351–354; *Othello,* III, 3:348–354; *Hamlet,* I, 4:40; *Macbeth,* V, 1:39; *Macbeth,* V, 1:55–56. (All references to Harrison edition.)

[2] John B. Gough, 1817–1886, was an effective temperance lecturer who drew his material from his own experiences.

mense influence; he speaks from his own experience, and warns and implores his hearers to avoid the evils from which he has suffered. Now if you had only been an habitual drunkard or if you had fallen once or twice, I could make an awful living example of you!

HAWKINS: Why, but Colonel Sellers, haven't you ever been drunk, yourself?

SELLERS, *sadly*: I haven't been drunk since we were last in Washington together—ten years ago —and then I was so *completely* drunk that, when I got sober I couldn't remember anything about it. (*He thinks a moment in silence.*) Wait—I have it—don't say anything! Yes, the first false step— that shall be my theme, and then I can present it with all the powerful aid of realistic art! Lafayette, have you any spirits about you? I've a bottle of pure alcohol on the mantel which I use in my experiments here, but that won't do. I must have a portable spirit—some soon-spreading gear that quickly as the hasty powder fired, may spread through all the veins—like brandy, for example.

HAWKINS, *hesitatingly*: I got a bottle at the druggist's before I left home, for use on the journey—

SELLERS: Got it with you?

HAWKINS, *drawing the flask out of his breast pocket*: Yes, here it is.

SELLERS: Ah, I am saved! Now, then, Lafayette, I am going to enter upon this career—for I shall hereafter devote my *whole life* to the cause of temperance—in a common sense, practical way. I am going to test in my own person the seductive effects of the first glass. (*He opens the bottle and winks.*) It's a very good article of brandy—for Hannibal.

HAWKINS: But the ladies, Colonel Sellers, it won't do to keep them waiting.

SELLERS: Oh, I shan't keep them waiting a minute. Women are never punctual. (*Tilts the bottle to his lips.*) A—a—a—h! That *is* good! That is good brandy, Lafayette. A good, pure medicinal brandy! Got it at Braden's?

HAWKINS: No, at Watson's.

SELLERS: Oh, I know—on the corner. Hannibal is a grand old town. And growing, too, they tell me, like a weed. (*Handing back the bottle.*) There, that will do! Just that one taste, has recalled the whole past to me! What a wonderful vehicle of memory the sense of taste is! Why Lafayette, I can recall the very sensation now, that I had when I tasted my first glass of brandy. It was on the old Pocahontas, coming down from Napoleon to St. Louis. I was merely a boy—a lad of twenty,

but I remember that first glass, the sense of degradation, of outlawry, and then as the infernal fumes mounted to my brain, the shameless exaltation! Oh, I can picture it all to them in words of fire! The orphan boy, on his first absence from home— of course, my parents were living, but an orphan is always so much more effective— The orphan tempted by evil associates—the first glass! *Glass!* (*Thoughtfully.*) I suppose I ought to have taken it from a glass—the bottle is such a different thing. If I am to study this situation at all, I must study it faithfully, Lafayette. Let me have that flask again. (*Looks about the mantel till he finds an old claret glass.*) Ah, here—here's one. Leg's broken off, but no matter. It doesn't have to stand up, anyway. (*Pours a full glass from the bottle.*) There! (*Drinks.*) That's something like! That is the real sensation! No degradation about that! No outlawry! *Nothing* but exaltation. I remember, now, there was nothing but exaltation at the time. And moderate drinking is *temperance*. The other is total abstinence—*fanaticism*. Make that point, and—k—ic—keep the distinction before their minds. Let the lesson, (*Pours out another glass and drinks.*) sink in!

HAWKINS, *nervously*: But ain't you afraid, Colonel Sellers that—

SELLERS: F—ic—fraid of what, Lafayette? I'm afraid of nothing in the world, nothing in the solar system! I will go before those ladies—I don't care *who* they are! And plead with them to shun the intoxicating bowl. I will ask them to b—ic— banish the social glass from their drawing rooms! How many a young man has taken the first downward step at the hand of beauty—at the glass in the hands of beauty—downward glass at the step —how many young men, I say, have taken the first glass from the downward steps of—how many— where was I, Lafayette! (*Drinks another glass.*) Lafayette, I've just thought of something! I'll tell you! I can't waste my time personally on this temperance lecturing; I must delegate it! There ought to be a dozen—there ought to be fifty lecturers started on the platform at the same time and attack the enemy in converging lines. Lafayette, I will materialize that corps of lecturers! What am I with my p—ic—petty experience of intoxication—what is Goff himself—to a corps of lecturers who have actually died of intemperance and filled the drunkard's grave? How their words would go home to the audience! At $200 each a night, my earnings with that corps alone would be $10,000 a night. And no expenses, no hotel bills, no car-fares—the whole thing clear gain! I will do it—I'll do it at once! Those are the lecturers who can depict the remorse of the hopeless drunkard!

Pours out a glass and drinks.

HAWKINS: O, don't take any more, Colonel Sellers—

SELLERS, *shaking his head sorrowfully*: The remorse, the remorse that gnaws the inebriate's soul! Remorse! (*Thoughtfully.*) Morse! Inventor of the electric telegraph. Why, Lafayette, if that invention were to be made in these days, it wouldn't attrack the slightest attention—not the slightest, ladies. Why, ladies, what is a trivial discovery like that compared with my electric materializer, Lafayette? If this meeting will adjourn to my house, I will show the honorable gentleman— gentleman of the jury and the court itself—I will show you a re-embodied spirit that will—where— where's that one-legged glass, Lafayette!

HAWKINS: You've got it there in your hands, Colonel. But do—on't take any more. Indeed, you musn't. You won't be fit to address the ladies.

SELLERS, *pouring out and drinking*: Yesh, yesh, I will. I'll show 'em what drink can bring a man to! Drink! Oh, that a man—

UNCLE DANIEL, *putting his head in at the door*: De ladies is all ready for you, Marse Sellers, dey's waitin'!

SELLERS: All right! I'm coming!

He attempts to pour another glass, but Hawkins gets it from him.

HAWKINS: No, no, Colonel Sellers, you musn't go! I'll excuse you to the ladies. You're not fit to go!

SELLERS: Get out of my way, Lafayette Hawkins, my child. I will fulfill my duty at any cost. My word is pledged. My honor is at stake—honor of a Southern gentleman. Finest type of gentleman in the Universe. Whashyou, whashyou been doin' with that door, Lafayette? Oh, here it is! Come round again just in the nick of time. I'm coming! Sigh no more, ladies, sigh no more!

He plunges out of the door followed by the desperate Hawkins.

HAWKINS: Oh, what shall I do?

CURTAIN

ACT III

SCENE I [1]: *Same as before. Time, evening. De Bohun and Mary sitting on sofa or adjacent chairs.*

DE BOHUN: I'm so glad you sent for me, my dear, I found my cousin quite in his usual state, and

[1] Act III, scene 1, appears only in the Yale copy.

sufficiently alive to send me about my business. In fact, *no* lives were lost in the fire at the Tolliver House beginning with my own, and the Honorable Mr. De Bohun was suffering from nothing worse than past enjoyment. He dined too well last night. And your father, you say he is sleeping now?

MARY: Yes. And the doctor thinks he'll be all right in a little while. It wasn't apoplexy, he says, but a kind of congestion that's very common and not the most dangerous. Oh! How often I wish that I were a man! Oh! If I were only a man!

DE BOHUN: Well, now, you know, my dear, I can't quite join you in that aspiration. No! No! It's *I* who must be a man and it's rather difficult after being brought up merely a gentleman. But there's one thing I'd quite made up my mind about; and that is about going home again. I'm going to stop here and do my best to be not only a man but an American. And you shall help me, I don't think I could make it out at all if you didn't. Now in the multiplicity of your father's inventions, don't you know—isn't there some hope of something—if it were properly managed? I shouldn't mind taking hold of something of the kind. I shouldn't, indeed! I should rather fancy "pushing a patent," as you say here. (*He wanders gingerly about looking carefully to his steps and staring at the various models.*) Which one of these things does your father happen to prefer himself, my dear?

MARY: Oh! Don't ask me. He prefers the wildest of course.

DE BOHUN: Of course, of course, with his love of the picturesque—the dramatic. But you don't altogether agree with him, I suppose?

MARY: *Agree* with him?

DE BOHUN: You don't believe a great deal in the sand-blast extinguisher, for instance?

MARY: I don't believe it would put out a candle. (*Sobbing.*) If it hadn't been for the steam cut-off, we should all have starved to death long ago. It's the only practical thing he ever invented and it's the only thing he never had the least faith in.

DE BOHUN: I'm afraid I don't understand. I don't believe I know what a steam cut-off is.

MARY: It's all that's saved us, or *me*, I mean. Father could always persuade mother that he had just made his fortune, and this dream of the Earldom—that's been as great a nightmare as any of the other dreams. I don't know how many times father hasn't had it in his grasp. I believe that if he could ever have raked and scraped together money enough to get there, he'd be in England now pressing his claim. When everything else failed, he fell back on that. I'm glad your cousin's alive—I'm glad that none of those poor creatures lost their lives in the fire—but, oh! I'm *so* thankful your cousin didn't. It will help to kill one more hope of that wretched Earldom, and father will *have* to fall back on the cut-off.

DE BOHUN, *impulsively*: And I'm sure if *you* believe in it— But would you mind telling me what a cut-off is?

MARY: Oh! I couldn't explain it, myself. But it's a little machine that they use on steam boilers, and it makes a little saving on each—so that every owner of an engine can afford to pay a few dollars royalty for it—and as there are thousands of engines in the country, if you can only get the owners to believe in it—

DE BOHUN: I see, and they won't believe in it?

MARY: Yes they will, they do, whenever it is brought to their notice. There is a man under contract with father now, who is to have one third of the patent right if he can get five hundred orders for it, and every now and then he sends us a little money on it, just enough to keep us from death's door. But he's terribly slow and father loses patience, and wants to sell it for any trifle, and goes off on some of his projects that are to give us a million to-morrow, and I lose all heart about it. I don't suppose it ever *will* come to anything.

DE BOHUN: Well! Well! I don't understand it at all, my dear, but it does look like a hope, and I wouldn't lose heart about it altogether. I really think I'd better go into it more definitely. Where is this agent of your father's at present?

MARY, *desperately*: He may be anywhere between here and the Rocky Mountains! We haven't heard from him for a week, now, and dear knows when we shall *ever* hear again.

DE BOHUN: But hasn't he some local address—some place where you can get at him somehow?

MARY: Oh! Yes, he has a brother at 3450 Pennsylvania Avenue,[1] but he's hardly ever in his office and we haven't seen him for I don't know how long. (*She goes up to the mantel and takes a pile of letters from it.*) Here's father's mail and not a letter opened, much less answered. We've been so excited to-day about the temperance address—and *you*—and I don't know what— Don't you want to help me open them?

1 Non-existent address.

DE BOHUN, *surprised*: Open your father's letters, my dear?

MARY, *tearing open the envelopes*: Yes—I'm his correspondence clerk. *He* would never open them. Sometimes I think it would be the best way *not* to open them, but I can't bear to let any chance escape me; you can't tell *what's* in them. (*She goes on distractedly tearing them open.*) Oh, I can't read them I'm so happy—I'm so miserable. (*She puts them back and he picks up one from the floor and hands it to her, she glances at it mechanically and then starts back.*) It's from *him!*

DE BOHUN: From him? From whom?

MARY, *wildly*: From the man—the agent—the cut-off— And he says—oh my love—my life—my darling—

She flings one arm around De Bohun's neck and presses the letter to his face.

DE BOHUN, *pulling his head back to get a focus on the letter; then reading*: "I shall be with you Thursday to close the contract. I've got the orders." Does he mean—

MARY: That it's a success, that we are saved—that you're not going to marry a beggar. (*Stopping.*) But *Thursday!* That was yesterday.

DE BOHUN: No, to-day is Thursday.

MARY: So it is. But it's been so long since morning that I thought it was a year ago.

DE BOHUN: What a surprise this will be for your father, my dear, what a joyful surprise.

MARY: Surprise! Oh! Dear, you don't know father. Nothing ever surprises him. No matter how astonishing a thing may happen, his mind is so constructed that he always thinks he has foreseen it. Really and truly it is just as I say—it is not possible to surprise him. Once he was struck by lightning. Why, he was just as calm as you are this minute—said he was expecting it.

DE BOHUN: Bless my soul! What a very remarkable old gentleman. Then you're going to tell him—

MARY: No, indeed! Not until I know that Mr. Simpson is here—here in Washington in this very house. (*Looking at the letter again.*) Oh dear! It's from Buffalo and it was dated day before yesterday. Oh! What if it was a hoax? What if he shouldn't come? What if he's been killed? How can I bear it? I know he won't come— It's Thursday night now, and he *hasn't* come.

DE BOHUN: Suppose I should go to his brother's office?

MARY: He wouldn't be there at this hour. No! I must wait.

DE BOHUN: Not at all, my dear, I can go to the man's house.

MARY: I don't know where he lives.

DE BOHUN: No matter; I can stop at the hotel and get his address from the directory. I don't remember his first name.

MARY: I forgot to tell you. Elijah—Elijah L. Simpson. But I can't let you leave me now. Don't go—

DE BOHUN, *kissing her*: I'll be back before you miss me.

MARY: Before I miss you? (*De Bohun runs out.*) He's gone—and I didn't think to tell him he could find a directory at any druggist's, without going to his hotel— Oh I know he'll never come back; why did I let him go? I must be crazy— everyone in this house is crazy.

Rushes out opposite door from De Bohun's exit.

SCENE II: *Sellers lies on a sofa in the moment of waking from a heavy sleep, with Mrs. Sellers seated beside his head. He rises to a sitting posture, and rubs his back.*

MRS. SELLERS: Does it hurt you, Mulberry? Have you pain there?

SELLERS, *crossly*: Pain? No! Where is my extinguisher? Who took off my extinguisher? Don't you understand, Polly, the risk we run every moment, without that extinguisher?

MRS. SELLERS: I'll get it for you, dear. It's just here at the foot of the sofa. We had to take it off when you were brought home. Ain't you too faint, yet, to have it on?

SELLERS: Faint? Brought home? What do you mean?

MRS. SELLERS: Why, don't you remember, dear, when you got out at the head of the temperance procession, to address the Sisters of Siloam just after you left the house, and had to be brought home in a hack? Lafayette was with you, and the poor boy was almost distracted. If it hadn't been for him, I don't know what would have become of you. He had to support you from the start—we saw you from the window! He says you must have poisoned yourself with some of the chemicals—

SELLERS: Oh, my head!

MRS. SELLERS: Are you dizzy, yet?

SELLERS: No—no—

MRS. SELLERS: He says you were wild and raving, and when you fell—

SELLERS: Did I fall?

MRS. SELLERS: Yes. A few blocks away from the house—he called a hack and put you into it and brought you home. You seemed to be in a kind of heavy stupor, and you've been dead asleep ever since. I never saw you so before.

SELLERS, *bowing his head upon his hands*: No, thank goodness, you never did! I was drunk, Polly.

MRS. SELLERS: Drunk, Mulberry?

SELLERS: Drunk, my dear, hopelessly, fatally drunk—drunk, to my everlasting disgrace and ruin. Oh, take me away from this town, Polly, and let me hide the shame that I've brought on these grey hairs! Oh, Polly.

He sobs.

MRS. SELLERS: Why, Mulberry, how came you—

SELLERS: Oh, as no man ever did before. From my wish to serve the sacred cause which my fall has made a hissing and a by-word. From my desire to speak from sad experience— Oh! How I could speak now! And tell my hearers what deadly ruin lurked in the first glass. I borrowed Lafayette's travelling flask of brandy—yes, I remember it all— and pursuing the idea from sip to sip, and from glass to glass— Oh Polly, Polly, Polly, what have I done to you and to poor Mary? We have suffered poverty, before, my poor girl—we have suffered hunger and cold—there have been times when we had scarcely rags to cover us—trouble and sorrow I have brought upon you time and again, and you have borne it like an angel, my dear old wife—but I never put you to shame before, to open, public shame!

MRS. SELLERS, *kneeling before him by the sofa, and pulling his head down upon her shoulder*: Oh, don't you cry, don't you cry! Don't you take on, Mulberry. I'd like to hear anybody but you, say you had brought me to shame! I'd *like* to hear them! What has the poverty, the hunger and cold been with you, you good, kind faithful heart? All joy, joy! And if I could bear shame for your sake, how happy I should be! But there is no shame. You acted from the highest, noblest motive, and I judge you by your motives, dear— I don't care what the deed is. I'm a poor, weak, silly old woman, but I'm your wife, Mulberry, and I feel that God lets me look at your heart as He does. (*Crying and kissing his head.*) There, there. Don't take on, any more. Let it all go. Nobody noticed—

SELLERS: Ah, don't deceive yourself. The town will be ringing with it in the morning; it will be in all the papers—

MRS. SELLERS: No; no; Lafayette says there was nothing but sympathy expressed by the ladies, and all the little boys cheered as the hack drove away!

They gave it three cheers, Lafayette says—yes. There, put on your extinguisher, dear, and cheer up. (*Bustling about and helping him to get it on.*) There might be a fire-alarm any moment, and you'd hate to miss it. Don't take on any more. You needn't be afraid about the papers. There have been three reporters here to get the particulars; but I've sent them all away. Don't you be troubled, Mulberry. (*She buckles the extinguisher around him, and he stands thoughtfully silent a moment.*) What is it, Berry, dear?

SELLERS,[1] *vehemently*: An idea! An immense, colossal, a mammoth idea! An idea destined to convulse the universal frame of things!

MRS. SELLERS, *apprehensively*: Oh, what can it be?

SELLERS: Polly, do you know what has hitherto wholly invalidated and neutralized the efficiency of this extinguisher?

MRS. SELLERS: Why, I thought it was the difficulty of carrying a portable sandblast to put out the fire when the extinguisher had concentrated it.

SELLERS: Folly, stuff, drivel, delirium!

MRS. SELLERS: What in the world can it be, then?

SELLERS: Simply, the want of fire-escapes to get at the fire on. Not one house in a thousand has them.

MRS. SELLERS: Well?

SELEERS: Well, I now propose to abolish all fire escapes! Abolish them! Abolish is the word, Polly!

MRS. SELLERS: What in the world would you use in their place, Berry?

SELLERS: Wings! My flying apparatus! I'm simply paralyzed that I shouldn't have thought of it before! All that I have to do is to fasten the wings to my shoulders, mount to the window of a burning house, and hover before it while I play the extinguisher upon the flames inside. Where *are* those wings, Polly? (*Runs about, looking.*) Ah, here they are! (*He drags out of a pile of rubbish, a pair of enormous wings, with the plumage considerably broken.*) Here, help me put them on. Hurry, my dear! We can't afford to lose a moment's time!

MRS. SELLERS: What are you going to do?

SELLERS: Don't talk! You'll see, Polly! Here, let me get my arms through those loops. (*Passes them through, and the wings are made fast.*) Now, then, my dear, open the window!

1 The following episode concerning the wings does not appear in the Yale copy.

MRS. SELLERS: The window?

SELLERS: Yes. Quick! I'm going to fly out of it, and hover before it while I play the extinguisher into the room, here.

MRS. SELLERS: Oh, mercy; you'll fall and kill yourself.

SELLERS: Nonsense! When did you ever know me to kill myself? Open the window, my dear.

MRS. SELLERS: Oh, Berry, love, don't try it! I know you'll get hurt.

She pinions him with her arms, while he struggles to get at the window.

SELLERS: I'll open it myself, if you don't.

MRS. SELLERS: No, no! Fly off of something low, first! This table; or a chair!

Clings about him.

SELLERS: Well, well; I must humor you, I suppose. Or no—wait! I'll fly *onto* the table. Get out of my way! (*Working his wings and failing to rise.*) Why don't you help me work them, Polly? Don't you see I've got the wind dead against me?

They both exert themselves violently, she working the wings behind him.

MRS. SELLERS: There, don't you rise a little?

SELLERS: Not a bit. It's the weight of the extinguisher. Never mind! It's better to fly *from* the table till I get some practice. Here, put the chair on it and give me a little more elevation.

MRS. SELLERS, *obeying*: Oh, do you think you'd better risk it, Berry?

SELLERS: What are you crying about? It's dead sure to succeed. I never saw such a discouraging woman! It's enough to take the heart out of *any* man. (*He mounts, while grumbling away; and at last stands upright in the chair.*) There! You see there's no danger. Now I shall merely spread my wings, and hover about under the ceiling as an illustration. I expect to make this invention pleasant as well as useful. I shall get this flying apparatus in various sizes and styles; ladies' wings, children's; large, roomy, and comfortable pinions for elderly and timid per— It's a triumphant success! The principle is fully vindicated! The wings buoy me up perfectly. (*Flapping them.*) Now just get out of the way, Polly, and I'll throw myself forward—

MRS. SELLERS: Wait, wait a minute, Mulberry; I've got something to tell you.

SELLERS, *faltering*: What is it?

MRS. SELLERS: Something very important! I almost forgot it in my excitement about you!

SELLERS, *impatiently*: Well, well! What is it?

MRS. SELLERS: I've got some good news for you

—some news that will make your heart sing for joy. You know that gentleman you left with us?

SELLERS: Yes—our honored guest—what—

MRS. SELLERS: Yes! Well, do you know who he was, Mulberry? Prepare yourself for a great surprise.

SELLERS: Who he was?

MRS. SELLERS: Yes!

SELLERS: Why, he was Mr. De Bohun.

Getting down from the chair.

MRS. SELLERS: Yes!

SELLERS: Our twentieth or thirtieth cousin from England.

MRS. SELLERS: Yes! Go on!

SELLERS: Our fellow claimant for the Earldom of Dover.

MRS. SELLERS: Yes!

SELLERS: Well?

MRS. SELLERS: Nothing more?

SELLERS: No, unless—unless you observed something peculiar about him—that he didn't eat any of the dried apples, or—

MRS. SELLERS: He ate more than all of us put together!

SELLERS: He *ate* you say? Ate dried apples? More than all of you? My goodness! Then there's a flaw in my calculations. I shall have to feed those fellows, and I didn't suppose they *could* eat! I'm out twenty or thirty millions a year.

MRS. SELLERS: Why, what in the world are you talking about, Mulberry?

SELLERS: About our cousin De Bohun. Do you know who and what he is, Polly?

MRS. SELLERS: That's what I was keeping—that's what I was going to tell you. He's the gentleman that saved our Mary's life that night in the river. There, I knew it would astonish you. Isn't it just like a theatre play? And Mary's so *happy*, poor thing! And he's just as happy as she is, and it's all made up between them and they're so fond of each other—I fill right up whenever I look at them; it reminds me of *our* young days, Mulberry.

SELLERS, *utterly aghast*: The gentleman who saved Mary's life—and she's so ha—happy—and it's all—made—up—between—them—and he's —just as—fond of—her—oh, my good gracious, where are they? Stop it, I say! Stop it! Stop it! This instant!

Rushing about and trying to get at the door.

MRS. SELLERS, *intercepting him*: Stop it? Why, Berry, are you crazy?

SELLERS: No, but you are! If there's anything

in materialization, he's a ghost; he's a *dead man*. He was burnt to death last night at the Tolliver House, and I materialized him this morning, don't you remember, to find out about the American claim to the Earldom. Oh my goodness! Oh, woman, woman! Mary's *happy* is she? Happy with a spectre, in love with a miserable fraud of an apparition! And that wretched, swindling dried-apple eating simulacrum is fond of her, hey? Oh, that I should have lived to see my child's affections placed upon—a—a—ma—materializee!

He bows his head upon his hands.

MRS. SELLERS: But why didn't you tell me? It all comes from your never telling me anything!

SELLERS: Tell you? Didn't I tell you I was going to materialize him? And didn't you run out of the room, scared to death when I began to work the materializer?

MRS. SELLERS: But why didn't you tell me you had done it? He came into the dining room just like any other gentleman, with his arm around Mary's waist.

SELLERS: Oh!

MRS. SELLERS: And she told me they were engaged—

SELLERS: Ow!

MRS. SELLERS: And he stepped up and kissed me as natural—

SELLERS: Ugh! Where are they?

MRS. SELLERS: Why Mary's in the kitchen, helping Aunt Sally with the supper and he—it—disappeared just after you were brought back. Said he was going to his hotel—

SELLERS: Of course! Saw that I had no power over him any longer. Disappeared—vanished! Oh, why did I ever leave him for an instant?

MRS. SELLERS: He said he would come back to supper.

SELLERS: Oh, of course, of course! You'll never see him again! A likely story! But I'll have him here again, if there's any virtue left in this materializer. I'll have that fellow back if I have to pull him out of the bottomless pit. Where's Lafayette! Lafayette! *Oh* Lafayette! (*Hawkins enters running.*) Here! Here! Look after these batteries, pile on the biggest current you can get, and think as hard as you can crack it on about De Bohun. I *want* him. But I'm going to inquire at the Tolliver House whether he's been back there, first. (*At telephone.*) [1] Hello. Give me the Tolliver Hotel. (*Pause.*) Bell? I never said anything about Bell—

[1] Compare Mark Twain's "A Telephonic Conversation."

I said give me the Tolliver Hotel—(*Pause.*)—No
—hotel—hotel—can't you hear? Ho—tel. (*Pause.*)
I never told you to go to any such place—I never
use such language. I said Toll-i-ver—Ho-tel—now
you get it? (*Pause.*) All right then. (*Pause.*) Hello
—is this the Tolliver Hotel? (*Pause.*) Are you
the clerk? (*Pause.*) O, call-boy. All right—you'll
do. Ask the clerk if Mr. Reginald De Bohun is
there. (*Pause.*) What—(*Pause.*) No. I never
said anything about a balloon. I said De Bohun
—I want to know if he's there—Mr. De
Bohun. (*Pause.*) What? (*Pause.*) Oh, n—no—
I ain't talking about spoons; I'm talking
about Mr. De Bohun—Reg—i—nald—De Bohun.
(*Pause. Very loud.*) Reg—i—what? (*Pause.*) O, all
right—De B, o, h, u, n. What? (*Pause.*) O, you've
got the last name, have you? Well, that's enough.
(*Pause.*) More than one in the hotel, you say?
(*Aside.*) Reginald—Reginald—I wonder what I
did with his card? That ain't as familiar to me as
his family name—however, I reckon I can manage
it. (*Aloud.*) Pay good attention, now, R—E—
(*Pause.*) No—, now G— I said E— (*Pause.
Louder.*) E. E. E—fourth letter of the alphabet—
R. E. double J— (*Pause.*) —no, not double K.
double J— (*Counting rapidly on his fingers to
himself a, b, c, d, e, f, g, h, i, j,*)—tenth letter of
the alphabet—(*Yelling now.*) R. E. double J, rej—
J, I, ji—rejji—what? (*Pause. Yelling.*)—I said R,
E, I, G, H, —rej—J, E, I, G, H, —ji—rejji—N,
O, U, L, D, nold—rejjinold—what? (*Pause.*)
—All right then—why didn't you say so before?
Let a man stand up here and spell all his teeth
loose when—what did you say? (*Pause.*) O, all
right—he's in his room, is he? Very good then—
that's all I wanted to know—how? (*Pause.
Louder.*) I said that's all I wanted to know—
which? (*Pause. Yelling.*) No. I never said anything about snow—(*Dumb show of profanity and
rage.*)—all I wanted to KNOW—(*Shouting.*)—
can't you hear anything? I said it's all I wanted
to—O go hang yourself. Good bye! (*Hangs up
the telephone with a slam, and steps away swabbing the perspiration away sorrowfully.*)—O, what
a sweet and gentle temper I had before they invented that deaf and dumb machine, and now
look at it! But at any rate, we've got him, Lafayette! He hadn't de-materialized yet, and I can
have him here in one quarter of a second. (*Enter
Uncle Daniel with a card.*) Ah, here he is now!
Stop the current, Lafayette! It's all right. He's
here. He's pretty prompt. Stands upon ceremony
to the last, though! But he was an Englishman—

that accounts for it. I reckon they send their
cards in to St. Peter. (*Gets out his glasses.*) Show
the gentleman in, Daniel. (*Reads the card.*)[1]
Lycurgus Suckers, representing The Washington
Standard-Post. Hello, this won't do! I can't see
anybody, Daniel! Tell him—

*He looks up as the reporter dodges in under
Daniel's arm.*

SUCKERS: He told me you were particularly engaged, but I knew you would see a representative
of *The Standard-Post*, Colonel Sellers. I used to
know you when you were here ten years ago, getting your Tennessee land purchase through Congress. I remember you.

SELLERS, *with dignity*: But I don't know you,
sir. And you have no right to push in here. This
is a private house!

SUCKERS: Yes, that's the theory. But in point of
fact there are no private houses in America, nor
private affairs. The public must and will know
everything. I am merely the servant of the public,
and I came to interview you as such.

SELLERS: Oh, if you came in a public cap-
pacity—

SUCKERS: Certainly.

SELLERS: Then, of course, I bow to the will of
the majority.

SUCKERS: I knew you would. They all do. The
fact is, they *wish* to be interviewed, from the start.
All that I wish to do is to ask you a few questions
in regard to your seizure in the street this afternoon. There are a great many rumors flying about,
and some painful reports may be telegraphed
through the Associated Press. (*He talks very glibly,
getting his note-book from his pocket and sharpen-
ing his pencil.*) I shall be glad to make any statement for you that you wish.

SELLERS: I was not well—excited all day—
wasn't right when I left the house—

HAWKINS: Colonel Sellers fell in the street when
about two blocks from the house and I brought
him home in the carriage. That's all.

SELLERS: And I have since been making a
triumphant experiment of my flying apparatus.

SUCKERS: Triumphant?

Looking doubtfully at the wings.

SELLERS: Yes, I can fly from the loftiest building—this is an old pair.

SUCKERS: Very good! First rate! (*Writes.*) And
now in regard to those reports of materialization

by means of stored electricity, which I heard on my way up. Anything in them?

SELLERS, *wildly enthusiastic in a moment*: Anything *in* them? Look at that battery! Look at these cells! That battery can store enough electricity in these cells to materialize all the dead men since Adam. Why look here, major—

SUCKERS: Suckers.

SELLERS: Major Suckers. I can tell you personally—in straight confidence in your capacity as a gentleman—

SUCKERS: Of course.

SELLERS: That this is an assured thing. There's nothing tentative, or experimental about it, any more. Why— (*Looking about him, and speaking in an undertone.*) I materialized a spirit here this morning!

SUCKERS: No!

Writes.

SELLERS: Yes, sir—a relation of mine. But, of course, I shouldn't wish the fact to go to the public.

SUCKERS: Certainly not.

Writes.

SELLERS: I can refer you to Mrs. Sellers and my nephew, who both lunched with the materializee —we shall have to coin a new word for the new fact.

SUCKERS: First-rate. Materializee is capital. (*Writes.*) Lunched with it, you say?

MRS. SELLERS: Yes, sir, on dried apples. We dine late, and make a light lunch at half past one. The materializee ate more than all of us put together.

SELLERS: But these details are confidential— between gentlemen.

SUCKERS, *writing*: Of course. Mr. Hawkins, present, you say?

SELLERS: Mr. Hawkins, and my daughter, also. The fact is, I don't mind telling you, Doctor Suckers, as an old friend, and not as an interviewer, that the materializee had saved my daughter's life when on earth a few months ago; and—it will add a pathetic interest to the narrative—for your ear alone, sir—

SUCKERS, *writing*: Yes!

SELLERS: To know that the young people were engaged, and that the poor girl could not disabuse herself of the impression that the materializee was a bona-fide old style flesh and blood lover. But that I shouldn't wish to get into print, Captain.

SUCKERS: Of course not.

Writing.

SELLERS: I haven't undeceived her, yet. She'll be heart-broken when I do. Well, I've no right to use names, but under the seal of secrecy, I don't mind telling you, Colonel Suckers, that this materializee was no other than—

SUCKERS, *writes*: No other than—

SELLERS: Mr. Reginald De Bohun who lost his life in the Tolliver House fire last night.

SUCKERS, *writing*: Is it possible?

SELLERS: He was my first cousin, the only son of the Earl of Dover; and the title and estates have therefore lapsed to *me!* My mother was a De Bohun. But, of course, these are family matters, and I wouldn't speak of them to everyone.

SUCKERS, *writing*: I understand. Shall you do anything further with your materializer on this side, Colonel?

SELLERS: Nothing that I wish made public, sir.

SUCKERS: Yes?

Writing.

SELLERS: But I shall probably pass it over to my nephew, here, Judge Hawkins, of Hannibal, Missouri—

HAWKINS: Oh, you really musn't, Uncle Sellers!

SELLERS, *waving him benignantly aside*: —whom I have instructed in its use, and who will be able to carry out my ideas of supplying materializees for policemen, poets, congressmen, presidents, financiers, and the other functionaries in whom the degeneration of the human species has left us comparatively weak. But as yet, I say nothing about this.

SUCKERS, *writing*: Yes.

SELLERS: As an English noble, I cannot go into trade, and so I shall leave the business to Judge Hawkins, and simply put up a little amateur materializer in the cinque ports at Dover, to amuse my guests with. But these are private matters.

SUCKERS, *writing*: I see. Well, now Colonel Sellers, I'm extremely obliged to you for being so frank with me, and I'll try not to abuse your confidence. Do you object to my asking you a few questions?

SELLERS: Certainly not.

SUCKERS: What is your opinion, Colonel Sellers, as an English nobleman, of the prospect of American pork in Europe?

SELLERS: We are destined to supply the world with pork, sir. The opposition of Prince Bismarck to our pork will be fatal to the German Empire if he continues it. I gave some attention to this question a few months ago, when I was coming on with my family from Missouri, and I addressed a meeting of gentlemen in the smoking-car—some of the leading minds of the West, sir, on this very point. The German people *will have* American pork. I predicted then, and predict now that if the senseless and soulless opposition of Bismarck continues, we shall have a republic in Germany in less than sixty days!

SUCKERS: Shall you advocate these views in the House of Lords?

SELLERS: Unquestionably. American pork and the spread of American principles go hand in hand—the pig and the eagle are one and inseparable.

SUCKERS: Colonel Sellers, in view of the fire of last night, do you wish to make any suggestion, as a philanthropist, concerning these too prevalent hotel disasters? You know, sir, they have crippled, and well-nigh ruined some of the best insurance com—

SELLERS, *interrupting*: They can stand it, sir—insurance companies can stand it perfectly. I suffer pangs, but not on their account. Ah, no—the thing that always distresses me about these hotel fires is that they invariably fall with such fatal certainty upon one particular class among us—I mean the actresses.

Reporter takes a rapid glance at Sellers.

SUCKERS, *aside*: Caesar's ghost, he's in earnest! I'll get a couple of columns out of this lunatic.

SELLERS: It always happens—always. Now there were five of them captured last night; and they're nice, good, industrious girls, every one of them—and one or two of them have made tolerably fair reputations, too. They had been living in cheap private boarding houses till yesterday; but of course, yesterday, of all days in the year, they must pack up and go to that hotel—why they might have known, by the whole history of their race, that it would burn down. Poor things! Why, do you know, between them they lost $160,000 worth of jewelry.

SUCKERS, *aside*: He actually believes that! Why, it's the same old gang that's always getting burnt out—if you let them tell it. The papers have a standing arrangement with them—always put them in the hotel fires—they pay by the year.

SELLERS: Yes, $160,000, and that's not all. That's only just what's reported—thus far. Wait till the reports are all in. You'll see. Why, sir, I haven't a doubt that there were as many as thirty-five actresses in that hotel last night— Why, they're the very children of sorrow; they flock to misfortune as to a feast. They flutter like moths to a burning hotel. You couldn't any more have a

hotel fire without burning out a battalion of actresses, than anything in the world. And they always lose their jewelry—they lose every button of it. They never put it in the hotel safe. They're the carelessest creatures! Misfortune? Why they can smell it across the globe! Why do you know, sir, actresses came from Europe—they came from Asia—they came from Africa—to get burnt out at the Chicago fire. Yes, sir, they did. They lost four hundred million dollars' worth of jewels in that one fire! It's true—perfectly true—I saw the estimate myself—it was in the papers—and mind you, no guess work, it named every actress and the—the—the—cargo she lost—came right out and named them. In print, you know, in print, conspicuously. They tried to keep it out, but it got in, somehow.

HAWKINS: Why didn't they sue the papers?

SELLERS: O, of course, they did threaten, but they hadn't any money left, and so they had to let it go. It's impossible for actresses to keep out of the papers to begin with, but to keep out of the papers and the fire both—

SUCKERS: Thank you. Do you believe that a state church should be established in this country?

SELLERS: As an American citizen I don't think it is adapted to the genius of our free institution! As an English noble, I believe the established church should be established everywhere.

SUCKERS: Colonel Sellers, shall you favor the international copyright treaty in the House of Lords?

SELLERS: No sir! The American people demand cheap literature, and they shall have it if they have to steal it. Let the English authors look out for themselves.

SUCKERS: As an American citizen do you favor the removal of the capital to St. Louis?

SELLERS: I do, sir. St. Louis is the political centre of the country, and will soon outstrip Chicago as the moral and religious centre.

SUCKERS: Do you believe in the immortality of the soul?

SELLERS: Certainly; I'm practically interested in the immortality of the soul. What becomes of materialization without it?

SUCKERS: Thank you. I think you are homeopathists, you and your lady?

SELLERS: Oh, dear no! We stick by the old practice.

SUCKERS: As a scientist, sir, what position do you take regarding the spots on the sun?

SELLERS: Well sir, I have given the subject a

great deal of attention and think it will be impossible to remove them with the present comparatively crude appliances of science. However, I do not mind stating to you, sir, in confidence, that I am working out in my mind a method which will—

SUCKERS: Remove the spots?

SELLERS: Yes sir.

SUCKERS: Stupendous! (Writes.) What will be the effect?

SELLERS: By my method I could remove them entirely, if I chose, and then the effects would be sure and permanent; but I shall also be able to retain the spots, and shift them from place to place on the sun's disk at will—and this I shall doubtless do, because there is more money in it.

SUCKERS: How?

SELLERS: It is the sun-spots, sir, that determine climate. It is their present position which makes Russia and the Arctic Circle frigid and the equator torrid. I can change all that. I shall establish a bureau and deal in climates.

SUCKERS: You actually propose to sell climates—or hire them out?

SELLERS: Yes sir, I will furnish to any country the climate it wants for cash. Explorers desiring it, shall make the northwest passage with no other baggage than a fig-leaf and a fan.

SUCKERS: You are leading a noble life, Colonel Sellers.

SELLERS: I am trying to do what good I can.

SUCKERS: Thank you. (Looking at his book.) That is about all. Oh! One thing more! Are you, or are you not, the Colonel Sellers who was tried for embezzlement in Ohio, a few months ago, and was acquitted on the ground of kleptomania?

SELLERS: No, sir.

SUCKERS: Ah, thanks. Well, now, Colonel Sellers, we always send a proof if possible to gentlemen who have been interviewed in *The Standard-Post*, but I shall not have time in your case. So I will read you what I propose to say. (Reads.) "Colonel Mulbery Sellers interviewed! A harvest of thought! Views of an extraordinary mind concerning religion, pork, materialization, hotel fires, international copyright, burnt-out actresses, the future state, distribution of climate by private enterprise—and kindred subjects!"

SELLERS: Very good—very good indeed.

SUCKERS, *reading*: "A report having been circulated that Colonel Mulberry Sellers, the eminent scientist, inventor and humanitarian, being overcome by emotion while riding at the head of a funeral procession, fell from his horse and was fatally injured, (*Dumb show of assent on the part of Sellers, and wondering surprise from his wife and Hawkins.*) one of our reporters was immediately dispatched to make inquiries, since two nations would be anxiously concerned—our own because of this great citizen's fame and many-sided usefulness, and England because of his immediate heirship to her oldest and richest dukedom—(*Dumb show as before.*) and his near relationship to the royal family. (*Hawkins and Mrs. Sellers dumb show of going to protest—Sellers gestures them down.*) The two countries will be grateful to know that the report was greatly exaggerated, as our reporter was able to testify from personal observation. The Duke is somewhat bruised, and will be confined to his mansion for a few days; but a consultation of the best physicians has resulted in the decision that, thanks to the careful nursing which his Excellency is receiving at the hands of his devoted wife and charming daughter, there is every reason to hope for the best. In the course of an extended interview during which the Duke wore not only his fire-extinguisher but a magnificent pair of India rubber wings, fledged with rough feathers, constituting the flying apparatus in which he had just descended in safety from the top of the Washington Monument. His Grace expressed the opinion, founded upon statistics and careful observation, that our imposition of a 30 per cent duty upon foreign pictures will affect us disastrously, because it will limit native art to the production of pork—"

SELLERS, *with enthusiasm*: It'll do it as sure as guns.

SUCKERS, *reading*: "—and at the same time Germany's attitude toward pork will help on the disastrous effects in a double way, for the reason that Germany, being almost the only foreign market for American art, the closing of her galleries against pork must inevitably result in the precipitation of our country into monarchy and the erection of a nihilist republic upon the ruins of the German Empire."

SELLERS, *excitedly*: I've foreseen it from the beginning!

SUCKERS: "Various matters were touched upon, during the interview—all of them of vast and vital importance to—(*Sellers is called out—reporter continues.*) such, for instance, as his scheme to reorganize the solar system, the shortening the orbits of comets, the addition of ten hours to the day, the bridging of the Atlantic—the annexation of the Milky Way—" ah, he's gone. Well, no matter, I can add a few trifles at the office—an interviewer that can't add a few trifles don't amount to anything.

Sellers returns.

SELLERS, *to reporter*: That is all right, sir; perfectly right; I congratulate you on the accuracy of your report. It is seldom, sir, that these things reach the public with any degree of correctness. I shall take occasion to express my sense of your disinterested devotion, sir, in a note to the managing editor of *The Standard-Post*. (*Wringing the reporter's hand.*) Hope to see you again. Call in when passing. Drop in of an evening and have a friendly cigar. (*Daniel approaches him with a card. Sellers glances at it, still keeping the reporter's hand.*) Ah, this is opportune! You musn't go, my dear sir—you must remain. This is one of the most satisfactory moments of my life. The materializee is here in person! Daniel, show the gentleman in. Don't be surprised, sir, (*to the reporter*) at his sending in his card, first; a gentleman is a gentleman always, dead or alive. (*De Bohun enters.*) Ah, my dear sir, I'm delighted to see you again—delighted.

Pressing his hand.

DE BOHUN: I'm sure you're very kind, Colonel Sellers. I ought to apologize for being so slow in responding to your friendly summons. I stopped at my hotel to get an address from the directory just at the moment you telephoned for me, and I had another errand before I came.

SELLERS: Don't mention it. I ought to apologize to you for leaving you to-day; but I was unavoidably called away. Mr. De Bohun, allow me to introduce you to Professor Suckers, one of our leading literary men— I may say the *first* literary man of our country—at present representing *The Standard-Post*—one of the proprietors of that flourishing journal, and one of our largest capitalists. (*De Bohun bows distantly; the reporter makes notes of his personal appearance.*) My nephew, Chief-justice Hawkins, of Missouri, I think you've met.

DE BOHUN: Oh yes. (*Aside to Hawkins.*) Ah—er by the way, Mr. Justice—er—Hawkins, would you mind at all telling me what it is our dear old friend has got on his back?

HAWKINS, *gravely*: His flying apparatus.

DE BOHUN: Oh—ah! Thanks. (*Surveying Sellers' wings.*) Most extraordinary! Thanks!

HAWKINS: Not at all.

DE BOHUN, *to Mrs. Sellers in undertone*: I really don't know what to say to you in explanation of my delay (*approaches her*) but perhaps we had better leave that to your daughter—

MRS. SELLERS, *shrinking back*: Oh, go away, go away! Don't touch me—don't come near me! You poor, dreadful, dreadful—

SELLERS, *shocked*: My dear, my dear! Remember! Remember the claims of hospitality. This—materializee—if he will excuse the expression—is under our roof; he is our guest—he has sat at our board, and partaken of our—our—simple luncheon.

MRS. SELLERS: I can't help it, Mulberry! If he touches me, I shall scream.

Throughout this scene the reporter must be moving from one character to another, actively taking notes of all that is said and done.

AUNT SALLY, *entering from room with Mary*: Don't you fret, don' you worry any! Marse De Bohun bound to come back. You jist ask your paw if he ain't.

MARY, *catching sight of De Bohun in the corner into which he has shrunk after Mrs. Sellers' rebuff*: Oh, there he is! There you are, my darling! I have you again. Oh, ugh, ugh, ugh, oh, oh, ha, ha!

Laughing and crying, she runs up and flings herself into De Bohun's arms.

MRS. SELLERS, *wildly*: Mary! Mulberry Sellers, will you stop that child?

SELLERS, *aghast*: Oh, you unhappy girl! Come away! Oh, poor, deluded child! Mary—let go, I say! Come away from it! It isn't a man!

MARY, *fiercely, coming forward*: Not a man!

SELLERS: No, it's a materializee!

MARY: Not a man! Oh, Rupert, Rupert, Rupert! Oh, my love, my darling! (*She drags him forward, wildly kissing and embracing him.*) If he isn't a man, then let me die! If he isn't a man, then I won't give him for all the men alive!

SELLERS, *shaken*: Who—who are you, sir?

DE BOHUN, *quietly*: Rupert De Bohun.

SELLERS: And you were, were you not, burned in the Tolliver House fire last night?

DE BOHUN: I was not. It was our poor cousin, Reginald De Bohun that the reports of the fire referred to. He was a cad, but I was sorry for him. I arrived in Washington this morning, and I've spent the afternoon looking up his ashes, but it was impossible—

SELLERS, *blandly*: To distinguish the different victims, I know. Don't trouble yourself about that, sir. I'll have all that attended to. I had arranged to send your remains home to your uncle. His will do just as well. I proposed in order to simplify the matter, and avoid any possible mistake to send all three of the victims home to the Earl of Dover.

DE BOHUN: That was very thoughtful of you, Colonel Sellers! But there seems to have been a mistake somewhere; it appears from what the people tell me at the Tolliver House, that there were *no* lives lost in the fire last night.

SELLERS: No lives lost?

DE BOHUN: No, and my cousin, whose end we've been lamenting very sincerely, I'm sure, has been confined to his room ever since dinner last night, from the effects of an American wine that he tested rather too thoroughly at dinner last night.

SELLERS: And this cousin of ours who has been getting himself into the papers as if he were a popular actress, and putting me to so much trouble and expense for materialization, who was he?

DE BOHUN: The heir of Dover.

SELLERS: The heir of Dover; and who would have been the heir if he were now an indistinguishable victim? [1]

DE BOHUN: I'm sorry to say that any one of five

[1] At this point the Barrett version stops, and only the Yale version has a satisfactory ending. The Barrett copy, however, shows some differences from the Mark Twain Estate version which in this instance gives another ending in Howells' hand beginning six speeches back.

SELLERS, *blandly*: Oh, don't trouble yourself about that, sir. I'll have all that attended to. And I have arranged to send your remains home to your uncle. His will do just as well. Another nephew?

DE BOHUN: No, his son.

SELLERS: His son?

DE BOHUN: His only son, and heir to the Earldom.

SELLERS: Bless my heart. And who is now the heir of Dover?

DE BOHUN, *taking Mary's hand, and drawing her to him*: You are, Colonel Sellers.

SELLERS: I? *I* the heir of Dover?

DE BOHUN: Yes, if you will give me this dear girl, in exchange for all the honor and glories of the Earldom. It was she whom I rescued from the sinking boat that night—

MRS. SELLERS: Why, you don't say. Well, I must shake hands now!

AUNT SALLY AND UNCLE DANIEL: Glory! Glory!

UNCLE DANIEL, *rocking his head round and crying*: Oh, Lord of Heaven!

AUNT SALLY, *jumping up and down*: Try on your robe in de mawning!

Repeats several times.

SELLERS, *recovering himself*: No, sir! Let justice be done, though the heavens fall! Stop that, Daniel! Stop that, Sally! *No,* sir! Take my child! You have won her fairly, and she is yours. Be good to her! She is the best girl in the solar system, and will be an ornament to every court! *(Wiping his eyes.)* But take the Earldom too! I am also sworn an American citizen, and America is good enough for me.

Clemens is to go on with this speech. As soon as Sellers sails in, the reporter comes round in front of him, drags up a table and chair, and reports furiously. Curtain falls on same grand period.

END OF PLAY

and twenty cousins in England—before either of us, my dear Colonel.

SELLERS: Exactly so! This is what I anticipated—this is what I foresaw from the start. It is utterly impossible for an American claimant to an English title to urge his right with any hope of success. Very well, then, we must for the present abandon the idea of the succession—and I must give my attention to some of these little experiments of mine. I'm glad to have my mind free for the purpose. I suppose the materializer—may be considered as yet too elemental in conception. Perhaps the extinguisher would be the most practical thing. With a little capital—

Uncle Daniel entering, gives name under breath.

UNCLE DANIEL: Mr. Simpson.

SELLERS: Simpson? What Simpson? Who's Simpson? I don't know any Simpson— He can't come in.

MARY: It's your agent, father—your agent for the cut-off. *(Rapturously.)* Oh! He's come, he's come, I know he's come. Send him in Dan'l, at once—yes—he's here, father, and we're saved. See! See! Here's his letter that came this morning and which I've just opened— *He's got the orders.*

SELLERS: Why, of course! I see nothing so extraordinary in that— That was to be expected— I always knew that cut-off could be counted upon. *(Enter Simpson.)* Ah, my dear sir, I'm glad to see you, powerful glad to see you. And you've succeeded in getting the little list of orders, eh?

SIMPSON: Twice—three times—four times the number. I've got two thousand orders.

SELLERS, *slowly*: Very good—very good indeed, but quite within the limit of my expectations.

SIMPSON: And that is not all. Encouraged by my success I have succeeded in interesting a wealthy boiler-maker who offers $100,000 for a ⅓ interest in the cut-off and sends this certified check for the amount subject to your order if you accept. This with your remaining interest and royalties should insure you a steady income of not less than $20,000 per annum.

SELLERS: Ah! Indeed! $20,000 per annum! That is a moderate sum, but perhaps I had better accept. It will serve to assist in developing more important matters. Here, Mary, my dear, you take charge of this check. I think you and your mother may need something in the way of wardrobe—and my remaining income will be sufficient for experiments. Besides from what I have seen lately I fancy there may be occasion for some little extras by way of a traveling outfit for you, Mary, if this young gentleman is of the same mind he was this morning.

Glances at De Bohun.

MARY: Oh! Father!

DE BOHUN: My dear Colonel and Mrs. Sellers; it should need no ghost come from the grave to tell you that my mind is on that theme. Were the Earldom mine, in fact, I would abandon it without a pang for the blessed privilege of standing here the accepted suitor of your daughter.

SELLERS: All right, my boy, all right! Take her and God bless you both. She's worth a dozen earldoms. And, by the way, if you should care to settle in this country and devote yourself to business, I should like to call your attention to one of my inventions which you have already noticed, but whose full capacity you cannot have comprehended. I allude to this little instrument.[1]

---

[1] This phonograph material was originally in the first act but was transferred to the third act. In the Mark Twain Estate manuscript version the phonograph also sang the following song as a parody on the popular Methodist hymn:

There is a boarding house, far, far away,
Where they have ham and eggs three times a day.
O, how those boarders yell,
When they hear that dinner bell—
They give that landlord (momentary outburst of terrific catfight which drowns out one word.)

Another Sellers invention which is included in the Barrett version and then crossed out and marked "omit" concerns sewer-gas.

SELLERS: Why, Lafayette, everything is useful—nothing ever ought to be wasted. Now look at sewer gas, for instance. Sewer gas has always been wasted, heretofore; nobody tried to save up sewer gas—you can't name me a man. Ain't that so, Lafayette? You know perfectly well it's so.

LAFAYETTE: Yes, it is so—but I never—er I don't quite see why a body—

SELLERS: Should want to save it? Well I'll tell you. Do you see this little invention here? It's a decomposer —I call it a decomposer. I give you my word of honor, that if you show me a house that produces a given quantity of sewer-gas in a day, I'll engage to set up my decomposer there and make that house produce a hundred times that quantity of sewer-gas, in less than an hour.

LAFAYETTE: Dear me, but why should you want to?

SELLERS: Want to? Listen, and you'll see. Lafayette, for illuminating purposes and economy combined, there's nothing in the world that begins with sewer-gas. And really, it don't cost a cent. You put in a good inferior article of plumbing—such as you find everywhere—and add my decomposer, and there you are. Just use the ordinary gas pipes—and there your expense ends. Think of it. Why Lafayette, in five years from now you won't see a house lighted with anything but sewer gas. Every physician I talk to recommends it; and every plumber.

LAFAYETTE: But isn't it dangerous?

SELLERS: O, yes, more or less, but everything is—coal gas, candles, electricity—there isn't anything that ain't.

LAFAYETTE: It lights up well, does it?

SELLERS: O, magnificently.

LAFAYETTE: Have you given it a good trial?

Pointing to phonograph.

DE BOHUN: Yes, Colonel. I have every reason to be grateful to that achievement of science as your daughter will testify; but pardon me, Colonel, if I do not seem to see what practical application can be made of it. In short, where is there any money in it?

SELLERS, *deprecatingly*: My friend—excuse me, but you haven't been long in this country and you don't as yet seem to "catch on," as we should remark in our current phraseology, with that alacrity which I could wish in a son-in-law. Practical application! Money! Why, my friend, there's a mint of money in it. Don't you understand? That is my grand adaptation of the phonograph to the marine service. You store up profanity in it for use at sea. You know that sailors don't fly around worth a cent unless you swear at them— so the mate that can do the best job of swearing is the most valuable man. In great emergencies his talent saves the ship. But the ship is a large thing, and he can't be everywhere at once; so there have been times where one mate has lost a ship which could have been saved if they had had a hundred. Prodigious storms, you know. Well, a ship *can't* afford a hundred mates; but she *can* afford a hundred cursing-phonographs, and distribute them all over the vessel—and there, you see, she's armed at every point. Imagine a big storm, and a hundred of my machines all cursing away at once—splendid spectacle, splendid—you couldn't hear yourself think. Ship goes through that storm perfectly serene—she's just as safe as she'd be in the harbor.

HAWKINS: Yes, I see—I see exactly. How do you prepare the thing?

SELLERS: Load it—simply load it.

HAWKINS: How?

SELLERS: Why, you just stand over it and swear into it.

HAWKINS: And that loads it, does it?

SELLERS: Certainly—because every word it collars, it keeps—keeps it forever. Never wears out.

SELLERS: Well, no, not a first rate one. Polly's prejudiced, and she won't let me put it in here; but I'm playing my cards to get it adopted in the President's house, and then it'll go—don't you doubt it. I shall not need this one for the present, Lafayette; you may take it around home with you, if you like, and give it a trial.

LAFAYETTE, *in discomfort*: You are—are—exceedingly kind, but—

SELLERS: O, not a word, not a word—I assure you I've not the least use for it for the present. Take it freely— take anything here that you want. There's plenty of things here.

Any time you turn the crank, out it'll come. In times of great peril, you can reverse it, and it'll swear backwards. That makes a sailor hump himself!

HAWKINS: Yes! And who loads it—the mate?

SELLERS: Yes, if he chooses, or I'll furnish them already loaded. I can hire an expert for $75 a month who will load a hundred and fifty phonographs in 150 hours, and do it easy. And an expert can furnish a stronger article, of course, than the mere average uncultivated mate can. Then you see all the ships of the world will buy them ready loaded—for I shall have them loaded in any language a customer wants. Lafayette, it will work the grandest moral reform of the 19th century. Five years from now, all the swearing will be done by machinery—on a ship. Lafayette, millions of dollars have been spent by the churches, in the effort to abolish profanity in the commercial marine. Lafayette, now think of it—my name will live forever in the affections of good men as the man, who, solitary and alone, accomplished this noble and elevating reform.

HAWKINS: You're right, Colonel. There is no two ways about *that*. How did you ever come to think of it? So simple, and so wonderful!

SELLERS: No, no! Lafayette! A mere trifle! The simplest toy! And yet it is complete in its result! If you want to load it up loud and strong, you stand right over it and shout. But if you leave it open, and all set, it'll eavesdrop, so to speak—that is to say, it will load itself up with any sounds that are made within six feet of it. Now I'll show you how it works. I had an expert come and load this one up, yesterday. (*Goes to it.*) Hello, it's been left open—it's too bad—still I reckon it hasn't had much chance to collect irrelevant stuff. All you do is to turn the crank—so. (*Turns it. Phonograph in a plaintive voice.*)

"A watcher sick and weary
Looks forth with anxious eye."

(*Pink trip slip. The wind waiting by. Stops turning.*) Hang it, that ain't it. Somebody's been singing around here. Try it again.

Turns crank.

PHONOGRAPH, *plaintive voice again, mingled with a low, gradually rising wail of cats slowly warming up towards a fight:*

"Are we almost there,
Are we almost there,
Said a dying girl as she drew near—"

meow, meow, pfst, meow, meow, meow! "Scat you devils"—(*And a rocket of flying missiles.*) bang—bang—bang—

Stops crank.

SELLERS: Well never mind—let it go. I've got some sailor profanity down in there somewhere, if I could get to it. But it isn't any matter; you see how the machine works.

HAWKINS, *with enthusiasm*: Works! It's a miracle! I know there's a hundred fortunes in it.

SELLERS: And mind, the Hawkins family get their share, Lafayette.

HAWKINS: Ah! It's the grandest invention of the age, of all the ages.

SELLERS: *Now* do you begin to see any money in it? Why, it's the grandest invention of the age.

DE BOHUN: It certainly is very interesting.

HAWKINS: Colonel, if Mr. De Bohun does not care to undertake the management of this great discovery, perhaps you would allow me a small interest in it.

SELLERS: Interest? Why, my boy, take it all. I have other great matters at stake— and can't devote myself to it— Why Lafayette, I expect to see you rolling in wealth inside of a year. The only thing I ask is that my name shall always be prominent in the grand moral reform which this machine is sure to produce.

HAWKINS: Oh! Thank you, thank you—a thousand times I thank you, Colonel.

DE BOHUN: And Colonel would you mind allowing me as your son-in-law to devote my time to the development of your remaining interest in the cut-off? I have a mechanical turn of mind and fancy I could greatly increase the value of your property.

SELLERS: Of course, of course—I shall be delighted to have you as a business partner. And come to think of it I guess you'll find it pleasanter than hanging round waiting for dead men's shoes —for after all what is an English earldom—a petty fragment of an effete monarchy compared to the glorious freedom of an American Citizen. Aunt Sally, bring me that striped banner, that beautiful emblem of our country. (*He waves the flag over all.*) Here my friends, my beloved family, I renounce all thought of an English abode and proclaim myself no longer the *Great American Claimant.*

CURTAIN

The Sleeping Car

[1882]

During some thirty-seven years of writing plays, Howells produced twenty-five one-act plays, twelve of which involve the same principal characters—the Robertses and the Campbells. With concern for some of their many personal problems, Howells follows these people and their friends through more than ten years of life together. It must have been a pleasant association, for using them Howells wrote some of his best one-act plays, and Howells' readers began to feel acquainted with these two young Boston couples. Although *The Sleeping Car* could not be called one of his best, it was in this play that Howells first introduced Mr. and Mrs. Roberts and her Aunt Mary— Mrs. Roberts, a sweet, completely sincere, well-meaning woman with a brain that scatters its effectiveness and is not so well developed as her conscience; Mr. Roberts, a writer, kindly, easily dominated, and noticeably ineffective in his dealings with that part of the world that exists, though quite vaguely for him, outside his far-reaching intellect; Aunt Mary, a capable old woman with a tongue and a mind that can be equally sharp. There is also Mrs. Roberts' elder brother, Willis Campbell, who seems in *The Sleeping Car* to be simply a rather sensible young man with some touches of the burlesque in his character, but who in later plays becomes the clearest thinker of the entire Roberts–Campbell entourage and also the most daring of jokers.

Like many a Howells farce, *The Sleeping Car* is lively and boisterous. John Hay wrote to Howells from France that this play was the "pearl" of the *Harper's Christmas* collection (December 20, 1882, Harvard Library). "I would give money to see it on the stage," he wrote. "There is a woman at the vaudeville who played in a French comedy . . . who would be the divinest Mrs. Roberts on earth, but it would be impossible here because a French sleeping car is a sad parody on our glorious institution. There's no sociableness, no promiscuity, no chance for love or war." Actually Howells' sleeping car is not a sleeping car but, as one of its passengers suggests, a "waking car," and the opportunities for love seem less remote than those for war, while sociableness is carried on under strained relationships. There might be some mischief aboard our glorious institution, but promiscuity, never—at least not in a Howells representation of it.

The Sleeping Car is, of course, farce and as obvious as Howells' primary technique of mistaken identity, which is repeated *ad absurdum*. Because Howells wanted mild boisterousness rather than vulgar violence, he chose his victim, the Californian, very carefully. Although he is a Californian and shows some of the characteristics of the legendary Westerner, he is genetically derived from the inhabitants of Louisburg Square or its surroundings. Of course, some of his Boston aristocratic modesty has disappeared and been replaced with a certain coarseness. But beneath that sartorial imperfection there is the heart of a Boston gentleman who for this play is much more of a gentleman than he has any reason to be.

Although Howells used mainly farce humor to accompany the farce action, some indications of the bright lines that were to figure in later plays exist in the clever speeches by minor characters, such as the man in the upper berth, and by Mrs. Roberts as she talks, talks, talks. And the stage directions, of which Howells was so proud, could not be omitted without some damage to the literary qualities of the play.

Odell's *Annals of the New York Stage* (XIII [New York: Columbia University Press, 1927–49], 396) lists two performances of *The Sleeping Car*: April 13 and 14, 1887, in the Chapel of the All Souls Universalist Church, South Tenth Street, New York City. Probably there were many more such amateur productions.

242

The Sleeping Car[1]

I.

SCENE: *One side of a sleeping-car on the Boston and Albany Road. The curtains are drawn before most of the berths: from the hooks and rods hang hats, bonnets, bags, bandboxes, umbrellas, and other travelling-gear; on the floor are boots of both sexes, set out for The Porter to black. The Porter is making up the beds in the upper and lower berths adjoining the seats on which a young mother, slender and pretty, with a baby asleep on the seat beside her, and a stout old lady, sit confronting each other— Mrs. Agnes Roberts and her Aunt Mary.*

MRS. ROBERTS: Do you always take down your back hair, aunty?

AUNT MARY: No, never, child; at least not since I had such a fright about it once, coming on from New York. It's all well enough to take down your back hair if it *is* yours; but if it isn't, your head's the best place for it. Now, as I buy mine of Madame Pierrot—

MRS. ROBERTS: Don't you *wish* she wouldn't advertise it as *human* hair? It sounds so pokerish— like human flesh, you know.

AUNT MARY: Why, she couldn't call it *inhuman* hair, my dear.

MRS. ROBERTS, *thoughtfully*: No—just *hair*.

AUNT MARY: Then people might think it was for mattresses. But, as I was saying, I took it off that night, and tucked it safely away, as I supposed, in my pocket, and I slept sweetly till about midnight, when I happened to open my eyes, and saw something long and black crawl off my bed and slip under the berth. *Such* a shriek as I gave, my dear! "A snake! a snake! oh, a snake!" And everybody began talking at once, and some of the gentlemen swearing, and the porter came running with the poker to kill it; and all the while it was that ridiculous switch of mine, that had worked out of my pocket. And glad enough I was to grab it up before anybody saw it, and say I must have been dreaming.

1 The text used here is from *The Sleeping Car and Other Farces*.

MRS. ROBERTS: Why, aunty, how funny! How *could* you suppose a serpent could get on board a sleeping-car, of all places in the world?

AUNT MARY: That was the perfect absurdity of it.

THE PORTER: Berths ready now, ladies.

MRS. ROBERTS, *to The Porter, who walks away to the end of the car, and sits down near the door*: Oh, thank you!— Aunty, do you feel nervous the least bit?

AUNT MARY: Nervous? No. Why?

MRS. ROBERTS: Well, I don't know. I suppose I've been worked up a little about meeting Willis, and wondering how he'll look, and all. We can't *know* each other, of course. It doesn't stand to reason that if he's been out there for twelve years, ever since I was a child, though we've corresponded regularly—at least *I* have—that he could recognize me; not at the first glance, you know. He'll have a full beard; and then I've got married, and here's the baby. Oh, *no!* he'll never guess who it is in the world. Photographs really amount to nothing in such a case. I wish we were at home, and it was all over. I wish he had written some particulars, instead of telegraphing from Ogden, "Be with you on the 7 A.M., Wednesday."

AUNT MARY: Californians always telegraph, my dear; they never think of writing. It isn't expensive enough, and it doesn't make your blood run cold enough, to get a letter, and so they send you one of those miserable yellow despatches whenever they can—those printed in a long string, if possible, so that you'll be *sure* to die before you get to the end of it. I suppose your brother has fallen into all those ways, and says "reckon" and "ornary" and "which the same," just like one of Mr. Bret Harte's characters.

MRS. ROBERTS: But it isn't exactly our not knowing each other, aunty, that's worrying me; that's something that could be got over in time. What is simply driving me distracted is Willis and Edward meeting there when I'm away from home. Oh, how *could* I be away! and why *couldn't* Willis have given us fair warning? I would have hurried from the ends of the earth to meet him. I don't believe poor Edward ever saw a Californian; and he's so quiet and pre-occupied, I'm sure he'd never get on with Willis. And if Willis is the least loud, he wouldn't like Edward. Not that I suppose he *is* loud; but I don't believe he knows anything about literary men. But you can see, aunty, can't you, how very anxious I must be? Don't you see that I ought to have been there when Willis and Edward met, so as to—to—well, to *break* them to each other, don't you know?

AUNT MARY: Oh, you needn't be troubled about that, Agnes. I dare say they've got on perfectly well together. Very likely they're sitting down to the unwholesomest hot supper this instant that the ingenuity of man could invent.

MRS. ROBERTS: Oh, do you *think* they are, aunty? Oh, if I could *only* believe they were sitting down to a hot supper together now, I should be *so* happy! They'd be sure to get on if they were. There's nothing like eating to make men friendly with each other. Don't you know, at receptions, how they never have anything to say to each other till the escalloped oysters and the chicken salad appear; and then how sweet they are as soon as they've helped the ladies to ice? Oh, thank you, *thank* you, aunty, for thinking of the hot supper! It's such a relief to my mind! You can understand, can't you, aunty dear, how anxious I must have been to have my only brother and my only—my husband—get on nicely together? My life would be a wreck, simply a wreck, if they didn't. And Willis and I not having seen each other since I was a child makes it all the worse. I do *hope* they're sitting down to a hot supper.

AN ANGRY VOICE, *from the next berth but one*: I wish people in sleeping-cars—

A VOICE, *from the berth beyond that*: You're mistaken in your premises, sir. This is a waking-car. Ladies, go on, and oblige an eager listener.

Sensation, and smothered laughter from the other berths.

MRS. ROBERTS, *after a space of terrified silence, in a loud whisper to her Aunt*: What horrid things! But now we really must go to bed. It *was* too bad to keep talking. I'd no idea my voice was getting so loud. Which berth will you have, aunty? I'd better take the upper one, because—

AUNT MARY, *whispering*: No, no; I must take that, so that you can be with the baby below.

MRS. ROBERTS: Oh, how good you are, Aunt Mary! It's too bad; it is really. I can't let you.

AUNT MARY: Well, then, you must; that's all. You know how that child tosses and kicks about in the night. You never can tell where his head's

going to be in the morning, but you'll probably find it at the foot of the bed. I couldn't sleep an instant, my dear, if I thought that boy was in the upper berth; for I'd be sure of his tumbling out over you. Here, let me lay him down. (*She lays the baby in the lower berth.*) There! Now get in, Agnes—do, and leave me to my struggle with the attraction of gravitation.

MRS. ROBERTS: Oh, *poor* aunty, how will you ever manage it? I *must* help you up.

AUNT MARY: No, my dear; don't be foolish. But you may go and call the porter, if you like. I dare say he's used to it.

Mrs. Roberts goes and speaks timidly to The Porter, who fails at first to understand, then smiles broadly, accepts a quarter with a duck of his head, and comes forward to Aunt Mary's side.

MRS. ROBERTS: Had he better give you his hand to rest your foot in, while you spring up as if you were mounting horseback?

AUNT MARY, *with disdain*: Spring! My dear, I haven't *sprung* for a quarter of a century. I shall require every fibre in the man's body. His hand, indeed! You get in first, Agnes.

MRS. ROBERTS: I will, aunty dear; but—

AUNT MARY, *sternly*: Agnes, do as I say. (*Mrs. Roberts crouches down on the lower berth.*) I don't choose that any member of my family shall witness my contortions. Don't you look.

MRS. ROBERTS: No, no, aunty.

AUNT MARY: Now, porter, are you strong?

PORTER: I used to be porter at a Saratoga hotel, and carried up de ladies' trunks dere.

AUNT MARY: Then you'll do, I think. Now, then, your knee; now your back. There! And very handsomely done; thanks.

MRS. ROBERTS: Are you really in, Aunt Mary?

AUNT MARY, *dryly*: Yes. Good-night.

MRS. ROBERTS: Good-night, aunty. (*After a pause of some minutes*) Aunty!

AUNT MARY: Well, what?

MRS. ROBERTS: Do you think it's perfectly safe?

She rises in her berth, and looks up over the edge of the upper.

AUNT MARY: I suppose so. It's a well-managed road. They've got the air-brake, I've heard, and the Miller platform, and all those horrid things. What makes you introduce such unpleasant subjects?

MRS. ROBERTS: Oh, I don't mean accidents. But, you know, when you turn, it does creak so awfully. I shouldn't mind myself; but the baby—

AUNT MARY: Why, child, do you think I'm going to break through? I couldn't. I'm one of the *lightest* sleepers in the world.

MRS. ROBERTS: Yes, I know you're a light sleeper; but—but it doesn't seem quite the same thing, somehow.

AUNT MARY: But it is; it's quite the same thing, and you can be perfectly easy in your mind, my dear. I should be quite as loath to break through as you would to have me. Good-night.

MRS. ROBERTS: Yes; good-night. —Aunty!

AUNT MARY: Well?

MRS. ROBERTS: You ought to just see him, how he's lying. He's a perfect log. *Couldn't* you just bend over, and peep down at him a moment?

AUNT MARY: Bend over! It would be the death of me. Good-night.

MRS. ROBERTS: Good-night. Did you put the glass into my bag, or yours? I feel so very thirsty, and I want to go and get some water. I'm sure I don't know why I should be thirsty. Are you, Aunt Mary? Ah! here it is. Don't disturb yourself, aunty; I've found it. It was in my bag, just where I'd put it myself. But all this trouble about Willis has made me so fidgety that I don't know where anything is. And now I don't know how to manage about the baby while I go after the water. He's sleeping soundly enough now; but if he should happen to get into one of his rolling moods, he might tumble out on to the floor. Never mind, aunty, I've thought of something. I'll just barricade him with these bags and shawls. Now, old fellow, roll as much as you like. If you should happen to hear him stir, aunty, won't you— Aunty! Oh, dear! she's asleep already; and what shall I do? (*While Mrs. Roberts continues talking, various notes of protest, profane and otherwise, make themselves heard from different berths.*) I know. I'll make a bold dash for the water, and be back in an instant, baby. Now, don't you move, you little rogue. (*She runs to the water-tank at the end of the car, and then back to her berth.*) Now, baby, here's mamma again. Are you all right, mamma's own?

A shaggy head and bearded face are thrust from the curtains of the next berth.

THE STRANGER: Look here, ma'am. I don't want to be disagreeable about this thing, and I hope you won't take any offence; but the fact is, I'm half dead for want of sleep, and if you'll only keep quiet now a little while, I'll promise not to speak above my breath if ever I find you on a sleeping-car after you've come straight through

from San Francisco, day and night, and not been able to get more than about a quarter of your usual allowance of rest—I will indeed.

MRS. ROBERTS: I'm very sorry that I've disturbed you, and I'll try to be more quiet. I didn't suppose I was speaking so loud; but the cars keep up such a rattling that you never can tell how loud you *are* speaking. Did I understand you to say that you were from California?

THE CALIFORNIAN: Yes, ma'am.

MRS. ROBERTS: San Francisco?

THE CALIFORNIAN: Yes, ma'am.

MRS. ROBERTS: Thanks. It's a terribly long journey, isn't it? I know quite how to feel for you. I've a brother myself coming on. In fact, we expected him before this. (*She scans his face as sharply as the lamplight will allow, and continues, after a brief hesitation.*) It's always such a silly question to ask a person, and I suppose San Francisco is a large place, with a great many people always coming and going, so that it would be only one chance in a thousand if you did.

THE CALIFORNIAN, *patiently*: Did what, ma'am?

MRS. ROBERTS: Oh, I was just wondering if it was possible—but of course, it isn't, and it's very flat to ask—that you'd ever happened to meet my brother there. His name is Willis Campbell.

THE CALIFORNIAN, *with more interest*: Campbell? Campbell? Yes, I know a man of that name. But I disremember his first name. Little low fellow—pretty chunky?

MRS. ROBERTS: I don't know. Do you mean short and stout?

THE CALIFORNIAN: Yes, ma'am.

MRS. ROBERTS: I'm sure I can't tell. It's a great many years since he went out there, and I've never seen him in all that time. I thought if you *did* happen to know him— He's a lawyer.

THE CALIFORNIAN: It's quite likely I know him; and in the morning, ma'am—

MRS. ROBERTS: Oh, excuse me. I'm very sorry to have kept you so long awake with my silly questions.

THE MAN IN THE UPPER BERTH: Don't apologize, madam. I'm not a Californian myself, but I'm an orphan, and away from home, and I thank you, on behalf of all our fellow-passengers, for the mental refreshment that your conversation has afforded us. *I* could lie here, and listen to it all night; but there are invalids in some of these berths, and perhaps on their account it will be as well to defer everything till the morning, as our friend suggests. Allow me to wish you pleasant dreams, madam.

THE CALIFORNIAN, *while Mrs. Roberts shrinks back under the curtain of her berth in dismay, and stammers some inaudible excuse, slowly emerges full length from his berth:* Don't you mind me, ma'am; I've got everything but my boots and coat on. Now, then. (*Standing beside the berth, and looking in upon the man in the upper tier.*) You! Do you know that this is a lady you're talking to?

THE UPPER BERTH: By your voice and your shaggy personal appearance I shouldn't have taken you for a lady—no, sir. But the light is very imperfect; you may be a bearded lady.

THE CALIFORNIAN: You never mind about my looks. The question is, Do you want your head rapped up against the side of this car?

THE UPPER BERTH: With all the frankness of your own Pacific Slope, no.

MRS ROBERTS, *hastily re-appearing:* Oh, no, no, don't hurt him! He's not to blame. I was wrong to keep on talking. Oh, please don't hurt him!

THE CALIFORNIAN, *to* The Upper Berth: You hear? Well, now, don't you speak another word to that lady to-night. Just go on, ma'am, and free your mind on any little matter you like. *I* don't want any sleep. How long has your brother been in California?

MRS. ROBERTS: Oh, don't let's talk about it now; I don't want to talk about it. I thought—I thought— Good-night. Oh, dear! I didn't suppose I was making so much trouble. I didn't mean to disturb anybody. I—

Mrs. Roberts gives way to the excess of her confusion and mortification in a little sob, and then hides her grief behind the curtains of her berth. The Californian slowly emerges again from his couch, and stands beside it, looking in upon the man in the berth above.

THE CALIFORNIAN: For half a cent I *would* rap your head up against that wall. Making the lady cry, and getting me so mad I can't sleep! Now see here, you just apologize. You beg that lady's pardon, or I'll have you out of there before you know yourself. (*Cries of* "Good!" "That's right!" *and* "Make him show himself!" *hail Mrs. Roberts's champion, and heads, more or less dishevelled, are thrust from every berth. Mrs. Roberts remains invisible and silent, and the loud and somewhat complicated respiration of her Aunt makes itself heard in the general hush of expectancy. A remark to the effect that* "The old lady seems to enjoy her rest" *achieves a facile applause.*

The Californian again addresses the culprit.) Come, now, what do you say? I'll give you just one-half a minute.

MRS. ROBERTS, *from her shelter:* Oh, please, *please* don't make him say anything! It was very trying in me to keep him awake, and I know he didn't mean any offence. Oh, *do* let him be!

THE CALIFORNIAN: You hear that? You stay quiet the rest of the time; and if that lady chooses to keep us all awake the whole night, don't *you* say a word, or I'll settle with you in the morning.

Loud and continued applause, amidst which The Californian turns from the man in the berth before him, and restores order by marching along the aisle of the car in his stocking feet. The heads vanish behind the curtains. As the laughter subsides, he returns to his berth, and after a stare up and down the tranquillized car, he is about to retire.

A VOICE: Oh, don't just bow! Speak!

A fresh burst of laughter greets this sally. The Californian erects himself again with an air of bated wrath, and then suddenly breaks into a helpless laugh.

THE CALIFORNIAN: Gentlemen, you're too many for *me*.

He gets into his berth, and after cries of "Good for California!" "You're all right, William Nye!" and "You're several ahead yet!" the occupants of the different berths gradually relapse into silence, and at last, as the car lunges onward through the darkness, nothing is heard but the rhythmical clank of the machinery, with now and then a burst of audible slumber from Mrs. Roberts's Aunt Mary.

II.

At Worcester, where the train has made the usual stop, The Porter, with his lantern on his arm, enters the car, preceding a gentleman somewhat anxiously smiling; his nervous speech contrasts painfully with the business-like impassiveness of The Porter, who refuses, with an air of incredulity, to enter into the confidences which the gentleman seems reluctant to bestow.

MR. EDWARD ROBERTS: This is the Governor Marcy,[1] isn't it?

1 William Learned Marcy, 1786–1857, was governor of New York for three terms (1833–38) and also served as Secretary of State under Polk and Pierce.

THE PORTER: Yes, sah.

MR. ROBERTS: Came on from Albany, and not from New York?

THE PORTER: Yes, sah, it did.

MR. ROBERTS: Ah! it must be all right. I—

THE PORTER: Was your wife expecting you to come on board here?

MR. ROBERTS: Well, no, not exactly. She was expecting me to meet her at Boston. But I— (*Struggling to give the situation dignity, but failing, and throwing himself, with self-convicted silliness, upon The Porter's mercy.*) The fact is, I thought I would surprise her by joining her here.

THE PORTER, *refusing to have any mercy*: Oh! How did you expect to find her?

MR. ROBERTS: Well—well—I don't know. I didn't consider. (*He looks down the aisle in despair at the close-drawn curtains of the berths, and up at the dangling hats and bags and bonnets, and down at the chaos of boots of both sexes on the floor.*) I don't know *how* I expected to find her.

Mr. Roberts's countenance falls, and he visibly sinks so low in his own esteem and an imaginary public opinion that The Porter begins to have a little compassion.

THE PORTER: Dey's so many ladies on board I couldn't find her.

MR. ROBERTS: Oh, no, no! of course not. I didn't expect that.

THE PORTER: Don't like to go routing 'em all up, you know. I wouldn't be allowed to.

MR. ROBERTS: I don't ask it; that would be preposterous.

THE PORTER: What sort of looking lady was she?

MR. ROBERTS: Well, I don't know, really. Not very tall, rather slight, blue eyes. I—I don't know what you'd call her nose. And—stop! Oh, yes, she had a child with her, a little boy. Yes!

THE PORTER, *thoughtfully looking down the aisle*: Dey was three ladies had children. I didn't notice whether dey was boys or girls, or *what* dey was. Didn't have anybody with her?

MR. ROBERTS: No, no. Only the child.

THE PORTER: Well, I don't know what you are going to do, sah. It won't be a great while now till morning, you know. Here comes the conductor. Maybe he'll know what to do.

Mr. Roberts makes some futile, inarticulate attempts to prevent The Porter from laying the case before The Conductor, and then stands guiltily smiling, overwhelmed with the hopeless absurdity of his position.

THE CONDUCTOR, *entering the car, and stopping before The Porter, and looking at Mr. Roberts*: Gentleman want a berth?

THE PORTER, *grinning*: Well, no, sah. He's lookin' for his wife.

THE CONDUCTOR, *with suspicion*: Is she aboard this car?

MR. ROBERTS, *striving to propitiate The Conductor by a dastardly amiability*: Oh, yes, yes. There's no mistake about the car—the Governor Marcy. She telegraphed the name just before you left Albany, so that I could find her at Boston in the morning. Ah!

THE CONDUCTOR: At Boston? (*Sternly*) Then what are you trying to find her at Worcester in the middle of the night for?

MR. ROBERTS: Why—I—that is—

THE PORTER, *taking compassion on Mr. Roberts's inability to continue*: Says he wanted to surprise her.

MR. ROBERTS: Ha—yes, exactly. A little caprice, you know.

THE CONDUCTOR: Well, that may all be so. (*Mr. Roberts continues to smile in agonized helplessness against The Conductor's injurious tone, which becomes more and more offensively patronizing.*) But I can't do anything for you. Here are all these people asleep in their berths, and I can't go round waking them up because you want to surprise your wife.

MR. ROBERTS: No, no; of course not. I never thought—

THE CONDUCTOR: My advice to *you* is to have a berth made up, and go to bed till we get to Boston, and surprise your wife by telling her what you tried to do.

MR. ROBERTS, *unable to resent the patronage of this suggestion*: Well, I don't know but I will.

THE CONDUCTOR, *going out*: The porter will make up the berth for you.

MR. ROBERTS, *to The Porter, who is about to pull down the upper berth over a vacant seat*: Ah! Er—I—I don't think I'll trouble you to make it up; it's so near morning now. Just bring me a pillow, and I'll try to get a nap without lying down.

He takes the vacant seat.

THE PORTER: All right, sah.

He goes to the end of the car, and returns with a pillow.

MR. ROBERTS: Ah—porter!

THE PORTER: Yes, sah.

MR. ROBERTS: Of course you didn't notice; but

you don't think you *did* notice who was in that berth yonder?

He indicates a certain berth.

THE PORTER: Dat's a gen'leman in dat berth, I think, sah.

MR. ROBERTS, *astutely*: There's a bonnet hanging from the hook at the top. I'm not sure, but it looks like my wife's bonnet.

THE PORTER, *evidently shaken by this reasoning, but recovering his firmness*: Yes, sah. But you can't depend upon de ladies to hang deir bonnets on de right hook. Jes' likely as not dat lady's took de hook at de foot of her berth instead o' de head. Sometimes dey takes both.

MR. ROBERTS: Ah! *(After a pause)* Porter!

THE PORTER: Yes, sah.

MR. ROBERTS: You wouldn't feel justified in looking?

THE PORTER: I couldn't, sah; I couldn't, indeed.

MR. ROBERTS, *reaching his left hand towards The Porter's, and pressing a half-dollar into his instantly responsive palm*: But there's nothing to prevent *my* looking if I feel perfectly sure of the bonnet?

THE PORTER: N-no, sah.

MR. ROBERTS: All right.

The Porter retires to the end of the car, and resumes the work of polishing the passengers' boots. After an interval of quiet, Mr. Roberts rises, and, looking about him with what he feels to be melodramatic stealth, approaches the suspected berth. He unloops the curtain with a trembling hand, and peers ineffectually in; he advances his head farther and farther into the darkened recess, and then suddenly dodges back again, with The Californian hanging to his neckcloth with one hand.

THE CALIFORNIAN, *savagely*: What do you want?

MR. ROBERTS, *struggling and breathless*: I—I—I want my wife.

THE CALIFORNIAN: Want your wife! Have *I* got your wife?

MR. ROBERTS: No—ah—that is—ah, excuse me —I thought you *were* my wife.

THE CALIFORNIAN, *getting out of the berth, but at the same time keeping hold of Mr. Roberts*: Thought I was your *wife*! Do I look like your wife? You can't play that on me, old man. Porter! Conductor!

MR. ROBERTS, *agonized*: Oh, I beseech you, my dear sir, don't—don't! I can explain it—I can

indeed. I know it has an ugly look; but if you will allow me two words—only two words—

MRS. ROBERTS, *suddenly parting the curtain of her berth, and springing out into the aisle, with her hair wildly dishevelled*: Edward!

MR. ROBERTS: Oh, Agnes, explain to this gentleman! *(Imploringly)* Don't you know me?

A VOICE: Make him show you the strawberry mark on his left arm.[1]

MRS. ROBERTS: Edward! Edward! *(The Californian mechanically loses his grip, and they fly into each other's embrace.)* Where did you come from?

A VOICE: Centre door, left hand, one back.

THE CONDUCTOR, *returning with his lantern*: Hallo! What's the matter here?

A VOICE: Train robbers! Throw up your hands! Tell the express-messenger to bring his safe.

The passengers emerge from their berths in various deshabille and bewilderment.

THE CONDUCTOR, *to Mr. Roberts*: Have *you* been making all this row, waking up my passengers?

THE CALIFORNIAN: No, sir, he hasn't. *I've* been making this row. This gentleman was peaceably looking for his wife, and I misunderstood him. You want to say anything to *me*?

THE CONDUCTOR, *silently taking The Californian's measure with his eye, as he stands six feet in his stockings*: If I did I'd get the biggest brakeman I could find to do it for me. *I've* got nothing to say except that I think you'd better all go back to bed again.

He goes out, and the passengers disappear one by one, leaving the Robertses and The Californian alone.

THE CALIFORNIAN, *to Mr. Roberts*: Stranger, I'm sorry I got you into this scrape.

MR. ROBERTS: Oh, don't speak of it, my dear sir. I'm sure we owe you all sorts of apologies, which I shall be most happy to offer you at my house in Boston, with every needful explanation. *(He takes out his card, and gives it to The Californian, who looks at it, and then looks at Mr. Roberts curiously.)* There's my address, and I'm sure we shall both be glad to have you call.

MRS. ROBERTS: Oh, yes, indeed. *(The Californian parts the curtains of his berth to re-enter it.)* Good-night, sir, and I assure you *we* shall do nothing more to disturb you—shall we, Edward?

[1] This is a reference to J. M. Morton's *Box & Cox* (1847).

MR. ROBERTS: No. And now, dear, I think you'd better go back to your berth.

MRS. ROBERTS: I couldn't sleep, and I shall not go back. Is this your place? I will just rest my head on your shoulder; and we must both be perfectly quiet. You've no idea what a nuisance I have been making of myself. The whole car was perfectly furious at me one time, I kept talking so loud. I don't know how I came to do it, but I suppose it was thinking about you and Willis meeting without knowing each other made me nervous, and I couldn't be still. I woke everybody up with my talking, and some of them were quite outrageous in their remarks; but I didn't blame them the least bit, for I should have been just as bad. That California gentleman was perfectly splendid, though. I can tell you *he* made them stop. We struck up quite a friendship. I told him I had a brother coming on from California, and he's going to try to think whether he knows Willis. (*Groans and inarticulate protests make themselves heard from different berths.*) I declare, I've got to talking again! There, now, I *shall* stop, and they won't hear another squeak from me the rest of the night. (*She lifts her head from her husband's shoulder.*) I wonder if baby will roll out. He *does* kick so! And I just sprang up and left him when I heard your voice, without putting anything to keep him in. I *must* go and have a look at him, or I never can settle down. No, no, don't you go, Edward; you'll be prying into all the wrong berths in the car, you poor thing! You stay here, and I'll be back in half a second. I wonder which is my berth. Ah! that's it; I know the one now. (*She makes a sudden dash at a berth, and pulling open the curtains is confronted by the bearded visage of The Californian.*) Ah! Ow! ow! Edward! Ah! I—I beg your pardon, sir; excuse me; I didn't know it was you. I came for my baby.

THE CALIFORNIAN, *solemnly*: I haven't got any baby, ma'am.

MRS ROBERTS: No—no—I thought *you* were my baby.

THE CALIFORNIAN: Perhaps I am, ma'am; I've lost so much sleep I could cry, anyway. Do I *look* like your baby?

MRS. ROBERTS: No, no, you don't. (*In distress that overcomes her mortification*) Oh, where *is* my baby? I left him all uncovered, and he'll take his death of cold, even if he doesn't roll out. Oh, Edward, Edward, help me to find baby!

MR. ROBERTS, *bustling aimlessly about*: Yes, yes; certainly, my dear. But don't be alarmed; we shall find him.

THE CALIFORNIAN, *getting out in his stocking feet*: We shall find him, ma'am, if we have to search every berth in this car. Don't you take on. That baby's going to be found if he's aboard the train, now, you bet! (*He looks about and then tears open the curtains of a berth at random.*) That your baby, ma'am?

MRS. ROBERTS, *flying upon the infant thus exposed*: Oh, *baby*, baby, baby! I thought I had lost you. Um! um! um!

> *She clasps him in her arms, and covers his face and neck with kisses.*

THE CALIFORNIAN, *as he gets back into his berth, sotto voce*: I wish I *had* been her baby.

MRS. ROBERTS, *returning with her husband to his seat, and bringing the baby with her*: There! Did you ever *see* such a sleeper, Edward? (*In her ecstasy she abandons all control of her voice, and joyfully exclaims.*) He has slept all through this excitement, without a wink.

A SOLEMN VOICE, *from one of the berths*: I envy him.

> *A laugh follows, in which all the passengers join.*

MRS. ROBERTS, *in a hoarse whisper, breaking a little with laughter*: Oh, my goodness! there I went again. But how funny! I assure you, Edward, that if their remarks had not been about me, I could have really quite enjoyed some of them. I wish there had been somebody here to take them down. And I hope I shall see some of the speakers in the morning before— Edward, I've got an idea!

MR. ROBERTS, *endeavoring to teach his wife by example to lower her voice, which has risen again*: What—what is it, my dear?

MRS. ROBERTS: Why, don't you see? How perfectly ridiculous it was of me not to think of it before! though I did think of it once, and hadn't the courage to insist upon it. But of course it is; and it accounts for his being so polite and kind to me through all, and it's the only thing that can. Yes, yes, it *must* be.

MR. ROBERTS, *mystified*: What?

MRS. ROBERTS: Willis.

MR. ROBERTS: Who?

MRS ROBERTS: This Californian.

MR. ROBERTS: Oh!

MRS. ROBERTS: No *stranger* could have been so

patient, and—and—attentive; and I know that he recognized me from the first, and he's just kept it up for a joke, so as to surprise us, and have a good laugh at us when we get to Boston. Of *course* it's Willis.

MR. ROBERTS, *doubtfully*: Do you think so, my dear?

MRS. ROBERTS: I *know* it. Didn't you notice how he looked at your card? And I want you to go at once and speak to him, and turn the tables on him.

MR. ROBERTS: I—I'd rather *not*, my dear.

MRS. ROBERTS: Why, Edward, what can you mean?

MR. ROBERTS: He's very violent. Suppose it *shouldn't* be Willis?

MRS. ROBERTS: Nonsense! It *is* Willis. Come, let's both go and just tax him with it. He can't deny it, after all he's done for me. (*She pulls her reluctant husband toward The Californian's berth, and they each draw a curtain.*) Willis!

THE CALIFORNIAN, *with plaintive endurance*: Well, ma'am?

MRS. ROBERTS, *triumphantly*: There! I knew it was you all along. How could you play such a joke on me?

THE CALIFORNIAN: I didn't know there'd been any joke; but I suppose there must have been, if you say so. Who am I now, ma'am—your husband, or your baby, or your husband's wife, or—

MRS. ROBERTS: How funny you are! You *know* you're Willis Campbell, my only brother. Now *don't* try to keep it up any longer, Willis.

VOICES, *from various berths*: Give us a rest, Willis! Joke's too thin, Willis! You're played out, Willis! Own up, old fellow—own up!

THE CALIFORNIAN, *issuing from his berth, and walking up and down the aisle, as before, till quiet is restored*: I haven't got any sister, and my name ain't Willis, and it ain't Campbell. I'm very sorry, because I'd like to oblige you any way I could.

MRS. ROBERTS, *in deep mortification*: It's I who ought to apologize, and I do most humbly. I don't know what to say; but when I got to thinking about it, and how kind you had been to me, and how sweet you had been under all my—interruptions, I felt perfectly sure that you couldn't be a mere stranger, and then the idea struck me that you must be my brother in disguise; and I was so certain of it that I couldn't help just letting you know that we'd found you out, and—

MR. ROBERTS, *offering a belated and feeble moral support*: Yes.

MRS. ROBERTS, *promptly turning upon him*: And *you* ought to have kept me from making such a simpleton of myself, Edward.

THE CALIFORNIAN, *soothingly*: Well, ma'am, that ain't always so easy. A man may mean well, and yet not be able to carry out his intentions. But it's all right. And I reckon we'd better try to quiet down again, and get what rest we can.

MRS. ROBERTS: Why, yes, certainly; and I will try—oh, I will *try* not to disturb you again. And if there's anything we can do in reparation after we reach Boston, we shall be *so* glad to do it!

They bow themselves away, and return to their seat, while The Californian re-enters his berth.

III.

The train stops at Framingham, and The Porter comes in with a passenger, whom he shows to the seat opposite Mr. and Mrs. Roberts.

THE PORTER: You can sit here, sah. We'll be in, in about half an hour now. Hang up your bag for you, sah?

THE PASSENGER: No, leave it on the seat here.

The Porter goes out, and the Robertses maintain a dejected silence. The bottom of the bag, thrown carelessly on the seat, is toward the Robertses, who regard it listlessly.

MRS. ROBERTS, *suddenly clutching her husband's arm, and hissing in his ear*: See! (*She points to the white lettering on the bag, where the name "Willis Campbell, San Francisco," is distinctly legible.*) But it can't be; it must be some other Campbell. I can't risk it.

MR. ROBERTS: But there's the name. It would be very strange if there were two people from San Francisco of exactly the same name. I will speak.

MRS. ROBERTS, *as wildly as one can in whisper*: No, no, I can't let you. We've made ourselves the laughing-stock of the whole car already with our mistakes, and I can't go on. I would rather perish than ask him. You don't suppose it *could* be? No, it couldn't. There may be twenty Willis Campbells in San Francisco, and there probably are. Do you think he looks like me? He has a straight nose; but you can't tell anything about the lower part of his face, the beard covers it so; and I can't make out the color of his eyes by this light. But of course, it's all nonsense. Still, if it *should* be! It would be very stupid of us to ride all the way from Framingham to Boston with that name staring one in the eyes. I *wish* he would turn it away. If it really turned out to *be* Willis, he would think we were awfully stiff and cold. But I can't help it; I *can't* go attacking every stranger I see, and accusing him of being my brother. No, no, I can't, and I *won't*, and that's all about it. (*She leans forward, and addresses the stranger with sudden sweetness.*) Excuse me, sir, but I *am* very much interested by the name on your bag. Not that I think you are even acquainted with him, and there are probably a great many of them there; but your coming from the same city, and all, *does* seem a little queer, and I hope you won't think me intrusive in speaking to you, because if you *should* happen, by the thousandth of a chance, to be the right one, I should be *so* happy!

CAMPBELL: The right what, madam?

MRS. ROBERTS: The right Willis Campbell.

CAMPBELL: I hope I'm not the wrong one; though after a week's pull on the railroad it's pretty hard for a man to tell which Willis Campbell he is. May I ask if your Willis Campbell had friends in Boston?

MRS. ROBERTS, *eagerly*: He had a sister and a brother-in-law and a nephew.

CAMPBELL: Name of Roberts?

MRS. ROBERTS: Every one.

CAMPBELL: Then you're—

MRS. ROBERTS, *ecstatically*: Agnes.

CAMPBELL: And he's—

MRS. ROBERTS: Mr. Roberts!

CAMPBELL: And the baby's—

MRS. ROBERTS: Asleep!

CAMPBELL: Then I *am* the right one.

MRS. ROBERTS: Oh, Willis! Willis! Willis! To think of our meeting in this way! (*She kisses and embraces him, while Mr. Roberts shakes one of his hands which he finds disengaged.*) How in the world did it happen?

CAMPBELL: Oh, I found myself a little ahead of time, and I stopped off with an old friend of mine at Framingham; I didn't want to disappoint you when you came to meet this train, or get you up last night at midnight.

MRS. ROBERTS: And I was in Albany, and I've been moving heaven and earth to get home before you arrived; and Edward came aboard at Worcester to surprise me, and— Oh, you've never seen the baby! I'll run right and get him this instant, just as he is, and bring him. Edward, you be explaining to Willis— Oh, my goodness! (*Looking wildly about*) I don't remember the berth, and I shall be sure to wake up that poor California gentleman again. What shall I do?

CAMPBELL: What California gentleman?

MRS. ROBERTS: Oh, somebody we've been stirring up the whole blessed night. First I took him for baby, and then Edward took him for me, and then I took him for baby again, and then we both took him for you.

CAMPBELL: Did he look like any of us?

MRS. ROBERTS: Like *us*? He's eight feet tall, if he's an inch, in his stockings—and he's always in them—and he has a long black beard and mustaches, and he's very lanky, and stoops over a good deal; but he's just as lovely as he can be, and live, and he's been as kind and patient as twenty Jobs.

CAMPBELL: Speaks in a sort of soft, slow grind?

MRS. ROBERTS: Yes.

CAMPBELL: Gentle and deferential to ladies?

MRS. ROBERTS: As pie.

CAMPBELL: It's Tom Goodall. I'll have him out of there in half a second. I want you to take him home with you, Agnes. He's the best fellow in the world. *Which* is his berth?

MRS. ROBERTS: Don't ask me, Willis. But if you'd go for baby, you'll be sure to find *him*.

MR. ROBERTS, *timidly indicating a berth*: I think that's the one.

CAMPBELL, *plunging at it, and pulling the curtains open*: You, old Tom Goodall!

THE CALIFORNIAN, *appearing*: I ain't any Tom Goodall. My name's Abram Sawyer.

CAMPBELL, *falling back*: Well, sir, you're right. I'm awfully sorry to disturb you; but, from my sister's description here, I felt certain you must be my old friend Tom Goodall.

THE CALIFORNIAN: I ain't surprised at it. I'm only surprised I *ain't* Tom Goodall. I've been a baby twice, and I've been a man's wife once, and once I've been a long-lost brother.

CAMPBELL, *laughing*: Oh, they've found *him*. I'm the long-lost brother.

THE CALIFORNIAN, *sleepily*: Has she found the other one?

CAMPBELL: Yes; all right, I believe.

THE CALIFORNIAN: Has *he* found what *he* wanted?

CAMPBELL: Yes; we're all together here. (*The Californian makes a movement to get into bed again.*) Oh, don't! You'd better make a night of it now. It's almost morning anyway. We want you to go home with us, and Mrs. Roberts will give you a bed at her house, and let you sleep a week.

THE CALIFORNIAN: Well, I reckon you're right, stranger. I seem to be in the hands of Providence to-night, anyhow. (*He pulls on his boots and coat, and takes his seat beside Campbell.*) I reckon there ain't any use in fighting against Providence.

MRS. ROBERTS, *briskly, as if she had often tried it and failed*: Oh, not the least in the world. I'm sure it was all intended; and if you had turned out to be Willis at last, I should be *certain* of it. What surprises me is that you shouldn't turn out to be anybody, after all.

THE CALIFORNIAN: Yes, it is kind of curious. But I couldn't help it. I did my best.

MRS. ROBERTS: Oh, don't speak of it. We are the ones who ought to apologize. But if you only had been somebody, it would have been such a good joke! We could always have had such a laugh over it, don't you see?

THE CALIFORNIAN: Yes, ma'am, it would have been funny. But I hope you've enjoyed it as it is.

MRS. ROBERTS: Oh, very much, thanks to you. Only I can't seem to get reconciled to your not being anybody, after all. You *must* at least be some one we've heard about, don't you think? It's so strange that you and Willis never even met. Don't you think you have some acquaintances in common?

CAMPBELL: Look here, Agnes, do you always shout at the top of your voice in this way when you converse in a sleeping-car?

MRS. ROBERTS: Was I talking loud again? Well, you can't help it, if you want to make people hear you.

CAMPBELL: But there must be a lot of them who don't want to hear you. I wonder that the passengers who are not blood-relations don't throw things at you—boots and hand-bags and language.

MRS. ROBERTS: Why, that's what they've *been* doing—language at least—and I'm only surprised they're not doing it now.

THE CALIFORNIAN, *rising*: They'd better not, ma'am.

He patrols the car from end to end, and quells some rising murmurs, halting at the rebellious berths as he passes.

MRS. ROBERTS, *enraptured by his championship*: Oh, he *must* be some connection. (*She glances through the window.*) I do believe that was Newton, or Newtonville, or West Newton, or Newton Centre. I must run and wake up baby, and get him dressed. I sha'n't want to wait an instant after we get in. Why, we're slowing up! Why, I do believe we're there! Edward, we're there! Only fancy being there already!

MR. ROBERTS: Yes, my dear. Only we're not quite there yet. Hadn't we better call your Aunt Mary?

MRS. ROBERTS: I'd forgotten her.

CAMPBELL: Is Aunt Mary with you?

MRS. ROBERTS: To be sure she is. Didn't I tell you? She came on expressly to meet you.

CAMPBELL, *starting up impetuously*: Which berth is she in?

MRS. ROBERTS: Right over baby.

CAMPBELL: And which berth is baby in?

MRS. ROBERTS, *distractedly*: Why, that's just what I can't *tell*. It was bad enough when they were all filled up; but now, since the people have begun to come out of them, and some of them are made into seats, I *can't* tell.

THE CALIFORNIAN: I'll look for you, ma'am. I should like to wake up all the wrong passengers on this car. I'd take a pleasure in it. If you could make sure of any berth that *ain't* the one, I'd begin on that.

MRS. ROBERTS: I can't even be sure of the wrong one. No, no; you mustn't— (*The Californian moves away, and pauses in front of one of the berths, looking back inquiringly at Mrs. Roberts.*) Oh, don't ask *me!* I can't tell. (*To Campbell*) Isn't he amusing? So like all those Californians that one reads of—so chivalrous and *so* humorous!

AUNT MARY, *thrusting her head from the curtains of the berth before which The Californian is standing*: Go along with you! What do you want?

THE CALIFORNIAN: Aunt Mary.

AUNT MARY: Go away. Aunt Mary, indeed!

MRS. ROBERTS, *turning toward her, followed by Campbell and Mr. Roberts*: Why, Aunt Mary, it *is* you! And here's Willis, and here's Edward.

AUNT MARY: Nonsense! How did they get aboard?

MRS. ROBERTS: Edward came on at Worcester, and Willis at Framingham, to surprise me.

AUNT MARY: And a very silly performance. Let them wait till I'm dressed, and then I'll talk to them. Send for the porter. (*She withdraws her head behind the curtain, and then thrusts it out again.*) And who, pray, may *this* be?

She indicates The Californian.

MRS. ROBERTS: Oh, a friend of ours from California, who's been so kind to us all night, and who's going home with us.

AUNT MARY: Another ridiculous surprise, I suppose. But he shall not surprise *me.* Young man, isn't your name Sawyer?

THE CALIFORNIAN: Yes, ma'am.

AUNT MARY: Abram?

THE CALIFORNIAN: Abram Sawyer. You're right there, ma'am.

MRS. ROBERTS: Oh! oh! I knew it! I knew that he must be somebody belonging to us. Oh, thank you, aunty, for thinking—

AUNT MARY: Don't be absurd, Agnes. Then you're my—

A VOICE, *from one of the berths*: Long-lost stepson. Found! found at last!

The Californian looks vainly round in an endeavor to identify the speaker, and then turns again to Aunt Mary.

AUNT MARY: Weren't your parents from Bath?

THE CALIFORNIAN, *eagerly*: Both of 'em, ma'am—both of 'em.

THE VOICE: O my prophetic soul, my uncle!

AUNT MARY: Then you're my old friend Kate Harris's daughter?

THE CALIFORNIAN: I might be her *son*, ma'am; but *my* mother's name was Susan Wakeman.

AUNT MARY, *in sharp disgust*: Call the porter, please.

She withdraws her head and pulls her curtains together; the rest look blankly at one another.

CAMPBELL: Another failure, and just when we thought we were sure of you. I don't know what we shall do about you, Mr. Sawyer.

THE VOICE: Adopt him.

CAMPBELL: That's a good idea. We will adopt you. You shall be our adoptive—

THE VOICE: Baby boy.

ANOTHER VOICE: Wife.

A THIRD VOICE: Brother.

A FOURTH VOICE: Early friend.

A FIFTH VOICE: Kate Harris's daughter.

CAMPBELL, *laying his hand on The Californian's shoulder, and breaking into a laugh*: Don't mind them. They don't mean anything. It's just their way. You come home with my sister, and spend Christmas, and let us devote the rest of our lives to making your declining years happy.

VOICES: Good for you, Willis! We'll all come! No ceremony! Small and early!

CAMPBELL, *looking round*: We appear to have fallen in with a party of dry-goods drummers. It makes a gentleman feel like an intruder. (*The train stops; he looks out of the window.*) We've arrived. Come, Agnes; come, Roberts; come, Mr. Sawyer—let's be going.

They gather up their several wraps and bags, and move with great dignity toward the door.

AUNT MARY, *putting out her head*: Agnes! If you must forget your aunt, at least remember your child.

MRS. ROBERTS, *running back in an agony of remorse*: Oh, baby, did I forget you?

CAMPBELL: Oh, aunty, did she forget you? (*He runs back, and extends his arms to his aunt.*) Let me help you down, Aunt Mary.

AUNT MARY: Nonsense, Willis. Send the porter.

CAMPBELL, *turning round and confronting The Porter*: He was here upon instinct. Shall he fetch a step-ladder?

AUNT MARY: He will know what to do. Go away, Willis; go away with that child, Agnes. If I should happen to fall on you— (*They retreat; the curtain drops and her voice is heard behind it addressing The Porter.*) Give me your hand; now your back; now your knee. So! And very well done, thanks.

The Register

[1883]

Of all his plays, the one that Howells felt was the most peculiarly American was *The Register*. In "A Letter to the Publisher," in *Minor Dramas* [Edinburgh: David Douglas, 1907], he commented on this work:

> The third in the series was written, one heavenly month of May, in Verona where an Italian friend had put me up at the Circolo Letterario, and had told me that I should find the most comfort and quiet in a certain large, round room, frequented mainly by ecclesiastics. These were for some reason then mostly in the country, and now and then one looked silently in on me, coming like a shadow and so departing, and I always felt that *The Register*, though such an arch-American love-story, and operated by an American mechanism which, I am afraid must make it unintelligible even to the English readers, ought to have been dedicated to the reverend clergy of Verona. If they would now allow me tardily to inscribe it to them, I should do so with regard for their cloth which I never failed to feel for it in Italy, or elsewhere.

The simplicity and straightforwardness of the action, as Howells portrays it, add greatly to the charm of what might have been a situation farce. Consequently, the homelike realism not only gives substance to the comedy and the romance but also shows most of the play to be quite believable. When it is not, one willingly suspends his disbelief. It would be impossible, for example, for Miss Reed to overhear through the register the talk of the gentlemen in the next apartment while Miss Spaulding practices the piano in the same room with her. But this is theater illusion, not actual life, and Howells realizes the distinction and credits his audience with understanding.

Although this contrivance—the register—is the vehicle of the play, the characterizations are important in whatever success the play achieves. Grinnidge is witty and he listens to Ransom; that is all the dramatist requires of him. Miss Spaulding is a similar type. That leaves Ransom and Miss Reed. Perhaps a man in love is entitled to be inconsistent; if so, one has no quarrel with the action here. Perhaps, too, the inconsistency exists only between the painter at Ponkwasset who lets his pride dictate to him and the man in Boston whose heart takes no commands. At any rate, no reader of Howells would expect Ransom to be able to contend with Miss Reed, a typical Howells girl who enjoys toying with her own emotions as well as those of others. She is an actress, and she acts her part well, dramatizing and overdramatizing her feelings. As usual with those plays not featuring the Campbells or the Robertses, the men are the weaker instruments— tamed, tuned, and played upon by such women as Miss Reed.

Probably this play never reached the professional stage, although amateur groups undoubtedly performed it. A letter to Howells from his brother Joseph A. Howells (August 12, 1886, Hayes Memorial Library) mentions a young lady who "says that they had 'The Register' for a church entertainment."

The Register[1]

I.

SCENE: *In an upper chamber of a boarding-house in Melanchthon Place, Boston, a mature, plain young lady, with every appearance of establishing herself in the room for the first time, moves about, bestowing little touches of decoration here and there, and talking with another young lady, whose voice comes through the open doorway of an inner room.*

MISS ETHEL REED, *from within*: What in the world are you doing, Nettie?

MISS HENRIETTA SPAULDING: Oh, sticking up a household god or two. What are you doing?

MISS REED: Despairing.

MISS SPAULDING: Still?

MISS REED, *tragically*: *Still!* How soon did you expect me to stop? I am here on the sofa, where I flung myself two hours ago, and I don't think I shall ever get up. There is no reason *why* I ever should.

MISS SPAULDING, *suggestively*: Dinner.

MISS REED: Oh, dinner! Dinner, to a broken heart!

MISS SPAULDING: I don't believe your heart is broken.

MISS REED: But I tell you it is! I ought to know when my own heart is broken, I should hope. What makes you think it isn't?

MISS SPAULDING: Oh, it's happened so often!

MISS REED: But this is a real case. You ought to feel my forehead. It's as *hot!*

MISS SPAULDING: You ought to get up and help me put this room to rights, and then you would feel better.

MISS REED: No; I should feel worse. The idea of household gods makes me sick. Sylvan deities are what *I* want; the great god Pan among the cat-tails and arrow-heads in the "ma'sh" at Ponkwasset; the dryads of the birch woods—there are no oaks; the nymphs that haunt the heights and hollows of the dear old mountain; the—

[1] The text used here is from *The Sleeping Car and Other Farces.*

MISS SPAULDING: Wha-a-at? I can't hear a word you say.

MISS REED: That's because you keep fussing about so. Why don't you be quiet, if you want to hear? (*She lifts her voice to its highest pitch, with a pause for distinctness between the words.*) I'm heart-broken for—Ponkwasset. The dryads—of the—birch woods. The nymphs—and the great—god—Pan—in the reeds—by the river. And all—that—sort of—thing!

MISS SPAULDING: You know very well you're not.

MISS REED: I'm not? What's the reason I'm not? Then, what am I heart-broken for?

MISS SPAULDING: You're not heart-broken at all. You know very well that he'll call before we've been here twenty-four hours.

MISS REED: Who?

MISS SPAULDING: The great god Pan.

MISS REED: Oh, how cruel you are, to mock me so! Come in here, and sympathize a little! Do, Nettie.

MISS SPAULDING: No; you come out here and utilize a little. I'm acting for your best good, as they say at Ponkwasset.

MISS REED: When they want to be disagreeable!

MISS SPAULDING: If this room isn't in order by the time he calls, you'll be everlastingly disgraced.

MISS REED: I'm that now. I can't be more so—there's that comfort. What makes you think he'll call?

MISS SPAULDING: Because he's a gentleman, and will want to apologize. He behaved very rudely to you.

MISS REED: No, Nettie; *I* behaved rudely to *him.* Yes! Besides, if he behaved rudely, he was no gentleman. It's a contradiction in terms, don't you see? But I'll tell you what I'm going to do if he comes. I'm going to show a proper spirit for once in my life. I'm going to refuse to see him. *You've* got to see him.

MISS SPAULDING: Nonsense!

MISS REED: Why nonsense? Oh, why? Expound!

MISS SPAULDING: Because he wasn't rude to me, and he doesn't want to see me. Because I'm plain, and you're pretty.

MISS REED: I'm *not!* You know it perfectly well. I'm hideous.

MISS SPAULDING: Because I'm poor, and you're a person of independent property.

MISS REED: *Dependent* property, I should call it: just enough to be useless on! But that's insulting to *him.* How can you say it's because I have a little money?

MISS SPAULDING: Well, then, I won't. I take it back. I'll say it's because you're young, and I'm old.

MISS REED: You're *not* old. You're as young as anybody, Nettie Spaulding. And you know I'm not young; I'm twenty-seven, if I'm a day. I'm just dropping into the grave. But I can't argue with you, miles off so, any longer. (*Miss Reed appears at the open door, dragging languidly after her the shawl which she had evidently drawn round her on the sofa; her fair hair is a little disordered, and she presses it into shape with one hand as she comes forward; a lovely flush vies with a heavenly pallor in her cheeks; she looks a little pensive in the arching eyebrows, and a little humorous about the dimpled mouth.*) Now I can prove that you are entirely wrong. Where were you?—This room *is* rather an improvement over the one we had last winter. There is more of a view—(*she goes to the window*) of the houses across the Place; and I always think the swell front gives a pretty shape to a room. I'm sorry they've stopped building them. Your piano goes very nicely into that little alcove. Yes, we're quite palatial. And, on the whole, I'm glad there's no fireplace. It's a pleasure at times; but for the most part it's a vanity and a vexation, getting dust and ashes over everything. Yes; after all, give me the good old-fashioned, clean, convenient register! Ugh! My feet are like ice. (*She pulls an easy-chair up to the register in the corner of the room, and pushes open its valves with the toe of her slipper. As she settles herself luxuriously in the chair, and poises her feet daintily over the register*) Ah, this is something like! Henrietta Spaulding, ma'am! Did I ever tell you that you were the best friend I have in the world?

MISS SPAULDING, *who continues her work of arranging the room*: Often.

MISS REED: Did you ever believe it?

MISS SPAULDING: Never.

MISS REED: Why?

MISS SPAULDING, *thoughtfully regarding a vase which she holds in her hand, after several times shifting it from a bracket to the corner of her* piano *and back*: I wish I could tell where you *do* look best!

MISS REED, *leaning forward wistfully, with her hands clasped and resting on her knees*: I wish you would tell me *why* you don't believe you're the best friend I have in the world.

MISS SPAULDING, *finally placing the vase on the bracket*: Because you've said so too often.

MISS REED: Oh, that's no reason! I can prove to you that you are. Who else but you would have taken in a homeless and friendless creature like me, and let her stay bothering round in demoralizing idleness, while you were seriously teaching the young idea how to drub the piano?

MISS SPAULDING: Anybody who wanted a room-mate as much as I did, and could have found one willing to pay more than her share of the lodging.

MISS REED, *thoughtfully*: Do you think so, Henrietta?

MISS SPAULDING: I know so.

MISS REED: And you're not afraid that you wrong yourself?

MISS SPAULDING: Not the least.

MISS REED: Well, be it so—as they say in novels. I will not contradict you; I will not say you are my *best* friend; I will merely say that you are my *only* friend. Come here, Henrietta. Draw up your chair, and put your little hand in mine.

MISS SPAULDING, *with severe distrust*: What do you want, Ethel Reed?

MISS REED: I want—I want—to talk it over with you.

MISS SPAULDING, *recoiling*: I knew it! Well, now, we've talked it over enough; we've talked it over till there's nothing left of it.

MISS REED: Oh, there's everything left! It remains in all its original enormity. Perhaps we shall get some new light upon it. (*She extends a pleading hand towards Miss Spaulding.*) Come, Henrietta, my only friend, shake!—as the "good Indians" say. Let your Ethel pour her hackneyed sorrows into your bosom. Such an uncomfortable image, it always seems, doesn't it, pouring sorrows into bosoms! Come!

MISS SPAULDING, *decidedly*: No, I won't! And you needn't try wheedling any longer. I won't sympathize with you on that basis at all.

MISS REED: What shall I try, then, if you won't let me try wheedling?

MISS SPAULDING, *going to the piano and opening it*: Try courage; try self-respect.

MISS REED: Oh, dear! when I haven't a morsel

of either. Are you going to practise, you cruel maid?

MISS SPAULDING: Of course I am. It's half-past four, and if I don't do it now I sha'n't be prepared to-morrow for Miss Robins: she takes this piece.

MISS REED: Well, well, perhaps it's all for the best. If music be the food of—umph-ump!—you know what!—play on.

They both laugh, and Miss Spaulding pushes back a little from the piano, and wheels toward her friend, letting one hand rest slightly on the keys.

MISS SPAULDING: Ethel Reed, you're the most ridiculous girl in the world.

MISS REED: Correct!

MISS SPAULDING: And I don't believe you ever were in love, or ever will be.

MISS REED: Ah, there you wrong me, Henrietta! I have been, and I shall be—lots of times.

MISS SPAULDING: Well, what do you want to say now? You must hurry, for I can't lose any more time.

MISS REED: I will free my mind with neatness and despatch. I simply wish to go over the whole affair, from Alfred to Omaha;[1] and you've got to let me talk as much slang and nonsense as I want. And then I'll skip all the details I can. Will you?

MISS SPAULDING, *with impatient patience*: Oh, I suppose so!

MISS REED: That's very sweet of you, though you don't look it. Now, where was I? Oh, yes; do you think it was forth-putting at all, to ask him if he would give me the lessons?

MISS SPAULDING: It depends upon why you asked him.

MISS REED: I asked him from—from— Let me see; I asked him because—from— Yes, I say it boldly; I asked him from an enthusiasm for art, and a sincere wish to learn the use of oil, as he called it. Yes!

MISS SPAULDING: Are you sure?

MISS REED: Sure? Well, we will say that I am, for the sake of argument. And, having secured this basis, the question is whether I wasn't bound to offer him pay at the end, and whether he wasn't wrong to take my doing so in dudgeon.

MISS SPAULDING: Yes, I think he was wrong. And the terms of his refusal were very ungentle-

[1] See Revelations, I:8.

manly. He ought to apologize most amply and humbly. (*At a certain expression in Miss Reed's face, she adds, with severity.*) Unless you're keeping back the main point. You usually do. Are you?

MISS REED: No, no. I've told you everything —everything!

MISS SPAULDING: Then I say, as I said from the beginning, that he behaved very badly. It was very awkward and very painful, but you've really nothing to blame yourself for.

MISS REED, *ruefully*: No-o-o!

MISS SPAULDING: What do you mean by that sort of "No"?

MISS REED: Nothing.

MISS SPAULDING, *sternly*: Yes, you do, Ethel.

MISS REED: I don't, really. What makes you think I do?

MISS SPAULDING: It sounded very dishonest.

MISS REED: Did it? I didn't mean it to.

Her friend breaks down with a laugh, while Miss Reed preserves a demure countenance.

MISS SPAULDING: What *are* you keeping back?

MISS REED: Nothing at all—less than nothing! I never thought it was worth mentioning.

MISS SPAULDING: Are you telling me the truth?

MISS REED: I'm telling you the truth and something more. You can't ask better than that, can you?

MISS SPAULDING, *turning to her music again*: Certainly not.

MISS REED, *in a pathetic wail*: O Henrietta! do you abandon me thus? Well, I will tell you, heartless girl! I've only kept it back till now because it was so extremely mortifying to my pride as an artist—as a student of oil. Will you hear me?

MISS SPAULDING, *beginning to play*: No.

MISS REED, *with burlesque wildness*: You shall! (*Miss Spaulding involuntarily desists.*) There was a moment—a fatal moment—when he said he thought he ought to tell me that if I found oil amusing I could go on; but that he didn't believe I should ever learn to use it, and he couldn't let me take lessons from him with the expectation that I should. There!

MISS SPAULDING, *with awful reproach*: And you call that less than nothing? I've almost a mind never to speak to you again, Ethel. How *could* you deceive me so?

MISS REED: Was it really deceiving? *I* shouldn't call it so. And I needed your sympathy so much, and I knew I shouldn't get it unless you thought I was altogether in the right.

MISS SPAULDING: You are altogether in the *wrong!* And it's *you* that ought to apologize to *him*—on your bended knees. How *could* you offer him money after that? I wonder at you, Ethel!

MISS REED: Why—don't you see, Nettie?—I did keep on taking the lessons of him. I did find oil amusing—or the oilist—and I kept on. Of course I had to, off there in a farmhouse full of lady boarders, and he the only gentleman short of Crawford's. Strike, but hear me, Henrietta Spaulding![1] What was I to do about the half-dozen lessons I had taken before he told me I should never learn to use oil? Was I to offer to pay him for these, and not for the rest; or was I to treat the whole series as gratuitous? I used to lie awake thinking about it. I've got some little tact, but I couldn't find any way out of the trouble. It was a box—yes, a box of the deepest dye! And the whole affair having got to be—something else, don't you know?—made it all the worse. And if he'd only—only— But he didn't. Not a syllable, not a breath! And there I was. I *had* to offer him the money. And it's almost killed me—the way he took my offering it, and now the way you take it! And it's all of a piece. (*Miss Reed suddenly snatches her handkerchief from her pocket, and buries her face in it.*) Oh, dear—oh, dear! Oh!—hu, hu, hu!

MISS SPAULDING, *relenting*: It was awkward.

MISS REED: Awkward! You seem to think that because I carry things off lightly I have no feeling.

MISS SPAULDING: You know I don't think that, Ethel.

MISS REED, *pursuing her advantage*: I don't know it from you, Nettie. I've tried and *tried* to pass it off as a joke, and to treat it as something funny; but I can tell you it's no joke at all.

MISS SPAULDING, *sympathetically*: I see, dear.

MISS REED: It's not that I care for him—

MISS SPAULDING: Why, of course.

MISS REED: For I don't in the least. He is horrid every way: blunt, and rude, and horrid. I never cared for him. But I care for myself! He has put me in the position of having done an unkind thing—an unladylike thing—when I was only

doing what I had to do. Why need he have taken it the way he did? Why couldn't he have said politely that he couldn't accept the money because he hadn't earned it? Even *that* would have been mortifying enough. But he must go and be so violent, and rush off, and— Oh, I never could have treated anybody so!

MISS SPAULDING: Not unless you were very fond of them.

MISS REED: What?

MISS SPAULDING: Not unless you were very fond of them.

MISS REED, *putting away her handkerchief*: Oh, nonsense, Nettie! He never cared anything for me, or he couldn't have acted so. But no matter for that. He has fixed everything so that it can never be got straight—never in the world. It will just have to remain a hideous mass of—of—I don't know what; and I have simply got to go on withering with despair at the point where I left off. But I don't care! That's one comfort.

MISS SPAULDING: I don't believe he'll let you wither long, Ethel.

MISS REED: He's let me wither for twenty-four hours already! But it's nothing to me, now, *how* long he lets me wither. I'm perfectly satisfied to have the affair remain as it is. I am in the right, and if he comes I shall refuse to see him.

MISS SPAULDING: Oh, no, you won't, Ethel!

MISS REED: Yes, I shall. I shall receive him very coldly. I won't listen to any excuse from him.

MISS SPAULDING: Oh, yes, you will, Ethel!

MISS REED: No, I shall not. If he wishes me to listen he must begin by humbling himself in the dust—yes, the dust, Nettie! I won't take anything short of it. I insist that he shall realize that I have suffered.

MISS SPAULDING: Perhaps he has suffered too!

MISS REED: Oh, *he* suffered!

MISS SPAULDING: You know that he was perfectly devoted to you.

MISS REED: He never said so.

MISS SPAULDING: Perhaps he didn't dare.

MISS REED: He dared to be very insolent to me.

MISS SPAULDING: And you know you liked him very much.

MISS REED: I won't let you say that, Nettie Spaulding. I *didn't* like him. I respected and admired him; but I didn't *like* him. He will never come near me; but if he does he has to begin by—by— Let me see, what shall I make him begin by doing? (*She casts up her eyes for inspiration while she leans forward over the register.*)

[1] "Eurybiades lifting up his staff as if he were going to strike, Themistocles said: 'Strike if you will, but hear.'" *Apothegms of Kings and Great Commanders, Themistocles,* translation of Plutarch by Dryden, 134.

Yes, I will! He has got to begin by taking that money!

MISS SPAULDING: Ethel, you *wouldn't* put that affront upon a sensitive and high-spirited man!

MISS REED: Wouldn't I? You wait and *see*, Miss Spaulding! He shall take the money, and he shall sign a receipt for it. I'll draw up the receipt now, so as to have it ready, and I shall ask him to sign it the very moment he enters this door—the very instant! *(She takes a portfolio from the table near her, without rising, and writes.)* "Received from Miss Ethel Reed one hundred and twenty-five dollars, in full, for twenty-five lessons in oil-painting." There—when Mr. Oliver Ransom has signed this little document he may begin to talk; not before!

She leans back in her chair with an air of pitiless determination.

MISS SPAULDING: But, Ethel, you don't mean to make him take money for the lessons he gave you after he told you you couldn't learn anything?

MISS REED, *after a moment's pause*: Yes, I do. This is to punish him. I don't wish for justice now; I wish for vengeance! At first I would have compromised on the six lessons, or on none at all, if he had behaved nicely; but after what's happened I shall insist upon paying him for every lesson, so as to make him feel that the whole thing, from first to last, was a purely business transaction on my part. Yes, a *purely*—BUSINESS—TRANSACTION!

MISS SPAULDING, *turning to her music*: Then I've got nothing more to say to you, Ethel Reed.

MISS REED: I don't say but what, after he's taken the money and signed the receipt, I'll listen to anything else he's got to say, very willingly.

Miss Spaulding makes no answer, but begins to play with a scientific absorption, feeling her way fitfully through the new piece, while Miss Reed, seated by the register, trifles with the book she has taken from the table.

II.

The interior of the room of Miss Spaulding and Miss Reed remains in view, while the scene discloses, on the other side of the partition wall in the same house, the bachelor apartment of Mr. Samuel Grinnidge. Mr. Grinnidge in his dressing-gown and slippers, with his pipe in his mouth, has the effect of having just come in; his friend Mr. Oliver

Ransom stands at the window, staring out into the November weather.

GRINNIDGE: How long have you been waiting here?

RANSOM: Ten minutes—ten years. How should I know?

GRINNIDGE: Well, I don't know who else should. Get back to-day?

RANSOM: Last night.

GRINNIDGE: Well, take off your coat, and pull up to the register, and warm your poor feet. *(He puts his hand out over the register.)* Confound it! somebody's got the register open in the next room! You see, one pipe comes up from the furnace and branches into a V just under the floor, and professes to heat both rooms. But it don't. There was a fellow in there last winter who used to get all my heat. Used to go out and leave his register open, and I'd come in here just before dinner and find this place as cold as a barn. We had a running fight of it all winter. The man who got his register open first in the morning got all the heat for the day, for it never turned the other way when it started in one direction. Used to almost suffocate—warm, muggy days—maintaining my rights. Some piano-pounder in there this winter, it seems. Hear? And she hasn't lost any time in learning the trick of the register. What kept you so late in the country?

RANSOM, *after an absent-minded pause*: Grinnidge, I wish you would give me some advice.

GRINNIDGE: You can have all you want of it at the market price.

RANSOM: I don't mean your legal advice.

GRINNIDGE: I'm sorry. What have you been doing?

RANSOM: I've been making an ass of myself!

GRINNIDGE: Wasn't that rather superfluous?

RANSOM: If you please, yes. But now, if you're capable of listening to me without any further display of your cross-examination wit, I should like to tell you how it happened.

GRINNIDGE: I will do my best to veil my brilliancy. Go on.

RANSOM: I went up to Ponkwasset early in September for the foliage.

GRINNIDGE: And staid till late in October. There must have been a reason for that. What was *her* name? Foliage?

RANSOM, *coming up to the corner of the chimney-piece, near which his friend sits, and talking to him directly over the register*: I think you'll have to get along without the name for the present. I'll tell you by and by. *(As Mr. Ransom pronounces these words, Miss Reed, on her side of the partition, lifts her head with a startled air, and, after a moment of vague circumspection, listens keenly.)* But she *was* beautiful. She was a blonde, and she had the loveliest eyes—eyes, you know, that could be funny or tender, just as she chose—the kind of eyes I always liked. *(Miss Reed leans forward over the register.)* She had one of those faces that always leave you in doubt whether they're laughing at you, and so keep you in wholesome subjection; but you feel certain that they're *good*, and that if they did hurt you by laughing at you, they'd look sorry for you afterward. When she walked you saw what an exquisite creature she was. It always made me mad to think I couldn't *paint* her walk.

GRINNIDGE: I suppose you saw a good deal of her walk.

RANSOM: Yes; we were off in the woods and fields half the time together.

He takes a turn towards the window.

MISS REED, *suddenly shutting the register on her side*: Oh!

MISS SPAULDING, *looking up from her music*: What is it, Ethel?

MISS REED: Nothing, nothing; I—I—thought it was getting too warm. Go on, dear; don't let me interrupt you.

After a moment of heroic self-denial she softly presses the register open with her foot.

RANSOM, *coming back to the register*: It all began in that way. I had the good fortune one day to rescue her from a—cow.

MISS REED: Oh, for shame!

MISS SPAULDING, *desisting from her piano*: What *is* the matter?

MISS REED, *clapping the register to*: This ridiculous book! But don't—don't mind me, Nettie. *(Breathlessly)* Go—go—on!

Miss Spaulding resumes, and again Miss Reed softly presses the register open.

RANSOM, *after a pause*: The cow was grazing, and had no more thought of hooking Miss [1]—

MISS REED: Oh, I didn't suppose he *would!*— Go on, Nettie, go on! The hero—*such* a goose!

[1] Howells might have built this incident on an experience familiar to him. In a letter dated December 26, 1885 (Harvard Library) he wrote to his father: "I dreamed of Vic [his sister] last night, my dream running back to the cow hooking episode. Give her my best love. I hope *that* cow is sold."

RANSOM: I drove her away with my campstool, and Miss—the young lady—was as grateful as if I had rescued her from a menagerie of wild animals. I walked home with her to the farmhouse, and the trouble began at once. *(Pantomime of indignant protest and burlesque menace on the part of Miss Reed)* There wasn't another well woman in the house, except her friend Miss Spaulding, who was rather old and rather plain.

He takes another turn to the window.

MISS REED: Oh! *(She shuts the register, but instantly opens it again.)* Louder, Nettie.

MISS SPAULDING, *in astonishment*: What?

MISS REED: Did I speak? I didn't know it. I—

MISS SPAULDING, *desisting from practice*: What is that strange, hollow, rumbling, mumbling kind of noise?

MISS REED, *softly closing the register with her foot*: I don't hear any strange, hollow, rumbling, mumbling kind of noise. Do you hear it *now?*

MISS SPAULDING: No. It was the Brighton whistle, probably.

MISS REED: Oh, very likely.

As Miss Spaulding turns again to her practice Miss Reed re-opens the register and listens again. A little interval of silence ensues, while Ransom lights a cigarette.

GRINNIDGE: So you sought opportunities of rescuing her from other cows?

RANSOM, *returning*: That wasn't necessary. The young lady was so impressed by my behavior, that she asked if I would give her some lessons in the use of oil.

GRINNIDGE: She thought if she knew how to paint pictures like yours she wouldn't need any one to drive the cows away.

RANSOM: Don't be farcical, Grinnidge. That sort of thing will do with some victim on the witness-stand who can't help himself. Of course I said I would, and we were off half the time together, painting the loveliest and loneliest bits around Ponkwasset. It all went on very well, till one day I felt bound in conscience to tell her that I didn't think she would ever learn to paint, and that if she was serious about it she'd better drop it at once, for she was wasting her time.

GRINNIDGE, *getting up to fill his pipe*: That was a pleasant thing to do.

RANSOM: I told her that if it amused her, to keep on; I would be only too glad to give her all the hints I could, but that I oughtn't to encourage her. She seemed a good deal hurt. I fancied at the time that she thought I was tired of having her with me so much.

MISS REED: Oh, *did* you, indeed! (*To Miss Spaulding, who bends an astonished glance upon her from the piano*) The man in this book is the most *conceited* creature, Nettie. Play chords—something very subdued—ah!

MISS SPAULDING: What *are* you talking about, Ethel?

RANSOM: That was at night; but the next day she came up smiling, and said that if I didn't mind she would keep on—for amusement; she wasn't a bit discouraged.

MISS REED: Oh!—Go on, Nettie; don't let my outbursts interrupt you.

RANSOM: I used to fancy sometimes that she *was* a little sweet on me.

MISS REED: You wretch!—Oh, scales, Nettie! Play scales!

MISS SPAULDING: Ethel Reed, are you crazy?

RANSOM, *after a thoughtful moment*: Well, so it went on for the next seven or eight weeks. When we weren't sketching in the meadows, or on the mountain-side, or in the old punt on the pond, we were walking up and down the farmhouse piazza together. She used to read to me when I was at work. She had a heavenly voice, Grinnidge.

MISS REED: Oh, you silly, silly thing!—Really this book makes me sick, Nettie.

RANSOM: Well, the long and the short of it was, I was hit—*hard*, and I lost all courage. You know how I am, Grinnidge.

MISS REED, *softly*: Oh, poor fellow!

RANSOM: So I let the time go by, and at the end I hadn't said anything.

MISS REED: No, sir! You *hadn't*!

Miss Spaulding gradually ceases to play, and fixes her attention wholly upon Miss Reed, who bends forward over the register with an intensely excited face.

RANSOM: Then something happened that made me glad, for twenty-four hours at least, that I hadn't spoken. She sent me the money for twenty-five lessons. Imagine how I felt, Grinnidge! What could I suppose but that she had been quietly biding her time, and storing up her resentment for my having told her she couldn't learn to paint, till she could pay me back with interest in one supreme insult?

MISS REED, *in a low voice*: Oh, how could you think such a cruel, vulgar thing?

Miss Spaulding leaves the piano, and softly approaches her, where she has sunk on her knees beside the register.

RANSOM: It was tantamount to telling me that she had been amusing herself with me instead of my lessons. It remanded our whole association, which I had got to thinking so romantic, to the relation of teacher and pupil. It was a snub—a heartless, killing snub; and I couldn't see it in any other light.

Ransom walks away to the window, and looks out.

MISS REED, *flinging herself backward from the register, and hiding her face in her hands*: Oh, it wasn't! it wasn't! it wasn't! *How* could you think so?

MISS SPAULDING, *rushing forward, and catching her friend in her arms*: What is the matter with you, Ethel Reed? What are you doing here, over the register? Are you trying to suffocate yourself? Have you taken leave of your senses?

GRINNIDGE: Our fair friend on the other side of the wall seems to be on the rampage.

MISS SPAULDING, *shutting the register with a violent clash*: Ugh! how hot it is here!

GRINNIDGE: Doesn't like your conversation, apparently.

MISS REED, *frantically pressing forward to open the register*: Oh, don't shut it, Nettie, dear! If you do I shall die! Do-o-n't shut the register!

MISS SPAULDING: Don't shut it? Why, we've got all the heat of the furnace in the room now. Surely you don't want any more?

MISS REED: No, no; not any more. But—but—Oh, dear! what shall I do?

She still struggles in the embrace of her friend.

GRINNIDGE, *remaining quietly at the register, while Ransom walks away to the window*: Well, what did you do?

MISS REED: There, there! They're commencing again! Do open it, Nettie. I *will* have it open!

She wrenches herself free, and dashes the register open.

GRINNIDGE: Ah, she's opened it again.

MISS REED, *in a stage-whisper*: That's the other one!

RANSOM, *from the window*: Do? I'll tell you what I did.

MISS REED: That's Ol—Mr. Ransom. And, oh, I can't make out what he's saying! He must have gone away to the other side of the room—and it's at the most important point!

MISS SPAULDING, *in an awful undertone*: Was

that the hollow rumbling I heard? And have you been listening at the register to what they've been saying? O *Ethel!*

MISS REED: I haven't been listening, exactly.

MISS SPAULDING: You have! You have been eavesdropping!

MISS REED: Eavesdropping is listening through a key-hole, or around a corner. This is very different. Besides, it's Oliver, and he's been talking about *me*. Hark! (*She clutches her friend's hand, where they have crouched upon the floor together, and pulls her forward to the register.*) Oh, dear, how hot it is! I wish they would cut off the heat down below.

GRINNIDGE, *smoking peacefully through the silence which his friend has absent-mindedly let follow upon his last words*: Well, you seem disposed to take your time about it.

RANSOM: About what? Oh, yes! Well—

MISS REED: 'Sh! Listen.

MISS SPAULDING: I won't listen! It's shameful: it's wicked! I don't see how you can do it, Ethel!

She remains, however, kneeling near the register, and she involuntarily inclines a little more toward it.

RANSOM: —It isn't a thing that I care to shout from the house-tops. (*He returns from the window to the chimney-piece.*) I wrote the rudest kind of note, and sent back her letter and her money in it. She had said that she hoped our acquaintance was not to end with the summer, but that we might sometimes meet in Boston; and I answered that our acquaintance had ended already, and that I should be sorry to meet her anywhere again.

GRINNIDGE: Well, if you wanted to make an ass of yourself, you did it pretty completely.

MISS REED, *whispering*: How witty he is! Those men are always so humorous with each other.

RANSOM: Yes; I didn't do it by halves.

MISS REED, *whispering*: Oh, *that's* funny, too!

GRINNIDGE: It didn't occur to you that she might feel bound to pay you for the first half-dozen, and was embarrassed how to offer to pay for them alone?

MISS REED: How he *does* go to the heart of the matter!

She presses Miss Spaulding's hand in an ecstasy of approval.

RANSOM: Yes, it did—afterward.

MISS REED, *in a tender murmur*: Oh, *poor* Oliver!

RANSOM: And it occurred to me that she was perfectly right in the whole affair.

MISS REED: Oh, how generous! how noble!

RANSOM: I had had a thousand opportunities, and I hadn't been man enough to tell her that I was in love with her.

MISS REED: How can he say it right out so bluntly? But if it's true—

RANSOM: I *couldn't* speak. I was afraid of putting an end to the affair—of frightening her—disgusting her.

MISS REED: Oh, how little they know us, Nettie!

RANSOM: She seemed so much above me in every way—so sensitive, so refined, so gentle, so good, so angelic!

MISS REED: There! *Now* do you call it eavesdropping? If listeners never hear any good of themselves, what do you say to that? It proves that I haven't been listening.

MISS SPAULDING: 'Sh! They're saying something else.

RANSOM: But all that's neither here nor there. I can see now that under the circumstances she couldn't as a lady have acted otherwise than she did. She was forced to treat our whole acquaintance as a business matter, and I had forced her to do it.

MISS REED: You *had*, you poor thing!

GRINNIDGE: Well, what do you intend to do about it?

RANSOM: Well—

MISS REED: 'Sh!

MISS SPAULDING: 'Sh!

RANSOM: —that's what I want to submit to you, Grinnidge. I must see her.

GRINNIDGE: Yes. I'm glad *I* mustn't.

MISS REED, *stifling a laugh on Miss Spaulding's shoulder*: They're actually *afraid* of us, Nettie!

RANSOM: See her, and go down in the dust.

MISS REED: My very words!

RANSOM: I have been trying to think what was the very humblest pie I could eat, by way of penance; and it appears to me that I had better begin by saying that I have come to ask her for the money I refused.

MISS REED, *enraptured*: Oh! doesn't it seem just like—like—inspiration, Nettie?

MISS SPAULDING: 'Sh! Be quiet, do! You'll frighten them away!

GRINNIDGE: And then what?

RANSOM: What then? I don't know what then. But it appears to me that, as a gentleman, I've got nothing to do with the result. All that I've got to do is to submit to my fate, whatever it is.

MISS REED, *breathlessly*: What princely courage! What delicate magnanimity! Oh, he needn't have the *least* fear! If I could only tell him that!

GRINNIDGE, *after an interval of meditative smoking*: Yes, I guess that's the best thing you can do. It will strike her fancy, if she's an imaginative girl, and she'll think you a fine fellow.

MISS REED: Oh, the horrid thing!

GRINNIDGE: If you humble yourself to a woman at all, do it thoroughly. If you go half-way down she'll be tempted to push you the rest of the way. If you flatten out at her feet to begin with, ten to one but she will pick you up.

RANSOM: Yes, that was my idea.

MISS REED: Oh, was it, indeed! Well!

RANSOM: But I've nothing to do with her picking me up or pushing me down. All that I've got to do is to go and surrender myself.

GRINNIDGE: Yes. Well; I guess you can't go too soon. I like your company; but I advise you as a friend not to lose time. Where does she live?

RANSOM: That's the remarkable part of it: she lives in this house.

MISS REED AND MISS SPAULDING, *in subdued chorus*: Oh!

GRINNIDGE, *taking his pipe out of his mouth in astonishment*: No!

RANSOM: I just came in here to give my good resolutions a rest while I was screwing my courage up to ask for her.

MISS REED: Don't you think he's *very* humorous? Give his good resolutions a rest! That's the way he *always* talks.

MISS SPAULDING: 'Sh!

GRINNIDGE: You said you came for my advice.

RANSOM: So I did. But I didn't promise to act upon it. Well!

He goes toward the door.

GRINNIDGE, *without troubling himself to rise*: Well, good luck to you!

MISS REED: How droll they are with each other! Don't you *like* to hear them talk? Oh, I could listen all day.

GRINNIDGE, *calling after Ransom*: You haven't told me your duck's name.

MISS REED: Is *that* what they call us? Duck! Do you think it's very respectful, Nettie? I don't believe I like it. Or, yes, why not? It's no harm —if I *am* his duck!

RANSOM, *coming back*: Well, I don't propose to go shouting it round. Her name is Miss Reed —Ethel Reed.

MISS REED: How *can* he?

GRINNIDGE: Slender, willowy party, with a lot of blond hair that looks as if it might be indigenous? Rather pensive-looking?

MISS REED: Indigenous! I should hope so!

RANSOM: Yes. But she isn't pensive. She's awfully deep. It makes me shudder to think how deep that girl is. And when I think of my courage in daring to be in love with her—a stupid, straightforward idiot like me—I begin to respect myself in spite of being such an ass. Well, I'm off. If I stay any longer I shall never go.

He closes the door after him, and Miss Reed instantly springs to her feet.

MISS REED: Now he'll have to go down to the parlor and send up his name, and that just gives me time to do the necessary prinking. You stay here and receive him, Nettie.

MISS SPAULDING: Never! After what's happened I can never look him in the face again. Oh, how low, and mean, and guilty I feel!

MISS REED, *with surprise*: Why, how droll! Now I don't feel the least so.

MISS SPAULDING: Oh, it's very different with *you*. *You're* in love with him.

MISS REED: For shame, Nettie! I'm *not* in love with him.

MISS SPAULDING: And you can explain and justify it. But I never can justify it to myself, much less to him. Let me go, Ethel! I shall tell Mrs. McKnight that we must change this room instantly. And just after I'd got it so nearly in order! Go down and receive him in the parlor, Ethel. I *can't* see him.

MISS REED: Receive him in the parlor! Why, Nettie, dear, you're crazy! I'm going to *accept* him: and how can I accept him—with all the consequences—in a public parlor? No, indeed! If you won't meet him here for a moment, just to oblige me, you can go into the other room. Or, no —you'd be listening to every word through the key-hole, you're so demoralized!

MISS SPAULDING: Yes, yes, I deserve your contempt, Ethel.

MISS REED, *laughing*: You will have to go out for a walk, you poor thing; and I'm not going to have you coming back in five or ten minutes. You have got to stay out a good hour.

MISS SPAULDING, *running to get her things from the next room*: Oh, I'll stay out till midnight!

MISS REED, *responding to a tap at the door*: Ye-e-s! Come in!—You're caught, Nettie.

A MAID-SERVANT, *appearing with a card*: This gentleman is asking for you in the parlor, Miss Reed.

MISS REED: Oh! Ask him to come up here, please. —Nettie! Nettie! (*She calls to her friend in the next room.*) He's coming right up, and if you don't run you're trapped.

MISS SPAULDING, *re-appearing, cloaked and bonneted*: I don't blame *you*, Ethel, comparatively speaking. You can say that everything is fair in love. He will like it, and laugh at it in you, because he'll like everything you've done. Besides, you've no principles, and I *have*.

MISS REED: Oh, I've lots of principles, Nettie, but I've no practice!

MISS SPAULDING: No matter. There's no excuse for me. I listened simply because I was a woman, and couldn't help it; and, oh, what will he think of me?

MISS REED: I won't give you away; if you really feel so badly—

MISS SPAULDING: Oh, *do* you think you can keep from telling him, Ethel dear? Try! And I will be your slave forever! (*Steps are heard on the stairs outside.*) Oh, there he comes!

She dashes out of the door, and closes it after her, a moment before the maid-servant, followed by Mr. Ransom, taps at it.

III.

Miss Reed opens the door, and receives Mr. Ransom with well-affected surprise and state, suffering him to stand awkwardly on the threshold for a moment.

SHE, *coldly*: Oh!—Mr. Ransom!

HE, *abruptly*: I've come—

SHE: Won't you come in?

HE, *advancing a few paces into the room*: I've come—

SHE, *indicating a chair*: Will you sit down?

HE: I must stand for the present. I've come to ask you for that money, Miss Reed, which I refused yesterday, in terms that I blush to think of. I was altogether and wholly in the wrong, and I'm ready to offer any imaginable apology or reparation. I'm ready to take the money and to sign a receipt, and then to be dismissed with

whatever ignominy you please. I deserve anything —everything!

SHE: The money? Excuse me; I don't know—I'm afraid that I'm not prepared to pay you the whole sum to-day.

HE, *hastily*: Oh, no matter! no matter! I don't care for the money now. I merely wish to—to assure you that I thought you were perfectly right in offering it, and to—to—

SHE: What?

HE: Nothing. That is—ah—ah—

SHE: It's extremely embarrassing to have people refuse their money when it's offered them, and then come the next day for it, when perhaps it isn't so convenient to pay it—*very* embarrassing.

HE, *hotly*: But I tell you I don't want the *money*! I never wanted it, and wouldn't take it on any account.

SHE: Oh! I thought you said you came to get it?

HE: I said—I didn't say—I meant—that is—ah—I—

He stops, open-mouthed.

SHE, *quietly*: I could give you part of the money now.

HE: Oh, whatever you like; it's indifferent—

SHE: Please sit down while I write a receipt. (*She places herself deliberately at the table, and opens her portfolio.*) I will pay you now, Mr. Ransom, for the first six lessons you gave me—the ones before you told me that I could never learn to do anything.

HE, *sinking mechanically into the chair she indicates*: Oh, just as you like!

He looks up at the ceiling in hopeless bewilderment, while she writes.

SHE, *blotting the paper*: There! And now let me offer you a little piece of advice, Mr. Ransom, which may be useful to you in taking pupils hereafter.

HE, *bursting out*: I never take pupils!

SHE: Never take pupils! I don't understand. You took *me*.

HE, *confusedly*: I took you—yes. You seemed to wish—you seemed—the case was peculiar—peculiar circumstances.

SHE, *with severity*: May I ask *why* the circumstances were peculiar? I saw nothing peculiar about the circumstances. It seemed to me it was a very simple matter. I told you that I had always had a great curiosity to see whether I could use oil paints, and I asked you a very plain question, whether you would let me study with you. Didn't I?

HE: Yes.

SHE: Was there anything wrong—anything queer about my asking you?

HE: No, no! Not at all—not in the least.

SHE: Didn't you wish me to take the lessons of you? If you didn't, it wasn't kind of you to let me.

HE: Oh, I was perfectly willing—very glad indeed, very much so—certainly!

SHE: If it wasn't your *custom* to take pupils, you ought to have told me, and I wouldn't have forced myself upon you.

HE, *desperately*: It wasn't forcing yourself upon me. The Lord knows how humbly grateful I was. It was like a hope of heaven!

SHE: Really, Mr. Ransom, this is very strange talk. What am I to understand by it? *Why* should you be grateful to teach me? Why should giving me lessons be like a hope of heaven?

HE: Oh, I will tell you!

SHE: Well?

HE, *after a moment of agony*: Because to be with you—

SHE: Yes?

HE: Because I wished to be with you. Because —those days in the woods, when you read, and I—

SHE: Painted on my pictures—

HE: Were the happiest of my life. Because— I loved you!

SHE: Mr. Ransom!

HE: Yes, I must tell you so. I loved you; I love you still. I shall always love you, no matter what—

SHE: You forget yourself, Mr. Ransom. Has there been anything in my manner—conduct—to justify you in using such language to me?

HE: No—no—

SHE: Did you suppose that because I first took lessons of you from—from—an enthusiasm for art, and then continued them for—for—amusement, that I wished you to make love to me?

HE: No, I never supposed such a thing. I'm incapable of it. I beseech you to believe that no one could have more respect—reverence—

He twirls his hat between his hands, and casts an imploring glance at her.

SHE: Oh, respect—reverence! I know what they mean in the mouths of men. If you respected, if you reverenced me, could you dare to tell me,

after my unguarded trust of you during the past months, that you had been all the time secretly in love with me?

HE, *plucking up a little courage*: I don't see that the three things are incompatible.

SHE: Oh, then you acknowledge that you did presume upon something you thought you saw in me to tell me that you loved me, and that you were in love with me all the time?

HE, *contritely*: I have no right to suppose that you encouraged me; and yet—I can't deny it now —I was in love with you all the time.

SHE: And you never said a word to let me believe that you had any such feeling toward me!

HE: I—I—

SHE: You would have parted from me without a syllable to suggest it—perhaps parted from me forever? (*After a pause of silent humiliation for him*) Do you call that brave or generous? Do you call it manly—supposing, as you hoped, that *I* had any such feeling?

HE: No; it was cowardly, it was mean, it was unmanly. I see it now, but I will spend my life in repairing the wrong, if you will only let me.

He impetuously advances some paces toward her, and then stops, arrested by her irresponsive attitude.

SHE, *with a light sigh, and looking down at the paper, which she has continued to hold between her hands*: There was a time—a moment—when I might have answered as you wish.

HE: Oh! then there will be again. If you have changed once, you may change once more. Let me hope that some time—any time, dearest—

SHE, *quenching him with a look*: Mr. Ransom, I shall *never* change toward you! You confess that you had your opportunity, and that you despised it.

HE: Oh! *not* despised it!

SHE: Neglected it.

HE: Not wilfully—no. I confess that I was stupidly, vilely, pusillan—pusillan—illani—

SHE: 'Mously—

HE: Thanks—'mously unworthy of it; but I didn't despise it; I didn't neglect it; and if you will only let me show by a lifetime of devotion how dearly and truly I have loved you from the first moment I drove that cow away—

SHE: Mr. Ransom, I have told you that I should never change toward you. That cow was nothing when weighed in the balance against your being willing to leave a poor girl, whom you supposed interested in you, and to whom you had paid the most marked attention, without a word to show her that you cared for her. What is a cow, or a whole herd of cows, as compared with obliging a young lady to offer you money that you hadn't earned, and then savagely flinging it back in her face? A yoke of oxen would be nothing—or a mad bull.

HE: Oh, I acknowledge it! I confess it.

SHE: And you own that I am right in refusing to listen to you now?

HE, *desolately*: Yes, yes.

SHE: It seems that you gave me lessons in order to be with me, and if possible to interest me in you; and then you were going away without a word.

HE, *with a groan*: It was only because I was afraid to speak.

SHE: Oh, is *that* any excuse?

HE: No; none.

SHE: A man ought always to have courage. (*After a pause, in which he stands before her with bowed head*) Then there's nothing for me but to give you this money.

HE, *with sudden energy*: This is too much! I—

SHE, *offering him the bank-notes*: No; it is the exact sum. I counted it very carefully.

HE: I won't take it; I can't! I'll never take it!

SHE, *standing with the money in her outstretched hand*: I have your word as a gentleman that you will take it.

HE, *gasping*: Oh, well—I will take it—I will— (*He clutches the money, and rushes toward the door.*) Good-evening; ah—good-by—

SHE, *calling after him*: The receipt, Mr. Ransom! Please sign this receipt!

She waves the paper in the air.

HE: Oh, yes, certainly! Where is it—what—which— (*He rushes back to her, and seizing the receipt, feels blindly about for the pen and ink.*) Where shall I sign?

SHE: Read it first.

HE: Oh, it's all—all right—

SHE: I insist upon your reading it. It's a business transaction. Read it aloud.

HE, *desperately*: Well, well! (*He reads.*) "Received from Miss Ethel Reed, in full, for twenty-five lessons in oil-painting, one hundred and twenty-five dollars, and her hand, heart, and dearest love forever." (*He looks up at her.*) Ethel!

SHE, *smiling*: Sign it, sign it!

HE, *catching her in his arms and kissing her*: Oh, yes—here!

SHE, *pulling a little away from him, and laughing*: Oh, oh! I only wanted *one* signature! Twenty autographs are too many, unless you'll let me trade them off, as the collectors do.

HE: No; keep them all! I couldn't think of letting any one else have them. One more!

SHE: No; it's quite enough! (*She frees herself, and retires beyond the table.*) This unexpected affection—

HE: *Is* it unexpected—seriously?

SHE: What do you mean?

HE: Oh, nothing!

SHE: Yes, tell me!

HE: I hoped—I thought—perhaps—that you might have been prepared for some such demonstration on my part.

SHE: And why did you think—hope—perhaps—*that*, Mr. Ransom, may I ask?

HE: If I hadn't, how should I have dared to speak?

SHE: Dared? You were obliged to speak! Well, since it's all over, I don't mind saying that I *did* have some slight apprehensions that something in the way of a declaration might be extorted from you.

HE: Extorted? Oh!

He makes an impassioned rush toward her.

SHE, *keeping the table between them*: No, no.

HE: Oh, I merely wished to ask why you chose to make me suffer so, after I had come to the point.

SHE: Ask it across the table, then. (*After a moment's reflection*) I made you suffer—I made you suffer—so that you might have a realizing sense of what you had made *me* suffer.

HE, *enraptured by this confession*: Oh, you angel!

SHE, *with tender magnanimity*: No; only a woman—a poor, trusting, foolish woman! (*She permits him to surround the table, with imaginable results. Then, with her head on his shoulder*) You'll *never* let me regret it, will you, darling? You'll never oblige me to punish you again, dearest, will you? Oh, it hurt *me* far worse to *see* your pain than it did you to—to—feel it! (*On the other side of the partition, Mr. Grinnidge's pipe falls from his lips, parted in slumber, and shivers to atoms on the register.*) Oh! (*She flies at the register with a shriek of dismay, and is about to close it.*) That wretch has been listening, and has heard every word!

HE, *preventing her*: What wretch? Where?

SHE: Don't you hear him, mumbling and grumbling there?

GRINNIDGE: Well, I swear! Cash value of twenty-five dollars, and untold toil in coloring it.

RANSOM, *listening with an air of mystification*: Who's that?

SHE: Gummidge, Grimmidge—whatever you called him. Oh! (*She arrests herself in consternation.*) Now I *have* done it!

HE: Done what?

SHE: Oh—nothing!

HE: I don't understand. Do you mean to say that my friend Grinnidge's room is on the other side of the wall, and that you can hear him talk through the register? (*She preserves the silence of abject terror. He stoops over the register, and calls down it.*) Grinnidge! Hallo!

GRINNIDGE: Hallo, yourself!

RANSOM, *to Miss Reed*: Sounds like the ghostly squeak of the phonograph. (*To Grinnidge*) What's the trouble?

GRINNIDGE: Smashed my pipe. Dozed off and let it drop on this infernal register.

RANSOM, *turning from the register with impressive deliberation*: Miss Reed, may I ask *how* you came to know that his name was Gummidge, or Grimmidge, or whatever I called him?

SHE: Oh, dearest, I *can't* tell you! Or—yes, I had better. (*Impulsively*) I will judge you by myself. I could forgive *you* anything!

HE, *doubtfully*: Oh, could you?

SHE: Everything! I had—I had better make a clean breast of it. Yes, I had. Though I don't like to. I—I listened!

HE: Listened?

SHE: Through the register to—to—what—you —were saying before you—came in here.

Her head droops.

HE: Then you heard everything?

SHE: Kill me, but don't look *so* at me! It was accidental at first—indeed it was; and then I recognized your voice; and then I knew you were talking about me; and I had so much at stake; and I did love you so dearly! You *will* forgive me, darling? It wasn't as if I were listening with any bad motive.

HE, *taking her in his arms*: Forgive you? Of course I do. But you must change this room at once, Ethel; you see you hear everything on the other side, too.

SHE: Oh, not if you whisper on this. You couldn't hear *us*? (*At a dubious expression of his*)

You *didn't* hear us? If you did, I can never forgive you!

HE: It was accidental at first—indeed it was; and then I recognized your voice; and then I knew you were talking about me; and I had so much at stake; and I did love you so dearly!

SHE: All that has nothing whatever to do with it. How much did you hear?

HE, *with exemplary meekness*: Only what you were saying before Grinnidge came in. You didn't whisper then. I had to wait there for him while—

SHE: While you were giving your good resolutions a rest?

HE: While I was giving my good resolutions a rest.

SHE: And that accounts for your determination to humble yourself so?

HE: It seemed perfectly providential that I should have known just what conditions you were going to exact of me.

SHE: Oh, don't make light of it! I can tell you it's a very serious matter.

HE: It was very serious for me when you didn't meet my self-abasement as you had led me to expect you would.

SHE: Don't make fun! I'm trying to think whether I can forgive you.

HE, *with insinuation*: Don't you believe you could think better if you put your head on my shoulder?

SHE: Nonsense! Then I should forgive you without thinking. (*After a season of reflection*) No, I *can't* forgive you. I never could forgive eavesdropping. It's *too* low.

HE, *in astonishment*: Why, you did it yourself!

SHE: But you began it. Besides, it's very different for a man. Women are weak, poor, helpless creatures. They have to use finesse. But a man should be above it.

HE: You said you could forgive me anything.

SHE: Ah, but I didn't know what you'd been doing!

HE, *with pensive resignation, and a feint of going*: Then I suppose it's all over between us.

SHE, *relenting*: If you could think of any reason *why* I should forgive you—

HE: I can't.

SHE, *after consideration*: Do you suppose Mr. Grumage, or Grimidge, heard too?

HE: No; Grinnidge is a very high-principled fellow, and wouldn't listen; besides, he wasn't there, you know.

SHE: Well, then, I will forget you on these

grounds. (*He instantly catches her to his heart.*) But these alone, remember.

HE, *rapturously*: Oh, on any!

SHE, *tenderly*: And you'll always be devoted? And nice? And not try to provoke me? Or neglect me? Or anything?

HE: Always! Never!

SHE: Oh, you dear, sweet, simple old thing— how I *do* love you!

GRINNIDGE, *who has been listening attentively to every word at the register at his side*: Ransom, if you don't want me to go stark mad, *shut the register!*

RANSOM, *about to comply*: Oh, poor old man! I forgot it was open!

MISS REED, *preventing him*: No! If he has been vile enough to listen at a register, let him suffer. Come, sit down here, and I'll tell you just when I began to care for you. It was long before the cow. Do you remember that first morning after you arrived—

She drags him close to the register, so that every word may tell upon the envious Grinnidge, on whose manifestations of acute despair, a rapid curtain descends.

A Sea Change or Love's Stowaway

[1884]

Lyrics by W. D. Howells; Music by George Henschel

Although as a dramatist Howells concentrated on light, realistic sketches, occasionally he abandoned his throne of realism to frolic with wits and jesters on the stage of make-believe. Rather than being realistic and truthful in theme or detail, A Sea Change is romantic and exaggerated, but Howells saw a need for fantasy and burlesque and recognized it in Criticism and Fiction (New York: Harper & Bros., 1891): "The fiction that aims merely to entertain—the fiction that is to serious fiction as the opéra bouffe, the ballet and the pantomime are to the true drama—need not feel the burden of this obligation [to be truthful] so deeply. . . ." Essentially A Sea Change is opéra bouffe, and it is quite possible that Howells had his own opera in mind when he wrote this comment.

As opéra bouffe, the tone of A Sea Change is strictly farcical and vaudevillian, employing an obvious extravagance in its humor and other artistic decoration. There is some slight suggestion of the more characteristic social humor of Howells, but even this is broad and blunt in contrast to his dialogue in other plays. Here there is no depth; nothing is intended to be taken seriously. The poetry itself, although interesting in its variety of form and attaining a certain effectiveness, is mainly a burlesque imitation of the lyrical and fast-moving words of W. S. Gilbert, just as Henschel's music suggests that of Arthur Sullivan, even to one song in the Handelian manner.

At the time he wrote A Sea Change Howells was an established writer, and Sir George Henschel (1850–1934), who composed the music, was demonstrating his musical ability as the first conductor of the Boston Symphony Orchestra, a post he retained from 1881 until 1884. It was during the winter and spring of this last year that the two men collaborated on the operetta. (See the New York Tribune, June 22, 1884, "Mr. Howells's Operetta. How it came to be written.") It was slow, queer work for Howells, as he wrote to his father (March 23, 1884, Harvard Library), but amusing—amusing, that is, until the production plans met an unforseeable disaster. In a letter to Henry James (August 22, 1884, Life in Letters, I, 367), Howells described the unfortunate circumstances that prevented immediate production of the opera: "I don't know whether I've bragged to you of all the work I've done the past winter. One piece of it was an opera which Henschel set to music, and we had a contract with the Bijou Theatre for its production in November. The other night the manager with whom we contracted, in trying to get aboard his yacht in the fog, fell and fractured his skull, poor man. He died and with him our legal hold upon a potential future. I dare say the Theatre will still want it; but I wait for the return of the puissant Osgood, who put our contract through, before knowing." But the Bijou, which was to have produced the opera November 10 under the direction of a Mr. Neuendorff, did not continue its interest. One reason was undoubtedly the staging that the authors contemplated. The New York Times reviewer for the later orchestral reading commented on some of the opera's quite impossible requirements: "The stage furniture of 'A Sea Change' includes not only a big portion of the deck of an ocean steamship, but also an iceberg, big enough to be the habitation of a chorus, which must float alongside the vessel and be lashed to her. The paraphernalia of the piece is, to tell the truth, almost fantastically extravagant, and would strain the resources of a large and well appointed theatre."

After rejection by the Bijou Theatre, the authors took their opera to Mr. Field of the Boston Museum, who after much consideration consented to perform it with his orchestra of sixteen pieces. Thus on the forenoon of January 27, 1885, before a small number of invited friends, there was an orchestra reading of the opera. The *Times* reviewer described it: "The rehearsal consisted of a performance at sight of the instrumental parts of the whole work by the band of the Museum, under the direction of Mr. Purdy. The band is not a brilliant one, and the reading was exceedingly crude; but with the aid of a pianoforte score, one with a quick fancy and some ability in reading music was able to get a good idea of the music which Mr. Henschel has written to Mr. Howells's words." "The purpose of the private rehearsal today," wrote the reviewer, "was to help Mr. Field, of the Museum, to make up his mind whether or not to undertake the production of the piece. . . . Mr. Field has not yet made up his mind further than to say that he thinks well of the piece and has not yet rejected it. Mr. Duff, of the *Standard*, in New-York, has requested the use of the score for inspection, and it will be sent to him. It is possible, therefore, that if it is found practicable, Messrs. Field and Duff may bring it out simultaneously." But this did not happen, and interest in the opera practically disappeared.

With the manager's lack of interest becoming more and more apparent, Howells' enthusiasm waned. "I say let us publish the confounded thing and be rid of it," he wrote to Osgood (February 5, 1885, Harvard Library). But Henschel was not so anxious, because in their private agreement Henschel was to get no royalty from the sale of the text in book form. The operetta actually had been published simultaneously by Trübner & Co. in London and James R. Osgood & Co. in 1884, to preserve the authors' rights against plagiarism; but, the New York *Times* reviewer confided, only a very few copies had been released. It was not until July 15, 1887 (Harvard Library), that Henschel wrote to Howells: "Since there is no possibility for producing the opera from the words alone or the music alone I think there would be no danger in having the words published as a book. . . ." The following year A *Sea Change* appeared in *Harper's Weekly* and in book form by Ticknor. These texts are distinct from each other—numerous additions having been made after the *Harper's Weekly* publication—and differ markedly from the earlier Osgood version. For example, as Theron prepares to leave with the Ice Princess, the Osgood text includes a rather long dialogue between Muriel and the Steward, and a song by the Steward in which he confesses that he is Truth's Stowaway. In the Harvard Library there is another printed version of the opera which seems to be a page-proof text—because the printer's spacing sometimes shows—of this first publication by Osgood and Trübner. Perhaps this was intended for use as a prompt copy, for there are numerous stage directions and textual changes in Howells' hand. Characteristic are his comments on the manner in which he would like to have a scene played: "The seaman comes on dancing a hornpipe, with his back constantly to the audience, entering at one side, and going out at the other. The hornpipe is played *pianissimo*, and his dances must be absolutely noiseless. He wears a straw hat trimmed with blue ribbons, like a shepherd's. He disappears at the end of the hornpipe. Then Muriel speaks."

With these publications and the failure of the rehearsal to stimulate the hoped-for response came the end of any serious consideration for a stage production of A *Sea Change*. There was some slight revival of interest at different times, but it was casual. Evidently, early in 1892 B. H. Ticknor found someone who inquired about A *Sea Change*, for Howells wrote him a note (March 1, 1892, Library of Congress) saying that he should be very glad to have an offer for the stage rights of the play: "I will refuse nothing that is at all reasonable." Then on May 5, 1916 (Harvard Library), Henschel wrote that a Mr. Tyler was interested in the play. But nothing came of either of these inquiries. The nearest thing to a public performance of A *Sea Change* was the BBC production of February 4 and 6, 1929. Miss Georgie Henschel, daughter of Sir George Henschel, wrote me on December 26, 1955 that A *Sea Change* had been given twice by the BBC, first in 1929 and again in 1930. Grove's *Dictionary of Music and Musicians* mentions 1930 as the only BBC date. The Music Librarian of the BBC notes that their registry contains a program of the 1929 production but has no evidence of a repeat in 1930.

271

A Sea Change or Love's Stowaway[1]

A LYRICATED FARCE

ACT I
LOVE'S STOWAWAY

SCENE: *The promenade-deck of the steamer Meso-potamia, two days out from Boston. It is morning, before breakfast. A group of sailors are hauling at a sheet; and a sail is seen rising, with an audible clucking of the tackle.*

CHORUS OF SEAMEN

If I had a sweetheart, and she was a rover,
  Haul away, boys, haul away!
I'd follow her all the wide world over,
  Haul away, boys, haul away!

If she said yes, I never would leave her,
  Haul away, boys, haul away!
If she said no, I would go and grieve her,
  Haul away, boys, haul away!

For the will of a girl there is never any knowing,
  Haul away, boys, haul away!
She would want me to stay if she saw me going.
  Haul away, boys, haul away!

Then, never say die; keep a stiff upper lip, boys;
  Haul away, haul, haul away!
The wind is fair, and we've got a good ship, boys,
  Haul away, haul, haul away!

> [*The Seamen straggle forward over the deck, singing. Then Theron Gay steals from the door of the smoking-room, peering fearfully about him.*]

THERON

> [*Recitative.*]

A surmise or suspicion,
I know not which to call it,
Possesses me, that, without my intending,
I am this very moment emulating
The resolute behavior
Of the heroic and ideal lover
Whose bold philosophy has been indicated
In the soul-stirring accents of the chorus.

Four nights ago, sitting among the flowers
In Mr. Vane's conservatory,
I told my love to Muriel his daughter.
With what result will doubtless be conjectured
When I have added that I took my passage
By the first steamer I could get for Europe
Early the following morning.

And now, there are circumstances
Which lead me to imagine
That Muriel, flying from my hated presence,
Has taken passage on this very steamer.
Such is the simple and probable situation!
But, since we started, we have all been sea-sick,
And hardly any of us has been able
To leave his state-room;
And it has been impossible to make certain
Of what may be at last a mere conjecture.
Yet now I can no longer bridle
My wild impatience,
And I will ask the first of the ship's people
Whom I encounter;
And *apropos* of that, just as it happens
Always upon the stage at such a juncture,
When they would hold the mirror up to nature,
Here comes the very man, above all others,
Who can relieve my mind.

> [*The Deck-Steward appears with a waiter, and a tumbler of lemonade on it.*]

I will accost him. Steward!

STEWARD: Yes, sir. Beg your pardon, sir?

THERON: What's this? The sea's like glass; the ship's as steady as a rock; nobody's sick this morning, surely?

STEWARD, *confusedly*: You're quite right, sir. It's—it's the force of 'abit, sir. I'm so used to bringin' lemonade to the ladies stretched about 'ere on deck in hevery hattitude of hagony, that I just came hup this mornin', sir—

THERON, *sternly*: Without the surgeon's orders? What do the rules and regulations say, which are printed, glazed, and framed, and hung up in all the state-rooms?

STEWARD, *dropping on his knees, and extending his waiter imploringly, from which Theron mechanically takes the lemonade, and drinks it, set-*

---

[1] The text used here is the Ticknor and Company edition. Title: See *The Tempest*, I, 2:400.

ting back the empty glass: Don't report me, sir!
It was merely the force of 'abit.

THERON

                                        [*Aside.*]
Now, whether, having got him in my power,
'Twere better throw myself upon his mercy,
And tell him all,
Or rather try *finesse*,
And lead him on,
He knows not how or whither,
To tell me what I wish?
I have an inspiration;
And, as might naturally be expected
Under the unexpected circumstances,
It takes the lyric form; and I will sing it.

THERON
An Inspiration

Victim of what box soever,
   Wait and think a little, pray,
Ere the last frail tie you sever,
   Binding you to silence! Stay,
   Do not give yourself away!

If the simple world believes you
   Wiser, richer, better, say,
Than you are, although it grieves you,
   Do not undeceive it! Stay,
   Do not give yourself away!

If you have upon your conscience,
   Sins that struggle to the day,
Stay! Confession would be nonscience;
   (So pronounced for the rhyme's sake, pray!)
   Do not give yourself away!

If your note falls due to-morrow,
   And your heart sinks in dismay,
Try to beg or steal or borrow,
   Ere you own you cannot pay.
   Do not give yourself away!

If you adore some lovely being,
   And you long to tell her, stay,
Since there can be no foreseeing
   That she will not answer nay!
   Do not give yourself away!

If, in short, the cards are shuffled,
   So that you hold but deuce or trey
In life's game, with front unruffled
   Wait, and let your opponent play.
   Do not give yourself away!

THERON

                                        [*Aside.*]
I cannot say just whence this inspiration
Came, and some precepts in it
Certainly strike me as being rather lurid.
I might go on considerably farther;
But I have said enough already
Quite to decide me not to tell this steward
Aught of myself, but rather seek to pump him.
   Steward!

STEWARD: Beg your pardon, sir?
THERON: For the present I will spare you. And
now, can you tell me—(I must manage this with
great subtlety, so as to throw him off his guard)
—if there is a Miss Muriel Vane of Boston on
board?
STEWARD: Well, that, sir, is a question which I
can honly hanswer in one way, sir.
THERON: How is that?
STEWARD: In a haria, sir.
THERON: What is a haria?
STEWARD: Haria? Why, haria is the Hitalian
for hair, sir.
THERON: Hair?
STEWARD: Yes, sir; in a hair, sir. A song, sir.
THERON: Of course. I expected you to do that.
People always do. Well?

STEWARD
Haria

I am a simple deck steward,
Life has left me to leeward!
   I am hold, I am gray,
   I am sad, well-a-day!
But my 'eart shall be hopen to youward.

Welcome were sixpence or shilling;
Ready the 'and, sir, and willing;
   Yet the truth must be told,
   Though for touch of the gold
The palm may be throbbing and thrilling.

THERON: And what am I to infer from this
oracular rubbish?
STEWARD: I 'adn't quite finished, you know, sir.

   I cannot be quite explicit
   As to the fact you'd elicit.
      There's so many aboard,
      If I wentured the word,
   I might 'it, and again I might miss, it.

That is, I can't say positively, sir. Most of the
ladies 'as kept their berths, sir. Sh! Somebody
comin', sir.

THERON: Then, I must conceal myself! It is the only way.

He re-enters the door of the smoking-room. From the door of the saloon gangway appear two maids, carrying shawls, rugs, and wraps of every kind, with pillows and cushions; Mrs. Vane with a Willoughby pug and smelling-bottle; and Mr. Vane with a foot-stool, a sun-umbrella, and a steamer-chair. He wearily places the chair, and the maids arrange the wraps and cushions about it, while the old people advance and sing.

MR. AND MRS. VANE

Two long days and nights of dread commotion,
   Tossing on a couch of sleepless anguish,
Victim of the wild unresting ocean,
   We have seen our hapless daughter languish.
     [They take hands, and chassez gravely, with a dignified dancing-step. The maids, having finished their work, sing sotto-voce, looking over the shoulders of Mr. and Mrs. Vane.]

THE MAIDS

Two long days and nights of whim and notion,
   Twisting, turning, scolding, crying, fretting,
We have seen her a perpetual motion
   Of unreal wants and vain regretting.
     [They make a saucy dancing-step on each side of the old people.]

MR. AND MRS. VANE

He who would persistently adore her,
   When he might have seen she could not pity,
Left her with no choice but flight before her
   From her country and her native city.
     [They dance as before.]

THE MAIDS

Spoiled and selfish thing, we hope 'twill please her,
   Now she's left her true and faithful lover.
We should have been willing, just to tease her,
   If it had been rough the whole way over.
     [They dance as before.]

MRS. VANE: Have you finished, Mary?

MARY: Yes'm.

MRS. VANE: Is every thing ready, Sarah?

SARAH: Quite ready, ma'am.

MRS. VANE: I feel as if nothing had been done for the poor child, after all. What have we done, Matthew?

MR. VANE: We have secured the captain's room for her.

MRS. VANE: Well?

MR. VANE: We have secured the purser's room for ourselves, so as to be constantly near her.

MRS. VANE: Well?

MR. VANE: We have secured the seat on the captain's right at table for her.

MRS. VANE: Well?

MR. VANE: We have secured the exclusive attendance of the head stewardess.

MRS. VANE: Well?

MR. VANE: We have secured the whole time and services of the assistant surgeon.

MRS. VANE: Well?

MR. VANE: In short, as nearly as possible, we have secured the entire ship in every way.

MRS. VANE, *sighing*: It seems very little.

MR. VANE: It *is* very little, but it's all we could do.

MRS. VANE: Well, let us go and see if Muriel can be persuaded to come up. Oh, when I think of what the child has undergone! And all from that wretch! And all for nothing!

MR. VANE: Well, my dear, I have cheerfully joined you in censuring the young man in song and dance; but I really can't see that he was so very much to blame. He is a person of respectable standing in society.

MRS. VANE: Yes.

MR. VANE: He was graduated at Harvard with three honors: Reading, Writing, and Arithmetic, I believe they were.

MRS. VANE: Yes.

MR. VANE: He is very talented, with an ambition to shine as the scholar in politics.

MRS. VANE: Yes.

MR. VANE: To this end he has already secured a position on a Sunday paper as reporter, with a salary of ten dollars a week. It is not a vast sum; but, having a great deal of our own, we naturally despise money in others.

MRS. VANE: Yes.

MR. VANE: As such things go, he is in the way to promotion. In less than twenty-five years he might hope to be an Own Correspondent, with fifteen dollars a week.

MRS. VANE: Yes.

MR. VANE: He is a person of unblemished character and exceptionally pleasing manners. In dress he is a gentleman,—an American gentleman of English pattern.

MRS. VANE: Yes.

MR. VANE: He was very much in love with Muriel, and it is customary with young men to tell their love.

MRS. VANE: But wholly unnecessary! *All* the young men were in love with Muriel, but none of them thought it necessary to tell it. Why should *he*?

MR. VANE, *with conviction*: True!

MRS. VANE: He might have seen how sensitive, how high-spirited, how delicately constituted she was, how little calculated to know her own mind.

MR. VANE: Very true!

MRS. VANE: He might have known that it would be extremely repulsive and completely prostrating.

MR. VANE: I see.

MRS. VANE: But he was not even satisfied with telling Muriel that he loved *her*. He insisted upon knowing whether she loved *him*.

MR. VANE: That was certainly going too far.

MRS. VANE: The child had no alternative but flight, and—here we are!

MR. VANE: Perfectly true! He was obviously wrong. But what should he have done?

MRS. VANE: He should have waited.

MR. VANE: Waited?

MRS. VANE: Yes.

MR. VANE: What for?

MRS. VANE: For—for a more fitting opportunity.

MR. VANE: Oh! How long?

MRS. VANE: Indefinitely. Women sometimes have to wait all their lives. Why shouldn't men?

MR. VANE: There's a great deal in that.

MRS. VANE: Muriel is not exacting. Gratify her wishes, few and simple as they always are, and she asks nothing more. But come, Matthew! The child will be distracted at our absence. What are you stopping for?

MR. VANE: Oh, nothing! Merely an appropriate little ode that I thought I might repeat. But no matter!

MRS. VANE: Is it *very* appropriate?

MR. VANE: Quite.

MRS. VANE, *with resignation*: Perhaps you had better repeat it, then. You would never feel easy if you didn't.

MR. VANE: I think you are right, my dear.

MR. VANE
A Little Ode
There was a youth,
    He loved a maid.
He spoke the truth,
    She fled affrayed.

Had he forborne
    A little space,

Fate might have worn
    Another face.

In later mood
    It might have fared,
That she had wooed,
    And he been scared!

MRS. VANE: I don't think any thing of the kind would have happened with Muriel.

MR. VANE: Very possibly. I merely throw out the suggestion.

MRS. VANE: Yes, it has a very plausible sound; but it's much more probable that she would never have wooed him.

MR. VANE: You think not? But why?

MRS. VANE: Because, in that case, there would have been no opera.

MR. VANE: That hadn't occurred to me.

MRS. VANE: Well, come now! Muriel will be *so* impatient!

As the Vanes go below, Theron dashes from his concealment, and clutches the Steward by the arm.

THERON, *wildly*: Who—who—is this young lady?

STEWARD: What young lady, sir?

THERON: Don't trifle with me! The one who is coming up.

STEWARD: The one who 'as taken the captain's room?

THERON: Yes! Her name!

STEWARD: I 'aven't 'appened to 'ear 'er name, sir: but I 'ave a list of the cabin-passengers 'ere in my pocket, sir; and if you'll kindly 'old this waiter a moment, sir, I'll read it for you.

THERON, *taking the waiter*: Be quick! I am of a very impulsive nature, though trained in the school of indifferentism at our leading university; and I may not be able to restrain my impatience.

STEWARD: All right, sir! I've got it! 'Ere it is! I won't keep you a moment, sir (*unfolding the list*). Perhaps you would like to 'ave me sing it, sir?

THERON: Do you ordinarily sing it?

STEWARD: Well, yes, sir, we do, sir, on this ship, sir. The Mesopotamia is one of the *new* Retarders, you know, sir.

THERON: Very good, then! I should much prefer you to sing it.

He takes a shilling from his pocket, and gives it to him with a great show of secrecy, which the Steward emulates in receiving it.

STEWARD: Thank you kindly, sir. You won't

forget the pound ten at the hend of the voyage, *will* you, sir? Let me see a moment, sir. Oh, yes! "List of saloon-passengers per steamship Mesopotamia, sailing from Boston to Liverpool, April 1, 1884.

"Mr. Julian Ammidown.
Mr. and Mrs. Rufus Brown.
Major Connelly.
Colonel Donnelly.
Mrs. Susan Dewell.
Dr. Jacob Ewall.
Mr. and Mrs. Follansbee.
Mrs. 'Arris, Miss 'Arrises (three)"—
Goin' hout to heducate 'er daughters in Paris, and leavin' Mr. Haitch to supply the funds at 'ome, I suppose.

THERON: It is the national custom. Go on.

STEWARD: All right, sir.

"Mr. Ingham and Mr. Jones"—

THERON: No, no! Stop: I thought I could bear it for the sake of the effect, and the resemblance to Leporello's list in Don Giovanni; but I can't. Skip the rest of the alphabet, and get down to the V's at once!

STEWARD

"Mr. and Mrs. Matthew Vane"—

THERON

O my heart, burst not in twain!

STEWARD

"Miss Muriel Vane, two maids and pug.
Rev. Dr. Silas Wrugg."

THERON, *dropping the waiter*: Wait! Stop! Hold on! It is she! I knew it as soon as I recognized her parents' voices in my place of concealment.

STEWARD, *starting back*: Then you are—

THERON: A stowaway!

STEWARD: Very sorry, sir; but I shall be obliged to report you.

He picks up the fragments of the tumbler, and replaces them on the waiter.

THERON: *Report* me! And after I have spared *you?*

STEWARD: Well, you see, sir, a stowaway is very different, sir. The rules are very strict about reportin' 'em, sir. You'll be put in hirons, and sent back from Liverpool by the first return steamer.

He winks, and wags his hand behind him for money.

THERON: Irons? Are you open to bribery? (*The Steward turns round, wagging his hand. Theron continues aside.*) And am I the slave of this corrupt person? Subject to the beck and call of a deck steward? A thought strikes me! (*Aloud*) But I am not a common stowaway,—not one of those pitiful wretches, who, dying of poverty and homesickness in a foreign land, basely seek to return to friends and country at the expense of the company. My passage has been fully paid, and I occupy Berth 81 on the saloon-deck. Listen, and I will tell you all. I—

STEWARD: I beg your *pardon*, sir!

THERON: Well?

STEWARD: I *beg* your pardon, sir; but don't you think you'd better sing it? It's rather more the custom, sir. I *beg* your pardon!

THERON: Of course. I ought to have thought of that myself.

STEWARD: It would be a little more in keepin', sir. A great many gentlemen 'ave confided their 'eart 'istories to me, sir; and they halways sung them, sir. Many's the 'alf crown I've 'ad from them, sir, for listenin'.

THERON, *giving him money*: Very well. (*He sings*)

I am Love's Stowaway—

STEWARD, *interrupting*: I *beg* your pardon, sir; but don't you think you'd better wait for the chorus? It's just comin' hup, sir. The lookout 'as sighted a hiceberg, and the chorus is comin' hup to see it.

THERON: But I thought I heard a chorus at the beginning of the piece.

STEWARD: So you did, sir. That was the Chorus of Seamen. We've got two choruses on the Mesopotamia. The hold boats honly 'ad one. *This* chorus is a Chorus of Passengers.

THERON: Oh, well! if it's a chorus of *saloon*-passengers—

STEWARD: It is, sir.

THERON: Then, I don't mind waiting a reasonable time for them; but they mustn't be long.

STEWARD: They won't keep you a moment, sir. 'Ere they come now, sir.

Enter Chorus of Passengers, singing by groups.

GROUP OF GENTLEMEN PASSENGERS

We are lawyers and physicians,
Bankers, brokers, electricians,
Publishers and politicians,

Editors, professors, students
Of all kinds, whom our imprudence,
  In the mad pursuit of wealth,
Has compelled, for relaxation,
To endure a brief vacation;
  And we all are going over for our health.

But whatever be our station,
Our profession or vocation,
  Our politics, our objects, our ideals, and the rest,
Love alone, and love supremely,
Love alone, and love extremely,
  Is our life's great interest!

ALL
Yes, our life's great interest!

GROUP OF FASHIONABLE LADIES
We are daughters, wives, and mothers
To these gentlemen and brothers,
Whom, with very many others,
Our expensive tastes and passions,
Our caprices and our fashions,
  Goaded in pursuit of wealth;
But, worn out with the enjoyment
Which has formed our sole employment,
  Now we all are going over for our health;
And whatever be the notion
Of womanhood's devotion
  To such objects and ambitions as have our souls
    possest,
Love alone, and love supremely,
Love alone, and love extremely,
  Is our life's great interest.

ALL
Yes, our life's great interest!

GROUP OF MERCHANTS RETURNING FROM
THE BOSTON FOREIGN EXHIBITION
Russians, Polacks, Turks, Armenians,
Hindoos, Arabs, and Athenians,
Chinese, Japs, and Abyssinians,
Germans, Frenchmen, and Egyptians,
Orientals of all descriptions,
  From the mad pursuit of wealth,
In the city of the Yankees,
Hardly richer ev'n in Thank'ees,
  We are flying homeward for our health.
But whatever be the fraction,
Division or subtraction,
  Of the general sum-total as in numerals exprest,
Love alone, and love supremely,
Love alone, and love extremely,
  Is our life's great interest.

ALL
Yes, our life's great interest!

GROUP OF SHOP-GIRLS
We are some of the salesladies—
Minnies, Mamies, Susies, Sadies—
From the famous house whose trade is
The distinction and the glory
Of all modern retail story;
  And from its abundant wealth,
As a novel advertisement
Of ingenious devisement,
  It is sending us all over for our health.
But whatever were its motive,
A business one or votive,
  In despatching us so unexpectedly upon this
    quest,
Love alone, and love supremely,
Love alone, and love extremely,
  Is our life's great interest.

ALL
Yes, our life's great interest!

ALL THE LADIES: But we see no iceberg!
STEWARD: It's pretty low down yet, ladies. (To Theron) Now's your time, sir! I told you they wouldn't be long, sir!
THERON, *giving him money*: I shall never forget your thoughtful kindness in procuring me this sympathetic audience.

ONE OF THE LADIES
[*Recitative.*]
And who, pray, is this gentleman we see here,—
With us, although apparently not of us?

THERON: Ladies, if you will allow me, I will introduce myself.

A Confession
I am Love's Stowaway!
  Love lured me from my home,
  And far across the wandering foam
He bade me stray.

I am Love's Stowaway!
  He chose the fated bark;
  And, darkly plotting in the dark,
He did betray.

I am Love's Stowaway!
  And, where my love was hid,
  I followed blind, as blind Love bid:
I must obey.

I am Love's Stowaway!
  And here my love and I
  Together from each other fly,
The self-same way!

> [*Theron is about to continue his song, when enter Muriel with her father and mother, maids and pug.*]

ONE OF THE CHORUS
[*Recitative.*]
Wait! Stop! Excuse the seeming interruption!
We think the lady wishes to say something.

MURIEL
[*Recitative.*]
Merely to make a personal explanation,
Such as, in good society, is usual
On mingling with a company of strangers.

MURIEL
A *Statement*
I am a member of that Aristocracy,
  Wholly composed of the lovelier sex,
Which, in the heart of our New-World Democracy,
  Reigns, the observer to please and perplex.

Since I was born, well, I do not think, really,
  That I have been of the least use on earth:
All has been done that could *be* done, ideally,
  Utterly useless to make me from birth.

Never a wish that was not at once gratified;
  Nothing refused me that money could buy;
All my opinions respected and ratified,
  Since I could utter the first in a cry;

Flattered, deferred to, obeyed in society
  Like a young princess come into her own;
Free to do all that I would to satiety;
  Law to myself, first and last, and alone;

Dressed like one born to the purple imperial;
  Housed like a duchess, and served like a lord;
And, like the heroine of a cheap serial,
  By all that looked at me wildly adored;

I am a member of that Aristocracy,
  Wholly composed of the lovelier sex,
Which, in the heart of our New-World Democracy
  Reigns, the observer to please and perplex.

And the great wonder is, not that I'm odious—

CHORUS OF ALL THE MEN
No, we don't think you so! Nobody could!
No, we make protest in accents melodious!

MURIEL
Thanks. You are all, I am sure, very good.

Well, then, the miracle is, that the wealthily
Born and conditioned American girl,
Placed, as to all things that spoil, so unhealthily,
  Never's the Oyster, but always the Pearl.

> *She sinks into her steamer-chair, where the two maids elaborately arrange her. Theron stealthily retires toward the door of the smoking-room, and the Chorus gradually withdraw. Muriel remains with her party and the Steward.*

MRS. VANE: How do you feel now, dear?

MURIEL: So much better, mamma, thank you. How nice the air is! Mamma!

MRS. VANE: Yes, dear?

MURIEL: Would you mind just looking in my jewelry-case for poor Carlino's best collar? He's so shabby in this old thing!

MRS. VANE, *kissing her*: I'm *so* glad to see you taking an interest in life again. I'll be back instantly. (*Exit.*)

MR. VANE: Are you sure you're perfectly comfortable, my child?

MURIEL: Oh, perfectly, papa! Papa!

MR. VANE: Yes, my child?

MURIEL: I hate to be so much bother; but there's no one else I could trust to bring me— let me see!—my other earrings. I put on these drops never thinking, and diamonds are shocking before breakfast. (*She takes them out, and hands them to her father.*) It's too bad, sending you, papa!

MR. VANE: My child (*kissing her*), you know how happy it makes me to do any thing for you. (*Exit.*)

MURIEL: Sarah!

SARAH: Yes, Miss Muriel?

MURIEL, *taking a bracelet from her wrist, and giving it to Sarah*: I've been a great deal of trouble to you. Here's a little thing— I know you admire it. I've seen you looking at it.

SARAH: O Miss Muriel! what shall I do? (And me been saying such awful things about the poor, dear, pretty creature!)

MURIEL: Nothing, please. Sarah!

SARAH: Yes, Miss Muriel?

MURIEL: Do you suppose you could—wait a moment till I can think. Oh!—find me a lighter handkerchief? This is so heavy! It fatigues me.

SARAH: Why, Miss Muriel, I'd jump overboard for you! (*Exit.*)

MURIEL: Mary!

MARY: Yes, Miss Muriel?

MURIEL, *taking a brooch from her neck, and handing it to her*: Don't thank me, please. And— Mary!

MARY: Yes, Miss Muriel?

MURIEL: Do you think you could go away, and stay a little while, without any particular excuse? It's so tiresome making them!

MARY: Why, of course I can, Miss Muriel. And you're the sweetest, sensiblest, untroublesomest young lady in *this* world! And I won't come about the whole day again! *(Exit.)*

MURIEL, *with a sigh*: Now, Steward, we are alone. Have you any first name?

STEWARD: Why, miss, I 'aven't 'ardly any *last* name. I'm Robert, miss.

MURIEL: Well, Robert, I can see that you have a heart.

STEWARD: I 'ave, miss. *Hall* the stewards on the Mesopotamia 'as 'em, miss. The captain, and the hofficer on duty, and the 'ole crew, 'as 'em. 'Earts, and electric lights, set bowls, and annuncihators in all the state-rooms. Any little thing I could bring you, miss?

MURIEL: No, Robert, not at present. I have no appetite.

STEWARD: But your happetite will come back now. You won't be hill any more. Was you pretty bad, miss?

MURIEL: The sea-sickness was the least part of it *(sighing)*; though I *was* sick. Yes. But, Robert!

STEWARD: Yes, miss?

MURIEL: What were all those people doing here when I came up?

STEWARD: It was honly the chorus of passengers, miss, who 'ad come hup to see the hiceburg.

MURIEL: Oh! And who was the young gentleman who appeared to be singing to them?

STEWARD: Why, he was tellin' hall about 'imself, miss, in the song.

MURIEL: Oh, I dare say! But you never can make out the words, and I had no libretto. *(After a moment, musingly)* There was something strangely familiar in his voice and figure. But, of course, it could not be.

A Misgiving

I must not, I dare not, imagine it he,
  In his love and his sorrow forsaken;
Though, if we were not such a distance at sea,
  I should say that I was not mistaken.

The form and the face were the same; but, ah, me!
  Divided by many a billow,

I make my moan to the pitiless sea,
  And he sighs under the willow.

My moans cannot reach him, my love, where he sighs
  In metaphor under the willow:
The voice of his sorrow inaudible dies,
  Where I toss on the wandering billow.

But I thought for a moment—a breath,—it might be
  That I really was not mistaken,
Although such a very great distance at sea,
  In my pride and my folly forsaken.

He sang very well, I fancied.

STEWARD, *with musical reluctance*: Well, honly tolerable, miss. We've 'ad a great many tenors on the Mesopotamia.

MURIEL: Yes; but his voice had a certain sympathetic quality,—a *brio*, a *timbre*—

STEWARD: Very true, miss; but it was very thin in the hupper notes.

MURIEL: Oh, it wasn't perfect, I suppose! Do you happen to know his name, Robert?

STEWARD: Well, no, miss, I don't know 'is *name*: but I've got my list of the passengers 'ere; and if you'll kindly 'old my waiter, miss *(he gives it to her, with the fragments of the tumbler on it)*, I'll read it hover to you.

MURIEL: You are very good, Robert.

STEWARD: Or, what do you say, as you seem to be a connyshure, miss, to my singin' it?

MURIEL: Do you sometimes sing it?

STEWARD: Yes, miss, I *generally* sing it.

MURIEL: I shall be delighted.

STEWARD

[Singing.]

"Mr. Julian Ammidown.
Mr. and Mrs. Rufus Brown.
Major Connelly.
Colonel Donnelly.
Mrs. Susan Dewell.
Dr. Jacob Ewall.
Mr. and Mrs. Follansbee.
Mrs. 'Arris, Miss 'Arrises (three)"—

Oh! Beg your pardon, miss! 'Ere's a name I missed once before between the Hefs and the Haitches,—

"Mr. Theron Gay"—

MURIEL, *flinging the waiter from her, and bursting wildly from her chair, with her hands to her temples*: Theron!

THERON, *rushing from the door of the smoking-room*: Muriel!

They fly into each other's arms, and sing.

A Collision.

MURIEL

Oh, if you be some fond and dear illusion,
　Some blessed dream,
Born of the brain's fantastical confusion,
　Be what you seem!
　　Stay with me, stay,
　　Fade not away,
Oh, dearly loved illusion!

THERON

I am no vision, no hallucination:
　Be not afraid!
Wholly unchanged in substance and formation,
　I could not fade,
　　My love, my bride,
　　Ev'n if I tried,
Like an hallucination!

MURIEL, *with dignity*: Then, if you are really Mr. Theron Gay, of Boston, Mass., I must ask you, as a gentleman, to leave me.

THERON, *astounded*: Leave you, Muriel? But you just requested me to remain!

MURIEL: That was under the impression that you were a pleasing unreality. I was very explicit.

THERON: And, as a reality, am I so unpleasing?

MURIEL: That is not the question. You must release me.

THERON: If you insist. But why?

MURIEL: For one thing, it is essential to the plot.

THERON, *releasing her*: Oh! if it is essential to the plot, of course I must yield. The literary instinct teaches that.

MURIEL: And, besides, you have no right to be here. You had no right to follow me. Especially on the same steamer.

THERON: But, my love, I didn't know you were on board. That is the strangest part of it. I fled, in my madness and despair, by the first steamer I could get. It happened to be the very ship you had embarked in. (*Tenderly*) Cannot you recognize some design of Fate in this coincidence, Muriel?

MURIEL: If it is, as you say, purely an accident—

THERON: Oh, it is!

MURIEL: Then I forgive you, but on condition that you go ashore instantly.

THERON: Why, but, Muriel—

MURIEL: Don't reply! I simply ask you, as a gentleman, to go ashore, and not persist in attentions which you must see are very disagreeable. (*She returns to her steamer-chair, and talks while he makes her comfortable in it with the shawls, cushions, and wraps.*) I will not ask you how it is that you came to choose this ship—

THERON: It was a fatality. Will you have this shawl over your feet?

MURIEL: Yes, thank you. And I will not imply that you knew very well I was on board.

THERON: Oh, I swear to you that it would be doing me serious injustice! I had scarcely any idea of it. (*Fitting a cushion to her shoulders*) Is that comfortable?

MURIEL: Perfectly, thanks. I will not insinuate that you have been planning this interview ever since you knew I was here, helpless and defenceless.

THERON: Oh, never! Will you have the pug in your lap, or in your arms?

MURIEL: In my arms, please. You are very kind, I'm sure, and I'm quite ashamed to give you so much trouble; but I will merely say, that, if you have a spark of honorable feeling, you will go ashore at once. I will be calm, I will be reasonable; but you must go.

THERON: Why, but, Muriel, it's quite impossible! We are forty-eight hours out from Boston; and, even at the comparatively low rate of speed characteristic of the Retarders, we must be two or three hundred miles at sea. I would do any thing to oblige a lady, any thing to gratify my dearest love; but, at the moment, I find it quite impracticable to go ashore.

MURIEL: You will not?

THERON: I cannot!

MURIEL: Then, I shall simply go wild.

MURIEL, THERON, STEWARD

A Delirium
　　Yes, I shall go wild!
　　Befooled, beguiled,
Followed afar in my flight by insolent treason,
I call, with the last ray of reason,
　　Papa!
　　Mamma!
Come to your child!

THERON

No, do not go wild:
You are not beguiled!
Hear me, my loved one, my only one, listen to
    reason!
    I am wholly guiltless of treason.
        Papa!
        Mamma!
    Come to your child!

STEWARD

They both will go wild.
He, unjustly reviled,
Cannot convince her that he is guiltless of treason,
Cannot make her listen to reason.
        Papa!
        Mamma!
    Come to your child!
    [*Mr. and Mrs. Vane rush distractedly on
    deck, with the Chorus of Passengers, all
    bringing life-preservers.*]

MR. VANE

Mamma!

MRS. VANE

Papa!

BOTH

We come to you, child!

CHORUS

Papa!
Mamma!
Come to your child!

MRS. VANE

Oh! what is it, my precious one?

MR. VANE

My child, what is it?

CHORUS

Is it an iceberg?
        [*They get out their opera-glasses.*]

THERON
                            [*With exasperation.*]
No: it is an ice girl!

CHORUS

A nice girl?

THERON

Yes, an ice girl!

CHORUS

Oh, no puns!
We are not the ones
To be amused with trivial word-play of that kind.

THERON
                            [*Furiously.*]
    I said a girl of ice,
    Not a girl that is nice.
To any sort of jesting I am not now inclined.

MURIEL, *clinging to a hand of each*: O papa!
O mamma! See! It's Theron!

MRS. VANE, *putting on her glasses*: It is indeed!
Wretch! How came he here?

MR. VANE, *putting on his glasses*: Upon my
word, so it is. Mr. Gay, you must be aware that
this is very—very—

MRS. VANE: Use some violent expression, Matthew!

MR. VANE: I will, my dear,—unexpected!

THERON: I know it, Mr. Vane. It's quite unintentional.

MRS. VANE: Oh! Unintentional!

MURIEL, *faintly*: Don't be harsh with him,
mamma. But when I simply asked him, as a
gentleman, to go ashore, and leave me—

MRS. VANE: He refused?

MURIEL: He said he couldn't.

MRS. VANE: A likely story! Where is the captain? I will see the captain about this. (*Running,
and shaking her parasol at the man at the wheel*)
Oh—ah! My good man!

MAN AT THE WHEEL, *looking round*: Ay, ay,
ma'am!

MRS. VANE: Where is the captain?

MAN AT THE WHEEL: He's down in the boiler-
room, ma'am, takin' the reck'nin'.

MRS. VANE: Send him here at once.

MAN AT THE WHEEL: Ay, ay, ma'am!
                    [*Recitative down speaking-tube.*]

Captain, you're wanted here! And I may hadd,
    sir,
Seems a young lady, taken wery bad, sir.
I can't just tell you if there's need to worry,
But the young lady's mother says to 'urry.
        [*The Captain appears on deck instantly, with
        a sextant in his hands, a telescope under one
        arm, and a speaking-trumpet under the other.*]

CAPTAIN
An Explanation
I am the Mesopotamia's very obliging commander;
    And I will say it, with whom boasting was never
        the wont,

No swifter craft than this has swum the seas since
    Leander
Executed his famed feat on the dark Hellespont.

No, the Mesopotamia is not an old-time Retarder,
    Such as we read of once in the American press,
Flabby and flat in *cuisine,* and frowsy in state-
    room and larder,
    With (as in classical art) nothing at all in ex-
    cess.

Passengers here may converse with officers on and
    off duty,
    And will especially, please, talk with the man
    at the wheel;
Honor, obscurity, riches, poverty, homeliness,
    beauty,
    Constitute equal parts here of the same com-
    monweal.

Such are the company's rules; and I think you
    will easily gather
    From my behavior thus far, that the particular
    part
I would assume toward you all, is the part of
    affectionate father,
    With the more delicate ones' interests chiefly
    at heart.

Well, ladies, which of you sent for me?

MRS. VANE: It was I, captain, on behalf of my
daughter.

MR. VANE: On behalf of our daughter—yes!

CAPTAIN: And what can I do for you, miss?

MURIEL: Nothing. But the man at the wheel
makes me giddy, turning it round so.

CAPTAIN, *through his trumpet, to the Man at
the Wheel:* Lash your wheel!

MAN AT THE WHEEL, *obeying:* Ay, ay, sir! (*Attempting to sing*)

        I am the—

CAPTAIN, *sternly:* Belay that! (*To Muriel*) Anything more, miss?

MURIEL: No,—only the ship seems to tremble a
good deal.

CAPTAIN, *to the Man at the Wheel:* Tell the
officer on duty to send me the engineer.

MAN AT THE WHEEL: Ay, ay, sir! (*Down speak-
ing-tube*) Engineer!

ENGINEER
[*Appearing instantly, and attempting to sing.*]
        I am the—

CHORUS
Oh, stow it!
We know it.

CAPTAIN
We've had enough of explanation, and we'll show
it.

A Suggestion

If you wish to deliver some long explanation,
    Mainly in honor and praise of yourself,
Be not deceived with the fond expectation,
    That the world, which it brings neither glory
    nor pelf,
        Will list to your call:
    The right way for you is to hire a hall!
    Yes, hire a hall!

If your tongue should be long, and be hung in
    the middle,
    And it chance that you be of the lovelier sex,
With a gift beyond symphony, cymbals, or fiddle,
    The soul of your husband to pierce and to vex,
        And you *must* caterwaul,
    The right way for you is to hire a hall!
    Yes, hire a hall!

If you are a poet, and lately have written
    Some verses you fancy uncommonly fine;
If you are a lover, just given the mitten,—
    And no one will hearken, you should not repine.
        'Tis the fortune of all;
    The right way for you is to hire a hall!
    Yes, hire a hall!

If you're a pianist, and have a fell passion
    For banging away at the keys by the hour,
Allow me! There is a more merciful fashion
    Than socially making displays of your power,—
        A fashion for all:
    The right way for you is to hire a hall!
    Yes, hire a hall!

If you are a statesman or ward politician,
    A man with a grievance, a maid with a grief,
An agent, a dentist, a soul with a mission,
    Beware how your turn to your friends for relief.
        I'll be frank with you all:
    The right way for you is to hire a hall!
    Yes, hire a hall!

If you are a—

CHORUS
Oh, hire a hall!

CAPTAIN: I bow to the will of the—Remnant.
(*To the Engineer*) Go down, and stop the engines.

ENGINEER: Ay, ay, sir! (*Exit.*)

CAPTAIN, *to Muriel*: Is that all, miss?

MURIEL, *reluctantly*: Y-e-e-e-e-s.

MRS. VANE: Muriel, I must speak, if *you* will not. Captain, she is annoyed by the presence of one of the young gentlemen on board, who refuses to go ashore.

CAPTAIN: Which young gentleman is it, ma'am?

MRS. VANE: Shall I indicate him more particularly, Muriel?

MURIEL, *veiling her eyes with her hand*: I suppose you must, mamma. But don't be harsh!

MRS. VANE: I will be firm. It is Mr. Gay.

CAPTAIN, *to Theron, sternly*: I have not had the pleasure of seeing you before, sir, I think.

THERON: Very true. I have lately been describing myself in song to the ladies and gentlemen present as Love's Stowaway. So far as relates to the payment of my passage, the term is not perfectly accurate. The purser will tell you that my ticket was quite regular. I occupy Berth 81 on the saloon-deck; but I called myself Love's Stowaway because I was here without the knowledge of a young lady who was flying on your ship from a hemisphere which my attentions had rendered insupportable to her. I will not spare myself, sir—

MURIEL, *to Mrs. Vane*: Oh, how generous, how magnanimous, he is!

MRS. VANE: Hush, my child! If you give way, the affair must end here.

MURIEL: Well, I will be patient, then.

THERON: I will not shrink from saying that I told her my love at a moment when it was surprising, and perhaps painful, to her. I also fled; and, by a series of accidents, I found myself on the same ship with Miss Vane. If you had been on deck immediately after the opening chorus, you could have heard me state the same facts in recitative. Now, do with me as you will. I am, strictly speaking, Love's Unintentional Stowaway. But I am a stowaway, and I do not shrink from the penalty. Put me in irons.

MRS. VANE, *to Muriel, who is weeping*: Remember, if you yield now, you spoil every thing.

CAPTAIN: Well, ma'am, there are practical difficulties in the way of Mr. Gay's going ashore. I have just been taking an observation in the boiler-room, and we are twenty-three miles from land. It is a very quick run: we are only two days out.

MURIEL: But, captain, you could turn the ship round, and go back with him, couldn't you?

CAPTAIN: Yes, miss, we could do that; but it would postpone our arrival in Europe almost indefinitely. It would be simpler to throw him overboard.

MURIEL: I don't think I could quite consent to that. It would be inhuman, wouldn't it?

CAPTAIN: It would be unusual; but, as I understand, it is an extreme case.

MURIEL: Yes, it is. It is very provoking. Is there no other way?

CAPTAIN: Yes. If you could wait, miss, we might transfer him to the first homeward-bound ship we met.

MURIEL: Perhaps we had better wait.

CAPTAIN: In the meantime I will just have him loaded with chains.

MURIEL, *starting forward*: With chains?

CAPTAIN: Yes, miss, as a stowaway by his own confession.

MURIEL: Oh, yes! (*She sinks back in her chair.*) Of course!

THERON

A Defiance

Yes, load me with chains!
    What are your iron links
To the bonds in which my last hope wanes,
    My spirit sinks?

Yes, load me with chains!
    Spare not, do not delay!
Soon I shall lie, 'neath the suns and the rains,
    Death's Stowaway!

> [*A group of Seamen appear with handcuffs and heavy chains. At the end of each stanza they dance some steps of the Sailor's Hornpipe.*]

THE SEAMAN'S PROTEST

Oh! don't you think it's hard on the sympathetic sailor,
    Whose heart is in his hand, and whose hand is on his hip,
To make him play the part of policeman or of jailer,
    And render him detestable to all aboard the ship?

For our natural disposition we refer you to the pictures,
    And the story-books the landsmen write about the jolly tar;
Though we might make, of course, our suggestions and our strictures,
    You must go to them, if really you would know us as we are.

'Tis our ordinary habit to sing of Sue and Polly
  As we lightly climb aloft, to reef the topsail in
    the gale;
We are all opposed, on principle, to care and
    melancholy;
  We love to catch the shark, and harpoon the
    sleeping whale.

Then, when all the toils and dangers of the day
    are safely over,
  'Tis our custom to lie basking before the fo'c's'le
    fire,
Spinning yarns and piping ditties of maiden and
    of lover,
  And watch the cheery flames till they flicker
    and expire.

And nothing more repugnant to the feelings of a
    sailor,
  Than loading of a gentleman with chains can
    be conceived;
And that we should have to play the policeman
    or the jailer
  On this ship's, a thing that none of us would
    ever have believed.

                    [*They load Theron with chains.*]

MURIEL, *sobbing convulsively*: But, captain, suppose we don't meet any homeward-bound ship?

CAPTAIN: Then, miss,—the idea has just occurred to me,—we could put him off on an iceberg. We are now entering the region of floating ice, and we may encounter a suitable iceberg at any moment. They are continually drifting toward the coast of Labrador; and the chances are, that within a week, or ten days at the farthest, he would find himself within the Straits of Belle Isle, from whence he could easily make his way by the Intercolonial Railway to Halifax, and so by boat to Boston.

MURIEL: Do you think an iceberg is preferable to a homeward-bound merchant-vessel?

CAPTAIN: It's about an even thing, miss.

MURIEL, *thoughfully*: It would be more romantic on an iceberg.

CAPTAIN: Yes, it would certainly be more romantic.

MURIEL: I should think Theron would prefer it. Well, then, let it be whichever we meet first.

CAPTAIN: All right, miss. Steward!

STEWARD: Yes, sir?

CAPTAIN: Tell the third officer in charge of the passengers' luggage to have Mr. Gay's boxes brought up out of the hold; and go and fetch his valise out of his state-room yourself. Not a moment is to be lost.

STEWARD: Yes, sir. (*Exit.*)

A derrick is seen lifting Theron's trunk through a bulkhead in the deck. The Steward re-appears with Theron's bag and travelling-shawls. The latter removes his Glengarry cap, and puts on his silk hat, as if going ashore. The Chorus, now fully realizing the horror of the situation, start forward in protest.

CHORUS

What is this, O dread commander
  Of the Mesopotam-i-a?
If we rightly understand her,
  We are filled with wild dismay.

In default of home-bound vessel,
  Would she see her true-love, pray,
Left with the winds and waves to wrestle,
  On an iceberg cast away?

CAPTAIN

Yes; for, if I understand her,
  She will brook no more delay.

MURIEL

Only because, O dread commander!
  You can think of no other way.

THERON

Yes, fond friends and sympathizing,
  Truly there is no other way
In the scope of our surmising;
  And, as a gentleman, I obey.

MR. VANE

This is politeness most surprising.

MRS. VANE

It is the least that he could say!

MR. VANE

Were I readier at devising,
  He should never be cast away.

STEWARD

I am worse by the thirty shilling
  'E would have given me, I dare say,
At the hend of the voyage!

CHORUS
Thrilling,
Far beyond our feeble lay,
Is the existing situation.
No one, we think, will say us nay,
When we add an execration
Of the Fates that still betray.
But since nothing can be more certain
Than that there seems no other way,
Dropping over our grief a curtain,
Let us be light, let us be gay!
[They dance.]

CAPTAIN, STEWARD, AND MR. AND MRS. VANE
[Dancing together.]
Let us be light, let us be gay!

THERON
[Dancing alone.]
Let them be light, let them be gay!

MURIEL
[Keeping time with her head.]
Let him be light, let him be gay!

But in the meantime, Theron, if you have any thing to say in justification of your strange conduct, I cannot refuse to hear it; though, of course, it won't affect the final result.

THERON: No, Muriel, I understand that perfectly. Do you mean my conduct in finding myself on the same ship with you?

MURIEL: No: that is all past, now!

THERON: Oh! Then, you mean my conduct in offering myself to you. Well, there is nothing I would like to say; but there is something I would like to sing.

MURIEL: Could you make it short? I am really quite worn out. I have been so *terribly* sea-sick, Theron! And I haven't literally slept a wink since I came on board. Singing seems to string the ideas out so! And there has been so much of it! And then, if there happens to be an *encore*, there's no living through it.

THERON: I will try to boil it down.

MURIEL: Do! And I hope the music isn't abrupt or dramatic? I really couldn't bear it, in my exhausted state.

THERON: No: it's a simple, pleasing air,—rather soothing, than otherwise, I believe.

MURIEL: Well, then, sit down by me while you sing, Theron, and take my hand in yours. We may part so soon! *(He obeys.)*

THERON
A Justification
You ask me why? We both were young;
And round our lives the rosy air
Full of divine expectance hung,
Like the soft light that everywhere
Clings to the leafless branches bare,
In March while yet the trees are bare.

You ask me why? It was the time
The bird begins to build its nest,
And all the world is filled with rhyme
Of soul to soul, and breast to breast;
With rapture wild, and sweet unrest,
With spring-time's wild and sweet unrest.

You ask me why? It was the hour
When Doubt is lulled, and Hope awakes,
And certain tender dreams have power
Upon us for their own sweet sakes;
And all such different seeming takes,
Such mystic midnight seeming takes.

You ask me why? It was the place
Of many a summer-breathing flower;
The rose's bloom, the lily's grace,
Drooped o'er us in the mimic bower,
Around the fountain's gush and shower,
The tiny fountain's gush and shower.

You ask me why? We sat alone.
In distant rooms we heard the waltz
Throb dully; and, in undertone,
You bade me tell you of your faults;
Amid the pulses of the waltz,
You bade me tell you of your faults.
[While he sings, she drowses, unseen by him. Her head sinks on her breast.]

THERON
Muriel, love? She weeps!

CHORUS
No, no, she sleeps!
The aching heart, the weary brain,
At last are free from pain.
Muriel sleeps.

MR. AND MRS. VANE
Yes, yes, she sleeps!
Be silent, oh! and make no stir,
Lest you awaken her.
Muriel sleeps.

CAPTAIN
[*Through his trumpet.*]
Ay, ay, she sleeps!
The wretch who dares to breath a word
Henceforth, goes overboard.
Muriel sleeps.

MAN AT THE WHEEL
[*Sounding the whistle.*]
Ay, ay, she sleeps!
Oh, softly, whistle, softly sigh
The news afar and nigh!
Muriel sleeps.

THERON
Oh, joy! She sleeps!
It was my song that brought surcease
Of pain to her, and peace.
Muriel sleeps.

MURIEL
[*Stirring in her sleep.*]
Come back! *I* love you too!

CHORUS OF ALL THE VOICES
Hush, hush!
Our Muriel dreams.
A tender flush
Bepaints her cheek, and seems
The light of dreams.

Hush, hush!
Our Muriel raves.
Oh, cease your roar and rush,
Ye winds and waves!
Our Muriel raves.

Hush, hush!
Of love she raves,
And parting; and a gush
Of hot tears steals
From underneath her fallen lids, and laves
Her pale, worn cheeks,
And eloquently speaks
The sorrow that she feels,
Even while she sleeps!
Even while she sleeps,
She weeps!

[*The scene is slowly darkened until all the figures become invisible, while the Chorus continues.*]

CURTAIN

ACT II

MURIEL'S DREAM

The scene is the same; but the deck is now gorgeously decorated with rich stuffs in various colors, hanging from the shrouds and yards, and forming a pavilion, open at the back, so as to show the other guard of the steamer, and the sea beyond. The front of the house is wreathed with flowers, enormous rosettes adorn all the upright surfaces, the masts and funnels are likewise garlanded, and the mouths of the funnels are filled with vast bouquets, through which the smoke is seen escaping. There is a touch of something fantastic in all these decorations, and in the dress of all the persons present, who are in ball-costume.

CHORUS
[*Promenading arm in arm.*]
Ladies and gentlemen,
If at all singular
In our appearance
Some of us seem,
Let us enlighten you:
We are not really
People, but only
Things in a dream,—
Muriel's dream!

All this magnificent
Paraphernalia
That you will notice
Here, if you please,
Is but the scenery
That quite subjectively,
As in a vision
Dreaming she sees,—
Muriel sees!

And though the opera
May appear tedious
In its performance,
Yet it is plain
All its occurrences
Are simultaneous,
All in an instant
Flashed on the brain,—
Muriel's brain!

MURIEL, *magnificently dressed, promenading arm in arm with Theron:* And so we're going to have a ball! How perfectly fascinating! Do you know, Theron, I've often wondered they didn't have them oftener on the Retarders? It would certainly be an attraction.

THERON: Yes, I think it would. How do you like the decorations?

MURIEL, *pausing a moment to glance up at them, with her hands clasped through his arm*: Beautiful! A little peculiar, perhaps?

THERON: No: I don't think so.

MURIEL: Well, perhaps not. Who did them?

THERON: They were designed by the Society for the Prevention of Decorative Art. The piano is from the establishment of Messrs. Chickerway & Steining.

He pauses, and takes up in his hand a toy grand piano.

MURIEL: Oh, yes! It's one of their new Baby Grands. But *(regarding it critically)* isn't it rather small?

THERON, *walking on*: It *is* small; but it will grow.

MURIEL: Oh, certainly! It will grow—in time.

THERON: Yes: it will grow old.

MURIEL: That was what I meant. There are to be refreshments, I suppose?

THERON: Well, very light. *Bouillon* for the ladies, and chocolate-creams and chewing-gum for the salesladies.

MURIEL: Perfect! Who suggested the ball?

THERON: Why, to tell the truth, *I* thought of it.

MURIEL: But how came you to have such a fortunate inspiration? You're so stupid, usually, you know. (It doesn't seem to be quite what I meant to say!)

THERON: Well, I don't know. I thought it would be a graceful little attention to the steerage-passengers if I got up a sort of *fête* for them in celebration of my approaching departure.

MURIEL, *fondly*: How *like* you, Theron! But *(looking about)* I don't see any of the steerage-passengers here.

THERON: No: they're rather a low set. Of course we couldn't have them present.

MURIEL: Of course not. Theron!

THERON: Yes, dearest?

MURIEL: I never thought! But where did the flowers come from? So far at sea, you know.

THERON: Oh! The flowers are artificial.

MURIEL: Why, so they are! But they looked as unnatural as the real ones.

THERON: The captain has them watered with cologne from time to time, and that keeps them fresh. Here comes the man, now.

A seaman appears with garden-hose, and

sprinkles the flowers, executing, at the same time, some steps of the Hornpipe.

MURIEL: I never saw any thing so lavish! And how characteristic of a seaman, to dance!

THERON: The captain has spared no expense, and the crew all enter into the spirit of the affair.

MURIEL, *with an uneasy sigh*: I suppose the decorations are all right; but don't you think the company is rather queer?

THERON: I see nothing queer about them.

MURIEL: Well, if I didn't know that I was awake, I should certainly think I was dreaming. Those Arab gentlemen, now: they seem to have become quite dark since I first saw them.

THERON: Yes, they are Arabian Nights now.

MURIEL: That accounts for it. Well, it must be right. But why do the gentlemen all keep their bonnets on?

THERON: To prevent the bees in them from escaping. They've got bees in their bonnets, to a man!

MURIEL: I see. Theron!

THERON: Well?

MURIEL: I don't like to ask so many questions, but *why* has the captain got on an over-skirt?

THERON, *carelessly*: Oh, I suppose he's heard of the secretary of the treasury issuing a steamboat-captain's commission to that lady in Mississippi, and wishes to be ready for the change.[1]

MURIEL: How stupid of me not to think! But *do* you like papa in mamma's fichu?

THERON: I think it's rather becoming.

MURIEL, *thoughtfully*: Perhaps the color is. But now—mamma in a dress-coat! Do you think it's quite the thing?

THERON: Why, it's very common, you know.

MURIEL: Yes. What have they *all* got on?

THERON: Their life-preservers.

MURIEL: Oh! I see. But is it safe, having them round the knees?

THERON: Well, they do less harm there, probably. They can take them off if any thing happens.

MURIEL: True. Why have they got all these signs stuck about, "Keep off the grass"? I don't see any grass.

THERON: No: it isn't up yet. But there'll be plenty of it before we get to Liverpool,—sea-grass, you know. The Mesopotamia is generally covered with it when it comes into port. It's very decorative.

[1] In 1884 Mrs. Mary A. Miller of Louisiana was issued a license to command a Mississippi steamboat by Kenneth Raynor, the Solicitor of the Treasury.

MURIEL: I dare say. I would like to speak with the steward, please.

STEWARD, *instantly appearing, with his left hand developed into a spacious waiter*: Yes, miss?

MURIEL, *staring*: Ugh! Oh! I merely wished to see the captain a moment. Robert!

STEWARD: Yes, miss?

MURIEL, *indicating his hand*: Is it—comfortable?

STEWARD: Perfectly, miss. It's convenient; and it can't fly hout of your 'old in rough weather, miss, like the hold style of waiter.

MURIEL: Yes, there's that to be said. And—Robert!

STEWARD: Yes, miss?

MURIEL: You don't notice any thing odd about the company, do you?

STEWARD: Nothing whatever, miss.

MURIEL, *in bewilderment*: Yes: that's what Theron said. Well, send me the captain. (*The Steward vanishes, and the Captain appears.*) Oh! I have been waiting for you. But (*severely*) I wish you wouldn't flash upon me in that disagreeable manner. One would think you were something at the theatre, coming up out of the floor.

CAPTAIN: Well, miss, I'm greatly pressed for time. I've to get this ball over before breakfast.

MURIEL: It seems to me it's a very droll time for a ball.

CAPTAIN: It's a *matinée*; to let the steerage-passengers go to their work in season. Besides, I dare say you've been at a great many balls where you had to hurry to get through before breakfast.

MURIEL: That is perfectly true. But now tell me frankly, captain, do you notice any thing strange about your guests?

CAPTAIN, *looking round*: Well, no, miss. They seem dressed as people usually are at a dancing-party.

MURIEL, *in despair*: Oh, dear! But Theron, now: why does Theron wear that enormous bow on the small of his back? Whisper it, please.

CAPTAIN, *glancing from Theron to the pug, which is similarly equipped, and then replying through his trumpet*: Because the other one has it, I suppose.

MURIEL, *bursting into tears*: Oh, don't turn the poor fellow into ridicule at the last moment! It's inhuman! (*She runs to him, and, detaching the bow, flings it into the sea. Then a thought seems to strike her.*) Theron!

THERON: Yes, Muriel?

MURIEL: Why, you are still here!

THERON: Yes. We haven't met any home-bound vessel yet.

MURIEL: Well, it won't do. We have made all our preparations for parting, and we must part.

Duet of Resignation

MURIEL

Yes, we must part, for parting comes to all:
  It is the thought that poisons love's delight;
In rapture's cup it is the drop of gall;
  At noon it is the shadow of the night.

THERON

Yes, we must part. We only live to part:
  The bird must leave its native sky afar,
The leaf its bough, the rose its stem, the heart
  Its hope; the day must lose its morning star.

BOTH

Yes, we must part, O love! or soon or late,
  Whether we laugh or weep, or smile or sigh,
It is of all that lives the common fate;
  And love itself at last must fade and die.

MURIEL, *sobbing*: But what about the iceberg, Theron? The captain promised me, that, if we met no home-bound vessel, you should be put off on an iceberg!

THERON, *sobbing*: The lookout hasn't sighted any iceberg yet.

LOOKOUT, *on top of the house*: Sail, ho!

CAPTAIN, *through his trumpet*: Where away?

LOOKOUT: On the port-quarter, sir.

CAPTAIN: Heave to!

LOOKOUT: Ay, ay, sir!

CAPTAIN: Cast the log!

LOOKOUT: Ay, ay, sir!

CAPTAIN: Reef the starboard watch!

LOOKOUT: Ay, ay, sir!

CAPTAIN: Eight bells!

LOOKOUT: Eight bells it is, sir!

CAPTAIN: Yare!

LOOKOUT: Ay, ay, sir!

CAPTAIN: Luff!

LOOKOUT: Ay, ay, sir!

CHORUS

Oh, how excessively
Novel and interesting!
Let us be writing
  Letters to send—
If he will pardon us

Offering to trouble him
With their conveyance—
Home by our friend.
[*They all take out postal-cards, and write.*]

LOOKOUT: Little mistake, sir!

CAPTAIN: Well?

LOOKOUT: It isn't a sail, sir. It's a hiceberg.

CHORUS, *getting out their glasses*: An iceberg!

THERON: Muriel!

MURIEL: Theron!

They fly into each other's arms.

CHORUS OF ALL THE GENTLEMEN PASSENGERS

Cruel girl! Can nothing move you
    From the deed that you would do?
If it be worthy death to love you,
    Know that we are guilty too.
Put us off on the iceberg too!

CHORUS OF ALL THE LADY PASSENGERS

Shameless thing! If we could only
    Do what we would like to do,
His exile should not be lonely.
    Let these wretches stay with you!
We would go on the iceberg too.

THERON
[*Soothing Muriel.*]

Nay, kind ladies, do not chide her:
    She but does what she must do.
I am willing to abide her
    Final wish in the premises. You
      Must not think of coming too.
No, kind ladies, it would not do!

MURIEL: That is very sweet of you, Theron. Not that I care for them. But I'm sure you won't suffer much, if any. It's coming summer, and the iceberg will be cool and pleasant. You will be abundantly provided with food, fuel, cigars, and reading-matter. You'll soon drift ashore somewhere. But, in any case, it can't be helped. You must go. There's no other way of getting rid of you. Don't you see, dearest?

THERON: Oh, yes! I see, Muriel. You're quite right. I dare say I shall do very well.

MURIEL: Captain, we don't seem to be approaching very rapidly.

CAPTAIN: That's because we're going *towards* the iceberg. If we were sailing *from* it, you would see how soon we should overhaul it.

MURIEL: Oh, yes! I forgot that this was one of the Retarders.

Sound of distant singing is heard.

CAPTAIN: But, even as it is, we sha'n't be long. There, you can hear the people on the iceberg already.

MR. VANE: Are they usually inhabited, captain?

CAPTAIN: Yes, usually, but not always.

MR. VANE: How very odd!

MRS. VANE: And are the inhabitants like us?

CAPTAIN, *with some embarrassment*: Well, ma'am, that depends upon what you mean by *us*. If you mean *me*,—well, no: they're not precisely like us. They're fairies.

MURIEL: Fairies?

CAPTAIN: Yes, miss. And there's another difference. They're all beautiful young ladies. Yes, it's a singular fact, but one well known to science, that the inhabitants of icebergs are all fairies, all young, all beautiful, and all ladies.

MURIEL, *with misgiving*: O Theron, dear! do you think you'd *better* go? If any thing should happen to you, I could never forgive myself.

THERON: Don't be troubled, Muriel. I shall be perfectly safe, I've no doubt.

CAPTAIN: There, miss, you can hear them quite distinctly now.

CHORUS OF THE ICEBERG FAIRIES
[*As they sing, the iceberg approaches; and they are seen scattered over its peaks and slopes, draped in flowing white and blue, and wearing fillets of frosted silver in their hair. The iceberg softly touches the side of the steamer, and the seamen make it fast. They place a staging from the rail to the deck.*]

Out of the frozen realms of the North,
    From the dreamless solitudes
    Where immemorial silence broods
Over a world that is white and whist
    As is the pale, dead moon,
    Singing a mystic rune,
Clad all in pearl and amethyst,
Life out of Death, we have wandered forth.

Out of the beautiful northern sky,
    From the eerie flash and play
    Of lights that fairer than the day
Paint the long night of half a year,
    We may describe ourselves
    As some auroral elves,
Who, having left their normal sphere,
Through the world are wandering far and nigh.

MR. VANE: This is very interesting, very definite, and, upon the whole, satisfactory. But I'm rather surprised that they should adopt that scientific view of the moon's condition. From fairies I should expect something more poetical.

CAPTAIN: Oh! science has penetrated everywhere; and I may say that Iceberg Fairies are, as a rule, nothing if not scientific.

MR. VANE, *with conviction*: True. (*From moment to moment, various inscriptions reveal themselves on the sides of the iceberg, as "St. Jacob's Oil Conquers Pain," "Anti-Fat," "Burdock Blood Bitters," "Rock and Rye," etc.*) I observe that they seem to have adopted several of our popular remedies at the North Pole.

CAPTAIN: There's a great deal of rheumatism there, and, with an exclusive meat-diet, the blood needs purifying in the spring. You'll find the whole North Pole painted over with patent-medicine advertisements in the American fashion.

MR. VANE: Ah! that's an additional motive for not discovering it. Well, Muriel, I suppose there's no occasion for further delay. Shall I speak to these ladies, or will you?

MURIEL: Perhaps *I* had better, papa, as they seem strangers. (*She advances to the rail of the steamer next the iceberg.*) Hmm! Let me see! Whom shall I ask for? Oh! Why, of course! Ladies, can any of you tell me if the queen is at home?

THE ICE PRINCESS, *advancing politely*: Miss Vane?

MURIEL: Yes. The Ice Princess?

THE ICE PRINCESS, *smiling*: Yes. Mamma will be *so* sorry to miss you. But she's confined to her cavern with a cold today.

MURIEL: Oh, I'm very sorry! I hope it isn't any thing serious?

THE ICE PRINCESS: Oh, no! Merely a cold in the head. But, of course, it's trying. Could I give her any message from you?

MURIEL: You're very kind. I don't know that I ought to trouble you with a business-matter. Er—won't you come aboard?

THE ICE PRINCESS, *complying, with all her fairies*: Oh, thank you! And I shall be only too glad if I can do any thing for you.

MURIEL: It's nothing. Merely a young gentleman whom I would like to have you take with you, and put ashore somewhere on the American coast. If you don't actually touch anywhere, it don't matter: he could swim a few miles. I suppose I needn't go into details; but it's quite necessary he should leave the steamer. Theron! (*She extends her hand behind her; and Theron, with his travelling-shawl over his arm, and carrying his valise, approaches, and takes it.*) The Ice Princess, Mr. Gay! (*They bow in acknowledgment of the introduction.*) It is Mr. Gay whom I wish to have go with you.

THE ICE PRINCESS, *politely*: Oh, yes! (*She examines him through her pince-nez as he retires.*) Isn't he rather good-looking?

MURIEL: Yes,—rather.

THE ICE PRINCESS: And amiable?

MURIEL: Yes,—rather amiable.

THE ICE PRINCESS: Well, you see, we are all ladies, and, mamma not being at all well, do you think it would be very nice?

MURIEL: Oh, perfectly! There are so many of you!

THE ICE PRINCESS: That is true. But he is a Harvard man, I suppose; and none of us ever learned Greek.

MURIEL: Oh! they don't *learn* Greek at Harvard. If you will read the College Fetich, you will see that they only *study* it. I dare say *he* didn't learn *any* thing. (*To Theron, who seems to have spoken.*) What? (*To the Ice Princess, as if explaining.*) Oh, yes! Athletics, of course, and modern languages,—the german; it's one of those languages that you dance, you know.

THE ICE PRINCESS: Well, that's very nice. What are his principles?

MURIEL: I don't quite understand you. Do you mean his political principles? He is a Protectionist.

THE ICE PRINCESS: We are Protectionists too.

MURIEL, *with fine reluctance*: Oh! I don't think he's an extreme one.

THE ICE PRINCESS: We are moderate too. We believe in a tariff for revenue; for we must have pocket-money, you know. At the same time, we are Protectionists. As ladies, we have to be protected, of course. But I referred not so much to his political principles, as his theories of life.

MURIEL: I believe, that, at one time, he thought it was hardly worth while. He had been reading a little of Mallock.[1] But he told me he had got over that in his junior year. He is very earnest now.

THE ICE PRINCESS: I am glad of that. We are very earnest too.

MURIEL: When you say *we*, do you mean yourself individually, or all the fairies?

THE ICE PRINCESS: Both. Is he literary, or scientific?

[1] William H. Mallock (1849–1923), best known as the author of *The New Republic*, 1877, wrote various studies of social and economic life directed against the doctrine of socialism.

MURIEL: Scientific, I *think*. At any rate, he's written a novel.

THE ICE PRINCESS: Oh, indeed! *We* have written novels too. Is he of the old romantic school, with real heroes and heroines, or the modern analytic, photographic school, with just common people?

MURIEL: I'm sure I can't say: *I* couldn't read it.

THE ICE PRINCESS: Nobody can read ours either. Is he sceptical?

MURIEL: *No*, indeed! That's *quite* gone by. Are you?

THE ICE PRINCESS: Well, we're rather scientific, you know.

MURIEL: Why, you might as well—let me see! —you might as well wear a tie-back as to talk agnosticism *now*.

THE ICE PRINCESS, *thoughtfully*: I hadn't heard. Mr. Gay could convert us, perhaps. And you say his character is irreproachable?

MURIEL: Quite.

THE ICE PRINCESS, *sighing*: He is certainly very handsome. He's been abroad?

MURIEL: Of course. But he isn't at all Europeanized, if that's what you mean.

THE ICE PRINCESS: I'm glad of that. Oh! One thing more, please. I hope he isn't a Bostonian. Their manners are so cold. They chill us.

MURIEL: I shouldn't have thought they could chill *Ice* Fairies.

THE ICE PRINCESS: They can chill *any* thing. And precisely because we *are* Ice Fairies, we pine for warmth.

An Illustration

The rose that in some winter room
  So fraily grows, so palely blows,
Knows in its heart a brighter bloom,
  And longs to be a summer rose,—
    In sun and shower, a summer rose.

The song each silent soul within
  That weakly tries, that meekly dies,
For utterance that it may not win,
  From poet-lips would scale the skies,—
    A poet's song would scale the skies.

The love that lurks in every breast,
  So kind a thing, so blind a thing,
If with a smile or word caressed,
  Would wake, and rise, and be a king,—
    Of life and death the lord and king.

MURIEL: Yes, I admit all that; but it stands to reason, that, if the manners of the Bostonians are cold, their hearts are warm. Theron, what should you say in evidence of the hidden warmth of the Bostonians? For they certainly *do* hide it.

THERON: Very little. I know there has been a good deal of talk about our manners; but I ask. what if we do seem cold?

MURIEL, *to the Princess*: Yes, what if we do?

THERON: We make no pretence of being warm.

MURIEL: No one could deny that!

THERON: And that is more than you could say of people whose manner is more cordial.

MURIEL, *fondly*: O Theron, *be* a popular orator! Be very, very classic! And affective!

THERON: Muriel, I will! Two or three points have occurred to me; and, if her Highness will give me her attention for a few moments, I think she will admit their force.

THE ICE PRINCESS: Why, certainly, Mr. Gay. I will listen, with pleasure.

THERON
A Rejoinder

It is not where the greatest smoke is,
  That the fiercest fire is seen:
It is not where the finest joke is,
  That the longest laugh comes in.

It is not where the winds are coldest,
  That you find the deepest snow:
It is not where the word is boldest,
  That you feel the heaviest blow.

It is not where the surf is loudest,
  That the great sea-serpents hide:
It is not where the throng is proudest,
  That you meet the blushing bride.

THE ICE PRINCESS: Yes: I see, and it may all be as Mr. Gay says; but we have never had a young gentleman among us yet, and I must take time to think it over.

MURIEL: There's no hurry. Of course I didn't expect you to decide immediately.

THE ICE PRINCESS: No. And, while we are thinking, we should like to dance a little ballet, as people always do when anything important is pending. Perhaps it would amuse you?

MURIEL: It will be very good of your Highness. Imperial, or royal, by the way?

THE ICE PRINCESS: Imperial, please. The queen is an empress, you know.

MURIEL: Oh, yes! Like Victoria. We shall be perfectly delighted to have you dance.

BALLET AND SONG BY THE ICE FAIRIES
With the tender chords all muted,
Fairy-voiced and fairy footed,
    Let us trip, and let us glide,
        Gleaming,
            Sparkling,
        Dreaming,
            Darkling,
    O'er the ocean's frozen tide.

Down the crystal ice-peaks swarming,
On the crystal ice-field forming,
    Let us drift like falling snow,
        Swirling,
            Sweeping,
        Curling,
            Creeping,
    Like the lightly falling snow.

Then let silence, deep and hollow,
On our merry uproar follow:
    Let us all, like shapes of snow,
        Brightly
            Shimmer,
        Lightly
            Glimmer,
    Stop as if all frozen so!
                    [*They all stop instantly.*]

MURIEL: How perfectly charming! What do you call it?

THE ICE PRINCESS: Frost on the Window-Panes. Isn't it a pretty name?

MURIEL: Lovely! And so significant! I think— if you'll excuse my proposing it—the passengers would like to dance a little now, to show their appreciation and gratitude.

THE ICE PRINCESS: Oh! we shall be charmed, I'm sure.

BALLET AND SONG BY THE PASSENGERS
With a burst of music flashing
Lightning-like and thunder-crashing
    On the stilly, startled air,
        Quickly
            Forming,
        Thickly
            Storming,
    Fill the wide deck everywhere!

Swains and nymphs of every nation,
Recking naught of race or station,
    Mingle in the merry dance,
        Widely
            Straying,
        Idly
            Playing,
    Back and forth, retire, advance!

Then, like leaves that whisk and rustle,
When the winds of autumn hustle
    Through the woodlands bare and gray,
        Hither
            Hieing,
        Thither
            Flying,
    Flit and flutter and fleet away!

THE ICE PRINCESS: Delicious! And what do you call *this*, pray?

MURIEL: Oh! it's merely a little pastoral. I forget the name. Theron, what do they call this dance?

THERON: The Grasshopper; or, The United Gayeties Sociable.

THE ICE PRINCESS, *with mortification*: Why, certainly! I ought to have recognized it. By the way, it reminds me of a little thing of our own, which I should like to have the fairies dance for you if—

CHORUS OF PASSENGERS: Oh, no! Miss Muriel would want *us* to dance again, and we've had quite enough of it.

CAPTAIN: Yes: give us a rest!

A Demand
Give us a rest, for life at best is brief;
    For life is full of weariness, at best:
Give to the troubled heart and brain relief,
    Give us, with strife and loss and grief opprest,
        Give us a rest!

Nepenthe does not grow on every bush,
    Nor wealth await all young men who go West:
Then, from the world's unending shove and push,
    The idle turmoil, and the useless quest,
        Give us a rest!

From all endeavor to provoke *encores*,
    From plays on words, from puns with wit unblest,
From all the sad variety of bores,
    And hobbies of peculiar interest,
        Give us a rest!

MR. VANE: Isn't this very much to the same purpose as the song you sang in the first act in regard to hiring a hall?

CAPTAIN: Yes, it is. But it suggests a less expensive method of relief. Sometimes it costs a great deal of money to hire a hall, but you can simply *stop*, any time, for nothing.

MR. VANE: I had not looked at it in that light.

CAPTAIN: Naturally. You have probably never been at sea before.

MRS. VANE: I hope you're satisfied now, Matthew! Exposing your thoughtlessness before everybody!

THE ICE PRINCESS, *to Muriel*: I noticed that Mr. Gay seemed to dance very well.

MURIEL: He reverses nicely.

THE ICE PRINCESS: Well, I have thought it all over very seriously, and I have concluded to take him.

She passes her hand through his arm.

MURIEL, *faintly*: Thank you. Of course you will be kind to him?

THE ICE PRINCESS: Very kind.

MURIEL: If he should be homesick—

THE ICE PRINCESS: I will read to him, or sing; or the fairies will dance.

MURIEL: And if he should be ill—so far from a doctor—

THE ICE PRINCESS: We have all the popular remedies. Besides, mamma understands sickness perfectly,—she's ill so much, herself,—and he shall have the best of care.

MURIEL: And if—if—he should be unhappy? If he should ask—for—for—me?

THE ICE PRINCESS, *with dignity*: I think his interests may be safely intrusted to me, in every way. And it shall be my special charge to see that my husband *doesn't* ask for you. I should like to hear him!

MURIEL, *aghast*: Your husband! But you're not going to marry him?

THE ICE PRINCESS: Certainly. In fact,—we Ice Fairies are very frank; perhaps too much so,— I find upon reflection, that I have always loved him.

MURIEL: You have always loved him? But you have never met him before!

THE ICE PRINCESS: That makes no difference. Though I'm not so sure about not meeting him.

A Reminiscence

Somewhere before our lives began,
Ere I was maid, or he was man,
  Somewhere in shapeless space,
Ideas of what was to be,

But wholly unembodied, we
  Met somehow, face to face.

That he was he, and I was I,
We inly knew, but knew not why,
  Though that we loved we knew:
Something within us or without,
Taught us to feel beyond a doubt,
  That we were one, though two.

And still I feel that nameless thrill
That trembled through me then, and still
  The hope that then I felt.
The strange, dim rapture of that hour,
I feel again its heavenly power,
  I pant, I burn, I melt!

MR. VANE, *interrupting*: Excuse me, your Imperial Highness, but isn't that rather dangerous— *for you?*

THE ICE PRINCESS: What dangerous?

MR. VANE: Er—melting.

THE ICE PRINCESS: Not at all. For, if I were to thaw altogether, I should re-form again immediately. I am a Reformer.

MR. VANE: Civil Service?

THE ICE PRINCESS: Certainly!

MRS. VANE: Of course she is, Matthew! Don't be absurd!

MURIEL: Is there any more?

THE ICE PRINCESS: Only one more stanza:—

  And as it once was, æons since,
  It shall be ever, æons hence,
    Whether we live or die.
  In depths below, in heights above,
  To love we live, we die to love,
    We, we; he, he; I, I!

For these reasons I propose to marry him at once.

MURIEL, *politely*: But you must allow us to offer you some refreshments first. They are just coming up.

A train of table-stewards, in red and yellow tights and the ordinary stewards' jackets, appears, bearing trays with cups of bouillon, and plates of chocolate-creams, and sticks of chewing-gum. They keep time to a march from Lohengrin blent with Yankee Doodle.

THE ICE PRINCESS: You're *very* kind!

MURIEL: Theron, what is it reminds one so of Lohengrin? Something about the music—

THERON: No: that reminds me rather more of our national anthem.

MURIEL: Or the dress of the stewards—

THERON: It's the ordinary dress of table-stewards.

> *The stewards serve the bouillon to the passengers. Muriel takes a cup from a tray, and hands it to the Princess.*

MURIEL: Will your fairies have bouillon, or some of the chocolate-creams and chewing-gum?

THE ICE PRINCESS: Oh! chewing-gum, please. *They* were all salesladies once; and they're very nervous still, poor things!

MURIEL, *looking anxiously round*: It doesn't seem to be going off very well, Theron. Don't they generally sing at a banquet? It seems to me that they ought to clink their cups of bouillon together, and sing.

THERON: Yes: I don't see why they don't! It's very odd.

CHORUS OF LADY AND GENTLEMEN PASSENGERS: We are keeping our breath to cool our broth.

CHORUS OF FAIRIES AND SALESLADIES: How can we sing, with our mouths full of chewing-gum?

MURIEL, *with pique*: Oh, very well! We can't oblige you to sing, of course; though I think the effect would be better.

THE CHORUS
[*Clinking their cups, suddenly burst forth.*]
A song, a song,
For the brave bouillon,
For the bouillon hot and steaming!
We sing its praise
As our cups we raise,
With bouillon sparkling and gleaming.

Beef-tea, beef-tea,
The champagne of the sea!
For every sort of weather,
Or smooth or rough,
This is the stuff!
Touch again, and drink it together!

MURIEL: Ah, I thought you would have to do it! Thank you very much, indeed. (*To the Princess*) Well, I have been thinking it over too; and I don't wish you to *marry* Theron. I wish you merely to transport him to the nearest point on the American coast, and—drop him.

MRS. VANE, *severely*: That is all you are expected to do; and perhaps if you had been as sensitive in regard to others as you profess to be in regard to yourself it wouldn't be necessary to call your attention to a very well-known fact. And, oh! if I had the trump of doom—

STEWARD, *appearing with a banjo in his hand*: The captain's mislaid the trump of doom, ma'am; but 'ere's the cook's banjo.

MRS. VANE, *examining it*: Well, the banjo will do very nicely, Robert. Now, then! *Con espressione*, please. (*The Steward strikes the cadence on the banjo at the end of each two lines.*)

An Observation
Oh! never yet in castle-hall or bower
    Was high-born dame, or simple damozel,
That dreamt the banished victim of her power
    Might find another he could love as well.

She ever saw him wandering unconsoled,
    Alike in throngèd streets and deserts dim:
She never thought that there could be so bold
    A woman as to wish to comfort him.

If she could have imagined such a thing,
    So very unexpected, mean, and low,
That should with shame her sex's bosom wring,
    She had thought twice before she let him go.

THE ICE PRINCESS: I am very sorry, but the only arrangement I can make with regard to Theron is to marry him. I should be compromised by any other. Mamma would not hear of it.

> *They move toward the iceberg.*

MURIEL, *decisively*: Very well, then, Theron cannot go with you.

THERON, *advancing*: Yes, Muriel, I must go. I have always loved the princess. I shall marry her, and run the iceberg between New York and Liverpool in competition with the refrigerator-steamships for the transportation of Chicago beef. Now that I am engaged, my sole thought is to provide for my family; and in this I am sure all the gentlemen present will sympathize with me. I understand that the Ice Princess is an American fairy.

THE ICE PRINCESS: I am. I was born in St. Louis.

THERON: I thought I could not be mistaken in the accent. She will, therefore, be expensive.

CHORUS OF GENTLEMEN: She will!

THERON: But she will be worth the money.

CHORUS OF GENTLEMEN: She will!

THERON: Precisely. And for this reason I will explain my new departure.

A New Departure
I am a family-man,—
    A provident family-man!
And as a member of that great plutocracy,

Sprung from the heart of our New-World Democracy
    I get all the money I can!

    Formerly I was a youth,
    Dreaming of Beauty and Truth,
Tender and hopeful, and somewhat æsthetical,
With an ideal both high and poetical.
    (Perhaps it was *too* high in sooth!)

    Now a more practical aim
    I loudly and proudly proclaim;
And whether the prize you have drawn in love's
    lottery
Be of an origin earthly or watery,
    Yours I imagine the same.

    I am a family-man,—
    A provident family-man!
And as a member of that great plutocracy,
Sprung from the heart of our New-World De-
mocracy,
    I get all the money I can!

MR. VANE: Excuse me, Mr. Gay, but isn't this
last song of yours rather too much like some of
Gilbert and Sullivan's things?

THERON: There *is* a slight resemblance. But, if
the Princess intends to have me, she must have
"Patience" with me.

CHORUS, *in great anguish*: Oh!

STEWARD, *holding out his hand, still more en-
larged!* Don't forget the steward, sir!

THERON: Have you change for a hundred-dollar
bill?

STEWARD: I could *keep* the change, sir!

THERON: On second thoughts, I will send you
an order on the Treasurer of the Iceberg Transportation Company. Well, Muriel, my former
love, I must say adieu, I suppose. The princess
is getting impatient. Good-morning. (*He bows
distantly, and gets over the rail on to the iceberg.*)
Now, love! (*He extends his hand toward the
Princess, who mounts the rail.*) Will you jump,
dearest?

THE ICE PRINCESS: Into your arms, sweet!

THERON, *extending his arms*: Well, then, darling! One, two, three! And here you are!
    *She leaps, and he catches her in his arms.
    The fairies follow.*

MURIEL, *hiding her face in her hands*: Oh—
h—h—h!

CHORUS OF ICE FAIRIES

We who, till now, scarce knew that we were
    women,

Perceive, each one, we always did adore
Some one among the passengers or seamen,
    And shall forevermore.
    [*They return to the iceberg.*]

CHORUS OF GENTLEMEN PASSENGERS AND SEAMEN
And we, who always knew that we were human,
    To our first, last, and only loves are true:
Never yet beings in the form of woman
    Attracted us, save you!
    [*They cross the deck, as if to follow the
    fairies, while the Steward tries to collect his
    fees from them.*]

STEWARD: Don't forget the steward, gentlemen!

MRS. VANE, *detaining Mr. Vane*: Matthew,
don't you dare to speak to that nasty queen of
theirs!

MR. VANE, *freeing himself*: My dear, the queen
is ill, and in low spirits. Besides, I have loved
her from childhood.

A Discovery
Ah, yes! unknown, unseen,
    And wholly unsuspected,
She was my bosom's queen,
    Adored, though undetected,—
Unknown, unseen,
    And wholly unsuspected!

Her image filled my breast
    With rapture and devotion;
Though, it must be confessed,
    I had not any notion
What filled my breast
    With rapture and devotion.

Around my path through life,
    Without the slightest warning,
My less and more than wife,
    She poured celestial morning,—
Around my life
    She poured celestial morning!

And now to her I go
    In spite of every danger:
I feel that I should know
    So intimate a stranger.
To her I go,
    In spite of every danger.

Farewell, O true and tried,
    And now at last forsaken!
I fancied you my bride,
    But find I was mistaken.

She was my bride,
And I was quite mistaken.
[*He gets over the ship's side on to the iceberg.*]

MURIEL: Well, then, papa, if you must go, be good to poor Theron! Theron, take care of papa!

An Adjuration
Be kind to each other!
Whatever betide,
Your heart-burnings smother,
Your enmities hide.

It seems to me I was going to say something else. Oh, yes!

Be kind to each other!
Be truthful, and be
Both father and brother
Reciprocally.

No, that isn't it, either. Let me see:—

To your loved ones be tender
At all times; and, oh!
Endeavor to render
A kiss for a blow.

It isn't in the least what I wanted to say! I was going to warn them against those horrid things, and here I am actually encouraging them to behave affectionately toward them! I must try again!

Be the harsh word unspoken,
Upbraid not, nor chide:
For a frown oft has broken
The heart of a bride.

What perfectly disgusting rubbish! I don't know where I could have got hold of it.

To those fond hearts and lonely
Be husband and son
Together, but only
Be careful which one.

It is getting worse and worse. Really, it makes me sick!

Look before, not behind, you!
For loves that are dead
Let no vain sorrow blind you,
No vain tears be shed.

Why, how atrocious! It is the most pessimistic thing I ever heard of!

Then, away with remembrance,
Away with regret;
Turn from parting, Death's semblance,
Turn, live, and forget.

(Bursting into tears.) Oh, dear! The wrong words keep coming in spite of every thing. What shall I do?

MRS. VANE: I know what *I* shall do. Captain, I invoke, I demand, your protection. Stop Mr. Vane!

CAPTAIN: Stop him? My dear madam, I am going myself.

CHORUS OF LADY PASSENGERS
Is it thus, unkind commander
Of the Mesopotam-i-a,
That you leave your ship to wander
On the ocean as it may?
Is it thus that you abandon,
Is it thus that you betray,
Us, without a glimpse of land on
Either side? Stay with us, stay!

CAPTAIN: No, ladies: under the circumstances I must leave you. I have always loved one of these Iceberg Fairies. I don't know which, as yet. You will be perfectly safe on the Mesopotamia. The head-stewardess understands the working of the ship; and I have no doubt, that in a month, or two months at the farthest, you will be in Liverpool. Although usually the last to leave the ship, I shall leave it now, and leave it firmly.

An Advertisement
Though tempests drive the shuddering wreck
Through the long night till morn,
The captain keeps the reeling deck
To which his truth was sworn.

Though masts be toppled in the sea,
Shrouds snapped, and canvas torn,
To his ship, as if his bride were she,
He keeps the fealty sworn.

Woe if he falters! For the press
Will hold him up to scorn
If he leave the ship in her distress,
To which his truth was sworn.

But this is a wholly different case. The weather is good, the ship is in perfect trim; and I've no doubt you'll have a comfortable voyage. Mrs. Vane, will you kindly post this note for my former wife when you reach Liverpool? It informs her of the facts of this singular case.

MRS. VANE, *politely taking the letter*: Certainly, captain: I shall be very glad.

CAPTAIN: You are very kind. (*He gets over the ship's side upon the iceberg.*)

CHORUS OF PASSENGERS

[*Following him.*]

We are lawyers and physicians,
Bankers, brokers, electricians,
Publishers, and politicians,
Russians, Polacks, Turks, Armenians,
Hindoos, Arabs, and Athenians,
Chinese, Japs, and Abyssinians,
Germans, Frenchmen, and Egyptians,
Orientals of all descriptions,
Editors, professors, students
Of all kinds, whom their imprudence
  In the mad pursuit of wealth,
Has compelled, for relaxation,
To endure a brief vacation,
  Which we come to spend among you for our
    health.

[*They rush up the slopes and peaks of the iceberg, and clasp the Ice Fairies in their arms.*]

CHORUS OF ICE FAIRIES

Welcome, lawyers and physicians,
Bankers, brokers, electricians,
Publishers, and politicians,
Russians, Polacks, Turks, Armenians,
Hindoos, Arabs, and Athenians,
Chinese, Japs, and Abyssinians,
Germans, Frenchmen, and Egyptians,
Orientals of all descriptions,
Editors, professors, students
Of all kinds, whom your imprudence
  In the mad pursuit of wealth,
Has compelled, for relaxation,
To endure a brief vacation,
  Welcome, welcome to our iceberg for your
    health!

[*The seamen on the iceberg cast loose from the steamer, and they begin to drift apart, the Chorus of Lady Passengers thronging the rail, in tears.*]

CHORUS OF SEAMEN

Dry your tears, little dears,
Left alone aboard the ship;
Needless all your anxious sighs;
Cease to pipe your pretty eyes!

We do not blame our lot,
Though we leave you on the ship:
With these hearts that love us, we,
Safe and merry all will be!

MURIEL: And do I understand that you are really going off with that creature, Theron?

THERON: Yes, Muriel, I am perfectly serious about it; that is, as serious as I can be under the circumstances. Of course I can't help smiling. I am very happy, but I am serious. The steward remains with you, and perhaps—

MURIEL, *in reproach*: Oh, this from you, Theron! (*To the Steward, sharply.*) You here, Robert? What are you doing? Why don't you go with the gentlemen?

STEWARD: Well, miss, I 'ave a delicacy in statin' the true reason, miss—

MURIEL: Poor Robert! And do you *love* me, Robert?

STEWARD: Yes, I have always loved you.

MURIEL: And you are sure you're not actuated by any mercenary motive?

STEWARD: Quite, miss.

MURIEL: And you will always be kind to my poor, grass-widowed mother?

STEWARD: Always, miss.

MURIEL: Well!—But you would never be able to put on the ring with that ridiculous hand of yours!

STEWARD: No, miss. But I could take up the collection in it.

MURIEL: True. Well, then, take me, Robert! But wait a moment till I bid poor Theron farewell.

A Despair

Ah, truant love! to whom I cannot send
  The broken heart I bear,
This cry I send, and would that I might wend
  As swiftly with it through the trackless air.

For, oh! so heavy, heavy, heavy lies
  Upon my soul some spell,
That on my lips, in mute eclipse,
  Trembles and faints the secret they would tell.

A formless cry I send athwart the deep,
  For none can help but you!
Nay, save me from the demon of my sleep!
  Come back, O love, come back! I love you too!

THERON
A Regret

O loved and lost! to whom I look and long,
   The deep yawns at our feet:
Wild memories throng, and tremble into song,
   On lips where once your kiss had been so sweet.

But never, never, never may I know
   Bliss once my soul's desire:
The flame sinks low that filled me with its glow,
   And nothing may revive the dying fire.

In vain you send your cry across the sea:
   For, if I would be true,
It is, you see, impossible for me;
   For her Imperial Highness loves me too!

CHORUS OF LADY PASSENGERS
[*Turning suddenly upon Muriel, who runs across the deck towards the iceberg, and intercepting her.*]

Ah, heartless, fickle one!
For you we are undone!
   If it had not been for you,
All our husbands and our brothers,
Sons, and very many others,
   Had continued true.
   Now, what shall we do?
Follow! Catch her!
Seize her! Scratch her!
   Fickle and untrue!
[*They pursue Muriel round the deck; she flies, singing.*]

MURIEL

They will catch me!
Seize me! Scratch me!
Fickle and untrue!
Theron, love, I come to you!
[*She mounts the rail, and leaps after the iceberg, with a shriek.*]
   Ah—h—h!
[*The scene darkens till all is lost to sight, the Chorus singing.*]
   Hush, hush,
   Our Muriel raves!
Oh, cease your roar and rush,
   Ye winds and waves!
   Our Muriel raves!

   A horrid anguish seems
   To fill her dreams!
But from her dreams she breaks:
   Our Muriel wakes!
   Lo, Muriel wakes!

EPILOGUE

The scene is gradually illumined again. Muriel is discovered seated in her steamer-chair, as at the close of the first act; and everything is restored to its former state.

THERON, *tenderly*: Then, you *do* love me, Muriel?

MURIEL, *eagerly*: Oh, *yes*, indeed! Where—where is the steward?

STEWARD: 'Ere I ham, miss.

MURIEL, *gasping*: Well—well—ugh! Go away, please! No; show me your hand first. (*He shows it of its normal size and shape, and she examines it carefully.*) Why, I thought it had turned into a waiter!

STEWARD: What waiter, miss?

MURIEL: Oh, do go away! Where is the iceberg?

ALL: What iceberg?

MURIEL: And the fairies?

ALL: What fairies?

MURIEL: And that shameless princess?

ALL: What shameless princess?

MURIEL: But the ball? And the decorations? The flowers? The bow on Theron's back? And Carlino's? The Baby Grand piano? And the refreshments?

ALL: What ball, decorations, flowers, bow, piano, and refreshments?

MURIEL: And the—

ALL: What?

MURIEL, *with a sigh*: Yes! I must have been dreaming.

THERON: I thought you were dreaming, from a remark that you made.

MURIEL: Don't—don't leave me, Theron.

THERON: Never, Muriel, till the church has made you mine.

MURIEL: But there are no clergymen on board.

CHORUS OF CLERGYMEN, *suddenly emerging from the crowd*: Plenty! Sore throat, you know!
   They retire immediately.

MURIEL: Well! Don't you think you had better wait till after breakfast, Theron? I am quite faint.

THERON: Perhaps I had.

MURIEL: Papa!

MR. VANE: Yes, my child?

MURIEL: Shake hands with Theron.

MR. VANE, *complying*: Yes, my child.

MURIEL: Mamma!

MRS. VANE: Yes, dear?

MURIEL: Kiss Theron!

MRS. VANE, *obeying*: Certainly, dear.

MURIEL: Theron!

THERON: Yes, love?

MURIEL: Kiss—let me see! Oh, yes! (*By a sudden inspiration lifting the pug.*) Kiss Carlino!

THERON, *wildly embracing Muriel*: Oh, my love!

MURIEL: Well, don't *eat* me, Theron,—at least, not till *I* have had something.

The breakfast-bell is heard from below.

THERON AND MURIEL
A Conclusion

THERON

The breakfast-bell! The breakfast-bell!
  It is the happy, happy sound,
That, at the hour which each knows well,
  The whole huge hungry world goes round.
    In keep and tower,
    In hut and bower,
  In street and wood, in field and fell,
  We list the merry breakfast-bell.

CHORUS

We list the merry breakfast-bell!

MURIEL

The breakfast-bell! The breakfast-bell!
  It rings for one, it rings for all.
On land or sea, if human, we
  Obey its merry, merry call.
    Fond love may burn,
    And o'er her urn
The tears of sorrow rise and fall:
The breakfast-bell rings for us all!

CHORUS

The breakfast-bell rings for us all!

[*They go out dancing,—Muriel and Theron together, Mr. and Mrs. Vane, two maids, the Captain and Steward, and the Chorus of Passengers, in couples. The Chorus of Seamen haul up a sail, and sing.*]

If I had a sweetheart, and she was a rover,
  Haul away, boys, haul away!
I'd follow her all the wide world over,
  Haul away, boys, haul away!

If she said yes, I never would leave her,
  Haul away, boys, haul away!
If she said no, I would go and grieve her,
  Haul away, boys, haul away!

For the will of a girl there is never any knowing,
  Haul away, boys, haul away!
She would want me to stay if she saw me going,
  Haul away, boys, haul away!

Then, never say die; keep a stiff upper lip, boys;
  Haul away, haul, haul away!
The wind is fair, and we've got a good ship, boys,
  Haul away, haul, haul away!

The Elevator

[1884]

Although this is the second of the dozen plays dramatizing the activities of the Robertses or the Campbells or both, it is the first time that the reader is introduced to the little circle of friends who appear or are referred to in the various plays. It has been a year since Willis Campbell arrived in *The Sleeping Car*, and he is now reasonably well established in this group, although Dr. Lawton does not recall him by his first name. Aunt Mary has also been with the Robertses for the same length of time, but there does not seem to have been a dinner like this one before, because old Mr. Bemis has not seen her for twenty years. The Somerses are mentioned (in earlier editions of this play Howells used the name Summers) but the delightful Amy will not appear with the group for another two years. With the Curwens, the Millers, Miss Lawton, and young Mr. Bemis, the circle is complete; others will come and go, but in this play Howells has presented the primary characters with whom he will work in most of his one-act dramas for the next ten years.

Dr. Lawton will always be the brilliant conversationalist, the intellectual wit who takes advantage of his age to speak out frankly in ways that might not be tolerated in a younger person. Throughout the plays Mrs. Curwen remains a flirt; Lou Lawton a quiet, shy creature (soon to marry the somewhat stuffy young Mr. Bemis); and old Mr. Bemis a kindly respectable old man.

The characterizations of Mrs. Roberts, her Aunt Mary, and her brother Willis Campbell are here clearly consistent with their appearance in *The Sleeping Car*. But Mr. Roberts is neither like the person by that name in the previous farce nor like the Edward Roberts in subsequent plays—an absent-minded, utterly unresourceful individual, easily confused, and a ready target for

Campbell's teasing jokes and inventive mischief. In *The Elevator* he is witty, clever in his conversation, and somewhat cavalier in his attitude toward those in the elevator. Dr. Lawton even refers to him as a joker, something which Edward Roberts decidedly is not. In this play he is a calming, stabilizing influence, a resourceful person to whom Dr. Lawton looks to get the people out of the elevator; and he does have ideas. An interesting person, certainly, but he is not the Edward Roberts of the other plays.

Better than most of his farces, *The Elevator* shows Howells' twin concern for the commonplace incidents of life and current advancements in technology. The situation for the play, he revealed in "A Letter to the Publisher," in *Minor Dramas*, was based on an elevator experience in a fashionable Boston apartment house. Perhaps it happened to him; one cannot know. However, Howells did have a serious apprehension concerning elevators, and ten years after publishing this drama he wrote to Mildred Howells (July 11, 1894, Harvard Library): "I thought of this elevator, after I wrote you this morning, and so telegraphed you to be careful of it. Get the porter to show you how to *stop* it, and *send it down* after you have *started it up*; and *up*, after you have started it *down*. Wear your glasses when you get out and in, and watch not to get your dress, or hairdo, or foot caught." In addition to apprehension over it, Howells would seem also to have had some understanding of this new invention, the elevator. His reference to the air cushion is accurate, and Campbell's solution for the elevator problem is logically based on the fact that a hydraulic elevator could descend by its own weight without use of pressure such as a steam elevator would require. It is interesting, too, in connection with the elevator, that Howells

300

should bolster his realism with reference to a contemporary event. W. Sloan Kennedy in "The Vertical Railway," *Harper's Monthly* (November, 1882), describes an elevator experiment that Dr. Lawton builds into an exciting incident in the play. "At the Chicago exposition in 1880," wrote Kennedy, "the ropes of a car weighing 2800 lbs. were cut, a number of visitors having entered it. The car fell 109 feet; the passengers walked out smiling. . . . In other experiments baskets of eggs taken into the car were unbroken, and persons held in their hands glasses of water, not a drop of which was spilled."

Although the staging of this play might have caused some difficulty in amateur theatricals, there is evidence that it was quite widely appreciated by both amateur and professional performers. One group produced it in Streator, Illinois, sometime in 1885, with George "Honey-Boy" Evans—song writer, minstrel, vaudeville performer—as the elevator boy.

The Elevator [1]

I.

SCENE: *Through the curtained doorway of Mrs. Edward Roberts's pretty drawing-room, in Hotel Bellingham, shows the snowy and gleaming array of a table set for dinner, under the dim light of gas-burners turned low. An air of expectancy pervades the place, and the uneasiness of Mr. Roberts, in evening dress, expresses something more as he turns from a glance into the dining-room, and still holding the portière with one hand, takes out his watch with the other.*

MR. ROBERTS, *to Mrs. Roberts entering the drawing-room from regions beyond*: My dear, it's six o'clock. What can have become of your aunt?

MRS. ROBERTS, *with a little anxiety*: That was just what I was going to ask. She's never late; and the children are quite heart-broken. They had counted upon seeing her, and talking Christmas a little before they were put to bed.

ROBERTS: Very singular her not coming! Is she going to begin standing upon ceremony with us, and not come till the hour?

MRS. ROBERTS: Nonsense, Edward! She's been detained. Of course she'll be here in a moment. How impatient you are!

ROBERTS: You must profit by me as an awful example.

MRS. ROBERTS, *going about the room, and bestowing little touches here and there on its ornaments*: If you'd had that new cook to battle with over this dinner, you'd have learned patience by this time without any awful example.

ROBERTS, *dropping nervously into the nearest chair*: I hope she isn't behind time.

MRS. ROBERTS, *drifting upon the sofa, and disposing her train effectively on the carpet around her*: She's before time. The dinner is in the last moment of ripe perfection now, when we must still give people fifteen minutes' grace.

1 The text used here is from *The Sleeping Car and Other Farces.*

302

She studies the convolutions of her train absent-mindedly.

ROBERTS, *joining in its perusal*: Is that the way you've arranged to be sitting when people come in?

MRS. ROBERTS: Of course not. I shall get up to receive them.

ROBERTS: That's rather a pity. To destroy such a lovely pose.

MRS. ROBERTS: Do you like it?

ROBERTS: It's divine.

MRS. ROBERTS: You might throw me a kiss.

ROBERTS: No; if it happened to strike on that train anywhere, it might spoil one of the folds. I can't risk it.

A ring is heard at the apartment door. They spring to their feet simultaneously.

MRS. ROBERTS: There's Aunt Mary now! (*She calls into the vestibule.*) Aunt Mary!

DR. LAWTON, *putting aside the vestibule portière, with affected timidity*: Very sorry. Merely a father.

MRS. ROBERTS: Oh! Dr. Lawton? I am so glad to see you! (*She gives him her hand.*) I thought it was my aunt. We can't understand why she hasn't come. Why! where's Miss Lawton?

LAWTON: That is precisely what I was going to ask you.

MRS. ROBERTS: Why, she isn't here.

LAWTON: So it seems. I left her with the carriage at the door when I started to walk here. She called after me down the stairs that she would be ready in three seconds, and begged me to hurry, so that we could come in together, and not let people know I'd saved half a dollar by walking.

MRS. ROBERTS: *She's* been detained too!

ROBERTS, *coming forward*: Now you know what it is to have a delinquent Aunt-Mary-in-law.

LAWTON, *shaking hands with him*: O Roberts! Is that you? It's astonishing how little one makes of the husband of a lady who gives a dinner. In my time—a long time ago—he used to carve. But nowadays, when everything is served *à la Russe*, he might as well be abolished. Don't you think, on the whole, Roberts, you'd better not have come?

ROBERTS: Well, you see, I had no excuse. I hated to say an engagement when I hadn't any.

LAWTON: Oh, I understand. You *wanted* to come. We all do, when Mrs. Roberts will let us. (*He goes and sits down by Mrs. Roberts, who has taken a more provisional pose on the sofa.*) Mrs. Roberts, you're the only woman in Boston who could hope to get people, with a fireside of their own—or a register—out to a Christmas dinner. You know I still wonder at your effrontery a little?

MRS. ROBERTS, *laughing*: I knew I should catch you if I baited my hook with your old friend.

LAWTON: Yes, nothing would have kept me away when I heard Bemis was coming. But he doesn't seem so inflexible in regard to me. Where is he?

MRS. ROBERTS: I'm sure I don't know. I'd no idea I was giving such a formal dinner. But everybody, beginning with my own aunt, seems to think it a ceremonious occasion. There are only to be twelve. Do you know the Millers?

LAWTON: No, thank goodness! One meets some people so often that one fancies one's weariness of them reflected in their sympathetic countenances. Who are these acceptably novel Millers?

MRS. ROBERTS: Do explain the Millers to the doctor, Edward.

ROBERTS, *standing on the hearth-rug, with his thumbs in his waistcoat pockets*: They board.

LAWTON: Genus. That accounts for their willingness to flutter round your evening lamp when they ought to be singeing their wings at their own. Well, species?

ROBERTS: They're very nice young newly married people. He's something or other of some kind of manufactures. And Mrs. Miller is disposed to think that all the other ladies are as fond of him as she is.

MRS. ROBERTS: Oh! That is not so, Edward.

LAWTON: You defend your sex, as women always do. But you'll admit that, as your friend, Mrs. Miller may have this foible.

MRS. ROBERTS: I admit nothing of the kind. And we've invited another young couple who haven't gone to housekeeping yet—the Curwens. And *he* has the same foible as Mrs. Miller.

Mrs. Roberts takes out her handkerchief, and laughs into it.

LAWTON: That is, if Mrs. Miller has it, which we both deny. Let us hope that Mrs. Miller and

Mr. Curwen may not get to making eyes at each other.

ROBERTS: And Mr. Bemis and his son complete the list. Why, Agnes, there are only ten. You said there were twelve.

MRS. ROBERTS: Well, never mind. I meant ten. I forgot that the Somerses declined. (*A ring is heard.*) Ah! that's Aunt Mary. (*She runs into the vestibule, and is heard exclaiming without.*) Why, Mrs. Miller, is it you? I thought it was my aunt. Where is Mr. Miller?

MRS. MILLER, *entering the drawing-room arm in arm with her hostess*: Oh, he'll be here directly. I had to let him run back for my fan.

MRS. ROBERTS: Well, we're very glad to have you to begin with. Let me introduce Dr. Lawton.

MRS. MILLER, *in a polite murmur*: Dr. Lawton. (*In a louder tone*) O Mr. Roberts!

LAWTON: You see, Roberts? The same aggrieved surprise at meeting you here that I felt.

MRS. MILLER: What in the world do you mean.

LAWTON: Don't you think that when a husband is present at his wife's dinner party he repeats the mortifying superfluity of a bridegroom at a wedding?

MRS. MILLER: I'm *sure* I don't know what you mean. I should never think of giving a dinner without Mr. Miller.

LAWTON: No? (*A ring is heard.*) There's Bemis.

MRS. MILLER: It's Mr. Miller.

MRS. ROBERTS: Aunt Mary at last! (*As she bustles toward the door*) Edward, there *are* twelve —Aunt Mary and Willis.

ROBERTS: Oh, yes. I totally forgot Willis.

LAWTON: Who's Willis?

ROBERTS: Willis? Oh, Willis is my wife's brother. We always have him.

LAWTON: Oh, yes, Campbell.

MRS. ROBERTS, *without*: Mr. Bemis! So kind of you to come on Christmas.

MR. BEMIS, *without*: So kind of you to ask us houseless strangers.

MRS. ROBERTS, *without*: I ran out here, thinking it was my aunt. She's played us a trick, and hasn't come yet.

BEMIS, *entering the drawing-room with Mrs. Roberts*: I hope she won't fail altogether. I haven't met her for twenty years, and I counted so much upon the pleasure— Hello, Lawton!

LAWTON: Hullo, old fellow! (*They fly at each other, and shake hands.*) Glad to see you again.

BEMIS, *reaching his left hand to Mr. Roberts*,

while Mr. Lawton keeps his right: Ah! Mr. Roberts.

LAWTON: Oh, never mind *him*. He's merely the husband of the hostess.

MRS. MILLER, *to Roberts*: What *does* he mean?

ROBERTS: Oh, nothing. Merely a joke he's experimenting with.

LAWTON, *to Bemis*: Where's your boy?

BEMIS: He'll be here directly. He preferred to walk. Where's your girl?

LAWTON: Oh, she'll come by and by. She preferred to drive.

MRS. ROBERTS, *introducing them*: Mr. Bemis, have you met Mrs. Miller?

She drifts away again, manifestly too uneasy to resume even a provisional pose on the sofa, and walks detachedly about the room.

BEMIS: What a lovely apartment Mrs. Roberts has.

MRS. MILLER: Exquisite! But then she has such perfect taste.

BEMIS, *to Mrs. Roberts, who drifts near them*: We were talking about your apartment, Mrs. Roberts. It's charming.

MRS. ROBERTS: It *is* nice. It's the ideal way of living. All on one floor. No stairs. Nothing.

BEMIS: Yes, when once you get here! But that little matter of five pair up—

MRS. ROBERTS: You don't mean to say you *walked* up! Why in the world didn't you take the elevator?

BEMIS: I didn't know you had one.

MRS. ROBERTS: It's the only thing that makes life worth living in a flat. All these apartment hotels have them.

BEMIS: Bless me! Well, you see, I've been away from Boston so long, and am back so short a time, that I can't realize your luxuries and conveniences. In Florence we *always* walk up. They have *ascenseurs* in a few great hotels, and they brag of it in immense signs on the sides of the building.

LAWTON: What pastoral simplicity! We are elevated here to a degree that you can't conceive of, gentle shepherd. Has yours got an air-cushion, Mrs. Roberts?

MRS. ROBERTS: An air-cushion? What's that?

LAWTON: The only thing that makes your life worth a moment's purchase in an elevator. You get in with a glass of water, a basket of eggs, and a file of the "Daily Advertiser." They cut the elevator loose at the top, and you drop.

BOTH LADIES: Oh!

LAWTON: In three seconds you arrive at the ground-floor, reading your file of the "Daily Advertiser"; not an egg broken nor a drop spilled. I saw it done in a New York hotel. The air is compressed under the elevator, and acts as a sort of ethereal buffer.

MRS. ROBERTS: And why don't we always go down in that way?

LAWTON: Because sometimes the walls of the elevator shaft give out.

MRS. ROBERTS: And what then?

LAWTON: Then the elevator stops more abruptly. I had a friend who tried it when this happened.

MRS. ROBERTS: And what did he do?

LAWTON: Stepped out of the elevator; laughed; cried; went home; got into bed: and did not get up for six weeks. Nervous shock. He was fortunate.

MRS. MILLER: I shouldn't think you'd want an air-cushion on *your* elevator, Mrs. Roberts.

MRS. ROBERTS: No, indeed! Horrid! (*The bell rings.*) Edward, *you* go and see if that's Aunt Mary.

MRS. MILLER: It's Mr. Miller, I know.

BEMIS: Or my son.

LAWTON: My voice is for Mrs. Roberts's brother. I've given up all hopes of my daughter.

ROBERTS, *without*: Oh, Curwen! Glad to see you! Thought you were my wife's aunt.

LAWTON, *at a suppressed sigh from Mrs. Roberts*: It's one of his jokes, Mrs. Roberts. Of course it's your aunt.

MRS. ROBERTS, *through her set teeth, smilingly*: Oh, if it *is*, I'll make him suffer for it.

MR. CURWEN, *without*: No, I hated to wait, so I walked up.

LAWTON: It is Mr. Curwen, after all, Mrs. Roberts. Now let me see how a lady transmutes a frown of threatened vengeance into a smile of society welcome.

MRS. ROBERTS: Well, look! (*To Mr. Curwen, who enters, followed by her husband*) Ah, Mr. Curwen! So glad to see you. You know all our friends here—Mrs. Miller, Dr. Lawton, and Mr. Bemis?

CURWEN, *smiling and bowing, and shaking hands right and left*: Very glad—very happy—pleased to know you.

MRS. ROBERTS, *behind her fan to Dr. Lawton*: Didn't I do it beautifully?

LAWTON, *behind his hand*: Wonderfully! And so unconscious of the fact that he hasn't his wife with him.

MRS. ROBERTS, *in great astonishment, to Mr. Curwen*: Where in the world is Mrs. Curwen?

CURWEN: Oh—oh—she'll be here. I thought she *was* here. She started from home with two right-hand gloves, and I had to go back for a left, and I—I suppose— Good heavens! (*Pulling the glove out of his pocket*) I ought to have sent it to her in the ladies' dressing-room.

He remains with the glove held up before him, in spectacular stupefaction.

LAWTON: Only imagine what Mrs. Curwen would be saying of you if she *were* in the dressing-room.

ROBERTS: Mr. Curwen felt so sure she was there that he wouldn't wait to take the elevator, and walked up. (*Another ring is heard.*) Shall I go and meet your aunt *now*, my dear?

MRS. ROBERTS: No, indeed! She may come in now with all the formality she chooses, and I will receive her excuses in state. (*She waves her fan softly to and fro, concealing a murmur of trepidation under an indignant air, till the portière opens, and Mr. Willis Campbell enters. Then Mrs. Roberts breaks in nervous agitation.*) Why, Willis! Where's Aunt Mary?

MRS. MILLER: And Mr. Miller?

CURWEN: And Mrs. Curwen?

LAWTON: And my daughter?

BEMIS: And my son?

MR. CAMPBELL, *looking tranquilly round on the faces of his interrogators*: Is it a conundrum?

MRS. ROBERTS, *mingling a real distress with an effort of mock-heroic solemnity*: It is a tragedy! O Willis dear! it's what you see—what you hear; a niece without an aunt, a wife without a husband, a father without a son, and another father without a daughter.

ROBERTS: And a dinner getting cold, and a cook getting hot.

LAWTON: And you are expected to account for the whole situation.

CAMPBELL: Oh, I understand! I don't know what your little game is, Agnes, but I can wait and see. *I'm* not hungry.

MRS. ROBERTS: Willis, do you think I would try and play a trick on you, if I could?

CAMPBELL: I think you can't. Come, now, Agnes! It's a failure. Own up, and bring the rest of the company out of the next room. I suppose almost anything is allowable at this festive season, but this is pretty feeble.

MRS. ROBERTS: Indeed, indeed, they are not there.

CAMPBELL: Where are they, then?

ALL: That's what we don't know.

CAMPBELL: Oh, come, now! that's a little too thin. You don't know where *any* of all these blood-relations and connections by marriage are? Well, search me!

MRS. ROBERTS, *in open distress*: Oh, I'm sure something must have happened to Aunt Mary!

MRS. MILLER: I can't understand what Ellery C. Miller means.

LAWTON, *with a simulated sternness*: I hope you haven't let that son of yours run away with my daughter, Bemis?

BEMIS: I'm afraid he's come to a pass where he wouldn't ask *my* leave.

CURWEN, *re-assuring himself*: Ah, she's all right, of course. I know that—

BEMIS: Miss Lawton?

CURWEN: No, no—Mrs. Curwen.

CAMPBELL: Is it a true bill, Agnes?

MRS. ROBERTS: Indeed it is, Willis. We've been expecting her for an hour—of course she always comes early—and I'm afraid she's been taken ill suddenly.

ROBERTS: Oh, I don't think it's that, my dear.

MRS. ROBERTS: Oh, of course you never think anything's wrong, Edward. My whole family might die, and—(*Mrs. Roberts restrains herself, and turns to Mr. Campbell, with hysterical cheerfulness.*) Who came up in the elevator with you?

CAMPBELL: Me? *I* didn't come in the elevator. I had my usual luck. The elevator was up somewhere, and after I'd pressed the annunciator button till my thumb ached, I watched my chance and walked up.

MRS. ROBERTS: Where was the janitor?

CAMPBELL: Where the janitor always is—nowhere.

LAWTON: Eating his Christmas dinner, probably.

MRS. ROBERTS, *partially abandoning and then recovering herself*: Yes, it's perfectly spoiled! Well, friends, I think we'd better go to dinner—that's the only way to bring them. I'll go out and interview the cook. (*Sotto voce to her husband*) If I don't go somewhere and have a cry, I shall break down here before everybody. Did you ever know anything so strange? It's perfectly—pokerish.

LAWTON: Yes, there's nothing like serving dinner to bring the belated guest. It's as infallible as going without an umbrella when it won't rain.

CAMPBELL: No, no! Wait a minute, Roberts,

You might sit down without one guest, but you can't sit down without five. It's the old joke about the part of Hamlet. I'll just step round to Aunt Mary's house—why, I'll be back in three minutes.

MRS. ROBERTS, *with perfervid gratitude*: Oh, how *good* you are, Willis! You don't know how *much* you're doing! What presence of mind you have! Why couldn't we have thought of sending for her? O Willis, I can never be grateful enough to you! But you always think of everything.

ROBERTS: I accept my punishment meekly, Willis, since it's in your honor.

LAWTON: It's a simple and beautiful solution, Mrs. Roberts, as far as your aunt's concerned; but I don't see how it helps the rest of us.

MRS. MILLER, *to Mr. Campbell*: If you meet Mr. Miller—

CURWEN: Or my wife—

BEMIS: Or my son—

LAWTON: Or my daughter—

CAMPBELL: I'll tell them they've just one chance in a hundred to save their lives, and that one is open to them for just five minutes.

LAWTON: Tell my daughter that I've been here half an hour, and everybody knows I drove here with her.

BEMIS: Tell my son that the next time I'll walk, and let him drive.

MRS. MILLER: Tell Mr. Miller I found I had my fan after all.

CURWEN: And Mrs. Curwen that I've got her glove all right.
He holds it up.

MRS. ROBERTS, *at a look of mystification and demand from her brother*: Never mind explanations, Willis. They'll understand, and we'll explain when you get back.

LAWTON, *examining the glove which Curwen holds up*: Why, so it *is* right!

CURWEN: What do you mean?

LAWTON: Were you sent back to get a *left* glove?

CURWEN: Yes, yes; of course.

LAWTON: Well, if you'll notice, this is a right one. The one at home is left.

CURWEN, *staring helplessly at it*: Gracious powers! what shall I do?

LAWTON: Pray that Mrs. Curwen may *never* come.

MR. CURWEN, *dashing through the door*: I'll be back by the time Mr. Campbell returns.

MRS. MILLER, *with tokens of breaking down*

visible to Mrs. Roberts: I wonder what could have kept Mr. Miller. It's so very mysterious, I—

MRS. ROBERTS, *suddenly seizing her by the arm, and hurrying her from the room*: Now, Mrs. Miller, you've just got time to see my baby.

MR. ROBERTS, *winking at his remaining guests*: A little cry will do them good. I saw as soon as Willis came in instead of her aunt, that my wife couldn't get through without it. They'll come back as bright as—

LAWTON: Bemis, should you mind a bereaved father falling upon your neck?

BEMIS: Yes, Lawton, I think I should.

LAWTON: Well, it *is* rather odd about all those people. You can say of one or two that they've been delayed, but five people can't have been delayed. It's too much. It amounts to a coincidence. Hello! What's that?

ROBERTS: What's what?

LAWTON: I thought I heard a cry.

ROBERTS: Very likely you did. They profess to deaden these floors so that you can't hear from one apartment to another. But I know pretty well when my neighbor overhead is trying to wheel his baby to sleep in a perambulator at three o'clock in the morning; and I guess our young lady lets the people below understand when she's wakeful. But it's the only way to live, after all. I wouldn't go back to the old up-and-down-stairs, house-in-a-block system on any account. Here we all live on the ground-floor practically. The elevator equalizes everything.

BEMIS: Yes, when it happens to be where you are. I believe I prefer the good old Florentine fashion of walking upstairs, after all.

LAWTON: Roberts, I *did* hear something. Hark! It sounded like a cry for help. There!

ROBERTS: You're nervous, doctor. It's nothing. However, it's easy enough to go out and see. (*He goes out to the door of the apartment, and immediately returns. He beckons to Dr. Lawton and Mr. Bemis, with a mysterious whisper.*) Come here both of you. Don't alarm the ladies.

II.

In the interior of the elevator are seated Mrs. Roberts's Aunt Mary (Mrs. Crashaw), Mrs. Curwen, and Miss Lawton; Mr. Miller and Mr. Alfred Bemis are standing with their hats in their hands. They are in dinner costume, with their overcoats on their arms, and the ladies' draperies and ribbons show from under their outer wraps, where they are caught up, and held with that caution which characterizes ladies in sitting attitudes which they have not been able to choose deliberately. As they talk together, the elevator rises very slowly, and they continue talking for some time before they observe that it has stopped.

MRS. CRASHAW: It's very fortunate that we are all here together. I ought to have been here half an hour ago, but I was kept at home by an accident to my finery, and before I could be put in repair I heard it striking the quarter past. I don't know what my niece will say to me. I hope you good people will all stand by me if she should be violent.

MILLER: In what a poor man may with his wife's fan, you shall command me, Mrs. Crashaw.
He takes the fan out, and unfurls it.

MRS. CRASHAW: Did she send you back for it?

MILLER: I shouldn't have had the pleasure of arriving with you if she hadn't.

MRS. CRASHAW, *laughing, to Mrs. Curwen*: What did you send *yours* back for, my dear?

MRS. CURWEN, *thrusting out one hand gloved, and the other ungloved*: I didn't want two rights.

YOUNG MR. BEMIS: Not even women's rights?

MRS. CURWEN: Oh, so young and so depraved! Are all the young men in Florence so bad? (*Surveying her extended arms, which she turns over*) I don't know that I need have sent him for the other glove. I could have explained to Mrs. Roberts. Perhaps she would have forgiven my coming in one glove.

MILLER, *looking down at the pretty arms*: If she had seen you without.

MRS. CURWEN: Oh, you were looking! (*She rapidly involves her arms in her wrap. Then she suddenly unwraps them, and regards them thoughtfully.*) What if he should bring a ten-button instead of an eight! And he's quite capable of doing it.

MILLER: Are there such things as ten-button gloves?

MRS. CURWEN: You would think there were ten-thousand button gloves if you had them to button.

MILLER: It would depend upon whom I had to button them for.

MRS. CURWEN: For Mrs. Miller, for example.

MRS. CRASHAW: We women are too bad, always sending people back for something. It's well the men don't know *how* bad.

MRS. CURWEN: 'Sh! Mr. Miller is listening. And he thought we were perfect. He asks nothing better than to be sent back for his wife's fan. And he doesn't say anything even under his breath when she finds she's forgotten it, and begins, "Oh, dearest, my fan"—Mr. Curwen does. But he goes all the same. I hope you have your father in good training, Miss Lawton. You must commence with your father, if you expect your husband to be "good."

MISS LAWTON: Then mine will never behave, for papa is perfectly incorrigible.

MRS. CURWEN: I'm sorry to hear such a bad report of him. Shouldn't *you* think he would be "good," Mr. Bemis?

YOUNG MR. BEMIS: I should think he would try.

MRS. CURWEN: A diplomat, as well as a punster already! I must warn Miss Lawton.

MRS. CRASHAW, *interposing to spare the young people*: What an amusing thing elevator etiquette is! Why should the gentlemen take their hats off? Why don't you take your hats off in a horse-car?

MILLER: The theory is that the elevator is a room.

YOUNG MR. BEMIS: We were at a hotel in London where they called it the Ascending Room.

MISS LAWTON: Oh, how amusing!

MILLER, *looking about*: This is a regular drawing-room for size and luxury. They're usually such cribs in these hotels.

MRS. CRASHAW: Yes, it's very nice, though I say it that shouldn't of my niece's elevator. The worst about it is, it's so slow.

MILLER: Let's hope it's sure.

YOUNG MR. BEMIS: Some of these elevators in America go up like express trains.

MRS. CURWEN, *drawing her shawl about her shoulders, as if to be ready to step out*: Well, I never get into one without taking my life in my hand, and my heart in my mouth. I suppose every one really expects an elevator to drop with them, some day, just as everybody really expects to see a ghost some time.

MRS. CRASHAW: Oh, my dear! what an extremely disagreeable subject of conversation.

MRS. CURWEN: I can't help it, Mrs. Crashaw. When I reflect that there are two thousand elevators in Boston, and that the inspectors have just pronounced a hundred and seventy of them unsafe, I'm so desperate when I get into one that I could—flirt!

MILLER, *guarding himself with the fan*: Not with me?

MISS LAWTON, *to young* Mr. Bemis: How it *does* creep!

YOUNG MR. BEMIS, *looking down fondly at her*: Oh, does it?

MRS. CRASHAW: Why, it doesn't go at all! It's stopped. Let us get out.

They all rise.

THE ELEVATOR BOY, *pulling at the rope*: We're not there, yet.

MRS. CRASHAW, *with mingled trepidation and severity*: Not there? What are you stopping, then, for?

THE ELEVATOR BOY: I don't know. It seems to be caught.

MRS. CRASHAW: Caught?

MISS LAWTON: Oh, dear!

YOUNG MR. BEMIS: Don't mind.

MILLER: Caught? Nonsense!

MRS. CURWEN: *We're* caught, I should say.

She sinks back on the seat.

THE ELEVATOR BOY: Seemed to be going kind of funny all day!

He keeps tugging at the rope.

MILLER, *arresting the boy's efforts*: Well, hold on—stop! What are you doing?

THE ELEVATOR BOY: Trying to make it go.

MILLER: Well, don't be so—violent about it. You might break something.

THE ELEVATOR BOY: Break a wire rope like that!

MILLER: Well, well, be quiet now. Ladies, I think you'd better sit down—and as gently as possible. I wouldn't move about much.

MRS. CURWEN: Move! We're stone. And I wish for my part I were a feather.

MILLER, *to the boy*: Er—a—er—where do you suppose we are?

THE ELEVATOR BOY: We're in the shaft between the fourth and fifth floors.

He attempts a fresh demonstration on the rope, but is prevented.

MILLER: Hold on! Er—er—

MRS. CRASHAW, *as if the boy had to be communicated with through an interpreter*: Ask him if it's ever happened before.

MILLER: Yes. Were you ever caught before?

THE ELEVATOR BOY: No.

MILLER: He says no.

MRS. CRASHAW: Ask him if the elevator has a safety device.

MILLER: Has it got a safety device?

THE ELEVATOR BOY: How should I know?

MILLER: He says he don't know.

MRS. CURWEN, *in a shriek of hysterical laughter*: Why, he understands English!

MRS. CRASHAW, *sternly ignoring the insinuation*: Ask him if there's any means of calling the janitor.

MILLER: Could you call the janitor?

THE ELEVATOR BOY, *ironically*: Well, there ain't any telephone attachment.

MILLER, *solemnly*: No, he says there isn't.

MRS CRASHAW, *sinking back on the seat with resignation*: Well, I don't know what my niece will say.

MISS LAWTON: Poor papa!

YOUNG MR. BEMIS, *gathering one of her wandering hands into his*: Don't be frightened. I'm sure there's no danger.

THE ELEVATOR BOY, *indignantly*: Why, she can't *drop*. The cogs in the runs won't let her!

ALL: Oh!

MILLER, *with a sigh of relief*: I knew there must be something of the kind. Well, I wish my wife had her fan.

MRS. CURWEN: And if I had my left glove I should be perfectly happy. Not that I know what the cogs in the runs are!

MRS. CRASHAW: Then we're merely caught here?

MILLER: That's all.

MRS. CURWEN: It's quite enough for the purpose. Couldn't you put on a life-preserver, Mr. Miller, and go ashore and get help from the natives?

MISS LAWTON, *putting her handkerchief to her eyes*: Oh, dear!

MRS. CRASHAW, *putting her arm around her*: Don't be frightened, my child. There's no danger.

YOUNG MR. BEMIS, *caressing the hand which he holds*: Don't be frightened.

MISS LAWTON: Don't leave me.

YOUNG MR. BEMIS: No, no; I won't. Keep fast hold of my hand.

MISS LAWTON: Oh, yes, I will! I'm ashamed to cry.

YOUNG MR. BEMIS, *fervently*: Oh, you needn't be! It is perfectly natural you should.

MRS. CURWEN: I'm too badly scared for tears. Mr. Miller, you seem to be in charge of this expedition—couldn't you do something? Throw out ballast, or let the boy down in a parachute? Or I've read of a shipwreck where the survivors, in an open boat, joined in a cry, and attracted the notice of a vessel that was going to pass them. We might join in a cry.

MILLER: Oh, it's all very well joking, Mrs. Curwen—

MRS. CURWEN: You call it joking!

MILLER: But it's not so amusing, being cooped up here indefinitely. I don't know how we're to get out. We can't join in a cry, and rouse the whole house. It would be ridiculous.

MRS. CURWEN: And our present attitude is so eminently dignified! Well, I suppose we shall have to cast lots pretty soon to see which of us shall be sacrificed to nourish the survivors. It's long past dinner-time.

MISS LAWTON, *breaking down*: Oh, *don't* say such terrible things.

YOUNG MR. BEMIS, *indignantly comforting her*: Don't, don't cry. There's no danger. It's perfectly safe.

MILLER, *to the Elevator Boy*: Couldn't you climb up the cable, and get on to the landing, and—ah!—get somebody?

THE ELEVATOR BOY: I could, maybe, if there was a hole in the roof.

MILLER, *glancing up*: Ah! true.

MRS. CRASHAW, *with an old lady's serious kindness*: My boy, can't you think of anything to do for us?

THE ELEVATOR BOY, *yielding to the touch of humanity, and bursting into tears*: No, ma'am, I can't. And everybody's blamin' me, as if I done it. What's my poor mother goin' to do?

MRS. CRASHAW, *soothingly*: But you said the runs in the cogs—

THE ELEVATOR BOY: How can I tell! That's what they say. They hain't never been tried.

MRS. CURWEN, *springing to her feet*: There! I knew I should. Oh—

She sinks fainting to the floor.

MRS. CRASHAW, *abandoning Miss Lawton to the ministrations of young Mr. Bemis, while she kneels beside Mrs. Curwen and chafes her hand*: Oh, poor thing! I knew she was overwrought by the way she was keeping up. Give her air, Mr. Miller. Open a— Oh, there isn't any window!

MILLER, *dropping on his knees, and fanning Mrs. Curwen*: There! there! Wake up, Mrs. Curwen. I didn't mean to scold you for joking. I didn't, indeed. I—I—I don't know what the deuce I'm up to. (*He gathers Mrs. Curwen's inanimate form in his arms, and fans her face where it lies on his shoulder.*) I don't know what my wife would say if—

MRS. CRASHAW: She would say that you were doing your duty.

MILLER, *a little consoled*: Oh, do you think so? Well, perhaps.

YOUNG MR. BEMIS: Do you feel faint at all, Miss Lawton?

MISS LAWTON: No, I think not. No, not if you say it's safe.

YOUNG MR. BEMIS: Oh, I'm sure it is!

MISS LAWTON, *renewing her hold upon his hand*: Well, then! Perhaps I hurt you?

YOUNG MR. BEMIS: No, no! You couldn't.

MISS LAWTON: How kind you are!

MRS. CURWEN, *opening her eyes*: Where—

MILLER, *rapidly transferring her to Mrs. Crashaw*: Still in the elevator, Mrs. Curwen. (*Rising to his feet*) Something must be done. Perhaps we *had* better unite in a cry. It's ridiculous, of course. But it's the only thing we can do. Now, then! Hello!

MISS LAWTON: Papa!

MRS. CRASHAW: Agne-e-e-s!

MRS. CURWEN, *faintly*: Walter!

THE ELEVATOR BOY: Say!

MILLER: Oh, that won't do. All join in "Hello!"

ALL: Hello!

MILLER: Once more!

ALL: Hello!

MILLER: *Once* more!

ALL: Hello!

MILLER: Now wait a while. (*After an interval*) No, nobody coming. (*He takes out his watch.*) We must repeat this cry at intervals of a half-minute. Now, then!

They all join in the cry, repeating it as Mr. Miller makes the signal with his lifted hand.

MISS LAWTON: Oh, it's no use!

MRS. CRASHAW: They don't hear.

MRS. CURWEN: They *won't* hear.

MILLER: Now, then, three times!

ALL: Hello! hello! hello!

III.

Roberts appears at the outer door of his apartment on the fifth floor. It opens upon a spacious landing, to which a wide staircase ascends at one side. At the other is seen the grated door to the shaft of the elevator. He peers about on all sides, and listens for a moment before he speaks.

ROBERTS: Hello yourself.

MILLER, *invisibly from the shaft*: Is that you, Roberts?

ROBERTS: Yes; where in the world are you?

MILLER: In the elevator.

MRS. CRASHAW: We're *all* here, Edward.

ROBERTS: What! You, Aunt Mary!

MRS. CRASHAW: Yes. Didn't I say so?

ROBERTS: Why don't you come up?

MILLER: We can't. The elevator has got stuck somehow.

ROBERTS: Got stuck? Bless my soul! How did it happen? How long have you been there?

MRS. CURWEN: Since the world began!

MILLER: What's the use asking how it happened? We don't know, and we don't care. What we want to do is to get out.

ROBERTS: Yes, yes! Be careful! (*He rises from his frog-like posture at the grating, and walks the landing in agitation.*) Just hold on a minute!

MILLER: Oh, *we* sha'n't stir.

ROBERTS: I'll see what can be done.

MILLER: Well, see quick, please. We have plenty of time, but we don't want to lose any. Don't alarm Mrs. Miller, if you can help it.

ROBERTS: No, no.

MRS. CURWEN: You *may* alarm Mr. Curwen.

ROBERTS: What! Are *you* there?

MRS. CURWEN: Here? I've been here all my life!

ROBERTS: Ha! ha! ha! That's right. We'll soon have you out. Keep up your spirits.

MRS. CURWEN: But I'm *not* keeping them up.

MISS LAWTON: Tell papa I'm here too.

ROBERTS: What! You too, Miss Lawton?

MRS. CRASHAW: Yes, and young Mr. Bemis. Didn't I *tell* you we were all here?

ROBERTS: I couldn't realize it. Well, wait a moment.

MRS. CURWEN: Oh, you can trust us to wait.

ROBERTS, *returning with Dr. Lawton, and Mr. Bemis, who join him in stooping around the grated door of the shaft*: They're just under here in the well of the elevator, midway between the two stories.

LAWTON: Ha! ha! ha! You don't say so.

BEMIS: Bless my heart! What are they doing there?

MILLER: We're not doing anything.

MRS. CURWEN: We're waiting for you to do something.

MISS LAWTON: Oh, papa!

LAWTON: Don't be troubled, Lou, we'll soon have you out.

YOUNG MR. BEMIS: Don't be alarmed, sir. Miss Lawton is all right.

MISS LAWTON: Yes, I'm not frightened, papa.

LAWTON: Well, that's a great thing in cases of this kind. How did you happen to get there?

MILLER, *indignantly*: How do you suppose? We came up in the elevator.

LAWTON: Well, why didn't you come the rest of the way?

MILLER: The elevator wouldn't.

LAWTON: What seems to be the matter?

MILLER: We don't know.

LAWTON: Have you tried to start it?

MILLER: Well, I'll leave that to your imagination.

LAWTON: Well, be careful what you do. You might—

MILLER, *interrupting*: Roberts, who's that talking?

ROBERTS, *coming forward politely*: Oh, excuse me! I forgot that you didn't know each other. Dr. Lawton, Mr. Miller.

Introducing them.

LAWTON: Glad to know you.

MILLER: Very happy to make your acquaintance, and hope some day to see you. And now, if you have completed your diagnosis—

MRS. CURWEN: None of us have ever had it before, doctor; nor any of our families, so far as we know.

LAWTON: Ha! ha! ha! Very good! Well, just keep quiet. We'll have you all out of there presently.

BEMIS: Yes, remain perfectly still.

ROBERTS: Yes, we'll have you out. Just wait.

MILLER: You seem to think we're going to run away. Why shouldn't we keep quiet? Do you suppose we're going to be very boisterous, shut up here like rats in a trap?

MRS. CURWEN: Or birds in a cage, if you want a more pleasing image.

MRS. CRASHAW: How are you going to get us out, Edward?

ROBERTS: We don't know yet. But keep quiet—

MILLER: Keep quiet! Great heavens! we're afraid to stir a finger. Now don't say "keep quiet" any more, for we can't stand it.

LAWTON: He's in open rebellion. What are you going to do, Roberts?

ROBERTS, *rising and scratching his head*: Well, I don't know yet. We might break a hole in the roof.

LAWTON: Ah, I don't think that would do. Besides you'd have to get a carpenter.

ROBERTS: That's true. And it would make a

racket, and alarm the house— (*Staring desperately at the grated doorway of the shaft*) If I could only find an elevator man—an elevator builder! But of course they all live in the suburbs, and they're keeping Christmas, and it would take too long, anyway.

BEMIS: Hadn't you better send for the police? It seems to me it's a case for the authorities.

LAWTON: Ah, there speaks the Europeanized mind! They always leave the initiative to the authorities. Go out and sound the fire-alarm, Roberts. It's a case for the Fire Department.

ROBERTS: Oh, it's all very well to joke, Dr. Lawton. Why don't you prescribe something?

LAWTON: Surgical treatment seems to be indicated, and I'm merely a general practitioner.

ROBERTS: If Willis were only here, he'd find some way out of it. Well, I'll have to go for help somewhere—

MRS. ROBERTS AND MRS. MILLER, *bursting upon the scene*: Oh, what is it?

LAWTON: Ah, you needn't go for help, my dear fellow. It's come!

MRS. ROBERTS: What are you all doing here, Edward?

MRS. MILLER: Oh, have you had any bad news of Mr. Miller?

MRS. ROBERTS: Or Aunt Mary?

MILLER, *calling up*: Well, are you going to keep us here all night? Why don't you do something ?

MRS. MILLER: Oh, what's that? Oh, it's Mr. Miller! Oh, where are you, Ellery?

MILLER: In the elevator.

MRS. MILLER: Oh! and where is the elevator? Why don't you get out? Oh—

MILLER: It's caught, and we can't.

MRS. MILLER: Caught? Oh, then you will be killed—killed—killed! And it's all my fault, sending you back after my fan, and I had it all the time in my own pocket; and it comes from my habit of giving it to you to carry in your overcoat pocket, because it's deep, and the fan can't break. And of course I never thought of my own pocket, and I never *should* have thought of it at all if Mr. Curwen hadn't been going back to get Mrs. Curwen's glove, for he'd brought another right after she'd sent him for a left, and we were all having such a laugh about it, and I just happened to put my hand on my pocket, and there I felt the fan. And oh, *what* shall I do?

Mrs. Miller utters these explanations and self-reproaches in a lamentable voice, while

crouching close to the grated door to the elevator shaft, and clinging to its meshes.

MILLER: Well, well, it's all right. I've got you another fan, here. Don't be frightened.

MRS. ROBERTS, *wildly*: Where's Aunt Mary, Edward? Has Willis got back? (*At a guilty look from her husband*) Edward! *don't* tell me that *she's* in that elevator! Don't do it, Edward! For your own sake don't. Don't tell me that your own child's mother's aunt is down there, suspended between heaven and earth like—like—

LAWTON: The coffin of the Prophet.

MRS. ROBERTS: Yes. *Don't* tell me, Edward! Spare your child's mother, if you won't spare your wife!

MRS. CRASHAW: Agnes! don't be ridiculous. I'm here, and I never was more comfortable in my life.

MRS. ROBERTS, *calling down the grating*: Oh! Is it you, Aunt Mary?

MRS. CRASHAW: Of course it is!

MRS. ROBERTS: You recognize my voice?

MRS. CRASHAW: I should hope so, indeed! Why shouldn't I?

MRS. ROBERTS: And you know me? Agnes? Oh!

MRS. CRASHAW: Don't be a goose, Agnes.

MRS. ROBERTS: Oh, it *is* you, aunty. It *is*! Oh, I'm *so* glad! I'm *so* happy! But keep perfectly still, aunty dear, and we'll soon have you out. Think of baby, and don't give way.

MRS. CRASHAW: I shall not, if the elevator doesn't, you may depend upon that.

MRS. ROBERTS: Oh, what courage you *do* have! But keep up your spirits! Mrs. Miller and I have just come from seeing baby. She's gone to sleep with all her little presents in her arms. The children did want to see you so much before they went to bed. But never mind that now, Aunt Mary. I'm only too thankful to have you at all!

MRS. CRASHAW: I wish you did have me! And if you will all stop talking and try some of you to do something, I shall be greatly obliged to you. It's worse than it was in the sleeping-car that night.[1]

MRS ROBERTS: Oh, do you remember it, Aunt Mary? Oh, how funny you are! (*Turning heroically to her husband*) Now, Edward, dear, get them out. If it's necessary, get them out over my dead body. Anything! Only hurry. I will be calm; I will be patient. But you must act instantly. Oh, here comes Mr. Curwen! (*Mr. Curwen*

---

1 This is a reference to activity in *The Sleeping Car*.

mounts the stairs to the landing with every sign of exhaustion, as if he had made a very quick run to and from his house.) Oh, *he* will help—I know he will! Oh, Mr. Curwen, the elevator is caught just below here with my aunt in it and Mrs. Miller's husband—

LAWTON: And my girl.

BEMIS: And my boy.

MRS. CURWEN, *calling up*: And your wife!

CURWEN, *horror-struck*: And my wife! Oh, heavenly powers! what are we going to do? How shall we get them out? Why don't they come up?

ALL: They can't.

CURWEN: Can't? Oh, my goodness!

He flies at the grating, and kicks and beats it.

ROBERTS: Hold on! What's the use of that?

LAWTON: You couldn't get at them if you beat the door down.

BEMIS: Certainly not.

They lay hands upon him and restrain him.

CURWEN, *struggling*: Let me speak to my wife! Will you prevent a husband from speaking to his own wife?

MRS. MILLER, *in blind admiration of his frenzy*: Yes, that's just what I said. If some one had beaten the door in at once—

MRS. ROBERTS: Oh, Edward, dear, let him speak to his wife. *(Tearfully)* Think if *I* were there!

ROBERTS, *releasing him*: He may speak to his wife all night. But he mustn't knock the house down.

CURWEN, *rushing at the grating*: Caroline! Can you hear me? Are you safe?

MRS. CURWEN: Perfectly. I had a little faint when we first stuck—

CURWEN: Faint? Oh!

MRS. CURWEN: But I am all right now.

CURWEN: Well, that's right. Don't be frightened! There's no occasion for excitement. Keep perfectly calm and collected. It's the only way— What's that ringing?

The sound of an electric bell is heard within the elevator. It increases in fury.

MRS. ROBERTS AND MRS. MILLER: Oh, isn't it dreadful?

THE ELEVATOR BOY: It's somebody on the ground-floor callin' the elevator!

CURWEN: Well, never mind him. Don't pay the slightest attention to him. Let him go to the deuce! And, Caroline!

MRS. CURWEN: Yes?

CURWEN: I—I—I've got your glove all right.

MRS. CURWEN: Left, you mean, I hope?

CURWEN: Yes, left, dearest! I *mean* left.

MRS. CURWEN: Eight-button?

CURWEN: Yes.

MRS. CURWEN: Light drab?

CURWEN, *pulling a light yellow glove from his pocket*: Oh!

He staggers away from the grating and stays himself against the wall, the mistaken glove dangling limply from his hand.

ROBERTS, LAWTON, AND BEMIS: Ah! ha! ha! ha!

MRS. ROBERTS: Oh, for shame! to laugh at such a time!

MRS. MILLER: When it's a question of life and death. There! The ringing's stopped. What's that? *(Steps are heard mounting the stairway rapidly, several treads at a time. Mr. Campbell suddenly bursts into the group on the landing with a final bound from the stairway.)* Oh!

CAMPBELL: I can't find Aunt Mary, Agnes. I can't find anything—not even the elevator. Where's the elevator? I rang for it down there till I was black in the face.

MRS. ROBERTS: No wonder! It's here.

MRS. MILLER: Between this floor and the floor below. With my husband in it.

CURWEN: And my wife!

LAWTON: And my daughter!

BEMIS: And my son!

MRS. ROBERTS: And aunty!

ALL: And it's stuck fast.

ROBERTS: And the long and short of it is, Willis, that we don't know how to get them out, and we wish you would suggest some way.

LAWTON: There's been a great tacit confidence among us in your executive ability and your inventive genius.

MRS. ROBERTS: Oh, yes, we know you can do it.

MRS. MILLER: If you can't, nothing can save them.

CAMPBELL, *going to the grating*: Miller!

MILLER: Well?

CAMPBELL: Start her up!

MILLER: Now, look here, Campbell, we are not going to stand that; we've had enough of it. I speak for the whole elevator. Don't you suppose that if it had been possible to start her up we—

MRS. CURWEN: We shouldn't have been at the moon by this time.

CAMPBELL: Well, then, start her *down!*

MILLER: I never thought of that. *(To the Elevator Boy)* Start her down. *(To the people on the landing above)* Hurrah! She's off!

CAMPBELL: Well, *now* start her up!

A JOINT CRY FROM THE ELEVATOR: Thank you! we'll *walk* up this time.

MILLER: Here! let us out at this landing!

They are heard precipitately emerging, with sighs and groans of relief, on the floor below.

MRS. ROBERTS, *devoutly*: O Willis, it seems like an interposition of Providence, your coming just at this moment.

CAMPBELL: Interposition of common sense! These hydraulic elevators weaken sometimes, and can't go any farther.

ROBERTS, *to the shipwrecked guests, who arrive at the top of the stairs, crestfallen, spent, and clinging to one another for support*: Why didn't you think of starting her down, some of you?

MRS. ROBERTS, *welcoming them with kisses and hand-shakes*: I should have thought it would occur to you at once.

MILLER, *goaded to exasperation*: Did it occur to any of *you?*

LAWTON, *with sublime impudence*: It occurred to *all* of us. But we naturally supposed you had tried it.

MRS. MILLER, *taking possession of her husband*: Oh, what a fright you have given us!

MILLER: *I* given you! Do you suppose I did it out of a joke, or voluntarily?

MRS. ROBERTS: Aunty, I don't know what to say to you. *You* ought to have been here long ago, before anything happened.

MRS. CRASHAW: Oh, I can explain everything in due season. What I wish you to do now is to let me get at Willis, and kiss him. (*As Campbell submits to her embrace*) You dear, good fellow! If it hadn't been for your presence of mind, I don't know how we should ever have got out of that horrid pen.

MRS. CURWEN, *giving him her hand*: As it isn't proper for *me* to kiss you—

CAMPBELL: Well, I don't know. I don't wish to be *too* modest.

MRS. CURWEN: I think I shall have to vote you a service of plate.

MRS. ROBERTS: Come and look at the pattern of mine. And, Willis, as you are the true hero of

the occasion, you shall take me in to dinner. And I am not going to let anybody go before you.

She seizes his arm, and leads the way from the landing into the apartment. Roberts, Lawton, and Bemis follow stragglingly.

MRS. MILLER, *getting her husband to one side*: When she fainted, she fainted *at* you, of course! What did you do?

MILLER: Who? I! Oh! (*After a moment's reflection*) She came to!

CURWEN, *getting his wife aside*: When you fainted, Caroline, who revived you?

MRS. CURWEN: Who? *Me?* Oh! How should I know? I was insensible. (*They wheel arm in arm, and meet Mr. and Mrs. Miller in the middle. Mrs. Curwen yields precedence with an ironical courtesy.*) After you, Mrs. Miller!

MRS. MILLER, *in a nervous, inimical twitter*: Oh, before the heroine of the lost elevator?

MRS. CURWEN, *dropping her husband's arm, and taking Mrs. Miller's*: Let us split the difference.

MRS. MILLER: Delightful! I shall never forget the honor.

MRS. CURWEN: Oh, don't speak of honors! Mr. Miller was *so* kind through all those terrible scenes in the elevator.

MRS. MILLER: I've no doubt you showed yourself duly grateful.

They pass in, followed by their husbands.

YOUNG MR. BEMIS, *timidly*: Miss Lawton, in the elevator you asked me not to leave you. Did you—ah—mean—I *must* ask you; it may be my only chance; if you meant—never?

MISS LAWTON, *dropping her head*: I—I—don't —know.

YOUNG MR. BEMIS: But if I *wished* never to leave you, should you send me away?

MISS LAWTON, *with a shy, sly upward glance at him*: Not in the elevator!

YOUNG MR. BEMIS: Oh!

MRS. ROBERTS, *re-appearing at the door*: Why, you good-for-nothing young things, why don't you come to— Oh! excuse me! (*She re-enters precipitately, followed by her tardy guests, on whom she casts a backward glance of sympathy.*) Oh, you *needn't* hurry!

A Foregone Conclusion

[1884–1885]

W. D. Howells and William Poel

This early Howells novel was dramatized by three different men and produced in each version with little success. During the spring of 1884 William Poel, English dramatist and actor, adapted the novel for the stage, calling his work *Priest or Painter*, "One Passionate Love, One Mortal Sorrow," and played the part of the priest in the Royal Olympic Theatre production on July 11, 1884. The previous year Howells had been in England and may have conferred with Poel on the dramatization. Beerbohm Tree, however, had expressed an interest in Poel's adaptation as early as April 11, 1884 (letter to Poel, Kansas University Library), and by August of that year was enthusiastic about playing the part of the priest. At this time Poel was revising after the July production and was also asking Howells' opinion on certain points—a development that disturbed Tree, who felt that Howells was "not greatly gifted with dramatic instinct" (letter to Poel, August 6, 1884, Kansas University Library). But Tree was willing to work with Howells and was anxious that Howells rewrite the death scene "poetically" and look over a new scheme he had for the third act. The extent of Howells' interest is not known, but the English people seemed to be looking for collaboration on the play when the whole situation suddenly changed. On August 22, 1884, Howells wrote to Henry James (*Life in Letters*, I, 367): "The Madison Square people have bought the London dramatization of *A Foregone Conclusion*, and have sent it to me for revision. As yet we have not got beyond the point of refusing to do it for nothing." Although the Mallory brothers had apparently bought out Poel's interest, as late as February 15, 1885 (letter

from Edmund Gosse to Howells, Harvard Library), Tree was still attracted by the Venetian play. Eventually F. R. Benson did produce the play in England; and George Alexander, English actor (undated letter to Howells, Harvard Library), once asked if he might act Howells' version in England, but there is no evidence that he ever did.

The version of the play purchased by the Madison Square people was the one acted at the Olympic Theatre. Working from that typescript copy, Howells soon adapted it to fit his own ideas concerning *A Foregone Conclusion*. It is this adaptation by Howells of Poel's typescript—now in the possession of William White Howells—that is printed here. Essentially Howells wrote a new first act for the play; made Poel's Act I his own Act II, adding several pages of dialogue; changed the Poel Act II to Act III, omitting scene 3 of the Poel material and adding several pages to introduce scene 2 in this act; and created a new and final Act IV. The Poel Act III, which took place at a picture exhibit in New York two years after the previous action, Howells omitted. In the main it merely told of the action that Howells dramatized in his Act IV and brought Ferris and Florida happily together. In the Poel Act II, scene 3, after the priest said good-by to the departing Vervains, he was stabbed by a gondolier who suspected him of betraying Venice to the Austrians. Although Poel invented an American sculptor, Will James, this character appeared only in his Act III. Howells used a sculptor named Billings throughout, but omitted the landlord who played a conspicuous part in the Poel drama. The Enthoven Collection of the

Victoria and Albert Museum in England contains six other Poel versions of this play, most of them complete or nearly complete. One such version, obviously a previous copy of the play purchased by the Madison Square Theatre, used paste-ups from Howells' novel. Later versions place a major interest of the play in the attitude of the Venetians toward the priest as a spy for the Austrians; consequently they employ the first act to show why the gondolier hates the priest and to make probable the priest's death as a result of the stabbing which in these versions becomes the climax of the play.

Howells' dramatization of A *Foregone Conclusion* began its rather brief and inauspicious stage career as one of A. M. Palmer's authors' matinees series on November 18, 1886. In a letter to his father (November 21, 1886, Harvard Library), Howells gave his opinion: "I went to New York and saw the trial performance of my play at the Madison Square Theatre on Thursday. The house was a splendid one, and the applause was incessant; it was a great success, I thought, but the newspapers, without a dissenting voice, pronounce the play bad. What the managers will do with it I don't know, and I am not anxious; but I thoroughly respect the play." The newspaper reviewers were, as Howells noted, severe. Odell (*Annals*, XIII, 218) summed up the current opinion when he wrote that "the conviction of the time that a successful novelist could not write a good play was justified by this effort." But the play, probably with revision by Howells, continued to be performed. The New York *Times* of Sunday, January 2, 1887, noted that A *Foregone Conclusion* would be performed the following Thursday. In *These Many Years* (p. 282), Brander Matthews mentioned that after the Palmer matinee the play was repeated frequently on a summer trip to Chicago, where from July 11–15, 1887, the company played eight performances at the McVicker's Theatre. At that time, according to the reviewer in the Chicago *Tribune*, July 12, 1887, the play had five acts, the fifth act having to do with the happiness or unhappiness of Ferris, an issue that the reviewer considered a matter of indifference once the priest's fate had been decided. Probably, then, Poel's Act III furnished the situation for Howells' Act V. The reviewer also felt that the play would have been improved if Acts I and V had been omitted. Otherwise, Howells' reception in Chicago was better than in New York. One of the final performances of the play was in the Tremont Theatre in Boston on November 5, 1889. Again the newspaper reviewers were unimpressed, but Henry Austin Clapp in *Reminiscences of a Dramatic Critic* (Boston: Houghton Mifflin Co., 1902, p. 182), although noting the obvious lack of skill in its construction, remembered the play for its gay wit, lavish humor, broad human sympathies, and literary distinction.

The third dramatist to use A *Foregone Conclusion* was Edward M. Alfriend of Richmond, Virginia, better known as coauthor with A. C. Wheeler of *The Great Diamond Robbery*. Alfriend's dramatization was first produced in Richmond during the week of May 26, 1890, as part of the celebration connected with the unveiling of the Lee Monument. A. M. Palmer had brought the actors from New York, and the reviewer in the Richmond *Dispatch* of May 27, 1890, noted that the play was well received. According to this reviewer the play was adapted from Howells' novel, and "it is evident that the dialogue is mainly from Mr. Alfriend's pen, only the mere outline of the plot and a few incidents being taken from the novel." But when the play was taken to New York to the Palmer Theatre, the reviewers (*Dramatic Mirror*, June 28, 1890) considered it more of a failure than Howells' version. Consequently it was played little, and the manuscript is now lost.

A Foregone Conclusion[1]

A Drama by
W. D. Howells and William Poel

SCENE, VENICE. 1863.

PERSONS

DON IPPOLITO, a priest.

HENRY FERRIS, American Consul and painter.

HIRAM BILLINGS, sculptor.

CANONICO (who does not speak), uncle to Don Ippolito.

MRS. VERVAIN, of Providence, R. I.

FLORIDA, her daughter.

MARINA, servant to Ferris.

NINA, servant to Mrs. Vervain.

VENERANDA, servant to Don Ippolito.

ACT I

SCENE: *The American Consulate at Venice, which is also the studio of Henry Ferris, consul and painter. An easel with a canvas on it; table with tubes of colors, palette, etc.; canvases faced against the wall. Ferris going about decorating the consular book-case and shield with large and small American flags, and whistling The Star Spangled Banner. His friend, Billings, the sculptor, watching him from the window, near which he sits with his hat on.*

FERRIS, *retiring for the effect, and dusting his fingers*: Well, what do you say to that?

BILLINGS: Looks like the Fourth of July. What are you doing it for, in April?

FERRIS: Well, I don't know. Obscure motives of patriotism. Can't have too much American flag round in a Consulate when those fellows are hammering away at it in the South.

BILLINGS: I suppose that's so. Well, sometimes I don't know whether to go to Florence and

open a studio, or go home and open a sutler's shop.

FERRIS: You would make a first-class private, Billings.

BILLINGS: I don't know. I don't want to look *too* high. Well! (*Rises with a yawn.*) I must be going.

FERRIS: What's the hurry?

Still studying the decorations, and rearranging points here and there.

BILLINGS: There *isn't any* hurry in Venice. That's the trouble. If you don't make the start yourself, you never get off from a place. I sat talking three hours to Mrs. Vervain, at her hotel last night, simply because I didn't know what to do if I stopped. What a lovely old soul she is! Well, I suppose, you might call her a fool, for short; but I shall feel disappointed if I don't find a good many like her in heaven.

FERRIS: You won't find her where you're going, Billings, but if there's any world where good will out values the intellect, I guess she'll be among the first there, with that winning, weak-headed desire of hers to make every one happy.

BILLINGS, *sighing*: I wish Mrs. Vervain would *adopt* me. I feel the need of a protector. I should like some one to bring me up.

FERRIS: What *you* want is to get yourself adopted by an improved thrashing-machine. That would bring out your good qualities, or kill you in the attempt. How did you find the Vervains?

BILLINGS: The old lady was about as usual. And so was the young one, for that matter. She's got a brisk little temper of her own.

FERRIS, *coldly*: Umph!

BILLINGS: Oh, I suppose she doesn't use it on you. But it's my opinion that the late Colonel

[1] This play has not been published previously.

Vervain, U. S. A. must have been rather an uncomfortable person to differ with and that his temper has come down to his daughter on a larger scale than she knows how to manage. She looks white-hot with that ashen-blond hair of hers. She's sweet on you, Ferris.

FERRIS: She dissembles her love.

BILLINGS: Ah, I dare say. (*He goes and looks at a picture on Ferris' easel.*) Why that is not half as bad as some of your things, Ferris.

FERRIS: Don't be fulsome, Billings.

BILLINGS: Oh, I don't mind scattering a few roses in a fellow artist's path. Good-bye.

FERRIS: Good-bye. Stop in again, two or three weeks from now.

BILLINGS: Well, I will—you're so pressing.

Exit. Ferris resumes his whistling and the inspection of his flags. The bell rings, and his servant puts her head in at the door.

FERRIS: Well, Marina, who is it?

MARINA: A gentleman who wishes to see the Signore Console alone.

FERRIS: Very well, I am alone. Show him in.

He stands with his hands on his hips, fronting the door, which reopens, and admits Don Ippolito, who hesitates, then comes forward, and removing his hat, makes a low, graceful bow.

DON IPPOLITO: The Signore Console?

FERRIS, *politely*: I am the Consul.

DON IPPOLITO: I may be disturbing, or detaining the Signore Console?

FERRIS: No, I am quite at leisure. How can I have the honor of serving you?

DON IPPOLITO, *wiping his forehead with his handkerchief, and then nervously twisting it in his hands*: I suppose that the Signore Console gives passports?

FERRIS, *suspiciously*: Sometimes.

DON IPPOLITO, *with increased perturbation*: Could the Signore Console give a passport for America to me?

FERRIS, *coldly*: Are you an American citizen?

DON IPPOLITO: American citizen?

FERRIS: Yes, subject to the American republic.

DON IPPOLITO, *sadly*: No, surely; I have not that happiness. We Venetians are Austrian subjects, as you know.

FERRIS, *relentingly*: Then I can't give you a passport. No government can give passports to foreign subjects.

DON IPPOLITO: But I thought that to go to America an American passport would be needed.

FERRIS: In America they don't care a fig for passports. You come and you go, and nobody meddles. But if you are a Venetian and want to pass the frontier, you must get a passport from the Austrian governor—if you can.

DON IPPOLITO, *dejectedly*: Precisely! Patience! Signore Console, I ask your pardon for the trouble I have given.

He bows low in parting.

FERRIS, *following him toward the door*: I'm very sorry. Perhaps there is something else in which I could be of use to you?

DON IPPOLITO, *stopping*: Ah, I hardly know. I really had a kind of hope in coming to you, but now it seems a mere stupidity. I was so ignorant about the passports, that doubtless I am also quite deluded in this.

FERRIS: As to that, of course, I can't say, but I hope not.

DON IPPOLITO: Why, listen, signore! I had something that I had thought of offering to your honored government for its advantage in this deplorable rebellion.

FERRIS, *coldly*: Oh, indeed!

DON IPPOLITO, *eagerly*: I have with me the model of a weapon of my contrivance which I thought the government of the North might employ in cases where its batteries were in danger of capture by the secessionists.

FERRIS: Yes? Will you let me see it?

DON IPPOLITO: You do me honor. (*He takes from his pocket the model of a breech loading cannon.*) You perceive, Signore Console, that this is nothing very new as a breech loader. The grand feature of my invention is this secret chamber in the breech, which is intended to hold an explosive of high potency, with a fuse coming out here below. The gunner finding his piece in danger, ignites this fuse and takes refuge in flight. At the moment the enemy seizes the gun the contents of the secret chamber explode, demolishing this piece and destroying its captor. (*He becomes constantly more animated as he goes on, and he dramatizes the final passages with great vividness.*) Behold, Signore Console!

He hands Ferris the model.

FERRIS, *turning it over in his hand*: It's certainly very curious. Did you make this model yourself?

DON IPPOLITO: Surely. I have no money to spend on artisans; and as you might infer, signore, I am not well seen by my superiors and associates on account of these amusements of mine, and I keep them to myself as much as I can. (*He laughs nerv-*

ously.) What do you think, signore? If this invention were brought to the notice of your generous government, would it not patronize my labors? I have read that America is the land of enterprises. Who knows but your government might invite me to take some service under it in which I could employ these little gifts that Heaven— But tell me, signore, how this invention appears to you!

FERRIS: Have you had any practical experience in gunnery?

DON IPPOLITO: Why certainly not!

FERRIS: Neither have I. (*He keeps turning the model over in his hand.*) But I was wondering whether the explosives in this secret chamber would not become so heated by the discharges that it would go off and kill our own artillerymen without waiting for the secessionists?

Don Ippolito's countenance falls; his head sinks on his breast.

DON IPPOLITO: You are right! It is another failure!

FERRIS: Oh, I don't say that. I don't really know any more of the matter than you do. Have you any acquaintances among the Austrian officers to whom you could show your model?

DON IPPOLITO: I don't consult with the military. (*Bitterly.*) Besides, what would be thought of a *priest* who showed such an invention to an officer of our paternal government?

FERRIS, *laughing*: I suppose it would surprise the officers somewhat. (*After a moment.*) May I ask whether you have employed yourself with other inventions?

Lays the model on his table.

DON IPPOLITO, *dejectedly*: I have attempted a great many.

FERRIS: Are they all of this—warlike character?

DON IPPOLITO: No, they are mainly all of peaceful intention. It was the wish to produce something of immediate utility that set me about this cannon. These good friends of mine who have done me the honor of looking at my attempts had blamed me for the uselessness of my inventions. They allowed that they were ingenious, but they said that even if they were practicable, they would not be what the world cares for. I knew very little about the world. Do you think, Signore Console, that if I could get a passport to leave Venice, and should succeed in reaching America— (*Ferris slowly shakes his head.*) Ah! (*Sighing.*) Signore Console, I thank you infinitely for your kindness, I beg your pardon for the intrusion, and I take my leave.

He bows.

FERRIS, *detaining him*: Ah—don't—ah—go. That is, I have been thinking I might assist— But perhaps you don't wish me—

DON IPPOLITO: Oh, I shall be most truly grateful for any suggestion that you can make me. If you will be my adviser—my friend—

FERRIS: It isn't in regard to your inventions. But—the long and the short of it is—there are two American ladies, friends of mine, in Venice, who expect to be here till mid-summer. They are mother and daughter, and the young lady wants to speak and read Italian with somebody a few hours each day. The question is whether it is quite out of your way—I ask it at a venture—to give her lessons of this kind. I suppose no harm is done, if you can't—

DON IPPOLITO, *seizing his hand in both of his own*: Heaven! Oh, you don't know what you do for me! You lift me out of despair! I had reached one of those passes that seem the last bound of endeavor. But you give me new life. Now I can go on with my experiment. I can attest my gratitude by possessing your country of the weapon I had designed for it. I am sure of the principle; some slight improvement; perhaps the use of a new explosive— Yes, it can be done, and I shall yet see America! God bless you, my dear son— I mean—sir—

FERRIS: Wait—hold on—not so fast! Are you sure you can do what they want?

DON IPPOLITO: Oh perfectly! Listen! I have already been the instructor of a noble lady here; and I can bring the testimonial of her family to my efficiency! Adieu! I will go at once for them. I will return within an hour.

FERRIS: But remember! I make no engagement for the ladies. You must see them before anything is settled.

DON IPPOLITO: Surely, surely! I understand! Do not come to the door! I will return soon! Remain well! Adieu!

He rushes impetuously from the room, leaving Ferris planted in the middle of the floor and frowning dubiously.

FERRIS: He goes off with all the violence of one of his own inventions. If we could explode *him* in a mass of secessionists—(*His eye wanders to the model of the cannon left on his table.*) Hello! He's left it! (*He seizes it and rushes to the door.*) Marina! Marina!

MARINA, *appearing*: Behold me, signore!

FERRIS: Call him back! He's left his confounded cannon here!

MARINA: Who, signore?

FERRIS: Who? That gentleman, who just went out! That priest—(*The door bell rings.*) Ah! There he is now! He's come back for it. Take it to him. Run! (*Exit Marina.*) I wouldn't have had that machine left here on any account. It might take *me* for a secessionist.

MARINA, *re-entering*: The American ladies, signore.

Exit; and enter Mrs. and Florida Vervain.

MRS. VERVAIN: Ah, Mr. Ferris, I'm so glad we found you in. I *know* we're encroaching on your very valuable time, and I'm quite ashamed to do it. But isn't it a heavenly day? What *I* call a perfect day, just right every way; none of these disagreeable extremes. It's so unpleasant to have it too hot, for example. I'm the greatest person for moderation, Mr. Ferris, and I carry the principle into everything; but I do think the breakfasts of these Italian hotels are too light altogether. I like our American breakfasts, don't you? To be sure, you oughtn't to think of such a thing as eating in a place like Venice, all poetry; but a sound mind in a sound body, *I* say. We're perfectly wild over it. Don't you think it's a place that grows upon you, very much, Mr. Ferris? All these associations—Bridge of Sighs, and all that—it does seem too much; and the gondoliers everywhere. But I'm afraid the gondoliers cheat us; and in the stores I never feel safe a moment. No such a thing as corals! Florida is extremely fond of them, and we've just bought a set in the Piazza, and I know we paid too much for them. Florida—you *must* see them, Mr. Ferris—where *are* those corals?

FLORIDA: In your pocket, Mother. You put the box there.

MRS. VERVAIN: Why, so I did. (*She searches in her pocket; pulling out her handkerchief, she flits out upon the floor the model of the cannon.*) Good gracious! What is that?

FERRIS, *picking it up*: Merely a breech loading cannon, Mrs. Vervain. How in the world did *you* come by it?

MRS. VERVAIN: Your servant forced something into my hands as I came in, and I supposed it was something I had dropped, and put it into my pocket.

FERRIS: Ah, ha, ha, ha! Ho, ho, ho! Ha, ha, ha!

MRS. VERVAIN: And what are you doing with breech loading cannons about your house? Is it something you've been inventing? How ingenious you painters are! But there was Leonardo da Vinci, invented chain pumps, and everything, and I'm not the least surprised.

FERRIS: But I didn't invent this, Mrs. Vervain. It was invented by an interesting heretic who has just left me. A priest, of all things in the world, who proposes that I shall get it into the hands of the government, and who wanted a passport to go to America, and settle down there in the profession of inventor.

FLORIDA, *snubbingly*: I don't see anything so very strange in that.

FERRIS: Oh, don't you? I'm very glad. I've just engaged him to give you those lessons in Italian.

MRS. VERVAIN: Nonsense! What *do* you mean?

FERRIS: Not exactly what I say, of course. But sit down, Mrs. Vervain! Miss Florida! (*Offering them seats. Florida goes to window and looks out.*) And I will try to explain. This priest—

MRS. VERVAIN: You don't really *mean* a priest?

FERRIS: This time I really *do* mean it. This priest came to me on the errand I've described, and he forgot the model. I sent Marina after him with it, and as you were coming in she naturally gave it to you.

MRS. VERVAIN: I see. But what is it about engaging him to give Florida lessons?

FERRIS: Why, of course, I haven't exactly engaged him. I found him a cultivated and agreeable man—most of the Venetian priests are such a snuffy lot—and I asked him if he thought he could do it. He jumped at the chance. He's poor; and he thinks you will pay him enough to take him to America.

MRS. VERVAIN: What stuff! Now I know you're joking!

FLORIDA, *from the window*: One can be sure of Mr. Ferris's taste, even when there's still question of his wit.

FERRIS: In matters of taste I sit at your feet, Miss Florida. (*To Mrs. Vervain.*) I *didn't* promise him anything. I said I would leave the affair to you, and in the meantime he's dashed off to get testimonials to his efficiency and good moral character from a noble lady of Venice, whose instruction he's had charge of. I think her name was Desdemona.

MRS. VERVAIN: No! Was it really?

FLORIDA, *turning*: I think we had better be going, mother.

MRS. VERVAIN: Not at all! I'm very comfortable here, and I haven't talked this matter out with Mr. Ferris yet. I'm sure he's very good to interest himself, and I don't know what we should do if it were not for the consuls. I always feel as if consuls were one of the family.

FERRIS, *bowing with mock humility*: You do us too much honor, Mrs. Vervain.

MRS. VERVAIN: Roland Vervain being in the army, you know. Florida thinks we impose upon them; but I always say, what are they there for, if not for American ladies to impose on them?

FERRIS: What do we exist for? You're quite right, Mrs. Vervain.

MRS. VERVAIN: There! Florida, I knew he would agree with me. (*To Ferris.*) And so it came perfectly natural to me to ask you to get us a teacher. And you think this priest would do? What do you know about him?

FERRIS: What I've told you. He came to me with this cannon and he wanted me to give him a passport for America, so that he could offer it to our government.

MRS. VERVAIN: Oh, nonsense! It's one of your jokes!

FERRIS: You overpraise me, Mrs. Vervain. If I could make such jokes as that priest was, I should set up for a great American humorist. He had the touch of pathos that all true pieces of humor ought to have. He made me melancholy. (*Florida turns from the window to listen.*) His face haunts me. I dare say he was commonplace enough, though he didn't look it. Spare your romance, Miss Vervain!

FLORIDA: I see as little romance as joke in it.

FERRIS, *bitterly regarding her*: It was a cannon that would make it lively for the Southerners—if they had it. Poor fellow! I suppose he thought I would give him a letter to Lincoln and the whole Army of the Potomac would be turned out to receive him at Washington. Too bad, isn't it?

MRS. VERVAIN: And you think he would do for a teacher?

FERRIS: Ah, that's for you to decide, Mrs. Vervain.

MRS. VERVAIN: Well, one great difficulty with Florida's teachers has been that they all fall in love with her.

FLORIDA: Mother!

MRS. VERVAIN: You know they did, Florida! Pestachiavi, and Schulze, and that horrid old Fleuron. We've had them everywhere, and they've all done it!

FERRIS: A priest would be professionally debarred.

MRS. VERVAIN: Yes, there's something in that. Really, I don't know why he wouldn't do. What do you say yourself, Florida?

FLORIDA, *turning to the window again*: Whatever you wish, mother.

MRS. VERVAIN: Well, I wish somebody had a decided opinion. Then I should be able to decide.

FERRIS: Ah, ha, ha, ha!

MRS. VERVAIN: What are you laughing at, Mr. Ferris? Something I've been saying?

FERRIS: No, something I've been thinking.

FLORIDA, *indignantly*: No doubt it was ridiculous.

FERRIS: I was thinking of you, Miss Vervain.

MRS. VERVAIN: How you two do keep sparring! Well, about this priest, now, seriously.

FERRIS: Seriously, I've told you all I know about him.

MRS. VERVAIN, *rising and putting on her pincenez to scrutinize his expression*: Seriously?

Her glasses leap from her nose, and lodge in Ferris's waistcoat.

FERRIS, *with mock solemnity*: Allow me! (*He restores them with a bow. Florida breaks into a helpless laugh.*) Thank you, Miss Vervain.

FLORIDA: Oh, I detest—buffoonery.

FERRIS: I was afraid you were going to say me. I'm glad that I'm an earnest person.

MRS. VERVAIN: Well, I want you to come and lunch with us, Mr. Ferris. And we can talk him over, then.

FERRIS: I can't come, Mrs. Vervain.

MRS. VERVAIN: Nonsense! Why not?

FERRIS: Very sorry. Affairs of state—rebel privateer—Alabama seen on the Grand Canal, this morning, running down an oyster-boat.

MRS. VERVAIN: Stuff! You *shall* come. Go and get this priest of yours, and bring him with you. Then we can judge from his looks.

FERRIS: I don't know where he lives.

MRS. VERVAIN: What's his name?

FERRIS: Bless my soul, I don't *know* his name.

MARINA, *throwing open the door*: Don Ippolito Rondinelli, signore!

DON IPPOLITO, *entering*: A thousand excuses, Signore Console. I have returned to relieve you of that poor model of mine, which I did not remember leaving here till I reached my own house. (*At sight of the ladies.*) But I intrude—

FERRIS, *handing it to him*: Not at all. Here it is. And let me introduce you, Don Ippolito, to the ladies of whom I was speaking to you. Mrs. Vervain—

MRS. VERVAIN, *coming forward and taking his hand*: And my daughter. (*Don Ippolito and Florida bow to each other.*) I hope you will be able to come to us?

DON IPPOLITO: Thanks, madama, but I have not yet furnished myself with the testimonials.

MRS. VERVAIN: Oh, no testimonials are necessary. As a friend of Mr. Ferris, (*Ferris makes a gesture of astonishment and despair.*) we shall be only too glad to have you come on any conditions.

DON IPPOLITO: You overwhelm me with your goodness, madama. If I thought I could be useful to you—

MRS. VERVAIN: I'm sure you can. My daughter will tell you. Florida, explain our ideas to Don Ippolito. (*To Ferris while Florida and Don Ippolito talk in dumb show.*) So very odd calling a priest *Don*.

FERRIS: It's the custom of this ridiculous country, Mrs. Vervain.

MRS. VERVAIN: I thought they said *Padre*. Don sounds so Spanish. Don Rodrigo, you know. And do you think he'll do?

FERRIS: Well, it's rather late to ask that, now. You've engaged him.

MRS. VERVAIN: Nonsense! Why Florida is just talking it over with him. But I dare say we *shall* engage him. (*Looking through her glasses at them.*) How beautiful his manners are!

FERRIS: Very.

MRS. VERVAIN: How young he is!

FERRIS: Very.

MRS. VERVAIN: And how handsome!

FERRIS: Very.

MRS VERVAIN: How exquisitely respectful to her he is. (*Fondly.*) I can see that he admires her—everybody does! I hope they'll like each other.

FERRIS, *quickly*: Ah, I hope not!

MRS. VERVAIN: What do you mean?

FERRIS, *in a loud tone*: Nothing, Mrs. Vervain! Will you never understand that I never mean anything?

Don Ippolito and Florida come forward. The Curtain falls.

ACT II

SCENE: *Entrance Hall in a Venetian palace—octagonal shape and openings C. and R.; terrace and balustrade; steps R. 2nd. E. with wing of large church adjoining. Back cloth a panorama of Grand Canal. Oak chairs and table up stage. Statues and columns; a door into private apartment L. 2nd E. Entrances R. and L. 1st E. Mosaic pavement floor-cloth—amber lime lights from openings, Florida and Priest discovered; Florida seated at small table R.; Priest standing near her, back to audience. Florida is looking intently into the face of the Priest.*

DON IPPOLITO: Shall we go on with the reading, madamigella?

FLORIDA, *closing book*: No, we shall not read any more today. (*Priest moves to go L.; Florida calls softly.*) Don Ippolito. (*Don Ippolito returns.*) Why didn't you like to walk in the procession of Corpus Domini yesterday?

DON IPPOLITO: I have not said that I did not like to do so.

FLORIDA: No, that is true.

DON IPPOLITO: It is a strange question to ask a priest, as I remembered I was when you asked it.

FLORIDA: Don't you always remember that?

DON IPPOLITO: No; sometimes I am suffered to forget it. (*Pause. Moves up stage, then returns.*) It is in this house that I forget my priesthood, for you have been willing to see the man in me, and let me forget the priest. Do you know what it is to be a priest in this most unhappy city? To be haunted by the strict espionage of all your own class? To be shunned as a spy by all who are not of it? But you and your good moother have not put up that barrier which everywhere shuts me out from my kind.

FLORIDA: Why did you become a priest?

DON IPPOLITO: It is a long story. I will not trouble you with it now—some other time.

Moves to go.

FLORIDA: No, now. (*Rises and comes down to Don Ippolito.*) We should be very unhappy if we could not respect you, not trust you as we have done. And how could we, if we knew you were not true to yourself in being what you are.

DON IPPOLITO: Are all the priests of your faith devotees?

FLORIDA: They cannot be. But are none of yours so?

DON IPPOLITO: Heaven forbid that I should say *that*; my poor uncle is a saint in his way; my ambition and my attempted inventions are a scandal to him; he starves himself, and goes cold and faint that God may have mercy and turn my heart to the things on which his own is fixed. He loves my soul, but not me, and we are scarcely friends. (*Don Ippolito turns up stage. Florida sits by fountain. Don Ippolito returns to her.*) We are of the people, my family, and in each generation we have sought to honor our blood by devoting one of the race to the church. When I was a child I used to divert myself by making little figures out of wood and pasteboard, and I drew rough copies of the pictures I saw at church. My mother was a widow; one day she brought my uncle to see me. My uncle called me to him and asked me whether I should like to be a priest when I grew up; I said "Oh yes," as children do. That will be very well,

I thought to myself; the priests have very little to do, and they gain money with their masses; and I shall be able to make whatever I like. My inclination was purely secular. Through my uncle's influence I was placed in the Seminary of the Salute. Once, for an uncommon pleasure, they took us to the Arsenal, and let us see the shipyards and the museum. You know the wonderful things that are there; the flags and the guns captured from the Turks; the strange weapons of all devices; the famous suits of armor. I came back half-crazed; I wept that I must leave the place. But I set to work the best I could to carve out in wood an invention which the model of one of the antique galleys had suggested to me. They found it—nothing can be concealed in such a school—and they carried me with my contrivance before the superior. "My son," said he, "do you wish to be a priest?" "Surely, Reverend Father," I answered, "Why not?" "Because these things are not for priests. Their thoughts must be on other things." And saying this, he took my poor plaything, and thrust it down among the coals of his *scaldino*, and so turned again to his book. My mother was by this time dead, but I could hardly have gone to her if she had been living. "These things are not for priests!" kept repeating itself night and day in my brain. I was in despair, I was in a fury to see my uncle. I poured out my heart to him, and tried to make him understand the illusions and vain hopes in which I had lived. He received coldly my sorrow and the reproaches which I did not spare him; he warned me against the scandal of attempting to withdraw now from the path marked out for me. I said that I never would be a priest. "And what will you do?" he asked. Alas! what could I do? I went back to my prison, and in due course I became a priest. Poor helpless, friendless wretch, I cannot see how I was to blame! You have asked why I became a priest. Perhaps I have not told you why, but I have tried, and that is all I can do. If the guilt was mine, I have suffered for it. If it was not mine, still I have suffered for it. Some ban seems to have rested upon whatever I have attempted. My work—oh, I know it well enough!—has been cursed with futility. My labors are miserable failures, or contemptible successes. I have had my unselfish dreams of blessing mankind by some great discovery or invention; but my life has been *barren—barren—barren!*

FLORIDA, *rises*: It seems very strange, almost like some dream that you should be saying all this to me, Don Ippolito, and I do not know why I should have asked you anything.

DON IPPOLITO: It was due to the truth in you that I should seem to you what I am.

FLORIDA: But surely you can somehow help yourself. Are men just as powerless after all as women, when it comes to real trouble? Is a man—

DON IPPOLITO: I cannot answer. I am only a priest.

FLORIDA: Yes, but a priest should be a man, and so much more. If you— It's strange that I should be saying this to you, and it must seem presumptuous in me; but if you were to pray—

DON IPPOLITO: To what, madamigella?

FLORIDA: To what? To God. (*Don Ippolito shakes his head.*) You must excuse me. I ought to have remembered that in your church—

DON IPPOLITO, *turning from Florida*: I have no church.

FLORIDA: Oh!

   Shrinking in horror. Don Ippolito turns to her.

DON IPPOLITO: It is terrible, I know it. Now you see how black and deadly a lie my life is; but believe me, dear young lady, that I at least have the grace to abhor myself. Do not wholly condemn me.

FLORIDA: I do not condemn you; that is not for me; but oh, I wish I could help you.

DON IPPOLITO: You cannot help me, but I thank you for your compassion. I shall never forget it. (*Bell rings.*) Permit me, madamigella, to take my leave.

FERRIS, *enters* R.: Oh, good afternoon, Miss Vervain.

   Gives her a bunch of hyacinths. Nina enters 1st. E. R. Florida and Ferris are R. C. upstage; the Priest is watching them from down stage R. with back to audience.

FLORIDA: Did you mean them for me?

FERRIS: I didn't, but I do; I bought them in ignorance, but I understand now, what they were meant for by nature.

FLORIDA: I will go and put them in water.
   Exits.

FERRIS: Ah, Don Ippolito! Good morning. (*Shaking hands.*) How are the lessons going? Did I disturb you?

DON IPPOLITO, *embarrassed*: No, no.

FERRIS: I haven't seen you for nearly a week, and my portrait of you is suffering. But I suppose you are very busy. How are you getting on with your cannon? Have you hit upon that new explosive yet?

DON IPPOLITO: No, I have not touched the cannon since I came to you that day. I suppose it is the distraction of my new occupation, and of the new acquaintances I have made in your amiable countrywomen, which hinder me from going about anything in earnest. They are real angels, and madama is a true original.

FERRIS: Mrs. Vervain is rather peculiar; she is a woman who has had affliction enough to turn a stronger head than hers could ever have been. But she has the best heart in the world.

DON IPPOLITO: Yes, she is good. And madamigella is good. As *good* as she is beautiful. (*Pause.*) Why do you not marry madamigella?

FERRIS, *amused*: Really, I don't know, I don't want to marry anybody. Besides it's possible that Miss Vervain might not—want to marry me.

DON IPPOLITO: As to that you never can tell. All young girls desire to be married, I suppose. Do you not think she is very beautiful? And good?

FERRIS: Oh, all you like! Perhaps a trifle of temper—

DON IPPOLITO: They must be very rich to live as they do.

FERRIS: I don't know about that; Americans spend and save in ways different from the Italians. I dare say the Vervains find Venice very cheap after London, and Paris and Berlin.

DON IPPOLITO: Perhaps if they were rich you would be in a position to marry her?

FERRIS: I should not marry Miss Vervain for her money.

DON IPPOLITO: No, but if you loved her, the money would enable you to marry her.

FERRIS: I never said that I loved Miss Vervain, and I don't know how you feel warranted in speaking to me about the matter. (*Rises.*) She is beautiful, and I believe she's good, but if men had to marry because women were beautiful and good, there isn't one of us could live a single day. Besides, I'm the victim of another passion; I'm laboring under an unrequited affection for art.

DON IPPOLITO, C. *eagerly*: Then you do *not* love her?

FERRIS, *coming up from L. and looking Don Ippolito full in the face*: So far as I'm advised at present, no I don't.

DON IPPOLITO: It is strange.

Enter Billings.

BILLINGS: Hello, national representative!

FERRIS: Hello, Billings!

BILLINGS: Glad you could come, old man.

FERRIS: You'll be sorry I can't stay then. I only dropped in with some flowers. Do you often give these breakfast parties?

BILLINGS: Well, this is the first of the succession. Don Ippolito does us the favor to come to it on that account; though he's almost as much one of the family as I am. You've never seen my studio in the garden yet, have you? Greatest piece of luck I've had—Mrs. Vervain's offering me her pavilion. Best soul in the world! She's *always* having *me* to breakfast. Seems to like my looks. Well, I guess she's adopted me.

Enter Nina.

NINA: Madama prays Don Ippolito to do her the pleasure to pass.

BILLINGS: Oh, yes, I forgot, Don Ippolito. They want you to help arrange the brush.

DON IPPOLITO: The brush?

BILLINGS: Yes, the flowers—on the table. Brush, for short, you know.

DON IPPOLITO: Ah, I come instantly.

Exit.

FERRIS, *looking after him*: You're quite a happy family.

BILLINGS: Well, yes. Doves and white rabbits. No poisonous reptiles, as yet. Chance for you, Ferris!

FERRIS, *after an absent-minded pause*: What do you suppose that priest there meant by asking me why I didn't marry Miss Vervain?

BILLINGS: Ha, ha, ha! Did he ask you that?

FERRIS: Yes.

BILLINGS: Well, it *was* rather intimate. But these Dutch—I call 'em all Dutch; it's shorter—are rather queer. They regard marriage strictly from the business point of view. I suppose he wanted to know. Did you tell him why? I hope you were frank with the poor fellow, and told him it was because she wouldn't have you?

Enter Nina.

NINA: Signore Sculptor—

BILLINGS: Ah, *I'm* wanted, too. I knew they couldn't get along without me. Bye, Ferris.

Exit. Enter Florida L. 2nd. E. She enters slowly as if she were thinking of something.

FLORIDA: Mother will be here directly; I am sorry she has been so long detained, Mr. Ferris. Have you seen our garden?

FERRIS: I came through it. You're fortunate to find a house with a garden in Venice. And yours is so particularly satisfactory with these ruinous old statues in it. The worst of it is you can't take home the sentiment of these things.

FLORIDA, *looking through window into garden*: I thought it was the business of painters to send home the sentiment of them in pictures.

FERRIS: Oh yes, a poor, faded out reproduction of their sentiment which is as moonlight unto sunlight when compared with the real thing. Ah, would you mind holding still a moment?

Takes out his sketch book.

FLORIDA: Do you want to draw me? I'm not worth it.

FERRIS: Don't disparage my subjects. Suppose I did that Gothic window with you looking out. Would our friends at home understand it? A whole history must be left unexpressed. To be sure they might praise the grade of your pose, if I were so lucky as to catch it, and your way of putting your hand under the elbow that supports your chin, but they wouldn't know what it all meant, and couldn't imagine that you were inspired by that time-stained garden out there to sigh longingly over the wicked past.

FLORIDA: Excuse me, I'm not sighing over it. I don't want it back. I can't understand how you and Don Ippolito can speak so tolerantly of what no one can respect.

FERRIS: Oh, Don Ippolito is a pagan, and I'm a painter; and I've a weakness for dilapidation; I wish I could paint it but I can't.

FLORIDA, *moves away but still appearing absorbed in thought*: How are you getting on with the portrait of Don Ippolito?

FERRIS: Slowly—in fact I've made one failure already, and I'm pretty well on with a second. You see, I am trying to paint a Venetian priest so that you'd know him without a bit of conventional Venice near him.

FLORIDA: But why do you paint him simply as a priest? I should think you would want to make him the center of some famous or romantic scene.

FERRIS: No, I doubt if you think, or you'd see that a Venetian priest doesn't need tawdry accessories. What I should like to paint *at* is the lingering pagan in the man. I want to show that baffled aspiration, apathetic despair, and rebellious longing which you catch in his face when he's off his guard, and that suppressed look which is the characteristic expression of all *Austrian* Venice. Then I should work in that small suspicion of Jesuit which there is in every priest.

FLORIDA: You won't make it Don Ippolito if you put in all that. He has the simplest and openest look in the world.

Crossing to L.C.

FERRIS: Excuse me, I don't think you know. I can convince you— But before I begin talking Don Ippolito over with you I wish to tell you that I've been talking you over with him. But I've the grace to say that I'm ashamed of myself.

FLORIDA: Why need you be ashamed? We shall say no harm of him. Did you of me?

FERRIS: Not exactly; but I think you can't let people alone too much. One ought never to speak of the faults of one's friends. They can never be the same afterwards.

FLORIDA: So you have been talking of my faults? Perhaps you could tell me of them to my face?

FERRIS: I don't know that you have any faults. They may be virtues in disguise. (*Pause.*) Well, I did say that I thought you had a quick temper. (*Movement of Florida.*) But now I see that I was mistaken.

FLORIDA: May I ask what else you said?

FERRIS: Oh, that would be a betrayal of confidence.

FLORIDA: Then why have you mentioned the matter to me at all?

FERRIS: I wanted to clear my conscience, I suppose, and sin again.

FLORIDA: I thought you wanted to talk of Don Ippolito.

FERRIS: I do, and I hardly know how to put what I want to say. He puzzles me to begin with. You know I feel somewhat responsible for him, as I discovered him for you.

FLORIDA: Yes.

FERRIS: I recommended him to you, and in that I acted in the teeth of a bitter Venetian prejudice against priests. They believe that priests are full of guile and deceit, that they are spies for the Austrians, and altogether evil.

FLORIDA: I should not be afraid of him in any case, but I can't believe any wrong of him.

FERRIS: I don't want you to do that; I don't myself. I've bungled the matter, as I might have known I would. I was trying to put into words an undefined uneasiness of mine, but I've made a mess of it. Besides, I ought to have spoken to Mrs. Vervain.

FLORIDA, *alarmed*: Oh no, don't. Little things wear upon my mother so. I'm glad you didn't speak to her. What do you want me to do?

FERRIS: Don't do anything; dismiss all my

stupid talk from your mind. I feel as if I had been guiltily trying to set you against a man whom I like very much, and who thinks me his friend. Only a Venetian family would not use a priest with the frank hospitality you've shown; perhaps because they would be afraid of other Venetian tongues.

FLORIDA: We shall not be troubled. We don't care for Venetian tongues.

FERRIS: I'm going.

FLORIDA: Won't you wait and see my mother?

FERRIS: No, I just dropped in for a moment, as it were, to blast an innocent man's reputation and destroy a young lady's peace of mind.

FLORIDA, *anxiously*: What you've said is true, isn't it?

FERRIS: Yes it is, and it isn't. It is true that there is a great distrust of the priests among the Italians, but I suspect the largest number of all those who talk loudest against the priests are really subject to them.

FLORIDA: There must be some priests who have been induced to enter the church before they've seriously thought about it, and then don't know how to escape from the path that has been marked out for them from their childhood. Should you see such a priest as that, shouldn't you be very sorry for him?

FERRIS: I should, indeed, if I liked him. If I didn't, I'm afraid I shouldn't.

FLORIDA: If you were that kind of priest, what would *you* do?

FERRIS: Upon my word I don't know, I can't imagine it. Why, think what a helpless creature a priest is in everything but his priesthood, more helpless than a woman even.

Rises.

FLORIDA: You haven't answered my question.

FERRIS: Oh yes I have. I have told you it wasn't a supposable case.

FLORIDA: But suppose it was?

Rises.

FERRIS: Well, if I must, with my unfortunate bringing up, I couldn't say less than that such a man ought to get out of his priesthood at any hazard. He should cease to be a priest, if it cost him kindred, friends, good fame, country, everything. Yes, I should say decidedly he ought to get out of it by all means.

Enter Mrs. Vervain, with Billings and Don Ippolito.

MRS. VERVAIN: You don't mean to say you're going without even speaking to me, Mr. Ferris!

(Comes forward to shake hands. Florida runs to her and straightens her cap.) Have I got it on skewy, after all my fuss? *(To Ferris.)* I tell Florida that any one would take her for the *old* lady; she doesn't take half the trouble to keep up appearances that I do.

FERRIS: And yet she has quite the effect of a stylish person in the bloom of youth.

MRS. VERVAIN: Yes, that is true. And Venice is agreeing with *both* of us, wonderfully. Really, the gondolas are too much for anything. But I do think they ought to paint them some cheerfuller color.

FERRIS: Blue or pink, Mrs. Vervain?

MRS. VERVAIN: Anything! I never was in color since I was a girl and I have such a horror of black. I was married in my mourning for my last sister. First a brother then a sister, it was very strange how they kept going that way. And these gondolas with that poky top to them. What did Byron call it?

FERRIS: I thought it was time for Byron. He called it a coffin clapped in a canoe.

Billings and Don Ippolito talking.

MRS. VERVAIN: Exactly, I always feel as if I was going to my own funeral when I get into one. But now you *must* tell me how you like our apartment, Mr. Ferris! Isn't it perfect? And only 300 francs a month! Did you ever hear of anything so cheap?

FERRIS: It's only about twice as much as you ought to pay. And it's very cheap, as you say.

MRS. VERVAIN: It isn't at all cheap if we've been imposed upon! Florida, this is shameful.

FLORIDA: Oh, never mind, mother. Look at this. *(Showing Ferris's sketch.)* Do you know it? Mr. Ferris just did it.

MRS. VERVAIN, *coming to table*: Why it's Florida. How very nicely you do sketch, Mr. Ferris.

FERRIS: Thanks, Mrs. Vervain; you're always flattering me.

MRS. VERVAIN: No, but seriously, I wish that I had paid more attention to my drawing when I was a girl, and now Florida—she won't touch a pencil. I wish you'd talk to her, Mr. Ferris.

FERRIS: Oh, people who are pictures needn't trouble themselves to be painters.

Looking pointedly at Florida.

MRS. VERVAIN, *looking at the sketch through her tubed hand*: But you've made her too proud, Mr. Ferris. She doesn't look like that.

FERRIS: Yes she does—to those unworthy of her kindness. I have taken Miss Vervain in the act of scorning the Venetian past and its humble admirer, me, with it.

MRS. VERVAIN: Well, you've made her too proud.

FERRIS: It can't be helped now, Mrs. Vervain. The sketch is irretrievably immortal. I'm sorry, but it's too late.

MRS. VERVAIN: Oh stuff! As if you couldn't turn up the corners of the mouth a little, or something.

FERRIS: And give her the appearance of laughing at me? Never!

MRS. VERVAIN: Don Ippolito, what do you think of Mr. Ferris's sketch? *You* don't think she has this proud look?

FLORIDA: Mother, the subject isn't an important one.

MRS. VERVAIN: Oh yes, it is, my dear. At least it is important to me if it isn't to you; I must insist, Don Ippolito. Now, did you *ever* see Florida look so proud?

DON IPPOLITO: I never saw her look so proud with you, madama. In all her relations to you, madamigella has seemed to me—

FLORIDA, *starting forward*: You are not asked to comment on my behavior to my mother; you are not invited to speak of my conduct at all. What is it to you how *I* treat my mother?

Don Ippolito remains motionless. Billings and Ferris walk together to one side.

MRS. VERVAIN: Florida!

BILLINGS, *to Ferris*: Pretty rough on the reverend father?

FERRIS: It makes me sick. The girl's a brute.

MRS. VERVAIN, *after a pause*: Well now, let us all go to breakfast. Mr. Ferris, you have *got* to stay!

FERRIS: No, really, Mrs. Vervain, I can't.

MRS. VERVAIN: Well, good bye, then. You shall not keep me from breakfast, you see. You must stay, or go.

FERRIS: I'm going.

MRS. VERVAIN: Don Ippolito; Mr. Billings! Come!

Exeunt together.

FERRIS, *coldly*: Good morning, Miss Vervain.

FLORIDA, *coming impetuously toward him*: Wait! I want to speak with you about Don Ippolito. What shall I do to him for my rudeness? You *must* tell me! You *shall!* You are older than I am!

FERRIS: Thanks. I was afraid you were going to say wiser. Well, I should think your own sense of justice, your own sense of—

FLORIDA: Decency. Say it! It *was* indecent! That was it!

FERRIS: —would tell you what to do. And you had better do it at once. I will call him. (*Goes to the door.*) Don Ippolito! Favor me a moment!

He bows to Florida and goes out before Don Ippolito enters.

DON IPPOLITO, *looking about confusedly*: The Signore Console—

FLORIDA: It's I who wished to see you, Don Ippolito. I want to tell you that I'm sorry; I want to ask your pardon. How can you ever forgive me for what I said?

DON IPPOLITO: Oh!

He takes her hand, and after a moment, presses it to his breast.

FLORIDA: I don't know how I could be rude to you. I—we all—like you so much, and I feel so sorry for you. Oh, Don Ippolito! I *do* wish to be your friend.

DON IPPOLITO: Your wish makes all this world my friend.

FLORIDA: No, no! Don't say that. I can do very little for you. I'm a helpless girl. I don't know how to begin what I want to say. I am so young, and so very ignorant of the world. Oh, I wish there was someone who had the right to speak to you.

DON IPPOLITO: No one has so much the right as you.

FLORIDA: It may be all wrong, all wrong. Besides, how do I know you are a good man, Don Ippolito? How do I know that you've been telling me the truth? This is in Venice and you may be leading me on to say things to you that will make trouble for my mother and me. You may be a spy.

DON IPPOLITO: Oh, no! No! God forbid, madamigella, I would rather die than be false to you in a single breath or thought.

FLORIDA: I know it, I know it! How could I say such a cruel thing.

DON IPPOLITO, *moving towards her as if to seize her hand, but checking himself*: Not cruel. No, madamigella, not cruel.

FLORIDA: But—but is there no escape for you?

DON IPPOLITO: Yes, there is *one* way of escape. I have often thought of it, but it is beset with many great dangers, and to be a priest makes one timid and insecure.

FLORIDA: That's nothing. You must think again of that way of escape, and never turn from it till you have tried it. Only take the first step and you can go on. Friends will rise up everywhere and make it easy for you. Come, you must promise.

DON IPPOLITO: If I should take this *only* way of escape, and it seemed desperate to *all* others, would you *still* be my friend?

FLORIDA: I will be your friend if the whole world turn against you.

DON IPPOLITO: Would you be my friend if this way of escape were for me to be no longer a priest?

FLORIDA: Oh yes, yes! Why not?

DON IPPOLITO: Then it does not seem terrible to you?

FLORIDA: Terrible? No! I don't see how you can rest till it's done!

DON IPPOLITO: Is it true then that you *urge* me to this step which indeed I have so long desired to take?

FLORIDA: Yes, it is true. It is the very thing that I hoped you would do. You will never regret it.

DON IPPOLITO: But it will cost much.

FLORIDA: No matter; such a man as you ought to leave the priesthood at any risk or hazard. You should cease to be a priest if it cost you kindred, friends, good fame, country, everything. Why need you be downhearted? Leave Venice! There are other places. Think how inventors succeed in America.

DON IPPOLITO: In America! Ah, how long I have desired to be there!

FLORIDA: You must go, and you shall not be a stranger even at first. We are going home soon; you shall come with us there, and make our house your home. Everything will be easy. God is good, and you may be sure He will befriend you.

DON IPPOLITO: Someone has already been very good to me; I thought it was you, but I will call it God.

FLORIDA: Hush! You musn't say such things. (*Pause.*) But we must go to my mother now. Take time to think, but not too much time. Only, be true to yourself.

DON IPPOLITO: Thanks, madamigella, thanks!

FLORIDA: I don't know; I am frightened. You must do nothing for me; I cannot let you. I am not *fit* to advise you. Is there no one else? I mean, can't you speak—to Mr. Ferris? He is so true, honest and just.

DON IPPOLITO: I will speak with him.

FLORIDA: Remember, I take nothing back. No matter what happens, I will be your friend.

The priest bends over Florida's hand, then takes it in his, and leads her from the room.

CURTAIN

ACT III

SCENE 1: *Henry Ferris's studio at the Consulate of the United States. Pictures and sketches about the room. Ferris is discovered before an easel, painting the portrait of Don Ippolito who is seated in a large Gothic chair. It is afternoon.*

DON IPPOLITO: I wish I could speak to you, dear friend, of some matters that concern me very dearly. Do you remember when I first came to you?

FERRIS: Certainly! Is it of that matter you want to speak to me? I'm very sorry to hear it, for I don't think it practical.

DON IPPOLITO: Practical, practical! Nothing is practical till it has been tried. And why should I not go to America?

FERRIS: Because you can't get your passport, for one thing.

DON IPPOLITO: I have thought of that. I can get a passport for Italy from the Austrian authorities here, and at Milan there must be ways in which I could change it for one from the king of Italy that would carry me through France into England.

FERRIS: That is quite true. Why hadn't you thought of that when you first came to me?

DON IPPOLITO: I did not know I could get a passport for Italy till to-day.

FERRIS, *both silent; Ferris fills his pipe, goes to table*: Well, I'm very sorry, I'm afraid you're dooming yourself to many bitter disappointments in going to America. What do you expect to do there?

DON IPPOLITO: Why, with my inventions—

FERRIS: I suppose—(*putting a lighted match to his pipe*) that a painter must be a poor sort of American: *his* first thought is of coming to Italy; I know very little whether an inventor has any prospect of making a living. Most of them can never bring their ideas to the public notice at all. You have asked me why you should not go to America. Well, because I think you would starve there.

DON IPPOLITO: I am used to that; and besides, until some of my inventions became known, I could give lessons in Italian.

FERRIS: Oh, bravo! You prefer instant death then?

DON IPPOLITO: But madamigella seemed to believe that my success as an inventor would be assured there.

FERRIS, *ironical laugh*: A lady's knowledge of

business is limited. When did you talk with her about it? You had not spoken of it to me, of late, and I thought you were more contented than you used to be.

DON IPPOLITO: It is true. Sometimes within the last weeks I have almost forgotten it.

FERRIS: And what has brought it so forcibly to your mind again?

DON IPPOLITO: That is what I so greatly desire to tell you. (*Priest gives an appealing look at the painter's face and moistens his lips a little, waiting further questions from Ferris. Ferris does not speak.*) Even though I have not said so in words to you, dear friend, has it not appeared to you that I have no heart in my vocation?

FERRIS: Yes, I have sometimes fancied that; I had no right to ask you why.

DON IPPOLITO: Some day I will tell you, when I have the courage. It is partly my own fault, but more my miserable fortune. Wherever the wrong lies, it has at last become intolerable to me. I cannot endure it any longer and live. I must go away. I must fly from it.

Priest rises. Pause. Ferris shrinks from him instinctively, as if from one who has set himself upon some desperate attempt.

FERRIS: Do you mean, Don Ippolito, that you are going to renounce your priesthood? (*Don Ippolito opens his hands and lets his priesthood drop, as it were, to the ground. Pause.*) You never spoke of this before, when you talked of going to America; though, to be sure—

DON IPPOLITO: Yes, yes! (*With vehemence.*) But now an angel has appeared and shown me the blackness of my life! An angel, yes, an angel, whose truth has mirrored my falsehood in all its vileness and distortion—to whom, if it destroys me, I cannot devote less than a truthfulness like hers!

FERRIS: Hers—hers? (*With a sudden pang.*) Whose? Don't speak in these riddles! Whom do you mean?

DON IPPOLITO: Whom can I mean but only one? Madamigella!

FERRIS: Miss Vervain? Do you mean to say that Miss Vervain has advised you to renounce your priesthood?

DON IPPOLITO: She has bidden me forsake it, at the cost of kindred, friends, good fame, country, everything!

FERRIS, *passes his hand confusedly over his face:* May I ask (*in a hard, dry voice*) how she came to advise such a step?

DON IPPOLITO: I can hardly tell. Something had already moved her to learn from me the story of my life. Her pure heart was torn by the thought of my wrong and of my error!

FERRIS, *bites stem of his pipe, and turns away, ordering the color-tubes and pencils on a table against the wall, setting them close together in very neat, straight rows*: Perhaps Miss Vervain also advised you to go to America?

DON IPPOLITO: Yes, she has thought of everything. She has promised me a refuge under her mother's roof there, until I can make my inventions known; and I shall follow them at once.

FERRIS: Follow them?

DON IPPOLITO: They are going, she told me. Madama does not grow better. They are homesick. They—but you must know all this already?

FERRIS: Oh, not at all, not at all. (*With a bitter smile.*) You are telling me news. Pray go on.

DON IPPOLITO: There is no more. She made me promise to come to you and listen to your advice before I took any step. I must not trust to her alone, she said; but if I took this step, then, whatever happened, she would be my friend. Ah, dear friend, may I speak to you of the hope that these words gave me? You have seen—have you not?—seen that—(*Priest falters, Ferris stares at him helplessly. Priest anxiously draws nearer to him, laying an imploring touch upon his arm.*) I love her!

FERRIS: You? You! A priest!

DON IPPOLITO, *violently*: Priest! Priest! From this day I am no longer a priest! From this hour I am a man, and I can offer her the honorable love of a man! (*Ferris looks very coldly at Don Ippolito. Don Ippolito meets it with a glance of tremulous perplexity; his hand drops from Ferris's arm, and he moves some steps from him.*) What is it, dear friend? Is there something that offends you? I came to you for counsel, and you meet me with a repulse little short of enmity! I do not understand. Do I intend doing anything wrong, without knowing it? Oh, I beseech you to speak plainly!

FERRIS: Wait! Wait a minute— (*Waves his hand as if in a passing pain.*) I am trying to think. What you say is—I cannot imagine it!

DON IPPOLITO: Not imagine it? Not imagine it? And why? Is she not beautiful?

FERRIS: Yes.

DON IPPOLITO: And good?

FERRIS: Yes.

DON IPPOLITO: And young?

FERRIS: Yes.

DON IPPOLITO: And yet wise beyond her years? And true, and yet angelically kind?

FERRIS: It is all as you say, Heaven knows. But— a priest—

Goes up to Gothic chair.

DON IPPOLITO: Always that word! (*Returning and standing over painting.*) And at heart, what is a priest, then, but a man? Has he not blood and nerves like you? Has he not eyes to see what is fair, and ears to hear what is sweet? Can he live near so divine a flower, and not know her grace, not inhale the fragrance of her soul, not adore her beauty? Oh, great Heaven! And if at *last* he would tear off the stifling mask, and escape from prison, return from exile, would you gainsay him?

FERRIS: No. (*Priest moves. Ferris sinks in Gothic chair, rests his head against its high back, looks at Priest across the room. Pause. With strong effort.*) Don Ippolito, I am ready to befriend you to the utmost of my power. What was it you intended to ask me? I have told you truly what I thought of your scheme of going to America, but I may very well be mistaken. Was it about that, Miss Vervain desired you to consult me? Or did she wish me to advise you about the renunciation of your priesthood? You must have thought that carefully over for yourself.

DON IPPOLITO: Yes, I do not think you could make me see that as a greater difficulty than it has appeared to me. (*Pauses with confused and daunted air, as if some important point had slipped his mind.*) But I must take the step; the burden of the double part I play is unendurable, is it not?

FERRIS: You know better than I.

DON IPPOLITO, *going up to Ferris*: But if you were such a man as I, should you not cease to be a priest?

FERRIS: I advise you nothing. I could not counsel another in such a case.

DON IPPOLITO: But you think and feel as I do, and I am right then?

FERRIS: I do not say you are wrong. (*Rises. Pause. Ferris is silent, Don Ippolito moves up and down the room slowly.*) Don Ippolito, I suppose you did not speak idly to me of your—feelings for Miss Vervain, and that I may speak plainly to you in return.

DON IPPOLITO, *pausing in his walk, and fixing his eyes on Ferris*: Surely, it was to you, as the friend of both, that I spoke of my love, and my hope—which is oftener my despair!

FERRIS: Then you have not much reason to believe that she returns your—feeling?

DON IPPOLITO: How could she return it? I have hitherto been a priest to her, but hereafter, if I can prove myself a man, if I can win my place in the world— No, even now, why should she care so much for my escape from these bonds, if she did not care for me more than she knew?

FERRIS: Are you sure that it is not concern for what seems to Miss Vervain, your terrible position, that has made her show so much anxiety on your account?

DON IPPOLITO: Do I not know that well? Have I not felt the balm of her most heavenly pity?

FERRIS: And may she not be only trying to appeal to something in you as high as the impulse of her own heart?

DON IPPOLITO, *almost angrily*: As high! Can there be any higher thing in heaven and on earth, than love for such a woman?

FERRIS: Yes; both in heaven and on earth.

DON IPPOLITO, *with a puzzled stare*: I do not understand you! (*Ferris makes no reply, falls into a reverie, in which he seems to forget Don Ippolito, and the whole affair. Pause.*) Have you nothing to say to me, signore?

FERRIS: I! What is there to say?

Sitting on table, turns.

DON IPPOLITO: Do *you* know any reason why I should not love her, save that I am—have *been*—a priest?

FERRIS: No, I know none.

DON IPPOLITO: Ah! There is something on your mind that you will not speak! I beseech you not to let me err! I love her so well that I would rather die than let my love offend her! If you can be my friend in this, so far as to advise or warn me; if you can be her friend—(*Ferris abruptly rises, crosses in front of Priest, then comes back and looks dizzily at Priest, then sits on stool.*) Will you not answer me, signore?

FERRIS: What do you wish? You tell me you are resolved to renounce the priesthood and go to America; and I have answered you to the best of my power. You tell me that you are in love with Miss Vervain. What can I have to say about that?

DON IPPOLITO, *sadly*: Nothing. (*Moves two paces, leans on chair, looks over left shoulder.*) I ask your pardon for troubling you with my affairs. It was my ignorance which I pray you to excuse. I shall not trouble you again. I take my leave, signore—

He goes out, and Ferris remains watching

*the door by which he has vanished. A bell
sounds, and then voices are heard without.*

MRS. VERVAIN: Why, Don Ippolito, is that you?
It's so dark in this passage one can't see their hand
before their face.

DON IPPOLITO: Yes, yes; it is I, madama. But I
cannot wait. I am pressed—give me leave—

MRS. VERVAIN, *entering*: Ah, Mr. Ferris, I'm so
glad to find you at home, though it's a wonder any
one lives to get through that dark entry of yours.
How do you do?

FERRIS, *absently*: Well; very well—

MRS. VERVAIN, *looking at him*: You don't *look*
well. You ought to let me take you in hand—or
take you away. You're killing yourself with work.
Now, I'll tell you what, Mr. Ferris: You come
with us!

MR. FERRIS: Come with you?

MRS. VERVAIN: Yes. I've got the greatest news
for you. Is that your Don Ippolito?

Looking at picture through her glasses.

FERRIS: Till some one buys it.

MRS. VERVAIN: How mercenary! It's very good
—capital! But you can't sell it to me if that's
what you mean. Because we are going to have the
original! *(Ferris starts back.)* Guess what I've come
to tell you!

FERRIS, *sinking weakly into a chair*: I can't, Mrs.
Vervain. I haven't the strength.

MRS. VERVAIN: Well, I've come to tell you for
one thing that you are going to dine with us
today. But the other thing you *must* guess!

FERRIS: I am not good at guessing. I'd rather
not know what it is, than have to guess it.

MRS. VERVAIN: You won't try once even? Well,
you are going to be rid of us soon! We are going
away.

FERRIS: Yes, I know that. Don Ippolito told me
so.

MRS. VERVAIN: And is that all you have to say?
Isn't it rather sad? Isn't it sudden? Come, Mr.
Ferris, do be a little complimentary for once!

FERRIS: It is sudden, and I can assure you it's
sad enough—*for me.*

MRS. VERVAIN: Well, so it is for us. You have
been very good to us, and we shall never forget it.
Florida has been speaking of it, too, and she's extremely grateful, and thinks we've quite imposed
upon you.

FERRIS: Thanks.

MRS. VERVAIN: I suppose we have; but as I always say, you're the representative of the country
here. However, that's neither here nor there; we

both, I think, will be better at home; for I am
sorry to say that though I don't complain of Venice—it's really a beautiful place, and all that; not
the least exaggerated—still, I don't think it's
done my health much good; or at least I don't
seem to gain, don't you know, I *don't seem to
gain.*

FERRIS: I am very sorry to hear it, Mrs. Vervain.

MRS. VERVAIN: Yes, I am sure you are; but *you*
see, don't you, that we must go? We are going
next week. When we've once made up our minds,
there's no object in prolonging the agony. (Mrs.
*Vervain adjusts her glasses with thumb and finger
of her right hand, peeps into Ferris's face with
a gay smile.)* But the greatest part of the surprise
is—(*lowering her voice a little*)—that Don Ippolito is going with us.

FERRIS, *sharply*: Ah!

MRS. VERVAIN: I knew I should surprise you!
(*Laughs.*) We've been having a regular confab—
clave, I mean—about it here, and he's all on fire
to go to America; though it must be kept a secret,
on his account, poor fellow. He's to join us in
France, and then he can easily get into England
with us. You know, he's to give up being a priest,
and is going to devote himself to inventions, when
he gets to America! Now, what *do* you think of
it, Mr. Ferris? Quite strikes you dumb, doesn't it?
(*Ferris gasps, as though about to speak, but says
nothing.*) He's so enthusiastic about it, and yet he
breaks down every little while, and seems quite to
despair of the undertaking. But shedding tears,
now! It's dreadful in a man, isn't it? I wish Don
Ippolito wouldn't do that. It makes one creep! I
can't feel that it's manly; can you?

FERRIS: Oh, these things are different with the
Latin races!

MRS. VERVAIN: At any rate, I'm glad that *Amer-
icans* don't shed tears, as a general *rule.* Now,
Florida—you'd think she was the man all through
this business; she's so perfectly heroic about it!
Has she ever spoken to you about Don Ippolito?
She does think so highly of your opinion, Mr.
Ferris!

FERRIS: She does me too much honor.

MRS. VERVAIN: Oh, I don't think so. She told
me this morning that she'd made Don Ippolito
promise to speak to you about it. Florida told me
beforehand that I mustn't press him. She said he
must be left entirely to himself in that matter,
and—

FERRIS: He spoke to me about it.

MRS. VERVAIN: Then why in the world did you let me run on? I suppose you advised him against it?

FERRIS: I certainly did.

MRS. VERVAIN: Well, there's where I think woman's intuition is better than man's reason! (*Ferris bows his head.*) Yes, I'm quite woman's rights in that respect.

FERRIS: Oh, without doubt!

MRS. VERVAIN: I'm perfectly delighted at the idea of Don Ippolito's giving up the priesthood, and I've told him he must get married to some American girl. You ought to have seen how the poor fellow blushed! But really, you know, there are lots of nice girls that would *jump* at him—so handsome, and sad-looking, and a genius! (*Ferris stares helplessly at Mrs. Vervain.*) Yes, I think he's a genius, and I'm determined that he shall have a chance! I suppose we've got a job on our hands, but I'm not sorry. I'll introduce him into society, and if he needs money, he shall have it! What does God give us money for, Mr. Ferris, but to help our fellow-creatures? (*Ferris laughs at this outburst of piety.*) What are you laughing at? Something I've been saying? Well, you won't have me to laugh at much longer! I do wonder whom you'll have next. Oh, but there isn't time to talk about that now; I want you to come back with me and stop to dinner. We dine early!

FERRIS: Thank you, I can't. Indeed I can't, Mrs. Vervain.

MRS. VERVAIN: Really? Then you must come in after dinner.

FERRIS: I can't promise.

MRS. VERVAIN: You are *not* well!

FERRIS: Oh yes!

MRS. VERVAIN: You look perfectly worn-out. Well, we shall miss you a great deal, Mr. Ferris.

FERRIS: Thanks.

MRS. VERVAIN: Yes, we shall be quite lost without you!

FERRIS: You are too good.

MRS. VERVAIN: Yes, I really think I am considering that we are going to leave Venice so soon, and you won't come to dinner with me—very good indeed!

FERRIS: I—I'll come in after dinner.

MRS. VERVAIN: I *knew* you would! We shall all be at home—Florida, Don Ippolito and myself—and then we can have a good talk. Good-bye for the present. Never mind the door. Don't trouble to come down!

Ferris is standing still, as if stupefied. After

Mrs. Vervain exits, he takes up the portrait of the priest, looks at it for some seconds, then throws it on the ground and sinks in chair, burying his face in his hands.

SCENE II: *Mrs. Vervain's garden. Moonlight. A fountain, surrounded by statues, with seats near it. Enter Ferris and Billings from opposite sides.*

BILLINGS: Hello, Ferris! Is that you? I thought it was Don Ippolito.

FERRIS, *sinking wearily on one of the benches*: Don Ippolito?

BILLINGS: Yes, he's in the garden somewhere with Miss Vervain.

FERRIS: With Miss Vervain?

BILLINGS: "By heaven, he echoes me, as if there were some monster in his thought too hideous to be seen." [1] Why shouldn't he be with her?

FERRIS: Oh, no reason in the world.
    Rises feebly.

BILLINGS: What's the matter with you? You seem to be sicklied over with the pale cast of something or other.

FERRIS: No—

BILLINGS: You're not—jealous of that poor devil?

FERRIS: Excuse me, Mr. Billings; I haven't thrust my confidence upon you.

BILLINGS: So much the worse for you. If you had, I could have told you long ago that the girl's as much in love with you as you are with her—and *that's* spoons enough! They're going to take this priest to America with them, and give him a chance for his life. But that's all. And don't you forget it. How did you get in here?

FERRIS, *recovering himself*: By the water-gate. But do you really think, Billings,—do you believe —are you sure—

BILLINGS: As guns! Come into my shanty here —I call Mrs. Vervain's pavilion a shanty for short —and take a look at my head of Miss Florida by candle-light, now you've got the chance, and then we'll go up to the house and join the folks. I guess she'll have got back with Don Ippolito by that time. Come along, old man, brace up!

    Exeunt, arm in arm. Enter Don Ippolito and Florida.

FLORIDA: You must not give way to despair; you will succeed, I am sure, for you will deserve success!

1 *Othello*, III, 3:106–108. Howells quotes inaccurately.

DON IPPOLITO: It is all your goodness, madamigella. (*Sighs.*) And at the bottom of my heart, I am afraid that all the hope and courage I have are also yours.

FLORIDA: You shall never want for hope and courage then. We believe in you, and we honor your purpose, and we will be your steadfast friends. But now you must think only of the present and how you are to get away from Venice. Oh, I can understand how you hate to leave it! (*Sinking in one of the seats.*) What a beautiful night! I seem to have spent my whole life in this garden. When we're settled in Providence, I'm going to have mother send back for some of these statues. We shall have a fountain just like this, over there; you shall make it and you shall be the first to set it playing, and then we'll sit down by it and imagine ourselves in the garden of Casa Vervain at Venice.

DON IPPOLITO: No; let me be the last to set it playing here!

Stoops to a pipe and turns on the water.

FLORIDA, *touching his shoulder*: You musn't! The *padrone* doesn't like to waste the water.

DON IPPOLITO: Oh, we'll pray the saints to rain it back on him. (*Stands with folded arms watching the play of the fountain; then turns abruptly to Florida.*) Is Providence your native city?

FLORIDA: Oh no! I was born at St. Augustine in Florida!

DON IPPOLITO: Yes, I forgot; madama has told me about it. Providence is her city, but the two are near together?

FLORIDA: No. (*Compassionately.*) They are a thousand miles apart.

DON IPPOLITO: A thousand miles apart! What a vast country!

FLORIDA: Yes, it's a whole world.

DON IPPOLITO, *softly*: Ah, a world, indeed! I shall never comprehend it!

FLORIDA: You never will, if you do not go about it more practically.

DON IPPODITO: Practically! Practically! What a word with you Americans! That is the consul's word—*practical*.

FLORIDA: Then you have seen him today? (*With eagerness.*) I wanted to ask you—

DON IPPOLITO: Yes, I went to consult the oracle, as you bade me.

FLORIDA: Don Ippolito—

DON IPPOLITO: And he was averse to my going to America. He said it was not practical.

FLORIDA, *murmurs*: Oh!

DON IPPOLITO, *with vehemence*: I think that Signore Ferris is no longer my friend!

FLORIDA: Did he treat you coldly—harshly? (*With a note of indignation in her voice.*) Did he know that I—that you came?

DON IPPOLITO: Perhaps he was right. Perhaps I shall indeed go to ruin there. Ruin! Ruin! Do I not live in ruin here?

FLORIDA: What did he say? What did he tell you?

DON IPPOLITO: No, no, not now, madamigella! I do not want to think of that man now. I want you to help me once more to realize myself in America, where I shall never have *been* a priest, where I shall at least battle even-handed with the world! He could not see me save in this robe—in this figure that I abhor!

FLORIDA: Oh! It was strange. It was not like him; it was cruel! What did he say?

DON IPPOLITO: In everything but words, he bade me despair; he bade me look upon all that makes life dear and noble as impossible to me!

FLORIDA: Oh, how—how could he! Perhaps he did not understand you. No, he did not understand you! What did you say to him, Don Ippolito? Tell me!

She leans towards him in anxious emotion.

DON IPPOLITO, *the priest has in his visage sublimity, and the terror of a man who puts everything to the risk*: How will it really be with me, yonder? As it is with other men, whom their past life, if it has been guiltless, does not follow to that new world of freedom and justice!

FLORIDA: Why should it not be so? Did *he* say it would not?

DON IPPOLITO: Need it be known there that I have been a priest? Or if I tell it, will it make me appear a kind of monster—different from other men?

FLORIDA: No, no! Your story would gain friends and honor for you everywhere in America! Did *he*—

DON IPPOLITO: Will it ever be possible for me to win something more than honor and friendship there? (*Florida looks up inquiringly and confusedly.*) If I am a man, and the time should ever come that a face, a look, a voice, shall be to me what they are to other men, will *she* remember it against me that I have been a priest, when I tell her—say to her—how dear she is to me, offer her my life's devotion, ask her to be my wife? (*Florida rises and confronts him in helpless silence. He does not seem to notice, he suddenly clasps his hands together and desperately stretches them towards her.)* Oh, my hope, my trust—my life! If it were *you* that I loved?

FLORIDA, *recoils, shuddering, and with almost a shriek*: What! You? A priest!

DON IPPOLITO, *gives a low cry—half sob*: His words! His words! It is true! I cannot escape. I must die as I have lived!

He drops his face into his hands and stands with his head bowed before her. Neither speaks for a long time, or moves.

FLORIDA: Yes, I see it all—how it has been— *(Relapses into silence and stares as if at a procession of the scenes of the past months. She then moans to herself.)* Oh, oh, oh! *(She wrings her hands and draws nearer the priest. She lifts her hands to his, gently takes them away from his face, and looks into his hopeless eyes.)* Oh, Don Ippolito, what shall I say to you? What can I do for you now?

DON IPPOLITO: You cannot help me; there is no help for an error like mine. Sometime, if ever the thought of me is a greater pain than it is at this moment, you can forgive me. Yes, you can do that for me!

FLORIDA: But who will ever forgive me *(drops his hands)* for my blindness! Oh, you must believe—I never thought, I never dreamt—

DON IPPOLITO: I know it well! It was your fatal truth that did it—truth too high and fine for me to have discerned save through this agony! You too, loved my soul—and you would have had me no priest for the reason that he would have had me a priest—I see it! But you had no right to love my soul, and not *me!* A woman must not love the soul and not the man!

FLORIDA, *piteously*: Yes, yes! But you were a priest to me!

DON IPPOLITO: Yes! And now I see that I never could be otherwise! Ah, the wrong began many years before we met! I was trying to blame you a little.

FLORIDA: Blame me, blame me—do!

Takes his hands.

DON IPPOLITO: But there is no blame! Think that it was another way of asking your forgiveness! Oh my God! My God! My God! *(He utters this cry under his breath, with his face lifted upwards. He looks at her again.)* Madamigella, if my share of this misery gives me the right to ask of you—

FLORIDA: Oh! Ask anything of me!

DON IPPOLITO, *faltering*: You do not love me!

(Abruptly.) Is there someone else you love? *(Florida doesn't answer.)* Is it——he? *(Florida hides her face.)* I knew it! *(With a groan.)* I knew that, too!

Turns away.

FLORIDA: Don Ippolito! *(She springs towards him.)* Is this the way you leave me? What will you do now?

DON IPPOLITO: Did I not say? I am going to die a priest?

FLORIDA: Is there nothing that you will let me hope for you?

DON IPPOLITO: Nothing! *(Enter Ferris and Billings. Priest seizes her hands imploringly extended towards him, and clasps them together and kisses them both.)* Adieu— *(He whispers, then opens them and passionately kisses either palms.)* Adieu! Adieu!

A great wave of sorrow and compassion and despair for him sweeps through Florida. She follows him, touches his shoulder, and as he turns round, takes his head in her hands and kisses his forehead. Then she suddenly puts her hands against his breast, thrusts him away, turns, and runs. Exit Priest.)

FERRIS: So, *this* is the girl who— *(Struggling to release himself.)* Let go of me, Billings! Let go, I say! Do you think I shall follow her? Or him! My God! Will you let me go?

BILLINGS: No, no! Hold on! There's some mistake.

FERRIS: The old mistake—as old as the world. A man trusting a woman! *(Wrenching himself free as the curtain falls.)* But I'm done with it.

CURTAIN

ACT IV

SCENE: *A large room in the house of Don Ippolito. In the background a wide arched doorway, closed by portières of heavy stuff.*

MRS. VERVAIN: How slow Don Ippolito is in getting well! It's six weeks now since we came here to take care of him, and he isn't able to walk yet. If we wait for him, I don't know when we shall get home. Really, Florida, I think we'd better push on without him, and let him follow at his leisure. I could leave him money—

FLORIDA: Don Ippolito isn't going to America, mother.

MRS. VERVAIN: Not going to America!

FLORIDA: Yes, he told me so, today. He will not leave Venice; he will remain a priest.

MRS. VERVAIN: Not leave Venice! Remain a priest! Florida, you astonish me! But I am not the least surprised, not the least in the world. I thought Don Ippolito would give out, all along. I always doubted if he would succeed in America; he is too much of a dreamer. But this really goes a little beyond everything. I never expected this. What did he say, Florida? How did he excuse himself?

FLORIDA: He didn't try. He said that his inventions were all a vain dream; he has had them broken up; his uncle burnt them yesterday in his laboratory.

MRS. VERVAIN: Yes, he's quite under his uncle's thumb again, and I can see that he was really a priest at heart all the time. It sounds perfectly natural to hear him calling you *daughter*, now, though it did seem odd at first.

FLORIDA, *sadly*: Yes.

MRS. VERVAIN: I suppose it's all for the best. I'm sure it was ordered so. But that doesn't relieve Don Ippolito from the charge of black ingratitude. He's quite made fools of us.

FLORIDA: He was not to blame. It was a very great step for him.

MRS. VERVAIN: I know that. But he ought not to have talked of it till he knew his own mind fully; that's the only safe way. Well, then, there's nothing to prevent our going tomorrow. Have you been crying, Florida? Well, of course, you can't help feeling sorry for such a man. There's a great deal of good in Don Ippolito. But when you come to my age, you won't cry so easily, my dear. Besides, Don Ippolito's out of all danger, now. (*After a pause.*) What I think of is Mr. Ferris. I can't bear to leave Venice without seeing him again, and there's no telling *when* he'll be back. Shouldn't you like to see him before we go, Florida?

FLORIDA, *coldly*: No, I don't care for him.

MRS. VERVAIN: You never did appreciate Mr. Ferris, my dear, from the first. You were always squabbling. But he just suited me—saying such funny things to you, and keeping you so light. Florida, my dear, I *wish* you had liked Mr. Ferris. He was quite my ideal—yes! Not that he was the *best* ideal! He was as real as—as a piece of bread. But he was *very* nice, and he was as good as a son to me—no son could have been better. How kind he was! At one time I thought he had a fancy for you, Florida.

FLORIDA: Mother!

MRS. VERVAIN: Yes! I did! And I did hope you would get to like him.

FLORIDA: Mother!

MRS. VERVAIN: But I soon saw it was no use. You both got worse and worse, and that last day, you behaved as if you perfectly hated each other.

FLORIDA, *sobbing into her handkerchief, and running from the room*: O, mother, mother, mother!

> Mrs. Vervain remains looking after her in perplexity, till she turns at the sound of Billings's entrance from the other side.

MRS. VERVAIN: Have you heard anything of Mr. Ferris, yet, Mr. Billings?

BILLINGS: No more than I've told you. He's been in Vienna ever since that night. Probably he had to go on some official business. I've sent every day to the Consulate, and I'm expecting Veneranda back from there now.

MRS. VERVAIN: So very strange, his running away in that manner.

BILLINGS: Very.

MRS. VERVAIN: It *must* be consular business. Though Mr. Ferris is very eccentric, don't you think so, Mr. Billings?

BILLINGS: Oh, greatest ass in the world—

MRS. VERVAIN: Well, I don't know about that, exactly.

BILLINGS: Of course not, I merely say ass for short; but I *mean* eccentric.

MRS. VERVAIN: He's a very *good* man; and very, very kind. That makes his deserting us at such an important moment all the harder to bear. But of course he didn't know of Don Ippolito's sickness, or he wouldn't have gone. We shouldn't have known of it ourselves, if we hadn't sent you here with the money for Florida's lessons.

BILLINGS: No.

MRS. VERVAIN, *shaking her head*: I never expected to see Don Ippolito rise from that bed again. And now that he's over his fever, how changed he is! He's lost all his ambition to go to America, and won't hear of it, and that old uncle of his, the canonico, is with him every moment, and the house is like a church; and he calls Florida *daughter*; and he's burnt all his inventions; and you wouldn't know him for the same creature: But *he's* good, too; don't you think so, Mr. Billings?

BILLINGS: Good as gold.

MRS. VERVAIN: Well, I must run off to him

again. But do let me know if you have any news
of Mr. Ferris. I know how sorry he'll be when
he knows what's happened.

BILLINGS: I'll keep you posted, Mrs. Vervain.
(*Exit Mrs. Vervain. Enter Veneranda from opposite side. Impatiently.*) Well, well?

VENERANDA, *breathlessly*: The Signore Console
has returned; the Signore Console is coming.

BILLINGS: Coming?

VENERANDA: Yes, here, at once. At first he would
hardly speak to me, or look at me; and I couldn't
pronounce your name, Signore Billini, so that he
knew who had sent me; but he understood at
last; and then I told him that Don Ippolito had
been very sick, poor thing, but that he had his
senses now again, and that he had something to
say that it greatly concerned the Signore Console
to hear, and begged him to come to him as soon
as he could. And when he said he would come,
I made myself very bold, and begged him to
come instantly, for my master was still so weak
that a little disappointment might kill him; and
then he said he would come at once and— (*Bell
rings; Veneranda runs to window and looks out.*)
Ah! It is the Signore Console! He has come already. (*Calling out.*) The door is open; do me the
pleasure to come upstairs. (*Running to door and
admitting Ferris.*) Enter Signore Console! Behold,
the Signore Billini. I go to advise my master.

> *Exit. Enter Ferris. He is pale, and nervous,
> and greatly changed. He shakes hands mechan-
> ically with Billings.*

FERRIS: Well?

BILLINGS: Well, I'm glad to see you, old man.

FERRIS: I don't know why the sight of me should
bring you joy, but if it does, you're welcome,
Billings. I feel like a fool coming here. What does
Don Ippolito want to say to me? Where is he?

BILLINGS: You'll see him directly. But he isn't
a monument of physical strength, yet. I suppose
the old woman's gone to tell him you're here,
and they'll wheel him in, directly.

FERRIS: Wheel him in?

BILLINGS: Yes. He can't walk yet. But they
push him about in a reclining chair—one of
his own inventions; the only one that's survived
the general conflagration he's made of them.

FERRIS: Umph.

BILLINGS: I think Don Ippolito's got religion.

FERRIS: Umph.

> *He sits down.*

BILLINGS: Well, how are you, yourself?

FERRIS: Not disposed to general conversation.

BILLINGS: Well, that's frank, anyway. Seen anything of the Vervains?

FERRIS: No.

BILLINGS: Heard anything?

FERRIS: No.

BILLINGS: Like to?

FERRIS: No; I never want to see or hear anything of them again.

BILLINGS: Why, I don't see what you have
against *Mrs.* Vervain, Ferris.

FERRIS: She's the mother of her daughter.

BILLINGS, *after a pause*: Well, Ferris, if I didn't
know you to be a pretty good sort of fellow,
when you're off your guard, I should say you
were about the greatest ruffian alive. For short.

FERRIS: If you got me here to say this, Mr.
Billings, make it shorter still. Good morning, sir.

> *Down to the door.*

BILLINGS, *running and placing himself against
the door*: They're in this house!

FERRIS: Then it's a trap! It's a wretched bit of
stage-play! Let me out of this, or I'll throw you
into the canal!

BILLINGS: No, you won't, old man! Now, you
listen! You're all mistaken about this thing. I
came here a few days after that night, and found
Don Ippolito in a brain fever; and then Mrs.
Vervain and Miss Florida came and took care of
him like a couple of angels; and if you call that
a trap set for such game as you— Pshaw! You
make me sick! You ain't worth the trouble of
setting right, but I'll tell you you were all mistaken
about what you saw. I want you to be right for
her sake; for she loves you—I don't know why—

FERRIS: I've had enough of this. Will you get
away from that door?

BILLINGS: No! Not till you've seen Don Ippolito!

> *They confront each other threateningly.
> Slow music. The portière parts and Don Ippo-
> lito is wheeled in, by his uncle, the canonico,
> and Veneranda.*

DON IPPOLITO, *extending his hand to Ferris*: Ah,
I had made you wait too long? You were going?

FERRIS, *coming back and taking his hand*: No—
no—

DON IPPOLITO: You were very good, to come.
I have wished so much to speak with you. (*To
the canonico.*) Dear uncle, this is the kind friend
of whom I told you. You know what I wished to
say to him. (*The canonico bows to Ferris, and
retires without speaking.*) My good Veneranda,
you will come when I sound this bell. (*Exit

Veneranda.) And you, Signore Billings, may I crave a moment with our friend here alone?

BILLINGS: Well, I don't advise you to waste *much* breath on him in *your* state, Don Ippolito. It's bad enough for a *well* man to fool away his eloquence on him.

Exits.

DON IPPOLITO, *to Ferris*: I have sent for you so often—every day since I recovered my mind. You will know how to forgive the impatience of a man not yet quite master of himself. I thank you for coming. I have been very sick as you see; I did not think to live. I did not care. I am very weak now; let me say to you quickly what I want to say. (*He speaks brokenly, with an effort; now he fixes his eyes on Ferris's face, and his voice becomes steadier.*) Dear friend, I spoke to her that night after I parted from you. (*Ferris turns his face away.*) I spoke without hope, and because I must. I spoke in vain; all was lost, all was past in a moment. (*Pause.*) Even if I had not been a priest, I should still have been impossible to her! She— (*He stops from weakness.*) But now everything is over with me on earth. I thank the Infinite Compassion for the sorrows through which I have passed. I also have proved the miraculous power of the church, potent to save in the ages. (*He takes a crucifix from his pillow, and kisses it.*) Many merciful things have befallen me on my bed of pain. My uncle, whom the long years of my darkness divided from me, is now more at peace with me. Even yonder poor old woman, whom I sent to call you, and who used to scorn me with horror as a false priest, has grown decrepit with her cares and vigils in my sickness. Yes, I have had many and signal marks of the Divine Pity. (*Pauses, panting.*) They tell me that the danger of this sickness is past. But none the less I have died in it. When I rise from this bed, it shall be to take the vows of a Carmelite friar. When I first owned to—to madamigella—the falsehood in which I once lived, she besought me to try if I might not find consolation in the holy life to which I had been devoted. I have come to understand that this refuge, this comfort, awaits me in the cell of the Carmelite. I have brought so much trouble into her life, that I would fain have her know that I have found peace where she bade me seek it, that I have mastered my affliction by reconciling myself to it. She does not know this as yet, and it is for you, my friend, to tell her.

FERRIS, *turning upon him*: For *me*?

DON IPPOLITO: Yes—say to her that but for

her pity and fear for me, I must have died in my sins.

FERRIS, *after a moment, coldly*: I am glad that your mind is at rest concerning the doubts which have so long troubled you; as you say, it is the privilege of your church to work miracles in all ages. As to Miss Vervain, I am sorry that I cannot promise to give her your message. I shall never see her again.

DON IPPOLITO, *raising his head*: You will never see her again! Oh bereft! Oh, deaf and blind! It was *you* that she loved. She confessed it to me that night—

FERRIS, *trying to steady his voice*: I was in the garden that night—by an evil chance—and I saw how she parted from the man she did not love. I saw—

DON IPPOLITO, *in a hapless whisper*: You saw— you saw! (*Then in a louder tone.*) And how shall I make you believe that what you saw was not a woman's love, but an angel's heavenly pity for me? Does it seem hard to believe this of her?

FERRIS, *doggedly*: Yes; it is hard.

DON IPPOLITO: And yet it is the very truth. Oh, you do not know her—you never knew her! In the same moment that she denied me her love she divined the anguish of my soul, and with that embrace she sought to console me for the friend-lessness of a whole life, past and to come. But I know that I waste my words on you! You never would see me as I was; you would find no singleness in me, and yet I had a heart full of loyalty to you. In what was I ever false to you?

FERRIS, *moved*: You never were false to me, Don Ippolito, and God knows I was true to you, and at what cost! We might well curse the day we met, for we have only done each other harm. But I never meant you harm. And now I ask you to forgive me if I cannot believe you are right in what you say. I cannot—yet. I am of another race from you, slow to suspect, also to trust. Give me a little time; let me see you again. I want to go away and think; I will come again tomorrow. May I?

DON IPPOLITO: Surely, surely! You will do me the greatest pleasure. Yes, come again—but very soon. You know that my time in the world is short, and that when I enter the convent— Adieu! To meet again! (*He takes Ferris's hand, and draws him down toward him; then he kisses him on both cheeks.*) It is our Italian custom, you know, among *friends*. Farewell!

FERRIS: And I am your friend, Don Ippolito, and have always been so! Adieu! To meet again!

(With a burst of passion.) Oh! It isn't you that I doubt! If it were only you!

DON IPPOLITO, *mystified*: I do not understand.

FERRIS: I'm afraid you haven't understood! I'm afraid that the same deceit has tricked us both!

DON IPPOLITO: The same deceit?

FERRIS: That the same cruel and senseless vanity has played with your heart as it has with mine—

DON IPPOLITO: Do you mean—madamigella? *(Ferris nods.)* And can you so blaspheme her heavenly truth? Man, man! You are *not* man! You are harder than stone, for if you were of stone, you must tremble to your knees and ask God's pardon for your wrong to one of His whitest ministers. What shall I say—what shall I do to soften you? Ah, if it were you alone! But she—her heart is set on you; and, yes! You *shall* believe in her. *(His voice has risen.)* Heaven grant it!

Enter Florida.

FLORIDA: Were you calling, Don Ippolito? *(Seeing Ferris she shrinks back.)* Ah!

DON IPPOLITO: Yes! I was calling upon Heaven, and *you* came! No, do not go, my daughter—stay! *(She stops.)* Here—this unhappy man—this poor soul, who was once my friend and yours, but who is not even his own friend now—wishes to ask you something.

FERRIS: I have nothing to ask.

Turning away.

DON IPPOLITO, *to Florida*: But you—you have something to tell him?

FLORIDA: I have nothing to tell him.

Averting her face, and hiding it in her hands.

DON IPPOLITO: Then let me ask for him and answer for you. You, who have guarded me back from the Valley of the Shadow into life again, and have won from Heaven a chance for me to retrieve my erring past—he accuses you! Do you know of what? Of making his love your pastime while you mocked at mine!

FLORIDA, *turning and looking Ferris in the face*: Oh! Did you think I was such a wicked girl as that?

FERRIS, *broken*: I loved you, Florida! I *love* you! I have no other reason or defense.

FLORIDA: You thought that I could be so false and cruel—

FERRIS: Yes, yes! I thought it all—God help me!

FLORIDA: When I was only sorry for him, when it was you that I—

FERRIS: Oh, I know it, he has told me so!

FLORIDA: And you would not believe him? *(Ferris silent.)* Do you believe *me* now?

FERRIS: When I look at you, I can't believe I ever doubted you.

FLORIDA: Ah, I *cannot* forgive you—

FERRIS: I do not deserve your forgiveness!

FLORIDA: I don't care that you have doubted me; but if you ever loved me—

FERRIS: *Loved* you!

FLORIDA: You have disgraced *yourself* by such a thought, and that I *can't* forgive.

FERRIS: I know it—I don't ask it. But think sometimes that I had the decency to abhor myself. I had a sacred sorrow, but I have been unworthy of it. Let me take myself out of your sight. Farewell, again, Don Ippolito. I shall not come tomorrow. *(Don Ippolito does not heed him.)* I am going to hide myself!

He turns to go.

FLORIDA, *tenderly*: Good-bye—Henry!

FERRIS, *stopping*: Florida!

FLORIDA: My mother will be sorry— She—she —always loved you—

FERRIS: I always behaved like a brute to her. Tell her I was not fit to say good-bye to her. I am not fit to say good-bye to you, and yet— good-bye.

FLORIDA: Good-bye.

He moves slowly toward the door.

DON IPPOLITO, *who has lain silent*: My daughter! *(He stretches his hand toward Florida, who takes it.)* My son! *(Ferris takes his outstretched hand. Don Ippolito places Florida's hand in Ferris's, and they falter to their knees on either side of his couch.)* God bless you and keep you, my children!

He sinks back.

FLORIDA, *springing to her feet*: He is fainting.

FERRIS, *bending over him*: So, he is only—

DON IPPOLITO, *faintly*: Dying! Farewell! May you be happy!

FLORIDA: Oh, you *shall* not die! Veneranda! Mr. Billings! Mother! Come quick!

They all rush in and crowd about him.

DON IPPOLITO: Where are you all, dear friends? It grows so dark! *(Solemnly.)* Where is the image of our blessed Lord?

MRS. VERVAIN, *pressing the crucifix to his lips*: Here, here, my poor child!

She holds his head on her breast.

DON IPPOLITO: Thank you—my mother! Ah, now it is light again!

His head sinks down. They all kneel. Solemn music without.

CURTAIN

The Garroters

[1885]

In "A Letter to the Publisher" which prefaced *Minor Dramas* Howells confided to his readers that he built *The Garroters* "from the experience of a friend in Boston Common." He also noted in this "Letter" that his play was almost identical in plot with a farce—probably *Who Stole the Pocket Book; or, A Dinner For Six*, in one act, 1852—by the English dramatist John Maddison Morton. Several times in his career Howells had used situations from real life in his plays, but this time, as Morton's use of a similar plot indicates, he had a particularly good farce idea, and *The Garroters* became one of Howells' few plays that can boast a dramatic and stageworthy plot. Other plays may be more humorous or may have better dialogue; certainly a number are more effective in their satire of Boston society. But this play has a reasonable, well worked-out plot that progresses dramatically and with effective embellishments from the initial situation through the various incidents to the final situation.

Although Howells called *The Garroters* a farce, G. B. Shaw called it a farce comedy, and William Archer applied the term *comedietta* to it. Most of the action, of course, and the characterizations of Willis and Roberts are farcical. Tormented with awkward possibilities and faced with a ridiculous plan of rescue, Roberts in his completely passive, unthinking manner illustrates effectively the farce character; had he thought, he could never have agreed to Willis' plan. But the other characters are different—they think. In general they move the plot rather than being moved by it and manifest the humor and demeanor of the comic character as opposed to the farce character. Further evidence of comic characteristics in *The Garroters* is shown by the background of social conventions. Occasionally there are sparkling bits of conversation as the dialogue

moves smoothly and rapidly among these people who handle themselves as convention demands and good breeding dictates. Such background implies that there can be no real doubt as to how the play must end, but in the process of reaching his end Howells gives a humorous portrayal of people of a certain social level handling an emergency in a way that, omitting the farcical Campbell–Roberts contrivance, shows their good manners.

"This is the only one of all the farces," Howells wrote in "A Letter to the Publisher," "which has got seriously upon the stage. A young Canadian lady, living in London, gave it London circumstance throughout, and it was played there once or twice, and then lingered for more than two years in provincial theatres." Mildred Howells (*Life in Letters*, II, 173) identifies the lady as Emeretta Lawrence.

Both George Bernard Shaw and William Archer commented on the London performances—in which the title of the play was changed to *A Dangerous Ruffian*—in a manner deserving quotation. Shaw wrote:

By the way, I have discovered, quite by accident, an amusing farcical comedy. Somebody told me that there was a farce by Mr. W. D. Howells at the Avenue Theatre. I looked in the daily paper, but could find no mention of the name of Mr. Howells. However, it was evidently quite possible that the management had never heard of Mr. Howells, just as they had apparently never heard of me. So I went, and duly found the name "Howells" on the programme. The little piece showed, as might have been expected, that with three weeks' practice the American novelist could write the heads off the poor bunglers to whom our managers generally appeal when they want a small bit of work to amuse the people who come at eight. But no doubt it is pleasanter to be a novelist, to have an intelligent circle of readers comfortably seated by their firesides or swinging sunnily in hammocks in their gardens, to be pleasantly diffuse, to play with your work, to be independent of time and space, than to conform to the stern conditions of the stage and fight with stupidity before and behind the curtain. (*Dramatic Opinions and Essays*, I [New York: Brentano's, 1907], 266–67.)

Archer commented:

An ingenious and humorous comedietta by Mr. W. D. Howells now precedes *Mrs. Ponder-*

burg's Past at the Avenue (November 30, 1895–January 2, 1896). It is entitled *A Dangerous Ruffian*, and deals with the exploit of an absent-minded professor who knocks down and robs an inoffensive old gentleman, under the impression that he is recovering his watch from a daring pickpocket. The principal character, however, is not the Professor, but his hysterically adoring spouse, who is cleverly played by Miss Florence Harrington." (*The Theatrical 'World' of 1895* [London: Walter Scott, 1896], p. 373.)

Doubtless the play had a wide acceptance in America on the amateur stage. Odell lists one production in the Chapel of the All Souls Universalist Church, South Tenth Street, December 22, 1886 (*Annals of the New York Stage*, XIII, 394).

The Garroters[1]

PART FIRST

At the window of her apartment in Hotel Bellingham, Mrs. Roberts stands looking out into the early nightfall. A heavy snow is driving without, and from time to time the rush of the wind and the sweep of the flakes against the panes are heard. At the sound of hurried steps in the anteroom, Mrs. Roberts turns from the window, and runs to the portière, through which she puts her head.

MRS. ROBERTS: Is that you, Edward? So dark here! We ought really to keep the gas turned up all the time.

MR. ROBERTS, *in a muffled voice, from without:* Yes, it's I.

MRS. ROBERTS: Well, hurry in to the fire, do! Ugh, what a storm! Do you suppose anybody will come? You must be half frozen, you poor thing! Come quick, or you'll certainly perish! (*She flies from the portière to the fire burning on the hearth, pokes it, flings on a log, jumps back, brushes from her dress with a light shriek the sparks driven out upon it, and continues talking incessantly in a voice lifted for her husband to hear in the anteroom.*) If I'd dreamed it was any such storm as this, I should never have let you go out in it in the world. It wasn't at all necessary to have the flowers. I could have got on perfectly well, and I believe *now* the table would look better without them. The chrysanthemums would have been quite enough; and I know you've taken more cold. I could tell it by your voice as soon as you spoke; and just as quick as they're gone to-night I'm going to have you bathe your feet in mustard and hot water, and take eight of aconite, and go straight to bed. And I don't want you to eat very much at dinner, dear, and you must be sure not to drink any coffee, or the aconite won't be of the least use. (*She turns and encounters her husband, who enters through the portière, his face pale, his eyes wild, his white necktie pulled out of knot, and his shirt front rumpled.*) Why, Edward, what

[1] The text used here is from *The Mouse Trap and Other Farces.*

in the world is the matter? What has happened?

ROBERTS, *sinking into a chair:* Get me a glass of water, Agnes—wine—whiskey—brandy—

MRS. ROBERTS, *bustling wildly about:* Yes, yes. But what— Bella! Bridget! Maggy!—Oh, I'll go for it myself, and I *won't* stop to listen! Only—only don't die! (*While Roberts remains with his eyes shut, and his head sunk on his breast in token of extreme exhaustion, she disappears and reappears through the door leading to her chamber, and then through the portière cutting off the dining-room. She finally descends upon her husband with a flagon of cologne in one hand, a small decanter of brandy in the other, and a wineglass held in the hollow of her arm against her breast. She contrives to set the glass down on the mantle and fill it from the flagon, then she turns with the decanter in her hand, and while she presses the glass to her husband's lips, begins to pour the brandy on his head.*) Here! this will revive you, and it'll refresh you to have this cologne on your head.

ROBERTS, *rejecting a mouthful of the cologne with a furious sputter, and springing to his feet:* Why, you've given me the cologne to *drink*, Agnes! What are you about? Do you want to poison me? Isn't it enough to be robbed at six o'clock on the Common, without having your head soaked in brandy, and your whole system scented up like a barber's shop, when you get home?

MRS. ROBERTS: Robbed? (*She drops the wineglass, puts the decanter down on the hearth, and carefully bestowing the flagon of cologne in the wood-box, abandons herself to justice.*) Then let them come for me at once, Edward! If I could have the heart to send you out in such a night as this for a few wretched rose-buds, I'm quite equal to poisoning you. Oh, Edward, *who* robbed you?

ROBERTS: That's what I don't know. (*He continues to wipe his head with his handkerchief, and to sputter a little from time to time.*) All I know is that when I got—phew!—to that dark spot by the Frog Pond, just by—phew!—that little group of—phew!—evergreens, you know—phew!—

MRS. ROBERTS: Yes, yes; go on! I can bear it, Edward.

ROBERTS: —a man brushed heavily against me, and then hurried on in the other direction. I had unbuttoned my coat to look at my watch under the lamp-post, and after he struck against me I clapped my hand to my waistcoat, and—phew!—

MRS. ROBERTS: Waistcoat! Yes!

ROBERTS: —found my watch gone.

MRS. ROBERTS: What! your watch? The watch Willis gave you? Made out of the gold that he mined himself when he first went out to California? Don't ask me to believe it, Edward! But I'm only too glad that you escaped with your life. Let them have the watch and welcome. Oh, my dear, dear husband! (She approaches him with extended arms, and then suddenly arrests herself.) But you've got it on!

ROBERTS, with as much returning dignity as can comport with his dishevelled appearance: Yes; I took it from him. (At his wife's speechless astonishment) I went after him and took it from him. (He sits down, and continues with resolute calm, while his wife remains standing before him motionless.) Agnes, I don't know how I came to do it. I wouldn't have believed I could do it. I've never thought that I had much courage—physical courage; but when I felt my watch was gone, a sort of frenzy came over me. I wasn't hurt; and for the first time in my life I realized what an abominable outrage theft was. The thought that at six o'clock in the evening, in the very heart of a great city like Boston, an inoffensive citizen could be assaulted and robbed, made me furious. I didn't call out. I simply buttoned my coat tight round me and turned and ran after the fellow.

MRS. ROBERTS: Edward!

ROBERTS: Yes, I did. He hadn't got half a dozen rods away—it all took place in a flash—and I could easily run him down. He was considerably larger than I—

MRS. ROBERTS: Oh!

ROBERTS: —and he looked young and very athletic; but these things didn't seem to make any impression on me.

MRS. ROBERTS: Oh, I wonder that you live to tell the tale, Edward!

ROBERTS: Well, I wonder a little at myself. I don't set up for a great deal of—

MRS. ROBERTS: But I always knew you had it! Go on. Oh, when I tell Willis of this! Had the robber any accomplices? Were there many of them?

ROBERTS: I only saw one. And I saw that my only chance was to take him at a disadvantage. I sprang upon him, and pulled him over on his back. I merely said, "I'll trouble you for that watch of mine, if you please," jerked open his coat, snatched the watch from his pocket—I broke the chain, I see—and then left him and ran again. He didn't make the slightest resistance, nor utter a word. Of course it wouldn't do for him to make any noise about it, and I dare say he was glad to get off so easily. (With affected nonchalance) I'm pretty badly rumpled, I see. He fell against me, and a scuffle like that doesn't improve one's appearance.

MRS. ROBERTS, very solemnly: Edward! I don't know what to say! Of course it makes my blood run cold to realize what you have been through, and to think what might have happened; but I think you behaved splendidly. Why, I never heard of such perfect heroism! You needn't tell me that he made no resistance. There was a deadly struggle—your necktie and everything about you shows it. And you needn't think there was only one of them—

ROBERTS, modestly: I don't believe there was more.

MRS. ROBERTS: Nonsense! There are always two! I've read the accounts of those garrotings. And to think you not only got out of their clutches alive, but got your property back—Willis's watch! Oh, what will Willis say? But I know how proud of you he'll be. Oh, I wish I could scream it from the house-tops. Why didn't you call the police?

ROBERTS: I didn't think—I hadn't time to think.

MRS. ROBERTS: No matter. I'm glad you have all the glory of it. I don't believe you half realize what you've been through now. And perhaps this was the robbers' first attempt, and it will be a lesson to them. Oh yes! I'm glad you let them escape, Edward. They may have families. If every one behaved as you've done, there would soon be an end of garroting. But, oh! I can't bear to think of the danger you've run. And I want you to promise me never, never to undertake such a thing again!

ROBERTS: Well, I don't know—

MRS. ROBERTS: Yes, yes; you must! Suppose you had got killed in that awful struggle with those reckless wretches tugging to get away from you! Think of the children! Why, you might have burst a blood-vessel! Will you promise, Edward? Promise this instant, on your bended knees, just as if you were in a court of justice! (Mrs. Roberts's *excitement mounts, and she flings herself at her husband's feet, and pulls his face down to hers with the arm she has thrown about his neck.)* Will you promise?

MRS. CRASHAW, *entering unobserved*: Promise you what, Agnes? The man doesn't smoke *now*. What more can you ask? *(She starts back from the spectacle of Roberts's disordered dress.)* Why, what's happened to you, Edward?

MRS. ROBERTS, *springing to her feet*: Oh, you may well ask that, Aunt Mary! Happened? You ought to fall down and worship him! And you *will* when you know what he's been through. He's been robbed!

MRS. CRASHAW: Robbed? What nonsense! Who robbed him? *Where* was he robbed?

MRS. ROBERTS: He was attacked by two garroters—

ROBERTS: No, no—

MRS. ROBERTS: Don't speak, Edward! I *know* there were two. On the Common. Not half an hour ago. As he was going to get me some rosebuds. In the midst of this terrible storm.

MRS. CRASHAW: Is this true, Edward?

MRS. ROBERTS: Don't answer, Edward! One of the band threw his arm round Edwards' neck—so.

She illustrates by garroting Mrs. Crashaw, who disengages herself with difficulty.

MRS. CRASHAW: Mercy, child! What *are* you doing to my lace?

MRS. ROBERTS: And the other one snatched his watch, and ran as fast as he could.

MRS. CRASHAW: Willis's watch? Why, he's got it on.

MRS. ROBERTS, *with proud delight*: Exactly what I said when he told me. *(Then, very solemnly)* And do you know *why* he's got it on?—'Sh, Edward! I *will* tell! Because he ran after them and took it back again.

MRS. CRASHAW: Why, they might have killed him!

MRS. ROBERTS: Of *course* they might. But *Edward* didn't care. The idea of being robbed at six o'clock on the Common made him so furious that he scorned to cry out for help, or call the police, or anything; but he just ran after them—

ROBERTS: Agnes! Agnes! There was only *one*.

MRS. ROBERTS: Nonsense, Edward! How could you tell, so excited as you were?—And caught hold of the largest of the wretches—a perfect young giant—

ROBERTS: No, no; not a *giant*, my dear.

MRS. ROBERTS: Well, he was *young, anyway!*—And flung him on the ground.

She advances upon Mrs. Crashaw in her enthusiasm.

MRS. CRASHAW: Don't you fling *me* on the ground, Agnes! I won't have it.

MRS. ROBERTS: And tore his coat open, while all the rest were tugging at him, and snatched his watch, and then—and then just walked coolly away.

ROBERTS: No, my dear; I ran as fast as I could.

MRS. ROBERTS: Well, *ran*. It's quite the same thing, and I'm just as proud of you as if you had walked. Of course you were not going to throw your life away.

MRS. CRASHAW: I think he did a very silly thing in going after them at all.

ROBERTS: Why, of course, if I'd thought twice about it, I shouldn't have done it.

MRS. ROBERTS: Of course you wouldn't, dear! And that's what I want him to promise, Aunt Mary: never to do it again, no matter *how* much he's provoked. I want him to promise it right here in your presence, Aunt Mary!

MRS. CRASHAW: I think it's much more important he should put on another collar and—shirt, if he's going to see company.

MRS. ROBERTS: Yes; go right off at once, Edward. How you *do* think of things, Aunt Mary! I really suppose I should have gone on all night and never noticed his looks. Run, Edward, and do it, dear. But—kiss me first! Oh, it *don't* seem as if you could be alive and well after it all! Are you sure you're not hurt?

ROBERTS, *embracing her*: No; I'm all right.

MRS. ROBERTS: And you're not injured internally? Sometimes they're injured internally—aren't they, Aunt Mary?—and it doesn't show till months afterwards. Are you sure?

ROBERTS, *making a cursory examination of his ribs with his hands*: Yes, I think so.

MRS. ROBERTS: And you don't feel any bad effects from the cologne *now*? Just think, Aunt Mary, I gave him cologne to drink, and poured the brandy on his head, when he came in! But I was determined to keep calm, whatever I did. And if I've poisoned him I'm quite willing to die for it—oh, quite! I would gladly take the blame of it before the whole world.

MRS. CRASHAW: Well, for pity's sake, let the man go and make himself decent. There's your bell now.

MRS. ROBERTS: Yes, do go, Edward. But—kiss me—

MRS. CRASHAW: He *did* kiss you, Agnes. Don't be a simpleton!

MRS. ROBERTS: Did he? Well, kiss me again, then, Edward. And now do go, dear. M-m-m-m.

The inarticulate endearments represented by these signs terminate in a wild embrace, protracted halfway across the room, in the height of which Mr. Willis Campbell enters.

WILLIS, *pausing in contemplation*: Hello! What's the matter? What's she trying to get out of you, Roberts? Don't you do it, anyway, old fellow.

MRS. ROBERTS, *in an ecstasy of satisfaction*: Willis! Oh, you've come in time to see him just as he is. Look at him, Willis!

In the excess of her emotion she twitches her husband about, and with his arm fast in her clutch, presents him in the disadvantageous effect of having just been taken into custody. Under these circumstances Roberts's attempt at an expression of diffident heroism fails; he looks sneaking, he looks guilty, and his eyes fall under the astonished regard of his brother-in-law.

WILLIS: What's the matter with him? What's he been doing?

MR. ROBERTS: 'Sh, Edward!—What's he been doing? What does he look as if he had been doing?

MRS. CRASHAW: Agnes—

WILLIS: He looks as if he had been signing the pledge. And he—smells like it.

MRS. ROBERTS: For shame, Willis! I should think you'd sink through the floor. Edward, not a word! I *am* ashamed of him, if he *is* my brother.

WILLIS: Why, what in the world's up, Agnes?

MRS. ROBERTS: Up? He's been *robbed!*—robbed on the Common, not five minutes ago! A whole gang of garroters surrounded him under the Old Elm—or just where it used to be—and took his watch away! And he ran after them, and knocked the largest of the gang down, and took it back again. He wasn't hurt, but we're afraid he's been injured internally; he may be bleeding internally *now*— Oh, do you think he is, Willis? Don't you think we ought to send for a physician?—That, and the cologne I gave him to drink. It's the brandy I poured on his head makes him smell so. And he all so exhausted he couldn't speak, and I didn't know what I was doing, either; but he's

promised—oh yes, he's promised!—never, never to do it again.

She again flings her arms about her husband, and then turns proudly to her brother.

WILLIS: Do you know what it means, Aunt Mary?

MRS. CRASHAW: Not in the least! But I've no doubt that Edward can explain, after he's changed his linen—

MRS. ROBERTS: Oh yes, do go, Edward! Not but what I should be proud and happy to have you appear just as you are before the whole world, if it was only to put Willis down with his jokes about your absent-mindedness, and his boasts about those California desperadoes of his.

ROBERTS: Come, come, Agnes! I *must* protest against your—

MRS. ROBERTS: Oh, I know it doesn't become me to praise your courage, darling! But I should like to know what Willis would have done, with all his California experience, if a garroter had taken his watch?

WILLIS: I should have let him keep it, and pay five dollars a quarter himself for getting it cleaned and spoiled. Anybody but a literary man would. How many of them were there, Roberts?

ROBERTS: I only saw one.

MRS. ROBERTS: But of course there were more. How could he tell, in the dark and excitement? And the one he did see was a perfect giant; so you can imagine what the rest must have been like.

WILLIS: Did you really knock him down?

MRS. ROBERTS: Knock him down? Of course he did.

MRS. CRASHAW: Agnes, *will* you hold your tongue, and let the men alone?

MRS. ROBERTS, *whimpering*: I can't, Aunt Mary. And you couldn't, if it was yours.

ROBERTS: I pulled him over backwards.

MRS. ROBERTS: There, Willis!

WILLIS: And grabbed your watch from him?

ROBERTS: I was in quite a frenzy; I really hardly knew what I was doing—

MRS. ROBERTS: And he didn't call for the police, or anything—

WILLIS: Ah, that showed presence of mind! He knew it wouldn't have been any use.

MRS. ROBERTS: And when he had got his watch away from them, he just let them go, because they had families dependent on them.

WILLIS: I should have let them go in the first

place, but you behaved handsomely in the end, Roberts; there's no denying that. And when you came in she gave you cologne to drink, and poured brandy on your head. It must have revived you. I should think it would wake the dead.

MRS. ROBERTS: I was all excitement, Willis—

WILLIS: No, I should think from the fact that you had set the decanter here on the hearth, and put your cologne into the wood-box, you were perfectly calm, Agnes. (*He takes them up and hands them to her.*) Quite as calm as usual.

The doorbell rings.

MRS. CRASHAW: Willis, *will* you let that ridiculous man go away and make himself presentable before people begin to come?

The bell rings violently, peal upon peal.

MRS. ROBERTS: Oh, my goodness, what's that? It's the garroters—I know it is; and we shall all be murdered in our beds!

MRS. CRASHAW: What in the world can it—

WILLIS: Why don't your girl answer the bell, Agnes? Or I'll go myself.

The bell rings violently again.

MRS. ROBERTS: No, Willis, you sha'n't! Don't leave me, Edward! Aunt Mary!—Oh, if we *must* die, let us all die together! Oh, my poor children! Ugh! What's that?

The servant-maid opens the outer door, and uttering a shriek, rushes in through the drawing-room portière.

BELLA, THE MAID: Oh, my goodness! Mrs. Roberts, it's Mr. Bemis!

MRS. ROBERTS: Which Mr. Bemis?

ROBERTS: What's the matter with him?

MRS. CRASHAW: Why doesn't she show him in?

WILLIS: Has *he* been garroting somebody too?

BEMIS, *appearing through the portière*: I—I beg your pardon, Mrs. Roberts. I oughtn't to present myself in this state—I— But I thought I'd better stop on my way home and report, so that my son needn't be alarmed at my absence when he comes. I— (*He stops, exhausted, and regards the others with a wild stare, while they stand taking note of his disordered coat, his torn vest, and his tumbled hat.*) I've just been robbed—

MRS. ROBERTS: Robbed? Why, *Edward* has been robbed too.

BEMIS: —coming through the Common—

MRS. ROBERTS: Yes, *Edward* was coming through the Common.

BEMIS: —of my watch—

MRS. ROBERTS, *in rapturous admiration of the coincidence*: Oh, and it was Edward's *watch* they took!

WILLIS: It's a parallel case, Agnes. Pour him out a glass of cologne to drink, and rub his head with brandy. And you might let him sit down and rest while you're enjoying the excitement.

MRS. ROBERTS, *in hospitable remorse*: Oh, what am I thinking of! Here, Edward—or no, you're too weak, you mustn't. Willis, *you* help me to help him to the sofa.

MRS. CRASHAW: I think you'd better help him off with his overcoat and his arctics. (*To the maid*) Here, Bella, if you haven't quite taken leave of your wits, undo his shoes.

ROBERTS: *I'll* help him off with his coat—

BEMIS: Careful! careful! I may be injured internally.

MRS. ROBERTS: Oh, if you only *were*, Mr. Bemis, perhaps I could persuade Edward that he was too: I *know* he is. Edward, don't exert yourself! Aunt Mary, will you *stop* him, or do you all wish to see me go distracted here before your eyes?

WILLIS, *examining the overcoat which Roberts has removed*: Well, you won't have much trouble buttoning and unbuttoning this coat for the present.

BEMIS: They tore it open, and tore my watch from my vest pocket—

WILLIS, *looking at the vest*: I see. Pretty lively work. Were there many of them?

BEMIS: There must have been two, at least—

MRS. ROBERTS: There were half a dozen in the gang that attacked Edward.

BEMIS: One of them pulled me violently over on my back—

MRS. ROBERTS: Edward's put *his* arm round his neck and choked him.

MRS. CRASHAW: Agnes!

MRS. ROBERTS: I *know* he did, Aunt Mary.

BEMIS: And the other tore my watch out of my pocket.

MRS. ROBERTS: *Edward's*—

MRS. CRASHAW: Agnes, I'm thoroughly ashamed of you. *Will* you stop interrupting?

BEMIS: And left me lying in the snow.

MRS. ROBERTS: And then he ran after them, and snatched his watch away again in spite of them all; and he didn't call for the police, or anything, because it was their first offence, and he couldn't bear to think of their suffering families.

BEMIS, *with a stare of profound astonishment*: Who?

MRS. ROBERTS: Edward. Didn't I *say* Edward, all the time?

BEMIS: I thought you meant me. I didn't think

of pursuing them; but you may be very sure that if there had been a policeman within call—of course there wasn't one within cannon-shot—I should have handed the scoundrels over without the slightest remorse.

ROBERTS: Oh!

He sinks into a chair with a slight groan.

WILLIS: What is it?

ROBERTS: 'Sh! Don't say anything. But—stay here. I want to speak with you, Willis.

BEMIS, *with mounting wrath*: I should not have hesitated an instant to give the rascal in charge, no matter *who* was dependent upon him—no matter if he were my dearest friend, my own brother.

ROBERTS, *under his breath*: Gracious powers!

BEMIS: And while I am very sorry to disagree with Mr. Roberts, I can't help feeling that he made a great mistake in allowing the ruffians to escape.

MRS. CRASHAW, *with severity*: I think you are quite right, Mr. Bemis.

BEMIS: Probably it was the same gang attacked us both. After escaping from Mr. Roberts they fell upon me.

MRS. CRASHAW: I haven't a doubt of it.

ROBERTS, *sotto voce to his brother-in-law*: I think I'll ask you to go with me to my room, Willis. Don't alarm Agnes, please. I—I feel quite faint.

MRS. ROBERTS, *crestfallen*: I can't feel that Edward was to blame. Ed— Oh, I suppose he's gone off to make himself presentable. But Willis —Where's Willis, Aunt Mary?

MRS. CRASHAW: Probably gone with him to help him.

MRS. ROBERTS: Oh, he *saw* how unstrung poor Edward was! Mr. Bemis, I think you're quite prejudiced. How could Edward help their escaping? I think it was quite enough for him, single-handed, to get his watch back. (*A ring at the door, and then a number of voices in the ante-room.*) I do believe they're all there! I'll just run out and prepare your son. He would be dreadfully shocked if he came right in upon you. (*She runs into the anteroom, and is heard without.*) Oh, Dr. Lawton! Oh, Lou dear! *Oh*, Mr. Bemis! How can I ever tell you? Your poor father! No, no, I *can't* tell you! You mustn't ask me! It's too hideous! And you wouldn't believe me if I did.

CHORUS OF ANGUISHED VOICES: What? what? what?

MRS. ROBERTS: They've been robbed! Garroted on the Common! And, *oh*, Dr. Lawton, I'm so glad *you've* come! They're both injured internally, but I *wish* you'd look at Edward first.

BEMIS: Good heavens! Is that Mrs. Roberts's idea of preparing my son? And his poor young wife!

He addresses his demand to Mrs. Crashaw, who lifts the hands of impotent despair.

PART SECOND.

In Mr. Roberts's dressing-room, that gentleman is discovered tragically confronting Mr. Willis Campbell, with a watch uplifted in either hand.

WILLIS: Well?

ROBERTS, *gasping*: My—my watch!

WILLIS: Yes. How comes there to be two of it?

ROBERTS: Don't you understand? When I went out I—didn't take my watch—with me. I left it here on my bureau.

WILLIS: Well?

ROBERTS: Oh, merciful heavens! don't you see? Then I couldn't have been robbed!

WILLIS: Well, but whose watch did you take from the fellow that didn't rob you, then?

ROBERTS: His own! (*He abandons himself powerlessly upon a chair.*) Yes; I left my own watch here, and when that person brushed against me in the Common, I missed it for the first time. I supposed he had robbed me, and ran after him, and—

WILLIS: Robbed *him!*

ROBERTS: Yes.

WILLIS: Ah, ha, ha, ha! I, hi, hi, hi! O, ho, ho, ho! (*He yields to a series of these gusts and paroxysms, bowing up and down, and stamping to and fro, and finally sits down exhausted, and wipes the tears from his cheeks.*) Really, this thing will kill me. What are you going to do about it, Roberts?

ROBERTS, *with profound dejection and abysmal solemnity*: I don't know, Willis. Don't you see that it must have been—that I must have robbed —Mr. Bemis?

WILLIS: Bemis! (*After a moment for tasting the fact*) Why, so it was! Oh, Lord! oh, Lord! And was poor old Bemis that burly ruffian? that blood-thirsty gang of giants? that—that—oh, Lord! oh, Lord! (*He bows his head upon his chair-back in complete exhaustion, demanding, feebly, as he gets breath for the successive questions.*) What are you going to d-o-o-o? What shall you s-a-a-a-y? How can you expla-a-ain it?

ROBERTS: I can do nothing. I can say nothing. I can never explain it. I must go to Mr. Bemis and make a clean breast of it; but think of the absurdity—the ridicule!

WILLIS, *after a thoughtful silence*: Oh, it isn't *that* you've got to think of. You've got to think of the old gentleman's sense of injury and outrage. Didn't you hear what he said—that he would have handed over his dearest friend, his own brother, to the police?

ROBERTS: But that was in the supposition that his dearest friend, his own brother, had intentionally robbed him. You can't imagine, Willis—

WILLIS: Oh, I can imagine a great many things. It's all well enough for you to say that the robbery was a mistake; but it was a genuine case of garroting, as far as the assault and taking the watch go. He's a very pudgicky old gentleman.

ROBERTS: He is.

WILLIS: And I don't see how you're going to satisfy him that it was all a joke. Joke? It *wasn't* a joke! It was a real assault and a *bona fide* robbery, and Bemis can prove it.

ROBERTS: But he would never insist—

WILLIS: Oh, I don't know about that. He's pretty queer, Bemis is. You can't say what an old gentleman like that will or won't do. If he should choose to carry it into court—

ROBERTS: Court!

WILLIS: —it might be embarrassing. And anyway, it would have a very strange look in the papers.

ROBERTS: The papers! Good gracious!

WILLIS: Ten years from now, a man that heard you mentioned would forget all about the acquittal, and say: "Roberts? Oh yes! Wasn't he the one they sent to the House of Correction for garroting an old friend of his on the Common?" You see it wouldn't do to go and make a clean breast of it to Bemis.

ROBERTS: I see.

WILLIS: What will you do?

ROBERTS: I must never say anything to him about it. Just let it go.

WILLIS: And keep his watch? I don't see how you could manage that. What would you do with the watch? You might sell it, of course—

ROBERTS: Oh no, I *couldn't* do that.

WILLIS: You might give it away to some deserving person; but if it got him into trouble—

ROBERTS: No, no; that wouldn't do, either.

WILLIS: And you can't have it lying around; Agnes would be sure to find it, sooner or later.

ROBERTS: Yes.

WILLIS: Besides, there's your conscience. Your conscience wouldn't *let* you keep Bemis's watch away from him. And if it would, what do you suppose Agnes's conscience would do when she came to find it out? Agnes hasn't got much of a head—the want of it seems to grow upon her; but she's got a conscience as big as the side of a house.

ROBERTS: Oh, I see; I see.

WILLIS, *coming up and standing over him, with his hands in his pockets*: I tell you what, Roberts, you're in a box.

ROBERTS, *abjectly*: I know it, Willis; I know it. What do you suggest? You *must* know some way out of it.

WILLIS: It isn't a simple matter like telling them to start the elevator down when they couldn't start her up.[1] I've got to think it over. (*He walks to and fro, Roberts's eyes helplessly following his movements.*) How would it do to— No, that wouldn't do, either.

ROBERTS: What wouldn't?

WILLIS: Nothing. I was just thinking— I say, you might— Or, no, you couldn't.

ROBERTS: Couldn't what?

WILLIS: Nothing. But if you were to— No; up a stump that way too.

ROBERTS: Which way? For mercy's sake, my dear fellow, don't seem to get a clew if you haven't it. It's more than I can bear. (*He rises, and desperately confronts Willis in his promenade.*) If you see any hope at all—

WILLIS, *stopping*: Why, if you were a different sort of fellow, Roberts, the thing would be perfectly easy.

ROBERTS: Very well, then. What sort of fellow do you want me to be? I'll be any sort of fellow you like.

WILLIS: Oh, but you couldn't! With that face of yours, and that confounded conscience of yours behind it, you would give away the whitest lie that was ever told.

ROBERTS: Do you wish me to lie? Very well, then, I will lie. What is the lie?

WILLIS: Ah, now you're talking like a man! I can soon think up a lie, if you're game for it. Suppose it wasn't so very white—say a delicate blonde!

ROBERTS: I shouldn't care if it were as black as the ace of spades.

WILLIS: Roberts, I honor you! It isn't everybody who could steal an old gentleman's watch, and then be so ready to lie out of it. Well, you *have* got courage—both kinds—moral and physical.

[1] A reference to *The Elevator*.

ROBERTS: Thank you, Willis. Of course I don't pretend that I should be willing to lie, under ordinary circumstances; but for the sake of Agnes and the children— I don't want any awkwardness about the matter; it would be the death of me. Well, what do you wish me to say? Be quick; I don't believe I could hold out for a great while. I don't suppose but what Mr. Bemis would be reasonable, even if I—

WILLIS: I'm afraid we couldn't trust him. The only way is for you to take the bull by the horns.

ROBERTS: Yes?

WILLIS: You will not only have to lie, Roberts, but you will have to wear an air of innocent candor at the same time.

ROBERTS: I—I'm afraid I couldn't manage that. What is your idea?

WILLIS: Oh, just come into the room with a laugh, when we go back, and say, in an off-hand way, "By the way, Agnes, Willis and I made a remarkable discovery in my dressing-room; we found my watch there on the bureau. Ha, ha, ha!" Do you think you could do it?

ROBERTS: I—I don't know.

WILLIS: Try the laugh now.

ROBERTS: I'd rather not—now.

WILLIS: Well, try it, anyway.

ROBERTS: Ha, ha, ha!

WILLIS: Once more.

ROBERTS: Ha, ha, ha!

WILLIS: Pretty ghastly; but I guess you can come it.

ROBERTS: I'll try. And then what?

WILLIS: And then you say, "I hadn't put it on when I went out, and when I got after that fellow and took it back, I was simply getting somebody else's watch!" Then you hold out both watches to her, and laugh again. Everybody laughs, and crowds round you to examine the watches, and you make fun and crack jokes at your own expense all the time, and pretty soon old Bemis says, "Why, this is my watch, now!" and you laugh more than ever—

ROBERTS: I'm afraid I couldn't laugh when he said that. I don't believe I could laugh. It would make my blood run cold.

WILLIS: Oh no, it wouldn't. You'd be in the spirit of it by that time.

ROBERTS: Do you think so? Well?

WILLIS: And then you say, "Well, this is the most remarkable coincidence I ever heard of. I didn't get my own watch from the fellow, but I got yours, Mr. Bemis"; and then you hand it over to him and say, "Sorry I had to break the chain in

getting it from him," and then everybody laughs again, and—and that ends it.

ROBERTS, with a profound sigh: Do you think that would end it?

WILLIS: Why, certainly. It'll put old Bemis in the wrong, don't you see? It'll show that instead of letting the fellow escape to go and rob him, you attacked him and took Bemis's property back from him yourself. Bemis wouldn't have a word to say. All you've got to do is to keep up a light, confident manner.

ROBERTS: But what if it shouldn't put Bemis in the wrong? What if he shouldn't say or do anything that we've counted upon, but something altogether different?

WILLIS: Well, then, you must trust to inspiration, and adapt yourself to circumstances.

ROBERTS: Wouldn't it be rather more of a joke to come out with the facts at once?

WILLIS: On you it would; and a year from now —say next Christmas—you could get the laugh on Bemis that way. But if you were to risk it now, there's no telling how he'd take it. He's so indignant he might insist upon leaving the house. But with this plan of mine—

ROBERTS, in despair: I couldn't, Willis. I don't feel light, and I don't feel confident, and I couldn't act it. If it were a simple lie—

WILLIS: Oh, lies are never simple; they require the exercise of all your ingenuity. If you want something simple, you must stick to the truth, and throw yourself on Bemis's mercy.

ROBERTS, walking up and down in great distress: I can't do it; I can't do it. It's very kind of you to think it all out for me, but— (struck by a sudden idea) Willis, why shouldn't you do it?

WILLIS: I?

ROBERTS: You are good at those things. You have so much aplomb, you know. You could carry it off, you know, first-rate.

WILLIS, as if finding a certain fascination in the idea: Well, I don't know—

ROBERTS: And I could chime in on the laugh. I think I could do that if somebody else was doing the rest.

WILLIS, after a moment of silent reflection: I should like to do it. I should like to see how old Bemis would look when I played it on him. Roberts, I will do it. Not a word! I should like to do it. Now you go on and hurry up your toilet, old fellow; you needn't mind me here. I'll be rehearsing.

MRS. ROBERTS, knocking at the door, outside: Edward, are you never coming?

ROBERTS: Yes, yes; I'll be there in a minute, my dear.

WILLIS: Yes, he'll be there. Run along back, and keep it going till we come. Roberts, I wouldn't take a thousand dollars for this chance.

ROBERTS: I'm glad you like it.

WILLIS: Like it? Of course I do. Or, no! Hold on! Wait! It won't do! No; you must take the leading part, and I'll support you, and I'll come in strong if you break down. That's the way we have got to work it. You must make the start.

ROBERTS: Couldn't you make it better, Willis? It's your idea.

WILLIS: No; they'd be sure to suspect me, and they can't suspect you of anything—you're so innocent. The illusion will be complete.

ROBERTS, *very doubtfully*: Do you think so?

WILLIS: Yes. Hurry up. Let me unbutton that collar for you.

PART THIRD.

Mrs. Roberts, surrounded by her guests, and confronting from her sofa Mr. Bemis, who still remains sunken in his arm-chair, has apparently closed an exhaustive recital of the events which have ended in his presence there. She looks round with a mixed air of self-denial and self-satisfaction to read the admiration of her listeners in their sympathetic countenances.

DR. LAWTON, *with an ironical sigh of profound impression*: Well, Mrs. Roberts, you are certainly the most lavishly hospitable of hostesses. Every one knows what delightful dinners you give; but these little dramatic episodes which you offer your guests, by way of appetizer, are certainly unique. Last year an elevator stuck in the shaft with half the company in it,[1] and this year a highway robbery, its daring punishment and its reckless repetition—what the newspapers will call "A Triple Mystery" when it gets to them—and both victims among our commensals! Really, I don't know what more we could ask of you, unless it were the foot-padded footpad himself as a commensal. If this sort of thing should become *de rigueur* in society generally, I don't know what's become of people who haven't your invention.

MRS. ROBERTS: Oh, it's all very well to make fun now, Dr. Lawton; but if you had been here when they first came in—

YOUNG MRS. BEMIS: Yes, indeed, I think so too,

Mrs. Roberts. If Mr. Bemis—Alfred, I mean—and papa hadn't been with me when you came out there to prepare us, I don't know what I should have done. I should certainly have died, or gone through the floor.

She looks fondly up into the face of her husband for approval, where he stands behind her chair, and furtively gives him her hand for pressure.

YOUNG MR. BEMIS: Somebody ought to write to the Curwens [2]—Mrs. Curwen, that is—about it.

MRS. BEMIS, *taking away her hand*: Oh yes, papa, *do* write!

LAWTON: I will, my dear. Even Mrs. Curwen, dazzling away in another sphere—hemisphere—and surrounded by cardinals and all the other celestial lights there at Rome, will be proud to exploit this new evidence of American enterprise. I can fancy the effect she will produce with it.

MRS. ROBERTS: And the Millers—what a shame they couldn't come! How excited they would have been!—that is, Mrs. Miller. Is their baby very bad, Doctor?

LAWTON: Well, vaccination is always a very serious thing—with a first child. I should say, from the way Mrs. Miller feels about it, that Miller wouldn't be able to be out for a week to come yet.

MRS. ROBERTS: Oh, how ridiculous you are, Doctor!

BEMIS, *rising feebly from his chair*: Well, now that it's all explained, Mrs. Roberts, I think I'd better go home; and if you'll kindly have them telephone for a carriage—

MRS. ROBERTS: *No*, indeed, Mr. Bemis! We shall not let you go. Why, the *idea*! You must stay and take dinner with us, just the same.

BEMIS: But in this state—

MRS. ROBERTS: Oh, never mind the *state*. You look perfectly well; and if you insist upon going I shall know that you bear a grudge against Edward for not arresting him. Wait! We can put you in perfect order in just a second. (*She flies out of the room, and then comes swooping back with a needle and thread, a fresh white necktie, a handkerchief, and a hair-brush.*) There! I can't let you go to Edward's dressing-room, because he's there himself, and the children are in mine, and we've had to put the new maid in the guest-chamber—

---

[1] A reference to *The Elevator*.

[2] The Curwens are members of the social group in which the Robertses and the Campbells figure prominently. The Millers are also friends. See *The Elevator*.

you *are* rather cramped in flats, that's true; that's the worst of them—but if you don't mind having your toilet made in public, like the King of France—

BEMIS, *entering into the spirit of it*: Not the least; but—

He laughs, and drops back into his chair.

MRS. ROBERTS, *distributing the brush to young Mr. Bemis, and the tie to his wife, and dropping upon her knees before Mr. Bemis*: Now, Mrs. Lou, you just whip off that crumpled tie and whip on the fresh one, and, *Mister* Lou, you give his hair a touch, and I'll have this torn button-hole mended before you can think.

She seizes it and begins to sew vigorously upon it.

MRS. CRASHAW: Agnes, you are the most ridiculously sensible woman in the country.

LAWTON, *standing before the group, with his arms folded and his feet well apart, in an attitude of easy admiration*: The Wounded Adonis, attended by the Loves and Graces. Familiar Pompeiian fresco.

MRS. ROBERTS, *looking around at him*: I don't see a great many Loves.

LAWTON: She ignores us, Mrs. Crashaw. And after what you've just said!

MRS. ROBERTS: Then why don't you do something?

LAWTON: The Loves *never* do anything—in frescoes. They stand round and sympathize. Besides, we are waiting to administer an anæsthetic. But what I admire in this subject even more than the activity of the Graces is the serene dignity of the Adonis. I have seen my old friend in many trying positions, but I never realized till now all the simpering absurdity, the flattered silliness, the senile coquettishness, of which his benign countenance was capable.

MRS. ROBERTS: Don't mind him a bit, Mr. Bemis; it's nothing but—

LAWTON: Pure envy. I own it.

BEMIS: All right, Lawton. Wait till—

MRS. ROBERTS, *making a final stitch, snapping off the thread, and springing to her feet, all in one*: There, have you finished, Mr. and Mrs. Lou? Well, then, take this lace handkerchief, and draw it down from his neck and pin it in his waistcoat, and you have—

LAWTON, *as Mr. Bemis rises to his feet*: A Gentleman of the Old School. Bemis, you look like a miniature of yourself by Malbone. Rather flattered, but—recognizable.

BEMIS, *with perfectly recovered gayety*: Go on, go on, Lawton. I can understand your envy. I can pity it.

LAWTON: Could you forgive Roberts for not capturing the garroter?

BEMIS: Yes, I could. I could give the garroter his liberty, and present him with an admission to the Provident Wood-yard, where he could earn an honest living for his family.

LAWTON, *compassionately*: You *are* pretty far gone, Bemis. Really, I think somebody ought to go for Roberts.

MRS. ROBERTS, *innocently*: Yes, indeed! Why, what in the world can be keeping him? (*A nursemaid enters and beckons Mrs. Roberts to the door with a glance. She runs to her; they whisper; and then Mrs. Roberts, over her shoulder*) That ridiculous great boy of mine says he can't go to sleep unless I come and kiss him goodnight.

LAWTON: Which ridiculous great boy, I wonder?—Roberts, or Campbell? But I didn't know they had gone to bed!

MRS. BEMIS: You are too bad, papa! You know it's little Neddy.

MRS. ROBERTS, *vanishing*: Oh, I don't mind his nonsense, Lou. I'll fetch them both back with me.

LAWTON, *after making a melodramatic search for concealed listeners at the doors*: Now, friends, I have a revelation to make in Mrs. Roberts's absence. I have found out the garroter—the assassin.

ALL THE OTHERS: What!

LAWTON: He has been secured—

MRS. CRASHAW, *severely*: Well, I'm very glad of it.

YOUNG BEMIS: By the police?

MRS. BEMIS, *incredulously*: Papa!

BEMIS: But there were several of them. Have they all been arrested?

LAWTON: There was only one, and none of him has been arrested.

MRS. CRASHAW: Where is he, then?

LAWTON: In this house.

MRS. CRASHAW: Now, Dr. Lawton, you and I are old friends—I shouldn't like to say *how* old—but if you don't instantly be serious, I—I'll carry my rheumatism to somebody else.

LAWTON: My *dear* Mrs. Crashaw, you know how much I prize that rheumatism of yours! I will be serious—I will be only too serious. The garroter is Mr. Roberts himself.

ALL, *horror-struck*: Oh!

LAWTON: He went out without his watch. He thought he was robbed, but he wasn't. He ran after the supposed thief, our poor friend Bemis here, and took Bemis's watch away, and brought it home for his own.

YOUNG BEMIS: Yes, but—

MRS. BEMIS: But, papa—

BEMIS: How do you know it? I can see how such a thing might happen, but—how do you know it *did?*

LAWTON: I divined it.

MRS. CRASHAW: Nonsense!

LAWTON: Very well, then, I read of just such a case in the *Advertiser* a year ago. It occurs annually—in the newspapers. And I'll tell you what, Mrs. Crashaw—Roberts found out his mistake as soon as he went to his dressing-room; and that ingenious nephew of yours, who's closeted with him there, has been trying to put him up to something—to some game.

MRS. CRASHAW: Willis has too much sense. He would know that Edward couldn't carry out any sort of game.

LAWTON: Well, then, he's getting Roberts to let *him* carry out the game.

MRS. CRASHAW: Edward couldn't do that either.

LAWTON: Very well, then, just wait till they come back. Will you leave me to deal with Campbell?

MRS. CRASHAW: What are you going to do?

YOUNG BEMIS: You mustn't forget that he got us out of the elevator, sir.

MRS. BEMIS: We might have been there yet if it hadn't been for him, papa.

MRS. CRASHAW: I shouldn't want Willis mortified.

BEMIS: Nor Mr. Roberts annoyed. We're fellow-sufferers in this business.

LAWTON: Oh, leave it to me, leave it to me! I'll spare their feelings. Don't be afraid. Ah, there they come! Now don't say anything. I'll just step into the anteroom here.

ROBERTS, *entering the room before Campbell, and shaking hands with his guests*: Ah, Mr. Bemis; Mrs. Bemis; Aunt Mary! You've heard of our comical little coincidence—our—Mr. Bemis and my—

He halts, confused, and looks around for the moral support of Willis, who follows hilariously.

WILLIS: Greatest joke on record! But I won't spoil it for you, Roberts. Go on! (*In a low voice to Roberts*) And don't look so confoundedly down in the mouth. They won't think it's a joke at all.

ROBERTS, *with galvanic lightness*: Yes, yes—such a joke! Well, you see—you see—

MRS. CRASHAW: See *what*, Edward? *Do* get it out!

WILLIS, *jollily*: Ah, ha, ha!

ROBERTS, *lugubriously*: Ah, ha, ha!

MRS. BEMIS: How funny! Ha, ha, ha!

YOUNG MR. BEMIS: Capital! capital!

BEMIS: Excellent!

WILLIS: Go on, Roberts, do! or I shall die! Ah, ha, ha!

ROBERTS, *in a low voice of consternation to Willis*: Where was I? I can't go on unless I know where I was.

WILLIS, *sotto voce to Roberts*: You weren't anywhere! For Heaven's sake, make a start!

ROBERTS, *to the others, convulsively*: Ha, ha, ha! I supposed all the time, you know, that I had been robbed, and—and—

WILLIS: Go on! *go on!*

ROBERTS, *whispering*: I can't do it!

WILLIS, *whispering*: You've got to! You're the beaver that clomb the tree. Laugh naturally, now!

ROBERTS, *with a staccato groan, which he tries to make pass for a laugh*: And then I ran after the man—

He stops, and regards Mr. Bemis with a ghastly stare.

MRS. CRASHAW: What is the matter with you, Edward? Are you sick?

WILLIS: Sick? No! Can't you see that he can't get over the joke of the thing? It's killing him. (*To Roberts*) Brace up, old man! You're doing it splendidly.

ROBERTS, *hopelessly*: And then the other man—the man that had robbed me—the man that I had pursued—ugh!

WILLIS: Well, it *is* too much for him. I shall have to tell it myself, I see.

ROBERTS, *making a wild effort to command himself*: And so—so—this man—man—ma—

WILLIS: Oh, good Lord—(*Dr. Lawton suddenly appears from the anteroom and confronts him.*) Oh, the devil!

LAWTON, *folding his arms, and fixing his eyes upon him*: Which means that you forgot I was coming.

WILLIS: Doctor, you read a man's symptoms at a glance.

LAWTON: Yes; and I can see that you are in a bad way, Mr. Campbell.

WILLIS: Why don't you advertise, Doctor? Patients need only enclose a lock of their hair, and the color of their eyes, with one dollar to pay the cost of materials, which will be sent, with full directions for treatment, by return mail. Seventh son of a seventh son.

LAWTON: Ah, don't try to jest it away, my poor friend. This is one of those obscure diseases of the heart—induration of the pericardium—which, if not taken in time, result in deceitfulness above all things, and desperate wickedness.

WILLIS: Look here, Dr. Lawton, what are you up to?

LAWTON: Look here, Mr. Campbell, what is your little game?

WILLIS: I don't know what you're up to.

He shrugs his shoulders and walks up the room.

LAWTON, *shrugging his shoulders and walking up the room abreast of Campbell*: I don't know what your little game is.

They return together, and stop, confronting each other.

WILLIS: But if you think I'm going to give myself away—

LAWTON: If you suppose I'm going to take you at your own figure—

They walk up the room together, and return as before.

WILLIS: Mrs. Bemis, what is this unnatural parent of yours after?

MRS. BEMIS, *tittering*: Oh, I'm sure I can't tell.

WILLIS: Aunt Mary, you used to be a friend of mine. Can't you give me some sort of clew?

MRS. CRASHAW: I should be ashamed of you, Willis, if you accepted anybody's help.

WILLIS, *sighing*: Well, this is pretty hard on an orphan. Here I come to join a company of friends at the fireside of a burgled brother-in-law, and I find myself in a nest of conspirators. (*Suddenly, after a moment*) Oh, I understand. Why, I ought to have seen at once. But no matter—it's just as well. I'm sure that we shall hear Dr. Lawton leniently, and make allowance for his well-known foible. Roberts is bound by the laws of hospitality, and Mr. Bemis is the father-in-law of his daughter.

MRS. BEMIS, *in serious dismay*: Why, Mr. Campbell, what do you mean?

WILLIS: Simply that the mystery is solved—the double garroter is discovered. I'm sorry for you, Mrs. Bemis; and no one will wish to deal harshly with your father when he confesses that it was he who robbed Mr. Roberts and Mr. Bemis. All that they ask is to have their watches back. Go on, Doctor! How will that do, Aunt Mary, for a little flyer?

MRS. CRASHAW: Willis, I declare I never saw anybody like you!

She embraces him with joyous pride.

ROBERTS, *coming forward, anxiously*: But, my dear Willis—

WILLIS, *clapping his hand over his mouth, and leading him back to his place*: We can't let you talk now. I've doubt you'll be considerate, and all that, but Dr. Lawton has the floor. Go on, Doctor! Free your mind! Don't be afraid of telling the whole truth! It will be better for you in the end.

He rubs his hands gleefully, and then thrusting the points of them into his waistcoat-pockets, stands beaming triumphantly upon Lawton.

LAWTON: Do you think so? (*With well-affected trepidation*) Well, friends, if I must confess this—this—

WILLIS: High-handed outrage. Go on.

LAWTON: I suppose I must. I shall not expect mercy for myself; perhaps you'll say that, as an old and hardened offender, I don't deserve it. But I had an accomplice—a young man very respectably connected, and who, whatever his previous life may have been, had managed to keep a good reputation; a young man a little apt to be misled by overweening vanity and the ill-advised flattery of his friends; but I hope that neither of you gentlemen will be hard upon him, but will consider his youth, and perhaps his congenital moral and intellectual deficiencies, even when you find your watches—on Mr. Campbell's person. (*He leans forward, rubbing his hands, and smiling upon Campbell.*) How will that do, Mr. Campbell, for a flyer?

WILLIS, *turning to Mrs. Crashaw*: One ahead, Aunt Mary?

LAWTON, *clasping him by the hand*: No, generous youth—even!

They shake hands, clapping each other on the back with their lefts, and joining in the general laugh.

BEMIS, *coming forward, jovially*: Well, now, I gladly forgive you both—or whoever did rob me—if you'll only give me back my watch.

WILLIS: I haven't got your watch.

LAWTON: Nor I.

ROBERTS, *rather faintly, and coming reluctantly forward*: I—I have it, Mr. Bemis. (*He produces it from one waistcoat-pocket and hands it to Bemis. Then visiting the other*) And what's worse, I have my own. I don't know how I can ever explain it, or atone to you for my extraordinary behavior. Willis thought you might finally see it as a joke, and I've done my best to pass it off lightly—

WILLIS: And you succeeded. You had all the lightness of a sick hippopotamus.

ROBERTS: I'm afraid so. I'll have the chain mended, of course. But when I went out this evening I left my watch on my dressing-table, and when you struck against me in the Common I missed it, and supposed I had been robbed, and I ran after you and took yours—

WILLIS: Being a man of the most violent temper and the most desperate courage—

ROBERTS: But I hope, my dear sir, that I didn't hurt you seriously?

BEMIS: Not at all—not the least. (Shaking him cordially by both hands) I'm all right. Mrs. Roberts has healed all my wounds with her skilful needle; I've got on one of your best neckties, and this lace handkerchief of your wife's, which I'm going to keep for a souvenir of the most extraordinary adventure of my life—

LAWTON: Oh, it's an old newspaper story, Bemis, I tell you.

WILLIS: Well, Aunt Mary, I wish Agnes were here now to see Roberts in his character of moral hero. He "done" it with his little hatchet, but he waited to make sure that Bushrod was all right before he owned up.

MRS. ROBERTS, appearing: Who, Willis?

WILLIS: A very great and good man—George Washington.

MRS. ROBERTS: I thought you meant Edward.

WILLIS: Well, I don't suppose there is much difference.

MRS. CRASHAW: The robber has been caught, Agnes.

MRS. ROBERTS: Caught? Nonsense! You don't mean it! How can you trifle with such a subject? I know you are joking! Who is it?

YOUNG BEMIS: You never could guess—

MRS. BEMIS: Never in the world!

MRS. ROBERTS: I don't wish to. But oh, Mr. Bemis, I've just come from my own children, and you must be merciful to his family!

BEMIS: For your sake, dear lady, I will.

BELLA, between the portières: Dinner is ready, Mrs. Roberts.

MRS. ROBERTS, passing her hand through Mr. Bemis's arm: Oh, then you must go in with me, and tell me all about it.

The Mouse Trap

[1886]

When Howells wrote this play, he was obviously using the word mousetrap, as the Elizabethans sometimes used it, to mean a device intended to catch a person suspected of scheming. There is no mouse and no trap, only poor Campbell, who is caught by one of his bright ideas and held fast. Like the imaginary mouse, he protests, flounders wildly in the limited space of the drawing room and is clearly stunned by the illogical actions of the women. They, on the other hand, although somewhat hysterical, understand the situation completely and escape whenever they wish, leaving Campbell still confused and still caught.

The part of the play that is haunted by the ghostly mouse is pure farce, building both on the awkward situation in which the ladies find themselves and on the "mouse" stories that they tell to make their situation appear even more horrible. The beginning and the end of the play suggest a comedy of manners with a theme as old as comedy: man's ever unsuccessful attempt to understand woman. Campbell's wit and logic are impotent against an aroused Mrs. Somers. When he defers to an expedient action, however, he only makes her appear ridiculous before herself. Then he is faced with the problem of allowing and even helping her to talk herself out of a rather silly position in a manner which will be wholly agreeable to herself. If it were not for the finesse and true wisdom of Mrs. Somers, he would fail; for the schemer must be exposed for what he is, and the unfair advantage which he pre-empted must be turned upon him in his suffering. Effective here is Howells' portrayal of a well-bred woman's ability to see that she has been too severe, to evade completely the point in question, and to satisfy the man she has abused without apologizing to him.

Although evidence presented here must be only partial, *The Mouse Trap* enjoyed a wide popularity among amateur theatrical groups in America and was performed professionally both here and in England. Amateur productions are, in the main, quite untraceable, but occasional fly-leaf comments in copies of *The Mouse Trap*—"New York, Aug. 16, 1891 'To Jane—compliments of Willis Campbell' F. P. H., (a picture of a mouse)"—are perhaps some indication of the current popularity of the play for charity shows and church parlor dramatics. Odell lists two performances of Howells' farce in his *Annals of the New York Stage*: a benefit for the Greenpoint YMCA during the 1887–88 theater season (XIII, 601) and an actors' fund matinee on April 11, 1894 (XV, 589). Odell suggested Wallack's as the place of the second production, but a Howells letter to Sally Norton (April 10, 1894, Harvard Library) inviting her to the performance mentions the Star Theatre and the Lyceum Theatre Company. Elsewhere in America *The Mouse Trap* was performed by the Chicago School of Acting, November 21, 1895 (information from the files of Professor Napier Wilt, University of Chicago); and in a letter to his sister Aurelia, December 29, 1901 (Harvard Library), Howells mentioned that the Carnegie Lyceum was to perform the play for a charity.

There is evidence, too, that this drama was performed a number of times in England. On February 16, 1895 (Harvard Library), Howells had a request from a certain J. Percival Wheatley of Carlisle, England, to perform the play in public. Although the records in the Lord Chamberlain's Office show only one performance—Theatre Royal in Edinburgh, 1897—in "A Letter to the Publisher," in *Minor Dramas*, Howells states that *The Mouse Trap* "has been twice played in London for great and dignified charities, with an all-star cast, including such planetary splendors as Miss Terry and Mrs. Kendal, the last of whom, indeed, especially adapted it to the appreciation of the British public." Actually it was not quite so simple as this. When Howells heard that *The Mouse Trap* had been performed without his permission, he sent a severe letter to Madge Kendal, who replied that the performance had been for charity and that she had not thought she needed permission (letter in Harvard Library, n.d.). She went on to say that although she had had to "cut it ruthlessly," it had been a most successful performance with Genevieve Ward, Beerbohm Tree, Ellen Terry, and herself, and that many others had done the play since their performance. It is difficult to say when Mrs. Kendal's production took place; but probably when Howells next went to England he met her, and in mentioning the fact in a letter to his wife (April 24, 1904, *Life in Letters*, II, 198) he explained: "Madge Kendal and I wept tears of forgiveness on each other's shoulders; and she told me all about *The Mouse Trap*."

The Mouse Trap[1]

In her drawing-room, Mrs. Amy Somers, young, pretty, stylish, in the last evanescent traces of widowhood, stands confronting Mr. Willis Campbell. She has a newspaper in her hand, folded to the width of a single column, which she extends towards him with an effect of indignant menace.

MRS. SOMERS: Then you acknowledge that it is yours?

CAMPBELL: I acknowledge that I made a speech before the legislative committee on behalf of the anti-suffragists. You knew I was going to do that. I don't know how they've reported it.

MRS. SOMERS, *with severity*: Very well, then; I will read it. "Willis Campbell, Esq., was next heard on behalf of the petitioners. He touched briefly upon the fact that the suffrage was evidently not desired by the vast majority of educated women."

CAMPBELL: You've always said they didn't want it.

MRS. SOMERS: That is not the point. (*Reading*) "And many of them would feel it an onerous burden, and not a privilege."

CAMPBELL: Well, didn't you—

MRS. SOMERS: Don't interrupt! (*Reading*) "Which would compel them, at the cost of serious sacrifices, to contend at the polls with the ignorant classes who would be sure to exercise the right if conferred."

CAMPBELL: That was your own argument, Amy. They're almost your own words.

MRS. SOMERS: That isn't what I object to. (*Reading*) "Mr. Campbell then referred in a more humorous strain to the argument, frequently used by the suffragists, that every tax-payer should have the right to vote. He said that he objected to this, because it implied that non-tax-payers should not have the right to vote, which would deprive of the suffrage a large body of adoptive citizens, who voted at all the elections with great promptness and assiduity. He thought the exemption of women from some duties required of men by the State fairly offset the loss of the ballot in their case, and that until we were prepared to send ladies to battle we ought not to oblige them to go to the polls. Some skirmishing ensued between Mr. Campbell and Mr. Willington, on the part of the suffragists, the latter gentleman affirming that in great crises of the world's history women had shown as much courage as men, and the former contending that this did not at all affect his position, since the courage of women was in high degree a moral courage,[2] which was not evoked by the ordinary conditions of peace or war, but required the imminence of some extraordinary, some vital emergency."

CAMPBELL: Well, what do you object to in all that?

MRS. SOMERS, *tossing the paper on the table, and confronting him with her head lifted and her hands clasped upon her left side*: Everything! It is an insult to women.

CAMPBELL: *Woman*, you mean. I don't think *women* would mind it. Who's been talking to you, Amy?

MRS. SOMERS: Nobody. It doesn't matter who's been talking to me. That is not the question.

CAMPBELL: It's the question I asked.

MRS. SOMERS: It isn't the question *I* asked. I wish simply to know what you mean by that speech.

CAMPBELL: I wish you knew how pretty you look in that dress. (*Mrs. Somers involuntarily glances down at the skirt of it on either side, and rearranges it a little, folding her hands again as before.*) But perhaps you do.

MRS. SOMERS, *with dignity*: Will you answer my question?

CAMPBELL: Certainly. I meant what I said.

MRS. SOMERS: Oh, you did! Very well, then! When a woman stands by the bedside of her sick child, and risks her life from contagion, what kind of courage do you call that?

CAMPBELL: Moral.

---

1 The text used here is the Harper & Brothers 1894 edition. Title: see *Hamlet,* III, 2:247.

2 Compare Campbell's thoughts with Mark Twain's ideas in "The Temperance Crusade and Woman's Rights," 1873.

MRS. SOMERS: And when she remains in a burning building or a sinking ship—as they often do—and perishes, while her child is saved, what kind of courage is it?

CAMPBELL: Moral.

MRS. SOMERS: When she seizes an axe and defends her little ones against a bear or a wolf that's just bursting in the cabin door, what kind of courage does she show?

CAMPBELL: Moral.

MRS. SOMERS: Or when her babe crawls up the track, and she snatches it from the very jaws of the cow-catcher—

CAMPBELL: Oh, hold on, now, Amy! Be fair! It's the engineer who does that: he runs along the side of the locomotive, and catches the smiling infant up, and lays it in the mother's arms as the train thunders by. His name is usually Hank Rollins. The mother is always paralyzed with terror.

MRS. SOMERS: Of course she is. But in those other cases how does her courage differ from a man's? If hers is always moral, what kind of courage does a man show when he faces the cannon?

CAMPBELL: Immoral. Come, Amy, are you trying to prove that women are braver than men? Well, they are. I never was in any danger yet that I didn't wish I was a woman, for then I should have the courage to face it, or else I could turn and run without disgrace. All that I said in that speech was that women haven't so much nerve as men.

MRS. SOMERS: They have more.

CAMPBELL: Nerves—yes.

MRS. SOMERS: No, nerve. Take Dr. Cissy Gay, that little, slender, delicate sensitive thing; what do you suppose she went through when she was studying medicine, and walking the hospitals, and all those disgusting things? And Mrs. J. Plunkett Harmon: do you mean to say that *she* has no nerve, facing all sorts of audiences, on the platform, everywhere? Or Rev. Lily Barber, living down all that ridicule, and going quietly on in her work—

CAMPBELL: Oh, *they've* been talking to you.

MRS. SOMERS: They have *not*! And if they have, Dr. Gay is as much opposed to suffrage as you are.

CAMPBELL: As *I*? Aren't you opposed to it too?

MRS. SOMERS: Of course I am. Or I was till you made that speech.

CAMPBELL: It wasn't exactly intended to convert you.

MRS. SOMERS: It has placed me in a false position. Everybody knows, or the same as knows, that we're engaged—

CAMPBELL: Well, *I'm* not ashamed of it, Amy.

MRS. SOMERS, *severely*: No matter! And now it will look as if I had no ideas of my own, and was just swayed about any way by you. A woman is despicable that joins with men in ridiculing women.

CAMPBELL: Who's been saying that?

MRS. SOMERS: No one. It doesn't matter who's been saying it. Mrs. Mervane has been saying it.

CAMPBELL: Mrs. Mervane?

MRS. SOMERS: Yes, Mrs. Mervane, that you're always praising and admiring so for her good sense and her right ideas. Didn't you say she wrote as logically and forcibly as a man?

CAMPBELL: Yes, I did.

MRS. SOMERS: Very well, then, she says that if anything could turn her in favor of suffrage, it is that speech of yours. She says it's a subtle attack upon the whole sex.

CAMPBELL: Well, I give it up! You are all alike. You take everything personally, in the first place, and then you say it's an attack on all women. Couldn't I make this right by publishing a card to acknowledge your physical courage before the whole community, Amy? Then your friends would have to say that I had recognized the pluck of universal womanhood.

MRS. SOMERS: No, sir; you can't make it right now. And I'm sorry, sorry, *sorry* I signed the anti-suffrage petition. Nothing will ever teach men to appreciate women till women practically assert themselves.

CAMPBELL: That sounds very much like another quotation, Amy.

MRS. SOMERS: And they must expect to be treated as cowards till they show themselves heroes. And they must first of all have the ballot.

CAMPBELL: Oh!

MRS. SOMERS: Yes. Then, and not till then, men will acknowledge their equality in all that is admirable in both. Then there will be no more puling insolence about moral courage and vital emergencies to evoke it.

CAMPBELL: I don't see the steps to this conclusion, but the master-mind of Mrs. J. Plunkett Harmon reaches conclusions at a bound.

MRS. SOMERS: It *wasn't* Mrs. Harmon.

CAMPBELL: Oh, well, Rev. Lily Barber, then. You needn't tell me *you* originated that stuff, Amy. But I submit for the present. Think it over, my dear, and when I come back to-morrow—

MRS. SOMERS: Perhaps you had better not come back to-morrow.

CAMPBELL: Why?

MRS. SOMERS: Because—because I'm afraid we are not in sympathy. Because if you thought that I needed some vital emergency to make me show that I was ready to die for you any moment—

CAMPBELL: *Die* for me? I want you to live for me, Amy.

MRS. SOMERS: —and the emergency never came, you would despise me.

CAMPBELL: Never!

MRS. SOMERS: If you have such a low opinion of women generally—

CAMPBELL: *I* a low opinion of women!

MRS. SOMERS: You said they were cowards.

CAMPBELL: I didn't say they were cowards. And if I seemed to say so, it was my misfortune. I honestly and truly think, Amy, that when a woman is roused, she isn't afraid of anything in heaven or on—

He stops abruptly, and looks towards the corner of the room.

MRS. SOMERS: What is it?

CAMPBELL: Oh, nothing. I thought I saw a mouse.

MRS. SOMERS: A mouse! (*She flings herself upon him, and clutches him with convulsive energy. Then suddenly freeing him, she leaps upon a chair, and stoops over to hold her train from the floor.*) Oh, drive it out, drive it *out!* Don't *kill* it. Oh—e-e-e-e! *Drive* it out! Oh, what shall I do? Oh, Willis, love, jump on a chair! Oh, horrid little dreadful reptile! Oh, *drive* it out! (*In uttering these appeals Mrs. Somers alternately looses her hold upon her train in order to clasp her face in her hands, and then uncovers her face to seize her train.*) Oh, is it *gone?* Come here, Willis, and let me hold your hand! Or no! Drive it, drive it, *drive it out!*

CAMPBELL, *going about the room in deliberate examination*: I can't find it. I guess it's gone into its hole again.

MRS. SOMERS: No, it hasn't! It hasn't got any hole here. It must have come in from somewhere else. Oh, I *hope* I shall have a little wisdom *some* time, and never, never, never have cake and wine brought into the drawing-room again, no matter *how* faint with walking any one is. Of course it was the smell of the fruit and crumbs attracted it; and they might just as well take the horse-cars, but they said they had walked all the way to get me to sign the suffrage petition, and when I said

I'd signed the anti-suffrage, of course I had to offer them something; I couldn't do less. Have you driven it out?

CAMPBELL: I've done my best. But I can't find it, and I can't drive it out till I *do* find it.

MRS. SOMERS: It's run into the fire-place. Rattle the tongs! (*Campbell goes to the fire-place and rattles the tongs against the shovel, Mrs. Somers meanwhile covering her face.*) Ow—ugh—e-e-e-e! Is it gone?

She uncovers her eyes.

CAMPBELL: It never was there.

MRS. SOMERS: Yes, it was, Willis. Don't tell me it wasn't! Where else was it if it wasn't there? Look under that book-table!

CAMPBELL: Which one?

MRS. SOMERS: That one with the shelf coming down almost to the carpet. Poke under it with the poker! (*As Campbell obeys, she again hides her face.*) U-u-u-gh! Is it gone *now?*

CAMPBELL: It wasn't there.

MRS. SOMERS: Poke hard! Bang against the mop-board! Bang!

CAMPBELL, *poking and banging*: There! I tell you it never was there.

MRS. SOMERS, *uncovering her face*: Oh, what shall I do? It must be somewhere in the room, and I never can breathe till you've found it. Bang again!

CAMPBELL: Nonsense! It's gone long ago. Do you suppose a mouse of any presence of mind or self-respect would stay here after all this uproar?

He restores the tongs to their stand with a clash.

MRS. SOMERS, *responsive to the clash*: Ow!

CAMPBELL, *advancing towards her and extending his hand*: Come, Amy; get down now. I must be going.

MRS. SOMERS, *in horror*: Get down? Going?

CAMPBELL: Certainly. I can't stay here all day. I've got to follow that mouse out into the street and have him arrested. It's a public duty.

MRS. SOMERS: Don't throw ridicule on it! (*After a moment*) You know I can't let you go till I've seen that mouse leave this room. Go all round, and stamp in the corners. (*She covers her face again.*) Ugh!

CAMPBELL: How are you going to see him leave the room if you won't look? He's left long ago. I wouldn't stay if I was a mouse. And I've got to go, anyway.

MRS. SOMERS, *uncovering her face*: No! I beg, I *command* you to stay, or I shall never get out of this room alive. You *know* I sha'n't. (*A ring at the street door is heard.*) Oh, *dear,* what shall I do? I've told Jane I would see anybody that called, and now I daren't step my foot to the floor! What *shall* I do?

CAMPBELL, *with authority*: You must get down. There's no mouse here, I tell you; and if people come and find you standing on a chair in your drawing-room, what will they think?

MRS. SOMERS: I can kneel on it. (*She drops to her knees on the chair.*) There!

CAMPBELL: That's no better. It's worse.

MRS. SOMERS, *listening to the party at the door below, which the maid has opened*: 'Sh! I want to make out who it is. 'Sh! Yes—it is! (*After listening*) Yes; it's Mrs. Miller and Lou Bemis and Mrs. Curwen! I don't see how they happen to come together, for Mrs. Miller and Mrs. Curwen perfectly hate each other. Oh yes! I know! They're all on the way to Mrs. Ransom's reception,[1] he's showing his pictures and some of her things— horrid daubs; I don't see how she can have the face—and they've met here by accident. 'Sh! She's showing them into the reception-room. Yes, that's quite right. (*Mrs. Somers delivers these sentences in a piercing whisper of extreme volubility.*) Now, as soon as she brings up their cards, I'll say I'm not at all well—that I'm engaged— just going out. No, that won't do. I *must* be sick. Anything else would be perfectly insulting after saying that I was at home; and Jane has got to go back and tell them she forgot that I had gone to bed with a severe headache. (*As Jane appears at the drawing-room door, and falters at sight of Mrs. Somers kneeling on her chair, that lady beckons her to her, frowning, shaking her head, and pressing her finger on her lip to enforce silence, and takes the cards from her, while she continues in whisper*) Yes. All right, Jane! Go straight back and tell them you forgot I had gone to bed with a perfectly blinding headache; and don't let another soul into the house. Mr. Campbell saw a mouse, and I can't get down till he's caught it. Go!

JANE, *after a moment of petrifaction*: A mouse! In the room, here? Oh, my goodness gracious me!

She leaps upon the chair next to Mrs. Somers, who again springs to her feet.

MRS. SOMERS: Did you *see* it? Oh, e-e-e-e!

JANE: W-o-o-o-o! I don't know! Where was it? Oh yes, I thought—

[1] A reference to characters in *The Register.*

They clutch each other convulsively, and blend their cries, at the sound of which the ladies in the reception-room below come flocking up-stairs into the drawing-room.

THE LADIES, *at sight of Mrs. Somers and her servant*: What is it? what is it?

MRS. SOMERS: Oh, there's a *mouse* in the room! Oh, jump on chairs!

MRS. MILLER, *vaulting into the middle of the sofa*: A mouse!

MRS. LOU BEMIS, *alighting upon a slight reception-chair*: Oh, not in *this* room, Mrs. Somers! Don't say it!

MRS. CURWEN, *with a laugh of mingled terror and enjoyment, from the top of the table where she finds herself*: Where is it?

MRS. SOMERS: I don't know. I didn't see it. But, oh! it's here somewhere. Mr. Campbell saw it, and Jane did when she came up with your cards, and he's been trying to drive it out, but he can't even *budge* it; and—

CAMPBELL, *desperately*: Ladies, there isn't any mouse here! I've been racketing round here with the shovel and tongs all over the room, and the mouse is gone. You can depend upon that. You're as safe here as you would be in your own rooms.

MRS. SOMERS: How can you say such a thing? No, I won't be responsible if anything happens. The mouse is in this room. No one has seen it go out, and it's here still.

MRS. BEMIS, *balancing herself with difficulty on her chair*: Oh dear! how tippy it is! I'm sure it's going to break.

MRS. CURWEN: Get up here with me, Mrs. Bemis. We can protect each other.

MRS. MILLER: You would both fall off. Better come here on the sofa, Mrs. Bemis.

MRS. CURWEN: The mouse could run up that ottoman sofa as easily as the ground.

MRS. MILLER, *covering her face*: Oh, how can you say such a thing?

MRS. BEMIS: Oh, I know I'm going to fall!

MRS. SOMERS: Willis, for shame! Help her!

CAMPBELL: But how—how can I help—

MRS. SOMERS: Get her another chair.

CAMPBELL: Oh!

He pushes a large arm-chair towards Mrs. Bemis, who leaps into it with a wild cry, spurning the reception-chair half across the room in her flight.

MRS. BEMIS: Oh, thank you, thank you, Mr Campbell! Oh, I shall always bless you!

MRS. CURWEN: Yes, you have saved all our lives. Where there's a man, I don't care for a thousand mice.

MRS. MILLER: Oh, how very frank!

MRS. CURWEN: Yes, I'm nothing if not open-minded.

CAMPBELL, *surveying her with amusement and interest*: I don't believe you're very much scared.

MRS. BEMIS: Oh yes, she is, Mr. Campbell. She keeps up that way, and then the first thing she faints.[1]

MRS. CURWEN: Not on centre-tables, my dear; there isn't room.

CAMPBELL, *with increasing fascination*: Why don't you get down, and set the rest an example of courage?

MRS. CURWEN: I prefer to set the example here: it's safer.

CAMPBELL: You look like the statue of some goddess on her altar—or saint—

MRS. CURWEN: Thank you. If you will say victim, I will agree with you. Say Iphigenia. But the others are too much. I draw the line at goddesses and saints.

CAMPBELL: And *you're* afraid of mice, too?

MRS. CURWEN: To be sure I am.

CAMPBELL: Well, there is no mouse down here —nothing but a miserable man. Now, will you get down?

MRS. SOMERS: Mrs. Curwen, don't think of it! He's just *saying* it. The mouse *is* there. (*To Campbell*) You are placing us all in a very ridiculous position.

CAMPBELL: I am sorry for that; I am, indeed. I give you my word of honor that I don't believe there's any mouse in the room.

MRS. SOMERS: Jane just saw it.

CAMPBELL: She *thought* she saw it, but I don't think she did. A lion would have been scared out by this time.

A ring at the door is heard.

MRS. SOMERS: There, Jane, there's some one ringing! You must go to the door.

JANE, *throwing her apron over her head*: Oh, please, Mrs. Somers, I can't go! I'm so afraid of mice!

MRS. SOMERS: Nonsense! you *must* go. It's perfectly ridiculous your pretending not.

JANE: Oh, I couldn't, Mrs. Somers! I was always so from a child. I can't bear 'em.

MRS. SOMERS: This is disgraceful! Do you mean

[1] A reference to action in *The Elevator*.

to say that you won't do what I ask you? Very well, then; you can *go!* You needn't stay the week out; I will pay you, and you go at once. Do you understand?

JANE: Yes, I do, and I'd be glad to go this very minute, but I don't dare to get down.

MRS. SOMERS: But why shouldn't you get down? There isn't the least danger. Is there any danger now, Mr. Campbell?

CAMPBELL: Not the least in the world. Mouse gone long ago.

MRS. SOMERS: There!

JANE: I can't help it. There are so many in the dining-room—

MRS. SOMERS: In *my* dining-room? Oh, my goodness! why didn't you tell me before?

JANE: And one ran right over my foot.

MRS. SOMERS: Your foot? Oh, I wonder that you live to tell it! Why haven't you put traps? Where's the cat?

JANE: The cook's spoiled the cat, feeding it so much.

MRS. MILLER: Yes, that's the worst of cooks: they always spoil cats.

MRS. BEMIS: They overfeed them.

MRS. MILLER: And then, of course, the cats are worth nothing as mousers. I had a cat—

The bell sounds again.

MRS. SOMERS: There! Some one *must* go.

CAMPBELL: Why, *I'll* go to the door.

MRS. SOMERS: And leave *us* here? Never! How can you propose such a thing? If you dare to go, I shall die. Don't think of such a thing.

JANE: The cook will go, if they keep ringing. Oh! ugh! hu, hu! When ever shall I get out of this?

MRS. SOMERS: Stop crying, Jane! Be calm! You're perfectly safe. You may be glad it's no worse. 'Sh! There's the cook going to the door at last. Who can it be? Listen!

JANE, *clutching Mrs. Somers*: Oh! ugh! Wo-o-o-o!

ALL THE LADIES: E-e-e-e!

MRS. SOMERS: What's the *matter*, Jane? Let me go! *What's* the matter?

JANE: Oh, I thought I was falling—right down in among it!

MRS. AGNES ROBERTS, *calling up from below*: What in the world *is* it, Amy?

CAMPBELL: Oh, my prophetic soul, my sister!

MRS. SOMERS, *shouting*: Is that you, Agnes? Don't come up! Don't come up, for your *life!*

Don't come up, unless you wish to perish instantly. Oh, it's dreadful, your coming now. Keep away! Go right straight out of the house, unless you wish to fling your life away.

THE OTHER LADIES: Don't come! Don't come! Keep away! It will do no good.

MRS. ROBERTS, *mounting the stairs, as if lured to her doom by an irresistible fascination*: Not come? Keep away? Who's talking? What is it? Oh, *Amy*, what is it? (*As she reaches the stair-landing space before the drawing-room and looks in, where Campbell stands in the middle of the floor with his hands in his pockets and despair in his face*) You here, Willis? What are you doing? What is it? (*Her eye wanders to the ladies trembling in their several refuges, and a dawning apprehension makes itself seen in her face.*) What is— Oh, it is—it isn't—it isn't a—mouse! Oh, *Amy*! Amy! Amy! Oh, how *could* you let me come right into the room with it? Oh, I never can forgive you! I thought it was somebody getting killed. Oh, why didn't you *tell* me it was a mouse?

She alights on the piano-stool, and keeps it from rocking by staying herself with one hand on the piano-top.

CAMPBELL: Now look here, Agnes—

MRS. ROBERTS: Hush! Don't speak to me, Willis! You unnatural, cruel, heartless— Why did *you* let me come in? I wonder at you, Willis! If you had been *half* the brother you ought to be— Oh dear, dear! I know how you will go away and laugh now, and tell everybody. I suppose you think it corroborates that silly speech of yours before the legislative committee that's wounded all your best friends so, and that I've been talking myself perfectly dumb defending you about. (*Mrs. Roberts unconsciously gives a little push for emphasis, and the stool revolves with her.*) E-e-e-e! Oh, Amy, how can you have one of these old-fashioned, horrid, whirling things, fit for nothing but boarding-house parlors!

MRS. SOMERS, *with just pique*: I'm very sorry you don't like my piano-stool, Agnes. I keep it because it was my poor mother's; but if you'll give me due notice another time, I'll try to have a different—

MRS. ROBERTS, *bursting into tears*: Oh, don't say another word, Amy dear! I'm so ashamed of myself that I can hardly breathe now!

CAMPBELL: And I'm ashamed of you too, Agnes! Get down off that stool, and behave yourself like a sensible woman. (*He goes towards her as if to lift her down.*) The mouse is gone long

ago. And if it was here, it wouldn't bite you.

MRS. ROBERTS, *repelling him with one hand while she clings insecurely to the piano with the other*: Bite? Do you suppose I care for a mouse's biting, Willis? I wouldn't care for the bite of an elephant. It's the *idea*. Can't you understand?

THE OTHER LADIES: Oh yes, it's the idea.

MRS. SOMERS: Yes, I told him in the first place, Agnes, that it was the *idea* of a mouse.

MRS. CURWEN: It's the innate repugnance.

CAMPBELL: It's the enmity put between the mouse that tempted Eve and the woman—

MRS. ROBERTS: Don't be—sacrilegious, Willis! Don't, for your own sake!

MRS. SOMERS: Yes, it's very easy to make fun of the Bible.

MRS. ROBERTS: Or woman. And the wit is equally contemptible in either case.

MRS. MILLER: Other animals feel about mice just as we do. I was reading only the other day of an elephant—your mentioning an elephant reminded me of it, Mrs.—

MRS. ROBERTS: Oh!

THE OTHER LADIES: E-e-e-e!

MRS. SOMERS: What is it?

MRS. ROBERTS: Nothing. I thought I was going to fall. Go on, Mrs. Miller.

MRS. MILLER: Oh, it's merely that the elephant was asleep, and a mouse ran up its trunk—

ALL THE LADIES: Horrors!

MRS. MILLER: And the poor creature sprang up in the greatest alarm, and bellowed till it woke the whole menagerie. It simply shows that it isn't because women are nervously constituted that they're afraid of mice, for the nervous organism of an elephant—

MRS. SOMERS: The first time I went to Europe I found a mouse in one of *my* trunks. It was a steamer trunk, that you push under the berth, and I've perfectly loathed them ever since.

MRS. BEMIS: Once in a farm-house where we were staying the summer, a mouse ran right across the table.

ALL THE LADIES: Oh!

MRS. CURWEN: One morning I found one in the bath-tub.

ALL THE LADIES: *Oh*, Mrs. Curwen!

MRS. CURWEN: We'd heard it scrambling round all night. It was stone-dead.

ALL THE LADIES: Hideous!

CAMPBELL: Why, bless my soul! if the mouse was dead—

MRS. SOMERS: Then it was ten times as bad as

if it was alive. Can't you understand? It's the *idea*. But, oh, don't let's talk of it any more, ladies! Let's talk of something else. Agnes, are you going to Mrs. Ransom's?

MRS. ROBERTS: I've been. Nearly everybody's coming away.

MRS. MILLER: Why, what time is it, Mrs. Somers?

MRS. SOMERS: I don't know.

CAMPBELL, *looking at his watch*: It's ten minutes of six, and I've missed my appointment.

MRS. CURWEN: And if we don't go now we shall miss the reception.

MRS. BEMIS: Papa was very particular I should go, because he couldn't.

MRS. MILLER: We must go at once.

MRS. SOMERS: Oh, I'm so sorry! Jane, go down with the ladies.

JANE: Oh, *please*, Mrs. Somers!

MRS. MILLER: But how are we to go? We are imprisoned here. We cannot get away. You must do something.

MRS. CURWEN: It is your house, Mrs. Somers. You are responsible.

MRS. SOMERS: But what can I do? I can't get down myself. And if I did, what good would it do?

MRS. ROBERTS: For shame, Willis, to laugh!

CAMPBELL: I wasn't laughing. I was merely smiling aloud.

MRS. ROBERTS: It's the same thing. You ought to think of something.

MRS. SOMERS: Oh yes, do, Willis. Think of something for my—for goodness' sake, and I will always thank you. You're so ingenious.

CAMPBELL: Well, in the first place, I don't believe there's any mouse in the room.

MRS. SOMERS: That is nonsense; Jane saw it. Is that all your ingenuity amounts to?

MRS. ROBERTS, *electrically*: Amy, I have an idea!

MRS. SOMERS: Oh, Agnes! How *like* you!

MRS. ROBERTS: Not at all. It's the simplest thing in the world. It's the only way. And no thanks to Willis, either.

ALL THE LADIES: Well? Well? Well?

MRS. ROBERTS: It's just this: all make a rush, one after another, and the rest scream. And Willis must keep beating the floor.

MRS. SOMERS: How perfectly magnificent! Well, Agnes, you *have* got your wits about you! It is the very thing! Now, Mrs. Curwen, if you will jump down and make a rush—

MRS. CURWEN: It's for you to make the rush first, Mrs. Somers. You are the hostess.

MRS. SOMERS: Yes, but I'm not going, don't you see? I've sent my card to Mrs. Ransom.

MRS. CURWEN: Then, Mrs. Miller, will you, please—

MRS. MILLER: Mrs. Bemis is nearest the door. I think she will wish to start first.

MRS. BEMIS: No; I will wait for the rest.

MRS. SOMERS: That is a good idea. They ought to all rush together, not one after another. Don't you think so, Agnes?

MRS. ROBERTS: Yes, that was what I meant. And we ought to all scream just before they start, so as to scare it.

MRS. SOMERS: Oh, how capital! You *have* got a brain, Agnes! *Now* I begin to believe we shall live through it. And Mr. Campbell ought to beat the floor first, oughtn't he?

CAMPBELL: I haven't got anything to beat it with. (*He looks about the room.*) But I can go down and get my cane.

ALL: No!

MRS. SOMERS: Jane will go down and get it for you.

JANE: Oh, I couldn't, Mrs. Somers!

CAMPBELL: Perhaps the poker—but it would spoil your carpet.

MRS. SOMERS: No matter for the carpet; you can beat it into—pulp. (*Campbell gets the poker and beats the carpet in different places.*) Harder! Beat harder!

MRS. ROBERTS: You're not beating at all, Willis. You're just—temporizing.

Campbell wildly thrashes the carpet.

MRS. SOMERS: There! that is something like. Now scream, Agnes! Scream, Mrs. Curwen! Mrs. Miller, Lou, scream, please!

ALL: E-e-e-e!

MRS. SOMERS: But nobody started!

MRS. CURWEN: I didn't believe the rest would start, and so *I* didn't.

MRS. MILLER: I was sure no one else would start.

MRS. BEMIS: So was I.

MRS. ROBERTS: We must have faith in each other, or else the plan's a failure. Now all scream!

They scream.

MRS. SOMERS: E-e-e-e! Keep beating the carpet, Willis! Hard, hard, hard! (*The other ladies all leap down from their perches, and rush screaming out of the drawing-room, followed by Jane, with a whoop that prolongs itself into the depths of the basement, after the retreating wails and hysterical laughter of the ladies have died out of the street* door.) Oh, wasn't it splendid? It was a perfect success.

CAMPBELL, *leaning on his poker, and panting with exhaustion*: They got out alive.

MRS. SOMERS: And it was all Agnes's idea. Why, Agnes is gone too!

CAMPBELL: Yes, Agnes is gone. I think it was a ruse of hers to save her own life. She's quite capable of it.

MRS. SOMERS, *with justice*: No, I don't think that. She was just carried away by the excitement of the moment.

CAMPBELL: At any rate, she's gone. And now, Amy, don't you think you'd better get down?

MRS. SOMERS, *in astonishment*: Get *down*? Why, you must be crazy. How can I get down if it's still there?

CAMPBELL: What?

MRS. SOMERS: The mouse.

CAMPBELL: But it *isn't* there, my dear. You saw for yourself that it wasn't there.

MRS. SOMERS: Did you see it run out?

CAMPBELL: No; but—

MRS. SOMERS: Very well, then, it's there still. Of course it is. I wouldn't get down for worlds.

CAMPBELL: Oh, good heavens! Do you expect to spend the rest of your life up there in that chair?

MRS. SOMERS: I don't know. I shall not get down till I see that mouse leave this room.

CAMPBELL, *desperately*: Well, then, I must make a clean breast of it. There never was any mouse here.

MRS. SOMERS: What do you mean?

CAMPBELL: I mean that when we were talking —arguing—about the physical courage of women, I thought I would try a mouse. It's succeeded only too well. I'll never try another.

MRS. SOMERS: And could you really be guilty of such a cruel—

CAMPBELL: Yes.

MRS. SOMERS: Shameless—

CAMPBELL: I was.

MRS. SOMERS: Despicable deception?

CAMPBELL: It was vile, I know, but I did it.

MRS. SOMERS: I don't believe it. No, rather than believe that of *you*, Willis, I would believe there were a million mice in the room.

CAMPBELL: Amy, indeed—

MRS. SOMERS: No; if you could deceive me then, you can deceive me now. If you could say there was a mouse in the room when there wasn't, you are quite capable of saying there isn't when there

is. You are just saying it now to get me to get down.

CAMPBELL: Upon my honor, I'm not.

MRS. SOMERS: Oh, don't talk to me of honor! The honor of a man who could revel—yes, *revel*—in the terrors of helpless women—

CAMPBELL: No, no; I'd no idea of it, Amy.

MRS. SOMERS: You will please not address me in that way, Mr. Campbell. You have forfeited all right to do so.

CAMPBELL: I know it. What I did was very foolish and thoughtless.

MRS. SOMERS: It was very low and ungentlemanly. I suppose you will go away and laugh over it with your—associates.

CAMPBELL: Why not say my ruffianly accomplices at once, Amy? No, I assure you that unless you tell of the affair, nobody shall ever hear of it from me. It's too disastrous a victory. I'm hoist by my own petard, caught in my own mouse-trap. There is such a thing as succeeding too well.

MRS. SOMERS: I should *think* you would be ashamed of it. Suppose you *have* shown that women are nervous and excitable, does that prove anything?

CAMPBELL: Nothing in the world.

MRS. SOMERS: Very likely some of us will be sick from it. I dare say you think that would be another triumphant argument.

CAMPBELL: I shouldn't exult in it.

MRS. SOMERS: I don't know when I shall ever get over it myself. I have had a dreadful shock.

CAMPBELL: I'm sorry with all my heart—I am, indeed. I had no conception that you cared so much for mice—despised them so much.

MRS. SOMERS: Oh yes, laugh, do! It's quite in character. But if you have such a contempt for women, of course you wouldn't want to *marry* one.

CAMPBELL: Yes, I should, my dear. But *only* one.

MRS. SOMERS: Very well, then! You can find some *other* one. All is over between *us*. Yes! I will send you back the precious gifts you have lavished upon me, and I will thank you for mine. A man who can turn the sex that his mother and sister belong to into ridicule can have no real love for his wife. I am glad that I found you out in time.

CAMPBELL: Do you really mean it, Amy?

MRS. SOMERS: Yes, I mean it. And I hope it will be a lesson to you. If you find any other poor, silly, trusting creature that you can impose yourself upon for a gentleman as you have upon me,

I advise you to reserve your low, vulgar, boyish tricks till after she is helplessly yours, or she may tear your hateful ring from her finger and fling it— (*She attempts to pull a ring from her finger, but it will not come off.*) Never mind! I will get it off with a little soapsuds; and then—

CAMPBELL: Oh no, my dear! Come, I can allow for your excitement, but I can't stand everything, though I admit everything. When a man has said he's played a silly part he doesn't like to be told so, and as for imposing myself upon you for a gentleman—you must take that back, Amy.

MRS. SOMERS: I do. I take it back. There hasn't been any imposture. I *knew* you were not a gentleman.

CAMPBELL: Very good! Then I'm not fit for a lady's company, and I don't deny, though you're so hard upon me, that you're a lady, Amy. Goodbye.

He bows and walks out of the room.

MRS. SOMERS, *sending her voice after him in a wail of despair*: Willis!

CAMPBELL, *coming back*: Well?

MRS. SOMERS: I can't let you go. (*He runs towards her, but she shrinks back on her chair against the wall.*) No, no!

CAMPBELL, *hesitating*: Why did you call me back, then?

MRS. SOMERS: I—I didn't call you back; I just said—Willis.

CAMPBELL: This is unworthy—even of *you.*

MRS. SOMERS: Oh!

CAMPBELL: Do you admit that you have been too severe?

MRS. SOMERS: I don't know. What did I say?

CAMPBELL: A number of pleasant things; that I was a fraud, and no gentleman.

MRS. SOMERS: Did I say that?

CAMPBELL: Yes, you did.

MRS. SOMERS: I must have been very much incensed against you. I beg your pardon for—being so angry.

CAMPBELL: That won't do. I don't care how angry you are if you don't call me names. You must take them back.

MRS. SOMERS: Do you see my handkerchief anywhere about on the carpet?

CAMPBELL, *looking about, and then finding it*: Yes; here it is. (*He hands it to her, and she bends forward and takes it from him at arm's-length, whipping it nervously out of his hand.*) What's the matter?

MRS. SOMERS: Oh, nothing—nothing! Will you please give me my fan from the table there? (*He obeys, and she catches it from him as she has caught the handkerchief.*) Thank you! Keep away, please!

CAMPBELL, *angrily*: Really this is too much. If you are afraid of touching me—

MRS. SOMERS: No, I don't mind touching you; that isn't it. But if you stood so near, don't you see, it might run up *you*, and jump on to *me*.

CAMPBELL: What might?

MRS. SOMERS: You know. The mouse.

CAMPBELL: The mouse! There *is* no mouse.

MRS. SOMERS: That's what you said before.

CAMPBELL: Well, it's true. There isn't any mouse, and there never was.

MRS. SOMERS: There's the *idea*. And that's all I ever cared for.

CAMPBELL: Well, what are you going to do? I can't kill the idea of a mouse, and I can't drive it out of the room.

MRS. SOMERS: I don't know what I'm going to do. I suppose I shall die here. (*She presses her handkerchief to her eyes.*) I shall never get out of the room alive. Then I hope you will be satisfied.

CAMPBELL: Amy, how can you say such things to me?

MRS. SOMERS: Oh, I suppose you're fond of me, in your contemptuous way. I never denied that. And I'm sorry, I'm sure, if I wounded your feelings by anything I said.

CAMPBELL: Then you admit that I am a gentleman?

MRS. SOMERS: I didn't say that.

CAMPBELL: And I can't be satisfied with less. I'll own that I've been stupid, but I haven't been ungentlemanly. I can't remain unless you do.

MRS. SOMERS: And do you think threatening me is gentlemanly?

CAMPBELL: That isn't the question. Do you think I'm a gentleman?

MRS. SOMERS: You're what the *world* calls a gentleman—yes.

CAMPBELL: Do *you* think I'm one?

MRS. SOMERS: How can I tell? I can't think at all, perched up here.

CAMPBELL: Why don't you get down, then?

MRS. SOMERS: You know very well why.

CAMPBELL: But you'll have to get down some time. You can't stay there always.

MRS. SOMERS: Why should you care?

CAMPBELL: You know I do care. You know that I love you dearly, and that I can't bear to see you in distress. Shall I beat the carpet, and you scream and make a rush?

MRS. SOMERS: No; I haven't the strength for that. I should drop in a faint as soon as I touched the floor.

CAMPBELL: Oh, good heavens! What am I going to do, then?

MRS. SOMERS: I don't know. You got me into the trouble. I should think you could get me out of it.

CAMPBELL, *after walking distractedly up and down the room*: There's only one way that I can think of, and if we're not engaged any longer, it wouldn't do.

MRS. SOMERS, *yielding to her curiosity, after a moment's hesitation*: What is it?

CAMPBELL: Oh, unless we're still engaged, it's no use proposing it.

MRS. SOMERS: Can't you tell me without?

CAMPBELL: Impossible.

MRS. SOMERS, *looking down at her fan*: Well, suppose we are still engaged, then? (*Looking up*) Yes, say we *are* engaged.

CAMPBELL: It's to carry you out.

MRS. SOMERS, *recoiling a little*: Oh! do you think that would be very nice?

CAMPBELL: Yes, I think it would. We can both scream, you know.

MRS. SOMERS: Yes?

CAMPBELL: And then you fling yourself into my arms.

MRS. SOMERS: Yes?

CAMPBELL: And I rush out of the room with you.

MRS. SOMERS, *with a deep breath*: I would never do it in the world.

CAMPBELL: Well, then, you must stay where you are.

MRS. SOMERS, *closing her fan*: You're not strong enough. (*She puts her handkerchief into her pocket.*) You would be sure to fall. (*She gathers her train in one hand.*) Well, then, look the other way! (*Campbell turns his face aside and waits.*) No, I can't do it.

CAMPBELL, *retiring wrathfully to the other side of the room*: What shall we do, then?

MRS. SOMERS, *after reflection*: I don't know what we shall do. But if I were a man—

CAMPBELL: Well, if you were a man—

MRS. SOMERS: Don't you think Mrs. Curwen is fascinating?

CAMPBELL: *She* does.

MRS. SOMERS: You must admit she's clever? And awfully stylish?

CAMPBELL: I don't admit anything of the kind. She's always posing. I think she made herself ridiculous standing there on the table.

MRS. SOMERS, *fondly*: Oh, do you think so? You are very severe.

CAMPBELL: Come, now, Amy, what has all this got to do with it?

MRS. SOMERS: Nothing. But if I were a man—

CAMPBELL: Well?

MRS. SOMERS: Well, in the first place, I wouldn't have got you wrought up so.

CAMPBELL: Well, but if you had! Suppose you had done all that I've done, and that I was up there in your place standing on a chair, and wouldn't let you leave the room, and wouldn't get down and walk out, and wouldn't allow myself to be carried, what should you do?

MRS. SOMERS, *who has been regarding him attentively over the top of her fan, which she holds pressed against her face*: Why, I suppose if you wouldn't let me help you willingly—*I should use violence.*

CAMPBELL: You witch!

As he makes a wild rush upon her, the curtain, which in the plays of this author has a strict regard for the convenances, *abruptly descends.*

THE END

Five O'Clock Tea

[1887]

Among those who have discussed Howells' plays in print, there is general agreement that *Five O'Clock Tea* is one of his most effective comedies. The dialogue is as clever as any he ever wrote for the stage. The social satire, the gentle and humorous unveiling of human weaknesses, the variety of humor from the farcical to the sophisticated—all show Howells at his best. At the same time the play points up some of Howells' inadequacies in dramatic technique; a major problem here is the exposition. Until the play is nearly a fifth of the way through, the reader has little idea of its main theme. Not even from preceding plays does the reader know that Amy and Willis are in love. (*The Mouse Trap*, although printed earlier, follows *Five O'Clock Tea* in stage action.) However, Howells once excused some of the plays of Edward Harrigan with the comment that people did not want plot and technical mastery, but simply his "delicious characters." It would then, perhaps, be appropriate to consider mainly the excellence of Howells' characterizations and dialogue.

The conversation in *Five O'Clock Tea* is particularly delightful. It is gay, fast moving, witty—excellent for stage comedy. From the beginning the repartee of Campbell and Mrs. Somers sets the pace of polite small talk, having no objective other than that the participants entertain themselves, their friends, and the audience. Scattered liberally throughout this dialogue are mostly good humored, though sometimes stinging, satirical comments on Boston society. On society women in particular—their variety, their social code, their superficial conversation, their attitudes toward each other—Howells exercises his acute powers of observation and his wit. He seems to feel that many women instinctively dislike other women and tolerate one another only for social reasons or for the opportunity to react emotionally to stimuli that only women can provide. To be proper and polite—two requirements of this society—Mrs. Somers must invite Mrs. Curwen to the tea, but she does not have to like her; Howells presents a wonderful scene in which the two ladies are politely obnoxious to each other while Campbell contributes to the joy of one and the discomfiture of the other. Delicate scenes such as Amy's return to the group to announce her engagement, after she has applied sufficient powder to "hide the traces of her tears from everyone but the ladies," reveal the penetrating dramatization of human nature of which Howells was capable. As in other plays, Howells tosses a few barbs at the English, but because this play is essentially a portrayal of a woman's ability to make up her mind, he reserves most of his comment for the ladies.

Five O'Clock Tea[1]

Mrs. Amy Somers, in a lightly floating tea-gown of singularly becoming texture and color, employs the last moments of expectance before the arrival of her guests in marching up and down in front of the mirror which fills the space between the long windows of her drawing-room, looking over either shoulder for different effects of the drifting and eddying train, and advancing upon her image with certain little bobs and bows, and retreating from it with a variety of fan practice and elaborated courtesies, finally degenerating into burlesque, and a series of grimaces and "mouths" made at the responsive reflex. In the fascination of this amusement she is first ignorant, and then aware, of the presence of Mr. Willis Campbell, who on the landing space between the drawing-room and the library stands, hat in hand, in the pleased contemplation of Mrs. Somers's manœuvres and contortions as the mirror reports them to him. Mrs. Somers does not permit herself the slightest start on seeing him in the glass, but turns deliberately away, having taken time to prepare the air of gratification and surprise with which she geets him at half the length of the drawing-room.

MRS. SOMERS, *giving her hand*: Why, Mr. Campbell! How very nice of you! How long have you been prowling about there on the landing? So stupid of them not to have turned up the gas!

CAMPBELL: I wasn't much incommoded. That sort of pitch-darkness is rather becoming to my style of beauty, I find. The only objection was that I couldn't see you.

MRS. SOMERS: Do you often make those pretty speeches?

CAMPBELL: When I can found them on fact.

MRS. SOMERS: What can I say back? Oh! That I'm sorry I couldn't have met you when you were looking your best.

CAMPBELL: Um! Do you think you could have borne it? We might go out there.

MRS. SOMERS: On second thoughts, no. I shall ring to have them turn up the gas.

CAMPBELL: No; let me. (*He prevents her ringing, and going out into the space between the library and drawing-room, stands with his hand on the key of the gas-burner.*) Now how do I look?

MRS. SOMERS: Beautiful!

CAMPBELL, *turning up the gas*: And now?

MRS. SOMERS: Not *half* so well. Decidedly pitch-darkness is becoming to you. Better turn it down again.

CAMPBELL, *rejoining her in the drawing-room*: No; it isn't so becoming to you; and I'm not envious, whatever I am.

MRS. SOMERS: You are generosity itself.

CAMPBELL: If you come to phrases, I prefer magnanimity.

MRS. SOMERS: Well, *say* magnanimity. Won't you sit down—while you have the opportunity?

She sinks upon the sofa, and indicates with her fan an easy-chair at one end of it.

CAMPBELL, *dropping into it*: Are there going to be so many?

MRS. SOMERS: You never can tell about five o'clock tea. There mayn't be more than half a dozen; there may be thirty or forty. But I wished to affect your imagination.

CAMPBELL: You had better have tried it in some other kind of weather. It's snowing like—

MRS. SOMERS, *running to window, and peeping out through the side of the curtain*: It is! like—cats and dogs!

CAMPBELL: Oh no! You can't say that! It only rains that way. I was going to say it myself, but I stopped in time.

MRS. SOMERS, *standing before the window with clasped hands*: No matter! There will simply be nobody but bores. *They* come in any sort of weather.

CAMPBELL: Thank you, Mrs. Somers. I'm glad I ventured out.

MRS. SOMERS, *turning about*: What? (*Then realizing the situation*) Oh, *poor* Mr. Campbell!

[1] The text used here is the Harper & Brothers 1894 edition. "The supposed time of the action antedates that of 'The Mouse-Trap,' published in *Harper's Magazine* for December 1886." (Howells' footnote.)

CAMPBELL: Oh, don't mind *me!* I can stand it if you can. I belong to a sex, thank you, that doesn't pretend to have any tact. I would just as soon tell a man he was a bore as not. But I thought it might worry a lady, perhaps.

MRS. SOMERS: Worry? I'm simply aghast at it. Did you ever hear of anything worse?

CAMPBELL: Well, not much worse.

MRS. SOMERS: What can I do to make you forget it?

CAMPBELL: I can't think of anything. It seems to me that I shall always remember it as the most fortunate speech a lady ever made to me—and they have said some flattering things to me in my time.

MRS. SOMERS: Oh, don't be entirely heartless. Wouldn't a cup of tea blot it out? With a Peak & Frean? (*She advances beseechingly upon him.*) Come, I will give you a cup at once.

CAMPBELL: No, thank you; I would rather have it with the rest of the bores. They'll be sure to come.

MRS. SOMERS, *resuming her seat on the sofa*: You are implacable. And I thought you said you were generous.

CAMPBELL: No; merely magnanimous. I can't forget your cruel frankness; but I know *you* can, and I ask you to do it. (*He throws himself back in his chair with a sigh.*) And who knows? Perhaps you were right.

MRS. SOMERS: About what?

CAMPBELL: My being a bore.

MRS. SOMERS: I should think *you* would know.

CAMPBELL: No; that's the difficulty. Nobody would be a bore if he knew it.

MRS. SOMERS: Oh, *some* would, I think.

CAMPBELL: Do you mean me?

MRS. SOMERS: Well, no, then. I don't believe you would be a bore, if you knew it. Is that enough? Or do you expect me to say something more?

CAMPBELL: No, it's quite enough, thank you.

He remains pensively silent.

MRS. SOMERS, *after waiting for him to speak*: Bores for bores, don't you hate the silent ones most?

CAMPBELL, *desperately rousing himself*: Mrs. Somers, if you only knew how disagreeable I was going to make myself just before I concluded to hold my tongue!

MRS. SOMERS: Really? What were you going to say?

CAMPBELL: Do you actually wish to know?

MRS. SOMERS: Oh no; I only thought you wished to tell.

CAMPBELL: Not at all. You complained of my being silent.

MRS. SOMERS: Did I? I was wrong. I will never do so again.

She laughs in her fan.

CAMPBELL: And I complain of your delay. You can tell me now, just as well as two weeks hence, whether you love me enough to marry me or not.

MRS. SOMERS: You promised not to recur to that subject without some hint from me. You have broken your promise.

CAMPBELL: Well, you wouldn't give me any hint.

MRS. SOMERS: How can I believe you care for me if you are false in this?

CAMPBELL: It seems to me that my falsehood is another proof of my affection.

MRS. SOMERS: Very well, then; you can wait till I know my mind.

CAMPBELL: I'd rather know your heart. But I'll wait. (*After a pause*) Why do you carry a fan on a day like this? I ask, to make general conversation.

MRS. SOMERS, *spreading the fan in her lap, and looking at it curiously*: I don't know. (*After a moment*) Oh yes; for the same reason that I shall have ice-cream after dinner to-day.

CAMPBELL: That's no reason at all. (*After a moment*) Are you going to have ice-cream to-day after dinner?

MRS. SOMERS: I might. If I had company.

CAMPBELL: Oh, I couldn't stay after hinting. I'm too proud for that. (*He pulls his chair nearer and joins her in examining the fan in her lap.*) What is so very strange about your fan?

MRS. SOMERS: Nothing. I was just seeing how a fan looked that was the subject of gratuitous criticism.

CAMPBELL: I didn't criticise the *fan.*

He regards it studiously.

MRS. SOMERS: Oh! *Not* the fan?

CAMPBELL: No; I think it's extremely pretty. I like big fans.

MRS. SOMERS: So good of you! It's Spanish. That's why it's so large.

CAMPBELL: It's hand-painted, too.

MRS. SOMERS, *leaning back, and leaving him to the inspection of the fan*: You're a connoisseur, Mr. Campbell.

CAMPBELL: Oh, I can tell hand-painting from machine-painting when I see it. 'Tisn't so good.

MRS. SOMERS: Thank you.

CAMPBELL: Not at all. Now, that fellow— cavalier, I suppose, in Spain—making love in that attitude, you can see at a glance that *he's* hand-painted. No *machine*-painted cavalier would do it in that way. And look at the lady's hand. Who ever saw a hand of that size before?

MRS. SOMERS, *unclasping the hands which she had folded at her waist, and putting one of them out to take up the fan*: You said you were not criticizing the fan.

CAMPBELL, *quickly seizing the hand, with the fan in it*: Ah, I'm wrong! Here's another one no bigger. Let me see which is the largest.

MRS. SOMERS, *struggling not very violently to free her hand*: Mr. Campbell!

CAMPBELL: Don't take it away! You must listen to me now, Amy.

MRS. SOMERS, *rising abruptly, and dropping her fan as she comes forward to meet an elderly gentleman arriving from the landing*: Mr. Bemis! How very heroic of you to come such a day! Isn't it too bad?

BEMIS: Not if it makes me specially welcome, Mrs. Somers. (*Discovering Campbell*) Oh, Mr. Campbell!

CAMPBELL, *striving for his self-possession as they shake hands*: Yes, another hero, Mr. Bemis. Mrs. Somers is going to brevet everybody who comes to-day. She didn't *say* heroes to me, but—

MRS. SOMERS: You shall have your tea at once, Mr. Bemis. (*She rings.*) I was making Mr. Campbell wait for his. You don't order up the teapot for one hero.

BEMIS: Ha, ha, ha! No, indeed! But I'm very glad you do for two. The fact is—(*rubbing his hands*) I'm half frozen.

MRS. SOMERS: Is it so very cold? (*To Campbell, who presents her fan with a bow*) Oh, thank you. (*To Mr. Bemis*) Mr. Campbell has just been objecting to my fan. He doesn't like its being hand-painted, as he calls it.

BEMIS: That reminds me of a California gentleman whom I found looking at an Andrea del Sarto in the Pitti Palace at Florence one day—by-the-way, *you've* been a Californian too, Mr. Campbell; but you won't mind. He seemed to be puzzled over it, and then he said to me—I was standing near him—"Hand-painted, I presume?"

MRS. SOMERS: Ah! ha, ha, ha! How very good! (*To the maid, who appears*) The tea, Lizzie.

CAMPBELL: You don't think he was joking?

BEMIS, *with misgiving*: Why, no, it never occurred to me that he was.

CAMPBELL: You can't always tell when a Californian's joking.

MRS. SOMERS, *with insinuation*: Can't you? Not even adoptive ones?

CAMPBELL: Adoptive ones never joke.

MRS. SOMERS: Not even about hand-painted fans? What an interesting fact! (*She sits down on the sofa behind the little table on which the maid arranges the tea, and pours out a cup. Then, with her eyes on Mr. Bemis*) Cream and sugar both? Yes? (*Holding a cube of sugar in the tongs*) How many?

BEMIS: One, please.

MRS. SOMERS, *handing it to him*: I'm so glad you take your tea *au naturel*, as I call it.

CAMPBELL: What do you call it when they don't take it with cream and sugar?

MRS. SOMERS: *Au unnaturel*. There's only one thing worse: taking it with a slice of lemon in it. You might as well draw it from a bothersome samovar at once, and be done with it.

CAMPBELL: The samovar is picturesque.

MRS. SOMERS: It is insincere. Like Californians. Natives.

CAMPBELL: Well, I can think of something much worse than tea with lemon in it.

MRS. SOMERS: What?

CAMPBELL: No tea at all.

MRS. SOMERS, *recollecting herself*: Oh, poor Mr. Campbell! Two lumps?

CAMPBELL: One, thank you. Your pity is so sweet!

MRS. SOMERS: You ought to have thought of the milk of human kindness, and spared my cream-jug too.

CAMPBELL: You didn't pour out your compassion soon enough.

BEMIS, *who has been sipping his tea in silent admiration*: Are you often able to keep it up in that way? I was fancying myself at the theatre.

MRS. SOMERS: Oh, *don't* encore us! Mr. Campbell would keep saying his things over indefinitely.

CAMPBELL, *presenting his cup*: Another lump. It's turning bitter. *Two!*

BEMIS: Ha, ha, ha! Very good—very good indeed!

CAMPBELL: Thank you kindly, Mr. Bemis.

MRS. SOMERS, *greeting the new arrivals, and leaning forward to shake hands with them as they come up, without rising*: Mrs. Roberts! How very good of you! And Mr. Roberts!

ROBERTS: Not at all.

MRS. ROBERTS: Of course we were coming.

MRS. SOMERS: Will you have some tea? You see I'm installed already. Mr. Campbell was so greedy he wouldn't wait.

CAMPBELL: Mr. Bemis and I are here in the character of heroes, and we had to have our tea at once. You're a hero too, Roberts, though you don't look it. Any one who comes to tea in such weather is a hero, or a—

MRS. SOMERS, *interrupting him with a little shriek:* Ugh! How hot that handle's getting!

CAMPBELL: Ah, I dare say. Let me turn out my sister's cup. (*Pouring out the tea and handing it to Mrs. Roberts*) I don't see how you could reconcile it to your No. Eleven conscience [1] to leave your children in such a snow-storm as this, Agnes.

MRS. ROBERTS, *in vague alarm:* Why, what in the world could happen to them, Willis?

CAMPBELL: Oh, nothing to *them.* But suppose Roberts got snowed under. Have some tea, Roberts?

He offers to pour out a cup.

MRS. SOMERS, *dispossessing him of the teapot with dignity:* Thank you, Mr. Campbell; *I* will pour out the tea.

CAMPBELL: Oh, very well. I thought the handle was hot.

MRS. SOMERS: It's cooler now.

CAMPBELL: And you won't let me help you?

MRS. SOMERS: When there are more people you may hand the tea.

CAMPBELL: I wish I knew just how much that meant.

MRS. SOMERS: Very little. As little as an adoptive Californian in his most earnest mood.

While they talk—Campbell bending over the teapot, on which Mrs. Somers keeps her hand—the others form a little group apart.

BEMIS, *to Mrs. Roberts:* I hope Mr. Roberts's distinguished friend won't give us the slip on account of the storm.

ROBERTS: Oh no; he'll be sure to come. He may be late. But he's the most amiable of Englishmen, and I know he won't disappoint Mrs. Somers.

BEMIS: The most unamiable of Englishmen couldn't do that.

ROBERTS: Ah, I don't know. Did you meet Mr. Pogis?

BEMIS: No; what did he do?

1 A No. Eleven conscience refers to a seaman working a round trip who does not intend to jump ship.

ROBERTS: Why, he came—to the Hibbens's dinner—in a sack coat.

MRS. ROBERTS: I thought it was a Cardigan jacket.

BEMIS: I heard a Norfolk jacket and knickerbockers.

MRS. SOMERS: Ah, there is Mrs. Curwen! (*To Campbell, aside*) And without her husband!

CAMPBELL: Or any one else's husband.

MRS. SOMERS: For shame!

CAMPBELL: You began it.

MRS. SOMERS, *to Mrs. Curwen, who approaches her sofa:* You are kindness itself, Mrs. Curwen, to come on such a day.

The ladies press each other's hands.

MRS. CURWEN: You are goodness in person, Mrs. Somers, to say so.

CAMPBELL: And I am magnanimity embodied. Let me introduce myself, Mrs. Curwen!

He bows, and Mrs. Curwen deeply courtesies.

MRS. CURWEN: I should never have known you.

CAMPBELL, *melodramatically, to Mrs. Somers:* Tea, ho! for Mrs. Curwen—impenetrably disguised as kindness.

MRS. CURWEN: What shall I say to him?

MRS. SOMERS, *pouring the tea:* Anything you like, Mrs. Curwen. Aren't we to see Mr. Curwen to-day?

MRS. CURWEN, *taking her tea:* No, I'm his insufficient apology. He's detained at his office—business.

CAMPBELL: Then you see they don't *all* come, Mrs. Somers.

MRS. CURWEN: All what?

CAMPBELL: Oh, all the—heroes.

MRS. CURWEN: Is that what he was going to say, Mrs. Somers?

MRS. SOMERS: You never can tell what he's going to say.

MRS. CURWEN: I should think you would be afraid of him.

MRS. SOMERS, *with a little shrug:* Oh no; he's quite harmless. It's just a little way he has. (*To Mr. and Mrs. Miller, Mr. and Mrs. Alfred Bemis, and Dr. Lawton, who all appear together*) Ah, how do you do? So glad to see you! So very kind of you! I didn't suppose *you* would venture out. And you too, Doctor?

She begins to pour out tea for them, one after another, with great zeal.

DR. LAWTON: Yes, I too. It sounded very much as if I were Brutus also. (*He stirs his tea and stares round at the company.*) It seems to me that I have met these conspirators before. That's what makes Boston insupportable. You're always meeting the same people!

CAMPBELL: We all feel it as keenly as you do, Doctor.

LAWTON, *looking sharply at him*: Oh! *you* here? I might have expected it. Where is your aunt?

MRS. CRASHAW, *appearing*: If you mean me, Dr. Lawton—

LAWTON: I do, my dear friend. What company is complete without you?

MRS. SOMERS, *reaching forward to take her hand, while with her disengaged hand she begins to pour her a cup of tea*: None in *my* house.

MRS. CRASHAW: Very pretty. (*Taking her tea*) I hope it isn't complete, either, without the English painter you promised us.

MRS. SOMERS: No, indeed! And a great many other people besides. But haven't you met him yet? I supposed Mrs. Roberts—

MRS. CRASHAW: Oh, I don't go to *all* of Agnes's fandangoes. I was to have seen him at Mrs. Wheeler's—he is being asked everywhere, of course—but he didn't come. He sent his father and mother instead. They were very nice old people, but they hadn't painted his pictures.

LAWTON: They might say his pictures would never have been painted without them.

BEMIS: It was like Heine's going to visit Rachel by appointment. She wasn't in, but her father and mother were; and when he met her afterwards he told her that he had just come from a show where he had seen a curious monster advertised for exhibition—the offspring of a hare and a salmon. The monster was not to be seen at the moment, but the showman said here was monsieur the hare and madame the salmon.

MRS. ROBERTS: What in the world did Rachel say?

LAWTON: Ah, that's what these brilliant anecdotes never tell. And I think it would be very interesting to know what the victim of a witticism has to say.

MRS. CURWEN: I should think you would know very often, Doctor.

LAWTON: Ah, now I should like to know what the victim of a compliment says!

MRS. CURWEN: He bows his thanks.

DR. LAWTON *makes a profound obeisance, to which Mrs. Curwen responds in burlesque.*

MILLER: We all envy you, Doctor.

MRS. MILLER: Oh yes. Mrs. Curwen never makes a compliment without meaning it.

MRS. CURWEN: I can't say that quite, my dear. I should be very sorry to mean all the civil things I say. But I never flatter gentlemen of a certain age.

MRS. MILLER, *tittering ineffectively*: I shall know what to say to Mr. Miller after this.

MRS. CRASHAW: Well, if you haven't got the man, Mrs. Somers, you *have* got his picture, haven't you?

MRS. SOMERS: Yes; it's on my writing-desk in the library. Let me—

LAWTON: No, no; don't disturb yourself! We wish to tear it to pieces without your embarrassing presence. Will you take my arm, Mrs. Crashaw?

MRS. BEMIS: Oh, let us all go and see it!

ROBERTS: Aren't you coming, Willis?

CAMPBELL, *without looking round*: Thank you, I've seen it.

MRS. SOMERS, *whom the withdrawal of her other guests has left alone with him*: How could you tell such a fib?

CAMPBELL: I could tell much worse fibs than that in such a cause.

MRS. SOMERS: What cause?

CAMPBELL: A lost one, I'm afraid. Will you answer my question, Amy?

MRS. SOMERS: Did you ask me any?

CAMPBELL: You know I did—before those people came in.

MRS. SOMERS: Oh, *that!* Yes. I should like to ask *you* a question first.

CAMPBELL: Twenty, if you like.

MRS. SOMERS: Why do you feel authorized to call me by my first name?

CAMPBELL: Because I love you. Now will you answer me?

MRS. SOMERS, *dreamily*: I didn't say I would, did I?

CAMPBELL, *rising, sadly*: No.

MRS. SOMERS, *mechanically taking the hand he offers her*: Oh! What—

CAMPBELL: I'm going; that's all.

MRS. SOMERS: So soon?

CAMPBELL: Yes; but I'll try to make amends by not coming back soon—or at all.

MRS. SOMERS: You mustn't!

CAMPBELL: Mustn't what?

MRS. SOMERS: You mustn't keep my hand. Here come some more people. Ah, Mrs. Canfield! Miss Bayly! So very nice of you, Mrs. Wharton! Will you have some tea?

MRS. WHARTON: No, thank you. The only objection to afternoon tea is the tea.

MRS. SOMERS: I'm so glad you don't mind the weather. (*With her hand on the teapot, glancing up at Miss Bayly*) And do you refuse too?

MISS BAYLY: I can answer for Mrs. Canfield that *she* doesn't, and I *never* do. *We* object to the weather.

MRS. SOMERS, *pouring a cup of tea*: That makes it a little more difficult. I can keep from offering Mrs. Wharton some tea, but I can't stop its snowing.

MISS BAYLY, *taking her cup*: But you're so amiable; we know you would if you could, and that's quite enough. We're not the first and only, are we?

MRS. SOMERS: *Dear*, no! There are multitudes of flattering spirits in the library, stopping the mouth of my portrait with pretty speeches.

MISS BAYLY, *vividly*: Not your *Bramford* portrait?

MRS. SOMERS: My Bramford *portrait*.

MISS BAYLY, *to the other ladies*: Oh, let us go and see it too!

They flutter out of the drawing-room, where Mrs. Somers and Campbell remain alone together as before. He continues silent, while she waits for him to speak.

MRS. SOMERS, *finally*: Well?

CAMPBELL: Well, what?

MRS. SOMERS: Nothing. Only I thought you were—you were going to—

CAMPBELL: No; I've got nothing to say.

MRS. SOMERS: I didn't mean that. I thought you were going to—go.

She puts up her hand and hides a triumphant little smile with it.

CAMPBELL: Very well, then, I'll go, since you wish it.

He holds out his hand.

MRS. SOMERS, *putting hers behind her*: You've shaken hands once. Besides, who said I wished you to go?

CAMPBELL: Do you wish me to stay?

MRS. SOMERS: I wish you to—hand tea to people.

CAMPBELL: And you won't say anything more?

MRS. SOMERS: It seems to me that's enough.

CAMPBELL: It isn't enough for me. But I suppose beggars mustn't be choosers. I can't stay merely to hand tea to people, however. You can say yes or no now, Amy, as well as at any other time.

MRS. SOMERS: Well, no, then—if you wish it so much.

CAMPBELL: You know I don't wish it.

MRS. SOMERS: You gave me my choice. I thought you were indifferent about the word.

CAMPBELL: You know better than that, Amy.

MRS. SOMERS: Amy again! Aren't you a little previous, Mr. Campbell?

CAMPBELL, *with a sigh*: Ah, that's for you to say.

MRS. SOMERS: Wouldn't it be impolite?

CAMPBELL: Oh, not for *you*.

MRS. SOMERS: If you're so sarcastic, I shall be afraid of you.

CAMPBELL: Under what circumstances?

MRS. SOMERS, *dropping her eyes*: I don't know. (*He makes a rush upon her.*) Oh! here comes Mrs. Curwen! Shake hands, as if you were going.

MRS. CURWEN: What! is Mr. Campbell going, *too*?

MRS. SOMERS: Too? *You're* not going, Mrs. Curwen?

MRS. CURWEN: Yes, I'm going. The likeness is perfect, Mrs. Somers. It's a speaking likeness, if there ever was one.

CAMPBELL: Did it do all the talking?

MRS. CURWEN: It would—if Mrs. Roberts and Dr. Lawton hadn't been there. Well, I must go.

CAMPBELL: So must I.

MRS. SOMERS, *in surprise*: Must you?

CAMPBELL: Yes; these drifts will be over my ears directly.

MRS. CURWEN: You poor man! You don't mean to say you're *walking*?

CAMPBELL: I shall be, in about half a minute.

MRS. CURWEN: Indeed you shall not! You shall be driving—with me. I've a vacancy in the coupé, and I'll set you down wherever you like.

CAMPBELL: Won't it crowd you?

MRS. CURWEN: Not at all.

CAMPBELL: Or incommode you in any way?

MRS. CURWEN: It will oblige me in every way.

CAMPBELL: Then I will go, and a thousand thanks. Good-by again, Mrs. Somers.

MRS. CURWEN: Good-by, Mrs. Somers. Poor Mrs. Somers! It seems too bad to leave you here alone, bowed in an elegiac attitude over your teaurn.

MRS. SOMERS: Oh, not at all! Remember me to Mr. Curwen.

MRS. CURWEN: I will. Well, Mr. Campbell—

MRS. SOMERS: Mr. Campbell—

CAMPBELL: Well?

MRS. CURWEN: To which?

CAMPBELL: Both.

MRS. SOMERS: Neither!

MRS. CURWEN: Ah! ha, ha, ha! Mr. Campbell, do you know much about women?

CAMPBELL: I had a mother.

MRS. CURWEN: Oh, a *mother* won't do.

CAMPBELL: Well, I have an only sister who is a woman.

MRS. CURWEN: A sister won't do, *either*—not your own. You can't learn a woman's meaning in that way.

CAMPBELL: I will sit at your feet, Mrs. Curwen, if you'll instruct me.

MRS. CURWEN: I shall be delighted. I'll begin now. Oh, you needn't really prostrate yourself! (*She stops him in a burlesque attempt to do so.*) And I'll concentrate the wisdom of the whole first lesson in a single word.

CAMPBELL, *with clasped hands of entreaty*: Speak, blessed ghost!

MRS. CURWEN: Stay! Ah! ha, ha, ha! (*She flies at Mrs. Somers and kisses her.*) You can't say I'm ill-natured, my dear, whatever I am!

MRS. SOMERS, *pursuing her exit with the word*: No, merely atrocious.

> A *pause ensues, in which Campbell stands irresolute.*

CAMPBELL, *finally*: Did you wish me to stay, Amy?

MRS. SOMERS, *airily*: I? Oh no! It was Mrs. Curwen.

CAMPBELL: Then I think I'll accept her kind offer of a seat in her coupé.

MRS. SOMERS: Oh! I thought, of course, you'd stay—at *her* request.

CAMPBELL: No; I shall only stay at yours.

MRS. SOMERS: And I shall not ask you. In fact, I warn you not to.

CAMPBELL: Why?

MRS. SOMERS: Because, if you urge me to speak now, I shall say—

CAMPBELL: I wasn't going to urge you.

MRS. SOMERS: No matter! I shall say it now without being urged. Yes, I've made up my mind. I can't marry a flirt.

CAMPBELL: I can, Amy.

MRS. SOMERS: Sir!

CAMPBELL: You know very well you sent those people into the other room to keep me here and torment me—

MRS. SOMERS: *Now* you've *insulted* me, and all *is* over.

CAMPBELL: To tantalize me with your loveliness, your beauty, your grace, Amy!

MRS. SOMERS, *softening*: Oh, that's all very well—

CAMPBELL: I'm glad you like it. I could go on at much greater length. But you know I love you dearly, Amy, and why should you delight in my agonies? But only marry me, and you shall delight in them as long as you live, and—

MRS. SOMERS: You must hold me very cheap to think I would take you from that creature.

CAMPBELL: Confound her! I wasn't hers to give. I offered myself first.

MRS. SOMERS: She offered you last, and—no, thank you, please.

CAMPBELL: Do you really mean it?

MRS. SOMERS: I shall not say. Or, yes, I *will* say. If that woman, who seems to have you at her beck and call, had not intermeddled, I might have made you a very different answer. But now my eyes are opened, and I see what I should have to expect, and—no, thank you, please.

CAMPBELL: And if she hadn't offered me—

MRS. SOMERS, *drawing out her handkerchief and putting it to her eyes*: I was feeling kindly towards you—I was such a little fool—

CAMPBELL: Amy!

MRS. SOMERS: And you knew how much I disliked her.

CAMPBELL: Yes, I saw by the way you kissed each other.

MRS. SOMERS: Nonsense! You knew that meant nothing. But if it had been anybody else in the world but her, I shouldn't have minded it. And now—

CAMPBELL: Now—

MRS. SOMERS: Now all those geese are coming back from the other room, and they'll see that I've been crying, and everybody will know everything. Willis—

CAMPBELL: *Willis?*

MRS. SOMERS: Let me go! I must bathe my eyes! You stay here and receive them! I'll be back at once!

> *She escapes from the arms stretched towards her, and out of the door, just before her guests enter from the library, and Campbell remains to receive them. The ladies, in returning, call over one another's heads and shoulders.*

MRS. ROBERTS: Amy, it's *lovely!* But it doesn't *half* do you justice.

YOUNG MRS. BEMIS: It's too sweet for *anything*, Mrs. Somers.

MRS. CRASHAW: Why did you let the man put you into that ridiculous seventeenth-century dress? Can't he paint a modern frock?

MRS. WHARTON: But what exquisite coloring, Mrs. Somers!

MRS. MILLER: He's got just your lovely turn of the head.

MISS BAYLY: And the way you hold your fan— what character he's thrown into it!

MRS. ROBERTS: And that fall of the skirt, Amy; that shirt is *full* of character! (*She discovers Mr. Campbell behind the tea-urn. He has Mrs. Somers's light wrap on his shoulders, and her fan in his hand, and he alternately hides his blushes with it, and coquettishly folds it and pats his mouth in a gross caricature of Mrs. Somers's manner. In rising he twitches his coat forward in a similar burlesque of a lady's management of her skirt.*) Why, where is Amy, Willis?

CAMPBELL: Gone a moment. Some trouble about—the hot water.

LAWTON: Hot water that you've been getting into? Ah, young man, look me in the eye!

CAMPBELL: Your glass one, Doctor?

YOUNG MR. BEMIS: Why, my dear, has your father got a glass eye?

MRS. BEMIS: Of *course* he hasn't! What an idea! I don't know what Mr. Campbell means.

LAWTON: I've no doubt he wishes I had a glass eye—two of them, for that matter. But that isn't answering my question. Where is Mrs. Somers?

CAMPBELL: That was my sister's question, and I did answer it. Have some tea, ladies? I'm glad you like my portrait, and that you think he's got my lovely turn of the head, and the way I hold my fan, and the character of my skirt; but I agree with you that it isn't half as pretty as I am.

THE LADIES: Oh, what shall we do to him? Prescribe for us, Doctor.

CAMPBELL: No, no! I want the Doctor's services myself. I don't want him to give me his medicines. I want him to give me away.

LAWTON: You're tired of giving yourself away, then?

CAMPBELL: It's of no use. They won't have me.

LAWTON: Who won't?

CAMPBELL: Oh, I'll leave Mrs. Somers to say.

MRS. SOMERS, *radiantly reappearing*: Say what? (*She has hidden the traces of her tears from every one but the ladies by a light application of powder, and she knows that they all know she has been crying, and this makes her a little more smiling.*) Say what?

She addresses the company in general rather than Campbell.

CAMPBELL, *with caricatured tenderness*: Say yes.

MRS. SOMERS: What does he mean, Doctor?

LAWTON: Oh, I'm afraid he's past all surgery. I give him over to you, Mrs. Somers.

CAMPBELL: There, now. She wasn't the last to do it!

MRS. SOMERS, *with the resolution of a widow*: Well, I suppose there's nothing else for it, then. I'll see what can be done for your patient, Doctor.

She passes her hand through Campbell's arm, where he continues to stand behind the tea-table.

MRS. ROBERTS, *falling upon her and kissing her*: Amy, you don't *mean* it!

MRS. BEMIS, *embracing her in turn*: I never can believe it.

MRS. CRASHAW: It is ridiculous! What, Willis?

MRS. MILLER: It does seem too nice to be true.

BEMIS: You astonish us!

ROBERTS: We never should have dreamed of it.

YOUNG MR. BEMIS: You *must* give us time to realize it.

MRS. WHARTON: Is it *possible*?

MISS BAYLY: *Is* it possible?

They all shake hands with Mrs. Somers in turn.

ROBERTS: Isn't this rather sudden, Willis?

CAMPBELL: Well, it is—for Mrs. Somers, perhaps. But *I've* found it awfully gradual.

MRS. SOMERS: Nonsense! It's an old story for both of us.

CAMPBELL: Well, what I like about it is, it's *true*. Founded on fact!

MRS. ROBERTS: Really? [1] *I* can't believe it!

CAMPBELL: Well, I don't know whom all this charming incredulity's intended to flatter, but if it's I, I say no, *not* really, at all! It's merely a little *coup de théâtre* we've been arranging.

LAWTON, *patting him on the shoulder*: One ahead, as usual.

MRS. SOMERS: Oh, thank you, Doctor! There are two of us ahead now.

LAWTON: I believe you, at any rate. Bravo!

He initiates an applause in which all the rest join, while Campbell catches up Mrs. Somers's fan and unfurls it before both their faces.

THE END

1 All other editions omit "Really?"

A Likely Story

[1888]

In "A Letter to the Publisher," Howells made this defense of A Likely Story:

> In default of stirring dramatic incident in it, character might be ascribed to it, and the point on which it turns, that of putting two letters in the wrong envelopes, has lately been verified to me in the most expressive manner. One day last summer, when I was wondering why I did not get notice from an editress that the manuscript of a farce I had sent her was received, there came a letter from her, addressed to me on the cover, but within requesting a well-known artist to make pictures for my piece. In the meantime, he had got a letter assuring him of the arrival of it, and telling him it was "delicious." But Nature, when she gets her capital N on, is always trying to imitate Art, and that is one of the reasons why I think Art should have the decency, at least occasionally, to imitate Nature.

Howells even suggested that the play would be effective on the stage if it were given a chance. But he probably would have been disappointed, because A Likely Story is primarily a situation sketch.

The believability of this play idea is, of course, its focal point. It *is* difficult to believe. The whole thing is farce, a *likely* story! And as with most likely stories, a successful outcome demands a certain amount of contrivance by the persons involved. Actually the force behind the likely story is Amy Campbell, whose womanly nature prompts the action, while her womanly wiles relieve the tension and facilitate the solutions, at the same time that her womanly conscience quietly absolves itself of any blame. All the characters agree that the incident is a rather unlikely story, but only the women understand it. "Dansons!" they cry, and they lead; the men to follow, presumably forever.

What probably made this play particularly pleasing to Howells was its commonplace realism, its sprightly quality, and an informality which is quietly emphasized by Howells' comments on the poor, real life that he loves. He seems to enjoy his role as relaxed commentator in this play, and through his plot he points particularly toward the woman in society. There is woman's intuitive knowledge of the effectiveness of a well-chosen tearful moment; there is woman's uncontrollable desire to bring "two lovely young creatures together"; there is woman's enthusiasm for romantic intrigue; and there is woman's miraculous ability to circumvent the actual. Says Miss Greenway, "Truth is bad enough for *you* to carry off. Promise me that you will always leave the other thing to me." So Howells demonstrates for us that women are gay and convincing deceivers.

A Likely Story[1]

MRS. CAMPBELL: Now this, I think, is the most exciting part of the whole affair, and the pleasantest. (*She is seated at breakfast in her cottage at Summering-by-the-Sea. A heap of letters of various stylish shapes, colors, and superscriptions lies beside her plate, and irregularly straggles about among the coffee-service. Vis-à-vis with her sits Mr. Campbell behind a newspaper.*) How prompt they are! Why, I didn't expect to get half so many answers yet. But that shows that where people have nothing to do *but* attend to their social duties they are always prompt—even the men; women, of course, reply early anyway, and you don't really care for them; but in town the men seem to put it off till the very last moment, and then some of them call when it's over to excuse themselves for not having come after accepting. It really makes you wish for a leisure class. It's only the drive and hurry of American life that make our men seem wanting in the *convenances*; and if they had the time, with their instinctive delicacy, they would be perfect: it would come from the heart: they're more truly polite now. Willis, just *look* at this!

CAMPBELL, *behind his paper*: Look at what?

MRS. CAMPBELL: These replies. Why, I do believe that more than half the people have answered already, and the invitations only went out yesterday. That comes from putting on R.S.V.P. I knew I was right, and I shall always do it, I don't care what *you* say.

CAMPBELL: You didn't put on R.S.V.P. after all I said?

He looks round the edge of his paper at her.

MRS. CAMPBELL: *Yes*, I did. The idea of your setting up for an authority in such a thing as that!

CAMPBELL: Then I'm sorry I didn't ask you to do it. It's a shame to make people say whether they'll come to a garden-party from four till seven or not.

MRS. CAMPBELL: A shame? How can you provide if you don't know how many are coming? I should like to know that. But of course I couldn't expect you to give in gracefully.

CAMPBELL: I should give in gracefully if I gave in at all, but I don't. (*He throws his paper down beside his chair.*) Here, hand over the letters, and I'll be opening them for you while you pour out the coffee.

MRS. CAMPBELL, *covering the letters with her hands*: Indeed you won't!

CAMPBELL: Well, pour out the coffee, then, anyway.

MRS. CAMPBELL, *after a moment's reflection*: No, I shall not do it. I'm going to open them every one before you get a drop of coffee—just to punish you.

CAMPBELL: To punish me? For what? (*Mrs. Campbell hesitates, as if at a loss what to say.*) There! you don't know.

MRS. CAMPBELL: Yes, I do: for saying I oughtn't to have put on R.S.V.P. Do you take it back?

CAMPBELL: How can I till I've had some coffee? My mind won't work on an empty stomach. Well—

He rises and goes round the table towards her.

MRS. CAMPBELL, *spreading both arms over the letters*: Willis, if you dare to touch them, I'll ring for Jane, and then she'll see you cutting up.

CAMPBELL: Touch what? I'm coming to get some coffee.

MRS. CAMPBELL: Well, I'll give you some coffee; but don't you touch a single one of those letters—after what you've said.

CAMPBELL: All right! (*He extends one hand for the coffee, and with the other sweeps all the letters together, and starts back to his place. As she flies upon him*) Look out, Amy; you'll make me spill this coffee all over the tablecloth.

MRS. CAMPBELL, *sinking into her seat*: Oh, Willis, how can you be so base? *Give* me my letters. *Do!*

CAMPBELL, *sorting them over*: You may have half.

[1] The text used here is the Harper & Brothers 1894 edition.

375

MRS. CAMPBELL: No; I shall have all. I insist upon it.

CAMPBELL: Well, then, you may have all the ladies' letters. There are twice as many of them.

MRS. CAMPBELL: No; I shall have the men's, too. Give me the men's first.

CAMPBELL: How can I tell which are the men's without opening them?

MRS. CAMPBELL: How could you tell which were the ladies'? Come, now, Willis, don't tease me any longer. You know I hate it.

CAMPBELL, *studying the superscriptions, one after another*: I want to see if I can guess who wrote them. Don't you like to guess who wrote your letters before you open them?

MRS. CAMPBELL, *with dignity*: I don't like to guess who wrote other people's letters.

She looks down at the tablecloth with a menace of tears, and Campbell instantly returns all the notes.

CAMPBELL: There, Amy; you may have them. I don't care who wrote them, nor what's in them. And I don't want you to interrupt me with any exclamations over them, if you please.

He reaches to the floor for his newspaper, and while he sips his coffee, Mrs. Campbell loses no time in opening her letters.

MRS. CAMPBELL: I shall do nothing *but* exclaim. The Curwens accept, of course—the very first letter. That means Mrs. Curwen; that is one, at any rate. The New York Addingses do, and the Philadelphia Addingses don't; I hardly expected they would, so soon after their aunt's death, but I thought I ought to ask them. Mr. and Mrs. Roberts, naturally; it was more a joke than anything, sending their invitation. Mrs. and the Misses Carver regret very much; well, *I* don't. Professor and Mrs. Traine are very happy, and so am I; he doesn't go everywhere, and he's awfully nice. Mr. and Mrs. Lou Bemis are very happy, too, and Dr. Lawton is very happy. Mrs. Bridges Dear Mrs. Campbells me, and is very sorry in the first person; she's always nice. Mr. Phillips, Mr. Rangeley, Mr. Small, Mr. Peters, Mr. Staples, Mr. Thornton, *all* accept, and they're all charming young fellows.

CAMPBELL, *around his paper*: Well, what of that?

MRS. CAMPBELL, *with an air of busy preoccupation*: Don't eavesdrop, please; I wasn't talking to you. The Merrills have the pleasure, and the Morgans are sorrow-stricken; the—

CAMPBELL: Yes, but why should you care whether those fellows are charming or not? Who's going to marry them?

MRS. CAMPBELL: *I* am. Mrs. Stevenson is bowed to the earth; Colonel Murphree is overjoyed; the Misses Ja—

CAMPBELL, *putting his paper down*: Look here, Amy. Do you know that you have one little infinitesimal ewe-lamb of a foible? You think too much of young men.

MRS. CAMPBELL: *Younger* men, you mean. And *you* have a multitude of perfectly mammoth peccadilloes. You interrupt. (*She goes on opening and reading her letters.*) Well, I didn't expect the Macklines *could*; but everybody seems to be coming.

CAMPBELL: You pay them too much attention altogether. It spoils them; and one of these days you'll be getting some of them in love with you, and *then* what will you do?

MRS. CAMPBELL, *with affected distraction*: What *are* you talking about? I'd refer them to you, and you could kill them. I suppose you killed lots of people in California. That's what you always gave me to understand.

She goes on with her letters.

CAMPBELL: I never killed a single human being that I can remember; but there's no telling what I might do if I were provoked. Now, there's that young Welling. He's about here under my feet all the time; and he's got a way lately of coming in through the window from the piazza that's very intimate. He's a nice fellow enough, and sweet, as you say. I suppose he has talent, too, but I never heard that he had set any of the adjacent watercourses on fire; and I don't know that he could give the Apollo Belvedere many points in beauty and beat him.

MRS. CAMPBELL: *I* do. Mrs. and Miss Rice accept, and her friend Miss Greenway, who's staying with her, and—yes! here's one from Mr. Welling! Oh, how glad I am! Willis, dearest, if I *could* be the means of bringing those two lovely young creatures together, I should be *so* happy! *Don't* you think, now, he *is* the most delicate-minded, truly refined, exquisitely modest young fellow that ever was?

She presses the unopened note to her corsage, and leans eagerly forward entreating a sympathetic acquiescence.

CAMPBELL: Well, as far as I can remember my own youth, no. But what does he say?

MRS. CAMPBELL, *regarding the letter*: I haven't looked yet. He writes the *most* characteristic hand, for a man, that I ever saw. And he has the divinest taste in perfumes! Oh, I wonder what *that* is? Like a memory—a regret.

She presses it repeatedly to her pretty nose, in the endeavor to ascertain.

CAMPBELL: Oh, hello!

MRS. CAMPBELL, *laughing*: Willis, you *are* delightful. I should like to see you really jealous once.

CAMPBELL: You won't, as long as I know my own incomparable charm. But give me that letter, Amy, if you're not going to open it. I want to see whether Welling is going to come.

MRS. CAMPBELL, *fondly*: Would you *really* like to open it? I've half a mind to let you, just for a reward.

CAMPBELL: Reward! What for?

MRS. CAMPBELL: Oh, I don't know. Being so nice.

CAMPBELL: That's something I can't help. It's no merit. Well, hand over the letter.

MRS. CAMPBELL: I should have thought you'd insist on *my* opening it, after that.

CAMPBELL: Why?

MRS. CAMPBELL: To show your confidence.

CAMPBELL: When I haven't got any?

MRS. CAMPBELL, *tearing the note open*: Well, it's no use trying any sentiment with you, or any generosity either. You're always just the same; a teasing joke is your ideal. You can't imagine a woman's wanting to keep up a little romance all through; and a character like Mr. Welling's, who's all chivalry and delicacy and deference, is quite beyond you. That's the reason you're always sneering at him.

CAMPBELL: I'm not sneering at him, my dear. I'm only afraid Miss Rice isn't good enough for him.

MRS. CAMPBELL, *instantly placated*: Well, she's the only girl who's anywhere *near* it. I don't say she's faultless, but she has a great deal of character, and she's very practical; just the counterpart of his dreaminess; and she *is* very, *very* good-looking, don't you think?

CAMPBELL: Her bang isn't so nice as his.

MRS. CAMPBELL: No; and aren't his eyes beautiful? And that high, serious look! And his nose and chin are perfectly divine. He looks like a young god!

CAMPBELL: I dare say; though I never saw an old one. Well, is he coming? I'm not jealous, but I'm impatient. Read it out loud.

MRS. CAMPBELL, *sinking back in her chair for*

the more luxurious perusal of the note: Indeed I shall not. (She opens it and runs it hastily through, with various little starts, stares, frowns, smiles of arrested development, laughs, and cries) Why—why! What does it mean? Is he crazy? Why, there's some mistake. No! It's his hand—and here's his name. I can't make it out. (She reads it again and again.) Why, it's perfectly bewildering! Why, there must be some mistake. He couldn't have meant it. Could he have imagined? Could he have dared? There never has been the slightest thing that could be tortured into— But of course not. And Mr. Welling, of all men! Oh, I can't understand it! Oh, Willis, Willis, Willis! What *does* it mean?

She flings the note wildly across the table, and catching her handkerchief to her face, falls back into her chair, tumultously sobbing.

CAMPBELL, *with the calm of a man accustomed to emotional superabundance, lifting the note from the toast-rack before him*: Well, let's see. (He reads aloud) "Oh, my darling! How can I live till I see you? I will be there long *before* the hour! To think of your *asking* me! You should have said, 'I permit you to come,' and I would have flown from the ends of the earth. The presence of others will be nothing. It will be sweet to ignore them in my heart, and while I see you moving among them, and looking after their pleasure with that beautiful thoughtfulness of yours, to think, 'She is mine, mine, mine!'

Oh, young lord lover, what sighs are those
For one that can never be thine? [1]

I thank you, and thank you a thousand times over, for this proof of your trust in me, and of your love—*our* love. You shall be the sole keeper of our secret—it is so sweet to think that no one even suspects it!—and it shall live with you, and if you will, it shall die with me. Forever yours, Arthur Welling." (Campbell turns the note over, and picking up the envelope, examines the address.) Well, *upon* my word! It's to you, Amy—on the outside, anyway. What do you suppose he means?

MRS. CAMPBELL, *in her handkerchief*: Oh, I don't know; I *don't* know why he should address such language to me!

CAMPBELL, *recurring to the letter*: I never did. "*Oh, my darling—live till I see you—ends of the earth—others will be nothing—beautiful thought-*

1 Tennyson, *Maud*, I, XXII, V, 29.

378 THE COMPLETE PLAYS OF WILLIAM DEAN HOWELLS

fulness—mine, mine, mine—our love—sweet to think no one suspects it—forever yours." Amy, these are pretty strong expressions to use towards the wife of another, and she a married lady! I think I had better go and solve that little problem of how he can live till he sees you by relieving him of the necessity. It would be disagreeable to him, but perhaps there's a social duty involved.

MRS. CAMPBELL: Oh, Willis, *don't* torment me! What do you suppose it means? Is it some—mistake? It's for somebody else!

CAMPBELL: I don't see why he should have addressed it to you, then.

MRS. CAMPBELL: But don't you see? He's been writing to some other person at the same time, and he's got the answers mixed—put them in the wrong envelopes. Oh dear! I wonder who she is!

CAMPBELL, *studying her with an air of affected abstraction*: Her curiosity gets the better of her anguish. Look here, Amy! *I* believe you're *afraid* it's to some one else.

MRS. CAMPBELL: Willis!

CAMPBELL: Yes. And before we proceed any further I must know just what you wrote to this—this Mr. Welling of yours. Did you put on R.S.V.P.?

MRS. CAMPBELL: Yes; and just a printed card like all the rest. I did want to write him a note in the first person, and urge him to come, because I expected Miss Rice and Miss Greenway to help me receive; but when I found Margaret had promised Mrs. Curwen for the next day, I knew she wouldn't like to take the bloom off that by helping me first; so I didn't.

CAMPBELL: Didn't what?

MRS. CAMPBELL: Write to him. I just sent a card.

CAMPBELL: Then these passionate expressions *are* unprovoked, and my duty is clear. I must lose no time in destroying Mr. Welling. Do you happen to know where I laid my revolver?

MRS. CAMPBELL: Oh, Willis, what are you going to do? You see it's a mistake.

CAMPBELL: Mr. Welling has got to prove that. I'm not going to have young men addressing my wife as Oh their darling, without knowing the reason why. It's a liberty.

MRS. CAMPBELL, *inclined to laugh*: Ah, Willis, how funny you are!

CAMPBELL: Funny? I'm furious.

MRS. CAMPBELL: You know you're not. Give me the letter, dearest. I know it's for Margaret Rice, and I shall see her, and just feel round and find out if it isn't so, and—

CAMPBELL: What an idea! You haven't the slightest evidence that it's for Miss Rice, or that it isn't intended for you, and it's my duty to find out. And nobody is authority but Mr. Welling. And I'm going to him with the *corpus delicti*.

MRS. CAMPBELL: But how can you? Remember how sensitive, how shrinking he is. Don't, Willis; you mustn't. It will kill him!

CAMPBELL: Well, that may save me considerable bother. If he will simply die of himself, I can't ask anything better.

He goes on eating his breakfast.

MRS. CAMPBELL, *admiring him across the table*: Oh, Willis, how perfectly delightful you are!

CAMPBELL: I know; but why?

MRS CAMPBELL: Why, taking it in the nice, sensible way you do. Now, some husbands would be so stupid! Of course you *couldn't* think—you couldn't *dream*—that the letter was really for me; and yet you might behave very disagreeably, and make me very unhappy, if you were not just the lovely, kind-hearted, magnanimous—

CAMPBELL, *looking up from his coffee*: Oh, hello!

MRS. CAMPBELL: Yes; that is what took my fancy in you, Willis: that generosity, that real gentleness, in spite of the brusque way you have. Refinement of the heart, *I* call it.

CAMPBELL: Amy, what are you after?

MRS. CAMPBELL: We've been married a whole year now—

CAMPBELL: Longer, isn't it?

MRS. CAMPBELL: —And I haven't known you do an unkind thing, a brutal thing.

CAMPBELL: Well, I understand the banging around hardly ever begins much under two years.

MRS. CAMPBELL: How *sweet* you are! And you're so funny always!

CAMPBELL: Come, come, Amy; get down to business. What is it you do want?

MRS. CAMPBELL: You won't go and tease that poor boy about his letter, will you? Just hand it to him, and say you suppose here is something that has come into your possession by mistake, and that you wish to restore it to him, and then—just run off.

CAMPBELL: With my parasol in one hand, and my skirts caught up in the other?

MRS. CAMPBELL: Oh, how good! Of course I was imagining how *I* should do it.

CAMPBELL: Well, a man can't do it that way. He would look silly. (*He rises from the table, and comes and puts his arm round her shoulders.*) But you needn't be afraid of my being rough with him. Of course it's a mistake; but he's a fellow who will enter into the joke too; he'll enjoy it; he'll— (*He merges his sentence in a kiss on her upturned lips, and she clings to his hand with her right, pressing it fondly to her cheek.*) I shall do it in a man's way; but I guess you'll approve of it quite as much.

MRS. CAMPBELL: I know I shall. That's what I like about you, Willis: your being so helplessly a man always.

CAMPBELL: Well, that's what attracted me to you, Amy; your manliness.

MRS. CAMPBELL: And I liked your *finesse*. You are awfully inventive, Willis. Why, Willis, I've just thought of something. Oh, it would be *so* good if you only would!

CAMPBELL: Would what?

MRS. CAMPBELL: Invent something now to get us out of the scrape.

CAMPBELL: What a brilliant idea! *I'm* not in any scrape. And as for Mr. Welling, I don't see how you could help him out unless you sent this letter to Miss Rice, and asked her to send yours back—

MRS. CAMPBELL, *springing to her feet*: Willis, you are inspired! Oh, how perfectly delightful! And it's so delicate of you to think of that! I will just enclose his note—give it here, Willis— and he need never know that it ever went to the wrong address. Oh, I always felt that you were *truly* refined, anyway. (*He passively yields the letter, and she whirls away to a writing-desk in the corner of the room.*) Now, I'll just keep a copy of the letter—for a joke; I think I've a perfect right to—(*scribbling furiously away*) and then I'll match the paper with an envelope—I can do that perfectly—and then I'll just imitate his hand—such fun!—and send it flying over to Margaret Rice. Oh, *how* good! Touch the bell, Willis. (*and then—as the serving-maid appears*) Yes, Jane! Run right across the lawn to Mrs. Rice's, and give this letter for Miss Margaret, and say it was left here by mistake. Well, it *was*, Willis. Fly, Jane! Oh, Willis, love! Isn't it perfect! Of course she'll have got his formal reply to my invitation, and be all mixed up by it, and now when this note comes, she'll see through it all in an instant, and it will be such a relief to her; and oh, she'll think that he's directed *both* the

letters to her because he couldn't think of any one else! Isn't it lovely? Just like anything that's nice, it's ten times as nice as you expected it to be; and—

CAMPBELL: But hold on, Amy! (*He lifts a note from the desk.*) You've sent your copy. Here's the original now. She'll think you've been playing some joke on her.

MRS. CAMPBELL, *clutching the letter from him, and scanning it in a daze*: What! Oh, my goodness! It is! I have! Oh, I shall die! Run! Call her back! Shriek, Willis! (*They rush to the window together.*) No, no! It's too late! She's given it to their man, and now nothing can save me! Oh, Willis! Willis! Willis! This is all your fault, with that fatal suggestion of yours. Oh, if you had only left it to me I never should have got into such a scrape! She will think now that I've been trying to hoax her, and she's perfectly implacable at the least hint of a liberty, and she'll be ready to kill me. I don't know *what* she won't do. Oh, Willis, how *could* you get me into this!

CAMPBELL, *irately*: Get you into this! Now, Amy, this is a little too much. You got yourself into it. You urged me to think of something—

MRS. CAMPBELL: Well, do, Willis, *do* think of something, or I shall go mad! Help me, Willis! Don't be so heartless—so unfeeling.

CAMPBELL: There's only one thing now, and that is to make a clean breast of it to Welling, and get him to help us out. A word from him can make everything right, and we can't take a step without him; we can't move!

MRS. CAMPBELL: I can't let you. Oh, isn't it horrible!

CAMPBELL: Yes; a nice thing is always ten times nicer than you expected it to be!

MRS. CAMPBELL: Oh, how can you stand there mocking me? Why don't you go to him at once, and tell him the whole thing, and beg him, implore him, to help us?

CAMPBELL: Why, you just told me I mustn't!

MRS. CAMPBELL: You didn't expect me to say you might, did you? Oh, how cruel!

She whirls out of the room, and Campbell stands in a daze, in which he is finally aware of Mr. Arthur Welling, seen through the open window, on the veranda without. Mr. Welling, with a terrified and furtive air, seems to be fixed to the spot where he stands.

CAMPBELL: Why, Welling, what the devil are you doing there?

WELLING: Trying to get away.

CAMPBELL: To get away? But you sha'n't, man! I won't let you. I was just going to see you. How long have you been there?

WELLING: I've just come.

CAMPBELL: What have you heard?

WELLING: Nothing—nothing. I was knocking on the window-casing to make *you* hear, but you seemed preoccupied.

CAMPBELL: Preoccupied! convulsed! cataclysmed! Look here: we're in a box, Welling. And you've got us into it. (*He pulls Welling's note out of his pocket, where he has been keeping his hand on it, and pokes it at him.*) Is that yours?

WELLING, *examining it with bewilderment mounting into anger*: It's mine; yes. May I ask, Mr. Campbell, how you came to have this letter?

CAMPBELL: May I ask, Mr. Welling, how you came to write such a letter to my wife?

WELLING: To your wife? To Mrs. Campbell? I never wrote any such letter to her.

CAMPBELL: Then you addressed it to her.

WELLING: Impossible!

CAMPBELL: Impossible? I think I can convince you, much as I regret to do so. (*He makes search about Mrs. Campbell's letters on the table first, and then on the writing-desk.*) We have the envelope. It came amongst a lot of letters, and there's no mistake about it. (*He continues to toss the letters about, and then desists.*) But no matter; I can't find it; Amy's probably carried it off with her. There's no mistake about it. I was going to have some fun with you about it, but now you can have some fun with me. Whom did you send Mrs. Campbell's letter to?

WELLING: Mrs. Campbell's letter?

CAMPBELL: Oh, pshaw! your acceptance or refusal, or whatever it was, of her garden fandango. You got an invitation?

WELLING: Of course.

CAMPBELL: And you wrote to accept it or decline it at the same time that you wrote this letter here to some one else. And you addressed two envelopes before you put the notes in either. And then you put them into the wrong envelopes. And you sent this note to my wife, and the other note to the other person—

WELLING: No, I didn't do anything of the kind!

He regards Campbell with amazement, and some apparent doubt of his sanity.

CAMPBELL: Well, then, Mr. Welling, will you allow me to ask what the deuce you did do?

WELLING: I never wrote to Mrs. Campbell at all. I thought I would just drop in and tell her

why I couldn't come. It seemed so formal to write.

CAMPBELL: Then will you be kind enough to tell me whom you *did* write to?

WELLING: No, Mr. Campbell, I can't do that.

CAMPBELL: You write such a letter as that to my wife, and then won't tell me whom it's to?

WELLING: No! And you've no right to ask me.

CAMPBELL: I've no right to ask you?

WELLING: No. When I tell you that the note wasn't meant for Mrs. Campbell, that's enough.

CAMPBELL: I'll be judge of that, Mr. Welling. You say that you were not writing two notes at the time, and that you didn't get the envelopes mixed. Then, if the note wasn't meant for my wife, why did you address it to her?

WELLING: That's what I can't tell; that's what I don't know. It's as great a mystery to me as it is to you. I can only conjecture that when I was writing that address I was thinking of coming to explain to Mrs. Campbell that I was going away to-day, and shouldn't be back till after her party. It was too complicated to put in a note without seeming to give my regrets too much importance. And I suppose that when I was addressing the note that I did write I put Mrs. Campbell's name on because I had her so much in mind.

CAMPBELL, *with irony*: Oh!

MRS. CAMPBELL, *appearing through the portière that separates the breakfast-room from the parlor beyond*: Yes! (*She goes up and gives her hand to Mr. Welling with friendly frankness.*) And it was very nice of you to think of me at such a time, when you ought to have been thinking of some one else.

WELLING, *with great relief and effusion*: Oh, thank you, Mrs. Campbell! I was sure you would understand. You couldn't have imagined me capable of addressing such language to you; of presuming—of—

MRS. CAMPBELL: Of course not! And Willis has quite lost his head. I saw in an instant just how it was. I'm so sorry you can't come to my party—

CAMPBELL: Amy, have you been eavesdropping?

MRS. CAMPBELL: There was no need of eavesdropping. I could have heard you out at Loon Rock Light, you shouted so. But as soon as I recognized Mr. Welling's voice I came to the top of the stairs and listened. I was sure you would do something foolish. But now I think we had better make a clean breast of it, and tell Mr. Welling just what we've done. We knew, of course, the letter wasn't for me, and we thought we wouldn't vex you about it, but just send it to the one it *was* meant for. We've surprised your secret, Mr. Welling, though we didn't intend to; but if you'll accept our congratulations—under the rose, of course—we won't let it go any further. It does seem so perfectly ideal, and I feel like saying, Bless you, my children! You've been in and out here so much this summer, and I feel just like an elder sister to Margaret.

WELLING: Margaret?

MRS. CAMPBELL: Well, Miss Rice, then—

WELLING: Miss Rice?

MRS. CAMPBELL, *with dignity*: Oh, I'm sorry if we seem to presume upon our acquaintance with the matter. We couldn't very well help knowing it under the circumstances.

WELLING: Certainly, certainly—of course: I don't mind that at all: I was going to tell you, anyway: that was partly the reason why I came instead of writing—

CAMPBELL, *in an audible soliloquy*: I supposed he *had* written.

MRS. CAMPBELL, *intensely*: Don't interrupt, Willis! Well?

WELLING: But I don't see what Miss Rice has to do with it.

MRS. CAMPBELL: You don't see! Why, isn't Margaret Rice the one—

WELLING: What one?

MRS. CAMPBELL: The one that you're engaged —the one that the note was really *for?*

WELLING: No! What an idea! Miss Rice? Not for an instant! It's—it's her friend—Miss Greenway—who's staying with her—

MRS. CAMPBELL, *in a very awful voice*: Willis! Get me some water—some wine! Help me! Ah! Don't touch me! It was you, *you* who did it all! Oh, *now* what shall I do?

She drops her head upon Campbell's shoulder, while Welling watches them in stupefaction.

CAMPBELL: It's about a million times nicer than we could have expected. That's the way with a nice thing when you get it started. Well, young man, you're done for; and so are we, for that matter. We supposed that note which you addressed to Mrs. Campbell was intended for Miss Rice—

WELLING: Ho, ho, ho! Ah, ha, ha! Miss Rice? Ha—

CAMPBELL: I'm glad you like it. You'll enjoy the rest of it still better. We thought it was for

Miss Rice, and my wife neatly imitated your hand on an envelope and sent it over to her just before you came in. Funny, isn't it? Laugh on! Don't mind *us!*

WELLING, *aghast*: Thought my note was for Miss Rice? Sent it to her? Gracious powers! (*They all stand for a moment in silence, and then Welling glances at the paper in his hand.*) But there's some mistake. You haven't sent my note to Miss Rice: here it is now!

CAMPBELL: Oh, that's the best of the joke. Mrs. Campbell took a copy—(*Mrs. Campbell moans.*) she meant to have some fun with you about it, and it's ten times as much fun as I expected; and in her hurry she sent off her copy and kept the original. Perhaps that makes it better.

MRS. CAMPBELL, *detaching herself from him and confronting Mr. Welling*: No; worse! She'll think we've been trying to hoax her, and she'll be in a towering rage; and she'll show the note to Miss Greenway, and you'll be ruined. Oh poor Mr. Welling! Oh, what a fatal, fatal—mix!

She abandons herself in an attitude of extreme desperation upon a chair, while the men stare at her, till Campbell breaks the spell by starting forward and ringing the bell on the table.

MRS. CAMPBELL: What are you doing, Willis?

CAMPBELL: Ringing for Jane. (*As Jane appears*) Did you give Miss Rice the note?

JANE: No, sir; I gave it to the man. He said he would give it to Miss Rice.

CAMPBELL: Then it's all up. If by any chance she hadn't got it, Amy, you might have sent over for it, and said there was a mistake.

JANE: He said Miss Rice was out driving with Miss Greenway in her phaeton, but they expected her back every minute.

MRS. CAMPBELL: Oh, my goodness! And you didn't come to tell me? Oh, if we had only known! We've lost our only chance, Willis.

JANE: I did come and knock on your door, ma'am, but I couldn't make you hear.

CAMPBELL: There's still a chance. Perhaps she hasn't got back yet.

JANE: I know she ain't, sir. I've been watching for her every since. I can always see them come, from the pantry window.

MRS. CAMPBELL: Well, then, don't stand there talking, but run at once! Oh, Willis! Never tell me again that there's no such thing as an overruling providence. Oh, what an interposition! Oh,

I can never be grateful and humble enough—
Goodness me, Jane! why don't you go?

JANE: Go where, ma'am? I don't know what
you want me to do. I'm willing enough to do anything if I know what it is, but it's pretty hard to
do things if you don't.

CAMPBELL: You're perfectly right, Jane. Mrs.
Campbell wants you to telegraph yourself over to
Mrs. Rice's, and say to her that the letter you
left for Miss Rice is not for her, but another lady,
and Mrs. Campbell sent it by mistake. Get it and
bring it back here, dead or alive, even if Mrs.
Rice has to pass over your mangled body in the
attempt.

JANE, *tasting the joke, while Mrs. Campbell
gasps in ineffective efforts to reinforce her husband's instructions*: I will that, sir.

CAMPBELL: And now, while we're waiting, let's
all join hands and dance round the table. You're
saved, Welling. So are you, Amy. And so am I—
which is more to the point.

MRS. CAMPBELL, *gayly*: Dansons! *(She extends
her hands to the gentlemen, and as they circle
round the breakfast-table she sings.)*

> Sur le pont d'Avignon,
> Tout le monde y danse en rond.

*(She frees her hands and courtesies to one gentle-
man and the other.)*

> Les belles dames font comme ça;
> Les beaux messieurs font comme ça.

*(Then she catches hands with them again, and
they circle round the table as before, singing.)*

> Sur le pont d'Avignon,
> Tout le monde y danse en rond.

Oh, dear! Stop! I'm dizzy—I shall fall.
    *She spins into a chair, while the men con-
    tinue solemnly circling by themselves.*
CAMPBELL: It is a sacred dance:

> Sur le pont d'Avignon—

WELLING: It's an expiation:

> Tout le monde y danse en rond.

MRS. CAMPBELL, *springing from her chair and
running to the window*: Stop, you crazy things!
Here comes Jane! Come right in here, Jane! Did
you get it? Give it to me, Jane!

WELLING: *I* think it belongs to me, Mrs. Campbell.

CAMPBELL: Jane, I am master of the house—
nominally. Give me the letter.

JANE, *entering, blown and panting, through the
open window*: Oh, how I did run—

MRS. CAMPBELL: Yes, yes! But the letter—

WELLING: Did you get it?

CAMPBELL: Where is it?

JANE, *fanning herself with her apron*: I can't
hardly get my breath—

MRS. CAMPBELL: Had she got back?

JANE: No, ma'am.

CAMPBELL: Did Mrs. Rice object to giving it
up?

JANE: No, sir.

WELLING: Then it's all right?

JANE: No, sir. All wrong.

WELLING: All wrong?

CAMPBELL: How all wrong?

MRS. CAMPBELL: What's all wrong, Jane?

JANE: Please, ma'am, may I have a drink of
water? I'm so dry I can't speak."

MRS. CAMPBELL: Yes, certainly.

CAMPBELL: Of course.

WELLING: Here.

    *They all pour glasses of water and press
    them to her lips.*

JANE, *pushing the glasses away, and escaping
from the room*: They thought Mrs. Campbell
was in a great hurry for Miss Rice to have the
letter, and they sent off the man with it to meet
her.

MRS. CAMPBELL: Oh, merciful goodness!

WELLING: Gracious powers!

CAMPBELL: Another overruling providence. Now
you *are* in for it, my boy! So is Amy. And so am I
—which is still more to the point.

MRS. CAMPBELL: Well, now, what shall we do?

CAMPBELL: All that we can do now is to await
developments: they'll come fast enough. Miss Rice
will open her letter as soon as she gets it, and she
won't understand it in the least; how *could* she
understand a letter in your handwriting, with
Welling's name signed to it? She'll show it to
Miss Greenway—

WELLING: Oh, don't say that!

CAMPBELL: —Greenway; and Miss Greenway
won't know what to make of it either. But she's
the kind of girl who'll form some lively conjec-
tures when she reads that letter. In the first place,
she'll wonder how Mr. Welling happens to be
writing to Miss Rice in that affectionate strain—

MRS. CAMPBELL, *in an appealing shriek*: Willis!

CAMPBELL: —And she naturally won't believe he's done it. But then, when Miss Rice tells her it's your handwriting, Amy, she'll think that you and Miss Rice have been having your jokes about Mr. Welling; and she'll wonder what kind of person you are, anyway, to make free with a young man's name that way.

WELLING: Oh, I assure you that she admires Mrs. Campbell more than anybody.

MRS. CAMPBELL: Don't try to stop him; he's fiendish when he begins teasing.

CAMPBELL: Oh, well! If she admires Mrs. Campbell and confides in you, then the whole affair is very simple. All you've got to do is to tell her that after you'd written her the original of that note, your mind was so full of Mrs. Campbell and her garden-party that you naturally addressed it to her. And then Mrs. Campbell can cut in and say that when she got the note she knew it wasn't for her, but she never dreamed of your caring for Miss Greenway, and was so sure it was for Miss Rice that she sent her a copy of it. That will make it all right and perfectly agreeable to every one concerned.

MRS. CAMPBELL: And I can say that I sent it at your suggestion, and then, instead of trying to help me out of the awful, awful—box, you took a cruel pleasure in teasing me about it! But I shall not say anything, for I shall not see them. I will leave you to receive them and make the best of it. Don't *try* to stop me, Willis.

She threatens him with her fan as he steps forward to intercept her escape.

CAMPBELL: No, no! Listen, Amy! You *must* stay and see those ladies. It's all well enough to leave it to me, but what about poor Welling? *He* hasn't done anything—except cause the whole trouble.

MRS. CAMPBELL: I am very sorry, but I can't help it. I must go. (*Campbell continues to prevent her flight, and she suddenly whirls about and makes a dash at the open window.*) Oh, very well, then! I can get out this way. (*At the same moment Miss Rice and Miss Greenway appear before the window on the piazza.*) Ugh! E—e—e! How you frightened me! But—but come in. So gl—glad to see you! And you—you too, Miss Greenway. Here's Mr. Welling. He's been desolating us with a story about having to be away over my party, and just getting back for Mrs. Curwen's. Isn't it too bad? Can't some of you young ladies—or all of you—make him stay?

As Mrs. Campbell talks on, she readjusts her

spirit more and more to the exigency, and subdues her agitation to a surface of the sweetest politeness.

MISS RICE, *entering with an unopened letter in her hand, which she extends to Mrs. Campbell:* What in the world does it all mean, Mrs. Campbell, your sending your letters flying after *me* at this rate?

MRS. CAMPBELL, *with a gasp:* My letters? (*She mechanically receives the extended note, and glances at the superscription.*) Mrs. Willis Campbell. Ah!

She hands it quickly to her husband, who reads the address with a similar cry.

CAMPBELL: Well, well, Amy! This is a pretty good joke on you. You've sealed up one of your own notes, and sent it to Miss Rice. Capital! Ah, ha, ha!

MRS. CAMPBELL, *with hysterical rapture:* Oh, how delicious! What a ridiculous blunder! I don't wonder you were puzzled, Margaret.

WELLING: What! Sent her your own letter, addressed to yourself?

MRS. CAMPBELL: Yes. Isn't it amusing?

WELLING: The best thing I ever heard of.

MISS RICE: Yes. And if you only knew what agonies of curiosity Miss Greenway and I had suffered, wanting to open it and read it anyway, in spite of all the decencies, I think you would read it to us.

CAMPBELL: Or at least give Miss Rice her own letter. What in the world did you do with that?

MRS. CAMPBELL: Put it in my desk, where I thought I put mine. But never mind it now. I can tell you what was in it just as well. Come in here a moment, Margaret.

She leads the way to the parlor, whither Miss Rice follows.

MISS GREENWAY, *poutingly:* Oh, mayn't I know, too? I think that's hardly fair, Mrs. Campbell.

MRS. CAMPBELL: No; or—Margaret may tell you afterwards; or Mr. Welling may, *now!*

MISS GREENWAY: How very formidable!

MRS. CAMPBELL, *over her shoulder, on going out:* Willis, bring me the refusals and acceptances, won't you? They're up-stairs.

CAMPBELL: Delighted to be of any service.

Behind Miss Greenway's back he dramatizes over her head to Welling his sense of his own escape, and his compassion for the fellow-man whom he leaves in the toils of fate.

WELLING: Nelly!

He approaches, and timidly takes her hand.

MISS GREENWAY: Arthur! That letter was addressed in your handwriting. Will you please explain?

WELLING: Why, it's very simple—that is, it's the most difficult thing in the world. Nelly, can you believe *anything* I say to you?

MISS GREENWAY: What nonsense! Of course I can—if you're not too long about it.

WELLING: Well, then, the letter in that envelope was one I wrote to Mrs. Campbell—or the copy of one.

MISS GREENWAY: The copy?

WELLING: But let me explain. You see, when I got your note asking me to be sure and come to Mrs. Curwen's—

MISS GREENWAY: Yes?

WELLING: —I had just received an invitation from Mrs. Campbell for her garden-party, and I sat down and wrote to you, and concluded I'd step over and tell her why I couldn't come, and with that in mind I addressed your letter—the one I'd written you—to her.

MISS GREENWAY: With my name inside?

WELLING: No; I merely called you "darling"; and when Mrs. Campbell opened it she saw it couldn't be for her, and she took it into her head it must be for Miss Rice.

MISS GREENWAY: For Margaret? What an idea! But why did she put your envelope on it?

WELLING: She made a copy, for the joke of it; and then, in her hurry, she enclosed that in my envelope, and kept the original and the envelope she'd addressed to Miss Rice, and—and that's all.

MISS GREENWAY: What a perfectly delightful muddle! And how shall we get out of it with Margaret?

WELLING: With Margaret? I don't care for her. It's you that I want to get out of it with. And you do believe me—you do forgive me, Nelly?

MISS GREENWAY: For what?

WELLING: For—for— I don't know what for. But I thought you'd be so vexed.

MISS GREENWAY: I shouldn't have liked you to send a letter addressed darling to Mrs. Curwen; but Mrs. Campbell is different.

WELLING: Oh, how archangelically sensible! How divine of you to take it in just the right way!

MISS GREENWAY: Why, of course! How stupid I should be to take such a thing in the wrong way!

WELLING: And I'm so glad now I didn't try to lie to you about it.

MISS GREENWAY: It wouldn't have been of any use. You couldn't have carried off anything of that sort. The truth is bad enough for *you* to carry off. Promise me that you will always leave the other thing to *me.*

WELLING: I will, darling; I will, indeed.

MISS GREENWAY: And now we must tell Margaret, of course.

MISS RICE, *rushing in upon them, and clasping Miss Greenway in a fond embrace*: You needn't. Mrs. Campbell has told me; and oh, Nelly, I'm so happy for you! And isn't it all the greatest mix?

CAMPBELL, *rushing in, and wringing Welling's hand*: You needn't tell me, either; I've been listening, and I've heard every word. I congratulate you, my dear boy! I'd no idea she'd let you up so easily. You'll allow yourself it isn't a very likely story.

WELLING: I know it. But—

MISS RICE: That's the very reason no one could have made it up.

MISS GREENWAY: *He* couldn't have made up even a likely story.

CAMPBELL: Congratulate you again, Welling. Do you suppose she can keep so always?

MRS. CAMPBELL, *rushing in with extended hands*: Don't answer the wretch, Mr. Welling. Of course she can with *you.* Dansons!

She gives a hand to Miss Greenway and Welling each; the others join them, and as they circle round the table she sings,

Sur le pont d'Avignon,
Tout le monde y danse en rond.

THE END

The Albany Depot

[1889]

Howells, interested as he was in everyday domestic happenings, frequently used slight situations in his plays. He was neither very adept at nor interested in plot, and the made-to-order situation relieved him of a problem; thus he could focus his attention on dialogue and lesser, detailed actions—both of which he enjoyed. Usually he found his plot in some friend's experience, but in *The Albany Depot* he confessed to being his own model. "This play," he wrote in "A Letter to the Publisher," in *Minor Dramas*, "grew from an incident of my own domestic experience, which I could not, at the time, have hoped to see ripen into its present form, so brief was then my 'expectation of life' in the perilous circumstances." Hamlin Garland in *Roadside Meetings* (New York: The Macmillan Co., 1930) also notes that Howells once told him that *The Albany Depot* was suggested by an experience of his own in hiring a cook for Mrs. Howells.

Although a native Bostonian of 1889 would be aware of Howells' artistic license, he would have had no trouble identifying the scene. When this play was written, the station for the Boston & Albany Railroad (leased to the New York Central system in 1900 for ninety-nine years) was located on Kneeland Street, which was probably only a ten-minute coupé ride from Stearns' Department Store, then in its first year of business in a new location at the corner of Tremont Street and Temple Place. In preparing his train schedule for *The Albany Depot*, Howells arbitrarily added a few train departures to build the scenic illusion of a railroad station and to break up the action with interruptions by "the colored man who calls the trains." The train times, then, are often inaccurate, and the listing of station stops is occasionally confused. But Howells realistically distinguishes between the Main Line and the Circuit Line trains and accurately describes the train to which the Robertses commit themselves as the 3:50 to Auburndale on the Main Line. The departure time is slightly changed, and Howells omits two towns, but the official timetable of the Boston & Albany Railroad Company, issued on June 24, 1895, lists Train #35, "West Newton, Auburndale, Riverside, Wellesley Farms, Wellesley Hills, Wellesley, Natick, So. Framingham, Express to West Newton."

The Albany Depot[1]

(THE ACTION PASSES IN BOSTON)

MRS. ROBERTS, *with many proofs of an after-noon's shopping in her hands and arms, appears at the door of the ladies' room, opening from the public hall, and studies the interior with a search-ing gaze, which develops a few suburban shoppers scattered over the settees, with their bags and packages, and two or three old ladies in the rock-ing-chairs. The Chorewoman is going about with a Saturday afternoon pail and mop, and profiting by the disoccupation of the place in the hour be-tween the departures of two great expresses, to wipe up the floor. She passes near the door where Mrs. Roberts is standing, and Mrs. Roberts ap-peals to her in the anxiety which her failure to detect the object of her search has awakened*: Oh, I was just looking for my husband. He was to meet me here at ten minutes past three; but there don't seem to be any gentlemen.

THE CHOREWOMAN: Mem?

MRS. ROBERTS: I was just looking for my hus-band. He was to meet me here at ten minutes past three; but there don't seem to be any gentlemen. You haven't happened to notice—

THE CHOREWOMAN: There's a gentleman over there beyant, readin', that's just come in. He seemed to be lukun' for somebody.

She applies the mop to the floor close to Mrs. Roberts's skirts.

MRS. ROBERTS, *bending to the right and to the left, and then, by standing on tip-toe, catching sight of a hat round a pillar*: Then it's Mr. Rob-erts, of course. I'll just go right over to him. Thank you ever so much. Don't disturb yourself! (*She picks her way round the area of damp left by the mop, and approaches the hat from behind.*) It is you, Edward! What a horrid idea I had! I was just going to touch your hat from behind, for fun; but I kept myself from it in time.

ROBERTS, *looking up with a dazed air from the magazine in his hand*: Why, what would have happened?

MRS. ROBERTS: Oh, you know it mightn't have been *you*.

ROBERTS: But it *was* I.

MRS. ROBERTS: Yes, I know; and I was per-fectly sure of it; you're always so prompt, and I always wonder at it, such an absent-minded crea-ture as you are. But you came near spoiling every-thing by getting here behind this pillar, and bury-ing yourself in your book that way. If it hadn't been for my principle of always asking questions, I never should have found you in the world. But just as I was really beginning to despair, the Chore-woman came by, and I asked her if she had seen any gentleman here lately; and she said there was one now, over here, and I stretched up and saw you. I had such a fright for a moment, not seeing you; for I left my little plush bag with my purse in it at Stearns's, and I've got to hurry right back; though I'm afraid they'll be shut when I get there, Saturday afternoon, this way; but I'm going to rattle at the front door, and perhaps they'll come —they always stay, some of them, to put the goods away; and I can tell them I don't want to buy any-thing, but I left my bag with my purse in it, and I guess they'll let me in. I want you to keep these things for me, Edward, and I'll leave my shopping-bag; I sha'n't want it any more. Don't lose any of them. Better keep them all in your lap here together, and then nobody will come and sit on them. (*She disburdens herself of her packages and parcels, and arranges them on her husband's knees, while she goes on talking.*) I'm almost ready to drop, I'm so tired, and I do believe I should let you go up to Stearns's for me; but you couldn't describe the bag so they would recognize it, let alone what was in it, and they wouldn't give it to you, even if they would let you in to inquire: they're much more likely to let a lady in than a gentleman. But I shall take a coupé, and tell the driver simply to fly, though there's plenty of time to go to the ends of the earth and back before our train starts. Only I should like to be here to receive the Campbells, and keep Willis from buying tickets for Amy and himself, and us, too, for that matter; he has that vulgar passion—I don't know

---

[1] The text used here is the Harper & Brothers edition.

where he's picked it up—for wanting to pay everybody's way; and you'd never think of your Hundred-Trip ticket-book till it was too late. Do take your book out and hold it in your hand, so you'll be sure to remember it, as soon as you see Willis. You had better keep saying over to yourself, "Willis—Hundred-Trip Tickets—Willis —Hundred-Trip Tickets"; that's the way I do. Where *is* the book? I have to remember everything! *Do* keep your ticket-book in your hand, Edward, till Willis comes.

ROBERTS: But I want to read, Agnes, and I've got to hold my *Pop. Sci.* with one hand and keep your traps in my lap with the other. Did you find a cook?

MRS. ROBERTS, *with rapturous admiration of him*: Well, Edward, you *have* got a brain! I declare, the cook had utterly gone out of my mind. Forgetting that plush bag makes me forget everything. I've got a splendid one—a perfect treasure. She won't do any of the wash, and we'll have to put that out; and she's been used to having a kitchen-maid; but she said we were such a small family that she could shell the peas herself. She's the most respectable-looking old thing you ever saw; and she's been having ten dollars a week from the last family she was in; but she'll come the summer with us for six. I was very fortunate to get her; all the good girls are snapped up for the sea-side in May, and they won't go into the country for love or money. It was the greatest chance! She's such a neat, quiet, lady-like person, and all the better for being Irish and a Catholic: Catholics *do* give so much more of a flavor; and I never could associate that Nova Scotia, sunken-cheeked leanness of Maria's with a cook. This one's name is—well, I forget what her name is; Bridget, or Norah, or something like that—and she's a perfect little butter-ball. She's coming to go out on the same train with us; and she'll get the dinner to-night; and I sha'n't have the mortification of sitting down to a pick-up meal with Amy Campbell, the first time she has visited us; she's conceited enough about her house-keeping as it is, I'm sure, and I wouldn't have her patronizing and pitying me for worlds. The cook will be here at half-past three precisely; I had to pretend the train started a little earlier than it does so as to make her punctual; they *are* such uncertain things! and I don't suppose I shall be back by that time, quite, Edward, and so you must receive her. Let me see! (*She glances up at the clock on the wall.*) It's just quarter-past now, and our train

goes at ten minutes to four— My goodness! I'll have to hurry.

THE COLORED MAN, *who cries the trains, walking half-way into the room and then out*: Cars ready for Cottage Farms, Longwood, Chestnut Hill, Brookline, Newton Centre, Newton Highlands, Waban, Riverside, and all stations between Riverside and Boston. Circuit Line train now ready on Track No. 3.

MRS. ROBERTS, *in extreme agitation*: Good gracious, Edward, that's our train!

ROBERTS, *jumping to his feet and dropping all her packages*: No, no, it isn't, my dear! That's the Circuit Line train: didn't you hear? Ours doesn't go till ten to four, on the Main Line.

MRS. ROBERTS: Oh yes, so it does. How ridiculous! But now I *must* run away and leave you, or I never shall get back in time. Be sure to speak to the cook as soon as she comes in, or she'll get discouraged and go away again; you can't depend on them for an instant; I told her *you* would be here to meet her, if I wasn't—I thought I might be late; and you musn't let her slip. And if the Campbells happen to get here before I'm back, don't you give them the least inkling of our having just engaged a cook. I'm going to smuggle her into the house without Amy's knowing it; I wouldn't have her know it for the world. She prides herself on keeping that impudent, spoiled thing of hers, with her two soups; and she would simply never stop crowing if she knew I'd had to change cooks in the middle of the summer.

ROBERTS, *picking up and dropping the multitudinous packages, and finally sitting down with them all in his lap, very red and heated*: I'll be careful, my dear.

MRS. ROBERTS: How flushed you are, bending over! You're so stout now, you ought to bend sidewise; it's perfect folly, your trying to bend *straight* over; you'll get apoplexy. But now I *must* run, or I shall never be back in the world. Don't forget to look out for the cook!

ROBERTS, *at whom she glances with misgiving as she runs out, holding the parcels on his knees with both elbows and one hand, and contriving with the help of his chin to get his magazine open again*: No, no; I won't, my dear.

He loses himself in his reading, while people come and go restlessly. A gentleman finally drops into the seat beside him, and contemplates his absorption with friendly amusement.

CAMPBELL: Don't mind *me*, Roberts.

ROBERTS, *looking up*: Heigh? What! Why, Willis! Glad to see you—

CAMPBELL: Now that you *do* see me, yes, I suppose you are. What have you got there that makes you cut all your friends? (*He looks at Roberts's open page.*) Oh! *Popular Science Monthly*. Isn't Agnes a little afraid of your turning out an agnostic? By-the-way, where *is* Agnes?

ROBERTS: She left her purse at Stearns's, and she's gone back after it. Where's Amy?

CAMPBELL: Wherever she said she wouldn't be at the moment. I expected to find her here with you and Agnes. What time did you say your train started?

ROBERTS: At ten minutes to four. And, by-the-way—I'd almost forgotten it—I must keep an eye out for the cook Agnes has been engaging. She was to meet us here before half-past two, and I shall have to receive her. You mustn't tell Amy; Agnes doesn't want her to know she's been changing cooks; and I've got to be very vigilant not to let her give us the slip, or you won't have any dinner to-night.

CAMPBELL: Is that so? Well, that interests *me*. Were you expecting to find her in the *Pop. Sci.?*

ROBERTS: Oh, I'd only been reading a minute when you came in.

CAMPBELL: I don't believe you know how long you'd been reading. Very likely your cook's come and gone.

ROBERTS, *with some alarm*: She couldn't. I'd only just opened the book.

CAMPBELL: I dare say you *think* so. But you'd better cast your eagle eye over this assemblage now, and see if she isn't here; though probably she's gone. What sort of looking woman is she?

ROBERTS, *staring at him in consternation*: Bless my soul! I don't know! I never saw her!

CAMPBELL: Never saw her?

ROBERTS: No; Agnes engaged her at the intelligence-office, and told her we should meet her here, and she had to go back for her purse, and left me to explain.

CAMPBELL: Ha, ha, ha! Ha, ha, ha! How did she expect you to recognize her?

ROBERTS: I—I don't know, I'm sure. She—she was very anxious I shouldn't let her get away.

CAMPBELL, *laughing*: You poor old fellow! What are you going to do?

ROBERTS: I'm sure I've no idea. Agnes—

CAMPBELL: Agnes ought to have a keeper. You know what I've always thought of *your* presence of mind, Roberts; but Agnes—I'm really surprised at Agnes. This is too good! I must tell Amy this. She'll never get over this. Ah, ha, ha, ha!

ROBERTS: No, no! You mustn't, Willis. Agnes would be very much provoked with me, if you told Amy she had been engaging a cook. She expects to smuggle her into the house without Amy's knowing.

CAMPBELL: And she left you to meet her here, and keep her—a cook you'd never set eyes on! Ha, ha, ha, ha! Ah, ha, ha, ha! What's her name?

ROBERTS: Agnes couldn't remember her last name—one never remembers a cook's last name. Her first name is Norah or Bridget.

CAMPBELL: Maggie, perhaps; they all sound alike. Ah, ha, ha! Ha, ha ha! This improves.

ROBERTS: Don't, Willis; you'll attract attention. What—what shall I do? If Agnes comes back, and finds I've let the cook get away, she'll be terribly put out.

CAMPBELL: Perfectly furious, you poor old fellow!—the rage of a disappointed pigeon! I wouldn't be in your shoes for anything. Oh my! I wish Amy was here. Did—did—Agnes—(*he struggles with his laughter, and explodes from time to time between syllables*)—did she tell you how the woman looked?

ROBERTS: She said she was a very respectable-looking old thing—a perfect butter-ball. I suppose she was stout.

CAMPBELL: That covers the ground of a great many cooks. They're apt to look respectable when they're off duty and they're not in liquor, and they're apt to be perfect butter-balls. Any other distinctive traits?

ROBERTS, *ruefully*: I don't know. She's Irish, and a Catholic.

CAMPBELL: They're apt to be Irish, and Catholics too. Well, Roberts, I don't see what you can ask better. All you've got to do is to pick out a respectable butter-ball of that religion and nationality, and tell her you're Mrs. Roberts's husband, and you're to keep her from slipping away till Mrs. Roberts gets here.

ROBERTS: Oh, pshaw, now, Willis! What would you do?

CAMPBELL: *There's* a respectable butter-ball over in the corner by the window there. You'd better go and speak to her. She's got a gingham bundle, like a cook's, in her lap, and she keeps looking about in a fidgety way, as if she expected somebody. I guess that's your woman, Roberts. Better not let her give you the slip. You'll never hear the last of it from Agnes if you do. And who'll get our dinner to-night?

ROBERTS, *looking over at the woman in the corner, with growing conviction*: She does answer to the description.

CAMPBELL: Yes, and she looks tired of waiting. If I know anything of that woman's character, Roberts, she thinks she's been trifled with, and she's not going to stay to be made a fool of any longer.

ROBERTS, *getting to his feet*: Do you think so? What makes you think so? Would you go and speak to her?

CAMPBELL: I don't know. She seems to be looking this way. Perhaps she thinks she recognizes *you*, as she never saw you before.

ROBERTS: There can't be any harm in asking her? She does seem to be looking this way.

CAMPBELL: Pretty blackly, too. I guess she's lost faith in you. It wouldn't be any use to speak to her now, Roberts.

ROBERTS: I don't know. I'm afraid I'd better. I must. How would you introduce the matter, Willis?

CAMPBELL: Oh, I wouldn't undertake to say! I must leave that entirely to you.

ROBERTS: Do you think I'd better go at it boldly, and ask her if she's the one; or—or—approach it more gradually?

CAMPBELL: With a few remarks about the weather, or the last novel, or a little society gossip? Oh, decidedly.

ROBERTS: Oh, come, now, Willis! What would you advise? You must see it's very embarrassing.

CAMPBELL: Not the least embarrassing. Simplest thing in the world!

THE COLORED MAN, *who calls the Trains, coming and going as before*: Cars for Newton, Newtonville, West Newton, Auburndale, Riverside, Wellesley Hills, Wellesley, Natick, and South Framingham. Express to Newton. Track No. 5.

CAMPBELL: Ah, she's off! She's going to take the wrong train. She's gathering her traps together, Roberts!

ROBERTS: I'll go and speak to her.

He makes a sudden dash for the woman in the corner. Campbell takes up his magazine, and watches him over the top of it, as he stops before the woman, in a confidential attitude. In a moment she rises, and with a dumb show of offence gathers up her belongings and marches past Roberts to the door, with an angry glance backward at him over her

shoulder. He returns crestfallen to Campbell.

CAMPBELL, *looking up from his magazine, in affected surprise*: Where's your cook? You don't mean to say she was the wrong woman?

ROBERTS, *gloomily*: She wasn't the right one.

CAMPBELL: How do you know? What did you say to her?

ROBERTS: I asked her if she had an appointment to meet a gentleman here.

CAMEBELL: You *did*? And what did she say?

ROBERTS: She said "No!" very sharply. She seemed to take it in dudgeon; she fired up.

CAMPBELL: I should think so. Sounded like an improper advertisement.

ROBERTS, *in great distress*: Don't, Willis, for Heaven's sake!

CAMPBELL: Why, you must see it had a very clandestine look. How did you get out of it?

ROBERTS: I didn't. I got into it further. I told her my wife had made an appointment for me to meet a cook here that she'd engaged—

CAMPBELL: You added insult to injury. Go on!

ROBERTS: And that she corresponded somewhat to the description; and—and—

CAMPBELL: Well?

ROBERTS: And she told me she was no more a cook than my wife was; and she said she'd teach me to be playing my jokes on ladies; and she grabbed up her things and flew out of the room.

CAMPBELL: Waddled, *I* should have said. But this is pretty serious, Roberts. She may be a relation of John L. Sullivan's. I guess we better get out of here; or, no, we can't! We've got to wait for Amy and Agnes.

ROBERTS: What—what would you do?

CAMPBELL: I don't know. Look here, Roberts: would you mind sitting a little way off, so as to look as if I didn't belong with you? I don't want to be involved in this little row of yours unnecessarily.

ROBERTS: Oh, come now, Willis! You don't think she'll make any trouble? I apologized. I said everything I could think of. She *must* think I was sincere.

CAMPBELL: In taking her for a cook? I've no doubt she did. But I don't see how that would help matters. I don't suppose she's gone for an officer; but I suspect she's looking up the largest Irishman of her acquaintance, to come back and interview you. I should advise you to go out and get on some train; I'd willingly wait here for Amy and Agnes; but you see the real cook might come here, after you went, and I shouldn't know her from Adam—or Eve. See?

ROBERTS, *desperately*: I see— Good heavens! Here comes that woman back; and a man with her. Willis, you must help me out.

Roberts gets falteringly to his feet, and stands in helpless apprehension, while Mr. and Mrs. McIlheny bear down upon him from the door. Mr. McIlheny, a small and wiry Irishman, is a little more vivid for the refreshment he has taken. He is in his best black suit, and the silk hat which he wears at a threatening slant gives dignified impressiveness to his figure and carriage. With some dumb-show of inquiry and assurance between himself and his wife, he plants himself in front of Roberts, in an attitude equally favorable for offence and defence.

MCILHENY: And are ye the mahn that's after takun' my wife for yer cuke?

MRS. MCILHENY, *indicating Campbell, absorbed in his magazine*: And there's the other wan I saw jokun' wid um, and puttun' um up to it.

MCILHENY, *after a swift glance at Campbell's proportions and self-possession*: That's what ye're after thinkun', Mary; but I haven't got annything to do with what ye're after thinkun'. All I wannt to know is what this mahn meant by preshumin' to speak to a lady he didn't know, and takun' her for a cuke. (*To Roberts*) Will ye tell me that, ye—

ROBERTS, *in extreme embarrassment*: Yes, yes, certainly; I shall be very glad to explain, if you'll just step here to the corner. We're attracting attention where we are—

MCILHENY: Attintion! Do ye suppose I care for attintion, when it's me wife that's been insulted?

He follows Roberts up, with Mrs. McIlheny, as he retires to the corner where she had been sitting, out of the way of the people coming and going. Campbell, after a moment, closes his magazine, and joins them.

ROBERTS: Insulted? By no manner of means! Nothing was further from my thoughts. I—I— can explain it all in a moment, my dear sir, if you will have patience; I can indeed. I have the highest respect for the lady, and I'm quite incapable of offering her an affront. The fact is— I hardly know how to begin—

MCILHENY: Go ahn, sor; or I'll have to do the beginnun' meself, pretty soon.

He shifts himself from one foot to another with a saltatory briskness.

ROBERTS: The fact is, my wife had engaged a cook, up-town, and she had sent her down here to meet me, and go out with me to our summer place at Weston.

MCILHENY: An' fwhat has all that rigamarole to do wid your speakin' to a lady ye'd never been inthrojuced to? Fwhat had yer wife's cuke to do with Mrs. McIlheny?

ROBERTS: Why, I didn't know the cook by sight, you see. My wife had engaged her up-town, and appointed her to meet me here, without reflecting that I had never seen her, and wouldn't know who she was, when I *did* see her; she partly expected to be here herself, and so I didn't reflect, either.

MCILHENY, *with signs of an amicable interest*: An' she lift ye to mate a lady ye never had seen before, and expicted ye to know her by soight?

ROBERTS: Precisely.

MCILHENY, *smiling*: Well, that's loike a wooman, Mary; ye can't say it ain't.

MRS. MCILHENY, *grinning*: It's loike a mahn, too, Mike, by the same token.

MCILHENY: Sure it's no bad joke on ye, sor.

CAMPBELL, *interposing*: I was having my laugh at him when your good lady here noticed us. You see, I know his wife—she's my sister—and I could understand just how she would do such a thing, and—ah, ha, ha, ha, ha! Ha, ha, ha! I don't think I shall ever get over it.

MCILHENY: Sure it *is* good! Hu, hu, hu, hu! Mary, it's what ye'd call a bull, if it was Irish, I'm thinkun'; an' it's no bad bull as it is, my dear.

MRS. MCILHENY, *laughing*: Ye're right there, Mike. It's as fine a bull as ever there was.

CAMPBELL: And my friend here insisted on going over and speaking to the lady, in hopes she could help him out of the difficulty. I suppose he bungled it; he only wanted to ask her if she'd seen a cook here, who had an appointment to go out of town with a gentleman. I'd been joking him about it, and he thought he must do something; and I fancy he made a mess of it. He was a good deal worked up. Ha, ha, ha! Ah, ha, ha, ha!

Mr. and Mrs. McIlheny join in his laugh, and finally Roberts himself.

THE COLORED MAN, *who calls the Trains, coming and going*: Cars for Auburndale, Riverside, Pine Grove, and Newton Lower Falls. Express to Auburndale, Track No. 7.

MRS. MCILHENY: There's our train. Mike! Come!

MCILHENY: So 'tis, Mary! Well, I'm hawpy to make yer acquaintance, gentlemen; and if ye're ever in the City Hahl when the Council is sittun', and ye'll send in yer names to Mike McIlheny, I'll be pl'ased to show ye ahl the attintion in me power. Ye must excuse me now; we're jist runnun' out to the Fahls to pass Sunday at a cousin's of Mrs. McIlheny's.

He shakes hands with Roberts and Campbell, and runs out, followed by his wife.

CAMPBELL: Distinguished public character. Well, we're out of that, Roberts. I had to crowd the truth a little for you, but I fetched the belligerent McIlheny. What are you going in for next?

ROBERTS: I—upon my word, I haven't the least idea. I think I shall give up trying to identify the cook. Agnes must do it herself when she comes here.

CAMPBELL: Oh no! *That* won't do, old fellow. The cook may come here and give you the slip before Agnes gets back.

ROBERTS: What would you do?

CAMPBELL: Well, I don't know; I don't like to advise, exactly; but it seems to me you've got to keep trying. You've got to keep your eye out for respectable butter-balls, and not let them slip through your fingers.

ROBERTS: You mean, go up and speak to them? I *couldn't* do that again.

CAMPBELL: Well, of course you didn't make a howling success with Mrs. McIlheny; but it wasn't a dead-failure either. But you must use a little more diplomacy—lead up to the subject gently. Don't go and ask a women if she's a cook, or had an appointment to meet a gentleman here. *That* won't do. I'll tell you! You might introduce the business by asking if she had happened to see a lady coming in or going out; and then describe Agnes, and say you had expected to meet her here. And she'll say she hadn't seen her here, but such a lady had just engaged her as a cook. And then you'll say you're the lady's husband, and you're sure she'll be in in a moment. And there you are! That's the way you ought to have worked it with Mrs. McIlheny. Then it would have come out all right.

ROBERTS, *pessimistically*: I don't see how it would have made her the cook.

CAMPBELL: It couldn't have done that, of course; but it would have done everything short of that. But we're well enough out of it, anyway. It was mighty lucky I came in with my little amendment just when I did. There's all the

difference in the world between asking a lady whether she *is* a cook and whether she's *seen* a cook. That difference just saved the self-respect of the McIlheny's, and saved your life. It gave the truth a slight twist in the right direction. You can't be too careful about the truth, Roberts. You can't offer it to people in the crude state; it's got to be prepared. If you'd carried it through the way I wanted you to, the night you and old Bemis garroted each other,[1] you'd have come out perfectly triumphant. What you want is not the *real* truth, but the *ideal* truth; not what you *did*, but what you *ought* to have done. Heigh? Now, you see, those McIlhenys have gone off with their susceptibilities in perfect repair, simply because I substituted a *for* for an *if*, and made you inquire *for* a cook instead of *if* she was a cook. Perhaps you did ask for instead of ask if?

ROBERTS: No, no. I asked her if she *was* a cook.

CAMPBELL: Well, I'm glad the McIlhenys had too much sense to believe that. They're happy, anyway. They're enjoying the hobble that you and Agnes are in, with lofty compassion. They—hello! here's that fellow coming back again!

ROBERTS: Who? Which? Where?

He starts nervously about, and confronts Mr. McIlheny bearing down upon him with a countenance of provisional severity.

MCILHENY: Just wan word more wid you, sor. Mrs. McIlheny has been thinkun' it oover, and she says you didn't ask her if she was after *seeun'* a cuke, but whether she was after *beun'* a cuke? Now, sor, which wahs ut? Out wid ut! Don't be thinkun' ye can throw dust in our eyes because we're Irishmen! (*A threatening tone prevails in Mr. McIlheny's address at the mounting confusion and hesitation in Roberts.*) Come! are ye deaf, mahn?

ROBERTS, *in spite of Campbell's dumb-show inciting him to fiction*: I—I—if you will kindly step apart here, I can explain. I was very confused when I spoke to Mrs. McIlheny.

MCILHENY, *following him and Willis into the corner*: Fwhat made ye take my wife for a cuke? Did she luke anny more like a cuke than yer own wife? Her family is the best in County Mayo. Her father kept six cows, and she never put her hands in wather. And ye come up to her in a public place like this, where ye're afraid to spake aboove yer own breath, and ask her if she's after beun' the cuke yer wife's engaged. Fwhat do ye mane by ut?

ROBERTS: My dear sir, I know—I can under-

1 A reference to *The Garroters*.

stand how it seems offensive; but I can assure you that I had no intention—no—no—

He falters, with an imploring glance at Campbell, who takes the word.

CAMPBELL: Look here, Mr. McIlheny, you can appreciate the feelings of a gentleman situated as my friend was here. He had to meet a lady whom he had never seen before, and didn't know by sight; and we decided—Mrs. McIlheny was so pleasant and kindly looking—that he should go and ask here if she had seen a lady of the description he was looking for, and—

MCILHENY: Yessor! I can appreciate ahl *that*. But fwhy did he ask her if *she* was the lady? Fwhy did he ask her if she was a cuke? That's what I wannt to know!

CAMPBELL: Well, now, I'm sure you can understand that. He was naturally a good deal embarrassed at having to address a strange lady; his mind was full of his wife's cook, and instead of asking her if she'd *seen* a cook, he bungled and he blundered, and asked her—I suppose—if she *was* a cook. Can't you see that? how it would happen?

MCILHENY, *with conviction*: Yessor, I can. And I'll feel it an hannor if you gintlemen will join me in a glass of wine on the carner, across the way—

CAMPBELL: But your train?

MCILHENY: Oh, domn the thrain! But I'll just stip aboord and tell Mrs. McIlheny I've met a frind, an' I'll be out by the next thrain, an' I'll be back wid you in a jiffy.

He runs out, and Campbell turns to Roberts.

ROBERTS: Good heavens, Willis! what are we going to do? Surely, we can't go out and drink with this man?

CAMPBELL: I'm afraid we sha'n't have the pleasure. I'm afraid Mrs. McIlheny is of a suspicious nature; and when Mr. Mac comes back, it'll be to offer renewed hostility instead of renewed hospitality. I don't see anything for us but flight, Roberts. Or, *you* can't fly, you poor old fellow! You've got to stay and look out for that cook. I'd be glad to stay for you, but, you see, I should not know her.

ROBERTS: I don't know her either, Willis. I was just thinking whether you couldn't manage this wretched man rather better alone. I—I'm afraid I confuse you; and he gets things out of me—admissions, you know—

CAMPBELL: No, no! Your moral support is everything. That lie of mine is getting whittled

away to nothing; we shall soon be down to the bare truth. If it hadn't been for these last admissions of yours, I don't know what I should have done. They were a perfect inspiration. I'll tell you what, Roberts! I believe you can manage this business twice as well without me. But you must keep your eye out for the cook! You mustn't let any respectable butter-ball leave the room without asking her if she's the one. You'll know how to put it more delicately now. And I won't complicate you with McIlheny any more. I'll just step out here—

ROBERTS: No, no, no! You musn't go, Willis. You mustn't indeed! I shouldn't know what to do with that tipsy nuisance. Ah, here he comes again!

CAMPBELL, *cheerily, to the approaching McIlheny*: I hope you didn't lose your train, Mr. McIlheny!

MCILHENY, *darkly*: Never moind my thrain, sor! My wife says it was a put-up jahb between ye. She says ye were afther laughun', and lukun' and winkun' at her before this mahn stipped up to spake to her. Now what do ye make of that?

CAMPBELL: We were laughing, of course. I had been laughing at my friend's predicament, in being left to meet a lady he'd never seen before. You laughed at it yourself.

MCILHENY: I did, sor.

ROBERTS, *basely truckling to him*: It was certainly a ludicrous position.

CAMPBELL: And when we explained it, it amused your good lady too. She laughed as much as yourself—

MCILHENY: She did, sor. Ye're right. Sure it would make a cow laugh. Well, gintlemen, ye must excuse me. Mrs. McIlheny says I mustn't stop for the next thrain, and I'll have to ask you to join me in that glass of wine some other toime.

CAMPBELL: Oh, it's all right, Mr. McIlheny. You've only got about half a minute.

He glances at the clock, and McIlheny runs out, profusely waving his hand in adieu.

ROBERTS, *taking out his handkerchief and wiping his forehead*: Well, thank Heaven! we're rid of him at last.

CAMPBELL: I'm not so sure of that. He'll probably miss the train. You may be sure Mrs. McIlheny is waiting for him outside of it, and then we shall have them both on our hands indefinitely. We shall have to explain and explain. Fiction has entirely failed us, and I feel that the truth is giving way under our feet, I'll tell you what, Roberts!

ROBERTS, *in despair*: What?

CAMPBELL: Why, if McIlheny should happen to come back alone, we mustn't wait for him to renew his invitation to drink; we must take him out ourselves, and get him drunk; so drunk he can't remember anything; stone drunk; dead drunk. Or, that is, *you* must. I haven't got anything to do with him. I wash my hands of the whole affair.

ROBERTS: You mustn't, Willis! You know I can't manage without you. And you know I can't take the man out and get him drunk. I couldn't. I shouldn't feel that it was right.

CAMPBELL: Yes, I know. You'd have to drink with him; and you've got no head at all. You'd probably get drunk first, and I don't know what I should say to Agnes.

ROBERTS: That isn't the point, Willis. I couldn't ask the man to drink; I should consider it immoral. Besides, what should you do if the cook came while I was away? You wouldn't know her.

CAMPBELL: Well, neither would you, if you stayed.

ROBERTS: That's true. There doesn't seem to be any end of it, or any way out of it. I must just stay and bear it.

CAMPBELL: Of *course* you must stay. And when McIlheny comes back, you'd better ask him out to look upon the wine when it is red.[1]

ROBERTS: No; that's impossible, quite. I shouldn't mind the association—though it isn't very pleasant; but to offer drink to a man already— Do you suppose it would do to ask him out for a glass of soda? Plain soda would be good for him. Or I could order claret in it, if the worst came to the worst.

CAMPBELL: Claret! What Mr. McIlheny requires is forty-rod whiskey in a solution of sulphuric acid. You must take that, or fourth-proof brandy straight, with him.

ROBERTS, *miserably*: I couldn't; you know I couldn't.

CAMPBELL: What are you going to do, then?

ROBERTS: I don't know; I don't know. I—I'll give him in charge to a policeman.

CAMPBELL: And make a scandal here?

ROBERTS: Of course it can't be done!

CAMPBELL: Of *course* it can't. Give a councilman in charge? The policeman will be Irish too, and then what'll you do? You're more likely to be carried off yourself, when the facts are ex-

plained. They'll have an ugly look in the police report.

ROBERTS: Oh, it can't be done! Nothing can be done! I wish Agnes would come!

THE COLORED MAN, *who calls the Trains*: Cars ready for South Framingham, Whitneys, East Holliston, Holliston, Metcalf's, Braggville, and Milford. Express to Framingham. Milford Branch. Track No. 3."

MRS. ROBERTS, *rushing in and looking about in a flutter, till she discovers her husband*: Good gracious, Edward! Is that our train? I ran all the way from the station door as fast as I could run, and I'm perfectly out of breath. Did you ever hear of anything like my meeting Amy on the very instant? She was getting out of her coupé just as I was getting out of mine, and I saw her the first thing as soon as I looked up. It was the most wonderful chance. And the moment we pushed our way through the door and got inside the outer hall, I heard the man calling the train— he calls so distinctly—and I told her I was sure it was our train; and then we just simply flew, both of us. I had the greatest time getting my plush bag. They were all locked up at Stearns's as tight as a drum, but I saw somebody inside, moving about, and I rattled the door, and made signs till he came; and then I said I had left my plush bag; and he said it was against the rules, and I'd have to come Monday; and I told him I knew it was, and I didn't expect him to transgress the rules, but I wished very much to have my plush bag, because there were some things in it that I wished to have, as well as my purse; for I'd brought away my keys in it; and I knew Willis— how d'ye do, Willis?—would want wine with his dinner, and you'd have to break the closet open if I didn't get the key; and so he said he would see if the person who kept the picked-up things was there yet; and it turned out he was, and he asked me for a description of the bag and its contents; and I described them all, down to the very last thing; and he said I had the greatest memory he ever saw. And now I think everything is going off perfectly, and I shall be able to show Amy that there's something inland as well as at the seaside. Why don't you speak to her, Edward? What is the matter? What are you looking at? (*She detects him in the act of craning his neck to this side and that, and peering over people's heads and shoulders in the direction of the door.*) Hasn't Norah—Bridget, I mean—come yet?

She frowns significantly, and cautions him

[1] Proverbs, 23 : 31, 32.

concerning Mrs. Campbell by pressing her finger to her lip.

ROBERTS: Yes—yes, she's here; I suppose she's—she's here. How do you do, Amy? So glad—

He continues his furtive inspection of the door-way, and Willis turns away with a snicker.

MRS. CAMPBELL: Willis, what are you laughing at? Is there anything wrong with my bonnet? Agnes, *is* there? He would let me go about looking like a perfect auk. Did I bang it getting out of the coupé? Do tell me, Willis!

MRS. ROBERTS, *to her husband*: You don't mean to say you haven't *seen* her yet?

ROBERTS, *desperately*: Seen her? How should I know whether I've seen her? I never saw her in my life.

MRS. ROBERTS: Then what are you looking for, in that way?

ROBERTS: I—I'm looking for her husband.

MRS. ROBERTS: Her husband?

ROBERTS: Yes. He keeps coming back.

Campbell bursts into a wild shriek of laughter.

MRS. ROBERTS, *imploringly*: Willis, what *does* it mean?

MRS. CAMPBELL, *threateningly*: Willis, if you don't behave yourself—

MRS. ROBERTS, *with the calm of despair*: Well, then, she isn't coming! She's given us the slip! I might have known it! Well, the cat might as well come out of the bag first as last, Amy, though I was trying to keep it in, to spare your feelings; I knew you'd be so full of sympathy. (*Suddenly to her husband*) But if you saw her husband—Did he say she sent him? I didn't dream of her being married. How do you know it's her husband?

ROBERTS: Because—because she went out and got him! Don't I tell you?

MRS. ROBERTS: Went out and got him?

ROBERTS: When I spoke to her.

MRS. ROBERTS: When you spoke to her? But you said you didn't see her!

ROBERTS: Of *course* I didn't see her. How should I see her, when I never saw her before? I went up and spoke to her, and she said she wasn't the one. She was very angry, and she went out and got her husband. He was tipsy, and he's been coming back ever since. I don't know what to do about the wretched creature. He says I've insulted his abominable wife!

CAMPBELL, *laughing*: O Lord! Lord! This will be the death of me!

MRS. CAMPBELL: This is one of your tricks, Willis; one of your vile practical jokes.

CAMPBELL: No, no, my dear! I couldn't invent anything equal to *this*. Oh my! oh my!

MRS. CAMPBELL, *seizing him by the arm*: Well, if you don't tell, instantly, what it is—

CAMPBELL: But I *can't* tell. I promised Roberts I wouldn't.

ROBERTS, *wildly*: Oh, tell, tell!

CAMPBELL: About the cook, too, Agnes?

MRS. ROBERTS: Yes, yes; everything! Only tell!

CAMPBELL, *struggling to recover himself*: Why, you see, Agnes engaged a cook, up-town—

MRS. ROBERTS: I didn't want you to know it, Amy. I thought you would be troubled if you knew you were coming to visit me just when I was trying to break in a new cook, and so I told Edward not to let Willis know. Go on, Willis.

MRS. CAMPBELL: And I understand just how you felt about it, Agnes; you knew he'd laugh. Go on, Willis.

CAMPBELL: And she sent her down here, and told Roberts to keep her till she came herself.

BOTH LADIES: Well?

CAMPBELL: And I found poor old Roberts here, looking out for a cook that he'd never seen before, and expecting to recognize a woman that he'd never met in his life.

He explodes in another fit of laughter. The ladies stare at him in mystification.

MRS. ROBERTS: I would have stayed myself to meet her, but I'd left my plush bag with my purse in it at Stearns's, and I had to go back after it.

MRS. CAMPBELL: She *had* to leave him. What is there to laugh at?

MRS. ROBERTS: I see nothing to laugh at, Willis.

CAMPBELL, *sobered*: You *don't*?

BOTH LADIES: No.

CAMPBELL: Well, by Jove! Then perhaps you don't see anything to laugh at in Roberts's having to guess who the cook was; and going up to the wrong woman, and her getting mad, and going out and bringing back her little fiery-red tipsy Irishman of a husband, that wanted to fight Roberts; and my having to lie out of it for him; and their going off again, and the husband coming back four or five times between drinks, and having to be smoothed up each time—

BOTH LADIES: No!

MRS. ROBERTS: It was simply horrid.

MRS. CAMPBELL: It wasn't funny at all; it was simply disgusting. Poor Mr. Roberts!

CAMPBELL: Well, by the holy poker! This knocks me out! The next time I'll marry a man, and have somebody around that can appreciate a joke. The Irishman said himself it would make a cow laugh.

MRS. CAMPBELL: I congratulate you on being of the same taste, Willis. And I daresay you tried to heighten the absurdity, and add to poor Mr. Roberts's perplexity.

ROBERTS: No, no! I assure you, Amy, if it hadn't been for Willis, I shouldn't have known how to manage. I was quite at my wits' end.

MRS. CAMPBELL: You are very generous, I'm sure, Mr. Roberts; and I suppose I shall have to believe *you*.

ROBERTS: But I couldn't act upon the suggestion to take the man out and treat him; Willis was convinced himself, I think, that that wouldn't do. But I confess I was tempted.

MRS. ROBERTS: Treat him?

ROBERTS: Yes. He was rather tipsy already; and Willis thought he would be more peaceable perhaps if we could get him quite drunk; but I really couldn't bring my mind to it, though I was so distracted that I was on the point of yielding.

BOTH LADIES: Willis!

MRS. ROBERTS: You wanted poor Edward to go out and drink with that wretched being, so as to get him into a still worse state?

MRS. CAMPBELL: You suggested that poor Mr. Roberts should do such a thing as that? Well, Willis!

MRS. ROBERTS: Well, Willis! (*She turns from him more in sorrow than in anger, and confronts a cook-like person of comfortable bulk, with a bundle in her hand, and every mark of hurry and exhaustion in her countenance.*) Why, here's Bridget now!

THE COOK: Maggie, mem! I was afraid I was after missun' you, after all. I couldn't see the gentleman anywhere, and I've been runnin' up and down the depot askun' fur um; and at last, thinks I, I'll try the ladies' room; and sure enough here ye was yourself. It was lucky I thought of it.

MRS. ROBERTS: Oh! I forgot to tell you he'd be in the ladies' room. But it's all right now, Maggie; and we've just got time to catch our train.

CAMPBELL, *bitterly*: Well, Agnes, for a woman that's set so many people by the ears, you let your-self up pretty easily. By Jove! here comes that fellow back again!

They all mechanically shrink aside, and leave Roberts exposed to the approach of McIlheny.

MCILHENY: Now, sor, me thrain's gahn, and we can talk this little matter oover at our aise. What did ye mane, sor, by comin' up to the Hannorable Mrs. Michael McIlheny and askun' her if she was a cuke? Did she luke like a person that'd demane herself to a manial position like that? Her that never put her hands in wather, and had hilpers to milk her father's cows? What did ye mane, sor? Did she luke like a lady, or did she luke like a cuke? Tell me that!

THE COOK, *bursting upon him from behind Roberts, who eagerly gives place to her*: I'll tell ye that meself, ye impidint felly! What's to kape a cuke from lukun' like a lady, or a lady from lukun' like a cuke? Ah, Mike McIlheny, ye drunken blaggurd, is it *me* ye're tellin' that Mary Molloy never put her hands in wather, and kept hilpers to milk her father's cows! Cows indade! It was wan pig under the bed; and more shame to them that's ashamed to call it a pig, if ye *are* my cousin! *I'm* the lady the gentleman was lukin' for, and if ye think I'm not as good as Mary Molloy the best day she ever stipped, I'll thank ye to tell me who is. Be off wid ye, or I'll say something ye'll not like to hear!

MCILHENY: Sure I was jokin', Maggie! I was goun' to tell the gintleman that if he was lukun' for a cuke, I'd a cousin out of place that was the best professed cuke in Bahston. And I'm glad he's got ye: and he's a gintleman every inch, and so's his lady, I dar' say, though I haven't the pleasure of her acquaintance—

THE COLORED MAN, *who calls the Trains*: Cars ready for West Newton, Auburndale, Riverside, Wellesley, Natick, and South Framingham. Train for South Framingham. Express to West Newton. Track No. 5.

MRS. ROBERTS: That's our train, Amy! We get off at Auburndale. Willis, Edward, Maggie—come!

They all rush out, leaving McIlheny alone.

MCILHENY, *looking thoughtfully after them*: Sure, I wonder what Mary'll be wantun' me to ask um next!

THE END

A Letter of Introduction

[1892]

Everyone is occasionally absent-minded; therefore Howells needed no particular source for his main situation in *A Letter of Introduction*, but concerning a lesser incident in the play he had this to say in "A Letter to the Publisher" (*Minor Dramas*):

> Once a lady gave me the fact of her having rung the fire alarm before her door in an effort to post her letter in the alarm-box, which, with us, so much resembles a mail-box. But when I warned her that this fact would probably be traced home to her, she withdrew it. Within a week I had the satisfaction of sending her a newspaper cutting from New York where a lady had done exactly that thing, and brought the whole fire department about the house, and narrowly escaped fine and imprisonment, and I do not know what else.

Making obvious use of situations, *A Letter of Introduction* is primarily farce, but to call it such without very important qualifications is to malign one of Howells' more successful attempts at satirizing fashionable society in his one-act drama. Occasionally he strikes at that lesser society south of Boston; Campbell, professing some difficulty in establishing the nationality of Westgate, says, ". . . and he had so much of that English brogue, when he spoke, that I thought he must be a New Yorker." Boston, however, remains a principal target for Howells. There is Campbell's contrived scene of "a cultivated Boston family, at home with itself, and at peace with the whole *human* family." Later, Howells uses Campbell again to poke fun at the reputation for snobbery that prevailed among Boston's Back Bay aristocracy: ". . . and for a real, unadulterated diffidence, a shrinking, deprecatory little misgiving as to the existence of the outside universe, I think Mr. Westgate will find that Boston takes the cake. In California people don't *know* they're modest, but in Boston they *do*. That's the difference."

The English, represented by Mr. Westgate, also receive their share of Howells' satiric fun; however, despite Roberts' comments on Westgate's "insular manner," his being "nationally English" but personally nice, and his being necessarily offensive as an Englishman, Westgate comes out rather well at the end of the play. Throughout it all, Howells is never bitter or mean in his ridiculing conversation, although sometimes he is biting. His method is clear and acute observation; his object seems to be an ironic playfulness which he as both an insider and an outsider in Boston society could well enjoy.

A Letter of Introduction[1]

MRS. ROBERTS, *looking in upon her husband from the door of the library in their apartment at the Hotel Bellingham*: Well, you've got rid of him, Edward.

ROBERTS: Yes, at last, thank Heaven! (*He continues writing at his table, without looking up, as he answers his wife.*) But I thought he never would go, at one time. He isn't a bad kind of fellow, for an Englishman, and if I hadn't been so busy with this paper, I shouldn't have minded his staying. Of course he was nationally English, but personally he was rather nice. Still it was a terrible interruption, just at this moment.

MRS. ROBERTS: Why didn't you hint to him, somehow, to go away?

ROBERTS: Well, I couldn't do that, you know. I really liked him. He was so very amiable.

MRS. ROBERTS: Oh, his being amiable is no excuse. You're amiable yourself, Edward—*too* amiable, if anything. I don't call it amiable to take up almost a full hour of your precious time. I should think any one who came in and saw how busy you were, now, would go away if he had a heart of *stone*. No, I can't believe he was truly amiable; and I must really do something to protect you from these constant interruptions. How do you think I'd better do it?

ROBERTS, *writing*: Do what?

MRS. ROBERTS, *sinking into a chair, and folding her hands in her lap*: Protect you from these interruptions.

ROBERTS, *writing*: Protect *who*?

MRS. ROBERTS: You, Edward. My heart bleeds for you, to see you so driven with your work, and then people coming in and sitting down, and talking to you. I must *stop* it.

ROBERTS, *writing*: Oh yes. Stop what?

MRS. ROBERTS: These perfectly killing interruptions. I should think you would go crazy.

ROBERTS, *writing*: Who?

MRS. ROBERTS: Why you, you poor thing. I

1 The text used here is the Harper & Brothers edition.

think it's worse than cruelty to animals.

ROBERTS, *writing*: Worse than cruelty to animals. Worse— Why, what nonsense is this you've made me write, Agnes? (*He looks up at her in a daze.*) What *do* you want, Agnes? And *do* state it succinctly, my dear!

MRS. ROBERTS: Why, I didn't know but you'd asked him to stay to lunch.

ROBERTS, *writing again*: No; I didn't really feel that I could give the time. I should have liked to do so, and I suppose it was rather shabby not to. It was the least he could have expected. (*He continues writing.*) But I've done the next best thing. I've given him a letter of introduction to Uncle Philip, and he will glut him with all kinds of hospitality when he gets to New York.

MRS. ROBERTS: Yes. (*After a moment*) Do you think it was quite right, Edward?

ROBERTS, *looking up*: Right? What right?

MRS. ROBERTS: To put him off on your uncle, if you didn't like him yourself?

ROBERTS: But I *did* like him. I liked him as well as it's possible to like any Englisman on short notice. You have to know an Englishman several days before you're sure you like him; but this one was really very pleasant, and I told Uncle Philip he would probably find him so, unless I was greatly deceived. But now, Agnes, you must really let me go on—

MRS. ROBERTS: Surely, Edward, you didn't put that into a letter of introduction?

ROBERTS, *laughing*: That I would have to leave open for him to read? Well, I'm not quite so bad as *that*, Agnes. I wrote a letter to Uncle Philip, to go through the post, and I told him that as soon as he got through the crust of a rather insular manner, and a most unaccountable enthusiasm for Americans, I'd no doubt he'd find my Englishman charming. You couldn't suppose I'd put all that in a letter of introduction?

MRS. ROBERTS: Of course not. But you know you *are* so absent-minded, my dear, and I couldn't help being a little afraid—

ROBERTS: Your fears come too late, my dear.

The Englishman is gone, and both the letters with him. Now you *must* let me finish this—

MRS. ROBERTS, *rising to her feet in amazement*: Both the letters with him?

ROBERTS: Yes; I knew he would pass the letter-box on the corner, and I asked him to drop Uncle Philip's letter in it.

MRS. ROBERTS: Wasn't that rather peculiar, Edward?

ROBERTS, *with vexation*: Peculiar? No! What was peculiar about it?

The Voices, in the anteroom, without, of Mr. and Mrs. Willis Campbell:—

HE: In the library? Well, we'll just push right in on them.

SHE: And Mrs. Roberts is there too?

ROBERTS: Oh, good heavens! Go out, Agnes, and stop them! Take them into the parlor a moment, do, till I get this—

MRS. ROBERTS: You *know* I can't do that, Edward! (*To Mrs. Campbell, at the door*) Ah! Come in, Amy! I'm *so* glad to see you.

The ladies kiss, and Campbell follows his wife in.

CAMPBELL: And so is Roberts; but he doesn't look it. Hope I don't interrupt you, Roberts, as people say when they know they do.

ROBERTS, *who has pushed away his writing, and risen to greet the intruders with forced gayety*: How do you do, Amy? No; I was just getting to the end of my morning's work, Willis.

CAMPBELL: Well, it'll do you good to break off before you reach the very tip, then. Keep you from having that tired feeling, you know. What you need is a little dynamite to blast you out of your chair, here, every morning at half past twelve. If you keep on writing close up to lunch, you'll spoil your digestion.

ROBERTS: Well, I sha'n't this morning. I've had an Englishman here for the last hour, and I feel as if I could digest almost anything.

MRS. CAMPBELL: Why, it must have been *your* Englishman, then, whom we met at the corner, as we came here! There, Willis! I told you it was an Englishman!

CAMPBELL: I couldn't believe it: he was so confoundedly agreeable, and he had so much of that English brogue, when he spoke, that I thought he must be a New Yorker.

MRS. ROBERTS: Why, how came he to talk with you?

CAMPBELL: Well, he was hanging round a telegraph pole, trying to post a letter in the fire-alarm box. He said he'd been asked to post it by a gentleman who had told him there was a letter-box at the first corner, and the fire-alarm looked like it. I had to take him by the elbow, and steer him across the street to the green box on the lamp post. He didn't seem to like the way it opened its mouth at the top like a dying frog, but he risked his letter in it, anyway.

MRS. ROBERTS: There, Edward!

CAMPBELL: Hello! Where does Roberts come in? (*Mrs. Roberts maintains a reproachful silence, and Campbell turns to Roberts.*) Look here, Roberts, what have you been doing? It wasn't *you* who gave that poor young Englishman that letter to post?

ROBERTS, *trying to put a bold face upon it*: Nonsense! Certainly I did. I had given him a letter of introduction to Uncle Philip—he thinks he may go on to New York to-night, by the boat—and I asked him to post the letter I wrote to advise Uncle Philip of his coming. That's all.

MRS. ROBERTS: Of course it was all right. But it seemed a little odd when Edward first told me.

CAMPBELL: Did you make your uncle the usual little confidences about the introducee, in your letter of advice?

ROBERTS: I told him I knew he would like him after he had got through his insular manner.

CAMPBELL: And then you got him to post the letter! Well, it *was* something like seething the kid in its mother's milk,[1] Agnes.

MRS. CAMPBELL: What a disgusting idea! Mr. Roberts, don't mind him! He isn't *worth* it. His one idea is to tease.

ROBERTS: I see what you mean, Campbell. But of course he couldn't know what was in it, and it seemed very simple and natural to get him to drop it in the box.

CAMPBELL: It *was* simple, and it was *very* natural. A less absent-minded man's wife might have told him it wasn't exactly delicate, even if the fellow couldn't have known what was in it.

MRS. CAMPBELL: And in *you* it *would* have been indelicate; but with Mr. Roberts it's a very different thing.

CAMPBELL: Oh yes; I know! Absent-mindedness. Well, Roberts, you'll get yourself into an awful mess with your absent-mindedness some day. How do you know he didn't know what was in the letter to your uncle?

ROBERTS, *with some scorn*: Why, simply because I sealed it before I gave it to him.

1 Compare Exodus, 23 :19.

CAMPBELL: And did you seal the letter of introduction?

ROBERTS: Of course not!

CAMPBELL: Oh, you didn't! Then how do you know that you didn't seal up the letter of introduction, and give him the letter of advice to carry with him?

ROBERTS: Because I *know* I didn't.

CAMPBELL: Oh, *that's* no reason! Now be careful. Would you swear you didn't? Suppose you were on the witness stand!

MRS. CAMPBELL: No, don't suppose it, Mr. Roberts. Don't suppose anything of the kind.

CAMPBELL, *without regarding her*: This sort of thing is done every day. People are always getting letters mixed, and shuffling them into the wrong envelopes. Amy did something of the kind herself down at the Shore, last summer and nearly broke off the engagement between young Welling and Miss Greenway.[1] And if she hadn't been the most sensible kind of a girl, Amy *would* have done it, too. And as it was, I had to do some of the tallest lying this side of the Pacific slope. Perfect *sequoias*—made our place, down there, look like the Yosemite Park, when those fables began to tower up.

MRS. CAMPBELL, *faltering*: It's true, Agnes. I told you about it, you remember.

MRS. ROBERTS: Yes, I know. But that doesn't prove that Edward—

CAMPBELL: Oh, doesn't it! If Amy, who has her few wits always about her, could do such a thing, it stands to reason that Roberts, whose multitudinous mind is always off somewhere else when it's wanted, would do it nine times out of ten. Think how absent-minded he is! Remember how he got aboard the sleeping-car that night, and went prying round in all the berths to find you?[2]

MRS. CAMPBELL: Don't be offensive, Willis!

CAMPBELL: I'm simply veracious! And then think how he left his watch in his room, and thought poor old Bemis was a garroter that had taken it from him, and ran after him on the Common, and grabbed Bemis's watch from him, and nearly killed him.[3] And then his going to meet a cook that he'd never seen at the Albany depot, and getting into that scrape with Mrs. McIlheny.[4]

1 A reference to *A Likely Story.*
2 A reference to *The Sleeping Car.*
3 A reference to *The Garroters.*
4 A reference to *The Albany Depot.*

MRS. ROBERTS: That was *my* fault, Willis. I sent him; and I ought to have remembered that he'd never seen the cook.

CAMPBELL: Oh! And what ought Roberts to have remembered? I tell you, he's put that Englishman's letter of introduction into the sealed envelope, and the letter of advice into the open one, beyond the shadow of a doubt.

ROBERTS, *with rising alarm*: Oh, pshaw! You know you don't think so, Willis.

CAMPBELL: Think so? I know it! Where was he sitting?

ROBERTS: Where you are now.

CAMPBELL: In this chair? When you wrote the letters, which did you finish first?

ROBERTS: The letter of introduction, I think.

CAMPBELL: You think! He can't even remember *that!* Well, can you remember which you *gave* him first?

ROBERTS: No, I can't; but it must have been the letter of introduc—

CAMPBELL: Did you put both letters in their envelopes before you gave them to him, or did you hand him first one and then the other?

ROBERTS: I'm sure I can't say! But my impression is—

CAMPBELL, *waving his conjecture scornfully aside*: Agnes, you see how thoroughly mixed up he is.

MRS. CAMPBELL: Yes, and you've *mixed* him up. I declare—

MRS. ROBERTS: Yes, Willis.

CAMPBELL: Oh, very well, then! If I've mixed him up, I'll let him unmix himself. Then he can't complain. If he didn't blunder with the letters, I suppose my merely *asking* him won't create the fact. I didn't make him do it.

MRS. CAMPBELL: And he didn't do it.

CAMPBELL: He ought to know.

MRS. ROBERTS: And you *do* know, don't you, Edward?

ROBERTS: Why, of course. But anything's possible. And now that Willis has suggested it, why, I can't take my oath—

CAMPBELL, *to the ladies*: You see!

ROBERTS: What—what can I do, Willis? The mere supposition of such a thing—

CAMPBELL: Oh, I don't know. Go after the Englishman, I suppose, and try to run him down before he reads your letter of advice. (*He bursts into a loud, unfeeling laugh, while Roberts begins to walk the floor in agitation.*) Can you recall any of the expressions you used? Perhaps they weren't so bad.

ROBERTS, *pausing and rubbing his forehead*: I think I can. I told Uncle Phil not to mind his insular manner; that he was necessarily offensive as an Englishman; but that he seemed to have a great many good qualities, and was quite American in some of his feelings and ideas, and had an enthusiasm for us worthy of a better cause. I said I had only met him once, but I had no doubt he would prove worthy of any kindness that was shown him.

CAMPBELL: Patronizing and insulting to the last degree! Well, you've done it, Roberts!

ROBERTS: I know—I see! But I didn't mean to be offensive. The fact is, I wrote very hastily; I wanted to get rid of him; my mind was half on my article, here—

CAMPBELL: And it was in the same divided condition when you put the letters into their envelopes! What could you expect?

ROBERTS: Look here, Willis! Couldn't *you*—

CAMPBELL: Oh, no! This isn't a thing that *I* can interfere in. If it were a case for ground-and-lofty lying, you might call me in; but where it's principally *tact* that's needed, I'd better leave it to you, my dear fellow.

He claps Roberts on the shoulder, and breaks down in another laugh.

MRS. CAMPBELL: Now look here, Willis! This is perfectly outrageous. You haven't the slightest proof in the world that Mr. Roberts has mixed the letters, and it's just your wicked teasing that makes you say he has. If you have any feeling at all, you will stop. *I* think it's gone beyond a joke.

MRS. ROBERTS: And I do, too, Amy. Of course I think Edward was wrong to send the man to his uncle just to get rid of him; but that's no reason Willis should torment him so.

ROBERTS: No, no! There's only too great reason to suppose he's right. Good heavens! What shall I do about it?

CAMPBELL: Well, if I might venture a little suggestion without being denounced as a heartless reprobate—

ROBERTS: I haven't denounced you, Willis!

CAMPBELL: My wife and sister have in your interest, and just when I had thought how to help you out.

MRS. ROBERTS: Oh, how, Willis?

MRS. CAMPBELL: Tell it, instantly, Willis!

CAMPBELL: You'd better look him up at his hotel, and pretend you thought you gave the wrong address on the letter to your uncle.

ROBERTS: That's all very well, but I don't know where he's stopping.

CAMPBELL: Well, that does rather cut the ground from under us. (*A ring at the door is heard.*) Ah, there he is now, coming back to have it out with Roberts. He's read that letter of advice, and he wants to know what it means. We must go, Roberts. I'm sorry to leave you in this fix, but—

BELLA, THE MAID, *coming in with a card for Roberts*: The elevator boy brought it up. The gentleman is waiting below, sir.

ROBERTS:, *glancing at the card*: Merciful powers! Willis is right! It is the man himself!

MRS. ROBERTS: Oh, Edward, what do you suppose he wants? But don't be alarmed, dearest! *I* don't agree with Willis in his pessimistic views. I know you can easily explain it.

CAMPBELL: Oh, *can* he? Well, I think I'll just wait, then, and hear his explanation.

MRS. CAMPBELL: Willis! You must advise him what to do. You must invent some plan.

CAMPBELL: *Thank* you! I don't deny that I'm pretty ingenious, and all that; but what you want here is the invention of a Thomas A. Edison. Nothing short of it will ever get Roberts out of *this* scrape.

ROBERTS, *trying to pluck up courage*: But I deny that there *is* any scrape. The whole affair is purely hypothetical. There's nothing in the world to prove that I've mixed up the letters, and I deny that I did. The man has simply come back because he's forgotten something, or wishes to make some little inquiry, or—

CAMPBELL: Then why don't you have him up at once, instead of letting him cool his heels down there in your front hall? Have him up! It's uncivil to keep him waiting.

MRS. ROBERTS: No, no. (*To the maid*) Stop, Bella! No, Willis; we must provide for contingencies. I think Edward is perfectly right, and I know he didn't mix the letters up; but oughtn't we to guard against any chances, Willis?

CAMPBELL: I should say you ought. And you'd better ring for a policeman to do it. He's an awfully athletic-looking fellow. Those Englishmen often are.

MRS. ROBERTS: Then, Bella, you must tell the boy to say that Mr. Roberts has just gone out; and that Mrs. Roberts is very sorry—

ROBERTS: No, Agnes, that won't do, my dear. I can't allow that. If I've done this thing, I must face the consequences.

MRS. ROBERTS: Yes, that's what I say. We must provide for contingencies.

CAMPBELL: He may want to fight you, Roberts, like McIlheny, you know, when you asked his wife whether she was a cook.[1]

MRS. CAMPBELL: Everything depends upon what kind of humor he's in, of course.

MRS. ROBERTS: Of course. If he's very—boisterous, you musn't have anything to say to him; but if he's pleasant, or if he's merely cold, or hurt, in his manner, why, I suppose you must ask him to lunch. And Willis and Amy can stay, and help make it go off.

CAMPBELL: Oh, thank you, Agnes! The Roberts family seems to have a gift for patronizing offensiveness; I don't mind it myself, but if I was an Englishman that Roberts had told to his face that he was nationally detestable—

ROBERTS: Told to his face?

CAMPBELL: It's the same thing—it would take a good deal more than lunch to pacify *me*. I should want *dinner*, and not merely a *family* dinner, a snap-shot, accidental thing, but a regular formal affair, with the best people asked, and the chance of other invitations. The least *you* can do, Roberts, is to send for this Englishman's baggage, and make him stay a fortnight with you.

MRS. ROBERTS: I *had* thought of that, Willis.

CAMPBELL: You *said—lunch*.

MRS. ROBERTS: But our flat is so small, and the children are in the guest-chamber—

CAMPBELL: And in the meantime, the Englishman is waiting below in the select society of the janitor.

MRS. ROBERTS: Oh, my goodness, I forgot all about him!

ROBERTS: Yes. We *must* have him up at once, and then act accordingly.

CAMPBELL: Oh yes; you musn't give yourself away. If you don't *happen* to have mixed the letters up, you don't want to begin apologizing. You will have to judge from his manner.

ROBERTS: But he was so extremely flattering, so very enthusiastic about us, I'm afraid we can't tell from his manner.

CAMPBELL: You must draw him out, specifically. Did you ask him how he liked America?

ROBERTS: No; I was ashamed to ask him when he told me he had just arrived this morning.

CAMPBELL: Well, then, Amy can ask him. She isn't ashamed to ask anything. And if he begins to abuse us, up hill and down dale—

1 A reference to *The Albany Depot*.

MRS. CAMPBELL: He had better *not* abuse us! I shouldn't allow it.

MRS. ROBERTS: Oh yes, Amy; bear anything! We *must* try to pacify him somehow.

CAMPBELL: And Roberts had better go out, and meet him in that anteroom of yours—it's as *dark* as a pocket—and make him take off his overcoat—he mustn't allow any refusal—and then kind of linger behind him a moment after you've received him at the door here, and search his overcoat pockets. Very probably he's put the letter into one of them.

MRS. ROBERTS: Do you think that would be very nice, Willis?

CAMPBELL: Well, I don't know: about as nice as having Amy truckle to his abuse of the country.

MRS. CAMPBELL: It isn't at all the same thing.

CAMPBELL: It's exactly the same thing. (A *ring at the door summons Bella away*.) He's getting impatient. Well, I shouldn't like to be kept waiting so long myself.

BELLA, *returning*: It's the gentleman below, ma'am. The boy says he'd like to know if you got his card.

CAMPBELL: I thought so. You must let him come up, or you must send word that you're not at home. You can't prolong the suspense indefinitely.

MRS. CAMPBELL: No, Agnes, you can't, really!

ROBERTS: We must decide, my dear!

MRS. ROBERTS, *desperately*: Well, then, tell the janitor to send him up, Bella! (As *Bella goes*) And we haven't thought at all how we shall act!

CAMPBELL: Well, I know *one* thing: if Roberts lets his knees knock together, *so as to be heard*, I won't stand it. I'll leave the house. It'll be *too* disgraceful. Courage, Roberts! I wouldn't miss seeing how you'll carry this thing off for any money! I know you're a perfect moral hero on all ordinary occasions, but in a predicament like this I don't envy you. And the worst of it is, that if the fellow's a gentleman—and he looked like one, in the English way—you won't be able to judge from his acts how he feels! You'll have to grope your way in the dark, and— There he is! (A *ring is heard*.) Now let's all look unconcerned, as if we were not expecting any one. Amy, you be turning over those photographic views of the White Mountains, in your pretty, careless way. Agnes, you be examining some object with the microscope. Here, Roberts, you sit down to your writing again. And I'll be tuning up the family phonograph. That'll give him an idea of a cultivated

Boston family, at home with itself, and at peace with the whole *human* family. And we must all be extremely deferential and—complimentary—so's to take the bad taste of Roberts's letter out of his mouth. (*Campbell delivers these instructions in a rapid whisper. As Bella opens the door to admit the stranger to the anteroom, he continues in a loud, didactic voice.*) As you very justly observed, in our present uncertainty as to whether the peculiar parallel markings of the planet Mars are marine canals, or merely magic-lantern displays of the Martians to attract the attention of the telescope man on Boston Common—

BELLA, *announcing the Englishman at the library door*: Mr. Westgate.

WESTGATE, *to Roberts*: Ah, I beg your pardon! It's really very ridiculous, and I'm quite ashamed to trouble you again, Mr. Roberts. Your letter—

ROBERTS, *coming eagerly forward*: Oh, I'm so glad to see you again, Mr. Westgate. You're just in time for lunch; and I hope you can sit down with us. Mrs. Roberts, Mr. Westgate. My wife hadn't the pleasure of—ah—meeting you before, I think. Let me take your overcoat. You'll find it very hot in our American houses, I'm afraid.

WESTGATE: Oh, not at all! I'm sure I shall like it. I should *so* like to see one of your furnaces! But I only came back a moment to show you a little mistake—if it *is* a mistake—

MRS. ROBERTS, *eagerly*: I'm so sorry we've only steam heat, and can't show you a furnace; but you'll find it quite hot; and you *must* take off your coat.

WESTGATE: Why, you're very good, I'm sure. But only for a moment.

ROBERTS: Allow me!

> *He possesses himself of Westgate's hat and coat, and rushes out into the anteroom with them.*

MRS. ROBERTS: Let me introduce you to my sister, Mrs. Campbell; and my brother, Mr. Campbell, Mr. Westgate.

> *Westgate bows to the lady, and then shakes hands with Campbell.*

WESTGATE: Ah! how do you do? I'd no idea—I'm very glad to meet you, I'm sure. I don't know what I should have done with the letter Mr. Roberts intrusted to me—

CAMPBELL: Oh, that was nothing. I saw that you were on the point of doing something desperate, and I just stepped in. There's nothing I like better than saving human life; and as I've often tried to post my wife's letters in the fire-alarm box, at two o'clock in the morning, and never succeeded yet, I had a fellow-feeling for you.

WESTGATE: H'm! Yes! You see your post-boxes are so very different to ours—

MRS. CAMPBELL: Oh, your London post-boxes are simply delightful! They're just *like* posts—fat ones; and they take in whole packages. But—I hope you *like* America, Mr. Westgate!

MRS. ROBERTS: Yes, we are always so glad when your countrymen—

CAMPBELL: We aim to please.

WESTGATE: Well, I can't say I like your post-boxes exactly.

MRS. CAMPBELL: Oh, neither do we!

WESTGATE: And I'd always heard you had clear winter weather. I've never seen it more overcast at home.

MRS. ROBERTS: That is true. It's going to snow, I think. I'm afraid you won't like our snow!

CAMPBELL: Well, perhaps, we might have some with the chill off.

WESTGATE, *regarding him fixedly for a moment*: Ow! Ah! I see! Very good! Ah, ha, ha, ha! Ha, ha, ha! And—ha, ha, ha! Ah, ha, ha!—you meant, *coming home from the club!* I hadn't understood your American humor, at first. I fancy there's no hope of any good Samaritan to show you to the post-box at two o'clock in the morning hour! Ah, ha, ha!

MRS. ROBERTS: I've been scolding my husband for troubling you with that letter, Mr. Westgate!

WESTGATE: No, really? But I always heard the American ladies were so amiable, you know.

MRS. CAMPBELL: Oh, we *are*, Mr. Westgate! But we have to maintain discipline in the family, you know.

WESTGATE: Of course. But—(*to Campbell*) what did you mean exactly, by having snow with the chill off? Such a delightful expression.

CAMPBELL: Well, I don't know. Some sort of joke, I suppose.

WESTGATE: I was sure you did! Ah, ha, ha! Your countrymen are so delightfully humorous—so funny, you know. You know we think you're *such* fun.

CAMPBELL: Do you think so? I don't think we're half so funny as Englishmen.

MRS. CAMPBELL: We think you're *twice* as funny as we are, Mr. Westgate.

WESTGATE: Ow, but really, now!

MRS. CAMPBELL: I don't know how we should have done without your Mr. Gilbert.

WESTGATE: But isn't he rather exaggerated? I

much prefer your Joshua Billings. And your after-dinner speakers! Mr. Depew, for instance!

MRS. ROBERTS: But the Prince of Wales, you know.

WESTGATE: Ow! Do you regard him as a humorist? He says some neat things, occasionally. But your California humor, now: we've nothing like *that*, you know!

MRS. CAMPBELL: I'm afraid you will make my husband intolerably conceited.

WESTGATE: Really? Is Mr.—ah—Campbell a Californian? How very delightful! And is that peculiar dialect used by your California writers spoken in the cities? I should so much like to hear it. I don't think we ever quite get the right accent in reading it.

CAMPBELL: You'd hear it everywhere in California. I'm a little out of practice now, myself; I speak Bostonese, at present; but I recollect very well how the ladies in San Francisco used to say, "Well, I got the dead wood onto you, that time," and "How're you makin' it, pard?" and "You bet," and "You git!" You mean that sort of thing?

WESTGATE: Exactly. How delightful! So very picturesque, you know. So imaginative!

CAMPBELL: Yes, I suppose there's more imagination to the acre in California than you'll find anywhere else in the United States.

MRS. CAMPBELL: And more modesty, Mr. Westgate; more unconscious merit.

CAMPBELL: Well, I shouldn't like to boast before a foreigner. There's Chicago. And for a real, unadulterated diffidence, a shrinking, deprecatory little misgiving as to the existence of the outside universe, I think Mr. Westgate will find that Boston takes the cake. In California people don't *know* they're modest, but in Boston they *do*. That's the difference.

MRS. ROBERTS: I hope Mr. Westgate will stay with us long enough to find out that everything you say is a wicked slander, Willis. Why must you rush off to New York at once, Mr. Westgate?

WESTGATE: You're very good, I'm sure. But I'm afraid— Ha, ha, ha! Ha, ha, ha! (*To Campbell*) That was a very amusing expression of yours! Imagination to the acre! As if it were some kind of crop! Very good! Capital! Ah, ha, ha! And would you be kind enough to explain that expression, "take the cake"?

CAMPBELL: Oh, it comes from the cake walk, you know.

WESTGATE: Ow!

CAMPBELL: Yes. Where the darkies try to see

which can put on the most style in a kind of walk-round, and there's a cake up for a prize, and the greatest swell takes it.

WESTGATE: How very amusing!

CAMPBELL: Amusing? It's more fun than a goat!

MRS. CAMPBELL: Willis!

WESTGATE: Oh, but really! *Don't* stop him! It's quite what I came to America for—those delightful expressions! I don't know why you're all so shy of using them when you come over! We get them in print, but we seldom hear them.

CAMPBELL: You should go to a ladies' lunch here! You wouldn't hear anything else.

WESTGATE: Ow! And just what is a ladies' lunch?

CAMPBELL: It's the social entertainment of the future. The race is running to girls so, in Massachusetts, that they've got to having these lunches without asking men, so as to see how it will feel when there are no men to ask. Often it's merely a hen feed, where they would like to have men if they could get them; just as a stag dinner is a good time that women would like to come to if they could. Sometimes it's a virtue, sometimes it's a necessity. But it's always a joke.

MRS. ROBERTS: You mustn't believe him, Mr. Westgate. He's never been at a ladies' lunch, and he doesn't know how charming they are.

WESTGATE: Yes, I understand gentlemen are not asked. But—ah, ha, ha! Ha, ha, ha!—that was a very droll expression of Mr. Campbell's about a goat. More—more amusing than a goat, I think it was. Will you ladies kindly tell me why a goat should be considered so very amusing? You see I'm beginning to be afraid I can't trust Mr. Campbell.

MRS. ROBERTS: I'm afraid you must, in this case. I'm sure we don't know why a goat should be more entertaining than any other animal.

WESTGATE: Ow! Then you're not *all* humorists, over here? We get that idea, you know. We think you're such *jokers*. But really, you know, I think that some people who do that kind of thing, you know, and have Americans a great deal, don't see the point of their jokes at all times; or not *at once*. Your humor is so different to ours, you know. I've often had the meaning of an American joke occur to me some time after, you know, when I've had leisure to think it out. Still, it *is* very amusing.

MRS. CAMPBELL: But *we* think the English humor so refined—so high-bred.

MRS. ROBERTS: Oh yes! Your jokes bear the

stamp of such an old civilization, my husband says.

CAMPBELL: So polished with use.

WESTGATE: Ah, well! I don't know about that, you know. There may be something in it. But I'm inclined to think— Ah, ha, ha, ha! Very good! Excellent! I didn't catch your meaning, at first. *Used so often!* I see! Ha, ha, ha! You ought to come over to us, Mr. Campbell. We've a great many charming Americans; but most of them are quite like ourselves.

CAMPBELL: Is it so bad as that?

WESTGATE: Yes; it's really quite vexing, you know. So very tiresome.

MRS. ROBERTS: I hope Mr. Westgate will stay with us long enough to see that we've something besides humor—in Boston, at least. You must let us send to the hotel for your trunk—boxes, I *should* say.

WESTGATE: Ow no! Ow no! I *much* prefer *trunk.*

MRS. CAMPBELL: And *we* prefer *boxes.*

WESTGATE: No, really?

MRS. ROBERTS: You must be our guest long enough at least to see something of Boston. Mr. Roberts will take you to the Art Club Exhibition.

WESTGATE: You're really very good. But I'd really no idea— I only came back a moment on account of a little mistake I think Mr. Roberts made in the let—

MRS. ROBERTS, *hastily*: We think Boston is quite an art centre, now. Amy, I want Mr. Westgate to see the little Monet in the p— drawing-room.

WESTGATE: Oh, *do* say parlor! I think it's so much nicer. And without the *u*, please.

MRS. CAMPBELL: I see you're determined to be pleased with everything American, Mr. Westgate, and I'm sure you'll like this Monet.

WESTGATE: But I beg your pardon! Isn't he French?

CAMPBELL: All the American pictures we buy are by Frenchmen.

MRS. CAMPBELL: But *we* much prefer English pictures, Mr. Westgate. You have so much more technique than the French, so much more *school.* I adore Tadema, myself.

WESTGATE: But—yes—ah—I think he's Dutch, though?

MRS. CAMPBELL: Well, as Mr. Campbell was saying, *our* paintings are all by Frenchmen—all that we buy. If you will come with me, Mr. Westgate—

MRS. ROBERTS: What in the world has happened to Edward?

CAMPBELL: He can't have been searching the man's coat-pockets all this time. Perhaps he's cut open the lining. Or he's found the wrong letter, and has gone off and hid somewhere. *(Roberts shows himself at the door.)* No; there he is now. I didn't know but he'd committed suicide. Well, Roberts! Come in, old fellow! The coast is clear, for the moment! *(Roberts advances spectrally into the room.)* What's the matter?

They all speak throughout the scene in hoarse whispers, and from time to time the voices of Mrs. Campbell and Mr. Westgate penetrate to them from the drawing-room.

ROBERTS: Is he gone?

MRS. ROBERTS: 'Sh! No. He's in the parlor, with Amy. She's showing him the pictures. He couldn't go without his hat and overcoat, you know.

ROBERTS: Yes. I didn't think of that.

CAMPBELL: 'Sh! Have you been through his clothes? 'Sh!

ROBERTS: No; I hadn't the courage.

CAMPBELL: 'Sh! Then where *have* you been? 'Sh!

ROBERTS: Sitting out there in the anteroom.

MRS. ROBERTS: Oh, poor Edward! 'Sh! Did you listen? He still seems very amiable. 'Sh! I don't think he's angry about anything. I don't believe you've made any serious mistake.

CAMPBELL: Unless he's—'sh!—dissembling. They're awfully double-faced fellows, Englishmen are. 'Sh! I think he's dissembling. 'Sh!

MRS. ROBERTS: 'Sh! Nonsense, Willis! He says you made some mistake with the letter; but—

CAMPBELL: 'Sh! Of course you mixed them! He's just lying low. You'd better keep out of his way, Roberts. 'Sh!

WESTGATE, *without*: Then I suppose you've quite a large school of resident artists in Boston?

MRS. CAMPBELL, *without*: Well, no. But we've a very large school of *non-*resident Boston artists. Our painters all have to go to New York to get a living.

WESTGATE, *without*: Ow! Then I suppose New York is the artistic centre of your country?

MRS. CAMPBELL, *without*: Not at all. We have the critics here.

WESTGATE, *without*: Then you consider criticism more essential than painting in an artistic centre?

CAMPBELL: 'Sh! He's getting sarcastic. He's tuning up for you, Roberts. He's tearing off the mask of amiability. Better get out into the anteroom again, Roberts. Agnes can say you were too sick to come to lunch, and we can carry it off somehow. Oh, but—hello! She's asked him to let her send for his boxes—such a delightful expression!—and come and stay with you. I think you'd better be suddenly called out of town. There's no other way for it!

ROBERTS, *with a tremendous effort of moral heroism*: No; I must stay and face it out. It would be cowardly to shirk it.

MRS. ROBERTS: Oh, Edward, what courage you *do* have! But what will you say to him? Willis, *can't* you think of something for Edward to say? You know he's never good on the spur of the moment, and you *are*. 'Sh!

CAMPBELL: 'Sh! Don't say anything at all, till he opens up. But keep treating him beautifully, and then he'll see that Roberts *couldn't* have meant anything by those insulting and patronizing expressions. He'll think it's just our Yankee awkwardness and vulgarity.

MRS. ROBERTS, *willingly accepting the suggestion*: Yes, just our Yankee awkwardness and vulgarity. I know he'll excuse it, Edward. You musn't be alarmed. Remember how much *real* courage you always have!

ROBERTS: I can't let him excuse it on that ground. No; I must grapple with it frankly.

CAMPBELL: All right! Only let him grapple first. Don't give yourself away.

MRS. ROBERTS: 'Sh! They're coming back. 'Sh!

CAMPBELL: 'Sh! Now, Roberts, brace up. 'Sh! Be a man! Be an American! And deny everything!

WESTGATE: Your Monet is beautiful, Mrs. Roberts. You know, I think you Americans are so much more open-minded than we are, and you take up with the new things so much sooner. I don't think the impressionists are to the fore with us yet.

MRS. ROBERTS: Oh, but I can't allow you to say anything against England, Mr. Westgate!

MRS. CAMPBELL: No, indeed; you would find no sympathizers in that, Mr. Westgate.

CAMPBELL: We gamble on the mother-country every time, here in Boston, at least, and in New York you'll feel as if you'd just got back to London.

WESTGATE: Well, you know, I should be rather sorry to do that. I came over to see Americans.

CAMPBELL: Well, you're barking up the wrong tree.

WESTGATE: Barking up— What a delightful expression! Would you mind saying— Ah, ha, ha! Ha, ha, ha! Very good! I see! You mean in stripping the bark off for the birch canoes, I suppose.

These figurative phrases are so vigorous. And you have so many of them. I've heard Americans use some of them at home. Do you suppose that expression originated with your Indians, perhaps?

CAMPBELL: No; they originated the expression, Good Indians, dead Indians. But if you have a fancy for these expressions, Roberts, here, can fill you up with a lot of them.

ROBERTS: Yes—that is—I do hope you can spend a few days with us before you push on to New York.

WESTGATE: Why, you're very good, I'm sure. But that reminds me of the letter of introduc—

CAMPBELL: You stay on here, and Roberts will paint the town red for you.

MRS. ROBERTS: You must allow us to send for your boxes.

MRS. CAMPBELL: Your luggage—yes.

WESTGATE: Ow, but I'd so much rather you'd say *baggage!* I've had it sent to the railway—

MRS. ROBERTS: Station? That doesn't the least matter.

WESTGATE: Ow, but it does! I'd *so* much rather say *deepo*, as you do.

ROBERTS: We can get it perfectly well, if you'll give us your transfer—

CAMPBELL: Don't say *checks*, Roberts! There must be some *English* word!

WESTGATE: No, really; I must go on to New York. My plans are all made. But on my return from the West I shall be most happy to remember your kindness. I've only ventured to trouble Mr. Roberts in regard to the mistake he seems to have made with—

ROBERTS: I beg you won't suppose—

MRS. ROBERTS, *at the same time*: You musn't regard it, indeed, Mr. Westgate!

MRS. CAMPBELL, *at the same time*: Mr. Roberts is *so* absent-minded!

CAMPBELL, *at the same time*: Roberts is *all* absence of mind!

WESTGATE: Ha, ha, ha! But you know— Ah, ha, ha! Ha, ha, ha! I see! Capital! Oh, excellent. *English* word for checks! Excellent. Ah—would you be good enough to say just what you mean by painting a place red?

CAMPBELL: Roberts will show you, if you'll only stay!

WESTGATE: It's quite impossible, now, at all events. *(To Roberts)* But the letter you kindly gave me to your uncle—

ROBERTS: Yes—Yes—

MRS. ROBERTS: You'll like Uncle Philip *so*

much! And he'll appreciate the favor Edward's done him in sending—

MRS. CAMPBELL, *at the same time*: He's so fond of the English!

CAMPBELL, *at the same time*: And he's right on to Roberts's jokes. They're always at it together. Back and forth, all the time. If Roberts has put up any little job, Uncle Phil will catch on like lightning.

WESTGATE: Oh, what extremely delightful expressions! I'm sure I sha'n't remember the half of them! But this letter—do you really think—

He takes it from his pocket.

ROBERTS: Yes—yes. I'm quite certain he'll—

MRS. ROBERTS, *at the same time*: Oh yes, indeed! My husband was with him so much at one time! They're almost of the same age.

WESTGATE: Oh, indeed! I fancied an old gentleman! Then you think that he'll understand—

MRS. CAMPBELL: Uncle Philip understands Mr. Roberts and all his ways perfectly. They have such fun when they're together.

MRS. ROBERTS, *at the same time*: It doesn't matter what Edward has written, he'll take it just in the right way.

CAMPBELL, *at the same time*: Yes, he'll know it's *some* kind of a joke.

WESTGATE: Well, you know, I thought perhaps, myself, it was one of your pieces of American humor.

MRS. ROBERTS: Oh, it *was*, Mr. Westgate, I assure you it was! Just one of our pieces of American humor—

MRS. CAMPBELL: Yes, indeed; you can depend upon that, Mr. Westgate!

WESTGATE: Ah well! If it had been Mr. Campbell, here, I should have felt sure of it. But I couldn't be quite so certain that Mr. Roberts—

CAMPBELL: Oh, when it comes to joking, Americans are all alike. Roberts is a little more alike than the rest of us; that's all. So's Uncle Philip, for that matter. He'd take it right even if Roberts hadn't written anything at all.

WESTGATE: But that's just what Mr. Roberts has done!

ALL THE OTHERS: What!

WESTGATE, *handing the envelope to Roberts, who finds it empty, and passes it to his wife, who in turn hands it silently to Mrs. Campbell*: Of course I wished to read the kind things you'd said of me, as soon as possible, and I was greatly surprised to find no letter in this envelope. I wasn't sure whether you intended me simply to present the envelope to your uncle, or whether— At all events, I decided I'd better come and ask.

CAMPBELL, *who has possessed himself of the envelope*: Why, look here, Roberts! You put both letters in that sealed envelope I kept Mr. Westgate from posting in the fire-alarm box.

ROBERTS: Why, so I must! Really, Mr. Westgate, I don't know what to say!

MRS. ROBERTS: Yes, Edward, I don't know what you *will* say!

CAMPBELL: Roberts, you're incorrigible! When *will* you give up this habit of practical joking? Really, old fellow, you ought to stop it. You and Uncle Phil have kept it up long enough. And *I* think you owe Mr. Westgate an apology. The joke's on Uncle Phil, of course; but you ought to see that it's rather embarrassing to Mr. Westgate to find himself the bearer of an empty envelope instead of a letter of introduction. Come, now, *you must explain*; and we'll all apologize for you. (*Roberts waits with a foolish face of deprecation, turning to horror, at the suggestion of an explanation.*) Come! You owe it to yourself, as a joker.

WESTGATE, *amiably*: Ow, now! Not at all. No apologies. I shouldn't be able to forgive myself if I couldn't allow a man his joke. But I *should* like an explanation, you know. Your humor is so *very* different to ours, and I don't believe any one at home, if I said you had given me an empty envelope to carry to your uncle, *could* feel the spirit of it. And these things are so tiresome, you know, when they happen to fall flat. I hope you won't think me importunate if I say I should like to know just where the laugh comes in on a thing of that kind?

CAMPBELL: Out with it, Roberts!

MRS. ROBERTS: Don't you think— Oh, I'm sure you'll spoil it, Edward!

MRS. CAMPBELL: Don't you think you'd better leave it to Uncle Philip?

CAMPBELL: Well, that's an inspiration, Amy. Leave it to Uncle Phil, Roberts!

ROBERTS, *with a deep sigh of relief*: Yes, that will be best. My Uncle Philip will tell you, if you don't mind.

BELLA, *at the door*: Lunch is served, Mrs. Roberts.

MRS. ROBERTS, *gayly*: I'm going to lead the way, with Mr. Westgate. Edward, bring Amy. And, Willis, you can—

CAMPBELL: Oh, come, now! None of your little unconscious jokes, Agnes! I won't stand it from my own sister.

WESTGATE: Ow! Do the American ladies often make jokes without knowing it, Mrs. Roberts? *(To Campbell)* But what is just the point of— Ow, I see! Very good! Ha, ha, ha! And shall we have some distinctively American dishes, Mrs. Roberts? You know I'm so very, very curious about your chowder, and doughnuts, and maple syrup, and buckwheat cakes, and corn-dodgers, and hoe-downs. Such delightful names. They really make one's mouth water.

He goes out with Mrs. Roberts.

CAMPBELL, *lingering, and detaining his wife and Roberts*: Roberts, can't you dance a hoe-cake for him? You ought to do it on your knees, you miserable sinner!

THE END

Evening Dress

[1892]

Everyone loses things, even dress suits, but not everyone has Willis Campbell to help him find what he has lost, or a wife like Agnes Roberts to make the hunt impossible from the beginning. It is not strange, then, that in "A Letter to the Publisher" Howells states that *Evening Dress* was founded on fact. To Mrs. Roberts, the embarrassed wife, a social duty is a sacred thing even if the social obligation is to someone she does not like: "But that's just the kind of people that you're a perfect slave to!" Hence, though health be endangered and happiness all but destroyed, Mr. Roberts must attend Mrs. Miller's musicale—any other action would not be understood. And, of course, one must be properly attired.

The title suggests farce, and one could classify the play in no other way, yet certain distinctive qualities such as speech patterns, homely attitudes, and an emphasis on truth mark it clearly as a Howells farce. Because she is a Howells woman of the commonplace world, Mrs. Roberts has a mind littered with pins, head scarves, handkerchiefs, wifely devotion, and homely idioms. She also adheres strictly to truth as she understands it and as her society qualifies it; Howells has a great deal of fun with this social concept of truth. Victimized by his place in the world, Roberts cannot allow his wife to send a note saying that he is sick, because "It wouldn't be the truth." Yet he *is* dead tired and nearly ill. What would the truth be? Ironically, in that society, the nearer to the actual truth one is, the more open to sus-

picion one may become. Later in the play, in spite of knowing that she is fibbing, the maid Bella tells two obvious lies for which both ladies praise her. Behind the scenes Howells laughs at society's confused attitude toward truth as it becomes a comic combination of the appalling and the appealing.

In "A Letter to the Publisher" prefacing *Minor Dramas*, Howells mentioned that *Evening Dress* had been played in New York for charities. But the only performance recorded in Odell's *Annals of the New York Stage* (XV, 568–69) was a matinee at the Empire Theatre on March 27, 1894. Odell states: "The austere critic of the *Dramatic Mirror* considered the Howells' item very thin, dealing, as it did, with the efforts of two men to find the suit dramatically; the next thing, he thought, might be a play about a lady shopper who found she had left her purse at home." Francis Hyde Bangs mentions (in a letter to me of March 28, 1957) that early in 1894 John Kendrick Bangs performed the part of Mr. Roberts in a private production of *Evening Dress* at Bangs's home, 453 North Broadway in Yonkers, New York. About sixty persons were present. During the play the most humorous line came not from Bangs, but from J. K. Bangs, Jr., age six, who had been allowed to stay up for the performance. When Bangs, as Roberts, said: "I solemnly assure you I haven't touched a drop of it [whiskey]!" his son's small voice was heard: "Oh, yes, you have, papa!" Master Bangs was then removed from the room.

Evening Dress [1]

I

MRS. EDWARD ROBERTS: Now, my dear, Amy and I will get there early, so as to make up for your coming a little late, but you *must* be there for the last half, at least. I would excuse you altogether if I could, for I know you must be dead tired, up all night, that way, on the train, but Mrs. Miller is one of those people who never *can* listen to reason, and she would take deadly offence if you missed her musicale, and wouldn't forgive us the longest day she lived. So you see? (*Mrs. Roberts addresses herself to her husband in the library of their apartment in Hotel Bellingham, at Boston, as she stands before the fire pulling on a long glove and looking at him across his desk, where he has sunk into a weary heap in his swivel chair.*) You *are* dreadfully used up, Edward, and I think it's cruel to make you go out; but what can I do? If it was anybody but Mrs. Miller I wouldn't *think* of having you go; I'm sure I never want to have her about, anyway. But that's just the kind of people that you're a perfect slave to! Now, dear, I've let the two girls go out, and you must remember that you're in the place alone with the children; but you needn't be troubled, because nobody will come after this hour till Willis does, and the girls will be back before that. Willis is to come and get you on his way to the Millers', and it's all been arranged for you, and you needn't think of a thing till Willis comes. You'll have to dress, of course; but you needn't begin that at once, and you can just sit here in your chair and rest. (*Mr. Roberts stretches his arms wildly abroad, and, throwing back his head, permits himself a yawn that eclipses his whole face. Mrs. Roberts lets both her arms fall at her side in token of extreme despair.*) Edward! If you *should* go to sleep!

ROBERTS, *pulling himself together, with a gigantic effort*: No, no! You needn't be afraid, my dear. But, oh! what *wouldn't* I give for a chance to!

MRS. ROBERTS, *who sinks into a chair and regards the unhappy man with a look of tender compassion*: You poor thing, I've almost a mind to let you!

ROBERTS, *heroically*: No, it wouldn't do, Agnes. I must—ow, ugh, ow—go. Ugh, ow, ugh!

He abandons himself to a succession of abysmal yawns, in which the sequence of his ideas is altogether lost.

MRS. ROBERTS: Well, then, I shall have to trust you. (*She gathers her train up for departure, and moves slowly towards the door.*) I don't think I've forgotten anything. Let me see: fan, handkerchief, both gloves; pins, because you're never sure that they've put enough, and you don't know where you'll come apart; head scarf, yes, I've got that on; fur boots, I've got *them* on. I really believe I'm all here. But I shouldn't be, Edward, if it were not for the system I put into everything; and I do wish, dear, that you'd try it once, just to please me!

ROBERTS, *very drowsily*: Try what, Agnes?

MRS. ROBERTS: Why, getting what you have to do by heart, and repeating it over. If you could *only* bring yourself to say: *Both girls out; me alone with the children; Willis at ten; mustn't go to sleep; last half, anyway; Mrs. Miller awfully angry.* There! If you could say that after me, I could go feeling so *much* easier! Won't you do it, Edward? I know it has a ridiculous sound, but—

ROBERTS, *yawning*: How am I to dress?

MRS. ROBERTS: Edward! Well, I always *will* say that you're perfectly inspired! To think of my forgetting the most important thing, after all! Oh, I do believe there *is* an overruling Providence, I don't *care* what the agnostics pretend. Why, it's to be evening dress for the men, of course! Mrs. Miller would do it to be different from Mrs. Curwen, who let you come in your cutaways, even if it wasn't the regular thing; and she's gone around ever since saying it was the most rowdy, Bohemian thing she ever heard of, and she might as well have had beer, at once.

ROBERTS: Who?

MRS. ROBERTS: Why, Mrs. Miller.

ROBERTS: Mrs. Miller going to have beer?

MRS. ROBERTS: Oh, Edward, I don't see how you *can* be so— But there! I won't blame you, dearest. I know you're just literally expiring for want of sleep, and it seems to me I must be the cruellest thing in the world to make you go. And if you'll say the word, I'll smash off a note now at the eleventh hour—though it's two hours of eleven yet!—and just *tell* Mrs. Miller that you've got home down sick, and I've had to stay and take care of you. Will you?

ROBERTS: Oh no, Agnes. It wouldn't be the truth.

MRS. ROBERTS, *in a rapture of admiration and affection*: Oh, who *cares* for the truth in such a cause, you poor heroic angel, you? Well, if you insist upon going, I suppose we must; and now the only way is for you to keep everything clearly in mind. You'd better say it over backward, now, and begin with evening dress, because that's the most important. Now! *Evening dress; Mrs. Miller awfully angry; last half, anyway; mustn't go to sleep; Willis at ten; me alone with the children; both girls out.* Now, do you think— Ow— e—e—e! (A *ring at the door extorts a shriek from Mrs. Roberts, who simultaneously gathers her robes about her, in order to fall with decency in the event of burglars or fire, while her husband rises and goes to open the apartment door.*) Who can it be, at this hour? Oh! Amy!

MRS. WILLIS CAMPBELL, *in the doorway*: Oh, Amy, indeed! How d' y' do, Edward! Glad to see you back alive, and just in time for Agnes to kill you with Mrs. Miller's musicale. May I ask, Agnes, how long you expected me to freeze to death down in that coupé before you came?

MRS. ROBERTS: Oh, Amy, dear, you must forgive me! I was just staying to give Edward his charges —you know he's so terribly forgetful—and I forgot all about you!

MRS. CAMPBELL: Then I wish, the next time, he'd give *you* some charges, my dear. But come, now, do! We shall be rather late, anyway, and that simpleton will be perfectly furious.

MRS. ROBERTS: Yes, that's just what I was saying to Edward. She'll never forgive you. If it was anybody else, I shouldn't think of dragging him out to-night.

MRS. CAMPBELL: The worst of a bore like her is that she's sure to come to all *your* things, and you can't get off from *one* of hers. Willis declares

he's going to strike, and I couldn't have got him out to-night if I hadn't told him you were going to make Edward go.

MRS. ROBERTS: Oh, isn't it perfectly wicked, Amy! I know he's just going to have the grippe. See how drowsy he is! That's one of the first symptoms.

MRS. CAMPBELL: It's one of the symptoms of having passed the night on a sleeping-car, too.

MRS. ROBERTS: That's true, and thank you, Amy. I forgot all about that. But now, Edward, dear, you *will* remember, won't you? If I could only stay with you—

ROBERTS, *who has been drowsily drooping in his chair during the exchange of these ideas between the ladies*: Oh, I'm all right, Agnes. Or— ow, ugh, ow!—I should be if I had a cup of tea.

MRS. ROBERTS: There! I *knew* it. If I had been worth anything at all as a wife I should have had you a cup of tea long ago. Oh, how heartless! And I've let both the girls go, and the fire's all out in the range, anyway. But I'll go and start it with my own hands—

MRS. CAMPBELL: In those gloves! You're crazy, Agnes! Edward, I'll tell you what Willis does, when he's out of sorts a little: he takes a taste of whiskey-and-water. He says nothing freshens him up like it.

ROBERTS: That's a good idea.

MRS. ROBERTS, *bustling into the dining-room and reappearing with a tumbler and a decanter*: The very thing, Amy! And thank you *so* much. Trying to make Edward remember seems to put everything out of my head! I might have thought of *whiskey*, though! If it's only loss of sleep, it will wake him up, and if it's grippe, it's the most nourishing thing in the world.

ROBERTS: I'm not going to have the grippe, Agnes.

MRS. ROBERTS: Edward! Don't boast! You may be stricken down in an instant. I heard of one person who was taken so suddenly she hadn't time to get her things off, and tumbled right on the bed. You must put some water in it, of course; and hot water is very soothing. You can use some out of the pipes; it's perfectly good.

MRS. CAMPBELL: Agnes, are you *never* coming?

ROBERTS: Yes, go along, Agnes, do! I shall get on quite well, now. You needn't wait.

MRS. ROBERTS: Oh, if I could only stay and think *for* you, dearest! But I can't, and you must do the best you can. Do keep repeating it all over! It's the only way—

MRS. CAMPBELL, *from the door*: Agnes!

MRS. ROBERTS: Amy, I'm coming instantly.

MRS. CAMPBELL: I declare I shall go without you!

MRS. ROBERTS: And I shouldn't blame you a bit, Amy! And *if* it turns out to be the grippe, Edward, don't lose an instant. Send for the doctor as fast as the district messenger [1] can fly; give him his car fare, and let one come for me; and jump into bed and cover up warm, and keep up the nourishment with the whiskey; there's another bottle in the sideboard; and perhaps you'd better break a raw egg in it. I heard of one person that they gave three dozen raw eggs a day to in typhoid fever, and even *then* he died; so you must nourish yourself all you can. And—

MRS. CAMPBELL: Agnes! I'm going!

MRS. ROBERTS: I'm coming! Edward!

ROBERTS: Well?

MRS. ROBERTS: There is something else, very important. And I can't think of it!

ROBERTS: Liebig's extract of beef? [2]

MRS. ROBERTS, *distractedly*: No, no! And it wasn't oysters, either, though they're very nourishing, too. Oh, dear! What—

MRS. CAMPBELL: Going, Agnes!

MRS. ROBERTS: Coming, Amy! Try to think of something else that I ought to remember, Edward!

ROBERTS: Some word to the girls when they come in?

MRS. ROBERTS: No!

ROBERTS: About the children, something?

MRS. ROBERTS: No, no!

ROBERTS: Willis, then; what Amy wants him to do?

MRS. ROBERTS: Oh, no, no! I shall surely die if I can't think of it!

MRS. CAMPBELL, *at the door of the apartment*: Gone!

MRS. ROBERTS, *flying after her, as the door closes with a bang*: Oh, Amy! how can you be so heartless? She's driven it quite out of my head!

---

1 Either on a single call basis or as a subscriber, a person had a messenger on call for a great variety of duties, sometimes as an escort. ". . . they will send a nice messenger boy to take an unprotected female to a party, and come for her, at a charge of 25 cents each way, and it is quite proper." (WDH to Aurelia, December 29, 1901, Harvard Library.)

2 In a letter to his father, April 6, 1892 (Harvard Library) Howells wrote some advice for caring for the grippe: "Take a table spoon of whiskey, in a half tumbler of milk, filled with soup made by dissolving a teaspoonful of Leibig's extract of beef in hot water, salted to your taste."

II

MR. WILLIS CAMPBELL: Hello, hello, hello! *Oh*, hello, hello, hello! Wake up, in there! Roberts, wake up! Sound the loud timbrel! [3] Fire, murder, and sudden death! *Wake* up! Monday morning, you know; here's Tuesday, Wednesday, Thursday, Friday, Saturday, all gone and nothing done! Come, arouse thee, my merry Swiss boy! Take thy pail and to labor away! All aboard! Train for Newton, West Newton, Newtonville, Auburndale, Riverside, and Newton Lower Falls, on track No. 5. Express to Newton.[4] Wake up, Roberts! Here's McIlheny, out here, wants to know why you took his wife for a cook. Hurry up! he can't wait. Wake up, you old seven-by-nine sleeper, you, or Mrs. Miller's musicale will just simply expire on the spot. Come! It's after ten o'clock now, or it will be in about five minutes. Hurry up! Hello, hello, hello! (*Campbell accompanies his appeals with a tempest of knocks, thumps, and bangs on the outside of Roberts's chamber door. Within, Roberts is discovered, at first stretched on his bed in profound repose, which becomes less and less perfect as Campbell's blows and cries penetrate to his consciousness. He moves, groans, drops back into slumber, groans again, coughs, sits up on the bed, where he has thrown himself with all his clothes on, and listens.*) I say, aren't you going to Mrs. Miller's? If you are, you'd better get out of bed some time before the last call for breakfast. Now ready in the dining-car!

ROBERTS, *leaping out of bed and flinging open the door*: Why, I've *been* to Mrs. Miller's!

CAMPBELL, *entering with his hat on, and his overcoat on his arm*: Oh no, you haven't, you poor, suffering creature! That was a heavenly dream! Why, good gracious, man, you're not dressed! (*Campbell is himself in perfectly appointed evening-dress, and he stares in dismay at the travelling-suit which Roberts still wears.*) You can't go in that figure, you know. You might to Mrs. Curwen's, but you'd give Mrs. Miller deadly offence; she'd think the Curwen had put you up to it. Didn't Agnes tell you I'd be here at ten for you? What have you been doing with yourself? I supposed I should find you walking up and down here, fuming with impatience.

ROBERTS: I was dead tired, and after Agnes went, I just threw myself down here for a moment's rest, and I was off before I knew it—

---

3 Thomas Moore, *Sound the Loud Timbrel*.

4 A reference to *The Albany Depot*.

CAMPBELL: Well, then, hustle! There's no time to lose. We shall be late, but I guess we can get there in time to save Agnes's life if we hump ourselves. Are you shaved?

ROBERTS: Yes, I thought I'd better shave before I lay down—

CAMPBELL: Well, then, that's half the battle, and you ought to be into your dress-suit in five minutes; but you're an intellectual man, and your fingers are all thumbs, and so I'll give you ten minutes. Hello! What's this? (*In speaking of shaving, Campbell has mechanically cast his eye towards the bureau, and has gradually become aware of the half-tumbler of water and the decanter of whiskey which Roberts has left standing there. He pounces upon the decanter, pulls out the stopple, and applies his nose to the mouth.*) Ah, ha! *This* is the milk in the cocoanut, is it? No wonder you slept soundly, and had sweet dreams? Well, Roberts!

ROBERTS: No, no, Willis! I solemnly assure you I haven't touched a drop of it!

CAMPBELL: Oh yes! I know! That's what they always say!

ROBERTS: But I tell you, Willis—

CAMPBELL: Oh, all right, my boy! I don't blame you! You have never fallen before, probably, but you're down this time, old man. You have every appearance of being grossly intoxicated, as the reporters say, at this instant. Look how red your eyes are!

ROBERTS: It's loss of sleep. I tell you I haven't tasted the whiskey.

CAMPBELL: But it's half gone! (*He lifts the decanter and shows.*) Well, I hope Agnes may never know it, and your poor children, Roberts—

ROBERTS: Nonsense! Agnes knows all about it. She brought me the decanter herself. She and Amy thought it would freshen me up. But I distrusted it; I was afraid the effect would be soporific—

CAMPBELL: And it seems you were perfectly right. Events have proved it. But come, now, don't sit there all night, old fellow. (*Roberts has sunk upon the edge of the bed.*) We've got to be off to this scene of maddening gayety at Mrs. Miller's. Want a wet towel round your head? Nothing like it, you know!

ROBERTS, *with dignity*: Thank you, I don't need any wet towel, and I'll be with you in a few moments, if you'll kindly wait.

He moves towards the door of his dressing-room.

CAMPBELL, *cheerfully*: Oh, I'll stay by, Roberts; you needn't be afraid. There's nothing mean about me, and you'll want somebody to pull you together, now and then, and I know just what to do; I've been through this kind of thing with lots of fellows in California. I know the haughty and self-helpful stage. You're all right, Roberts. But don't lose time. What's the matter now?

Roberts has come back from his dressing-room and is staring vacantly at Campbell.

ROBERTS: I was trying to think where I'd put my dress-suit.

CAMPBELL, *triumphantly*: Exactly! And *now* do you expect me to believe you haven't been at that decanter? Where do you suppose you put it?

ROBERTS: Where I always do; on a hook in my closet.

CAMPBELL: You hang up your dress-suit? Why, it must look like a butler's! You ought to fold your clothes and lay them in a bureau drawer. Don't you know that? Very likely Agnes has got onto that while you've been away, and put them in here.

He looks towards the bureau, and Roberts tries to pull open one drawer after another.

ROBERTS: This seems locked. I never lock my drawers.

CAMPBELL: Then that's proof positive that your dress-suit is in there. Agnes has put it in, and locked it up, so as to keep it nice and fresh for you. Where's your key?

ROBERTS: I don't know. I always leave it in the key-hole of one of the drawers. Haven't you got a key-ring, Willis?

CAMPBELL: I've got a key-ring, but I haven't got it about me, as Artemus Ward said of his gift for public speaking. It's in my other trousers pockets. Haven't you got a collection of keys? Amy has a half-bushel, and she keeps them in a hand-bag in the bath-room closet. She says Agnes does.

ROBERTS: So she does! I'll just look. (*While he is gone, Campbell lays down his hat and overcoat, and tries the bureau drawers. Roberts returns to find him at this work.*) No; she must have put them somewhere else. I know she always used to put them there.

CAMPBELL: Well, then we've got to pick the locks. Have you got a boot-buttoner? There's nothing like a boot-buttoner to pick locks. Or, hold on a minute! We've got to go about this thing systematically. Now, I don't think you can tell in your condition whether your dress-coat's in your closet or not, Roberts. We must bring your clothes all out here and lay them on the bed, and see. That dress-suit may turn up yet. You probably thought it was something like an ulster. I know how a man's ideas get mixed, after a little too much freshening up.

ROBERTS, *unmindful of his joke*: You're right, Willis. I may have overlooked it. I'll bring out everything. (*He disappears, and reappears with a business-suit of black diagonal, which he throws on the bed.*) That isn't it.

CAMPBELL, *inspecting it*: No; but it isn't so far off. Some of the young chaps have their dress-coats made of diagonal. Try again, Roberts; you'll fetch it yet. (*Roberts disappears, and reappears with a frock-coat of blue and checked trousers.*) Oh, *that* won't do, Roberts. Don't give way like that. Who ever saw a man in evening-dress with check trousers on? Now, what have we next? (*As Roberts goes and comes, Campbell receives his burdens and verifies them.*) A velvet jacket won't do, either, unless you're a travelling Englishman. Three pairs of summer pantaloons are all very well in their way; but they're out of season, and stripes are not the thing for evening wear any more. Beautiful bath gown, but more adapted for amateur dramatics than for a musicale. Two waistcoats and a Norfolk jacket mean well, but are not adapted to the purpose. Exemplary light overcoat, but still not quite the thing. Double-breasted reefer and Canada homespun trousers; admirably fitted for a sea-voyage and camping out. Armload of semi-detached waistcoats and pantaloons; very suggestive, but not instantly available. Pajamas not at all the thing. Elderly pair of doeskin trousers and low-cut waistcoat—Why, hello, Roberts! here's part of your dress-suit now! Where's the coat?

ROBERTS, *dropping into a chair and wiping his forehead, while he surveys the tangled heap of garments on the bed*: Given away. Got too small for me, three years ago. Agnes kept the waistcoat and trousers for the sake of association, because I told her I wore them at the party where we first met. They won't go half round me now.

CAMPBELL, *scrutinizing them critically as he holds them*: Well, look here, Roberts, we may have to come to these yet. Stand up, old fellow. (*Roberts mechanically stands up, and Campbell tries the top of the trousers against his waistband.*) May need a little slitting down the back, so as to let them out a third, or two-thirds, or so. But I guess we'll try an ice-pick first.

He flings the clothes on the bed, and touches the electric bell.

ROBERTS: Ice-pick?

CAMPBELL: Yes; nothing like it for prying open bureau drawers. (*To Bella, the maid, who appears at the door in answer to his ring*) The ice-pick, please.

BELLA: Ice-pick, sir?

CAMPBELL: Yes. The—ice—pick—here—quick.

BELLA, *vanishing, with a gesture of wonder at the pile of clothing on the bed*: All right, sir.

ROBERTS: But, Willis! Won't it bruise and deface the bureau? Agnes is very careful of this bu—

CAMPBELL: Not at all. You just set the pick in here over the lock, and pry. I sha'n't leave a scratch. (*They stoop down together in front of the bureau, and Campbell shows him how.*) But what are you going to do? You've got to have your clothes if you're going to the musicale. Ah, here we are! Thanks. (*As Bella comes with the ice-pick, which he pushes in over the lock of the lowest drawer.*) We'll begin with the lowest, because that's where Amy keeps mine, and if Agnes has got onto it through her, she'll be sure to do exactly the same. Now, then, I just scratch the bolt down with my knife, and Open, Sesame! What do you say to bruising your old bureau now?

ROBERTS, *as Campbell pulls out the drawer and sets it on a chair*: Perfect! Only—(*he lifts the things from the drawer, and places them on another chair*) there don't seem to be anything here but underclothes.

CAMPBELL: Well, then, we must get the next out. No time to lose. Come! Keep shoving the pick in, and I'll scratch the bolt down with my knife. See? It's nothing.

They pull the drawer out and set it on the floor, and Roberts ruefully contemplates it.

ROBERTS: Nothing but shirts, collars, cuffs and neckties.

CAMPBELL: Ah, I don't know that. It's a deep drawer—(*he begins taking the linen out, and laying it on the floor*) and the dress-suit may be at the bottom. No! Nothing here. You're right, Roberts. Well, now for the top drawer and the last. If we'd taken that out first, we needn't have taken out the second; we could have seen it in place. You ought to have thought of that, Roberts.

ROBERTS, *with injury*: You suggested taking out the lowest first, yourself, Willis. You said Agnes would be sure to have put them there.

CAMPBELL: Did I? Well, I knew I must have

a reason for it. But come along now, Roberts, and push the ice-pick in. (*After a season of experiment with the pick and the penknife*) The bolt won't scratch down. What are you going to do now, Roberts?

ROBERTS: I don't know.

CAMPBELL: But you've got to do something, you know. We can't just give it up. Where are those dress-trousers and waistcoat? (*He begins tumbling the things on the bed, laying some on chairs, letting others drop to the floor.*) Ah, here they are! Now, I'll tell you what, Roberts, you've got to wear these. Go into your dressing-room there and put them on, and then we can tell how much they have to be slit up the back.

ROBERTS: But where's the coat, even if I could get the other things on?

CAMPBELL: We'll think about that later. We haven't got any time to lose in talk. We can pin back the skirts of your frock-coat, as the travelling Americans used to do when they went to the opera in London. Hurry up! (*He gives Roberts the garments, and pushes him into the door of his dressing-room, and walks impatiently up and down amidst the chaos of clothing till Roberts reappears.*) Why, that isn't bad!

ROBERTS: Bad? I can't breathe; I feel as if I were being cut in two!

CAMPBELL: Nonsense! That's the way every woman feels when she's laced. It gives you a beautiful waist, Roberts! Ah, ha, ha, ha! Ha, ha, ha! O Lord! Oh, mercy! Ah, ha, ha, ha!

ROBERTS: Now, look here, Willis—

CAMPBELL, *turning him round, and surveying him from different points*: No, no! Don't mind *me!* It's just my way, you know. I don't mean anything by it. I think these things look first-rate on you. There's no mistake about their giving you a youthful figure; we can just let them out a few stitches, and you'll be perfectly comfortable. The only thing now is the coat. I'm afraid that pinning back wouldn't do. We'd better try something else. I'll tell you! Send down and borrow Merrick's coat! He's still on the floor below you, I suppose?

ROBERTS: Yes, but he's so thin—

CAMPBELL: The very thing! Those thin fellows always have their things made roomy—

ROBERTS: But he's tall.

CAMPBELL: That's all right. If you keep these things on you've got to give in some direction, and you're probably going to stretch.
  He rings the bell.

ROBERTS: But it's very late. He must be in bed.

CAMPBELL: I'll fix that. (*To Bella, as she appears*) Bella, I want you to go down to the gentleman under here, and ask him if he won't lend Mr. Roberts his dress-coat. Tell him Mrs. Roberts has gone off to a party, and Mr. Roberts doesn't know where to find his coat.

ROBERTS: Oh, do you think she'd better tell him that, Willis?

CAMPBELL: Why, certainly! You must account for the request in some way. It'll appeal to his sympathy, and put him into a good-humor if he happens to have to get out of bed to oblige you.

BELLA: They're all up yet, sir. I saw their cook on the back stairs when I came in. They've been giving a dinner—

CAMPBELL: Well, run then. (*To Roberts, as Bella vanishes*) Merrick can take it right off his back. But whilst she's gone we'll just give this lock another chance. (*They work jointly at the bureau drawer.*) No, it won't scrape down. It's probably rusted in. You must get this lock oiled, Roberts. (*As Bella returns with a dress-coat in her hand*) Ah, here we are! That's very nice of Merrick. What did he say?

BELLA: I didn't see him, sir. The girl brought it.

CAMPBELL: Well, that's all, Bella. (*He shakes out the coat as she goes, and looks down at it.*) I suppose it amused Merrick. He's got a good deal of humor, Merrick has. I hope he won't give it to the press.

ROBERTS: Good heavens, Willis! You don't—

CAMPBELL: Oh, he wouldn't give real names. Merrick's too much of a gentleman for that. Come, try it on. We've got to hurry, now. (*Roberts backs towards him with extended arms and Campbell slips the coat-sleeves on them.*) Easy, easy! It may be a little narrow for you in the back—No, sir! It fits you like a glove. (*He stands off and surveys Roberts, after smoothing the coat across the shoulders.*) Yes, sir, like a glove— a glove that the pretty shop-girl has put on for you, after she's peppered it full of that white stuff to make it go on, and told you that you could easily wear a size smaller. (*He begins to laugh as he lifts each of Roberts's limp arms, with the sleeves dangling below his hands, and touches the skirt, which descends to the calf of his leg.*) The most youthful figure I ever saw! Looks like a boy in his father's coat. Merrick *is* a tall fellow. I'd no idea—

ROBERTS, *looking ruefully over his shoulder*: You see it won't do, Willis.

CAMPBELL: No, no! I don't say that, quite.

But perhaps we'd better try something else. Who's overhead now?

ROBERTS, *desperately*: Baker. And he's short and fat—

CAMPBELL: Short and fat isn't at all bad. (*Touching the annunciator.*) He's probably had his coat made rather long and snug. It'll be the very thing for you. We mustn't leave a stone unturned, or a coat untried. (*To Bella, appearing at the door, and putting her apron up to control herself at sight of Mr. Roberts's figure*) Do you know whether Mr. Baker's people have gone to bed?

BELLA: No, sir. I heard their second girl saying on the stairs that Mrs. Baker was up with a bad toothache.

CAMPBELL: What a piece of luck! Run right up, will you, and borrow Mr. Baker's dress-coat. (*To Roberts, on Bella's disappearance*) Baker's coat will be all right; but still we'd better work away at this bureau drawer again. Drive the ice-pick in a little farther, now.

> They struggle with lock as before, until Bella returns, Roberts absent-mindedly keeping Merrick's coat on, and from time to time taking a turn about the room to rest his back.

ROBERTS: Let's give it up, Willis. We can't get it open. It's no use!

CAMPBELL, *desisting*: Well, we'll leave that to the last, then. But I've the liveliest confidence in Baker's coat. Ah, here it is! Saved! Saved! (*He takes the garment from Bella at the threshold.*) Now, then, the great thing is to get Merrick's coat off in one piece. I thought I heard a ripping sound in the back of it when you were straining at that drawer. But I guess it was merely fancy. Easy, easy!

> He helps Roberts get the coat off, and examines it.

ROBERTS, *anxiously*: Is it all right?

CAMPBELL: Yes, it's perfectly sound. You may have started the seams a little, but it's nothing that Merrick will ever notice. Now for Baker! There! Goes on like an old shoe! (*He retires a few steps and surveys Roberts's back, which Roberts is craning his neck round to get a view of in the glass.*) There's space! Gives you a mighty fine, portly figure, Roberts; it looks *grand* on you, it does indeed! I call that the back of a leading citizen in very comfortable circumstances. Something magisterial about it. Perhaps it's a little full; but that's a good fault; it must set awfully easy. Sleeves are a trifle short, maybe, but not too much to show your cuff-buttons; I hate a coat that don't do that. Yes, I should call that a very nice fit.

ROBERTS, *tearing off the coat, and flinging it on the bed*: You know it won't do, Willis. And now I must give the whole thing up. You'd better hurry off and explain to Agnes why I could not come.

CAMPBELL: Oh no, I can't leave you in the lurch that way, my dear fellow. Besides it would break Agnes all up. We must *do* something. I think either one of those coats would go perfectly well; but if you're so particular about your personal appearance, there's only one thing left. We *must* get this drawer open. Look here. We'll shove the ice-pick in a little farther, so's to give the bolt the slightest possible catch, and then we'll both pull, you on one handle, and I on the other. It won't hurt the bureau. And besides, it's the only chance left. I suppose these coats *don't* look as if they were made for you. What do you say?

ROBERTS, *disconsolately*: Oh, I suppose we'd better try. It can't be much worse.

> He casts a hopeless glance around the confused and tumbled room.

CAMPBELL, *absently*: Yes. Might as well be hung for a sheep as a lamb, you know. Agnes won't be able to express her feelings anyway when she sees this room. It looks as if a small cyclone had been joking round here; but she'll like your devotion in doing your utmost.

ROBERTS: Do you think so? I'm not so sure. But we'll try it.

> He pushes the ice-pick in with all his strength.

CAMPBELL: That's it! Now then! (*They each grasp a handle of the drawer and pull.*) One, two, three—pull! Once more—pull! Now the third time—pull! And *out* she comes!

> The bolt suddenly gives and the drawer drops violently to the floor, scattering its contents in every direction, while the two men totter backward and cling to each other to keep their balance. At the same moment the voices of Mrs. Roberts and Mrs. Campbell make themselves heard without in vague cries of astonishment, question, and apprehension, mounting into a wild shriek as the drawer crashes to the floor.

III

MRS. ROBERTS, *without*: Oh, Edward, *is* it a burglar?

MRS. CAMPBELL, *without*: Is it a mouse, Willis?

MRS. ROBERTS: Ring for the district telegraph— call for a policeman, Edward! Press the ratchet down three times!

MRS. CAMPBELL: Don't *kill* him, Willis; don't you *dare* to kill him. Take him up with the tongs and fling him out of the window!

MRS. ROBERTS: Don't trust him, Edward: get Willis to hold him, and press the ratchet quick!

MRS. CAMPBELL: Keep him from getting back into his hole, for then you never can tell whether he's there or not!

MRS. ROBERTS: Why don't you answer, Edward? Oh, dear, perhaps he's garroted Edward. I *know* he has!

MRS. CAMPBELL: Willis, if this is any of your tricks—if it's one of your miserable practical jokes—

MRS. ROBERTS: Oh, I wonder what they're keeping so quiet for! Edward, are you safe? Do you need *me?* If you do, just speak, and I will—go for a policeman, myself!

MRS. CAMPBELL: If you don't answer, Willis— (*Whimpering*) Oh, he just wants to make me take my life in my hand! He wouldn't like anything better.

> The two men, during this rapid colloquy, *remain silently aghast, staring at each other and at the scene of confusion around them.*

MRS. ROBERTS: Well, then, do it, Amy! You have so much more courage than I have, and you have no children; and if you'll only go to the door and peep in I'll stay here, and keep screaming as loud as ever I can. I'll begin now—

ROBERTS: No, no; don't call out, Agnes. It's all right. We've just had a little accident with one of the bureau drawers. It's perfectly safe; but don't come in till we—

> He dashes madly about the room, trying to *put it in shape. Both ladies instantly show themselves at the door.*

MRS. ROBERTS, *in dismay at the spectacle*: Why, what in the world has happened, Edward?

MRS. CAMPBELL: It's something Willis has put him up to. I knew it was from the way he kept so still. Where is he?

CAMPBELL, *coming boldly forward out of Roberts's dressing-room, where he had previously taken refuge*: I've saved Roberts's life. If it hadn't been for me he couldn't have moved hand or foot. He was dead asleep when I came here, and I've been helping him look for his dress-suit. (*At these words*

Mrs. Roberts abandons herself to despair in one of the chairs overflowing with clothes.) Hello! What's the matter with Agnes?

MRS. ROBERTS: I never can look any one in the face again! To think of my doing such a thing when I've always prided myself on being so thoughtful, and remembering things so perfectly! And here I've been reproaching Edward and poor Willis the whole evening for not coming to that horrid musicale, and accusing them of all kinds of things, and all the time I knew I'd forgotten something and couldn't think what it was! Oh, dear! I shall simply never forgive myself! But it was all because I wanted him to look so nice in it, and I got it pressed while he was away, and I folded it up in the tissue-paper myself, and took the greatest care of it; and then to have it turn out the way it has!

CAMPBELL: What in the world are you talking about?

MRS. ROBERTS: Why, Edward's dress-suit, of course!

MRS. CAMPBELL: Of course she is. But you always have to have things put in words of one syllable for you.

CAMPBELL: No irrelevant insults, Mrs. Campbell, if you please! Now, Agnes, try to collect yourself. When you had folded his dress-suit in tissue-paper so nicely, what did you do with it?

MRS. ROBERTS: Why, I wrapped it in my white Chuddah shawl, and put it away back on the top shelf in his closet, and I forgot to tell him where it was. (*Visible sensation on all sides*) And if Edward were to say now that he couldn't forgive me, I should just simply fall down and worship him.

CAMPBELL: He can forgive you, probably, but he cannot *forget;* we must leave *that* to women. And here we were, searching every nook and corner of the house, and every hole and cranny, for that dress-suit, which you'd poked away in tissue-paper and Chuddah, while you were enjoying yourself at Mrs. Miller's.

MRS. CAMPBELL: We weren't enjoying ourselves. It was the deadliest thing that ever was, and you were very lucky to escape.

CAMPBELL: That is all very well; but the credit of that belongs entirely to a merciful Providence. What I want to know is how Agnes is going to excuse herself for hiding her husband's clothes, so that if this musicale had been the most delightful affair of the season he would have missed it just the same.

MRS. ROBERTS, *regarding her husband's strange figure in the youthful waistcoat and trousers*: Why, Edward, dear, what in the world have you got on?

CAMPBELL: She doesn't even remember the dress-suit in which poor Roberts first met her! Well, Agnes, you're a pretty wife and mother! Look at that man! (*He takes Roberts by the elbow and turns him round.*) Did you ever see devotion like that? He's buttoned in so tight that he can't draw a full breath to save him, but he would have gone to the party, if he had expired to slow music after he got there; only he couldn't find the coat. You'd given that away.

MRS. CAMPBELL, *fishing up a garment from the tempestuous sea of clothes*: Why, here's a dress-coat, now!

CAMPBELL: Yes, that's Merrick's. It was rather snug for Roberts.

MRS. ROBERTS: And here's another!

CAMPBELL: Yes, that's Baker's. It was rather roomy for Roberts.

MRS. ROBERTS: But how did you get them?

CAMPBELL, *lightly*: Oh, we sent and borrowed them.

ROBERTS, *less lightly*: We had to do *something*, Agnes. I knew you would be terribly anxious if I didn't come—

MRS. ROBERTS, *with abject contrition*: Oh, don't speak a word, you poor suffering martyr!

CAMPBELL: We should have borrowed every coat in the block if you hadn't got back.

MRS. CAMPBELL: Yes, and I've no doubt you'd have taken a perfectly fiendish enjoyment in every failure.

CAMPBELL, *with a wild, spluttering laugh*: Well, the disappointments certainly had their compensations. Roberts, just let them see how well you look in Merrick's coat! Or, no: try Baker's first; I think Baker's is a little more swell on you, if anything.

BELLA, *at the door*: Supper is served, Mrs. Roberts.

CAMPBELL: Supper?

MRS. ROBERTS: Oh, yes! Mrs. Miller never gives you anything but ice-cream; and I thought we should all need something hot when we got back, and so I had a few— But I forgot all about the supper!

CAMPBELL: I'm glad Bella didn't. Better let Bella put Roberts's clothes away, after this.

MRS. ROBERTS, *in extreme dejection*: Yes, I think I really had, Willis. I'm not fit to be Edward's wife, if I behave that way to him.

CAMPBELL: Well, well, he must have a divorce, then; but not till after supper.

MRS. CAMPBELL: Yes, never mind now, Agnes. It's all turned out well, as it is: Edward has been spared a fearful bore, and nobody will ever be any the wiser about your putting away his evening dress—

CAMPBELL: Oh, indeed! *Won't* they? When Baker and Merrick meet at the club, and exchange notes about Agnes locking up Roberts's clothes—

MRS. ROBERTS, *with horror*: Edward! You didn't send that word to them!

ROBERTS: Why—why—I'm afraid we did, something like it, my dear. We had to explain our request, somehow—

MRS. ROBERTS, *relaxing into a chair*: Then I simply never can hold up my head again.

She lets it fall in typical despair.

MRS. CAMPBELL, *pressing the annunciator, with the energy of a lioness at bay*: I don't believe it's as bad as that. It simply can't be. It would be too abominable. (*As Bella appears in answer to the bell*) Did you tell the gentlemen, when you went to borrow the coats for Mr. Roberts, that Mrs. Roberts had locked up his dress-suit?

BELLA: Why, that's what Mr. Campbell said to say, ma'am, but I didn't believe Mrs. Roberts would quite like it, ma'am, and so I said—

She hesitates, and Mrs. Roberts springs to her feet, with arms outstretched to her.

MRS. ROBERTS: *What*, Bella?

BELLA: Why, you know, ma'am, I couldn't help thinking how things fly about a house like this.

MRS. ROBERTS: Yes, yes!

MRS. CAMPBELL: Go on!

BELLA: I didn't believe the gentlemen would have sent word like that themselves, if they'd thought of it; and so—

MRS. ROBERTS: And so?

MRS. CAMPBELL: So?

BELLA: I know you like to have me always speak the truth, and so I do, to you, ma'am, and every lady I ever lived with; but I wasn't going to have that young waitress of Mrs. Baker's and that nasty cook of Mrs. Merrick's laughing at us.

CAMPBELL: Well, and what did you do?

MRS. ROBERTS: Yes, Bella!

BELLA: I told Mrs. Merrick's cook that the gentlemen were getting up some charades; and

I told Mr. Baker's second girl that the tailor hadn't sent Mr. Roberts's coat home.

MRS. CAMPBELL: Well, you *were* inspired, Bella.

MRS. ROBERTS, *to Bella*: Oh, you—angel!

CAMPBELL: Well, that isn't quite what they call the father of them. Who was the father of what? But we won't dispute about terms. The great thing now is to get at that little supper. Come on, Roberts!

MRS. ROBERTS: Yes, Edward, take out Amy—

ROBERTS, *putting himself in evidence*: But don't you see, my dear, I can't draw a full breath now; and if I were to eat anything—

MRS. ROBERTS: Oh, well, go and change them at once. We won't wait for you, dear, but I'll see to keeping it hot for you.

CAMPBELL, *as he follows the ladies out of one door, while Roberts vanishes into his dressing-room through the other*: Yes, just slip on anything that will fit you. It's so near morning now that we won't insist on evening dress.

THE END

The Unexpected Guests

[1893]

If one were to select the best of Howells' farce-comedies, *The Unexpected Guests* would necessarily be high on the list. In the first place it is his only play that is almost pure social comedy. Founded on fact ("A Letter to the Publisher," *Minor Dramas*) and having a single artificial convention for its central issue, it is a witty portrayal of the fashionable Boston Back Bay aristocracy that Howells knew well. Here, perhaps better than in any other of his plays, he demonstrates his penetrating knowledge of the way in which women face society and react to the various confusions that society frequently provokes. And Howells not only represents but gently satirizes the social conventions as well as the bewildered and bewildering members of society.

Poor Mrs. Campbell! She is completely upset by the unexpected arrival of the Belforts and will go through the dinner "like a stone." It is a disaster! All must be changed! "And I'd got the violets scattered so carelessly," she says. "Now I shall just *fling* them on. I don't care how they look." This is the fashionable society that Howells delights in portraying. It is a society where people sometimes dislike each other, where the less scrupulous may take cruel advantage of others, but where the genteel do what propriety dictates and good breeding demands.

Using the convention of polite lying as his main theme, Howells produced one of his best plays in *The Unexpected Guests*. If one does not want to see another person, does one simply tell him so, or does one give the conventional lie which accomplishes one's purpose while not injuring the pride of one's visitor? Must, then, fashionable society be either untruthful or hypocritical? Or is there some middle ground on which one may stand secure? Mrs. Campbell maintains that truth is a female virtue; yet as her dinner guests arrive late with varying excuses, she immediately soothes each visiting conscience with the appropriate social untruth. Not all members of this society are blind to its foibles, however. Behind the benign countenance of Dr. Lawton and the mischievous eyes of Willis Campbell, there is a clear understanding, but though they have opinions, they have no answers to the questions. Throughout the action Howells' use of the phonograph constantly keeps the idea of truth before the audience. A ghostly chant, something like the voice over the telephone in *The Impossible*, it becomes almost prophetic: "Truth crushed to earth shall rise again."

The Unexpected Guests[1]

Mrs. Willis Campbell's Drawing-Room

DR. LAWTON: Then truth, as I understand you, Mrs. Campbell, is a female virtue.

MRS. CAMPBELL: It is one of them.

DR. LAWTON: Oh! You have several?

MRS. CAMPBELL: Legions, Dr. Lawton.

DR. LAWTON: What do you do with them all?

MRS. CAMPBELL: Oh, we just keep them. You may be sure we don't waste them on *men*. What would be the use, for instance, of always telling Willis the truth? He wouldn't believe it, to begin with.

CAMPBELL: You had better try me once, Amy. My impression is that it's the other thing I can't get away with. And yet I'm a great deal more accustomed to it!

MRS. CAMPBELL: That is neither here nor there. But what I say, and what I insist, is that the conventional lies that people tell are just as much lies as any—just as wicked, and altogether unnecessary. Why should I send word to the door that I'm not at home, or that I'm engaged, when I'm not, merely to get out of seeing a person?

CAMPBELL: Because you are such a liar, my love.

DR. LAWTON: No! Excuse me, Campbell! I don't wish to intercept any little endearments, but really I think that in this case Mrs. Campbell's sacrifice of the truth is a piece of altruism. She knows how it is herself; she wouldn't like to be in the place of the person she wants to get out of seeing. So she sends word that she is not at home, or that she's engaged.

MRS. CAMPBELL: Of course I do. Willis's idea of *truth* would be to send word that he didn't want to see them.

DR. LAWTON, *laughing*: I haven't the least doubt of it.

CAMPBELL: Well, you hoary-headed impostor, what would yours be?

DR. LAWTON: Mine? I have none! I have been a general practitioner for forty years. But what time did you ask me for, Mrs. Campbell?

1 The text used here is the Harper & Brothers edition.

MRS. CAMPBELL: Seven. I don't see what's keeping them all.

CAMPBELL: The women are not coming.

MRS. CAMPBELL: Why?

CAMPBELL: Because they said they were. Truth is a female virtue.

MRS. CAMPBELL: I must say, I don't see why they're so late. I can't understand, when every woman knows the anxiety of a hostess, how any one can be late. It's very heartless, I think.

Mrs. Campbell is in dinner dress; she remains tranquilly seated on the sofa while she speaks, but the movement of her alternately folded and expanded fan betrays the agitation of her spirits. Dr. Lawton, lounging at large ease in a low chair, regards her with a mixture of admiration and scientific interest. Her husband walks up and down with a surcharge of nervous energy which the husband of a dinner-giver naturally expends when the guests are a little late.

CAMPBELL: They will probably come in a lump—if they come at all. Don't be discouraged, Amy. If they don't come, I shall be hungry enough, by-and-by, to eat the whole dinner myself.

MRS. CAMPBELL: That is a man's idea; you think that the great thing about a dinner is to get it eaten.

DR. LAWTON: Oh, not *all* of us, Mrs. Campbell!

MRS. CAMPBELL: Well, I will except you, Dr. Lawton.

CAMPBELL: And what is a woman's idea of a dinner, I should like to know?

MRS. CAMPBELL: To get it over.

CAMPBELL: In this instance, then, I think you're going to fail. I see no prospect of your getting it over. The people are not coming. I guess you wrote Thursday when you meant Tuesday; didn't you, Amy? Your Tuesdays always look like Thursdays, anyway.

MRS. CAMPBELL: Now, Willis, if you begin your teasing!

CAMPBELL: Well, what I want you to do is to tell them what you really think of them when

420

they do come. I don't want any hollow-hearted pretence that it isn't at all late, and that you did not expect them before, and all that kind of thing. You just say, *Yes, you are rather behind time;* and, *No, I didn't write half-past seven; I wrote seven.* With all your devotion to truth, I'll bet you wouldn't dare to speak it once.

MRS. CAMPBELL: What will you bet? Come, now! Dr. Lawton will hold the stakes.

CAMPBELL: Ah, *I* should have to pay, whichever lost, and Lawton would pocket the stakes.

DR. LAWTON: Try me!

CAMPBELL: I'd rather not. It would be too expensive. *(A ring is heard; and then voices below and on the stairs.)* The spell is broken! I hear the stentorian tones of my sister Agnes.

MRS. CAMPBELL: Yes, it *is* Agnes; and now they'll all come. *(She runs out to the space at the top of the stairs which forms a sort of passageway between the drawing-room and library.)* Oh, Agnes! I'm *so* glad to see you! And Mr. Roberts!

She says this without, and the shock of kisses penetrates to the drawing-room, where Campbell and Dr. Lawton remain.

MRS. ROBERTS, *without*: Amy, I'm quite ashamed of myself! I'm afraid we're late. I think Edward's watch must be slow.

MRS. CAMPBELL, *without*: Not at all! I don't believe it's seven yet. I've only just got into my gown.

CAMPBELL: It *is* a female virtue, Doctor!

DR. LAWTON: Oh, there's no doubt of its sex.

MRS. CAMPBELL, *without*: You'll find Willis in the drawing-room with Dr. Lawton, Mr. Roberts.

CAMPBELL, *as Roberts meekly appears*: Hello, Roberts! You're late, old fellow. You ought to start Agnes dressing just after lunch.

ROBERTS: No, I'm afraid it's my fault. How do you do, Dr. Lawton? I think my watch is losing time.

CAMPBELL: You didn't come your old dodge of stealing a garroter's watch on your way through the Common?[1] That was a tremendous exploit of yours, Roberts.

DR. LAWTON: And you were at your best that night, Campbell. For a little while I wasn't sure but truth was a boy.

CAMPBELL: I don't believe old Bemis has quite forgiven Roberts to this day. By-the-way, Bemis is late, too. Wouldn't have helped much to grab his watch to-night, Roberts. Hold on! That's his voice, now! *(As Mr. Bemis enters)* Good-evening,

Mr. Bemis. Roberts and I were just talking of that night when you tried to garrot him in the Common, and he got away with your watch.

MR. BEMIS, *reluctantly*: Oh! very good. Ha, ha, ha!

ROBERTS, *cringingly*: Ha, ha, ha! Capital!

MR. BEMIS: Talking of watches, I hope I'm not late.

CAMPBELL: About half an hour.

MRS. CAMPBELL, *re-entering and giving her hand*: Don't believe a word of it, Mr. Bemis. You're just in time. Why, even Aunt Mary is not here yet!

AUNT MARY CRASHAW, *without*: Yes, I am, my dear—half-way up your ridiculous stairs.

MRS. CAMPBELL: Oh, Aunt Mary!

She runs out to meet her.

CAMPBELL, *to Dr. Lawton*: You see! she can't tell the truth even by accident.

ROBERTS: What in the world do you mean, Willis?

CAMPBELL: 'Sh! It's a bet. *(To Mrs. Crashaw, coming in with his wife)* You *are* pretty well blown, Aunt Mary.

MRS. CRASHAW: Blown? I wonder I'm alive to reproach Amy for these stairs. Why don't you live in a flat?

CAMPBELL: I am going to put in an elevator here, and you can get stuck in it.[2]

MRS. CRASHAW: I dare say I shall, if *you* put it in. What a frightful experience! I shall never forget that night. How d'ye do, Edward? *(She shakes hands with Roberts and Mr. Bemis.)* How do you do, Mr. Bemis? I *know* how Dr. Lawton does, without asking.

DR. LAWTON, *gallantly*: All the better for—

MRS. CRASHAW: *Don't* say, for seeing me! We may *be* chestnuts, doctor, but we needn't speak them. *(To Mrs. Campbell)* Are you going to have the whole elevator company, as usual?

MRS. CAMPBELL: Yes—all but Mr. and Mrs. Miller. I asked them, but they had an engagement.

MRS. CRASHAW: So much the worse for them. Mrs. Curwen will be very much disappointed not to see—Mrs. Miller. *(The men laugh. She shakes her fan at them.)* You ought to be ashamed to provoke me to say such things. Well, now, since I'm here, I wish the others would come. I'm rather hungry, and it's late, isn't it?

MRS. CAMPBELL: Not at all! I don't see why you all think it's late. I'm sure it's very early. Ah, Mrs. Curwen! *(She advances upon this lady, who enters*

[1] A reference to *The Garroters.*

[2] A reference to *The Elevator.*

with her husband behind her.) So glad you could come. And Mr. Curwen! I didn't hear you coming!

MRS. CURWEN: That proves you didn't eavesdrop at the head of the stairs, my dear. We were quarrelling all the way up to this threshold. After I'd answered it, I mislaid your invitation, and Mr. Curwen was sure we were asked for Wednesday. But I knew better. As it is, I'm afraid we're rather late.

MRS. CAMPBELL, *forcing a laugh*: We rarely sit down before eight. Oh, Mrs. Bemis! How do you do, Mr. Bemis!

She greets young Mr. and Mrs. Bemis with effusion, as they come in with an air of haste.

MRS. BEMIS: Oh, I *know* we're frightfully late!

BEMIS: Yes, it's quite shocking—

MRS. CAMPBELL: Not at all! Really, I think it must be a conspiracy. Everybody says they are late, and I don't know why.

CAMPBELL: I do; but I don't like to tell.

DR. LAWTON: Much safer, my dear boy! Much!

MRS. CAMPBELL, *ignoring this passage*: If I should make you wait, just to *show* you that it was early, I don't think it would be more than you deserve.

CAMPBELL: Probably, if you did that, Miss Reynolds would get here too soon.

MRS. CAMPBELL: Yes; and she's usually so prompt.

MRS. CURWEN: I'm beginning to have the courage of my convictions, Mrs. Campbell. Are you *sure* you didn't say half-past?

MRS. CAMPBELL: I'm sure I can't say. Very likely I may have done so in your note. But I don't see why we are so inflexible about dinner engagements. *I* think we ought to give people at least three-quarters of an hour's grace, instead of that wretched fifteen minutes that keeps everybody's heart in their mouth. *(The door-bell sounds.)* Ah! That's Miss Reynold's ring, and—

CAMPBELL: We are saved! I was afraid we were going to be thirteen at table.

MRS. ROBERTS: Thirteen! What do you mean, Willis?

CAMPBELL: Why, one from twelve, you know.

MRS. ROBERTS: Oh, yes.

The others laugh.

MRS. CAMPBELL: Don't notice him, Agnes. He's in one of his very worst ways to-night.

MRS. ROBERTS: But I don't see what the joke is!

MRS. CAMPBELL: Neither do I, Agnes. I—

A GHOSTLY VOICE, *as of an asthmatic spectre speaking through an imperfectly attached set of artificial teeth, makes itself heard from the library*: Truth crushed to earth will rise again. For God's eternal years are hers—er—r—r—ck—ck—cr—cr —cr—ee—ck— [1]

MRS. CRASHAW: Good heavens, Willis, what in the world is that?

THE VOICE: This is the North America Company's perfected phonograph, invented by Thomas A.—cr—cr—cr—ee—ee—ck—ck—ck—New Jersey. This cylinder was—cr—cr—elocutionist—ee —ee—ck—Cullen Bryant— Truth crushed to— cr—cr—ck—ck—

CAMPBELL: Don't be alarmed, Aunt Mary. It's just a phonograph that I had got in to amuse you after dinner. It don't seem to be exactly in order. Perhaps the cylinder's got dry, or Jim hasn't got quite the right pressure on—

MRS. CRASHAW: Is Jim in there?

MRS. CAMPBELL: Yes; Agnes has lent him to us to-day. I adore boys, and Jim has been angelic the whole afternoon.

MRS. ROBERTS: Oh, you're *too* good, Amy!

MRS. CRASHAW: I don't wonder he's been angelic, with a thing like that to play with. I should be angelic myself. Why can't we go and be amused with it a little before dinner, Willis?

THE OTHERS, *respectively*: Oh, yes. Do. By all means. I never heard one before. We really can't wait. Let us hear it now, Mr. Campbell! Do make him, Mrs. Campbell.

CAMPBELL: Well, all right. I'll go with you— *(He stops, feeling himself significantly clutched by the wrist, and arrested in mid-career, by Mrs. Campbell.)* Or, Jim can show it off. It'll do him so much good. I'll let Jim. *(The guests follow one another out with cries of real and simulated interest, and Campbell turns to his wife.)* What in the world is it, Amy?

MRS. CAMPBELL: What is it? I shall die, Willis!

CAMPBELL: Well, speak first.

MRS. CAMPBELL: Something's happened to the dinner, I know. And I'm afraid to go and see. The cook's so cross!

CAMPBELL: Well, shall *I* go?

MRS. CAMPBELL: And if you keep up this teasing of yours, you'll simply kill me.

CAMPBELL: Well, I won't, then. But it's very lucky your guests are belated too, Amy. Now, if

[1] Bryant, "The Battle-Field," stanza 9. (Incorrect quotation)

you *could* get the dinner on in about ten minutes, we should be just right. But you've told them all they were so early that they'll believe the delay is all yours.

MRS. CAMPBELL: They won't believe anything of the kind! They know better. But I don't dare—

JANE, *the waitress, appearing through the portière of the drawing-room*: Dinner is ready, Mrs. Campbell.

MRS. CAMPBELL: Oh, well, then, do get them started, Willis! Don't forget, it's young Mrs. Bemis you're to take down—*not* Mrs. Curwen.

CAMPBELL: Oh, no! I sha'n't forget that. I hope Mrs. Curwen won't. Hello! There's another ring. Who in the world is that?

MRS. CAMPBELL: 'Sh! If that horrid, squeaking phonograph—

THE PHONOGRAPH, *from the library*: Truth crushed to earth will—

MRS. CAMPBELL: Good gracious! I can't hear a word. Hark! It's Miss Reynolds talking with some one in the reception-room, and it sounds like—but it can't be—no, it can't—it—it *is*—yes! And that's *his* voice too, Willis! What does it mean? Am I losing my five senses? Or am I simply going stark, staring mad?

CAMPBELL: You don't say the Millers have come?

MRS. CAMPBELL: The Millers? No! Who cares anything about the Millers? 'Sh!

She listens.

CAMPBELL, *listening*: Why, it's the Belforts!

MRS. CAMPBELL: How can you *dare* to say it, Willis? Of course it's the Belforts. Hark!

She listens.

CAMPBELL, *listening*: But I thought you said they declined, too.

MRS. CAMPBELL: They did. It's some frightful mystery. Be still, do, Willis!

CAMPBELL: Why, I'm not making any noise. It's the froufrou of that dress of yours.

MRS. CAMPBELL: It's your shirt bosom. You always *will* have them so stiff; and you keep breathing so.

CAMPBELL: Oh, well, if you don't want me to breathe!

MRS. CAMPBELL, *desperately*: It doesn't matter. It wouldn't help now if you *never* breathed again. Don't joke, Willis! I can't bear it. If you do, I shall scream.

CAMPBELL: I wasn't going to joke. It's too serious. What are you going to do?

MRS. CAMPBELL: I don't know. We must do anything to keep them from finding out that they weren't expected.

CAMPBELL: But how do you suppose it's happened, Amy?

MRS. CAMPBELL: I don't know. They meant to decline somewhere else and accept here, and they mixed the letters. It's always happening. But be still now! They're coming up, and all we can do is to keep them in the dark as well as we can. You must help me, Willis.

CAMPBELL: Oh, there's nothing I like better than throwing dust in people's eyes. It's my native element.

MRS. CAMPBELL: Of course it puts the table all out, and we've got to rearrange the places, and think who is going to take out who again as soon as we can get rid of them. Be making up some pretext, Willis. We've got to consult together, or else we are completely lost. You'll have to stay and keep talking, while I run down and make them put another leaf into the table. I don't believe there's room enough now, and I'm not certain about the quails. The cook said she didn't believe they were all nice. How can people be so careless about notes! I think it's really criminal. There ought to be something done about it. If people won't read their notes over they ought to be told about it, and I've the greatest mind to say at once that they sent a refusal, and I wasn't expecting them. It would serve them right.

CAMPBELL: Yes, and it would be such a relief to your feelings. I wish you *would* do it, Amy. Just for once.

MRS. CAMPBELL: I shall have to take the table-cloth off if I put another leaf in, and the whole thing has got to be rearranged, decorations and everything; and I'd got the violets scattered so carelessly. Now I shall just *fling them on*. I don't care how they look. I'm completely discouraged, and I shall just go through it all like a stone.

CAMPBELL: Like a precious stone. You *are* such a perfect little brick, Amy.

MRS. CAMPBELL: I guess you wouldn't like it yourself, Willis. And the Belforts are just the people I should have liked to do my best before, and now their being here spoils everything.

CAMPBELL, *smiling*: It *is* a complication!

MRS. CAMPBELL: Oh, yes, giggle, do! I suppose you'd expect me to be logical, as you call it, with my dying breath.

CAMPBELL: No, I shouldn't, Amy; but I know you'd be delightful under any circumstances. You always get there just the same, whether you take the steps or not. But brace up now, dear, and you'll come out all right. Tell them the truth and I'll stand by you. I don't want any better fun.

He slips behind his wife, who gives him a ghastly glance over her shoulder as the Belforts enter the room with Miss Reynolds.

MRS. CAMPBELL: Oh, how do you do, Maria? *(She kisses Miss Reynolds, and then, with gay cordiality, gives her hand to Mrs. Belfort.)* I'm so glad to see you! *(She shakes hands with Belfort.)* So kind of you to come.

MISS REYNOLDS: I'm sorry to be a little late, Amy; but better late than never, I suppose.

MRS. BELFORT: I'm not so sure of that. Dear Mrs. Campbell! I wish you would be quite frank with me!

MRS. CAMPBELL: Late? Frank? What do you mean, both of you? You know you're never late, Maria; and why should I be frank with you, Mrs. Belfort?

CAMPBELL: What do you take us for?

MRS. BELFORT, *holding Mrs. Campbell's hand clasped between both of hers*: For the very nicest and kindest people in the world, who wouldn't let me have the mortification of deranging them on any account. Did you expect us this evening?

MRS. CAMPBELL: Expect you? What a strange question! Why in the world shouldn't we expect you?

CAMPBELL: What an extraordinary idea!

MRS. BELFORT: Because I had to hurry away from Mrs. Miller's tea when I went home to dress, and when I told her we were coming here to dinner, she said, "Oh, you are *going*, then?" in such a way that, though she covered it up afterwards, and said she didn't mean anything, and she didn't know why she had spoken, I felt sure there must be some misunderstanding, and I've come quite ready to be sent away again if there is. Didn't you get my note?

MRS. CAMPBELL: Your note? Why, of course I did!

MRS. BELFORT: Then it's all right. *Such* a relief! Now I feel that I can breathe freely again.

MR. BELFORT: I assure you, Mrs. Campbell, it's a relief to me, too. I've never seen my wife of quite so many minds as she's been for the last hour and a half. She was quite encyclopedic.

CAMPBELL: Oh, I know how that is, my dear boy. I've known Mrs. Campbell change hers as often as an unabridged dictionary in great emergencies.

MRS. BELFORT: But really, the only thing for us to do was to come, as I felt from the beginning, in spite of my doubts what to do. I thought I could depend upon you to send us away if we weren't wanted; but if we were, and didn't come, you couldn't very well have sent for us.

MRS. CAMPBELL, *gayly*: Indeed I should!

CAMPBELL, *gallantly*: The dinner would have been nothing without you.

MRS. BELFORT: I don't know about that, but I'm sure we should have been nothing without the dinner. We were *so* glad to come. I waited a little while about answering, till I could see whether we could be free of a sort of provisional engagement we had hanging over us. Even after we got here, though, I'd half a mind to run away, and we've been catechising poor Miss Reynolds down in the reception-room till she wouldn't stand it any longer, and so here we are.

MRS. CAMPBELL: And I'm perfectly delighted. If you had yielded to any such ridiculous misgiving, I should never have forgiven you. I'm sure I don't know what Mrs. Miller could have—

THE PHONOGRAPH, *in the library*: Truth crushed to earth will cr—cr-r-r-r—ck—ck—cr—

MRS. BELFORT: A phonograph! Oh, have you got one? I *must* hear it!

CAMPBELL: Well, won't you come into the library? My nephew is in there, driving everybody mad with it. He'll be perfectly delighted with a fresh victim.

MRS. BELFORT: And I shall be charmed to offer myself up. Come, Miss Reynolds. Come, Roger.

CAMPBELL: Yes, come along, Belfort.

He leads the way to the door, and then adroitly slips back to his wife, who has abandoned herself wildly upon the sofa.

MRS. CAMPBELL: Well, now, what are you going to do, Willis?

CAMPBELL: *I'm* not going to do anything. I haven't been flying in the face of Providence. If ever there was a woman offered a clean and safe way out! But since you preferred to remain in this labyrinth—this Black Forest of improbabilities—

MRS. CAMPBELL: Oh, don't torment me, Willis! Don't you see that her taking it that way made it all the more impossible for me to tell her of the blunder she had committed? I simply couldn't do it, then.

CAMPBELL: I don't see how you could help doing it, then.

MRS. CAMPBELL: When she behaved so magnanimously about it, and put herself in my power? I would sooner have died, and she knew it perfectly well. That's the reason she *was* so magnanimous. You wouldn't have done it yourself after that. But it's no use talking about that now. We've got to do something, and you've got to think what we shall do. Now think!

CAMPBELL: What about?

MRS. CAMPBELL: Oh, don't tease, dearest! About the trouble—and who shall take out who—and the quails. You know what!

CAMPBELL: Well, I think if we leave those people alone much longer, they'll all come out here and ask if they weren't mistaken in supposing they were expected.

MRS. CAMPBELL, *whimpering*: Oh, there you go! How perfectly heartless!

MRS. ROBERTS, *showing herself at the door*: Amy, dear, what *is* the matter? Didn't you tell me the Belforts were not coming? Is that what's keeping you out here? I just knew it was!

MRS. CAMPBELL: Yes, Agnes; but do go back to them, and keep them amused. Willis and I are trying to think what to do. I've got to rearrange the whole table, you know, and I'm not sure whether there'll be quails enough to go round.

MRS. ROBERTS: Don't worry about that, Amy. I won't take any, and I'll give Edward a hint about them.

CAMPBELL: And Roberts is capable of asking you before the whole company why you don't want him to take quail. There's nothing like Roberts for presence of mind and any little bit of *finesse* like that. No, it won't do for the entire connection to fight shy of quail. Mrs. Belfort has got her suspicions roused, and she'd be on to a thing of that kind like lightning. She's got the notion that she wasn't expected, somehow, and she's been making it hot for Amy—trying to get her to own up, and all that. If it hadn't been for me, Amy *would* have owned up, too. But I kept my eye on her, and she lied out of it like a little man.

MRS. CAMPBELL: It isn't so, Agnes. He *wanted* me to tell the truth about it, as he calls it—

MRS. ROBERTS: What an idea! You might as well have died at once. I don't see what you could have been thinking of, Willis!

MRS. CAMPBELL: Yes, he can't understand yet why I shouldn't, when Mrs. Belfort asked me if there wasn't some mistake, and literally **threw** herself on my mercy. She had no business to do

it, and I shall always think it was taking a mean advantage; but I wasn't going to let myself be outdone in magnanimity. I shouldn't have thought she would be capable of it.

MRS. ROBERTS: It wasn't very nice, but I suppose she was excited. We mustn't blame her, and you did the only thing that any human creature could do. I'm surprised at Willis; or, rather, I'm *not* surprised.

CAMPBELL: Well, don't let it keep you away from our other guests, Agnes.

MRS. CAMPBELL: Oh, yes; *do* go back to them, Agnes, dear! I have got to arrange all over again now, about who's to go out with who, you know. I shall want you to let Edward take Mrs. Curwen, and—

MRS. ROBERTS: Oh, Amy, you know I'd do anything for you, especially in a case like this; but I *can't* let Edward take Mrs. Curwen out. I don't mind her flirting; she does that with every one; but she always gets Edward to laughing so that it attracts the attention of the whole table, and—

CAMPBELL: That's a very insignificant matter. I'll take out Mrs. Curwen, myself—

MRS. CAMPBELL: No, indeed you won't! You always get *her* laughing, and that's a great deal worse.

CAMPBELL: Well, well, I won't, then. But we can arrange that afterwards.

MRS. CAMPBELL: No, we'll settle it now, if you please; and I don't want you to go *near* Mrs. Curwen. She'll be sure to see that there's something wrong from the delay, and she'll try to find it out, and if she should I shall simply perish on the spot. She'll try to get round you and make you tell, and I want you to promise me, Willis, on your bended knees, that you won't let it out. She's insufferable enough as it is, but if she got to sympathizing with me, or patronizing me about such a thing, as she'd be sure to do, I don't know what I *should* do. Will you promise?

CAMPBELL: Oh, I promise. Look out you don't tell her yourself, Amy! But now I've got to see that there's enough to eat, under this new deal, and the great question is about the quail, and I've thought how to manage that. I'll just run down to the telephone, and send to the club for them. We can have them here inside of a half-hour, and never turn a feather.

MRS. CAMPBELL: Oh, Willis, you *are* inspired. Well, I shall always say that when there is any real thinking to be done— But hurry back, do, dear, and Agnes and I will be trying to settle who shall take out— Oh, I'm afraid you won't get back in time to help us! It takes so long to telephone the simplest thing.

CAMPBELL: I'll be back in one-quarter of a second.

He rushes out, brushing by Mrs. Crashaw, who enters at the same moment from the library.

MRS. CRASHAW: Amy, child, what in the world has happened? What are you staying out here away from your company for? Where's Willis going? What's Agnes doing here? It's perfectly scandalous to leave all those people alone!

MRS. CAMPBELL: Oh, Aunt Mary, if you only knew, you wouldn't scold us! Don't you see the Belforts have come?

MRS. CRASHAW: Yes, of course they've come, and after they declined; I understand that. But it's only a matter of two plates more at the table—

MRS. CAMPBELL: Oh, is it? And am I to let *him* go down with *her*? The whole affair has got to be planned over, and another leaf put in, and the table rearranged, and I don't know what all.

MRS. ROBERTS: And Willis has gone down to telephone to the club for more quails.

MRS. CRASHAW, *to Mrs. Campbell*: You don't mean that you only got just quails enough?

MRS. CAMPBELL, *indignantly*: A dinner for ten is not a dinner for twelve. I may not have kept house so long as you, Aunt Mary, but I'm not *quite* a child! (*At this critical moment Campbell returns.*) Well, will they send them?

CAMPBELL: Yes, yes. It's all right. I couldn't get the club, just now; Central was busy; but I've primed Green's man, down below, and he'll call them up in a minute. He understands it. I thought I'd hurry back and see if I could be of use. Well, have you got things all straight?

MRS. CRASHAW: No; we've spent the time in getting them crookeder, if possible. I've insinuated that Amy didn't know how to order her dinner, and she's told me I'm an old woman. I *am* an old woman, Amy, and you mustn't regard me. I think my mind's going.

She kisses Mrs. Campbell, who clasps her in a forgiving embrace.

MRS. CAMPBELL: Mine's *gone*, Aunt Mary, or I never could have taken anything amiss from *you*! I don't see how I shall live through it. I don't know what to do; it seems to get worse every moment.

MRS. CRASHAW: Why, you don't suppose the Belforts *suspect* anything, do you?

MRS. CAMPBELL: That's the worst of it. I thought I ought to let the Millers know who had failed when I asked them so late; and the Belforts were there at tea this afternoon, and Mrs. Miller let out her surprise that they were coming. So, of course, I had a double duty.

CAMPBELL: But, thank goodness, she was equal to it, Aunt Mary. I've had to do some tall lying in my time, but I never soared to the heights that Amy reached with the Belforts, in my palmiest days.

MRS. CRASHAW: Well, then, if she convinced them that their supicions were wrong, it's all right; and if the quails are coming from the club, I don't see what there is to worry about. We must be thankful that you could get out of it so easily.

MRS. CAMPBELL: But we're *not* out of it. The table has to be rearranged, but I can have that done now somehow, while we're waiting for the quails. The great thing is to manage about the going out. It happens very fortunately that if I tell all the other men whom they're to take out, Mr. Belfort can't suppose that he was an after-thought. But I can't seem to make a start with a new arrangement, in my own mind.

CAMPBELL: You've used up all your invention in convincing the Belforts that they were expected. Good gracious, here's Dr. Lawton! What do you want here, you venerable opprobrium of science?

DR. LAWTON, *standing at ease on the threshold of the drawing-room*: Nothing. I merely got tired of hearing the praises of truth chanted in there, and came out here for—a little change.

CAMPBELL: Well, you can't stay. You've got to go back, and help keep the Belforts from supposing they weren't expected, if it takes all your hoarded wisdom as a general practitioner for forty years.

MRS. CAMPBELL: Oh yes; do go back, doctor!

DR. LAWTON: What has been the treatment up to the present time?

CAMPBELL: The most heroic kind. Amy has spared neither age nor sex, in the use of whoppers. You know what she is, doctor, when she has a duty to perform.

DR. LAWTON: But whoppers, as I understand, are always of one sex. They may be old; they often are, I believe; but they are invariably masculine.

CAMPBELL: Oh, that doesn't prevent women's using them. They use all of us.

DR. LAWTON: Well, then, there's no need of my going back on that account. In fact, I may congratulate Mrs. Campbell on the most complete success. The Belforts are thoroughly deceived.

MRS. CAMPBELL, *with tremulous eagerness*: Oh, do you *think* so, doctor? If I could only believe that, how happy I should be!

DR. LAWTON: You may be sure of it, Mrs. Campbell. Belfort doesn't count, of course?

MRS. CRASHAW: Of course not; men will believe anything that's told them.

DR. LAWTON: And I don't allude to *him*. But Mrs. Belfort got me to one side as soon as she saw me, and told me she had been afraid there was something wrong, but Mrs. Campbell had assured her that she had got her note of acceptance, and now she was going to give her whole mind to the phonograph's beautiful rendering of Bryant's poem on truth.

MRS. ROBERTS: There, Amy, you see there's no reason to worry about that!

MRS. CRASHAW: No; the only thing now is to get your dinner on the table, child, and let us eat it as soon as possible.

CAMPBELL: Yes, if Lawton's telling the truth.

THE LADIES: Willis!

DR. LAWTON: Don't mind him, ladies! The experiences of his early life in California, you know, must have been very unfavorable to a habit of confidence in his fellow-men. I pity him.

MRS. CURWEN, *appearing with young Mr. Bemis*: Dr. Lawton, I wish you would go and bring your daughter here. She's flirting outrageously with my husband.

In making this accusation, Mrs. Curwen casts the eye of experienced coquetry at young Mr. Bemis, who laughs foolishly.

DR. LAWTON: Oh, I dare say he won't mind; he must be so used to it.

MRS. CURWEN: What do you mean, Dr. Lawton? What does he mean, Mr. Campbell?

CAMPBELL: I couldn't imagine, for the life of me.

MRS. CURWEN: Can *you* tell, Mrs. Campbell?

MRS. CAMPBELL: Oh, I *never* tell—such things.

MRS. CURWEN: What mysteries! Well, can you tell me what makes Mrs. Belfort so uncommonly gay, this evening? She seems to be in the greatest spirits, laughing with everybody—Mr. Bemis *père*, and Mr. Roberts.

MRS. CAMPBELL: Mrs. Belfort?

MRS. CURWEN: Yes. She seems a little hysterical. I wonder if anything's happened?

MRS. CAMPBELL, *sweeping the circle of her*

confidants with a look of misery: What could have happened?

DR. LAWTON: It's merely the pleasure of finding herself in your company, Mrs. Curwen.

MRS. CURWEN: Oh, thank you, Dr. Lawton. I know that I scatter sunshine in my path, but not to that extent, I think. (*With winning appeal*) Oh, what *is* the cat in the meal, doctor? (*To young Mr. Bemis, archly*) Do make them tell me, Mr. Bemis!

YOUNG MR. BEMIS, *with the air of epigram*: I'm sure I don't know.

He chokes with flattered laughter.

MRS. CURWEN: How cruel of you not even to try! (*She makes eyes at young Mr. Bemis, and then transfers them rapidly to Campbell.*) Won't you just whisper it in my ear, Mr. Campbell? Mrs. Roberts, you can't imagine what nice things your husband's been saying to me! I didn't know he paid compliments. And now I suppose he's devoting himself to Mrs. Belfort. Perhaps it was that made her so lively. He began at once. He's *so* amusing. I envy you having such a husband always about.

YOUNG MR. BEMIS, *in the belief that he is saying something gallant*: I'm sure we're none of us so hard-hearted as to envy *you*, Mrs. Curwen.

MRS. CURWEN: Oh, *thank* you, Mr. Bemis! I shall really be afraid to tell Mr. Curwen *all* you say. (*She laughs, and Campbell joins her, even under the reproachful gaze of his wife and sister. Mrs. Curwen turns coaxingly to him.*) Do tell!

CAMPBELL: Tell what?

MRS. CURWEN: Well— (*She pauses thoughtfully, and then suddenly adds.*) Who's going to take me out to dinner?

MRS. CAMPBELL, *surprised into saying it*: Why, it's all disarranged now by the Belforts—

She stops, and a thrill of dismay at her self-betrayal makes itself apparent in the spectators.

MRS. CURWEN, *with clasped hands*: Don't say by the Belforts coming unexpectedly! Oh, *dear* Mrs. Campbell, I know how to pity you! That very thing happened to me last winter. Only, it was Mrs. Miller who came after she'd declined; she said Mr. Miller wouldn't come without her. But why do you mind it? *We* all went out pellmell. Such fun! But it must have taken all Mr. Campbell's ingenuity to keep them from suspecting.

CAMPBELL: More, too. I was nowhere.

MRS. CURWEN, *with caressing deference to Mrs.*

Campbell: Of course you were not needed. But isn't it shocking how one has to manage in such an emergency? I really believe it would be better to tell the truth sometimes. Don't you?

MRS. CAMPBELL: It's all very well telling the truth if they don't suspect anything. But when people tax you with their mistakes, and try to make you own up that they've blundered, then of course you *have* to deny it.

MRS. ROBERTS: You simply *have* to.

MRS. CRASHAW: There's no other way, in that case, even if you'd prefer to tell the truth.

MRS. CURWEN: Oh, in that case, yes, indeed. *Poor* Mrs. Campbell! I can imagine how annoying it must have been; but I *should* have liked to hear you getting out of it! What *did* you say? *I'm* so transparent, people see through me at once.

CAMPBELL: Are you?

DR. LAWTON: Don't you think you're a little hard on yourself, Mrs. Curwen?

MRS. CURWEN, *with burlesque meekness and sincerity*: No, not the least. It's simple justice. (*Mr. Curwen enters with Roberts.*) You can ask my husband if you don't believe *me*. Or no, I'll put the case to him myself. Fred, dear, if people whom I didn't expect to dinner, came, *could* I keep them from discovering that they weren't expected? You know how awkward I am about such things—little fibs, and all that?

CURWEN: Well, I don't know—

MRS. CURWEN, *shaking her fan at him during the general laugh*: Oh, what a wicked husband! *You* don't believe I could fib out of such a thing, do you, Mr. Roberts?

ROBERTS, *gallantly*: If I knew what the thing was?

MRS. CURWEN: Why, like the Belforts— Oh, *poor* Mrs. Campbell! I *didn't* mean to let it out!

MRS. CAMPBELL: Oh, it doesn't matter. Would you like to go and tell the Belforts themselves? Or, you needn't go: they're coming here.

MRS. BELFORT, *returning from the library, followed by her husband and the elder Mr. Bemis*: How perfectly the phonograph renders that piece, Mr. Campbell! I've never heard anything like it.

CAMPBELL: It's all in practice. You wouldn't hear anything else here, Mrs. Belfort. It's my favorite poem. And I'm happy to find that Mrs. Curwen likes it as much as I do.

MRS. CURWEN: I adore it!

THE PHONOGRAPH, *within*: Truth crushed to earth will rise again.

CAMPBELL: Every time! But I wish Jim would change the cylinder. I like a little vari—

A SOUND, *from the regions below, something like*: Woor, roor, roor; woor, roor, roor! *and then a voice*: Hello! Is that you, Central? Well, give me two hundred and forty-one, please! Yes, two, four, one: Iroquois Club.[1] Yes! What? Yes, Iroquois Club—two forty-one. Well, hurry up! Is that you, Iroquois? Yes? Busy? Well, that won't work. I don't care if you *are* busy. You've got to take my message, and take it right away. Hear that?

CAMPBELL: Hear it? I should think they could! That confounded fool has left the closet-door open!

He rushes out and down the stairs, while the others assume various attitudes of sympathy and dismay, and Mrs. Curwen bows herself into her fan, and the voice below continues.

THE VOICE: Well, why don't you send them quails you promised half an hour ago? What? Who is it? It's Mr. Campbell. C, a, m, Cam, m, e, l, mel, Campbell. One hump! What? Oh, hump yourself! It's Mr. Cam—

CAMPBELL'S VOICE, *from below*: Why the deuce don't you shut that closet-door? Shut it! Shut it! We can hear you all over the house, the way you yell. Don't you know how to use a telephone? Shut that door, anyway!

THE VOICE: Oh, I beg your pardon, sir, I didn't think about the door. I didn't know it was open. All right, sir. (*There is the sound of a closing door, and then, as Campbell rejoins his guests with a flushed face, the woor-roor-rooring of the electric bell begins again.*) Iroquois! Is this Iroquois? No, I don't want you; I want Iroquois. Well, is that Iroquois now? (*The words are at first muffled; then they grow more and more distinct, in spite of the intervening door.*) Yes, quails! A dozen roast quails. You got the order half an hour ago. There's a lot of folks come that they didn't expect, and they got to have some more birds. Well, hurry up, then! Good-by! Woor-roor!

CAMPBELL, *amid the consternation of the company, while Mrs. Belfort fixes his wife with an eye of mute reproach*: Now, my dear, this is so awful that nothing can be done about it on the old lines.

MRS. CAMPBELL: Yes; I give it up. Mrs. Belfort,

[1] Probably a favorite eating place of Howells, as a letter to his sister Aurelia suggests (December 14, 1902, Harvard Library).

I tried my very best to keep you from suspecting, and even when you did suspect, I'm sure you must say that I did all I could. But fate was against me.

MRS. CURWEN: Oh, *poor* Mrs. Campbell! *Must* you own up?

MRS. BELFORT: But I don't understand. You got my note of acceptance, didn't you?

MRS. CAMPBELL: But it *wasn't* a note of acceptance: it was a note of regret!

MRS. BELFORT: Indeed it was not!

MRS. CAMPBELL: I knew just how it had happened as soon as I saw you this evening, and I determined that wild horses should not get the truth out of me. (*Campbell and Dr. Lawton exchange signals of admiration.*) You must have been writing two notes, declining somewhere else, and then got them mixed. It's always happening.

CAMPBELL: It's one of the commonest things in the world—on the stage; and ever since a case of the kind happened to Mrs. Campbell down at the Shore,[1] one summer, she's known how to deal with it.

MRS. BELFORT: But I *didn't* write two notes and get them mixed. I wrote but one, to tell Mrs. Campbell how very glad I was to come. Do you happen to have kept my note?

MRS. CAMPBELL: They are all here in this desk, and—(*running to it, and pulling it open*) here is yours. (*She reads.*) "Dear Mrs. Campbell, I am very sorry to be so late in answering. An out-of-town engagement for the tenth, which has been hanging over us in a threatening way for the past fortnight—"

Mrs. Campbell turns the leaf, and continues reading in a murmur that finally fades into the silence of utter dismay.

CAMPBELL: Well, my dear?

MRS. CRASHAW: What in the world is it, child?

MRS. ROBERTS: Amy!

MRS. CURWEN: Oh, not *another* mystery, I hope!

CAMPBELL: Go on, Amy, or shall I—

MRS. CAMPBELL, *reading desperately on*: "—for the past fortnight, is happily off at last, and I am very glad indeed to accept your kind invitation for dinner at seven on that day, for Mr. Belfort and myself—"

She lets her hands, with the letter stretched between them, fall dramatically before her.

[1] A reference to *A Likely Story*.

CAMPBELL: Well, my dear, there seems to be a pretty clear case against you, and unless you can plead mind-transference, or something like that—

MRS. ROBERTS: I'm sure it's mind-transference, Amy! I've often been through the same experience myself. Just take the opposite of what's said.

MRS. CAMPBELL, *in a daze*: But I don't see—Yes, now I begin to remember how it must have been—how it was. I know now, but I don't know how I can ever forgive myself for such carelessness, when I'm always so particular about notes—

CAMPBELL: Yes, I've even heard you say it was criminal to read them carelessly. I can bear witness for you there.

MRS. ROBERTS: I'm sure I could too, Amy, in a court of justice.

MRS. CAMPBELL: Yes, I was just going out when your note came, Mrs. Belfort, and I read the first page—down to "for the past fortnight"—and I took it for granted that the opening regret meant a refusal, and just dropped it into my desk and gave you up. It's inexcusable, perfectly inexcusable! I'm quite at your feet, Mrs. Belfort, and I shall not blame you at all if you can't forgive me. What shall I say to you?

MRS. BELFORT, *amiably*: Nothing, my dear, except that you will let me stay, now I'm here!

MRS. CAMPBELL: How sweet you are! You shall *live* with us!

CAMPBELL: Truth crushed to earth! It's perfectly wonderful! Mrs. Campbell can't get away from it when she tries her best. She tells it in spite of herself. She supposed she wasn't telling it when she said there was no mistake on your part; but she *was*. Well, it *is* a feminine virtue, doctor.

DR. LAWTON: Unquestionably, I think that it came into the world with woman.

MRS. CAMPBELL, *with mounting courage*: Yes a pretty predicament I should have been in, Willis, if I had taken your advice, and told the truth, as you call it, in the beginning. But now we won't wait any longer. The quails will come in their own good time. My dear, will you give Mrs. Belfort your arm? And, Mr. Belfort, will you give me yours?

MRS. CURWEN: And all the rest of us?

MRS. CAMPBELL: Oh, you can come out pell-mell.

MRS. CURWEN: Oh, *dear* Mrs. Campbell!

THE END

Bride Roses

[1893]

This little play, which Laurence Hutton labeled one of Howells' best (*Harper's Monthly*, XCIV [April, 1897], 818), seems perhaps at first glance to be primarily a contrived sketch with a liberal amount of sentiment included. Careful reading of the play, however, reveals a tenderness on Howells' part and a definite skill in development that gives the piece moderate but real dramatic stature and a seriousness which is lacking in most of his plays. Henry Arthur Jones called it "a delicate piece of tragedy" (letter to Howells, December 17, 1906, Harvard Library). Although tragedy is not an apt term, this is Howells' first one-act play in which, using dramatic irony, he treats a serious theme built around the upsetting idea that death comes to the young.

An ironic tone pervades the entire play from the time the first lady requests her flowers—tall, ethereal, fragile, with the faintest tinge of color. The Bride rose itself embodies a rather symbolic irony; each person describes it as "cold," yet each gives it because it seems most nearly expressive of the young lady. For social happiness, personal love, or great sorrow there is the Bride rose. But only when the first lady places her final order does the reader feel the full irony: "Open, fragile-looking ones, with long stems. . . ."

Howells shows his dramatic skill most clearly in this play by his characterization of the florist, his use of irony, and his ability to bring clearly before his readers and audience the connection between the three purchasers of Bride roses. Mr. Eichen-laub is an unobtrusive character who might seem purely functional, but he is named—a matter of some significance since he is the only one in the play with a name—and he is so skillfully drawn that he is a focal point of the play. In one sense, as his name suggests, he is a part of nature, a simple man absorbed in his perfunctory task as a vendor of flowers, indifferent to the struggles and conflicts of mankind all around him. Like his flowers—the Bride rose in particular—he serves everywhere with equal effectiveness: weddings, parties, funerals, or receptions. Innocent as his flowers, unconscious of the drama before him, neither curious nor questioning in his attitude, only existing and making his flowers available, the florist seems almost a personification of nature which, as in his final action—a shrug, comments on man. Perhaps this analysis extends the meaning beyond Howells' concept; nevertheless, Mr. Eichenlaub is not merely a clerk in a flowershop but a meaningful figure in the drama.

In his *Annals of the New York Stage* (XV, 558), Odell mentions that James A. Herne's *Shore Acres* was given in Daly's Theatre, March 5, 1894, as a benefit for unemployed actors. Along with this play, Howells' *Bride Roses* was performed. According to the *Dramatic Mirror* Howells' play failed; it was in no way effective. Yet Odell went on to say: "We shall see before this season ends that the new era is beginning with productions of plays by Ibsen, Sudermann, Hauptmann, Herne, and Howells."

Bride Roses[1]

SCENE

A LADY, *entering the florist's with her muff to her face, and fluttering gayly up to the counter, where the florist stands folding a mass of loose flowers in a roll of cotton batting*: Good-morning, Mr. Eichenlaub! Ah, put plenty of cotton round the poor things, if you don't want them frozen stiff! You have no idea what a day it is, here in your little tropic.

She takes away her muff as she speaks, but gives each of her cheeks a final pressure with it, and holds it up with one hand inside as she sinks upon the stool before the counter.

THE FLORIST: Dropic? With icepergs on the wintows?

He nods his head toward the frosty panes, and wraps a sheet of tissue-paper around the cotton and the flowers.

THE LADY: But you are not near the windows. Back here it is midsummer!

THE FLORIST: Yes, we got a rhevricherator to keep the rhoces from sunstroke. (*He crimps the paper at the top, and twists it at the bottom of the bundle in his hand.*) Hier! (*He calls to a young man warming his hands at the stove.*) Chon, but on your hat, and dtake this to— Holt on! I forgot to but in the cart. (*He undoes the paper, and puts in a card lying on the counter before him; the lady watches him vaguely.*) There! (*He restores the wrapping and hands the package to the young man, who goes out with it.*) Well, matam?

THE LADY, *laying her muff with her hand in it on the counter, and leaning forward over it*: Well, Mr. Eichenlaub. I am going to be very difficult.

THE FLORIST: That is what I lige. Then I don't feel so rhesbonsible.

THE LADY: But to-day, I *wish* you to feel responsible. I want you to take the whole responsibility. Do you know why I always come to you, instead of those places on Fifth Avenue?

THE FLORIST: Well, it is a good teal cheaper, for one thing—

1 The text used here is the Houghton, Mifflin and Company edition.

THE LADY: Not at all! That isn't the reason, at all. Some of your things are dearer. It's because you take so much more interest, and you talk over what I want, and you don't urge me, when I haven't made up my mind. You let me consult you, and you are not cross when I don't take your advice.

THE FLORIST: You are very goodt, matam.

THE LADY: Not at all. I am simply just. And now I want you to provide the flowers for my first Saturday: Saturday of this week, in fact, and I want to talk the order all over with you. Are you very busy?

THE FLORIST: No; I am qvite at your service. We haf just had to egsegute a larche gommission very soddenly, and we are still in a little dtisorder yet; but—

THE LADY: Yes, I see. (*She glances at the rear of the shop, where the floor is littered with the leaves and petals of flowers, and sprays of fern and evergreen. A woman, followed by a belated smell of breakfast, which gradually mingles with the odor of the plants, comes out of a door there, and begins to gather the larger fragments into her apron. The lady turns again, and looks at the jars and vases of cut flowers in the window, and on the counter.*) What I can't understand is how you know just the quantity of flowers to buy every day. You must often lose a good deal.

THE FLORIST: It gomes out about rhighdt, nearly always. When I get left, sometimes, I can chenerally work dem off on funerals. Now, that bic orter hat I just fill, that wass a funeral. It usedt up all the flowers I hat ofer from yesterday.

THE LADY: Don't speak of it! And the flowers, are they just the same for funerals?

THE FLORIST: Yes, rhoces nearly always. Whidte ones.

THE LADY: Well, it is too dreadful. I am not going to have roses, whatever I have. (*After a thoughtful pause, and a more careful look around the shop*) Mr. Eichenlaub, why wouldn't orchids do?

THE FLORIST: Well, they would be bretty dtear.

431

You couldn't make any show at all for less than fifteen tollars.

THE LADY, *with a slight sigh*: No, orchids wouldn't do. They are fantastic things, anyway, and they are not very effective, as you say. Pinks, anemones, marguerites, narcissus—there doesn't seem to be any great variety, does there?

THE FLORIST, *patiently*: There will be more, lader on.

THE LADY: Yes, there will be more sun, later on. But now, Mr. Eichenlaub, what do you think of plants in pots, set around?

THE FLORIST: Balmss?

THE LADY, *vaguely*: Yes, palms.

THE FLORIST: Balmss would to. But there would not be very much golor.

THE LADY: That is true; there would be no color at all, and my rooms certainly need all the color I can get into them. Yes, I shall have to have roses, after all. But not white ones!

THE FLORIST: Chacks?

THE LADY: No; Jacks are too old-fashioned. But haven't you got any other very dark rose? I should like something almost black, I believe.

THE FLORIST, *setting a vase of roses on the counter before her*: There is the Matame Hoste.[1]

THE LADY, *bending over the roses, and touching one of them with the tip of her gloved finger*: Why, they *are* black, almost! They are nearly as black as black pansies. They are really wonderful! (*She stoops over and inhales their fragrance.*) Delicious! They are beautiful, but—(*abruptly*) they are hideous. Their color makes me creep. It is so unnatural for a rose. A rose—a rose ought to be —rose-colored! Have you no rose-colored roses? What are those light pink ones there in the window?

THE FLORIST, *going to the window and getting two vases of cut roses, with long stems, both pink, but one kind a little larger than the other*: That is the Matame Watterville, and this is the Matame Cousine. They are sister rhoces; both the same, but the Matame Watterville is a little bigger, and it is a little dtearer.

THE LADY: They are both exquisite, and they are such a tender almond-bloom pink! I think the Madame Cousine is quite as nice; but of course the larger ones are more effective. (*She examines them, turning her head from side to side, and then withdrawing a step, with a decisive sigh.*) No;

1 All of the names by which Howells calls his roses are authentic.

they are too pale. Have you nothing of a brighter pink? What is that over there?

She points to a vase of roses quite at the front of the window, and the florist climbs over the mass of plants and gets it for her.

THE FLORIST: That is the Midio.

THE LADY: The what?

THE FLORIST: The Midio.

THE LADY: You will think I am very stupid this morning. Won't you please write it down for me? (*The florist writes on a sheet of wrapping-paper, and she leans over and reads.*) Oh! *Meteor!* Well, it is very striking—a little *too* striking. I don't like such a vivid pink, and I don't like the name. Horrid to give such a name to a flower. (*She puts both hands into her muff, and drifts a little way off, as if to get him in a better perspective.*) Can't you suggest something, Mr. Eichenlaub?

THE FLORIST: Some kind off yellow rhoce? Dtearhoces?

THE LADY, *shaking her head*: Tea-roses are ghastly. I hate yellow roses. I would rather have black, and black is simply impossible. I shall have to tell you just what I want to do. I don't want to work up to my rooms with the flowers; I want to work up to the young lady who is going to pour tea for me. I don't care if there isn't a flower anywhere but on the table before her. I want a color scheme that shall not have a false note in it, from her face to the tiniest bud. I want them to all *come together*. Do you understand?

THE FLORIST, *doubtfully*: Yes. (*After a moment*) What kindt looking yo'ng laty iss she?

THE LADY: The most ethereal creature in the world.

THE FLORIST: Yes; but what sdyle—fair or tark?

THE LADY: Oh, fair! Very, very fair, and very, very fragile-looking; a sort of moonlight blonde, with those remote, starry-looking eyes, don't you know, and that pale saffron hair; not the least ashen; and just the faintest, faintest tinge of color in her face. I suppose you have nothing like the old-fashioned blush-rose? That would be the very thing.

THE FLORIST, *shaking his head*: Oh, no; there noding like that in a chreen-house rhoce.

THE LADY: Well, that is exactly what I want. It ought to be something very tall and ethereal; something very, very pale, and yet with a sort of suffusion of color.

She walks up and down the shop, looking at all the plants and flowers.

THE FLORIST, *waiting patiently*: Somet'ing beside rhoces, then?

THE LADY, *coming back to him*: No; it must be roses, after all. I see that nothing else will do. What do you call those?

She nods at a vase of roses on a shelf behind him.

THE FLORIST, *turning and taking them down for her*: Ah, those whidte ones! That is the Pridte. You sait you wouldn't haf whidte ones.

THE LADY: I may have to come to them. Why do they call it the Pride?

THE FLORIST: I didn't say Bridte; I said Pridte.

THE LADY: Oh, Bride! And do they use Bride roses for—

THE FLORIST: Yes; and for weddtings, too; for everything.

The lady leans back a little and surveys the flowers critically. A young man enters, and approaches the florist, but waits with respectful impatience for the lady to transact her affairs. The florist turns to him inquiringly, and upon this hint he speaks.

THE YOUNG MAN: I want you to send a few roses—white ones, or nearly white—(*He looks at the lady.*) Perhaps—

THE LADY: Oh, not at all! I hadn't decided to take them.

THE FLORIST: I got plenty this kindt; all you want. I can always get them.

THE YOUNG MAN, *dreamily regarding the roses*: They look rather chilly. (*He goes to the stove, and drawing off his gloves, warms his hands, and then comes back.*) What do you call this rose?

THE FLORIST: The Pridte.

THE YOUNG MAN, *uncertainly*: Oh! (*The lady moves a little way up the counter toward the window, but keeps looking at the young man from time to time. She cannot help hearing all that he says.*) Haven't you any white rose with a little color in it? Just the faintest tinge, the merest touch.

THE FLORIST: No, no; they are whidte, or they are yellow; dtea-rhoces; Marshal Niel—

THE YOUNG MAN: Ah, I don't want anything of that kind. What is the palest pink rose you have?

THE FLORIST, *indicating the different kinds in the vases, where the lady has been looking at them*: Well, there is nothing lighder than the Matame Cousine, or the Matame Watterville, here; they are sister rhoces—

THE YOUNG MAN: Yes, yes; very beautiful; but too dark. (*He stops before the Madame Hoste.*) What a strange flower! It is almost *black!* What is it for? Funerals?

THE FLORIST: No; a good many people lige them. We don't sell them much for funerals; they are too cloomy. They uce whidte ones for that: Marshal Niel, dtea-rhoces, this Pridte here, and other whidte ones.

THE YOUNG MAN, *with an accent of repulsion*: Oh! (*He goes toward the window, and looks at a mass of Easter lilies in a vase there. He speaks as if thinking aloud.*) If they had a little color— But they would be dreadful with color! Why, you ought to have *something!* (*He continues musingly, as he returns to the florist.*) Haven't you got something very delicate, and slender, about the color of pale apple blossoms? If you had them light enough, some kind of azaleas—

THE LADY, *involuntarily*: Ah!

THE FLORIST, *after a moment, in which he and the young man both glance at the lady, and she makes a sound in her throat to show that she is not thinking of them, and had not spoken in reference to what they were saying*: The only azaleas I haf are these pink ones, and those whidte ones.

THE YOUNG MAN: And they are too pink and too white. Isn't there anything tall, and very delicate? Something, well—something like the old-fashioned blush-rose? But with very long stems!

THE FLORIST: No, there is noding lige that which gomes in a crheenhouse rhoce. We got a whidte rhoce here—(*he goes to his refrigerator, and brings back a long box of roses*) that I didn't think of before. (*He gives the lady an apologetic glance.*) You see there is chost the least sdain of rhet on the etch of the leafs.

THE YOUNG MAN, *examining the petals of the roses*: Ah, that is very curious. It is a caprice, though.

THE FLORIST: Yes, it is a kind of sbordt. That rhoce should be berfectly whidte.

THE YOUNG MAN: On the whole, I don't think it will do. I will take some of those pure white ones. Bride, did you call them?

THE FLORIST: Yes, Pridte. How many?

THE YOUNG MAN: Oh, a dozen—two dozen; I don't know! I want very long, slender stems, and the flowers with loose open petals; none of those stout, tough-looking little buds. Here! This, and this, and all these; no, I don't want any of those at all. (*He selects the different stems of roses, and while the florist gets a box, and prepares it with a lining of cotton and tissue-paper, he leans over and writes on a card. He pauses and puts up his pencil; then he takes it out again and covers the card with writing. He gives it to the florist.)* I wish that to go into the box where it will be found the first thing. *(He turns away, and encounters the lady's eyes as she chances to look toward him.)* I beg your pardon! But—

THE LADY, *smiling, and extending her hand*: I felt almost *sure* it was you! But I couldn't believe my senses. All the other authorities report you in Rome.

THE YOUNG MAN: I returned rather suddenly. I just got in this morning. Our steamer was due yesterday, but there was so much ice in the harbor that we didn't work up till a few hours ago.

THE LADY: You will take all your friends by surprise.

THE YOUNG MAN: I'm a good deal taken by surprise myself. Two weeks ago I didn't dream of being here. But I made up my mind to come, and —I came.

THE LADY, *laughing*: Evidently! Well, now you must come to my Saturdays; you are just in time for the first one. Some one you know is going to pour tea for me. That ought to be some consolation to you for not having stayed away long enough to escape my hospitalities.

THE YOUNG MAN, *blushing and smiling*: Oh, it's a very charming welcome home. I shall be sure to come. She is—everybody is—well, I hope?

THE LADY: Yes, or everybody *was* on Monday when I saw them. Everybody is looking very beautiful this winter, lovelier than ever, if possible. But so spiritual! *Too* spiritual! But that spirit of hers will carry her—I mean everybody, of course! —through everything. I feel almost wicked to have asked her to pour tea for me, when I think of how much else she is doing! Do you know, I was just ordering the flowers for my Saturday, and I had decided to take her for my key-note in the decorations. But that made it so difficult! There doesn't seem anything delicate and pure and sweet enough for her. There ought to be some flower created just to express her! But as yet there isn't.

THE YOUNG MAN: No, no; there isn't. But now I must run away. I haven't been to my hotel yet; I was just driving up from the ship, and I saw the flowers in the window, and—stopped. Good-by!

THE LADY: Good-by! What devotion to some-body—everybody! Don't forget my Saturday!

THE YOUNG MAN: No, no; I won't. Good-by!

He hurries out of the door, and his carriage is heard driving away.

THE FLORIST: I wondter if he but the attress on the cart? No; there is noding! *(He turns the card helplessly over.)* What am I coing to do about these flowers?

THE LADY: Why, didn't he say where to send them?

THE FLORIST: No, he rhon away and dtidn't leaf the attress.

THE LADY: That was *my* fault! I confused him, poor fellow, by talking to him. What are you going to do?

THE FLORIST: That is what I lige to know! Do you know what hotel he stobs at?

THE LADY: No; he didn't say. I have no idea where he is going. But wait a moment! I think I know where he meant to send the flowers.

THE FLORIST: Oh, well; that is all I want to know.

THE LADY: Yes, but I am not certain. *(After a moment's thought)* I know he wants them to go at once; a great deal may depend upon it—everything. *(Suddenly)* Could you let me see that card?

THE FLORIST, *throwing it on the counter before her*: Why, soddonly; if he is a frhiendt of yours—

THE LADY, *shrinking back*: Ah, it isn't so simple! That makes it all the worse. It would be a kind of sacrilege! I have no right—or, wait! I will just glance at the first word. It may be a clew. And I want you to bear me witness, Mr. Eichenlaub, that I didn't read a word more. *(She catches up a piece of paper, and covers all the card except the first two words.)* Yes! It is she! Oh, how perfectly delightful! It's charming, charming! It's one of the prettiest things that ever happened! And I shall be the means—no, not the means, quite, but the accident—of bringing them together! Put the card into the box, Mr. Eichenlaub, and don't let me see it an instant longer, or I shall read every word of it, in spite of myself!

She gives him the card, and turns, swiftly, and makes some paces toward the door.

THE FLORIST, *calling after her*: But the attress, matam. You forgot.

THE LADY, *returning*: Oh, yes! Give me your pencil. *(She writes on a piece of the white wrapping-paper.)* There! That is it. *(She stands irresolute, with the pencil at her lip.)* There was something else that I seem to have forgotten.

THE FLORIST: Your flowers?

THE LADY: Oh, yes, my flowers. I nearly went

away without deciding. Let me see. Where are those white roses with the pink tinge on the edge of the petals? (*The florist pushes the box towards her, and she looks down at the roses.*) No, they won't do. They look somehow—cruel! I don't wonder he wouldn't have them. They are totally out of character. I will take those white Bride roses, too. It seems a fatality, but there really isn't anything else, and I can laugh with her about them, if it all turns out well. (*She talks to herself rather than the florist, who stands patient behind the counter, and repeats, dreamily.*) Laugh with her!

THE FLORIST: How many shall I sendt you, matam?

THE LADY: Oh, loads. As many as you think I ought to have. I shall not have any other flowers, and I mean to toss them on the table in loose heaps. Perhaps I shall have some smilax to go with them.

THE FLORIST: Yes; or cypress wine.

THE LADY: No; that is too crapy and creepy. Smilax, or nothing; and yet I don't like that hard, shiny, varnishy look of smilax either. You wouldn't possibly have anything like that wild vine, it's scarcely more than a golden thread, that trails over the wayside bushes in New England? Dodder, they call it.

THE FLORIST: I nefer heardt off it.

THE LADY: No, but that would have been just the thing. It suggests the color of her hair; it would go with her. Well, I will have the smilax too, though I don't like it. I don't see why all the flowers should take to being so inexpressive. Send all the smilax you judge best. It's quite a long table, nine or ten feet, and I want the vine going pretty much all about it.

THE FLORIST: Perhaps I better sendt somebody to see?

THE LADY: Yes, that would be the best. Good-morning.

THE FLORIST: Goodt-morning, matam. I will sendt rhoundt this afternoon.

THE LADY: Very well.

She is at the door, and she is about to open it, when it is opened from the outside, and another lady, deeply veiled, presses hurriedly in, and passes down the shop to the counter, where the florist stands sorting the long-stemmed Bride roses in the box before him. The first lady does not go out; she lingers at the door, looking after the lady who has just come in; then, with a little hesitation, she

slowly returns, as if she had forgotten something, and waits by the stove until the florist shall have attended to the new-comer.

THE SECOND LADY, *throwing back her veil, and bending over to look at the box of roses*: What beautiful roses! What do you call these?

THE FLORIST: That is a new rhoce: the Pridte. It is jost oudt. It is coing to be a very bopular rhoce.

THE SECOND LADY: How very white it is! It seems not to have the least touch of color in it! Like snow! No; it is too cold!

THE FLORIST: It *iss* gold-looging.

THE SECOND LADY: What do they use this rose for? For—for—

THE FLORIST: For everything! Weddtings, theatre barties, afternoon dteas, dtinners, funerals—

THE SECOND LADY: Ah, that is shocking! I can't have it, then. I want to send some flowers to a friend who has lost her only child—a young girl—and I wish it to be something expressive—characteristic—something that won't wound them with other associations. Have you nothing—nothing of that kind? I want something that shall be significant; something that shall be like a young girl, and yet— Haven't you some very tall, slender, delicate flowers? Not this deathly white, but with a little color in it? Isn't there some kind of lily?

THE FLORIST: Easder lilies? Lily-off-the-valley? Chonquils? Azaleas? Hyacinths? Marcuerites?

THE SECOND LADY: No, no; they won't do, any of them! Haven't you any other kind of roses, that won't be so terribly—terribly—

She looks round over the shelves and the windows banked with flowers.

THE FLORIST: Yes, we haf dtea-rhoces, all kindts; Marshal Niel; Matame Watterville and Matame Cousine—these pink ones; they are sister rhoces; Matame Hoste, this plack one; the Midio, here; Chacks—

THE SECOND LADY: No, no! They won't any of them do. There ought to be a flower invented that would say something—pity, sympathy—that wouldn't hurt more than it helped. Isn't there anything? Some flowering vine?

THE FLORIST: Here is the chasmin. That is a very peautiful wine, with that sdtar-shaped flower; and the berfume—

THE SECOND LADY, *looking at a length of the jasmine vine which he trails on the counter before her*: Yes, that is very beautiful; and it is girlish, and like— But no, it wouldn't do! That perfume is heartbreaking! Don't send that!

THE FLORIST, *patiently*: Cypress wine? Smilax?

THE SECOND LADY, *shaking her head vaguely*: Some other flowering vine.

THE FLORIST: Well, we have cot noding in, at present. I coult get you some of that other chasmin —kindt of push, that gifs its berfume after dtark—

THE SECOND LADY: At night? Yes, I know. That might do. But those pale green flowers, that are not like flowers—no, they wouldn't do! I shall have to come back to your Pride roses! Why do they call it Pride?

THE FLORIST: It is Pridte, not Bridte, matam.

THE SECOND LADY, *with mystification*: Oh! Well, let me have a great many of them. Have you plenty?

THE FLORIST: As many as you lige.

THE SECOND LADY: Well, I don't want any of these hard little buds. I want very long stems, and slender, with the flowers fully open, and fragile-looking—something like *her*. (*The first lady starts.*) Yes: like this—and this—and this. Be sure you get them all like these. And send them—I will give you the address. (*She writes on a piece of the paper before her.*) There, that is it. Here is my card. I want it to go with them.

She turns from the florist with a sigh, and presses her handkerchief to her eyes.

THE FLORIST: You want them to go rhighdt away? (*He takes up the card, and looks at it absently, and then puts it down, and examines the roses one after another.*) I don't know whether I cot enough of these oben ones on handt, already—

THE SECOND LADY: Oh, you mustn't send them to-day! I forgot. It isn't to be till to-morrow. You must send them in the morning. But I am going out of town to-day, and so I came in to order them now. Be very careful not to send them to-day!

THE FLORIST: All rhighdt. I loog oudt.

THE SECOND LADY: I am so glad you happened to ask me. It has all been so dreadfully sudden, and I am quite bewildered. Let me think if there is anything more! (*As she stands with her finger to her lip, the first lady makes a movement as if about to speak, but does not say anything.*) No, there is nothing more, I believe.

THE FLORIST, *to the First Lady*: Was there somet'ing?

THE FIRST LADY: No. There is no hurry.

THE SECOND LADY, *turning towards her*: Oh, I beg your pardon! I have been keeping you—

THE FIRST LADY: Not at all. I merely returned to— But it isn't of the least consequence. Don't let me hurry you!

THE SECOND LADY: Oh, I have quite finished, I believe. But I can hardly realize anything, and I was afraid of going away and forgetting something, for I am on my way to the station. My husband is very ill, and I am going South with him; and this has been so sudden, so terribly unexpected. The only daughter of a friend—

THE FIRST LADY: The only—

THE SECOND LADY: Yes, it is too much! But perhaps you have come— I ought to have thought of it; you may have come on the same kind of sad errand yourself; you will know how to excuse—

THE FIRST LADY, *with a certain resentment*: Not at all! I was just ordering some flowers for a reception.

THE SECOND LADY: Oh! Then I beg your pardon! But there seems nothing else in the world but—death. I am very sorry. I beg your pardon!

She hastens out of the shop, and the first lady remains, looking a moment at the door after she has vanished. Then she goes slowly to the counter.

THE LADY, *severely*: Mr. Eichenlaub, I have changed by mind about the roses and the smilax. I will not have either. I want you to send me all of that jasmine vine that you can get. I will have my whole decorations of that. I wonder I didn't think of that before. Mr. Eichenlaub! (*She hesitates.*) Who was that lady?

THE FLORIST, *looking about among the loose papers before him*: Why, I dton't know. I cot her cart here, somewhere.

THE LADY, *very nervously*: Never mind about the card! I don't wish to know who she was. I have no right to ask. No! I won't look at it. (*She refuses the card, which he has found, and which he offers to her.*) I don't care for her name, but— Where was she sending the flowers?

THE FLORIST, *tossing about the sheets of paper on the counter*: She dtidn't say, but she wrhote it down here, somewhere—

THE LADY, *shrinking back*: No, no! I don't want to see it! But what right had she to ask me such a thing as that? It was very bad taste; very obtuse,—whoever she was. Have you—ah— found it?

THE FLORIST, *offering her a paper across the counter*: Yes; here it iss.

THE LADY, *catching it from him, and then, after a glance at it, starting back with a shriek*: Ah-h-h! How terrible! But it can't be! Oh, I don't know what to think— It is the most dreadful thing that ever— It's impossible! (*She glances at the paper again, and breaks into a hysterical laugh.*) Ah, ha, ha, ha, ha! Why, this is the address that I wrote out for that young gentleman's flowers! You have made a terrible mistake, Mr. Eichenlaub—you have almost killed me. I thought —I thought that woman was sending her funeral flowers to—to— (*She holds her hand over her heart, and sinks into the chair beside the counter, where she lets fall the paper.*) You have almost killed me.

THE FLORIST: I am very sorry. I dtidn't subbose— But the oder attress must be here. I will fint it—

He begins tossing the papers about again.

THE LADY, *springing to her feet*: No, no! I wouldn't look at it now for the world! I have had *one* escape. Send me all jasmine, remember.

THE FLORIST: Yes, all chasmin.

The lady goes slowly and absently toward the door, where she stops, and then she turns and goes back slowly, and as if forcing herself.

THE LADY: Mr. Eichenlaub.

THE FLORIST: Yes, matam.

THE LADY: Have you—plenty—of those white— Bride roses?

THE FLORIST: I get all you want of them.

THE LADY: Open, fragile-looking ones, with long, slender stems?

THE FLORIST: I get you any kindt you lige!

THE LADY: Send me Bride roses, then. I don't care! I will not be frightened out of them! It is too foolish.

THE FLORIST: All rhighdt. How many you think you want?

THE LADY: Send all you like! Masses of them! Heaps!

THE FLORIST: All rhighdt. And the chasmin?

THE LADY: No; I don't want it now.

THE FLORIST: You want the smilax with them, then, I subbose?

THE LADY: No, I don't want any smilax with them, either. Nothing but those white Bride roses! (*She turns and goes to the door; she calls back.*) Nothing but the roses, remember!

THE FLORIST: All rhighdt. I don't forget. No chasmin; no smilax; no kindt of wine. Only Pridte rhoces.

THE LADY: Only roses.

THE FLORIST, *alone, thoughtfully turning over the papers on his counter*: That is sdrainche that I mage that mistake about the attress! I can't find the oder one anwhere; and if I lost it, what am I coing to do with the rhoces the other lady ortert? (*He steps back and looks at his feet, and then stoops and picks up a paper, which he examines.*) Ach! here it iss! Zlipped down behindt. Now I don't want to get it mixed with that oder any more. (*He puts it down at the left, and takes up the address for the young man's roses on the right; he stares at the two addresses in a stupefaction.*) That is very sdrainche too. Well!

He drops the papers with a shrug, and goes on arranging the flowers.

A Masterpiece of Diplomacy

[1894]

This is one of the few farces for which there is proof that Howells took a basic situation–idea from real life. In a letter to Miss Grace Ashburner in Cambridge (September 1, 1893, Sedgwick Collection, Historical Room, Stockbridge Library, Stockbridge, Mass.), he explains his play and requests her permission to use the story:

> A good many years ago—fifteen at least—you told me, or at least I think it was you who told me, of some people who found themselves in an awful case by having called two doctors in succession, and had them both arrive, and had them on their hands, to be held apart and in ignorance of each other's presence, till they could be got out of the house again. This has, from time to time, seemed to me a good farce motive, and in fact I have now written a farce, transacting it, of course, with my everlasting Robertses and Campbells. But before I print it, I want to make sure that its appearance would not, directly or indirectly, annoy you, if it was really you who told me the story, and I should be very greatly obliged if you would kindly reply at once.

Although the play situation is farcical, it is interesting to see the dramatic imagination Howells brings to this simple plot, which he complicates advantageously with his doctors of differing medical persuasions and his characters whose efforts at persuasion meet with varying degrees of success. As this is the eleventh of the twelve plays involving the Robertses and the Campbells, they would be well known to a Howells audience. In this play, however, Howells emphasizes only those characteristics of his play friends that tend to identify them with farce: the slow and somewhat confused father, the highly excitable mother, the more reasonable female friend, the clever contriver, and the wise and fun-loving doctor. With these characters and his basic idea, Howells builds a successful farce by introducing various bits of satire and low humor, a pair of double dealers, a play within a play, and a small boy who is more hungry than sick and not much of either. In one way this play differs from his others because Howells gives it a title which goes beyond simple identification of scene or action. Diplomacy is necessary, but the word *masterpiece* in the title adds a delightful touch.

438

A Masterpiece of Diplomacy[1]

The scene is in the summer cottage of Mr. and Mrs. Edward Roberts, in a Boston suburb, and the space where they encounter from opposite doors at the moment the action opens is a square hallway, with the stairs climbing out of one corner of it, and a fireplace in the other, after a fashion no longer very novel in the architecture of summer cottages. It is rather a close morning in August, but all the windows are shut, and a fire is briskly burning on the hearth.

ROBERTS, *at sight of his wife*: Well, Agnes?

MRS. ROBERTS, *at sight of her husband*: Well, Edward?

ROBERTS: How is the child?

MRS. ROBERTS: Where is the doctor?

ROBERTS: He wasn't at home.

MRS. ROBERTS: Not at home! Oh! then I'm sure you'll approve of what I've done. And I was so afraid I had made a mistake.

ROBERTS: A mistake?

MRS. ROBERTS: Yes. About the doctor. He was in such a violent perspiration that I couldn't help being alarmed about him, though of course I know that perspiration is generally a very good thing. But it simply rolls off him, and he keeps begging for something to eat.

ROBERTS: The doctor?

MRS. ROBERTS: The doctor! No! Haven't you just told me he wasn't at home?

ROBERTS: Yes, but I left word for him to come as soon as he could, and I thought perhaps he had got my message and run. The perspiration, you know!

MRS. ROBERTS: Yes, poor little Rob, he's in a perfect drip, and he keeps wanting to have his clothes on. But you're perspiring yourself, Edward; and *you've* been running. I don't know what I shall do! I've made the fire, here, so as to keep Robby from taking cold; and I don't dare to put the window up, for fear of the draught, and you must be just simply expiring. Why *did* you run so, dear?

ROBERTS: I didn't run. But it's like an oven, out-of-doors. And I walked rather fast, for I wanted to get back and see how the child was, especially when I found the doctor wasn't at home.

MRS. ROBERTS: Yes, you did just as I should have done, and I'm so glad now that I telephoned for Dr. Lawton.

ROBERTS: Dr. Lawton?

MRS. ROBERTS: Yes; as soon as this terrible perspiration set in I felt that we oughtn't to wait another instant, for it might be a case of life and death, and I knew you wouldn't want to take any risks; and when I remembered that you mightn't find Dr. Williams at home, I was perfectly wild, and I telephoned at once for Dr. Lawton to come instantly; and it was very well I did so, for *he* wasn't at home, either. But Lou Bemis was there, and she told me to keep up courage, and as soon as her father came in she would send him flying. Did you leave word for Dr. Williams to hurry?

ROBERTS: Yes, I left a very urgent message on his slate. I—

MRS. ROBERTS: I hope you underlined it, Edward! You never *will* underline things, even the most important!

ROBERTS: Well, I underlined this, my dear.

MRS. ROBERTS: How many times? Three times?

ROBERTS: I think it was three times—

MRS. ROBERTS: Because if you don't do it three times, it isn't the least use in the world. Are you sure it was three times?

ROBERTS: Yes, I think so—

MRS. ROBERTS: And did you put an exclamation after it? Three?

ROBERTS: I don't know—

MRS. ROBERTS: Oh, how *could* you be so careless, Edward? If you didn't put three exclamations, you might as well not have gone. He'll just take his time to it, and Robby may be in a collapse by the time he gets here. He's furious now. Listen!

A WRATHFUL VOICE, *from above*: I want to get up! I want to have my clothes on! I want my breakfast!

MRS. ROBERTS: There, that's the way he's been going on the whole time since you left! Dear, dear!

[1] The text used here is from *Harper's Monthly*, February 1894, LXXXVIII, 371–85.

I wish the doctor would come. I don't see what keeps them all! It's as much as Amy can do to hold him in bed. He's as strong as a lion, and I know it's just his delirium. They're always so when they're delirious.

THE WRATHFUL VOICE, *again*: No, I don't love you a bit, and you're a hateful old thing! And I want my clothes. I won't have the doctor! I ain't sick, and I'm going to get up! I am, too! When Uncle Willis comes, I'll tell him how you've acted. I'm hungry, and I want my breakfast!

MRS. ROBERTS: There!

ROBERTS: I'll go up to him—

MRS. ROBERTS: No, no, Edward! You'll be sure to give way to him, and Amy can manage him nicely. And I want you to be here to receive the doctor. I'll run back and relieve Amy; she must be perfectly worn out, poor thing. He fights so.

ROBERTS: But if he's in a perspiration, Agnes—

MRS. ROBERTS: But it isn't a *common* perspiration, Edward! Of course if it were any other time, and they were not quarantining everybody everywhere, and almost firing on them in New York,[1] I might think it was a very good thing; but as it *is*, I can't do anything till the doctor comes; and if he doesn't come pretty soon, I don't know what we shall do with the child. I wish you had put three exclamations after the hurry! I'm sure I've done my part. I've kindled the fire here, and shut every window in the house, so that the heat can all go up into his room, and I've got the flannels all ready heating in the oven, so that if the collapse does come, I can swathe him in them from head to foot: and I don't see how you could be so heartless, Edward, as not to put three exclamations, when you were about it!

ROBERTS: Well, perhaps Dr. Lawton will get here at once—

MRS. ROBERTS: Yes, and it's fortunate I happened to think of him! I don't know what would happen, if I didn't keep my mind on everything and everywhere at once. I don't mean to reproach you, Edward; and I know that you're perfectly devoted to the children, but if you only could have had the forethought to put three excla—

THE FURIOUS VOICE: Ya-a-a-a! I will, I will, I will! You sha'n't keep me in bed! I want my clothes! I want my breakfast! I want my Poppa!

MRS. ROBERTS: Yes, dear—

[1] The reference here is undoubtedly to the cholera epidemic in New York the year before this play was published, probably while Howells was writing it; there was considerable excitement in New York, and various infected ships in the harbor were quarantined.

ROBERTS: Yes, Bob—

MRS. ROBERTS, *in an awful voice*: Edward, I'm astonished at you! Just when we had got him nicely quieted down, and he's in the wildest delirium!

THE FURIOUS VOICE: I want my Poppa!

ROBERTS: But the child is calling me! What shall I do, Agnes?

MRS. ROBERTS: Do! Stay where you are, Edward, if you are *half* a father! You must be here, and receive the doctor. And be sure to keep him, so that I can come down and tell him the history of the case before he sees Robby, or he'll be all prejudiced, especially if it's Dr. Lawton; you know how headstrong he always is, and wants to see the patient before you can get in a word. Oh, dear! I almost wish I hadn't called him.

ROBERTS: Perhaps Dr. Williams will get here first.

MRS. ROBERTS: Oh, how *good* you are, Edward, and how *thoughtful!* Of *course* he'll be here first, and I never thought of it.

THE FURIOUS VOICE: Poppa! Poppa! Poppa! I want my Poppa!

MRS. ROBERTS: Yes, darling! in a moment! Papa's coming! Oh, Edward, how can you let me lie so to the poor darling, and perhaps he's in the last stages!

ROBERTS, *in a stifled voice*: But what shall I do, Agnes? You won't let me go to him, or answer him; and—

MRS. ROBERTS: Oh, yes, put it all on me, dear! And when I've been through so much already— There! (*At the sound of a step on the veranda Mrs. Roberts shrinks together for flight, and with one foot on the stair and her skirts gathered in her hand, she turns to her husband with a stage-whisper.*) It's the doctor, and I don't care which doctor it is, you must keep him here till I can make Robby a little presentable and throw on something so that I sha'n't be such a *perfect* fright, and dash the comb through my hair. Don't let him come till I send Amy down to let you know when. I'm not going to have the doctor find her there, and pretending to care more for the child then his own mother; she'd like to, well enough. Don't wait for Bella to open the door. Open it yourself, and—U-u-u-gh! (*This cry feebly represents the emotion of Mrs. Roberts as the steps on the veranda approach, and the door is flung open without any pull at the bell, revealing the face and figure of Mr. Willis Campbell.*) Willis! How could you?

CAMPBELL: Could what?

MRS. ROBERTS: I thought it was the doctor! I was *sure* it was!

CAMPBELL: Well, perhaps it is. What do you want with the doctor? Who's sick?

MRS. ROBERTS: 'Sh! Robby—

CAMPBELL: What's the matter with Bob, this time? Cholera?

MRS. ROBERTS, *whimpering*: Oh, there you are! I don't see how you can say such a thing. He's been in the most frightful agony, and he's had a nap since, and now he's all in a cold perspiration, and he insists upon getting up and putting on his clothes and having his breakfast, and it's as much as Amy and I can do to manage him: he struggles like a maniac. She's almost exhausted, poor thing.

CAMPBELL: What's she doing?

THE WRATHFUL VOICE, *from above*: She's holding me in bed, Uncle Willis, and she's keeping me from having my clothes on, and getting any breakfast! Oh, uncle, uncle! Come up here and make her stop!

CAMPBELL: *I* can't make her stop, Bob—

MRS. ROBERTS: 'Sh! for shame, Willis, spoiling everything! He musn't know you're here, or we can't do a thing with him, and we *must* keep him in bed, now, till the doctor comes, or it may be as much as his life is worth.

CAMPBELL: What doctor have you sent for?

ROBERTS: I've just been to get Dr. Williams, but he wasn't at home, and I left word—

MRS. ROBERTS: And I got so anxious that I couldn't wait any longer, and I telephoned for Dr. Lawton, and Lou Bemis is going to send him the instant he comes in. They can consult together, if the case is very dangerous, and I'm sure I never saw anything like it: perfectly bathed in an ice-cold perspiration, rolling off him in great beads.

CAMPBELL: Who?

MRS. ROBERTS: Robby!

CAMPBELL: I thought you meant Roberts. He looks as if he was ready to float away. What have you got a fire for on a day like this?

MRS. ROBERTS: It's to send the heat into Robby's room, and prevent his taking cold, in the perspiration.

CAMPBELL: Well, if you want to send the heat up into his room, why don't you open the doors and windows down here, and make a draught?

MRS. ROBERTS: Do you think that would do it?

CAMPBELL: Of course it would; and besides, it's a great deal hotter outside than it is here. What's the matter with Bob, anyway? Been eating something?

MRS. ROBERTS: He's been eating everything!

MRS. CAMPBELL, *from above*: Agnes! Agnes! I can't manage this boy any longer!

MRS. ROBERTS, *flying up the stairs*: I'm coming, Amy! I don't see how I could be so heartless as to leave you alone with him so long, anyway. But I had to stop and ask Edward about the doctor, and tell him about the case so that he could explain it; and then Willis came in, and I've been advising with him; but I know you must be dropping dead, and I'm thoroughly ashamed of myself, and I shall never be grateful enough to you for it, the longest day I—

Her voice gradually loses itself in the regions above, which she vanishes into before it becomes wholly inaudible.

CAMPBELL, *calling after her*: I'll stay here with Roberts and help him explain when the doctors come. We'll have a doctor apiece to explain to, if they happen to come together.

ROBERTS: Good heavens, Willis! You don't suppose they'll come together?

CAMPBELL: Well, I don't know what's to prevent them.

ROBERTS: But wouldn't it be rather awkward?

CAMPBELL: It would be deucedly awkward, my dear fellow; but you ought to have thought of that before you called them both. If they happen here together, and the case turns out to be a rather simple one not calling for a consultation of physicians, the doctors may be a little bit put out about it. You know how peppery old Lawton is where professional etiquette is concerned.

ROBERTS: Is he? I didn't know—

CAMPBELL: And I suppose he'll wonder why you should have called in a stranger, when your old family physician was in the neighborhood. Lawton will be hurt. But you can easily make it right with him. You can tell him you prefer homeopathy for your children: some people do, you know; it's milder.

ROBERTS: Do you think that would do, Willis?

CAMPBELL: Yes; it's the only way; and I'll tackle Williams. I'll tell him it was such a trifling case, you thought you wouldn't call in a regular practitioner. That'll give him confidence in himself.

ROBERTS: I don't think that would do, Willis—

CAMPBELL: Well, perhaps it wouldn't. Perhaps we'd better trust to inspiration. But we've got to take one apiece, and see what Providence will do for us. What makes Agnes think Bob is so very bad?

ROBERTS: I don't know, I'm sure. He was in a good deal of pain, when I left, and now he's in a profuse perspiration.

CAMPBELL: Well, that sounds rather threatening, but I think when the doctor comes you'd better not give him the history of the case. I think you'd better devote yourself to explaining why you called another doctor. Now, if they both come together, which doctor do you think you had better take? Do you think you could manage best with that cranky old Lawton, with his punctilious medical etiquette, and his contempt of homeopathy, or little Williams, with his sensitiveness, and conceit, and quick temper, and his—

ROBERTS: I—I don't know which I had better take, Willis.

CAMPBELL: I'd willingly take old Lawton, but he never believes a word I say: and I'd take Williams, but he's got a notion that I'm always laughing at him. I'm afraid I can't be of much use to you, Roberts.

ROBERTS: Oh, but surely, Willis, you're not going to back out altogether?

CAMPBELL: No, not back out. I'll stay by, and throw in a word or two, when I see it's needed. You'll get on swimmingly. (To Mrs. Campbell, who appears on the stairs somewhat disheveled and very heated-looking) Hello, Amy!

Mrs. Campbell descends the stairs, and reaches the level of the hallway while she is speaking.

MRS. CAMPBELL: What is that you are trying to put Edward up to, Willis? I insist upon knowing.

CAMPBELL: What's the matter, Amy? You look as though you had been having a little flirtation with a cyclone.

MRS. CAMPBELL: Never mind how I look, or what I've been flirting with. What have you been putting Edward up to?

CAMPBELL: Oh, very well, if you don't want him to do what I say, you can take the case in hand yourself. The simple fact is that he's called in Williams, and Agnes has called in Lawton, and the two doctors are going to arrive here together as mad as hornets, and I was just telling Roberts how to manage them. But I don't want to force my advice on any one.

MRS. CAMPBELL: How do you know they'll arrive together, and be as mad as hornets?

CAMPBELL: Well, my dear, as soon as you *see*

them arrive together, you watch out whether they're as mad as hornets or not. That's all! What do you want Roberts here to say to them when they both come in together?

MRS. CAMPBELL: They won't both come together. (She goes to one of the windows and looks out.) There, I knew they wouldn't! There comes Dr. Williams, and he's quite alone. There's not another soul in sight, and he's hurrying like everything.

CAMPBELL: Well, then, you must smuggle him out of the way, as quick as he gets into the house, and leave the coast clear for Dr. Lawton. Perhaps old Lawton hasn't started at all, yet, and you can stop him. Can't you call up Mrs. Bemis, and tell her that Rob is all right, and her father needn't come?

MRS. CAMPBELL: But what if he isn't all right?

CAMPBELL: Why, then, here's Dr. Williams to make him so!

MRS. CAMPBELL: That is so—

ROBERTS: Yes, do speak to her, Amy, and Willis and I will meet Dr. Williams here—

MRS. CAMPBELL: Well, I will if *you* wish it, Edward, but I'm not sure. (She goes to the telephone in another room and is heard ringing, and then conducting the one-sided dialogue of the telephone.) Is that you, Lou? Yes, well! It's Mrs. Bemis I want. Are you Mrs. Bemis? Yes, well! This is Mrs. Campbell—Mrs. Willis Campbell. Amy, you know. Well, I'm speaking for Mrs. Roberts. Robby is much better. He's quite well, and if your father hasn't started yet— What? Is that you, Mrs. Bemis! Hello! Who is that! Lou? Yes, well! If Dr. Lawton hasn't started yet, Mrs. Roberts thinks it isn't worth while for him to come, and— What? Oh, my goodness, Willis!— (she rushes into the hallway again as she pronounces the dreadful words) he's started as fast as he can drive, and he'll be here before we can turn round. What shall we do?

CAMPBELL: Well, then, I'll tell you what! Roberts, here, has got to use a little—finesse, a little diplomacy.

MRS. CAMPBELL: You know he can't!

ROBERTS: You know I'm never up to that sort of thing, Willis. I really can't help thinking, although I value your kindness so much, Willis, and appreciate your wish to help me, that perhaps it would be best, after all, to treat the matter frankly.

CAMPBELL: How, frankly?

ROBERTS: Why, simply tell both of the doctors, when they come, that we called one because we didn't think the other would get here in time, and—and—throw ourselves on their mercy, don't you know.

CAMPBELL: Oh, a nice time you would have on old Lawton's mercy! It would never do in the world, Roberts. You would make the most fearful mess of it.

ROBERTS: I'm afraid we should make a fearfuler mess of it the other way. I do indeed. I'm not at all equal to it, Willis. You know how to carry these things off naturally, but I—

MRS. CAMPBELL: And I think you are quite right, Edward. It's much better to be honest about things.

CAMPBELL: You wouldn't know how to be honest about a thing if you tried, Amy. You leave Roberts to me.

ROBERTS: No, Willis, I don't know how—I can't—

CAMPBELL: Well, in this instance, you have simply *got* to; or you'll have the awfulest row— By George, Amy, why shouldn't *you* use the finesse, or the diplomacy? You'd be the very one for a thing of that kind. I don't say it to flatter you, but when it comes to a little fibbing—in a good cause, of course—

MRS. CAMPBELL, *after a moment of apparent fascination with the notion*: No, I shall have nothing to do with it. I shouldn't mind the fibbing— for the cause *is* good—but I should know that you had something underhanded in it, and were just trying to get me into a scrape. No, Willis, I can't trust you, even in a case of life and death.

CAMPBELL: Well, better put up your hair, anyway, Amy; and there's something stringing out of your neck— 'Sh! There's his step on the piazza!

Mrs. Campbell runs to the mirror in the corner of the hallway, and hastily reorders her dress and hair, and turns again to her husband.

MRS. CAMPBELL: Will that do?

CAMPBELL, *laughing*: Perfectly.

MRS. CAMPBELL: I don't believe it; unless you're just laughing to tease me.

CAMPBELL: I'm not, Amy, indeed. And now as soon as he rings, Roberts and I will get out of this, and let you receive him, and then you'll know that I haven't put up any job on you. Now my plan is that Roberts shall stay in the library, on one side of the hall, here, and I'll stay in the dining-room on the other side. If old Lawton comes before you get Williams out of the house, I'll receive him in the dining-room, and prime

him with a little sherry, and talk round him, and keep him amused till Williams is gone. And you must smuggle him down the back way, and Roberts will be there in the library, and shut the door, and then I'll steal out, and get up stairs with Lawton, and then Roberts can open the door, and hustle the other fellow out, and get him into his buggy, and have him off, and old Lawton will never suspect anything. (*He glances out of the window.*) By George, there comes Lawton down the road now, and there isn't an instant to lose! Poke Williams right into the library there with Roberts, the instant he appears, and shut the door on them, and—'Sh! There's his step! He's crossing the veranda! He's ringing! (*The bell is heard.*) Come, Roberts! (*Roberts starts to follow Campbell into the dining-room.*) No, no! You're to be in the library, you know. (*He turns Roberts about in the right direction by main force.*) And remember, you're to take him up out of the door at the other end of the library, and then get him out of the house by the back stairs.

He closes the library door upon Roberts, and retreats to the dining-room. At the same moment Mrs. Campbell opens the hall door to Dr. Williams.

MRS. CAMPBELL: We don't stand upon ceremony this morning, doctor; I don't know where the maids all are. We've been terribly frightened about poor little Robby, and I don't know what you'll think of him. But we've kept him in bed till you came, though he's been perfectly furious to get up and have his clothes on.

DR. WILLIAMS, *standing with his hat in one hand, and his case of medicines in the other*: Get up and have his clothes on?

MRS. CAMPBELL: Yes; his mother is afraid he may be a little delirious. But won't you just step in here, and speak with Mr. Roberts? He would like to see you first.

She throws open the library door, and Dr. Williams disappears within, looking mystified. As she closes the door on him, and turns away, Campbell shows himself at the dining-room door, and addresses her in a stage-whisper.

CAMPBELL: Splendid, Amy! I couldn't have done it better myself. Now, if you'll only manage old Lawton half as well, our lives will be saved.

MRS. CAMPBELL, *whispering*: Dr. Lawton will be more difficult. Willis, I believe I shall let you receive Dr. Lawton.

CAMPBELL: No, no! You musn't think of it. You are doing magnificently, Amy! It will be such a joke on old Lawton when we're all safely out of it! Say the first thing that comes into your head, and it will be right. (*He runs to the window, and peeps.*) He's there! He's hitching his horse, and he'll be at the door in half a minute. Courage, Amy, and luck to you.

MRS. CAMPBELL: No, Willis! Don't leave me! You know I shall be perfectly helpless in Dr. Lawton's hands. You know how merciless he is if he suspects anything.

CAMPBELL: Old Lawton? Well, Amy, if you couldn't manage old Lawton! All you have got to do is to send him in to me, and I'll keep him from going up stairs till Edward gets the other fellow out of the house, and the coast is clear.

MRS. CAMPBELL: Willis, you *mustn't* go. Stay and receive him with me.

CAMPBELL: I tell you I can't. It will spoil everything. He'll be sure to smell a rat if I'm with you.

MRS. CAMPBELL, *in a lamentable voice*: He *always* smells a rat!

CAMPBELL: Well, he won't this time. There he is, coming up the veranda steps. Now, keep your wits about you, Amy, do! And send him right in here to me.

He retreats toward the dining-room door.

MRS. CAMPBELL: Oh, how can you be so cruel, unkind, and inconsiderate! Well, now, I don't care *how* badly I manage, and I shall just be glad of it if I make a mess of the whole thing. (*The bell rings, and she pulls the door open, and admits Dr. Lawton.*) Oh, how very kind of you, doctor! Agnes has been worried to death, asking you to come in your vacation. But poor little Rob has been acting so strangely that she couldn't help feeling alarmed, and she knew there was no one like you, and she telephoned you on the impulse of the moment; and it's *so* good of you to come. (*She glances round at the dining-room door, and catches a glimpse of Campbell making frantic gestures of approval and encouragement.*) Won't you sit down a moment, and I'll go and tell—

DR. LAWTON: No. I'd better see the patient at once, if he's in an alarming condition.

MRS. CAMPBELL: Oh, he is! But hadn't I better get you a fan, or a lemonade, or something? It's so very warm this morning.

DR. LAWTON: I should think it was—in here. What have you got a fire for this morning?

MRS. CAMPBELL: Why, Agnes kindled it. She thought that Rob might take cold, he's in such a drip of perspiration, and she didn't realize how hot it was outdoors. She wanted to send the heat up into his room.

DR. LAWTON, *throwing open the windows*: Well, she hasn't succeeded, then. And it's a very good thing she hasn't. It's enough to kill the child, let alone the doctor. By-the-way, whose horse is that out there?

MRS. CAMPBELL, *with dismay, which she tries to make pass for astonishment*: Horse?

DR. LAWTON: Yes; I didn't say *cow*, Mrs. Campbell.

MRS. CAMPBELL, *looking resolutely away from the window in the direction of the dining-room door, which Campbell closes*: Is there any horse besides yours, there, Dr. Lawton?

DR. LAWTON: Yes, there is another doctor's horse. The signs are unmistakable. Who's in the dining-room, there?

MRS. CAMPBELL: Dining-room? Why, I suppose the maids—

DR. LAWTON, *darting suddenly upon her*: Isn't Mr. Campbell in there? (*As she hesitates, he smiles, and continues in a rapid whisper.*) I see. They called another doctor first, and when he didn't come at once, they telephoned to me. That is all perfectly natural, and all perfectly right. I suppose you're afraid I shall be vexed at finding another doctor here. I think it's the jolliest kind of fix for Roberts, but I haven't the heart to tease him about it. If it was your husband, Mrs. Campbell, I shouldn't mind doing it. He's always teasing somebody. Tell me, now, what's his little game at present? Concealment is impossible, you know, and you might as well be honest as not.

MRS. CAMPBELL, *allured by the fact*: I suppose I really might.

She whispers throughout, and so does Dr. Lawton.

DR. LAWTON: Better. What is he up to, in there?

MRS. CAMPBELL: Will you ever tell him I told you?

DR. LAWTON: Never!

MRS. CAMPBELL: Well, it would really be such a good joke on Willis, and I should like to see him come up with, once.

DR. LAWTON: Dear lady, if you will only tell me, he shall be come up with as he never was in his life before!

MRS. CAMPBELL: But wouldn't it be a little wrong, doctor? I shouldn't want you to tease him *very* much!

DR. LAWTON: Not so as to injure him, of course;

but just to give him a little lesson. You can safely trust me. I am your family physician, you know, and I will be responsible for the result.

MRS. CAMPBELL, *reflectively*: That is true. And it would be just serving him right, wouldn't it, for leaving me here to take the brunt of it with you, and to try to keep you in the dark.

DR. LAWTON: It would be your duty, Mrs. Campbell, in an event of that kind.

MRS. CAMPBELL: And perhaps it would cure him of his teasing, if he could feel how it was himself.

DR. LAWTON: It would be the saving of him. It would bring out all his good and noble qualities. What is his game?

MRS. CAMPBELL: I have the greatest mind in the world to tell you, only I don't like to do anything that a man would think underhand.

DR. LAWTON: A man would think it the frankest kind of a thing. A woman might think it underhand, but—

MRS. CAMPBELL: Oh, I don't care what a woman would think. And it would be such a good joke on Willis! Well, you see—you see—

DR. LAWTON: Yes, yes!

MRS. CAMPBELL: You see, Dr. Williams—

DR. LAWTON: Oh; little pills! [1] Well, he isn't such a bad sort of fellow. Go on!

MRS. CAMPBELL: Agnes sent for him, and then, while Edward was gone, Robby broke into such a profuse perspiration that she got frightened, and telephoned for you. And when Willis found out what they had done, he began to tease, and to try to make them believe it was something awful, and that you would both be so angry that you would never forgive it—

DR. LAWTON, *rubbing his hands*: Capital! Just as I suspected. Oh, I'll fool him to the top of his bent! [2] Go on!

MRS. CAMPBELL: And poor Edward *wanted* to tell the truth about it, as soon as you came, and Willis wouldn't let him. And he said Edward must go into the library, and receive Dr. Williams, and let him see the child, and then smuggle him out the back way, and he would be waiting in the dining-room, and I was to show you in there to him—

DR. LAWTON: Glorious! Oh, young man, how I will block your game!

1 Lawton, like Dr. O. W. Holmes, was not a homeopathist; see *Literary Friends and Acquaintance*, 140, 161–62, for reference to the Holmes-Stowe argument concerning homeopathy.

2 *Hamlet*, III, 2:401.

MRS. CAMPBELL: And he would keep you amused there till Dr. Williams was safely out of the house, and then let you go up stairs, and you would never know anything about it.

DR. LAWTON: Oh, *won't* I? Well, Mrs. Campbell, now I'm going to begin. You say, *Just step into the dining-room, doctor, and I'll call Mr. Roberts.*

MRS. CAMPBELL, *aloud*: Yes, Mr. Roberts would like to see you first, and if you'll step into the dining-room a moment out of this terrible heat, and won't mind its being in a little disorder—

DR. LAWTON, *whispering*: Is any one in the library now?

MRS. CAMPBELL, *opening the door, to peep in*: No.

DR. LAWTON: All right. (*Aloud*) Thank you. I'll wait in the library, if you please, and look at a word I want to see in Roberts's dictionary.

He goes into the library, and closes the door after him, and at the same instant Campbell flings open the dining-room door, and flies out upon his wife.

CAMPBELL: Great heavens, Amy, what in the world are you up to? Don't you know that Roberts is in there with Dr. Williams? You showed them in there yourself, half a minute ago.

Campbell is obliged to speak in an impassioned whisper, so that he shall not be heard in the library.

MRS. CAMPBELL: Why, so I did! What shall I do?

CAMPBELL: Oh, do! You can't do anything now. The die is cast, the jig is up, the fat's in the fire, the milk's spilt.

MRS. CAMPBELL, *mysteriously*: I don't believe it is.

CAMPBELL: Don't believe it is! What do you mean?

MRS. CAMPBELL: 'Sh! Willis, I have a great mind to tell you something.

CAMPBELL: Tell me something?

MRS. CAMPBELL: 'Sh! Yes, it would be such a joke on Dr. Lawton!

CAMPBELL: On Lawton! Out with it, Amy! I'm round paying a heavy premium for jokes on Lawton.

MRS. CAMPBELL: What will you give me if I tell you?

CAMPBELL: Oh, anything! Everything! A kiss.

MRS. CAMPBELL: Stuff! Will you ever let any human being know that I told you?

CAMPBELL: Red-hot pincers couldn't get it out of me.

MRS. CAMPBELL: Well, I peeped before I let him go in, and made sure Dr. Williams had gone up stairs. He wants to block your game, Willis. But I don't think it was very nice of him to try to get a wife to join against her husband; do you?

CAMPBELL: Oh, that was very wrong indeed! I wonder at Lawton. What did he want you to do?

MRS. CAMPBELL: If it wasn't for that, I don't believe I should tell you.

CAMPBELL: I know you wouldn't, Amy. It's your sense of duty that obliges you to speak.

MRS. CAMPBELL: If I were sure that it was my sense of duty—

CAMPBELL: You may bet anything it is, Amy. I can tell when you're doing a thing because you're mad, and when you're doing it from a sense of duty. You look altogether different.

MRS. CAMPBELL: And it isn't at all for the joke—

CAMPBELL: *Joke*, Amy? *You* joke! You would rather perish. You wouldn't know how, even if you wanted to. What is it?

MRS. CAMPBELL: Oh, then you think women have no sense of humor?

CAMPBELL: I? I think they are so truly humorrous that they needn't joke to show it, and that if you saw anything funny in giving Dr. Lawton away, you wouldn't do it. What is the old reprobate up to, Amy?

MRS. CAMPBELL: Well, then, I'll tell you, if you won't give *me* away, as you call it.

CAMPBELL: Amy!

MRS. CAMPBELL: He made me confess—or the same as confess—that there was another doctor here, and you were going to keep it from him, till we could get Dr. Williams out of the house, and then let him go up and see Rob, and he would never know anything about it. And I know he's going to bounce out of the library in a minute, and pretend to be furious, and block your game, as he calls it.

CAMPBELL: Oh, *is* he! I guess two can play at blocking that game!

MRS. CAMPBELL: And I'm not going to stay, Willis, and you may get out of the boggle the best way you can.

CAMPBELL: You are an angel, Amy, and nothing proves it more than your wanting to sneak out of the difficulty that your perfidy has got two men into. Angels of your description always do that.

MRS. CAMPBELL: Well, if that's the way you talk, Willis, I'll take back everything I've said. Dr. Lawton doesn't know anything about my telling you. Now, how do you feel?

CAMPBELL: Terribly. But I think I'll act just as if he did. Go, my love; leave me to my fate.

MRS. CAMPBELL: I shall not do it, now, because I see that you really wish me to. I shall stay, and see what a miserable mess you will make of it. I shall stay, and triumph over both of you. And I shall laugh and laugh. Oh, how I shall la— Wo-o-o! Oh, my goodness, he's coming?

At the sound of the knob turning in the library door Mrs. Campbell starts in fright, and with a backward glance at Dr. Lawton as he emerges, she flies from the scene.

CAMPBELL, *gayly*: Ah, Dr. Lawton!

DR. LAWTON, *grimly*: Ah, Mr. Campbell!

CAMPBELL: Awfully good of you to let them disturb you in your vacation, this way. Roberts will be down in a moment. He wants to see you before you go up to Rob. Agnes wants him to explain the case to you. It's rather a peculiar case—

DR. LAWTON: I don't think I'll wait to see Mr. Roberts, Mr. Campbell. I will ask you to say to Mrs. Roberts that I preferred not to wait—simply that.

CAMPBELL, *with affected consternation*: Why, Dr. Lawton, I hope you don't mind having had to wait a few moments for Roberts. I'll run right up stairs for him. I know he'll be extremely mortified and distressed.

DR. LAWTON, *as before*: The waiting is nothing. I don't mind the waiting—

CAMPBELL, *with affected humility*: Then may I ask—

DR. LAWTON, *as before*: Yes, sir, you may ask, and I have not the slightest objection to answering. Another physician has been called here, before me.

CAMPBELL: Oh, but, Dr. Lawton, I assure you—

DR. LAWTON, *always with the greatest sternness*: Don't attempt to trifle with me, sir. When I hitched my horse before the door, I found another doctor's horse hitched there: an unmistakable doctor's horse, chewing the top of the post, and drowsing as peacefully as the flies would let him.

He turns aside to conceal a laugh.

CAMPBELL: Well, I recognize the type, doctor, but I think you must be mistaken—

DR. LAWTON: No, sir. I am not mistaken. How should I be mistaken?

CAMPBELL: Well, the grocer's horse behaves that way, too, I believe.

DR. LAWTON: But grocers don't drive round in top-buggies!

CAMPBELL: That is true.

He appears to fall into extreme dejection.

DR. LAWTON: Besides, the motive for this delay that I have been subjected to is not sufficiently accounted for on the ground that Mr. Roberts wishes to explain a case to me that I can judge of a great deal better than he can. No, sir! They have another doctor up there with the patient, and they are waiting to smuggle him out of the house before they let me go up. I suspect your hand in this, Mr. Campbell, and I will not suffer you to trifle with me. You are keeping me here until Dr. Williams can be got out of the house, and then you are to let me go through the farce of prescribing for the patient.

CAMPBELL, *with simulated deprecation*: Now, Dr. Lawton—

DR. LAWTON, *with every token of suppressed fury*: Well, sir?

CAMPBELL: If I were to give you my honor that there was not another doctor in this house?

DR. LAWTON: I advise you not to do so. (*He seizes Campbell by the arm, and pulls him to the window.*) Look there, sir! What do you say to that? Do you see my horse hitched at one end of that rail, out there, and do you see Dr. Williams's horse hitched at the other end of the rail? What do you say to that?

CAMPBELL: Why, Dr. Lawton, if you force me to be frank, I say that I didn't suppose you began so early in the morning. I don't object to a modest eye-opener, but if a man takes so many as to make him see double—

DR. LAWTON: Don't prevaricate, Mr. Campbell! Do you see two doctors' horses there, or don't you?

CAMPBELL: I see *one* doctor's horse, there.

DR. LAWTON, *releasing him, and anxiously scanning his face*: Ah! my poor young friend! This is worse than the simple drunkenness you accuse me of. Are you aware that there is a very serious brain disorder which causes the victim to see but half of a given object, and of two objects to see but one?

CAMPBELL: No; is there? Then we had better get another doctor to judge between us, or appeal from Philip after to Philip before his second eye-opener. Come, now, doctor, hadn't you better go home! I'll excuse you to the family, and account for you some way. I don't believe Amy noticed anything; and when you get back, you can sleep it off, and nobody will be the wiser. It isn't habitual with you, and we can hush it up for this once if you'll only go—

DR. LAWTON, *with a fresh access of pretended rage*: No, sir, I will not go! I insist upon seeing Mr. Roberts, and upon verifying the presence of another doctor in this house.

CAMPBELL, *with a shrug*: Well, I suppose if you *see* double there's nothing to prevent you from *thinking* double. But if the solemn assurance of one of your oldest and truest friends—

THE VOICE FROM OVERHEAD, *making itself heard through the closed door*: I won't, I won't, I won't! I don't want any medicine! I know it's nasty. Go away, doctor! I ain't sick!

The voice dies away into the indistinct murmur of other persuasive and menacing voices, and the sound of a struggle, terminating in a wild yell.

DR. LAWTON: There, sir, what do you say to that?

CAMPBELL: Say to what?

DR. LAWTON: To that outcry, that uproar, that plain proclamation of Dr. Williams's presence!

CAMPBELL: Why, did you hear anything, doctor?

DR. LAWTON, *with a compassionate shake of his head*: Hearing affected, too! This is very interesting. Will you let me examine your eye, Mr. Campbell?

CAMPBELL: Oh, certainly. (*After the doctor has lifted the lid, and peered earnestly into his eye*) Anything green, there?

DR. LAWTON: What do you mean, sir?

CAMPBELL: Oh, nothing, only I think you are doing it splendidly, and it's a pity you shouldn't know how fully I appreciate it. My game is completely blocked. Go on!

DR. LAWTON, *after a moment*: Who told you?

CAMPBELL: Amy.

DR. LAWTON, *with mock tragedy*: Then I have been betrayed.

CAMPBELL: I've been betrayed, too. She told you that I was going to put up a job on you.

DR. LAWTON: She did. Mrs. Campbell is truth itself.

CAMPBELL: I should say deceit personified.

DR. LAWTON: You are Mrs. Campbell's husband. What shall we do now?

CAMPBELL, *offering his hand*: Shake.

DR. LAWTON, *taking it*: And then?

CAMPBELL: Keep the thing up with increased fervor. Bite the biter; deceive the deceiver; outshine the truth itself in candor.

DR. LAWTON: Ah, that might be difficult—for some of us! But still I think we had better make the attempt. But first: there isn't anything serious the matter with Rob, is there?

CAMPBELL: He's hungry, as I infer from a remark that I heard him make.

DR. LAWTON: That's a trouble that can always be reached, happily, in our condition of life. Well, where did we leave off?

CAMPBELL: Oh, I think at Rob's giving Dr. Williams's presence away.

DR. LAWTON: I remember! Well, here goes, then! (*He bursts out furiously.*) *No, sir, I will not be put off with any such excuse. It is a matter which touches my personal and professional dignity. Where is Mr. Roberts, I say?* (*In a natural tone*) How will that do?

CAMPBELL: First rate! Perhaps it was a little too emphatic. I'm afraid Amy will begin to suspect something. Now I'll reply in persuasive accents: *My dear Dr. Lawton, you know that Roberts is incapable of offering you a personal or a professional affront. If you will give me a little time, I can explain—*

DR. LAWTON: Well, now, I'll retort in a tone of biting sarcasm: *I fancy you will not only want a little time; you will want a little eternity to explain a thing like this. But if Mr. Roberts will not come to me, I will go to Mr. Roberts!*

CAMPBELL, *naturally*: Oh, that's capital! That will fetch them. 'Sh! They're opening the door a little. That's Agnes. I suppose Roberts must have got Williams down the back stairs. Now I'll throw myself in your way, here, and attempt to prevent your going up. That will simply madden you. I'll place myself at the foot of the stairs, with folded arms, and say, in a voice choked with a sense of duty, *Dr. Lawton, if you so far forget yourself as to attempt to mount a single step toward the room where my poor nephew lies in a drip of perspiration, I will—* Now, you go on, in a perfect frenzy.

DR. LAWTON: *You will what, sir? Do you mean to say that you will use physical force to prevent me?* (*Naturally*) How will that do?

CAMPBELL: The very thing! Now I'll come in: *I don't know what you call it, but I shall keep you from going up stairs.*

DR. LAWTON, *dramatically*: Stand aside, sir!

CAMPBELL: Not so loud, quite. They're listening. I'll give you the right pitch: *I will not stand aside. If you mount these stairs, it will be over my body, dead or alive.* About like that, you know. Now, we must both stamp our feet, and that will bring them.

They both stamp their feet, and a sound of swishing dresses and suppressed voices is heard on the little gallery that looks down into the hallway from above. The dresses and the voices are those of Mrs. Roberts and Mrs. Campbell; Mrs. Campbell restrains Mrs. Roberts by main force from rushing down and interfering with the quarrel of the men.

MRS. CAMPBELL, *in bated breath*: Now, do control yourself, Agnes! I tell you they're just trying to fool each other. Oh, dear! I wish I hadn't put them up to it! This comes from not sticking to the exact truth. Edward's way is the best; yes, it is, and I shall always stick to it after this, if it kills me.

MRS. ROBERTS: Oh, but are you *sure* they're trying to fool each other, Amy? Perhaps you're not telling the truth, *now*! If they should be in earnest, I should surely die! (*The men continue to dramatize a struggle on the floor below.*) Oh, look at them! I can't bear to look at them! Oh, are you sure you're not mistaken, Amy?

MRS. CAMPBELL: Don't I *tell* you I put them up to it myself?

MRS. ROBERTS: Oh, I wish Edward would come back, and separate them! I don't see what he's doing with Dr. Williams so long! Of course he had to make the excuse of the garden when he took him down the back way, but he could have shown him every leaf in it by this time, I should think. Amy, I can't think they're joking. They do struggle so fearfully. There! They've let each other go, at last, but it's simply from exhaustion!

CAMPBELL, *proudly placing himself at the foot of the stairs again, and addressing Dr. Lawton, with feigned hauteur*: I think you are satisfied now, that you can't go up stairs, Dr. Lawton.

DR. LAWTON, *dramatically*: We will see, Mr. Campbell. I have kept one little argument in reserve.

He advances upon Campbell with lifted hand, as if to strike.

CAMPBELL, *dramatically*: What! A blow, Dr. Lawton?

DR. LAWTON, *dramatically*: Several, Mr. Campbell, *if you insist upon it. Will you stand aside?*

CAMPBELL, *dramatically putting himself into a posture of self-defence*: Never! And beware, Dr. Lawton! You are an old man, but I will not be answerable for the consequences if you strike me. I will not take a blow from you, much as I respect you, and would like to gratify you. I allow no one to strike me but Mrs. Campbell.

MRS. ROBERTS: Oh, Amy! Is it true? Do you ever strike poor Willis?

MRS. CAMPBELL: Don't be a goose, Agnes! Doesn't that show you that he's just making fun.

MRS. ROBERTS: Oh, do you *think* he is? If I could only believe you, Amy, I should bless you, the longest day you lived. Is Dr. Lawton making fun, too?

MRS. CAMPBELL: Yes, up to a certain point. But he doesn't seem to be making as much fun as Willis is.

MRS. ROBERTS: Oh, I'm sure he's in the bitterest earnest. See, he's just struck at Willis!

MRS. CAMPBELL: Yes, and Willis has warded off the blow nicely.

MRS. ROBERTS: Oh, don't look! (*She hides her eyes in her hands.*) What are they doing now?

MRS. CAMPBELL: He keeps striking at Willis, and Willis wards off his blows, without returning one of them. Oh, isn't he glorious! That's his fencing. He can outfence anybody, Willis can. He mustn't strike *him*, but if he lets him strike HIM, I will never speak to him again!

MRS. ROBERTS: Oh, stop them, somebody, do! Oh, Willis—

DR. LAWTON, *advancing with lifted hand*: I demand to see Mr. Roberts!

MRS. ROBERTS, *in wild appeal*: Oh, but he isn't here, Dr. Lawton! Indeed he isn't! He's out in the garden with Dr. Williams, and as soon as he can get rid of him he'll come right back and explain everything. It all happened through my being so anxious, and telephoning for you after he had gone for Dr. Williams, because we hated so to disturb you in your vaca— Oh, my goodness, he doesn't hear a word I say! (*The men renew their struggle.*) Oh, Amy, do you think they're still in fun?

MRS. CAMPBELL, *with misgiving*: I don't believe they're as much in fun as they were at first. I—

MRS. ROBERTS, *wringing her hands*: Oh, well, then, speak to Willis, do, and see if you can make him hear you!

MRS. CAMPBELL, *with great but faltering stern-*ness: Willis! Willis! I want you to stop that absurd nonsense! You will give me a nervous headache if you keep on. You know that Dr. Lawton doesn't mean anything, and you're just trying to frighten us, and I think it's a shame. Stop, Willis! Oh, dear! he doesn't hear me, or he just pretends he doesn't. I don't know what I shall do.

MRS. ROBERTS: Well, then, we must both scream as loud as ever we can scream.

MRS. CAMPBELL: Yes, that's the only thing we can do now.

They both scream at the tops of their voices. Campbell and Dr. Lawton desist, and look smilingly up at them, with an air of great ap-.parent surprise and interest. At the same moment Roberts and Dr. Williams burst wildly in through the door from the veranda.

ROBERTS, *with shuddering dismay*: What's the matter? What are you screaming for? Is Robby in a relapse? Willis—Dr. Lawton—what is it?

CAMPBELL, *with great calm*: What is what? Have you noticed anything, Dr. Lawton?

DR. LAWTON, *with kindly serenity*: I'm sure I couldn't say. Has there been anything unusual going on?

MRS. ROBERTS AND MRS. CAMPBELL: They have been struggling violently together, and we screamed.

MRS. ROBERTS: Dr. Lawton was trying to come up stairs to speak with you, and Willis wouldn't let him.

MRS. CAMPBELL: They were just fooling us, and I will settle with Willis when we get home.

MRS. ROBERTS: We were terribly frightened.

MRS. CAMPBELL: I was not frightened, but I was never so indignant in my life.

CAMPBELL: Do you understand all this, Dr. Lawton?

MRS. CAMPBELL: Willis! I will *not* stand this any longer, and if you keep it up, I shall go into hysterics. Now you just tell Edward the truth!

CAMPBELL: Well, Amy, I will. You see, Roberts, that as soon as Dr. Lawton got here he suspected another physician, and he taxed Amy with it when she let him in, and instead of confessing at once, as any one else would have done, that he had been called simply because Roberts hadn't found Dr. Williams at home—

MRS. CAMPBELL: Oh!

CAMPBELL: —she invented a cock and bull story, and then, because it wouldn't work, she told him that I was trying to play it on him; and they arranged it between them that they would let me do it—

MRS. CAMPBELL: And I think I was perfectly justifiable. You're always doing such things to me.

DR. LAWTON: You were simply acting for his best good, Mrs. Campbell.

CAMPBELL: Then she gave Lawton away to me, the first chance she had. But as soon as Lawton and I got together we saw through each other in a minute, and we concluded to let her have as much of her game as she wanted. That's all. Sorry to disturb Agnes, but that couldn't be helped. Of course we had to make some noise in the course of our little drama—

ROBERTS: Fortunately, Dr. Williams hadn't driven away; and when I heard the alarming uproar here, I called him in again. I thought Robby might—

CAMPBELL: Well, that's pretty rough on Dr. Lawton.

DR. LAWTON: Yes, Roberts, you might have remembered I was here. Well, I forgive you! Dr. Williams, shall we go up together and see if our patient is in a relapse?

He offers Dr. Williams his hand.

DR. WILLIAMS, *taking it, and meaning to say something civil*: I think I can safely leave him to you, *now*, doctor. There's nothing really the matter—

DR. LAWTON: Oh, you're very good!

CAMPBELL: *You* seem to be getting compliments on all hands, Lawton. What's the matter with a few words of modest praise for your fellow-conspirator?

MRS. ROBERTS, *to the waitress, who looks out from the dining-room door*. What is it, Bella? Breakfast? Well, now, you must both stay to breakfast with us, and if you decide that Robby can have something, and will only consult together and say what he shall have—

DR. LAWTON, *looking up the stairs at a forlorn little figure, very much dishevelled and imperfectly attired, which appears on the landing*: Suppose we let Robby decide for himself! Would you like some watermelon, Bob?

DR. WILLIAMS: Or ice-cream?

DR. LAWTON: Or August sweetings?

DR. WILLIAMS: Or soda-water?

DR. LAWTON: Or candy?

DR. WILLIAMS: Or peaches and cream?

CAMPBELL: Or all together?

MRS. CAMPBELL: Ah, don't tease the child!

ROBBY, *looking wistfully from one to the other as he descends to the floor, and fixing his eyes on his mother at last*: If you'll let me come to the table, mamma—I couldn't find all my clothes—I'd like a little milk-toast and tea.

MRS. ROBERTS, *stooping and putting his arms round her neck*: Oh, you poor little dirty angel! You shall have anything you want on the table. You won't mind his coming just as he is?

She turns with Robby to her guests, who take him into their arms one after another.

DR. LAWTON: If Rob had another rag on him, I shouldn't feel good enough for his company.

DR. WILLIAMS: I consider him perfect, just as he is.

MRS. CAMPBELL: And I will never hold him in bed again!

ROBBY, *after a moment*: You couldn't.

CAMPBELL, *catching him up on his shoulder, and dancing into the dining-room with him*: I knew she was just shamming when she pretended to do it.

A Previous Engagement

[1895]

Few of Howells' one-act farces and comedies received critical attention by his contemporary reviewers; therefore, it is significant that Laurence Hutton devoted one of his "Literary Notes" in *Harper's Monthly* (April, 1897, XCIV, supp. 1, 818) to *A Previous Engagement*. It reads in part:

The element of comedy, especially the element of what is known as light comedy, pervades all the dramatic works which Mr. Howells has been producing of late season in his Theatre of Bric-a-Brac and upon his stage of Imaginative Style. There was, it is true, more of the sentiment of tears than of laughter in *Bride Roses*, one of the best of Mr. Howells's little plays . . .; but *A Previous Engagement* is comedy pure and simple. . . . [The characters] hold a series of dialogues, all of them bright and sparkling; and the point of the plot turns upon what Mr. Howells himself once termed "hen-mindedness," as it is exhibited in the character of the heroine. "How should girls know their own minds?" asks Mrs. Winton. "They are brought up *not* to know their own minds. That is supposed to be pretty, and refined, and delicate!"

We miss a number of familiar names and faces in the present drama. Mr. Campbell and Mrs. Roberts have no parts assigned to them; but although Mrs. Roberts is not announced in the cast, in letters large or small, there are to be found many traces of that delightfully inconsequent creature in the Leading Lady whose characteristic hen-mindedness is displayed in her scattering uncertainty as to whether she wants to wear Bride Roses or to wreck her happiness upon the ground of A Previous Engagement.

There is no actual evidence that this play was ever produced; however, the Samuel French publication indicates that it probably was. There is also other circumstantial evidence. Minnie Maddern Fiske wrote to Howells (n.d., Harvard Library): "I have just had the great pleasure of reading your little play *A Previous Engagement* which you so kindly sent me. It is charming and I am delighted with it. With your permission I shall look forward to presenting it at the first opportunity. The part of Phillippa attracts me tremendously & I'll play it well—you'll see!" Another letter from Mrs. Fiske dated June 28, 1900 (Harvard Library), praises the little play and notes that she still wants to do it on the stage. The English dramatist Henry Arthur Jones, writing to Howells on August 13, 1907 (Harvard Library), also indicated his enjoyment of *A Previous Engagement* and noted that he would see Samuel French to arrange for English amateur performances. Whether anything came from the enthusiasm of these two writers, one cannot say.

A Previous Engagement[1]

MRS. WINTON: I shall have to begin somehow, Mr. Camp, and I can't begin worse, I suppose, than by saying that Philippa is peculiar.

MR. CAMP: It isn't at all a bad beginning, Mrs. Winton. I should have had no criticism to offer even if you had begun by saying she was unique.

He smiles and she laughs a little. They are sitting in the parlor of Mrs. Winton's cottage on the southern Long Island shore: she with the air of having just come down to meet him, and he with the effect of not having so freshly arrived but that he has had time to accumulate most of the books on the table near which he sits in the vain effort to amuse the impatience of waiting; they lie in a straggling heap next his elbow, some half open. He has one glove off; with the gloved hand he rests his straw hat upon his knee.

MRS. WINTON: Ah, I shouldn't have gone so far as that; and I'm quite ashamed to have kept you so long; but—we had a little controversy as to whether I should be allowed to see you at all or not. Philippa insisted that it was altogether her own affair, and she ought to see you first.

MR. CAMP: I hardly know what to say. Between the joy of seeing Miss Winton and the desolation of not seeing you—

MRS. WINTON, *laughing*: Of course it's difficult, and I won't make you go on. But I felt that I ought to come, for it might be now or never—

MR. CAMP: *Oh,* Mrs. Winton!

MRS. WINTON: I don't mean it's so bad as that —unless *you* choose.

MR. CAMP: *I* choose!

MRS. WINTON: I certainly shouldn't have allowed you to be got down here and then driven off again by any act of ours.

MR. CAMP: Oh, *Mrs.* Winton!

MRS. WINTON: Spare your raptures; or, rather, postpone them, till you know whether you can really indulge them. Philippa says that before she can consent to anything like an engagement, she must tell you something.

MR. CAMP: What *is* it, Mrs. Winton?

1 The text used here is the Harper & Brothers edition.

MRS. WINTON: Oh, *that* would be telling. And although she has seen at last that it is proper for me to come and—and prepare you, so far as you can *be* prepared, she insists absolutely upon telling you herself. And she's all the more determined because it's an ordeal.

MR. CAMP: For me?

MRS. WINTON: For her—she *thinks.*

She laughs.

MR. CAMP, *musingly:* Oh, for both, then! *(He preserves a thoughtful silence for a moment.)* Miss Winton has rather a fondness for—ordeals?

MRS. WINTON, *with candor:* No, no. I can't say that she has—exactly. But when it comes to a question of duty— But why do you ask *me?* You know what Philippa is!

MR. CAMP, *sighing:* She is an angel. But sometimes I doubt if I know just what *kind* of angel.

MRS. WINTON: Yes, there are angels and angels, I suppose.

MR. CAMP: Do you think we ought to be afraid of angels, Mrs. Winton?

MRS. WINTON: Not if we are good, I think.

MR. CAMP: Well, sometimes I'm afraid I'm afraid of Philippa. Does that mean that I'm not good? Of course I know I'm not good enough for *her.*

MRS. WINTON: Oh, in this case it's just the other way, I believe. She thinks she may not be good enough for you.

MR. CAMP: Now you *do* alarm me. Who is to judge?

MRS WINTON: You are!

MR. CAMP: I? Does she say that? Then there is no hope! It must be something desperately bad, if I'm fit to judge of it. Is it something desperately bad, Mrs. Winton?

MRS. WINTON: Well, *I* shouldn't think so.

She checks herself in a laugh.

MR. CAMP: Oh, why stop laughing? It gives me new life! Now I shall have to get on with the old—what there is of it. Mrs. Winton, what *is* it that Philippa wishes to tell me?

He edges forward on his chair in his eager-ness.

MRS. WINTON, *falling back in hers*: Why, it's merely that— No, no! I mustn't tell you. I promised her. How can you ask me?

MR. CAMP: I don't ask you to tell me what it is. I meant merely to ask you what it was *like*.

MRS. WINTON: And I can't tell you that, either.

MR. CAMP: Did you promise her that, too?

MRS. WINTON: I promised that I would not even approach the subject.

MR. CAMP: Oh! *(After a moment)* And how were you expecting to prepare me? It seems to me that you are taking the very course to unprepare me, if I understand such things.

MRS. WINTON: I don't see how you can say that. I think I have been very reassuring.

MR. CAMP: How?

MRS. WINTON: By my manner.

MR. CAMP: What has your manner been?

MRS. WINTON: Light, cheerful, gay, almost frivolous.

MR. CAMP, *with a sigh*: That's true. But it's always that.

MRS. WINTON: Mr. Camp!

MR. CAMP: Oh! I mean you're always so good. And you think I ought to take courage from your manner?

MRS. WINTON: I mustn't say that. It would be treachery to Philippa. There! I can hear her walking impatiently to and fro overhead! *(They both listen.)* Can't you?

MR. CAMP: That silken sweeping? That swift, soft footing, like a caged—

MRS. WINTON: Yes—

MR. CAMP: But isn't this a kind of eavesdropping? Ought we to overhear the play of Philippa's emotions, as expressed in her circumambulations?

MRS. WINTON: No; we ought *not*. You're quite right! It is a kind of eavesdropping.

She rises.

MR. CAMP, *springing to his feet*: Oh, don't leave me, Mrs. Winton! I feel dreadfully unprepared. I—I feel—yes, I feel unaneled. Do you know what aneling is?

MRS. WINTON: I haven't the least notion, except that it's something Shakespearian. I must go—

MR. CAMP: One word! One little monosyllabic vocable! I think I've been a pretty average sort of man, Mrs. Winton. But a fellow doesn't live till thirty without getting *some* dust on his youthful bloom. Girls are so strange nowadays; and Philippa is so—unique; and if she should ask me—

MRS. WINTON, *fondly*: You poor man! She isn't going to *ask* you anything! She's going to *tell* you something.

MR. CAMP: Oh! Do you think that will be any better?

MRS. WINTON: That I can't say. 'Sh! I hear her stopping! She's stopping at the door!

MR. CAMP: Do you think she's coming down?

MRS. WINTON, *listening*: No; she's walked away again! What do you wish to say more, Mr. Camp?

MR. CAMP: Oh yes! I wish to say— But do resume your light, cheerful, gay, almost frivolous manner, or I shall have no courage at all!

MRS. WINTON, *laughing*: Well, there!

MR. CAMP: Well—where was I?

MRS. WINTON: I'm sure I don't know *where* you were.

MR. CAMP: Do you know where *you* were?

MRS. WINTON: No! 'Sh! But I know where Philippa is! She's just slammed to her dressing-table drawer, and that means she's put some finishing touch on, and she's not going to wait any longer! 'Sh! She's crossing the room—she's at the door. Don't try to keep me, Mr. Camp! You mustn't! Why, are you crazy? If Philippa found me here— There she is on the stairs!

She releases the hand to which Camp is clinging, and flashes into the next room through the sliding-doors, which with one motion she opens and shuts as Philippa reaches the bottom of the stairs and enters the parlor.

PHILIPPA: I wish to tell you, before we go one word farther, Mr. Camp—

MR. CAMP: Even before we say good-morning?

PHILIPPA: Good-morning, if you insist. It's a decency, and I suppose it doesn't matter that it's now afternoon—

MR. CAMP: It's before dinner.

PHILIPPA: Yes—it's that. *(She is a dark girl, with a thin, impassioned face, and an intense look in her starry eyes, which have a strange remoteness of glance, as if their rays might be some minutes in traversing space before reaching the object they fall upon. She is so tall that her eyes are nearly on a level with the parting of Mr. Camp's blond hair; but then, Mr. Camp is not very tall, and he stands a little inclined towards her, in the tentative and provisional attitude he has taken at her entrance.)* Will you sit down?

MR. CAMP: Can we shake hands after we sit down?

PHILIPPA: I don't wish to shake hands—yet.

MR. CAMP: But we don't meet as enemies?

PHILIPPA: We meet as—neutrals. (*She takes the chair lately occupied by her aunt. With a faint sigh, and a slight shrug, Camp resumes his own. There is a moment's silence, while Philippa fingers the arm of her chair and with an effort governs the tremor of her hand.*) Mr. Camp, I wish to tell you that I have been engaged before.

Her tone is thick with emotion, but she holds her voice firm.

MR. CAMP, *making a joyful start towards her*: Before? Then you mean that now—

PHILIPPA: Wait, please. Let—let me go on. Don't misunderstand me. I mean—nothing but what I say. I would have told you this sooner— I would have told you at the beginning, if I had imagined— But it has all been so unexpected!

MR. CAMP: Not to me, Philippa! I expected it the first moment I saw you. In fact, I knew it.

PHILIPPA: That makes it so much the worse for me. I ought to have known it; I can only say that I didn't; and that's saying nothing. Your letter—your offer—was a perfect surprise; but as soon as it came I was resolved that you should know everything. I would have come—don't interrupt me, please—I would have come to tell you; that would have been the right way; but they wouldn't let me; and I was forced to send for you here. I have made you travel a long distance—

MR. CAMP: It was only a few hours; and they'd a parlor-car on!

PHILIPPA: No matter! It was wrong. And now you have the full right to reject me—

MR. CAMP: Reject you? Philippa, if you'll let me follow you round on my knees the rest of my life—

PHILIPPA: I mean—I was going to say—after you've heard all.

MR. CAMP: All? Is there any more? You've told me you were engaged before—

PHILIPPA: I was wrong to say that; it implied that I thought myself engaged now.

MR. CAMP: I wish you did! I shouldn't care for your being engaged before. Only be engaged now, Philippa, and—

PHILIPPA: You don't know all yet, and I can't let you say anything till you do. And I can't let you call me Philippa.

MR. CAMP: Miss Winton, then. I take back the Philippa.

PHILIPPA: You are very good—you are like *him* in that. We were very young when we met—I was only seventeen. I don't tell you to excuse myself. But life had just begun for me, and I found my world in him. My world? My heaven! He had no tie to this earth except in me—I dragged him down as low as such a spirit could descend. If I am good in anything, he made me so.

MR. CAMP: I think you may have had a hand in it, too. A little hand!

He looks at hers.

PHILIPPA, *ignoring him*: We were engaged, and we were to have been married, although I was so young—he was only six years older himself— as soon as he got a parish—

MR. CAMP: He was—excuse me; I don't want to seem intrusive—a clergyman, then?

PHILIPPA: Yes.

A silence follows, unbroken by her.

MR. CAMP: Well, if that is all— But of course! (*After a moment*) And you said— You wished to say something more?

PHILIPPA: Yes—everything. I broke off the engagement. I tired of him.

MR. CAMP: Oh!

PHILIPPA: I was too light for any serious love—

MR. CAMP: I don't think that follows, necessarily. Do you mean that he bored you?

PHILIPPA, *tragically*: I tired of him. Yes, *say* bored. The time came when he bored me. But if I had been true, and high, and worthy, he would never have bored me. I saw that afterwards. Distinctly.

MR. CAMP: Do you mean that you—wanted to have it on again?

PHILIPPA: Oh, never! If I had, I could have forgiven myself. But the relief was too great, too disgraceful, too wicked. You had better know the worst of me. It was a perfect joy to have him out of the country.

MR. CAMP: He went away?

PHILIPPA: To India. He is a missionary there.

MR. CAMP, *subduing a laugh into a respectful smile*: Well, I don't pretend to be very superhuman; and I confess that if he had been where we were likely ever to meet him—and the world's so small!—I would just as soon it had not happened. I suppose a man likes to be the first, though I really don't know why; but if the other fel—the other one—is so far off, why, it's practically the same as if I *were* the first.

PHILIPPA: Do you really think so?

MR. CAMP: Yes, I'm quite sure of it.

PHILIPPA: But if you were to meet him—

MR. CAMP: Then it would be a little—creepy.

PHILIPPA: I am glad to hear you say that. I couldn't have l—honored you if you hadn't.

She hesitates.

MR. CAMP: And was that all?

PHILIPPA: Yes—all. (*She sighs. He makes a movement towards her.*) No!

MR. CAMP, *restraining himself*: But if that's all, and I don't mind it in the least, why in Heaven's name aren't we engaged, Philippa?

PHILIPPA, *looking steadily at him*: Because—because—if I could tire of him, if I am so fickle and variable as that, I'm not sure that I'm worthy of you.

MR. CAMP: Oh, let me be judge of that!

PHILIPPA: I'm not so generous as you—so wide-minded. If *you* had told *me* such a thing, I don't believe I could have cared nothing for it.

MR. CAMP: Oh!

PHILIPPA: No, not even if I loved you.

MR. CAMP: Even if you loved me! Don't you love me, Philippa?

PHILIPPA: How should I know?

MR. CAMP: Well, if you shouldn't, who should? Do you feel no peculiar emotion towards me? If you wish a diagnosis!

PHILIPPA: I think you are charming—

MR. CAMP: Philippa!

PHILIPPA: Yes, from the very first I felt a strange fascination in your presence. I feel it now! (*He starts towards her.*) Don't touch me! I think —I *think*—I love you. Wait! But I want to think it *over*. Just now I'm—blinded. You seem very good—I hope you're not too good for me! I'm going down to the sea-shore to think it all over.

MR. CAMP: I hoped you had thought it over, Philippa, by this time.

PHILIPPA: I mean your not minding. I haven't had time to think that over yet. I wish to see it in every light.

MR. CAMP: May I go, too, and help you?

PHILIPPA: Are you going to stay for dinner?

MR. CAMP: They haven't asked me yet. But I dare say they will, if all goes well.

PHILIPPA: Will you wait till I come back?

MR. CAMP: If you won't let me come to meet you!

PHILIPPA: You can come to meet me.

MR. CAMP: When—how soon?

PHILIPPA: By-and-by. That is, if I make up my mind. If I want you, I'll put my handkerchief on the point of my parasol, and wave it. You'll see it over the bank.

MR. CAMP: Well.

PHILIPPA, *after a pause*: We may never see each other again. Should you like to— Do you think me a very strange girl, Mr. Camp?

MR. CAMP: Bless me, no! Like all of them! Only in a different way.

PHILIPPA: Then—we may not meet again.

MR. CAMP: Oh, don't say that! Not if you put your handkerchief on your parasol?

PHILIPPA: In that case, yes. But if I don't—if I think it's best not to—

MR. CAMP, *eagerly*: Yes!

PHILIPPA: I shouldn't wish you to think I didn't care for you—

MR. CAMP: Oh, Philippa!

PHILIPPA: But because I wasn't sure I ought— that it was right—

MR. CAMP: Oh!

PHILIPPA: But I want you to believe that I do care for you, and I'm only anxious to find out how and why—in this new light; and if I couldn't find out, I should be very, very sorry for you; sorrier even than I was for myself; and I thought— And—and should you—should you like to kiss me before I go?

MR. CAMP, *with a burst of honesty*: Philippa, I don't know! I thought I would have given the world to kiss you. But now—

PHILIPPA: Will you let me kiss *you*?

MR. CAMP: Oh, if it comes to that!

PHILIPPA: Good-bye, then—perhaps forever.

MR. CAMP: Oh, *no!*

PHILIPPA: It might be better so—for both of us.

She goes up to him, and puts a hand on either of his shoulders. His arms hang at his sides. She looks earnestly into his eyes, and then she kisses him, and he remains standing so after she has left the room.

MRS. WINTON, *flashing the sliding-doors apart*: Congratu—

MR. CAMP: Good heavens, Mrs. Winton! Have you been—

MRS. WINTON: Not an instant! I've been sitting most conscientiously beyond ear-shot, and almost perishing of my own virtue. I've just this moment come in from the very farthest end of the veranda. What's the matter? Isn't it settled?

MR. CAMP: Not in the least.

MRS. WINTON: But didn't I hear—the only thing I *did* hear?

MR. CAMP: You heard a kiss.

MRS. WINTON: And doesn't *that* settle it?

MR. CAMP: Not always.

MRS. WINTON: But if you kissed her—

MR. CAMP: I didn't kiss her. She kissed me—more shame to me!

MRS. WINTON: Oh! Is it such a disgrace?

MR. CAMP: I shouldn't have thought so—once. But now—

MRS. WINTON: The weight of such questions used to be with women; but now they seem to be with men. Could you be a little less mysterious, Mr. Camp?

MR. CAMP: It would be difficult. Mrs. Winton, it seems to me that I've had a look into Philippa's soul!

MRS. WINTON: Oh, indeed! And what was it like?

MR. CAMP: Heaven!

MRS. WINTON: And is that what makes you so dreary—not to say, paralytic? Suppose we sit down.

MR. CAMP, *sinking into his chair again*: Yes; it was rather overawing. Earth is gayer. (*He sighs.*) The trouble with me is, so far as I can make out, that I didn't have a glimpse of Philippa's soul on the same level. I had to look up. It's given me a moral crick in the neck.

MRS. WINTON: Now you're beginning to be yourself again.

MR. CAMP: That's comparatively easy. The difficulty is to be somebody else; and that's what I fancy Philippa has a right to, in my case.

MRS. WINTON: Why, you *are* a little dislocated! Won't you try to let me help you?

MR. CAMP: There isn't anything to tell—if that's what you're after.

MRS. WINTON: I couldn't admit it for worlds!

MR. CAMP: She seemed to wish me to know that she had once been engaged to a—

MRS. WINTON: Yes, I supposed it was that. Why, she was a mere child at the time! But of course it flattered her vanity; and she did take it very seriously—for a while.

MR. CAMP: She broke it off because she got tired of him.

MRS. WINTON: Did she tell you that? Yes, she got tired of him, that is the plain truth. But I must say he was a man of very high ideals. He had a beautiful nature; he was noble.

MR. CAMP, *leaning forward in pathetic entreaty*: Was he so very, *very* noble, Mrs. Winton?

MRS. WINTON, *laughing against her fan*: Yes, his nobleness was of the deepest dye. But he wasn't the least amusing.

MR. CAMP: You think I have a melancholy advantage of him there?

MRS. WINTON: Yes. He made you feel that there could not be such a thing as joking in heaven.

MR. CAMP: Thank you, Mrs. Winton. You don't think you're flattering me?

MRS. WINTON, *with a cry of laughter*: Not at all! You are exactly what Philippa needs; and if she doesn't— But what did you say when she told you of her engagement?

MR. CAMP: That it didn't make any difference to me.

MRS. WINTON: Surely she didn't complain of that?

MR. CAMP: No. But it seemed to make a difference to *her*. She complained of *that*. She accused me of being too good for her, and she said she must go down to the beach and think it over. She asked if you had asked me to stay to dinner—

MRS. WINTON: I have—now!

MR. CAMP: But she seemed to think it was just as well you hadn't; for she intimated that she might not get back from the beach before I was gone. And she bade me a provisional farewell. I wanted to go down to the beach with her, and help her think; but she said she would put her handkerchief on the point of her parasol and wave it over the bank if she needed assistance— Good heavens! She may be needing it, she may be waving it, now! (*He rushes to the window, while Mrs. Winton falls back in her chair in shrieks of laughter, and he stares long and earnestly towards the sea.*) No. It's only a four-masted schooner in the offing; not a handkerchief at all! And then she asked if she might—kiss me. I don't know how I ever came to allow it.

MRS. WINTON: Ah, ha, ha! Ah, ha, ha! Really I shall die.

MR. CAMP, *ruefully*: Mrs. Winton, what do you suppose she did it for?

MRS. WINTON, *wiping the tears from her eyes*: For the usual reason—if it's a reason. Such things used to go by favor, I believe.

MR. CAMP: I can't flatter myself of it, in this case; I'm afraid Philippa is—peculiar.

MRS. WINTON: Why, that's what I said in the first place. You assented, but I could see you didn't believe me.

MR. CAMP: One must sometimes give people the benefit of a reasonable doubt. I didn't believe she was *so* peculiar, then.

MRS. WINTON: And I don't believe she is, now.

MR. CAMP: What do you mean?

MRS. WINTON: I mean that Philippa is a girl, like all the rest of them.

MR. CAMP: That's exactly what I said myself.

MRS. WINTON: Oh, that's why you don't believe it. But it's true, all the same.

MR. CAMP: Well, I'll admit she's a girl, but not like the rest of them. What do you think she meant? Don't you really think she knew her own mind, and just—

MRS. WINTON: How should a girl know her own mind?

MR. CAMP: That's true!

MRS. WINTON: They're brought up not to know their own minds. That is supposed to be pretty, and refined, and delicate. Tell me, now; should you respect Philippa so much if you thought she had known her own mind when you asked her to marry you?

MR. CAMP: I don't know—

MRS. WINTON: There, you see!

MR. CAMP: But Philippa being what she is, what should you do if you were in my place? What should you do now?

MRS. WINTON: I shouldn't let her wave her handkerchief a great while unseen.

MR. CAMP: Oh, do you think— (He rushes frantically to the window, and peers out. After a moment, with a deep sigh) No; it's still the four-masted schooner.

MRS. WINTON: Nothing else in sight?

MR. CAMP: Nothing but Winton. He's coming up the road towards the gate.

MRS. WINTON: Oh, that's nice. He'll be so glad to see you.

MR. CAMP: Will he? It's awfully good of him. Still—do you know, Mrs. Winton?—I don't feel exactly like meeting company.

MRS. WINTON: So glad you don't make a stranger of me, Mr. Camp.

MR. CAMP: Oh, you're different. Winton's a man, don't you know. I can't help feeling that I'm in a very tender and precarious condition, till this affair is decided, and Winton might jar upon me. You understand?

MRS. WINTON: I've no doubt Mr. Winton will, when I tell him. I'm not a man, myself.

MR. CAMP: You're better.

MRS. WINTON: Oh, I know that!

MR. CAMP: And if you don't mind, I'll just slip out of the side-door on to the veranda, here, and fetch a compass round about your shrubbery, and get away without meeting Winton, just now.

MRS. WINTON: How delightful! Why, it's quite like something improper!

MR. CAMP: Yes, isn't it? And it's so perfectly innocent, too. If Winton asks after me, you might say I've just gone down towards the beach to look at the shipping. I want to keep an eye on that four-masted schooner, you know.

MRS. WINTON: Yes, there's no telling what moment it may turn into a handkerchief on a parasol.

MR. CAMP: That is my idea. And you really think there's a chance?

MRS. WINTON: A fighting chance.

MR. CAMP: Oh, bless you, bless you! (He slips out through the sliding-doors, kissing his hand to her.) One gets into the habit of these things, really. But it's only my hand, Mrs. Winton.

He pulls the doors to while Mrs. Winton sinks back into her chair in another fit of laughter. While she still has her handkerchief to her eyes, Winton enters in jacket and knickerbockers, with the dust of a long ramble upon him. He stands looking at her a moment before he speaks.

WINTON: Wasn't that Camp I saw going out of the side gate?

MRS. WINTON: Yes, poor fellow; he was in hopes you wouldn't see him.

WINTON: Poor fellow? Isn't Philippa going to have him?

MRS. WINTON: She's gone down to the beach to find out.

WINTON: And he's going to help her look?

MRS WINTON: Not unless he sees her wave her handkerchief on the point of her parasol.

WINTON: Oh, that's the arrangement, is it?

He sits down in the chair that Camp has lately occupied, and stretches his legs out with a groan of fatigue, pushing his hands into his pockets.

MRS. WINTON: Philippa was sure to have some arrangement, and that's the one in the present case.

WINTON: Well, I suppose she has a right to think it over, and to think it over more than once, if she chooses. I've often felt that if I were to receive an offer of marriage, even after a woman had been courting me the better part of a summer, I should want a good deal of time to think it over. I couldn't decide at once. I should want to view her in the new light of a fiancée before I accepted her.

MRS. WINTON: It seems to be a family trait, the inability to decide upon an offer of marriage.

WINTON: I should be glad to think I took after Philippa in anything. But really, I don't see how you women ever make up your minds. How did you make up *your* mind, Bessie, for example?

MRS. WINTON: I shouldn't call it exactly a mental operation, now. Besides, it was too long ago.

WINTON: It was a good while. But it rather freshens up those associations to have something of the kind going on in the house. Is Camp very much annoyed by the suspense?

MRS. WINTON: Not annoyed, I should say, so much as awed—he thinks he is awed. You had better know all about it, Frederick. It's been very peculiar.

WINTON: Ah, Philippa is peculiar. Was that what you had been crying about when I came in?

MRS. WINTON: It's what I'd been laughing about.
She begins laughing again, and continues to laugh.

WINTON: It seems to have been *very* like Philippa.

MRS. WINTON: It was more like her than anything that's happened yet. It's Philippa gone farther.

WINTON: I didn't know Philippa could go any farther. But I should like to hear how. Only, if it's practicable, I wish you wouldn't make light of her, or rather of *it*. After all, Philippa is—Philippa.

MRS. WINTON: I will try to spare you. I didn't understand why she wanted to have him down here, for I thought she could make up her mind about him just as well at a distance; but as soon as he appeared, I found out. She wished to tell him of her former engagement, and then, as nearly as I could make out, let him take her or leave her.

WINTON: Ah, don't put it in that way!

MRS. WINTON: That's the way it was, and that's the way I must put it. I pleaded with her not to be so foolish: I told her that it couldn't possibly make any difference to him; that it would be extremely awkward, and might be offensive; that she could tell him after they were engaged; but nothing would do but she must tell him now. She wouldn't even let me tell him, and put it in the right light. The most she would let me do was to go down and prepare him for it, after we had kept him waiting fifteen minutes; and she wouldn't let me say more than that there was something she wished to tell him.

WINTON: That was hard on you, Bessie. Did you keep your word?

MRS. WINTON: Of course I kept my word. I am not a man. He entered into the spirit of it at once, and was in the right mood, at least, for her revelation. He wasn't afraid because she was going to tell him something, but he thought she might be going to ask him something.

WINTON: That might have been more embarrassing.

MRS. WINTON: But I reassured him on that point, and, as a matter of fact, she didn't ask him anything whatever. She simply told him about her engagement, and he told her, of course, that it didn't make the slightest difference. But it seems that didn't satisfy her, and she insisted that she must go away and think it over. He naturally wished to go with her, but she forbade him, and said that if she wanted him she would wave her handkerchief on the point of her p-p-parasol. (*Mrs. Winton breaks down laughing.*) And then—then—when he consented to that, she offered in view of their not—not meeting again, and as a slight token of her regret, to—to—k-k-kiss him, and she did actually kiss him!
She hides her face in her handkerchief, and bows herself forward in a paroxysm of laughter.

WINTON: Were you by?

MRS. WINTON: By? No! Of course not. I was by as far as hearing the kiss was concerned, for I was just coming back to them when it—happened.

WINTON, *after a moment of frowning silence*: Sometimes I think Philippa is a fool.

MRS. WINTON, *recovering herself, with seriousness*: I don't think she's a fool. I think she knows very well what she's about.

WINTON: What do you mean?

MRS. WINTON: It would be no use to say. You wouldn't understand, and you're so silly about the girl that you would take it the wrong way. You never can understand that women can't go about things as men do, and you think if they use a little finesse with themselves, they are doing something criminal and false.

WINTON: What do you mean by using finesse with themselves?

MRS. WINTON: I said you wouldn't understand. (*She follows him with laughing eyes, still wet with tears, as he rises and walks up and down the room.*) Women not only have to hoodwink men; they have to hoodwink themselves too. A girl—such a girl as Philippa—enjoys putting herself through her paces before a man; she likes to exploit her emotions, and see how he takes it; though she may not know it!

WINTON: I believe women think worse of women than men do.

MRS. WINTON: Oh. that may be.

WINTON: But in this case your subtlety has deceived you. I would stake my life that Philippa meant no more by what she did than pity for the man. He happens to be a pretty decent fellow—as men go. If he were like the carrion some men are, I think I should go after him and—bury him.

He stops before his wife, and looks down furiously into her face.

MRS. WINTON: Don't bury *me*, my dear!

WINTON: Don't laugh, then. It's a shame to laugh.

MRS. WINTON: At such a fool as Philippa? Really, you're all alike, you men! Mr. Camp wouldn't let me laugh, either, at first. Why shouldn't women be all alike, too? At any rate, whatever Philippa fancies, I hope you can see that she's committed.

WINTON: How committed?

MRS. WINTON: Young ladies don't go about kissing young men without giving them a well-founded expectation that they are going to marry them; and if I were Mr. Camp I should not wait for a handkerchief on the point of a parasol. I should go down to the beach, and do a little of the thinking myself.

WINTON: Camp won't.

MRS. WINTON: No; he is peculiar too. There is a pair of them. I shouldn't have thought it of him. Outside of my own family, no one has made me feel so much like a reprobate. He wasn't so abrupt as you are, my dear, but he was quite as severe in his way. Really, it makes one wish to talk the matter over with a human being or two.

WINTON: Did you ask Camp to stay to dinner?

MRS. WINTON: Provisionally, I did. Everything has to be done provisionally in this house till Philippa has thought it over. If she comes to an unfavorable conclusion, I don't suppose Mr. Camp would wish to stay.

WINTON: I suppose not. I must go up and take a little of the dust off. Why, Philippa!

He starts back from the door, which he was about to lay his hand upon, when it opens, and Philippa enters from the hall.

PHILIPPA, *to her uncle:* Mr. Camp—where is he?

WINTON: I haven't seen him, Philippa—

MRS. WINTON: How long did you expect him to wait? He's gone—

PHILIPPA, *with a start, turning to her aunt:* Gone?

MRS. WINTON: Ah, I see you would have been sorry! He's gone to look after a four-masted schooner that he saw in the offing. He hadn't the courage to look after a handkerchief on the point of a parasol.

PHILIPPA: I knew you would make him tell you. Well, I don't care! (*In proof of her indifference the tears come into her eyes, and her chin trembles. She controls herself in turning again to her uncle.*) I don't know whether I have done exactly right, Uncle Fred. Aunt Elizabeth, might I see Uncle Frederick alone? I wish to ask him something.

MRS. WINTON: By all means! I seem to be turned out of the room on *all* occasions. You won't mind my listening at the key-hole?

She looks back laughing from the door before she disappears.

PHILIPPA, *with the severity of looking at her aunt still in her eyes:* Why does she think it is such a laughing matter?

WINTON: I rather think she regards *you* as the laughing matter, Philippa.

PHILIPPA: Do *you?*

WINTON: No; we're of the same family, Philippa, and that's more than being of the same sex, as far as understanding each other goes.

PHILIPPA: Ah, if it were only you, Uncle Fred, that I had to talk with! (*After a moment's pause*) Uncle Fred, what sort of man is Mr. Camp?

WINTON: Bless my soul! How should I know? He's what you see, I suppose: he's amiable—and kind—and amusing. I think he's an uncommonly clever fellow. He's sure to get on. He works hard at his lawing. Every one likes him, I believe; at any rate, I never heard any one say a word against him.

PHILIPPA: Yes, but what is he *really?* What is his life?

WINTON: His life? Who knows what another man's life is? I shrink from knowing my own!

PHILIPPA: And ought a girl to marry a man whose life she doesn't know, and make it *her* life, as she must if she truly loves him?

WINTON: No, my child, I don't think she ought. But, as a general thing, I should say she had to. She's no worse off than he is, though.

PHILIPPA: Yes she is, if she has told him everything, and he has told her nothing.

WINTON: Ah, in that case, yes.

PHILIPPA, *with tears:* Uncle, why are you so cold, so hard with me? You say you understand me: do you blame me for anything?

WINTON: Well, no, not blame; that isn't the word. But you're very impulsive, Philippa, and impulse—is always liable to misinterpretation.

PHILIPPA: I know what you mean; Aunt Bessie has been telling you, and laughing at me. But it was not an impulse; it was a decision.

WINTON: Oh! Now I *don't* understand, I believe.

PHILIPPA: No, in this case it isn't sufficient to be of the same family. But my mother, if she were alive, would understand, and she wouldn't keep me from opening my heart to her.

WINTON: Open your heart to me, Philippa! I shall listen with all the sympathy in the world. You know that I have always encouraged you to think for yourself, and act for yourself. I don't believe in the Chinese foot-binding of women, physically or psychically. I like your notions, and I will stand by you. Now go on and tell me whatever you wish.

PHILIPPA: No, I can't, now. The time is past. I shall have to think for myself, and act for myself.

WINTON: And you're sure you're not cold and hard with *me*, now?

PHILIPPA: No, no, Uncle Fred. But you understand how a thing can be possible one instant, and impossible the next. You can understand that, can't you?

WINTON: I can understand how it can be so with you, Philippa. It may be queer, what you do; but it won't be wrong. Act for yourself, and if you need any standing-by, let me do it for you.

PHILIPPA, *a little absently, a little ruefully, as she goes out*: Thank you, Uncle Fred.

Winton remains looking anxiously after her, and then begins walking meditatively up and down. A tap at the sliding-doors arrests him. They open, and Mrs. Winton peers in.

MRS. WINTON: Merely to say that Mr. Camp is coming up the road towards the house. Oh, you're alone! (*She comes in, and shuts the doors behind her.*) Well?

WINTON, *briefly*: She says it was a decision, and not an impulse.

MRS. WINTON: Her fond farewell?

WINTON: Yes—or fond *au revoir*. I suppose she meant that. It wasn't put into words.

MRS. WINTON: I thought so from the beginning. A girl is always a girl, even when she's a Philippa.

WINTON: What do you mean?

MRS. WINTON: You will see. But I'll go on duty now, and relieve you. I'll see Mr. Camp.

WINTON: Not at all. I'm going to see Camp myself. I want to talk with him.

MRS. WINTON: Well, you mustn't. He doesn't want to see *you*. He went away to avoid seeing you. He said he was in a very tender condition, and if you jarred upon him, it might be fatal.

WINTON: I guess Camp will have to take the risk. I'm in a very tender condition myself, and I'm in danger too, and I'll have to risk it. But I don't believe we shall hurt each other, and I believe we shall help Philippa.

MRS. WINTON: Are you going to give her away?

WINTON: Give her away?

MRS. WINTON: Give him a hint—tell him it was a decision?

WINTON: Certainly not. I'm not sure that it was a decision—in that sense of the term. She meant that it was deliberate.

MRS. WINTON: Stuff!

WINTON: As much as you please. But if there's to be any giving away, it's Camp who's got to do it.

MRS. WINTON: Very well, then, I hope there won't be any throwing away, either. Mr. Camp is one chance in a thousand.

WINTON: So is Philippa—in a million.

MRS. WINTON: I hope you'll make him think so. But I wash my hands of it. (*There is a ring at the door, and Mrs. Winton prepares to make her escape; but she launches a Parthian arrow at her husband over her shoulder as she flies.*) And don't flatter yourself that you understand Philippa, or that you are helping her when you are helping her to do what she wants, or that you are even pleasing her. That is all.

WINTON, *shaking hands with Camp*: Ah, glad to see you, Camp. I know all about it, and I am not going to jar upon you if I can avoid it.

MR. CAMP: Then Mrs. Winton—

WINTON: Has told me. So has Philippa, for that matter.

MR. CAMP: And their stories agree?

WINTON: Wonderfully, as far as the facts are concerned.

MR. CAMP: That's a good deal. I wish you could say as much for their opinions. I didn't find Miss Winton on the beach.

WINTON: No; she had come up here, I fancy, to find you.

MR. CAMP: Do you mean it?

WINTON: Yes; she wishes to see you again.

MR. CAMP: Oh! (*After a moment*) Would you allow yourself to become the sport of reviving hopes for that reason?

WINTON: Well, I don't know, really. It seems to me that the thing depends very much upon yourself—what you are. Camp, what are you? What sort of fellow?

MR. CAMP: Bless me, how should I know?

WINTON: Of course. But are you frank? Are you capable of being frank?

MR. CAMP: It's difficult.

WINTON: But not impossible?

MR. CAMP: If there were something to be gained by it—

WINTON: Philippa's to be gained by it. And to tell you the truth, I don't believe she's to be gained by anything else. And it must be the real thing.

MR. CAMP: The real thing? And you don't call that jarring? How far must it go?

WINTON: All lengths, I should say. If you were not entirely frank, and she found it out afterwards, I should say it might be unpleasant.

MR. CAMP: And if she found everything out at once, that might be unpleasant too!

WINTON: It's a risk you've got to take, my dear fellow. It's quite worth while, it seems to me. Philippa's worth while.

MR. CAMP, thoughtfully: Ah, there can't be two minds about that—in me, at least. Have you any idea what she is going to want me to be frank about?

WINTON: I have a general idea, yes.

MR. CAMP: But you don't feel authorized to impart it?

WINTON: I think she would prefer to impart it —that is, she would think it better. And I wish to stand by Philippa. I know she's queer, but I think she's generally right. She's noble, and she's high-minded. I won't say any more; I'm not sure I ought to have said so much. But we all like you, and I couldn't help wishing you luck. The affair is in your own hands. If you don't feel equal to it, why I really think you had better go away.

MR. CAMP: Go away?

WINTON: Yes: what is the use of seeing her again? I could make it right with her—that is, I could account for your going away.

MR. CAMP: I don't think I shall go away, Mr. Winton.

WINTON: I hoped you wouldn't; but I thought I would give you the chance. I will send her to you. She wishes to have some serious talk with you.

MR. CAMP: Oh! At once?

WINTON: Why, hadn't you better have it over?

MR. CAMP: If it were well over, yes. But if one is dead, it is for such a long time! Well!

WINTON, wringing his hand: All right, then. Courage—and candor!

MR. CAMP: I'll try to have the candor, even if I haven't the courage.

WINTON: I'm not sure but Philippa would prefer that.

He leaves Camp sunk in a kind of daze, in the chair he has mechanically taken at the corner of the table, his elbow leant upon it, and his head resting on his hand. He starts to his feet at the light approach of Philippa, who glides in at the door which her uncle has left ajar.

MR. CAMP: I—I beg your pardon. I—didn't notice you—at first. Perhaps I oughn't to be here, but—Mr. Winton said there was something you wished to say to me.

PHILIPPA: Sit down, Mr. Camp. I hoped there was something you wished to say to me.

She sits down at the corner of the table farthest from him.

MR. CAMP: About—

PHILIPPA, gently: Yourself.

MR. CAMP: Do you think there's anything I could say to my advantage?

PHILIPPA: You musn't joke! I'm very serious.

MR. CAMP: So am I. If I don't seem so, I assure you it isn't because I don't feel so. Seriously, I will tell you anything you ask.

PHILIPPA: Must I ask? I hoped, down there by the sea, that if we met again you would have thought there was something you would tell me without asking. Why were you so indifferent when I told you that I had been engaged?

MR. CAMP: Why? I suppose I didn't care.

PHILIPPA: That is what I understood when you said a man always liked to be the first. And it doesn't all of it suggest anything?

MR. CAMP: Well, I can't say—

PHILIPPA: Then I will ask you something. Were you ever in love, before? (He hesitates.) I told you I had been!

MR. CAMP: Why, of course! One is always more or less in love. That is, not dangerously, but provisionally, potentially. People take one's fancy; and it's over in a day—or a week—or a summer. You can't govern your fancy. But it doesn't really mean anything. I suppose there's a certain amount of flirtation has to go on.

PHILIPPA: Yes. Should you like to think of my flirting with some one for a day, a week, a summer?

MR. CAMP: Well, no. And I can't imagine it.

But with a man, you know, that sort of thing is different.

PHILIPPA: You mean that you flirt with other men?

MR. CAMP: No, I didn't mean that, exactly.

PHILIPPA: Oh, then you flirt with women. Do you respect the women you flirt with?

MR. CAMP: It isn't a question of respect. It's— Well, then, no! One doesn't respect them! But still, I can't think there's so great harm in it. That is— Yes, it isn't the thing, quite. No, you can't say you respect the woman you flirt with. But it's even, as far as that goes. She doesn't respect you, either. Why, Philippa—I beg your pardon—

PHILIPPA: Oh, call me Philippa. What difference does it make? I can call you Leonard.

MR. CAMP: Will you?

PHILIPPA: Since you say you don't respect the women you flirt with, you can't mind what I do.

MR. CAMP: Well, I don't see the relation, exactly.

PHILIPPA: No, not now. And you say they never came to anything, the flirtations?

MR. CAMP: No-o-o—except—once. Philippa, I was once engaged before, too. The thing is so perfectly dead and gone that I can hardly believe in it. She was an abominable flirt.

PHILIPPA: Is that what she says of you?

MR. CAMP, *reproachfully*: Philippa! (*After a moment's reflection*) I don't blame her altogether. I was to blame, too. Yes, I think I was quite as much to blame as she was. These things are not done from one side only. But—I was very much in love with her at last. I'll say that for myself. It's about the only thing I can say.

PHILIPPA, *closing her eyes to a fine line, as if trying to see the affair critically*: The same kind of love that you feel—that you say you feel—for me?

MR. CAMP: Well— (*He stops, and then with a burst.*) I might distinguish, but I was certainly in love with her. It's the only saving grace about it.

PHILIPPA, *as before*: But you didn't respect her?

MR. CAMP: I loved her. There's no question of anything else in it.

PHILIPPA: There is with a woman. Do you think she would have liked to know that you loved her without respecting her?

MR. CAMP: I don't believe she would have minded.

He takes out his handkerchief and mops his forehead. He rises and looks out of the window. Then he comes back, and faces her stand-ing. She remains seated, playing with the leaves of the book half open on the table. There is a silence.

PHILIPPA: Is she living?

MR. CAMP: Yes, she's living.

PHILIPPA: Where?

MR. CAMP: In New York. (*Philippa remains with downcast eyes, turning the leaves of the book with the fingers of one hand.*) But she's married, and has two or three children. It's all as if it never had been. You need never know her—you wouldn't be likely to meet her—

PHILIPPA, *opening her eyes and looking up at him*: Had you meant to tell me about your engagement?

MR. CAMP, *anxiously*: Yes, certainly—

PHILIPPA: When?

MR. CAMP: I don't know. I wished to tell you at once—

PHILIPPA: Before I told you?

MR. CAMP: I thought it would do any time. I didn't see it very seriously. And then, when I found how seriously you looked at it in your own case, I couldn't—at once. (*With a deep breath*) I think that's the truth of the matter.

PHILIPPA: After we were engaged, and I couldn't break with you, or when we were married, and I couldn't help myself, you meant to tell me.

MR. CAMP: Well—

He stops.

PHILIPPA: And if *I* hadn't told you till then, what would you have thought of me?

MR. CAMP: Thought of you?

PHILIPPA: Shouldn't you have blamed me?

MR. CAMP, *after a pause, desperately*: Yes; I should have blamed you. But in my own case, I don't believe, honestly, that I thought so far as that. My hopes were not so confident—

PHILIPPA, *looking down again as before*: When I kissed you, I meant to marry you—

MR. CAMP: Ah, Philippa!

PHILIPPA: I only wanted to go away and think. If you had come after me to the beach—

MR. CAMP: I didn't dare, after you forbade me. If I could only have imagined— Surely you don't blame me for that!

PHILIPPA: Oh, no! I don't blame you for anything. (*Jumping to her feet, and flinging the book across the room*) That is all, Mr. Camp: you can go, now.

MR. CAMP: No, now I *can't* go, Miss Winton.

He has risen, too.

PHILIPPA: Then I will go. (*She dashes out of the room, but almost immediately returns.*) May I ask *why* you can't go, when I wish you to?

MR. CAMP: How can I go when you are feeling that you have been unjust to me?

PHILIPPA: *I* unjust? *How* unjust?

MR. CAMP: I will leave you to say. Or now, if you like, I will go away without troubling you to say, for I see that you *have* the feeling.

PHILIPPA: This is trifling.

MR. CAMP: Do you think I am trifling with you?

PHILIPPA: No. (*After a moment*) But if you were not trifling, you would tell me how you think I have been unjust to you.

MR. CAMP: No, you know I wouldn't. I couldn't.

They stand looking at each other for an appreciable time before Philippa speaks.

PHILIPPA: The worst thing was your confessing you might not have told me until after we were married.

MR. CAMP: There's something worse than that. I would have very gladly never told you. I'm not proud of it.

PHILIPPA: Oh, don't think you can move me by owning the truth!

MR. CAMP: I don't. I saw that the truth didn't move you before. But I'm not anxious to move you. I'm not on trial now.

PHILIPPA: I am not on trial, either. You accusation doesn't put me on trial.

MR. CAMP: My accusation?

PHILIPPA: I know what you mean. That I had no right to make you speak of yourself. But I had.

MR. CAMP: Yes—in a certain case.

PHILIPPA: I should despise myself if I pretended not to know what you mean. You mean that if I didn't intend to forgive you, no matter what you said, I had no right to make you speak. Is that what you mean? (*Camp makes as if to speak, but does not speak.*) I know that you could say I had encouraged you, and that when I began to feel myself caring for you, I ought to have tried to find out what sort of person you were. But how could I do that? Of course you will say that you couldn't tell me at the start—

MR. CAMP: I don't know that I shall say that—or anything. My trial's over. I've been condemned and executed.

PHILIPPA: Who condemned you?

MR. CAMP: You told me I might go.

PHILIPPA: And you didn't go. So it's the same as if you hadn't been condemned. (*She waits a moment as if for him to answer.*) Then if every-thing is at an end, and you have no more to say, I don't see why we should continue the conversation. (*She goes out, but comes back at once.*) I suppose you will think that I got you down here to trap you, and humiliate you, and then cast you off.

MR. CAMP: I might be base enough to think that, but not base enough to think it of you, Philippa.

PHILIPPA: Oh! And you think that my telling you of my own engagement was simply a ruse to get you to tell me of yours?

MR. CAMP: I don't think even that.

PHILIPPA: You know that I never dreamed of asking you anything about yourself; and I went down to the beach admiring your magnanimity, and all at once it occurred to me that you had some good reason for it. I dare say you blame me for suspecting you, although you were guilty.

MR. CAMP: I've told you I don't blame you for anything.

PHILIPPA: It's all very well to say that. (*She stops, with a dazed air.*) I know what makes you despise me. It was my kissing you.

MR. CAMP: Phillipa, will you believe one thing I say? I hold that kiss sacred. It came from your angelic goodness of heart—from your—

PHILIPPA: Oh, it's too late, it's too late! I suppose you think I hurried back to make sure of you, because I had kissed you, when—when the sight of you would be a perpetual reminder of it.

MR. CAMP: My imagination doesn't rise to such heights as that.

PHILIPPA: Then, what is it you accuse me of?

MR. CAMP: Nothing.

PHILIPPA, *after a moment*: You—you are very generous.

MR. CAMP: Ah, even *your* saying that doesn't make me believe it; and I should like very much to go away believing something to my credit. Come, Philippa! I told you the worst I know about my past. I've tried to be honest, and I think I've succeeded pretty well, though it isn't easy for me. I know I've made myself thoroughly detestable in the attempt. I wish you'd say, before I go, that you think I've been honest with you. Will you?

PHILIPPA: I think you've been honest.

MR. CAMP: Thank you. Before I go I wish to ask you something else. Do you think *you've* been honest?

PHILIPPA: I?

MR. CAMP: Oh, you've been honest enough with

me—terribly honest. You've told me, if not just in so many words, that you think I meant to act a base and cowardly part—

PHILIPPA: No—

MR. CAMP: You've made me feel that you do. And you have made me feel that there must be something very squalid in me if I could flirt with a woman and become engaged to her when I didn't respect her; and I haven't even the poor consolation of thinking that I broke with her. She broke with me, or else I should have married her.

PHILIPPA: I don't think that is bad.

MR. CAMP: Ah, now you are beginning to be honest—honest with yourself; and that's what I wished you to be. *I'm* not worth your honesty, but *you* are. And now, tell me! Don't you think that to insist upon our having lived up to each other's ideals before we knew each other would be something a little unreal, a little factitious, a little affect—

PHILIPPA: Mr. Camp!

MR. CAMP: Oh, I've had glimpses, visions, during this bad quarter of an hour, of possibilities of character—conduct—that I never dreamt of before. I've imagined going through life worthily, because *you* wished it. My ideals have been lower than yours; I'm ashamed of it, I'm glad of it, for I like to look up to you. But don't you think that for you to demand that they should have been the same before I had your example would be something you fancied you ought to do, rather than *felt* you ought to do—would be a bit of pose?

PHILIPPA: Pose! Now, *now* I see that you *do* despise me, and that you have, all along! But you *know* that I abhor pose more than anything, and that rather—rather than have you believe I was capable of it, I would have you think I had never cared at all for your—being engaged before! *(Then, with a start, realizing what she has said)* That is, I don't mean—I mean—I mean—

MR. CAMP: I know what you mean, Philippa; and don't be afraid that I shall presume upon what you've merely said. I'm going, now; I won't trouble you any longer, but I shall always remember just how you looked, standing there by that table, with your head down, and your hand hanging at your side, and I shall wish—I shall wish—I had asked you to let me take your hand! *(Without lifting her head, she puts her hand out to him.)* Ah! Thank— Philippa—Philippa, may I kiss—your hand?

PHILIPPA, *faintly*: Yes.

MR. CAMP, *stooping at her side, and lifting her hand to his lips*: Good-bye, Philippa.

He offers to release her hand, but she clings mechanically to his.

PHILIPPA: I have made you say you were ashamed—

MR. CAMP: You've made me tell the truth.

PHILIPPA: The worst?

MR. CAMP: I can't think of anything worse.

PHILIPPA: Thank you. I only wished to know the worst. And you're not going away hating me?

MR. CAMP: No; loving you more than ever!

PHILIPPA, *with her face turned to him, and her eyes averted*: Why—what are you—going for?

MR. CAMP: Philippa!

He throws his arms about her, and clasps her to him. She suddenly frees herself.

PHILIPPA: I left my parasol! I left it on the beach. And my handkerchief.

MR. CAMP: Was it tied on the point of it?

PHILIPPA: I tied it on, going down.

MR. CAMP: Oh!

He offers to seize her in his arms again, but she escapes to the door, which she opens.

PHILIPPA, *calling up the stairs*: Aunt Elizabeth! Uncle Fred!

They are heard instantly descending the stairs, and they appear at the door with surprising promptness.

MRS. WINTON: Well, Philippa?

MR. CAMP: Oh, nothing! Philippa left her parasol on the beach, and we are going to look for it.

PHILIPPA: I thought I would tell you that Mr. Camp—Leonard—will stay to dinner.

MRS. WINTON: Oh, I'm so glad—

MR. CAMP: Yes, we'll be back before dinner.

MRS. WINTON: Don't hurry.

WINTON, *to Philippa*: You don't look as if you were very anxious about your parasol, Philippa.

PHILIPPA, *dropping her eyes*: Oh no. It's the handkerchief on it.

MRS. WINTON, *to Mr. Camp*: Then it wasn't the four-masted schooner, after all?

MR. CAMP: Why, not altogether. But we can't say, you see, till we've found the parasol.

MRS. WINTON: Oh, you're waiting for that. Well, you can't be too cautious.

MR. CAMP: No, but as soon as we find it, we'll wave it over the top of the bank. That is, Philippa will. *(He looks round.)* But where is Philippa?

She has, in fact, slipped out of the room.

MRS. WINTON, *going to the window*: She's running down towards the beach. Hadn't you better follow her this time, Mr. Camp?

She turns to find that Camp has vanished too, and that she is alone with her husband.

WINTON: Well?

MRS. WINTON: Well, *that's* over.

WINTON: Did we find it so?

MRS. WINTON: At any rate, you can see that it's a thorough reconciliation.

WINTON: Yes, it's evidently a reconciliation. (*After a moment*) I'm not sure it's a solution.

MRS. WINTON: If we can't have solutions, we'd better have reconciliations.

THE END

An Indian Giver

[1897]

In "A Letter to the Publisher" (*Minor Dramas*) Howells facetiously explained that an Indian giver was "what we used to call a regretful benefactor, from the Indian custom of taking back a present rashly bestowed; but now that there are so few Indians left the phrase is no longer much used." Howells also admitted in this "Letter" that he felt some partiality for *An Indian Giver* "because I fancied it had more character in it than the others, and I think it might have its little effect in representation, if it were given a chance." Unfortunately, it never got its chance on the professional stage, although Minnie Maddern Fiske once wrote to Howells (July 29, 1900, Harvard Library) that she greatly enjoyed reading the play and that sometime she wanted to do a Howells play; perhaps *An Indian Giver* would have been a success.

In *An Indian Giver* Howells displays his usual emphasis on propriety, truth, and morality. James Fairford, as Mrs. Wenham states, is "truth itself." He deeply resents being forced to act a lie by Mrs. Inglehart, and as a man of moral character he fails utterly in dealing with people who do not have his scruples. Yet the audience can clearly see that Expediency pushes Truth aside and that as the curtain falls Truth is not too unhappy about it. The interdependence of truth and morality that Howells emphasized in *Criticism and Fiction* is shown in Mrs. Inglehart's untruthfulness in the whole matter. Mrs. Wenham states emphatically: ". . . you [Mrs. Inglehart] have done a wrong and wicked thing, and you'll have to answer for the consequences." In *The Rise of Silas Lapham* an immoral or untruthful action forms the core of a situation for which there must be atonement. In this play Mrs. Inglehart is made to suffer through Miss Lawrence's desire to play the game as long as she can, and this action contributes to the dramatic effectiveness of the whole.

It is worth noting, too, that the renewal of love between Fairford and the young widow is perfectly proper according to Howells' ethics, as he portrayed comparable situations in such novels as *A Modern Instance* and *The Son of Royal Langbrith*. Fairford had been in love with her *before* her marriage to Mr. Inglehart, but he immediately left her after that event, to return only at her suggestion. He did not stain his reputation by loving a married woman; hence, he could marry her when she was free again. In this play one also perceives Howells' dual conception of truth: there are truth and propriety, frequently twisted and abused in the social world of love and afternoon teas; and there are truth and morality, for which Howells reserves a conservative or even Puritanical view.

An Indian Giver[1]

MRS. INGLEHART: My dear! I will not hear another word. He is *yours!* The idea of making such a fuss about a little thing like the gift of a young man!

MISS LAWRENCE: It's only that I was afraid you might want him yourself, Mrs. Inglehart. It would make me unhappy if I thought you had deprived yourself of a cousin you might regret. They don't grow on every bush, I believe.

MRS. INGLEHART: Such as Jim don't, I'll admit. But I hope I know the duties of a hostess, and the first of them is to get a young lady visitor engaged if possible. You've never seen Jim, have you?

MISS LAWRENCE: Never. What's he like?

MRS. INGLEHART: Are you very fond of tall men?

MISS LAWRENCE: Is he tall?

MRS. INGLEHART: Not so very. I should say he had more breadth and thickness than length.

MISS LAWRENCE: Oh, I like them broad and thick.

MRS. INGLEHART: Do you? *(She speaks with a certain intonation of misgiving, and then she has the effect of pulling herself together.)* Do you like them brown-complexioned and dark-eyed?

MISS LAWRENCE: Is *he* brown-complexioned and dark-eyed?

MRS. INGLEHART: He's brown-complexioned and blue-eyed.

MISS LAWRENCE: Oh, that sort of contradiction is adorable. The blue eyes always have such a funny look in the dark face. I shall like him, I know. When's he coming?

MRS. INGLEHART: Any moment, now.

MISS LAWRENCE: Oh!

She jumps to her feet. Mrs. Inglehart remains seated, but leans forward to look in through the door at the clock in the hall, from the veranda where, with a pretense of sewing in her lap, she is talking with her guest. To the right of this hall the windows of a wide drawing-room open to the floor, and people come and go through them as

[1] The text used here is the Houghton, Mifflin and Company edition.

if they were doors. From the veranda, which extends around three sides of the house, broad steps descend to a driveway curving in front of it. Beyond the road green lawns, wept over by drooping white birches, slope to the red rocks that keep Mrs. Inglehart's place from the sea.

MRS. INGLEHART: Or not *moment*, exactly. He promised to be here by the half past four, but he probably won't come till the five-ten; it's only four now.

MISS LAWRENCE: Time enough to prink, then. *(She sinks back into her chair, provisionally.)* Is Mr. Fairford punctilious about prinking?

MRS. INGLEHART: I see you would dread that.

MISS LAWRENCE: I don't know that I should. They have to have *some* fault.

MRS. INGLEHART: And you think that is a fault?

MISS LAWRENCE: I can't say that I do. Do you?

MRS. INGLEHART, *with an air of great candor*: To tell you the truth, I don't believe Jim cares about women's dress.

MISS LAWRENCE: Then he is the most dangerous kind. He'll not see anything, but he'll feel everything. I shall have to dress at his nerves.

MRS. INGLEHART: It's clear that you've made your observations, my dear.

MISS LAWRENCE: By twenty-six, one has.

MRS. INGLEHART: I should never have dreamt twenty-six.

MISS LAWRENCE: I haven't dreamt it myself. In my dreams I'm still sixteen. It's only in my waking moments that I'm twenty-six.

MRS. INGLEHART, *thoughtfully*: You have courage.

MISS LAWRENCE: I have conviction. It's best to be honest—unless the man prefers lies.

MRS. INGLEHART: Don't they all?

MISS LAWRENCE: Nearly all. But if Mr. Fairford should happen to be the exception that doesn't, will you please tell him I *owned* to twenty-six, but you don't *know* how much older I really am?

MRS. INGLEHART, *with open admiration and covert alarm*: You're a strange girl!

MISS LAWRENCE: Will that scare him? Should you advise me to be less strange?

MRS. INGLEHART, *with a sigh*: No; he will like you so.

MISS LAWRENCE, *laughing*: What despair! Poor Mrs. Inglehart! You're sorry already you gave him to me! Well, you may have him back.

MRS. INGLEHART, *with noble constancy*: No, no; you're the very one for him.

MISS LAWRENCE: Then our only hope is that he isn't the one for me.

MRS. INGLEHART: You think I'm not in earnest. Well, then, the only thing left is to convince you by practical—

MISS LAWRENCE: Demonstration? I don't see how it can be done. You can't pass this young man along to me without consulting his inclinations. Has he very decided inclinations?

MRS. INGLEHART: Yes, he has. That was the trouble, I suppose.

MISS LAWRENCE: So there *was* trouble.

She smiles intelligently.

MRS. INGLEHART: It was a great while ago. It was before I was—there was any—Mrs. Inglehart. And there would be the same trouble again, if I were not—there were not any—Mrs. Inglehart. So it's best to have it over before it begins.

MISS LAWRENCE: I see what you mean. He's one of those terrible creatures who know their own minds; or think they do; and—may I be a little critical of your gift? I know it seems ungracious!

MRS. INGLEHART: Not in the least. People change their wedding-presents, even.

MISS LAWRENCE: I shouldn't wish to change the present; only the name: Jim! If it were only Jack, now, I should know what to do. The Jacks are all alike. They smoke, they flirt desperately, but they are very warm-hearted, and conceal a great deal of sentiment under the mask of cynicism—like Thackeray's men. They would do anything for you—at least any little thing like jumping overboard from a yacht to fish your hat up, or marrying a girl that you've found out is in love with them, and you think they ought, though you're dying for them yourself. You can twist them round your fingers; but it must be different with Jims. Jim! It suggests something rather grim; perhaps it's because it rhymes with it. Jim! I should say one's little arts, one's little airs and graces, would be thrown away on Jim. He sounds like a person of convictions: he sounds like a person of opinions, too, and very stiff ones. I suspect that Jim is serious, and he likes seriousness in women. He has ideas of home and a wife, and of being master in his own house. All that could be easily taken out of him if he were Jack, of course; but being Jim, it couldn't. He's masterful; I feel that he's masterful. He has all sorts of preconceived notions. He would be very domestic, and intellectual, and he would rather read to you than talk to you. He would want to respect you, and if you wouldn't let him, he would—make it hot for you. Yes, I know the type: adoring, domineering, devoted, and utterly intolerable.

MRS. INGLEHART, *who has been leaning forward more and more, and edging almost out of her chair, in her intentness*: You've met him! You know him! You've been letting me give myself away!

MISS LAWRENCE: Mr. Fairford? You? I? You've given *him* away, but not yourself, at least to me, Mrs. Inglehart. I never saw Mr. Fairford in my life. I never heard of him till I came here.

MRS. INGLEHART: Then I don't know but it's worse, for you've guessed him. How you must dread the idea of him!

MISS LAWRENCE, *thoughtfully*: I don't know. I rather like the notion of grappling with such a—problem. It would be fun to get the better of it.

MRS. INGLEHART: And if you got the worse?

MISS LAWRENCE: I don't believe I should get the worse. But now, really, hadn't I better go and prink, Mrs. Inglehart? I don't believe Jim would like to find me unprepared.

MRS. INGLEHART: No. Go and prink.

MISS LAWRENCE, *going in through the open door*: If he should happen to come before I get down, I know I can trust him with you, Mrs. Inglehart.

She vanishes, with a smile over her shoulder at Mrs. Inglehart, who remains silent and motionless, apparently insensible of her withdrawal, though she keeps a mechanical smile of parting on her face. Her mother enters from the door that Miss Lawrence has passed through.

MRS. WENHAM: When do you expect James, Lilly?

MRS. INGLEHART, *with a deep sigh*: Oh, any time, now. He said he would be here at half past four.

MRS. WENHAM: Then he'll *be* here at half past four.

MRS. INGLEHART: Yes, I suppose he will,— with his tiresome punctuality.

MRS. WENHAM: Tiresome? If there is one thing

more than another that I like in James Fairford, it *is* his punctuality. It's something that I can thoroughly sympathize with him in. If it had not been for *my* habits of punctuality, where would you have been at this moment, Lillian?

MRS. INGLEHART: Perhaps not born. But now don't preach, mother. Advise. You'll like it almost as well.

MRS. WENHAM, *looking doubtful, but as if assenting for argument's sake*: Well?

MRS. INGLEHART: What do you think of Miss Lawrence?

MRS. WENHAM: What do you mean by thinking? If you've been behaving foolishly in any way, and want me to help you out of it by blaming Miss Lawrence—

MRS. INGLEHART: Blame? Who's talking of blame? I simply wish to know if you don't think she's something of a cat.

MRS. WENHAM: Cat? How, cat?

MRS. INGLEHART: I mean very purring, and sly, and velvety.

MRS. WENHAM: No, not at all.

MRS. INGLEHART: Well, then, very sharp and clawy.

MRS. WENHAM: What have you been doing, Lillian?

MRS. INGLEHART: Nothing. I've been *un*doing. How do you think she and Jim will like each other?

MRS. WENHAM: What difference how they like each other?

MRS. INGLEHART: One doesn't want one's guests to be at sword's points.

MRS. WENHAM: I don't know why you asked her when you knew he was coming.

MRS. INGLEHART: I'm sure they'll like each other. He'll respect her. I respect her myself. She has a great deal of character, and all that; but I think there's a vein of coarseness in her. Yes, she *is* coarse. She has a bold way of talking about men. It may be very modern, and the rest of it, but I don't like it, and I don't think it's nice.

MRS. WENHAM: What men has she been talking about?

MRS. INGLEHART: Oh,—none.

MRS. WENHAM: What has she been saying about them?

MRS. INGLEHART: Oh,—nothing. But girls seem to say anything, nowadays. Especially old ones! How old am I, mother?

MRS. WENHAM: You're twenty-seven. You know that well enough.

MRS. INGLEHART: And she's twenty-six, and looks every day of it. (*Vaguely after a moment*) I'm sure *I* don't know how I came to ask her here.

MRS. WENHAM: Why do you say that, *now*? Have you been making a fool of yourself, Lilly?

MRS. INGLEHART: I *won't* be scolded in my own house, mother!

MRS. WENHAM: Very well, if you call it scolding. (*Mrs. Wenham sits very erect in her chair, and gathers all her dignity about her; Mrs. Inglehart rocks to and fro in a reckless and distraught manner.*) May I ask a simple question?

MRS. INGLEHART: I suppose so.

MRS. WENHAM: Are you going to accept James?

MRS. INGLEHART: What an idea! No!

MRS. WENHAM: Then, if it isn't scolding, allow me to say that he will have a right to feel trifled with. Your letting him come here, after what's past, is tantamount to your saying you would marry him if he asked you—

MRS. INGLEHART: Very well, I'll keep him from asking me, then. There are ways of staving men off.

MRS. WENHAM: Not such men as James Langton Fairford. You haven't forgotten how he behaved when you tried it before—before your marriage.

MRS. INGLEHART: That was a great while ago. I considered him a mere boy, and he might have known it.

MRS. WENHAM: He was two years older than you.

MRS. INGLEHART: And how old was I, pray? Nineteen! A perfect chit! That proves that he was a boy. And he was very rude. If he had been a little more—thoughtful, and patient! You know how it was, mother. After Jim's outrageous conduct, I had no alternative but to marry Mr. Inglehart; and I am not going to have it said, now, after all I've been through on his account, that I was in love with him all along, and married him the minute I decently could. I trust I have too much regard for Mr. Inglehart's memory for *that*.

MRS. WENHAM: Then allow me to say, my dear, without scolding, that I don't know what you're after.

MRS. INGLEHART: I'm not after anything, if you prefer such a common expression. It's Jim that's after me; and I shall not feel in the least bound to be overtaken. I have other plans for him.

MRS. WENHAM: Other plans?

MRS. INGLEHART: He may fancy Roberta Lawrence. I'm sure I don't see what men find in her, all of them. But if it's frankness, as they call it, I wish them joy of it. Of all the detestable hypocrites in *this* world commend me to a frank woman. Why, it's nothing but mask upon mask, all the way through!

MRS. WENHAM: Is this why you are so down upon the poor girl?

MRS. INGLEHART: Down upon her? Well, yes; it may be hate to throw such a husband as Jim Fairford in her way. At any rate I've set my heart upon making a match between them. That will let me out and it will be such fun.

She expresses her exultation in rather a lugubrious note of laughter, and tries to escape the severe gaze which her mother fixes upon her.

MRS. WENHAM: Just one word, Lillian Inglehart! Does Miss Lawrence know anything of this fine scheme?

MRS. INGLEHART: No. That is, I have put it out of my power to accept Jim Fairford by telling Roberta Lawrence she may have him if she can get him. If she does, or can, that's the end of it; and it's the end of it anyway.

MRS. WENHAM: Well, Lillian, if you are in earnest in what you say, you are certainly the greatest fool— But perhaps you consider this scolding?

MRS. INGLEHART: Not at all. I call it reasoning. Go on.

MRS. WENHAM: Oh, I've nothing more to say. But if you have really told the girl—if you have put this idea into her head, you have done a wrong and wicked thing, and you'll have to answer for the consequences. It would be no more than you deserve if James *did* take a fancy to her, and I hope he will; and if you have a spark of generosity in your composition, you at least won't try to prejudice him against her.

MRS. INGLEHART: You have such a low opinion of me, mother, that I wonder you associate with me at all. But now I'm going to wring your bosom by an act of the most exemplary magnanimity you ever heard of. A splendid idea has just occurred to me. I'm going to send Roberta down to see Jim first and receive him. She's upstairs now, prinking, and I'm going straight to my room, and I'm going to be so slow getting ready that she'll have to go down, and she can have him all to herself for a first impression; and a girl of twenty-six knows how to make hay while the sun shines. *Now* what do you say?

MRS. WENHAM, *going in*: Humph!

MRS. INGLEHART: You don't believe I'll do it?

MRS. WENHAM: I *know* you won't.

MRS. INGLEHART, *calling after her*: Well, I'm so glad you approve of the idea, mother. I only wish you could see how expressive your back looks, as you disappear in the distance. It's everything that's appreciative and flattering. (*As Mrs. Wenham vanishes*) Well, I don't care. (*In the course of her two dialogues a great many sewing materials and appliances have dropped about Mrs. Inglehart on the floor; as she now rises, her scissors fall out of her lap, and as she stoops to pick them up she is reminded of the other things.*) What a bother! (*When she has got them all in her lap again, she turns to the door, but is arrested by the sound of a quick, decided footfall on the steps of the veranda. She looks round over her shoulder, and in this very pretty and engaging attitude she meets the blue eyes flashing out of the brown face of James Fairford. He has a robust hand-bag in one hand and an umbrella in the other; over his arm hangs a light overcoat. He is dressed in summer stuffs, but in no concession to the negligence of summer fashion; his shirt is white; his firm legs are cased in trousers that descend to his black shoes; his whole keeping is that of a man who despises the appearance of recreation, and puts business before pleasure.*) James! (*Mrs. Inglehart's exclamation expresses mingled pleasure, surprise, and dismay. She drops all the things out of her lap again.*) What are you doing here at this unearthly hour? You said you would be here at half past four!

She sinks back into her chair.

FAIRFORD: It's half past four now.

He sits heavily down in one of the veranda chairs, plants his bag before him, and then pushes it away with his foot, while he mops his forehead with his handkerchief.

MRS. INGLEHART: Did you walk?

FAIRFORD: Do I seem to have driven? And in what?

MRS. INGLEHART, *hiding a smile with her hand*: I wonder how you found the way.

FAIRFORD: They told me at the station.

MRS. INGLEHART, *gracefully sinking into a chair*: Did they tell you that if it hadn't been for your ridiculous punctuality you'd have been met at the train? Now you see what comes of being on time!

FAIRFORD: I dare say they would if they could have spared a moment from the celebration of your charms and virtues. You seem to have cast your confounded glamour over the neighborhood, as usual.

MRS. INGLEHART: Yes, it's new to me. It must have been the telegraph girl!

FAIRFORD: There was a girl, and there was a telegraph. I didn't see them in combination.

MRS. INGLEHART: They were one, all the same. Yes, I may say she's quite an ardent admirer.

FAIRFORD: So am I, Lillian.

MRS. INGLEHART: Oh yes. But you mustn't say it. I hope you weren't rude to the poor girl on that account?

FAIRFORD: Why mustn't I say it? I've come here to say it!

MRS. INGLEHART, *to gain time*: But you've said it before—and you ought to be a little more diversified in your remarks.

FAIRFORD, *getting to his feet*: Lillian, how can you trifle with me so? Surely you know what I must understand—must hope—from your allowing me to come here to-day? (*He starts toward her and stumbles over his bag; he kicks the bag: Mrs. Inglehart laughs.*) Oh, laugh at me, make a fool of me!

MRS. INGLEHART: You know you don't approve of me, Jim; you know you don't.

FAIRFORD: I believe you can make me approve of you if you choose. And if you don't choose, I want you anyway.

MRS. INGLEHART: Oh! Do you think that's very logical?

FAIRFORD, *bitterly*: No, I'm not proud of it. As you say, it isn't logical; it isn't reasonable; but I always wanted you; I wanted you long ago, before you were married.

MRS. INGLEHART: Why do people say you don't know how to flatter? I'm sure it's enough to turn *my* poor head to have a man say he isn't proud of caring for me, but he keeps on doing it regardless of consequences.

FAIRFORD: You know what I mean. I never pretended that you were my ideal in character, but—

MRS. INGLEHART: I thought it was customary to tell the lady that she *was* your ideal. That's what they always tell *me*!

FAIRFORD: I don't care what other people tell you. *I* tell you the truth; and I tell you that you are *not* my ideal.

MRS. INGLEHART: What am I, then, if I'm not your ideal?

FAIRFORD: You're—you're my love. But you know that.

MRS. INGLEHART: I've heard you say so. But I'm not sure that I know it.

FAIRFORD: Not sure!

MRS. INGLEHART: You may not be sure of your own mind.

FAIRFORD: This is trifling, Lillian. What do you say to me?

MRS. INGLEHART: What can I say till I'm convinced you're in earnest?

FAIRFORD: And what will convince you? It seems to me that it's proof enough of my sincerity that I'm here to offer myself to you and to ask you to be my wife. Didn't you know that I was coming to do that? What else do you expect? Do you want me to say that you *are* my ideal, that you are everything in nature and character that I have dreamed of, and that I would not have you different?

MRS. INGLEHART: You might try it. I don't know what effect it would have.

FAIRFORD: You wish me to minister to your vanity, to fill your head with nonsense. Well, I will never do it!

MRS. INGLEHART: Then I don't see how it's going to end. You might at least say you believe I could *become* your ideal.

FAIRFORD: But if I don't believe you could, and therefore I renounce my ideal; if I throw it away, and I tell you that you, whatever you are, are a thousand times dearer than anything I've ever imagined? And yet you might be all that I've ever dreamed of in woman, prompt, energetic, constant in purpose, with a high sense of duty, a devotion to noble—

MRS. INGLEHART: Another James Fairford. What egotism! Yes, I could easily be all that, if I wanted to. The trouble is I couldn't want to.

FAIRFORD: I know it, and I don't ask it of you. I ask you merely to be yourself,—and to be mine.

MRS. INGLEHART: Do you think that's so little, that you say *merely*? Asking a woman to be herself and to be yours is asking everything.

FAIRFORD: Then don't be yourself; don't be anything but mine.

MRS. INGLEHART: Now you are beginning to talk sense—

FAIRFORD, *starting toward her*: And you consent —you—

A sound as of a lifting window above the veranda roof is heard, and then, after a moment, the voice of Miss Roberta Lawrence.

MISS LAWRENCE: Mrs. Inglehart!

MRS. INGLEHART, *in a low key to Fairford*: Oh,

good gracious, I forgot all about her! *Now* what am I to do? *(In a high key to Miss Lawrence)* Yes?

MISS LAWRENCE, *with a nervous laugh*: Oh, it *is* you. I thought, I wasn't sure it was you I heard. What time is it, please?

MRS. INGLEHART: It's a little after four—a qarter—twenty minutes—

MISS LAWRENCE: Then there's time, yet.

There is a sound of a closing window.

FAIRFORD: Why did you say that, Lillian? You know it's twenty minutes of five.

MRS. INGLEHART: That's a very charming girl, Jim—a Miss Roberta Lawrence. I want you to meet her. But perhaps you have met her already—

FAIRFORD: No; but that isn't the point. Why did you say twenty minutes? I wish you hadn't, dear!

MRS. INGLEHART: Well, it *is* twenty minutes—and more too; it's twenty minutes of five. You said so yourself. Now don't tease, but go and prettify. That's what *she's* doing—

The sound of the lifting window is heard again, and then the voice of Miss Lawrence.

MISS LAWRENCE: Mrs. Inglehart! Are you still there?

MRS. INGLEHART, *in a high key*: Yes! *(In a low key to Fairford)* Now you must go! It's a shame for you to stay here eavesdropping. And making me, too; and you so conscientious! 'Sh!

MISS LAWRENCE: I'm in something of a dilemma. I don't know whether it had better be the green, or the blue.

MRS. INGLEHART: Oh—the blue, dear; or no, the green—blue, I mean. *(In a low key to Fairford)* Now you have spoilt everything, and disgraced me before my guest. I can never forgive you!

FAIRFORD: How have I done that? She has said nothing that compromises either of you—

MRS. INGLEHART: You've let her give herself away. You know that it's for you she's choosing between blue and green.

FAIRFORD: Bless my soul, how should I know such a thing?

MRS. INGLEHART: Don't you suppose I told her you were coming? And when she comes down and finds you here you won't be capable of seeming to have come just that instant.

FAIRFORD: If she asks—

MRS. INGLEHART: As if she would ask! She is too high-spirited, too noble-minded to go prying about; but it will kill her, all the same. You don't know how a girl like Roberta Lawrence, so frank herself, and so unsuspicious, will take such a thing. Of course, if it was I, I could laugh it off; but she will think that I did it purposely; she won't show it, but she will never believe that I was as innocent as she was in the matter.

FAIRFORD: It seems to me you're not painting a very frank and unsuspicious character.

MRS. INGLEHART: I mean I should in her place. You know what I mean. But if you prefer to vex me— She'll be asking something else in another minute!

FAIRFORD: But what do you want me to do?

MRS. INGLEHART: You must *think* what I want you to do. You have got me into this trouble, by your ridiculous promptness, and you must get me out.

FAIRFORD: Then let me go to my room, and I can't overhear anything more.

MRS. INGLEHART: Oh, you think it's so simple as that, do you? Wait a minute—I have it! You must go away! And you must come back in about ten minutes or so, as if you hadn't been here at all. And you must apologize for being late; say you missed the train, or something like that, and—

FAIRFORD, *sitting doggedly down*: No, I can't do anything of the kind.

MRS. INGLEHART: You can't?

FAIRFORD: Well, then, I won't. It would be acting a lie.

MRS. INGLEHART: You accuse me of wishing you to lie.

FAIRFORD: I don't think you do it knowingly. But, Lillian, you must see—

MRS. INGLEHART: 'Sh! There, she's putting up her window again!

MISS LAWRENCE, *from her window*: I've decided not to dress at him, Mrs. Inglehart. I am going to be perfectly passive, and let fate take its course. I'm going to wear my silver-gray.

MRS. INGLEHART: Perfect! *(In a low tone to Fairford, desperately)* It's too late for you to go away now. You might as well stay!

FAIRFORD: But I don't understand. Why should Miss Lawrence dress at me? Have *you* dressed at me, Lillian? You look heavenly in that—thing you've got on; I don't know what it is.

MRS. INGLEHART: Oh, much pleasure your compliments give me, when I know what a cold, hollow heart they come from! I may dress for you, but you won't gratify me in the smallest thing. Suppose your going away *does* have the appearance of deceit? Is a mere *appearance* so very killing, when it's for such a good object? Oh, Jim!

Do help me out! Think of the poor girl's feelings if she comes down and finds you here! She'll *know* you overheard her. If you really cared for me—

FAIRFORD, *rising with a groan, and gathering his bag up for going*: And if I go—if I do this against my reason and conscience, what shall you do with me when I come back?

MRS. INGLEHART: You'll be so interested in Miss Lawrence you won't care.

FAIRFORD: That won't do, Lillian. I shall want my answer when I come back. Will you promise it?

MRS. INGLEHART: It's very mean of you to make conditions! I'll *listen* to you. But I won't even do that if you stay. And if you think I'm asking you to act a lie, just think what a lie you've been making *me* act.

FAIRFORD: I? How?

MRS. INGLEHART: By letting me see you before you saw her, when I promised mamma I wouldn't.

FAIRFORD: But why did you promise that? What—

MRS. INGLEHART: That has nothing to do with it. A promise is a promise, and sacred. Will you go? And when you come back, and find Miss Lawrence here, will you ask after me as if you hadn't met me?

FAIRFORD: No, certainly not. I can't carry the deceit as far as that.

MRS. INGLEHART: Not to enable me to keep my promise? Very well, then, that shows that you don't trust me, and if you don't trust me, you can't care for me.

FAIRFORD: I don't trust you in the least, and I care all the world for you. For heaven's sake, Lillian, be candid with me, for once, and tell me what all this coil is! I know that whatever you've got in your head, there's nothing but truth in your heart, and if you would only be guided by that—

MRS. INGLEHART, *apparently fascinated by the idea*: Well, I will. I'll tell you all about it. You see that we were talking about your coming, and I said to Roberta Lawrence— 'Sh! There's her step! She's coming out of her room—she's on the stairs! Run, James, if you love me!

She pushes him towards the veranda steps, and without waiting to see him vanish round the corner of the house, she turns, and flies through the long window into the drawing-room, while Miss Lawrence emerges from the hallway, and Mrs. Wenham advances from the veranda on the side of the house opposite

that which has just hidden Fairford from view.

MISS LAWRENCE: Mrs. Inglehart! *(To Mrs. Wenham)* I thought Mrs. Inglehart was here!

MRS. WENHAM: And I thought I heard talking. But I must have dreamed it. I seem to have dozed over my book.

MISS LAWRENCE: Perhaps you heard me calling down to her. I was consulting her about Mr. Fairford's taste in colors. Isn't he very late?

She looks in at the clock in the hall, and Mrs. Wenham looks in too.

MRS. WENHAM: Yes, it's nearly five, and he promised to be here at half past four. Something must have detained him; he's usually so prompt.

MISS LAWRENCE, *smiling*: Yes, terribly prompt, I believe. At least that's the impression Mrs. Inglehart gives of him.

The ladies have seated themselves, and Miss Lawrence, reclining in her chair, indifferently studies the effect of a ring on her left hand.

MRS. WENHAM, *looking at her over her glasses*: You've never met my nephew, I believe?

MISS LAWRENCE: No; and I've no idea how he'll like me. You know it's very important he should like me. Mrs. Inglehart has given him to me.

MRS. WENHAM, *dryly*: Yes, I have been scolding Lillian for her nonsense. He is not hers to give.

MISS LAWRENCE: Oh! To keep, then!

MRS. WENHAM: I am not so sure. Miss Lawrence, I know that you are a very frank person—

MISS LAWRENCE: Some people say merely brutal.

MRS. WENHAM: No matter! I feel that I can speak frankly with you. Don't trust my daughter!

MISS LAWRENCE: This *is* frank.

MRS. WENHAM: She acts upon impulses that she regrets. She is in love with James Fairford, I believe, and I know that he is in love with her. He was, before she married Mr. Inglehart, and I think she was with him; but the affair never came to anything, because—because— It was Lillian's fault; she couldn't be serious with him.

MISS LAWRENCE: And now? Has he got over wanting her to be serious, or has she become so?

MRS. WENHAM: Lillian will never be serious— at least not like other people; and that is why I feel it my duty to be serious with you. No one knows Lillian as I do. If she saw that any one else wanted James, she would move heaven and earth to get him herself.

MISS LAWRENCE, *laughing*: Really, what you say rather inclines me to try for him. I should like to see Mrs. Inglehart moving heaven and earth.

MRS WENHAM: Don't, my dear! I should simply leave the house. There isn't a thing she wouldn't do if she saw you wanted him. (*Miss Lawrence laughs more and more.*) I know what nonsense she has been talking to you, and I made her promise, just to punish her, that she would let you meet him first, and have a chance to—I mean that she should be made to suffer a little for her wicked folly—

MISS LAWRENCE: Through some finesse of mine? Wouldn't that be rather too much theatre?

MRS. WENHAM: Yes, I don't know what she wouldn't do in her jealousy; for she'd be frantically, blindly, madly jealous if she thought he cared for you the least bit.

MISS LAWRENCE: Poor Mrs. Inglehart! I should like to see her jealous. It doesn't seem in character. But I'm greatly obliged to you for securing me the first innings. How do you propose to manage it?

MRS. WENHAM: That I shall leave entirely to Lillian. I suppose that as she's out of the way, and he's expected momentarily, she's actually keeping her word, and—

MISS LAWRENCE: I'm sitting here to intercept Mr. Fairfold on his way into the house! Isn't it rather cold-blooded? But I don't mind! You don't think he could manage to escape me, somehow?

MRS. WENHAM: I shall be sitting here too; and I dare say Lillian has given directions where he's to be received.

MISS LAWRENCE: Heroic Mrs. Inglehart! I begin to quake a little. Do you know, if I had been *she*, I should have broken my word. (*After a thoughtful moment*) If one were really meditating an assault upon Mr. Fairford's affections, what should you say was his weakest side, Mrs. Wenham?

MRS. WENHAM: James? (*Proudly*) He *has* no weak side.

MISS LAWRENCE: Oh, I didn't say weak, I said *weakest*. Where is he least strong?

MRS. WENHAM: Except for his inconceivable folly in regard to Lillian, I should say that James Fairford was equally strong at all points. He is truth itself; promptitude, sincerity, justice, honor—

MISS LAWRENCE, *with a deep breath*: He *is* formidable.

MRS. WENHAM: He despises anything like double-dealing, or prevarication, or even evasion. He will admire *you*, Miss Lawrence.

MISS LAWRENCE: Oh, thank you! I begin to have my doubts. (*Mrs. Inglehart appears at one of the long veranda windows, and looks through them, with her hands lifted to either side of the casement.*) Oh, come out, Mrs. Inglehart!

MRS. INGLEHART: It's very tempting. But I can't, and I've got to take my mother away too, and consult about some little changes in receiving Mr. Fairford. You must keep him here until I come.

MISS LAWRENCE: I wish he were here now. If he could only see you there as you're standing now! I wish you could see yourself, and you'd agree with me that there was never anything *quite* so graceful as that pose of yours.

MRS. INGLEHART: You must tell him about it when he does come; that will be such a nice pose for *you*.

MISS LAWRENCE, *rising and bobbing a courtesy to Mrs. Inglehart in acknowledgment of her little dig*: Thank you, so much! (*To Mrs. Wenham, who joins her daughter*) And you're actually going to leave me alone with Mr. Fairford!

MRS. WENHAM: You'll be in the best of hands, my dear. Remember what I told you.

MISS LAWRENCE: I shan't forget such a charge as that!

MRS. INGLEHART: A conspiracy? (*She looks from one to the other; then over her shoulder, as she vanishes within.*) Be sure to keep him; tell him he can't go to his room just yet.

MISS LAWRENCE, *calling after her*: Oh, I'll *keep* him. (*When Mrs. Inglehart and her mother are out of sight, she bows herself forward in silent laughter, and when she lifts her face out of her hands again, she confronts Fairford, who is stealthily mounting the veranda steps, with a manner the reverse of his earlier brusqueness and severity. At sight of him Miss Lawrence springs to her feet, and comes gayly toward him with outstretched hand.*) Mr. Fairford? Miss Lawrence! Mrs. Inglehart has commissioned me to welcome you in her place, and to keep you here, while she and Mrs. Wenham are taking counsel together about your room. Won't you sit down till they come?

FAIRFORD, *backing upon a chair, with his bag in his hand and his overcoat on his arm*: Thank you.

> *He falls into the chair and stares helplessly at her.*

MISS LAWRENCE: Was your train late, or did

you take a later one? You see the fame of your promptness has preceded you, and you were expected at half past four.

FAIRFORD: The train wasn't late; I'm late—I've been walking—

MISS LAWRENCE, *politely*: From the station!

FAIRFORD, *with a deep sigh of relief*: Yes—I walked—from the station, yes.

MISS LAWRENCE: Then that accounts for it. And it must take some time for the wayfarer who isn't personally conducted to find his way round to the entrance of Mrs. Inglehart's house. A house naturally fronts before, but if it has the sea in the rear, there's a certain temptation to front behind, and Mrs. Inglehart's house has yielded to the temptation. Don't you think it's like her? So full of—unexpectedness!

FAIRFORD: Yes; very singular. Very puzzling— if you've never been here before.

MISS LAWRENCE, *keenly*: And is this the first time you've been here?

FAIRFORD: I *(Desperately)* I've never been here before to-day.

MISS LAWRENCE: Do you mean, never before to-day, or never to-day before?

FAIRFORD: I mean, never before to-day; not to-day before.

MISS LAWRENCE: Then there *is* a difference! I'm so glad; I thought there wasn't when I asked. *(She muses aloud.)* Let me see! He has never been here before to-day; but he may have been here to-day before. Is that sense? Let me try it the other way! He has been here to-day before, but he has never been here before to-day. *(Fairford gazes uneasily at her.)* I can't make it out; but I'll ask Mrs. Inglehart when she comes; she'll know. I'll put it as a conundrum: If a gentleman has never been here before to-day, and yet has been here to-day before, when has the gentleman been here before? *(Fairford listens with signs of increasing terror, which culminate in a violent start when she turns suddenly upon him.)* Mr. Fairford, I'm tempted to make you a confidence! Oh—ha, ha, ha! Don't be frightened. It's only something psychical. But I have had such a strange impression in regard to you.

FAIRFORD, *in alarm*: Me?

MISS LAWRENCE: Yes. I wonder if I may venture to speak of it; but with your frankness—oh, all your virtues have anticipated you; every one was here promptly at half past four!—I'm sure you'll answer me. As you came up the veranda steps, just now, I had that weird sense of its all having happened before. You have had it: every one has; but at this instant it's so vivid with me that it seems as if you must *share* it with me. *(Laughingly)* Do you have a been-here-before feeling too?

FAIRFORD: I can't say—I— May I ask what you mean?

MISS LAWRENCE: I don't wonder you're surprised. But I'm so curious to know whether two persons could have that weird seizure at the same moment in regard to the same thing. Of course it's impossible, and I ought really to beg your pardon, but as you came up the veranda steps, just now, it flashed upon me, "He feels as if he had been here before." Perhaps it was a strange look— Excuse me; I'm odiously personal. Will you please to make a remark?

FAIRFORD: I! A remark?

MISS LAWRENCE: Yes; anything—anything to turn the conversation. I've made all the remarks up to this point. I see you don't like psychical confidences.

FAIRFORD: Yes—I like them very much. But I wish to say—I ought to tell you—I don't know how to—

He stops and stares at her.

MISS LAWRENCE, *looking down at her dress on either side of her, and twitching it*: Is there something on my gown? A bug? A caterpillar? No? *(Laughingly)* A woman always thinks something's wrong with her dress when people stare. But perhaps it's only the color? It's a very peculiar shade of gray; I've been told by flatterers that I look like a wraith in it, and you look—excuse me, really, Mr. Fairford! you look as if I *did* look like a wraith!

FAIRFORD: Not at all, I assure you. But I—but in regard to your psychical experience, I wish— I feel bound to say—

MISS LAWRENCE: Then you like that kind of thing! Do let me tell you another! It's apropos of this gown, which I wish you to notice particularly, so that you can corroborate me when I tell Mrs. Inglehart. *(She rises, and puts it in evidence by slowly turning in front of her chair; Fairford starts up, and backs away in vague alarm.)* Should you have thought I put it on for you?

FAIRFORD, *gasping*: For me?

MISS LAWRENCE: No? Didn't you know it? *(She fixes him with a piercing glance, and then sinks into her chair again, laughing, while he remains standing, aghast.)* It can't be the first time that you've been dressed at by a young lady; it's something that's always happening when men are expected in houses where girls are. Don't you know that?

FAIRFORD, *with relief*: I suppose—I dare say—

MISS LAWRENCE: But, *unless you know,* you never could imagine the rest of what I'm going to tell you. I've just had the most awful scare. A little while before you came, I was up in my room, which looks out over the roof of the veranda here, and I fell into a hopeless doubt between blue and green. Which should I wear? I couldn't decide, and as I had left Mrs. Inglehart sitting here alone, I indulged myself in a little impulse. I put up my window, and asked Mrs. Inglehart which it should be, and then after I had decided, I decided over again, and put up my window to tell her so. It was this last time that I had my fright. I thought—I fancied—I dreamed—that I heard another voice just before I spoke, and that this voice was a man's voice. Of course it was impossible, in the nature of things, even if it was so, but it served, for the time being. As soon as I could I reasoned myself out of it. Mrs. Inglehart couldn't be so ungenerous—so unkind—as to let me suppose she was here alone, and even if she could, the man would have insisted upon giving me some proof of his presence, if he was a gentleman. Of course if it were the groom, or the gardener, or some workman about the place, I needn't care; and so, as I said, I reasoned myself out of it. But it was a very pretty scare while it lasted, I can assure you. I really suppose it was this that gave me that been-here-before feeling when I saw you coming up the steps. Ah, here comes Mrs. Inglehart, and I'm off duty; but please don't speak to her of it, will you? I wish to tell her later myself. You promise?

FAIRFORD: Yes—

MISS LAWRENCE: Oh, thank you. I'll be back directly, Lilly. I've kept Mr. Fairford safely for you.

She waves her hand to Mrs. Inglehart as she appears at the parlor window, and vanishes through the door into the hall.

MRS INGLEHART, *coming out on the veranda*: What is it you are not to tell me?

FAIRFORD: Who is that, Lillian?

MRS. INGLEHART: It's Miss Lawrence, of course. Don't you like her?

FAIRFORD: Against my reason and conscience, I consented to go away and come back, in this disgraceful fashion, to spare your feelings, and hers; and the result is that I shall do neither, and that I shall not be able to hold up my head.

MRS. INGLEHART: Why, what in the world has happened?

FAIRFORD: That is what I can't tell you; that's what I promised I wouldn't tell. You can ask Miss Lawrence; I am going away.

MRS. INGLEHART: Going away!

FAIRFORD: I have been placed in a thoroughly false position. To oblige you, I have consented to act a falsehood, and I have done it so badly that—

MRS. INGLEHART: Of course you've done it badly. I expected that. But what of it? Did she get it out of you?

FAIRFORD: I must leave you to learn from Miss Lawrence what has passed. I have given my word, and I must keep it. Good-by!

He bows coldly, and goes toward the veranda steps.

MRS. INGLEHART, *running to intercept him*: But you are not actually going! You can't be so insane, so wicked as that!

FAIRFORD: You've made it impossible for me to stay. The truth must come out, and then you will see why.

MRS. INGLEHART: But no matter how bad the truth is, you'll only make it worse by going!

FAIRFORD: I must be judge of that. Will you please let me pass?

MRS. INGLEHART: Do you think this is treating me very nicely? What shall I say to Miss Lawrence? How shall I explain? Oh, Jim, dear! Don't be boyish! I've no doubt that as soon as I know what the trouble is, I can make it right. I might have known she would tangle you up, somehow; but it can't be bad enough to drive you from my house. Think how it will look!

FAIRFORD: I must leave appearances to you, hereafter; you can manage them better.

MRS. INGLEHART: Is that what *she* said of me?

FAIRFORD: Lillian!

MRS INGLEHART: I didn't mean that, Jim; indeed I didn't. But you can't imagine how awkward it will be for me if you go; what a false position it will place *me* in. Don't be selfish! Don't go. *I ask you to stay.*

She looks at him significantly.

FAIRFORD: It's too late. I'd have given the world to hear that from you a little while ago; but now—

He falters.

MRS INGLEHART: Very well; go, then! I know what the trouble is. She knew that you had been here before, and she could only have done it by eavesdropping.

FAIRFORD: No, Lillian; it was we who were eavesdropping.

MRS. INGLEHART: Then it's not eavesdropping to listen from a window, but it is from a veranda? She heard every word we were saying here, and her calling down to me was a mere ruse. I might have known it at the time. But of course, if you think I was capable of eavesdropping and she wasn't, that settles the matter, and I have no more to say. Don't let me keep you, Mr. Fairford.

She suddenly bursts into tears, and catching her handkerchief to her face, flies through the window and vanishes, at the same moment that Mrs. Wenham appears at the hallway door.

MRS. WENHAM, *coming forward to where Fairford remains standing motionless, bag in hand*: Why, James! You've got here at last. What in the world kept you? Have you just come?

FAIRFORD: I'm just going.

MRS. WENHAM: Going? Without seeing Lillian?

FAIRFORD: I have seen her, and—that's why I'm going.

MRS. WENHAM: She isn't sending you away!

FAIRFORD: No, no! Not in that sense of the word. We've quarreled. Aunt Harriet, I wish to tell you—

MRS. WENHAM: Oh, you needn't tell me! I know what it is. It's part of that miserable nonsense of hers about— But you haven't *seen* Miss Lawrence!

FAIRFORD, *in dull despair*: Yes, I've seen Miss Lawrence.

MRS. WENHAM: And Lillian was angry with you on that account, and in her ridiculous jealousy— Well, then, I'm glad she's lost you, James.

FAIRFORD: I'm not, Aunt Harriet. And I'm afraid it isn't just as you think it is. I must tell you something—I promised not to tell Lillian, but I may tell you—

MRS. WENHAM: You may tell *me anything*, James. Whom did you promise?

FAIRFORD: Miss Lawrence. I came at half past four as I promised, and I found Lillian on the veranda here—

MRS. WENHAM: Lillian? And where was Miss Lawrence?

FAIRFORD: I don't know—or I didn't then; but it seems somewhere overhead; and presently, while we were talking, she put up her window, and began calling down to Lillian, and asking her what she should wear. Lillian seemed to have forgotten about her—

MRS. WENHAM: Wretched child!

FAIRFORD: And when she remembered, she said she had promised you Miss Lawrence should see me first, and I must go away, and come back so as to give the impression that I hadn't been here.

MRS. WENHAM: But you never consented to such an outrageous imposition?

FAIRFORD: I didn't like it; but I thought Lillian was right in thinking Miss Lawrence would be annoyed if she knew that I had overheard her, and I consented—in violation of every principle of my life. When I came back, Miss Lawrence was here.

MRS. WENHAM: Well?

FAIRFORD: It was useless. She began to let me understand at once that she knew I had been here already, and—in short, the game was up. She kept the whole thing in such form that I could neither admit it nor deny it. When Lillian returned and Miss Lawrence left us, I threatened to go away, and she begged me to stay, and after we had some hot words, she told me to go, and—here I am. What is it all about, Aunt Harriet? Why should she promise you to let Miss Lawrence receive me, and why should Miss Lawrence wish to dress especially to please me?

MRS. WENHAM: I will tell you, James. But first sit down and put that bag somewhere. You're not going, and Lillian never meant you to go, any more than you meant to leave her when you threatened it. I'm glad I know just how the case stands, and I think I can make you see Lillian's behavior in the right light, though I am thoroughly ashamed of it myself, and disgusted with her, and I've told her so. You will always have to account for something that is wholly incomprehensible in Lillian, if you expect to understand her at all.

FAIRFORD, *patiently*: Yes, that is what I have always tried to do.

MRS. WENHAM: Well, then, you can easily imagine that when she had consented to your coming here to-day on terms that any one else would feel were the same as accepting you, she should feel the need of putting it out of her power to accept you—or rather that she would have to be in the greatest danger of losing you—before she was able to accept you.

FAIRFORD, *making an effort*: I think I can conceive of something like that. What has it to do with Miss Lawrence's trying to please my taste in dress?

MRS. WENHAM: Simply this. Before she could realize your loss, Lillian had to give you to some one else.

FAIRFORD, *after a moment's reflection*: If you wanted anything, would you put it out of your power, in order to realize your desire for it?

MRS. WENHAM: No, but Lillian would; and I should respect you a great deal more if you renounced her forever, and took a fancy to Miss Lawrence. But I hope you won't, for I know that Lillian is devotedly fond of you.

FAIRFORD: I'm afraid there's no danger of my renouncing her. Whom did she give me to?

MRS. WENHAM: Oh, you poor, single-minded man! To Miss Lawrence.

FAIRFORD: And did Miss Lawrence know it?

MRS. WENHAM: James, I don't wonder Lillian finds you rather trying at times. Of course she knew it! And I insisted upon her being allowed to meet your first, and to—to—to—

FAIRFORD: What?

MRS. WENHAM: My dear, you are enough to try the patience of a saint. Such innocence as yours is *criminal!*

> At this word, Mrs. Inglehart suddenly emerges from the drawing-room window upon the veranda.

MRS. INGLEHART: I will not have you abusing me to James, mother.

MRS. WENHAM: I was not speaking of you!

MRS. INGLEHART: You said criminal.

MRS. WENHAM: I said James was criminal—for being so good.

MRS. INGLEHART: Oh! And what have you been saying about me?

MRS. WENHAM: I've been explaining you.

MRS. INGLEHART: Very well, then, I won't *be* explained—above all to Mr. Fairford. (*She sits down and looks at her mother.*) I thought he was going.

FAIRFORD, *appealingly*: You know I couldn't go, Lillian—

MRS. INGLEHART, *ignoring him*: He *said* he was going; but perhaps that was a man's way of meaning that he wasn't. You never can tell what they mean from what they say. Do you know

where Miss Lawrence is, mother? I wish to tell her that Mr. Fairford has changed his mind, and is going to stay after all. She may not like to come to dinner in that case; or Mr. Fairford may not like to meet her. They seem both to be victims of the same deceit, poor dears. I'm sure I don't know who has tried to deceive them, except for their own good.

FAIRFORD: I never doubted your motive, Lillian. I know how generous you are. I only objected to the false position that I was placed in with reference to Miss Lawrence.

MRS. INGLEHART, *always ignoring him*: I hope you are satisfied, mother, with having insisted on my letting Miss Lawrence meet Mr. Fairford first, instead of receiving him myself as a hostess should.

MRS. WENHAM, *rising in virtuous indignation*: Lillian, I will not allow you to be so perverse! I don't care *how* old you are. You are acting like a naughty child, but I suppose it's because you're thoroughly ashamed of yourself. I've told James all about your wicked folly, and if I were he I should go away, and leave you to get out of it as you could. I wash my hands of the whole affair.

> Mrs. Wenham sweeps indoors and abandons the cousins to their own devices.

MRS. INGLEHART, *after a marked silence, very mildly and meekly*: Well, Jim!

FAIRFORD: Well, Lil!

MRS. INGLEHART: What do you think of me now?

FAIRFORD: I haven't changed my mind; but I *think* I understand you a little better than I did.

MRS. INGLEHART: And you still blame me? Remember I don't know what my mother's been saying about me.

FAIRFORD: Nothing that doesn't make you dearer to me. I think she was too hard upon you for a harmless joke like that.

MRS. INGLEHART: Oh, Jim, how sweet you are! Do you really mean it?

FAIRFORD: I wish you would let me prove it. I wish you could let me employ my life in proving it.

MRS. INGLEHART: Oh, you know I always trusted you. You're truth itself!

FAIRFORD: And I always trusted you, though—

MRS. INGLEHART: Though I'm not truth itself.

FAIRFORD: Something like that.

MRS. INGLEHART: How delicious! You know I always did think your candor was delicious. (*She puts up her hands to the back of her head, and tries to look round at the top of her chair.)* I seem to be caught—

FAIRFORD: Can I help you?

MRS. INGLEHART: Oh, no. *(But he comes to her and frees the knot of her hair from a loose fibre of the cane which has caught it.)* Thank you so much, James.

He does not go away, and he does not re- linquish the hand she had put up to help free her hair. He sits down on the arm of her chair, and scrutinizes her left-hand fingers critically.

MRS. INGLEHART: Well?

FAIRFORD: I thought I couldn't be mistaken in the size. May I try it on?

MRS. INGLEHART: Why, if you've taken all the trouble to bring it—

FAIRFORD: I ventured to do it.

MRS. INGLEHART, *looking fondly up into his eyes while he fits the ring on her finger*: It was no great risk.

FAIRFORD: Does it hurt? Is it too tight?

MRS. INGLEHART: It is too tight, but it doesn't— hurt! *(A sound of quick footfalls and rustling skirts makes itself heard within the drawing-room. Mrs. Inglehart jumps to her feet.)* Oh, good gracious! There's that detestable girl! I forgot all about her again! Run, Jim! Or no, it's too late now. Stay! *(The sound of the quick footfalls and the rustling skirts within grows vaguer.)* Yes, go now. She's executing a little manœuvre. She's seen us, but she's pretending she didn't, and she's gone back to give us time before she comes out through the hall door. That's all right. Run along now, dear, and leave me to manage with her. I don't think she'll get anything out of *me* that I don't want her to know. Why don't you go, James? Oh! Goose! *(She puts her arms round his neck, as he bends over her, and kisses him, and then pushes him decisively away. As he disappears round the corner of the veranda, she calls.)* Miss Law- rence! Roberta! Is that you?

MISS LAWRENCE, *within*: I am looking for a handkerchief I left— Oh, here it is! *(She appears at the door, and looks out.)* I thought Mr. Fair- ford—

MRS. INGLEHART: He was here a moment ago, but he's gone to his room—I suppose to his room. I've been so much interested in your psycho- logical experience, Roberta.

MISS LAWRENCE: Then he's told! I might have expected it.

MRS. INGLEHART: You'd have been disappointed if you had. Men needn't tell things. They've merely to say they won't, and then women are inspired with the facts. I guessed what had hap- pened as soon as I saw the kind of trouble he was in, and I envied you the opportunity you had of—rattling him. Do tell me just how you did it.

MISS LAWRENCE: Do you think that will be necessary?

MRS. INGLEHART: No, I don't know that I do. And I admire you for your reticence. I supposed frankness was your strong point.

MISS LAWRENCE: Isn't that always a forlorn hope with us? The pose of utter despair? The last resort?

MRS. INGLEHART: Perhaps it is. I was just going to try it with you. There seems nothing else for it.

MISS LAWRENCE: Ah, you pique my curiosity. What is it you *could* be frank about? I mean—

MRS. INGLEHART: I see what you mean. But you remember that a little while ago, here, I gave you James Fairford?

MISS LAWRENCE: Yes; and "the gods themselves cannot resume their gifts." [1]

MRS INGLEHART: I don't know about the gods, but I'm sure the goddesses could. My dear Roberta, I want him back. I must have him. Come, now, be very, very nice, and let me have him again! Won't you? I know that legally, and everything else, he belongs to you, and I suppose that in a court of justice I shouldn't have the slightest chance. But I throw myself on your mercy. See! *(She comes over to where the girl has seated herself, and drops on her knees before her.)* Let me have him, dear! I'd no idea I cared anything about him till I'd parted with him. Come! Say the word!

MISS LAWRENCE: And I, what am I to do with the wealth of affection that I had prepared to lavish upon him?

MRS. INGLEHART: Oh, give it to somebody else! Jim won't mind.

MISS LAWRENCE: Ah, that's just what I'm not so sure about! I've an idea that he is madly devoted to me. In fact, I can't give him up till I know from his own lips that he wishes to be given up. Yes, he must renounce me—

MRS. INGLEHART: Oh, but I assure you he doesn't care anything about you—

1 Tennyson, *Tithonus*, line 49.

MISS LAWRENCE: That I must know from himself. I insist upon his choosing between us!

MRS. INGLEHART, *rising*: Do you really mean it?

MISS LAWRENCE: Yes; I think it would be fun.

MRS. INGLEHART, *with genuine feeling*: I can't say it's my idea of a joke. Well, then, it may be very inhospitable, and all that, and I wish it could have come about a little more gracefully, but I have to tell you— Oh, have you hurt yourself? *(She takes note of the handkerchief which Miss Lawrence has wrapped around her left hand; the girl puts the hand behind her.)* Can't I give you something? Arnica? Pond's extract? How did you do it? *Putting up the window?*

MISS LAWRENCE, *in embarrassment*: No, no—

MRS. INGLEHART, *dryly*: I'm very sorry. Those window-catches are awkward things. I've caught my fingers when I've been thinking of something else.

MISS LAWRENCE: It wasn't the window-catch, I assure you, Mrs. Inglehart, and I don't know how to tell you what it is, exactly. I thought it would be so simple; but— I ought never to have let you give me Mr. Fairford.

MRS. INGLEHART: Oh, don't mind that. I've taken him back again.

MISS LAWRENCE: Oh, that doesn't make it right on my part. I meant to have told you before; but I couldn't get the chance; and then it seemed to get more and more complicated, and—

MRS. INGLEHART, *impatiently*: Well?

MISS LAWRENCE: Well!

She puts out her left hand to Mrs. Inglehart, and covers her eyes with the handkerchief she has caught from it.

MRS. INGLEHART, *clutching it wildly*: An engagement ring!

MISS LAWRENCE: Yes, we were engaged last week, and when you began to speak to me, and I didn't know quite how—I hadn't the courage—

MRS. INGLEHART, *flinging Miss Lawrence's hand from her*: Then it was all a trick from the beginning! And you let me make a fool of myself in that way, and all the time you were engaged! And you said you never met him before—

MISS LAWRENCE, *in amaze*: How could I say such a thing? We've known each other for years.

MRS. INGLEHART: So it appears. And I don't know how you could say you'd never seen him, but I know you did say it. Perhaps you'd like *two* engagement rings. You may have mine—

She tries to get it off.

MISS LAWRENCE: What *do* you mean? What are you doing? Whom are you talking about?

MRS. INGLEHART, *still struggling violently with the ring*: James Fairford. You may have both his rings—

MISS LAWRENCE: James Fairford! I don't want his rings—either of them. I'm engaged to Arthur Wayland! Do you think there's only one man in the world?

MRS. INGLEHART, *after a moment's daze*: Then you—you—I see—yes! Oh, you dear! Oh, I'm so happy for you! *(She falls upon Miss Lawrence's neck and clasps her to her heart.)* Arthur Wayland? He's charming, and he's a very lucky fellow, but he deserves you if any one does. Ah, ha, ha! Oh, hu, hu, hu!

Mrs. Wenham appears at one corner of the veranda, and Fairford at the other, from different sides of the house.

MRS. WENHAM, *sternly*: What is the matter, Lillian?

MRS. INGLEHART, *between tears and laughter*: Nothing, nothing! Roberta is engaged, and I'm merely congratulating her.

The Rise of Silas Lapham
[1898]

W. D. Howells and Paul Kester

Among the Howells materials in the Houghton Library at Harvard University are four typescript versions with manuscript emendations of *The Rise of Silas Lapham*, a drama in four acts, written by Howells and Paul Kester. As these typescripts are undated, I have arbitrarily designated them versions A, B, C, and D, in order that I may explain my choice of the text published here, the version Howells would have selected to publish had he had a choice but been unable to make alterations. (It is safe to say that with his fondness for perfect copy he would have found none of these ready for publication without revision.) Versions A and B follow the novel very closely. Both show Howells' changes and comments in the margins, but version B seems to have been made before version A, because manuscript corrections in B are quite generally typed in A. However, the two versions do overlap: A seems to have been worked over more than once, and the typescript in B is occasionally manuscript in A. Version D is not complete; it lacks, for example, a beginning for Act II and an ending for Act IV. It also adds the character of Dinwiddie from West Virginia to introduce Act I; however, D omits parts of speeches that are crossed out in A and includes in type the manuscript changes made in A. Version D also has many suggested changes in an unfamiliar hand which are carried out in version C, making the latter version a longer play with many drastic departures from the novel. For example, the beginning elaborates the Dinwiddie business as well as introducing more conversation between the employees in Lapham's office, and in this version Penelope goes to the Corey dinner. From his letters, one can be certain that Howells did not approve of these changes; when dealing with prospective producers he consistently asked Kester for their earlier versions of the play. Hence, the text printed in this volume is essentially version A, which is complete except for a few lines at the end of Act I, plus the obvious alterations indicated in version A that appear more clearly expressed in version D.

It is difficult to know just when or under what circumstances Howells became interested in dramatizing *The Rise of Silas Lapham*, but in all probability the suggestion came from Paul Kester (1870–1933), a young cousin of Howells on the Welsh side of the family who wrote his first play in 1892 and achieved some success. But no matter why Howells began the dramatization, there is no doubt that his objective was a stageworthy play. Even before he and Kester started writing, he tried to interest the actor W. H. Crane, who responded with an encouraging letter (February 3, 1896, Harvard Library). By the autumn of 1896 the Howells-Kester collaboration was evidently in progress, for Howells voiced his enthusiasm for the project to Kester (letter September 13, 1896, New York Public Library), but it was not until still another year that the work approached a finished form. In the meantime Howells must have made some arrangements with James A. Herne, for his letters during and after 1898 state that he and Kester were dramatizing the novel for Herne.

The period from the fall of 1897 through the summer of 1899 seems to have been the most critical for the dramatization of *Silas Lapham*. During this time Herne first became enthusiastic, then almost immediately demanded such drastic revision that Howells rebelled with some disgust, and finally rejected the play altogether. The story is an unhappy one as it appears in Howells' letters. Herne's first request for the play came in the fall of 1897, and Howells anxiously wrote to Kester (November 15, 1897, New York Public Library): "Will you bring it [Silas Lapham] here, if it is in a state to show him? Bring it anyway!" It would seem, however, that there was nothing to bring at that time, for on January 17, 1899 (letter, New York Public Library), Howells was still asking Kester for a scenario of Silas Lapham that he could show to Herne. For some reason Kester always seemed to have the play, but the method of the collaborators, as Howells explained it to his sister Aurelia (letter, May 1, 1898, Life in Letters, II, 91), was simple: "Paul gets it together and then I revise it." At the time he wrote this note he told Aurelia that they had completed only one act, but that he expected Kester to bring the second one that day.

Soon after Howells' request for the play from Kester he had what he described as a satisfactory talk with Herne (letter to Kester, January 22, 1898, New York Public Library), and by late spring the play was sufficiently near completion for Herne to suggest (letter, June 8, 1898, New York Public Library) that they meet to discuss revisions—revisions that were to become a very serious matter for Howells. In the letter Herne had a great many things to say—some good, some bad—the essence of which was that Howells had written a great book but that the book was not a play and that Howells' manuscript, "a transcript of the book," was also not a play. He found Mrs. Lapham weak, Silas without humor, the love of Tom and Irene very vague, and the climax poorly arranged. In other words, there was a lot of hard work necessary to make this material into a play, but Herne, with his wife, was ready to help: "The stage is sorely in need of plays—and there is a big one in Silas Lapham and we must get it out of that great book." In the face of all of this criticism Howells was upset and wrote to Kester (June 10, 1898, New York Public Library) that he would not undertake this "radical reconstruction," and that so far as Herne as producer was concerned, the matter was ended. Armed with Howells' permission to do anything short of recasting the entire play, Kester tried later to approach Herne, but he was not successful.

Time passed; Howells occasionally revived his interest, but the play was never produced, although an impressive number of theater managers had an opportunity to reject it. In the fall of 1902 (letter to Howells, November 30, 1902, New York Public Library), Alden Bass became interested in Silas Lapham and then gave it up. Howells' attempt (letter to Kester, June 15, 1903, New York Public Library) to get a "lady who has made one of my farces go for some years in England" to try the play was equally unsuccessful. A drama agent named Mrs. Woodward, engaged by Kester, seems to have been most effective, for it must have been she who interested both Crane and Frohman in the play manuscript (Crane to Woodward, February 4, 1903, New York Public Library). With this development Howells was pleased but still skeptical. On July 15, 1903 (New York Public Library), he wrote to Kester: "It is very nice about both Crane and Frohman. Between two such stools how can we fall to the ground? But I shall believe in S. Lapham when I see Crane doing him in a Frohman Theater!" But when Howells finally saw what he called the Woodward version [version C], he was definitely disturbed, although this work as a stageworthy play has definite advantages over the Howells–Kester version. It was, however, no longer an adaptation of the novel, and Howells immediately wrote to Kester (November 13, 1903, New York Public Library): "I have just been looking over the copy you sent me at Kittery Point, and I find it wonderfully bewitched by your collaborateuse. She has changed seven parts of it past all recognition and injected dreadful rubbish into its helpless body, so that I'm ashamed to show it to Mr. Frohman as it stands." Consequently, Kester sent an earlier version of the play to Howells, who with great optimism then submitted it to Frohman. But two months later, all was gloom again as Frohman rejected the play, saying that ". . . it would have to be put into more effective theatrical correlation" (letter to Howells, January 14, 1904, New York Public Library). Frohman's only qualification was a postscript in which he said that he might ask for the manuscript again later, but he did not, and Howells did not expect that he would (Howells to Kester, January 15, 1904, New York Public Library). Essentially, this was the end of any serious consideration of the play for the stage, although Howells never really gave up the idea and even relented to the point where he would have been glad to let anyone who wanted it have the Woodward version (Howells to Kester, March 27, 1907, New York Public Library).

The final chapter of the story of *The Rise of Silas Lapham* as a play has little to do with Howells. It concerns Lillian Sabine's dramatization, which was produced by the Actors' Guild at the Garrick Theatre in New York beginning on November 25, 1919, and lasted for forty-seven performances. Although Howells expressed concern for her version in a letter to Kester, August 25, 1916 (New York Public Library), and tried to interest her in his and Kester's dramatization, she adapted straight from the novel. Howells was skeptical of her succeeding, writing to Kester that "I hae me doots" (July 18, 1917, New York Public Library). The play was not, in fact, well received. Hamlin Garland saw it the first night and noted in *My Friendly Contemporaries* (New York: The Macmillan Co., 1932), p. 269, that he was "a bit disappointed," feeling that the lines lacked the clear strength of Howells' dialogue and that there was confusion in the plot.

Since the Sabine production, problems have arisen over the motion picture rights of the novel and the play. Originally, in a letter to Lillian Sabine, October 15, 1919 (files of W. W. Howells), Howells renewed Miss Sabine's dramatic rights for a two-year period, but this renewal has been misunderstood. As late as January 15, 1937 (letter to Mildred Howells, files of W. W. Howells), the Authors' League of America gave the opinion that because Mildred Howells had the picture rights and Miss Sabine the dramatic rights, the *talking* motion picture rights belonged to both. Others—Ferris Greenslet of Houghton Mifflin and Louise Sillcox of the Dramatists' Guild—have stated that Miss Sabine could claim neither movie nor dramatic rights of the novel. Presumably, a movie of *The Rise of Silas Lapham* would employ material from both dramatizations and the novel; certainly it would destroy the value of the dramatizations. In the spring of 1934 Mildred Howells, on a trip through the West, stopped with the Garlands in California and made some effort to interest the Fox Studios in *The Rise of Siles Lapham*. Hardesty Johnson, son-in-law of Garland and an employee of the Fox Studios, tried to promote the idea, and it was generally suggested that the picture might be a vehicle for Will Rogers. However nothing came of this venture.

The Rise of Silas Lapham[1]

A PLAY IN FOUR ACTS

W. D. Howells and Paul Kester

ACT I

SCENE: *Lapham's Office, Boston. The scene shows the dim and vast interior of Lapham's warehouse. The office is railed off at the right, the private office well down stage separated by a high partition from the counting room and clerks' offices that run R. U. E. Kegs, barrels and cans of paint fade away into the perspective of the warehouse. Windows light the office at the right high above the desks. A big, round faced clock ticks on the wall.*

Discovered: At rise Walker and Williams. Girl copying letters on her typewriter. Walker making entries in the books before him.

Enter Bartley Hubbard.

HUBBARD: Can I see Colonel Lapham?

WALKER: Well, he's busy just now. I'll take in your name.

HUBBARD: I've got an appointment with him. My name's Hubbard. I represent the Boston *Events*, and he's promised me an interview for our Solid Men of Boston series.

WALKER: Oh! Oh yes! Sit down just a moment, Mr. Hubbard, and the Colonel will be out. I know he was expecting you. He's engaged with his architect, but—

HUBBARD, *taking out his notebook*: His architect?

WALKER: Yes; Mr. Seymour—

HUBBARD, *writing*: Oh, yes. I know. What's he building?

WALKER: He's putting up a house on the waterside of Beacon Street—

HUBBARD, *writing*: Swell, I suppose?

WALKER: With Mr. Seymour to do the work, and the Colonel to furnish the funds—

HUBBARD: Ought to be!

1 This play has not been published previously.

LAPHAM, *heard off*: I presume you'll have the front parlor finished in black-walnut?

Enter Lapham and Seymour from L. Lapham has a large plan of the house in his hands.

SEYMOUR: Well, yes, if you like. Of course, you can *paint* black walnut, too.

LAPHAM, *gasping*: *Paint* black walnut?

SEYMOUR: Yes. White, or a little off-white.

LAPHAM: Well, I'm dummed! I presume you'll want Eastlake mantleshelves and tiles?

SEYMOUR: I was thinking perhaps a white marble chimney piece, treated in the refined Empire style would be the thing for that room.

LAPHAM: White marble? I thought that had gone out long ago. Hardwood floors?

SEYMOUR: In the music-room, of course.

LAPHAM: And in the parlors?

SEYMOUR: Carpet.

LAPHAM: And in the other rooms?

SEYMOUR: Carpet.

LAPHAM: Well, I'm . . . but I'll talk it over with Mis' Lapham. I'll just keep this plan.

Laying plan on table.

SEYMOUR: All right; good morning, Colonel Lapham.

LAPHAM: Good morning, sir.

Exit Seymour L.

LAPHAM, *looking after him*: That fellow's fifty years behind the times,—or ten years ahead. I wonder what Ongpeer style is? I hated to ask.

WALKER: Here's Mr. Hubbard, Colonel Lapham.

HUBBARD: From the *Events*.

LAPHAM: Oh, yes. That's all right. (*To Hubbard, nodding to door through which Seymour has passed.*) A fellow who's putting up a house for me on the waterside of Beacon, had to get rid of him first. I'll be with you in just half a minute. Walk right in. (*Leading the way to his private office down R. As Bartley sits he turns back to typewriter who hands him letters.*) Those Mexican orders?

GIRL: Yes, sir.

LAPHAM: There! (*Signing.*) William, I want these to go right away. (*Then turning back to*

Hubbard he sits in the chair facing him.) So you want my life, death and Christian sufferings, do you, young man?

HUBBARD: That's what I'm after; your money or your life!

LAPHAM: I guess you wouldn't want my life without the money.

HUBBARD: Take 'em both. Don't want your money without your life if you come to that.

LAPHAM, *thoughtfully*: I don't know as I know just where you want me to begin.

HUBBARD: Might begin with your birth; that's where most of us begin.

LAPHAM: I didn't know whether you wanted me to go quite so far back as that. But there's no disgrace in having been *born*, and I was born in the State of Vermont, pretty well up under the Canada line; so well up, in fact, that I came very near being an adoptive citizen: for I was bound to be an American of *some* sort, from the word *Go!* That was about, well, let me see, pretty near sixty years ago. Well—say I'm fifty-five years old; and I've *lived* 'em too; not an hour of waste time about me anywheres. I was born on a farm, and—

HUBBARD: Worked in the fields summers and went to school winters? Regulation thing?

LAPHAM, *dryly*: Regulation thing.

HUBBARD: Parents poor, of course? Any barefoot business? Early deprivation of any kind that would encourage the youthful reader to go and do likewise?

LAPHAM, *more dryly*: I guess if you see these things as a joke my life won't *interest* you.

HUBBARD: Oh, yes it will! You'll see it'll come out all right.

LAPHAM: We were poor, and there was hard work and plenty of it, but there wa'n't much complaining. Mother set the example and we all followed. Yes, sir, a man never sees all that his mother has been to him until it's too late to let her know that he sees it. Why, *my mother*— *(He pauses.)* It kind of gives me a lump in the throat! She was a little frail thing, not bigger than a good sized intermediate school-girl; but she did the whole work of a family of boys, and boarded the hired man besides. I don't know how she got any time to sleep. But I suppose she did. She got time to go to church and to teach us to read the Bible. She was *good*. But it ain't her on her knees in church that comes back to me so much like the sight of an angel as her on her knees before me at night washin' my poor,

dirty little feet, that I'd run bare in all day, and makin' me decent for bed. I can feel her hands on my feet yet. *(He pauses, looking down at his boots.)* We were patched all over, but we wa'n't ragged. I tell *you*, when I hear women complainin' nowadays that their lives are stunted and empty, I want to tell 'em about my *mother's* life. I could paint it out for 'em.

HUBBARD: And you say, Col. Lapham, that you discovered this mineral paint on the old farm yourself?

LAPHAM: *I* didn't discover it. My father found it one day in a hole made by a tree blowin' down. There it was, lyin' loose in the pit, and stickin' to the roots that had pulled up a big cake of dirt with 'em. *I* don't know what give him the idea that there was money in it, but he did think so from the start. It got to be a kind of joke with us, and I guess that paint mine did as much as any one thing to make us boys clear out as soon as we got old enough. All my brothers went West and took up land: but I've hung on to New England, and I've hung on to the old farm; not because the paint mine was on it, but because the old house was—and the graves. Of course it's turned out a good thing. I keep the old house up in good shape, and we spend a month or so there every summer; m'wife kind of likes it, and the girls. Pretty place. Sightly all round it. *(Rising and taking down a large photograph, and blowing upon it to clear it of dust.)* There we are, *all* of us!

HUBBARD, *pointing*: I don't need to look twice at *you*.

LAPHAM, *laughing*: Well, that's *Bill!* He's one of their leading lawyers out Dubuque way: been judge of the Common Pleas once or twice. That's his son—just graduated at Yale—alongside of my youngest girl. Good-looking chap.

HUBBARD: She's a good-looking chap. *(Colonel Lapham frowns and Hubbard changes his tone.)* What a beautiful creature she is! What a refined sensitive face! And she looks *good*, too.

LAPHAM, *placated*: She *is* good. My other daughter, *(touching the faces in the photograph)* Mis' Lapham. My brother Willard and his family; farm at Kankakee. Hazard Lapham and his wife— Baptist preacher in Kansas. Jim and his three girls—milling business at Minneapolis. Ben and his family—practicing medicine in Fort Wayne. I presume we sha'n't soon get together again, all of us.

Puts up photograph.

HUBBARD: And you say that you stayed right

along at the old place when the rest cleared out West?

LAPHAM: N-o-o-o-p. I cleared out West, too, first off. Went to Texas. But I got enough of the Lone Star in about three months, and I came back with the idea that Vermont was good enough for me.

HUBBARD: Fatted calf business?

LAPHAM, *with dignity*: I presume they were glad to see me. Mother (*gently*) died that winter, and I stayed on with father. I buried *him* in the spring; and then I came down to a little place called Lumberville and picked up what jobs I could get. Then I hired the tavern stand—and—well, to make a long story short, I got married. Yes. I married the school teacher. We did pretty well with the hotel, and my wife, she was always at me to paint up. Well, I put it off and *put* it off, till one day I give in, and says I, "Well, let's paint up. Why Pert"—m'wife's name's Persis—"I've got a whole paint mine on the farm. Let's go out and look at it." We brought back about a bushel of the stuff in the buggy-seat; and I tried it crude, and I tried it burnt, and I liked it. M'wife, she liked it, too. Well, sir, that tavern's got that coat of paint yet, and it hain't ever had any other, and I don't know as it ever will. When I got the first coat on, I called my wife out. I'd tried it on the back of the house, and she left her dishes. I can remember she came out with her sleeves rolled up, and set down alongside of me on the trestle, and says I—"What do you think, Persis?" and says she, "Well, you hain't got a paint mine, Silas Lapham; you've got a *gold* mine." I set to work and I got a man down from Boston; and I carried him out to the farm, and he analyzed it, and when he came to test it he found out that it contained about seventy-five per cent of peroxide of iron.

HUBBARD: Well; and what then?

LAPHAM: What then? Well, then, he told me, "You've got a paint, here, that's going to drive every other mineral paint out of the market. Why," says he, "it'll drive 'em right into the Back Bay!" Of course, I didn't know what the Back Bay was then—buildin' there now!—but I begun to open my eyes. Says he, "It'll mix easily with linseed oil, whether you want to use it boiled or raw; and it ai'n't a-goin' to crack or fade, and it ai'n't a-goin' to scale. You've got a paint that will stand like the everlastin' hills in every climate under the sun!" And every word

he said was gospel. Well, I ai'n't a-goin' to brag up my paint. I don't suppose you came here to hear me *blow—*

HUBBARD: Oh, yes, I did. That's what I want. The whole truth and—more!

LAPHAM: Oh, there isn't very much more to say about the paint itself. You can use it for almost anything when a paint is wanted, inside or out. It'll prevent decay, and it'll stop it after it's begun, in tin or iron. You can paint the inside of a cistern or a bath tub with it, and water won't hurt it; and you can paint a steam boiler with it, and heat won't. You can cover a brick wall with it, or a railroad car, or the deck of a steamboat. And you can't do a better thing for either.

HUBBARD: Never tried it on the human conscience, I suppose.

LAPHAM, *gravely*: No, sir. I guess you want to keep that as free from paint as you can, if you want much use of it. I never cared to try any of it on mine! There! (*Kicking one of the large casks that stands near.*) That's about our biggest package, and here— (*Pointing.*) This is our smallest.

HUBBARD: Hello! That's pretty.

LAPHAM: Yes, it's rather nice. It's our latest thing. Look here! (*Taking down a small jar from above his desk.*) The Persis Brand.

HUBBARD: Named for Mrs. Lapham?

LAPHAM: Got it up and put the first of it on the market her last birthday. She was pleased.

HUBBARD: I should think she might have been.

LAPHAM: I don't know about your mentioning it in your interview.

HUBBARD: That's going into the interview if nothing else does. I suppose you didn't let the grass grow under your feet after you found out what was in your paint?

LAPHAM: No, sir. I went right back to Lumberville and sold out everything and put all I could rake and scrape together into paint. And Mis' Lapham was with me, every time. I tell you she was a woman! If it hadn't been for her the paint wouldn't have come to anything. I used to tell her it wa'n't the seventy-five per cent of purr-ox-eyed of iron in the *ore*, that made that paint go; it was the seventy-five per cent of purr-ox-eyed of iron in *her*.

HUBBARD: Good.

LAPHAM: In less'n six months there wa'n't a board-fence, nor a barn, nor a face of rock in that whole region that didn't have "Lapham's Mineral Paint-Specimen" on it in the three colors we begun by making. I've heard a good deal of talk about the stove-blacking man and the kidney-cure man, because they advertised that way, but I don't see where the joke comes in, exactly. I never saw anything so very sacred about a big rock along a river or in a pasture, that it wouldn't do to put mineral paint on it in three colors. I wish some of the people that talk about the landscape, and write about it, had to bust one of them rocks out of the landscape with powder, or dig a hole to bury it in; I guess they'd sing a little different tune! Well—where was I?

HUBBARD: Decorating the landscape.

LAPHAM: Oh. Yes. I started right there at Lumberville, and it give the place a start too. You won't find it on the map, now; I give a pretty good lump of money to build a townhall, about five years back, and the first meeting they held in it they voted to change the name—Lumberville *wa'n't* a name—and it's Lapham now. I built my works there, and the fires that Mis' Lapham lighted in 'em hain't ever been out once, and it ain't likely they will be, in my time or yours. I've never cut wages, and I've never had a strike. I've known most of the men since I was a boy. I guess they didn't make any mistake when they called it Lapham. I guess the whole town's on my shoulder. When the war broke out, I went. Mis' Lapham said she guessed I had a country that was worth fighting for, and says she, "I'll look after the paint, Si." Well, I got through, and you can call me Colonel if you want to. Feel there! (*Touching his leg.*) Anything hard?

HUBBARD: Ball?

LAPHAM: Gettysburg. That's my thermometer. If it wa'n't for that, I shouldn't know enough to come in when it rains.

HUBBARD, *laughing in recognition of joke*: So you took hold of the paint and rushed it!

LAPHAM: Well, I took hold of the paint and rushed it all I *could*. My wife was at me all the time to take a partner—somebody with capital, but I couldn't seem to bear the idea. That paint was like my own blood to me. I saw it was the thing to do, but I tried to fight it off, and I tried to joke it off. Well, I had to come to it. I took a partner. He had money enough, but he didn't know anything about paint. We hung on together for a year or two, and then we quit.

HUBBARD: And he had the experience?

LAPHAM, *sullenly*: I had some of the experience, too.

HUBBARD: And since that, I suppose, you've played it alone.

LAPHAM: I've played it alone.

A *silence; Lapham sits gloomily.*

HUBBARD: You must ship some of this paint of yours to foreign countries, Colonel?

LAPHAM, *looking from his silence with a sigh*: We ship it to all parts of the world. It goes to South America, lots of it. It goes to Australia, and it goes to India and China, and it goes to the Cape of Good Hope. I believe that it's a blessing to the world. When folks come in, and kind of smell round, and ask me what I mix it with I always say, "Well, in the first place, I mix it with *Faith*; and after that I grind it up with the best quality of boiled linseed oil that money can buy!" (*Lapham rises. Mrs. Lapham, Penelope and Irene enter from L. Bartley Hubbard turns to go.*) Well, well, well! Father, mother, Aunt Hitty and all the folks! What do *you* want? Come down to see the Persis Brand at home? Set down, ladies, set down!

Forgetting Hubbard.

HUBBARD: Well, I guess we've got about through, Colonel—

LAPHAM, *taking his hand and holding it*: Well, I don't know but what we have. Come round again, some time. Like to ride after a good hoss?

HUBBARD: If I can handle the leathers myself.

LAPHAM, *clapping him on the shoulder*: That's right! Come round, and I'll let you see what my mare can do. Well, good day. Hold on! Let me introduce you to Mis' Lapham—and my daughters. (*Mrs. Lapham gives her hand; girls bow.*) Mr. Hubbard of *The Events*. He's been taking my measure for an interview. You won't know me when you see me in print.

HUBBARD: Mrs. Lapham, if I could show the Colonel *just as he is*, it would make my fortune with *The Events*.

MRS. LAPHAM: I'd rather you'd do that than flatter him up any. It's hard enough to manage him, as it is, and if he gets the notion he's somebody—

LAPHAM: *Your* wife talk to you that way? Well, I guess they're all alike.

They all laugh, and Hubbard exits, bowing. As he exits, Walker, William and typewriter put on coats, hats, etc. and go out to luncheon.

MRS. LAPHAM: Si, we stopped at the new house on the way, and we met Mr. Seymour and he told us about the plans you'd been making. You're putting more money into that house than you'll ever get out again. Now, you just stop at a hundred thousand, and don't you let him get you a cent over. Why, you're perfectly bewitched with the fellow! You've lost your head, Silas Lapham, and if you don't look out you'll lose your money, too.

LAPHAM, *laughing*: There's no call to feel anxious, Pert. I never had so much of it to spend before.

MRS. LAPHAM: *Spend* it, then. Don't *throw* it away. And how come you have so much more money than you know what to do with, Silas Lapham?

LAPHAM: Oh, I've made a very good thing in stocks lately.

MRS. LAPHAM: In stocks? When did you take up gambling for a living?

LAPHAM: Gambling? What gambling? Who said it was gambling?

MRS. LAPHAM: *You* have, many a time.

LAPHAM: Buyin' and sellin' on a margin—yes. But this was a bona fide transaction. I bought at forty-three for an investment, and I sold at a hundred and seven; and the money passed both times.

MRS. LAPHAM: Well, you better let stocks alone. Next time you'll buy at a hundred and seven and sell at forty-three. Then where'll you be?

LAPHAM: Left.

MRS. LAPHAM: You better stick to paint a while yet. I wish we were going to stick to the old house. I wish you had sold that lot on Beacon Street, Silas.

LAPHAM: I hain't.

MRS. LAPHAM: I am satisfied where we be, Si.

LAPHAM: Guess we could live on Beacon Street pretty much as we live at the South End. I guess we live as well as most of the Back Bay folks now, and set as good a table. And if you come to style, I don't know as anybody has got more right to put it on than we have!

PENELOPE, *advancing*: I don't see any use in not enjoying money if you've got it to enjoy. That's what it's for, I suppose; though you mightn't always think so.

LAPHAM: I guess the ayes has it, Pen. How would it do to let Irene and your mother stick in the old place, and us go into the new house?

PENELOPE: I don't believe you could get either of them to do it, Colonel. At any rate mother hasn't shaken the shavings of the *new* house off her back.

She goes round and picks several shavings off

her mother's skirt which she holds up and then drops on the floor. Lapham laughs with her.

MRS. LAPHAM: Did you let me come all the way down here with these shavings sticking to my dress? (*All laugh.*) Well, now you girls go out and look around the warehouse. I've got something to say to your father.

The girls exeunt.

LAPHAM: Pert, a man can be a man on Beacon Street as well as he can on Nankeen Square.

MRS. LAPHAM: Oh yes, you'll shovel off the snow yourself, and I'll do the wash, as I used to in Lumberville. I presume you'll let me have set-tubs, Si. You know I ain't so young any more. But that ain't the point; it ain't what I want to say, Silas. I see we've got to make the move, for the children's sake. If the girls are going to keep on living in Boston and marry here, I presume we ought to try to get them into society, some way, or do something.

LAPHAM: Well, who's ever done more for their children than we have? Don't they dress just as you say? I don't know what you mean. Why don't you get them into society? There's money enough!

MRS. LAPHAM: We ought to have gone out more. We ought to have invited company.

LAPHAM: Why don't you? If it's for the girls, I don't care if you have the house full the whole while.

MRS. LAPHAM: I don't know who to ask.

LAPHAM: Well, you can't expect *me* to tell you.

MRS. LAPHAM: No. We're both country people, and we've kept our country ways, and we don't either of us know what to do. You've had to work so hard, and your luck was so long coming, and then it came with such a rush, that we hadn't any chance to learn what to do with it. It's just the same with Irene's looks; I didn't expect she was going to have any! She was such a plain child, and, all at once, she's blazed out this way. As long as it was Pen, that didn't seem to care for society, I didn't give much mind to it. But I can see it's going to be different with Irene.

LAPHAM, *as Pen's voice is heard without laughing with Irene*: Listen to that! That girl can talk for twenty right straight along. She's better than a circus, any day. I guess it's lucky for Irene that she's got Pen to help her talk.

MRS. LAPHAM: I can't ever feel down, where Pen is.

LAPHAM: That's so, and I guess she's got about as much culture as any of them, don't you?

MRS. LAPHAM: She reads a great deal.

LAPHAM: She seems to be at it the whole while. I don't want she should get notions.

MRS. LAPHAM: I don't want she should injure her health.

LAPHAM: Oh, I guess Pen'll know how to take care of herself.

MRS. LAPHAM: She's got *sense* enough. But she ain't as practical as Irene. It's only when they get to talking that you can see that Pen's got twice as much brains. But that's nothing. (*Taking out an envelop from her purse.*) Here's a letter from Mrs. Bromfield Corey asking me to subscribe to the Charity Hospital.

LAPHAM, *taking letter and turning it in his hands, affecting uncertainty*: Mrs. Bromfield Corey? The one you met at Baie St. Paul and took care of when she was sick? Mother of young Corey you introduced to me at the new house last week? Didn't she call a while back?

MRS. LAPHAM: You know well enough whom I mean, Silas.

LAPHAM: Thought I should *die* at the account Pen gave of her call on you, and the way she acted it out! "Mrs. Corey didn't make me feel as if she'd bought me," says she, "and thought she'd given too much; and mother held up her head just as if she was all wool and a yard wide, and she would just like to have anybody deny it."

Laughs.

MRS. LAPHAM: Oh, Pen! It's easy enough for her to make fun. Of course, Mrs. Corey was a little stiff; that's their way; but I can tell you that if you think they're not the nicest people you ever saw you're mightily mistaken. And they're the very top of society.

LAPHAM, *looking at letter*: Want a cheque?

MRS. LAPHAM: I presume we'd better send something.

LAPHAM, *writing*: Will this do?

MRS. LAPHAM: *taking check then tearing it in two*: I will take a cheque for *one* hundred dollars, Silas Lapham, not *five* hundred.

LAPHAM: Why?

MRS. LAPHAM: Because a hundred is enough, and I don't want to show off before them.

LAPHAM, *writing again*: Oh, I thought maybe you *did*. Well, Pert, I guess you're about right. Do you know what business Corey's in?

MRS. LAPHAM: I guess he ai'n't in any business. They were very nice.

LAPHAM: Well, they'd ought to be; never done anything else.

MRS. LAPHAM: They didn't seem really stuck up.

LAPHAM: They'd no need to—with you— I could buy and sell Bromfield Corey twice over.

MRS. LAPHAM: Well, I guess I wouldn't try, Silas. I can't express it, Silas, but that *young* Mr. Corey had about perfect ways.

LAPHAM: Liked him myself, the other day; seemed to be stuck up on Irene—didn't he? If I had him in business with me I would make a man of him.

MRS. LAPHAM: I do believe you've got mineral paint on the brain. Do you suppose a young fellow like Corey would *touch* mineral paint with a ten foot pole?

LAPHAM: Why not?

MRS. LAPHAM: Well, if you don't know already there's no use trying to tell you.

LAPHAM: Too good for it? Well, perhaps he is. But I don't see how a fellow like that, that's had every advantage in this world, can hang round home and let his father support him.

MRS. LAPHAM: If his father has the money to support him, and don't complain of the burden, I don't see why *we* should.

LAPHAM: I don't like the principle. I like to see a man act like a man. Now, I suppose that fellow belongs to two or three clubs, and hangs round 'em all day lookin' out the window— I've seen 'em—instead of trying to hunt up something to do for an honest living.

The girls, arms in arm, and tilting stylishly about, while they stare up at the kegs and cans of paint, and put their faces together, and whisper and then laugh out, come forward past the side of the private office.

LAPHAM: There! Did you ever see much nicer girls anywhere?

Mrs. Lapham and Lapham remain looking fondly at the girls while they come down to the front and begin talking.

IRENE, *to Penelope*: Do you suppose Mr. Corey will think papa *always* talks in the bragging way he did the other day at the new house?

PENELOPE: He'll be right if he does. It's the way father always does talk. I guess if he can't make allowance for father's bragging he'll be a little *too* good. I enjoyed hearing the Colonel go on!

IRENE: I *know* you did. Didn't you think he looked very nice?

PENELOPE: Who? The Colonel?

IRENE: You know very well I don't mean papa!

PENELOPE: Oh! Mr. Corey! Why didn't you say Mr. Corey if you meant Mr. Corey? If I meant

Mr. Corey I should say Mr. Corey. It isn't swearing! Corey, Corey—Co—

IRENE: Will you *hush*, you wretched thing? The whole place can hear you! Did you like his nose?

PENELOPE: Ah, now you're coming to something. I don't know whether, if I had so much nose, I should want it *all* Roman.

IRENE: I don't see how you can expect to have a nose part one kind and part another.

PENELOPE: Oh, I do. Look at mine! Now my nose started Grecian, but changed its mind after it got over the bridge and concluded to be snub the rest of the way.

IRENE: You've got a very pretty nose, Pen!

PENELOPE: But you only say that in hopes of getting me to compliment *his*, Mrs. —C.

IRENE: You mean thing!

PENELOPE: Well, *D.* then. You've nothing to say against D? Though I think C. is just as nice an initial.

IRENE: Oh! Pen! Pen! You are just awful! Ow-w.

The girls put their heads together and laugh; then walk back into the warehouse. The parents begin again in Lapham's office.

LAPHAM: Rogers was here this morning before I came in.

MRS. LAPHAM, *with a violent start*: Rogers!

LAPHAM: Rogers. I thought he was dead!

MRS. LAPHAM: Oh, don't *say* such a thing! It sounds as if you wished it. (*Whimpering.*) I don't know how he always manages to appear just at the moment when he seems to have gone fairly out of our lives, and blight everything.

LAPHAM: What do you let him blight everything for?

MRS. LAPHAM: I can't help it. I don't know as his being dead would help it any. I can't see him without feeling just as I felt at first. I can't look at him without feeling as if you'd ruined him, Silas.

LAPHAM: Don't *look* at him then. I want you should recollect, Persis, that I never wanted a partner.

MRS. LAPHAM: If he hadn't put his money in when he did, you'd a' broken down.

LAPHAM: Well, he got his money out again, and more.

MRS. LAPHAM: He didn't want to take it out.

LAPHAM: I gave him his choice—buy out or sell out.

MRS. LAPHAM: You knew he couldn't buy out. It was no choice at all.

LAPHAM: It was a business chance.

MRS. LAPHAM: No. You'd better face the truth, Silas Lapham. You crowded him *out*. A man that *saved* you!

LAPHAM: I'm sick of this. If you'll tend to the house, I'll manage my business myself. Don't meddle. It was fifteen years ago.

MRS. LAPHAM: I *will* meddle. What has time got to do with it? I can't ever get you to own up the least bit about Rogers.

LAPHAM: What do you want I should own up to? I tell you he was a break on me from the word go, if I hadn't got him out he'd a ruined me. I was loaded up with a partner that didn't know anything, and I unloaded; that's all. I had a right to do it. I made the success.

MRS. LAPHAM: Yes. You made it with Rogers' money, and when you'd made it you took his share. (*After a pause.*) And don't you ask me to go to that new house with you any more. You can sell it for all me. I sha'n't live in it. There's *blood* on it.

Enter Rogers L.

LAPHAM: Hush, Persis. He's come back.

MRS. LAPHAM, *turning*: Why, Mr. Rogers! (*She hesitates.*) We didn't know you were in Boston. Is Mrs. Rogers with you?

ROGERS: No, Mrs. Rogers is still in Chicago.

MRS. LAPHAM: I presume you are quite settled out there?

ROGERS: No. We have left Chicago. Mrs. Rogers has merely remained to finish up a little packing.

MRS. LAPHAM: Oh, indeed—are you coming back to Boston?

ROGERS: I cannot say as yet. We some think of so doing.

Lapham turns away pretending to look at the plan of the house before him. There is an uneasy pause.

MRS. LAPHAM, *vaguely glancing at plan*: We are building a house.

ROGERS: Oh, indeed!

MRS. LAPHAM: If you come to Boston, I hope I shall see Mrs. Rogers.

ROGERS: She will be happy to have you call.

MRS. LAPHAM: My girls are waiting. Silas, I want you should meet us at the wharf in time for the two o'clock boat. (*To Rogers.*) We are down at our cottage at Nantasket for the summer—it's convenient for Mr. Lapham. (*To Lapham.*) We will all go down together.

LAPHAM: I won't keep you waitin'.

MRS. LAPHAM: Good morning, Mr. Rogers.

She joins the girls without and they are seen passing off together.

ROGERS: I hope I don't interrupt you, Col. Lapham. I called on a matter of business. I've brought some papers with me—securities I would like you to examine. I have a patent that I some think of going into, and I wish to raise money— and I naturally thought of you.

LAPHAM: You need money?

ROGERS: Yes.

LAPHAM: How much?

ROGERS: I need twenty thousand dollars to-day.

LAPHAM: Twenty thousand dollars!

ROGERS: I couldn't do with less. My securities are worth ten times as much.

LAPHAM: I'm not thinking of security. We haven't come to that. Twenty thousand, eh? Business is in a pretty bad shape just now. But we've had two or three such flurries, 'fore, and they didn't amount to much, and I don't see as it will apply to my paint anyway.

ROGERS: Then you can let me have the money?

LAPHAM: I don't know. I don't know as I see my way clear.

ROGERS: If I can't raise this money to-day or to-morrow I may be forced to the wall. If we hadn't parted—or if I had bought you out instead of selling out to you, you might be in my place to-day.

LAPHAM: I might, and I mightn't.

ROGERS: You didn't leave me any choice. You forced me out. But I didn't call to bring all that up. If you can't let me have the money—

LAPHAM: Sit down. Let me see those securities.

As Lapham examines the papers Walker, typewriter and William come in from luncheon, hang up their hats and resume work.

ROGERS: Milling property—saw mills, and timberlands, grist mills—plant worth at least a quarter of a million.

LAPHAM: I've heard of this property. But the income isn't the value of the property.

ROGERS: You see there are two railroads, rival concerns; it makes the carrying for the mills very reasonable; it makes the possible profits very large.

LAPHAM: But if these roads should consolidate where would the mills be? Suppose they should want to buy me out at their own price, some time? They could squeeze me dry.

ROGERS: They are rival corporations, belonging to different systems. The Grand Lacustrine and Polar would never consolidate with the P. Y. and X.

LAPHAM: Well, I don't know as I'm right to do it. *(Calls.)* Walker, lock up these securities in my private box in the safe. *(He turns to his desk and writes.)* There! Come in tomorrow and we can arrange the details. Rogers, I wouldn't have done this for any other man in the face of the market.

ROGERS: Thank you; much obliged. *(They shake hands.)* Well, good afternoon.

LAPHAM, *absently, as Rogers turns away*: Good afternoon. *(Exit Rogers L. Lapham looks after him, a pause.)* Well, that's over.

Takes off his coat. He seats himself in his shirt sleeves and begins writing at his desk. Enter Tom Corey without, L.

TOM: Is Mr. Lapham in?

WALKER, *after a moment's pause, nodding to Lapham's office*: Yes, he's in.

TOM: Will you ask him if he can see Mr. Corey.

WALKER, *at Lapham's door*: Mr. Corey.

LAPHAM: Mr. Corey?

WALKER: Yes, sir. Shall he come in?

LAPHAM: Yes. *(Rising and standing.)* Come in, Mr. Corey. You'll excuse me, I'm about roasted. How are you? Won't you sit down?

TOM, *as he enters the private office*: I wish you'd let me take off my coat.

LAPHAM: Why, take it off!

TOM: I will, if you ask me after I've talked with you two minutes. But perhaps you haven't got two minutes to give me.

LAPHAM: Oh, yes, I have; just two. I've got to catch the two o'clock boat for Nantasket. Family going down, and I'm going with 'em; Saturday, you know, and we close early.

TOM: All right; I'll be quick. I want you to take me into the mineral paint business, Colonel Lapham. *(After a long pause Lapham takes a jar of the Persis Brand from his desk and stares at it.)* What is it?

LAPHAM: Nothing. I was just thinkin' of Mis' Lapham. Go on!

TOM: I suppose I could have got several people whose names you know to back my industry and sobriety. But I thought I wouldn't trouble anybody for certificates till I found out whether there was a chance of your wanting me. So I came straight to you.

LAPHAM: How do you think I am going to take you on?

TOM: I haven't a very clear idea, I'm afraid. But I see that you are introducing your paint into the foreign markets, and there I really thought I might be of use to you.

LAPHAM: How?

TOM: Well, I know two or three languages pretty well. I know French and I know German, and I've got a fair sprinkling of Spanish.

LAPHAM: You mean you can talk them?

TOM: Yes; and I can write an intelligible letter in either of them. I know the countries where you want to introduce this paint of yours. I've been there. I've been in Germany and France, and I've been in South America and Mexico. I believe I could go to any of those countries and place it to advantage.

LAPHAM, *shaking his head*: Your salary and expenses would eat up about all we could make on it.

TOM: Yes, if you had to pay me any salary and expenses.

LAPHAM: You don't propose to work for nothing.

TOM: I propose to work for a commission. (*As the Colonel shakes his head.*) I haven't come to you without making some inquiries about the paint, and I know how it stands with those who know best.

LAPHAM, *slowly lifting his head and facing Corey*: It's the best paint in God's universe!

TOM: It's the best in the market. I believe in it.

LAPHAM: You believe in it!

TOM: You musn't let me outstay my two minutes. (*Rises.*) I don't expect you to give me a decided answer on the spot. All that I ask is that you'll consider my proposition.

LAPHAM: Don't hurry. Set down. (*Both sit.*) I want to tell you about this paint. I want to tell you all about it. Look here! (*Showing a photograph.*) Here's where we get it. This photograph don't half do the place justice. It's one of the sightliest places in this country, and here's the very spot where my father found that paint—more —than—forty—years—ago. Yes, sir! We've got to have another talk about this thing. It's a surprise to me, and I don't see exactly how you are going to make it pay.

TOM: I'm willing to take the chances.

LAPHAM: Look here, I like to get things over. Why don't you come down with me to Nantasket? I can give you a bed as well as not, and then we can finish up.

TOM: I should like to have it finished up myself.

LAPHAM: Well, we'll see. (*Calling.*) Dennis! (*To Corey.*) Want to send any word home?

TOM: No; my father and I go and come as we like—when my mother and sister are away. If I don't come home he knows I'm not there. That's all.

LAPHAM: Well, that's convenient. You'll find you can't do that when you're married. (*Calls.*) Never mind, Dennis. (*He pauses as Tom has risen.*) Just one thing! Do your people know of this?

TOM: I spoke of it to my uncle, James Bellingham.

LAPHAM: The banker? It isn't far to his bank. Go up there and tell him what we have been talking about. I don't want you should do anything rash. If he agrees, come back and we will have time for the two o'clock boat—or a later one.

TOM: It's a mere form.

LAPHAM: I'd feel better, if you did.

Enter Dinwiddie, pauses in outer office, speaks to Walker, sits on chair to wait.

TOM: I'll go. (*Seeing plan.*) I passed your new house to-day. It's getting on.

LAPHAM: Yes, sir. (*Expanding.*) There! We're going to throw out a bay-window here, so as to get the water all the way up and down. This is my girls' room. There ain't going to be an unpleasant room in the whole house, from top to bottom. I started out to build a forty-thousand-dollar house, and that fellow Seymour has got me in for more than eighty thousand already, and I doubt if I get out much under a hundred and fifty, but you can't have a nice house for nothing. Yes, sir, give an architect money enough and he will give you a nice house every time.

TOM: I've heard that they're sharp at getting money to realize their ideas.

LAPHAM: Well, I should say so, and they always manage to get you when your wife is around and then you're helpless. Yes, sir, it's about the sightliest view that I know of. I always did like the waterside of Beacon. Long before I owned property there, or ever expected to, m'wife and me used to ride down that way and stop the buggy to get that view over the water. When people talk to me about Commonwealth Avenue, I don't know what they mean. It don't hold a candle to the waterside of Beacon. You've got just as much wind on the house, and you've got just as much dust, and all the view you've got is the view across the street. No, sir, when you come to the Back Bay at all, give me the waterside of Beacon!

TOM: Oh, I think you're quite right. I must hurry or I shall miss my uncle at his bank. I'll be back in fifteen minutes.

LAPHAM: You'll find me here!

Exit Tom L.

WALKER, *at office door:* Can you see Mr. Din-widdie, Colonel Lapham?

LAPHAM: Mr. Dinwiddie?

WALKER: From Kanawha, West Virginia.

LAPHAM: Oh, yes—yes! Show him in. *(Enter Dinwiddie.)* Glad to see you, Mr. Dinwiddie. But if you've come for my yes or no, now, I can't give it.

DINWIDDIE: I haven't come for that, sir. I've just come in to leave these papers—and some fresh specimens of our paint ore—we want to make our case as strong as possible. Here's a statement of our facilities—received it from my brother out in Kanawha this morning. You'll see from it exactly what transportation we have—the cheapness of natural gas for burning the ore—the mining facil-ities—and just how we stand. We've got a good thing; all we need is a partner to put in more money.

LAPHAM: Yes, you have got a good thing, I've seen that from the first. I'll look over these papers, and I'll examine the ore, but I don't know as I ought to take anything more on my shoulders. I'll think it over. I won't say yes, and I won't say no. And I may go in and I may stay out. That's where I stand.

DINWIDDIE: Well, we're looking about.

LAPHAM: That's right, that's right.

DINWIDDIE: But we'd rather have you in with us than anyone else—if we must have someone.

LAPHAM: I know just how you feel. Hello! There's my wife and girls back for me!

Enter Penelope, Mrs. Lapham and Irene L.

DINWIDDIE: Well, good day, Colonel.

He passes into outer office, touching his hat to the ladies; as he goes out he turns and stares long at Irene.

PENELOPE, *laughing:* There's Mr. Corey's rival, Irene. What's his name?

IRENE: He looked at *you.*

PENELOPE: Well, he's cross-eyed then.

The girls walk down the warehouse.

MRS. LAPHAM, *within office:* Well, Silas Lap-ham—what did Rogers want of you? I couldn't wait till you come to the boat, that's why I come back for you.

LAPHAM: He came to borrow money of me, and I lent it. That's the short of it. The long—

MRS. LAPHAM: Go on!

LAPHAM: He had brought along a lot of stocks as security.

MRS. LAPHAM: You didn't take it, Silas!

LAPHAM: Yes I did, though. When we got through we shook hands. Well I don't know when it's done me so much good to shake hands with anybody.

MRS. LAPHAM: And you told him—you owned up to him that you were in the wrong, Silas?

LAPHAM: No, I didn't, for I wa'n't. I've lent him the money, and I've kept his stocks, and he got what he wanted out of me.

MRS. LAPHAM: Give him back his stocks!

LAPHAM: No I sha'n't. Rogers came to borrow. He didn't come to beg.

MRS. LAPHAM: Well, I'm satisfied. The Lord has been good to you, Silas. Oh, you may laugh if you choose but he's let you live to make it up to Rogers, and I've been afraid you'd die, Silas, before you got the chance—

LAPHAM: I'm glad he let me live, but I hadn't anything to make up to Milton K. Rogers. And if God has let me live for that—

MRS. LAPHAM: Oh, say what you please, Si, I sha'n't stop you! You've taken the one spot—the one speck—off you that was ever there, and I'm satisfied.

LAPHAM: There wan't ever any speck, and what I done I done for you, Persis.

MRS. LAPHAM: And I thank you for your own soul's sake, Silas.

LAPHAM: I guess my soul's all right.

MRS. LAPHAM: And I want you should promise me one thing more.

LAPHAM: I thought you said you were satisfied?

MRS. LAPHAM: I am. But I want you should promise me this: that you won't let anything tempt you—anything—to ever trouble Rogers for that money you lent him, no matter what hap-pens. Do you promise?

LAPHAM: Why, I don't ever expect to press him for it. That's what I said to myself when I lent it. I don't think I ever done Rogers any wrong, but if I did do it, if I *did*—I'm willin' to call it square, if I never see a cent of my money back again!

MRS. LAPHAM: Well, that's settled, and we've still got time for the boat. Why don't you put on your coat? What are you waiting for, Silas?

LAPHAM: Oh, I'm just waiting for young Corey.

MRS. LAPHAM: Young Corey?

LAPHAM: Yes, he's going down to Nantasket with us to-night.

MRS. LAPHAM: Young Corey! Don't joke! What's he coming for?

LAPHAM: Oh, I asked him.

MRS. LAPHAM: I don't believe a word of it. Did you urge him? Pshaw, you haven't seen him. If you urged him, I'll never forgive you, Silas. If he wants to see Irene, he can find out ways of doing it for himself.

LAPHAM: I didn't urge him. Seemed to want to come.

MRS. LAPHAM: Look out, Silas! Where did you see him?

LAPHAM: Here in the office.

MRS. LAPHAM: What office?

LAPHAM: This.

MRS. LAPHAM: Nonsense! What was he doing here?

LAPHAM: Oh, he *said* he wanted to go into the mineral paint business.

MRS. LAPHAM: Silas Lapham, if you try to get off any more of those things on me!

LAPHAM: Had a notion he could work it in South America. *I* don't know what he's up to.

MRS. LAPHAM: Never mind! I'll get even with you, yet!

LAPHAM: I told him he had better see his uncle, James Bellingham, and then come down with me and talk it over. But I knew he wouldn't touch it with a ten foot pole.

MRS. LAPHAM: Go on!

LAPHAM: Right thing to do, wa'n't it?

Enter Tom Corey in warehouse L.

MRS. LAPHAM: Well, I never believed it, and I don't now!

LAPHAM: You wait and see!

They watch Corey shaking hands with the girls without; he stops to talk with them.

TOM: I suppose you're all very much taken with your new house? Did you all help to plan it?

IRENE: Oh, no, the architect and mama did that.

PENELOPE: But they allowed the rest of us to agree, when we were *good*.

Goes into background and leaves Tom and Irene seated on two kegs of paint.

IRENE: We are going to have the back room upstairs for a music room and library.

TOM: Yes? I should think that would be charming.

IRENE: We expected to have book-cases, but the architect wants to build the shelves in.

TOM: They'd look like part of the room then. You can make them low and hang your pictures above them.

IRENE: Yes, that's what he said. I presume with nice bindings it will look very well.

TOM: Oh, nothing furnishes a room like books.

IRENE: There will have to be a good many of them.

TOM: It will depend on the size of the room.

IRENE: Of course, I presume we shall have Gibbon.

TOM: If you want to read him.

IRENE: We had a great deal about him at school. I used to get them mixed up with each other, and I couldn't tell the historians from the poets. Should you want to have poetry? We don't any of us like poetry. Do you like it?

TOM: I'm afraid I don't very much. But there was a time when Tennyson was a great deal more to me than he is now.

IRENE: We had something about him at school too. I think we ought to have *all* the American poets.

TOM: Five or six of the best; you want Longfellow and Byrant and Whittier and Holmes and Emerson and Lowell.

IRENE: And Shakespeare. Don't you like Shakespear's plays?

TOM: Oh, yes, very much.

IRENE: I used to be perfectly crazy about his plays. Don't you think *Hamlet* is splendid? Weren't you perfectly astonished when you found out how many other plays he wrote? I always thought there was nothing but *Hamlet* and *Romeo and Juliet*. Well, if we have a library we have got to have books in it. Pen says it's perfectly ridiculous having one. Of course, papa will buy them if we say so. But I don't see how I am ever going to tell him which ones.

TOM: Why, if you like I'll put down the names we've been talking about.

IRENE: Will you? Here, take one of my cards.

TOM, *sitting on a keg of paint beside Irene:* Thank you. (*He writes.*) Those are the ones we mentioned, but perhaps I'd better add a few others.

IRENE: Oh, thank you. He has got to get them in the nicest bindings, too. I shall tell him about their helping to furnish the room and then he can't object.

She pokes at a shaving on the floor before her with her parasol.

TOM: You seem to have a great passion for playing with shavings.

IRENE: Oh, I guess it must have stuck in mamma's dress when we were at the house and she brought it down here. Perhaps you don't approve of playing with shavings?

TOM: Oh, yes, I do. I admire it very much. But it seems rather difficult. I've a great ambition to put my foot on the shaving's tail and hold it down for you.

IRENE: Well.

TOM: Thank you. (*He puts his foot on the shaving. Irene runs her parasol through it.*) That was wonderful. Would you like to try it again?

IRENE: No, I thank you. I think once will do.

TOM: Don't you like the smell of fresh pine? It's delicious. (*Taking up the shaving.*) It's really like a flower. May I offer it to you?

IRENE: Oh, thank you, thank you!

She takes it and fastens it in her belt, both laughing. Through this scene Lapham has kept at his desk, Mrs. Lapham standing near him; gradually he has stopped his writing and has sat watching Irene and Tom with varying feelings. Penelope has watched them too, but has suddenly turned and moved away into the gloom of the warehouse. She returns just as Irene puts the shaving into her belt.

TOM: I'm sorry I haven't one for you, too, Miss Lapham!

PEN: One what?

TOM: A shaving from your new house. Your sister and I have just agreed that they are deliciously fragrant.

PEN: Oh! I believe I prefer mineral paint.

TOM: I believe I do, too!

IRENE: I'll tell papa that.

PEN: Don't. He's too proud, now. If he knew that Mr. Corey liked the smell of his paint better than the smell of shavings, I don't know what he *would* do. (*Pen goes into private office. As Pen enters office Lapham rises, letting the roller top of his desk fall with a bang, turning the key in the lock. In office.*) Well, Colonel, if you're through now, perhaps you'll let Dennis shut up the shop and let us try for that two o'clock boat.

They come out into wareroom.

LAPHAM, *to Tom:* What did Mr. Bellingham say?

TOM: He's for it.

LAPHAM: Good. Then we'll talk over the details at Nantasket. (*To Mrs. Lapham, trumphantly.*) Well, mother, what do you say to the plan? Heigh?

Significantly.

MRS. LAPHAM: I say if you want to catch that boat—

LAPHAM: We've got ten minutes to try. (*Looking at watch.*) Time enough. I like to get aboard just as she moves out, and if she has the start a little I guess we can ketch her with a ten foot pole!

He nudges Mrs. Lapham, she strikes him playfully as all turn and exit.

CURTAIN

ACT II

SCENE: *The Corey's House. The scene shows a drawing room from which a dining room is separated by heavy curtains; the scene is so set that both rooms are virtually one when the curtains are drawn aside. A part of the hall with entrance through double doors opens from the drawing room. Doors lead to other rooms.*

Discovered: Mr. and Mrs. Corey, in evening dress. Mr. Corey has evening paper. Mrs. Corey has some flowers which she can arrange in vase or later take to the dining room.

MRS. COREY: Bromfield, I confess I wish this dinner were well over. It is all very distasteful to me.

COREY: Well, my dear, if it is any consolation to you, I think it is going to be as much of a trial to your Laphams as it is to you.

MRS. COREY: My Laphams!

COREY: Well, Tom's Laphams then. Come Anna, I thought you did not find them so bad at Baie St. Paul.

MRS. COREY: I hadn't seen them in Nankeen Square then.

COREY: You will see them on the waterside of Beacon Street before the winter is over.

MRS. COREY: Beacon Street is getting very common, Bromfield. When Tom first suggested going into this mineral paint business, why didn't you stop him? Tom need not earn his living—there is enough for us all.

COREY: I did urge it upon Tom, that with economy, and by cramping us a little, he need do nothing as long as he lived. But it appears that he wished to do something. I am afraid that Tom is selfish.

MRS. COREY: I feel very unhappy about it—it isn't the paint alone— (*Checks herself.*) I wish he had married someone.

COREY: With money? From time to time I have attempted Tom's corruption from that side, but he has a conscience against it, and I rather like him for it. I married for love myself.

MRS. COREY: What nonsense!

COREY: Besides, if you come to money, there's the Mineral Paint princess—she'll have plenty.

MRS. COREY: Oh, that's the worst of it! I suppose I could get on with the paint—

COREY: But not with the princess?

MRS. COREY: It troubles me, Bromfield. The child is very pretty.

COREY: Oh, you feel sure it's the pretty one, then? Tom says the plain one is very humorous; and there's a sense of humor as well as a sense of color in our family.

MRS. COREY: Nonsense! He couldn't think of that little black, pert thing. She was fairly saucy to me when I called on her mother.

COREY: You don't think you patronized them, Anna? I've seen the time when if I had been the subject of your condescension I should have sauced you myself. Well, let's hope it's neither of the princesses. You haven't sounded Tom on the subject?

MRS. COREY: No, I wish you could do so, Bromfield.

COREY: It's a delicate matter. You can't very well ask your son if he's in love, and which one besides!

MRS. COREY: It will have to be done sooner or later. I must go and give a glance at the table.

Exit through portieres to dining room. At the same moment enter Tom from left.

COREY: Ah, Tom! Your mother and I were just talking of you. (*Goes up and puts hands on son's shoulders, and gazes admiringly at him.*) Who's your tailor? I don't see how you can afford such nice clothes?

TOM: Why, you see, I have an indulgent father.

COREY: Ah, I wish *I* had. And sometimes I wish I was in the mineral paint line, like you; I should be more prosperous. But I must be satisfied to dine the mineral paint king. The royal family is disposed to make us do ante-chamber, it seems.

TOM: It's only a few minutes past eight. We must give them the quarter hour's grace.

COREY: Oh, yes. As all of them are coming they ought to have half an hour's grace, perhaps.

TOM: I'm not sure it was best to have them at all.

COREY: Your mother and I felt that we ought to.

TOM: I don't know quite what you mean.

COREY: I see you do, Tom.

TOM: No one can help feeling that they are people of good sense and right ideas.

COREY: Oh, that won't do. If society took in all the people of right ideas and good sense, it would expand beyond the calling capacity of its active members. Society is a very different sort of thing from good sense and right ideas. It is based upon them, of course, but the airy, graceful, winning superstructure which we all know demands different qualities. Have your friends got these qualities, which may be felt, but not defined?

TOM: To tell the truth, sir, I don't think they have the most elemental ideas of society as we understand it. I don't believe Mrs. Lapham ever gave a dinner.

COREY: With all that money!

TOM: I don't believe they have the habit of wine at table. I suspect that when they don't drink tea and coffee with their dinner, they drink ice-water.

COREY: Horrible!

TOM: I don't believe that I can make you see Colonel Lapham quite as I do. I don't know that we can judge him rightly by our standards.

COREY: Oh, one could make out a case. I suppose you know what you are about, Tom. I suspect this all comes of your winter in Texas. I am always saying that the Bostonian ought never to leave Boston. Then he knows—and then only—that there can be no standard but ours. One man goes to England and returns with the conception of a grander social life; another comes home from Germany with the notion of a more searching intellectual activity; a fellow just back from Paris has the absurdest ideas of art and literature; and you revert to us from the cowboys of Texas, and tell us to our faces that we ought to try Papa Lapham by a jury of his peers. It ought to be stopped, it ought, really. The Bostonian who leaves Boston ought to be condemned to perpetual exile.

Mrs. Corey enters. Tom goes to her.

MRS. COREY: Tom—

TOM: Mother, do you really think this dinner is going to be a trial for the Laphams?

MRS. COREY: No. No. I can't say it is, but I confess I wish it were well over. It's all very distasteful to me, Tom.

TOM: I'm sorry, mother, but you know I never suggested this dinner. I'm sure it is the right thing. I—I've forgotten my handkerchief.

Exit.

MRS. COREY: If the dinner only ended it!

COREY: We will not despond, my dear. If Tom is really in love with one of the Misses Lapham, or even both of them, we have the consolation of knowing that we couldn't help it.

Enter Nanny Corey.

NANNY: Poor Tom! I met him on the stairs. He's so troubled about his Laphams. Perhaps it won't be so bad.

MRS. COREY: She seemed an affectionate little thing with her mother, and really so pretty.

NANNY: Oh, she'll be an affectionate little thing with Tom, too, you may be sure. She'll make him think we were all against her from the beginning.

MRS. COREY: She has no cause for that, and we shall not give her any. I can't imagine what he finds to talk about with her.

NANNY: Oh, that's very simple; they talk about themselves, with occasional references to each other. I have heard people go on, on the hotel piazzas. She's embroidering, or knitting, and he says she seems quite devoted to needlework, and she says yes, she has a perfect passion for it, and everybody laughs at her for it; she always was so from a child, and supposes she always shall be— with remote and minute particulars. And she ends by saying that perhaps he does not like people to knit or embroider, or whatever. And he says, oh, yes, he does; what could make her think such a thing? But for his part he likes boating rather better. Then she lets him take up one corner of her work, and perhaps touch her fingers; and that encourages him to say that he supposes nothing could induce her to drop her work long enough to go down on the rocks, or out among the huckleberry bushes: and she puts her head on one side and says she doesn't know really. And then they go, and he lies at her feet on the rocks, or picks huckleberries and drops them in her lap, and they go on talking about themselves, and comparing notes to see how they differ from each other and—

MRS. COREY: That will do, Nanny. Disgusting!

NANNY: Disgusting? Not at all. It's very amusing when you see it, and when you do it!

MRS. COREY: It's always a mystery what people see in each other.

NANNY: The most that we can do is to hope for the best till we know the worst.

MRS. COREY: Of course, we shall make the best of the worst when it comes.

Exeunt Mr. and Mrs. Corey, R. Enter Tom, L.

NANNY: Tom, we've been talking about you!

TOM: That's what father told me before. What have you been saying?

NANNY: Very nice things. That she's very sweet and good, and that if you *must* be happy, we hope you may be *very* happy!

TOM: Oh, thank you, Nan. It's a little premature—

NANNY: I dare say. But it isn't the less certain on that account. I don't know that I should have chosen to go to Nankeen Square for a sister; but I don't think I could have found a more beautiful one, anywhere.

TOM: Beautiful? Well, I don't know. Charming, yes; and quaint; but beautiful—

NANNY: Why, where are your eyes? She's divine —if that's all you want.

TOM: Do you think so, Nan? That's very sweet of you—

NANNY: I do, indeed. And her name suits her beauty so exactly. It's royal; though they don't know how to pronounce it. You must teach them to say, I-re-ne.

TOM, *aghast*: I-re-ne!

NANNY, *amazed*: You don't mean to say it's—

TOM: Penelope? Of course, I do! How could you dream of anything else? I never thought of Irene for a moment. She's pretty, and she's good, as you say; but Penelope is—I was in love with her from the first moment. She fascinated me!

NANNY: Oh, Tom, Tom, Tom!

TOM: What?

NANNY: Do you think *they* know it?

TOM: Know it? Of course, they know it! What do you mean?

NANNY: I'm afraid they don't. I'm afraid they think it's Irene. Oh, Tom, how could you! We all thought it was Irene.

TOM: You thought it was Irene! Nanny—

NANNY: Hush! They're coming down stairs at last. Come! (*She seizes his hand and pulls him through door, R.*) They mustn't find us here!

Enter Lapham, pulling off his gloves; and Mrs. Lapham after him.

MRS. LAPHAM: I declare, Silas Lapham, you're pulling off those gloves again! Can't you do one way or another? You'll drive me wild with your fussing. Why didn't you find out whether you have to wear 'em or not?

LAPHAM, *putting on gloves*: Haven't I tried? I read all the behavior books, and they didn't say a word about it; and I asked the girl in the store where I bought 'em, and *she* couldn't tell, either. Just kept on peppering in that powdered soap to make 'em slip on, and split up the front or back till I got this pair. (*Glances down at them.*) My Lord, I don't know what to do. *One* while, I thought I'd ask Tom Corey—

MRS. LAPHAM: If you had, Silas Lapham, I'd

have *left* you. What's keeping her, I wonder. And you made me accept for Penelope, you said it wouldn't make any difference whether she came or not; and now I'm afraid it will, and I shan't know *what* to say. Oh, I wish we'd never *thought* of coming. And we're too old to learn to be like them.

LAPHAM: The children ain't. I wish Pen had come. She could talk for twenty.

MRS. LAPHAM: She was set against it from the first. She said they wanted to see Irene. They didn't want *her*.

LAPHAM: I guess they wanted her or they wouldn't have asked her. Of course, if young Corey's taken with Irene—

MRS. LAPHAM: Irene'll be a lucky girl to get him, if she wants him. But there! I'd ten times rather she was going to marry such a fellow as you were, Si, that had to make every inch of his own way, and she had to help him. (*Looking anxiously at Lapham and then starting back.*) Silas, you've got something more than your *gloves* and your cravat on your mind!

LAPHAM: Yes, I have, Persis.

MRS. LAPHAM, *tenderly*: Is it anything you can tell me about, Silas?

LAPHAM: I haven't ever hid anything from you, Persis, when you asked me, and it's too late to begin now. I'm in a kind of fix. Things have been dull all fall, but I thought they'd brisk up come winter. They haven't. There's been a lot of failures and some of them owed me, and some of them had me on their paper, and—

MRS. LAPHAM: And what?

LAPHAM: And then—Rogers.

MRS. LAPHAM: I didn't want you should get in any deeper with him.

LAPHAM: No. And you didn't want I should press him either, and I had to do one or the other. And so I got in deeper.

MRS. LAPHAM: Silas, I'm afraid I made you!

LAPHAM: It's all right, Persis, as far forth as that goes. It'll all come out right in the end. Only pretty near everybody but the fellows that owe me money seem to expect me to do a cash business all of a sudden.

MRS. LAPHAM: Do you mean you've got payments to make, and that people are not paying you?

LAPHAM: Something like that. I ain't going to let the grass grow under my feet, though, especially while Rogers digs the ground away from the roots.

MRS. LAPHAM: What are you going to do?

LAPHAM: If it has to come to that, I'm going to squeeze him. Milton K. Rogers is a rascal, if you want to know; or else all the signs fail. But I guess he'll find he's got his come-uppance.

MRS. LAPHAM: What's he done?

LAPHAM: What's he done? He's been dabbling in every sort of fool thing you can lay your tongue to; wild-cat stocks, patent-rights, land speculations, oil claims—till he's run through about everything. But he did have a big milling property out on the line of the P. Y. & X., saw-mills and grist mills and timber lands: and for the last years he's been doing a land office business with them— business that would have made anybody else rich. But you can't make Milton K. Rogers rich any more than you can fat a hide bound colt. It ain't in him. He'd run through Vanderbilt, Rocke- feller and Astor rolled into one in less than six months, give him a chance, and come out and want to borrow money of you. Well, he won't borrow any more of *me*; and if he thinks I don't know as much about that milling property as he does he's mistaken. I've taken his mills for security, and I guess I've got the inside track. Bill's kept me posted; and now I'm going out there to see how I can unload; and I shan't mind a great deal if Rogers is under the load when it's off once.

MRS. LAPHAM: I don't understand you, Silas.

LAPHAM: Why, it's just this. The G. L. & P. has leased the P. Y. & X. for ninety-nine years— bought it practically—and it's going to build car works right by those mills, and it wants the mills. And Milton K. Rogers knew it when he turned 'em in on me.

MRS. LAPHAM: Well, if the road wants the mills you can get what you ask for them.

LAPHAM: Can I? The G. L. & P. is the only road that runs within fifty miles of the mills, and you can't get a foot of lumber or a pound of flour to market any other way. As long as he had a little local road like the P. Y. & X. to deal with, Rogers could manage; but when it comes to a big through line like the G. L. & P. he couldn't stand any chance at all. If such a road as that takes a fancy to his mills, do you think it will pay what he asked? No, sir! He must take what the road offers, or else the road will tell him to carry his flour and lumber to market himself.

MRS. LAPHAM: And do you suppose he knew the G. L. & P. wanted the mills when he turned them in on you?

LAPHAM: Well, when Milton K. Rogers don't know which side his bread's buttered on!

MRS. LAPHAM: Well, I want you should ask yourself whether Rogers would ever have gone wrong if it hadn't been for your forcing him out of the business when you did. I want you should think whether you're not responsible for everything he's done since.

LAPHAM: You go and fetch Irene. I guess I can take care of myself and Milton K. Rogers, too.

Pulling off his gloves.

MRS. LAPHAM: Oh, *don't* take them off again. (*He puts them on. Enter Irene.*) Oh, there you are at last. Your father's fairly driving me distracted about his gloves.

IRENE: I think papa looks splendid!

LAPHAM: Good for you, Irene! My Lord, but you're pretty in that dress. It'll go off all right about Pen, Persis; you'll see. And I tell you what. You two just go in there, and see whether the men have got gloves on, and then one of you pretend you've forgot something and come out and tell me.

IRENE: Well, that's a good idea, papa. Come along, mama!

Mrs. Lapham with a gesture of despair goes out R. to library with Irene; while James Bellingham [1] *enters L.*

BELLINGHAM: Ah, Colonel. Waiting for the ladies? They always make us do that.

LAPHAM, *looking at tie, aside*: Black! (*Observing that he has no gloves, pulls his off and puts them into his coat tail pocket.*) Well, well—not exactly. They're in there, (*nodding R*) but I—I'm mighty glad to see you a moment alone, Mr. Bellingham. Your nephew, Tom Corey, has been talking to me about putting some money into the business and I've kind of fought off from him. I'll tell you why. Between you and me, I've got caught a little in stocks, and I've lent money to an old partner of mine. Well, it's all right. It ain't anything that I can't swing with one hand tied behind me. But when I let your nephew put in his money, I don't want him to take the least risk in the world—nor the shadow of it. Understand?

BELLINGHAM: It's what I should have expected

---

[1] At first Howells used both Charles and James Bellingham; then he combined the two into one character without making changes consistent throughout the typescript.

---

of you, Colonel Lapham. (*Offering hand.*) Not that I think there's the least risk, but—

LAPHAM, *swelling*: Not the least in the world! I can raise $100,000—on my own house any day,—and— But you know how I feel?

BELLINGHAM: I'm proud to say I do, Colonel Lapham—

Mrs. Lapham enter from R.

MRS. LAPHAM: Well, Colonel Lapham, ain't you *ever* coming? (*Seeing Bellingham.*) Oh, *excuse* me!

LAPHAM: Introduce you to Mrs. Lapham, Mr. Bellingham.

They bow and all go toward library R. whence issues Mrs. Corey followed slowly by the others. Mr. Corey, Mr. Seymour, Irene, Tom, Miss Kingsbury and Nanny.

TOM, *advancing, shaking hands with Lapham*: Ah, Colonel Lapham, very glad to see you. Mother—

Introducing Mrs. Corey to Lapham.

MRS COREY, *advancing and shaking hands*: General Lapham?

LAPHAM: No, ma'am, only Colonel.

COREY, *to Lapham*: I am very glad to see you again.

LAPHAM, *observing Corey's white tie, beaming with satisfaction, aside*: White!

Nanny holds Irene's hand a moment; Mrs. Corey turns to Mrs. Lapham.

MRS. COREY: Can I send any one to be of use to Miss Lapham?

MRS. LAPHAM: She isn't upstairs. (*Bluntly.*) She didn't feel just like coming tonight. I don't know as she's feeling very well.

MR. COREY: Oh! (*Very coldly; with offense.*) I'm very sorry. It's nothing serious, I hope. (*To Mr. Corey.*) I think we are all here then.

Mr. Corey crosses and gives his arm to Mrs. Lapham, the curtains are drawn back opening the dining room into the scene. Mrs. Corey slips her hand through Lapham's arm and detains him as he would start forward. They follow the others into the dining room and all sit at the table. Lapham on Mrs. Corey's right. Mrs. Lapham beside Mr. Corey. Irene beside Tom. Seeing James Bellingham tuck his napkin in his collar Lapham does likewise, then as none of the others do it he takes it out again.

BELLINGHAM, *to Miss Kingsbury*: I'm such an uncertain shot with a spoon. I defend my practice on the ground of neatness and commonsense.

The servants move about with the courses, filling the glasses. Lapham watches the others, and tastes his wine.

TOM, *to Irene*: I can't tell you how sorry I am that your sister could not come. She is not really very ill, I hope?

IRENE: No, only a bad headache.

TOM: I don't believe Miss Lapham cares much for society. Do you know I sometimes imagine that she even avoids me. She doesn't dislike me?

IRENE: Oh, no, no! How can you think such a thing? Why Pen is lovely.

TOM: I know that!

They converse together silently.

MRS. COREY, *to Lapham*: We have been so interested in watching your house grow, across the way. Mr. Seymour has done wonders.

SEYMOUR: If I have been able to make a nice thing of it, I owe it all to the practical sympathy of my client.

COREY: Practical sympathy is good. Does he bleed your husband, Mrs. Lapham? He's a terrible fellow for appropriations.

MRS. LAPHAM: I guess the Colonel knows how to take care of himself.

COREY, *leaning back in his chair*: Well, after all, you can't say, with all your modern fuss about it, that you do much better now than the old fellows who built such houses as this.

SEYMOUR: Ah, nobody can do better than well. Your house is in perfect taste; you know I've always admired it; and I don't think it's at all the worse for being old-fashioned. But I think we may claim a better feeling for structure. We use better material, and more wisely; and by and by we shall work out something more characteristic and original.

COREY: With your chocolate and your olive greens and your clutter of bric-a-brac?

SEYMOUR: All that's bad, of course. I don't wish to make you envious of Colonel Lapham, and modesty prevents my saying that his house is prettier—though I may have my convictions—but it's better built. All the new houses are better built. Now your house—

COREY: Mrs. Corey's house! *My* ancestral halls are in Salem, and I'm told you couldn't drive a nail into their timbers; in fact, I don't know that you would want to.

SEYMOUR: I should consider it a species of sacrilege; and I shall be far from pressing the point I was going to make against a house of Mrs. Corey's.

COREY, *as all laugh*: Well, you architects and musicians are the only true artistic creators; somehow or other you do evolve the camel out of your inner consciousness!

SEYMOUR: I will not deny the soft impeachment.

COREY: I dare say, and you'll own that it's very handsome of me to say this, after your unjustifiable attack on Mrs. Corey's property.

BELLINGHAM, *to Mrs. Lapham*: You mustn't listen to Miss Kingsbury. She's worse, when it comes to appropriations than Seymour himself. Depend upon it, Mrs. Lapham, she will give you no peace of your mind, now she's met you, from this out.

COREY: Beware of her and all her works. She calls them works of charity; but Heaven knows whether they are. It don't stand to reason that she gives the poor *all* the money she gets out of people. I have my own belief—(*in an audible whisper*) that she spends it for champagne and cigars.

MISS KINGSBURY: You shall be asked to the very next debauch of the committee, Mr. Corey; then you won't dare expose us.

BELLINGHAM: I wonder you haven't been down upon Corey to go to the Chardon Street home and talk with your indigent Italians in their native tongue. I saw in the *Transcript* the other night that you wanted someone for the work.

MISS KINGSBURY: We did think of Mr. Corey, but we reflected that he probably wouldn't talk with them at all; he would make them keep still to be sketched, and forget all about their wants.

COREY, *as the others laugh*: There is one charity that is so difficult, I wonder it hasn't occurred to a lady of your courageous invention.

MISS KINGSBURY: Yes? What is that?

COREY: The occupation, by deserving poor of neat habits, of all the beautiful, airy, wholesome houses that stand empty the whole summer long while their owners are away in their lowly cots beside the sea.

MISS KINGSBURY: Yes. It's terrible. I have often thought of our great, cool houses standing useless, and the thousands of poor creatures stifling in their holes and dens, and the little children dying for wholesome shelter. How cruelly selfish we are!

COREY: That is a very comfortable sentiment, Miss Kingsbury, and must make you feel almost as if you had thrown open No. 31 to the whole North End.

MRS. COREY: Surely, Bromfield, you don't consider what havoc such people would make with the furniture of a nice house.

COREY: That's true! I never thought of that.

LAPHAM, *to Mrs. Corey*: Picture of your daughter, I presume?

MRS. COREY: No, my daughter's grandmother. It's a Stewart Newton—he painted a great many Salem beauties; she was a Miss Polly Burroughs. My daughter *is* like her, don't you think? Those pretty old-fashioned dresses are coming in again—I'm not surprised you took it for her.

LAPHAM, *to Nanny Corey*: It's a good thing to have a grandmother handsome enough to be painted in your place, Miss Corey.

COREY: Why, that's true, Colonel Lapham, I hadn't thought of it before.

BELLINGHAM, *to Mrs. Lapham*: Does your husband often make those pretty speeches to young ladies, Mrs. Lapham?

MRS. LAPHAM: I guess he don't often have such a good chance.

NANNY: Spare my grandmother's blushes! I'm sure if she could speak, she would say: you ought to have seen both of Miss Irene's grandmothers.

They all laugh. Mrs. Corey rises.

MRS. COREY: I suppose you will want your coffee here?

COREY: Yes; we'll join you at tea.

All the ladies rise, Lapham starts to follow Mrs. Corey, then pauses seeing the gentlemen remain. Tom opens the door for his mother. The ladies exeunt. The gentlemen light their cigars and re-seat themselves.

COREY, *as servant offers cigars*: Try this one, Colonel Lapham. These are new. I had an Englishman here the other day who was smoking *old* cigars in the superstition that tobacco improved with age, like wine.

LAPHAM: Anybody who had ever lived off a tobacco country could tell him better than that. I guess I like a good cigar about as well as anybody.

BELLINGHAM, *coming to Lapham's side as he smokes, half turned in his seat*: Colonel Lapham, weren't you with the 96th Vermont when they charged across the river in front of Pickensburg, and the rebel battery opened fire on them in the water? (*Lapham slowly closing his eyes, and nodding his head in assent as he smokes.*) I thought so. I was with the 85th Massachusetts, and I sha'n't forget that slaughter. We were all new to it still. Perhaps that's why it made such an impression.

COREY: I don't know. Was there anything much more impressive afterward? I recollect the talk of some old army men at the time. They said that death-rate couldn't be beaten.

LAPHAM: About one in five of us got out safe.

He breaks the ashes from his cigar. Bellingham fills his glass.

COREY: What astonishes the craven civilian in all these things is the abundance—the superabundance—of heroism. The cowards were the exception; the men that were ready to die, the rule.

LAPHAM: The woods were full of them!

BELLINGHAM, *to Corey*: I don't see why you claim the credit of being a craven civilian, Bromfield. A man who was out with Garibaldi in '48!

COREY: Oh, a little amateur red-shirting. What has become of all the heroism? Tom, how many club men do you know who would think it sweet and fit to die for their country?

TOM: I can't think of a great many at the moment, sir!

BELLINGHAM: And I couldn't in '61. Nevertheless they were there. It's the occasion that's wanting, and I'm glad of it.

LAPHAM: So am I. I don't want to see any more men killed in my time.

COREY: We non-combatants were notoriously reluctant to give up fighting. But I incline to think Colonel Lapham and James may be right. I dare say we shall have the heroism again if we have the occasion.

LAPHAM: Heroism? I want to tell you about a fellow I had in my own company when we first went out. We were all privates to begin with; after a while they elected me captain—I'd had the tavern stand and most of 'em knew me. But Jim Millon never got to be anything more than corporal; corporal when he was killed. I can't say he went into the thing from the highest motives, altogether. I suppose Jim Millon's wife was enough to account for his going, herself. She was a pretty bad assortment. And she used to lead Jim *one* kind of life. Well, sir, that fellow used to save every cent of his pay and send it to that woman. Used to get me to do it for him. I tried to stop him. "Why Jim," said I, "you know what she'll do with it." "That's so, Cap," says he, "but I don't know what she'll do without it." And it did keep her straight, straight as a string—as long as Jim lasted. Seemed as if there was something mysterious about it. They had a little girl—about as old as my oldest girl—and Jim used to talk to me about her. Guess he done it as much for her as for the mother; and he said to me before the last action he went into, "I should like to turn tail and run, Cap. I ain't comin' out o' this one. But I don't suppose it would do." "Well, not for *you*, Jim," said I. "I want to live," says he, and he bust out crying right there in my tent. "I want to live for poor Molly and Zarilla"—that's what they called the little one—I dunno where they got the name. "I ain't ever had half a chance; and now Molly's doin' better, and I believe we should get along after this." He set there cryin' like a baby. But he wan't no baby when he went into action. I hated to look at him when it was over, not so much because he'd got a ball that was meant for me by a sharp-shooter—he saw the devil takin' aim, and he jumped to warn me—as because he didn't look like Jim; he looked like—fun, all desperate and savage. I guess he died hard. Now I say—

He pauses flushed with wine—staring ahead.

BELLINGHAM: Apollinaris?

LAPHAM: Thanks. I will take some of this wine. (*Pouring himself a glass.*) What—what's I sayin'?

BELLINGHAM: You were speaking of one of your men—Jim Millon.

LAPHAM, *with tipsy suspicion*: What's—what's Jim Millon got to do with it?

BELLINGHAM: Oh, nothing, I believe. We were speaking of the—of heroism in the war, and you were illustrating—

LAPHAM, *with a returning gleam*: Oh, yes. Well, what I want to say about Jim, is this— (*He stops again, and stares blankly around with a hiccough. He reaches for the wine again. Tom Corey pretends to take some for himself, and puts the bottle beyond his reach. Bromfield Corey comes nearer, in hopes of diverting him. Lapham regards him in surprise.*) Wa'—wan't you over there just now?

COREY: Yes, but I came round to speak with you about my boy. I hope, Colonel Lapham, that you are able to make Tom useful to you?

LAPHAM, *steadying himself, and sobered a little by the chance of bragging*: Well, sir, I guess it will be our fault if we don't. I don't like to say it to his face—I don't like the principle—but since you ask me about it, I'd just as lief say that I've never had any young man take hold equal to your son. I don't know as you care—

COREY: You make me very happy. I've always had the idea that there was something in my son, if he could only find the way to work it out. And

he seems to have gone into your business for the love of it.

LAPHAM: He went to work in the right way, sir. He told me about it. He looked into the paint, first. And that paint is a thing that will bear looking into.

COREY: You might think he had invented it if you heard him celebrating it.

LAPHAM: Is that so? Well, there ain't any other way. You've got to believe in a thing before you can put any heart in it. Why I had a partner in this thing once, along back just after the war, and he used to be always wanting to tinker with something else. "Why," says I, "you've got the best thing in God's universe now. Why ain't you satisfied?" I had to get rid of him at last. I stuck to my paint, and that fellow's drifted round pretty much all over the whole country, whittling his capital down all the while, till here a couple of months ago I had to lend him twenty thousand dollars to start new, and I've had to keep him going ever since. I was tellin' your brother— (*nods at James Bellingham*) just before we come in to dinner that Rogers has done his best to get me into a hole lately. I felt pretty blue, one while, but I'm all right now. No, sir, you've got to believe in a thing, and I believe in your son, and I don't mind telling you that so far as he's gone he's a success!

TOM: That's very kind of you.

LAPHAM, *to Corey*: Yes, sir, when your son proposed to take hold I didn't have much faith in his ideas, that's the truth. But I had faith in him, and I saw that he meant business from the start. I could see it was born in him; anyone could!

COREY: I'm afraid he didn't inherit it directly from me.

LAPHAM: Well, sir, we can't help those things. Some of us have got it and some of us haven't. The idea is to make the most of what we have got.

COREY: Oh yes, that's the idea.

LAPHAM: And you can't ever tell what's in you till you try. Why, when I started this thing I didn't more than half understand my own strength. I wouldn't have said, looking back, that I could have stood the wear and tear of what I've been through. But I developed as I went along. His going through college won't hurt him, he'll soon slough all that off—and his society bringing up, won't; don't you be anxious about it. Your son will get along.

COREY: Thank you.

LAPHAM: He'll get along. He's a good business man and a fine fellow. If you ever like to ride after a good horse—

COREY: Oh no, no, no; thank you! The better the horse the more I should be scared. Tom has told me of your driving.

LAPHAM: Ha! Ha! Ha! Well, everyone to his taste. But you must run up to Lapham with me some day, and see the works. (*Raising his voice and striking the arm of his chair with his hand as the wine goes more and more to his head.*) Those works are worth seeing! They're what brought me to Boston, and they're what have kept me here! They're what's building my house there across the street on the waterside of Beacon. They're what has built my fortune! And they're going to build it bigger and bigger. (*As Lapham gets tipsy, he reaches out for more wine in every direction. Tom Corey now tries to substitute a bottle of apollinaris for the madeira before him. Savagely.*) What's that?

TOM: I thought you wanted the apollinaris, Colonel.

LAPHAM, *with drunken dignity*: I guess I know what I want, young man. When I want apollinaris, I'll ask for it. Where was I? Oh, yes; up at Lapham. (*Raising his voice again and addressing Corey.*) Yes, sir, the fires that Mrs. Lapham lighted in the works when they first opened hain't been out once day or night in all these years, and they never shall go out in my time! I tell you, Corey, that paint brought me to Boston ten years ago a little worse off than nothing at all, for I was in debt for the money that I bought out my partner with. And here I am now worth my million, and meeting you gentlemen like one of you, and every cent of it is honest money—no speculation—every copper of it for value received. I've got more money than I know what to do with. Why, when your wife sent to mine for that charity, a while back, I wrote my cheque for five hundred dollars but my wife wouldn't take more than one hundred; said she wasn't going to show off before Mrs. Corey. I call that a pretty good joke on Mrs. Corey. I must tell her how Mrs. Lapham done her out of a cool four hundred dollars—(*He looks about, and discovers that the ladies are gone.*) Why—why—what's got all the women?

He starts up.

TOM: The ladies are in the drawing room, sir. We are going to join them in a moment.

LAPHAM: I want to see Mis' Corey *now*. This joke won't keep. I keep forgettin' things so, tonight—

COREY: I'll remind you of it, Colonel. Do sit down again.

BELLINGHAM: I want some more coffee, Bromfield. Wouldn't you like another cup, Colonel?

LAPHAM, *dropping back in his chair*: That's about it. I've got such a buzzin'—and this coffee goes to the right spot. I must get Mis' Corey to tell my wife how she makes it. I guess Irene could do it. She's the greatest little cook! Now Pen, she's more for readin', but Irene—

BELLINGHAM, *listening*: Isn't that a fire near here? I thought I heard an engine.

LAPHAM, *not regarding*: Gentlemen, I *like* you! (*To James Bellingham.*) It always was my ambition to know *you*; yes, sir. If anyone had said when I first come to Boston that in less than ten years I would be hob-nobbing here with Jim Bellingham, I would have told that person he lied; I would have told anybody he lied that had told me ten years ago that a son of Bromfield Corey would have come and asked me to take him into business!

TOM, *going to window*: The engines are here in the street.

A light is seen beyond the window, the engines are heard throbbing and pulsing in the street below. A sound of distant bells and voices. An engine crashes by.

SEYMOUR: There comes another! (*To Corey.*) May I—

COREY: By all means!

Exit Seymour for ladies. All crowd to the window, save Lapham who remains seated.

BELLINGHAM: It seems to be quite near.

Enter Seymour with Mrs. Lapham, Mrs. Corey, Miss Kingsbury, Irene and Nanny. All crowd to the window.

NANNY: Oh, isn't it perfectly magnificent! If you lean out you can see the flames!

MISS KINGSBURY: I wouldn't have missed it on any account. Thank you, Mr. Seymour, for bringing us out!

SEYMOUR: Oh, it's Mr. Corey's fire.

COREY: Ah, I thought you'd like it. I wish I could afford to have one for you every time you dined here.

MISS KINGSBURY: Oh, do you think you would if I came again?

MRS. LAPHAM: Irene!

IRENE: Papa! Papa!

MRS. LAPHAM, *looks from window*: Silas Lapham! Look! It's our house!

IRENE: Papa!

LAPHAM, *starting to window*: My house! (*All draw back, he stands in the now open window looking out, the curtains moving in the wind about him. The pulsing of the engines and the shouts and sounds of crackling—breaking glass—and flames sound nearer. Lapham puts his hand up to his forehead and steps back. Mrs. Lapham goes to him.*) Persis, our new house is gone!

The crash of engines, the shouts and the sounds of fire continue.

MRS. LAPHAM: Oh, Silas, it was insured?

LAPHAM: I had a buildin' risk on it, and it expired last week. It's a dead loss, and I guess I done it.

CURTAIN

ACT III

SCENE: *Lapham's house in Nankeen Square. Parlor as described in novel. Irene and Penelope talking before the fire.*

IRENE: The whole dinner went off splendidly; he sat next to me, although he went out with that Miss Kingsbury, but after he just said a few words to her he talked to me. Oh, Pen! How well he *does* talk! It made me feel ashamed. I shouldn't have had a word to say if he hadn't talked about you.

PEN, *listlessly*: About me?

IRENE: Yes, he talked about you nearly the whole while, and that gave me a chance, especially when he asked questions. Oh, you can't think how well he looks in evening dress! I could hear papa bragging away at his end of the table, and I knew he was feeling good at the way mamma was getting on; and if you had been there he would have been too proud for anything. You ought to have come, Pen! (*Pen rises and moves nervously about.*) You don't care a bit for what I'm saying! What's the matter?

PEN: Oh, nothing—nothing. But I can't help thinking about the Colonel. I'm troubled, Irene. How *did* he act when he saw it was our house burning up?

IRENE: Oh, that was awful. But I guess it was just his disappointment about having to build it all over again. Now, I want to tell what Mr. Corey said to Miss Kingsbury—

PEN: I can't fix my mind on it, now, Irene. I can't get it off of poor father. I wonder—

Enter Mrs. Lapham.

MRS. LAPHAM: Girls, I want you should let your father have the parlor this morning. He ain't going to his office—he's not feeling just right—and there'll be a lot of people coming here to see him. Go into the sitting room, or—

PEN: What's the matter with the Colonel, mother? Is he in trouble?

MRS. LAPHAM: Trouble—(*Checking herself.*) No, there's nothing particular the matter. Of course, the house burning up, he feels that terribly; it's an awful trial to him; you know how he sets his heart on anything— There! That's his step on the stairs now! Don't stand talking! I don't want him to find you girls here. If he does—

She pushes them out of the room, and as they go Lapham enters by other door, walking heavily.

LAPHAM: Persis!

MRS. LAPHAM: Well, Silas?

LAPHAM: I don't know where to turn. Where am I goin' to *begin* to raise two hundred thousand dollars?

MRS. LAPHAM: Well, Silas Lapham! When I hear *you* talk that way! I guess you *are* sick. I don't believe you're fit to be about. You're sick abed, I guess.

LAPHAM, *sinking into chair*: Where am I goin' to begin—

MRS. LAPHAM, *indignantly*: You make me lose all patience! Begin!

LAPHAM: Yes, I'm at the end of my string, Persis. (*Maid comes to the door; Mrs. Lapham meets her in dumb show.*) What's that?

MRS. LAPHAM: It's the messenger from the bank. Mr. Bellingham hasn't come down yet.

LAPHAM: Tell him to go back and wait for Bellingham till he does come.

Lapham rises from his chair with a groan and paces the room restlessly. Mrs. Lapham follows him with her eyes.

MRS. LAPHAM: Now, Silas Lapham, I want you should tell me just how you stand! Has it come to the worst?

LAPHAM: I'll know before noon. There wasn't any danger as long as I had the house, but now I've only got the lot left, and this house—and Rogers' mills, and they're as good as worthless if the railroad makes an offer. If I can't go in with these Kanawha paint men, I'm as good as gone. You won't let me do anything with those mills?

MRS. LAPHAM: Oh, yes, I'll let you, now.

LAPHAM: You know I can't do anything now if you *do*. Oh, my Lord!

MRS. LAPHAM: Yes, I'm to blame for it! I made you give Rogers all that money. I forced you to it.

LAPHAM: I don't want to blame anybody.

MRS. LAPHAM: I don't suppose but what there's plenty would help you, if they knew you wanted it, Si.

LAPHAM: They would if they knew I didn't need it.

MRS. LAPHAM, *a bell rings*: I guess that's Tom Corey, now. Shall I send him in if it is?

LAPHAM: Yes, send him in.

Exit Mrs. Lapham; enter Corey and Walker.

WALKER: I'm sorry you're not well, Colonel Lapham—

LAPHAM: That's all right. You brought my letters? (*He opens letters and runs them through.*) From my broker. (*He pauses, a bitter smile on his face.*) Another offer for my house that was burnt last night. (*He drops the letter. Enter Rogers. Lapham turns to him, and stares at him.*) What do *you* want?

ROGERS: William told me at the office that you would not be down, and I took the liberty of calling here.

LAPHAM: What for?

ROGERS, *seating himself while Tom and Walker draw back*: I want to know what you are going to do.

LAPHAM: I'll tell you first what I've *done*. I've been investigating at Dubuque and I've found out all about that milling property you turned in on me. Did you know that the G. L. & P. had leased the P. Y. & X.?

ROGERS: I some suspected that it might.

LAPHAM: When you turned the property in on me, did you know that the G. L. & P. wanted to buy the mills?

ROGERS: I presumed the road would give a fair price for them.

LAPHAM: You lie. You knew the road wouldn't give a fair price for the mills. You know it would give what it chose, and that I couldn't help myself. You're a thief, Milton K. Rogers, and you stole the money I lent you! You've bled me every time, and all I've got to show for it is a milling property on a line of road that can squeeze me, whenever it wants to, as dry as it pleases. And you want to know what I'm going to do? I'm going to squeeze *you*. I'm going to sell those collaterals

of yours, and I'm going to let the mills go for what they'll fetch! *I* ain't going to fight the G. L. & P.

He turns his back on Rogers.

ROGERS, *slowly and calmly*: There are some English parties here who have been making inquiries in regard to those mills, and—

LAPHAM: I guess you're lying, Rogers.

ROGERS: Well, all that I have to ask is that you will not act hastily in regard to my securities.

LAPHAM: You don't think I'm in earnest. (*Facing Rogers.*) You think I'm fooling, do you? (*He takes a bunch of keys from his pocket.*) Walker, go back to the office, and open my safe. You'll find a bundle of railroad securities marked "Rogers." Take them to Gallop and Paddock's in State Street, and tell 'em to sell 'em right away for what they'll fetch. (*He has crossed and scribbled a line at the table which he gives Walker. Exit Walker. Turning to Rogers.*) Now go!

ROGERS, *rising calmly*: Then, I understand that you will take no action in regard to the mills until I have seen the parties I speak of?

LAPHAM, *baffled*: I *wonder* what you're up to, Rogers? I *should* like to know. Here! You bring me a party that will give me enough for those mills to clear me of you, and I'll *talk* to you. But don't you come here with any man of straw; and I'll give you until noon to prove yourself a swindler again!

ROGERS, *unruffled*: I think the matter can be arranged.

Exit Rogers.

LAPHAM, *after a long pause, turning to Tom Corey who advances*: Well! was I *drunk* last night? (*There is a pause.*) Was I drunk? I ask you because I was never touched by drink in my life before, and I don't know.

TOM: That is what everyone understood, Colonel Lapham. Everyone saw how it was. Don't—

LAPHAM: Did they talk it over after I left?

TOM: You were among gentlemen.

LAPHAM: I know it, don't I? I was the only one there that wasn't a gentleman. I disgraced you. What did I say? What did I do?

TOM: There was nothing. It was purely a misfortune, an accident.

LAPHAM: I wa'n't fit to be there. Do you want to leave?

TOM: Leave?

LAPHAM: Yes; quit the business, cut the whole connection?

TOM: I haven't the remotest idea of it! Why in the world should I?

LAPHAM: Because you're a gentleman, and I'm not, and it ain't right I should be over you. I will give you up if you want to go before anything worse happens, and I shan't blame you. I can help you to do something better than I can offer you, and I will.

TOM: There's no question of my going unless you wish it. If you so—

LAPHAM: Will you tell your father that I had a notion all the time that I was acting the drunken braggard? Will you tell him I don't want him to notice me if we ever meet, and that I know I'm not fit to associate with gentlemen in anything but a business way, if I am that?

TOM: Certainly I shall do nothing of the kind. I can't listen to you any longer; what you say is shocking to me, shocking in a way you can't think.

LAPHAM: Why, man! If I can stand it, you can!

TOM: No, that doesn't follow. You can denounce yourself if you will, but I have my reasons for refusing to hear you, my reasons why I can't hear you. If you say another word, I must go away.

LAPHAM: I've disgusted you—but I didn't mean to. I take it back.

TOM: There wasn't one person present last night who didn't understand the matter precisely as my father and I did, and that fact must end it between us.

LAPHAM: Well, sit down. I want to talk to you. I'd ought to tell you you're wasting your time with me. I spoke about your placing yourself better. There ain't going to be the outcome for the paint in the foreign markets that we expected.

Enter Mr. Dinwiddie.

DINWIDDIE, *pausing in doorway*: The maid said I should find you here, Colonel.

LAPHAM: All right! Come right in, Mr. Dinwiddie. This is our Mr. Corey. (*Handshaking.*) You can talk before him.

DINWIDDIE: I've come to make you our final offer and get your decision. We want to close up matters to-day. There are other parties willing to go in but we'd rather deal with you if we could.

LAPHAM: I have always said you had a good thing; I should have to fight you hard; but the question is whether we had better go on and make a heavy loss for both sides by competition, or whether we had better form a partnership to run both paints and command the whole market.

DINWIDDIE: What do you propose, sir?

LAPHAM: I've three propositions: To sell out to you; to buy you out; or to join forces and go in

together. Name a figure which you will buy at; a figure which you will sell at; a figure which we could combine at. In other words, the amount of capital you need.

DINWIDDIE: It's out of the question to talk of buying you out, Colonel Lapham, and neither my brothers nor I want to sell our interests.

LAPHAM: How much capital do you want?

DINWIDDIE: Over a hundrd thousand dollars. I should have to telegraph to my brothers.

LAPHAM: Telegraph to your brothers, then.

DINWIDDIE: I'll come back in two hours for your answer, Colonel; I must close the transaction to-day.

LAPHAM: In two hours all right.

DINWIDDIE: If you don't go in, it will leave me time to see the other parties. Good morning, sir!

LAPHAM: Good morning. (*Exit Dinwiddie. Looking after him.*) He don't see it, but he has the game all in his hands. He will know that before evening. If I can't combine with them—

TOM: Colonel Lapham, I want to propose again what I proposed the other day, I want to put my money into the business.

LAPHAM, *tempted*: Your money. Oh, Lord!

TOM: I've got about thirty thousand dollars that I could put in, and if you don't want to consider me a partner, you can let me regard it as an investment.

LAPHAM, *after a pause*: No, not yours! I'll stake everything I have, but I won't imperil a cent that ain't mine. (*Enter Walker. Turning eagerly to him.*) Well, what did Gallop and Paddock do with those securities?

WALKER: Nothing, sir. They would not offer them.

LAPHAM: What did they mean?

WALKER: They said it would be as good as throwing them away, sir.

LAPHAM: They would have brought twenty thousand—

WALKER: Not five, sir.

LAPHAM, *taking securities*: Perhaps Bellingham can do better when he comes. (*He stands silent.*) You go back to the office, Walker, and see if there are any more letters for me and bring them here just as soon as the mail comes in. (*Exit Walker. As Walker exits, Lapham turns to Tom, speaking slowly.*) Corey, I want you should send a telegram for me. I want *you* should do it, and not Walker. I want you should telegraph to Lapham and tell them to put the fires out in the works.

As he speaks Mrs. Lapham enters behind him pausing at his words. Lapham sits down as if to write out the telegram himself.

TOM, *softly*: Not yet—Colonel Lapham!

LAPHAM, *about to fill out the telegraph blank, but stops*: They ain't once been out in all these years since Persis lit 'em—she wasn't more than a girl then—we had it all plain before us—now we're both old; and those fires—(*Tries to write, he can't do it—breaks down. To Tom.*) Write it yourself, Corey, I can't.

MRS. LAPHAM, *advancing*: Oh, Silas!

LAPHAM, *turning*: Persis— I didn't want you should hear!

TOM, *at door*: You wish me to come back?

LAPHAM: Yes. This is only the beginning.

Exit Tom, taking his hat.

MRS. LAPHAM: Oh, Silas! Silas!

LAPHAM, *after a pause*: What's the use? There wan't anything to do but to shut down, and I've shut down.

MRS. LAPHAM: I don't know what's going to become of the hands in the middle of the winter, this way.

LAPHAM, *grimly*: They've shared my luck; now let 'em share the other thing. (*He crosses the room.*) I'm up a stump, as soon as Rogers fails; and he *will*. Then I'll call a meeting of my creditors tomorrow and put myself in their hands. If there's enough left to satisfy *them*, *I'm* satisfied.

MRS. LAPHAM: Do you mean that it's all over with you?

LAPHAM: I guess there ain't any doubt about it, Persis.

MRS. LAPHAM: Will—will everything go?

LAPHAM: I can't tell yet. But if it comes to the worst, they shall have a chance at everything, every dollar, every cent. I'm sorry for you, Persis—and the girls.

MRS. LAPHAM: Oh, don't talk of us. What did I ever care for the money? I've had a happy home with you ever since we were married, and I guess I shall have as long as you live, whether we go on the Back Bay, or go back to the old home at Lapham.

LAPHAM, *musingly*: If this had happened when I was younger— I wan't afraid of anything once! But I noticed that after I passed fifty, I began to get scared easier. I don't believe I could pick up from a regular knockdown, now.

MRS. LAPHAM, *proudly*: Pshaw! *You* scared, Silas Lapham! I should like to see the thing that ever scared you; or the knockdown that *you* couldn't pick up from.

LAPHAM, *his face lighting*: Is that so, Persis?

MRS. LAPHAM: Yes, it's so!

LAPHAM, *thoughtfully*: There's a chance that Rogers may come to time, after all.

MRS. LAPHAM: What chance?

LAPHAM: One in ten million. He says there are some English parties after him to buy those mills.

MRS. LAPHAM: Well?

LAPHAM: Well, I gave him till this afternoon to prove himself a liar.

MRS. LAPHAM: You don't believe there are any such parties?

LAPHAM: Not in *this* world.

MRS. LAPHAM: But if there were?

LAPHAM: Then I'd let them have the mills at the price Rogers turned 'em in on me; I don't want to make anything on 'em. But I guess I shall hear from the G. L. & P. first, and when they make their offer I guess I shall have to accept it, whatever it is.

MRS. LAPHAM: If you could get your price from those English parties before they knew that the G. L. & P. wanted to buy the mills, would it let you out with Rogers?

LAPHAM: Just about.

MRS. LAPHAM: Then I know he'll move heaven and earth to bring it about. I know you won't be allowed to suffer for doing him good, Silas. Why should he pretend to have any such parties in view if he hasn't? Don't you be down-hearted, Si. You'll see that he'll be round with them by the afternoon. (*As she speaks, Lapham, who has seated himself, sits staring ahead; at first with a look of hope; then gradually expression after expression follows across his face; as Mrs. Lapham ceases speaking there is a long pause. Then they turn and look at each other. Slowly.*) Well, Si?

LAPHAM, *slowly*: Persis, I've been thinking about those English parties of Rogers'—

MRS. LAPHAM: So've I!

LAPHAM: And I can't make out but what I'd be just as bad as Rogers every bit and grain, if I let them have the mills and didn't tell 'em what the chances were with the G. L. & P.

MRS. LAPHAM: I thought of that, too!

LAPHAM, *after a pause*: Well, you wouldn't be afraid to have me do it, Persis?

MRS. LAPHAM, *sobbing*: Oh, Silas! Oh, Silas!

LAPHAM, *his arm about her*: Hush, hush, Persis,

the girls'll hear you if you keep on this way. Don't cry any more; you musn't.

MRS. LAPHAM: Oh, let me cry, Silas. It does seem too hard that you have to give up this chance when Providence fairly raised it up for you.

LAPHAM: I guess it wan't *Providence* raised it up. Most likely Rogers was lyin' and there ai'n't any such parties; but if there are, they can't have the mills from me without the whole story.

Enter Penelope.

PEN: Mother told me you were in trouble, Colonel, and I couldn't stay away any longer. I thought I'd come and cheer you up a little. I shall not talk, the sight of me will be enough.

LAPHAM, *laughs*: Trouble? Nothing of the sort. I was pretty blue a while ago, but I guess I was more scared than hurt. Don't you be worried about me, Pen.

PEN: I'm more worried about mother now. I do believe she's been crying.

LAPHAM: You just leave your mother to me, Pen. Crying? I guess not. I ain't seen her cry since the day we buried our boy, more'n twenty years ago, and I guess she ain't going to begin now just because things look a bit ugly to-day. I guess we're not going to let ugly looks scare us— eh, Persis?

MRS. LAPHAM, *smiling through her tears*: No, Si, no!

LAPHAM: That's right, no hang back about you. No, sir! You'll be with me in this as you've been with me every time. Don't you be troubled, Pen, we're goin' to pull through all right.

He moves toward the door leading Mrs. Lapham, his arm still about her. Exit Lapham and Mrs. Lapham.

PEN, *looking after them*: Poor mother—poor father!

Enter Tom.

TOM, *as he sees her*: Oh! I hope you're better to-day, Miss Lapham.

PEN: Better? *(Recollecting.)* Oh, yes, thank you, Mr. Corey. I'm quite well this morning.

TOM: We all missed you very much last night.

PEN: I'm afraid you wouldn't have missed me if I had been there.

TOM: You make fun of everything. Miss Irene was telling me last night about you.

PEN: Then it's no use for me to deny it. I must give Irene a talking to.

TOM: I hope you won't forbid her to talk about you!

PEN: Does Irene talk about me?

TOM: Perhaps I make her talk about you. You must blame *me* if it's wrong.

PEN: Oh, I didn't say it was wrong. But I hope if you said anything very bad of me you'll let me know what it was, so that I can reform.

TOM: No, don't change, please—

PEN: What did you say about me?

TOM: Everything. I have to talk *of* you, because I get to talk *to* you so seldom.

PEN: You mean that I do all the talking when we are—together?

TOM: We're so seldom together.

PEN: I don't know what you mean.

TOM: Sometimes I've thought—I've been afraid —that you avoided me.

PEN: Avoided you? Mother and Irene will be sorry to miss you. *(Then as he advances and takes her hand.)* I didn't mean to send you away.

TOM, *as he holds her hand*: Oh, I'm not going. I wanted to say—to say that I make your sister talk about you, because—to say I—there is something I want to say to you! I've said it so often to myself that I feel as if you must know it. You must know—she must have told you—she must have guessed—I—I didn't expect—I hoped to have seen your father—but I must speak now— whatever happens—I love you!

PEN, *starting away*: Me!

TOM: Yes, you. *(With a smile.)* Who else?

PEN: I thought—I—it was— Oh, what have you done?

TOM: Upon my soul I don't know. I hope no harm.

PEN: Oh, don't laugh, unless you want me to think you the greatest wretch in the world.

TOM: I? For loving you! For Heaven's sake tell me what you mean?

PEN: You know, I can't tell you. Can you say— can you put your hand on your heart and say that —you—say you never meant—that you meant *me* —all along?

TOM: Yes! Yes! Who else? You must have known it. You must have seen it— I've been abrupt, I know, and I've startled you; but if you love me, you can forgive my loving you so long before I spoke.

PEN: If it's true—what you say—you must go; and you must never come any more. Do you promise that?

TOM: Certainly not. Why should I promise such a thing—so abominably wrong? I could obey if you didn't love me.

PEN: Oh, I don't, indeed I don't. Now, will you obey?

TOM: No. I don't believe you.

PEN: Oh!

TOM: My love—my dearest—what is this trouble, that you can't tell it?

PEN: Oh. You don't understand.

TOM: No, I don't. You must tell me.

PEN: Well then— No! No! I can't. You must go.

TOM: I will not go.

PEN: You said you—loved me. If you do, you will go.

TOM: I will obey you, Penelope.

PEN: As if you were never to see me again? As if I were dying?

TOM: I will do what you say. But I shall see you again; and don't talk of dying. This is the beginning of life—

PEN: No. It's the end, it's the end of life for me. You—you must never come here again. I can't tell you why, and you must never try to know.

TOM: But you must try to tell me! There is nothing under Heaven—no calamity, no sorrow—that I wouldn't gladly share with you, or take all upon myself if I could.

PEN: I know. But this you can't— Oh, my—

TOM: Dearest—wait—think—let me ask your mother—your father—

PEN: No. If you do that you will make me hate you—will you—promise?

TOM: Oh, I promise!

PEN: Good-bye! (*She suddenly flings her arms about his neck pressing her cheek close to his. Then drawing back covering her face.*) Oh, Irene! Irene!

TOM: Irene! You don't mean!

PEN: Hush— Father's coming! Go!

Pen thrusts Tom out at one door as Lapham enters by another.

LAPHAM: Has Mr. Corey been back?

PEN: Father! Father!

She goes to him clinging to him.

LAPHAM, *trying to joke*: Father? Reduced to the ranks, eh, Pen? Not Colonel any more— (*Seriously as he looks in her face.*) Why, what's the matter with you? What have you been crying about?

PEN: Have I been crying?

LAPHAM: Yes.

PEN: It wasn't for you, father.

LAPHAM: Your cheeks are all wet.

PEN: I thought they were on fire. Well, I'll tell you what's happened. (*Crossing and closing door.*) I don't want Irene here. There's nothing the matter. Only Mr. Corey has offered himself to me. (*As he starts.*) Oh, I'm not a ghost! I wish I *was*. Father—you've got to know all about it.

LAPHAM: Go on!

PEN: I could almost say I had dreamt it, but I guess it really happened. Why don't you blame me, father? Why don't you say that I led him on, and tried to get him away from Irene? Don't you believe I did?

LAPHAM, *slowly*: Do you think that he got the idea you cared for him? *Did* you care for him any, Pen?

PEN: He knew it. How could I keep it from him? I said I didn't, at first.

LAPHAM: It was no use. You might as well said you did. (*Pause.*) It couldn't help Irene any way, if you didn't.

PEN: I always tried to help her with him, even when I— But, you never thought of me! I was nobody. I couldn't feel! No one cared for me!

LAPHAM, *humbly*: No. We didn't think of you. When did you—begin to care for him?

PEN: How do I know? What difference does it make? It's all over now, no matter when it began. What will you say to Irene? What will you do?

LAPHAM: I don't know what to do. I don't see as anything can be done. She's pretty enough, and she's capable and I've got the money— I don't know what I'm saying.

Pause.

PEN: Do you want me to go to Irene and tell her that I've got him away from her?

LAPHAM: Oh, good Lord! What do you want I should do, Pen?

PEN: Nothing for me. Do the best you can for Irene.

LAPHAM: She's nothing but a child. It's only a fancy with her. She'll get over it. She hain't really got her heart set on him.

PEN: She *has* got her heart set on him, father. She's got her whole life set on him; you know that.

LAPHAM: Yes, that's so.

PEN: If I could give him to her I would. But he isn't mine to give. He isn't mine to keep!

LAPHAM: She has got to bear it. She's got to bear her share of the trouble.

PEN: You're not going to *tell* Irene?

LAPHAM: Yes, I am. If she's a woman grown, she can bear a woman's burden.

PEN: I can't let you tell Irene; not *Irene!* I'm afraid to let you. How can I ever look at her again?

LAPHAM, *gently*: Why, you haven't done anything, Pen.

PEN: Yes, I must have done something! I *did* care for him from the first, and I must have tried to make him like me. Even now—when he came in. It was the first time I ever had him all to myself, for myself. Perhaps I could have kept him from saying that he cared for me; but when I saw he did—I must have seen it—I couldn't. I never thought he cared for me, I never expected him to. But I liked him. Yes. I did like him. Tell her that, or else I will.

LAPHAM: If it was to tell her he was dead—

PEN: How easy it would be! But he's worse than dead to her, and so am I!

LAPHAM, *firmly*: If there's to be any giving up, let it be by the one that sha'n't make anybody but herself suffer. There's trouble and sorrow enough in the world, without making it on purpose.

PEN: Irene shall not give up. She shall be happy.

Enter Irene.

IRENE, *as she enters*: Don't mind me, papa; I'm going out and I'm going to take Pen. I guess I shall get one of those pins that Nanny Corey had in her hair. I think it would become me, don't you, Pen?

PEN: Yes—I don't know— No. But I can't go out, Irene. You go.

IRENE: I wanted you to see the pin first; I want it just like Nanny Corey's.

PEN: Yes, but Irene—

LAPHAM: I don't like to have you go on so about the Coreys, unless—till Tom Corey's said something to show—

IRENE, *turning to him*: Papa! What do you mean?

LAPHAM: Irene, there's something you have got to bear. It's a mistake we've all made. He don't care anything for you. He never did. He told Pen so to-day. He cares for *her*. (*A long pause.*) Why don't you say something?

PEN: Do you want to kill me, Irene?

IRENE, *dazed*: Why should I want to hurt you, Pen? There's nothing to say.

PEN, *reaching toward her*: O 'Rene! 'Rene! 'Rene!

IRENE, *holding her off*: Don't—and don't you fret about me, Pen. I shall get along.

LAPHAM: I don't like to see you keeping up so, Irene. It'll be all the worse for you when you do break. Better give way a little at the start.

IRENE: I sha'n't break and I've given way all

I'm going to. I don't want you should say anything, or *look* anything, and whatever I do, I don't want you should try to stop me. Don't, Pen! You've never done a thing, or thought a thing to wrong me. I know just what I've got to bear.

PEN: Oh, Irene!

IRENE: Don't touch me—I'm going out. I'm choking here!

Exit Irene.

LAPHAM: Oh, my Lord!

PEN: I'll never see him again!

LAPHAM: That won't help Irene any. If he wants you, and you care for him, I don't see but what you've a right to each other. I wouldn't say but what you had a perfect right if you was to marry him to-day—

PEN: Father!

LAPHAM: No, I couldn't. There ain't any one to blame. He's behaved like a gentleman. Well, marry him, then; he's got the right, and so have you.

PEN: Never! It would come back to me as long as I breathed that I'd stolen him from her.

Enter Irene.

IRENE, *advancing to Penelope with the shaving, etc. in her hands*: There's that box I got last week because it was like his sister's. It won't become a dark person so well, but you can have it. There's his button-hole bouquet. He left it by his plate last night and I stole it. (*Dropping the shaving tied with ribbon in Pen's lap she turns and totters toward the door.*) There's what he gave me that day in father's office. (*After a pause.*) Pen, I want you should tell him all about it. If he's half a man, he won't give you up till he knows why you won't have him; and he has a right to know.

PEN: It won't make any difference, I couldn't have him after—

IRENE: That's for you to say. But if you don't tell him about *me*—I—will. Yes. You needn't say I cared for him. But you can say that you all thought he—cared for me!

PEN: Oh, Irene!

Moving toward her.

IRENE: Don't! You are all right, Pen—you haven't done anything—you helped me all you could—but I can't touch you—yet!

Exit.

PEN: Irene! Irene!

Exit Pen following Irene weeping.

LAPHAM, *looking after them*: If I'd lost my money a year ago—they'd have been spared this.

Enter Bellingham.

BELLINGHAM: I'm sorry, Colonel Lapham, to come so late—but business kept me at the bank. There are failures right and left to-day. You need to raise money?

LAPHAM: Yes. (*Handing the bundle of papers Walker brought back to Bellingham.*) What are these worth?

BELLINGHAM, *running through the papers hastily*: You couldn't raise five thousand on them as the market stands. In a week they may go up to thirty thousand.

LAPHAM: I can't wait a week. I can't wait a day.

BELLINGHAM: How much do you want to tide you over?

LAPHAM: I need above a hundred thousand dollars.

BELLINGHAM: How soon?

LAPHAM: Before the banks close.

BELLINGHAM: It's impossible. Sell out to the West Virginian firm.

LAPHAM, *firmly*: There ain't enough money in this country to buy out my paint!

BELLINGHAM: If the West Virginians get their paint into the market, yours won't be worth as much as that.

LAPHAM, *brokenly*: I know it! I must combine with them or make an assignment, and I can't raise the capital. I could raise something on this house and the lot on Beacon Street but it ain't enough.

BELLINGHAM: You forget the mills on the G. L. & P. You can raise something on them.

LAPHAM: The G. L. & P. want the mills—at their own price.

BELLINGHAM: You haven't received an offer?

LAPHAM: Not yet.

BELLINGHAM: Then you need not regard that fact. Offer the mills!

LAPHAM, *as voices are heard in hall*: There's Rogers now with his man. He says he has a purchaser. I want to tell you about it, Bellingham, before I see them. I want you should advise me.

> *Exit Lapham and Bellingham. Enter Rogers and English agent.*

AGENT: Now there must be some arrangement about my interest in the transaction if I close with you for my principals. I don't 'aggle about the figure— We pay Colonel Lapham the top price—

ROGERS: Hush! Here's his wife!

> *Enter Mrs. Lapham.*

MRS. LAPHAM: Mr. Lapham will be here in a minute, Mr. Rogers.

ROGERS, *presenting agent*: This is the gentleman who represents the rich English parties who propose purchasing the mills. Mr. Acroyd stands ready to close the bargain the moment Colonel Lapham names the figure. (*Enter Lapham and Bellingham.*) I have brought Mr. Acroyd, Colonel Lapham. He is prepared to take the mills at a just valuation. (*To agent.*) I believe the figure named was a hundred thousand dollars.

ACROYD: My principals wouldn't 'aggle at that figure for the property.

LAPHAM, *after a pause*: Do you know that those mills are wanted by the G. L. & P. and that they can make them worthless to anybody else?

ACROYD: I have 'ad the property investigated, and I'm satisfied with the appearance of things. I am willing to assume the risks you point out.

LAPHAM, *twisting his head in the direction of Rogers*: Has this fellow been telling you it's part of my game to say this? I can tell you on my side, there isn't a slipperier rascal than Milton K. Rogers.

ACROYD: No offer 'as been made yet as I understand.

LAPHAM: Not yet.

ROGERS: I have brought you gentlemen together as a friend of all parties. I ask nothing and expect nothing except the small sum which shall accrue to me after the discharge of my obligations to Colonel Lapham.

ACROYD: And if you 'ave any scruple in allowin' me to assume this risk, Colonel Lapham, perhaps you can console yourself with the fact that the loss, if there is to be any, will fall upon people who are able to bear it—upon an association of rich and charitable people. But we're quite satisfied there will be no loss. All you 'ave to do is to name your price and we will do our best to meet it. We sha'n't dispute about a few pounds more or less. If Mr. Lapham's, I beg your pardon, Colonel Lapham's, figure should be a little 'igher than ours, I've no doubt he'll not be too 'ard upon us in the end.

LAPHAM: Look here! You've come here to ask me to be a partner in a swindle. You want I should divide the profits with you! Well, you can't have the mills!

ROGERS: Mr. Acroyd is a Christian gentleman. You told me you would sell to him if I brought him. I want you should consider me a little in this business too. You're not the only one that's concerned. It's my only chance; if you don't sell, my wife and children will be beggared.

LAPHAM: So will mine, or the next thing to it.

ROGERS: I want you to give me this chance to get on my feet again. You've no right to deprive me of it; it's unchristian. You don't know that the road will ever want the mills.

MRS. LAPHAM, *wavering*: Silas—perhaps—

LAPHAM: Persis!

ROGERS: I don't even want that you should sell to Mr. Acroyd.

LAPHAM: What *do* you want?

ROGERS: I want you should sell to *me*. I want that property and I've got the money to buy it. What will you take for it? If it's the price you're standing out for—

MRS. LAPHAM: Think, Si!

LAPHAM: Persis—*shut up!* (*To Rogers.*) I see you want me to help you whip the devil round the stump. As soon as I sold to you, you would sell to this man.

ROGERS: You will not be responsible for what happens after you have sold.

Enter Walker with letter in his hand.

WALKER: Colonel Lapham—a letter from the G. L. & P.

ROGERS, *starting forward as Lapham takes the letter from Walker*: Don't open that letter till you give me your answer— If you break that seal, I wouldn't dare—

Enter Dinwiddie with telegram in hand.

DINWIDDIE: We accept your offer to join forces, Colonel Lapham. I've just got word from Kanawha. We'd rather go in with you than fight you with more capital.

LAPHAM, *stands irresolute. After a pause*: There won't be any fight, Mr. Dinwiddie. (*Tears open the envelope.*) I have failed to raise the sum I named. (*Hands letter to Bellingham.*)

ROGERS, *furious. Turns to Acroyd in despair*: You've ruined me.

LAPHAM, *to Bellingham*: I'm in your hands now, Mr. Bellingham, but I'll pay up dollar for dollar. (*He turns to Mrs. Lapham.*) Persis, I want we should go back to Lapham and begin again!

CURTAIN

ACT IV

SCENE: *Back at Lapham. The scene shows the exterior of the old farm house at Lapham with the porch and garden. In the distance are seen the rocks and barns with "Lapham's Mineral Paint, Specimen" upon their sides, disappearing in the rugged hillside perspective. Steps lead from the garden to the porch. A path leads to an old gate at C. There are seats near the well, and a garden bench before the house. At rise Penelope enters through the gate; she wears a summer dress and hat; she carries some letters in her hand. She comes to bench near well—sits down and begins to go through the pile assorting them and reading as she does so.*

PEN: Silas Lapham, Esq., Col. Lapham. Colonel —Colonel— (*Etc. ad lib.*) Mrs. Silas Lapham. (*Pauses with letter in hand.*) From Irene. (*Looks at it for a while then resumes as before.*) For the Colonel, Colonel, Colonel—

Again ad lib. until she comes upon her own letter from Tom. She takes it up quickly with joy lighting up her whole face, is about to tear it open hastily, but stops suddenly. The look of joy fades from her face and gives way to pensiveness, her hands drop into her lap still holding the letter at which she continues to stare. Mrs. Lapham enters from house, freshly and prettily dressed. She sees Penelope and watches her listless attitude for a moment, then says rather sharply.

MRS. LAPHAM: Well, Penelope Lapham! I do declare—

PEN, *jumps to her feet with a startled cry, the letters all scatter on the floor except her own which she has clasped tightly to her bosom*: Oh, mother. (*Then she falls back on bench and begins to laugh.*) I thought—it was my ghost.

MRS. LAPHAM, *abandoning her evident intention to scold her on seeing her hysterical condition, says more kindly*: What letters you got, Pen?

PEN, *gathering up the letters from the ground. Sitting on the bench*: All these for the Colonel; and here's one—from—Irene for you.

MRS. LAPHAM, *taking letters*: Your father's going down to the train to meet Mr. Bellingham and Mr. Dinwiddie: I hain't seen him so like his old self since I don't know when. Wants me to go with him; I don't know as I shall, if he drives that crazy cold of his. (*Suddenly.*) What you got there?

PEN: Nothing. Just a letter. For me.

MRS. LAPHAM: From Tom Corey?

PEN: How do I know? I haven't opened it yet.

MRS. LAPHAM: Then I should think you would.

PEN: Maybe I shall—some time. Better go down to the train with father.

MRS. LAPHAM: I guess I sha'n't go, if that's what you're waiting for. You know what your father's planned out? He's been waiting for Mr. Bellingham and Dinwiddie to light the fires in the works. Just like his showing off! Wants I should light up one furnace, and you one—and it most kills him not to have Irene here to light the other.

PEN: Poor Irene! What does she say, mother?

MRS. LAPHAM: I declare, I forgot her letter. (*Opens, and reads to herself.*) Well, there's a great lot. But she says she's about got through her visit. Had enough of Dubuque, and she'll be home almost any day, now. "But don't expect me till you see me," she says.

PEN: If she could only have got here for today!

MRS. LAPHAM: I don't see why your father couldn't have waited! There he comes! Don't you be down in the mouth, Pen! You just cheer up. I sha'n't let you do anything to cross him today.

PEN: Oh, I'll cheer up for the Colonel, any day, if that's all you want, mother.

Lapham enters from the house; he meets Pen as she goes up the steps to the porch.

LAPHAM: Hello, Pen! Any letters?

PEN: Mother's got them. You'll want to send a freight car for your mail, if it keeps on at this rate, Colonel.

LAPHAM: They can't get along without the paint, heigh? (*Running letters through his hands.*) Yes—orders! They have waked up, sure enough. One while, I didn't think we could work the old stock off. But it's gone now, and it's the Persis Brand that's done it; that's what's kept Lapham's paint in the market; and that's what's going to light the fires at Lapham again. They can't make the fine grades at Kanawha, and that's why they want to go in with me, after all. (*To Mrs. Lapham.*) Well, mother, you most ready to go down and light the fires in the works? You and Pen, and— My, I wish Irene was here! (*Exit Pen, furtively.*) I guess you'll have to light two of 'em, Pen— Hello!

Looks round.

MRS. LAPHAM: Never mind Pen, Silas. *She's* got a letter that she wants to read by herself, I guess.

LAPHAM, *significantly*: From?

MRS. LAPHAM: Yes! And here's one from Irene. Want to hear it? Or are you in such a fidge to get to the train.

LAPHAM: Time enough when she whistles for the bridge. What's Irene say?

They sit together on the bench before the house.

MRS. LAPHAM: Read it yourself, Si. (*She gives him the letter as they sit side by side.*) I guess it's going to come out all right. If Irene had only fixed it up with one of your brother Bill's boys, she'd be off Pen's mind; and I don't know but she has. Irene keeps *doing*; and she keeps with people; but Pen just sits and mopes. She don't even read. I came out just now to scold her about the state the house was in—you can see that Irene's away by the perfect mess; but when I saw her I hadn't the heart.

LAPHAM: I don't want you should ever be anyways ha'sh with Pen, Persis. (*Reading letter.*) "Tell Pen I don't want she should be foolish." That's like Irene!

MRS. LAPHAM: Irene's showing twice the character that Pen is, this very minute.

LAPHAM: Irene's got the easiest part, the way I look at it.

MRS. LAPHAM: What do you want Pen should do, if her letter *is* from him? I never could make it seem right if she took him.

LAPHAM: It *would* be right.

MRS. LAPHAM: Yes. I know. But it don't *seem* so.

LAPHAM, *sighing*: It's the only bitter drop in my cup. But he's going out to Mexico again for the Kanawha paint— He was going for mine, once! But then I got them to take him, and he put his money in with them— He'll do well for them out there.

MRS. LAPHAM: Mexico— It seems a long way off, Silas.

LAPHAM: A long way off for Pen.

MRS. LAPHAM: Silas Lapham! You going to let her marry him?

As they speak Pen is seen in the doorway coming from the house. She hears what they say of Tom's going out to Mexico. As Lapham looks up and sees her, a distant whistle is heard.

PEN, *from the porch*: That's your train whistling for the bridge, Colonel.

LAPHAM, *at gate*: I guess it's whistling for me. Come, Persis.

MRS. LAPHAM: I'm not going to the train with you, Silas. I've got enough to do to get ready for your visitors before they come. If Irene was here—

LAPHAM, *severely*: Persis! None o' that!

MRS. LAPHAM: Well, I won't. I only meant— Oh, *do* hurry, or you'll be too late to meet 'em.

LAPHAM, *going out*: I guess I sha'n't be too late. (*Calling Pen to his side.*) Pen!

PEN: Yes, Colonel.

Goes up to him to gate.

LAPHAM, *leaning over gate*: Is he coming here?

PEN: Yes, father.

LAPHAM: I want to read you a bit of Irene's letter—would you care to hear what she says?

PEN: Yes, father!

LAPHAM: She says. (*Reading letter.*) "Tell Pen I don't want she should be foolish." Well then, you remember what Irene says and don't you be!

Exit at gate.

MRS. LAPHAM: Your father says he's going to Mexico again for the Kanawha paint.

PEN: Yes. That's what he says in his letter. (*Pause.*) He's coming here on this train with his uncle and Mr. Dinwiddie.

MRS. LAPHAM: Pen!

PEN: He wants me to tell him before he goes back.

MRS. LAPHAM, *pause*: What you going to do?

PEN: I don't know yet. It depends a good deal upon what he does. I wish he wasn't coming.

MRS. LAPHAM: Well, he *is* coming.

PEN: Oh, yes—yes, he is. (*Listening to the rumble of the train in the valley.*) The train is coming in. Father'll be late— There! It's stopped at the station; you can hear the steam. They are getting off. Oh, mother—what shall I do? I feel like a thief—a thief that hasn't been caught yet. He belonged to Irene.

MRS. LAPHAM: It isn't the same as it was. You can see that Irene's all over it.

PEN: That's no credit to me. I'm as ashamed as ever.

MRS. LAPHAM: You've no need ever to be ashamed.

PEN: That's true, too, mother, but it doesn't help. There's no more reason now and no less than there ever was why I should say yes or why I should say no. Everything else changes, but this is just where it was a year ago. It don't go backward, and it don't go forward— If I could only take the bit in my teeth— If I could be *sentenced* to marry him!

MRS. LAPHAM: Penelope Lapham! I'm ashamed of you! Will you never be a woman?

Exit Mrs. Lapham into house.

PEN: That's just what I'm afraid of being!

Tom enters at back. Pen turns and sees him. He comes forward and they meet at the gate.

TOM: Penelope! I met your father in the village;

he is taking my uncle and Mr. Dinwiddie over the works— I came on—to see you—it's been so long—

He tries to take her hand.

PEN, *leading the way to the garden seats*: Sit down, Mr. Corey. There's no reason why we shouldn't talk it over quietly; for I know you'll think I'm right.

TOM: I've only come to do whatever you say, and not to be an—annoyance to you— I've thought it over and over. I can see now, how I must have seemed to be seeking her out. It's all been a dreadful mistake. But there's no mistake about my loving you, Penelope.

PEN: That only makes it worse.

TOM: Oh no. It makes it better. It makes it right. How is it worse— How is it wrong?

PEN: I can never forgive myself. I can see, now, how I must have been trying to get you away from her. I can't endure it. The only way is for me never to see you again. (*Laughing forlornly.*) That would be pretty hard on you if you cared.

TOM: I do care—all the world!

PEN: You won't, long.

TOM: Is this all, then? Is this the end?

PEN: I can't get over the thought of Irene.

TOM: You have been true to her. From the first time I saw you there at the new house that afternoon, you filled my fancy; then I only thought how charming you were—now I only think how good you are.

PEN: Don't!

TOM: We have not done any wrong—if you love me you won't deny me the happiness that I have done nothing to forfeit. I will never give you up. I will wait as long as you please for the time when you feel free from this mistake.

PEN: Time won't change anything. Don't you see that there's no hope for us!

TOM: No, I don't, and you will see it differently, too. You will let me take you with me when I go to Mexico.

PEN: No. No. Never. Never. Never. You must never try to see me again. You must promise never to come again—or write to me—or think of me.

TOM: You are cruel—cruel to yourself—cruel to me!

Tom turns from her in despair. Irene enters at the gate; Pen turns and sees her, utters a startled cry.

PEN: Why, Irene!

IRENE, *advancing*: Well, Pen. (*She kisses her.*) How do you do, Mr. Corey. (*Shakes hands.*) I thought I'd give father a little surprise; and I wanted to help you and mother light those fires. (*Turning to Tom.*) I came on the same train with you; I was in the last car. (*To Pen.*) I couldn't wait, Pen, to come up with father; he's been showing off the works to Mr. Dinwiddie and Mr. Bellingham. He's showing off the colt now. Where's mama?

PEN: She's in the house.

TOM: I—I think I'll go and meet Colonel Lapham.

Exit Tom through gate.

IRENE, *going straight to Pen*: Penelope Lapham, have you been such a ninny as to send that man away on my account? If you have, I'll thank you to bring him back again. I'm not going to have him thinking that I'm dying for one that never cared for me. It's insulting, and I'm not going to stand it. Now, you just stop it!

PEN: Oh, I will, 'Rene.

IRENE: Well, then! You go right after him. *He* don't want to meet Colonel Lapham!

Exit Pen. Enter Mrs. Lapham from the house.

MRS. LAPHAM: Irene Lapham!

IRENE: Yes, I'm here! I got tired and I came. That's all. We all came up on the same train.

MRS. LAPHAM, *after pause*: The same train! Have you seen *him?*

IRENE: Yes, with Pen here, just now.

MRS. LAPHAM: It's the first time Pen's seen him since we came back to Lapham.

IRENE: I hope it won't be the last time.

MRS. LAPHAM: 'Rene!

IRENE: That's all over, mother.

As they speak, Lapham, Bellingham, Mr. Dinwiddie and Bartley Hubbard appear and enter through the gate.

HUBBARD, *pausing and looking up the hillside at the barns and rocks with the signs upon them*: Still improving the face of nature, Colonel Lapham? Rouging up her cheeks a bit?

LAPHAM, *looking up the hillside as Dinwiddie comes down with Bellingham to Mrs. Lapham and Irene*: That was put on years ago. It don't fade, and it don't wash off, and it don't scale off in the sun. It'll stay there as long as the rocks stay, and I guess it'll keep the weather boarding on the barns till the crack of doom. That's the only thing that'll ever crack *it.*

MRS. LAPHAM, *to Bellingham*: We didn't expect Irene. She's given us a little surprise. You remember my daughter? (*To Dinwiddie.*) I don't

know as you met my daughter before, Mr. Dinwiddie?

DINWIDDIE: I never spoke to her, but I have seen her before. I don't suppose she remembers when, but I do.

They greet smilingly and talk apart.

HUBBARD: And I suppose you've forgotten our last meeting, Mrs. Lapham, but I haven't. I'm after the Colonel for the *Events* again. We've heard that you're going to light up here, and begin to paint the Universe with the Persis Brand!

MRS. LAPHAM: Anything the Colonel can tell you, you won't have to beg very hard to get out of him.

LAPHAM: I guess you're about right, Persis. But get on your things, all you girls, and come on down to the works. The men and their families are down there now, and they want to see the smoke go up the old flues again. I don't want you should keep them waiting. Where's Pen?

MRS. LAPHAM: Never you mind Pen. Come along, Irene.

Exit Mrs. Lapham and Irene into the house.

HUBBARD: Well, now about that talk for the *Events*, Colonel Lapham, when can we have it?

LAPHAM: What do you want I should talk about?

HUBBARD: Well, about the outlook for the paint when you combine with the Kanawha mills; you don't want to say anything about the terms under which you go in?

LAPHAM: Not yet. It's going to depend on the paint itself. The transfer will lift the last load of debt off, and when the papers are signed I won't owe any man a cent. You don't know what that means, young man—you never want to. I'll have an interest in the whole concern and the exclusive control of the works here in Lapham. Young blood's the thing we need, and Mr. Dinwiddie and his brothers, and Mr. Corey make a perfect team out at Kanawha.

DINWIDDIE: Hurrah for Colonel Lapham!

LAPHAM, *to Hubbard*: I presume you wanted my opinion on them, too? Well, as for myself, I presume that I've made mistakes as who hasn't? I can see just where they were—now—put my finger right on them—now— But there's one thing I can say; every cent I had has gone to the men I owed; I have come out of the smash with clean hands.

BELLINGHAM: I can certify to that, Mr. Hubbard.

HUBBARD: I hear that Mr. Rogers who turned

in those mills to you is doing well with his patent right.

LAPHAM: Well, I hope so.

Mrs. Lapham and Irene re-enter coming from the house.

MRS. LAPHAM: We're all ready, Si.

LAPHAM: Did you get the matches out of that old match box mother used over the mantel?

MRS. LAPHAM: Yes, Si.

LAPHAM: Then we'll go down and light the fires. It'll be good to see the smoke coming up from the valley again, eh Pert?

MRS. LAPHAM: It used to blow across here and spoil the wash sometimes—but I guess we can stand that, Silas.

LAPHAM: I guess we can stand it, Persis.

Irene and Mr. Dinwiddie pass out at the gate following Bellingham and Hubbard who stroll on slowly ahead. Irene pauses to gather a rose which Dinwiddie puts in his coat; at the gate Lapham pauses.

LAPHAM: Persis!

MRS. LAPHAM: Well?

LAPHAM, *looking after them*: Maybe it ain't going to be one of Bill's boys after all.

MRS. LAPHAM: Don't you be silly, Si.

LAPHAM: Where's Pen? She's got to come, too.

MRS. LAPHAM: Yes, she's coming, she's coming directly.

LAPHAM: I want she should be there. Persis, I want that we should all have a hand in bringing the good times back to Lapham. This thing begins to *suit* me!

As they speak, exit Lapham and Mrs. Lapham following the others. As they go Pen comes to the door and stands looking after them, she moves as if to follow, then sinks down on the steps, sitting there staring vacantly ahead. Tom comes to the gate. She looks up and sees him. Neither speaks. He comes in quietly and stands by her.

TOM: I came back, Penelope, because I couldn't give you up. I can't. I want you!

PEN, *looking up, slowly*: You can't want a girl who cheated and betrayed her own sister.

TOM: I want *you*.

PEN: Very well, then. You can't *have* me.

TOM: Is this your answer?

PEN: Yes.

TOM: I must submit. If I asked too much of you I was wrong, and—good-bye.

He holds out his hand, she puts hers in it.

PEN: You think I'm capricious and fickle. I can't

help it. I don't know myself. But it's right for us to part. Yes, it must be, I shall try to remember that. Good-bye! You won't care, very soon. I didn't mean that, no; I know how true you are, but you will soon feel differently. Good-bye! (*Clinging to his hand.*) I am not at all what they would like— your family; I always felt that. I am little, and black, and homely, and they don't understand my way of talking. No. I'm not fit. Good-bye! You're quite right, not to have patience with me any longer. I ought to be willing to marry you against their wishes if you want me to; but I can't make the sacrifice—I'm too selfish for that. (*Suddenly she throws herself upon his breast.*) Oh, I can't even give you up! I shall never dare look anyone in the face again. Go! Go! But—*take me with you!*

TOM: Penelope!

Lapham enters at the back, pausing in the gate, a hand upon either post.

LAPHAM, *calling*: Pen, ain't you coming? The fires are lit. Oh, ho!

TOM: Colonel Lapham!

Pen clings to him without looking up.

PEN: Oh, father—I've *stolen* him!

LAPHAM: No, Pen, as far forth as I know, you haven't stolen anything, and whatever you've got belongs to you!

A faint cheer is heard in the distance. Lapham listens and turns away.

PEN, *turning from Tom to him*: It's the men— at the works—cheering! For you—father! You came back for me— You ran away from the glory!

The cheering continues from the valley.

LAPHAM: Look, Pen! There's the first streak of smoke coming out of the valley now!

TOM, *at gate*: Mrs. Lapham—they have all— followed you home—

Mrs. Lapham and Bellingham followed slowly by Hubbard and Dinwiddie and Irene come up the hill from the village straggling in. Irene and Dinwiddie pausing at the gate. Mrs. Lapham crosses toward the house.

MRS. LAPHAM, *seeing Tom*: Why, Mr. Corey!

LAPHAM: Persis, I guess Mr. Corey'll stay to supper.

HUBBARD: When shall we expect to see you in Boston, again, Colonel?

LAPHAM: Maybe some of these days, when I can build again on the waterside of Beacon Street.

HUBBARD: I guess you could have been building there now if you'd wanted to.

LAPHAM: Well, I don't know. Suppose I could if I'd held my tongue.

MRS. LAPHAM, *from the porch*: Do it now, Silas, till we're at the table. Supper is waiting.

As Lapham follows the others toward the house, Bartley Hubbard turns to him again.

HUBBARD: There's just one little psychological point, Colonel. I don't want it for the *Events*. I've heard a good deal of talk about what you did. Some say it was merely common honesty, and some say it wasn't business. My point is, do you ever have any regrets?

LAPHAM: About what I done? *(Thoughtfully.)* Well, it don't always seem as if *I* done it. Seems sometimes as if it was a hole opened for me and I crept out of it. I don't know as I should always say it paid; but if I done it, and the thing was to do over again, right in the same way, I guess I should have to do it.

The twilight deepens, the lights show through the windows of the house—some are already seated at the table, the smoke drifts up in the distance—the cheering comes faintly —at intervals—far away. They turn to the house.

CURTAIN

The Smoking Car

[1898]

With *The Smoking Car* Howells ended his railroad drama, having stepped aboard *The Parlor Car* twenty-two years before, spent a restless night in *The Sleeping Car*, and put in a rather hectic half-hour of waiting at *The Albany Depot*. Howells admitted in "A Letter to the Publisher" prefacing *Minor Dramas* that *The Smoking Car* was not the logical car in which to end his railroading, for in his day it was coupled nearer to the engine than to the last car of the train. Nevertheless, the end had come; but for reasons other than "trainsmanship," or whatever it might be called, *The Smoking Car* is not the best finale one might wish for an old Boston-to-New-York commuter. It lacks the romance of *The Parlor Car*, the intrigue of *The Sleeping Car*, and the action and excitement of *The Albany Depot*.

When Howells was writing *A Counterfeit Presentment*, he at first tried to introduce certain action with a Yankee landlady, but soon had to confess to Lawrence Barrett that he could not do the Yankee character. This was, of course, more than twenty years before *The Smoking Car*, which was written after such novels as *A Modern Instance*, *The Minister's Charge*, and *The Landlord at Lion's Head*, in which Howells acquired skill in drawing his Yankees. In these novels, however, it is with older Downeasters that Howells shows talent in characterization. In fact, it is with the old man, the "by-hecker," that Howells achieves his greatest success; with the young country lad who has come to the city, his treatment is of the traditional Jonathan character. Generally, his young Yankee girls might just as well have come from Newton or Milton or any place outside cultured Boston as from their native place. And so it is with the young woman from Bangor, Maine, in *The Smoking Car*. She has some of the upper New Englander's speech mannerisms, but in both dialect and personality she fails as a far Downeaster, and her weakness is a dominant weakness of the play itself.

The Smoking Car[1]

In the smoking-car of a suburban train on the Boston and Albany Railroad, in the Albany Depot at Boston. Mr. Edward Roberts is seated, deeply absorbed in a book which he is reading. He has a pile of newspapers and magazines beside him, and he rests an absent hand on them. The seat in front is opened toward him, and he keeps a foot against its edge with the effect of laying claim to it, while a Young Mother, with a child in her arms, enters hastily and looks distractedly about. There is no one else in the car, and after walking its length she returns and addresses herself anxiously to Mr. Roberts.

THE YOUNG MOTHER: Is this the car for Newton Centre?

ROBERTS, *starting wildly from his book*: Newton Centre? Why, I don't know; I presume so; yes. Yes, I think so. I'm going to Newton Centre myself. It *is* the car for Newton Centre, isn't it?

THE YOUNG MOTHER: The brakeman said it was.

ROBERTS: Oh, well, then, it must be. Why—

THE YOUNG MOTHER: Because my husband's coming to go with me and I didn't want to get into the wrong car. He had to run back to the store for some things. (*She approaches Roberts, and looks down at the seats before and beside him.*) But if you're going there, it must be all right. Is this seat occupied?

ROBERTS: Well, not at present. I'm expecting some friends, but—

THE YOUNG MOTHER: Oh, well, all right, then. Should you mind if I put my baby down by you here a minute?

ROBERTS, *reluctantly, but more absently than reluctantly*: Why, no; I suppose not.

THE YOUNG MOTHER, *with an air of explanation*: You see, I've got to go and get my bag. I had it sent over from the boat—we just got in this morning, off the boat, you know—the Bangor boat; and it's so heavy—I'll have to hunt it up

at the express office, any way—that it don't seem as if I could manage both at the same time; and I don't know but what I'll telegraph to my husband's folks that we've got here, too. I wouldn't ask to leave her with you, but there don't seem to be anybody else I *can* ask, and I don't believe she'll make you any *great* trouble. May I?

ROBERTS: Why, yes; of course—that is, certainly, if—

THE YOUNG MOTHER: Oh, I don't believe she'll cry, and I shan't be gone but a minute, any way. (*Roberts does not offer to remove the papers at his side, and the young mother, after smoothing the baby's dress carefully under her, puts her down on top of them.*) Now, baby, don't you cry. Mamma will be back in a minute. Good-by! Good-by! (*She retreats a few steps, and flutters her hand at the baby.*) Goo, goo! Smile a little! Smile for the gentleman! There! She'll be all right, and I'll be right back. Do you know where the baggage-express office is?

ROBERTS, *in a daze*: It's in the station, I think.

THE YOUNG MOTHER: Right close to the place where the New York train stops?

ROBERTS: Yes, yes—I think so, I believe so—yes, it is.

THE YOUNG MOTHER: That's what the black man that calls the trains said; but I thought I'd better make sure, because there ain't much time to lose. Don't you topple over, baby! (*She runs forward and saves the baby from falling against the side of the seat from the top of the magazines.*) There! Mamma just caught you, didn't she? (*To Roberts*) If you don't mind, I'll just throw these things on to the seat in front of you, and then she'll sit steadier. (*She lifts the baby, and flings Roberts's papers upon the other seat, and then replaces the baby at his side.*) Now she'll do nicely. I'm so glad I happened to think of it before I went, for she might have fallen forward just as well as sideways; and it—*would* you mind putting your hand round her a *little* mite so as to keep her up? She *is* so wiggly! (*Roberts glares stupidly up through his glasses*

1 The text used here is the Houghton, Mifflin and Company edition.

and she takes hold of his arm and passes it round the baby.) If you'll excuse me! There! Now she *will* do. *(She moves backward to the door of the car again, waving her hand at the baby.)* By-by, precious! Don't you be afraid! Mamma'll be back as soon as she's got her bag. Goo, goo! Goo, goo! *(She disappears through the door, but instantly reappears.)* Do you know how soon it starts?

ROBERTS, *stupidly*: What starts?

THE YOUNG MOTHER: Why, the car?

ROBERTS: Oh! Oh, yes! The train! I don't know.

THE YOUNG MOTHER: Does it start at half past nine, exactly?

ROBERTS: I'm sure, I don't know. Yes, yes! I believe it does. Yes, my friends were to take the 9:30.

THE YOUNG MOTHER, *laughing*: You seem to be pretty easy for a person that was to meet friends. I sh'd been in a perfect fidge to know whether I'd got the right train. *(Roberts makes no response to her remark, and a doubt rushes visibly into the young mother's face.)* You're sure it *is* the car for Newton Centre?

ROBERTS, *with some spirit*: I think I said that I was going to Newton Centre myself.

THE YOUNG MOTHER: Yes, that's what you *said*. But you might have got the wrong car. I *guess* it's all right, though. And you think this is the one that goes at half past nine?

ROBERTS, *looking mechanically at his watch*: Yes, yes! Half past nine!

THE YOUNG MOTHER: Good gracious! Is it half past nine already? Then there won't be time to—

ROBERTS: No, no! It isn't half past nine; it's only ten minutes past.

THE YOUNG MOTHER: Well, that's nice. And this is the half past nine *train*?

ROBERTS: Yes, that's what I meant.

THE YOUNG MOTHER, *returning a few steps within*: I questioned the black man that calls out the trains in the waiting-room pretty close up about it, and he said it *was*. But he might have made a mistake, because he has to keep so many on his mind. I asked him if he didn't, oftentimes; but he says that's just the reason he never does. I told *him* that I should go perfectly distracted; and I cautioned him about my husband coming to meet me on the 9:30 train, and he said there couldn't be any mistake about it. Do you suppose there could?

ROBERTS: About what?

THE YOUNG MOTHER: About the train.

ROBERTS: Oh, none whatever; not the least in the world. It's the train for Newton Centre, I'm quite certain.

THE YOUNG MOTHER: The 9:30?

ROBERTS: Yes, the 9:30.

THE YOUNG MOTHER: And what time did you say it was now?

ROBERTS: I'm sure I don't know.

THE YOUNG MOTHER: Why, you just looked at your watch!

ROBERTS: Did I? I thought you wanted to know what train it was.

THE YOUNG MOTHER, *after a moment's doubt, in a burst of kindly perception and confidence*: Well, I guess your friends *better* come! But it's like John, half the time, and I guess most men are just so, if the truth was known. It's a comfort to feel that you can be trusted in spite of yourselves. Won't you see what time it is again, please?

ROBERTS, *looking at his watch again*: Ten minutes after nine.

THE YOUNG MOTHER, *easily*: Oh, well, then! *(She returns and pulls the baby's clothing straight over the toes of her small shoes, kisses her, hugs her, and kisses her again.)* There! Now, I *will* go! And if my husband *should* happen to come in while I'm gone, will you tell him I'm just out hunting for my bag?

ROBERTS: Yes, yes. I shan't forget.

THE YOUNG MOTHER, *in a burst of good feeling*: I *guess* I can trust you. I should like to tell your wife about your looking at your watch for the day of the week, if it's her that's coming to meet you, and have a real good laugh with her. *(She beams kindly though somewhat patronizingly upon Roberts, as she retreats once more toward the door.)* By-by, baby! I'll be right back. I don't know but I'd better tell *her* to look after *you*.

She laughs toward Roberts, as if this were a joke which he must enjoy with her, and vanishes through the door of the car just as Mr. Willis Campbell enters by the door at the other end. He walks down the car toward Roberts, approaching him from behind.

CAMPBELL: Hello, Roberts! What are you doing in the smoker? *(He leans over Roberts to put various parcels into the rack, without observing the baby.)* You'll be taking to drink next.

ROBERTS, *vaguely*: Is this the smoker?

CAMPBELL: It's going to be, as soon as I can light a cigar. But I don't know what you'll say to Agnes when she finds you here, wreathed in a cloud of tobacco. She's coming with Amy, isn't she?

ROBERTS: Yes, I think she said so.

CAMPBELL: Well, I'll tell you what, Roberts: you think too much; you ought to *know* something. Now, even *I* know that those two women are coming down here to join us, and they'll go flying about like a couple of distracted hens when they don't find you. They'll never think of looking for you here, and they don't want me, and they'll be in an awful flutter.

ROBERTS, *anxiously*: Perhaps I'd better go into another car.

CAMPBELL: No; this would be a good place to have it out with them. There won't be anybody else here, probably, and it will be quite like your own fireside. One of the few advantages of going home with you and Agnes, when you've been in over night with us, is that you can have the smoker all to yourself in the morning. The commuters don't begin going out till afternoon, and probably there won't be a soul at this hour to interrupt a family row. Still, I don't know but it would be safest to divide up, and you go into another car, as you don't smoke.

He continues to fit parcels into the racks as he talks.

ROBERTS: Yes; I really think it would, but I don't know what to do with this—

He glances down at the baby.

CAMPBELL, *heaving a final bundle into the rack*: There! That's done for. (*He turns about and follows Roberts's glance.*) Hello! What's that? Why, I was just going to sit on it! Did you find it here?

ROBERTS: No, no; it was left here—it was put in my charge—that is—

CAMPBELL: Who left it?

ROBERTS, *with spirit*: Who left it? Why, its mother, of course!

CAMPBELL: Its mother? Where is she?

ROBERTS: I'm sure I don't know. She went out to get her bag at the express office, and she'll be back directly.

CAMPBELL, *sitting down in the seat before Roberts and the baby, and confronting Roberts and the baby with a hard, judicial aspect*: How long has she been gone?

ROBERTS: She went out just as you came in. She hasn't been gone a moment.

CAMPBELL: And she asked if she might leave the baby here with you while she was gone?

ROBERTS: Yes.

CAMPBELL: And you said she might.

ROBERTS: I couldn't very well refuse. I let her leave it, of course.

CAMPBELL: Of course. (*He relents so far as to make a silent inventory of the baby's features and draperies.*) It's rather a nice little thing.

ROBERTS, *with relief*: Yes, and it's been very good.

CAMPBELL: Oh, it hasn't had time to be bad yet, if its mother's just gone out. (*After a moment*) Besides, it's probably drugged.

ROBERTS, *in alarm*: Drugged?

CAMPBELL: They usually drug them when they leave them that way.

ROBERTS: What do you mean by "leave them that way"?

CAMPBELL: Oh, nothing. Hello! it's going off!

ROBERTS, *grappling with the child*: Going off! Good heavens! She was *afraid* I should let it fall.

CAMPBELL: I don't mean that. It's going to sleep; don't you see? It *is* drugged! No wonder it's so good. Well, I congratulate you, Roberts.

ROBERTS, *angrily*: Congratulate me? What do you mean, Willis?

CAMPBELL: I don't know what Agnes will say to your taking such a responsibility without consulting her, but if you would *do* it, why I don't believe you could have adopted a prettier child.

ROBERTS: Adopted!

CAMPBELL: Do you mean to say you didn't know what you were about? In this paragraphic age, when every other day you might read of young mothers getting unwary strangers to hold their babies a moment, and then walking off and never coming back, do you mean to tell me you didn't know what game that woman was playing? Well, *you* ought to be left with somebody, and I've half a mind to adopt you myself. That's all.

He falls back against the seat, opens a newspaper, and makes a show of reading it. Roberts leans forward and desperately rends it from him.

ROBERTS: Willis, do you suppose—do you think—

CAMPBELL: Oh, I let *you* do the thinking. I simply *know*. I don't go beyond that. I leave thinking to men of intellect. I'm nothing but a businessman.

ROBERTS: And what do you know?

CAMPBELL: Oh, nothing. Merely that you're in for it!

ROBERTS, *sternly*: Do you mean that—that—poor creature has abandoned her child, and isn't coming back any more?

CAMPBELL: Well, not if you ask it in that threatening way, my dear fellow. I didn't put her up to it.

ROBERTS: Well, it's preposterous! She could hardly tear herself from it. She came back again and again, to kiss it, and—

CAMPBELL: Oh, I dare say! The natural feeling would assert itself at the last moment. I suppose I should do just so myself if I were a mother and meant to abandon my child. You couldn't expect less of her.

ROBERTS: But what possible motive could she have for abandoning her child? Why should she do such a monstrous—

CAMPBELL: Oh, well, there are various reasons. Perhaps her husband had abandoned *her*; or she may have been a young widow with no means of supporting it. There are always good grounds for a mother's deserting her infant when she does do it. What sort of a looking person was she?

ROBERTS: I don't know. Very good-looking, I believe.

CAMPBELL: Oh!

ROBERTS: And young—and nicely dressed—very respectable in appearance—

CAMPBELL: Ah!

ROBERTS: And smiling, and—

CAMPBELL: Of course; she had to put that on, poor thing! It wouldn't have done to let you see how heartbroken she really was. That would have roused even *your* misgivings. Was she what you would have called a lady?

ROBERTS, *thoughtfully*: Not—not exactly: not in the society sense, that is. I should say she was a nice village person—the wife of a prosperous mechanic. She spoke of her husband's "folks."

CAMPBELL: Precisely. Well, all you've got to do now is to reconcile Agnes to the inevitable. She'll come round in time, but of course—

ROBERTS, *with an effort for lightness*: Oh, come now, Willis; there's enough of this. I don't mind a joke, but there's such a thing as carrying it too far.

CAMPBELL: Ah, that's what you ought to have said to the unnatural mother. (*He leans forward and looks closely at the infant.*) Do you suppose there's any mark on its clothing, or any little note tucked in anywhere that would form a clew?

ROBERTS, *faltering*: I don't know. I never thought—

CAMPBELL: Then, for once, you ought to have thought. Better look—

ROBERTS: But I can't. I am afraid that if I disturb her she may—

CAMPBELL: Cry? Very likely. But you must do something, you know. Couldn't you pass your hand—I don't believe you'll wake her—softly over her, and if anything crackles like paper— (*Roberts acts upon this suggestion, so far as may be without risk to the child's tranquillity.*) No! All is silent. Well, then, the only thing is, should you know the mother again if you saw her?

ROBERTS: I don't believe I should. Would you—would you go out and look for her?

CAMPBELL: But if you wouldn't know her when you saw her?

ROBERTS: That's true! But something must be done! What would *you* do?

CAMPBELL: Why, if you don't really want to keep the poor little thing, or if you don't suppose Agnes—

ROBERTS: No, no; impossible! It isn't to be thought of!

He has got to his feet, and is standing over Campbell in great excitment, while Campbell remains calm.

CAMPBELL: Then, I'll tell you what you can do, and it's the only thing you can do. You'd better take the baby, and run through the crowd; and perhaps, if the mother sees you,—she'll be hanging about remorsefully—she may relent and want it back.

ROBERTS, *catching up the child from the seat*: Would you—would you—try leaving it with the brakeman, first? He might have noticed what sort of looking person she was, and—

CAMPBELL, *tolerantly*: Yes, you might try that. (*Roberts rushes from the car with the little one, while Campbell fastens his face to the car window, and expresses in vivid pantomime his pleasure in some spectacle without. He turns as Roberts reënters the car, with the child in his arms.*) Well?

ROBERTS, *breathlessly*: He won't do it. He says it isn't his business to look out for passengers' children, and I'd better find its mother, if I can!

CAMPBELL: The heartless ruffian! But you see, now, don't you?

ROBERTS: Yes, yes! I see! You're probably right. But what would you do now?

CAMPBELL: I don't see what's left, except to do what the brakeman and I have advised.

ROBERTS: And if I can't find her?

CAMPBELL: Then you'll have to bring the baby back, and throw yourself on Agnes's mercy. Or, hold on! Yes, I think you might try that; you might try leaving it at the package window. Very likely they'd take charge of it there, if you checked it, and keep it till the mother called for it. But most probably you'll find her, and when she sees that you are determined not to be put upon, perhaps—

ROBERTS: And—and—you don't think it would be better for me to leave the baby here with you, and run out and look for its mother myself?

CAMPBELL: I *know* it wouldn't. The whole moral effect upon her would be lost without the baby. Besides, how would you know her? You must take the baby for the moral effect upon her.

ROBERTS, *with despairing conviction*: That is true!

He rushes out again, and again Campbell attaches himself to the window, while from the other end of the car Mrs. Roberts and Mrs. Campbell advance falteringly and doubtfully toward him, with many diffident looks to the right and left. They seem to decide simultaneously that the figure at the window is Campbell, for they start vividly forward.

MRS. CAMPBELL: Willis!

MRS. ROBERTS: Where is Edward? We've been all through the train, and—

MRS. CAMPBELL: We can't find him anywhere. We knew we should find *you* in the smoking-car, and so I brought Agnes right in. Haven't you seen him?

CAMPBELL: Why, certainly. Haven't you?

He turns and faces them hardily.

MRS. CAMPBELL: Of course we haven't. Do you think we'd ask if we had?

MRS. ROBERTS: What do you mean, Willis? Has he been here?

CAMPBELL: Yes, I thought you must have met him. He hasn't been gone a moment. He's just gone out with the baby.

MRS. ROBERTS: The baby? What baby?

CAMPBELL: That's just what Roberts is going to find out if he can. He's looking for the mother.

MRS. ROBERTS: Willis, dear, don't tease! What do you mean by the mother?

CAMPBELL: What does anybody mean by the mother? The mother of the baby. Roberts is out looking for the mother who left the baby. Isn't that plain enough?

MRS. CAMPBELL, *pouncingly*: No, Willis, that is *not* enough! And I want you to stop your teasing, and tell us what you mean by a mother leaving her baby. Where did she leave it?

CAMPBELL: Here.

MRS. CAMPBELL: When?

CAMPBELL: About ten minutes ago.

MRS. CAMPBELL: What for?

CAMPBELL: Ah, there you have me.

MRS. CAMPBELL: Willis, if you don't answer me, I shall make a scene and disgrace you before the whole car. I am not going to be trifled with any longer.

CAMPBELL: I don't blame you, Amy. I shouldn't like it myself. As long as there's nobody but Agnes in the car I shan't mind your making a scene, and as we're likely to have the smoker to ourselves on a 9:30 train, why not sit down and wait here till Roberts gets back?

MRS. CAMPBELL, *firmly*: No, we shall not sit down, or anything, till you explain yourself. Now, don't go on with that nonsense about the mother and the baby, because we won't *stand* it.

CAMPBELL: Then what *shall* I go on with?

MRS. ROBERTS: Oh, go on with *anything*, Willis!

CAMPBELL: Very well, then, all that I can say is that I found Roberts here, five minutes ago, in charge of a baby—or child of a year—which he said had been left with him by its mother, while she went out to look up her baggage at the express office.

BOTH LADIES: Well?

CAMPBELL: Well, after a few moments' conversation with me he took the child and went out to look up the mother.

MRS. CAMPBELL: But why did he do that?

MRS. ROBERTS: Why didn't he simply wait till she came back?

CAMPBELL: Perhaps he thought she wasn't coming back.

MRS. ROBERTS: Oh, nonsense, Willis!

CAMPBELL: Oh, very well!

MRS. CAMPBELL, *visibly shaken*: They really do it sometimes, Agnes. I've read about it myself. But—

MRS. ROBERTS: Well, they never do it in the world. It doesn't stand to reason, Amy. If Willis were a mother himself he wouldn't even suggest such a thing!

MRS. CAMPBELL, *with conviction*: Of course he wouldn't. And if this is one of his miserable jokes—

CAMPBELL: Well, I don't pretend to be a mother, but I hope I understand the feelings of a man, and I assure you that I wouldn't joke on such a subject.

MRS. CAMPBELL: Then what *are* you joking about?

CAMPBELL: I am not joking at all.

MRS. ROBERTS, *visibly daunted*: I can't believe the wretched creature would really do it. Why didn't you ask the brakeman if he had noticed where she went?

CAMPBELL: Well, that's what Roberts did, and he wanted to leave the baby with him, but the brakeman said he had better find the mother himself—if he could. Roberts came back to report, and then he went out again. I suppose if he *can't* find her, you'll have to keep it, Agnes. It's a pretty little creature, and it seemed good. Hello! Here it comes, bringing Roberts with it! (*Roberts enters the car flustered and dazed, with the signs of anxiety and disappointment filling his face, and drops of perspiration starting from his brow.*) Well, where *was* she?

MRS. CAMPBELL: Did you find her? What did she say?

MRS. ROBERTS: Why didn't you leave the baby with her?

MRS. CAMPBELL: Why didn't she come back with you?

ROBERTS, *frantically*: Because I didn't find her. I've been to the express office and everywhere.

CAMPBELL, *to Mrs. Roberts*: You see!

MRS. ROBERTS: But you *must* find her, Edward!

CAMPBELL: Did you try leaving it at the package window?

ROBERTS: No; I couldn't quite bring myself to that.

MRS. CAMPBELL: Of course you couldn't! And nobody but Willis could have the heart to suggest such an inhuman thing. The package window! (*She drops on one knee before Roberts, who sits supporting the baby in his lap, and begins to study it.*) Poor little creature! How good it is; and it's perfectly lovely, with those big blue eyes; and it's as clean as a pin. Why, it's charming, and it isn't the least afraid. Just see it, Agnes!

CAMPBELL: Yes, Roberts said its mother had beautiful eyes and an attractive smile, and was nicely dressed. He seemed to have noticed everything about her.

MRS. CAMPBELL, *still considering the baby*: You can see what a good mother she is. Of course she isn't rich, but it's all the better cared for on that account. She hasn't left it to any horrid shirk of a nurse. It's as sweet as a little pink, isn't it, Agnes?

MRS. ROBERTS, *leaning forward in some distraction*: Oh, yes; it shows the mother's touch. Was she young, Edward?

ROBERTS: I don't know—I think so—I didn't notice—quite girlish, I should say. She kept coming back to take leave of it.

CAMPBELL: I tell him that was the remorse working in her.

MRS. CAMPBELL: Nonsense! She never meant to leave it in the world.

CAMPBELL: Then why doesn't she come back? It's twenty minutes past nine, now.

MRS. CAMPBELL: Very well, then; something has happened to her!

MRS. ROBERTS: Oh, something *must* have happened to her. Why doesn't someone go out and look for her? It seems so terrible for us to be keeping her baby here and not knowing what has happened to her.

CAMPBELL: But if nothing has happened—

MRS. CAMPBELL: Don't *hint* such a thing. You *know* there has. You ought to go out and see!

CAMPBELL: I? Roberts ought to go and see. I shouldn't know her if I found her.

MRS. ROBERTS: Oh, do go, Willis! Poor Edward is all worn out. Look at him!

Roberts has fallen back in extreme dejection and exhaustion, and he supports the baby on his knee with so lax a hand that it topples forward. The ladies scream, and Campbell catches it from him.

CAMPBELL: Look what you're about, Roberts! You're not fit to have an abandoned child left with you. Bless my soul, it's off again!

THE LADIES: Off?

CAMPBELL: Yes, it's going to sleep.

MRS. CAMPBELL: So it is, poor little forsaken soul! Let me take it.

MRS. ROBERTS: The little darling! (*As Mrs. Campbell possesses herself of the baby*) Be careful, Amy!

CAMPBELL: It was asleep when Roberts went out with it. Roberts thinks it's drugged.

ROBERTS: No, no, Willis; you suggested that. Though it is strange it sleeps so much. She said they were right off the boat, and perhaps they didn't sleep well during the night.

MRS. CAMPBELL, *pressing her face into the baby's*: To be sure they didn't, poor things!

CAMPBELL: And the mother may have fallen asleep in the express office with her bag in her arms. That would account for her not coming back.

MRS. CAMPBELL, *not minding him*: If she doesn't come back I shall keep it myself.

CAMPBELL: Not if I know it, Mrs. Campbell. That baby is *my* property.

MRS. ROBERTS: But if her mother left her with Edward—

CAMPBELL: It was because I hadn't come in yet. She'd never have left her with Roberts if she'd seen *me*. What shall we call her, Amy?

MRS. CAMPBELL: No, no! We mustn't think of it, till we've left no stone unturned. You must go out and look for her, Willis, and if you don't find her—

CAMPBELL: But haven't I told you that I shouldn't know her if I saw her?

MRS. CAMPBELL: It doesn't matter about your not knowing her. She'll know you if you have the baby with you.

CAMPBELL: Have the baby with me? Ha, ha, ha! I think I see myself running about with a baby in my arms asking people for its mother!

MRS. CAMPBELL: You made Edward do it.

CAMPBELL: That was another thing. She left it with him.

MRS. CAMPBELL: But you said she would have left it with you if she had seen you first, and now you must take it.

She tries to push it into his arms.

CAMPBELL: Oh, come, now! You don't want to make me ridiculous, Amy!

MRS. ROBERTS: You wouldn't really be ridiculous. I'm sure that any one who saw you, and knew what you were doing to save a poor woman from despair, would praise you up to the skies for it.

ROBERTS: I really think you could manage it better than I, Willis; you are so ready, and you know how to take people so cleverly. Nobody would think of making a joke of you.

CAMPBELL: Oh *wouldn't* they!

MRS. CAMPBELL: And if they did, it oughtn't to make the least difference to you. You ought to be glad of it. And, at any rate, you've got to go.

She makes him take the child from her.

MRS. ROBERTS: Yes, Willis, you *must*! Poor Edward is perfectly gone.

CAMPBELL: Well, so am I.

He suddenly drops the baby into Roberts's lap, and makes a start toward the door. The two ladies fling themselves in his way with one cry of protest and despair.

MRS. ROBERTS and MRS. CAMPBELL: Willis!

MRS. ROBERTS: You won't refuse such a *little* thing, Willis!

MRS. CAMPBELL: If he does, I will never speak to him again!

CAMPBELL: Oh, very well, then, if it comes to that! Here, give her to me.

He seizes the baby from Roberts and dashes from the car, laughing.

MRS. ROBERTS: There, I knew he would, if we could only appeal to his better nature.

MRS. CAMPBELL: I *hope* it's his better nature. But I didn't like his laughing.

ROBERTS: That may have been merely nervous; it made *me* nervous. But Willis manages these things so well; he's so full of resource. I feel quite sure he'll find her.

MRS. ROBERTS, *pressing to the window and looking out*: He's disappeared already! I shouldn't like to look for anyone in that crowded station. He *is* energetic.

MRS. CAMPBELL, *joining her*: He knew that I was in earnest. But I don't want to make him feel ridiculous. If I'd thought he really cared— But something had to be done, and done instantly. Did they laugh at *you*, Mr. Roberts?

ROBERTS: Well, I can't say laugh, exactly. No, I don't think I could say they laughed outright. But when I ran about, and asked if they had seen anybody—any lady—who had left her baby with a gentleman in the smoking-car, while she went out to look up her bag at the express office, they smiled.

MRS. CAMPBELL: I suppose it did amuse them; men are so peculiar. I hope I wasn't too precipitate with poor Willis. But I knew that he could do something if he was forced to it.

ROBERTS: Yes, he'll come out of it all right, with his tact and invention. He'll find her, easily enough.

MRS. ROBERTS, *in a transport of triumph*: He *has* found her! There he is, coming back, without the baby!

MRS. CAMPBELL: Where? Oh, yes; I see him! I do believe he *has* found her; and now I owe him any reparation that he chooses to ask. I'll confess that I was wrong to send him. He *is* good, isn't he, Agnes?

MRS. ROBERTS: He's beautiful! And you are just the wife for him, Amy. You do appreciate him.

ROBERTS: Willis is magnificent. I envy him his executive ability.

ALL THREE, *as Campbell enters the car, turning from the window*: Well?

MRS. CAMPBELL: Where did you find her?

MRS. ROBERTS: What did she say?

ROBERTS: How did you know her?

CAMPBELL: Nowhere; and nothing; and I didn't.

MRS. CAMPBELL: Then what did you do?

MRS. ROBERTS: Where is the baby?

ROBERTS: How did you get rid of it?

CAMPBELL: The way you ought to have done, my dear fellow. I left it with the matron—or whatever she is—of the ladies' waiting-room.

MRS. ROBERTS: Oh Willis!

MRS. CAMPBELL: And here we had been praising you so, and I was sorry that I had made you go! Well, that is what I get for ever regretting that I treated you badly.

ROBERTS: You think it will occur to the mother to inquire of the matron—

CAMPBELL: She won't make any inquiries! Or if, by one chance in a thousand, she wants her baby again, and makes a row for it after our train's gone, the matron is the very first person she'll be sent to. I thought it all out. In the other event, it will be handed over to the proper authorities and sent to the Derelict Infants' Home—or something. At any rate, it's off *our* hands.

MRS. CAMPBELL: Indeed it isn't. If she doesn't come for her baby, I'm going to keep it myself.

CAMPBELL: You? Why you're worse than Roberts.

MRS. CAMPBELL: I don't care who I'm worse than. Agnes doesn't want it, for she's got children of her own, and so you may go straight and bring it back here. Do, Willis! I'm truly in earnest. If that poor thing should come here for her baby before you brought it back, I don't know what I should say to excuse you.

CAMPBELL: Oh, I could trust you to think of something.

MRS. CAMPBELL: Don't tease, dearest, and *do* run!

MRS. ROBERTS: Yes, Willis, you must. It would be shocking to have her come for it, and we have to make some sort of lame explanation. Hurry as fast as you can. It must be nearly train time.

ROBERTS, *looking at his watch*: Yes, it's five minutes of it. But that's plenty of time for Willis—if he doesn't delay.

CAMPBELL: Oh, hello! Don't *you* join in, Roberts. It was you who got us all into this trouble, and now I'm going to let you go and get the baby from the matron yourself. There's plenty of time for you, if you don't stand here dilly-dallying.

ROBERTS: But the matron wouldn't know me, and she wouldn't give it to me.

CAMPBELL: I guess she'll give it to anybody that asks for it.

MRS. CAMPBELL: Very well, then I'll go for it myself. After this, don't pretend that you have the least regard for me. Don't try to stop me!

CAMPBELL, *interposing himself between his wife and the door*: Only over my prostrate form, Amy. I'm going. Your reasoning has convinced me; but you know that if we adopt this child I am not going to take care of it.

MRS. CAMPBELL: No, no, Willis. I shall never ask you. I assume the whole responsibility. Oh, how sweet you are! You always come round in the end.

CAMPBELL: I always listen to reason, even when I'm going to make a fool of myself. But suppose somebody's got it away from the matron on false pretences, and I can't bring it?

MRS. CAMPBELL: Don't come back without it!

CAMPBELL: Oh, very well.

He rushes out.

MRS. CAMPBELL, *watching him through the window*: He did hate to go! (*Turning to Mrs. Roberts*) Perhaps I've been rash, Agnes.

MRS. ROBERTS: No, not in the least, Amy. I should have been just so with Edward, and he would have hated it quite as much as Willis; wouldn't you, Edward?

ROBERTS: Oh, quite. It would have been extremely disagreeable.

MRS. CAMPBELL: Then I wish you had spoken before, Mr. Roberts. I didn't want to treat Willis worse than Agnes would have treated you. I am sure we have both, Willis and I, tried to consider you in the matter.

ROBERTS: Of course. You certainly have, and I am very grateful for your kindness. But you know I didn't like to interfere, exactly.

MRS. ROBERTS: Edward is always very careful in such matters.

MRS. CAMPBELL: Oh, I am sure he meant well.

But if Willis had been in his place and you in mine, I think Willis would have said something to stop me—or you, I mean.

MRS. ROBERTS: I hope you don't blame poor Edward, Amy, if you have been a little harsh with Willis.

MRS. CAMPBELL: Then you think I *have* been harsh! Well, I must say I didn't expect this of you, Agnes, when I was doing it all to relieve Edward of a difficulty.

MRS. ROBERTS: You know I didn't mean to reproach you, Amy.

ROBERTS: And we both thoroughly appreciate what you and Willis have done. I'm sure I don't know what would have become of *me* without your help—or his.

MRS. CAMPBELL: Oh, I assume nothing for myself. (*She takes out her handkerchief and wipes her eyes with a swift dash, and then runs it back into her pocket.*) Don't regard *me*, please! But I wish the next time you think I am making Willis make a fool of himself, you wouldn't hesitate to say so.

MRS. ROBERTS, *glancing out of the window*: There! There he is coming back.

MRS. CAMPBELL, *springing to the window beside her*: Don't tell me he isn't bringing the baby! Yes, yes! He's got it. And now I forgive him everything. I'm sure I don't know what we shall do with it.

MRS. ROBERTS: Why, I thought you wanted to adopt it, Amy.

MRS. CAMPBELL: Not if it's been the cause of my making Willis make a fool of himself. I should always detest the sight of it. (*She turns to encounter her husband, as he enters the car, red and perspiring, with the child in his arms.*) Had she come for it? Did the matron give it up willingly? Were you very ridiculous, Willis? Did she laugh at you? What did you say to her?

CAMPBELL, *sinking breathless into the seat beside her*: One thing at a time, my dear, and nothing till I've got my wind. (*He pursues, panting.*) There hadn't been any rush for her, not even on the part of the unnatural mother, and I dare say I was more a fool than I looked.

MRS. ROBERTS, *fondly and proudly*: Oh, you *couldn't* be, Willis, dear!

CAMPBELL: Thank you, Agnes, you are always so flattering. But the main point is that I got the baby back for you, and here it is, Amy, and the sooner you take it— Hello!

They all start into listening postures, while an excited and anxious woman's voice makes itself heard from without in apparent parley with the brakeman on the platform.

THE WOMAN'S VOICE: Is this the half past nine o'clock train for Newton Centre?

THE BRAKEMAN'S VOICE: Well, for that and about twenty other places.

THE WOMAN'S VOICE: The half past nine?

THE BRAKEMAN'S VOICE: Yes, ma'am.

THE WOMAN'S VOICE: You're sure it hasn't gone?

THE BRAKEMAN'S VOICE: Well, I won't be, in about two minutes.

THE WOMAN'S VOICE: Oh, my gracious! Which is the smoking-car?

THE BRAKEMAN'S VOICE: This is.

THE WOMAN'S VOICE: And was there a lady, here, about half an hour ago, that came out and told you she had left her baby in the car with a strange gentleman, and asked you whether you thought it would be safe, and said she would be back in about a minute, and asked you to tell her just how soon the train started, and said she was going to get her bag at the express office, and asked you if you would look in now and then and see how the baby was getting along, and asked how she should know the car again, and you said it was the smoking-car, and she would know it by that, and—

THE BRAKEMAN'S VOICE: Yes, ma'am.

THE WOMAN'S VOICE: Goodness! Then there ain't a minute to lose!

CAMPBELL: The unnatural mother! What are you going to say to her when she comes in to rob you of your adoptive child?

MRS. CAMPBELL: I shall know what to say. I hope *you* will.

CAMPBELL: I hope Roberts will.

THE YOUNG MOTHER, *at the door, peering down the aisle till she catches sight of the baby, which Campbell has expeditiously transferred to Roberts's knee, and then running toward the group*: Oh, there were so many, I was afraid I never should get to the right one. But it *is* the car, and there you are, baby, as bright as a biscuit! Did you think mamma had forgotten her precious? Oh, you darling! (*She catches the baby from Campbell, and crushes it to her breast and face; and then turns to Roberts.*) I don't know what you'll think of my being gone so long, but I have had such a time! First off, I thought I'd telegraph to his folks that we'd got here safe, but I couldn't seem to find the right place to send the dispatch to very easy—they live back in the country, a little ways—and then after I got it off, I went to the express office for my bag, and lo! and behold it wasn't there, and they said the baggage from the Bangor boat wasn't in yet, and I thought I *should* go through the floor; and who should I see but John himself, just about as wild as I was, looking for me and baby; and he's gone back to look after my bag on the boat, and we've concluded to stay till he gets it. He said he'd been all through the cars looking for baby and me, and he couldn't find us."

CAMPBELL: He probably didn't look into the smoking-car.

THE YOUNG MOTHER: Well, there, I guess you're right; and I don't know as I blame him any, for I didn't intend to get into it myself, and the gentleman here—(*she nods down at Roberts*) didn't tell me it was a smoking-car when I left baby with him, and—

CAMPBELL: Oh, that's just his way. He didn't know it himself.

THE YOUNG MOTHER: Well, he did seem pretty absent-minded, so't I didn't feel exactly right about leaving baby with him, but I had to leave her with somebody, and—

CAMPBELL: You couldn't have chosen better.

THE YOUNG MOTHER: I'm sure I'm ever so much obliged—

CAMPBELL: Don't mention it; we've all helped —my wife here, and my sister—and we've all taken such a fancy to your baby—

MRS. ROBERTS: Yes, indeed! Such a *good* little thing!

MRS. CAMPBELL: Perfect little angel!

CAMPBELL: We almost hoped you wouldn't come back for it, and we were just quarreling about which family it belonged to when you came in.

THE YOUNG MOTHER: Well, I guess when I tell John that he'll be ashamed of the way he talked to me about leavin' it with a perfect stranger. But I see by the gentleman's looks that it would be all right, and so I told John. I hope he didn't think I was never coming back, by the way I stayed.

CAMPBELL: Not for an instant! He's a brother-in-law of mine, and I took him in hand as soon as I came into the car, and we said we knew you'd be right back, and if you didn't come before the train left we'd get off.

THE YOUNG MOTHER: Well, I wish you good morning! And if any of you *do* ever come down Bangor way—

THE BRAKEMAN'S VOICE, *without*: All aboard!

THE YOUNG MOTHER, *vanishing through the door*: Oh, my good gracious, I shall get left, after all!

CAMPBELL, *as the car starts*: Well, Roberts lied us out of that pretty well, didn't he? (*He puts his arm across Roberts's shoulders.*) But he saved the mother's feelings by it; and I shall never think the worse of you for your fibs, old fellow!

A Hazard of New Fortunes

[1899]

Not long after James A. Herne rejected the dramatization of *The Rise of Silas Lapham*, Howells received a letter (late April 1899) from a young New York newspaperman named Frank Cornelius Drake requesting his permission to dramatize *Lapham*. Amused at the coincidence, Howells suggested that Drake try to adapt *A Hazard of New Fortunes* for the stage (letter, May 2, 1899, New York Public Library). To Drake, this was a flattering suggestion, especially since Howells pledged his co-operation, and Drake immediately went to work.

(Drake, 1872–1922, was a writer for the New York *Herald*, of which he was at one time Sunday editor, and an artist on the New York *Tribune* and the New York *World*. When he wrote to Howells, his only successful play was a brief piece called *Raspberry Shrub*. Later he found little time for the drama.)

In the New York *Herald* of May 30, 1920, Drake described his work with Howells in an article entitled "W. D. Howells's Kindly Help to a Young Writer a Score of Years Ago." (Reprinted, "William Dean Howells Helped This Young Man Write a Play," *The Literary Digest*, LXV [June 19, 1920], 56–58.) Their "literary partnership," as Drake called it, did not last long —only seven months—and the result of their labor appears to have been lost, but their correspondence gives some indication of their method in adapting a novel for the stage and of Howells' dramatic skill. For his part, Drake's first step was to write a scenario of his play, which he talked over with Howells, who suggested the same system of writing a play by mail that he had used with Paul Kester during the previous two years. "I should write him a clean, wide-spaced typewritten copy of each act as I finished it," Drake recorded in the New York *Herald*,

"and . . . while he was revising and rewriting it I would be getting another act ready for him; and he whole-heartedly insisted that I could write him fully and freely whenever I found myself 'stuck' over a situation. Then, as each act came back with his revision, I was to retype it, with further revisions of my own, and remail it to him for final consideration; and so on, until the play suited 'us,' as he so democratically put it."

From the beginning of their work, Howells' letters provided numerous suggestions and countersuggestions: Lindau should not be omitted, but should be almost the protagonist (May 4, 1894, New York Public Library); the setting could not be a Riverside Drive veranda because "it is out of key with the book and with the society facts" (May 27, 1899, New York Public Library); and servants should not be used to introduce Act I (September 2, 1899, New York Public Library). To suggestions from Drake involving serious departures from the text of the novel, Howells was much more liberal than he had been when dramatizing *The Rise of Silas Lapham* with Paul Kester. When Drake, with much diffidence, suggested a radical change for the ending of the play, Howells seemed to sense the greater drama in this new denouement and wrote an enthusiastic reply to Drake (August 29, 1899, New York Public Library):

I wrote you today suggesting that Act IV should end with the death of Lindau addressing the mob from the office window instead of Conrad. This will intensify the situation with Miss Vance, in whose arms Lindau dies. Now let Act V begin with that talk between old Dryfoos and his wife about going back to Moffitt (p. 300, Vol. I., Chap. 3). Toward the end Mela rushes in with 'Fawther, fawther! There's been somebody killed at the Every Other Week office! I do hope it ain't Conrad!' Scene with both father and mother. Dryfoos rushes distractedly out to verify the rumor. While he is gone, Conrad and Margaret come in, and tell of Lindau's death. Dryfoos returns, and in a burst of joy at finding his son alive is reconciled. C. and M. own their engagement, and Fulkerson and Miss Woodburn come in to announce theirs. This act can happily assemble all the characters. If you will contrive it and write in the dialogue as you think best I will go over it all carefully, and I think we shall have a strong close.

Drake did not abide completely by Howells' suggestion—with Howells' later approval he placed in Act I the talk between Mr. and Mrs. Dryfoos which Howells said should open Act V—but the letter illustrates Howells' zest for writing what he hoped would be a stageworthy play. There is also the suggestion of a change in his philosophy of drama. Undoubtedly influenced by his frequent unsuccessful relations with actors and stage managers, he had become more willing to adapt his work to the stage and, if necessary, to dilute his theory of realism.

By December 1899, except for some slight revisions, the play was finished. With these accomplished, it was submitted to Daniel Frohman, and then the anxious wait began. Two months later (letter to Drake, February 28, 1900, New York Public Library), Frohman rejected the play, saying: "There would be no success, financially, in a play of this kind, though it is interesting as reading matter and interesting from other points of view." Howells was disappointed but resigned, and there matters ended. Drake tried other managers, but no one was interested; by the time he wrote his *Herald* article in 1920, he did not even know where the manuscript of the play was.

Howells, too, lost whatever copies he had of the dramatization of *A Hazard of New Fortunes*. However, in the Hamlin Garland papers at the Library of the University of Southern California, there is a fragmentary dramatization of *A Hazard of New Fortunes* consisting of clippings of dialogue from the paperback first edition of the novel pasted on sheets and interspersed with some stage directions and considerable additional dia-

logue in Howells' hand. In the material, as it is printed in this volume, there are seven scenes: three each in Acts I and II and the first scene of Act III. Mr. Lloyd A. Arvidson, Curator of the American Literature Collection of the University of Southern California has intelligently guessed that Howells probably gave this fragmentary material to Garland as an example of how he might proceed in dramatizing *A Modern Instance*—a task which Garland completed to the extent of some one hundred pages of clippings from Howells' novel with his own handwritten interpolations. However, there is one major problem with this text of *A Hazard of New Fortunes*: it seems to be *all Howells' work*.

In the comments on procedure reported by Drake in the New York *Herald*, there was no mention of clippings from the novel, although this technique might have been employed. Because the Howells–Drake correspondence barely touches on the first three acts of the dramatization, there is little internal evidence of authorship one way or the other. Howells does mention that the Dryfoos conversation about returning to Moffitt appeared in Act I; yet in the form published here, the most logical place for that dialogue, identified only as Scene II in the University of Southern California fragment—if it *was* the same that Howells referred to in his letter—is in Act II. According to the correspondence, Howells deleted the servants from Act I, but Act I of this fragment takes place in a restaurant where there would be no necessity for servants. Perhaps Howells and Drake further changed the above scenes so that the comparison of texts has no importance. Perhaps, too, the play printed here bears no relation to the Howells–Drake dramatization of *A Hazard of New Fortunes*.

Of the seventy-five octavo sheets in the play fragment, twenty-four are entirely in Howells' hand, and nearly as many more contain a great number of his manuscript lines. Some of Howells' handwritten dialogue is new; some is taken from the novel. Essentially, with consideration for omissions, sudden transitions and interpolated conversation, it is possible to compare this play fragment with the novel. For example, Act I, scene 1, starts on page 71 of the Harper & Brothers Library Edition of the novel and ends on page 105, staying reasonably close to the novel text the whole time. Act I, scene 3, on the other hand, omits Mrs. March, introduces a lot of new dialogue, and skips around liberally from pages 172 through 255 of the novel.

In making this paste-up play fragment, Howells frequently inserted clippings straight from the novel without making the changes necessary for dramatic dialogue; therefore, in order to make this an intelligible play, it has been necessary first to standardize the style of punctuation and names of characters. In some places unnecessary words have been omitted and connectives supplied. Throughout the play fragment, verb tenses in the stage directions have been put into the present and descriptive phrases for particular speeches have been put into adverbial constructions.

A Hazard of New Fortunes[1]

ACT I

SCENE I

[First page of play missing]

MARCH: Yes, I remember now; but I'd totally forgotten it. How far back that goes! Who's Dryfoos?

FULKERSON: Dryfoos? (*Fulkerson, still smiling, tears off a piece of the half-yard of French loaf which had been supplied them, with two pale, thin disks of butter, and feeds it into himself.*) Old Dryfoos? Well, of course! I call him old, but he ain't so very. About fifty, or along there.

MARCH: No, that isn't very old—or not so old as it used to be.

FULKERSON: Well, I suppose you've got to know about him, anyway. And I've been wondering just how I should tell you. Can't always make out exactly how much of a Bostonian you really *are!* Ever been out in the natural gas country?

MARCH: No, I've had a good deal of curiosity about it, but I've never been able to get away except in summer, and then we always preferred to go over the old ground, out to Niagara and back through Canada, the route we took on our wedding journey. The children like it as much as we do.

FULKERSON: Yes, yes. Well, the natural gas country is worth seeing. I don't mean the Pittsburgh gas fields, but out in northern Ohio and Indiana around Moffitt—that's the place in the heart of the gas region that they've been booming so. Yes, you ought to see that country.

I rode along on the cars through those level black fields at corn-planting time, and every once in a while I'd come to a place with a piece of ragged old stove-pipe stickin' up out of the ground, and blazing away like forty, and a fellow ploughing all round it and not minding it any more than if it was spring violets. Horses didn't notice it either. Well, they've always known about the gas out

---

[1] This fragment has not been published previously.

there; they say there are places in the woods where it's been burning ever since the country was settled.

But when you come in sight of Moffitt—my, oh my! Well, you come in smell of it about as soon. That gas out there ain't odorless, like the Pittsburgh gas, and so it's perfectly safe; but the smell isn't bad—about as bad as the finest kind of benzene. Well, the first thing that strikes you when you come to Moffitt is the notion that there's been a good warm, growing rain, and the town's come up overnight. That's in the suburbs, the annexes, and additions. But it ain't shabby—no shanty-town business; nice brick and frame houses, some of 'em Queen Anne style, and all of 'em looking as if they had come to stay. And when you drive up from the depot you think everybody's moving. Everything seems to be piled into the street; old houses made over, and new ones going up everywhere.

I saw the place just when the boom was in its prime. I went out there to work the newspapers in the syndicate business, and I got one of their men to write me a real bright, snappy account of the gas; and they just took me in their arms and showed me everything. Well, it *was* wonderful, and it was beautiful too! To see a whole community stirred up like that was—just like a big boy, all hope and high spirits, and no discount on the remotest future; nothing but perpetual boom to the end of the time— I tell you it warmed your blood. Why, there were some things about it that made you think what a nice kind of world this would be if people ever took hold together, instead of each fellow fighting it out on his own hook, and devil take the hindmost. They made up their minds at Moffitt that if they wanted their town to grow they'd got to keep their gas public property. So they extended their corporation line so as to take in pretty much the whole gas region round there; and then the city took possession of every well that was put down, and held it for the common good. Anybody that's a mind to come to Moffitt and start any kind of manufacture can have all the gas he wants *free;* and for fifteen

532

dollars a year you can have all the gas you want to heat and light your private house. The people hold on to it for themselves, and, as I say, it's a grand sight to see a whole community hanging together and working for the good of all, instead of splitting up into as many different cutthroats as there are able-bodied citizens. See that fellow? (*Fulkerson breaks off, and indicates a tall, shabbily dressed, elderly man, who has just come in. He has the aquiline profile uncommon among Germans, and yet March recognizes him at once as German. His long, soft beard and mustache have once been fair, and they keep some tone of their yellow in the gray to which they have turned. His eyes are full, and his lips and chin shape the beard to the noble outline which shows in the beards the Italian masters liked to paint for their Last Suppers. His carriage is erect and soldierly, and March presently sees that he had lost his left hand. He takes his place at a table where the overworked waiter finds time to cut up his meat, and put everything in easy reach of his right hand.*) They say that fellow's a Socialist. I think it's a shame they're allowed to come here. If they don't like the way we manage our affairs, let 'em stay at home. They do a lot of mischief, shooting off their mouths round here. I believe in free speech and all that, but I'd like to see those fellows shut up in jail and left to jaw each other to death. We don't want any of their poison.

MARCH, *watching the old man*: They seem to have got a touch of it at Moffitt, from your account. Don't you know that you've been describing an ideal socialistic community?

FULKERSON: You don't say so! Well, they took me round everywhere in Moffitt, and showed me their big wells—lit 'em up for a private view, and let me hear them purr with the soft accents of a mass-meeting of locomotives. Why, when they let one of these wells loose in a meadow that they'd piped it into temporarily, it drove the flame away forty feet from the mouth of the pipe and blew it over half an acre of ground. They say when they let one of their big wells burn away all winter before they had learned how to control it, that well kept up a little summer all around it; the grass stayed green, and the flowers bloomed all through the winter. *I* don't know whether it's so or not. But I can believe anything of natural gas. My! but it was beautiful when they turned on the full force of that well and shot a Roman-candle into the gas—that's the way they light it—and a plume of fire about twenty feet wide and

seventy-five feet high, all red and yellow and violet, jumped into the sky, and that big roar shook the ground under your feet! You felt like saying, "Don't trouble yourself; I'm perfectly convinced." I believe in Moffitt. We-e-e-ll! That's where I met old Dryfoos.

MARCH: Oh yes!

He observes that the waiter has brought the old one-handed German a towering glass of beer.

FULKERSON, *laughing*: Yes. We've got round to Dryfoos again. I thought I could cut a long story short, but I seem to be cutting a short story long. If you're not in a hurry, though—

MARCH: Not in the least. Go on as long as you like.

FULKERSON: I met him there in the office of a real-estate man—speculator, of course; everybody was, in Moffitt; but a first-rate fellow, and public spirited as all get-out; and when Dryfoos left he told me about him. Dryfoos was an old Pennsylvania Dutch farmer, about three or four miles out of Moffitt, and he'd lived there pretty much all his life; father was one of the first settlers.

Everybody knew he had the right stuff in him, but he was slower than molasses in January, like those Pennsylvania Dutch. He'd got together the largest and handsomest farm anywhere around there; and he was making money on it, just like he was in some business somewhere; he was a very intelligent man; he took the papers and kept himself posted; but he was awfully old-fashioned in his ideas. He hung on to the doctrines as well as the dollars of the dads; it was a real thing with him. Well, when the boom began to come he hated it awfully, and he fought it. He used to write communications to the weekly newspaper in Moffitt—they've got three dailies there now—and throw cold water on the boom. He couldn't catch on noway. It made him sick to hear the clack that went on about the gas the whole while, and that stirred up the neighborhood and got into his family. Whenever he'd hear of a man that had been offered a big price for his land and was going to sell out and move into town, he'd go and labor with him and try to talk him out of it, and tell him how long his fifteen or twenty thousand would last him to live on, and shake the Standard Oil Company before him, and try to make him believe it wouldn't be five years before the Standard owned the whole region.

Of course he couldn't do anything with them. When a man's offered a big price for his farm, he don't care whether it's by a secret emissary from the Standard Oil or not; he's going to sell, and get the better of the other fellow if he can. Dryfoos couldn't keep the boom out of his own family, even. His wife was with him. She thought whatever he said and did was just as right as if it had been thundered down from Sinai. But the young folks were skeptical, especially the girls that had been away to school. The boy that had been kept at home because he couldn't be spared from helping his father manage the farm was more like him, but they contrived to stir the boy up with the hot end of the boom, too. So when a fellow came along one day and offered old Dryfoos a cool hundred thousand for his farm, it was all up with Dryfoos. He'd 'a liked to 'a kept the offer to himself and not done anything about it, but his vanity wouldn't let him do that; and when he let it out in his family, the girls outvoted him. They just *made* him sell.

MARCH: Of course! There's nothing like being the head of your family.

FULKERSON: I see you've *been* there. Well, Dryfoos wouldn't sell all. He kept about eighty acres that was off in one piece by itself, but the three hundred that had the old brick house on it, and the big barn—that went, and Dryfoos bought him a place in Moffitt, and moved into town to live on the interest of his money. Just what he had scolded and ridiculed everybody else for doing. Well, they say that at first he seemed like he would go crazy. He hadn't anything to do. He took a fancy to that land-agent, and he used to go and set in his office and ask him what he should do. "I hain't got any horses, I hain't got any cows, I hain't got any pigs, I hain't got any chickens, I hain't got anything to do from sunup to sundown." The fellow said the tears used to run down the old fellow's cheeks, and if he hadn't been so busy himself he believed he should 'a cried, too. But most o' people thought old Dryfoos was down in the mouth because he hadn't asked more for his farm, when he wanted to buy it back and found they held it at a hundred and fifty thousand. People couldn't believe he was just homesick and heartsick for the old place. Well, perhaps he *was* sorry he hadn't asked more; that's human nature, *too*.

After a while something happened. That land-agent used to tell Dryfoos to get out to Europe with his money and see life a little, or go and live in Washington, where he could *be* somebody; but Dryfoos wouldn't, and he kept listening to the talk there, and all of a sudden he caught on. He came into that fellow's one day with a plan for cutting up the eighty acres he'd kept into town lots; and he'd got it all plotted out so well, and had so many practical ideas about it, that the fellow was astonished. He went right in with him, as far as Dryfoos would let him, and glad of the chance; and they were working the thing for all it was worth when I struck Moffitt. Old Dryfoos wanted me to go out and see the Dryfoos & Hendry Addition—guess he thought maybe I'd write it up; and he drove me out there himself. Well, it was funny to see a town made; streets driven through; two rows of shade trees, hard and soft, planted; cellars dug and houses put up—regular Queen Anne style too, with stained glass—all at once. Dryfoos apologized for the streets because they were hand-made; said they expected their street-making machine Tuesday, and then they intended to *push* things.

MARCH, *ironically*: He ought to have been ashamed to let it go so late.

FULKERSON: That's what I told him, when we got intimate, after the first minute or two. He was mighty intelligent, and he questioned me up about my business as sharp as *I* ever was questioned; seemed to kind of strike his fancy; I guess he wanted to find out if there was any money in it. He was making money, hand over hand, then; and he never stopped speculating and improving 'till he'd scraped together three or four hundred thousand dollars: they said a million, but they like round numbers at Moffitt, and I guess half a million would lay over it comfortably and leave a few thousand to spare, probably. Then he came on to New York.

Fulkerson strikes a match against the ribbed side of the porcelain cup that holds the matches in the centre of the table, and lights a cigarette, which he begins to smoke, throwing his head back with a leisurely effect, as if he has got to the end of at least as much of his story as he means to tell without prompting.

MARCH: What in the world for?

FULKERSON, *taking out his cigarette and smiling*: To spend his money, and get his daughters into the old Knickerbocker society. Maybe he thought they were all the same kind of Dutch.

MARCH: And has he succeeded?

FULKERSON: Well, they're not social leaders yet. But it's only a question of time—generation or two—especially if time's money, and if *Every Other Week* is the success it's bound to be.

MARCH, *with a half-doubting, half-daunted laugh*: You don't mean to say, Fulkerson, that *he's* your Angel?

FULKERSON: That's what I mean to say. I ran onto him in Broadway one day last summer. If you ever saw anybody in your life, you're sure to meet him in Broadway again, sooner or later. That's the philosophy of the bunco business; country people from the same neighborhood are sure to run up against each other the first time they come to New York. I put out my hand, and I said, "Isn't this Mr. Dryfoos from Moffitt?" He didn't seem to have any use for my hand; he let me keep it; and he squared those old lips of his till his imperial stuck straight out. Ever see Bernhardt in *L'Étrangère?* Well, the American husband is old Dryfoos all over; no mustache, and hay-colored chin-whiskers cut slanting from the corners of his mouth. He cocked his little gray eyes at me, and says he: "Yes, young man. My name *is* Dryfoos, and I'm from Moffitt. But I don't want no present of Longfellow's works, illustrated; and I don't want to taste no fine teas; but I know a policeman that does; and if you're the son of my old friend Squire Strohfeldt, you'd better get out." "Well, then," said I, "how would you like to go into the newspaper syndicate business?" He gave another look at me, and then he burst out laughing, and he grabbed my hand, and he just froze to it. I never saw anybody so glad.

Well, the long and the short of it was that I asked him round here to Maroni's to dinner; and before we broke up for the night we had settled the financial side of the plan that's brought you to New York. I can see that you don't more than half like the idea of Dryfoos. It ought to give you more confidence in the thing than you ever had. Of course, if I hadn't had you in mind, and if I hadn't hoped to get you on here from Boston to edit the thing, I should never have thought of starting the magazine at all. But when I did think of it, I knew we [had to have someone] to furnish the capital. And here at Maroni's that day I just happened to tell Dryfoos what I wanted to go into when I could see my way to it, and he caught on of his own accord. The fact is I guess I'd better make a clean breast of it, now I'm at it. Dryfoos wanted to get something for that boy of his to do. He's in railroads himself, and he's in mines and other things, and he keeps busy, and he can't bear to have his boy hanging round the house doing nothing, like as if he was a girl. I told him that the great object of a rich man was

to get his son into just that fix; but he couldn't seem to see it, and the boy hated it himself. He's got a good head, and he wanted to study for the ministry when they were all living together out on the farm; but his father had the old-fashioned ideas about that. You know they used to think that any sort of stuff was good enough to make a preacher out of, but they wanted the good timber for business; and so the old man wouldn't let him. You'll see the fellow; you'll like him; he's no fool, I can tell you; and he's going to be our publisher, nominally at first, and actually when I've taught him the ropes a little.

MARCH: It's all right, my dear Fulkerson—

FULKERSON: It will be, after you've seen our Angel—I can't do him justice. You'll like the old fellow; I'm *sure* you'll like the young one. (*He pulls out his watch and glances at it.*) See here, how would you like to go up to Forty-sixth Street with me, and drop in on Dryfoos? Now's your chance. They'll all be glad to see you, and you'll understand things better when you've seen him and his family. I can't explain.

MARCH: Perhaps we'd better wait till Mrs. March comes on from Boston and let things take the usual course. The Dryfoos ladies will want to call on her as the last-comer, and if I treated myself *en garçon* now, and paid the first visit, it might complicate matters.

FULKERSON: Oh, no, it won't with the Dryfooses. They won't know any better. Come! I want you to see the Dryfoos ladies—Ma Dryfoos, and Christine, and Mely. I want you to see Mrs. Mandel.

MARCH: Who's Mrs. Mandel?

FULKERSON: She's an invention of mine—at least in her present capacity. She sent me a story for the syndicate, back in July some time, along about the time I first met old Dryfoos here. It was a little too long for my purpose, and I thought I could explain better how I wanted it cut in a call than I could in a letter. She gave a Brooklyn address, and I went to see her. I found her a perfect lady. She was living with her aunt over there; and she had seen better days, when she was a girl, and worse ones afterward. Well, she didn't strike me like a person that could make much headway in literature. Her story was well enough, but it hadn't much sand in it; kind of—well, academic, you know. I told her so, and she understood, and cried a little; but she did the best she could with the thing, and I took it and syndicated it. She kind of stuck in my mind, and the first time I went to see the Dryfooses—they were stopping at a sort of family hotel then till they could find a house—March, I just wish you could have known the Dryfooses last summer when I first saw them. My! Oh my! There was the native earth for you. Mely is a pretty wild colt now, but you ought to have seen her before she was broken to harness. And Christine? Ever see that black leopard they got up there in the Central Park? That was Christine. Well, I saw what they wanted. They all saw it—nobody is a fool in all directions, and the Dryfooses are in their right senses a good deal of the time. Well, to cut a long story short, I got Mrs. Mandel to take 'em in hand—the old lady as well as the girls. She was a born lady, and always lived like one till she saw Mandel; and that something academic that killed her for a writer was just the very thing for them. She knows the world well enough to know just how much polish they can take on, and she don't try to put on a bit more. See?

MARCH: Yes, I think I see.

FULKERSON: Well, she took hold at once, as ready as a hospital-trained nurse; and there ain't anything readier on *this* planet. She runs the whole concern, socially and economically, takes all the care of house-keeping off the old lady's hands, and goes round with the girls. Well, now, we'll go around and get Beaton to go up there with us. I promised to take him to call, too. By the way, how did Beaton strike you as an art editor, anyway?

MARCH: Is he going to be our art editor? I couldn't tell when we parted whether he had discharged me from the literary department, or I merely wanted to kick him.

FULKERSON: That didn't mean anything. Everybody wants to kick Beaton. It's his nature. But he'll make a rattling good art editor. Beaton has his times of being the greatest ass in the solar system, but he usually takes it out in personal conduct. When it comes to work, he's a regular horse.

MARCH: He appears to have compromised for the present by being a perfect mule.

FULKERSON: Well, he's in a transition state. He's the man for us. He really understands what we want. You'll see; he'll catch on. That lurid glare of his will wear off in the course of time. He's really a good fellow when you take him off his guard; and he's full of ideas. He's spread out over a good deal of ground at present, and so he's pretty thin; but come to gather him up into a lump, there's a good deal of substance to him.

Yes, there is. He's a first-rate critic, and he's a nice fellow with other artists. They laugh at his universality, but they all like him. He's the best kind of a teacher when he condescends to it; and he's just the man to deal with our work. Yes, sir, he's a prize. Well, we must go now.

He helps March on with his light overcoat, and the little stir they make for their departure catches the notice of the old German; he looks up from his beer at them. March is more than ever impressed with something familiar in his face. In compensation for his prudence in regard to the Dryfooses he now indulges an impulse. He steps across the room to where the old man sits, with his bald head shining like ivory under the gas jet, and his fine patriarchal length of bearded mask taking picturesque lights and shadows, and puts out his hand to him.

MARCH: Lindau! Isn't this Mr. Lindau?

The old man lifts himself slowly to his feet with mechanical politeness, and cautiously takes March's hand.

LINDAU, *slowly, while he scans March's face*: Yes, my name is Lindau. (*Then he breaks into a long cry.*) Ah-h-h-h-h, my dear poy! My yong friendt! My—my— Idt is Passil Marge—not zo? Ah, ha, ha, ha! How gladt I am to zee you! Why, I am gladt! And you rememberdt me? You remember Schiller, and Goethe, and Uhland? And Indianapolis? You still life in Indianapolis? It sheers my hardt to zee you. But you are lidtle oldt, too? Twenty-five years makes a difference. Ah, I am gladt! Dell me, idt is Passil Marge—no zo?

He looks anxiously into March's face, with a gentle smile of mixed hope and doubt.

MARCH: As sure as it's Berthold Lindau, and I guess it's you. And you remember the old times? You were as much of a boy as I was, Lindau. Are you living in New York? Do you recollect how you tried to teach me to fence? I don't know how to this day, Lindau. How good you were, and how patient! Do you remember how we used to sit up in the little parlor back of your printing-office, and read *Die Räuber*, and *Die Theilung der Erde*, and *Die Glocke*? And Mrs. Lindau? Is she with—

LINDAU: Deadt—deadt long ago. Right after I got home from the war—twenty years ago. But tell me, you are married? Children? Yes! Goodt! And how oldt are you now?

MARCH: It makes me seventeen to see you, Lindau, but I've got a son nearly as old.

LINDAU: Ah, ha, ha! Goodt! And where do you leefe?

MARCH: Well, I'm just coming to live in New York. (*March looks over at Fulkerson, who has been watching his interview with the perfunctory smile of sympathy that people put on at the meeting of old friends.*) I want to introduce you to my friend, Mr. Fulkerson. He and I are going into a literary enterprise here.

LINDAU, *with polite interest*: Ah! Zo?

He takes Fulkerson's proffered hand.

FULKERSON, *with another look at his watch*: Well, March, we're keeping Mr. Lindau from his dinner.

LINDAU: Dinner! Idt's better than breadt and meadt to see Mr. Marge!

MARCH: I must be going, anyway. But I must see you again soon, Lindau. Where do you live? I want a long talk.

LINDAU: And I. You will find me here at dinner time. It is the best place.

March fancies him reluctant to give another address.

MARCH, *to cover his consciousness, answers gayly*: Then, it's *auf Wiedersehen* with us. Well!

LINDAU: Also! (*The old man takes his hand, and makes a mechanical movement with his mutilated arm, as if he would have taken it in a double clasp. He laughs at himself.*) I wanted to gife you the other handt, too, but I gafe it to your gountry a goodt while ago.

MARCH, *with a sense of pain, and yet lightly, as if it were a joke of the old man's*: To *my* country? Your country too, Lindau!

LINDAU, *very grave, and, almost coldly*: What gountry hass a poor man got, Mr. Marge?

MARCH, *still humoring the joke*: Well, *you* ought to have a share in the one you helped to save for us rich men, Lindau.

LINDAU, *smiling sadly, but saying as he sits down again*: Auf Wiedersehen.

MARCH: *Auf Wiedersehen*, old friend!

FULKERSON: Well, sir, good night!

LINDAU: Goodt nighdt, sir.

He rises and bows as March and Fulkerson go out.

SCENE II: *The street outside. (This scene to be set for a few minutes; March and Fulkerson talk as they walk slowly across the stage before it.)*

FULKERSON: Seems to be a little soured. (*He is one of those Americans whose habitual conception of life is unalloyed prosperity. When any experience or observation of his goes counter to it, he suffers something like physical pain. He eagerly shrugs away the impression left upon his buoyancy by Lindau, and adds to March's continued silence.*) What did I tell you about meeting every man in New York that you ever knew before?

MARCH, *more to himself than to Fulkerson*: I never expected to meet Lindau in the world again. I had an impression that he had been killed in the war. I almost wish he had been.

FULKERSON: Oh, hello now!

MARCH, *laughs, but goes on soberly*: He was a man predestined to adversity, though. When I first knew him out in Indianapolis, he was starving along with a sick wife and a sick newspaper. It was before the Germans had come over to the Republicans generally, but Lindau was fighting the antislavery battle just as naturally at Indianapolis in 1858 as he had fought behind the barricades at Berlin in 1848. And yet he was always such a gentle soul! And so generous! He taught me German for the love of it; he wouldn't spoil his pleasure by taking a cent from me; he seemed to get enough out of my being young and enthusiastic, and out of prophesying great things for me. I wonder what the poor old fellow is doing here, with that one hand of his?

FULKERSON, *getting back some of his lightness*: Not amassing a very handsome pittance, I should say. There are lots of two-handed fellows in New York that are not doing much better, I guess. Maybe he gets some writing on the German papers.

MARCH: I hope so. He's one of the most accomplished men! He used to be a splendid musician—pianist—and knows eight or ten languages.

FULKERSON: Well, it's astonishing how much lumber those Germans can carry around in their heads all their lives, and never work it up into anything. It's a pity they couldn't do the acquiring, and let out the use of their learning to a few bright Americans. We could make things hum, if we could arrange 'em that way.

MARCH, *musingly*: Was this all that sweet, unselfish nature could come to? What a homeless old age at that meagre Italian *table d'hôte*, with that tall glass of beer for a half-hour's oblivion! That shabby dress, that pathetic mutilation! He must have a pension, twelve dollars a month, or eighteen, from a grateful country. But what else does he eke out with?

FULKERSON, *stopping short*: Why, look here,

March! Didn't you tell me Lindau knew forty or fifty different languages?

MARCH: Four or five, yes.

FULKERSON: Well, we won't quarrel about the number. The question is, why not work *him* in the field of foreign literature? If you carry out that notion of yours, of having a nice little translation in every number of the magazine, you'll want help looking up the [illegible word]. *You* can't go over all their reviews and magazines, and he could do the smelling for you, if you could trust his nose. Would he know a good thing?

MARCH, *on whom the scope of Fulkerson's suggestion gradually opens*: I think he would. He used to have good taste, and he must know the ground. Why, it's a capital idea, Fulkerson! Lindau wrote very fair English; and he could translate, with a little revision.

FULKERSON: And he would probably work cheap. Well, hadn't you better see him about it? I guess it'll be quite a windfall for him.

MARCH: Yes, it will. I'll look him up when we get started. Thank you for the suggestion, Fulkerson.

FULKERSON: Oh, don't mention it! *I* don't mind doing *Every Other Week* a good turn now and then when it comes in my way.

MARCH, *seizing his hand*: Fulkerson, you're the best father in the world! And you're modest, too. What a pity you're such a shameless charlatan!

FULKERSON: Look here! Which way are you rubbing me?

MARCH: And what are you going to do about Lindau's socialism?

FULKERSON: Well, it seems that I don't know what socialism is when I see it. Perhaps I'll like it as much in Lindau as I did in Moffitt.

He links his arm in March's, and they go out laughing.

SCENE III: *The house of the Dryfooses. The drawing-room is delicately decorated in white and gold, and furnished with a sort of extravagant good taste; there is nothing to object to [in] the satin furniture, the pale, soft, rich carpet, the pictures, and the bronze and china bric-a-brac, except that their costliness is too evident; everything in the room means money too plainly, and too much of it. Miss Christine and Miss Mela Dryfoos are discovered sitting before the fire with Mrs. Mandel. Miss Christine has a large black fan in her hand, which she waves, in talking, with a slow, watchful nervousness.*

MELA: Well, I declare! I never saw such an unsociable place as New York. We've been in this house three months, and I don't believe that if we stayed three years any of the neighbors would call. I think it was twice as much fun in Moffitt. I wish I was there now.

CHRISTINE: I reckon they'll call fast enough when it gets round how much father is worth.

MELA: Well, I wish it would hurry and do it, then. Here we dress up every night, and set and set, and not a soul ever comes near the house. Say, Christine—

MRS. MANDEL: My *dear* Miss Mela!

MELA: Well, how *shall* I call her, then?

CHRISTINE: Don't call me at all. I ain't across a ten acre lot. What do you want?

MELA: What do you spose that painter'll be like, when Mr. Fulkerson *does* bring him? If he *ever* does.

CHRISTINE: I don't know, and I don't care. He'll be a man, anyway.

MRS. MANDEL: Miss Dryfoos, really, I don't think you ought to allow yourself to say such things.

CHRISTINE: Why not? It's what every girl thinks. Do you suppose I'll let *him* know I think it?

MELA: Ah, I do hope he'll be young and handsome! But I don't believe Mr. Fulkerson'll *ever* bring him! I'm about sick waitin' for him. I wonder what he'll think of us? I hope Coonrod'll be here when he comes. Oh, here comes mother.

Her mother comes in with a slow step; her head shakes slightly as she looks about the room, perhaps from nervousness, perhaps from a touch of palsy. She looks about, and then goes to the open door, and calls through it.

MRS. DRYFOOS: Coonrod! Coonrod! You bring my shawl down with you.

MELA: Now, mother, Christine'll give it to you for not sending Mike.

MRS. DRYFOOS: Well, I don't know where he is, Mely, child. He ain't never around when he's wanted; and when he ain't wanted, it seems like a body couldn't git shet of him, nohow.

MELA, *enjoying the joke*: Well, you ought to ring for him.

MRS. MANDEL, *arranging an easy chair for her by the fire*: I hope you are feeling better, tonight, Mrs. Dryfoos. I'm so glad you could join us.

MRS. DRYFOOS: I'm just middlin'. I ain't never so well, nowadays. I tell fawther I don't believe it agrees with me very well here; but he says I'll git used to it.

She wavers on foot a moment before she sinks into the chair. She is a tall woman, who has been a beautiful girl, and her gray hair has a memory of blondness in it. She wears a simple silk gown, of Quakerly gray, and she holds a handkerchief folded square, as it had come back from the laundress.

MELA: Laws, mother! What you got that old thing on for? If I'd 'a known you'd 'a come down in *that!*

MRS. DRYFOOS: Coonrod said it was all right, Mely.

MELA, *laughing*: Mother was raised among the Dunkards, and she thinks it's wicked to wear anything but a gray silk even for dress up.

MRS. DRYFOOS: You ain't never heared o' the Dunkards, I reckon. Some folks calls 'em the Beardy Men, because they don't never shave; and they wash feet like they do in the Testament. My uncle was one. He raised me.

MRS. MANDEL: Isn't it a Pennsylvania German sect, something like the Quakers?

MRS. DRYFOOS: I dunno! But they're good people and the world'd be a heap better off if there was more like 'em. (*A ring at the door is heard.*) Good gracious, what's that?

MELA, *clapping her hands*: Callers!

MRS. DRYFOOS: Well, Mely, if it's company, I reckon I better go upstairs agin.

MELA: Laws! It cain't be anybody but Mr. Fulkerson, and you needn't be afraid of him. We don't know another soul in town.

FULKERSON, *without*: Ah, how d'ye do, Conrad? Brought our friend with me. (*A sound of putting off overcoats; Fulkerson appears in the doorway, with his feet set square and his arms akimbo.*) Ah! hello! hello! Regular gathering of the clans. How are you, Mrs. Dryfoos? How do you do, Mrs. Mandel, Miss Christine, Mela, Aunt Hitty, and all the folks? How you wuz?

He shakes hands gayly all round, and takes a chair next the old lady, whose hand he keeps in his own, and leaves Conrad to introduce Beaton and March.

CONRAD: This is my mother, Mr. March; and Mrs. Mandel. My sisters, Mr. March—and, (*presenting Beaton to all the ladies*) Mr. Beaton.

FULKERSON: Yes, here we are in full force—the whole staff of *Every Other Week*: literary editor brought in from Boston regardless of expense; art editor secured in New York after a sharp competition with the Ivory Soap men, and Pyles' pear line; affable manager in the person of Conrad; and

inspired advertising genius in the great and only Fulkerson. Where's the gentlemanly proprietor, the moneyed force, the financial angel?

MELA: Oh, how you do carry on, Mr. Fulkerson. If I was these gentlemen, I wouldn't let you.

FULKERSON: They like it. They know it's my way. But ain't we going to see your father?

MRS. DRYFOOS: I reckon fawther'll be down pretty soon. He always takes a nap after supper.

MELA: Well, mother, when you ever goin' to learn to say dinner? I do believe mother'll go on callin' lunch dinner, as long as she lives.

FULKERSON: Well, right. It's the good old way. I've brought Mr. Beaton along to-night, and I want you to make him feel at home, like you do me, Mrs. Dryfoos. He hasn't got any rheumatism to speak of; but his parents live in Syracuse, and he's a kind of an orphan, and we've just adopted him down at the office. When you going to bring the young ladies down there, Mrs. Mandel, for a champagne lunch? I will have some hydro-Mela and Christine it, heigh? How's that for a little starter? March was feeling a little kind of lost with his family still up in the wilds of Boston, and I let him come, too. Well, well, what a world it is! Miss Christine, won't you show Mr. Beaton that seal ring of yours? He knows about such things, and I brought him here to see it as much as anything. (*Explaining to March.*) It's an intaglio I brought from the other side, and I guess you'll like to look at it. Tried to *give* it to the Dryfoos family, and when I couldn't I sold it to 'em. Bound to see it on Miss Christine's hand somehow! Hold on! Let him see it where it belongs, first! (*Beaton and Christine remain talking in dumb show apart from the rest. Fulkerson goes on with an open travesty of the mother's habitual address.*) Well, Mely, child, and how are *you* getting along? Mrs. Mandel hold you up to the proprieties pretty strictly? Well, that's right. You know you'd be roaming all over the pasture if she didn't. Been to any of the theatres, or churches, or other places of entertainment, lately?

MELA: Oh, pshaw, now. You stop, Mr. Fulkerson! Well, we went to the opera the other night. Father took a box at the Metropolitan.

MARCH: Then you got a good dose of Wagner, I suppose?

MELA: What?

MRS. MANDEL: I don't think Miss Mela is very fond of Wagner's music. I believe you are all great Wagnerites in Boston?

MARCH: I'm a very bad Bostonian, Mrs. Mandel. I suspect myself of preferring Verdi.

MELA: That night we were there they had to turn the gas down all through one part of it, and the papers said the ladies were awful mad because they couldn't show their diamonds. I don't wonder, if they all had to pay as much for their boxes as we did. We had to pay sixty dollars.

MARCH: Well, I think I shall take my box by the month, then. It must come cheaper, wholesale.

MELA: Oh no, it don't. The people that own their boxes, and that had to give fifteen or twenty thousand dollars *apiece* for them, have to pay sixty dollars a night whenever there's a performance, whether they go or not.

MARCH: Then I should go every night.

MELA: Most of the ladies were low neck—

MARCH: Well, I shouldn't go low *neck*.

MELA, *breaking into a fondly approving laugh at his drolling*: Oh, I guess you love to train! Us girls wanted to go low neck, too; but father said we shouldn't, and mother said if we did she wouldn't come to the front of the box once. Well, she didn't, anyway. We might just as well 'a gone low neck. She stayed back the whole time, and when they had that dance—the ballet, you know—she just shut her eyes. Well, Conrad didn't like that part much either; but us girls and Mrs. Mandel, we brazoned it out right in the front of the box. We were about the only ones there that went high neck. Conrad had to wear a swallow-tail; but father hadn't any, and he had to patch out with a white cravat. You couldn't see what he had on in the back o' the box, anyway.

MRS. DRYFOOS: I say they ought to be all tarred and feathered and rode on a rail. They'd be drummed out of town in Moffitt.

MELA, *with a crowing laugh*: I should think they would! And they wouldn't anybody go low neck to the opera-house there, either—not low neck the way they do here, anyway.

MRS. DRYFOOS: And that pack of worthless hussies that come out on the stage and begun to kick—

MELA: Laws mother! I thought you said you had your eyes shut!

MRS. DRYFOOS: Well, I did, Mely, as soon as I could *believe* my eyes. I don't know what they're doin' in all their churches to let such things go on. It's a sin and a shame, *I* think. Don't you, Coonrod?

MRS. MANDEL, *attempting a diversion*: Have you heard any of our great New York preachers yet, Mr. March?

MARCH: No, I haven't.

CONRAD: There are a great many things here to take your thoughts off the preaching that you hear in most of the churches. I think the city itself is preaching the best sermon all the time.

MARCH: I don't know that I understand you.

MELA, *answering for him*: Oh, Conrad has got a lot of notions that nobody can understand. You ought to see the church he goes to when he does go. I'd about as lief go to a Catholic church myself; I don't see a bit o' difference. He's the greatest crony with one of their preachers; he dresses just like a priest, and he says he *is* a priest.

She laughs for enjoyment of the fact, and her brother casts down his eyes.

MARCH: Have you been to the fall exhibition?

MELA: The exhibition?

She looks at Mrs. Mandel.

MRS. MANDEL: The pictures of the Academy, you know. Where I wanted you to go the day you had your dress tried on.

MELA, *turning to March again*: No; we haven't been yet. Is it good?

MARCH: I believe the fall exhibitions are never so good as the spring ones. But there are some good pictures.

MELA: I don't believe I care much about pictures. I don't understand them.

MARCH: Ah, *that's* no excuse for not caring about them. The painters themselves don't, half the time.

MRS. DRYFOOS: I think it's a shame, some of the pictur's a body sees in the winders. They say there's a law ag'inst them things; and if there is, I don't understand why the police don't take up them that paints 'em. I hear tell, since I been here, that there's women that goes to have pictur's took from them that way by men painters.

FULKERSON: Oh, hello, hello, hello! Beaton, step up here, and defend yourself. Beaton, you're wanted here.

MELA, *looking around at Christine and Beaton with a laugh*: He seems to think he's wanted somewheres else, too!

BEATON, *coming forward*: What is it?

FULKERSON: Mrs. Dryfoos has got a crow to pick with the fine arts. But I guess we can let that go to another time. What do you think of Miss Christine's intaglio?

BEATON: It's an antique.

FULKERSON: Well, I'm glad to hear you say so. I didn't know but I'd got the better of the Dryfoos family on that trade.

CHRISTINE: I recken you *will* know it when you get the better of my father on a trade, Mr. Fulkerson.

MELA: Well, I just *bet* you will.

FULKERSON: Father's girls, every time! When I see you with that particular look on, Miss Christine, I feel like introducing you for the old gentleman! I never saw a girl take after her father more!

MELA: That's so; I tell her she's just the picture of father, Mr. Beaton.

BEATON, *to Christine*: If the portrait isn't flattered, your father must be.

MELA: Well, you can judge for yourself now! I hear him commin' downstairs.

FULKERSON: Well, then, just take Miss Christine to one side so March can know which is which when I introduce him to your father. (*Dryfoos enters shufflingly in his slippers, and glancing frowningly around in the stronger light at the different people present.*) Ah, here comes the head of the procession. (*He seizes Dryfoos's hand.*) March, I want to introduce you to our financial chief. Mr. Dryfoos, this is our literary chief, and here's Mr. Beaton, the head and front of our offending in the art-line. (*As Dryfoos shakes hands with the others, Fulkerson rattles on.*) I told you, fellows, you don't understand yet, what a big thing we've got in Mr. Dryfoos. (*To Dryfoos.*) Yes, sir, I'm going to strike everything that is imaginative and romantic in the newspaper soul with you and your history and your fancy for going in for this thing. I can start you in a paragraph that will travel through all the newspapers, from Maine to Texas and from Alaska to Florida. We have had all sorts of rich men backing up literary enterprises, but the natural gas man in literature is a new thing, and the combination of your picturesque past and your aesthetic present is something that will knock out the sympathies of the American public the first round. I feel, that *Every Other Week* is at a disadvantage before the public as long as it's supposed to be *my* enterprise, *my* idea. As far as I'm known at all, I'm known simply as a syndicate man, and nobody in the press believes that I've got the money to run the thing on a grand scale; a suspicion of insolvency must attach to it sooner or later, and the fellows on the press will work up that impression, sooner or later, if we don't give them something else to work up. Now, as soon as I begin to give it away to the correspondents that *you're* in it, with your untold millions—that, in fact, it was your idea from the start, that you originated it to give full play to the humanitarian tendencies of Conrad here, who's always had these theories of co-operation, and longed to realize them for the benefit of our struggling young writers and artists—

DRYFOOS: I suppose you understand this man's style, Mr. March. He's like what they used to call a blower, if they got a gas well in the old times when they were boring for salt.

He takes no further notice of Beaton, who turns away and begins talking to Christine in dumb show.

FULKERSON: Well, sir, the advertising department is the heart and soul of every business, and I like to keep my hand in with a little practice on the trumpet in private for the magazine's sake.

DRYFOOS: How much do you expect to get out of it the first year, if it keeps the start it's got?

FULKERSON, *to March with a delighted glance*: Comes right down to business, every time! (*To Dryfoos.*) Well, sir, if everything works right, and we get rain enough to fill up the springs, and it isn't a grasshopper year, I expect to clear above all expenses something in the neighborhood of twenty-five thousand dollars.

DRYFOOS: Humph! And you are all going to work a year—editor, manager, publisher, artists, writers, printers, and the rest of 'em—to clear twenty-five thousand dollars? I made that much in half a day in Moffitt once. I see it made in half a minute in Wall Street, sometimes.

The old man presents this aspect of the case with a good natured contempt, which includes Fulkerson and his enthusiasm in an obvious liking.

CONRAD: But when we make that money here, no one loses it.

DRYFOOS, *turning sharply upon him*: Can you prove that? Whatever is won is lost. It's all a game; it don't make any difference what you bet on. Business is business, and a businessman takes his risks with his eyes open.

FULKERSON, *insinuating with impudent persiflage*: Ah, but the glory! I hadn't got to the glory yet, because it's hard to estimate it; but put the glory at the lowest figure, Mr. Dryfoos, and add it to the twenty-five thousand, and you've got an annual income from *Every Other Week* of dollars enough to construct a silver railroad, double track, from this office to the moon. I don't mention any of the sister planets because I like to keep within bounds.

DRYFOOS, *showing his lower teeth for pleasure in Fulkerson's fooling*: That's what I like about you, Mr. Fulkerson; you always keep within bounds.

FULKERSON: Well, I *ain't* a shrinking Boston violet, like March here. More sunflower in my style of diffidence; but I am modest, I don't deny it. And I do hate to have a thing overstated.

DRYFOOS: And the glory—you do really think there's something in the glory that pays?

FULKERSON, *with a burlesque of generous disdain*: Not a doubt of it! I shouldn't care for the paltry return in money if it wasn't for the glory along with it.

DRYFOOS: And how should you feel about the glory, if there was no money along with it?

FULKERSON: Well, sir, I'm happy to say we haven't come to that, yet.

DRYFOOS, *with a sort of pathetic rancor*: Now, Conrad, here, would rather have the glory alone. I believe he don't even care much for your kind of glory either, Mr. Fulkerson.

FULKERSON: Oh, well, we know how Conrad feels about the things of this world, anyway. I should like to take 'em on the plane of another sphere, too, sometimes; but I noticed a good while ago that this was the world I was born into, and so I made up my mind that I would do pretty much what I saw the rest of the folks doing here below. And I can't see but what Conrad runs the thing on business principles in his department, and I guess you'll find it so, if you'll look into it. I consider that we're a whole team and big dog under the wagon with you to draw on for supplies, and March, here, at the head of the literary business, and Conrad in the counting-room, and me to do the heavy lying in the advertising part. Oh, and Beaton, of course, in the art. I 'most forgot Beaton—*Hamlet* with Hamlet left out.

DRYFOOS, *glancing off at Beaton in talk with Christine, and then turning to March and pointing at Conrad*: I want to make a regular New York businessman out of that fellow. You s'pose I'm ever going to do it?

MARCH, *trying to fall in with the joke*: Well, I don't know. Do you mean nothing but a businessman?

DRYFOOS, *laughing at whatever latent meaning he fancies in this*: You think he would be a little

too much for me there? Well, I've seen enough of 'em to know it don't always take a large pattern of a man to do a large business. But I want him to get the business training, and then if he wants to go into something else, he knows what the world is, anyway. Heigh?

MARCH, *with some compassion for the young man reddening patiently under his father's comment*: Oh, yes!

DRYFOOS, *going on as if his son were not in hearing*: Now that boy wanted to be a preacher. What does a preacher know about the world he preaches against, when he's been brought up a preacher? He don't know so much as a bad little boy in his Sunday-school; he knows about as much as a girl. I always told him: you be a man first, and then you be a preacher, if you want to. Heigh?

MARCH, *beginning to feel some compassion for himself in being witness of the young fellow's discomfort under his father's homily*: Precisely!

DRYFOOS: When we first come to New York, I told him: now here's your chance to see the world on a big scale. You know already what work and saving and steady habits and sense will bring a man to; you don't want to go round among the rich; you want to go among the poor, and see what laziness, and drink, and dishonesty, and foolishness will bring men to. And I guess he knows, about as well as anybody; and if he ever goes to preaching he'll know what he's preaching about.

FULKERSON, *talking and approaching*: I want these fellows to see that picture of yours, *Christ Breaking Bread*.[1] Copy of Titian—just the thing for a dining-room. Won't you show it to us, Mr. Dryfoos?

DRYFOOS: Yes, come along.

He shuffles toward the door.

FULKERSON: You come, too, Beaton.

Beaton excuses himself to Christine, and goes out with the other men.

MRS. DRYFOOS: Well, now, Mely, I reckon I'll go to bed. It's past the time.

MELA: Mrs. Mandel'll help you up, mother. Or, there! I see you want me to go with you. I reckon we'll both go, Mrs. Mandel.

MRS. MANDEL: I'm sure your mother will prefer that, Miss Mela.

MRS. DRYFOOS: Why, Mely, child, I don't want to take you away from the company.

[1] Titian did not paint a picture called "Christ Breaking the Bread"; however, there are two paintings by Titian which show Christ at the Last Supper: "Christ at Emmaus," and "Last Supper."

MELA: Christine'll stay. Now don't say another word, for it won't be any use. Here, Mrs. Mandel, you take her shawl, and I'll get her up. (*She fusses affectionately over her mother, helping her out of the room. Christine watches them go; then she passionately kisses the ring on her finger, again and again. While she is still gloating on it, Mela comes running back.*) What all did he say, Christine?

CHRISTINE: Who?

MELA: Who? Why that old stuck-up Mr. Beaton of yours!

CHRISTINE: He is proud.

MELA: Well, I reckon his pride'll have a fall. He's perfectly gone on you, Christine; and it gets round about father's money, he'll feel pretty small.

CHRISTINE: Father's money? What of that?

MELA: Why, you don't suppose he's going to let the first fellow leave— Well, I believe in my heart the girl's struck up on the fellow, already! Don't eat *me* anyway, Christine! I ain't said he should marry you!

CHRISTINE: When I want to marry, I reckon I'll marry the one I want to.

MELA: Well, I s'pose father'll have something to say.

CHRISTINE: He'll have to say yes.

She goes dreamily out, looking down at the ring on her hand.

MELA, *staring after her:* We-e-e-ll!

CURTAIN

(*A good deal of talk and banter between the sisters about Beaton, in which it appears that he has already been making love to Christine.*)

ACT II

SCENE I: *Room in a tenement house. A bed where Lindau sits propped up, with a coat over his shoulders and skull-cap on his head, reading a book. His hairy old breast shows through the night-shirt, which gapes apart; the stump of his left arm lies upon the book to keep it open. The door of the room stands ajar. March appears in the open doorway, and after a moment knocks softly on the jamb. Lindau stares at him over his spectacles.*

LINDAU, *joyously:* Ah, my tear yo'ng friendt! Passil! Marge! Iss it you?

MARCH: Why, are you sick, Lindau?

March anxiously scans his face in taking his hand.

LINDAU, *laughing:* No, I'm all righdt. Only a lidtle lazy, and a lidtle eggonomigal. Idt's jeaper to stay in pedt sometimes as to geep a fire a-goin' all the time. Don't wandt to gome too hardt on the *brafer Mann*, you know:

"Braver Mann, er schafft mir zu essen!" [1]

You remember? Heine? You readt Heine still? Who is your favorite boet now, Passil? You write some boetry yourself yet? No? Well, I am gladt to zee you. Brush those baperss off that jair. Well, idt is goodt for zore eyess. How didt you findt where I leeve?

MARCH: They told me at Maroni's. (*He tries to keep his eyes on Lindau's face, and not see the discomfort of the room, but he is aware of the frowsy bedding, the odor of stale smoke, and the pipes and tobacco shreds mixed with the books and manuscripts strewn over the leaf of the writing-desk. He lays down on the mass the pile of foreign magazines he has brought under his arm.*) They gave me another address first.

LINDAU: Yes. I have chust gome here. Idt is not very cay, heigh?

MARCH, *with a smile:* It might be gayer. (*Soberly.*) Still a good many people seem to live in this part of the town. Apparently they die here too, Lindau. There is crepe on your outside door downstairs. I didn't know but it was for you.

LINDAU, *in the same humor:* Nodt this time. Berhaps some other time. We geep the ondertakers bretty pusy down here.

MARCH: Well, undertakers must live, even if the rest of us have to die to let them. (*Lindau laughs, and March goes on.*) But I'm glad it isn't your funeral, Lindau. And you say you're not sick, and so I don't see why we shouldn't come to business.

LINDAU, *lifting his eyebrows:* Pusiness? You gome on pusiness?

MARCH: And pleasure combined. You know when I saw you that night at Maroni's I told you I was going into a literary enterprise here. It's a magazine, and we're going to print translations of short stories and sketches from the European periodicals. It seemed to us that you might be willing to do some work of that kind.

LINDAU: It is for you, you say, Passil?

MARCH: It's for my magazine.

LINDAU: Den, of course, I do it. It is hawnest work for the hawnest man. It is all righdt.

MARCH: Well, everything is understood, then;

[1] This line of Heine is from one of the poems from *Die Heimkehr;* its first line reads: "Gaben mir Rat and gute lehren."

and I don't know that I need add that if you ever want any little advance on the work—

LINDAU, *quietly*: I will ask you, and I thank you for that. But I can wait; I ton't needt any money just at bresent. (*As if he sees some appeal for greater frankness in March's eye, he goes on.*) I tidn't gome here begause I was too boor to life anywhere else, and I ton't stay in pedt begause I couldn't hafe a fire to geep warm if I wanted it. I'm a lidtle loaxurious, that is all. If I stay in pedt, it's zo I can fling money away on something else. Heigh?

MARCH, *smiling at the irony lurking in Lindau's words*: But what *are* you living here for, Lindau?

LINDAU: Well, you zee, I foundt I was begoming a lidtle too moch of an aristograt. I hadt a room oap in Greenvidge Willage, among dose pig pugs over on the west side, and I foundt— (*Lindau's voice loses its jesting quality, and his face darkens.*) that I was beginning to forget the boor.

MARCH, *with impartial interest*: I should have thought that you might have seen poverty enough, now and then, in Greenwich Village to remind you of its existence.

LINDAU: Nodt like here. Andt you must zee it all the dtime—zee it, hear it, smell it, dtaste it— or you forget it. That is what I gome here for. I was begoming a ploated aristograt. I thought I was nodt like these beople down here, when I gome down once to look aroundt; I thought I must be somethings else, ans zo I zaid I better take myself in time, and I gome here among my brothers—the beccars and the thiefs! (*A noise makes itself heard in the next room, as if the door were furtively opened, and a faint sound of tiptoe-ing and of hands clawing on a table.*) Thiefs! (*Lindau repeats with a shout.*) Lidtle thiefs, that gapture your breakfast. Ah! ha! ha! (*A wild scurry-ing of feet, joyous cries and tittering, and a slam-ming door follow upon his explosion, and he re-sumes in the silence.*) Idt is the children cot pack from school. They gome and steal what I leaf there on my daple. Idt's one of our lidtle chokes; we onderstand each other; that's all righdt. Once the goppler in the other room there he use to chase 'em; he couldn't onderstand their lidtle tricks. Now dot goppler's teadt, and he ton't chase 'em any more. He was a Bohemian. Gindt of grazy, I cuess.

MARCH: Well, it's a sociable existence. But perhaps if you let them have things without steal-ing—

LINDAU: Oh, no, no! Most nodt mage them too gonceitedt. They mostn't go and feel themselfs petter than those boor millionaires that hadt to steal their money.

MARCH, *smiling indulgently at his old friend's violence*: Oh, there are fagots and fagots, you know, Lindau; perhaps not all the millionaires are so guilty.

LINDAU, *pushing his book aside, and thrusting his skull-cap back from his forehead*: How much money can a man honestly earn without wronging or oppressing some other man?

MARCH: Well, I should say about five thousand dollars a year. I name that figure because it's my experience that I could never earn more; but the experience of other men may be different, and if they tell me that they can earn ten, or twenty, or fifty thousand a year, I'm not prepared to say they can't do it.

LINDAU: Not the most gifted man that ever lived, in the practice of any art or science, and paid at the highest rate that exceptional genius could justly demand from those who have worked for their money, could ever earn a million dollars. It is the landlords and the merchant princes, the railroad kings and the coal barons—the oppressors whom you instinctively give the titles of tyrants— It is these that *make* the millions, but no man *earns* them. What artist, what physician, what scientist, what poet was ever a millionaire?

MARCH, *amused by Lindau's tirade*: I can only think of the poet Rogers. But he was as excep-tional as the other Rogers, the martyr, who died with warm feet.[1] But you must allow, Lindau, that some of those fellows don't do so badly with their guilty gains. Some of them give work to armies of poor people—

LINDAU, *furiously interrupting*: Yes, when they have gathered their millions together from the hunger and cold and nakedness and ruin and despair of hundreds of thousands of other men, they "give work" to the poor! They *give* work! They allow their helpless brothers to earn enough to keep life in them! They give *work!* Who is it gives *toil*, and where will your rich men be when once the poor shall refuse to give toil? Why, you have come to give *me* work!

MARCH, *laughing outright*: Well, I'm not a mil-

1 Samuel Rogers, 1763–1855, was a wealthy poet though he gained his money as a banker rather than as a poet. John Rogers, 1500?–1555, was a Catholic priest who, after meeting William Tindal, abandoned the Roman Church and eventually was burnt alive on Feb-ruary 4, 1555, at Smithfield.

lionaire, anyway, Lindau, and I hope you won't make an example of me by refusing to give toil. I dare say the millionaires deserve it, but I'd rather they wouldn't suffer in my person.

LINDAU, *mildly, relaxing the fierce glare he had bent upon March*: No! No man deserves to suffer at the hands of another. I lose myself when I think of the injustice in the world. But I must not forget that I am like the worst of them.

MARCH: You might go up Fifth Avenue and live among the rich awhile, when you're in danger of that. At any rate, I wish you'd come some day and lunch with their emissary. I've been telling Mrs. March about you, and I want her and the children to see you. Come over with these things and report.

He puts his hand on the magazines as he rises.

LINDAU, *gently*: I will come.

MARCH: Shall I give you your book?

LINDAU: No, I gidt oap bretty soon.

MARCH: And—and—can you dress yourself?

LINDAU, *gloomily*: I vhistle, and one of those lidtle fellowss comess. We haf to dake gare of one another in a blace like this. Idt iss nodt like the worldt.

MARCH, *trying to cheer him up*: Oh, it isn't such a bad world, Lindau! After all, the average of millionaires is small in it. And I don't believe there's an American living that could look at that arm of yours and not wish to lend you a hand for the one you gave us all.

LINDAU, *smiling grimly*: You think zo? I wouldn't moch like to drost 'em. I've driedt idt too often. Besides, they owe me nothing. Do you think I knowingly gave my hand to save this oligarchy of traders and tricksters, this aristocracy of railroad wreckers and stock gamblers and mine-slave drivers and mill-serf owners? No; I gave it to the slave; the slave—ha! ha! ha!—whom I helped to unshackle to the common liberty of hunger and cold. And you think I would be the beneficiary of such a state of things?

This scene to conclude with the appearance of Margaret Vance, who is visiting a poor family in the tenement and knocks at Lindau's door to make inquiry about him. She and Lindau meet as old friends; they talk of the death in the poor family. Conrad Dryfoos, on charity work, also comes in.

SCENE II: *Late afternoon. Dryfoos on a lounge in his library, asleep. A sound of gay talk and laughter comes through the draperied door leading to the drawing-room, with snatches of song and banjo music. His wife sits in a deep chair before the fire, with her eyes on his face, waiting for him to wake.*

DRYFOOS, *starting up*: Who is that, out there?

MRS. DRYFOOS: I reckon it's just some visitor of the girls. Sounds like Mr. Beaton.

DRYFOOS: Was I snoring?

MRS. DRYFOOS: Not a bit. You was sleeping as quiet! I did hate to have 'em wake you, and I was just goin' out to shoo them. They've been playin' something, and that made them laugh.

DRYFOOS: I didn't know but I had snored.

MRS. DRYFOOS: So you didn't. But I wouldn't 'a blamed you any if you had. I wisht you could give up goin' down to Wall Street, the way you do. You always come home so beat out. (*Dryfoos lies down again, and his wife adds after a moment.*) Jacob, I been thinkun' about the old place out home since you been layun' there. Did it look just like it used to the last time you was out?

DRYFOOS: Yes, mostly. They're sinking the wells down in the woods pasture.

MRS. DRYFOOS: And—the children's graves?

DRYFOOS: They haven't touched that part. But I reckon we got to have 'em moved to the cemetery. I bought a lot.

MRS. DRYFOOS, *beginning to weep softly*: It does seem too hard that they can't be let to rest in peace, pore little things. I wanted you and me to lay there, too, when our time come, Jacob. Just there, back 'o the beehives, and under them shoomakes—my, I can see the very place! And I don't believe I'll ever feel at home anywheres else. I woon't know where I am when the trumpet sounds. I have to think before I can tell where the east is in New York; and what if I should get faced the wrong way when I raise? Jacob, I wonder you could sell it!

Her hand shakes, and the fire-light shines on her tears as she searches the folds of her dress for her pocket. A peal of laughter comes from the drawing-room, and then the sound of chords struck on the piano.

DRYFOOS: Hush! Don't you cry, 'Liz'beth! Here, take my handkerchief. I've got a nice lot in the cemetery, and I'm goin' to have a monument, with two lambs on it—like the one you always liked so much. It ain't the fashion, any more, to have family buryin' grounds; they're collectin' 'em into the cemeteries, all round.

MRS. DRYFOOS, *muffling her face in his handker-*

chief: I reckon I got to bear it. And I suppose the Lord kin find me, wherever I am. But I always did want to lay just there. You mind how we used to go out and set there, after milkin', and watch the sun go down, and talk about where their angels was, and try to figger it out?

DRYFOOS: I remember, 'Liz'beth.

The man's voice in the drawing-room sings a snatch of French song, insolent, mocking, salient; and then Christine's attempts the same strain, and another cry of laughter from Mela follows.

MRS. DRYFOOS: Well, I always did expect to lay there. But I reckon it's all right. It woon't be a great while, now, anyway, Jacob. I don't believe I'm a-goin' to live very long. I know it don't agree with me, here.

DRYFOOS: Oh, I guess it does, 'Liz'beth. You're just a little pulled down with the weather. It's coming spring, and you feel it; but the doctor says you're all right. I stopped in, on the way up; and he says so.

MRS. DRYFOOS: I reckon he don't know everything. I've been runnin' down ever since we left Moffitt, and I didn't feel any too well there, even. It's a very strange thing, Jacob, that the richer you git, the less you ain't able to stay where you want to, dead or alive.

DRYFOOS: It's for the children we do it. We got to give them their chance in the world.

MRS. DRYFOOS: Oh, the world! They ought to bear the yoke in their youth, like we done. I know it's what Coonrod would like to do.

DRYFOOS, *getting upon his feet*: If Coonrod'll mind his own business, and do what I want him to, he'll have yoke enough to bear. (*He gets up and begins to walk back and forth.*) If he wants to bear this yoke, why ain't he here with his sisters? What does all that work of his on the East side amount to? It seems as if he done it to cross me, as much as anything. Here, I've gone into this newspaper business, or whatever it is, on his account, and he don't seem any more satisfied than ever. I can see he hain't got his heart in it.

MRS. DRYFOOS: The pore boy tries; I know he does, Jacob; and he wants to please you. But he gave up a good deal when he give up bein' a preacher; I s'pose we ought to remember that.

DRYFOOS, *sneering*: A preacher! I reckon bein' a preacher wouldn't satisfy him now. He had the impudence to tell me that he would like to be a *priest*: and he threw it up to me that he never

could be, because I'd kept him from studyin'.

MRS. DRYFOOS, *wistfully*: He don't mean a Catholic priest—not a Roman one, Jacob. He's told me all about it. They ain't the kind o' Catholics we been used to; some sort of 'Piscopalians; and they do a heap o' good amongst the poor folks over there. He says we ain't got any idea how folks lives in them tenement houses, hundreds of 'em in one house, and whole families in a room; and it burns in his heart to help 'em like them Fathers, as he calls 'em, that gives their lives to it. He can't be a Father, he says, because he can't git the eddication, now; but he can be a Brother; and I can't find a word to say ag'inst it, when he gits to talkin', Jacob.

DRYFOOS: I ain't saying anything against his priests, 'Liz'beth. They're all well enough in their way; they've given up their lives to it, and it's a matter of business with them, like any other. But what I'm talking about now is Coonrod. I don't object to his doin' all the charity he wants to, and the Lord knows I've never been stingy with him about it. He might have all the money he wants, to give round any way he pleases.

MRS. DRYFOOS: That's what I told him once, but he says money ain't the thing—or not the only thing you got to give to them poor folks. You got to give your time, and your knowledge, and your love—I don't know what all—you got to give *yourself*, if you expect to help 'em. That's what Coonrod says.

DRYFOOS: Well, I can tell him that charity begins at home. And he'd better give himself to *us* a little—to his old father and mother. And his sisters. What's he doin' goin' off there, to his meetings, and I don't know what all, an' leavin' them here alone?

MRS. DRYFOOS: Why, ain't Mr. Beaton with 'em? I thought I heared his voice.

DRYFOOS: Mr. Beaton! Of course, he is! And who's Mr. Beaton, anyway?

MRS. DRYFOOS: Why, ain't he one of the men in Coonrod's office? I thought I heard—

DRYFOOS: Yes, he is! But *who* is he? What's he doing round here? Is he makin' up to Christine?

MRS. DRYFOOS: I reckon he is. From Mely's talk, she's about crazy over the fellow. Don't you like him, Jacob?

DRYFOOS: I don't know him, or what he is. Who brought him here? How'd he come to come, in the first place?

MRS. DRYFOOS: Mr. Fulkerson brung him the other night. Don't you remember?

DRYFOOS: Fulkerson! *(He snorts.)* Where's Mrs. Mandel. I should like to know? He brought *her*, too. Does she go traipsin' off this way, every afternoon?

MRS. DRYFOOS: No, she seems to be here pretty regular most o' the time. I don't know how we could ever git along without her, Jacob; she seems to know just what to do, and the girls would be ten times as outbreakin' without her. I hope you ain't thinkin' o' turnin' her off, Jacob?

DRYFOOS: It's all Fulkerson, Fulkerson, Fulkerson. It seems to me that Fulkerson about runs this family. He brought Mrs. Mandel, and he brought that Beaton, and he brought that Boston fellow! I'll learn Fulkerson that he can't have everything his own way. I don't want anybody to help me spend my money. I made it, and I can manage it. I guess Mr. Fulkerson can bear a little watching, now. He's been travelling pretty free, and he's got the notion he's driving, maybe. I'm a-goin' to look after that book a little myself.

MRS. DRYFOOS: You'll kill yourself, Jacob, tryin' to do so many things. And what is it all fur? I can't see as we've got a bit more comfort of our lives, Jacob, because we've got such piles and piles of money. I wisht to gracious we was back on the farm this minute. I wisht you had held out ag'inst the children about sellin' it; 'twould 'a bin the best thing fur 'em, I say. I believe in my soul they'll git spoiled, here in New York. I kin see a change in 'em a'ready—in the girls. I wisht we could go back, Ja—

DRYFOOS, *shouting fiercely*: We *can't* go back! There's no farm any more to go back to. The fields is full of gas wells and oil wells and hell holes generally; the house is tore down, and the barn's goin'—

MRS. DRYFOOS, *gasping*: The *barn!* Oh, my!

DRYFOOS: If I was to give all I'm worth this minute, we couldn't go back to that farm, any more than them girls in there could go back and be little children. I don't say we're any better off, for the money. I've got more of it now than I ever had; and there's no end to the luck; it pours in. But I feel like I was tied hand and foot. I don't know which way to move; I don't know what's best to do about anything. The money don't seem to buy anything but more and more care and trouble. We got a big house that we ain't at home in; and we got a lot of hired girls round under our feet that hinder and don't help. Our children don't mind us, and we got no friends or neighbors. But it had to be. I couldn't help but

sell the farm, and we can't go back to it, for it ain't there. So don't you say anything more about it, 'Liz'beth.

MRS. DRYFOOS: Pore Jacob! Well, I woon't, dear.

DRYFOOS: Don't then! I'm goin' into the parlor to see what they're all about in there.

SCENE III: *The Dryfoos drawing-room. Dryfoos enters. His feet, in their broad, flat slippers, make no sound on the dense carpet, and he comes unseen upon the little group there near the piano—Mela perched upon the stool with her back to the keys, and Beaton bent over Christine, who sits with a banjo in her lap, letting him take her hands and put them in the right place on the instrument. Her face is radiant with happiness, and Mela is watching her with foolish, unselfish pleasure in her bliss.*

BEATON: No, no. You must keep your hand and arm so. There! Now strike with your right hand. See?

CHRISTINE, *with a fond upward look at him*: I don't believe I can ever learn.

BEATON: Oh yes, you can.

He looks round and discovers Dryfoos, who nods confusedly to him. Beaton is not embarrassed. He is in evening dress, and his face, pointed with its brown beard, shows extremely handsome above the expanse of his broad white shirt front. He gives back as nonchalant a nod as he has got.

DRYFOOS: What you got there, Christine?

CHRISTINE, *without looking up*: A banjo.

MELA, *gurgling*: Mr. Beaton is learnun' her the first position.

DRYFOOS, *half jocosely, half suspiciously*: And is the banjo the fashion, now? In my day, nobody but nigger minstrels used to play it.

MELA: It's all the rage nowadays. Everybody plays it. Mr. Beaton borrowed this from a lady friend of his.

DRYFOOS: Humph! Pity I got you a piano, then. A banjo would have been cheaper.

BEATON, *to Mela*: Oh, won't you just strike those chords? (*As Mela wheels about and beats the keys, he takes the banjo from Christine and sits down with it.*) This way! (*He strums it, and murmurs the tune Dryfoos has heard him singing from the library, while he keeps his beautiful eyes floating on Christine's.*) You try that, now; it's very simple.

DRYFOOS, *trying to assert himself*: Where is Mrs. Mandel?

Neither of the girls seems to have heard him at first in the chatter they break into over what Beaton proposed.

MELA, *absently*: Oh, she had to go out to see one of her friends that's sick. (*She strikes the piano keys.*) Come; try it, Chris!

The two girls play and Beaton sings without taking further notice of Dryfoos, who looks on frowningly. At the end, Beaton abruptly offers his hand to each of the girls in succession.

BEATON: Good-day. Good-bye!

MELA: Oh, you got to go?

BEATON: Yes, good-bye.

He nods lightly to Dryfoos and goes rapidly out.

MELA: Well, ain't it just a shame, Chris? I s'pose he's goin' to dinner somewhere, and that's why he's in such a hurry. I reckon he was enjoyin' himself pretty well. Say, Chris—

DRYFOOS, *savagely*: What sort of fellow is he, any way? Hasn't he got any manners?

CHRISTINE: I don't know but he has. He's polite enough to *us*. I suppose he thought you didn't want him to speak to you, the way you acted. If you want to learn any manners, you better leave him some yourself, father.

DRYFOOS: What do you mean?

CHRISTINE: Oh, pshaw, now, father, you know well enough. You're just mad because everybody don't bow down before you. Do you think you can treat people the way you do him, and then expect him to go round on his hands and knees? You didn't hardly speak to him the other night and just now—

DRYFOOS: If he don't like the way I treat him, what does he come here for?

MELA, *laughing*: Because he likes the way Christine treats him. (*A ring is heard.*) My goodness, there goes the bell! I believe in my heart it's another caller. Well, they're just pourin' in! Now you clear out, father, with those old slippers on, and your hair every *which* way.

ACT III

SCENE I: *A reception at a literary house. People talking in groups. Gentlemen serving ladies with tea. Beaton and Miss Vance together.*

BEATON: (*This to be turned into dialogue.*) The house was one where people might chat a long time together without publicly committing themselves to an interest in each other except such as grew out of each other's ideas. Miss Margaret Vance was there because she united in her catholic sympathies or ambitions the objects of the fashionable people and of the aesthetic people who met there on common ground. It was almost the only house in New York where this happened often, and it did not happen very often there. It was a literary house, primarily, with artistic qualifications, and the frequenters of it were mostly authors and artists; Wetmore, who was always trying to fit everything with a phrase, said it was the unfrequenters who were fashionable. There was great ease there, and simplicity; and if there was not distinction, it was not for want of distinguished people, but because there seems to be some solvent in New York life that reduces all men to a common level, that touches everybody with its potent magic and brings to the surface the deeply underlying nobody. The effect for some temperaments, for consciousness, for egotism, is admirable; for curiosity, for hero-worship, it is rather baffling. It is the spirit of the street transferred to the drawing-room; indiscriminating, levelling, but doubtless finally wholesome, and witnessing the immensity of the place, if not consenting to the grandeur of reputations or presences.

Beaton now denied that this house represented a salon at all, in the old sense; and he held that the salon was impossible, even undesirable, with us, when Miss Vance sighed for it. At any rate, he said that this turmoil of coming and going, this bubble and babble, this cackling and hissing of conversation, was not the expression of any such civilization as had created the salon. Here, he owned, were the elements of intellectual delightfulness, but he said their assemblage in such quantity alone denied the salon; there was too much of a good thing. The French word implied a long evening of general talk among the guests, crowned with a little chicken at supper, ending at cock-crow. Here was tea, with milk or with lemon—baths of it—and claret-cup for the hardier spirits throughout the evening. It was very nice, very pleasant, but it was not the little chicken—not the salon. In fact, he affirmed, the salon descended from above, out of the great world, and included the aesthetic world in it. But our great world, the rich people, were stupid, with no wish to be otherwise; they were not even curious about authors and artists.

MARGARET, *speaking impartially*: It isn't altogether the rich people's fault. I don't believe that the literary men and the artists would like a salon that descended to them. Madame Geoffrin, you know, was very plebeian; her husband was a businessman of some sort.

BEATON, *impartially*: He would have been a howling swell in New York.

Wetmore comes up to their corner, with a scroll of bread and butter in one hand and a cup of tea in the other. Large and fat, and clean shaven, he looks like a monk in evening dress.

MARGARET: We were talking about salons.

WETMORE, *breathing thickly from the anxiety of getting through the crowd without spilling his tea*: Why don't you open a salon yourself?

MARGARET, *with a laugh*: Like poor Lady Barberina Lemon? What a good story? That idea of a woman who couldn't be interested in any of the arts because she was socially and traditionally the material of them! We can never reach that height of nonchalance in this country.

WETMORE: Not if we tried seriously? I've an idea that if the Americans ever gave their minds to that sort of thing, they could take the palm—or the cake, as Beaton here would say—just as they do in everything else. When we do have an aristocracy, it will be an aristocracy that will go ahead of anything the world has ever seen. Why don't somebody make a beginning, and go in openly for an ancestry, and a lower middle class, and an hereditary legislature, and all the rest? We've got the liveries, and crests, and palaces, and caste feeling. We're all right as far as we've gone, and we've got the money to go any length.

MARGARET, *with a smiling glance round at Beaton*: Like your natural gas man, Mr. Beaton?

WETMORE, *stirring his tea*: Ah! Has Beaton got a natural gas man?

BEATON, *ignoring Wetmore's question*: My natural gas man doesn't know how to live in his palace yet, and I doubt if he has any caste feeling. I fancy his family believe themselves victims of it.

They say—one of the young ladies does—that she never saw such an unsociable place as New York; nobody calls.

WETMORE: That's good! I suppose they're all ready for company, too: good cook, furniture, servants, carriages?

BEATON: Galore.

WETMORE: Well, that's too bad. There's a chance for you, Miss Vance. Doesn't your philanthropy embrace the socially destitute as well as the financially? Just think of a family like that, without a friend, in a great city! I should think common charity had a duty, there—not to mention the uncommon.

MARGARET: Oh, they seem to have Mr. Beaton.

BEATON: They have me because they partly own me. Dryfoos is Fulkerson's financial backer in *Every Other Week*.

WETMORE: Is that so? Well, that's interesting, too. Aren't you rather astonished, Miss Vance, to see what a pretty thing Beaton is making of that magazine of his?

MARGARET: Oh, it's so very nice, every way; it makes you feel as if you *did* have a country, after all. It's as *chic*—that destestable little word!—as those new French books.

WETMORE: Beaton modelled it on them. Look here, Beaton, when your natural gas man gets to the picture-buying stage in his development, just remember your old friend, will you? You know, Miss Vance, those new fellows have their regular stages. They never know what to do with their money, but they find out that people buy pictures, at one point. They shut your things up in their houses where nobody comes; and after a while they overeat themselves—they don't know what else to do—and die of apoplexy, and leave your pictures to a gallery, and then they see the light. It's slow, but it's pretty sure. Well, I see Beaton isn't going to move on, as he ought to do; and so I must. He always *was* an unconventional creature.

Wetmore goes.

MARGARET, *after the retreat of one of the comers and goers leaves her alone with Beaton again*: Do you think that these young ladies would like me to call on them?

BEATON: Those young ladies?

MARGARET: I mean the Miss Dryfooses. It seems really barbarous, if nobody goes near them. We do all kinds of things, and help all kinds of people in some ways, but we let strangers remain strangers unless they know how to make their way among us.

BEATON, *with a sort of dreamy absence in his tone*: The Dryfooses certainly wouldn't know how to make their way among you.

MARGARET: We defend ourselves by trying to believe that they must have friends of their own, or that they would think us patronizing, and wouldn't like being made the objects of social charity; but they needn't really suppose anything of the kind.

BEATON: I don't imagine they would. I think they'd be only too happy to have you come. But you wouldn't know what to do with each other, indeed, Miss Vance.

MARGARET, *bravely*: Perhaps we shall like each other and then we shall know. What church are they of?

BEATON: I don't believe they're of any. The father is a Mammon-worshipper, pure and simple. I suppose the young ladies go to church, but I don't know where. They haven't tried to convert me.

MARGARET: I'll tell them not to despair—after I've converted *them*. Will you let me use you as a *point d'appui*, Mr. Beaton?

BEATON: Any way you like. If you're really going to see them, perhaps I'd better make a confession. I left your banjo with them, after I got it put in order.

MARGARET: How very nice! Then we have a common interest already.

BEATON: Do you mean the banjo, or—

MARGARET: The banjo, decidedly. Which of them plays?

BEATON: Neither. But the eldest heard that the banjo was "all the rage," as the youngest says. Perhaps you can persuade them that good works are the rage, too. Yonder they are!

MARGARET: Really!

BEATON: I said I was the stand, here; you meet everybody. But who had them asked? It must have been Fulkerson.

MARGARET: Oh, take me to them—do!

BEATON: They're coming this way. I'll introduce you if you like.

MARGARET: By all means!

Room Forty-Five

[1899]

In this play Howells seems to be experimenting with the idea that anger, physical violence, and name-calling might pass for drama, but the result is disappointing. The farce characters present not a conflict but a simple response: anger. Although Howells apparently intends that the audience should feel some humorous sympathy for the main characters, the monotony of their response produces an effect which is humorous, but neither dramatic nor likely to create sympathy. The shrewish and loud Mrs. Trenmore is primarily a temper tantrum personified. Mr. Trenmore is simply weak and probably never will swear. Only the night clerk is worth the audience's sympathy. Compared with this man of feeling as well as humor, the Trenmores are harsh instruments of a single string whose constant plucking produces something less than music.

In spite of obvious weaknesses *Room Forty-Five* does have interesting features. For example, Howells shows his ingenuity when he describes the snoring of the gentleman in Room 45 with such phrases as "such queer lumps of sound" and "making hooks and hunks of noise." Even more inspired than his picturesque phrasing is the night clerk's admiring, almost poetic description of the gentleman snorer's accomplishments. One must understand, the clerk might say, that as a snorer this man is unexcelled, "a kind of *vox humana,*" a person of supreme talent. As his letters suggest in their frequent comments on his hotel experiences (to Mildred Howells, September 22, 1905, Harvard Library—waked at 2:00 A.M. by "the hotel dynamo under our room"; to Aurelia Howells, December 14, 1902, Harvard Library—"sick at my stomach with the smell of the soap-boiling in the basement") Howells was close to his subject in this play and, although able to laugh at the Trenmores' situation, a little disturbed about hotel management in general. Mainly, *Room Forty-Five* is a semidramatic sketch of what Howells considered a semihumorous anecdote.

Room Forty-Five[1]

FARCE

SCENE: *A room in the Summertop Hotel. A chambermaid is discovered putting the last touches to the bed which she has made up in an alcove. A stout gentleman appears at the door and looks in.*

I

THE STOUT GENTLEMAN: Putting anybody in here to-night, Mary? I'm just going to turn in below, and I've been out with some friends, and I guess I'm pretty tired. You all know how I am when I'm sleeping light; and I'm going to sleep *hard* to-night. I'm afraid I should make it lively for anybody over me.

THE CHAMBERMAID: Oh, that's all right, sor. There ain't annybody in by the last train but a gentleman and his wife, and the clerk's put *them* into No. 10. I'm just gettin' the room ready for a party that's comin' to-morrow morning for the day.

THE STOUT GENTLEMAN: Well, forewarned is forearmed. I thought I ought to tell you.

THE CHAMBERMAID: All right, sor. Slape as harred as ye pl'ase. Ye won't harrum annyone here. *(After a final glance round the room)* Don't you worry, sor.

THE STOUT GENTLEMAN, *going out*: No. I always leave that to *them*. Well, good-night, Mary.

THE CHAMBERMAID: Good-night, sor.

She follows him out.

II

MRS. TRENMORE: Yes, this will do nicely. I don't see why you didn't put us here at once. *(She looks about the room which the night clerk has shown her into, and sinks down upon a sofa with a deep sigh of satisfaction. Mr. Julian Trenmore, her husband, draws a fainter sigh of relief, and puts down on the table in the centre of the room his dress-suit case, and a bundle of shawls and*

[1] The text used here is the Houghton, Mifflin and Company edition.

umbrellas; he finally takes off his hat and places it beside them. The night clerk, who has stood near the door, burdened with a valise, two smaller handbags, a variety of wraps, a parasol, and a kodak camera, until Mrs. Trenmore shall have expressed her content with the room, now begins to place these things on the floor, and is about to retreat when her voice arrests him.) May I ask why you didn't put us here at once?

THE NIGHT CLERK: Put you here?

MRS. TRENMORE: Yes, put us here; give us this room in the first place, instead of the room you did give us? I should really like to know.

THE NIGHT CLERK: The other room was only one flight up, and—

MRS. TRENMORE, *with vehemence*: Right over the kitchen, where they were washing up the last dishes and singing and talking and clashing the crockery and knives! And if we kept the windows shut the heat was suffocating, and if we opened them we simply *died* of the smell of stale bread and warm dishwater. You heard us *say* that we had come for a quiet night, and a breath of pure air, and that we wanted a cool room away from all the noises—

MR. TRENMORE, *with spirit that does not seem constant in him*: You heard me say so when I registered.

MRS. TRENMORE: And yet you put us in that wretched place, where we began to swelter and stifle from the first instant, and the clatter gave me a headache that I shall not get over for a week.

MR. TRENMORE: You said that No. 10 was the only room you had left.

MRS. TRENMORE: And here, only one flight further up, was this delicious place, absolutely empty, and as cool and quiet as the grave; with windows opening on a garden, and every breath of air thick with the syringas, or honeysuckles, or whatever they are. Now, *why* didn't you do it in the first place? *(She has risen to verify her praises of the room by examining it in every part; she flings back the curtain of an alcove, and discloses a snowy bed.)* Oh, I could sleep for *ages* in that bed! (*Then she advances suddenly upon the night clerk, who retires before her demand.*) I should simply like to know *why* you didn't. Is it the rule of the house to keep people out of a good room if you can possibly find a bad one for them? Do you take a *pleasure* in thwarting and harassing people? When people come and tell you that they are sick with the noise and heat of New York, and that they have run out for a few nights simply to save their lives, and you see them fairly dropping dead before you, do you *like* to give them a room where a salamander couldn't breathe and an adder would be stunned?

MR. TRENMORE: You heard me say so when I registered, and you told me that No. 10 was the only—

MRS. TRENMORE, *passing swiftly from the plaintive note of self-pitying appeal to the tone of withering irony*: Or do you merely prefer to wait up till the porter and call-boys have gone to bed, and then move the people yourself into something decent, when they have got perfectly desperate, and won't stand it any longer? I should like to know what your motive really is. I should like to know whether you have been following a rule of the house, or whether there is some mystery about it all that you can't explain, or whether you simply did not care to tell the truth. And after what you have made us suffer, I think I have a *right* to know.

MR. TRENMORE: Yes! Why didn't you show us this room at once?

THE NIGHT CLERK, *backing into the doorway, and making good his retreat as he speaks*: I—I—forgot this room.

MRS. TRENMORE, *with contemptuous incredulity*: Forgot! Forgot, indeed! This is insulting, simply insulting. He never forgot it in the world, and now to have the impudence— He was keeping it for somebody whom he couldn't impose upon with such a wretched hole as No. 10! He saw that he could put off anything upon *you!* They always do. You never browbeat them or bully them, and so I always have to submit to any sort of— Oh, I wish *I* was a man, and had to do the registering! I don't think— Forgot this room! Call him back, Julian! I won't stand it. I can't. If he thinks that I am going to put up with any such paltry subterfuge— I'll call him myself.

She plunges towards the electric button in the wall, but before she can get her finger upon it, her husband intercepts her and restrains her in a coaxing embrace.

MR. TRENMORE: No, no, my dear! Let it go till morning and have it out with him then. We've got the room we want, and the best room in the house, and we haven't lost so very much time, after all. You didn't let the grass grow under your feet in No. 10: we're well out of it, and you've punished that poor fellow enough. Leave him to his little mystery, or his hotel convention, or his plain lie, for the night, and make him suffer a little more in the morning.

MRS. TRENMORE: But he won't be on duty in the morning; we can't see him again till to-morrow night, and—

MR. TRENMORE: Then we'll wait till to-morrow night, and see him. But remember, now, that we came out for a rest, and not for a fight, though I believe you'd rather fight than rest any time, you're such a little bundle of pluck.

MRS. TRENMORE, *half persuaded and with a touch of fondness*: Oh, if *you* had more pluck, dearest, *I* needn't have so *much*. You're always so mild and patient, and that makes me furious.

MR. TRENMORE: I know it does, and I assure you I appreciate it. But—

MRS. TRENMORE, *more and more softened*: It was for your sake that I wanted to do it. When I thought how worn out with the heat you were, and how you hadn't been sleeping for days and weeks almost, and then thought of the cruelty of that wretch in putting us into No. 10, when all the time he had this beautiful, big, cool, quiet room standing vacant and perfectly idle, I—

MR. TRENMORE: I understand, and I'm very grateful, but now I'm very sleepy, and—

MRS. TRENMORE: I'm not. I never was so wide awake in my life. I could sit up all night, just to enjoy the quietness and sweetness. I do believe it's rested me more to give that creature a piece of my mind than sleeping a month would. (*She goes to the window and looks out, while he drops into a chair.*) Oh, this lovely garden! And this divine silence! How do you suppose we didn't see the garden from No. 10? Or was that wretch keeping *it* a secret, too, along with this room? They don't often have a garden, even in a summer hotel. There was one in that hotel at Plattsburgh, don't you remember? But the locomotives at the station under the hill seemed to be scampering up and down the garden paths the whole night. And here it's so still! You can almost hear yourself think. Dearest, if you can't sleep here, I don't know where you *can* sleep. Just come and see this garden, and smell it.

She turns her face over her shoulder at him.

MR. TRENMORE, *yawning*: In the morning, my dear. We'll take the night clerk out among the roses and rub his nose into the pinks till he gives the true reason for putting us in No. 10. But now I'd rather go to bed.

MRS. TRENMORE, *returning to him*: You *are* sleepy! That's because you kept your temper. If you'd been as mad as I was— But I'm not angry, now, a bit. I'm simply bewildered. What *can* the mystery be? There must be some mystery! That fellow never forgot this room in the world. There must be something uncanny about it. Do you suppose it's haunted? Perhaps somebody's committed suicide in it! Do you suppose there's a back fence that will have cats on it later?

MR. TRENMORE: They'll have to get up early if they're going to be much later. (*He looks at his watch.*) It's nearly one o'clock.

MRS. TRENMORE, *going to the window and looking out again*: I can't see any back fence. (*She leans further over the window sill and peers down.*) We seem to be in a kind of wing, or L, here. We're off from the main building, and there's a room just under us, but the ground floor is an open veranda. I never heard of cats coming on verandas, and I don't believe that there can be anything to disturb us. It's as still as still can be, now, anyway. That perfume—(*she inhales it vigorously*) is from a honeysuckle that perfectly walls in one side of the veranda; you ought to see it in the moonlight; it looks as if it had been snowed on, it's so full of blossoms. (*While she talks, Mr. Trenmore drowses in his chair, and his head drops on his breast.*) No, there's not the least danger of cats; I'm satisfied of *that.* Perhaps cat-*birds*; but *they* don't caterwaul, do they? (*She looks round, and sees her husband asleep.*) Poor Julian! I don't see how he can be sleepy, such a lovely night as this, in this exquisite room, and with this delicious garden underneath, and this silence, that fairly sings in my ears. Not a sound, anywhere! The last train must be in, and the station is a mile from here, anyhow, and every one of those kitchen girls has giggled herself off to bed; there isn't a cat; and— (*She starts, and listens; she puts her head out and then draws it in and listens again.*) Julian, what's *that?*

TRENMORE, *staggering to his feet*: What's what?

He makes some vague passes through the air and tries to rouse himself.

MRS. TRENMORE, *listening*: That—sound. Don't you hear it? No, there it's stopped! Did you make it?

TRENMORE: Make what?

MRS. TRENMORE: The sound. (*Laughing*) Of course you did! You had just dropped off, and you were sno— Hark! There it is again! Then it *wasn't* you! Now it's stopped again. No, there it goes! I knew I couldn't be mistaken, and it can't be you, now. (*A low hissing noise, coming and going regularly, like the first respirations of a locomotive in starting, makes itself heard.*) Don't you hear it?

TRENMORE: Yes, certainly, I hear it. It's nothing but the engineer trying the steam in his boilers; they have to keep the steam going all night, in these hotels. The boilers are in the basement, and it's coming up outside.

MRS. TRENMORE: Why, of course! Well, it does take you to think things out, Julian! Do you suppose he'll keep doing it long?

TRENMORE: I don't believe so—

MRS. TRENMORE: There! He's stopped again, already. Now, he's beginning again. (*She listens.*) But he can't be going to keep it up long, and we mustn't mind it. *I'm* sleepy, too, and— He seems to be putting on coal, now! Doesn't that sound like putting on coal? (*A stertorous, broken noise is heard, and the hissing ceases.*) Such queer lumps of sound! I believe I prefer the hissing. It's stopped. It's all over. Now, my dear, it's high time that— Oh, what *is* he doing?

TRENMORE, *listening*: Sawing kindling-wood, I should say. (*Listening again*) That's it! But I don't see why he should be *planing* it. And the plane seems to catch in knots, and—(*He goes to the window and puts out his head.*) Everything's quiet outside. I thought they might be chopping ice under the window. I've been in hotels where they do it all night; but—

MRS. TRENMORE, *tragically*: It isn't coming in through the window. It's coming up through the floor!

TRENMORE: Through the floor?

MRS. TRENMORE: Yes, don't you hear it?

TRENMORE: Oh, that's merely the register, bringing the sound from the cellar.

MRS. TRENMORE: But there *is* no register. I tell you it's in the room under this. Don't you hear it?

TRENMORE, *listening carefully*: It does seem to be coming through the floor.

MRS. TRENMORE, *sternly*: What are they doing?

TRENMORE, *listening and reporting with ana-*

lytical conscientiousness: Well, they seem to be letting off steam. And—putting on coal. And—sawing kindling. And—planing it. And—catching the plane in knots. And—chopping ice. And—now, they're emptying out potatoes on the floor. And—making hooks and hunks of noise. And—choking, and catching their breath, and—

MRS. TRENMORE: They're killing somebody! I tell you they are; and we shall both be subpœnaed and cross-examined, and I don't know *what* all. Go down and— There, it's stopped again; it's all perfectly silent; they're every one of them dead! (*The noises slowly renew themselves in all their strange variety.*) There! They're beginning to struggle again. Oh, Julian, if you have any love for me at all, you will go— No, I can't let you! They will murder you too. But call—call that wretched night clerk, and make *him* go. I'll ring—

She whirls away to press the bell button, but he catches her by the wrist, and pulls her over towards the floor with him where he stoops listening.

TRENMORE: It isn't murder— It's something much worse— It's— Don't you hear? Listen!

She stoops and listens with him; then she lifts herself and faces him.

MRS. TRENMORE: You don't mean to tell me that it's some one—*snoring*? (*He nods solemnly.*) Julian, I can't believe it! That any human being is making those horrible sheets and spurts, and chips, and shavings, and lumps, and hooks, and bounces of noise in his *sleep*? (*He nods as before.*) Well, then, I can tell you it's nothing of the kind. It's not snoring; it's murder! It's—(*She listens again, stooping lower with her ear toward the floor, and then facing him with awful calm.*) I do believe it is—what you say. And now, what are you going to do about it?

TRENMORE, *in a ghostly whisper*: I don't see what we can do, exactly. I suppose we shall have to wait till he stops.

MRS. TRENMORE: And suppose he doesn't stop? Suppose he *never* stops? (*Trenmore shrugs.*) Don't tell me you're not going to do anything! That you're going to submit—that you're going to die down passively under the worst snoring that there ever was! Then *I'm* not! We shan't get a wink of sleep the whole night. It's an outrage, and I won't endure it! I'm going to ring for that—(*She makes another dash at the bell button, and he intercepts her again; the noises continue in their complexity.*) Let me go, Julian!

Now, I understand why he was so loath to give us this room, and I shall let him know what we think of his putting us—

TRENMORE: We don't want to make a scene, my dear. We don't want to be ridiculous. Let us think whether we can't do something ourselves to stop it. (*They both stand silent and motionless, trying to think; the noises continue as before.*) If there was only a register we might call down through it.[1]

MRS. TRENMORE: But there *is* no register. I told you there was no register in the beginning. Indeed, if there was a register, don't you suppose I would bang on it till he was *glad* to stop? Go down and knock on his door!

TRENMORE: Do you think that would do? I'm afraid it might rouse the house. I might go to the wrong door—the noise seems to come from everywhere, now, and what—what—

MRS. TRENMORE, *impatiently*: Well, what?

TRENMORE: What if it was a lady?

MRS. TRENMORE: Nonsense! No woman in the world could make such a noise as that. I tell you it's a man, and you're perfectly safe.

TRENMORE, *dubiously*: I don't know about the safety. If it's a woman it would be scandalous, and if it's a man it might be dangerous. He might come to the door to ask what I wanted, and then what could I say? You can't tell a man that he's been snoring, and you've waked him. And if it was a woman came to the door—I've heard them on the sleeping-cars sometimes, and if it *should* happen to be a woman—think of the talk! No, my dear, it won't do.

MRS. TRENMORE: Then we must thump on the floor!

TRENMORE: Thump on the floor? Oh, I don't know! That's rather serious. I rather think we'll have to have patience. He can't keep it up *all* night; he must wake himself by and by. Let's wait a while longer. I don't believe we've any right to thump on the floor.

MRS. TRENMORE: Right or wrong, I'm going to do it. Has *he* any right to keep on making noises that raise the roof and shake the whole house, and we not lift a hand against it? Give me those umbrellas!

She makes a dash for the umbrellas on the table, but he interposes.

TRENMORE: But if it *should* be a woman—

[1] This is a reference to *The Register* in which this trick was used.

MRS. TRENMORE: Oh, I wish it *was* a woman. Horrid thing! Will you let me have those umbrellas, Julian, or do you wish me to go home to mamma? What a shame to treat your own wife so! You care more for some horrible, vulgar, common creature, that destroys the peace and comfort of a whole hotel with her puffing and—(*She slips round behind him, and seizes the umbrellas.*) There! Now, I'll see if I can't do something to stop her making a perfect hippopotamus of herself.

TRENMORE: But I don't say she *is* a woman, my dear!

MRS. TRENMORE: No matter. I don't care whether she's a woman or a man. If I can only find the place right over his head, I shall thump so that she'll be glad to—

She goes about listening at different points in the room, and trying to locate the noises, bending over, and putting her ear to the floor; he follows her, adapting himself to her movements in vain entreaty of posture and gesture.

TRENMORE: Don't do it, my dear; don't do it! Consider the uproar it's going to make! We shall have people running in from all over the house asking what's the matter. It isn't *done*, my love! It *can't* be done. We're in a public house, and we have no right to make a noise and wake everybody up. They can arrest us, I believe. Don't, darling! Do have a little patience. He'll soon wake, I know he will!

MRS. TRENMORE, *unheeding*: The sound seems to be everywhere. Oh, how cruel, Julian, to leave it all to me! (*She rises and glares reproachfully at him.*) Help me to find the place right over the dreadful thing's head. She ought to be ashamed!

TRENMORE: But if she's a man, he'll make an awful row at being waked. Very likely he'll come up here and—

MRS. TRENMORE: Oh, I should just like to *have* her. (*She goes about as before, stooping and listening.*) I believe I've got the place now. (*She stoops lower and listens.*) Yes, this is it. He's right under it, and no thanks to *you*, Julian. And now I shall thump—

TRENMORE: But, consider, my dear!

MRS. TRENMORE, *desperately*: I shall *not* consider. I have a right to save my own life; and—Will you lift the rug, here, Julian, or must I do everything? Oh, very well then; I'll lift it.

TRENMORE, *reluctantly lifting the rug*: I'll do it, my dear; but—but—thump softly.

MRS. TRENMORE: Thump softly! *Snore* softly!

(*She raises the umbrella and brings the point down with all her force.*) There! I think that she'll hear that, unless she's dead, and I know she isn't dead. (*She batters furiously with the umbrella, which goes to pieces in her hands.*) Give me another umbrella, Julian.

TRENMORE: But hadn't you better wait and see, my dear, if he won't—

MRS. TRENMORE, *snatching the other umbrella from the table, and returning to her work*: It hasn't made the slightest impression on her. (*She beats and thumps on the floor till the second umbrella gives way; she flings the fragments from her.*) Oh, if I only had a poker! (*She glares around the room.*) But of course in a summer hotel, like this, there's no fireplace, and no poker nearer than the kitchen. Why didn't you think to bring your cane?

TRENMORE, *soothingly*: It wouldn't have done any good, my dear. If umbrellas won't wake him, canes—

MRS. TRENMORE: Then give me my parasol!

TRENMORE: But your parasol couldn't bear it a moment!

MRS. TRENMORE, *seizing it*: No matter. I can't either. There! (*She dispatches the parasol with a single blow, flings the fragments from her, and turns to her husband.*) Bring your dress-suit case! It's good and hard, and—

TRENMORE: But, my dear! I don't want to thump the floor with my dress-suit case. I—

MRS. TRENMORE, *with frenzy*: You want me to do it? Very well, then, I will.

She reaches for the dress-suit case, but he puts it behind him.

TRENMORE: There! I'll do it. Where is the place? You've ruined the floor!

MRS. TRENMORE: No matter about the floor. Thump. (*Trenmore blindly obeys.*) Now, that is something *like* thumping. If that won't wake her, nothing will. And if you had thought of your dress-suit case in the first place, I needn't have destroyed our two umbrellas and my Paris parasol. But, no! I have to think of everything. Thump with the corner! (*After half a dozen blows with the corner of the case, it springs open, and the dress suit, with a shirt, collars, cuffs, ties, and handerchiefs flies out over the floor.*) That comes of your not locking it! But never mind the things, now. I never wanted you to bring them, and I told you so; but you always will, even if you don't expect to meet a soul you know. Thump!

She sinks panting into a chair.

TRENMORE, *erecting himself and standing with*

the open empty case in his hand, listening: No. He's stopped.

MRS. TRENMORE: Listen! I do believe we have stopped her. I knew we could do it. Oh, we have! What a rest! How deliciously silent! Oh, Julian, I never can be grateful enough to you. *(He looks round at his scattered garments.)* I'll pick them up for you, as soon as I can get my breath.

TRENMORE: I wish you'd get *my* breath, too, while you're at it. *(He sinks panting into a chair.)* And look at my dress-suit case!

He gazes ruefully down at the ruin.

MRS. TRENMORE: Don't mind it, dearest. I'll get you a new one for your birthday. I've been saving up the money I've got from you, and I didn't know what I *should* get you, and now it's a perfect inspiration. Oh, how quiet it is! Doesn't it seem too good to be true, dearest? Now, won't you always trust my judgment after this, a little? I know that I'm impetuous at times, and I do take the whip hand and the bit in my teeth, now and then, but only when it's absolutely necessary. Better put down the window, dear. We're both overheated, and we ought to keep out of the draft till we cool off. Oh, *what* a rest! I really had begun to despair; and it *has* cost us something. Your umbrella is ruined, and so is mine; and my parasol is a *perfect* wreck; and I suppose the floor— But if it's a man we can make *him* pay for the floor, can't we? Or we can just pull back the rug over it. No? Well, I know how sensitive you are about such things, and I merely suggested it; I'm sure I don't want to do anything wrong about it, if you don't. Oh, I'm so *happy!* I'm not the least sleepy any more; I feel as if I could stay up all night and enjoy the quiet more and more, every minute. Oh, how still it is! Can't you fairly *hear* the stillness? *(Trenmore lifts his head and stands in a listening attitude.)* What is it?

TRENMORE: Nothing. I—

MRS. TRENMORE: You what?

TRENMORE: Nothing. But I—didn't you—*hear* something?

MRS. TRENMORE: Only the singing of the silence in my ears.

TRENMORE: Yes, it must be that. But—didn't it begin that way before?

MRS. TRENMORE: *It?* Oh, Julian you don't—

TRENMORE: No, no! It's stopped. It was the si— *(A low, hissing noise makes itself heard. It deepens, and passes into the effect of escaping steam. It becomes like the respiration of a locomotive in starting. It changes into the sound of*

stoking an engine. It changes again into the sound of sawing wood, of planing knotty lumber, of chopping ice, of pouring out potatoes, and ends in lumps and hooks and bounces of sound. Trenmore turns a ghastly face upon his wife; she hides her face in her hands and bursts into tears.) I suppose he merely turned over and got a new grip.

MRS. TRENMORE: Oh, dear, oh, dear! What shall we do now, Julian?

TRENMORE: Shall I thump again?

MRS. TRENMORE: It wouldn't be any use. She'd just turn over again and get *another* new grip. Oh, I *know* it's a woman, now, and she's doing it to spite us because we woke her. I shall die; yes, I shall die! Oh, who could have dreamt of such an awful thing? Did you ever hear anything like it before? Now *say* if you did?

She stretches her hands piteously toward him.

TRENMORE: Never! not even on a sleeping-car, and I've listened to a whole car-load of drummers before now. *(Suddenly)* But I'm not going to stand it! *(He dashes his empty dress-suit case wildly to the floor, and jumps up and down on the bare space, while she weeps silently.)* I'm getting a little mad myself now. *(The noises below continue unaffected by his activities, and he flies at the electric bell button.)* I'm going to have that scoundrelly clerk up! I am going to know why he puts two unoffending strangers into the loft of a boiler factory. I am going to make him send the proprietor. I am going to have the police. I am going to rouse the house. I am going to raise the roof. *(He strides furiously up and down, kicking the broken umbrellas and shirts and collars out of his way. He stops abruptly and invokes the unconscious sleeper beneath.)* Oh, blow away, you old grampus! Your time is short! Get in your work; let off your steam, put on your coal, saw your kindling, plane your boards, chop your ice, pour out your potatoes, make your hooks and hunks!

MRS. TRENMORE, *clasping her hands in admiration:* Oh, dearest you *are* mad, aren't you? How sweet it is of you! But Julian, couldn't you—I know it's against your principles, and you never have; but just for my sake—swear?

THE NIGHT CLERK, *tapping on the door jamb, and extending a pitcher through the open doorway:* Ice-water?

TRENMORE: Ice what?

THE NIGHT CLERK: Water. You rang three times.

TRENMORE: Did I? Then I meant to ring three

hundred times. What did you mean by putting us in here?

THE NIGHT CLERK: You didn't like No. 10, and I changed you to the only room we had. Ain't you comfortable?

TRENMORE: Comf—! Do you hear that? Don't pretend you *don't* hear it? I won't stand it! (*He seizes the clerk by the arm and pulls him over, so as to bring his head close to the floor.*) Now do you hear it?

THE NIGHT CLERK, *rising, as Trenmore releases him*: If you say so. Yes, sir, I think I did hear a noise of some kind.

TRENMORE: Oh, you did! And what do you think it is?

THE NIGHT CLERK: Well, sir, it's no use trying to disguise it, I suppose. It's the gentleman in Room 45, right under you here. That's the way he always does.

TRENMORE, *choking with rage*: And you put us in here, over a man that *always* does like that? Now, see here! You just go down to Room 45, and wake that man up, and tell him—

MRS. TRENMORE: I knew it *couldn't* be a *woman*. No woman could be so lost to shame.

TRENMORE, *harshly*: Never mind about that now. (*To the clerk*) You go down—

THE NIGHT CLERK: Oh, I couldn't do that. I wouldn't have the right to call up any guest that way.

TRENMORE: No right to call up a porpoise—

THE NIGHT CLERK: No, sir. Not if he was a guest. And especially No. 45. You see it's like this. He's here for the summer, and he told us fair and square, when he came, that he had this—habit; and we arranged to put him off here in the L, with nobody under him, and only this one room over him—you must have noticed that we came here through a sort of gallery; and he's really hired the whole wing, as you may say—

TRENMORE: And you mean to tell me that we're *trespassing* on a locomotive, wood-sawing, ice-chopping, potato-pouring stoker like that?

THE NIGHT CLERK: No, sir, not exactly; we can use this room at our own risk, and we do use it under certain conditions, when there's no other vacant. You see, there isn't much danger, if we can get a transient in here, and get him asleep before No. 45 comes in. Then the transient sleeps through, and No. 45 doesn't disturb him. But sometimes we do get stuck. Now, to-night, for instance: when I put you in here, I supposed 45 was out, and wouldn't be in for an hour, and that would give you plenty of time to get in ahead of him, but he must have stolen a march on me. I don't blame you for being mad; I should be just so myself, but it wasn't my fault. I did the best I could, and I had to take the chances with you. (*He listens and adds, sociably.*) He's in great form, to-night, ain't he? Whole band, as you may say. Notice how he gets in that trombone tremolo every now and then? It's grand—in its way, I mean. (*The clerk sits down and listens with an air of critical appreciation.*) Oh, he's an orchestra, and no mistake! *I* never heard anything like it. Whole Wagner opera, ain't he? (*He appeals for sympathy to Mrs. Trenmore, but failing, addresses himself to Trenmore.*) Well, sir, you won't hardly believe it, but there ain't anything I like better, when the house is all settled down, than to take my cigar and get into a good easy-chair on the veranda under him, and just *listen*. No danger of my dropping off to sleep and missing a bell! No, sir. He looks after that. It's the variety that does it—that keeps you interested. (*He listens.*) There's a kind of a *vox humana* stop that he gets in, now and then, after he's been dining pretty well, that beats everything. I wish he would just try it once so you could hear it. (*He listens.*) No, that ain't it; that's his æolian harp attachment. Some nights I've heard him do a symphony; kind of soft and low, to begin with, like the wind in the leaves, and shepherds dancing; then drums in the distance, and cannon firing; then the tramp of soldiers, and army wagons creaking and horses neighing; then musket-firing along the whole line, and peasants running off and women crying. That usually wakes him up, and he turns over for a fresh start. (*He listens.*) I don't know as I ever heard him get in more style than he is doing to-night. Kind of a diapason, ain't it? Notice those high notes? And that bass? Oh, it's rich! He must have been out with the boys, somewhere, to-night. What a *swing* he's got to him! Like the wedding march in *Lohengrin*, ain't it? There! By George, he's stopped, and I thought he was just coming to that passage in the Intermezzo; I was keeping it for a kind of surprise for you. He *is* such an undependable fellow, though. Never twice alike. He's so quiet you'd think he was dead now, wouldn't you?

He listens with a rapt air.

TRENMORE, *grimly*: Do you suppose he *is* dead? That he's stopped for good?

THE NIGHT CLERK, *shaking his head*: I wouldn't like to trust him. He may begin in another minute, or he may take a rest—like when the orchestra goes out for beer, you know—and you won't hear from him for a quarter of an hour, may be. But he's uncertain.

TRENMORE: And what do you propose to do with us?

THE NIGHT CLERK: Well, sir, I'm sorry, but there isn't anything else except No. 10. I guess that's all quiet now; in fact, I know it is; and I've had it airing—

TRENMORE: Oh, then, you expected we should have to go back, did you?

THE NIGHT CLERK: Not exactly. But I thought, in case anything happened— If he gets in his work first, they generally want to move.

MRS. TRENMORE: Well, it's a wicked imposition, and I'm not going to stand it. I'm going to stay here. Does he never stop for good?

THE NIGHT CLERK: He does sometimes; or as good as for good. He wakes himself up so that he can't sleep, and then he turns out and smokes a cigar, and that gives you a chance to drop off. He *may* have done it now. You can never tell; and if he *has* happened to have got up and started in for a smoke, why, you may drop off, you know, and make out a splendid night's rest yet. Guess you're so tired he wouldn't wake you, if you hurried. But, as I say, it's all a chance.

MRS. TRENMORE: Then we will take the chance, Julian. I am not going to be driven back to that noisy, pantry-smelling— Oh, he's beginning again!

She sinks into her chair with a desolate wail, and hides her face in her hands.

THE NIGHT CLERK, *sadly, while the noises successively make themselves heard in all their variety:* I was afraid of it. You see, if he's been dining more than usual, he can't quite wake himself; he makes a strike for it, and that gives you the idea that he *has* done it. But— (*He shakes his head compassionately.*) I can understand just how the lady feels, and I'm sorry—

MRS. TRENMORE, *springing to her feet, and confronting him:* Then *do* something! Julian, go with him, and see if it's quiet in No. 10, and see if it's cool; and if it is— No, don't take your things! You can come back for them, if it's all right, and then I can come. (*Trenmore and the night clerk fly at her command, and she remains alone amid the sounds from below. At first she is absorbed in the interest of her husband's quest; then she becomes aware of the sounds.*) Oh, yes, keep on, you heartless, shameless thing! Puff away, you cruel wretch! I wonder what you look like, anyway! I should just like to see what sort of fiend in human

shape you really are! Keep on, do! (*She stamps on the bare floor above the sleeper's head, while he steadily works away from locomotive fizzing to wood-sawing, ice-chopping, and potato-rolling.*) Some great, disgusting, bulbous, blubbery thing, with cheeks hanging down, and a red fat neck, and pudgy hands—oh, *I* know what you look like! And I hate you, hate you, hate you! If you had a spark of humanity, or the least remorse, or any gallantry at all, you'd *stop.* But you just take a pleasure in driving a helpless woman from her room, great oaf! (*She begins to gather up the broken umbrellas and to put Trenmore's things back into his dress-suit case, whimpering.*) You've made me break our two silk paragon frame umbrellas, that cost five dollars apiece, and my parasol that I brought from Paris; but much *you* care, you big, ugly—I don't know what! And Julian's dress-suit case is perfectly ruined, and we shall have to pay for the floor over your head, you hideous monster. Oh, rumble and puff and whistle away! If you had any self-respect— But I don't care what you do now. I'm going to get away from you, and you can't spoil my rest any more. I just like to listen to you and despise you; I take a pleasure in it; and I hope you'll go on snorting and wheezing to your heart's content. It doesn't matter to me, now; I'm safe. Keep on, and show how gross and vulgar you are! I just like to laugh at you. Ha, ha, ha! I only wish you knew I was listening to you. Oh, go on; go on! I shall leave you now and wait outside; you can have the place to yourself. (*She goes out, and instantly returns.*) But don't suppose I'm going to leave you sweetly sleeping. (*She takes up the water-pitcher, and smashes it on the floor.*) There! I guess that will make you turn over. (*She goes and returns again, to follow the pitcher with the bowl.*) And that, too. (*She goes out, and returns to break a chair on the place.*) See how you like that, for a change. (*She drags the washstand form the wall and bumps it up and down.*) And that, and that, and that! Oh, it hasn't troubled him a bit! I surely shall go mad, if this keeps on! Yes—Julian, Julian! Come back and save me! Where *are* you, Ju—

TRENMORE, *returning with the night clerk:* It's all right, my dear. No. 10 is as cool as a cucumber and as sweet as a pink.

MRS. TRENMORE, *frantically:* Oh, I don't care *what* it is! If they were washing all the dishes in the world under it, and it was as hot and stuffy and smelly as—as—the pantry of a steamer, I'd go. Only take me out of this! My spirit is broken.

She falls upon his shoulder and he slowly trails her from the room, while the night clerk gathers up their baggage and prepares to follow them, with a cursory glance at the wreckage.

THE NIGHT CLERK: She got in some good work, but she couldn't disturb *him*. Oh, he's a bird! Hullo!

The stout gentleman appears at the door in a varied deshabille of pajama jacket and black trousers; he wears a silk hat.

THE STOUT GENTLEMAN: What's been going on here?

THE NIGHT CLERK: Going on? Oh, nothing! Did you hear anything?

THE STOUT GENTLEMAN: I heard a cat-fight, or a cyclone!

THE NIGHT CLERK: Ha, ha, ha! Oh, no; oh, no! You must have been dreaming. Sorry you waked yourself up.

THE STOUT GENTLEMAN: I haven't been to sleep yet. But now, look here! I've been out with some friends to-night, and you know how I am. Better not put anybody in here. I should make it lively for them.

THE CLERK, *following him to the door*: Oh, I shan't put anybody in here. Don't be afraid of *that!* And I hope you won't hear any more cyclones or cat-fights—ah, ha, ha! Good-night, good-night, sir!

The Mother and the Father

[1900, 1902, 1906]

This trilogy of birth, marriage, and death as seen through the eyes of a mother and a father is one of the most meaningful of Howells' dramatic writings, not because it is great drama, for it is not, but because it reveals a depth and poetry of soul in Howells unparalleled in his other dramatic works. Of the three parts, the first has a particular interest in that it shows Howells doing a thorough job of revising his magazine text for book publication—a portion of the author's task that one is rarely privileged to observe in Howells. But the third section is by far the best, the most compelling, and the most significant. Throughout the trilogy, however, the reader is given glimpses of Howells' philosophy of life and death, the here and the hereafter, and the power of love—all in an irregular though frequently strong and moving blank verse.

In "The Mother" Howells tries to explain the meaning of the birth of a child for the Father and the Mother—for all fathers and all mothers. As these parents look down at their newborn baby girl, they are overcome with a feeling of life's mysteries: What does she know? Where did her soul come from? As they attempt to answer this question, the Mother in the *Harper's Monthly* version is pessimistic, even bitter, over her responsibility for taking the child from the security of heaven. Perhaps it was something closer to our hate than to our love that brought the children out of that unconsciousness, she felt. To which the Father answers, "What horrible blasphemy!" But this attitude is shaded and made milder in the published book. Another change occurs near the end of this first scene, where, with the new life within her, the Mother is aware of a new birth and a new world for herself. It seems important to Howells that the Mother's new world does not include the Father who, although he

accepts the fact, feels neither understanding nor satisfaction. But in the book version the happiness that Howells once saw for the Father is almost entirely omitted. As the new life begins, Father, Mother, and child suffer a change that involves both joy and pain.

Brand Whitlock was impressed by "The Mother" and wrote to Howells (December 2, 1902, Harvard Library): "I hesitate to say it, but has it ever occurred to you to do something in that same spirit about a baby that comes into the world only to go immediately away?" Perhaps Howells was influenced by this thought when he wrote the third section of the play, "Father and Mother, A Mystery." Most interesting in this scene is the argument concerning the strength of faith. Here the Father dominates the Mother and is more knowing: He matches his faith against her doubts—faith in the power of love. The philosophy of intuitive knowledge and feeling that pervades this part of the play has its source in Swedenborgianism and Quakerism—the only religious creeds Howells ever felt at all deeply. Essentially, Howells says that the dead live in love if we will only believe and that there is great satisfaction in this belief.

One cannot leave this play without some mention of the closeness of the Mother's and Father's thoughts—particularly the Father's—to those of Howells himself when his daughter Winifred died at the age of twenty-six: the feeling of lostness, despair, and love; the nobility of the one gone. During the years following, Howells became more interested in religion. In a letter to his father (July 14, 1889, Harvard Library) he wrote: "I have finished Taylor's book, which I found interesting to the end, and now I will send it to you. Notice what he says of the nature of the Deity, and how he shows that the Universe is necessarily the full expression of His power, while of His co-ordinate attributes—His wisdom, goodness, and justice—we have only glimpses. There is a great deal of suggestion, a great deal of comfort in it all." He also read that year Giles's *Man As A Spiritual Being* and more of Swedenborg's books, particularly *Heaven and Hell*. His long-lasting interest in spiritualism is evident from his novels and his short stories as well as from *Colonel Sellers* and *The Impossible*.

The Mother and the Father[1]

DRAMATIC PASSAGES

I

THE MOTHER

In the upper chamber of a village house a young mother lying in bed with her new-born baby on her arm. A nurse moving silently about the room, and putting the last touches of order to its disorder, opens the door softly, and goes out. The Mother looks up at The Father, who stands looking down on her.

THE MOTHER

Is the nurse gone now? And are we alone
At last?

THE FATHER

Yes, dearest, she is gone; and I
Must leave you, too. You must be quiet, now.

THE MOTHER

Yes, now I will be quiet.
[After a moment.]
Dear!

THE FATHER

[Turning at the door.]
Yes, dear?

THE MOTHER

See her, how cunningly she nestles down,
As naturally as if she had been used
To doing it for years. How old she looks! How wise!
[The Mother rubs her cheek softly against the baby's head, and then draws back her face to look at it. The Father comes and stands beside the bed, looking down on the child.]
How much do you suppose she really knows?

THE FATHER

If she has newly come from heaven, our home,
As Wordsworth says,[2] then she knows everything
We have forgotten, but shall know again,
When we go back to heaven with her.

THE MOTHER

Yes.
[She rubs her cheek on the baby's head again.]
Do you believe it?

1 The text used here is the Harper & Brothers edition.
2 Ode on The Intimations of Immortality, stanza V, lines 65–66.

THE FATHER

Why, of course I do.
Why, what a—

THE MOTHER

Nothing. Only, I was thinking
That earth was good enough for me, and wishing
That we might all go on forever here.

THE FATHER

[Laughing, and then anxiously.]
Well, I should not object. But now, my dear,
If you keep on this talking, I am afraid
You will excite yourself. The doctor said—

THE MOTHER

Why, I was never calmer in my life!
I seem all rolled and lapped in endless peace.
I feel as if there never could be pain,
Or trouble, or weakness, in the world again.
I am as strong! But, yes, I understand,
And, to please you, I will be quiet now.
[She sighs restfully. The Father stoops and kisses her and then the child.]
I wish that you could somehow make one kiss
Do for us both!

THE FATHER

Well, I should like to try,
Sometime, but now—

THE MOTHER

Yes, now I must be quiet.

[He turns toward the door.]

Go!
Dear!
[He turns again.]

THE FATHER

Yes, dearest!

THE MOTHER

But I shall not sleep.

THE FATHER

[Anxiously.]
You ought to sleep. The doctor said—

THE MOTHER

[Impatiently.]
The doctor!
I'd like to know what does the doctor know!
Does he expect I'll let him take from me

563

A moment of this bliss and give it up
To stupid sleep? Why, I want every instant,
To share it all with you, and keep it ours!
If I found I was drowsing, I should scream
And wake myself.

THE FATHER
                    Yes, dearest love, I know!
I understand just how you feel. I feel
Just so myself. But now, to keep it ours,
You must do nothing that will make you sick—

THE MOTHER
And die? Oh yes! But what if I should die?
I have had my baby! What if I should die?

THE FATHER
                    [Wringing his hands.]
Dearest, how can you?

THE MOTHER
                    Sometimes I thought I must.
But then I set my teeth, and would not die!
Nothing could make me die till I had seen her.
But now that I have seen her, I could die.
How do I know but life might take from love
Something that death would leave it!

THE FATHER
                    [Ruefully.]
                    But you said,
Only a moment since, that you were wishing
That we might all go on forever here.

THE MOTHER
Yes, there is that view of it. Do not be
Afraid! I shall not die. There, go away,
And I will try to sleep. Or no, sit down,
Here by the bed. I will not speak a word.
But it will be more quieting with you
Beside us, than if you were there, outside,
Where neither one of us could see you. She
Wants you as much as I.

THE FATHER
    [Doubtfully, drawing up a chair and then
    sinking into it.]
                    What an idea!

THE MOTHER
Can't you believe, that through each one of us
She sees and wishes for the other one?
Of course she does!

THE FATHER
                    Perhaps.

THE MOTHER
                    There's no perhaps.
She'll live her life outside of ours too soon;

And that is why I cannot bear to lose
An instant while she lives it still in ours.
I hate the thought of sleeping. I should like
To keep awake till she can talk and walk;
Then I could sleep forever.
    [She suddenly puts out the hand of the arm under
    the baby's head and clutches the father's hand.]
                    Where did she
Come from? I do not mean her body or its breath.
That came from us. But oh, her soul, her soul!
Where did that come from?
    [The Father is silent, and she pulls convulsively
    at his hand.]
                    Can't you answer me?

THE FATHER
                    [In distress.]
How can I tell you such a thing as that?
You know as well as I. Somewhere in space,
Somewhere in God, she was that which might be,
Amidst the unspeakable infinitude
Of those that dwell there in the mystery,
From everlasting unto everlasting.

THE MOTHER
                    [Without releasing her hold.]
                    Well?

THE FATHER
                    [With a groan.]
And then our love had somehow power upon her,
And blindly chose her, that she might become
A living soul, and know, feel, think like us.
It chose her, what she shall be to the end,
Or rather she was somehow chosen for it.

THE MOTHER
                    [Still clutching his hand.]
Out of that infinite beatitude,
Where there is nothing of the consciousness
That we call this and that, here, in the world?
That ignorantly suffers and that dies,
After the life-long fear of death, and goes
Helplessly into that unconsciousness
Again?

THE FATHER
                    She is under the same law as we.
But what the law is, or why it should be,
She knows no less or more than we ourselves.
Why do you make me say such things to you?

THE MOTHER
                    [Dreamily.]
You say our love compelled her to come here.
But, where our baby was, she was so safe!
And if there was no care for her in space,
Or any love, as here sometimes there seems
No care or love for us, where we are left
So to ourselves, our baby never knew it.

THE FATHER
[*In anguish.*]

You want to break my heart.

THE MOTHER

My own is broken.

THE FATHER

And are you sorry she has come to us?
You are not glad to have our baby here?
You would rather it had been some other life
Summoned to fill up other lives than ours?
You do not care, then, for our little one?

THE MOTHER
[*Solemnly.*]

So much that you cannot imagine it.
I was her life; and now she is my life,
My very life, so that if hers went out
Mine would go out with it in the same breath!
That's how I care.

THE FATHER
[*Beseechingly.*]
Oh, try for her sake, then,
If not for yours or mine, to keep from thinking
These dreadful thoughts!

THE MOTHER
It is not I who think.
It thinks itself. Perhaps the baby thinks it.

THE FATHER

I don't know what to say to you, my dear!
You are right to think; but if some other time—

THE MOTHER

When other children come? No, no! Now! now!
Another time would be no miracle,
And I must try to find the meaning out,
While this is still a miracle to me,
As much as morning or the springtime is.
You, if you wish, can drug your thoughts, and sleep;
But my thoughts are so precious that if I
Should lose the least of them— What time is it?
[*She follows him keenly, as he takes out his watch.*]

THE FATHER
[*With a sigh.*]
Daylight, almost. Hark! You can hear the cocks.

THE MOTHER
[*Smiling.*]
How sweet it is to hear them crowing so!
It is our own dear earth that seems to speak
In the familiar sound. If it were summer,
The birds would be beginning to sing, now.
I'm glad it is not summer. Is it snowing
As hard as ever? Look!

THE FATHER
[*Going to the window and peering out.*]
No, it is clear,
And the full moon is shining.

THE MOTHER
[*Lifting her head a little.*]
Let me see!
[*With a long sigh, as he draws the curtain.*]
Yes, it is the moon. The same old moon
We used to walk beneath when we were lovers.
Do you suppose that it was really we?
[*She lets her head drop.*]

THE FATHER

If this is we.

THE MOTHER
It seems a year, almost,
Since yesterday—for now this is to-morrow.
Does the time seem as long to you, I wonder?

THE FATHER
[*Coming back to her.*]
Longer. I had to see you suffer and not help you.

THE MOTHER
[*Taking his hand again.*]
I did not mind it; I was glad to suffer.
You must not mind it either.
[*After a moment.*]
If she could live
Forever on the earth, and we live with her,
I should not mind our having brought her here.
The life of earth, it seems so beautiful,
Far more than anything imaginable
Of any life elsewhere. They cannot hear
Anything like the crowing of the cocks
In heaven—so drowsy and so drowsing! Hark,
How thin and low and faint it is! Oh, sweet,
Sweeter than voices of antiphonal angels,
Answering one another in the skies,
They keep on calling in the dim, warm barns,
With the kind cattle underneath their roosts,
Munching the hay, and sighing, rich and soft.
I used to hear it when I was a child,
And the milk hoarsely drumming in the pails.
I hope that she will live to love these things,
Dear simple things of our dear simple earth.
Do not you, dearest?

THE FATHER
Yes, indeed I do.
And now if only you could get some sleep—

THE MOTHER

Well, I will try. I will be quiet now.
How quietly she sleeps! She wants to set
A good example to her wicked mother.
Mother! Just think of it!

THE FATHER

And father! Think
Of that!

THE MOTHER

Yes, I have thought of that too, dear.
Put your lips down and kiss her little head.
[As The Father bends over her.]
There, now, with your face between hers and mine,
You can be kissing both.
[As he lifts himself.]
I was just thinking,
What if, instead of our blind, ignorant love,
Choosing her out of the infinitude
Of those unconsciousnesses, as we call them—
She, in the wisdom she had right from God,
Had chosen us, in spite of knowing us
Better than we can ever know ourselves,
In all our wickedness and foolishness,
To be her father and her mother here,
Because she understood the good that she
Could do us, and be safe from harm of us:
Would you like that?

THE FATHER

Far better than to think
She came because we ignorantly willed.

THE MOTHER

Well, now, perhaps, that is the way it was.
Only—

THE FATHER

What, dearest?

THE MOTHER

Oh, I do not know
If I can make you understand. Men cannot.
But if she came from Him, and if He knew
That was her errand, why did He make no sign,
Or send some of His angels down to say?

THE FATHER

Perhaps she was herself His angel.

THE MOTHER

Now,
You have said it! I hoped you would say that.
It always seemed so commonplace, before,
But now, the rarest, the most precious truth.
It was not only wishing first to see her,
And willing not to die till I had seen her,
That helped me live through all that agony.
But in the very midst and worst of it
There was a kind of—I can never express it!—
Waiting and expectation of a message!
What will the message be?

THE FATHER

Something, perhaps,
That never can be put in words, on earth,
But that we still shall feel the meaning of.
And at the last shall come to understand
As we have always felt it.

THE MOTHER

[After a moment.]
There was something—
I wish that I could tell you—through it all,
Confusion, or transfusion, I do not know,
As if the child was I, and I was it,
And I myself was being born— You'll think
That I am crazy!

THE FATHER

No, indeed! Go on!

THE MOTHER

Oh, there is nothing more. I felt as if
It was I coming into another world,
Where I had never been before. And this,
This is the other world!

THE FATHER

I do not understand.

THE MOTHER

[Sadly.]
I was afraid of that. And I shall hurt you
If I explain.

THE FATHER

No, no! You will not hurt me,
Or, if you do, it will be for my good.

THE MOTHER

[After a moment.]
An hour ago, one little hour ago,
If it has been even an hour ago,
You were the whole of love, and now you are
The least and last of it, and lost in it.
It is as if you went out of that world,
With that old self of mine, when this new self
Came with our baby here. There, now, I knew it!
I knew that I should hurt you, darling!

THE FATHER

No.
I am not hurt, and I can understand.
I would not have it different. I should hate
Myself if I could make you care for me
In that old way. It did seem beautiful,
And pure, and holy, and it seemed unselfish.
But this—this!
[He bends over the mother and child, and
gathers them both into his arms.]

THE MOTHER

[*Putting her hand on his head, and
gently smoothing it.*]
There, you'll wake the baby, dearest.
How strange it seems, my saying that already!
But now I am so sleepy, and the doctor
Said that I ought to sleep. You will not mind
If baby and I drive you out of the room?
I must be quiet now. You are not wounded?

[*She stretches her hand toward him as he
rises and turns toward the door.*]

THE FATHER

[*Catching her hand to his mouth.*]
No, no. I am glad you are sleepy. Sleep is the best
thing.
The doctor said so—

THE MOTHER

[*Drowsily.*]
Then I will go to sleep.
Father, good-night!

THE FATHER

[*Joyously.*]
No, no; good-morning, mother!

II

THE FATHER AND THE MOTHER

*The best room of a village house, after the bride and
groom have gone, and the wedding guests have left the
father and the mother of the bride alone. They are a
pair in later middle life, with hair beginning to be gray.
The Father stands at the window staring out. The
Mother goes restively about noting this thing and that.*

THE MOTHER

I thought we never should be rid of them!
The laughing, and the screaming, and the chatter,
I thought, would drive me wild. Now they are gone,
And I can breathe a little while before
I begin putting things in place again.
But what confusion! I should think a whirlwind
Had swept the whole house through, up stairs and down.
It seemed as if those people had no mercy.
And she, before that wall of roses there,
Standing through all so patient and so gentle,
And smiling so on every one that came
To shake hands with her, or to kiss her—white
As the white dress she wore! Ah, no one knew,
As I knew, what it cost her to keep up.
I knew her heart was aching for the home
That she was leaving, so that when it came
To the good-bye, I almost felt it break
Against my own. Dearest, you do believe

He will be good to her? You do believe—
What are you looking at out of the window?

THE FATHER

[*Without turning.*]
At the old slippers they threw after her.
The rice lies in the road as thick as snow.

THE MOTHER

Those silly customs, how I hate them all!
But if they help to keep our thoughts away—
You do see something else!

THE FATHER

No, nothing else.
I was just wondering if I might not hear
The whistle of their train.

THE MOTHER

And you have heard it?

THE FATHER

Not yet.

THE MOTHER

Then come and sit down here by me,
And tell me how it was when we were married.

[*He comes slowly from the window and
stands before her.*]
Do you suppose I looked as pale as she did?
I know I did not! I was sure of you
For life and death. Why do you not sit down?

[*He sinks absently beside her on the sofa.
She pulls his arm round her waist.*]
There, now, I do not feel so much afraid!

THE FATHER

Afraid of what?

THE MOTHER

How can I tell you what?
Afraid for her of all that I was then
So radiantly glad of for myself.
Do you believe we really were so happy?
I was one craze of hope and trust in you,
But was that happiness? Do you believe
He will be good to her as you have been
To me?

THE FATHER

Oh yes.

THE MOTHER

Why do you answer so,
Sighing like that?

THE FATHER

Because men are not good,
As women are.

THE MOTHER

Yes, I kept thinking that
Through the whole service, when the promises
He made seemed broken in the very making.
How little we know about him! A few months
Since she first saw him, and we give her to him
As trustfully as if we had known him always.

THE FATHER

And we ourselves, *we* had not known each other
Longer than they when we were married.

THE MOTHER

Oh,
But that was different!

THE FATHER

No, it was the same
And it was like most of the marriages
That have been and that shall be to the end.
They liked the charm of strangeness in each other.

THE MOTHER

But men and women are quite strange enough,
Merely as men and women, to each other,
When they have lived their whole lives long together.
And we ourselves, we took too many chances.
I did not think you ever would be harsh,
And when you spoke the first harsh word to me—
I believe, if he is ever unkind to her,
That I shall know it, wherever it may be.
She will come to me somehow in her grief,
And let me comfort her poor ghost with mine,
For it would kill us both. Do you suppose—
Do you believe he ever will be harsh
With her?

THE FATHER

I almost think you ask me that
Just to torment me.

THE MOTHER

There, that is so like you!
You cannot talk of her as if she were
A woman after all. But, I can tell you,
She in her turn can bear all I have borne;
And though she seems so frail and sensitive,
She is not one to break at a mere touch.
But men are that way, I have noticed it;
They think their wives can endure everything,
Their daughters nothing. You are not listening!

THE FATHER

Yes, I am listening. What is it you mean?

THE MOTHER

You are tenderer of your children than your wives
Because you love what is yourselves in them,

And you must love somebody else in us.
Cannot you give me a moment's sympathy
Now when I have nobody left but you?
What are you thinking of, I'd like to know?

THE FATHER

[*Going back to the window, and kneeling
on the window-seat, with his forehead
against the pane.*]
The night when she was born.

THE MOTHER

I knew it! I
Was thinking of it too, and how it seemed
As if she had somehow chosen us to be
Her father and her mother.

THE FATHER

Why not him,
Then, for her husband, by a mystery
As sacred?

THE MOTHER

Oh, why do you ask? Because
There is no other world, now, as there was
Then, where the mystery could shape itself—
No hitherto, as there is no hereafter.
We have destroyed it for ourselves and her,
And love for all of us is as much a thing
Of earth as death itself.

THE FATHER

I never said
That world did not exist.

THE MOTHER

Oh no; you only
Said that you did not know, and I have only
Bettered your ignorance a little and said
I knew. Women must have some faith or other
Even if they make a faith of disbelief;
They cannot halt half-way in yes and no;
And she is more like me than you in that,
Though she is like you in so many things.
That shattered fantasy—or, what you please—
Cannot be mended now and used again;
And howsoever she has chosen him—
Or, if you like, he has been chosen for her—
The choice is made between his love and ours.
The home she seemed to bring, then, when she came,
Now she is gone, it lies here in the dust.
Oh, I can pick the house up, after while,
But never pick the home up, while I live!
Well, let it be! I suppose you will call it
Nature, and preach that cold philosophy
Of yours: that every home is founded on
The ruin of some other home and shall be
The ruin out of which still other homes
Shall grow in turn, and so on to the end.

I find no comfort in it, and my heart
Aches for the child that is not less my child
Because she is her husband's wife. Oh yes,
If we were two fond optimistic fools,
I dare say we should sit here in this horror,
And hold each other's hands and smile to think
Of what a brilliant wedding it had been;
How everybody said how well she looked,
And how he was so handsome and so manly;
And try to follow them in imagination
To their new house, and settle them in it;
And say how soon we should be hearing from her,
And then how soon they would come back to us
Next summer. But we have not been that kind.
We have always said the things we really thought,
And not shrunk from the facts; and now I face them,
And say this wedding— Hark! Was that their train?

THE FATHER

It is the freight mounting the grade. Their train
Is overdue, but it will soon be there.

THE MOTHER

If it would never come or never go!
If all the worlds that whir around the sun
Could stop, and none of them go on again!
Once I had courage for us both, and now
You ought to have it. Oh, say something, do,
To help me bear it!

THE FATHER
What is it I should say?

THE MOTHER

That it has been all my own doing! Say
That I would have it, and am like the mothers,
The stupid mothers, still uncivilized,
That wish their daughters married for the sake
Of being married: that would help me bear it.
If you blamed me then I could blame you too,
And say you wished it quite as much as I.

THE FATHER

We neither of us wished it, and I think
We have always blamed each other needlessly.

THE MOTHER

Yes, and I cannot bear it as I used
When she was with us. Now that she is gone
And you are all in all to me again,
Dearest, you must be very good to me.
Did you hear something?

THE FATHER
[Going to the window.]
Yes, I thought I heard
The coming of their train; but it was nothing.

THE MOTHER
[Unheedingly.]
The worst of all was having to part so—
Hurried and fluttered—up there in her room,
Where she had been so long our little child,
And with that hubbub going on down here,
Not realize that we were parting. Oh,
If we could only have had a little time
And quiet for it! Hark! What noise was that?

THE FATHER

What noise?

THE MOTHER

Something that sounded like a voice!
Her voice! I know it must have been her voice!
[She rushes to the window and stares out.]
I always knew within my heart that she
Would call for me, if any unhappiness
Greater than she could bear should come to her.

THE FATHER

But what unhappiness—

THE MOTHER

A tone, a look!

THE FATHER

With our arms round her yet? He could not. That
Would be against nature.

THE MOTHER

Nature! How you men
Are always talking about Nature! Little
You understand her! Nature flatters men.
She gives men mastery and health and life,
And women subjection, weakness, pain, and death.
We know what Nature is, and you know nothing.
She takes our youth and wastes it upon you,
She steals our beauty for you, and she uses
Our love itself to enslave us to you. Nature!

THE FATHER

Has it been really so with you and me?

THE MOTHER

How do I know? You may have been unlike
Other men.

THE FATHER

No, but quite like other men;
Not better. Shall she take her chance with him?
Speak out now from the worst you know of me,
And say if you would have her back again.

THE MOTHER

It keeps on calling! Can it be her voice?

THE FATHER

Then say it is her voice. What will you answer?
Shall she come home and be our child again?

THE MOTHER

You put it all on me!

THE FATHER

Then if I take
The burden all upon myself, and choose—

THE MOTHER

What?

THE FATHER

That her longing for us should have power
To bring her back?

THE MOTHER

To say good-bye again?

THE FATHER

To stay and never say good-bye again,
To leave her husband and to cleave to us.

THE MOTHER

I cannot let you choose! For oh! it seems
That it would really happen if you chose.
Wait, wait a minute, while I try to think
How would it be if she came back again,
And crept once more into this empty shell
Of life that has been lived! What is there here
But two old hearts that hardly have enough
Of love left for each other? And she needs
The whole of such love as I found in you
When I had given you all the love I had.
No, she must go with him as I with you.
Because she has been all in all to us
So long, and yet for such a little time,
We have come to think that she must be unlike
Others, and she must be above their fate.
But that is foolish. She must take her chance,
As I took mine, and as we women have
Taken our chance from the beginning. There!
I give her up for the first time and last!
Tell her— I talk as if you were with her
There, and not here with me!

THE FATHER

And I—I feel
As if we both were there with her and with
Each other here.

THE MOTHER

And so we shall be always;
And most with her when most we are alone.
See, they have mounted to their train together!
She stands a moment at the door and waves

The hand that is not held in his toward us—
And they are gone into their unknown world
To find our own past in their future there!

III

THE FATHER

In the parlor of a village house, with open doors and windows. The Father and The Mother, an elderly man and woman, sitting alone among chairs in broken rows. There is a piano with lifted lid; dust is tracked about the floor.

THE FATHER

Now it is over.

THE MOTHER

It is over, now,
And we shall never see her any more.

THE FATHER

Have you put everything of hers away?
If I found anything that she had worn,
Or that belonged to her, I think the sight
Would kill me.

THE MOTHER

Oh, you need not be afraid;
I have put everything away.

THE FATHER

Oh, me!
How shall we do without her! It is as if
One of my arms had been lopt off, and I
Must go through life a multilated man.
This morning when I woke there was an instant,
A little instant, when she seemed alive,
Before the clouds closed over me again,
And death filled all the world. Then came that stress,
That horrible impatience to be done
With what had been our child. As if to hide
The cold white witness of her absence were
To have her back once more!

THE MOTHER

I felt that, too.
I thought I could not rest till it was done;
And now I cannot rest, and we shall rest
Never again as long as we shall live.
Our grief will drug us, yes, and we shall sleep,
As we have slept already; but not rest.

THE FATHER

We must, I cannot help believing it,
See her again some time and somewhere else.

THE MOTHER

Oh, never any time or anywhere!

THE FATHER

You used to think we should.

THE MOTHER

I know I did.
But that is gone forever, that fond lie
With which we used to fool our happiness,
When we had no need of it. When we had
Each other safe we could not even imagine
Not having one another always.

THE FATHER

Yes,
It was a lie, a cruel, mocking lie!

THE MOTHER

Why did you ask me, then? Do you suppose
That if the love we used to make believe
Would reunite us, really had the power,
It would not, here and now, be doing it,
Now, when we need her more than we shall need her
Ever in all eternity, and she—
If she is still alive, which I deny—
Is aching for us both as we for her?
You know how lost and heartsick she must be,
Wherever she is, if she is anywhere;
And if her longing, and if ours could bring us
Together, as we used to dream it could,
How soon she would be here!

THE FATHER

I cannot bear it!

THE MOTHER

I shall not care, when we are very old,
Years hence, and we shall have begun to be
Forgetful, as old people are, about her,
And all her looks and ways—I shall not care
To see her then: I want to see her now,
Now while I still remember everything,
And she remembers, and has all her faults
Just as we have our own, to be forgiven.
But if we have to wait till she is grown
Some frigid, faultless angel, in some world
Where she has other ties, I shall not care
To see her; I should be afraid of her.

THE FATHER

She would not then be she, nor we be we.

THE MOTHER

I want to tell her how I grieve for all
I ever did or said that was unkind
Since she was born. But if we met above,
In that impossible heaven, she would not care.

THE FATHER

If she knows anything she knows that now
Without your telling.

THE MOTHER

I want her to say
She knows it.

THE FATHER

Yet, somehow she seems alive!
The whole way home she seemed to be returning
Between us as she used, when we came home
From walking, and she was a child.

THE MOTHER

Oh that
Was nothing but the habit of her; just
As if you really had lost an arm
You would have felt it there.

THE FATHER

Oh yes, I know.
[He lets his head hang in silence; then he looks
up at the window opening on the porch.]
This honeysuckle's sweetness sickens me.
[He rises and shuts the window.]
I never shall smell that sweetness while I live
And not die back into this day of death.
[He remains at the window staring out.]
How still it is outside! The timothy
Stands like a solid wall beside the swath
The men have cut. The clover heads hang heavy
And motionless.

THE MOTHER

I wish that it would rain,
And lay the dust. The house is full of dust
From the road yonder. They have tracked it in
Through all the rooms, and I shall have enough
To do, getting it out again.

THE FATHER

The sun
Pours down its heat as if it were raining fire.
But she that used to suffer so with cold,
She cannot feel it. Did you see that woman,
That horrible old woman, chewing dill
All through the services?

THE MOTHER

Oh, yes, I saw her,
You know her: Mrs. Joyce, that always comes
To funerals.

THE FATHER

I remember. She should be
Prevented, somehow.

THE MOTHER

Why, she did no harm.

THE FATHER

I could not bear to have them stand and stare
So long at the dead face. I hate that custom.

THE MOTHER

I wonder that you cared. It was not *her* face,
Nor the form hers; only a waxen image
Of what she had been. Nothing now is she!
There is no place in the whole universe
For her whose going takes all from the earth
That ever made it home.

THE FATHER

                    Yes, she is gone,
And it is worse than if she had never been—
Hark!

THE MOTHER

          How you startle me! You are so nervous!

THE FATHER

I thought I heard a kind of shuddering noise!

THE MOTHER

It was a shutter shaking in the wind.

THE FATHER

There is no wind.

THE MOTHER

                    [*After a moment.*]
          Go and see what it was.
It seemed like something in the room where she—

THE FATHER

It sounded like the beating of birds' wings.
There! It has stopped.

THE MOTHER

                    I must know what it was.
If you will not go, I will. I shall die
Unless you go at once.

THE FATHER

                    Oh, I will go.
[*He goes out and mounts the stairs, which
creak under his tread. His feet are heard on
the floor above. After a moment comes the
sound of opening and closing shutters.*]

THE MOTHER

                              [*Calling up.*]
What is it? Quick!

THE FATHER

                    [*Calling down.*]
          It was some kind of bird
Between the shutters and the sash.
[*He descends the stairs slowly, and comes
into the room where The Mother sits waiting.*]

                              I cannot
Imagine how it got there.

THE MOTHER

                    What bird was it?

THE FATHER

Some kind I did not know. I wish that I
Had let it in.

THE MOTHER

          What do you mean by that?
Everything living tries to leave the house;
We stay because we are part of death,
And cannot go.

THE FATHER

          It did not wish to go;
It was not trying to get out, but in.
I put it out once and it came again;
And now I wish that I had let it stay.

THE MOTHER

You are so superstitious; and you think . . .
          [*She stops, and they both sit silent for a time.*]

THE FATHER

It may be our despair that keeps her from us.

THE MOTHER

You think, then, that our hope could bring her to us?

THE FATHER

Not that, no.

THE MOTHER

          Or, that we could make her live
Again by willing it sufficiently?

THE FATHER

                    Oh no,
Not by our willing; by our loving, yes!
Not through our will, which is a part of us
And filled full of ourselves, but through our love,
Which is a part of some life else, and filled
With something not ourselves, but better, purer.

THE MOTHER

Well, try.

THE FATHER

I cannot. Your doubt palsies me.

THE MOTHER

I cannot help it. If she cannot come
Back to my doubt she cannot to my faith. . . .
Oh! What was that?

THE FATHER
The wind among the chords
Of the piano. They have left it open
After the singing.

THE MOTHER
But there is no wind!
You said yourself, just now, there was no wind!

THE FATHER
Perhaps it was our voices jarred the strings.

THE MOTHER
They could not do it; and it was not like
Anything that I ever heard before.
It was like something heard within my brain.
And there is something that I see within!
Hark! Look! Do you hear nothing? Do you see
Nothing? Or am I going wild?

THE FATHER
No, no!
I hear and see it too. Are you afraid?

THE MOTHER
No, not the least. But, oh, how strange it is!
What is it like—to you?

THE FATHER
I dare not say
For fear that it should not be anything.

THE MOTHER
Do you believe that we are dreaming it?
That we are sleeping and are dreaming it?

THE FATHER
He could not be so cruel!

THE MOTHER
He made death.

THE FATHER
There! You have hurt it, and it will not speak;
You have offended it. Speak to it!

THE MOTHER
Child,
I did not mean to grieve you. Oh, forgive
Your poor wild mother! Is she here yet, dearest?

THE FATHER
Yes, she is here! Yes, I am sure of it—

THE MOTHER
I seemed to have lost her— No, she is here again!
How natural she is! How strong and bright,
And all that sick look gone! It must be true
That it is she, but how shall we be sure

After it passes? Where is it you see her?
Where is it that you hear her speak?

THE FATHER
Within!
Within my brain, my heart, my life, my love!

THE MOTHER
Yes, that is where I see and hear her too.
And oh, I feel her! This is her dear hand
In mine! How warm and soft it is once more,
After that sickness! Yes, we have her back,
Dearest, we have our child again! But still
How strange it is that she is all within,
And nowhere outside of our minds. Can you
Make her nowhere but in yourself?

THE FATHER
In you—

THE MOTHER
And I in you! I see her in your mind;
I hear her speaking in your mind! That shows
How wholly we are one. Our love has done it,
And we must never quarrel any more.
It was your faith; I will say that for you!
But are your sure we are not dreaming it?

THE FATHER
How could we both be dreaming the same thing?

THE MOTHER
We could if we are both so wholly one.

THE FATHER
We must not doubt, or it will cease to be.
See! It is growing faint!

THE MOTHER
Oh no, my child!
I do believe that it is really you.
And, father, you must not keep saying *It*,
As if she were not living. Now she smiles,
And now she is speaking! Can you understand
What she is saying?

THE FATHER
It is not in words,
And yet I understand.

THE MOTHER
And so do I.
I wish that you could put it into words
So that we might remember it hereafter.

THE FATHER
But what she says cannot be put in words.
It is enough that we can understand
Better than if it were in words.

THE MOTHER

No, no!

Unless it is in words, I am not sure.
Unless she calls you Father and me Mother—
Hush! Did you hear her speak?

THE FATHER

I thought I heard her.

THE MOTHER

I am sure I heard her call us both, and now
I know it is not an hallucination.
Oh, I believe, and I am satisfied!
But, child, I wish that you could tell me something
About it—where you are! Is it like this?
In everything that I have read about it,
It seemed so vague—

THE FATHER

She answers hesitating,
As we used, when she was a little thing,
To answer her in something that we thought
She would be none the happier for knowing.
We are as children with her now, and she
As father and mother to us, and we must not
Question her.

THE MOTHER

Yes, I must; I will, I will!

THE FATHER

There, she is gone! No, she is here again!

THE MOTHER

No, we are somewhere else. What place is this?
Is this where she was? Did she bring us here?
It seems as if we now were merged in her
As she was merged in us before we came,
But all our wills are one. Oh, mystery!
I am so lost in this strange unity;
Help me to find myself, if you are here!
You are here, are not you?

THE FATHER

Yes, I am here,
But not as I was there. I seem a part
Of all that was and is and shall be. This is life
And that was only living yonder! I can find you,
I can find her, but not myself in it,
Or only as a drop of water may
Find itself in the indiscriminate sea.

THE MOTHER

I cannot bear it! I was not prepared!
Oh, save me, dearest! Save me, oh, my child!
Speak to me, father, in the words we knew,
And not in these intolerable rays
That leave the thought no refuge from itself.

I have not yet the strength to yield my own
Up to this universal happiness.
I still must dwell apart in my own life,
A prison if it need be, or a pang.
Come back with me, both of you, for a while. . . .

[She starts, and stares about her.]

Why, I am here again, and you are here!
This is our house, with dust in it, and death!
This is our dear, dear earthly home! But where
Is she? Call! Tell her we are here again!

THE FATHER

We could not make her come. I am bewildered;
I scarcely know if I am here myself.

[A moment passes in silence.]

THE MOTHER

Perhaps she never came at all, and we
Have only dreamed that we were somewhere else.
I feel as if I had awakened from sleep.
How long were we away?

THE FATHER

I cannot tell:
As long as life, or only for an instant.

THE MOTHER

It could not have been long, for there I see
The humming-bird poised at the honeysuckle
Still, that I noticed when we seemed to go.
Nothing has really happened; yet, somehow. . . .
I wonder what it was she said to us
That satisfied us so! Can you remember?

THE FATHER

Not in words, no. It did not seem in words,
And if we tried to put it into words—

THE MOTHER

They would be such as mediums use to cheat
Their dupes with, or to make them cheat themselves.
No, no! We ought not to be satisfied.
It is a trick our crazy nerves have played us.
The self-same trick has cheated both, or we
Have hypnotized each other. It is the same
As such things always have been from the first:
Our sorrow has made fools of us; we have seen
A phantom that our longing conjured up;
And heard a voice that had no sound; and thought
A meaning into mocking emptiness!

THE FATHER

Then, how could it have satisfied us so?

THE MOTHER

That was a part of the hallucination.
Nothing has happened, nothing has been proved!

THE FATHER

Not to our reason, no, but to our love
Everything.

THE MOTHER

Then, let her come back again!

THE FATHER

Twice would prove nothing more if once proved
    nothing.
We have had our glimpse of something beyond earth:
As every one who sorrows somehow has.
The world is not so hollow as it was.
There still is meaning in the universe;
But if it ever is as waste and senseless
As only now it seemed, and the time comes
When we shall need her as we needed her,
Then we shall be with her, or she with us,
Whether the time is somewhere else or here.
Come, mother—mother for eternity!—
Come, let us go, each of us, to our work.

I have been to blame for breaking you with grief
Which I should have supported you against.
Forgive me for it!

THE MOTHER

Oh, what are you saying?
There is no blame and no forgiveness for it
Between us two, nothing but only love.

THE FATHER

The love in which she lives.

THE MOTHER

I will believe it
If you believe it.

THE FATHER

Help me to believe!

THE END

Her Opinion of His Story

[1907]

Young love, the theme of *Her Opinion of His Story*, is a favorite topic for Howells, who uses it to show the sometimes wavering but nevertheless effective mastery of women over men. But in this play the girl as well as the man shows a charming ineptness in striving with the opposite sex. A more worldly heroine would have made a more suffering hero. But Howells simply had the lovers disturb each other emotionally, both becoming perplexed by their awkward reactions to an expected situation. And there Howells should have left his scene, but he kept on writing. With its obvious defects as a drama, the play can perhaps be best appreciated as a slight sketch which is talky, slow, and inconclusive, although not unexciting—as youthful courtship is in real life.

More interesting than the hoax which Holyford is trying to play on Lettice is the fun Howells has with the means of the hoax—the novel. Through the sometimes stupid, sometimes intelligent concern of Lettice and Holyford for the plot they are making, Howells alternately pokes fun at the old domestic sentimental romance and slyly applauds the distinction which realism brings to the novel. The plot is, actually, rather simple—so simple, in fact, that if the boy and girl in the story face the situation truthfully, they will get married and the story will be over; as Holyford says, "I can't have my story stop in the second chapter. . . ." Hence, romance steps in and the usual gamut of romantic experiences is paraded: adventure, shipwreck, hidden treasure, loss of money, broken health, and so on. But Howells makes it very clear that the romantic is not enough; Lettice constantly questions what a "real girl" would do. How Howells must have enjoyed the two suggested endings—death or marriage—which let the reader solve the problem for himself! And Holyford's inability to have the hero and heroine fully understand each other without saying anything must also have given Howells pleasure. At any rate, the manuscript novel serves as a clever gambit by which Holyford may introduce his suit, as well as an interesting object of Howells' serious and satiric comment.

Her Opinion of His Story[1]

MISS TEMPLE: Why is he coming so early?

MISS LETTICE TEMPLE: Why, Aunt Catherine, do you call it early?

MISS TEMPLE: Why is he coming so early? Gentlemen don't usually call at ten o'clock in the forenoon.

LETTICE: Oh, certainly, if you look at it in that light. (*She goes about the veranda of the cottage, opening seaward over a stretch of informal lawn, and closed at either end with meshes of honeysuckle in bloom.*) I think these flowers are rather oppressive, don't you? (*She gives a series of superfluous touches to the summer furnishings of the place, especially the arrangement of the cushions in a deep armchair.*) I suppose he'll hate them, anyway, and tumble them all on to the floor! (*She retires a step or two, and considers the cushions. Then she puts a willow table at the side of the chair, and regards it with a thoughtful glance.*) Or would you put it in front?

MISS TEMPLE, *looking austerely up from the needle she is threading over a lapful of work overflowing from a basket, held in place by an adamantine rigidity of the knees, and an iron compression of the lips*: What in the world are you doing, Lettice? And why don't you answer my question?

She pulls the thread out its full length, and knots it without removing her thumb and finger.

LETTICE: Well, of course he wouldn't naturally come so early. But—I said he might.

MISS TEMPLE: You said he might?

LETTICE: He asked if he mightn't.

MISS TEMPLE: Then it's an appointment!

LETTICE: I don't know whether I should call it an appointment.

MISS TEMPLE: It has every appearance of it. What's the table for? Are you going to give him afternoon tea at this hour of the morning?

LETTICE, *with a touch of indignation*: Tea! Certainly not! It's for his manuscript. He said he should like to bring it.

MISS TEMPLE: Really, this is mystery upon mystery. I don't know what to make of you, Lettice. What are you up to?

LETTICE: I don't like being supposed to be "up" to anything, Aunt Catherine. It's a very simple matter. Why do you make a mystery of it?

MISS TEMPLE: I'm only too glad to make anything at all of it. If you like I will go away.

LETTICE: How can you say such a thing, Aunt Catherine? I wouldn't have you, for anything. And I don't believe *he* would, either. You must certainly stay and receive him, at least.

MISS TEMPLE: Very well! It's a beautiful morning.

LETTICE: So it is. I hadn't noticed. (*She approaches with a somewhat wistful air. Not being encouraged in her advances by her aunt, who is sewing with a certain degree of resentment, she sinks into the chair next her, and dangles the fringe of its knotted scarf through her fingers.*) I think that was such a pretty custom, tying scarfs through the backs of chairs. He's put the time back in that period, you know. He thinks the middle eighteen-seventies was the most charming period of any. He got to telling me about it, just before we began to break up last night, and I thought it was very interesting, and he asked me if he might tell me *all* about it some time, and of course I said yes, and he asked if he mightn't come this morning, and of course I couldn't refuse. Do you think it was so very odd?

MISS TEMPLE: I haven't the least idea what you are talking about, my dear. (*She lifts her eyes from her sewing, and glances at her niece's face, which droops.*) What is it, and why should he want to tell you all about it?

LETTICE: Of course it must sound ridiculous to you, Aunt Catherine; but he said he wanted my criticism. He said that I had a great deal of insight; I'm sure I don't know what he meant. I never knew that I was much of a judge of stories.

MISS TEMPLE: What has that got to do with it?

LETTICE: Why, that's the whole thing. He's been writing a story. Well, it isn't the first one he's written, but it's the first he has any real chance of getting accepted, as he calls it. The

1 The text used here is from *Harper's Bazaar*, May 1907, XLI, 429–37.

editor sent back something he had done, with just a printed notice that editors use for such things, but he wrote with a pen at the bottom of the notice, and said that he should be glad to see anything else that Mr. Holyford did. Mr. Holyford said this was going pretty far, for an editor, and so he was doing his best, and he doesn't want to offer it till he's got it quite perfect. He's read it to a friend of his, but he says he would like a woman's view of it, and—and—he wants to submit it to me.

MISS TEMPLE: Oh! I thought Mr. Holyford was a lawyer.

LETTICE: This is just in the intervals of practice, he says. He's only just out of the law school. He writes fiction when he has nothing else to do.

MISS TEMPLE: Oh, that is the way.

LETTICE: Yes, that is the way. He says that if a man makes a hit in literature, it's a great thing, and a good deal better than the law is at the beginning. He would rather be a literary man, anyway.

MISS TEMPLE: Does he go round telling everybody that? I shouldn't think it would be very good for his law practice.

LETTICE, *thoughtfully*: I don't suppose he tells *every*body. But he got to talking, last night, and he said he wanted me to believe that he didn't often talk so much about himself. He said he was quite ashamed; but it was so seldom you met a listener—one who could understand at the first word—that he was tempted to go on before he knew it. He has very little sympathy in his own family, I think. He says his father says he had better go fishing in the intervals of practice. Of course he laughed when he told me, but I could see that he felt it. He has a great deal of humor; though this isn't a humorous story. He did write poetry at one time, but he's dropped that. He thinks that if a man has really anything to say he can say it best in prose.

MISS TEMPLE: Is he going to read his story to you?

LETTICE: No, he says he won't do that. But he is going to bring it, and refer to it. He's got it all typewritten, so that if it interests me, he can let me have it to read myself. That's the reason I wanted to arrange the table, so that he can open it conveniently when he wants to refer to it. Don't you think that's a good idea?

MISS TEMPLE, *rising, and gathering her sewing into her basket*: Well, you won't want me here listening.

LETTICE: Do you think you ought to go, Aunt Catherine? Well! (*She gathers up some of the sewing which has dropped from the basket, and holds it provisionally in her hand. Then, as if struck by a sudden inspiration*) Aunt Catherine! I believe he would rather have you stay. He said himself that two heads were better than one.

MISS TEMPLE: Yes, but three are not. Give me that, Lettice.

She indicates with a gesture of her chin where Lettice shall put the piece of sewing.

LETTICE, *putting it behind her*: No, I won't do it, Aunt Catherine. It looks as if I had no confidence in you.

MISS TEMPLE: Why, goodness, child! You talk as if you wanted my opinion of the young man himself! Now I wish you to tell me how far this has gone. When I asked you here, and promised your mother that I would take good care of you, I didn't expect— You are too young, altogether.

LETTICE: I don't see why I should be so very young. I'm eighteen. But that has nothing to do with it. He wishes my opinion of his story, and that is all. If you are suspicious of me, Aunt Catherine, you had better stay, decidedly. I shall not know where to look, now, when he's talking.

MISS TEMPLE: You had better look at him, then. At any rate, I shall not stay to see where you look, if you think I'm suspicious of you.

She rises, and moves proudly toward the door.

LETTICE, *placing herself quickly before her*: No, Aunt Catherine. I didn't mean that.

MISS TEMPLE: You said it. Let me pass, please. (*Lettice does not move.*) Do you hear me, Lettice?

LETTICE: You must stay here to receive him with me. Oh!

At the sound of a step on the veranda stairs she utters a nervous whoop, and with a sudden dash round her aunt's figure she vanishes indoors, while Mr. Holyford, with a flat parcel, as of manuscript, under his arm, comes toward Miss Temple. He extends his hand tentatively, but realizing that one of Miss Temple's hands is preoccupied with her sewing-basket and the other with her skirt, he converts his proposed greeting into a graceful gesticulation.

HOLYFORD: How do you do, Miss Temple? I am afraid you don't remember me: Mr. Holyford. I was here at the Kelp Inn, last summer.

MISS TEMPLE: Oh, yes, Mr. Holyford. Won't you sit down. My niece was expecting you.

She sits down herself, and waves him to the chair prepared for him.

HOLYFORD: Thank you, but won't you take this chair yourself? It's more comfortable.

MISS TEMPLE: This is my chair. *(She keeps her seat decisively.)* It's low, and nicer for sewing. *(She takes the piece of work from the top of her basket, and unfolds it.)* Besides, Lettice got that ready for you, with the table to put your manuscript on.

HOLYFORD: She has told you of my audacious proposition? I only brought it along for reference. It isn't so bad as if I were going to read it to her. She's told you—

MISS TEMPLE: That you were going to ask her criticism of your story. She's very much flattered. It isn't often that authors submit their work to Lettice.

HOLYFORD: So much the worse for authors, if they have the chance. I feel very much flattered myself. I think Miss Lettice's intuitions are—are most valuable. I only hope she won't find me and my story too tiresome, or my story alone.

MISS TEMPLE, *non-committally:* She seemed anxious to hear it?

HOLYFORD: Did she? I'm awfully glad. I proposed it on the impulse of the moment, yesterday evening, and I spent the rest of the night composing appropriate names for myself. I think some of them would have pleased my father. He doesn't go in much for my fiction.

Holyford attempts a gratuitous hilarity, and rather fails of imparting gayety to his laugh. At least it does not infect Miss Temple, who has resumed her sewing seriously.

MISS TEMPLE: May I ask what kind of story it is?

HOLYFORD: Well— Are you much opposed to psychological novels?

MISS TEMPLE: Is it a question of *my* opinion?

HOLYFORD, *laughing with rather more enjoyment:* Well, yes, provisionally.

MISS TEMPLE: You mean till Lettice comes?

HOLYFORD: I should be glad to have it, even after she comes.

MISS TEMPLE, *looking over her shoulder toward the door:* I'm sure I don't know what's keeping her. Ah! There she comes.

HOLYFORD: Just as they do in plays! A character is no sooner mentioned than the person comes in; I've often noticed it. And the others always hear them coming, and say they're coming. *(He goes forward, and offers Lettice his hand.)* You see how punctual I am. But if you are sorry, you know you

can have a headache. Only, you ought to have had it behind the scenes, and sent word. Now it will be doubly difficult to get rid of me. But say the word!

LETTICE, *embarrassed:* You know Mr. Holyford, Aunt Catherine?

HOLYFORD: I've been introducing myself as hard as I can, and trying to make her believe she remembers my being at the Kelp Inn last summer. I don't know whether I told you I had put the scene at the Kelp Inn?

LETTICE: Have you? I always thought it was so picturesque.

HOLYFORD: And such a good name. Yes; there, and at a cottage in the neighborhood. It works in nicely, and marks that pseudo-æsthetic period perfectly—or the beginning of it. I've made a very careful study of the period: got in Eastlake furniture and the last of the hoop skirts. It's just the end of the Franco-Prussian war, and I've had my fellow out there fighting on the French side.[1] He's an ardent Republican.

LETTICE: Republican?

HOLYFORD: Yes. He's an American, and after the fall of Louis Napoleon, he stays on through the seige of Paris, and helps fight the Germans.

LETTICE: Oh! *That* kind of Republican. I thought you meant a Roosevelt man.

HOLYFORD: How delightfully actual you are, Miss Temple! It almost makes me sorry I hadn't laid the scene in the present time. But as it is, I suspect I've got my heroine too modern. It's she I want to tell you about more particularly. I've tried to keep her back in that period, by having her rather *petite.* You know the latter-day girl is so tall.

LETTICE: Oh!

HOLYFORD, *laughing, and bowing to her:* Well, not invariably. But that was the time before tall girls came in so much. I make up for it by having the hero rather tall—quite tall, in fact.

As they stand confronting each other, he overtops her by a head.

LETTICE: Hadn't we better sit down? You can throw the cushions out if you don't want them. But I thought you would like a table to put your manuscript on.

HOLYFORD: Oh, thank you. But I sha'n't allow myself to use it for fear I might get to reading my story.

1 All of these identifying features—Eastlake furniture, last of the hoop skirts, end of the Franco-Prussian war—fit primarily into the 1870's.

Where he has sat down, he holds the tied-up parcel on his knees, with his hands nervously outspread on it, as if to keep it down.

LETTICE, *demurely, from where she sits diagonally from him, with her face three-quarters averted*: I'm sure I should be very glad to hear it.

HOLYFORD, *impulsively*: Should you really? You tempt me almost beyond my strength. But as I was saying— I don't remember just what I was saying!

LETTICE: That it was after the Franco-Prussian war.

HOLYFORD: Oh, thank you. He comes back and throws himself heart and soul into Civil Service Reform. He's seen the rottenness of the Second Empire, and he wants to save us from the same fate. But that's a detail. The main thing is that he hasn't a cent, and that when he sees Dorrance— Do you like the name? Dorrance?

LETTICE: Yes, it's so quaint! Is it a girl's name?

HOLYFORD: I'm sure I don't know. If it isn't I can change it. I don't know where I got it exactly. I think your *own* name is charming, Miss Temple. I beg your pardon! I don't mean to be personal.

LETTICE: Not at all. I like it myself. It's better than Gladys.

HOLYFORD, *with scorn*: Oh, Gladys! I'm so glad *my* name is plain Paul. Though I have seen the time when I had my yearnings for Lionel.

LETTICE: Lionel would go very nicely with Holyford.

HOLYFORD: Yes, I don't deny it. And I'm rather well satisfied with my surname.

LETTICE: I believe it was my grandmother's.

HOLYFORD: What! Holyford? Then we're cousins! *May* I call you cousin?

LETTICE: No, Lettice! I don't mean that you may call me Lettice, but that I was called Lettice for my grandmother. Wasn't I, Aunt Ca— (*She looks round to where Miss Temple has been sitting.*) Why, she's gone!

HOLYFORD, *in dismay*: So she is! I'm sorry, I didn't realize that I was sitting with my back to her. I'm really very much ashamed—

LETTICE: Not at all. She'll be back in a moment. And then?

HOLYFORD: And when?

LETTICE: When he hasn't a cent.

HOLYFORD: Oh, yes! Well, Dorrance has plenty of money, in her own right. Her father is a millionaire— I hope you don't mind her being a millionaire's daughter?

LETTICE: Oh, not in the least. I should like to be rich myself.

HOLYFORD: Well, these are not at all vulgar millionaires; it was when millionaires were just coming in; and when the father accidentally finds out that Paul—I mean Lionel; Hugh, I mean—Hugh Lionel is his name; at any rate provisionally, for if it strikes you as too romantic—

LETTICE: I think it's fine.

HOLYFORD: I'm so glad. When he finds out that Hugh is in love with his daughter, and won't offer himself because she's rich and he's poor, he argues with him and tries to convince him that he's a fool. I think I've got a great scene, there. I think it's something quite new in fiction, don't you?

LETTICE: *I* never heard of anything like it.

HOLYFORD: No. And it has to be delicately handled. At the same time it has to be boldly treated, too. I think I've got over it pretty well. I've managed it humorously, or semi-humorously. The father is Western, and he has all that grotesque Western humor, and argues it out with him, man to man—takes the bull by the horns, you know.

LETTICE: How perfectly original!

HOLYFORD: Yes, isn't it new? I should really like to read that scene to you, Miss Temple, if—

LETTICE: Oh, do! I should like it of all things.

HOLYFORD: Well, if I *must*! (*He rises to lay open his manuscript on the table, and confronts Miss Temple, at the door. He starts guiltily back.*) Oh!

LETTICE, *jumping to her feet*: Oh!

MISS TEMPLE: Oh! I just came to see if I had dropped a spool of—

HOLYFORD, *looking eagerly about the veranda*: Thread? Let me find it for you.

LETTICE, *joining in the search*: Where do you think you dropped it, Aunt Catherine?

MISS TEMPLE, *vanishing indoors*: If I knew, I shouldn't be looking for it. But it doesn't the least matter. I can get another. (*Then from within*) I've found it. Here it is.

LETTICE AND HOLYFORD: Oh!

HOLYFORD: Ought I to have urged her to stay?

LETTICE: No, no. It would have just bored her. Go on!

HOLYFORD: And bore you?

LETTICE: How can you? You know I didn't mean that. Now you shall read me every word, so as to prove that you don't think I meant anything.

HOLYFORD: Couldn't I convince you with a chapter or two? I understand just what you meant, but I'd really rather tell you about the story than read it. The fact is, that until I've had your judgment on some points, I shouldn't like to read it to you.

LETTICE: I don't believe my literary judgment is worth anything.

HOLYFORD: I can't let you say that. Besides, the points are points of psychology.

LETTICE: Psychology? Isn't that rather formidable?

HOLYFORD: Well, say natural history. It's about what a girl would do in a given case.

LETTICE: I don't believe any living girl could tell you. But what case?

HOLYFORD: Well, it's rather difficult. Why are we standing up? I don't want to go, yet!

LETTICE: And I don't want you to. (*They both laugh and sit down.*) Well?

HOLYFORD: Well, it's something that comes up, after the father has had his talk with the hero. The hero gives the heroine a hint of his position, and then, as they know each other's feeling— I'm afraid you'll think it's rather a daring experiment!

LETTICE: Oh, I like those daring things.

HOLYFORD: Do you, indeed? Do you think I could venture to have him perfectly frank with her, and tell her that the consciousness of his being poor and her being rich forbids him to think of her love?

LETTICE: She wouldn't understand him, and so she couldn't argue the point. But it would be very interesting if she could. If she really cared for him, she couldn't think of herself at all. Not if she was a *real* girl.

HOLYFORD: I want her to be a real girl. (*He muses a moment, before yielding to an impulse.*) Miss Lettice, I don't believe you girls know how terrible you are to us poor fellows. I mean how much we're afraid of you. I don't believe any man would have the courage to offer himself to a girl unless—unless—

LETTICE: But if the hero hasn't offered himself, how can he expect her to refuse him?

HOLYFORD: I wasn't thinking of that. I was thinking of the matter in the abstract.

LETTICE: I don't believe a real girl can do anything in the abstract. She has got to have an actual case. Does Dorrance convince Hugh that her money doesn't matter?

HOLYFORD: How nice of you to remember their names! Why, you see if she convinces him then they get married, and the story stops.

LETTICE, *thoughtfully*: That is true.

HOLYFORD: I can't have my story stop in the second chapter, and so I had fancied having him tell her that until he can come back to her with as much money as she has he can never ask her to be his.

LETTICE, *fired with the idea*: That would be *grand!* And then I suppose you have him go off, and have a lot of adventures, trying to make the money. It would be splendid to have him shipwrecked, somewhere, and find a hidden treasure on the island.

HOLYFORD: Well, yes. But I am afraid that would seem too easy. I have him go into business, and try to make the money. Of course, it would be slow work in any case; he isn't a very good businessman, and he's a good many years about it. Once or twice he loses his money, and has to begin over again. It gives me plenty of room for my story, but I'm afraid people won't like her marrying somebody else in the meanwhile.

LETTICE: A real girl would never do that in the world!

HOLYFORD: Wouldn't she? I'm sorry. You see, she has to be doing something, while they are both getting along in the thirties; and the gray hairs are beginning to show themselves. I *had* thought of her going into some sort of university settlement work, but it's hard to make that attractive, and it doesn't involve as much suffering as I should like to have in. As the story now stands, I have her marry and then, when he has lost his money the second time, and is prostrated by the blow, she comes to him—

LETTICE: Oh, do you think she would?

HOLYFORD: Well, that's just the question. I was in hopes you would think she might. It's rather a pet scene with me when they meet and argue it over the second time.

LETTICE: Of course, not explicitly; but with a perfect understanding?

HOLYFORD: Not exactly, or not absolutely. What should you think of my having him die, and leave the problem for each reader to solve in his own way?

LETTICE: I don't believe I should like that. Why couldn't they get married?

HOLYFORD: They do, in one of the endings. I've written two. That's the great point I wanted to submit to you. Of course people like a good ending, but I can't help feeling that it would be more artistic, and more powerful, to have him die.

LETTICE: But wouldn't it be nicer to have her marry him, when they suppose he's going to die, and then nurse him back to life and health?

HOLYFORD: The critics might say it was taking an advantage of his helplessness.

LETTICE: Oh, you oughtn't to mind the critics.

HOLYFORD: I shouldn't if I were sure of *your* approval.

LETTICE: Then you don't consider me a critic!

HOLYFORD: The best in the world. But I want you to be awfully frank. Do you honestly think I could leave it as I've got it?

LETTICE: Perhaps it would do. But I don't know that I ever heard of a story with two endings before.

HOLYFORD: I don't mean that part. (*Laughing*) That would be rather a joke. (*Seriously*) It mightn't be such a bad notion, though. It would certainly be novel. No, of course it wouldn't do. What I meant was, do you think I could have her come, and when she sees that he won't have the courage to offer himself—

LETTICE: I don't believe any girl would do it.

HOLYFORD: But this is a widow.

LETTICE, *thoughtfully*: That is true. Perhaps that does make a difference. Perhaps a widow might.

HOLYFORD: And I've got a great scene out of it. I make it the climax. But after all, that isn't the point, the psychological point.

LETTICE: Isn't it? I don't see how anything could be more psychological.

HOLYFORD: Well, you see the case is this. They have to understand each other fully before he comes to her and tells her that he can't marry her till he's as rich as she is, and I want to arrange it so that they shall understand each other without saying anything.

LETTICE, *falteringly*: I don't believe I know what you mean.

HOLYFORD: Miss Lettice, do you believe that a girl ever thinks a man cares for her before he tells her in so many words?

LETTICE: I—I don't believe— That is, I don't think—a real girl does.

HOLYFORD: That's discouraging. I've got to manage it somehow. She must know that he is in love with her, and yet he must not tell her so, till he tells her that he can't offer himself because she is rich and he is poor. If he has offered himself, in

so many words, and asked her to be his wife, already, then he can't tell her that she's too rich for him, without seeming to want to get out of it for some other reason. Besides, if she doesn't know that he cares for her, and that she cares for him, she might say, "Nobody asked you, sir."

LETTICE: That is true.

HOLYFORD: You see the point, don't you? It has to be very delicately contrived, somehow.

LETTICE: Oh, yes.

HOLYFORD: It was what I hoped you could help me about. But if you say it couldn't happen, I must give it up and try something else. You don't believe it could happen in some cases?

LETTICE: Oh, I don't say it couldn't happen. I suppose—

HOLYFORD: Suppose what?

LETTICE: Nothing!

HOLYFORD: Oh, but do suppose something, Miss Lettice! Make the case your own.

LETTICE: But how could I? I'm not rich.

HOLYFORD: Oh, but there are other things—more precious than riches, more—more— Can't you imagine that you—that is—that some one—some one very much attached to you might want to find out— Or, no, that isn't the point, either. (*He has been leaning forward in her direction, and speaking very rapidly, and stopping abruptly, and then beginning again. Now he falls back in his chair with a long breath.*) I don't see how it can be done.

LETTICE: I shouldn't give it up if I were you. It's so original.

HOLYFORD, *laughing ruefully*: It's *too* original, I'm afraid. You can't have a thing happen that actually never happened in the world before.

LETTICE: Not very well. But lots of things happen in stories that never happened in the world, don't they?

HOLYFORD: You might say that. But this that I've planned seems rather indelicate. If he finds out that she likes him without asking her, won't she think it's selfish and sneaking of him? Wouldn't she despise him for it?

LETTICE: I don't know whether she would despise him, exactly.

She gives the question apparently thoughtful attention, looking down at the toe of her slipper.

HOLYFORD: It's essential to the story that he should know she likes him, and that she should know he knows; or else it's impossible for her to take that step at the end, which forms the only possible dénouement, unless we have them both die.

LETTICE, *faintly*: You oughtn't to have them die.

HOLYFORD: No, it's begging the question. And I don't see how I can have them marry. Of course, she can't approach the subject, and he wouldn't have the courage.

LETTICE: He might, if he thought he was dying. I've read stories where they did. I don't believe but what you can make it come out all right.

HOLYFORD, *hopefully*: Don't you, Miss Lettice? And you think that I—if he, that is—I mean if—No, no, I don't mean that. I don't know where I was!

LETTICE: Then, why not begin at the beginning, and—

HOLYFORD: Oh, there never was any beginning, and there never will be any ending! I believe it was ordained from everlasting to everlasting. Lettice! Don't you see that it's you,—I mean that it's I—I mean, don't you know that I care all the world for you?

He starts toward her, and she rises phantom-like to her feet.

LETTICE, *in a ghostly whisper*: Then—then, it was all a pretence! You didn't want my opinion—

HOLYFORD: I wanted you!

LETTICE: You wanted to play upon me, and find out what a girl would do—would say—would—Oh!

HOLYFORD: Yes, indeed! What would you say if I told you what I *have* told you, and what would you do? Don't tell me you never can care for me.

LETTICE, *with a nervous burst*: Oh, it's all horrid, horrid! You've mixed me up so that I don't know which is which, and I never can look myself in the face again! How could you? How could you?

She dashes by him, as he tries to intercept her, and escapes down the steps and over the lawn. Holyford stands clutching his head with both hands. Miss Temple appears in the doorway from the house.

MISS TEMPLE: What is the matter? Why is Lettice running away?

HOLYFORD: Oh, Miss Temple! I've made such a fool of myself. I've tried to tell Miss Lettice that I— I began to tell her about my story. I didn't mean—to tell her—or not to-day; but it turned into that, before I knew it. I was tempted on and on, and now she says I've mixed her up so that she doesn't know which is which, and I know she loathes us both!

MISS TEMPLE: Both?

HOLYFORD: Yes—my story and me!

MISS TEMPLE: You? What have *you* got to do with it?

HOLYFORD, *stopping before her in distractedly rushing to and fro on the veranda*: Everything! Don't you understand that Lettice is all the world to me? And that I've told her so?

MISS TEMPLE: Be still a moment! And what did she say?

HOLYFORD: She said—she said my story was horrid.

MISS TEMPLE: What has your story got to do with it? Did you offer her your story or yourself?

HOLYFORD: Oh, don't laugh at me, Miss Temple! What shall I do? What would *you* do, in my place?

MISS TEMPLE, *grimly and somewhat contemptuously*: Well, if she simply said my story was horrid, I think I should go after her and ask her what she meant.

HOLYFORD: *Would* you, Miss Temple? Oh, bless you, bless you! And you don't think—

MISS TEMPLE: How do I know? But it's the only way.

HOLYFORD, *plunging wildly down the steps, and over the lawn toward Lettice, where she is seen in half-length above the rocks*: Bless—

MISS TEMPLE, *going to the edge of the veranda, and watching, till Holyford comes up to Lettice*: Simpleton! (*Then she starts back and runs indoors.*) Oh! Oh!

Saved, An Emotional Drama

[1908]

Here is a melodrama to end all melodramas built around the traditional cry of the heroine as she swoons in the arms of her lover. Only in Howells' play *everyone* is saved—and not just at the climax of the play, but periodically, continually, and monotonously throughout, in a kind of arithmetic progression. *Being saved* becomes the only excuse for *being*, and the action of *Saved, An Emotional Drama* reads like a listing of the most effective situations in late-nineteenth-century American melodrama: Through the efforts of a child a burglar repents; a woman barely escapes the fate of Lady Isabelle in *East Lynne*; a good man is tempted to crime because another holds his note which he cannot pay; and a rich old man demands a frightful price before he will aid the good man. The characters, too, from the lovable child to the handsome seducer, are traditional melodramatic characters. And the theme is everywhere: Saved! Saved! Saved!

Although Howells' melodrama with its exaggeration and compression of action is a ridiculous play, it is something more than simply absurd. On one level the play is a general satire on all aspects of melodrama from the idea of being "saved" to the confusion of exaggerated situations, the incomprehensible people involved, and the melodramatic language used. It is also a satire on human conduct—the selfishness of people and the way a man becomes honest. For example, it is a serious condemnation of society that no one

in the play is able to recognize values in life; throughout there is a striking inability on the part of anyone to distinguish morality, honesty, or uprightness. Indirectly and through this obvious void in character make-up, the play becomes a commentary on truth and morality. When Fortesque bemoans his cold, unchauffeured state and his inability to flee with Geraldine, the Mama rejoices and compares the situation to her own escape; then, the Burglar firmly but gently states: "Well, it's a little different case, ma'am, with a single lady." At another point the bright surface of this play reflects an autumn thought of Howells expressed in *The Unexpected Guests*. When young Frederic announces that he is not going to tell a single lie all year, the Father intones: "Then you must retire from society, my friend." But the climax provokes the most thought. Whose word must the reader take for all of this "saving"? Why the word of the Burglar, whose Machiavellian progress toward becoming an "honest man" causes one to question the moral hypocrisy shown by the Child, who is a leading force in the play, and the moral stupidity of the others. Probably in no other way could Howells have commented more severely on mankind than by portraying the Little Child as he does. Actually the whole play is dramatically effective as a double satire: no one is saved, and it is only a trap that anyone thinks he is.

Saved, An Emotional Drama[1]

In the library of a stately house, at four o'clock on a New-Year's morning, stands the Burglar, with his dark-lantern in his hand. He has collected in a neat group on the library table, around the large silver inkstand, the silver paper-cutter, the silver seal, the massive silver candlesticks from the mantel, various small bronzes from their brackets, several exquisite small paintings, and some delicate ivory carvings. He looks at these objects with an air of satisfaction, and then, in a spirit of tireless enterprise, with the purpose of amassing greater value, he makes the light of his lantern play vividly about the room. It falls at last on the figure of the Little Child, who has so softly opened the door from the hallway as to have entered unheard. She is in her nightgown, and as the light strikes her the Burglar starts back, while she puts her hand to her eyes to shield them from the glare. She speaks in the high, piping voice of children on the stage; the Burglar rolls a husky bass from his bearded lips.

THE LITTLE CHILD: Oh, dear! What a funny light! There must be somebody here, and I thought I could just steal down, and get a book to look myself sleepy at the pictures with, and not disturb a soul. (*She sees the Burglar.*) Why, it's a man! A strange man! Who in the world can it be? (*To the Burglar with attempted severity*) What are you doing here in my papa's library at this hour of the night?

THE BURGLAR, *embarrassed*: Well, you see, miss, that ain't so easy to say. I shouldn't want to frighten you, and I don't know exactly how to tell you. It *might* frighten you.

THE LITTLE CHILD: Oh, I don't believe it would frighten me, anything you say. I'm sure your voice sounds very nice and kind, if it *is* a little tiny mite hoarse. You *may* have a cold.

THE BURGLAR: It generally sounds that way, but I don't mean anything by it. I've got some little girls of my own.

1 This play was published only in *Harper's Weekly*, December 26, 1908, VII, 22–24.

THE LITTLE CHILD, *delighted*: Many?

THE BURGLAR: Well, I don't know as you'd call it many: five or six.

THE LITTLE CHILD: How perfectly splendid! Why, *my* papa only has *me*! And have you got any little boys?

THE BURGLAR: Don't ask! More than I want. They're a bad lot.

THE LITTLE CHILD: And have you got a wife?

THE BURGLAR: A sick one. If she was out of bed, once, them boys would dance to a different tune. And I shouldn't be here.

THE LITTLE CHILD: You must say *those* boys. I don't believe they *want* to be bad. But now sit down here, in papa's easy-chair, and tell me all about it. You don't mind my being in my nighty, do you? I didn't know there was anybody here, and I just slipped down for a picture-book to look myself sleepy with.

THE BURGLAR: Well, miss, I don't know as I've got the time just now—

THE LITTLE CHILD: Oh, yes, you have. It won't take you long. But I don't want you to hurry! There! (*She pushes him into the chair and climbs into his lap, and puts her arm round his neck with her head against his breast.*) Now, go ahead, and don't miss a single word. What about your boys, and why don't you want to be here?

THE BURGLAR: Well, them boys—

THE LITTLE CHILD: *Those* boys.

THE BURGLAR: All right, miss. They hain't really got anything to do with it. And I don't want to be here because I hain't got any business to be here; not honestly. The fact is, miss, I'm a burglar.

THE LITTLE CHILD, *suddenly lifting her head, and looking into his eyes*: A burglar? Yes, that's what I thought. But a burglar's something awful, isn't it? And you don't *look* awful!

THE BURGLAR: That's because I'm sorry for it, and I would like to stop it. If I hadn't a sick wife, and my little girls to provide for, I'd stop it right now. I *was* hoping to get enough in your house here to see my way to leave off with, and I've put together a few things on the table, that I can cash up on. God bless you! When it comes to working the goods off you can't get half their value; and house rent and butchers' meat going up all the time.

THE LITTLE CHILD, *with increasing sympathy*: I see. And if—

THE BURGLAR: And if you could just tell me where I could find the solid silver—none of your plated stuff—and some of your mammy's jewelry and your pappy's watch, I could get an advance on them, so that I could turn round and look for some steady work daytimes. I understand lock-smithing pretty well, and I could get a job at that, if I was free-handed and wasn't so weighed down with care.

THE LITTLE CHILD, *slipping from his knee*: I believe I can help you! And I'll get you my bank, too. There are five gold-pieces in it, but if you feel so bad at being a burglar, and want to stop it, I'd rather you had them than I. Now, you must stay right here, and not stir, till I come back. You must keep as still as a mouse. Will you?

THE BURGLAR: Trust me for that, my little dear. I won't move an eye-winker. But don't you be gone long. There ain't much time left before daylight, now.

THE LITTLE CHILD: I won't be gone a minute. As soon as I find mamma's diamonds and papa's watch, I'll be right back. (*She retreats towards the door which she came in at, looking at the burglar gayly over her shoulder, and kissing her hand to him. Suddenly she pauses, and comes nervously back.*) There's some one! I heard steps on the stairs!

THE BURGLAR, *in consternation*: And I didn't bring my gun! Save me, my little girl! Save me!

THE LITTLE CHILD: I *will* save you, poor man! (*She looks wildly about, and her eyes fix on a door, which she flings open.*) Here! There's nothing but old magazines in this closet, and it will do nicely. It's rather stuffy, but you can keep a crack open.

THE BURGLAR, *clasping his hands and lifting his eyes to heaven*: Saved!

> *He has barely time to hurl himself into the closet, and close the door on his fingers, with a bated "Ouch!" when the library door opens and the Papa, in his long dressing-gown and his tasselled smoking-cap, such as people have not worn for many years, enters stealthily, shading his lamp with his hand. He starts at sight of the Little Child.*

THE PAPA: You here, child! What are you doing in my library at this time of night?

THE LITTLE CHILD: It's almost morning, papa, and—

THE PAPA, *glancing at the clock*: True! And, well?

THE LITTLE CHILD: I just came down to get a picture-book, to look myself sleepy with. But, papa, dear! What are *you* doing here at this time in the morning? You know you don't usually breakfast till nine, and to-day's New-Year's, when you're always up later.

THE PAPA, *haggardly*: I? Oh, yes! I forgot. I— I couldn't sleep. And I came down—it must be done or we leave our happy home before the night returns— I came down to write a check.

THE LITTLE CHILD: To write a check? But why are you so gloomy about it? You have often written checks before. Why do you have to get up so early to do it?

THE PAPA, *with ghastly irony*: But this—this is a very difficult check to write. It requires care and—quiet. (*Suddenly lifting his head*) Child! (*He looks darkly at her.*) Do you know that your father is by way of becoming a great criminal?

THE LITTLE CHILD: A criminal? Isn't that some kind of wicked person?

THE PAPA, *desolately*: Yes, yes, a very wicked person. (*He pulls his chair to the table.*) Who has been messing up my desk? What are all these things heaped together here for? And this odd lantern? Whose lantern is it?

THE LITTLE CHILD: I was keeping it all for a surprise! (*She clasps her hands rapturously.*) Papa, it's the *burglar's* lantern! He's a good burglar; he's going to quit it.

THE BURGLAR, *flinging open the closet door, and coming out*: Yes, it *was* the burglar's lantern. Now it's the lantern of a honest man. This little kiddy has saved me!

THE PAPA, *dryly*: Oh! And may I ask whose things these are on my library table?

THE BURGLAR: Them things—

THE LITTLE CHILD, *softly correcting him*: Those things!

THE BURGLAR: Heigh? What? Oh, yes! Thank you, miss! Those 'ere things *was* mine; now they're yourn.

THE PAPA, *examining them*: I thought I recognized them. Had you collected any other—objects?

THE LITTLE CHILD: He hadn't *time*, papa. I surprised him before he could get the solid silver in the dining-room; and he *does* so want your watch and mamma's diamonds to live on while he's looking for some other kind of business, he says.

She gazes wistfully into her father's face.

THE PAPA, *to the Burglar*: Is this the truth?

THE BURGLAR: It's gospel truth!

THE PAPA: Well, well! I'll think about it. Don't bother me now. This is my busy day.

He takes a small check-book from the pocket of his dressing-gown, and after filling out a check, he carefully studies the signature of a letter which he has spread on the table before him.

THE LITTLE CHILD, *softly, to the Burglar*: Now!

The Burglar steals into the dining-room and returns with the solid silver in a bag hung over his shoulder. At the same moment, the Mamma, deeply veiled and wrapped in a seal-skin motoring-cloak, as if for an instant journey, appears from the hallway.

THE MAMMA: You here, Reginald?

THE PAPA, *glancing up at her*: Yes, I, Patricia. Are you going somewhere?

THE MAMMA: I am quitting your house forever, Reginald. I am leaving our home in ruins. Arthur will be at the door in a moment. Hark! That is his car, now: I know the familiar snuffle and joggle. You will learn to forgive me, Reginald. Be good to our child—of course I can't take her with me, much as I would like to. She will miss a mother's care; but Arthur wouldn't have her along on any account, and I love him, *love* him; and I must quit all for him. My darling child, my poor husband! My heart will remain with you. (*Turning sharply upon the Little Child whom she sees for the first time*) Child, what are you doing here, at this hour? Naughty, naughty, naughty! Do you want to spoil your mother's life?

THE LITTLE CHILD: Oh, mamma, don't be cross with me. I just came down to get a picture-book to look myself sleepy with.

THE MAMMA: Well, then, take it, and go right straight back to bed this instant. After all the pains I have taken with that child, to have her coming down into the library at five o'clock in the morning for picture-books! (*Suddenly recollecting herself*) Well, what does it matter now? (*She flings the little satchel she has been holding on the table, and abandons herself in a corner of the sofa.*) I declare, if I had known what a bother it was going to be, I should have let Arthur go with Mrs. Featherstaff. It would have served them *both* right.

THE PAPA, *speaking after a thoughtful muse*: And you love this Arthur of yours, my darling?

THE MAMMA: Of course. He wanted to marry me first, when I was quite a girl.

THE PAPA: And you love him more than me? Than our child?

THE MAMMA: If you'd had your patience tried with her as much as I have! And now, coming down into the library at all hours of the night!

THE PAPA: I see what you mean. Well, I have been thinking it all over, and under the circumstances, I don't believe you could do better than go. I won't be the one to prevent you. Arthur has nothing to fear from *me*. No pursuit; no violence; no scandal; a quiet little divorce, and there an end. My poor wife! I had *hoped* to make you happy. But now, good-by! Go, and may heaven's blessing attend you and Arthur. Go, go, go! If ever you repent, remember that your ruined home is always here.

He hides his face in his arms on the table. At the same moment, the Burglar starts forward and drops the bag of silver from his shoulders, with a clang.

THE BURGLAR: Don't you do it, sir! Don't you let her go! She'll come back fast enough, never fear, but that ain't it! *My* wife bolted once, and she come back all in good time, and she's been the best of wives and mothers ever since. But—it's never been the same; not *exactly* the same.

THE MAMMA, *starting to her feet*: Who is this man? Reginald! Child!

THE BURGLAR: Don't you mind *me*, ma'am. I *was* a burglar; but that little daughter of yourn, and that husband, have made a honest man of me. (*He pushes the bag of silver under a chair with his foot.*) Done it by kindness, and I'd die for them —*both* of 'em.

THE MAMMA, *faltering*: And—and she came back, you say? Why?

THE BURGLAR: Got sick of him. And tired of the whole job.

THE MAMMA, *hoarsely*: I see, I see! Arthur *is* terribly tedious at times. He's a frightful bore, with his etchings. Could I pass my whole broken life with those etchings, in Florence, or wherever I went with my indelible *tache*? No, no, no! A thousand times no! Better a thousand times the annoying peculiarities of Reginald—his slamming doors, when he comes in, his being late to dinner, his defective memory, his total want of initiative, his lack of masterfulness. Besides, Arthur is not on time. (*To the Burglar*) Man! Whoever you are, you have saved me! Saved me from *him*, from *myself*! Oh, I will bless you with my last gasp! (*She offers to fling her arms about his neck, but starts back, and flings them round her husband's.*) Reginald, I am your own Patricia again, now and forever! Child, kiss your poor mother in your father's arms, which shall clasp him while we both live. Not that cheek! The other! Oh, Reginald, Reginald! Pay this noble man for saving your wife!

THE PAPA, *starting petulantly and flinging down his pen*: There! You've spoiled it, and it was the only one I had got anywhere near right. Couldn't you see how I was occupied—absorbed?

THE MAMMA: Oh, forgive me, dearest! I didn't notice. And I am *so* happy at your having me back again. But what in the world are you doing?

She drops on one knee beside him, and peers over at the writing to which he has returned.

THE PAPA, *returning to his work*: I am drawing a check.

THE MAMMA, *playfully*: You queer boy! And is drawing a check so very hard? You've drawn many a one for your poor Pat.

THE PAPA, *absently*: But this isn't like those. This—is—very—difficult.

Writing slowly.

THE MAMMA: But why aren't you putting your own name to it? Why are you—why are you putting— *(Jumping to her feet in suffocating excitement)* Reginald! Reginald! *(She snatches the check from him.)* Reginald! Are you forging my father's signature? Oh, Reginald!

She drops the check and hides her face in her hands. The Burglar, placing his fingers on his lips and winking at the Little Child, who clasps her hands and hops delightedly up and down, possesses himself of the Mamma's satchel.

THE PAPA: I am certainly signing your father's name. I wouldn't call it forging, but you never measure your terms.

THE MAMMA: And *why* are you signing his name?

THE PAPA: Because, for one thing, he has more money in the bank than I have. I have overdrawn my account, and unless I have this money to-morrow my note will go to protest.

THE MAMMA: And why have you overdrawn your account?

THE PAPA: I shouldn't think you would like to ask. That motoring-cloak you have on took my last two thousand, and our former friend Arthur has turned the note for five thousand I gave him, payable on demand, into the bank.

THE MAMMA: Wretch! Oh, Reginald, what an escape I have had! But, dearest, you must not do this dreadful thing.

THE PAPA: Very well. Then the rent on this house won't be paid, and we shall all be set out on the sidewalk, with that new set of luxurious Mission furniture.

THE MAMMA: Wait! Stop! Let me think! Unless you forge my father's check all this will happen?

THE PAPA: It will.

THE MAMMA: And if you do, and it is found out, you will go—

THE PAPA: To State's prison.

THE MAMMA: For how long?

THE PAPA: For ten or fifteen years—or less on an indeterminate sentence. Why are you so particular about the time?

THE MAMMA: Don't interrupt! *(After a moment)* Well, I have thought, and I will save you, Reginald. *I* will forge my father's check, and take all the risks. But there will *be* no risks. I know his writing much better than you, and I can imitate his signature perfectly. Reginald, I will sacrifice myself for you just as you would have sacrificed yourself for me—

THE PAPA: Well, I don't know—

THE MAMMA: Yes, you would! And I will save you, save you, save you!

She pushes him from his place, and arranging the papers before her, takes up the pen, when the tall, bent figure of the Old Father shows itself at the door. He hobbles forward with the help of a stick, and speaks in a cackling falsetto.

THE OLD FATHER: Well, I am glad to see that we are going to have breakfast at a decent hour at last. In my young days we *always* had a six-o'clock breakfast, and my poor father had to pull me out of bed to it. Now, when I'm wide awake and hungry at four, I can't get a bite or sup before nine. But you seem to be turning over a new leaf with the new year. Well, better late than never— *(He stops, and bursts into a crowing laugh.)* No, by George! Better *early* than never! Ha, ha, ha; he, he, he! Oh dear!

He sinks into the sofa, coughing and gasping.

THE MAMMA: I wish you wouldn't make so much noise, father. It's very distracting. *(She continues the study of his handwriting, and then tries for his signature.)* There! You've made me spoil it, and I must begin all over again.

THE BURGLAR, *coming forward and taking his stick*: Let me relieve you of that heavy cane, sir.

THE OLD FATHER: Eh? What? Oh! It *is* rather

heavy, and I don't need it when I'm sitting down, that's a fact.

THE BURGLAR, *turning aside to the Little Child and speaking in a low voice*: Gold-headed, see?

THE LITTLE CHILD, *joyously*: And that will help you to be an honest man much sooner!

THE BURGLAR: Pretty nigh a week sooner.

THE OLD FATHER, *to the Papa*: Who is this obliging stranger, Reggy, my boy?

THE PAPA: Oh, he? Why, our little Gladys found him here. I believe he's a—a—a—

THE BURGLAR: Say it out, guvner! I'm a honest man now, but when this little angel found me here, I was a burglar, and no better than a thief. But she's saved me, bless her heart.

He embraces the Little Child.

THE OLD FATHER, *with a lack-lustre stare*: I don't believe I understand. What's *she* doing?

THE PAPA: Who? Patricia?

THE OLD FATHER: Ah. It *is* Patricia, ain't it? Then what's she doing?

THE PAPA, *lightly*: Oh, just writing.

THE OLD FATHER: What's she writing?

THE MAMMA, *petulantly*: Well, if you *must* know, I'm writing a check in your hand, and signing your name to it.

THE OLD FATHER: In joke?

THE MAMMA: No, in earnest. These *p's* and *q's* of yours are enough to make one tear one's hair.

THE OLD FATHER, *after an interval long enough to grasp the fact*: Then you're forging my name! What are you doing that for?

THE MAMMA, *flinging down her pen in exasperation*: For *money*. Reginald, here, is ruined, by my extravagance and a note that he owes Arthur Fortescue, and I am sacrificing myself to save him. He offered to let me elope with Arthur, if I wanted to very much, but Arthur didn't keep his appointment; and, *(indicating the burglar)* this honest man, as he calls himself, convinced me that I would be sick of the job, and saved me; and so I'm here, helping Reginald out. He was making the greatest mess of it.

THE OLD FATHER: And so are you, by all accounts. He, he, he!

THE MAMMA: Well, father, if you don't like it, suppose you do it yourself.

THE OLD FATHER, *feebly cackling*: Forge my own check? Come, I should like that.

THE PAPA: We should *all* like it, sir. We are in a real—box. If I don't pay my note to Arthur to-morrow, it will go to protest; and you know what that means to a businessman.

THE OLD FATHER, *sobered*: Is it as bad as that?

THE PAPA: Quite.

THE MAMMA: Worse I should say.

THE OLD FATHER: Well, as it's New-Year's morning, I don't mind forging my note for a few hundreds.

THE MAMMA: Hundreds won't do, father. You must make it thousands. *I* was. There is the note to Arthur, which the wretched cad has turned into the bank, and that's five thousand alone. And then we should like a little for incidental expenses, say eight or ten thousand more.

THE OLD FATHER, *whistling*: Fifteen thousand! I will see you—

THE MAMMA: Think, father! It is New-Year's Day! Make it a happy New-Year's for your children!

She flings herself at his feet.

THE OLD FATHER: And if I do this—this monstrous thing, when shall I have breakfast?

THE MAMMA, *coldly*: Why, at nine, I suppose. Nobody's up yet; the servants have been up all night, seeing the Old Year out, and you wouldn't have the cruelty to call them at *this* hour?

THE OLD FATHER, *firmly*: No breakfast, no check.

THE MAMMA: How very unkind of you! I'm sure I don't know what we shall do. *(She weeps.)* A six-o'clock breakfast! Who ever heard of such a thing in a civilized house? Why, if we begin that way on New-Year's we will have to go through the year so! You know people do.

THE OLD FATHER: No breakfast, no check, unless you write it yourself, and you know you can't. The cashier would push it back under his window at the first glance. I tell you I'm too faint to write a check without breakfast. You know I'm good for nothing till I've had my coffee.

THE MAMMA, *springing to her feet*: And would coffee do?

THE OLD FATHER: It would do to begin with.

THE MAMMA: Then, father, we will save you from your selfish, selfish—egotism. I will have you a cup made on the spirit-lamp. Or I would, if Geraldine were here; *she* would make it. Oh, Geraldine, Geraldine!

GERALDINE, *showing herself at the door*: Did you call me, Patricia?

THE MAMMA: Oh, surely, heaven has sent you! I want you to make father a cup of coffee on the spirit-lamp, so he can forge his check for us, and save us from despair. Quick, quick! There isn't an instant to lose. It's not only the check I'm trying to get out of him, but it's his dreadful selfishness that I want to save him from.

GERALDINE: I understand, Patricia. I can't see how, when his children are so generous and thoughtful of others, father should think only of himself. But that doesn't matter. He shall have his coffee, as soon as spirit can boil water. (*Tenderly, as she goes to him, and dropping on her knees beside him, takes his withered hand between her palms*) Poor father! I won't judge him! I suppose you *are* faint without it?

THE OLD FATHER: That, and my grapefruit, and cereal, and buckwheat cakes and country sausage. But I could make a shift to forge my check on coffee. I wish it was for you, child. Patricia is a cat.

GERALDINE, *thoughtfully*: She *is* a cat. But, father, this is New-Year's morning, when we ought to think of our own faults and not others'! I suppose Patricia can't help being a cat. If it's her nature.

THE OLD FATHER: She takes after her mother.

GERALDINE: And I, I am like you, father: all sweetness, gentleness, purity. I wish I could say circumspection, too. But I cannot, oh, I cannot! I have lain awake all night, thinking of the dreadful scrape I've got into by my heedlessness. It's with Mrs. Blair: I said I was engaged the day of her dinner, and I wasn't. But worse, oh, far worse! Her dinner isn't the 12th at all, it's the 13th, and I said the 12th in my note, and now she'll write back and say I've mistaken the day! How our sins find us out! I shall have to go, after all.

She bows her head on her father's hand.

THE OLD FATHER: Don't cry on it. I hate having my hands cried on; makes them so wet. And—and—where is my coffee, I should like to know?

GERALDINE, *rising, and fetching her breath convulsively*: Yes, yes. Instantly, father. It's only that sensitive conscience that I get from you. Oh! (*She starts at the sight of Fortescue standing in a long motoring-coat of costly furs, at the door.*) Arthur Fortescue!

THE MAMMA: Wretch!

THE PAPA: Hello, old man!

THE LITTLE CHILD: I mustn't ask if you've brought my New-Year's gift, Cousin Artie.

THE OLD FATHER, *with senile gayety*: Hello, Arthur! Come for that little balance of yours from Reggy? I wish you may get it!

THE BURGLAR, *coming forward, and removing his fur coat for him*. Let me relieve you of that hot coat, sir. (*To the Little Child, in a hoarse whisper*) Two more days off!

She dances in a transport of joy.

FORTESCUE, *to the Old Father*: I have not come for money! I have come for one who has played me false at every turn; who is made up of illusion; who is a compound of loveliness and lies!

GERALDINE: Oh, Arthur, how can you speak so to me? (*At the start of astonishment which he gives, she puts her finger to her lips and frowns at him with reference to Gladys, whispering very loud.*) Hush! The child! She must not know it is her mother. She must suppose it is her aunt.

FORTESCUE, *humoring the ruse*: Then why have you left me out there in the cold all this time?

GERALDINE: But I didn't know you were there! And I have been waiting and watching, oh, so long! Look at the clock, Arthur: you were to have been here at five o'clock sharp, and now it's half past. Do you call that punctual?

FORTESCUE: Your clock's three-quarters fast. I've been blowing my nails out there for half an hour, and the chauffeur has left in a huff and gone home. Where's my coat? Or no! I can't run the machine; the whole thing's off!

THE MAMMA: And a very good thing. She would have been awfully sick of the job.

She turns to the Burglar for confirmation.

THE BURGLAR: Well, it's a little different case, ma'am, with a single lady. (*To Fortescue*) I've done a little shoving in my time, sir: let me take your coat out, and these few other little things, and I'll have you where you want to go in a jiffy. (*He collects his various booty, and as he passes out of the door he speaks to the Little Child, whom he leaves enraptured.*) This takes the trick. I've got a friend outside, and when he's put these things up and cashed in on 'em I can begin being a honest man to-day.

GERALDINE, *softly to Fortescue*: I have *saved* you, Arthur, saved you from *yourself!* You were about to commit a very wicked action involving all sorts of prevarication. Now, now, dearest, you are mine, and with a clear conscience. You have always loved me! Say you have always loved me, loud enough for everybody to hear! Say it, for the sake of the Little Child, of my poor old father, of my sister's heart-broken husband, of Patricia herself, and of your own soul!

FORTESCUE, *softly*: There is something in your suggestion. And, Jerry, you *are* a prettier girl than Pat.

GERALDINE: Oh, Arthur, if you only knew how she makes up! And always did!

FORTESCUE, *loudly*: Geraldine, I have always loved you, and I had come here this morning to force you to keep your rash promise of eloping with me. But you have saved me! Saved me from this crime, this folly; and now in the presence of your whole family, I ask you to become my wife, with a house or a church wedding, as you choose, but as soon as possible. Will you be mine?

GERALDINE: Arthur, you *know* I will. And will you always love me, as Reginald has loved Patricia? Patricia, let Reginald clasp you in his arms and show Arthur how he has always loved you.

THE MAMMA, *sotto voce, in passing her on her way to her husband's mechanical embrace*: Snake! Reptile! Crocodile!

GERALDINE: Oh, how happy I am! And now, father, give Arthur the check for his money.

THE OLD FATHER: When I've had my coffee.

GERALDINE: Oh, bother your— Yes, yes, father, dear, you shall have it instantly. Here is Frederick, and I know he'll get the spirit-lamp and my little coffee-pot, to boil the water in; won't you, Frederick? You'd love to do it for father and sister!

She appeals to the half-grown boy with eyes of tender entreaty, as he advances into the room.

FREDERICK, *staring at them with a haggard face*: None of that! I'm going to cut out all that.

GERALDINE, *fondly*: All what, Frederick?

FREDERICK: Lies. And my name's Fred. Don't you go Fredericking me, if you want anything out of me.

GERALDINE: Why, Frederick—

FREDERICK: Stop that, don't I tell you? It's New-Year's, and I'm going to form a good resolution, that I'll keep all the year, not to tell a single lie—

GERALDINE: Fred!

FREDERICK: Nor to let anybody else tell lies for me—

THE PAPA: Then you must retire from society, my friend.

FREDERICK: And, if anybody tries it, to come right out and expose 'em—

THE MAMMA: And make everybody hate you!

FREDERICK: And no more Santa Claus business—

THE LITTLE CHILD: Oh, Uncle Freddy, you musn't say so or even think such a thing!

FREDERICK: Well, you just listen to my resolution, my New-Year's resolution—

FORTESCUE: Hold on, my boy! Let me save you from that madness. If you love truth and hate falsehood, don't put it into a New-Year's resolution, for that sort of reform was invented by the Father of Lies himself. Nobody ever kept a New-Year's resolution. It's morally impossible. Don't take that sin upon your young soul! Last New-Year's I swore never to trust a woman, and look at me, now!

GERALDINE, *with her arm round his neck*: You funny old dear!

THE OLD FATHER: Better give it up, Fred; the noes have it.

THE BURGLAR, *coming forward to Fortescue, while Frederick pauses irresolute*: All ready, sir.

FORTESCUE: Ready for what?

THE BURGLAR: For the Little Church round the Corner. Didn't you say so?

GERALDINE: Yes, yes! He did. You did, dearest?

FORTESCUE: Oh! All right. (*To the Burglar*) Where's my coat?

THE BURGLAR: It's right out here, sir, in the taxicab.

FORTESCUE, *bewildered*: Taxicab?

THE BURGLAR: Your shover come back, and said he'd got to take the automobile to the garage and mend it up some. (*To the Little Child, softly*) My pal's took it off with the silver and dimuns, and gold-headed cane, and I don't have to wait a minute longer; I'm an honest man *now*!

THE LITTLE CHILD, *softly*: Oh, how glad I am! And may I come and play with your little girls?

THE BURGLAR: Sure! (*To Fortescue*) So I've got you a taxicab. That all right?

FORTESCUE: It isn't the *red* kind? They put bombs in them.[1]

THE BURGLAR: Oh, no! I looked out for that. The strike's off, anyway. This way, sir!

The Little Child has stolen to the organ, and as Fortescue and Geraldine move forward, followed by the Papa and Mamma, she strikes up the Wedding March from "Lohengrin." Geraldine nervously halts the party.

GERALDINE: Father! You're *not* going to let Arthur go without his check?

THE OLD FATHER: I seem to be going without my coffee.

1 On March 29, 1908, a public gathering in Union Square, New York City, of unemployed people ended in a riot in which a bomb exploded killing one and hurting several. Presumably the mob's singing of "The Marseillaise" helped to identify the "reds," anarchists, and other agitators involved.

GERALDINE: How tiresome! But Fred will get that for you.

THE OLD FATHER: He'll get the check for Fortescue.

FORTESCUE, *nobly*: You are right, father—if I may venture to call you so, at last. Geraldine, your father is good for the check, isn't he? I'm right about your father?

GERALDINE: Yes, you will get it if he says so. But his insisting on the coffee at this last moment —Fred! Fred, dear! Where is Freddy? Why, what's the matter with father? He seems faint! Father!

> She rushes to support him on one side, and the Mamma rushes to support him on the other.

THE MAMMA: Father!

FORTESCUE AND THE PAPA: Father! Dad, dear! Here!

THE LITTLE CHILD: Oh, grandpappy, dear!

THE BURGLAR: All right, old gentleman: brace up!

GERALDINE: He's gasping; he wants air!

THE OLD FATHER, *fiercely, with a return of his vigor*: I want *coffee!* And here it comes. (*Fred appears with a steaming cup and runs to him.*) And Fred is bringing it. He's worth the whole pack of ye! He's saved me!

ALL: He's saved him!

FREDERICK: I've saved myself too. I've thought it all over, Mr. Fortescue, and no New-Year's resolutions for me. I'm going to take things as they come.

THE LITTLE CHILD, *in her high, piping stage voice, with her hands dropped, and her eyes devoutly raised*: Yes, and we've *all* been saved, this happy New-Year's morn: saved from robbery, from crime, from shame, from heedless fibbing, from good resolutions, from faintness for want of coffee!

THE BURGLAR, *solemnly from the centre of the stage picture*: You never said a truer thing, deary. Take the word of a honest man for that!

A True Hero: Melodrama

[1909]

This polemic on lying and proper conduct is another of Howells' plays having truth and morality as its central issue. The true, ideal hero, moves in an ideal world of his own dream making and lives by an uncomplicated set of values in which truth is clearly defined. As a part of his philosophy of realism, Howells always tried to show the strong Swedenborgian interdependence of truth and morality. But in this play it becomes obvious that there are no general rules governing what is true and what is false. A person may act from the highest personal standards of truth and right and yet be immoral because his own values are twisted. Therefore some traditional concepts become valueless, and man's only defense is his reason. The play, then, becomes an interesting discussion of Howells' theory of realism.

Soon after *A True Hero* was published, Howells expressed a fear that it was a bad play. The idea portrayed is interesting, although obvious, but the dramatic framework for the idea is weak. It is soon evident that the plot is incidental to the idea of truth involved, and that motivation of characters is secondary to the reactions which must be provoked one way or another in the hero, Charles Lannard. Consequently, Mrs. Roycroft is a tool for Howells' thesis and a simple personi-

fication of evil. Her only interesting action is her attempt to explain how a look in Lannard's eyes made her commit the crime—as a glance from Miriam influenced Donatello in Hawthorne's *The Marble Faun*. Dr. Tolboy, who is artistically related to Dr. Lawton of other plays, is another obvious tool of the author; his primary job is to distinguish certain values for Lannard and to show him what truth really is. Once the light of Howells' truth penetrates Lannard's consciousness, the play is done.

There is also a theme below the surface of truth and morality in which *A True Hero* becomes a satire on melodrama in general and on the true hero of melodrama in particular. Although most of the satire is at the expense of Charles Lannard, the activity and inconsistency of Mrs. Roycroft become a part of Howells' satire on the melodramatic villain. Lannard, of course, has all the characteristics of ideal manhood that the most romantic of writers could possibly load upon a hero. Self is nothing; woman, everything. It is man's "Duty, his right, his God-granted privilege" to save woman. But Howells shows the ridiculousness of such thinking by introducing a worthless woman. Then what will the hero do?

A True Hero: Melodrama[1]

REV. GEORGE HARTLEY: And you say you took these things?

MRS. ROYCROFT: Yes, I did. I must have taken them.

The two are in Hartley's study, which opens into his church, and the strains of organ practice reach them from time to time through the door standing slightly ajar; the sun through the painted window behind Mrs. Roycroft throws the colors on the floor between them. He sits fallen back in his armchair before his desk, and she droops forward from a low seat fronting him, with her clasped hands pressed between her knees, and her shoulders lifted in a figure of hopeless desolation. A necklace and some other trinkets glitter on the desk; Hartley lifts them and tosses them farther from him.

HARTLEY: Why do you say, "must have taken them"—that way? Don't you know?

MRS. ROYCROFT, *in a voice hardly above a husky whisper*: Yes. No. How can I tell? It is like a bad dream. (*After a moment*) I was very unhappy. I didn't know what I was doing.

HARTLEY: But why should your unhappiness—

MRS. ROYCROFT: Don't ask me. I can't explain.

HARTLEY: Hmmm! (*After a pause*) Was there any one near who could have seen you?

MRS. ROYCROFT: No. Yes. Must I tell you? Perhaps I ought.

HARTLEY: Not unless you wish. You are not a member of my society, Mrs. Roycroft. Why have you come to me?

MRS. ROYCROFT: Because—because you are good.

HARTLEY, *perceptibly moved*: You mustn't say that sort of thing.

MRS. ROYCROFT, *very humbly*: No, I know it. I came—I came because you were a friend of his.

HARTLEY: His? What do you mean? Whose friend?

MRS. ROYCROFT: Mr.—Lannard's.

She sinks yet more abjectly forward.

HARTLEY: Lannard's? What has that got to do with it?

1 This play was published only in *Harper's Monthly*, November 1909, CXIX, 866–75.

MRS. ROYCROFT: It was he—who was near me.

HARTLEY: And you think he saw you?

MRS. ROYCROFT: He made no sign of it. He wouldn't!

HARTLEY, *with quick and stern decision*: Well, there is only one thing—

MRS. ROYCROFT: Yes, yes. Advise me, do! I came for that!

HARTLEY, *still severely*: Then I advise you in common honesty and common sense to get these things back at once. Get them to the salesman who showed them to you, so that he may not be suspected. And for your soul's sake I advise you—

MRS. ROYCROFT, *dropping to her knees before him*: Yes, yes!

HARTLEY: I advise you to make confession as well as restitution. Go and tell Planet Brothers what you have done—

MRS. ROYCROFT, *springing to her feet*: Never! Is this your idea of advice? They would put me in prison. And I thought you were so good! Surely you can help me out some way! You will save me?

HARTLEY, *with a deep sigh*: Oh, I can "save" you, as you call it. I suppose I can keep these things, the body of your sin, and send them back to Planets' so that it will not be known who took them—

MRS. ROYCROFT: You were going to say *stole*. Say it! That is what the world would call it, though I expected from you—

HARTLEY: Oh, it doesn't matter about the words. It's the thing that matters. But before I meddle with it, you have got to make a clean breast of it.

MRS. ROYCROFT: How do you mean?

HARTLEY: How came you to notice that Lannard was near you?

MRS. ROYCROFT: He was at the same case; he was choosing a ring. (*Suddenly, with a pounce*) He has been here! You cannot deny it!

HARTLEY: But I do deny it; he has not been here. Mrs. Roycroft, I shall have to ask you a question, if I am to help you. Has Lannard's name been associated with yours?

MRS. ROYCROFT, *with joyous relief*: Mr. Lannard? Why, he's a boy! The idea is absurd. But I'm so glad you mentioned it, Mr. Hartley. Now I can tell my husband, and he'll see how ridiculous such things are. Why, I had motored to Planets' with Mr. Manvers, and left him in the car at the door, and the idea of my going to meet poor Charley Lannard—

HARTLEY: I didn't say you had gone to meet him, but I'm glad—though it doesn't relieve the affair of a very ugly aspect for him.

MRS. ROYCROFT: For Mr. Manvers?

HARTLEY: For Lannard. Don't you know that if he was there at the same showcase suspicion may fall on him?

MRS. ROYCROFT: On Charley Lannard? Why, he's the soul of honor. But I see! (*Her voice sinks to a low tragic murmur and she droops again upon her seat; then she suddenly starts from it.*) I must save him—even from suspicion. I will tell all. I will go to the detectives, and confess everything. I will put myself under arrest. Charles Lannard! (*She rushes toward the street door of the study, all excitement, but turns impetuously back to Hartley, who has vaguely risen, and appeals to him with clasped hands.*) And you will never, never let him know that I have done it?

HARTLEY, *in alarm*: But wait, Mrs. Roycroft. Your children—your husband—you must think of them!

MRS. ROYCROFT: Oh, he has an account there. And I could manage the detectives myself, if it came to that. But there is no time to be lost if they suspect poor Charley.

HARTLEY: Stop! Let us talk it over. You mustn't do anything rash.

He puts himself between her and the door.

MRS. ROYCROFT, *confronting him full height*: If you dare to hinder me, Mr. Hartley, if you don't let me pass instantly, I will scream, I will make a scene, I will go into hysterics; I don't know what I'll do. Will you—

She whips round him, and out of the doorway, and he remains staring at it, when Doctor Tolboy appears within it.

TOLBOY: Who was *that* perturbed female? Or do they all leave your study in some such state?

HARTLEY, *after a moment of silence*: Tolboy, I want your advice—

TOLBOY: Is it so bad as that? Then you want my approval.

HARTLEY: No, neither; your help. That was Mrs. Roycroft—

TOLBOY: I knew it, but I thought I would give you the benefit of the doubt. What's she been doing now?

HARTLEY: Oh, my dear fellow, she's been stealing—stealing from Planet Brothers. (*He waves his hand nervelessly toward the desk where the jewelry is lying. Tolboy goes toward it, and bends over it, whistling softly.*) And it's happened so that the suspicion may fall upon poor young Charles Lannard. But I must say that as soon as she realized that, she was horror-stricken, and she's rushed out to take the blame on herself. She's gone to the Planets' to confess—to tell the detectives, and take the consequence. I couldn't stop her. (*Tolboy listens with dismay that passes into something different, when Hartley concludes.*) She said she would manage them.

TOLBOY: I've no doubt she'll try it. (*He smiles not quite cheerfully.*) But what's Lannard got to do with it? Where does *he* come in?

HARTLEY: She says he was at the same showcase looking at rings. I suppose he was looking at wedding-rings; he's to be married next week.

TOLBOY: Did she seem to have known that?

HARTLEY: I can't say. But what do you mean?

TOLBOY: Do you imagine she meant suspicion to fall on him, and then was sorry for it?

HARTLEY: How do I know? Why should she have taken the things?

TOLBOY: Why should she have left them here, if she was going back to restore them and give herself up?

HARTLEY, *in despair*: I didn't think of that. What do you advise me to do?

TOLBOY: You ought to have stopped her going, till you could think it over.

HARTLEY: I did try, but she escaped.

TOLBOY: Well, I don't see what you can do now except wait developments. Poor old Roycroft! I don't envy *him* his job.

HARTLEY: Tolboy, I don't like the tone you take. I know that you think lightly of Mrs. Roycroft, and I'll own myself that I have no great— But this is a serious matter. It doesn't involve her alone; it involves Lannard.

TOLBOY: I should think Lannard was out of it, unless she repents of repenting, and decides to let him take the blame. Who's practising in there?

He nods toward the door giving into the church.

HARTLEY: It's Lamm, our new organist. But—

TOLBOY, *listening*: Rather nice, isn't it?

HARTLEY: Yes. I don't know. I suppose so. But, Tolboy, if Lannard—

TOLBOY, *recurring to him from the music*: What sort of fellow is Lannard?

HARTLEY: He's a noble fellow. He's his father all over again!

TOLBOY: And a little more? I always suspect your noble fellows, you know. But I hadn't seen Lannard for some time before I went abroad, and he may be all right in spite of you. Who's he going to marry?

HARTLEY: The finest girl in the world! Margaret Wilson.

TOLBOY: Nettie Devoe's daughter?

HARTLEY: Yes. And she's as like her mother as he is like his father. They—

A knock at the street entrance arrests him.

TOLBOY, *escaping toward the church entrance*: If it's Mrs. Roycroft coming back to say she can't find Sherlock Holmes—

HARTLEY, *seizing Tolboy*: You mustn't go, Tolboy! I can't let you—I need you— Come in! (*He releases Tolboy at sight of Charles Lannard; and taking the young man's hand affectionately, turns with him toward Tolboy.*) I'm so glad to see you, my dear Charles. (*The young man is very pale, and his eyes are wild under his disordered hair. He is a slender youth in the early twenties, with a delicate, clean-shaven face.*) You know Doctor Tolboy?

LANNARD, *laxly and inattentively shaking hands*: Oh, yes. I thought—you weren't back, yet. How do you do? Ah! (*He catches sight of the jewelry on Hartley's desk.*) Then she did, she did! I was praying she hadn't; I was hoping I had dreamed it!

HARTLEY: It's no dream, my poor boy, but it's bad enough for the worst nightmare. I've been telling Doctor Tolboy: we can speak freely before him. He's an old friend of Mr. Roycroft's, you know.

LANNARD, *without heeding*: Where is she?

HARTLEY: She's gone to Planets'. She came here and told me everything, and I advised her to make confession and restitution, as the only means of diverting suspicion from you.

LANNARD: From me?

HARTLEY: You were at the same show-case buying a ring—

LANNARD: My wedding-ring! Yes?

HARTLEY: And as soon as these things are missed, the suspicion must fall either on her or on you.

LANNARD: I see. (*He realizes the fact with visible horror.*) And she's gone to say she stole them. (*After another moment*) But she mustn't! You oughtn't to have let her, Mr. Hartley. Think of her family—her little children. Oh, I can't allow it! I will go and take the blame myself. I will declare that I stole the things, and you must bear me out.

TOLBOY, *who has been regarding him with a smile of scientific interest*: But why should you do that?

LANNARD, *with exaltation*: Why shouldn't I do it? I am a man, and she is a woman. She is a wife, and it will break her husband's heart; she is a mother, and her motherhood makes her sacred.

TOLBOY, *thoughtfully*: Yes, I know. There is that view of it.

LANNARD, *fiercely*: Is there any other?

TOLBOY: I was merely wondering whether her husband's fatherhood made *him* sacred.

LANNARD, *indignantly*: The holiest things can be turned into ridicule.

HARTLEY: No, no, my dear Charles. I'm sure Tolboy doesn't mean anything of that kind. I'm sure he'll help us if he can.

TOLBOY: I'm afraid I can't, Hartley, on the lines proposed. But—it seems to me it's the other way about. Motherhood doesn't make a woman sacred: it's the woman that makes motherhood sacred, just as a man makes fatherhood sacred if he is good and faithful and devoted. I don't say Mrs. Roycroft isn't that sort of mother. But there are mothers and mothers. In this case there's one consideration that Mr. Lannard seems to have overlooked, if he will allow me.

HARTLEY: Certainly, my dear Tolboy. Go on!

TOLBOY: It appears that Mrs. Roycroft took the things, and that Mr. Lannard didn't. Why should he say he did?

LANNARD, *as before*: To save her!

TOLBOY: By a lie?

LANNARD: A lie!

TOLBOY: What should you call it, Hartley? But perhaps if Mr. Lannard would explain why he wishes to assume Mrs. Roycroft's guilt—

LANNARD: Explain? Explain? But I have told you already! She is a woman, a wife, a mother. If her guilt is known it will ruin her husband's life, and blast her children's future. Society will be shocked, and will cast her out. I don't wish to reflect upon you, Doctor Tolboy, but I can't understand what your ideals of manhood are. The man who sees a woman in the toils of her own error, and doesn't feel it his duty, his right, his God-granted privilege to save her at any cost to himself, is a traitor to every tie that binds him to his mother, his sister, and—any one who is more precious than either.

HARTLEY: You must feel the force of that, Tolboy?

TOLBOY: I'll allow that it's the theory in such cases. Do you preach that doctrine from your pulpit?

HARTLEY: I preach self-sacrifice.

TOLBOY: Self-sacrifice founded on a lie?

LANNARD: You mustn't use that word, Doctor Tolboy. You are my father's old friend, but I can't suffer it. To save a woman from her sin at any cost to veracity is not lying.

HARTLEY: Tolboy, you distinguish in motives?

TOLBOY: What kind of motive can change the nature of falsehood?

LANNARD: Then you would leave Mrs. Roycroft to her fate? You would—

TOLBOY: My dear young friend, you are delightful. Let me ask you a question or two. You don't mind my sitting down, Hartley?

HARTLEY: My dear Tolboy! Do sit down, both of you.

LANNARD: I will stand. And we are losing time when there's not a moment—

TOLBOY, *comfortably seating himself*: I don't believe Mrs. Roycroft is hurrying. But suppose we leave her out of the question?

LANNARD: We can't. She *is* the question.

TOLBOY: Well, not the only one. You won't think it too great a freedom in an old friend of your father—and your mother too—if I tell you I'm greatly interested in your engagement?

LANNARD, *softened into momentary forgetfulness*: Not at all, doctor. It's very kind of you.

TOLBOY: I used to dance with her mother when we were both a little younger. So did your father; he danced better than I, and she danced charmingly. It's very pretty his son being engaged to her daughter.

LANNARD: Thank you, Doctor Tolboy.

TOLBOY, *musingly*: He was such a knightly spirit! He could have been a very rich man, at one time, if he had been willing to say the thing that was not—just a little. But he died poor.

LANNARD: My mother told me as soon as I was old enough to understand.

TOLBOY: Ah, your mother! I hope she's well?

I've been away so long. Ever since I gave up practice nearly five years ago. And your sister?

LANNARD: They're both well, thank you. They will like to know you asked for them.

TOLBOY: I hear you've done very well for yourself. You're not sorry your father left you to fight your own way?

LANNARD: He left me his name.

TOLBOY: And that was enough. (*Presently*) By the way, was Mrs. Roycroft alone when you met her at Planets' to-day?

LANNARD, *recurring to her with a start*: I believe Mr. Manvers had motored up with her. He didn't come in.

TOLBOY: How about that business, Hartley?

HARTLEY: I don't talk scandal, my dear Tolboy.

TOLBOY: Ah, it *is* scandal, then. I hoped it was only slander when I heard of it in Rome.

HARTLEY: Has it travelled so far? The affair was broken off at one time—Manvers went abroad. Wretched woman!

TOLBOY: Yes, it's a pity such a fool has any man's happiness in her keeping. But Roycroft married too late or she married too soon. (*To Lannard*) You thought of taking the blame of such a woman on yourself?

LANNARD: I wished to save her—and to save her husband too. If the matter got into court, it would be known that she had come with Manvers— But it's too late now to do anything. (*He sinks into a chair and bows his face in his hands.*) She'll be under arrest, by this time. How could you let her go, Mr. Hartley? If they bring her here, I'll accuse myself; I'll declare that I took the things.

TOLBOY: I doubt if that will save her; and as for saving Roycroft, is it saving a man to keep him from knowing that his wife is flirting with another man?

He refers the point to Hartley, with a glance.

HARTLEY, *after a moment*: I don't believe it was ever the slightest use in the world. She wouldn't repent because she was kept from disgrace, and he wouldn't be spared by the deception.

Hartley has the air of being surprised into these conclusions.

TOLBOY, *turning to Lannard*: But if you succeed in keeping Roycroft from knowing that his wife was out motoring with Manvers, by taking the infamy of her theft on yourself—it seems a long way about—you will also have the satisfaction of saving her and her family from disgrace. I see.

(After a pause) Does she—excuse me—know your fiancée?

LANNARD: They are acquainted.

TOLBOY: Not friends?

LANNARD: Margaret is much younger.

TOLBOY: She will have the severity of youth. How will she like your taking Mrs. Roycroft's sin upon yourself? She won't believe you guilty; but what will she think of your motive? Will she think you had any duty in the matter except to keep out of it? Will she be proud of your sacrificing yourself for a woman she doesn't respect? Won't she feel that you owed something—perhaps more—to her?

LANNARD, *desperately*: In this matter it's for me to act alone.

TOLBOY: That's the way it's looked at in the strange world where such sacrifices are common. But in *this* world we are entangled in ties. Suppose this young girl, to whom you've given your promise to be all in all to her, agreed to let you do this thing, what about your mother? Her love of you and pride in you are hallowed by the memory of your father, who refused fortune for truth's sake; but you propose to bring dishonor on her by helping a faithless woman hoodwink her trusting husband. You wish to cover yourself with disgrace for a creature who has not a rag of common honesty—

LANNARD: Oh, you don't understand! Don't you see that this isn't a thing that I choose, but a thing that I *must* do? That every instinct of my nature, every impulse of my soul forces me to it? Can I coldly choose between the noble and the ignoble part? Can I leave this woman to her fate because she is weak and wicked? All the more because she is weak and wicked I must shield her, at any cost to myself and those dear to me. Where —where have you learned your cold-blooded doctrine—excuse my speaking so to my father's old friend—your heartless philosophy? But no matter, I will be true to myself in spite of everything.

TOLBOY: Ah, but you can't be true to yourself in a lie. It's morally impossible. You can only be false.

LANNARD: Then I will be true to *her.*

TOLBOY: And false to all those others? *(In lifting their voices they have been unaware of a knocking at the street door, but in the pause they now make it timidly repeats itself.)* There's somebody there, Hartley. Probably Mrs. Roycroft in irons. I couldn't bear that. I'll just slip into your sanctuary, and listen to your organist—

As he escapes into the church by one door, the other slowly opens, and Mrs. Roycroft is seen leaning against one of the jambs, faint and alone.

MRS. ROYCROFT, *piteously*: Oh, I was afraid there was no one here! I kept knocking and knocking, and at last I had to open it myself. *(She starts at sight of Lannard.)* You here, Mr. Lannard?

HARTLEY, *with a certain severity*: Yes, he is here, Mrs. Roycroft, and he knows everything. But where—

MRS ROYCROFT, *coming forward and dropping into the low chair she occupied before*: I hadn't the courage. I thought I could do it, but I couldn't. I've been walking round and round, trying to, and coming back here, and going again, and coming back. Do you blame me? What will you think, Mr. Lannard, if the suspicion falls on you, and I let it? What will Margaret think? But *she* hates me already! Let me go—I will make another effort. Oh, how cold you both are! *(She tries feebly to rise, but sinks back in her chair, and leaning forward, puts her face in her hands.)* I can't! But Mr. Hartley will bear me witness that I *wanted* to have myself arrested, and you will believe, Mr. Lannard, that I exonerated you to him? *(They continue silent, and she confronts them vividly.)* Somebody's been talking to you about me! And you are against me—two against one! How unmanly! But men are always so! Oh, what shall I do? Won't you speak to me, Mr. Lannard? I know you think I'm bad.

HARTLEY, *with lessened sternness*: Didn't you say yourself, a few minutes ago, that you had taken them?

MRS. ROYCROFT: Taken what? Oh! *(With disdain for the jewelry toward which Hartley waves his hand)* Those! Of course I took them!

HARTLEY: Then I don't understand—

MRS. ROYCROFT, *with hardness*: I know you don't. May I speak with Mr. Lannard a moment? Alone, I mean. You can leave the door into the church open, if you like.

HARTLEY: Really I— But of course, if you wish it. The door can be shut.

MRS. ROYCROFT: I prefer it open—if you'll take Doctor Tolboy out of earshot. Oh, I know he's in there. I saw him coming here, and I didn't see him going away. You were discussing me, I suppose. But don't apologize. *(She turns her back on Hartley, who, after a moment of confusion, goes into the church, and then she startles Lannard from his daze.)* What was Doctor Tolboy saying about me?

LANNARD, *with a sudden access of courage*: I shall not tell you, Mrs. Roycroft.

MRS. ROYCROFT: It's because Margaret hates me. She's been talking against me, too.

LANNARD: You mustn't bring Margaret in, if you please. I am ready to suffer and make all those dear to me suffer, but I can't let you speak of Margaret so; I can't let you speak of her at all. Her name is sacred.

MRS. ROYCROFT: Oh! And may I ask why you intend to suffer and make those dear to you suffer?

LANNARD: As soon as I heard from Mr. Hartley that you had taken these things I resolved to save you, to accuse myself, and break Margaret's heart, and kill my mother, and besmirch with infamy the stainless name my father left me, because you are a woman—and a wife—and a mother.

MRS. ROYCROFT, *after a moment of reflection*: I see. (*With a burst*) Oh, how much better women would be if the world were full of such men! And I had just been classing you with that poor weakling Hartley, and that venomous old Tolboy. (*She sighs deeply.*) How much I have wronged you! (*After another silence*) But I—I can't accept this sacrifice. You shall not do this for me. I can be generous too, and I refuse it. And no one shall ever know the real reason why you would have saved me.

LANNARD: The real reason? Isn't it enough that I am a man, and that you are a woman—and a wife—and a mother?

MRS. ROYCROFT: Oh no; the world is full of women and wives and mothers, but men don't jump at the chance of saving them. Margaret would scratch my eyes out if she knew the real reason, but—(*very solemnly*) she shall never know. Your secret will be safe with me, Charles.

LANNARD, *stupefied*: Charles!

MRS. ROYCROFT: Yes, *Charles*. You have given me the right to call you so. You would do this thing for me only because you love me.

LANNARD, *in wild dismay*: Oh, Mrs. Roycroft! *Love* you? Love *you*?

MRS ROYCROFT: Yes, me. (*She speaks sadly but fearlessly.*) You can't deny it. I've known it for—ages. And when you were choosing your wedding-ring to-day I could see that death was in your heart.

LANNARD: Death? But I was out of my mind with *joy* till I saw—I saw— Then death was truly in my heart.

MRS. ROYCROFT: You have to say that, of course. But you needn't be afraid. You are safe. And it will be easy to keep your secret because I don't love *you*, Charles. No, I pity you, but I don't love you—

LANNARD: Oh, thank you, thank you for that, Mrs. Roycroft!

MRS. ROYCROFT: If I loved—if I *did* love you—nothing should have stood between us. All ties, oaths, promises, would have been threads of gossamer. I would have gone to the ends of the world with you—to Cairo, or Paris, or Florence, or any of those places where people go. But I don't love you, Charles. I love no one but my husband, no one; and I want to save him—save him from himself, from his mad jealousy. He is very unhappy about Frank—Mr. Manvers, I mean—and I had promised I wouldn't meet him, but he *would* join me, and he insisted on motoring with me to Planets', and— Where was I?

LANNARD: Where were you?

MRS. ROYCROFT: Oh, yes; now I know. When I caught that look in your eyes, I knew that I was safe—that I could ask anything of you.

LANNARD, *in distress*: But you're mistaken, Mrs. Roycroft. I had no such look in my eyes. When I saw you—taking those things—the horror of it—

MRS. ROYCROFT: I am not mistaken; I know that look so well; I have caught it in too many eyes! And now I'm going to put you to the proof. Margaret shall never dream of it. Listen!

LANNARD: But, Mrs. Roycroft, even if this were true—about that look—I don't yet understand why you took the things—

MRS. ROYCROFT: I was coming to that. How shall I say it? You owe me more than you think—you owe me reparation for my fatal error. You didn't mean to wrong me, but when I saw that look, I was so terrified, so confused, so bewildered, so sorry for you, Charles, thinking of poor Margaret, and everything, that I swept those wretched things into my bag and came off without realizing what I had done. I rushed into the street like a mad woman—by the side door—and left Manvers in the motor on the Avenue. I suppose he's there yet, and I don't know what he'll think has become of me. But I didn't care! I was crazed—crazed with pity for you, Charles, and for poor, poor Margaret!

LANNARD: But why did you accuse yourself to Mr. Hartley, if—

MRS. ROYCROFT: Let me think, let me collect myself! Yes, now I have it! I didn't know where I was going; I flew through the street, and when I came to Mr. Hartley's church, I had an inspiration—a perfect inspiration. I resolved to burst in upon him and tell all. That look in your eyes—

LANNARD: Oh, good heavens! You didn't tell him *that*, Mrs. Roycroft?

MRS. ROYCROFT: No, I spared you, Charles. When I found him so cold and repellant and stiff, I felt that I couldn't trust him with anything really holy, and I stopped with the dry, commonplace facts. I simply said that I had taken the things, and when he showed me how I was letting suspicion fall upon you, I saw all, and I said I would go and confess and square the detectives—

LANNARD: Square them? Do you mean buy them off?

MRS. ROYCROFT: What are they there for? But when it came to it. I hadn't the courage, though I was ready to make any sacrifice for you; and I would now, though you refuse me such a trifle as saying that you were there to meet me because you loved me so wildly. I would have done anything for you, and you won't do such a little thing for me. And that you call love!

LANNARD: No, I *don't* call it love. I was willing, and I *am* willing, to say that I took the things, and save you. But I cannot take a lie upon my soul, by saying that I love you when I don't. That would be altogether different.

MRS. ROYCROFT: Different from accusing yourself of stealing, and going to prison, and getting into the papers, and everything?

LANNARD: Yes, with a whole world's difference! For then Margaret would know I was innocent, but if I said I loved you she would always believe it. No, I can't do that, Mrs. Roycroft.

MRS. ROYCROFT: Say that you are afraid to do it! (*Desolately*) Well, let it go! I will never trust any man again. And I was so sure of you!

LANNARD, *shaken*: But, Mrs. Roycroft, why would it be better for your husband to think I was in love with you than to think Manvers was?

MRS. ROYCROFT: Why, don't you see? I could say, "That boy!" and it would throw dust into his eyes completely.

LANNARD, *stiffly*: Oh!

MRS. ROYCROFT: I only said "boy," as an illustration. I should really say, "What, the son of your old friend, who's always been in and out of our house like your own child? Why, he's devoted to Margaret Wilson, and he was there

choosing a wedding-ring." Ha, ha, ha! You see, don't you?

LANNARD: No, Mrs. Roycroft, I don't see.

MRS. ROYCROFT: Then you must trust to me, and my knowledge of the world, and my experience, and my being older than you, though I'm not so *very* much older than Margaret, after all; I hope she's told you *her* age.

LANNARD, *distractedly*: But how—when—am I to say what you want me to say?

MRS. ROYCROFT: How? When? (*After a silence, reproachfully*) I should think your love for me would dictate that if you truly loved me.

LANNARD: But I *don't*, Mrs. Roycroft. That is what I have said from the beginning. That's the very point. I don't. I should think it very wrong. I am willing to do anything else to save you. But I can't deceive Mr. Roycroft by pretending to be in love with you, and diverting his suspicions from Mr. Manvers.

MRS. ROYCROFT, *after listening inattentively*: I have it, and it all works in beautifully! You've said you would acknowledge that you had taken these things?

LANNARD, *reluctantly*: Yes.

MRS. ROYCROFT: Well, all you've got to do is to say that you wished to give them to Margaret, and that you hadn't the money with you, but you expected to send it after you got home; and then in the confusion of the moment you put them into my hand-bag; something like that. You can think the details out. It would prove to Mr. Roycroft that his jealousy of Mr. Manvers was quite unfounded. I call it perfect.

LANNARD: But what will Mr. Hartley say? And Doctor Tolboy? I've talked it over with them—

MRS. ROYCROFT: They *must* confirm what you say, and they will when they see that it's the only way out. It's all so simple: I followed you here, don't you know, when I saw what you had done, because I suspected that you would come and tell Mr. Hartley as soon as you realized your wicked act, and I told him that *I* had done it. You denied it, and waited to take the blame, and while we were disputing about it, Doctor Tolboy came in, and he decided that we ought to send for my husband, for he knows how jealous he's been of Mr. Manvers, and when he understood that it was only you who had been with me he would be so relieved that he would move heaven and earth to get you out of the trouble. It's as plain as day, and I'll telephone my husband at once.

She starts toward the telephone, but Lan-

nard stops her, clutching her wrist, and fetching his breath in gasps.

LANNARD: And if I do this, if I tell, if I live this dreadful lie, what will *you* do?

MRS. ROYCROFT, *gayly*: Oh, I'll square Margaret, if that's what you mean.

LANNARD, *after manifest throes of deep excitement*: I don't know how to begin. But—I won't do it!

MRS. ROYCROFT: You will not save me? You will not sacrifice yourself to save the honor of a guilty woman, and she a wife and mother?

LANNARD: Not if you were twenty mothers and a hundred wives and a thousand guilty women. I break my promises, one and all. I won't say I took the things, and I won't say I love you. I'll keep faith with Margaret and my mother and my father's memory, and I'll break faith with you. Thank God, there's time.

MRS. ROYCROFT, *advancing upon him where he stands palpitating, and hissing in his face*: Silly—boy!

She whirls away toward the street door, as Hartley and Tolboy appear from the church entrance.

HARTLEY: Mrs. Roycroft! Wait! Don't go!

He hurries to his desk and gathers up the jewelry, which he stretches toward her.

MRS. ROYCROFT, *turning*: Oh! You've been listening.

HARTLEY: We—we were—returning. But what shall I do with these? If the detectives—

MRS. ROYCROFT: The detectives? Oh! I paid for that rubbish before I came back. *(To Lannard)* Now you can really have them for Margaret—my engagement gift. *(She flashes out of the door, which she crashes to behind her, and then instantly reopens.)* No. Some sort of teacup will do; I'll get it. Mr. Hartley, if you're so anxious about those things you can send them to my house— I'm going home to tell my husband *all*. *(With a sob)* He will believe me!

She crashes the door to behind her again.

TOLBOY, *after a moment of mutual consternation*: I really suppose he will, if she tells him all— or half, poor fellow. What a wonderful woman! *(To Lannard)* But I congratulate you, my dear boy, on being out of her clutches. There's no use trying to blink the fact: we've heard every word. I wanted to, and Hartley thought it was his duty—

HARTLEY: But I still don't understand why she wished to make me believe she had stolen those things. What reason had she, what motive?

TOLBOY: Oh, well, as a woman she wouldn't need a reason; and who can ever say what a woman's motive is? Perhaps her nature demanded a novel play of emotion. *(To Lannard)* But whatever she meant, you've done the right thing, my dear boy. I don't know that I should have had the courage.

LANNARD, *brokenly*: I've fallen below my ideal.

TOLBOY: The ideal of a man who thinks such a woman does such things once in a way, and may be redeemed by a good round lying piece of self-sacrifice? But such a woman always does such things in every way, and she can only be shielded, never saved. No, no! Never regret that in this case you've looked out for yourself. You've shown yourself a true hero! Some day I hope we shall have you in the novels and the plays.

The Night Before Christmas

[1910]

In 1910 Howells published two plays, *The Night Before Christmas* and *The Impossible, A Mystery Play*, each involving the same characters, who were to appear in no other plays. In a way, Clarence and Lucy Fountain seem to be Willis and Amy Campbell grown older and more serious; the man still has Willis' wit, and there is the sentimental but intelligent charm of Amy in the woman. But they speak differently from the Campbells or any other of Howells' dramatic characters, and the dialogue plus the general atmosphere sets these plays apart from other Howells dramas. Neither play shows a close relationship to medieval drama, although the mystery play has religious and supernatural overtones, and *The Night Before Christmas* ponders a truthful morality of Christmas.

During most of the play, the Fountains simply toy with the idea that Christmas is an abuse that civilized mankind should not inflict upon itself, but they do not deeply disturb themselves with this idea. There is simply the suggestion that the pagan Christmas they celebrate is a sad mimicry of a Christian Christmas. For the tired and gloomy Fountains, Christmas is mainly a legal holiday, and when one giver suggests an answer to their problem—"Love the Giver"—they pass it by without recognizing the value that the idea should have for them.

As a play *The Night Before Christmas* succeeds mainly as it shows Howells' distrust of the Christmas gift and the giver, although it is difficult to establish clearly his point of view. In many passages, particularly Fountain's witty speeches, the tone is satirical, but Howells also suggests a pronounced disproportion between the Christian ideals of his rural childhood and the material reality of an industrial city. The play ends happily, it is true, but the happiness is all on the surface, the parents having sentimentalized a reason for Christmas which, though true and perhaps meaningful for them, does not penetrate beyond occasional hints to the real reasons for Christmas. This is a thoughtful play—something more than simple fun—close in spirit to "Christmas Every Day" and other Howells stories in which the materialistic view, the attitude toward gifts, the wish to do away with Christmas, and the tiredness and the hypocrisy are clearly shown. Perhaps Howells simply *is* satirizing the Fountains' inability to feel the meaning of Christmas, mitigated somewhat by an affection for the children, but there is evidence that he shares their attitudes toward the gifts, the givers, and the occasion.

The Night Before Christmas[1]

A MORALITY

MRS. CLARENCE FOUNTAIN, *backing into the room, and closing the door noiselessly before looking round*: Oh, you poor thing! I can see that you are dead, at the first glance. I'm dead myself, for that matter. (*She is speaking to her husband, who clings with one hand to the chimney-piece, and supports his back with the other; from this hand a little girl's long stocking lumpily dangles; Mrs. Fountain, turning round, observes it.*) Not finished yet? But I don't wonder! I wonder you've even begun. Well, now, I will take hold with you. (*In token of the aid she is going to give, Mrs. Fountain sinks into a chair and rolls a distracted eye over the littered and tumbled room.*) It's worse than I thought it would be. You ought to have smoothed the papers out and laid them in a pile as fast as you unwrapped the things; that is the way I always do; and wound the strings up and put them one side. Then you wouldn't have had to wade round in them. I suppose I oughtn't to have left it to you, but if I had let *you* put the children to bed you know you'd have told them stories and kept them all night over their prayers. And as it was each of them wanted to put in a special Christmas clause; I know what kind of Christmas clause *I* should have put in if I'd been frank! I'm not sure it's right to keep up the deception. One comfort, the oldest ones don't believe in it any more than we do. Dear! I did think at one time this afternoon I should have to be brought home in an ambulance; it would have been a convenience, with all the packages. I simply marvel at their delivery wagons getting them here.

FOUNTAIN, *coming to the table, where she sits, and taking up one of the toys with which it is strewn*: They haven't all of them.

MRS. FOUNTAIN: What do you mean by all of them?

FOUNTAIN: I mean half.

He takes up a mechanical locomotive and stuffs it into the stocking he holds.

[1] The text used here is from *The Daughter of the Storage.*

MRS. FOUNTAIN, *staying his hand*: What are you doing? Putting Jimmy's engine into Susy's stocking! She'll be perfectly insulted when she finds it, for she'll know you weren't paying the least attention, and you can't blame Santa Claus for it with *her*. If that's what you've been doing with the other stockings— But there *aren't* any others. Don't tell me you've just begun! Well, I could simply cry.

FOUNTAIN, *dropping into the chair on the other side of the table, under the shelter of a tall Christmas tree standing on it*: Do you call unwrapping a whole car-load of truck and getting it sorted, just beginning? I've been slaving here from the dawn of time, and I had to have *some* leisure for the ghosts of my own Christmases when I was little. I didn't have to wade round in the wrappings of my presents in those days. But it isn't the sad memories that take it out of you; it's the happy ones. I've never had a ghastlier half-hour than I've just spent in the humiliating multiplicity of these gifts. All the old birthdays and wedding-days and Fourth of Julys and home-comings and children's christenings I've ever had came trooping back. There oughtn't to be any gay anniversaries; they should be forbidden by law. If I could only have recalled a few dangerous fevers and funerals!

MRS. FOUNTAIN: Clarence! Don't say such a thing; you'll be punished for it. I know how you suffer from those gloomy feelings, and I pity you. You ought to bear up against them. If *I* gave way! You must think about something cheerful in the future when the happiness of the past afflicts you, and set one against the other; life isn't *all* a vale of tears. You must keep your mind fixed on the work before you. I don't believe it's the number of the packages here that's broken you down. It's the shopping that's worn you out; I'm sure I'm a mere thread. And I had been at it from immediately after breakfast; and I lunched in one of the stores with ten thousand suburbans who had come pouring in with the first of their unnatural trains: I did hope I should have some of the places to myself; but they were every one jammed. And you

603

came up from your office about four, perfectly fresh.

FOUNTAIN: Fresh! Yes, quite dewy from a day's fight with the beasts at Ephesus [1] on the eve of Christmas week.

MRS. FOUNTAIN: Well, don't be cynical, Clarence, on this, of all nights of the year. You know how sorry I always am for what you have to go through down there, and I suppose it's worse, as you say, at this season than any other time of year. It's the terrible concentration of everything just before Christmas that makes it so killing. I really don't know which of the places was the worst; the big department stores or the separate places for jewelry and toys and books and stationery and antiques; they were all alike, and all maddening. And the rain outside, and everybody coming in reeking; though I don't believe that sunshine would have been any better; there'd have been more of them. I declare, it made my heart ache for those poor creatures behind the counters, and I don't know whether I suffered most for them when they kept up a ghastly cheerfulness in their attention or were simply insulting in their indifference. I know they must be all dead by this time. "Going up?" "Going down?" "Ca-ish!" "Here, boy!" I believe it will ring in my ears as long as I live. And the whiz of those overhead wire things, and having to wait ages for your change, and then drag your tatters out of the stores into the streets! If I hadn't had you with me at the last I should certainly have dropped.[2]

FOUNTAIN: Yes, and what had become of your good resolutions about doing all your Christmas shopping in July?

MRS. FOUNTAIN: *My* good resolutions? Really, Clarence, sometimes if it were not cruelty to animals I should like to hit you. *My* good— You *know* that you suggested that plan, and it wasn't even original with you. The papers have been talking about it for years; but when you brought it up as such a new idea, I fell in with it to please you—

FOUNTAIN: Now, look out, Lucy!

MRS. FOUNTAIN: Yes, to please you, and to help you forget the Christmas worry, just as I've been doing to-night. You never spare *me*.

FOUNTAIN: Stick to the record. Why didn't you do your Christmas shopping in July?

1. I Corinthians, 15:32.
2 In a letter to his sister, Aurelia, December 23, 1906 (Harvard Library) Howells comments on Christmas shopping: "Elinor and I have fairly freed ourselves from Christmas shopping, but Pilla is still under the curse, and we have got together quite the usual truck."

MRS. FOUNTAIN: Why didn't I? Did you expect me to do my Christmas shopping down at Sculpin Beach, where I spent the whole time from the middle of June till the middle of September? Why didn't *you* do the Christmas shopping in July? You had the stores under your nose here from the beginning till the end of summer, with nothing in the world to hinder you, and not a chick or a child to look after.

FOUNTAIN: Oh, I like that. You think I was leading a life of complete leisure here, with the thermometer among the nineties nine-tenths of the time?

MRS. FOUNTAIN: I only know you were bragging in all your letters about your bath and your club, and the folly of any one going away from the cool, comfortable town in the summer. I suppose you'll say that was to keep me from feeling badly at leaving you. When it was only for the children's sake! I will let you take them the next time.

FOUNTAIN: While you look after my office? And you think the stores are full of Christmas things in July, I suppose.

MRS. FOUNTAIN: I never thought so; and now I hope you see the folly of that idea. No, Clarence. We must be logical in everything. You can't get rid of Christmas shopping at Christmastime.

FOUNTAIN, *shouting wrathfully*: Then I say get rid of Christmas!

WATKINS, *opening the door for himself and struggling into the room with an armful of parcels*: I'm with you there, Clarence. Christmas is at the root of Christmas shopping, and Christmas giving, and all the rest of it. Oh, you needn't be afraid, Lucy. I didn't hear any epithets; just caught the drift of your argument through the keyhole. I've been kicking at the door ever since you began. Where shall I dump these things?

MRS. FOUNTAIN: Oh, you poor boy! Here—anywhere—on the floor—on the sofa—on the table. (*She clears several spaces and helps Watkins unload.*) Clarence! I'm surprised at you. What are you thinking of?

FOUNTAIN: I'm thinking that if this goes on, I'll let somebody else arrange the presents.

WATKINS: If I saw a man coming into my house with a load like this to-night, I'd throw him into the street. But living in a ninth-story flat like you, it might hurt him.

MRS. FOUNTAIN, *reading the inscriptions on the packages*: "For Benny from his Uncle Frank." Oh, how sweet of you, Frank! And here's a kiss for his Uncle Frank. (*She embraces him with as little interruption as possible.)* "From Uncle Frank to Jim." Oh, I know what that is! *(She feels the package over.)* And this is for "Susy from her Aunt Sue." Oh, I knew she would remember her namesake. "For Maggie. Merry Christmas from Mrs. Watkins." "Bridget, with Mrs. Watkins's best wishes for a Merry Christmas." Both the girls! But it's like Sue; she never forgets anybody. And what's this for Clarence? I *must* know! Not a bathgown? *(Undoing it)* I simply *must* see it. Blue! His very color! *(Holding it up)* From you, Frank? *(He nods.)* Clarence!

WATKINS: If Fountain tries to kiss me, I'll—

FOUNTAIN: I wouldn't kiss you for a dozen bathgowns. *(Lifting it up from the floor where Mrs. Fountain has dropped it)* It *is* rather nice.

WATKINS: Don't overwhelm me.

MRS. FOUNTAIN, *dancing about with a long, soft roll in her hand*: Oh, oh, oh! She saw me gloating on it at Shumaker's! I do wonder if it *is*.

FOUNTAIN, *reaching for it*: Why, open it—

MRS. FOUNTAIN: You dare! No, it shall be opened the very last thing in the morning, now, to punish you! How is poor Sue? I saw her literally dropping by the way at Shumaker's.

WATKINS, *making for the door*: Well, she must have got up again. I left her registering a vow that if ever she lived to see another Christmas she would leave the country months before the shopping began. She called down maledictions on all the recipients of her gifts and wished them the worst harm that can befall the wicked.

MRS. FOUNTAIN: Poor Sue! She simply lives to do people good, and I can understand exactly how she feels toward them. I'll be round bright and early to-morrow to thank her. Why do you go?

WATKINS: Well, I can't stay here all night, and I'd better let you and Clarence finish up.

He escapes from her detaining embrace and runs out.

MRS. FOUNTAIN, *intent upon her roll*: How funny he is! I wonder if he did hear anything but our scolding voices? Where were we?

FOUNTAIN: I had just called you a serpent.

MRS. FOUNTAIN, *with amusement*: No, really? *(Feeling the parcel)* If it's that Spanish lace scarf I can tell her it was machine lace. I saw it at the first glance. But poor Sue has no taste. I suppose I must stand it. But I can't bear to think what she's given the girls and children. She means well. Did you really say serpent, Clarence? You never called me just *that* before.

FOUNTAIN: No, but you called me a laughing hyena, and said I scoffed at everything sacred.

MRS. FOUNTAIN: I can't remember using the word hyena, exactly, though I do think the way you talk about Christmas is dreadful. But I take back the laughing hyena.

FOUNTAIN: And I take back the serpent. I meant dove, anyway. But it's this Christmastime when a man gets so tired he doesn't know what he's saying.

MRS. FOUNTAIN: Well, *you're* good, anyway, dearest, whatever you say; and now I'm going to help you arrange the things. I suppose there'll be lots more to-morrow, but we must get rid of these now. Don't you wish nobody would do anything for us? Just the children—dear little souls! I don't believe but what we can make Jim and Susy believe in Santa Claus again; Benny is firm in the faith; he put him into his prayer. I declare, his sweetness almost broke my heart. *(At a knock)* Who's that, I wonder? Come in! Oh, it's you, Maggie. Well?

MAGGIE: It's Mr. Fountain's sisters just telephoned up.

MRS. FOUNTAIN: Have them come up at once, Maggie, of course. *(As Maggie goes out)* Another interruption! If it's going to keep on like this! Shouldn't you have thought they might have *sent* their presents?

FOUNTAIN: I thought something like it in Frank's case; but I didn't say it.

MRS. FOUNTAIN: And I don't know why *I* say it, now. It's because I'm so tired I don't know what I *am* saying. Do forgive me! It's this terrible Christmas spirit that gets into me. But now you'll see how nice I can be to them. *(At a tap on the door)* Come in! Come in! Don't mind our being in all this mess. So darling of you to come! You can help cheer Clarence up; you know his Christmas Eve dumps. *(She runs to them and clasps them in her arms with several half-open packages dangling from her hands and contrasting their disarray with the neatness of their silk-ribboned and tissue-papered parcels which their embrace makes meet at her back.)* Minnie! Aggie! To lug here, when you ought to be at home in bed dying of fatigue! But it's just like you, both of you. Did you ever see anything like the stores to-day? Do sit down, or swoon on the floor, or anything. Let me have those wretched bundles which are simply killing you. *(She looks at the different packages.)* "For Benny from Grandpa." "For a good girl, from Susy's grandmother." "Jim, from Aunt Minnie and Aunt Aggie." "Lucy, with love from

Aggie and Minnie." And Clarence! What hearts you *have* got! Well, I always say there never were such thoughtful girls, and you always show such taste and such originality. I long to get at the things. (*She keeps fingering the large bundle marked with her husband's name.*) Not—not—a—

MINNIE: Yes, a bath-robe. Unless you give him a cigar-case it's about the only thing you can give a man.

AGGIE: Minnie thought of it and I chose it. Blue, because it's his color. Try it on, Clarence, and if it's too long—

MRS. FOUNTAIN: Yes, do, dear! Let's see you with it on. (*While the girls are fussily opening the robe, she manages to push her brother's gift behind the door. Then, without looking round at her husband.*) It isn't a bit too long. Just the very— (*Looking*) Well, it can easily be taken up at the hem. I can do it to-morrow. (*She abandons him to his awkward isolation while she chatters on with his sisters.*) Sit down; I insist! Don't think of going. Did you see that frightful pack of people when the cab horse fell down in front of Shumaker's?

MINNIE: See it?

AGGIE: We were in the midst of it! I wonder we ever got out alive. It's enough to make you wish never to see another Christmas as long as you live.

MINNIE: A great many *won't* live. There will be more grippe, and more pneumonia, and more appendicitis from those jams of people in the stores!

AGGIE: The germs must have been swarming.

FOUNTAIN: Lucy was black with them when we got home.

MRS. FOUNTAIN: Don't pay the slightest attention to him, girls. He'll probably be the first to sneeze himself.

MINNIE: I don't know about sneezing. I shall only be too glad if I don't have nervous prostration from it.

AGGIE: I'm glad we got our motor-car just in time. Any one that goes in the trolleys now will take their life in their hand. (*The girls rise and move toward the door.*) Well, we must go on now. We're making a regular round; you can't trust the delivery wagons at a time like this. Good-by. Merry Christmas to the children. They're fast asleep by this time, I suppose.

MINNIE: I only wish *I* was!

MRS. FOUNTAIN: I believe you, Minnie. Good-by. Good night. Good night, Aggie. Clarence, go to the elevator with them! Or no, he can't in that ridiculous bath-gown! (*Turning to Fountain as the door closes*) Now I've done it.

FOUNTAIN: It isn't a thing you could have wished to phrase that way, exactly.

MRS. FOUNTAIN: And you made me do it. Never thanking them, or anything, and standing there like I don't know what, and leaving the talk all to me. And now, making me lose my temper again, when I wanted to be so nice to you. Well, it is no use trying, and from this on I won't. *Clarence!* (*She has opened the parcel addressed to herself and now stands transfixed with joy and wonder.*) See what the girls have given me! The very necklace I've been longing for at Planets', and denying myself for the last fortnight! Well, never will I say your sisters are mean again.

FOUNTAIN: You ought to have said that to them.

MRS. FOUNTAIN: It quite reconciles one to Christmas. What? Oh, that *was* rather nasty. You know I didn't mean it. I was so excited I didn't know what I was saying. I'm sure nobody ever got on better with sisters-in-law, and that shows my tact; if I do make a slip, now and then, I can always get out of it. They will understand. Do you think it was very nice of them to flaunt their new motor in my face? But of course anything *your* family does is perfect, and always was, though I must say this necklace is sweet of them. I wonder they had the taste. (*A tap on the door is heard.*) Come in, Maggie! (*Sotto voce.*) Take it off.

> *She snatches his bath-robe and tosses it behind the door.*

HAZARD: I suppose I can come in, even if I'm not Maggie. Catch, Fountain. (*He tosses a large bundle to Fountain.*) It's huge, but it isn't hefty.

> *He turns to go out again.*

MRS. FOUNTAIN: Oh, oh, oh! Don't go! Come in and help us. What have you brought Clarence! May I feel?

HAZARD: You can look, if you like. I'm rather proud of it. There's only one other thing you can give a man, and I said, "No, not a cigar-case. Fountain smokes enough already, but if a bath-robe can induce him to wash—"

> *He goes out.*

MRS. FOUNTAIN, *screaming after him through the open door*: Oh, how good! Come back and see it on him.

> *She throws the bath-robe over Fountain's shoulders.*

HAZARD, *looking in again*: Perfect fit, just as the Jew said, and the very color for Fountain.

He vanishes, shutting the door behind him.

MRS. FOUNTAIN: How coarse! Well, my dear, I don't know where you picked up your bachelor friends. I hope this is the last of them.

FOUNTAIN: Hazard's the only one who has survived your rigorous treatment. But he always had a passion for cold shoulder, poor fellow. As bath-robes go, this isn't bad. *(He gets his arms into it, and walks up and down.)* Heigh?

MRS. FOUNTAIN: Yes, it is pretty good. But the worst of Christmas is that it rouses up all your old friends.

FOUNTAIN: They feel so abnormally good, confound them. I suppose poor old Hazard half killed himself looking this thing up and building the joke to go with it.

MRS. FOUNTAIN: Well, take it off, now, and come help me with the children's presents. You're quite forgetting about them, and it'll be morning and you'll have the little wretches swarming in before you can turn round. Dear little souls! I can sympathize with their impatience, of course. But what are you going to do with these bath-robes? You can't wear *four* bath-robes.

FOUNTAIN: I can change them every day. But there ought to be seven. This hood is rather a new wrinkle, though, isn't it? I suppose it's for a voyage, and you pull it up over your head when you come through the corridor back to your stateroom. We shall have to go to Europe, Lucy.

MRS. FOUNTAIN: I would go to Asia, Africa, and Oceanica, to escape another Christmas. Now if there are any more bath-robes— Come in, Maggie.

MAGGIE, *bringing in a bundle*: Something a District Messenger brought. Will you sign for it, ma'am?

MRS. FOUNTAIN: You sign, Clarence. If I know anything about the look and the feel of a bundle, this *is* another bath-robe, but I shall soon see. *(While she is cutting the string and tearing the wrappings away. Fountain signs and Maggie goes. Mrs. Fountain shakes out the folds of the robe.)* Well, upon my word, I should think there was conspiracy to insult you, Clarence. I should like to know who has had the effrontery— What's on it?

FOUNTAIN, *reading from the card which had fallen out of the garment to the floor*: "With Christmas greetings from Mrs. Arthur J. Gibby."

MRS. FOUNTAIN, *dropping the robe and seizing the card*: Mrs. Arthur J. Gibby! Well, upon my word, this *is* impudence. It's not only impudence, it's indelicacy. And I had always thought she was the very embodiment of refinement, and I've gone about saying so. Now I shall have to take it back. The idea of a lady sending a bath-robe to a gentleman! What next, I wonder! What right has Mrs. Gibby to send you a bath-robe? Don't prevaricate! Remember that the truth is the only thing that can save you. Matters must have gone pretty far, when a woman could send you anything so— intimate. What are you staring at with that paper? You needn't hope to divert my mind by—

FOUNTAIN, *giving her the paper in which the robe came*: Seems to be for *Mrs.* Clarence Fountain.

MRS. FOUNTAIN, *snatching it from him*: What! It is, it is! Oh, poor dear Lilly! How can you ever forgive me? She saw me looking at it to-day at Shumaker's, and it must have come into her head in despair what else to get me. But it was a perfect inspiration—for it was just what I was longing for. Why—*(laughing hysterically while she holds up the robe, and turns it this way and that)* I might have seen at a glance that it wasn't a man's, with this lace on and this silk hood, and—*(she hurries into it, and pulls it forward, looking down at either side)* it's just the right length, and if it was made for me it couldn't fit me better. What a joke I *shall* have with Lilly, when I tell her about it. I sha'n't spare myself a bit!

FOUNTAIN: Then I hope you'll spare me. I have some little delicacy of feeling, and I don't like the notion of a lady's giving me a bath-robe. It's —intimate. I don't know where you picked up your girl friends.

MRS. FOUNTAIN, *capering about joyfully*: Oh, how funny you are, darling! But go on. I don't mind it, now. And you may be glad you've got off so easily. Only now if there are any more bath-robes— *(A timid rap is heard at the door.)* Come in, Maggie!

The door is slowly set ajar, then flung suddenly wide open, and Jim and Susy in their night-gowns rush dancing and exulting in.

SUSY: We've caught you, we've caught you.

JIM: I just bet it was you, and now I've won, haven't I, mother?

SUSY: And I've won, too, haven't I, father? *(Arrested at sight of her father in the hooded bath-gown)* He does look like Santa Claus, doesn't he, Jimmy? But the real Santa Claus would be all over snow, and a long, white beard. You can't fool *us!*

JIM: You can't fool *us!* We know you, we know you! And mother dressed up, too! There isn't any Mrs. Santa Claus, and that proves it!

MRS. FOUNTAIN, *severely*: Dreadful little things! Who said you might come here? Go straight back to bed, this minute, or— *Will* you send them back, Clarence, and not stand staring so? What are you thinking of?

FOUNTAIN, *dreamily*: Nothing. Merely wondering what we shall do when we've got rid of our superstitions. Shall we be the better for it, or even the wiser?

MRS. FOUNTAIN: What put that question into your head? Christmas, I suppose; and that's another reason for wishing there was no such thing. If I had my way, there wouldn't be.

JIM: Oh, mother!

SUSY: No Christmas?

MRS. FOUNTAIN: Well, not for disobedient children who get out of bed and come in, spoiling everything. If you don't go straight back, it will be the last time, Santa Claus or no Santa Claus.

JIM: And if we go right back?

SUSY: And promise not to come in any more?

MRS. FOUNTAIN: Well, we'll see how you keep your promise. If you don't, that's the end of Christmas in *this* house.

JIM: It's a bargain, then! Come on, Susy!

SUSY: And we do it for you, mother. And for you, father. We just came in for fun, anyway.

JIM: We just came for a surprise.

MRS. FOUNTAIN, *kissing them both*: Well, then, if it was only for fun, we'll excuse you this time. Run along, now, that's good children. *Clarence!*

FOUNTAIN: Well?

He looks up at her from where he has dropped into a chair beside the table strewn with opened and unopened gifts at the foot of the Christmas tree.

MRS. FOUNTAIN: What *are* you mooning about?

FOUNTAIN: What if it was all a fake? Those thousands and hundreds of thousands of churches that pierce the clouds with their spires; those millions of ministers and missionaries; those billions of worshipers, sitting and standing and kneeling, and singing and praying; those nuns and monks, and brotherhoods and sisterhoods, with their ideals of self-denial, and their duties to the sick and poor; those martyrs that died for the one true faith, and those other martyrs of the other true faiths whom the one true faith tortured and killed; those masses and sermons and ceremonies, what if they were all a delusion, a mistake, a mis-

understanding? What if it were all as unlike the real thing, if there is any real thing, as this pagan Christmas of ours is as unlike a Christian Christmas?

MRS. FOUNTAIN, *springing up*: I knew it! I knew that it was this Christmas giving that was making you morbid again. Can't you shake it off and be cheerful—like me? I'm sure I have to bear twice as much of it as you have. I've been shopping the whole week, and you've been just this one afternoon.

She begins to catch her breath, and fails in searching for her handkerchief in the folds of her dress under the bath-robe.

FOUNTAIN, *offering his handkerchief*: Take mine.

MRS. FOUNTAIN, *catching it from him, and hiding her face in it on the table*: You ought to help me bear up, and instead of that you fling yourself on my sympathies and break me down. (*Lifting her face*) And if it was all a fake, as you say, and an illusion, what would you do, what would you give people in place of it?

FOUNTAIN: I don't know.

MRS. FOUNTAIN: What would you have in place of Christmas itself?

FOUNTAIN: I don't know.

MRS. FOUNTAIN: Well, then, I wouldn't set myself up to preach down everything—in a blue bath-gown. You've no idea how ridiculous you are.

FOUNTAIN: Oh, yes, I have. I can see you. You look like one of those blue nuns in Rome.[1] But I don't remember any lace on them.

MRS. FOUNTAIN: Well, you don't look like a blue monk, you needn't flatter yourself, for there are none. You look like— What are you thinking about?

FOUNTAIN: Oh, nothing. What do you suppose is in all these packages here? Useful things, that we need, that we must have? You know without looking that it's the superfluity of naughtiness in one form or other. And the givers of these gifts, they *had* to give them, just as we've had to give dozens of gifts ourselves. We ought to have put on our cards, "With the season's bitterest grudges," "In hopes of a return," "With a hopeless sense of the folly," "To pay a hateful debt," "With impotent rage and despair."

MRS. FOUNTAIN: I don't deny it, Clarence. You're perfectly right; I almost wish we *had* put

[1] The Sisters of Charity (Filles de la Charité) of St. Vincent de Paul wear blue gowns, blue aprons, and stiff white hats called cornettes.

it. How it would have made them hop! But they'd have known it was just the way they felt themselves.

FOUNTAIN, *going on thoughtfully*: It's the capsheaf of the social barbarism we live in, the hideous hypocrisy. It's no use to put it on religion. The Jews keep Christmas, too, and we know what they think of Christianity as a belief. No, we've got to go further back, to the Pagan Saturnalia— Well, I renounce the whole affair, here and now. I'm going to spend the rest of the night bundling these things up, and to-morrow I'm going to spend the day in a taxi, going round and giving them back to the fools that sent them.

MRS. FOUNTAIN: And I'm going with you. I hate it as much as you do— Come in, Maggie!

MAGGIE: Something the elevator-boy says he forgot. It came along with the last one.

MRS. FOUNTAIN, *taking a bundle from her*: If this is another bath-robe, Clarence! It *is*, as I live. Now if it is a woman sending it— (*She picks up a card which falls out of the robe as she unfolds it.*) "Love the Giver," indeed! Now, Clarence, I insist, I demand—

FOUNTAIN: Hold on, hold on, my dear. The last bath-robe that came from a woman was for *you*.

MRS. FOUNTAIN: So it was. I don't know what I was thinking about; and I do beg your par— But this is a man's bath-robe!

FOUNTAIN, *taking the card which she mechanically stretches out to him*: And a man sends it— old Fellows. Can't you read print? Ambrose J. Fellows, and a message in writing: "It was a toss-up between this and a cigar-case, and the bath-robe won. Hope you haven't got any other thoughtful friends."

MRS. FOUNTAIN: Oh, very brilliant, giving me a start like this! I shall let Mr. Fellows know— What is it, Maggie? Open the door, please.

MAGGIE, *opening*: It's just a District Messenger.

FOUNTAIN, *ironically*: Oh, only a District Messenger.

He signs the messenger's slip, while his wife receives from Maggie a bundle which she regards with suspicion.

MRS. FOUNTAIN: "From Uncle Philip for Clarence." Well, Uncle Philip, if you have sent Clarence—*Clarence!* (*Breaking into a whimper*) It is, it is! It's another.

FOUNTAIN: Well, that only makes the seventh, and just enough for every day in the week. It's quite my ideal. Now, if there's nothing about a cigar-case— Hello! (*He feels in the pocket of the*

robe and brings out a cigar-case, from which a slip of paper falls.*) "Couldn't make up my mind between them, so send both. Uncle Phil." Well, this is the last stroke of Christmas insanity.

MRS. FOUNTAIN: His brain simply reeled under it, and gave way. It shows what Christmas really comes to with a man of strong intellect like Uncle Phil.

FOUNTAIN, *opening the case*: Oh, I don't know! He's put some cigars in here—in a lucid interval, probably. There's hope yet.

MRS. FOUNTAIN, *in despair*: No, Clarence, there's no hope. Don't flatter yourself. The only way is to bundle back all their presents and never, never, never give or receive another one. Come! Let's begin tying them up at once; it will take us the rest of the night. (*A knock at the door.*) Come, Maggie.

JIM AND SUSY, *pushing in*: We can't sleep, mother. May we have a pillow fight to keep us amused till we're drowsy?

MRS. FOUNTAIN, *desolately*: Yes, go and have your pillow fight. It doesn't matter now. We're sending the presents all back, anyway.

She begins frantically wrapping some of the things up.

SUSY: Oh, father, are you sending them back?

JIM: She's just making believe. Isn't she, father?

FOUNTAIN: Well, I'm not so sure of that. If she doesn't do it, I will.

MRS. FOUNTAIN, *desisting*: Will you go right back to bed?

JIM AND SUSY: Yes, we will.

MRS. FOUNTAIN: And to sleep, instantly?

JIM AND SUSY, *in succession*: We won't keep awake a minute longer.

MRS. FOUNTAIN: Very well, then, we'll see. Now be off with you. (*As they put their heads together and go out laughing*) And remember, if you come here another single time, back go every one of the presents.

FOUNTAIN: As soon as ever Santa Claus can find a moment for it.

JIM, *derisively*: Oh, yes, Santa Claus!

SUSY: I guess if you wait for Santa Claus to take them back!

MRS. FOUNTAIN: Tiresome little wretches. Of course we can't expect them to keep up the self-deception.

FOUNTAIN: They'll grow to another. When they're men and women they'll pretend that Christmas is delightful, and go round giving people the presents that they've worn their lives out in buying and getting together. And they'll work themselves up into the notion that they are really enjoying it, when they know at the bottom of their souls that they loathe the whole job.

MRS. FOUNTAIN: There you are with your pessimism again! And I had just begun to feel cheerful about it!

FOUNTAIN: Since when? Since I proposed sending this rubbish back to the givers with our curse?

MRS. FOUNTAIN: No, I was thinking what fun it would be if we could get up a sort of Christmas game, and do it just among relations and intimate friends.

FOUNTAIN: Ah, I wish you luck of it. Then the thing would begin to have some reality, and just as in proportion as people had the worst feelings in giving the presents, their best feeling would be hurt in getting them back.

MRS. FOUNTAIN: Then why did you ever think of it?

FOUNTAIN: To keep from going mad. Come, let's go on with this job of sorting the presents, and putting them in the stockings and hanging them up on the tree and laying them round the trunk of it. One thing: it's for the last time. As soon as Christmas week is over, I shall inaugurate an educational campaign against the whole Christmas superstition. It must be extirpated root and branch, and the extirpation must begin in the minds of the children; we old fools are hopeless; we must die in it; but the children can be saved. We must organize and make a house-to-house fight; and I'll begin in our own house. To-morrow, as soon as the children have made themselves thoroughly sick with candy and cake and midday dinner, I will appeal to their reason, and get them to agree to drop it; to sign the Anti-Christmas pledge; to—

MRS. FOUNTAIN: Clarence! I have an idea.

FOUNTAIN: Not a *bright* one?

MRS. FOUNTAIN: Yes, a bright one, even if you didn't originate it. Have Christmas confined entirely to children—to the very youngest—to children that believe firmly in Santa Claus.

FOUNTAIN: Oh, hello! Wouldn't that leave Jim and Susy out? I couldn't have *them* left out.

MRS. FOUNTAIN: That's true. I didn't think of that. Well, say, to children that either believe or *pretend* to believe in him. What's *that?* (*She stops at a faint, soft sound on the door.*) It's Maggie with her hands so full she's pushing with her elbow. Come in, Maggie, come in. *Come* in! Don't you hear me? Come in, I say! Oh, it isn't

Maggie, of course! It's those worthless, worthless little wretches, again. (*She runs to the door calling out,* Naughty, naughty, naughty! *as she runs. Then, flinging the door wide, with a final cry of* Naughty, I say! *she discovers a small figure on the threshold, nightgowned to its feet, and looking up with a frightened, wistful face.*) Why, Benny! (*She stoops down and catches the child in her arms, and presses him tight to her neck, and bends over, covering his head with kisses.*) What in the world are you doing here, you poor little lamb? Is mother's darling walking in his sleep? What did you want, my pet? Tell mudda, do! Whisper it in mudda's big ear! Can't you tell mudda? What? Whisper a little louder, love! We're not angry with you, sweetness. Now, try to speak louder. Is that Santa Claus? No, dearest, that's just dadda. Santa Claus hasn't come yet, but he will soon. What? Say it again. *Is there any* Santa Claus? Why, who else could have brought all these presents? Presents for Benny and Jim and Susy and mudda, and seven bath-gowns for dadda. Isn't that funny? Seven! And one for mudda. What? I can't quite hear you, pet. Are we going to send the presents back? Why, who ever heard of such a thing? Jim said so? And Susy? Well, I will settle with them, when I come to them. You don't want me to? Well, I won't, then, if Benny doesn't want mudda to. I'll just give them a kiss apiece, pop in their big ears. What? You've got something for Santa Claus to give them? What? Where? In your crib? And shall we go and get it? For mudda too? And dadda? Oh, my little angel! (*She begins to cry over him, and to kiss him again.*) You'll break my heart with your loveliness. He wants to kiss you too, dadda. (*She puts the boy into his father's arms; then catches him back and runs from the room with him. Fountain resumes the work of filling the long stocking he had begun with; then he takes up a very short sock. He has that in his hand when Mrs. Fountain comes back, wiping her eyes.*) He'll go to sleep now, I guess; he was half dreaming when he came in here. I should think, when you saw how Benny believed in it, you'd be ashamed of saying a word against Christmas.

FOUNTAIN: Who's said anything against it? I've just been arguing for it, and trying to convince you that for the sake of little children like Benny it ought to be perpetuated to the end of the world. It began with the childhood of the race, in the rejuvenescence of the spirit.

MRS. FOUNTAIN: Didn't you say that Christmas began with the pagans? How monstrously you prevaricate!

FOUNTAIN: That was merely a figure of speech. And besides, since you've been out with Benny, I've been thinking, and I take back everything I've said or thought against Christmas; I didn't really think it. I've been going back in my mind to that first Christmas we had together, and it's cheered me up wonderfully.

MRS. FOUNTAIN, *tenderly*: Have you, dearest? I *always* think of it. If you could have seen Benny, how I left him, just now?

FOUNTAIN: I shouldn't mind seeing him, and I shouldn't care if I gave a glance at poor old Jim and Susy. I'd like to reassure them about not sending back the presents.

He puts his arm round her and presses her toward the door.

MRS. FOUNTAIN: How sweet you are! And how funny! And good! (*She accentuates each sentiment with a kiss.*) And don't you suppose I felt sorry for you, making you go round with me the whole afternoon, and then leaving you to take the brunt of arranging the presents? Now I'll tell you: *next* year, I *will* do my Christmas shopping in July. It's the only way.

FOUNTAIN: No, there's a better way. As you were saying, they don't have the Christmas things out. The only way is to do our Christmas shopping the day after Christmas; everything will be round still, and dog-cheap. Come, we'll begin day after to-morrow.

MRS. FOUNTAIN: We will, we will!

FOUNTAIN: Do you think we will?

MRS. FOUNTAIN: Well, we'll *say* we will.

They laugh together, and then he kisses her.

FOUNTAIN: Even if it goes on in the same old way, as long as we have each other—

MRS. FOUNTAIN: And the children.

FOUNTAIN: I forgot the children!

MRS. FOUNTAIN: Oh, how delightful you are!

THE END

Parting Friends, Tragedy

[1910]

Toward the end of his playwriting career, Howells tended to burlesque the traditional dramatic forms—the melodrama, the satire, the tragedy, the mystery play, the realistic play, and the social comedy. The subtitle of *Parting Friends, Tragedy*, then, is a clue to Howells' objectives in writing this play. Obviously Howells is not serious, and in one sense he is laughing at himself and at his theories of commonplace tragedy. Here is a commonplace tragedy, one of those simple "tragic" incidents that seem overwhelmingly important at the time. But what is it really when viewed in the proper perspective? It is mainly humorous, something that years hence will be a very comic story when told to one's grandchildren. The title, for example, suggests the ironic humor and frustration of those who want desperately to be "parting sweethearts"; in fact, the distinction is everything to them.

Oscar Firkins, who did not care for most of Howells' plays, felt that in *Parting Friends* "the issue is sentimental and minute, and the characters all impress us as having been up too late the night before the action" (*William Dean Howells, A Study*, p. 245). Firkins' comment, however, is unfair. If the play were longer, it *would* be tiresome, but within this brief act, considering what he tries to do—to make a commonplace incident dramatic—Howells presents in sketch form an interesting conflict. Bostonians know that they must not make a show of their emotions. Young Bostonians who, so far as people know, are not engaged must be extremely careful. This is the basis of the play. Employ a shy Boston male as one of the lovers, and you have the situation for a Howells "tragedy." Then add frustrating and disturbing influences to antagonize further the two main characters, and the farce is on its way. Although the young sweethearts take advantage of every opportunity, they are constantly thwarted; as time speeds on, they become more and more psychologically overwhelmed by their helplessness, just as they are physically overwhelmed by the district messengers and the multitude of young well-wishers. From the beginning, the audience feels the frustration of the characters and, with them, momentarily sees Mrs. Farlane as a *deus ex machina*, but it is not to be so. Howells pushes his realism to a "cruel"ending which comes rapidly and dramatically. After what Miss Matthews and Mr. Wayland have suffered, the interception of Miss Matthews' good-bys by the one undesirable person in the plot makes a perfect denouement, clearly in keeping with the mood of the play.

Parting Friends, Tragedy[1]

EVELYN: But why, *why* did you put it off till last night—or this morning rather—when you knew I must sail to-day, and there would be no chance to—to—to— Oh, I don't see how I can ever forgive you! Didn't you *know?* Didn't I do everything that any human girl could, to *show* you?

WAYLAND: Yes, dearest, you did; and I can see it all, now, looking back. I knew, yes, but I didn't dare.

EVELYN: That's what I can't forgive you for; your want of faith in me—in yourself. If I were a man—

WAYLAND: Oh, *don't* be a man, darling, not for a single instant; not even to convince me that I was *not* a man. I own it, now, but I want you just as you are, just as another woman!

He presses her hand hard as it lies on the seat next him and tenderly crushes her arm and fingers intertwined with his. They are seated on one of the most restricted sofas in one of the remotest embrasures of the music-room on the Anglo-Teutonic-Batavian triple turbine wireless 30,000-ton Ritz restaurant steamer Merseyhaveldam, *which is to sail in half an hour. Around their feet, and bulking well up to their knees, lie packages and bundles of farewell offerings, the poignancy of grief in them subdued by the gay ribbons and silken cords of their wrappings; boxes and sheaves of flowers abandoned hopelessly on the floor exhale a rank sweetness. The music-room seats are all occupied by preoccupied passengers, and there is an incessant coming and going, and laughing and talking everywhere. Tides of leave-takers swell and choke the passages outside, and pass in and out of the music-room. From time to time a young man enters and passes round the place on an apparently unsuccessful tour of discovery, which the couple in the secret nook do nothing to promote. The young man is tall and gangling, with a face to match his figure and a smile of inexhaustible amiability. He carries aloft a long pasteboard box.*

1 The text used here is the Harper & Brothers edition.

EVELYN, *shuddering against the shoulder of Wayland with a deep sigh of escape, as the unsuccessful explorer makes one of his disappearances:* He's gone again! Well?

WAYLAND: Was I saying anything? I thought I was merely *feeling.* Oh yes! You do forgive me, don't you?

EVELYN, *smelling the bunch of violets which she presses to her nose with her free hand:* Oh yes, yes! A million times. I only had to have something against you to keep from simply melting and flowing away. Oh, dear, how nice you are, and how wise, even down to these violets! Any other flowers— 'Sh! There he is. No! He's gone again; he merely glanced in. I suppose, by the look of that long box, he's got long-stemmed roses—American Beauties, of course; possibly Jacks. He doesn't mean any harm, poor fellow.

WAYLAND: Oh no, he's just a wandering idiot, and I shall not kill him—at least till you're gone.

EVELYN: How funny you are! I didn't know you had so much humor—always so solemn and sententious, till last night. But last night you *were* funny! Do you suppose anybody ever made love before in a taxicab? Or not made it exactly, but worked up to it. With Aunt Bessie there, you couldn't really offer yourself, though I don't believe she'd have minded. She must have seen it was coming; she's always adored you; and I knew she asked to let us drop you just to give you a last chance. And when you came in to say good-night, and she went up-stairs *to put off her things* and left us in the reception-room, you didn't lose *much* time, did you, darling? It was simply an explosion, that was all. But how much time you *did* lose before the explosion! No, I can't forgive you.

WAYLAND: I don't expect it, I don't want it. If you forgave me you might forget me; the two always go together, and I want you to keep me in mind every breath, every pulse! I shall you, and I couldn't consent to excel you in anything; though I couldn't excel you if I did consent.

EVELYN: Well, then, don't let's talk of it any more. We've only these few minutes left, and we ought to talk about something vital—make every word hold a lifetime of meaning; don't you think so?

WAYLAND: Yes, and how perfectly you say it, how—

MRS. WELBY, *struggling through the riveted furniture of the music-room, and the flux and reflux of passengers and their laughing, shouting, and talking friends*: Ah! There you are at last! Oh, my dearest child, what a time I *have* had! I thought I never should find you, and the boat would carry you off and me with you. And Mr. Wayland, too! Well, I can certainly trust *him* to see that I don't get left. Guess what I've brought you! But no, you must wait to get off before you look. *(She disburdens herself of two boxes which she has been carrying, putting them into the eager hands of Wayland, and then recovering them from him as she sinks into an arm-chair facing Evelyn.)* Oh, thank you so much. The whole joke is in not looking, now. But where's Mrs. Farlane?

EVELYN: Taking time by the forelock down in her berth. She's so determined to be sick, you know, that she's not going to lose a moment. She says if she isn't sick, it will be just so much pure gain.

MRS. WELBY: Dear Mrs. Farlane, how funny she is! So much character, always. Has anybody brought you any of that new *mousse* chocolate yet? Not that—

EVELYN: I *love* it!

MRS. WELBY: I don't mind saying it's in one of them; but the other is strictly *between ourselves*, don't you know. Dear Mrs. Farlane! If I had only remembered her passion for seasickness, I should certainly have brought her some of those red tablets; I don't remember their name, but you know them by their being red. And now—*(flinging herself back into her chair with a long sigh of expectation)* tell me all about your where, when, and how. You don't mean that Mr. Wayland is the only one of your young men that's come to see you off?

WAYLAND: No, Mrs. Welby; only the first of them.

He exchanges a furtive hand-pressure with Evelyn.

MRS. WELBY: And I'm the second. Well, that's something. *Sally!* *(She launches this cry at a young girl, so long-legged that her skirts have not been able to reach her ankles, who has burst through the vermiculant crowd, and, flushed,* rumpled, and panting, comes lugging a large basket of very large grapefruit, and stumbles with it at the feet of Miss Matthews.)* Why in the world didn't you leave it with the steward?

SALLY, *indignantly*: What steward, I should like to know? There are a thousand stewards, and you can't catch one of them. And, besides, after I'd motored down with it in my lap from Sixty-seventh Street, and kept them from tumbling out with my own hands all the way, do you think I was going to let any steward gobble them? I don't call *you* much of a mother for suggesting such a thing. *(She casts herself upon Evelyn's neck, with many kisses and tender murmurs.)* I picked them out myself, and there's one for every kiss; and— How do, Mr. Wayland! I didn't see you.

She gives him her hand.

WAYLAND: Oh, I wasn't here—compared with E—

SALLY: What?

EVELYN, *hastening to cover his confusion*: And you were quite right, Sally, and how good and kind of you to think of grapefruit, of all things! My favorite fruit, and so refreshing, and the very thing at sea. How good and kind of you!

MRS. WELBY: Well, I must say she might have shown more originality. Why, child, don't you know that they fairly bathe you in grapefruit on these boats?

SALLY: But they're not your own grapefruit, and—

EVELYN, *pulling her down and kissing her*: And that makes all the difference. We'll have yours at lunch and dinner, and the boat's at breakfast.

SALLY, *irrelevantly*: I saw Mr. Framer on the outskirts somewhere, with a box as long and narrow as he is, that I guess had American Beauties in it; and I guess he was looking for you. Oh, there it is now!

She indicates the box, held above the press and making its way irregularly about, as if seeking a positive direction.

EVELYN: Oh, well, stoop, Sally dear, and don't let him see you! Let him go and leave it with the other things on the saloon table. Can't somebody tell him? Can't you, Ra— Or, no, that won't do! Oh, dear!

SALLY: There! He's gone again. He went out of the door; you needn't be afraid. But I don't wonder you were. Why, Nancy! Well, of all the people! What have *you* brought? But of course I'm not asking.

MRS. WELBY: No, you don't seem to be, and I'm very glad you're so thoughtful, Sally.

MRS. EFFINGER: Merely a trifling *en tout cas*, if you *must* know, Sally, before the grateful recipient does. (*To Miss Matthews*) No cards. I couldn't think of anything you'd hate to have worse, Evelyn, and I trotted out all your *bêtes noires* and counted them. Bob's coming with something at the last moment, I suppose, but I beat him here, and I feel pretty sure I've beaten him on the *en tout cas*. Oh, how do you do, Mr. Wayland? You're such a shrinking violet I didn't see you behind that basket of grapefruit. Are you holding all the things? Then why not the *en tout cas*? Evelyn doesn't seem disposed to grab it.

EVELYN: You haven't given me any chance to grab it yet, Nancy. Hand it over.

She reaches for it.

MRS. EFFINGER, *giving it*: There. But why we haven't left all our offerings on the altar in the dining-saloon, I can't understand.

MRS. WELBY: We have no confidence in the attendants of the temple. I feel that they'd have eaten up every bit of my chocolate *mousse*—

MRS. EFFINGER, *with a cry to Evelyn*: Chocolate *mousse*! Oh, give me one, you greedy thing! When you knew how I adored them! Actually keeping the box shut!

SALLY: Oh, there he comes again! Or *it* does!

MRS. EFFINGER: He? It?

SALLY: Mr. Framer, with a box of American Beauties, as long and lank as he is! See it moving through the air! It's coming this way. (*With a skilful reproduction of the motor-'bus conductor's manner*) "Elevated road! All keep your seats! Bat your heads!" There, he's gone again. Evelyn's saved!

MRS. EFFINGER: Do I understand that Miss Matthews doesn't wish to meet the bearers of gifts? It seems to me that this is a hint to me. Good-bye, you poor thing! *Bon voyage*; many returns of the same. (*She stoops over Evelyn and kisses her.*) Good-bye!

EVELYN: Oh, thank you, Nancy, so much!

MRS. EFFINGER: For going?

EVELYN: For the *en tout cas*. Stay and see whether Cousin Bob can beat it!

MRS. EFFINGER: For pure banality, it's inapproachable. But the fates may fight for Bob; he *may* bring you a shoe-bag!

MRS. WELBY: Oh, don't *say* such a thing!

She rises.

MRS. EFFINGER: He *may*. (*To Mrs. Welby and Sally*) Coming, girls? (*To Wayland*) Mr. Wayland?

WAYLAND: Yes, yes. As soon as I can catch a steward to give these things to.

MRS. EFFINGER, *subtly*: Oh.

MRS. WELBY AND SALLY, *kissing Evelyn*: Good-bye, dear. Don't be greedy with the chocolates. Eat all the grapefruit you can, Evelyn. It will do you good.

EVELYN: Oh, can you believe they're actually gone?

WAYLAND: It does seem too good to be true.

EVELYN: Well, now let's don't lose any time! (You don't mind my grammar, or ungrammar?) They'll be back in hordes in a moment. Where were we? (*She vividly presses his hand with each question.*) Where were we?

WAYLAND: I'm with you, wherever you—

EVELYN: Oh, don't triv—be trivial, I mean. You were saying something vital; what was it?

WAYLAND: That I love you better than anything in the universe.

EVELYN: And I you. But that goes without saying. Oh, I know, now!

WAYLAND: We must—*must*—MUST—somehow—before we part; I couldn't leave you without—It wouldn't be parting. But with these people—

EVELYN: Couldn't we bend our faces down—together—and pretend to be looking for something in this rubbish, and—

WAYLAND: Oh, you darling to think *how*!

EVELYN: And you don't despise me *for* thinking?

WAYLAND, *in inexpressible protest*: Oh!

They bend over, in pretended scrutiny of the packages at their feet; a loud, jovial voice arrests them.

EFFINGER: Hello! There you are at last! I thought you'd decided not to go, Evelyn; been all over the ship for you. Hello, Wayland! What are *you* doing here? *You're* not going?

WAYLAND, *fiercely*: Oh no, I'm just filling in the time between parting friends.

EFFINGER: Well, you won't have much time to fill in between *me*. Ship sails in about ten minutes.

EVELYN, *with a covert clutch of Wayland's hand*: Oh! In ten minutes?

EFFINGER: Well, about. Haven't you heard the warning voice of the steward?

EVELYN, *convulsively*: No!

WAYLAND, *indignantly*: How can we hear anything in this din?

EFFINGER, *glancing round at the dense laughing and shouting throng in the music-room*: They do seem to be having rather a good time. (*To Evelyn*) Guess what I'm holding behind my back, to comfort you on your long five days' voyage!

EVELYN, *wildly*: A shoe-bag?

EFFINGER: A shoe-bag! Is that some of Nancy's rot? Do I look like a man that would bring a shoe-bag to a lovely girl leaving friends and home on an oft-tried trip to the Old World? Why, they starve you on these boats: tea when you wake; breakfast at nine; bouillon at eleven; lunch at one; tea at four; dinner at seven-thirty: if you don't have something betweentimes, you simply perish. You can't live on flowers and chocolates and grapefruit and *en touts cases* (Nancy brought that, I'll bet); and I've been to Dream's, and got you one of his fairy copper baskets! (*He brings it round in front of him, and Evelyn clasps her hands in a feint of ecstasy as he lifts the lid.*) There! It's a Dream itself, isn't it?—full of dreams! Did you ever see such a load of indigesti-comestibles? Try one now—greatest prophylactic against seasickness, one of these gooey, frosted layer-cakes! No? Well, you'll come to it; I must be off; going ashore, Wayland? What's the matter?

WAYLAND, *with his eyes fastened on a tall form moving on the skirts of the crowd, with a long, narrow box borne aloft*: Yes, yes, I'm going—go—

EVELYN: Oh, what is it?

WAYLAND: It *is*!

EFFINGER: Framer? Why, he's been looking all over the ship for you. I'll just go and tell—

EVELYN: If you dare!

EFFINGER, *with intelligence*: Oh! Well, I won't then. Come along, Wayland. How do they put you ashore on this line? I've heard whistles and gongs and stewards—which sounds last? But no matter. Good-bye, Miss Matthews; good-bye to Mrs. Farlane, for me; good-bye, Wayl— Why, no, you're going ashore, too!

WAYLAND: Yes, yes, as soon as I've signed for these things. Don't wait for me. (*To a district messenger, bearing a large jar of California figs*) For Miss Matthews? (*And to a succession of messengers with arm-loads of tulips, branches of bananas, and baskets of oranges, grapes, and apples*) For Miss Matthews? For Miss Matthews? For Miss Matthews? (*Signing*) Well, why didn't you leave them with the steward?

CHORUS OF DISTRICT MESSENGERS: Couldn't find no steward!

EFFINGER, *merging himself with the crowd*: Well, if you won't!

EVELYN, *bitterly*: But everybody seems to find *us*! Oh, I wish I hadn't a friend on earth!

WAYLAND: Well, they can't hold out much longer. The boat starts now in less than six minutes.

EVELYN: Oh, I can't let you go!

WAYLAND: Nor I you. But I must, I must!

EVELYN: How cruel you are! Let me stay with you! I won't—I *can't* go!

WAYLAND: And I can't stay. I'm going with you.

EVELYN: No, no. I'll stay.

WAYLAND: But you can't stay now, dearest. Your *Not Wanted on the Voyage* luggage is all in the hold. You must go!

EVELYN: Why didn't you speak sooner—why didn't I make you, I mean? Now, to part only a few hours after we belong to each other. But I *won't* blame you, at the last minute, so!

WAYLAND: But you're not; I'm blaming myself.

EVELYN: But I can't let you leave me here alone—without Aunt Elizabeth, or anything. Oh, where *is* she? How *can* she be down in her berth at such a time!

WAYLAND: I'll call her—get her—

EVELYN: No, there isn't time! Oh, hear those dreadful gongs and whistles and stewards all shouting at you to go ashore! *Where* is Aunt Elizabeth? Oh, there you are—just dropped from heaven in the very nick of time! Oh, Aunt Elizabeth!

MRS. FARLANE: What are you doing here, you crazy things? Mr. Wayland, I'm astonished at you. Don't you know the boat's just starting? They'll be pulling up the gangway. Why don't you go? Everybody else is going, and I've come up here from a sick—a seasick—bed to send you. (*The screaming, laughing crowd is, in fact, melting and ebbing away from the music-room. Mr. Framer vanishes through the door with his tall box of American Beauty roses.*) What *are* you stopping for?

WAYLAND, *very seriously*: Mrs. Farlane, I am engaged to Evelyn—

MRS. FARLANE, *with astonishment*: Well, I should suppose so—after last night!

WAYLAND: I consider her my wife *now*; and yet—and yet—we must part like strangers.

MRS. FARLANE: How, like strangers? What do you mean? Evelyn, is this some nonsense of yours? (*With severity*) If it's a joke, Mr. Wayland—

EVELYN, *whimpering*: Oh, do you think he

could joke on such a subject? People have been heaping themselves on us ever since he's been here, and they stare so—stare so—

WAYLAND: That we can't part as we should. If you would just stand a little nearer, so that I could—could—without making a show of it—kiss her good-bye—just—once—

MRS. FARLANE: Oh, you poor, poor things! I'll stand as close as I can, and cluster round you as thick! Do you mean here?

She puts herself in position, and moves this way and that so as to intercept the view of the lingering witnesses in the music-room, and Evelyn and Wayland have risen for a parting embrace, when a joyous noise bursts upon them from a troop of young men and girls who come pushing into the place with incoherent cries.

THE GIRLS: There you are at last! Oh, Evelyn, such a time we've had finding you! And we'll be carried off with you, now. Here, last chance! All the latest publications! I knew you'd forget a steamer-chair cushion, and I've brought— Don't tell me anybody else has given you grapefruit! And a Dream basket? Oh, how cruel! But mine's nickel-plated, anyway! I packed it myself, Evelyn! There isn't a moment! Hurry, girls! Oh, good-bye.

They drop their gifts at Evelyn's feet, and crowd Wayland from her with their multitude and successive embraces, while the young men shake hands with Wayland and Mrs. Farlane.

THE YOUNG MEN: Never got such time out of three taxies before! We shall all be up for speeding. Real ambulance gait. Told the mounted cops we had run over these girls, and were taking them to the hospital. If I hadn't seen Wayland's head and shoulders through the window here, we should never have found you. Come! That's the last call! We shall all be left—carried off, that is. Come, come!

With wails from the girls and babbled and bubbled farewells, the party join in flight, and carry with them the tall figure of Mr. Framer,

who has haunted the background with his box of roses, and, without attempting to leave it now, involuntarily vanishes.

THE STEWARD: All ashore, all ashore.

EVELYN, *to Wayland*: Oh, go, go! *(She glances through the window.)* Oh, they're untying the gangway. Oh, dearest love, go! Don't wait for anything! Throw one to me from the pier! *(She pushes him wildly from her.)* Everybody's looking back, and waving. We can't. You mustn't! *(Wayland wavers frantically and then rushes distractedly away.)* Oh, oh! What have I done?

MRS. FARLANE: A very silly thing; and he's done another! You don't deserve each other.

EVELYN, *flying to the window*: Oh, there he is on the gangway, just behind Mr. Framer! And the sailors are lifting it and the men on the pier are pulling it down! How frightfully it swings in the air! Oh, I can't bear to look! But I must! I must! What a dreadful din the whistle makes! How can they? Look, look, Aunt Bessie! Can you see him from your window? Yes? I can't! Where is he—where is he?

MRS. FARLANE, *at the next window*: He's all right; he's on the pier, now. Don't you see him? Just beside that idiot with his box of roses.

EVELYN: Yes, oh yes, *I* see him. How good you are, aunty, to find him. And he sees *me!* Yes, he does, he does! And he's kissing his hand to me! Oh, he remembered! Oh, you darling! Oh, my dear love! And I'll kiss mine to you; I don't care now if the whole world sees me.

She kisses her hand; then she gives a cry of despair.

MRS. FARLANE: What is it, Evelyn? Are you crazy? What's the matter? Has he fallen in?

EVELYN: No. But Mr. Framer's got in front of him and he thinks I'm kissing my hand to *him;* and he's kissing his to me. Oh, oh, oh!

She bursts into tears, and cowers away from the window, hiding her face in her handkerchief. Mrs. Farlane strikes an attitude of helpless and hopeless compassion.

THE END

The Impossible, A Mystery Play

[1910]

In some ways *The Impossible, A Mystery Play* may be compared to Mark Twain's story, *The Man That Corrupted Hadleyburg*. The dramatic action begins humorously enough, and even after the first three-quarters of the play, the audience is still not aware of anything more serious than a dinner party that is to be without guests. And this situation certainly has its humorous side. Then the mysterious voice of science and the spirit speaks, and the play suddenly becomes a trap for mankind. The tenor of the play changes, and an atmosphere of bitter ridicule envelops the scene. Because the Fountains have been subject to certain conventional notions of fashionable acceptance, and because they are products of their society, their acts and thoughts have become twisted. Howells feels this deeply, and at the same time that he pleads the case of these socially acceptable people he condemns their existence. *What is Man?* asks Mark Twain, and Howells, too, sees man's basic selfishness. Man cannot escape the trap that he has set for himself; he is incapable of a purely generous and Christian act. It is impossible!

The voice on the telephone is further evidence of Howells' use of spiritualism as a dramatic device—observable in earlier plays such as *Bride Roses, The Mother and the Father*, and *The Night Before Christmas*. Death always made Howells more conscious of the spiritual being—Elinor Howells died the year *The Impossible* was written—but throughout his writings he often refers to phenomena beyond one's understanding. In a letter to Aurelia Howells (February 18, 1906, Harvard Library), he wrote of another life—"May we all have a new birth on some other tree of life!"—and mentioned a story he was writing concerning a girl who loses her memory but keeps her personality intact. "It [the story] is against the notion that in another world we are not the same unless we fully remember what we have been." Such unknowable things bothered him more, the older he grew—as in "Though One Rose from the Dead"—although it would seem that his deep concern began with the death of Winifred Howells. (In a letter to his father, December 22, 1889 [Harvard Library], Howells mentions going to the First Spiritual Temple.) Unlike Mark Twain in his more pessimistic thinking, Howells could not give up his hope; yet neither could he abandon his questioning.

This play, then, is a serious drama with comic overtones. But it is not so much the situation as it is the characters, and not so much the plot or the comedy as it is the questioning idea which makes this play assume a marked importance among Howells' dramatic writing. As the rich lord in Howells' Biblical source—Luke 14:21—Howells–Fountain is angry; society has failed him, and he is forced to send his servant into the streets of the city for dinner guests. But in spite of his anger he cannot completely reject the society that fails him, and as a part of this society he, too, fails. Perhaps it is an impossible problem. The one mitigating aspect of the entire episode is the consciousness on the part of Fountain that his action is not exactly what the voice over the telephone intended. This slight awareness is the one sign of hope for this society that Howells recognizes; yet as in "The Midnight Platoon" (Howells, *Literature and Life* [New York: Harper & Bros., 1902]), the hope is ironic, for although the upper class may see and feel the existence of a social wrong, it is also quite satisfied with its own ideas and behavior.

The Impossible, A Mystery Play[1]

MRS. FOUNTAIN, *sweeping into the drawing-room of her apartment in complete dinner toilette, her head held illustratively erect on a body bowed a little forward; while her left hand presses a lace handkerchief to her belt, and her right just lifts her skirt from the floor, freeing her feet for their gliding movement over the carpet, she advances with conscious challenge toward her husband:* Well?

FOUNTAIN: Well, what?

He sits with his feet stretched as far out in front of him as they will reach, showing the soles of his patent-leather shoes, and as he speaks he lifts his sunken head from the expanse of his shirt-front, and stares absently at his wife.

MRS. FOUNTAIN: Nothing. How do I look?

She presses her gown inward a little and glances down at it on either side, with graceful curves and turns, as if at a rehearsal of deportment.

FOUNTAIN: Don't you always look well?

MRS. FOUNTAIN: Sometimes I like to be told I do. Why *will* you sit on the small of your back? You are perfectly ruining your coat-skirts.

FOUNTAIN: But I'm keeping my trousers from kneeing. It's the only way.

MRS. FOUNTAIN: You could stand up. I'm sure *I* should like to fling myself down and never rise again. I thought I never could get away from the children. Jim and Sue insisted on seeing me in my dinner dress, and they kept me so long that they couldn't remember whether they had said their prayers, and I had to say them all over again with them to make sure; and then poor little Benny clung to me so, and wanted me to stay till he went to sleep, and he started awake every time I moved.

FOUNTAIN: Where was the nurse?

MRS. FOUNTAIN, *disdainfully:* Oh, the nurse! *(She looks at the softly ticking clock on the mantle.)* It's still a quarter of eight, though. Do you think it's going?

FOUNTAIN: It was, just before you came in. I haven't listened since. I wish *I* could have said Jim's and Susy's prayers with them, instead of spending this awful quarter of an hour here alone. My feelings have been worse than Christmas Eve.[2] Who hooked you up?

MRS. FOUNTAIN: The nurse, of course. I knew you wouldn't remember it, and I must say that she wasn't to blame for not saying the children's prayers with them. But if you are going to have those Christmas Eve feelings all through the dinner!

FOUNTAIN: I'm not. I'm as gay as a lark, now you've come.

MRS. FOUNTAIN: Oh, yes. You depend upon *me* for everything. What if *I* should expect *you* to keep *my* spirits up?

FOUNTAIN: You'd be awfully disappointed, my love. Give me a kiss for luck. You look as pretty as a pink. I don't wonder Benny wanted to hang on to you.

MRS. FOUNTAIN: I shall not. Well, there, then! *(She kisses him.)* But don't be silly. What made you so gloomy, I should like to know? Don't you think it's going to go off well?

FOUNTAIN: It's going to go off like—

MRS. FOUNTAIN: Don't! Unless you knock on wood. What makes you think it's going to go off so well?

FOUNTAIN: It's been so perfectly planned.

MRS. FOUNTAIN: We fought long enough over it. And if you'd had *your* way!

FOUNTAIN: Don't go back to that. It's perfect because it's a compromise of tastes and ideals. The ideals were mine and the tastes were yours. But we had wonderful material to work with. Fate seemed to play right into our hands.

MRS. FOUNTAIN: Yes, it certainly did. And now I don't suppose there was ever a dinner that combined the two elements like it, and just in that way that neither of the elements can object to the other. The *chic* and the *smart*, it will be unprecedented, if anything ever was. Twelve is just the right number. It's large enough to break up

[1] This play was published only in *Harper's Monthly*, December 1910, CXXII, 116–25.

[2] A reference to *The Night Before Christmas*.

into several talks, and it isn't so dangerously near thirteen as fourteen is if one drops out.

FOUNTAIN: Yes, but you can always get some fellow in, or ask him not to come; but if one drops out of ten, and you fail for a substitute, you can't come down to eight without—

MRS. FOUNTAIN: What makes you think anybody's going to drop out?

FOUNTAIN: Did I say I did? All I ask is that nobody will drop in.

MRS. FOUNTAIN: Don't give me a start, then. Let's go and look at the table. You be Mr. Reverdy, and I'll be me, and we'll go out together.

FOUNTAIN: I'd rather not be old Reverdy, even for the pleasure of going out with the beautiful Mrs. Fountain.

MRS. FOUNTAIN: Silly! Well, then, I'll be Mrs. Trail, and you will be you. You mustn't forget you're to take her out, and when you get her out, don't keep joking with Mrs. Warbeck. Don't joke at all; it's undignified; and just smile; don't laugh.

FOUNTAIN: I won't laugh at Mrs. Trail's jokes, anyway; I'm not sure I shall smile. If I don't cry it's all you can ask.

MRS. FOUNTAIN, *ignoring his buffoonery*: Remember that you're to talk with Mrs. Trail about her portrait; that will let you bring the Graces in; but don't *lug* them in, and don't put Mrs. Grace *at* her. I shall be on pins and needles to see how Mrs. Trail takes her, anyway. She may choose to be very snubbing, and poor Nelly has never met a real society leader before. I don't see how I ever had the courage to bring it about, but I'm glad I was perfectly honest about it. I said Mr. *and Mrs.* Grace distinctly in my note to Mrs. Trail; so I've nothing on my conscience, though of course Mrs. Trail comes solely on *his* account. I'm putting Mr. Brown next to Mrs. Nevil, and he'll be nice to her because Mr. Nevil has just taken his story. I think I've balanced it very nicely between the arts and the fashions. There is old Reverdy, who is pure worldly, though he's as harmless as a dove; there is Mrs. Trail, who's worldly to the tips of her toes; there is Mrs. Warbeck, who's betwixt and between, because she's both fashionable and artistic; there's Mr. Brown, who goes everywhere, and yet thinks he can write novels; there are the Graces, who are beginning to tack on through his portraits and her cleverness; and there are the Nevils, who are pure literature and undefiled. How many does that make? (*She counts them up on her fingers.*)

Eight, and we are ten. Oh, good gracious, I forgot the Murrays. That's just twelve. Now, let's look at the table. (*She pulls her husband toward the dining-room doors, but withdraws her hand from his arm in order to circle more freely round the table set for twelve persons, and delicately glimmering with glass, silver, and china in the subdued light from the drawing-room. She changes the position of some slim vases of flowers, and then restores them to their first places.*) No, they're all right as they are. It's simply perfect. (*Fountain stands looking at the table, with an air of mental reservation. His wife challenges him sharply.*) Well?

FOUNTAIN: Oh, nothing.

MRS. FOUNTAIN: Yes, you were thinking something—something provoking.

FOUNTAIN: I don't believe a few girls would have hurt.

MRS. FOUNTAIN: There! I knew it. And whenever I suggested a girl, you vetoed it, because you said their innocence would be a blight on conversation.

FOUNTAIN: Am I never to be allowed the least irony in my own house? That's what I said, but I don't know of anything girls don't talk of nowadays; they're always putting me to the blush. What I really meant was that if I agreed to any of your girls, you'd think I wanted to talk to them; and I supposed if I vetoed them, you would have the magnanimity to insist on them. Of course poor Brown will talk to Mrs. Nevil because Nevil is his editor; but I know old Reverdy would have liked a débutante or two; he's just the age for them, with his perennial youth! I suppose you can call Miss Murray a girl; she's at least not married. And her brother's rather sissyish. Come, it's not so bad.

MRS. FOUNTAIN, *without heeding him*: The two Walkers would have given their eyes to come! Well, you've spoiled my pleasure in the dinner. Now, try to think up something else agreeable. (*She returns to the drawing-room, and closes the doors of the dining-room; then she moves restively about.*) We could have had the Walkers just as well as not.

FOUNTAIN: Whom would you have left out? You know you couldn't have had them. You were bound to have the very people you've asked. Why don't you sit down and be comfortable?

He is himself again stretched out in the informal attitude which he had taken at first, and looks up at her with his hands clasped behind his head.

THE IMPOSSIBLE, A MYSTERY PLAY

MRS. FOUNTAIN: Because they'll be here in a moment, now. Why do you want to rumple your back hair?

FOUNTAIN: Nobody'll look at my back hair. You've still got the most beautiful hair I ever saw, Lucy. Don't you think you have? But why prowl? You have such a

"Tiger, tiger, burning bright,
In the forest of the night"

effect. But your prowling won't bring them. Even if they were hungry, they wouldn't come an instant under the fifteen-minutes-past-the-time limit. But they're not hungry, not a soul of them. They're every one loathing the very thought of the expensive food I've bought them; perhaps old Reverdy's wondering if we've got a trick-dish to pique his jaded appetite—something wild and strange—but no one else cares. I wish you'd sit down and share in a little philosophical reflection with me. I've just thought of something very curious. How is it we always ask people to dinner who don't want any dinner, and would pay anything to get out of it, and never ask people who do want dinner and really need it? I suppose there are lots of people in New York to-night who haven't had any breakfast, let alone luncheon. Why didn't we think to have ten of *them*? It would have been very interesting, my dear.

MRS. FOUNTAIN, *scornfully*: Do you know ten people who haven't had breakfast and luncheon to-day?

FOUNTAIN: Well, not personally. But they could be found—with the aid of the police. Or, we might send round the block to the Bread Line at the Vienna bakery, where a lot of our fellow creatures get a handout of rolls and coffee after midnight. It's only four hours now to midnight, and the line must be beginning to form. You have got to step lively, lady, if you want to get a place in it. To be sure, they're all men. I wonder why there are no ladies in the Bread Line. Now the *grande dames* are going in for the suffrage, why don't some of them join the Bread Line?

MRS. FOUNTAIN: Go on. You're certainly surpassing yourself. One would think it was the night before Christmas. Ha, ha, ha!

She laughs bitterly.

FOUNTAIN: Well, not so bad as that, quite. Is friend Jules on deck?

MRS. FOUNTAIN, *with quiet scorn*: He's been here since six o'clock.

FOUNTAIN: Of course. That's one comfort with Martello. His people are always so prompt, and they all have French names, no matter what their nationality is. Jules is certainly an ideal waiter, and he does the old family butler so perfectly that I always feel as if he had been in my service for generations; the grease from his dress suit has come down from the remotest antiquity. I bathe in his delicious respect, so perfectly tempered to my merit. He certainly earns his five-dollar tip. And how beautifully those things are arranged by Providence! If I had to give Jules his tip before dinner I should certainly cut him down to two dollars, but after the last gun of gratitude has been fired by the parting guest, and I go out in the glow of my surfeit, and thank Jules for the nice way he's managed, it's all I can do to keep from giving him ten. Hark? Is that the muffled roar, the dying groan of a taxicab at our door? It is, by all that's— Who do you bet it is? Don't hesitate! You know I'll have to pay whichever loses.

He runs toward the window, but is intercepted by Mrs. Fountain, who detains him by his lapels.

MRS. FOUNTAIN: Clarence! They'll see you at the window. Do you want to disgrace yourself?

FOUNTAIN: Is it any disgrace to be seen at the window? When it's pitch-dark, and we're twelve stories up? Very well, you can go and look yourself, then.

He returns to his attitude of extreme leisure, and Mrs. Fountain goes to the window and peers out through a slightly lifted curtain.

MRS. FOUNTAIN: I shall know how to manage, *at least*. Yes, it's certainly somebody for this house. But the Welbies are giving a dinner, too, to-night. Now, if it's somebody for the Welbies!

FOUNTAIN: The only way will be to cut the Welbies dead the next time you meet them in the elevator. (*They remain silently waiting. The telephone rings, and Fountain springs to his feet.*) It's for us, Lucy, and I've won. Now, I shall have to pay myself your bet.

MRS. FOUNTAIN, *in a fine attitude of dramatic attention*: Listen! Is that telephone simpleton actually calling their names up, when I told her at least a thousand times to send everybody up to-night without calling their names? I shall certainly perish of the mismanagement of this house!

A confused colloquy at the telephone ensues, and then Jules, with a heavy Alsatian accent of his English, appears between the dining-room doors.

JULES: Zomebody ask for you at the vone, matame.

MRS. FOUNTAIN: Me? Horrors! I can't go. Who's wanting *me*, I should like to know? Go and see, Clarence. Don't tease, dearest!

FOUNTAIN: Oh, well, there's nothing I like better than telephoning. *(He follows Jules out through the dining-room, and is heard at the telephone.)* Oh! Mrs. Grace! How do you do, Mrs. Grace. This is Mrs. Fountain's husband; she's sent me to the phone for her. Well, you might send Grace, you know, though I shouldn't like it so well. What? Beg pardon! I can't make out exactly— Oh, keep off! Who's that breaking in, Central? Can't you make them keep off? Oh, is that you, Mrs. Grace? Somebody broke in. Sick? Oh, I'm so sorry to hear it. And he can't— Oh, that's too bad! Oh, yes, we should! We want you both, but if he can't come, we want you, anyway. Oh, is it as bad as that? Well, well, we must submit, of course. Don't worry about us. We shall manage somehow with people in the house. Grippe has precedence, of course. We shall hope for some other time. Well, love to poor old Grace. Wish him well out of it from me. Good-by.

As Fountain reappears with an agitated air, Mrs. Fountain takes the word from his mouth.

MRS. FOUNTAIN: Some other time, indeed! No, Mrs. Grace has missed the one chance of her life, I can tell her that much. Grippe! Why couldn't he have had the grippe earlier in the day? Here it is, five minutes of eight, and what are we to do?

FOUNTAIN: Have the Walker girls.

MRS. FOUNTAIN: Clarence, you *are* inspired! Call right down to them. Tell them exactly how it is. Tell them they're just a stop-gap, and that we are flinging ourselves on their generosity, but if they will come, we shall be so meekly grateful that butter won't melt in our mouths! Or no, you'll spoil it; you'll overdo it, you're so extravagant in your language. I shall have to do it myself; I have to do everything. You stay here, and if anybody comes— Oh, what shall I do? *(She flies from the room, and then is heard at the telephone.)* Yes, the Miss Walkers—at once— immediately—both—either of them! Oh! Is that you, Annie? No? Jenny? Well, it doesn't matter. It's all one. Will you take pity on an abject creature, and come help eat her dinner at the eleventh hour? Two people have just dropped by the way—the Graces; he's got the grippe. A very

bad case indeed; we've just heard from them, and they're as broken-hearted as we are, but if you'll only come in their places, we won't care for them— What? Both of you? Oh, that's too bad! You couldn't give your tick— But of course! How absurd I am! Do forgive me! It's because I'm so sorry. Well, good-by! I know you'll enjoy it. What? I wouldn't have you on any account! Good-by, dear! *(As she returns to her husband)* Selfish things! Nothing but the theatre.

FOUNTAIN: But didn't I hear you urging them to go?

MRS. FOUNTAIN: Of course you did; their selfishness came out in saying they had tickets. I would have died before I said that. Did you suppose I could let them come after that? *(The telephone rings, and she starts, and then arrests herself.)* No, you may go, this time, and if she's still offering to give up the theatre, don't you let her. The idea, after telling me!

She walks excitedly to and fro, while Fountain goes to the telephone.

FOUNTAIN, *without, and talking into the transmitter*: Who? I didn't quite catch the name?

MRS. FOUNTAIN: It's Jenny Walker, of course. Don't let her come, now. Tell her we've just asked somebody else. I wouldn't for the world—

FOUNTAIN: It isn't Jenny Walker. Keep still, please, so I can make out— Oh, confound it! Oh, hello! It's you, is it? I thought I knew your voice.

MRS. FOUNTAIN: Who is it?

FOUNTAIN, *at the phone*: Yes, I know you all right, now. What's the trouble? Oh, you don't say so. Well, well. That *is* bad, but I hope—

MRS. FOUNTAIN, *calling to him*: Tell her that we appreciate their consideration, and we're awfully sorry, and they mustn't think us rude, but there was so little time that we had to ask at once, and we've filled the places now. Tell her that we hope they'll enjoy it as much as we did; that we never laughed so much in our lives. Say—

FOUNTAIN, *replying to her, but speaking all the time into the transmitter*: Oh, good heaven! How often have I told you not to talk to me when I'm at the phone! Don't you know I can't make out a single word if you keep up your— Oh, I beg your pardon, old fellow! I was talking to somebody else. What were you saying? Oh, no, it wasn't Mrs. Fountain. Ha, ha, ha! It was the caterer's man, bothering me about the wine. Well? Oh, no, really! Don't say grippe! Is it, though?

And so bad as that? Well, it's too bad. But couldn't you come, anyway?

MRS. FOUNTAIN, *calling to him*: Who are you talking to, Clarence? If it's anybody else pretending they've got the grippe, I'll never forgive them, I don't care who it is. Who is it?

FOUNTAIN, *still talking into the transmitter*: Haven't I begged and implored you to be still. You've made him think that I've been trying to shut *you* up and he'll be taking us off to everybody. Oh, I don't mean you, Nevil. It's that confounded man of Martello's bothering the soul out of me. Well, if you can't come, I'm awfully sorry, and sorrier yet for the cause. Give Mrs. Nevil our sympathy. She mustn't worry about us. We can always pick up two people in a thickly settled house like this. Good-by, good-by. (*He returns to Mrs. Fountain.*) Well, the Nevils are out of the story, this time. She's down with the grippe, and he won't come because he's afraid it will unbalance your table. As if we could rake in another couple at a minute's notice!

MRS. FOUNTAIN, *with spirit*: I can manage a great deal more simply than that. (*She passes into the dining-room, where she dimly appears, talking to Jules.*) No, take the chairs quite away, and rearrange the plates. Four people have dropped out, and there will only be eight of us. Try to make it look symmetrical, Jules. Take away four of those vases of flowers; and here, these glasses and napkins. There, that's all right. (*She returns to the drawing-room, where Fountain stands dismayed, and laughs mockingly.*) More Christmas Eve musings? Well, don't be downcast! We've merely got rid of four false friends, and we shall be all the cozier at dinner. You've always said eight was an ideal dinner.

FOUNTAIN: Yes, but if we fade away to seven or six—?

MRS. FOUNTAIN, *boldly*: We *can't*, now. It's past eight o'clock already.

FOUNTAIN: I don't see how that's to prevent—

MRS. FOUNTAIN: Oh, yes, insist upon the logicality, do. So like a man! I suppose if I were at the point of death you wouldn't let me take my last breath till I had taken the next to the last. Can't you use a little imagination—all you've got! (*A ring is heard.*) There's the telephone again. Listen!

FOUNTAIN: It isn't the telephone. It's the door.

MRS. FOUNTAIN: It's the telephone!

FOUNTAIN: Door!

MRS. FOUNTAIN: Then somebody's coming. Sit down, and be waiting as if you were quietly talking with me. Quick! You look so red and excited. Smooth down your back hair.

She goes and smooths it down for him, and then sinks into an attitude of smiling and hospitable expectance on the sofa. A muted colloquy takes place between Jules and some one at the door; there is a clumping of heavy shoes on the floor, and a sound of hard breathing; the door shuts and Jules appears.

JULES, *offering two notes on a tray*: Two mezzenger-boys. Dere is no anzwer. I rezeipted for dem.

MRS. FOUNTAIN: *Two* messenger-boys? Well, what in the world— (*She seizes the notes convulsively, and tears them open.*) Mrs. Trail, of course. She would be too well bred to telephone, and her note is dated at five o'clock, just before she was ordered to bed with the grippe. (*To Jules, very severely*) How does it happen that this note has been three hours coming?

JULES: I ton't know, matame. Der poy zaidt he pen to der wrhong attress.

FOUNTAIN, *while Mrs. Fountain remains piercing Jules with an eye of inarticulate indignation*: Whom is the other note from? Did that boy go to the wrong address too?

MRS. FOUNTAIN, *running the note through*: Well, they *have* got to the East Side with a vengeance. They used to telephone from their West Side house.

FOUNTAIN: Who did?

MRS. FOUNTAIN: Who? The Murrays, of course. Now, from East Sixty-fourth Street, they send by letter, after having considerately waited till the last moment to see whether they wouldn't be well enough to come! Of all the impertinent, patronizing— Very well, Mrs. Murray, you will be an older if not a wiser woman before you will show me so much consideration again!

FOUNTAIN: That reduces us to five. A convenient number at an oblong table. Let's go and see where we shall sit. There will be old Reverdy, and young Brown and Mrs. Warbeck: three men to two women; a most unscriptural ratio, and against all experience in the Atlantic States. It will task my powers to the utmost, competing for your favor with old Reverdy, for of course we'll have to give young Brown to Mrs. Warbeck— Oh, don't cry, my dear! It *is* trying. But *you* can make it go off all right; I've never seen the box yet that you couldn't get out of! Don't, *don't* cry!

He takes Mrs. Fountain gingerly into his arms so as not to disarray her, but she flings herself sobbing on his neck.

MRS. FOUNTAIN: Oh, I don't care *how* I look, now! Oh, hu, hu, hu!

FOUNTAIN: There, there, my love! Don't mind it, confound them! Don't cry, hang them! Brace up, dearest, the deuce take them all! Would you like me to say something worse?

MRS. FOUNTAIN, *lifting her head, and drying her tears while still in his arms*: It wouldn't do any good. But, Clarence, darling, do, *do* you think one of your sisters would come?

FOUNTAIN, *releasing her with a thrill of dismay*: Oh, my love!

MRS. FOUNTAIN: If we really got down on our knees to them, and told them just how it was, and how I wanted to have them from the beginning, but had to yield to these wretched social obligations that have played us so false, and served us exactly right? I would telephone myself, and they would recognize that I had been crying, and was truly humbling myself before them.

FOUNTAIN, *with unabated misgiving*: I—I don't know. You might try. But—which one?

MRS. FOUNTAIN, *desolately*: No, it's useless. They're both as hard as nether millstones, and as unforgiving as—as— (*A ring makes itself heard.*) Well, is that the door or the telephone, this time?

After a moment Jules appears between the dining-room doors.

JULES, *indiscriminately*: Zomebody wandt you at the delephone.

MRS. FOUNTAIN, *very meekly, very weakly*: Me, Jules?

JULES: I gouldn't mage oudt, matame.

FOUNTAIN: Oh, I'll go, my dear; if it's you I'll excuse you, and do the talking for you.

MRS. FOUNTAIN: Thank you, darling. Jules! You'll have to make another change in the table— Or, wait a moment—

JULES: Yes, matame.

FOUNTAIN, *making himself heard at the telephone*: Why, of course, we understand. We're only sorry for you. We can easily manage with somebody in the house. You mustn't worry about it; don't give it another thought. Yes, it seems to be a regular epidemic, this winter. Yes, yes, I'll explain to Mrs. Fountain. We shall miss you, of course, but she'll know how to make every allowance. Well, good-by.

He returns to the drawing-room, rather pale, and with apprehension in his eye, but with an air of preparation for the worst. Jules has passed him in going into the dining-room.

MRS. FOUNTAIN: Well?

Her tone is one of mixed challenge and imploring.

FOUNTAIN: Well, the table will balance rather better, and you'll have three men to yourself instead of two. Mrs. Warbeck is out of the story, now.

MRS. FOUNTAIN: Don't tell me *Mrs. Warbeck* has the grippe?

FOUNTAIN: Well, I won't. It's merely a sneaking device of hers to get out of coming to your dinner. But she *says* she has the grippe.

MRS. FOUNTAIN: Of course it's a device; and I shall know how to treat Mrs. Warbeck the next time she asks me to one of her old lunches. *I* can have the grippe, too. Really, it seems as if there was a conspiracy. I never heard anything like it. You might suppose five or six people could have it, but when it comes to seven or eight, it passes a joke.

FOUNTAIN: Unless that's the point where the joke begins.

MRS. FOUNTAIN: I don't see how you can take it so quietly. Are you doing it to vex me, or is it because its Mrs. Warbeck? Well, one thing: now you can't keep talking to her all the time.

FOUNTAIN: Not unless you have a telephonic attachment at the table. (*A bell rings.*) I'll bet it's the door!

MRS. FOUNTAIN: And I say it's the phone. I shall certainly have those bells changed so that you can know which from which. Why doesn't Jules go to the phone?

FOUNTAIN: Perhaps he's gone to the door.

MRS. FOUNTAIN: Well, you go to the phone, then.

FOUNTAIN, *going*: That will certainly cover the ground. (*Then he is heard at the phone.*) Mr. Reverdy? Oh, yes, yes. Well? The grippe? Oh, he mustn't think of it. We're sorry he can't come, of course, but he mustn't worry. We can fill up with some one in the house here. Give him our best regards, and tell him we're only sorry on his account. Call us up in the morning, and let us know how he is. (*He returns to Mrs. Fountain.*) It's Reverdy's man, talking from the station at the apothecary's. Reverdy's down with grippe, and has a tremendous temperature. The old hero wanted to come, whether or no, but I said he mustn't think of it; we could easily fill up from the house here.

MRS. FOUNTAIN: Yes, I heard you saying it to

all of them. (*With biting sarcasm*) And *whom* shall you fill up with?

FOUNTAIN: I haven't got as far as that yet. But if I can't think of anybody you won't have so many men to talk to. Perhaps you can think of a woman. That would make the table balance better. (*A bell rings.*) Hello! They're at it again. This is getting a little monotonous. But we can have some variety by my going to the door, this time, and letting Jules go to the phone. (*He goes to the apartment door, and returns to Mrs. Fountain just as Jules appears from the dining-room.*) Nobody at the door, anyway. What do you say, Jules?

JULES: The chentleman wishes to sbeak with you, sör.

FOUNTAIN: Oh, all right, Jules; nothing I like better than talking with gentlemen over the phone.

He goes out through the dining-room.

MRS. FOUNTAIN: Who was the gentleman, Jules?

JULES: Well, I gouldn't mage oudt the name, egzactly, matame. Zounded zomething lige—

MRS. FOUNTAIN: Oh, it doesn't make any difference! You will have to take away all the plates and chairs but three, now. Put mine at the head of the table, and one on each hand of me.

JULES: All righdt, matame—

MRS. FOUNTAIN: 'Sh!

FOUNTAIN, *without, speaking at the phone*: No, I don't catch the name exactly, but— Oh, yes! Brown! Now I know you, but your voice sounded so hoarse— Oh, you don't say so! I'm awfully sorry. But you mustn't worry on our account; we can fill up, somehow, from the house, here. You oughtn't to have come out in this weather. We want a lot more novels from you, you know. It's awfully nice of you, but if you were laid up, or anything, Mrs. Fountain would never forgive me. Now, you get home as fast as you can, and put on a porous plaster, and take something soothing, and go to bed. Good-by. (*Returning to the drawing-room*) Poor old Brown had come out in the wet to telephone, so hoarse I didn't know who it was at first. Well, *he's* out of the story. And now what?

He resumes his easy full-length attitude in his chair, and looks up at Mrs. Fountain.

MRS. FOUNTAIN: Well, that's the end of the story, isn't it? Suppose *you* say what!

FOUNTAIN, *rising vigorously*: Then what I say is, let us go out to dinner, Mrs. Fountain. We won't stand upon ceremony. Jules, serve the dinner. I'm going to enjoy myself, which I shouldn't have done if any of those people had come. I'd be so anxious about *their* enjoyment. Come!

He offers his arm, and Mrs. Fountain puts forward her hand to take it, and then suddenly draws back.

MRS. FOUNTAIN: Listen! What strange voice is that?

FOUNTAIN, *after listening*: It *is* rather strange. Kind of gasping, struggling sound, as if the telephone were talking in the air. Why, it *is* the telephone! What in the world—

MRS. FOUNTAIN: Oh, what's it saying? It sounds so dreadful—a telephone talking to itself, that way. Why, it's ghastly!

FOUNTAIN: Hush! Listen!

MRS. FOUNTAIN: Can you make out what it's saying?

FOUNTAIN: I begin to. Hark!

MRS. FOUNTAIN: It sounds like somebody reading a chapter of—

FOUNTAIN: 'Sh!

THE VOICE OF THE TELEPHONE: Go out quickly into the streets and lanes of the city, and bring in hither the poor and maimed and blind and lame!

The voice is stilled: Fountain runs to the telephone.

FOUNTAIN: Hello, hello! What's that? (*The voice repeats its message.*) Oh, come off! Who's working me? Who? What do you mean?

Again the voice repeats its message; Fountain runs back to his wife.

MRS. FOUNTAIN, *whimpering and clinging to her husband*: Oh, dearest, isn't it dreadful! What are you doing to do?

FOUNTAIN: I'm going to do what it says. There doesn't seem any other way. Jules!

JULES: Yes, sör.

FOUNTAIN: Do you suppose there's anybody in that Bread Line yet?

JULES: It begin to form since from eight o'glock.

FOUNTAIN: Well, go, and knock down the first ten men you come to, and drag them in here to dinner.

JULES: All rhighdt, sör.

MRS. FOUNTAIN: Do you think he ought to knock them down?

FOUNTAIN: When they understand it's for dinner they'll be glad of it. They're used to being kicked out instead of dragged in. If there'd been time to stand on ceremony, I might have told him to decimate them; that would have been a little more classic; but perhaps they wouldn't have appreciated it, and we'd have been delayed unnecessarily. The first ten will do. But come now, we must get ready for them.

MRS. FOUNTAIN: Do you mean them to come to the table?

FOUNTAIN: That's what the telephone seemed to imply.

MRS. FOUNTAIN: Well, but—

FOUNTAIN: They'll be hungry enough to eat their way through all the courses. It'll give us an appetite to see them. They won't be stopped by the grippe, if they happen to have it.

MRS. FOUNTAIN: That's true. (*Then as if the idea had won upon her*) Well, let us do it, then. It will serve those horrid things right. I only wish they could see whom we're putting in their places. It would show them how much we despise them, with their flimsy excuses. Come, and let's put back all the chairs and plates, so they needn't be kept a moment from their dinner, poor things. Oh, how I shall like to look on! Don't you think it would be a good idea for us to wait on them?

FOUNTAIN: That might be overdoing it. They're probably more used to having just a footman serve them. Think how you'd feel yourself if your host and hostess were to wait on you.

MRS. FOUNTAIN, *thoughtfully*: That's true. We don't want to embarrass them. Well, come on, come on! (*She seizes his hand, and they dance out into the dining-room together, where they are seen rearranging the table.*) Every one of those individual vases of pinks shall go back, and here, we'll put that bowl of roses in the middle, again. Shall you serve the three kinds of wine?

FOUNTAIN, *restoring the glasses from the sideboard to the table*: Why, certainly. I'm sorry the champagne's rather sweet; I know they'd prefer dry. Or perhaps they're dry enough themselves. But the Sauterne's all right, and the Bordeaux— (*Feeling the bottles*) Yes, Jules has got the temperature just right. They'd have hated to have their claret cold. They're pretty particular about their claret, I've noticed.

MRS. FOUNTAIN: If there are any old men among them, don't you think it would be more graceful if we put them at the head and foot of the table and took corner seats ourselves?

FOUNTAIN: Yes, it would, rather. And what a pity there are never any ladies in the Bread Line. But no matter. When we get votes for women,

they'll have every other place in the Bread Line. Now, they feel that woman's sphere is in the home, especially if there's no fire in it.

They retire a little way from the table, and with arms interlocked, regard it approvingly.

MRS. FOUNTAIN: Perfect! Now let's go and be ready to receive them. (*In the drawing-room, where they find Jules, just arriving*) Why, Jules! Didn't you get them?

JULES: Yes, matame, I got dem all rhighdt. Boat—

MRS. FOUNTAIN: But what? But what?

JULES: Dey wouldn't let dem gome up the front ellewator, here.

MRS. FOUNTAIN: Wouldn't let my guests come up the front el—

FOUNTAIN: Then why didn't you bring them up the back elevator?

JULES: That is what I tidt, sör. They are all in the kitchen now, sör.

FOUNTAIN: Very well; serve the dinner at once, then. Tell them to come out into the dining-room. Or, no. Bring them here, Jules. We'll receive them properly, my dear. (*He turns to Mrs. Fountain.*) And go out in due form.

MRS. FOUNTAIN: Wait; stop a moment, Jules! Clarence, we must draw the line! I shouldn't have minded going out to dinner with them, and even waiting upon them with my own hands— you heard me say it—if they had come up the front elevator. But, dearest, don't you see? We must distinguish! We couldn't sit down with people who had come up the back elevator, now, could we? You see yourself we couldn't. It would be impossible.

FOUNTAIN, *with a sigh, after a moment of reflection*: Yes, it would be impossible. You are right, darling. I see it all. It is impossible. But what shall we do? Jules, what shall we do?

JULES: Well, sör, as they are all in the kitchen—

FOUNTAIN: Why, let them eat there, of course!

MRS. FOUNTAIN: Yes, let them eat in the kitchen, Jules. They won't mind.

JULES, *with polite hesitation*: No, matame, *they* won't mind. But the servants—the gook and the maits—

MRS. FOUNTAIN: You are right, Jules. It would be impossible.

JULES: Qvite imbossiple, matame.

FOUNTAIN: But what *is* possible, then? Everything isn't impossible in the case of ten starving men, is it?

JULES: Well, sör, if you will egscuse my sog-chesting somet'ing: I could but dem up a nize lonch, and let dem dake it out, and eat it vhere they lige, ton'dt you know—vhere they usually eat—in the street.

MRS. FOUNTAIN: The very thing! And, Jules! (*She calls after him, as he goes out of the dining-room.*) Be sure you give them something of every dish.

JULES: Vhy, the soup, matame—

MRS. FOUNTAIN: Of course not the soup, Jules. That would be impossible. You must certainly make his tip five dollars for getting us out of it so nicely, my dear. And now let's have him serve our dinner first. I'm fairly starving.

She puts her hand through his arm, and pulls him toward the dining-room.

FOUNTAIN, *musingly*: It seems to be the only solution. But—I wonder what the voice of the telephone would say?

Self-Sacrifice, A Farce Tragedy

[1911]

Of all Howells' short plays—aside from *The Mother and the Father*—*Self-Sacrifice, A Farce Tragedy* is the only one in which the book version shows considerable change from the periodical text. Howells' letters at the time of publication indicate that he simply wanted to make the play shorter for the book. In a letter to Duneka, the editor (February 19, 1911, Harvard Library), Howells wrote: "If you haven't yet placed in an early number my farce, 'Self-Sacrifice' I can make it much better by making it shorter. Even if you have placed it, I should like a proof so as to revise it for the book we are meditating." But the work was "already almost in the process of printing" (Duneka to Howells, February 24, 1911, Harvard Library), and he settled for the book revision.

In this way Howells explained his revision, but in the latter text the principle behind the cutting is obvious. For example, Howells cut the following dialogue which appeared in *Harper's Monthly*:

> MISS RAMSEY: I wanted to ask what you thought of Geralda Bracy in her Thistledown Dance. One can't tell from the papers; they're so censorious.
>
> ASHLEY: I've not seen her.
>
> MISS RAMSEY, *regarding the smoking end of her cigarette with refined recklessness*: One hears such different opinions. Some people think her dancing is very spiritual; one man said that, anyway, her costuming was not very material. *(After a silence on Ashley's part)* Don't you think that was funny?
>
> ASHLEY: I'm afraid I'm no judge of humor.
>
> MISS RAMSEY, *inattentively*: I believe I shall get Geralda Bracy here to lunch, some day. I shall count upon you, Mr. Ashley. Say you'll come, and I'll fix a date. Have I offered you any tea?

ASHLEY: Thank you, I don't care for any.

He also omitted all references to the novel of passion, *A Mist of Blood and Tears*, as in this paragraph:

> ASHLEY: You were speaking of *A Mist of Blood and Tears*. Do you remember where he tears her from her husband, and leaps with her from the windows of the nursery where her child is sleeping, and runs along the house-roofs with her in his arms till he comes to a fire-escape and his automobile at the bottom of it before her father's door? She clasps him round the neck, and cries out: "Oh, Max, Max! Husband and children, father and mother, and all the world for love and you!" Isn't it splendid?
>
> MISS RAMSEY: I—I think it's horrid.
>
> ASHLEY: Horrid? *(He laughs boisterously.)* Now *you* are joking; *you* are making fun.

In the book version Howells corrected his mistake in his earlier creation of Miss Ramsey. In order to talk about Geralda Bracy or *A Mist of Blood and Tears*, Miss Ramsey would have had to have a certain knowledge which, however she acquired it, would not have been considered genteel in her social set. Her absurd attempts with cigarettes and cocktails only show her more clearly as a sweet and innocent girl who wants to be thought sophisticated and daring. Artistically, then, Howells improved his play by his revision, but it is interesting that the speeches ever got into the play in the first place. Of course, Howells always enjoyed vaudeville, and about 1910 exotic dancers were popular on the stage. He also must have entertained himself thoroughly as he narrated part of the plot of *A Mist of Blood and Tears*—a type of sentimental fiction that he warred against his entire life.

Self-Sacrifice, A Farce Tragedy[1]

MISS RAMSEY: And they were really understood to be engaged?

Miss Ramsey is a dark-eyed, dark-haired girl of nearly the length of two lady's umbrellas and the bulk of one closely folded in its sheath. She stands with her elbow supported on the corner of the mantel, her temple resting on the knuckle of a thin, nervous hand, in an effect of thoughtful absent-mindedness. Miss Garnett, more or less Merovingian in a costume that lends itself somewhat reluctantly to a low, thick figure, is apparently poising for departure, as she stands before the chair from which she has risen beside Miss Ramsey's tea-table and looks earnestly up into Miss Ramsey's absent face. Both are very young, but aim at being much older than they are, with occasional lapses into extreme girlhood.

MISS GARNETT: Yes, distinctly. I knew you couldn't know, and I thought you ought to. *(She speaks in a deep conviction-bearing and conviction-carrying voice.)* If he has been coming here so much.

MISS RAMSEY, *with what seems temperamental abruptness*: Sit down. One can always think better sitting down. *(She catches a chair under her with a deft movement of her heel, and Miss Garnett sinks provisionally into her seat.)* And I think it needs thought, don't you?

MISS GARNETT: That is what I expected of you.

MISS RAMSEY: And have some more tea. There is nothing like *fresh* tea for clearing the brain, and we certainly need clear brains for this. *(She pushes a button in the wall beside her, and is silent till the maid appears.)* More tea, Nora. *(She is silent again while the maid reappears with the tea and disappears.)* I don't know that he has been coming here so *very* much. But he has no right to be coming at all, if he is engaged. That is, in that *way*.

MISS GARNETT: No. Not unless—he wishes he wasn't.

MISS RAMSEY: That would give him *less* than no right.

[1] The text used here is from *The Daughter of The Storage.*

MISS GARNETT: That is true. I didn't think of it in that light.

MISS RAMSEY: I'm trying to decide what I ought to do if he does want to get off. She said herself that they were engaged?

MISS GARNETT: As much as that. Conny understood her to say so. And Conny never makes a mistake in what people say. Emily didn't say *whom* she was engaged to, but Conny felt that that was to come later, and she did not quite feel like asking, don't you know.

MISS RAMSEY: Of course. And how came she to decide that it was Mr. Ashley?

MISS GARNETT: Simply by putting two and two together. They two were together the whole time last summer.

MISS RAMSEY: I see. Then there is only one thing for me to do.

MISS GARNETT, *admiringly*: I knew you would say that.

MISS RAMSEY, *dreamily*: The question is what the thing is.

MISS GARNETT: Yes!

MISS RAMSEY: That is what I wish to think over. Chocolates?

She offers a box, catching it with her left hand from the mantel at her shoulder, without rising.

MISS GARNETT: Thank you; do you think they go well with tea?

MISS RAMSEY: They go well with anything. But we mustn't allow our minds to be distracted. The case is simply this: If Mr. Ashley is engaged to Emily Fray, he has no right to go round calling on other girls—well, as if he wasn't—and he has been calling here a great deal. That is perfectly evident. He must be made to feel that girls are not to be trifled with—that they are not mere toys.

MISS GARNETT: How splendidly you do reason! And he ought to understand that Emily has a right—

MISS RAMSEY: Oh, I don't know that I care about *her*—or not *primarily*. Or do you say primarily?

629

MISS GARNETT: I never know. I only use it in writing.

MISS RAMSEY: It's a clumsy word; I don't know that I shall. But what I mean is that I must act from a general principle, and that principle is that when a man is engaged, it doesn't matter whether the girl has thrown herself at him, or not—

MISS GARNETT: She certainly did, from what Conny says.

MISS RAMSEY: He must be shown that other girls won't tolerate his behaving as if he were *not* engaged. It is wrong.

MISS GARNETT: We must stand together.

MISS RAMSEY: Yes. Though I don't infer that he has been attentive to other girls generally.

MISS GARNETT: No. I meant that if he has been coming here so much, you want to prevent his trifling with others.

MISS RAMSEY: Something like that. But it ought to be more definite. He ought to realize that if another girl cared for him, it would be cruel to her, paying her attentions, when he was engaged to some one else.

MISS GARNETT: And cruel to the girl he is engaged to.

MISS RAMSEY: Yes. (*She speaks coldly, vaguely.*) But that is the personal ground, and I wish to avoid that. I wish to deal with him purely in the abstract.

MISS GARNETT: Yes, I understand that. And at the same time you wish to punish him. He ought to be made to feel it all the more because he is so severe himself.

MISS RAMSEY: Severe?

MISS GARNETT: Not tolerating anything that's the least out of the way in other people. Taking you up about your ideas and showing where you're wrong, or even silly. Spiritually snubbing, Conny calls it.

MISS RAMSEY: Oh, I like that in him. It's so invigorating. It braces up all your good resolutions. It makes you ashamed; and shame is sanative.

MISS GARNETT: That's just what I told Conny, or the same thing. Do you think another one would hurt me? I will risk it, anyway. (*She takes another chocolate from the box.*) Go on.

MISS RAMSEY: Oh, I was just wishing that I had been out longer, and had a little more experience of men. Then I should know how to act. How do you suppose people do, generally?

MISS GARNETT: Why, you know, if they find a man in love with them, after he's engaged to another girl, they make him go back to her, it doesn't matter whether they're in love with him themselves or not.

MISS RAMSEY: I'm *not* in love with Mr. Ashley, please.

MISS GARNETT: No; I'm supposing an extreme case.

MISS RAMSEY, *after a moment of silent thought*: Did you ever hear of anybody doing it?

MISS GARNETT: Not just in our set. But I know it's done continually.

MISS RAMSEY: It seems to me as if I had read something of the kind.

MISS GARNETT: Oh yes, the books are full of it. Are those mallows? They might carry off the effects of the chocolates.

Miss Ramsey passes her the box of marshmallows which she has bent over the table to look at.

MISS RAMSEY: And of course they couldn't get into the books if they hadn't really happened. I wish I could think of a case in point.

MISS GARNETT: Why, there was Peg Woffington—

MISS RAMSEY, *with displeasure*: She was an actress of some sort, wasn't she?

MISS GARNETT, *with meritorious candor*: Yes, she *was*. But she was a very *good* actress.

MISS RAMSEY: What did *she* do?

MISS GARNETT: Well, it's a long time since I read it; and it's rather old-fashioned now. But there was a countryman of some sort, I remember, who came away from his wife, and fell in love with Peg Woffington, and then the wife follows him up to London, and begs her to give him back to her, and she does it. There's something about a portrait of Peg—I don't remember exactly; she puts her face through and cries when the wife talks to the picture. The wife thinks it is a real picture, and she is kind of soliloquizing, and asking Peg to give her husband back to her; and Peg does, in the end. That part is beautiful. They become the greatest friends.

MISS RAMSEY: Rather silly, I should say.

MISS GARNETT: Yes, it *is* rather silly, but I suppose the author thought she had to do something.

MISS RAMSEY: And disgusting. A married man, that way! I don't see any comparison with Mr. Ashley.

MISS GARNETT: No, there really isn't any. Emily has never asked you to give him up. And besides, Peg Woffington really liked him a little—loved him, in fact.

MISS RAMSEY: And I *don't* like Mr. Ashley at all. Of course I respect him—and I admire his intellect; there's no question about his being handsome; but I have never thought of him for a moment in any other way; and now I can't even respect him.

MISS GARNETT: Nobody could. I'm sure Emily would be welcome to him as far as *I* was concerned. But he has never been about with me so much as he has with you, and I don't wonder you feel indignant.

MISS RAMSEY, *coldly*: I don't feel indignant. I wish to be just.

MISS GARNETT: Yes, that is what I mean. And poor Emily is so uninteresting! In the play that Kentucky Summers does, she is perfectly fascinating at first, and you can see why the poor girl's fiancé should be so taken with her. But I'm sure no one could say you had ever given Mr. Ashley the least encouragement. It would be pure justice on your part. I think you are grand! I shall always be proud of knowing what you were going to do.

MISS RAMSEY, *after some moments of snubbing intention*: I don't know what I am going to do myself, yet. Or how. What *was* that play? I never heard of it.

MISS GARNETT: I don't remember distinctly, but it was about a young man who falls in love with her, when he's engaged to another girl, and she determines, as soon as she finds it out, to disgust him, so that he will go back to the other girl, don't you know.

MISS RAMSEY: That sounds rather more practical than the Peg Woffington plan. What does she do?

MISS GARNETT: Nothing you'd like to do.

MISS RAMSEY: I'd like to do something in such a cause. What does she do?

MISS GARNETT: Oh, when he is calling on her, Kentucky Summers pretends to fly into a rage with her sister, and she pulls her hair down, and slams everything round the room, and scolds, and drinks champagne, and wants him to drink with her, and I don't know what all. The upshot is that he is only too glad to get away.

MISS RAMSEY: It's rather loathsome, isn't it?

MISS GARNETT: It *is* rather loathsome. But it was in a good cause, and I suppose it was what an actress would think of.

MISS RAMSEY: An actress?

MISS GARNETT: I forgot. The heroine is a distinguished actress, you know, and Kentucky could play that sort of part to perfection. But I don't think a lady would like to cut up, much, in the *best* cause.

MISS RAMSEY: Cut up?

MISS GARNETT: She certainly frisks about the room a good deal. How delicious these mallows are! Have you ever tried toasting them?

MISS RAMSEY: At school. There seems an idea in it. And the hero isn't married. I don't like the notion of a married man.

MISS GARNETT: Oh, I'm quite sure he isn't married. He's merely engaged. That makes the whole difference from the Peg Woffington story. And there's no portrait, I'm confident, so that you wouldn't have to do that part.

MISS RAMSEY, *haughtily*: I don't propose to do *any* part, if the affair can't be arranged without some such mountebank business!

MISS GARNETT: You can manage it, if anybody can. You have so much dignity that you could awe him into doing his duty by a single glance. I wouldn't be in his place!

MISS RAMSEY: I shall not give him a glance. I shall not see him when he comes. That will be simpler still. (*To Nora, at the door*) What is it, Nora?

NORA: Mr. Ashley, Miss Ramsey.

MISS RAMSEY, *with a severity not meant for Nora*: Ask him to sit down in the reception-room a moment.

NORA: Yes, Miss Ramsey.

MISS GARNETT, *rising and seizing Miss Ramsey's hands*: Oh, Isobel! But you will be equal to it! Oh! Oh!

MISS RAMSEY, *with state*: Why are you going, Esther? Sit down.

MISS GARNETT: If I only *could* stay! If I could hide under the sofa, or behind the screen! Isn't it wonderful—providential—his coming at the very instant? Oh, Isobel! (*She clasps her friend convulsively, and after a moment's resistance Miss Ramsey yields to her emotion, and they hide their faces in each other's neck, and strangle their hysteric laughter. They try to regain their composure, and then abandon the effort with a shuddering delight in the perfection of the incident.*) What shall you do? Shall you trust to inspiration? Shall you make him show his hand first, and then act? Or shall you tell him at once that you know all, and— Or no, of course you can't do that. He's not supposed to know that you know. Oh, I can imagine the freezing hauteur that you'll receive him with, and the icy indifference you'll let him understand that he isn't a *persona grata* with! If I were only as tall as you! He isn't as tall himself, and you can tower over him. Don't sit down, or bend, or anything; just stand with your head up, and glance carelessly at him under your lashes as if nobody was there! Then it will gradually dawn upon him that you know everything, and he'll simply go through the floor.

They take some ecstatic turns about the room, Miss Ramsey waltzing as gentleman. She abruptly frees herself.

MISS RAMSEY: No. It can't be as tacit as all that. There must be something explicit. As you say, I must *do* something to cure him of his fancy—his perfidy—and make him glad to go back to her.

MISS GARNETT: Yes! Do you think he deserves it?

MISS RAMSEY: I've no wish to punish him.

MISS GARNETT: How noble you are! I don't wonder he adores you. *I* should. But you won't find it so easy. You must do something drastic. It *is* drastic, isn't it? or do I mean static? One of those things when you simply crush a person. But now I must go. How I should like to listen at the door! We must kiss each other very quietly, and I must slip out— Oh, you dear! How I long to know what you'll do! But it will be perfect, whatever it is. You always *did* do perfect things. (*They knit their fingers together in parting.*) On second thoughts I won't kiss you. It might unman you, and you need all your strength. Unman isn't the word, exactly, but you can't say ungirl, can you? It would be ridiculous. Though girls are as brave as men when it comes to duty. Good-by, dear!

She catches Miss Ramsey about the neck, and pressing her lips silently to her cheek, runs out. Miss Ramsey rings and the maid appears.

MISS RAMSEY, *starting*: Oh! Is that you, Nora? Of course! Nora!

NORA: Yes, Miss Ramsey.

MISS RAMSEY: Do you know where my brother keeps his cigarettes?

NORA: Why, in his room, Miss Ramsey; you told him you didn't like the smell here.

MISS RAMSEY: Yes, yes. I forgot. And has he got any cocktails?

NORA: He's got the whole bottle full of them yet.

MISS RAMSEY: Full yet?

NORA: You wouldn't let him offer them to the gentlemen he had to lunch, last week, because you said—

MISS RAMSEY: What did I say?

NORA: They were vulgar.

MISS RAMSEY: And so they are. And so much the better! Bring the cigarettes and the bottle and some glasses here, Nora, and then ask Mr. Ashley to come. (*She walks away to the window, and hurriedly hums a musical comedy waltz, not quite in tune, as from not remembering exactly, and after Nora has tinkled in with a tray of glasses she lights a cigarette and stands puffing it, gasping and coughing a little, as Walter Ashley enters.*) Oh, Mr. Ashley! Sorry to make you wait.

MR. ASHLEY: The time *has* seemed long, but I could have waited all day. I couldn't have gone without seeing you, and telling you—

He pauses, as if bewildered at the spectacle of Miss Ramsey's resolute practice with the cigarette, which she now takes from her lips and waves before her face with innocent recklessness.

MISS RAMSEY, *chokingly*: Do sit down. (*She drops into an easy-chair beside the tea-table, and stretches the tips of her feet out beyond the hem of her skirt in extremely lady-like abandon.*) Have a cigarette.

She reaches the box to him.

ASHLEY: Thank you. I won't smoke, I believe.

He stands frowning, while she throws her cigarette into a teacup and lights another.

MISS RAMSEY: I thought everybody smoked. Then have a cocktail.

ASHLEY: A what?

MISS RAMSEY: A cocktail. So many people like them with their tea, instead of rum, you know.

ASHLEY: No, I didn't know.

He regards her with amaze, rapidly hardening into condemnation.

MISS RAMSEY: I hope you don't *object* to smoking. Englishwomen all smoke.

ASHLEY: I think I've heard. I didn't know that American ladies did.

MISS RAMSEY: They don't, *all*. But they will when they find how nice it is.

ASHLEY: And do Englishwomen all drink cocktails?

MISS RAMSEY: They will when they find how

nice it is. But why do you keep standing? Sit down, if it's only for a moment. There is something I would like to talk with you about. What were you saying when you came in? I didn't catch it quite.

ASHLEY: Nothing—now—

MISS RAMSEY: And I can't persuade you to have a cocktail? I believe I'll have another myself. (*She takes up the bottle, and tries several times to pour from it.*) I do believe Nora's forgotten to open it! That is a good joke on me. But I mustn't let her know. Do you happen to have a pocket-corkscrew with you, Mr. Ashley?

ASHLEY: No—

MISS RAMSEY: Well, never mind. (*She tosses her cigarette into the grate, and lights another.*) I wonder why they always have cynical persons smoke, on the stage? I don't see that the two things necessarily go together, but it does give you a kind of thrill when they strike a match, and it lights up their faces when they put it to the cigarette. You know something good and wicked is going to happen. (*She puffs violently at her cigarette, and then suddenly flings it away and starts to her feet.*) Will you—would you— open the window?

She collapses into her chair.

ASHLEY, *springing toward her*: Miss Ramsey, are you—you are ill!

MISS RAMSEY: No, no! The window! A little faint—it's so close— There, it's all right now. Or it will be—when—I've had—another cigarette. (*She leans forward to take one; Ashley gravely watches her, but says nothing. She lights her cigarette, but, without smoking, throws it away.*) Go on.

ASHLEY: I wasn't saying anything!

MISS RAMSEY: Oh, I forgot. And I don't know what we were talking about myself.

She falls limply back into her chair and closes her eyes.

ASHLEY: Sha'n't I ring for the maid? I'm afraid—

MISS RAMSEY, *imperiously*: Not at all. Not on any account. (*Far less imperiously*) You may pour me a cup of tea if you like. That will make me well. The full strength, please.

She motions away the hot-water jug with which he has proposed qualifying the cup of tea which he offers her.

ASHLEY: One lump or two?

MISS RAMSEY: Only one, thank you.

She takes the cup.

ASHLEY, *offering the milk*: Cream?

MISS RAMSEY: A drop. (*He stands anxiously beside her while she takes a long draught and then gives back the cup.*) That was perfect.

ASHLEY: Another?

MISS RAMSEY: No, that is just right. Now go on. Or, I forgot. You were not going on. Oh dear! How much better I feel. There must have been something poisonous in those cigarettes.

ASHLEY: Yes, there was tobacco.

MISS RAMSEY: Oh, do you think it was the tobacco? Do throw the whole box into the fire! I shall tell Bob never to get cigarettes with tobacco in them after this. Won't you have one of the chocolates? Or a mallow? I feel as if I should never want to eat anything again. Where was I?

She rests her check against the side of her chair cushion, and speaks with closed eyes, in a weak murmur. Mr. Ashley watches her at first with anxiety, then with a gradual change of countenance until a gleam of intelligence steals into his look of compassion.

ASHLEY: You asked me to throw the cigarettes into the fire. But I want you to let me keep them.

MISS RAMSEY, *with wide-flung eyes*: You? You said you wouldn't smoke.

ASHLEY, *laughing*: May I change my mind? One talks better. (*He lights a cigarette.*) And, Miss Ramsey, I believe I *will* have a cocktail, after all.

MISS RAMSEY: Mr. Ashley!

ASHLEY, *without noting her protest*: I had forgotten that I had a corkscrew in my pocket-knife. Don't trouble yourself to ring for one. (*He produces the knife and opens the bottle; then, as Miss Ramsey rises and stands aghast, he pours out a glass and offers it to her, with mock devotion. As she shakes her head and recoils*) Oh! I thought you liked cocktails. They are very good after cigarettes—very reviving. But if you won't— (*He tosses off the cocktail and sets down the glass, smacking his lips.*) Tell your brother I commend his taste—in cocktails and—(*puffing his cigarette*) tobacco. Poison for poison, let me offer you one of *my* cigarettes. They're milder than these.

He puts his hand to his breast pocket.

MISS RAMSEY, *with nervous shrinking*: No—

ASHLEY: It's just as well. I find that I hadn't brought mine with me. (*After a moment*) You are so unconventional, so fearless, that I should like your notion of the problem in a book I've just been reading. Why should the mere fact that a man is married to one woman prevent his being in love with another, or half a dozen others; or *vice versa?*

MISS RAMSEY: Mr. Ashley, do you wish to insult me?

ASHLEY: Dear me, no! But put the case a little differently. Suppose a couple are merely engaged. Does that fact imply that neither has a right to a change of mind, or to be fancy free to make another choice?

MISS RAMSEY, *indignantly*: Yes, it does. They are as sacredly bound to each other as if they were married, and if they are false to each other the girl is a wretch, and the man is a villain! And if you think anything I have said can excuse you for breaking your engagement, or that I don't consider you the wickedest person in the world, and the most barefaced hypocrite, and—and—I don't know what—you are very much mistaken.

ASHLEY: What in the world are you talking about?

MISS RAMSEY: I am talking about you and your shameless perfidy.

ASHLEY: My shameless perf— I don't understand! I came here to tell you that I love you—

MISS RAMSEY: How dare you! To speak to me of that, when— Or perhaps you *have* broken with her, and think you are free to hoodwink some other poor creature. But you will find that you have chosen the wrong person. And it's no excuse for you her being a little—a little—not so bright as some girls, and not so good-looking. Oh, it's enough to make any girl loathe her own looks! You musn't suppose you can come here red-handed—yes, it's the same as a murder, and any true girl would say so—and tell me you care for me. No, Walter Ashley, I haven't fallen so low as that, though I *have* the disgrace of your acquaintance. And I hope—I hope—if you don't like my smoking, and offering you cocktails, and talking the way I have, it will be a lesson to you. And yes!—I *will* say it! If it will add to your misery to know that I did respect you very much, and thought everything—very highly—of you, and might have answered you very differently before, when you were free to tell me *that*—now I have nothing but the utmost abhorrence—and—disapproval of you. And—and— Oh, I don't see how you can be so hateful!

She hides her face in her hands and rushes from the room, overturning several chairs in her course toward the door. Ashley remains staring after her, while a succession of impetuous rings make themselves heard from the street door. There is a sound of opening it, and then a flutter of skirts and anxieties, and Miss Garnett comes running into the room.

MISS GARNETT, *to the maid hovering in the doorway*: Yes, I must have left it here, for I never missed it till I went to pay my fare in the motor-bus, and tried to think whether I had the exact dime, and if I hadn't whether the conductor would change a five-dollar bill or not, and then it rushed into my mind that I had left my purse somewhere, and I knew I hadn't been anywhere else. (*She runs from the mantel to the writing-desk in the corner, and then to the sofa, where, peering under the tea-table, she finds her purse on the shelf.*) Oh, here it is, Nora, just where I put it when we began to talk, and I must have gone out and left it. I— (*She starts with a little shriek, in encountering Ashley.*) Oh, Mr. Ashley! What a fright you gave me! I was just looking for my purse that I missed when I went to pay my fare in the motor-bus, and was wondering whether I had the exact dime, or the conductor could change a five-dollar bill, and— (*She discovers, or affects to discover, something strange in his manner.*) What —what is the matter, Mr. Ashley?

ASHLEY: I shall be glad to have you tell me— or any one.

MISS GARNETT: I don't understand. Has Isobel—

ASHLEY: Miss Garnett, did you know I was engaged?

MISS GARNETT: Why, yes; I was just going to congrat—

ASHLEY: Well, don't, unless you can tell me whom I am engaged to.

MISS GARNETT: Why, aren't you engaged to Emily Fray?

ASHLEY: Not the least in the world.

MISS GARNETT, *in despair*: Then *what* have I done? Oh, what a fatal, fatal scrape! (*With a ray of returning hope*) But she told me *herself* that she was engaged! And you were together so much, last summer! (*Desperately*) Then if she isn't engaged to you, whom is she engaged to?

ASHLEY: On general principles, I shouldn't know, but in this particular instance I happen to know that she is engaged to Owen Brooks. They were a great deal more together last summer.

MISS GARNETT, *with conviction*: So they were! (*With returning doubt*) But why didn't she say so?

ASHLEY: I can't tell you; she may have had her reasons, or she may not. Can you possibly tell me, in return for my ignorance, why the fact of her engagement should involve me in the strange way it seems to have done with Miss Ramsey?

MISS GARNETT, *with a burst of involuntary candor*: Why, I did that. Or, no! What's she been doing?

ASHLEY: Really, Miss Garnett—

MISS GARNETT: How can I tell you anything, if you don't tell me everything? You wouldn't wish me to betray confidence?

ASHLEY: No, certainly not. What was the confidence?

MISS GARNETT: Well— But I shall have to know first what she's been doing. You must see that yourself, Mr. Ashley. *(He is silent.)* Has she—has Isobel—been behaving—well, out of character?

ASHLEY: Very much indeed.

MISS GARNETT: I expected she would. *(She fetches a thoughtful sigh, and for her greater emotional convenience she sinks into an easy-chair and leans forward.)* Oh dear! It *is* a scrape. *(Suddenly and imperatively)* Tell me exactly what she did, if you hope for any help whatever.

ASHLEY: Why, she offered me a cocktail—

MISS GARNETT: Oh, how good! I didn't suppose she would dare! Well?

ASHLEY: And she smoked cigarettes—

MISS GARNETT: How perfectly divine! And what else?

ASHLEY, *coldly*: May I ask why you admire Miss Ramsey's behaving out of character so much? I think the smoking made her rather faint, and—

MISS GARNETT: She would have let it *kill* her! Never tell me that girls have no moral courage!

ASHLEY: But what—what was the meaning of it all?

MISS GARNETT, *thoughtfully*: I suppose if I got her in for it, I ought to get her out, even if I betray confidence.

ASHLEY: It depends upon the confidence. What is it?

MISS GARNETT: Why— But you're sure it's my duty?

ASHLEY: If you care what I think of her—

MISS GARNETT: Oh, Mr. Ashley, you musn't think it strange of Isobel, on my bended knees you musn't! Why, don't you see? She was just doing it to disgust you!

ASHLEY: Disgust me?

MISS GARNETT: Yes, and drive you back to Emily Fray.

ASHLEY: Drive me ba—

MISS GARNETT: If she thought you were engaged to Emily, when you were coming here all the time, and she wasn't quite sure that she hated to have you, don't you see it would be her duty to sacrifice herself, and— Oh, I suppose she's heard everything up there, and—

She catches herself up and runs out of the room, leaving Ashley to await the retarded descent of skirts which he hears on the stairs after the crash of the street door has announced Miss Garnett's escape. He stands with his back to the mantel, and faces Miss Ramsey as she enters the room.

MISS RAMSEY, *with the effect of cold surprise*: Mr. Ashley? I thought I heard— Wasn't Miss Garnett—

ASHLEY: She was. Did you think it was the street door closing on *me?*

MISS RAMSEY: How should I know? *(Then, courageously)* No, I didn't think it was. Why do you ask?

She moves uneasily about the room, with an air of studied inattention.

ASHLEY: Because if you did, I can put you in the right, though I can't restore Miss Garnett's presence by my absence.

MISS RAMSEY: You're rather—enigmatical. *(A ring is heard; the maid pauses at the doorway.)* I'm not at home, Nora. *(To Mr. Ashley)* It seems to be very close—

ASHLEY: It's my having been smoking.

MISS RAMSEY: *Your* having?

She goes to the window and tries to lift it.

ASHLEY: Let *me.*

He follows her to the window, where he stands beside her.

MISS RAMSEY: Now, she's seen me! And you here with me. Of course—

ASHLEY: I shouldn't mind. But I'm so sorry if —and I will go.

MISS RAMSEY: You can't go now—till she's round the corner. She'll keep looking back, and she'll think I made you.

ASHLEY: But haven't you? Aren't you sending me back to Miss Fray to tell her that I must keep my engagement, though I care nothing for her, and care all the world for you? Isn't that what you want me to do?

MISS RAMSEY: But you're not engaged to her! You just—

ASHLEY: Just what?

MISS RAMSEY, *desperately*: You wish me to disgrace myself forever in your eyes. Well, I will; what does it matter now? I heard you telling Esther you were not engaged. I *over*heard you.

ASHLEY: I fancied you must.

MISS RAMSEY: I *tried* to overhear! I *eavesdropped!* I wish you to know that.

ASHLEY: And what do you wish me to do about it?

MISS RAMSEY: I should think any self-respecting person would know. I'm *not* a self-respecting person. (*Her wandering gaze seems to fall for the first time upon the tray with the cocktails and glasses and cigarettes; she flies at the bell-button and presses it impetuously. As the maid appears*) Take these things away, Nora, please! (*To Ashley when the maid has left the room*) Don't be afraid to say what you think of me!

ASHLEY: I think all the world of you. But I should merely like to ask—

MISS RAMSEY: Oh, you can ask anything of me now!

ASHLEY, *with palpable insincerity*: I should like to ask why you don't respect yourself?

MISS RAMSEY: Was that what you were going to ask? I know it wasn't. But I will tell you. Because I have been a fool.

ASHLEY: Thank you. Now I will tell you what I was really going to ask. Why did you wish to drive me back to Miss Fray when you knew that I would be false to her a thousand times if I could only once be true to you?

MISS RAMSEY: Now you *are* insulting me! And that is just the point. You may be a very clever lawyer, Mr. Ashley, and everybody says you are—very able, and talented, and all that, but you can't get round that point. You may torture any meaning you please out of my words, but I shall always say you brought it on yourself.

ASHLEY: Brought what on?

MISS RAMSEY: Mr. Ashley! I won't be cross-questioned.

ASHLEY: Was that why you smoked, and poured cocktails out of an unopened bottle? Was it because you wished me to hate you, and remember my duty, and go back to Miss Fray? Well, it was a dead failure. It made me love you more than ever. I am a fool too, as you call it.

MISS RAMSEY: Say anything you please. I have given you the right. I shall not resent it. Go on.

ASHLEY: I should only repeat myself. You must have known how much I care for you, Isobel. Do you mind my calling you Isobel?

MISS RAMSEY: Not in the least if you wish to humiliate me by it. I should like you to trample on me in every way you can.

ASHLEY: Trample on you? I would rather be run over by a steam-roller than tread on the least of your outlying feelings, dearest. Do you mind my saying dearest?

MISS RAMSEY: I have told you that you can say anything you like. I deserve it. But oh, if you have a spark of pity—

ASHLEY: I'm a perfect conflagration of compassion, darling. Do you object to darling?

MISS RAMSEY, *with starting tears*: It doesn't matter now.

   She has let her lovely length trail into the corner of the sofa, where she desperately reclines, supporting her elbow on the arm of it, and resting her drooping head on her hand. He draws a hassock up in front of her, and sits on it.

ASHLEY: This represents kneeling at your feet. One doesn't do it literally any more, you know.

MISS RAMSEY, *in a hollow voice*: I should despise you if you did, and—(*deeply murmurous*) I don't *wish* to despise you.

ASHLEY: No, I understand that. You merely wish *me* to despise *you.* But why?

MISS RAMSEY, *nervously*: You know.

ASHLEY: But I don't know—Isobel, dearest, darling, if you will allow me to express myself so fully. *How* should I know?

MISS RAMSEY: I've told you.

ASHLEY: May I take your hand? For good-by! (*He possesses himself of it.*) It seems to go along with those expressions.

MISS RAMSEY, *self-contemptuously*: Oh yes.

ASHLEY: Thank you. Where were we?

MISS RAMSEY, *sitting up and recovering her hand*: You were saying good-by—

ASHLEY: Was I? But not before I had told you that I knew you were doing all that for my best good, and I wish—I *wish* you could have seen how exemplary you looked when you were trying to pour a cocktail out of a corked bottle, between your remarks on passionate fiction and puffs of the insidious cigarette! When the venomous tobacco began to get in its deadly work, and you turned pale and reeled a little, and called for air, it made me mentally vow to go back to Miss Fray instantly, whether I was engaged to her or not, and cut out poor old Brooks—

MISS RAMSEY: Was it Mr. Brooks? I didn't hear the name exactly.

ASHLEY: When I was telling Miss Garnett? I

ought to have spoken louder, but I wasn't sure at the time you were listening. Though as you were saying, what does it matter now?

MISS RAMSEY: Did I say that?

ASHLEY: Words to that effect. And they have made me feel how unworthy of you I am. I'm not heroic—by nature. But I could be, if you made me—by art—

MISS RAMSEY, *springing to her feet indignantly*: Now, you are ridiculing me—you are making fun of me.

ASHLEY, *gathering himself up from his hassock with difficulty, and confronting her*: Do I look like a man who would dare to make fun of you? I am half a head shorter than you, and in moral grandeur you overtop me so that I would always have to wear a high hat when I was with you.

MISS RAMSEY, *thoughtfully*: Plenty of girls are that way, now. But if you are ashamed of my being tall—

Flashingly, and with starting tears.

ASHLEY: Ashamed! I can always look up to you, you can always stoop to me!

He stretches his arms toward her.

MISS RAMSEY, *recoiling bewildered*: Wait! We haven't got to that yet.

ASHLEY: Oh, Isobel—dearest—darling! We've got past it! We're on the home stretch, now.

ANNOTATED BIBLIOGRAPHY

Annotated Bibliography

THE PARLOR CAR
1. *The Atlantic Monthly*, XXXVIII (September, 1876), 290–300.
2. *The Railroad Conductor's Brotherhood Monthly Magazine*, (Omaha, Nebraska), I (September, 1876), 395–405.
3. James R. Osgood & Co., Boston, 1876.
4. Ticknor & Co., Boston, 1876.
5. Houghton Mifflin Co., Boston, 1889, 1901.
6. *The Sleeping Car and Other Farces*. Boston: Houghton Mifflin Co., 1889: THE PARLOR CAR, THE SLEEPING CAR, THE REGISTER, THE ELEVATOR.
7. *Minor Dramas*. 2 vols. Edinburgh: David Douglas, 1907. Volume I: THE PARLOR CAR, THE SLEEPING CAR, THE REGISTER, THE ELEVATOR, THE GARROTERS, THE MOUSE TRAP, FIVE O'CLOCK TEA, A LIKELY STORY, THE ALBANY DEPOT. Volume II: A LETTER OF INTRODUCTION, THE UNEXPECTED GUESTS, EVENING DRESS, ROOM FORTY-FIVE, A PREVIOUS ENGAGEMENT, A MASTERPIECE OF DIPLOMACY, BRIDE ROSES, AN INDIAN GIVER, THE SMOKING CAR, HER OPINION OF HIS STORY.
(There are a number of variant readings which distinguish the plays in *Minor Dramas* from other texts, but most of them indicate either a compositor's carelessness—there are, for example, eighteen omissions or slight changes in A MASTERPIECE OF DIPLOMACY—or a change to wording that would be better understood in England, as from *bug* to *beetle* in AN INDIAN GIVER. The texts in *Minor Dramas*, then, are not reliable.)
8. *The Parlor-Car and The Sleeping-Car*. Boston: Houghton Mifflin Co., 1918. (This text and that in *Minor Dramas* and *The Sleeping Car and Other Farces* are distinguished from others by four variant readings.)

OUT OF THE QUESTION
1. *Atlantic Monthly*, XXXIX (February, 1877), 195–208; (March, 1877), 317–29; (April, 1877), 447–61. (There are sixty-five variant readings that identify the *Atlantic Monthly* text as distinct from others.)
2. James R. Osgood & Co., Boston, 1877.
3. Ticknor & Co., Boston, 1877.
4. *Out of the Question and At the Sign of the Savage*. Edinburgh: David Douglas, 1882. (New type was set for this edition.)
5. Houghton Mifflin Co., Boston, 1905. (This text is identical with that of the Osgood and Ticknor publications.)

A COUNTERFEIT PRESENTMENT
1. *Atlantic Monthly*, XL (August, 1877), 148–61; (September, 1877), 296–305; (October,

1877), 448–60. (In three parts; there are forty-three variant readings that identify the *Atlantic Monthly* text as distinct from others. A prompt copy in the Harvard Library employs paste-ups in two kinds of type, one of which is the proof of the *Atlantic Monthly*.)
2. James R. Osgood & Co., Boston, 1877. (In three parts; reissued in four parts.)
3. Ticknor & Co., Boston, 1877. (In four parts.)
4. *A Counterfeit Presentment and The Parlor Car*. Edinburgh: David Douglas, 1882. (A COUNTERFEIT PRESENTMENT is in four parts.)
5. Houghton Mifflin Co., Boston, 1880, 1905. (In four parts; this text is identical with that of the Osgood and Ticknor publications.)

YORICK'S LOVE
Unpublished

PRISCILLA: A COMEDY
Unpublished

COLONEL SELLERS AS A SCIENTIST; *W. D. Howells and S. L. Clemens*
Unpublished

THE SLEEPING CAR
1. *Harper's Christmas* (1882), pp. 6–7.
2. James R. Osgood & Co., Boston, 1883.
3. Ticknor & Co., Boston, 1883.
4. Houghton Mifflin Co., Boston, 1911. (Volumes which collect this play show one variant reading distinct from the texts listed here.)

THE REGISTER
1. *Harper's Monthly*, LXVIII (December, 1883), 70–86. (This text includes seven variant readings which distinguish it from other texts.)
2. James R. Osgood & Co., Boston, 1884.
3. Ticknor & Co., Boston, n.d.
4. Houghton Mifflin Co., Boston, 1899, 1903. (Book texts listed here are alike, but show three distinct variant readings from this play when it appears in print with other Howells plays.)

A SEA CHANGE OR LOVE'S STOWAWAY, A LYRICATED FARCE; *Lyrics by W. D. Howells and music by George Henschel*
1. James R. Osgood & Co., Boston, 1884. (Harvard Library holds a paste-up version of this play which seems to be made from the page proof of the Osgood text. It was, perhaps, intended for use as a prompt copy, and it includes numerous stage directions and textual changes in Howells' handwriting.)

2. Trübner & Co., London, 1884. (Trübner and Osgood published simultaneously.)
3. *Harper's Weekly*, XXXII (July 14, 1888), 505; Supp. 521–24.
4. Ticknor & Co., Boston, 1888. (This text shows numerous substantial additions and changes from the publication in *Harper's Weekly*.)
5. Houghton Mifflin Co., Boston, 1884, 1888. (The text is identical with the Ticknor publication.)

THE ELEVATOR
1. *Harper's Monthly*, LXX (December, 1884), 111–25. (There are five variant readings which mark this text as distinct from others.)
2. James R. Osgood & Co., Boston, 1885.
3. Ticknor & Co., Boston, 1885.
4. Houghton Mifflin Co., Boston, 1896, 1913. (All book texts are identical except for publisher's device, name, title page, and publishing date. The 1913 publication used larger pages but the same printing plates.)

A FOREGONE CONCLUSION; W. D. *Howells and William Poel*
Unpublished

THE GARROTERS
1. *Harper's Monthly*, LXXII (December, 1885), 146–62.
2. Harper & Bros., New York, 1886, 1894. (This text has two variant readings which distinguish it from other texts.)
3. David Douglas, Edinburgh, 1897. (In an agreement dated February 23, 1892, Harper and Brothers were to publish Howells' plays for the next five years; hence, the 1897 Douglas date for plays first published by Harper and Brothers.)
4. Samuel French, New York, 1921. (French printed the Harper and Brothers 1886 text.)

THE MOUSE TRAP
1. *Harper's Monthly*, LXXIV (December, 1886), 64–75. (There is no division of scenes in this text.)
2. *The Mouse Trap and Other Farces*. New York: Harper & Bros., 1889: THE GARROTERS, FIVE O'CLOCK TEA, THE MOUSE TRAP, A LIKELY STORY. (Several issues; new plates but no substantive changes in 1909 issue.)
3. Harper & Bros., New York, 1894.
4. David Douglas, Edinburgh, 1897. (Douglas printed the plays as they appeared in *The Mouse Trap and Other Farces*.)
5. Samuel French, New York, 1921.

FIVE O'CLOCK TEA
1. *Harper's Monthly*, LXXVI (December, 1887), 86–96.
2. Harper & Bros., New York, 1894. (One variant reading distinguishes this from other texts.)
3. David Douglas, Edinburgh, 1897.
4. Samuel French, New York, 1921.

A LIKELY STORY
1. *Harper's Monthly*, LXXVII (December, 1888),

26–38. (*Harper's Monthly* has two variant readings which distinguish it from other texts.)
2. Harper & Bros., New York, 1894.
3. David Douglas, Edinburgh, 1897.
4. Samuel French, New York, 1921.

THE ALBANY DEPOT
1. *Harper's Weekly*, XXXIII (December 14, 1889), 989; Supp. 1005–1008.
2. Privately printed for stage use only—no place, no date, ca. October, 1891. (Probably printed by Harper & Bros.)
3. Harper & Bros., New York, 1892.
4. David Douglas, Edinburgh, 1897.
5. Samuel French, New York, 1921.

SAMSON
1. Charles D. Koppel, New York, 1889. (A Tragedy in five acts, by Ippolito D'Aste. Translated by W. D. Howells. With the English and Italian words, as performed by Signor Salvini, during his farewell American tour, under the direction of Mr. A. M. Palmer.)

A LETTER OF INTRODUCTION
1. *Harper's Monthly*, LXXXIV (January, 1892), 243–356.
2. Harper & Bros., New York, 1892.
3. David Douglas, Edinburgh, 1897.
4. Samuel French, New York, 1921.

EVENING DRESS
1. *Cosmopolitan*, XIII (May, 1892), 116–27. (The *Cosmopolitan* has six variant readings which distinguish it from other texts.)
2. Harper & Bros., New York, 1893.
3. *Der Gesellschafts-Anzug*, Einzige autorisierte Übersetzung von C.A.C. Petzel. Milwaukee: Germania Publishing Co., 1893.
4. David Douglas, Edinburgh, 1897.
5. Samuel French, New York, 1921.

THE UNEXPECTED GUESTS
1. *Harper's Monthly*, LXXXVI (January, 1893), 211–25. (*Harper's Monthly* has four variant readings which distinguish it from other texts.)
2. Harper & Bros., New York, 1893.
3. David Douglas, Edinburgh, 1897.
4. Samuel French, New York, 1921.

BRIDE ROSES
1. *Harper's Monthly*, XXXVII (August, 1893), 424–30.
2. Houghton Mifflin Co., Boston, 1900.

A MASTERPIECE OF DIPLOMACY
1. *Harper's Monthly*, LXXXVIII (February, 1894), 371–85.
2. *Cincinnati Medical Journal*, IX (1894), 79–92. (This text shows minor changes in wording from the *Harper's Monthly* text.)

A PREVIOUS ENGAGEMENT
1. *Harper's Monthly*, XCII (December, 1895),

29–44. (*Harper's Monthly* has two variant readings which distinguish it from other texts.)
2. Harper & Bros., New York, 1897.
3. Samuel French, New York, 1921.

AN INDIAN GIVER
    1. *Harper's Monthly*, XCIV (January, 1897), 235–52. (*Harper's Monthly* has one variant reading which distinguishes it from other texts. Also the title in this publication was simply: *Indian Giver.*)
    2. Houghton Mifflin Co., Boston, 1900.

THE RISE OF SILAS LAPHAM; *W. D. Howells and Paul Kester*
Unpublished

THE SMOKING CAR
    1. *Frank Leslie's Popular Monthly*, XLVII (December, 1898), 183–99. (*Frank Leslie's* has three variant readings which distinguish it from other texts.)
    2. Houghton Mifflin Co., Boston, 1900.

A HAZARD OF NEW FORTUNES
Unpublished

ROOM FORTY-FIVE
    1. *Frank Leslie's Popular Monthly*, XLIX (December, 1899), 132–48. (*Frank Leslie's* has two variant readings which distinguish it from other texts.)
    2. Houghton Mifflin Co., Boston, 1900.

THE MOTHER AND THE FATHER
    1. "Father and Mother, A Mystery," *Harper's Monthly*, C (May, 1900), 869–74.
"The Mother," *Harper's Monthly*, CVI (December, 1902), 21–26.
"After the Wedding," *Harper's Monthly*, CXIV (December, 1906), 64–69.
    2. *The Mother and the Father, Dramatic Pas-*

sages. New York: Harper & Bros., 1909. (There are additions, omissions, and substitutions: a total of sixty-eight variant readings between the book and the magazine publications.)

HER OPINION OF HIS STORY
    1. *Harper's Bazaar*, XIII (May, 1907), 429–37.

SAVED, AN EMOTIONAL DRAMA
    1. *Harper's Weekly*, VII (December 26, 1908), 22–24.

A TRUE HERO, MELODRAMA
    1. *Harper's Monthly*, CXIX (November, 1909), 866–75.

THE NIGHT BEFORE CHRISTMAS, A MORALITY
    1. *Harper's Monthly*, CXX (January, 1910), 207–16. (*Harper's Monthly* has one reading distinct from the book version.)
    2. *The Daughter of the Storage.* New York: Harper & Bros., 1916, pp. 319–52.

PARTING FRIENDS, TRAGEDY
    1. *Harper's Monthly*, CXXI (October, 1910), 670–77.
    2. Harper & Bros., New York, 1911.
    3. Samuel French, New York, 1921.

THE IMPOSSIBLE, A MYSTERY PLAY
    1. *Harper's Monthly*, CXXII (December, 1910), 116–25.

SELF-SACRIFICE, A FARCE TRAGEDY
    1. *Harper's Monthly*, CXXII (April, 1911), 748–57.
    2. *The Daughter of the Storage.* New York: Harper & Bros., 1916, pp. 283–316. (The play was shortened considerably for book publication; see p. 628.)

Index

Index